W9-BRQ-428

Fundamental Methods of Mathematical Economics

To Emily, Darryl, and Tracey

—Alpha C. Chiang

To Skippy and Myrtle

—Kevin Wainwright

About the Authors

Alpha C. Chiang received his Ph.D. from Columbia University in 1954, after earning a B.A. in 1946 from St. John's University (Shanghai, China) and an M.A. in 1948 from the University of Colorado. In 1954 he joined the faculty of Denison University in Ohio, where he assumed the chairmanship of the Department of Economics in 1961. From 1964 on, he taught at the University of Connecticut where, after 28 years, he became Professor Emeritus of Economics in 1992. He also held visiting professorships at New Asia College of the Chinese University of Hong Kong, Cornell University, Lingnan University in Hong Kong, and Helsinki School of Economics and Business Administration. His publications include another book on mathematical economics: *Elements of Dynamic Optimization,* Waveland Press, Inc., 1992. Among the honors he received are awards from the Ford Foundation and National Science Foundation fellowships, election to the presidency of the Ohio Association of Economists and Political Scientists, 1963–1964, and listing in *Who's Who in Economics: A Biographical Dictionary of Major Economists 1900–1994,* MIT Press.

Kevin Wainwright is a faculty member of the British Columbia Institute of Technology in Burnaby, B.C., Canada. Since 2001, he has served as president of the faculty association and program head in the Business Administration program. He did his graduate studies at Simon Fraser University in Burnaby, B.C., Canada, and continues to teach in the Department of Economics there. He specializes in microeconomic theory and mathematical economics.

Preface

This book is written for those students of economics intent on learning the basic mathematical methods that have become indispensable for a proper understanding of the current economic literature. Unfortunately, studying mathematics is, for many, something akin to taking bitter-tasting medicine—absolutely necessary, but extremely unpleasant. Such an attitude, referred to as "math anxiety," has its roots—we believe—largely in the inauspicious manner in which mathematics is often presented to students. In the belief that conciseness means elegance, explanations offered are frequently too brief for clarity, thus puzzling students and giving them an undeserved sense of intellectual inadequacy. An overly formal style of presentation, when not accompanied by any intuitive illustrations or demonstrations of "relevance," can impair motivation. An uneven progression in the level of material can make certain mathematical topics appear more difficult than they actually are. Finally, exercise problems that are excessively sophisticated may tend to shatter students' confidence, rather than stimulate thinking as intended.

With that in mind, we have made a serious effort to minimize anxiety-causing features. To the extent possible, patient rather than cryptic explanations are offered. The style is deliberately informal and "reader-friendly." As a matter of routine, we try to anticipate and answer questions that are likely to arise in the students' minds as they read. To underscore the relevance of mathematics to economics, we let the analytical needs of economists motivate the study of the related mathematical techniques and then illustrate the latter with appropriate economic models immediately afterward. Also, the mathematical tool kit is built up on a carefully graduated schedule, with the elementary tools serving as stepping stones to the more advanced tools discussed later. Wherever appropriate, graphic illustrations give visual reinforcement to the algebraic results. And we have designed the exercise problems as drills to help solidify grasp and bolster confidence, rather than exact challenges that might unwittingly frustrate and intimidate the novice.

In this book, the following major types of economic analysis are covered: statics (equilibrium analysis), comparative statics, optimization problems (as a special type of statics), dynamics, and dynamic optimization. To tackle these, the following mathematical methods are introduced in due course: matrix algebra, differential and integral calculus, differential equations, difference equations, and optimal control theory. Because of the substantial number of illustrative economic models—both macro and micro—appearing here, this book should be useful also to those who are already mathematically trained but still in need of a guide to usher them from the realm of mathematics to the land of economics. For the same reason, the book should not only serve as a text for a course on mathematical methods, but also as supplementary reading in such courses as microeconomic theory, macroeconomic theory, and economic growth and development.

We have attempted to retain the principal objectives and style of the previous editions. However, the present edition contains several significant changes. The material on mathematical programming is now presented earlier in a new Chap. 13 entitled "Further Topics in Optimization." This chapter has two major themes: optimization with inequality constraints and the envelope theorem. Under the first theme, the Kuhn-Tucker conditions are developed in much the same manner as in the previous edition. However, the topic has been enhanced with several new economic applications, including peak-load pricing and consumer rationing. The second theme is related to the development of the envelope theorem, the maximum-value function, and the notion of duality. By applying the envelope theorem to various economic models, we derive important results such as Roy's identity, Shephard's lemma, and Hotelling's lemma.

The second major addition to this edition is a new Chap. 20 on optimal control theory. The purpose of this chapter is to introduce the reader to the basics of optimal control and demonstrate how it may be applied in economics, including examples from natural resource economics and optimal growth theory. The material in this chapter is drawn in great part from the discussion of optimal control theory in *Elements of Dynamic Optimization* by Alpha C. Chiang (McGraw-Hill 1992, now published by Waveland Press, Inc.), which presents a thorough treatment of both optimal control and its precursor, calculus of variations.

Aside from the two new chapters, there are several significant additions and refinements to this edition. In Chap. 3 we have expanded the discussion of solving higher-order polynomial equations by factoring (Sec. 3.3). In Chap. 4, a new section on Markov chains has been added (Sec. 4.7). And, in Chap. 5, we have introduced the checking of the rank of a matrix via an echelon matrix (Sec. 5.1), and the Hawkins-Simon condition in connection with the Leontief input-output model (Sec. 5.7). With respect to economic applications, many new examples have been added and some of the existing applications have been enhanced. A linear version of the IS-LM model has been included in Sec. 5.6, and a more general form of the model in Sec. 8.6 has been expanded to encompass both a closed and open economy, thereby demonstrating a much richer application of comparative statics to general-function models. Other additions include a discussion of expected utility and risk preferences (Sec. 9.3), a profit-maximization model that incorporates the Cobb-Douglas production function (Sec. 11.6), and a two-period intertemporal choice problem (Sec. 12.3). Finally, the exercise problems have been revised and augmented, giving students a greater opportunity to hone their skills.

Fundamental Methods of Mathematical Economics

Fourth Edition

Alpha C. Chiang

Professor Emeritus
University of Connecticut

Kevin Wainwright

British Columbia Institute of
Technology and
Simon Fraser University

Boston   Burr Ridge, IL   Dubuque, IA   Madison, WI   New York   San Francisco   St. Louis
Bangkok   Bogotá   Caracas   Kuala Lumpur   Lisbon   London   Madrid   Mexico City
Milan   Montreal   New Delhi   Santiago   Seoul   Singapore   Sydney   Taipei   Toronto

The McGraw-Hill Companies

McGraw-Hill
Irwin

FUNDAMENTAL METHODS OF MATHEMATICAL ECONOMICS

Published by McGraw-Hill/Irwin, a business unit of The McGraw-Hill Companies, Inc.,
1221 Avenue of the Americas, New York, NY, 10020. Copyright © 2005, 1984, 1974, 1967 by

Some ancillaries, including electronic and print components, may not be available to customers outside the United States.

This book is printed on acid-free paper.

2 3 4 5 6 7 8 9 0 DOC/DOC 0 9 8 7 6 5

ISBN 0-07-010910-9

About the cover: The graph in Figure 20.1 on page 635 illustrates that the shortest distance between two points is a
straight line. We chose it as the basis for the cover design because such a simple truth requires one of the most
advanced techniques found in this book.

Publisher: *Gary Burke*
Executive editor: *Lucille Sutton*
Developmental editor: *Rebecca Hicks*
Editorial assistant: *Jackie Grabel*
Senior marketing manager: *Martin D. Quinn*
Senior media producer: *Kai Chiang*
Project manager: *Bruce Gin*
Production supervisor: *Debra R. Sylvester*
Designer: *Kami Carter*
Supplement producer: *Lynn M. Bluhm*
Senior digital content specialist: *Brian Nacik*
Cover design: Kami Carter
Typeface: *10/12 Times New Roman*
Compositor: *Interactive Composition Corporation*
Printer: *R. R. Donnelley*

Library of Congress Cataloging-in-Publication Data

Chiang, Alpha C., 1927-
    Fundamental methods of mathematical economics / Alpha C. Chiang, Kevin
Wainwright.—4th ed.
        p. cm.
    Includes bibliographical references and index.
    ISBN 0-07-010910-9 (alk. paper)
        1. Economics, Mathematical. I. Wainwright, Kevin. II. Title.
HB135.C47 2005
330'.01'51—dc22
                                                                    2004059546

www.mhhe.com

Acknowledgments

We are indebted to many people in the writing of this book. First of all, we owe a great deal to all the mathematicians and economists whose original ideas underlie this volume. Second, there are many students whose efforts and questions over the years have helped shape the philosophy and approach of this book.

The previous three editions of this book have benefited from the comments and suggestions of (in alphabetical order): Nancy S. Barrett, Thomas Birnberg, E. J. R. Booth, Charles E. Butler, Roberta Grower Carey, Emily Chiang, Lloyd R. Cohen, Gary Cornell, Harald Dickson, John C. H. Fei, Warren L. Fisher, Roger N. Folsom, Dennis R. Heffley, Jack Hirshleifer, James C. Hsiao, Ki-Jun Jeong, George Kondor, William F. Lott, Paul B. Manchester, Peter Morgan, Mark Nerlove, J. Frank Sharp, Alan G. Sleeman, Dennis Starleaf, Henry Y. Wan, Jr., and Chiou-Nan Yeh.

For the present edition, we acknowledge with sincere gratitude the suggestions and ideas of Curt L. Anderson, David Andolfatto, James Bathgate, C. R. Birchenhall, Michael Bowe, John Carson, Kimoon Cheong, Youngsub Chun, Kamran M. Dadkhah, Robert Delorme, Patrick Emerson, Roger Nils Folsom, Paul Gomme, Terry Heaps, Suzanne Helburn, Melvin Iyogu, Ki-Jun Jeong, Robbie Jones, John Kane, Heon-Goo Kim, George Kondor, Hui-wen Koo, Stephen Layson, Boon T. Lim, Anthony M. Marino, Richard Miles, Peter Morgan, Rafael Hernández Núñez, Alex Panayides, Xinghe Wang, and Hans-Olaf Wiesemann.

Our deep appreciation goes to Sarah Dunn, who served so ably and givingly as typist, proofreader, and research assistant. Special thanks are also due to Denise Potten for her efforts and logistic skills in the production stage. Finally, we extend our sincere appreciation to Lucille Sutton, Bruce Gin, and Lucy Mullins at McGraw-Hill, for their patience and efforts in the production of this manuscript. The final product and any errors that remain are our sole responsibility.

Suggestions for the Use of This Book

Because of the gradual buildup of the mathematical tool kit in the organization of this book, the ideal way of study is to closely follow its specific sequence of presentation. However, some alterations in the sequence of reading is possible: After completing first-order differential equations (Chap. 15) you can proceed directly to optimal control theory (Chap. 20). If going directly from Chap. 15 to Chap. 20, however, the reader may wish to review Sec. 19.5, which deals with two-variable phase diagrams.

If comparative statics is not an area of primary concern, you may skip the comparative-static analysis of general-function models (Chap. 8) and jump from Chap. 7 to Chap. 9. In that case, however, it would become necessary also to omit Sec. 11.7, the comparative-static portion of Sec. 12.5, as well as the discussion of duality in Chap. 13.

Alpha C. Chiang
Kevin Wainwright

Brief Contents

Contents

Introduction

Part 1

Chapter 1

The Nature of Mathematical Economics

Mathematical economics is not a distinct branch of economics in the sense that public finance or international trade is. Rather, it is an *approach* to economic analysis, in which the economist makes use of mathematical symbols in the statement of the problem and also draws upon known mathematical theorems to aid in reasoning. As far as the specific subject matter of analysis goes, it can be micro- or macroeconomic theory, public finance, urban economics, or what not.

Using the term *mathematical economics* in the broadest possible sense, one may very well say that every elementary textbook of economics today exemplifies mathematical economics insofar as geometrical methods are frequently utilized to derive theoretical results. More commonly, however, mathematical economics is reserved to describe cases employing mathematical techniques beyond simple geometry, such as matrix algebra, differential and integral calculus, differential equations, difference equations, etc. It is the purpose of this book to introduce the reader to the most fundamental aspects of these mathematical methods—those encountered daily in the current economic literature.

1.1 Mathematical versus Nonmathematical Economics

Since mathematical economics is merely an approach to economic analysis, it should not and does not fundamentally differ from the *non*mathematical approach to economic analysis. The purpose of any theoretical analysis, regardless of the approach, is always to derive a set of conclusions or theorems from a given set of assumptions or postulates via a process of reasoning. The major difference between "mathematical economics" and "literary economics" is twofold: First, in the former, the assumptions and conclusions are stated in mathematical symbols rather than words and in equations rather than sentences. Second, in place of literary logic, use is made of mathematical theorems—of which there exists an abundance to draw upon—in the reasoning process. Inasmuch as symbols and words are really equivalents (witness the fact that symbols are usually defined in words), it matters little which is chosen over the other. But it is perhaps beyond dispute that symbols are more convenient to use in deductive reasoning, and certainly are more conducive to conciseness and preciseness of statement.

The choice between literary logic and mathematical logic, again, is a matter of little import, but mathematics has the advantage of forcing analysts to make their assumptions explicit at every stage of reasoning. This is because mathematical theorems are usually stated in the "if-then" form, so that in order to tap the "then" (result) part of the theorem for their use, they must first make sure that the "if" (condition) part does conform to the explicit assumptions adopted.

Granting these points, though, one may still ask why it is necessary to go beyond geometric methods. The answer is that while geometric analysis has the important advantage of being visual, it also suffers from a serious dimensional limitation. In the usual graphical discussion of indifference curves, for instance, the standard assumption is that only *two* commodities are available to the consumer. Such a simplifying assumption is not willingly adopted but is forced upon us because the task of drawing a three-dimensional graph is exceedingly difficult, and the construction of a four- (or higher) dimensional graph is actually a physical impossibility. To deal with the more general case of 3, 4, or *n* goods, we must instead resort to the more flexible tool of equations. This reason alone should provide sufficient motivation for the study of mathematical methods beyond geometry.

In short, we see that the mathematical approach has claim to the following advantages: (1) The "language" used is more concise and precise; (2) there exists a wealth of mathematical theorems at our service; (3) in forcing us to state explicitly all our assumptions as a prerequisite to the use of the mathematical theorems, it keeps us from the pitfall of an unintentional adoption of unwanted implicit assumptions; and (4) it allows us to treat the general *n*-variable case.

Against these advantages, one sometimes hears the criticism that a mathematically derived theory is inevitably *unrealistic.* However, this criticism is not valid. In fact, the epithet "unrealistic" cannot even be used in criticizing economic theory in general, whether or not the approach is mathematical. Theory is by its very nature an abstraction from the real world. It is a device for singling out only the most essential factors and relationships so that we can study the crux of the problem at hand, free from the many complications that do exist in the actual world. Thus the statement "theory lacks realism" is merely a truism that cannot be accepted as a valid criticism of theory. By the same token, it is quite meaningless to pick out any one approach to theory as "unrealistic." For example, the theory of firm under pure competition is unrealistic, as is the theory of firm under imperfect competition, but whether these theories are derived mathematically or not is irrelevant and immaterial.

To take advantage of the wealth of mathematical tools, one must of course first acquire those tools. Unfortunately, the tools that are of interest to economists are widely scattered among many mathematics courses—too many to fit comfortably into the plan of study of a typical economics student. The service the present volume performs is to gather in one place the mathematical methods most relevant to the economics literature, organize them into a logical order of progression, fully explain each method, and then immediately illustrate how the method is applied in economic analysis. By tying together the methods and their applications, the relevance of mathematics to economics is made more transparent than is possible in the regular mathematics courses where the illustrated applications are predominantly tied to physics and engineering. Familiarity with the contents of this book (and, if possible, also its sequel volume: Alpha C. Chiang, *Elements of Dynamic Optimization,* McGraw-Hill, 1992, now published by Waveland Press, Inc.) should therefore enable you to comprehend most of the professional articles you will come across in such periodicals as the *American Economic Review, Quarterly Journal of Economics, Journal of Political Economy, Review of Economics and Statistics,* and *Economic Journal.* Those of you who, through this exposure, develop a serious interest in mathematical economics can then proceed to a more rigorous and advanced study of mathematics.

1.2 Mathematical Economics versus Econometrics

The term *mathematical economics* is sometimes confused with a related term, *econometrics.* As the "metric" part of the latter term implies, econometrics is concerned mainly with the measurement of economic data. Hence it deals with the study of *empirical* observations using statistical methods of estimation and hypothesis testing. Mathematical economics, on the other hand, refers to the application of mathematics to the purely *theoretical* aspects of economic analysis, with little or no concern about such statistical problems as the errors of measurement of the variables under study.

In the present volume, we shall confine ourselves to mathematical economics. That is, we shall concentrate on the application of mathematics to deductive reasoning rather than inductive study, and as a result we shall be dealing primarily with theoretical rather than empirical material. This is, of course, solely a matter of choice of the scope of discussion, and it is by no means implied that econometrics is less important.

Indeed, empirical studies and theoretical analyses are often complementary and mutually reinforcing. On the one hand, theories must be tested against empirical data for validity before they can be applied with confidence. On the other, statistical work needs economic theory as a guide, in order to determine the most relevant and fruitful direction of research.

In one sense, however, mathematical economics may be considered as the more basic of the two: for, to have a meaningful statistical and econometric study, a good theoretical framework—preferably in a mathematical formulation—is indispensable. Hence the subject matter of the present volume should be useful not only for those interested in theoretical economics, but also for those seeking a foundation for the pursuit of econometric studies.

Chapter 2

Economic Models

As mentioned before, any economic theory is necessarily an abstraction from the real world. For one thing, the immense complexity of the real economy makes it impossible for us to understand all the interrelationships at once; nor, for that matter, are all these interrelationships of equal importance for the understanding of the particular economic phenomenon under study. The sensible procedure is, therefore, to pick out what appeals to our reason to be the primary factors and relationships relevant to our problem and to focus our attention on these alone. Such a deliberately simplified analytical framework is called an *economic model,* since it is only a skeletal and rough representation of the actual economy.

2.1 Ingredients of a Mathematical Model

An economic model is merely a theoretical framework, and there is no inherent reason why it must be mathematical. If the model *is* mathematical, however, it will usually consist of a set of *equations* designed to describe the structure of the model. By relating a number of *variables* to one another in certain ways, these equations give mathematical form to the set of analytical assumptions adopted. Then, through application of the relevant mathematical operations to these equations, we may seek to derive a set of conclusions which logically follow from those assumptions.

Variables, Constants, and Parameters

A *variable* is something whose magnitude can change, i.e., something that can take on different values. Variables frequently used in economics include price, profit, revenue, cost, national income, consumption, investment, imports, and exports. Since each variable can assume various values, it must be represented by a symbol instead of a specific number. For example, we may represent price by P, profit by π, revenue by R, cost by C, national income by Y, and so forth. When we write $P = 3$ or $C = 18$, however, we are "freezing" these variables at specific values (in appropriately chosen units).

Properly constructed, an economic model can be solved to give us the *solution values* of a certain set of variables, such as the market-clearing level of price, or the profit-maximizing level of output. Such variables, whose solution values we seek from the model, are known as *endogenous variables* (originating from within). However, the model may also contain variables which are assumed to be determined by forces external to the model, and whose magnitudes are accepted as given data only; such variables are called *exogenous variables* (originating from without). It should be noted that a variable that is endogenous to one model may very well be exogenous to another. In an analysis of the market determination of wheat price (P), for instance, the variable P should definitely be endogenous; but in the framework of a theory of consumer expenditure, P would become instead a datum to the individual consumer, and must therefore be considered exogenous.

Variables frequently appear in combination with fixed numbers or constants, such as in the expressions $7P$ or $0.5R$. A *constant* is a magnitude that does not change and is therefore the antithesis of a variable. When a constant is joined to a variable, it is often referred to as the *coefficient* of that variable. However, a coefficient may be symbolic rather than numerical. We can, for instance, let the symbol a stand for a given constant and use the expression aP in lieu of $7P$ in a model, in order to attain a higher level of generality (see Sec. 2.7). This symbol a is a rather peculiar case—it is supposed to represent a given constant, and yet, since we have not assigned to it a specific number, it can take virtually any value. In short, it is a *constant* that is *variable!* To identify its special status, we give it the distinctive name *parametric constant* (or simply *parameter*).

It must be duly emphasized that, although different values can be assigned to a parameter, it is nevertheless to be regarded as a datum in the model. It is for this reason that people sometimes simply say "constant" even when the constant is parametric. In this respect, parameters closely resemble exogenous variables, for both are to be treated as "givens" in a model. This explains why many writers, for simplicity, refer to both collectively with the single designation "parameters."

As a matter of convention, parametric constants are normally represented by the symbols a, b, c, or their counterparts in the Greek alphabet: α, β, and γ. But other symbols naturally are also permissible. As for exogenous variables, in order that they can be visually distinguished from their endogenous cousins, we shall follow the practice of attaching a subscript 0 to the chosen symbol. For example, if P symbolizes price, then P_0 signifies an exogenously determined price.

Equations and Identities

Variables may exist independently, but they do not really become interesting until they are related to one another by equations or by inequalities. At this moment we shall discuss equations only.

In economic applications we may distinguish between three types of equation: definitional equations, behavioral equations, and conditional equations.

A *definitional equation* sets up an identity between two alternate expressions that have exactly the same meaning. For such an equation, the identical-equality sign $\equiv$ (read: "is identically equal to") is often employed in place of the regular equals sign $=$, although the latter is also acceptable. As an example, total profit is defined as the excess of total revenue over total cost; we can therefore write

$$\pi \equiv R - C$$

A *behavioral equation,* on the other hand, specifies the manner in which a variable behaves in response to changes in other variables. This may involve either human behavior (such as the aggregate consumption pattern in relation to national income) or nonhuman behavior (such as how total cost of a firm reacts to output changes). Broadly defined, behavioral equations can be used to describe the general institutional setting of a model, including the technological (e.g., production function) and legal (e.g., tax structure) aspects. Before a behavioral equation can be written, however, it is always necessary to adopt definite assumptions regarding the behavior pattern of the variable in question. Consider the two cost functions

$$C = 75 + 10Q \qquad\qquad \textbf{(2.1)}$$

$$C = 110 + Q^2 \qquad\qquad \textbf{(2.2)}$$

where Q denotes the quantity of output. Since the two equations have different forms, the production condition assumed in each is obviously different from the other. In (2.1), the fixed cost (the value of C when $Q = 0$) is 75, whereas in (2.2) it is 110. The variation in cost is also different. In (2.1), for each unit increase in Q, there is a constant increase of 10 in C. But in (2.2), as Q increases unit after unit, C will increase by progressively larger amounts. Clearly, it is primarily through the specification of the form of the behavioral equations that we give mathematical expression to the assumptions adopted for a model.

As the third type, a *conditional equation* states a requirement to be satisfied. For example, in a model involving the notion of equilibrium, we must set up an *equilibrium condition,* which describes the prerequisite for the attainment of equilibrium. Two of the most familiar equilibrium conditions in economics are

$$Q_d = Q_s \qquad \text{[quantity demanded = quantity supplied]}$$

and $\qquad\qquad S = I \qquad$ [intended saving = intended investment]

which pertain, respectively, to the equilibrium of a market model and the equilibrium of the national-income model in its simplest form. Similarly, an optimization model either derives or applies one or more *optimization conditions*. One such condition that comes easily to mind is the condition

$$\text{MC} = \text{MR} \qquad \text{[marginal cost = marginal revenue]}$$

in the theory of the firm. Because equations of this type are neither definitional nor behavioral, they constitute a class by themselves.

2.2 The Real-Number System

Equations and variables are the essential ingredients of a mathematical model. But since the values that an economic variable takes are usually numerical, a few words should be said about the number system. Here, we shall deal only with so-called real numbers.

Whole numbers such as 1, 2, 3, ... are called *positive integers;* these are the numbers most frequently used in counting. Their negative counterparts $-1, -2, -3, \ldots$ are called *negative integers;* these can be employed, for example, to indicate subzero temperatures (in degrees). The number 0 (zero), on the other hand, is neither positive nor negative, and is in that sense unique. Let us lump all the positive and negative integers and the number zero into a single category, referring to them collectively as the *set of all integers.*

Integers, of course, do not exhaust all the possible numbers, for we have *fractions,* such as $\frac{2}{3}, \frac{5}{4}$, and $\frac{7}{3}$, which—if placed on a ruler—would fall between the integers. Also, we have negative fractions, such as $-\frac{1}{2}$ and $-\frac{2}{5}$. Together, these make up the *set of all fractions.*

FIGURE 2.1

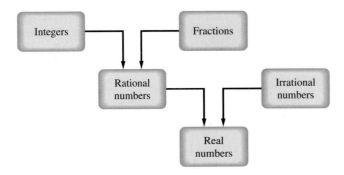

The common property of all fractional numbers is that each is expressible as a ratio of two integers. Any number that can be expressed as a ratio of two integers is called a *rational number.* But integers themselves are also rational, because any integer n can be considered as the ratio $n/1$. The set of all integers and the set of all fractions together form the *set of all rational numbers.* An alternative defining characteristic of a rational number is that it is expressible as either a terminating decimal (e.g., $\frac{1}{4} = 0.25$) or a repeating decimal (e.g., $\frac{1}{3} = 0.3333\ldots$), where some number or series of numbers to the right of the decimal point is repeated indefinitely.

Once the notion of rational numbers is used, there naturally arises the concept of *irrational numbers*—numbers that *cannot* be expressed as ratios of a pair of integers. One example is the number $\sqrt{2} = 1.4142\ldots$, which is a nonrepeating, nonterminating decimal. Another is the special constant $\pi = 3.1415\ldots$ (representing the ratio of the circumference of any circle to its diameter), which is again a nonrepeating, nonterminating decimal, as is characteristic of all irrational numbers.

Each irrational number, if placed on a ruler, would fall between two rational numbers, so that, just as the fractions fill in the gaps between the integers on a ruler, the irrational numbers fill in the gaps between rational numbers. The result of this filling-in process is a continuum of numbers, all of which are so-called real numbers. This continuum constitutes the *set of all real numbers,* which is often denoted by the symbol R. When the set R is displayed on a straight line (an extended ruler), we refer to the line as the *real line.*

In Fig. 2.1 are listed (in the order discussed) all the number sets, arranged in relationship to one another. If we read from bottom to top, however, we find in effect a classificatory scheme in which the set of real numbers is broken down into its component and subcomponent number sets. This figure therefore is a summary of the structure of the real-number system.

Real numbers are all we need for the first 15 chapters of this book, but they are not the only numbers used in mathematics. In fact, the reason for the term *real* is that there are also "imaginary" numbers, which have to do with the square roots of negative numbers. That concept will be discussed later, in Chap. 16.

2.3 The Concept of Sets

We have already employed the word *set* several times. Inasmuch as the concept of sets underlies every branch of modern mathematics, it is desirable to familiarize ourselves at least with its more basic aspects.

Set Notation

A *set* is simply a collection of distinct objects. These objects may be a group of (distinct) numbers, persons, food items, or something else. Thus, all the students enrolled in a particular economics course can be considered a set, just as the three integers 2, 3, and 4 can form a set. The objects in a set are called the *elements* of the set.

There are two alternative ways of writing a set: by *enumeration* and by *description*. If we let S represent the set of three numbers 2, 3, and 4, we can write, by enumeration of the elements,

$$S = \{2, 3, 4\}$$

But if we let I denote the set of *all* positive integers, enumeration becomes difficult, and we may instead simply describe the elements and write

$$I = \{x \mid x \text{ a positive integer}\}$$

which is read as follows: "I is the set of all (numbers) x, such that x is a positive integer." Note that a pair of braces is used to enclose the set in either case. In the descriptive approach, a vertical bar (or a colon) is always inserted to separate the general designating symbol for the elements from the description of the elements. As another example, the set of all real numbers greater than 2 but less than 5 (call it J) can be expressed symbolically as

$$J = \{x \mid 2 < x < 5\}$$

Here, even the descriptive statement is symbolically expressed.

A set with a finite number of elements, exemplified by the previously given set S, is called a *finite set*. Set I and set J, each with an infinite number of elements, are, on the other hand, examples of an *infinite set*. Finite sets are always *denumerable* (or *countable*), i.e., their elements can be counted one by one in the sequence 1, 2, 3, ... Infinite sets may, however, be either denumerable (set I), or *nondenumerable* (set J). In the latter case, there is no way to associate the elements of the set with the natural counting numbers 1, 2, 3, . . . , and thus the set is not countable.

Membership in a set is indicated by the symbol $\in$ (a variant of the Greek letter epsilon ϵ for "element"), which is read as follows: "is an element of." Thus, for the two sets S and I defined previously, we may write

$$2 \in S \quad 3 \in S \quad 8 \in I \quad 9 \in I \quad \text{(etc.)}$$

but obviously $8 \notin S$ (read: "8 is not an element of set S"). If we use the symbol R to denote the set of all real numbers, then the statement "x is some real number" can be simply expressed by

$$x \in R$$

Relationships between Sets

When two sets are compared with each other, several possible kinds of relationship may be observed. If two sets S_1 and S_2 happen to contain identical elements,

$$S_1 = \{2, 7, a, f\} \quad \text{and} \quad S_2 = \{2, a, 7, f\}$$

then S_1 and S_2 are said to be *equal* ($S_1 = S_2$). Note that the order of appearance of the elements in a set is immaterial. Whenever we find even one element to be different in any two sets, however, those two sets are not equal.

Another kind of set relationship is that one set may be a *subset* of another set. If we have two sets

$$S = \{1, 3, 5, 7, 9\} \qquad \text{and} \qquad T = \{3, 7\}$$

then T is a subset of S, because every element of T is also an element of S. A more formal statement of this is: T is a subset of S if and only if $x \in T$ implies $x \in S$. Using the set inclusion symbols $\subset$ (is contained in) and $\supset$ (includes), we may then write

$$T \subset S \qquad \text{or} \qquad S \supset T$$

It is possible that two given sets happen to be subsets of each other. When this occurs, however, we can be sure that these two sets are equal. To state this formally: we can have $S_1 \subset S_2$ and $S_2 \subset S_1$ if and only if $S_1 = S_2$.

Note that, whereas the $\in$ symbol relates an individual *element* to a *set,* the $\subset$ symbol relates a *subset* to a *set.* As an application of this idea, we may state on the basis of Fig. 2.1 that the set of all integers is a subset of the set of all rational numbers. Similarly, the set of all rational numbers is a subset of the set of all real numbers.

How many subsets can be formed from the five elements in the set $S = \{1, 3, 5, 7, 9\}$? First of all, each individual element of S can count as a distinct subset of S, such as $\{1\}$ and $\{3\}$. But so can any pair, triple, or quadruple of these elements, such as $\{1, 3\}$, $\{1, 5\}$, and $\{3, 7, 9\}$. Any subset that does *not* contain *all* the elements of S is called a *proper subset* of S. But the set S itself (with all its five elements) can also be considered as one of its own subsets—every element of S is an element of S, and thus the set S itself fulfills the definition of a subset. This is, of course, a limiting case, that from which we get the largest possible subset of S, namely, S itself.

At the other extreme, the smallest possible subset of S is a set that contains no element at all. Such a set is called the *null set,* or *empty set,* denoted by the symbol $\varnothing$ or $\{\ \}$. The reason for considering the null set as a subset of S is quite interesting: If the null set is not a subset of S ($\varnothing \not\subset S$), then $\varnothing$ must contain at least one element x such that $x \notin S$. But since by definition the null set has no element whatsoever, we cannot say that $\varnothing \not\subset S$; hence the null set is a subset of S.

It is extremely important to distinguish the symbol $\varnothing$ or $\{\ \}$ clearly from the notation $\{0\}$; the former is devoid of elements, but the latter does contain an element, zero. The null set is unique; there is only one such set in the whole world, and it is considered a subset of *any* set that can be conceived.

Counting all the subsets of S, including the two limiting cases S and $\varnothing$, we find a total of $2^5 = 32$ subsets. In general, if a set has n elements, a total of 2^n subsets can be formed from those elements.[†]

[†] Given a set with n elements $\{a, b, c, \ldots, n\}$ we may first classify its subsets into two categories: one with the element a in it, and one without. Each of these two can be further classified into two subcategories: one with the element b in it, and one without. Note that by considering the second element b, we double the number of categories in the classification from 2 to 4 ($= 2^2$). By the same token, the consideration of the element c will increase the total number of categories to 8 ($= 2^3$). When all n elements are considered, the total number of categories will become the total number of subsets, and that number is 2^n.

As a third possible type of set relationship, two sets may have no elements in common at all. In that case, the two sets are said to be *disjoint*. For example, the set of all positive integers and the set of all negative integers are mutually exclusive; thus they are disjoint sets.

A fourth type of relationship occurs when two sets have some elements in common but some elements peculiar to each. In that event, the two sets are neither equal nor disjoint; also, neither set is a subset of the other.

Operations on Sets

When we add, subtract, multiply, divide, or take the square root of some numbers, we are performing mathematical operations. Although sets are different from numbers, one can similarly perform certain mathematical operations on them. Three principal operations to be discussed here involve the union, intersection, and complement of sets.

To take the *union* of two sets A and B means to form a new set containing those elements (and only those elements) belonging to A, or to B, or to both A and B. The union set is symbolized by $A \cup B$ (read: "A union B").

Example 1

If $A = \{3, 5, 7\}$ and $B = \{2, 3, 4, 8\}$, then

$$A \cup B = \{2, 3, 4, 5, 7, 8\}$$

This example, incidentally, illustrates the case in which two sets A and B are neither equal nor disjoint and in which neither is a subset of the other.

Example 2

Again referring to Fig. 2.1, we see that the union of the set of all integers and the set of all fractions is the set of all rational numbers. Similarly, the union of the rational-number set and the irrational-number set yields the set of all real numbers.

The *intersection* of two sets A and B, on the other hand, is a new set which contains those elements (and only those elements) belonging to *both A and B*. The intersection set is symbolized by $A \cap B$ (read: "A intersection B").

Example 3

From the sets A and B in Example 1, we can write

$$A \cap B = \{3\}$$

Example 4

If $A = \{-3, 6, 10\}$ and $B = \{9, 2, 7, 4\}$, then $A \cap B = \varnothing$. Set A and set B are disjoint; therefore their intersection is the empty set—no element is common to A and B.

It is obvious that intersection is a more restrictive concept than union. In the former, only the elements *common to A and B* are acceptable, whereas in the latter, membership in *either A or B* is sufficient to establish membership in the union set. The operator symbols $\cap$ and $\cup$—which, incidentally, have the same kind of general status as the symbols $\sqrt{\ }$, $+$, $\div$, etc.—therefore have the connotations "and" and "or," respectively. This point can be better appreciated by comparing the following formal definitions of intersection and union:

Intersection: $\quad A \cap B = \{x \mid x \in A \quad \text{and} \quad x \in B\}$

Union: $\quad\quad\quad A \cup B = \{x \mid x \in A \quad \text{or} \quad x \in B\}$

FIGURE 2.2

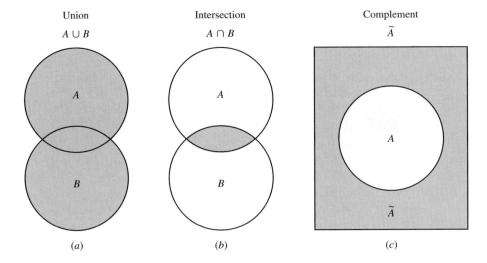

Union
$A \cup B$

Intersection
$A \cap B$

Complement
$\tilde{A}$

(a)   (b)   (c)

What about the *complement* of a set? To explain this, let us first introduce the concept of the *universal set*. In a particular context of discussion, if the only numbers used are the set of the first seven positive integers, we may refer to it as the universal set U. Then, with a given set, say, $A = \{3, 6, 7\}$, we can define another set $\tilde{A}$ (read: "the complement of A") as the set that contains all the numbers in the universal set U that are not in the set A. That is,

$$\tilde{A} = \{x \mid x \in U \quad \text{and} \quad x \notin A\} = \{1, 2, 4, 5\}$$

Note that, whereas the symbol $\cup$ has the connotation "or" and the symbol $\cap$ means "and," the complement symbol $\sim$ carries the implication of "not."

Example 5   If $U = \{5, 6, 7, 8, 9\}$ and $A = \{5, 6\}$, then $\tilde{A} = \{7, 8, 9\}$.

Example 6   What is the complement of U? Since every object (number) under consideration is included in the universal set, the complement of U must be empty. Thus $\tilde{U} = \varnothing$.

The three types of set operation can be visualized in the three diagrams of Fig. 2.2, known as *Venn diagrams*. In diagram *a*, the points in the upper circle form a set A, and the points in the lower circle form a set B. The union of A and B then consists of the shaded area covering both circles. In diagram *b* are shown the same two sets (circles). Since their intersection should comprise only the points common to both sets, only the (shaded) overlapping portion of the two circles satisfies the definition. In diagram *c*, let the points in the rectangle be the universal set and let A be the set of points in the circle; then the complement set $\tilde{A}$ will be the (shaded) area outside the circle.

Laws of Set Operations

From Fig. 2.2, it may be noted that the shaded area in diagram *a* represents not only $A \cup B$ but also $B \cup A$. Analogously, in diagram *b* the small shaded area is the visual

FIGURE 2.3

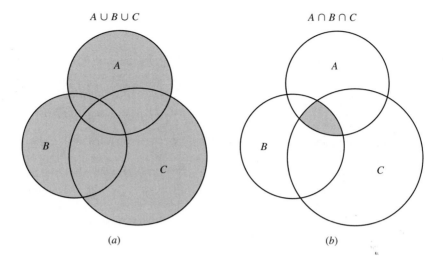

$A \cup B \cup C$ $A \cap B \cap C$

(a)   *(b)*

representation not only of $A \cap B$ but also of $B \cap A$. When formalized, this result is known as the *commutative law* (of unions and intersections):

$$A \cup B = B \cup A \qquad A \cap B = B \cap A$$

These relations are very similar to the algebraic laws $a + b = b + a$ and $a \times b = b \times a$.

To take the union of three sets A, B, and C, we first take the union of any two sets and then "union" the resulting set with the third; a similar procedure is applicable to the intersection operation. The results of such operations are illustrated in Fig. 2.3. It is interesting that the order in which the sets are selected for the operation is immaterial. This fact gives rise to the *associative law* (of unions and intersections):

$$A \cup (B \cup C) = (A \cup B) \cup C$$

$$A \cap (B \cap C) = (A \cap B) \cap C$$

These equations are strongly reminiscent of the algebraic laws $a + (b + c) = (a + b) + c$ and $a \times (b \times c) = (a \times b) \times c$.

There is also a law of operation that applies when unions and intersections are used in combination. This is the *distributive law* (of unions and intersections):

$$A \cup (B \cap C) = (A \cup B) \cap (A \cup C)$$

$$A \cap (B \cup C) = (A \cap B) \cup (A \cap C)$$

These resemble the algebraic law $a \times (b + c) = (a \times b) + (a \times c)$.

Example 7
Verify the distributive law, given $A = \{4, 5\}$, $B = \{3, 6, 7\}$, and $C = \{2, 3\}$. To verify the first part of the law, we find the left- and right-hand expressions separately:

Left: $A \cup (B \cap C) = \{4, 5\} \cup \{3\} = \{3, 4, 5\}$

Right: $(A \cup B) \cap (A \cup C) = \{3, 4, 5, 6, 7\} \cap \{2, 3, 4, 5\} = \{3, 4, 5\}$

Since the two sides yield the same result, the law is verified. Repeating the procedure for the second part of the law, we have

Left: $A \cap (B \cup C) = \{4, 5\} \cap \{2, 3, 6, 7\} = \emptyset$

Right: $(A \cap B) \cup (A \cap C) = \emptyset \cup \emptyset = \emptyset$

Thus the law is again verified.

To verify a law means to check by a specific example whether the law actually works out. If the law is valid, then any specific example ought indeed to work out. This implies that if the law does not check out in as many as one single example, then the law is invalidated. On the other hand, the successful verification by specific examples (however many) does not in itself prove the law. To *prove* a law, it is necessary to demonstrate that the law is valid for all possible cases. The procedure involved in such a demonstration will be illustrated later (see, e.g., Sec. 2.5).

EXERCISE 2.3

1. Write the following in set notation:
   (a) The set of all real numbers greater than 34.
   (b) The set of all real numbers greater than 8 but less than 65.

2. Given the sets $S_1 = \{2, 4, 6\}$, $S_2 = \{7, 2, 6\}$, $S_3 = \{4, 2, 6\}$, and $S_4 = \{2, 4\}$, which of the following statements are true?
   (a) $S_1 = S_3$
   (b) $S_1 = R$ (set of real numbers)
   (c) $8 \in S_2$
   (d) $3 \notin S_2$
   (e) $4 \notin S_3$
   (f) $S_4 \subset R$
   (g) $S_1 \supset S_4$
   (h) $\emptyset \subset S_2$
   (i) $S_3 \supset \{1, 2\}$

3. Referring to the four sets given in Prob. 2, find:
   (a) $S_1 \cup S_2$
   (b) $S_1 \cup S_3$
   (c) $S_2 \cap S_3$
   (d) $S_2 \cap S_4$
   (e) $S_4 \cap S_2 \cap S_1$
   (f) $S_3 \cup S_1 \cup S_4$

4. Which of the following statements are valid?
   (a) $A \cup A = A$
   (b) $A \cap A = A$
   (c) $A \cup \emptyset = A$
   (d) $A \cup U = U$
   (e) $A \cap \emptyset = \emptyset$
   (f) $A \cap U = A$
   (g) The complement of $\tilde{A}$ is A.

5. Given $A = \{4, 5, 6\}$, $B = \{3, 4, 6, 7\}$, and $C = \{2, 3, 6\}$, verify the distributive law.

6. Verify the distributive law by means of Venn diagrams, with different orders of successive shading.

7. Enumerate all the subsets of the set $\{5, 6, 7\}$.

8. Enumerate all the subsets of the set $S = \{a, b, c, d\}$. How many subsets are there altogether?

9. Example 6 shows that $\emptyset$ is the complement of U. But since the null set is a subset of *any* set, $\emptyset$ must be a subset of U. Inasmuch as the term "complement of U" implies the notion of being *not in U*, whereas the term "subset of U" implies the notion of being *in U*, it seems paradoxical for $\emptyset$ to be both of these. How do you resolve this paradox?

2.4 Relations and Functions

Our discussion of sets was prompted by the usage of that term in connection with the various kinds of numbers in our number system. However, sets can refer as well to objects other than numbers. In particular, we can speak of sets of "ordered pairs"—to be defined presently—which will lead us to the important concepts of relations and functions.

Ordered Pairs

In writing a set $\{a, b\}$, we do not care about the order in which the elements a and b appear, because by definition $\{a, b\} = \{b, a\}$. The pair of elements a and b is in this case an *unordered pair*. When the ordering of a and b does carry a significance, however, we can write two different *ordered pairs* denoted by (a, b) and (b, a), which have the property that $(a, b) \neq (b, a)$ unless $a = b$. Similar concepts apply to a set with more than two elements, in which case we can distinguish between ordered and unordered triples, quadruples, quintuples, and so forth. Ordered pairs, triples, etc., collectively can be called *ordered sets;* they are enclosed with parentheses rather than braces.

Example 1
To show the age and weight of each student in a class, we can form ordered pairs (a, w), in which the first element indicates the age (in years) and the second element indicates the weight (in pounds). Then (19, 127) and (127, 19) would obviously mean different things. Moreover, the latter ordered pair would hardly fit any student anywhere.

Example 2
When we speak of the set of all contestants in an Olympic game, the order in which they are listed is of no consequence and we have an unordered set. But the set {gold-medalist, silver-medalist, bronze-medalist} is an ordered triple.

Ordered pairs, like other objects, can be elements of a set. Consider the rectangular (Cartesian) coordinate plane in Fig. 2.4, where an x axis and a y axis cross each other at a right angle, dividing the plane into four quadrants. This xy plane is an infinite set of points, each of which represents an ordered pair whose first element is an x value and the second element a y value. Clearly, the point labeled (4, 2) is different from the point (2, 4); thus ordering is significant here.

FIGURE 2.4

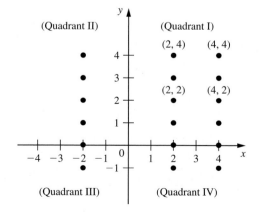

With this visual understanding, we are ready to consider the process of generation of ordered pairs. Suppose, from two given sets, $x = \{1, 2\}$ and $y = \{3, 4\}$, we wish to form all the possible ordered pairs with the first element taken from set x and the second element taken from set y. The result will, of course, be the set of four ordered pairs (1, 3), (1, 4), (2, 3), and (2, 4). This set is called the *Cartesian product* (named after Descartes), or *direct product,* of the sets x and y and is denoted by $x \times y$ (read: "x cross y"). It is important to remember that, while x and y are sets of numbers, the Cartesian product turns out to be a set of ordered pairs. By enumeration, or by description, we may express this Cartesian product alternatively as

$$x \times y = \{(1, 3), (1, 4), (2, 3), (2, 4)\}$$

or
$$x \times y = \{(a, b) \mid a \in x \text{ and } b \in y\}$$

The latter expression may in fact be taken as the general definition of Cartesian product for any given sets x and y.

To broaden our horizon, now let both x and y include all the real numbers. Then the resulting Cartesian product

$$x \times y = \{(a, b) \mid a \in R \text{ and } b \in R\} \qquad \textbf{(2.3)}$$

will represent the set of all ordered pairs with real-valued elements. Besides, each ordered pair corresponds to a *unique* point in the Cartesian coordinate plane of Fig. 2.4, and, conversely, each point in the coordinate plane also corresponds to a *unique* ordered pair in the set $x \times y$. In view of this double uniqueness, a *one-to-one correspondence* is said to exist between the set of ordered pairs in the Cartesian product (2.3) and the set of points in the rectangular coordinate plane. The rationale for the notation $x \times y$ is now easy to perceive; we may associate it with the crossing of the x axis and the y axis in Fig. 2.4. A simpler way of expressing the set $x \times y$ in (2.3) is to write it directly as $R \times R$; this is also commonly denoted by R^2.

Extending this idea, we may also define the Cartesian product of three sets $x, y,$ and z as follows:

$$x \times y \times z = \{(a, b, c) \mid a \in x, b \in y, c \in z\}$$

which is a set of ordered triples. Furthermore, if the sets $x, y,$ and z each consist of all the real numbers, the Cartesian product will correspond to the set of all points in a three-dimensional space. This may be denoted by $R \times R \times R$, or more simply, R^3. In the present discussion, all the variables are taken to be real-valued; thus the framework will generally be R^2, or $R^3, \ldots,$ or R^n.

Relations and Functions

Since any ordered pair associates a y value with an x value, any collection of ordered pairs—any subset of the Cartesian product (2.3)—will constitute a *relation* between y and x. Given an x value, one or more y values will be specified by that relation. For convenience, we shall now write the elements of $x \times y$ generally as (x, y)—rather than as (a, b), as was done in (2.3)—where both x and y are variables.

Example 3

The set $\{(x, y) \mid y = 2x\}$ is a set of ordered pairs including, for example, (1, 2), (0, 0), and $(-1, -2)$. It constitutes a relation, and its graphical counterpart is the set of points lying on the straight line $y = 2x$, as seen in Fig. 2.5.

FIGURE 2.5

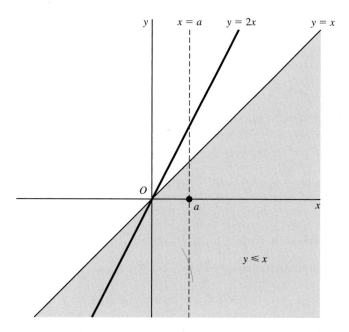

Example 4

The set $\{(x, y) \mid y \leq x\}$, which consists of such ordered pairs as $(1, 0)$, $(1, 1)$, and $(1, -4)$, constitutes another relation. In Fig. 2.5, this set corresponds to the set of all points in the shaded area which satisfy the inequality $y \leq x$.

Observe that, when the x value is given, it may not always be possible to determine a *unique* y value from a relation. In Example 4, the three exemplary ordered pairs show that if $x = 1$, y can take various values, such as 0, 1, or -4, and yet in each case satisfy the stated relation. Graphically, two or more points of a relation may fall on a single vertical line in the xy plane. This is exemplified in Fig. 2.5, where many points in the shaded area (representing the relation $y \leq x$) fall on the broken vertical line labeled $x = a$.

As a special case, however, a relation may be such that for each x value there exists only *one* corresponding y value. The relation in Example 3 is a case in point. In such a case, y is said to be a *function* of x, and this is denoted by $y = f(x)$, which is read as "y equals f of x." [*Note:* $f(x)$ does *not* mean f times x.] A function is therefore a set of ordered pairs with the property that any x value *uniquely* determines a y value.[†] It should be clear that a function must be a relation, but a relation may not be a function.

Although the definition of a function stipulates a unique y for each x, the converse is not required. In other words, more than one x value may legitimately be associated with the same y value. This possibility is illustrated in Fig. 2.6, where the values x_1 and x_2 in the x set are both associated with the same value (y_0) in the y set by the function $y = f(x)$.

A function is also called a *mapping,* or *transformation;* both words connote the action of associating one thing with another. In the statement $y = f(x)$, the functional notation f

[†] This definition of *function* corresponds to what would be called a *single-valued function* in the older terminology. What was formerly called a *multivalued function* is now referred to as a *relation* or *correspondence.*

FIGURE 2.6

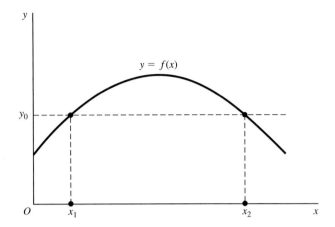

may thus be interpreted to mean a rule by which the set *x* is "mapped" ("transformed") into the set *y*. Thus we may write

$$f : x \rightarrow y$$

where the arrow indicates mapping, and the letter *f* symbolically specifies a rule of mapping. Since *f* represents a *particular* rule of mapping, a different functional notation must be employed to denote another function that may appear in the same model. The customary symbols (besides *f*) used for this purpose are g, F, G, the Greek letters ϕ (phi) and ψ (psi), and their capitals, Φ and Ψ. For instance, two variables y and z may both be functions of x, but if one function is written as $y = f(x)$, the other should be written as $z = g(x)$, or $z = \phi(x)$. It is also permissible, however, to write $y = y(x)$ and $z = z(x)$, thereby dispensing with the symbols *f* and *g* altogether.

In the function $y = f(x)$, x is referred to as the *argument* of the function, and y is called the *value* of the function. We shall also alternatively refer to x as the *independent variable* and y as the *dependent variable*. The set of all permissible values that x can take in a given context is known as the *domain* of the function, which may be a subset of the set of all real numbers. The y value into which an x value is mapped is called the *image* of that x value. The set of all images is called the *range* of the function, which is the set of all values that the y variable can take. Thus the domain pertains to the independent variable x, and the range has to do with the dependent variable y.

As illustrated in Fig. 2.7a, we may regard the function *f* as a rule for mapping each point on some line segment (the domain) into some point on another line segment (the range). By placing the domain on the x axis and the range on the y axis, as in Fig. 2.7b, however, we immediately obtain the familiar two-dimensional graph, in which the association between x values and y values is specified by a set of ordered pairs such as (x_1, y_1) and (x_2, y_2).

In economic models, behavioral equations usually enter as functions. Since most variables in economic models are by their nature restricted to being nonnegative real numbers,[†] their domains are also so restricted. This is why most geometric representations in

---

[†] We say "nonnegative" rather than "positive" when zero values are permissible.

FIGURE 2.7

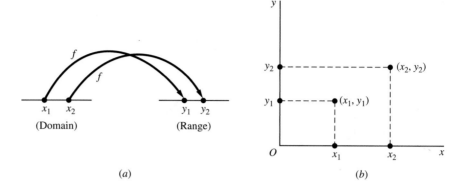

(a)   (b)

economics are drawn only in the first quadrant. In general, we shall not bother to specify the domain of every function in every economic model. When no specification is given, it is to be understood that the domain (and the range) will only include numbers for which a function makes economic sense.

Example 5

The total cost C of a firm per day is a function of its daily output Q: $C = 150 + 7Q$. The firm has a capacity limit of 100 units of output per day. What are the domain and the range of the cost function? Inasmuch as Q can vary only between 0 and 100, the domain is the set of values $0 \leq Q \leq 100$; or more formally,

$$\text{Domain} = \{Q \mid 0 \leq Q \leq 100\}$$

As for the range, since the function plots as a straight line, with the minimum C value at 150 (when $Q = 0$) and the maximum C value at 850 (when $Q = 100$), we have

$$\text{Range} = \{C \mid 150 \leq C \leq 850\}$$

Beware, however, that the extreme values of the range may not always occur where the extreme values of the domain are attained.

EXERCISE 2.4

1. Given $S_1 = \{3, 6, 9\}$, $S_2 = \{a, b\}$, and $S_3 = \{m, n\}$, find the Cartesian products:
   (a) $S_1 \times S_2$ (b) $S_2 \times S_3$ (c) $S_3 \times S_1$
2. From the information in Prob. 1, find the Cartesian product $S_1 \times S_2 \times S_3$.
3. In general, is it true that $S_1 \times S_2 = S_2 \times S_1$? Under what conditions will these two Cartesian products be equal?
4. Does any of the following, drawn in a rectangular coordinate plane, represent a function?
   (a) A circle   (c) A rectangle
   (b) A triangle   (d) A downward-sloping straight line
5. If the domain of the function $y = 5 + 3x$ is the set $\{x \mid 1 \leq x \leq 9\}$, find the range of the function and express it as a set.

6. For the function $y = -x^2$, if the domain is the set of all nonnegative real numbers, what will its range be?

7. In the theory of the firm, economists consider the total cost C to be a function of the output level Q: $C = f(Q)$.

   (*a*) According to the definition of a function, should each cost figure be associated with a unique level of output?

   (*b*) Should each level of output determine a unique cost figure?

8. If an output level Q_1 can be produced at a cost of C_1, then it must also be possible (by being less efficient) to produce Q_1 at a cost of $C_1 + \$1$, or $C_1 + \$2$, and so on. Thus it would seem that output Q does not uniquely determine total cost C. If so, to write $C = f(Q)$ would violate the definition of a function. How, in spite of the this reasoning, would you justify the use of the function $C = f(Q)$?

2.5 Types of Function

The expression $y = f(x)$ is a general statement to the effect that a mapping is possible, but the actual rule of mapping is not thereby made explicit. Now let us consider several specific types of function, each representing a different rule of mapping.

Constant Functions

A function whose range consists of only one element is called a *constant function*. As an example, we cite the function

$$y = f(x) = 7$$

which is alternatively expressible as $y = 7$ or $f(x) = 7$, whose value stays the same regardless of the value of x. In the coordinate plane, such a function will appear as a horizontal straight line. In national-income models, when investment I is exogenously determined, we may have an investment function of the form $I = \$100$ million, or $I = I_0$, which exemplifies the constant function.

Polynomial Functions

The constant function is actually a "degenerate" case of what are known as *polynomial functions*. The word *polynomial* means "multiterm," and a polynomial function of a single variable x has the general form

$$y = a_0 + a_1x + a_2x^2 + \cdots + a_nx^n \tag{2.4}$$

in which each term contains a coefficient as well as a nonnegative-integer power of the variable x. (As will be explained later in this section, we can write $x^1 = x$ and $x^0 = 1$ in general; thus the first two terms may be taken to be a_0x^0 and a_1x^1, respectively.) Note that, instead of the symbols $a, b, c, \ldots$, we have employed the subscripted symbols a_0, $a_1, \ldots, a_n$ for the coefficients. This is motivated by two considerations: (1) we can economize on symbols, since only the letter a is "used up" in this way; and (2) the subscript helps to pinpoint the location of a particular coefficient in the entire equation. For instance, in (2.4), a_2 is the coefficient of x^2, and so forth.

Depending on the value of the integer n (which specifies the highest power of x), we have several subclasses of polynomial function:

Case of $n = 0$: $y = a_0$ [*constant* function]

Case of $n = 1$: $y = a_0 + a_1 x$ [*linear* function]

Case of $n = 2$: $y = a_0 + a_1 x + a_2 x^2$ [*quadratic* function]

Case of $n = 3$: $y = a_0 + a_1 x + a_2 x^2 + a_3 x^3$ [*cubic* function]

and so forth. The superscript indicators of the powers of x are called *exponents*. The highest power involved, i.e., the value of n, is often called the *degree* of the polynomial function; a quadratic function, for instance, is a second-degree polynomial, and a cubic function is a third-degree polynomial.[†] The order in which the several terms appear to the right of the equals sign is inconsequential; they may be arranged in descending order of power instead. Also, even though we have put the symbol y on the left, it is also acceptable to write $f(x)$ in its place.

When plotted in the coordinate plane, a linear function will appear as a straight line, as illustrated in Fig. 2.8a. When $x = 0$, the linear function yields $y = a_0$; thus the ordered pair $(0, a_0)$ is on the line. This gives us the so-called y intercept (or *vertical intercept*), because it is at this point that the vertical axis intersects the line. The other coefficient, a_1, measures the *slope* (the steepness of incline) of our line. This means that a unit increase in x will result in an increment in y in the amount of a_1. What Fig. 2.8a illustrates is the case of $a_1 > 0$, involving a positive slope and thus an upward-sloping line; if $a_1 < 0$, the line will be downward-sloping.

A quadratic function, on the other hand, plots as a *parabola*—roughly, a curve with a single built-in bump or wiggle. The particular illustration in Fig. 2.8b implies a negative a_2; in the case of $a_2 > 0$, the curve will "open" the other way, displaying a valley rather than a hill. The graph of a cubic function will, in general, manifest two wiggles, as illustrated in Fig. 2.8c. These functions will be used quite frequently in the economic models subsequently discussed.

Rational Functions

A function such as

$$y = \frac{x - 1}{x^2 + 2x + 4}$$

in which y is expressed as a ratio of two polynomials in the variable x, is known as a *rational function*. According to this definition, any polynomial function must itself be a rational function, because it can always be expressed as a ratio to 1, and 1 is a constant function.

A special rational function that has interesting applications in economics is the function

$$y = \frac{a}{x} \qquad \text{or} \qquad xy = a$$

which plots as a *rectangular hyperbola,* as in Fig. 2.8d. Since the product of the two variables is always a fixed constant in this case, this function may be used to represent that special demand curve—with price P and quantity Q on the two axes—for which the total

---

[†] In the several equations just cited, the last coefficient (a_n) is always assumed to be nonzero; otherwise the function would degenerate into a lower-degree polynomial.

FIGURE 2.8

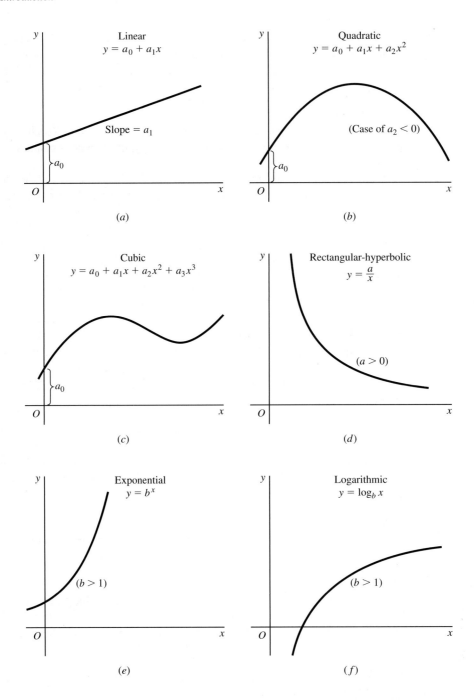

(a) Linear $y = a_0 + a_1x$; Slope $= a_1$; a_0

(b) Quadratic $y = a_0 + a_1x + a_2x^2$; (Case of $a_2 < 0$); a_0

(c) Cubic $y = a_0 + a_1x + a_2x^2 + a_3x^3$; a_0

(d) Rectangular-hyperbolic $y = \dfrac{a}{x}$; $(a > 0)$

(e) Exponential $y = b^x$; $(b > 1)$

(f) Logarithmic $y = \log_b x$; $(b > 1)$

expenditure PQ is constant at all levels of price. (Such a demand curve is the one with a unitary elasticity at each point on the curve.) Another application is to the average fixed cost (AFC) curve. With AFC on one axis and output Q on the other, the AFC curve must be rectangular-hyperbolic because AFC $\times$ Q($=$ total fixed cost) is a fixed constant.

The rectangular hyperbola drawn from $xy = a$ never meets the axes, even if extended indefinitely upward and to the right. Rather, the curve approaches the axes *asymptotically:* as y becomes very large, the curve will come ever closer to the y axis but never actually reach it, and similarly for the x axis. The axes constitute the *asymptotes* of this function.

Nonalgebraic Functions

Any function expressed in terms of polynomials and/or roots (such as square root) of polynomials is an *algebraic function.* Accordingly, the functions discussed thus far are all algebraic.

However, *exponential functions* such as $y = b^x$, in which the independent variable appears in the exponent, are *nonalgebraic.* The closely related *logarithmic functions,* such as $y = \log_b x$, are also nonalgebraic. These two types of function have a special role to play in certain types of economic applications, and it is pedagogically desirable to postpone their discussion to Chap. 10. Here, we simply preview their general graphic shapes in Fig. 2.8*e* and *f.* Other types of nonalgebraic function are the *trigonometric* (or *circular*) *functions,* which we shall discuss in Chap. 16 in connection with dynamic analysis. We should add here that nonalgebraic functions are also known by the more esoteric name of *transcendental functions.*

A Digression on Exponents

In discussing polynomial functions, we introduced the term *exponents* as indicators of the power to which a variable (or number) is to be raised. The expression 6^2 means that 6 is to be raised to the second power; that is, 6 is to be multiplied by itself, or $6^2 \equiv 6 \times 6 = 36$. In general, we define, for a positive integer n,

$$x^n \equiv \underbrace{x \times x \times \cdots \times x}_{n \text{ terms}}$$

and as a special case, we note that $x^1 = x$. From the general definition, it follows that for positive integers m and n, exponents obey the following rules:

Rule I $\qquad x^m \times x^n = x^{m+n} \qquad$ (for example, $x^3 \times x^4 = x^7$)

PROOF $\qquad x^m \times x^n = \Big(\underbrace{x \times x \times \cdots \times x}_{m \text{ terms}}\Big)\Big(\underbrace{x \times x \times \cdots \times x}_{n \text{ terms}}\Big)$

$$= \underbrace{x \times x \times \cdots \times x}_{m+n \text{ terms}} = x^{m+n}$$

Note that in this proof, we did not assign any specific value to the number x, or to the exponents m and n. Thus the result obtained is *generally* true. It is for this reason that the demonstration given constitutes a proof, as against a mere verification. The same can be said about the proof of Rule II which follows.

Rule II $\qquad \dfrac{x^m}{x^n} = x^{m-n} \qquad (x \neq 0) \qquad \left(\text{for example, } \dfrac{x^4}{x^3} = x\right)$

PROOF $\qquad \dfrac{x^m}{x^n} = \dfrac{\overbrace{x \times x \times \cdots \times x}^{m \text{ terms}}}{\underbrace{x \times x \times \cdots \times x}_{n \text{ terms}}} = \underbrace{x \times x \times \cdots \times x}_{m-n \text{ terms}} = x^{m-n}$

because the n terms in the denominator cancel out n of the m terms in the numerator. Note that the case of $x = 0$ is ruled out in the statement of this rule. This is because when $x = 0$, the expression x^m/x^n would involve division by zero, which is undefined.

What if $m < n$, say, $m = 2$ and $n = 5$? In that case we get, according to Rule II, $x^{m-n} = x^{-3}$, a *negative power* of x. What does this mean? The answer is actually supplied by Rule II itself: When $m = 2$ and $n = 5$, we have

$$\frac{x^2}{x^5} = \frac{x \times x}{x \times x \times x \times x \times x} = \frac{1}{x \times x \times x} = \frac{1}{x^3}$$

Thus $x^{-3} = 1/x^3$, and this may be generalized into another rule:

Rule III $\qquad\qquad\qquad\qquad x^{-n} = \dfrac{1}{x^n} \qquad (x \neq 0)$

To raise a (nonzero) number to a power of *negative n* is to take the *reciprocal* of its nth power.

Another special case in the application of Rule II is when $m = n$, which yields the expression $x^{m-n} = x^{m-m} = x^0$. To interpret the meaning of raising a number x to the zeroth power, we can write out the term x^{m-m} in accordance with Rule II, with the result that $x^m/x^m = 1$. Thus we may conclude that any (nonzero) number raised to the zeroth power is equal to 1. (The expression 0^0 is undefined.) This may be expressed as another rule:

Rule IV $\qquad\qquad\qquad\qquad\qquad x^0 = 1 \qquad (x \neq 0)$

As long as we are concerned only with polynomial functions, only (nonnegative) integer powers are required. In exponential functions, however, the exponent is a variable that can take noninteger values as well. In order to interpret a number such as $x^{1/2}$, let us consider the fact that, by Rule I, we have

$$x^{1/2} \times x^{1/2} = x^1 = x$$

Since $x^{1/2}$ multiplied by itself is x, $x^{1/2}$ must be the square root of x. Similarly, $x^{1/3}$ can be shown to be the cube root of x. In general, therefore, we can state the following rule:

Rule V $\qquad\qquad\qquad\qquad\qquad x^{1/n} = \sqrt[n]{x}$

Two other rules obeyed by exponents are

Rule VI $\qquad\qquad\qquad\qquad\qquad (x^m)^n = x^{mn}$

Rule VII $\qquad\qquad\qquad\qquad\qquad x^m \times y^m = (xy)^m$

EXERCISE 2.5

1. Graph the functions
   (a) $y = 16 + 2x$ $\qquad\qquad$ (b) $y = 8 - 2x$ $\qquad\qquad$ (c) $y = 2x + 12$
   (In each case, consider the domain as consisting of nonnegative real numbers only.)
2. What is the major difference between (a) and (b) in Prob. 1? How is this difference reflected in the graphs? What is the major difference between (a) and (c)? How do their graphs reflect it?

3. Graph the functions

   (a) $y = -x^2 + 5x - 2$ (b) $y = x^2 + 5x - 2$

   with the set of values $-5 \leq x \leq 5$ constituting the domain. It is well known that the sign of the coefficient of the x^2 term determines whether the graph of a quadratic function will have a "hill" or a "valley." On the basis of the present problem, which sign is associated with the hill? Supply an intuitive explanation for this.

4. Graph the function $y = 36/x$, assuming that x and y can take positive values only. Next, suppose that both variables can take negative values as well; how must the graph be modified to reflect this change in assumption?

5. Condense the following expressions:

   (a) $x^4 \times x^{15}$ (b) $x^a \times x^b \times x^c$ (c) $x^3 \times y^3 \times z^3$

6. Find: (a) x^3/x^{-3} (b) $(x^{1/2} \times x^{1/3})/x^{2/3}$

7. Show that $x^{m/n} = \sqrt[n]{x^m} = (\sqrt[n]{x})^m$. Specify the rules applied in each step.

8. Prove Rule VI and Rule VII.

2.6 Functions of Two or More Independent Variables

Thus far, we have considered only functions of a single independent variable, $y = f(x)$. But the concept of a function can be readily extended to the case of two or more independent variables. Given a function

$$z = g(x, y)$$

a given pair of x and y values will uniquely determine a value of the dependent variable z. Such a function is exemplified by

$$z = ax + by \qquad \text{or} \qquad z = a_0 + a_1 x + a_2 x^2 + b_1 y + b_2 y^2$$

Just as the function $y = f(x)$ maps a point in the domain into a point in the range, the function g will do precisely the same. However, the domain is in this case no longer a set of numbers but a set of ordered pairs (x, y), because we can determine z only when *both x and y* are specified. The function g is thus a mapping from a point in a two-dimensional space into a point on a line segment (i.e., a point in a one-dimensional space), such as from the point (x_1, y_1) into the point z_1 or from (x_2, y_2) into z_2 in Fig. 2.9a.

If a vertical z axis is erected perpendicular to the xy plane, as is done in diagram b, however, there will result a three-dimensional space in which the function g can be given a graphical representation as follows. The domain of the function will be some subset of the points in the xy plane, and the value of the function (value of z) for a given point in the domain—say, (x_1, y_1)—can be indicated by the height of a vertical line planted on that point. The association between the three variables is thus summarized by the ordered triple (x_1, y_1, z_1), which is a specific point in the three-dimensional space. The locus of such ordered triples, which will take the form of a *surface,* then constitutes the graph of the function g. Whereas the function $y = f(x)$ is a set of ordered *pairs,* the function $z = g(x, y)$ will be a set of ordered *triples.* We shall have many occasions to use functions of this type

FIGURE 2.9

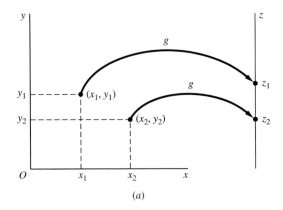

(a)

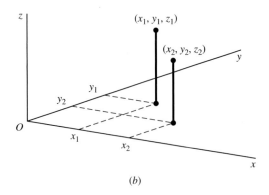

(b)

in economic models. One ready application is in the area of production functions. Suppose that output is determined by the amounts of capital (K) and labor (L) employed; then we can write a production function in the general form $Q = Q(K, L)$.

The possibility of further extension to the cases of three or more independent variables is now self-evident. With the function $y = h(u, v, w)$, for example, we can map a point in the three-dimensional space, (u_1, v_1, w_1), into a point in a one-dimensional space (y_1). Such a function might be used to indicate that a consumer's utility is a function of his or her consumption of three different commodities, and the mapping is from a three-dimensional commodity space into a one-dimensional utility space. But this time it will be physically impossible to graph the function, because for that task a four-dimensional diagram is needed to picture the ordered quadruples, but the world in which we live is only three-dimensional. Nonetheless, in view of the intuitive appeal of geometric analogy, we can continue to refer to an ordered quadruple (u_1, v_1, w_1, y_1) as a "point" in the four-dimensional space. The locus of such points will give the (nongraphable) "graph" of the function $y = h(u, v, w)$, which is called a *hypersurface*. These terms, viz., point and hypersurface, are also carried over to the general case of the n-dimensional space.

Functions of more than one variable can be classified into various types, too. For instance, a function of the form

$$y = a_1 x_1 + a_2 x_2 + \cdots + a_n x_n$$

is a *linear* function, whose characteristic is that every variable is raised to the first power only. A *quadratic* function, on the other hand, involves first and second powers of one or more independent variables, but the sum of exponents of the variables appearing in any single term must not exceed 2.

Note that instead of denoting the independent variables by x, u, v, w, etc., we have switched to the symbols $x_1, x_2, \ldots, x_n$. The latter notation, like the system of subscripted coefficients, has the merit of economy of alphabet, as well as of an easier accounting of the number of variables involved in a function.

2.7 Levels of Generality

In discussing the various types of function, we have without explicit notice introduced examples of functions that pertain to varying levels of generality. In certain instances, we have written functions in the form

$$y = 7 \qquad y = 6x + 4 \qquad y = x^2 - 3x + 1 \qquad \text{(etc.)}$$

Not only are these expressed in terms of numerical coefficients, but they also indicate specifically whether each function is constant, linear, or quadratic. In terms of graphs, each such function will give rise to a well-defined unique curve. In view of the numerical nature of these functions, the solutions of the model based on them will emerge as numerical values also. The drawback is that, if we wish to know how our analytical conclusion will change when a different set of numerical coefficients comes into effect, we must go through the reasoning process afresh each time. Thus, the results obtained from specific functions have very little generality.

On a more general level of discussion and analysis, there are functions in the form

$$y = a \qquad y = a + bx \qquad y = a + bx + cx^2 \qquad \text{(etc.)}$$

Since parameters are used, each function represents not a single curve but a whole family of curves. The function $y = a$, for instance, encompasses not only the specific cases $y = 0$, $y = 1$, and $y = 2$ but also $y = \frac{1}{3}$, $y = -5, \ldots$, ad infinitum. With parametric functions, the outcome of mathematical operations will also be in terms of parameters. These results are more general in the sense that, by assigning various values to the parameters appearing in the solution of the model, a whole family of specific answers may be obtained without having to repeat the reasoning process anew.

In order to attain an even higher level of generality, we may resort to the general function statement $y = f(x)$, or $z = g(x, y)$. When expressed in this form, the function is not restricted to being either linear, quadratic, exponential, or trigonometric—all of which are subsumed under the notation. The analytical result based on such a general formulation will therefore have the most general applicability. As will be found below, however, in order to obtain economically meaningful results, it is often necessary to impose certain qualitative restrictions on the general functions built into a model, such as the restriction that a demand function have a negatively sloped graph or that a consumption function have a graph with a positive slope of less than 1.

To sum up the present chapter, the structure of a mathematical economic model is now clear. In general, it will consist of a system of equations, which may be definitional, behavioral, or in the nature of equilibrium conditions.[†] The behavioral equations are usually in the form of functions, which may be linear or nonlinear, numerical or parametric, and with one independent variable or many. It is through these that the analytical assumptions adopted in the model are given mathematical expression.

In attacking an analytical problem, therefore, the first step is to select the appropriate variables—exogenous as well as endogenous—for inclusion in the model. Next, we must translate into equations the set of chosen analytical assumptions regarding the human, institutional, technological, legal, and other behavioral aspects of the environment affecting the working of the variables. Only then can we attempt to derive a set of conclusions through relevant mathematical operations and manipulations and to give them appropriate economic interpretations.

[†] Inequalities may also enter as an important ingredient of a model, but we shall not worry about them for the time being.

Part 2

Static (or Equilibrium) Analysis

Chapter 3

Equilibrium Analysis in Economics

The analytical procedure outlined in Chap. 2 will first be applied to what is known as *static analysis,* or *equilibrium analysis.* For this purpose, it is imperative first to have a clear understanding of what *equilibrium* means.

3.1 The Meaning of Equilibrium

Like any economic term, *equilibrium* can be defined in various ways. According to one definition, an equilibrium is "a constellation of selected interrelated variables so adjusted to one another that no inherent tendency to change prevails in the model which they constitute."[†] Several words in this definition deserve special attention. First, the word *selected* underscores the fact that there do exist variables which, by the analyst's choice, have not been included in the model. Hence the equilibrium under discussion can have relevance only in the context of the particular set of variables chosen, and if the model is enlarged to include additional variables, the equilibrium state pertaining to the smaller model will no longer apply.

Second, the word *interrelated* suggests that, in order for equilibrium to occur, all variables in the model must simultaneously be in a state of rest. Moreover, the state of rest of each variable must be compatible with that of every other variable; otherwise some variable(s) will be changing, thereby also causing the others to change in a chain reaction, and no equilibrium can be said to exist.

Third, the word *inherent* implies that, in defining an equilibrium, the state of rest involved is based only on the balancing of the internal forces of the model, while the external factors are assumed fixed. Operationally, this means that parameters and exogenous variables are treated as constants. When the external factors do actually change, there will be a new equilibrium defined on the basis of the new parameter values, but in defining the new equilibrium, the new parameter values are again assumed to persist and stay unchanged.

[†] Fritz Machlup, "Equilibrium and Disequilibrium: Misplaced Concreteness and Disguised Politics," *Economic Journal,* March 1958, p. 9. (Reprinted in F. Machlup, *Essays on Economic Semantics,* Prentice Hall, Inc., Englewood Cliffs, N.J., 1963.)

In essence, an equilibrium for a specified model is a situation characterized by a lack of tendency to change. It is for this reason that the analysis of equilibrium (more specifically, the study of what the equilibrium state is like) is referred to as *statics.*

The fact that an equilibrium implies no tendency to change may tempt one to conclude that an equilibrium necessarily constitutes a desirable or ideal state of affairs, on the ground that only in the ideal state would there be a lack of motivation for change. Such a conclusion is unwarranted. Even though a certain equilibrium position may represent a desirable state and something to be striven for—such as a profit-maximizing situation, from the firm's point of view—another equilibrium position may be quite undesirable and therefore something to be avoided, such as an underemployment equilibrium level of national income. The only warranted interpretation is that an equilibrium is a situation which, if attained, would tend to perpetuate itself, barring any changes in the external forces.

The desirable variety of equilibrium, which we shall refer to as *goal equilibrium,* will be treated later in Part 4 as optimization problems. In the present chapter, the discussion will be confined to the *nongoal* type of equilibrium, resulting not from any conscious aiming at a particular objective but from an impersonal or suprapersonal process of interaction and adjustment of economic forces. Examples of this are the equilibrium attained by a market under given demand and supply conditions and the equilibrium of national income under given conditions of consumption and investment patterns.

3.2   Partial Market Equilibrium—A Linear Model

In a static-equilibrium model, the standard problem is that of finding the set of values of the endogenous variables which will satisfy the equilibrium condition of the model. This is because once we have identified those values, we have in effect identified the equilibrium state. Let us illustrate with a so-called partial-equilibrium market model, i.e., a model of price determination in an isolated market.

Constructing the Model

Since only one commodity is being considered, it is necessary to include only three variables in the model: the quantity demanded of the commodity (Q_d), the quantity supplied of the commodity (Q_s), and its price (P). The quantity is measured, say, in pounds per week, and the price in dollars. Having chosen the variables, our next order of business is to make certain assumptions regarding the working of the market. First, we must specify an equilibrium condition—something indispensable in an equilibrium model. The standard assumption is that equilibrium occurs in the market if and only if the excess demand is zero ($Q_d - Q_s = 0$), that is, if and only if the market is cleared. But this immediately raises the question of how Q_d and Q_s themselves are determined. To answer this, we assume that Q_d is a decreasing linear function of P (as P increases, Q_d decreases). On the other hand, Q_s is postulated to be an increasing linear function of P (as P increases, so does Q_s), with the proviso that no quantity is supplied unless the price exceeds a particular positive level. In all, then, the model will contain one equilibrium condition plus two behavioral equations which govern the demand and supply sides of the market, respectively.

FIGURE 3.1

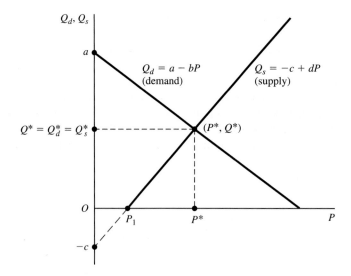

Translated into mathematical statements, the model can be written as

$$Q_d = Q_s$$
$$Q_d = a - bP \qquad (a, b > 0) \qquad\qquad \textbf{(3.1)}$$
$$Q_s = -c + dP \qquad (c, d > 0)$$

Four parameters, a, b, c, and d, appear in the two linear functions, and all of them are specified to be positive. When the demand function is graphed, as in Fig. 3.1, its vertical intercept is at a and its slope is $-b$, which is negative, as required. The supply function also has the required type of slope, d being positive, but its vertical intercept is seen to be negative, at $-c$. Why did we want to specify such a negative vertical intercept? The answer is that, in so doing, we force the supply curve to have a positive horizontal intercept at P_1, thereby satisfying the proviso stated earlier that supply will not be forthcoming unless the price is positive and sufficiently high.

The reader should observe that, contrary to the usual practice, quantity rather than price has been plotted vertically in Fig. 3.1. This, however, is in line with the mathematical convention of placing the *dependent* variable on the vertical axis. In a different context in which the demand curve is viewed from the standpoint of a business firm as describing the average-revenue curve, $AR \equiv P = f(Q_d)$, we shall reverse the axes and plot P vertically.

With the model thus constructed, the next step is to solve it, i.e., to obtain the solution values of the three endogenous variables, Q_d, Q_s, and P. The solution values are those values that satisfy the three equations in (3.1) simultaneously; i.e., they are the values which, when substituted into the three equations, make the latter a set of true statements. In the context of an equilibrium model, those values may also be referred to as the *equilibrium values* of the said variables.

Many writers employ no special symbols to denote the solution values of the endogenous variables. Thus, Q_d is used to represent either the quantity-demanded variable (with a whole range of values) or its solution value (a specific value); and similarly for the symbols

Q_s and P. Unfortunately, this practice can give rise to possible confusions, especially in the context of comparative-static analysis (e.g., Sec. 7.5). To avoid such a source of confusion, we shall denote the solution value of an endogenous variable with an asterisk. Thus, the solution values of Q_d, Q_s, and P, are denoted by Q_d^*, Q_s^*, and P^*, respectively. Since $Q_d^* = Q_s^*$, however, they can even be replaced by a single symbol Q^*. Hence, an equilibrium solution of the model may simply be denoted by an ordered pair (P^*, Q^*). In case the solution is not unique, several ordered pairs may each satisfy the system of simultaneous equations; there will then be a solution set with more than one element in it. However, the multiple-equilibrium situation cannot arise in a linear model such as the present one.

Solution by Elimination of Variables

One way of finding a solution to an equation system is by successive elimination of variables and equations through substitution. In (3.1), the model contains three equations in three variables. However, in view of the equating of Q_d and Q_s by the equilibrium condition, we can let $Q = Q_d = Q_s$ and rewrite the model equivalently as follows:

$$Q = a - bP$$
$$Q = -c + dP \qquad \textbf{(3.2)}$$

thereby reducing the model to two equations in two variables. Moreover, by substituting the first equation into the second in (3.2), the model can be further reduced to a single equation in a single variable:

$$a - bP = -c + dP$$

or, after subtracting $(a + dP)$ from both sides of the equation and multiplying through by -1,

$$(b + d)P = a + c \qquad \textbf{(3.3)}$$

This result is also obtainable directly from (3.1) by substituting the second and third equations into the first.

Since $b + d \neq 0$, it is permissible to divide both sides of (3.3) by $(b + d)$. The result is the solution value of P:

$$P^* = \frac{a + c}{b + d} \qquad \textbf{(3.4)}$$

Note that P^* is—as all solution values should be—expressed entirely in terms of the parameters, which represent given data for the model. Thus P^* is a determinate value, as it ought to be. Also note that P^* is positive—as a price should be—because all the four parameters are positive by model specification.

To find the equilibrium quantity $Q^* (= Q_d^* = Q_s^*)$ that corresponds to the value P^*, simply substitute (3.4) into *either* equation of (3.2), and then solve the resulting equation. Substituting (3.4) into the demand function, for instance, we can get

$$Q^* = a - \frac{b(a + c)}{b + d} = \frac{a(b + d) - b(a + c)}{b + d} = \frac{ad - bc}{b + d} \qquad \textbf{(3.5)}$$

which is again an expression in terms of parameters only. Since the denominator $(b + d)$ is positive, the positivity of Q^* requires that the numerator $(ad - bc)$ be positive as well. Hence, to be economically meaningful, the present model should contain the additional restriction that $ad > bc$.

The meaning of this restriction can be seen in Fig. 3.1. It is well known that the P^* and Q^* of a market model may be determined graphically at the intersection of the demand and supply curves. To have $Q^* > 0$ is to require the intersection point to be located above the horizontal axis in Fig. 3.1, which in turn requires the slopes and vertical intercepts of the two curves to fulfill a certain restriction on their relative magnitudes. That restriction, according to (3.5), is $ad > bc$, given that both b and d are positive.

The intersection of the demand and supply curves in Fig. 3.1, incidentally, is in concept no different from the intersection shown in the Venn diagram of Fig. 2.2b. There is one difference only: Instead of the points lying within two circles, the present case involves the points that lie on two lines. Let the set of points on the demand and supply curves be denoted, respectively, by D and S. Then, by utilizing the symbol $Q (= Q_d = Q_s)$, the two sets and their intersection can be written

$$D = \{(P, Q) \mid Q = a - bP\}$$
$$S = \{(P, Q) \mid Q = -c + dP\}$$

and
$$D \cap S = (P^*, Q^*)$$

The intersection set contains in this instance only a single element, the ordered pair (P^*, Q^*). The market equilibrium is unique.

EXERCISE 3.2

1. Given the market model
   $$Q_d = Q_s$$
   $$Q_d = 21 - 3P$$
   $$Q_s = -4 + 8P$$
   find P^* and Q^* by (a) elimination of variables and (b) using formulas (3.4) and (3.5). (Use fractions rather than decimals.)

2. Let the demand and supply functions be as follows:
   (a) $Q_d = 51 - 3P$ (b) $Q_d = 30 - 2P$
         $Q_s = 6P - 10$ $Q_s = -6 + 5P$
   find P^* and Q^* by elimination of variables. (Use fractions rather than decimals.)

3. According to (3.5), for Q^* to be positive, it is necessary that the expression $(ad - bc)$ have the same algebraic sign as $(b + d)$. Verify that this condition is indeed satisfied in the models of Probs. 1 and 2.

4. If $(b + d) = 0$ in the linear market model, can an equilibrium solution be found by using (3.4) and (3.5)? Why or why not?

5. If $(b + d) = 0$ in the linear market model, what can you conclude regarding the positions of the demand and supply curves in Fig. 3.1? What can you conclude, then, regarding the equilibrium solution?

3.3   Partial Market Equilibrium—A Nonlinear Model

Let the linear demand in the isolated market model be replaced by a quadratic demand function, while the supply function remains linear. Also, let us use numerical coefficients rather than parameters. Then a model such as the following may emerge:

$$Q_d = Q_s$$
$$Q_d = 4 - P^2 \tag{3.6}$$
$$Q_s = 4P - 1$$

As previously, this system of three equations can be reduced to a single equation by elimination of variables (by substitution):

$$4 - P^2 = 4P - 1$$

or

$$P^2 + 4P - 5 = 0 \tag{3.7}$$

This is a quadratic equation because the left-hand expression is a quadratic function of variable P. A major difference between a quadratic equation and a linear one is that, in general, the former will yield two solution values.

Quadratic Equation versus Quadratic Function

Before discussing the method of solution, a clear distinction should be made between the two terms *quadratic equation* and *quadratic function*. According to the earlier discussion, the expression $P^2 + 4P - 5$ constitutes a quadratic *function*, say, $f(P)$. Hence we may write

$$f(P) = P^2 + 4P - 5 \tag{3.8}$$

What (3.8) does is to specify a rule of mapping from P to $f(P)$, such as

P	$\cdots$	-6	-5	-4	-3	-2	-1	0	1	2	$\cdots$
$f(P)$	$\cdots$	7	0	-5	-8	-9	-8	-5	0	7	$\cdots$

Although we have listed only nine P values in this table, actually *all* the P values in the domain of the function are eligible for listing. It is perhaps for this reason that we rarely speak of "solving" the equation $f(P) = P^2 + 4P - 5$, because we normally expect "solution values" to be few in number, but here all P values can get involved. Nevertheless, one may legitimately consider each ordered pair in the table—such as $(-6, 7)$ and $(-5, 0)$—as a solution of (3.8), since each such ordered pair indeed satisfies that equation. Inasmuch as an infinite number of such ordered pairs can be written, one for each P value, there is an infinite number of solutions to (3.8). When plotted as a curve, these ordered pairs together yield the parabola in Fig. 3.2.

In (3.7), where we set the quadratic function $f(P)$ equal to zero, the situation is fundamentally changed. Since the variable $f(P)$ now disappears (having been assigned a zero value), the result is a quadratic *equation* in the single variable P.[†] Now that $f(P)$ is

---

[†] The distinction between quadratic function and quadratic equation just discussed can be extended also to cases of polynomials other than quadratic. Thus, a cubic equation results when a cubic function is set equal to zero.

FIGURE 3.2

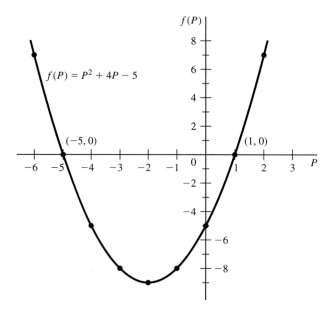

$$f(P) = P^2 + 4P - 5$$

restricted to a zero value, only a select number of P values can satisfy (3.7) and qualify as its solution values, namely, those P values at which the parabola in Fig. 3.2 intersects the horizontal axis—on which $f(P)$ is zero. Note that this time the solution values are just P values, not ordered pairs. The solution P values are often referred to as the *roots* of the quadratic *equation $f(P) = 0$*, or, alternatively, as the *zeros* of the quadratic *function $f(P)$*.

There are two such intersection points in Fig. 3.2, namely, (1, 0) and (−5, 0). As required, the second element of each of these ordered pairs (the *ordinate* of the corresponding point) shows $f(P) = 0$ in both cases. The first element of each ordered pair (the *abscissa* of the point), on the other hand, gives the solution value of P. Here we get two solutions,

$$P_1^* = 1 \quad \text{and} \quad P_2^* = -5$$

but only the first is economically admissible, as negative prices are ruled out.

The Quadratic Formula

Equation (3.7) has been solved graphically, but an algebraic method is also available. In general, given a quadratic equation in the form

$$ax^2 + bx + c = 0 \quad (a \neq 0) \tag{3.9}$$

there are two roots, which can be obtained from the *quadratic formula*:

$$x_1^*, x_2^* = \frac{-b \pm (b^2 - 4ac)^{1/2}}{2a} \tag{3.10}$$

where the + part of the ± sign yields x_1^* and the − part yields x_2^*.

Also note that as long as $b^2 - 4ac > 0$, the values of x_1^* and x_2^* would differ, giving us two distinct real numbers as the roots. But in the special case where $b^2 - 4ac = 0$, we would find that $x_1^* = x_2^* = -b/2a$. In this case, the two roots share the identical value; they are referred to as *repeated roots*. In yet another special case where $b^2 - 4ac < 0$, we would have the task of taking the square root of a negative number, which is not possible in the real-number system. In this latter case, no real-valued roots exist. We shall discuss this matter further in Sec. 16.1.

This widely used formula is derived by means of a process known as "completing the square." First, dividing each term of (3.9) by a results in the equation

$$x^2 + \frac{b}{a}x + \frac{c}{a} = 0$$

Subtracting c/a from, and adding $b^2/4a^2$ to, both sides of the equation, we get

$$x^2 + \frac{b}{a}x + \frac{b^2}{4a^2} = \frac{b^2}{4a^2} - \frac{c}{a}$$

The left side is now a "perfect square," and thus the equation can be expressed as

$$\left(x + \frac{b}{2a}\right)^2 = \frac{b^2 - 4ac}{4a^2}$$

or, after taking the square root on both sides,

$$x + \frac{b}{2a} = \pm\frac{(b^2 - 4ac)^{1/2}}{2a}$$

Finally, by subtracting $b/2a$ from both sides, the result in (3.10) is obtained.

Applying the formula to (3.7), where $a = 1$, $b = 4$, $c = -5$, and $x = P$, the roots are found to be

$$P_1^*, P_2^* = \frac{-4 \pm (16 + 20)^{1/2}}{2} = \frac{-4 \pm 6}{2} = 1, -5$$

which check with the graphical solutions in Fig. 3.2. Again, we reject $P_2^* = -5$ on economic grounds and, after omitting the subscript 1, write simply $P^* = 1$.

With this information in hand, the equilibrium quantity Q^* can readily be found from either the second or the third equation of (3.6) to be $Q^* = 3$.

Another Graphical Solution

One method of graphical solution of the present model has been presented in Fig. 3.2. However, since the quantity variable has been eliminated in deriving the quadratic equation, only P^* can be found from that figure. If we are interested in finding P^* and Q^* simultaneously from a graph, we must instead use a diagram with Q on one axis and P on the other, similar in construction to Fig. 3.1. This is illustrated in Fig. 3.3. Our problem is of course again to find the intersection of two sets of points, namely,

$$D = \{(P, Q) \mid Q = 4 - P^2\}$$

and

$$S = \{(P, Q) \mid Q = 4P - 1\}$$

FIGURE 3.3

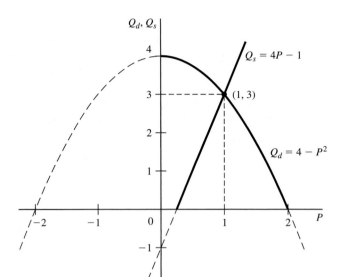

If no restriction is placed on the domain and the range, the intersection set will contain two elements, namely,

$$D \cap S = \{(1, 3), (-5, -21)\}$$

The former is located in quadrant I, and the latter (not drawn) in quadrant III. If the domain and range are restricted to being nonnegative, however, only the first ordered pair $(1, 3)$ can be accepted. Then the equilibrium is again unique.

Higher-Degree Polynomial Equations

If a system of simultaneous equations reduces not to a linear equation such as $(3.3)^{\dagger}$ or to a quadratic equation such as (3.7) but to a cubic (third-degree polynomial) equation or quartic (fourth-degree polynomial) equation, the roots will be more difficult to find. One useful method which may work is that of *factoring* the function.

Example 1

The expression $x^3 - x^2 - 4x + 4$ can be written as the product of three factors $(x - 1)$, $(x + 2)$, and $(x - 2)$. Thus the cubic equation

$$x^3 - x^2 - 4x + 4 = 0$$

can be written after factoring as

$$(x - 1)(x + 2)(x - 2) = 0$$

In order for the left-hand product to be zero, at least one of the three terms in the product must be zero. Setting each term equal to zero in turn, we get

$$x - 1 = 0 \quad \text{or} \quad x + 2 = 0 \quad \text{or} \quad x - 2 = 0$$

These three equations will supply the three roots of the cubic equation, namely,

$$x_1^* = 1 \quad x_2^* = -2 \quad \text{and} \quad x_3^* = 2$$

---

† Equation (3.3) can be viewed as the result of setting the linear function $(b + d)P - (a + c)$ equal to zero.

Example 1 illustrates two interesting and useful facts about factoring. First, given a third-degree polynomial equation, factoring results in three terms of the form $(x - \text{root})$, thus yielding three roots. Generally, an nth-degree polynomial equation should yield a total of n roots. Second, and more important for the purpose of root search, we note the following relationship between the three roots $(1, -2, 2)$ and the constant term 4: Since the constant term must be the product of the three roots, each root must be a divisor of the constant term. This relationship can be formalized in the following theorem:

Theorem I Given the polynomial equation

$$x^n + a_{n-1}x^{n-1} + \cdots + a_1 x + a_0 = 0$$

where all the coefficients are integers, and the coefficient of x^n is unity, if there exist integer roots, then each of them must be a divisor of a_0.

Sometimes, however, we encounter fractional coefficients in the polynomial equation, as in

$$x^4 + \tfrac{5}{2}x^3 - \tfrac{11}{2}x^2 - 10x + 6 = 0$$

which does not fall under the provision of Theorem I. Even if we multiply through by 2 to get rid of the fractions (ending in the form shown in Example 2 which follows), we still cannot apply Theorem I, because the coefficient of the highest-degree term is not unity. In such cases, we can resort to a more general theorem:

Theorem II Given the polynomial equation with integer coefficients

$$a_n x^n + a_{n-1}x^{n-1} + \cdots + a_1 x + a_0 = 0$$

if there exists a rational root r/s, where r and s are integers without a common divisor except unity, then r is a divisor of a_0, and s is a divisor of a_n.

Example 2 Does the quartic equation

$$2x^4 + 5x^3 - 11x^2 - 20x + 12 = 0$$

have rational roots? With $a_0 = 12$, the only possible values for the numerator r in r/s are the set of divisors $\{1, -1, 2, -2, 3, -3, 4, -4, 6, -6, 12, -12\}$. And, with $a_n = 2$, the only possible values for s are the set of divisors $\{1, -1, 2, -2\}$. Taking each element in the r set in turn, and dividing it by each element in the s set, respectively, we find that r/s can only assume the values

$$1, -1, \frac{1}{2}, -\frac{1}{2}, 2, -2, 3, -3, \frac{3}{2}, -\frac{3}{2}, 4, -4, 6, -6, 12, -12$$

Among these candidates for roots, many fail to satisfy the given equation. Letting $x = 1$ in the quartic equation, for instance, we get the ridiculous result $-12 = 0$. In fact, since we are solving a quartic equation, we can expect at most four of the listed r/s values to qualify as roots. The four successful candidates turn out to be $\frac{1}{2}, 2, -2,$ and -3. According to the factoring principle, we can thus write the given quartic equation equivalently as

$$(x - \tfrac{1}{2})(x - 2)(x + 2)(x + 3) = 0$$

where the first factor can also be written as $(2x - 1)$ instead.

In Example 2, we rejected the root candidate 1 because $x = 1$ fails to satisfy the given equation; i.e., substitution of $x = 1$ into the equation does not produce the identity $0 = 0$ as required. Now consider the case where $x = 1$ indeed is a root of some polynomial equation. In that case, since $x^n = x^{n-1} = \cdots = x = 1$, the polynomial equation would reduce to the simple form $a_n + a_{n-1} + \cdots + a_1 + a_0 = 0$. This fact provides the rationale for the following theorem:

Theorem III Given the polynomial equation

$$a_n x^n + a_{n-1} x^{n-1} + \cdots + a_1 x + a_0 = 0$$

if the coefficients $a_n, a_{n-1}, \ldots, a_0$ add up to zero, then $x = 1$ is a root of the equation.

EXERCISE 3.3

1. Find the zeros of the following functions graphically:
   (a) $f(x) = x^2 - 8x + 15$ (b) $g(x) = 2x^2 - 4x - 16$
2. Solve Prob. 1 by the quadratic formula.
3. (a) Find a cubic equation with roots 6, -1, and 3.
   (b) Find a quartic equation with roots 1, 2, 3, and 5.
4. For each of the following polynomial equations, determine if $x = 1$ is a root.
   (a) $x^3 - 2x^2 + 3x - 2 = 0$ (c) $3x^4 - x^2 + 2x - 4 = 0$
   (b) $2x^3 - \frac{1}{2}x^2 + x - 2 = 0$
5. Find the rational roots, if any, of the following:
   (a) $x^3 - 4x^2 + x + 6 = 0$ (c) $x^3 + \frac{3}{4}x^2 - \frac{3}{8}x - \frac{1}{8} = 0$
   (b) $8x^3 + 6x^2 - 3x - 1 = 0$ (d) $x^4 - 6x^3 + 7\frac{3}{4}x^2 - \frac{3}{2}x - 2 = 0$
6. Find the equilibrium solution for each of the following models:
   (a) $Q_d = Q_s$ (b) $Q_d = Q_s$
       $Q_d = 3 - P^2$ $Q_d = 8 - P^2$
       $Q_s = 6P - 4$ $Q_s = P^2 - 2$
7. The market equilibrium condition, $Q_d = Q_s$, is often expressed in an equivalent alternative form, $Q_d - Q_s = 0$, which has the economic interpretation "excess demand is zero." Does (3.7) represent this latter version of the equilibrium condition? If not, supply an appropriate economic interpretation for (3.7).

3.4 General Market Equilibrium

The last two sections dealt with models of an isolated market, wherein the Q_d and Q_s of a commodity are functions of the price of that commodity alone. In the actual world, though, no commodity ever enjoys (or suffers) such a hermitic existence; for every commodity, there would normally exist many substitutes and complementary goods. Thus a more realistic depiction of the demand function of a commodity should take into account the effect not only of the price of the commodity itself but also of the prices of related commodities. The same also holds true for the supply function. Once the prices of other commodities are brought into the picture, however, the structure of the model itself must be broadened so as to be able to yield the equilibrium values of these other prices as well. As a result, the price and quantity variables of multiple commodities must enter endogenously into the model en masse.

In an isolated-market model, the equilibrium condition consists of only one equation, $Q_d = Q_s$, or $E \equiv Q_d - Q_s = 0$, where E stands for excess demand. When several interdependent commodities are simultaneously considered, equilibrium would require the absence of excess demand for each and every commodity included in the model, for if so much as *one* commodity is faced with an excess demand, the price adjustment of that commodity will necessarily affect the quantities demanded and quantities supplied of the related commodities, thereby causing price changes all around. Consequently, the equilibrium condition of an *n*-commodity market model will involve *n* equations, one for each commodity, in the form

$$E_i \equiv Q_{di} - Q_{si} = 0 \qquad (i = 1, 2, \ldots, n) \qquad \textbf{(3.11)}$$

If a solution exists, there will be a set of prices P_i^* and corresponding quantities Q_i^* such that all the *n* equations in the equilibrium condition will be simultaneously satisfied.

Two-Commodity Market Model

To illustrate the problem, let us discuss a simple model in which only two commodities are related to each other. For simplicity, the demand and supply functions of both commodities are assumed to be linear. In parametric terms, such a model can be written as

$$\begin{aligned}
Q_{d1} - Q_{s1} &= 0 \\
Q_{d1} &= a_0 + a_1 P_1 + a_2 P_2 \\
Q_{s1} &= b_0 + b_1 P_1 + b_2 P_2 \\
Q_{d2} - Q_{s2} &= 0 \\
Q_{d2} &= \alpha_0 + \alpha_1 P_1 + \alpha_2 P_2 \\
Q_{s2} &= \beta_0 + \beta_1 P_1 + \beta_2 P_2
\end{aligned} \qquad \textbf{(3.12)}$$

where the a and b coefficients pertain to the demand and supply functions of the first commodity, and the α and β coefficients are assigned to those of the second. We have not bothered to specify the signs of the coefficients, but in the course of analysis certain restrictions will emerge as a prerequisite to economically sensible results. Also, in a subsequent numerical example, some comments will be made on the specific signs to be given the coefficients.

As a first step toward the solution of this model, we can again resort to elimination of variables. By substituting the second and third equations into the first (for the first commodity) and the fifth and sixth equations into the fourth (for the second commodity), the model is reduced to two equations in two variables:

$$\begin{aligned}
(a_0 - b_0) + (a_1 - b_1)P_1 + (a_2 - b_2)P_2 &= 0 \\
(\alpha_0 - \beta_0) + (\alpha_1 - \beta_1)P_1 + (\alpha_2 - \beta_2)P_2 &= 0
\end{aligned} \qquad \textbf{(3.13)}$$

These represent the two-commodity version of (3.11), after the demand and supply functions have been substituted into the two equilibrium conditions.

Although this is a simple system of only two equations, as many as 12 parameters are involved, and algebraic manipulations will prove unwieldy unless some sort of shorthand is introduced. Let us therefore define the shorthand symbols

$$c_i \equiv a_i - b_i \qquad (i = 0, 1, 2)$$
$$\gamma_i \equiv \alpha_i - \beta_i$$

Then, after transposing the c_0 and γ_0 terms to the right-hand side, we get

$$c_1 P_1 + c_2 P_2 = -c_0$$
$$\gamma_1 P_1 + \gamma_2 P_2 = -\gamma_0 \qquad \textbf{(3.13')}$$

which may be solved by further elimination of variables. From the first equation, it can be found that $P_2 = -(c_0 + c_1 P_1)/c_2$. Substituting this into the second equation and solving, we get

$$P_1^* = \frac{c_2 \gamma_0 - c_0 \gamma_2}{c_1 \gamma_2 - c_2 \gamma_1} \qquad \textbf{(3.14)}$$

Note that P_1^* is entirely expressed, as a solution value should be, in terms of the data (parameters) of the model. By a similar process, the equilibrium price of the second commodity is found to be

$$P_2^* = \frac{c_0 \gamma_1 - c_1 \gamma_0}{c_1 \gamma_2 - c_2 \gamma_1} \qquad \textbf{(3.15)}$$

For these two values to make sense, however, certain restrictions should be imposed on the model. First, since division by zero is undefined, we must require the common denominator of (3.14) and (3.15) to be nonzero, that is, $c_1 \gamma_2 \neq c_2 \gamma_1$. Second, to assure positivity, the numerator must have the same sign as the denominator.

The equilibrium prices having been found, the equilibrium quantities Q_1^* and Q_2^* can readily be calculated by substituting (3.14) and (3.15) into the second (or third) equation and the fifth (or sixth) equation of (3.12). These solution values will naturally also be expressed in terms of the parameters. (Their actual calculation is left to you as an exercise.)

Numerical Example

Suppose that the demand and supply functions are numerically as follows:

$$
\begin{aligned}
Q_{d1} &= 10 - 2P_1 + P_2 \\
Q_{s1} &= -2 + 3P_1 \\
Q_{d2} &= 15 + P_1 - P_2 \\
Q_{s2} &= -1 \qquad + 2P_2
\end{aligned}
\qquad \textbf{(3.16)}
$$

What is the equilibrium solution?

Before answering the question, let us take a look at the numerical coefficients. For each commodity, Q_{si} is seen to depend on P_i alone, but Q_{di} is shown as a function of both prices. Note that while P_1 has a negative coefficient in Q_{d1}, as we would expect, the coefficient of P_2 is positive. The fact that a rise in P_2 tends to raise Q_{d1} suggests that the two commodities are substitutes for each other. The role of P_1 in the Q_{d2} function has a similar interpretation.

With these coefficients, the shorthand symbols c_i and γ_i will take the following values:

$$c_0 = 10 - (-2) = 12 \qquad c_1 = -2 - 3 = -5 \qquad c_2 = 1 - 0 = 1$$
$$\gamma_0 = 15 - (-1) = 16 \qquad \gamma_1 = 1 - 0 = 1 \qquad \gamma_2 = -1 - 2 = -3$$

By direct substitution of these into (3.14) and (3.15), we obtain

$$P_1^* = \tfrac{52}{14} = 3\tfrac{5}{7} \qquad \text{and} \qquad P_2^* = \tfrac{92}{14} = 6\tfrac{4}{7}$$

And the further substitution of P_1^* and P_2^* into (3.16) yields

$$Q_1^* = \tfrac{64}{7} = 9\tfrac{1}{7} \qquad \text{and} \qquad Q_2^* = \tfrac{85}{7} = 12\tfrac{1}{7}$$

Thus all the equilibrium values turn out positive, as required. In order to preserve the exact values of P_1^* and P_2^* to be used in the further calculation of Q_1^* and Q_2^*, it is advisable to express them as fractions rather than decimals.

Could we have obtained the equilibrium prices graphically? The answer is yes. From (3.13), it is clear that a two-commodity model can be summarized by two equations in two variables P_1 and P_2. With known numerical coefficients, both equations can be plotted in the $P_1 P_2$ coordinate plane, and the intersection of the two curves will then pinpoint P_1^* and P_2^*.

n-Commodity Case

The previous discussion of the multicommodity market has been limited to the case of two commodities, but it should be apparent that we are already moving from *partial-equilibrium* analysis in the direction of *general-equilibrium* analysis. As more commodities enter into a model, there will be more variables and more equations, and the equations will get longer and more complicated. If all the commodities in an economy are included in a comprehensive market model, the result will be a Walrasian type of general-equilibrium model, in which the excess demand for every commodity is considered to be a function of the prices of all the commodities in the economy.

Some of the prices may, of course, carry zero coefficients when they play no role in the determination of the excess demand of a particular commodity; e.g., in the excess-demand function of pianos the price of popcorn may well have a zero coefficient. In general, however, with n commodities in all, we may express the demand and supply functions as follows (using Q_{di} and Q_{si} as function symbols in place of f and g):

$$\begin{aligned} Q_{di} &= Q_{di}(P_1, P_2, \ldots, P_n) \\ Q_{si} &= Q_{si}(P_1, P_2, \ldots, P_n) \end{aligned} \qquad (i = 1, 2, \ldots, n) \qquad \textbf{(3.17)}$$

In view of the index subscript, these two equations represent the totality of the $2n$ functions which the model contains. (These functions are not necessarily linear.) Moreover, the equilibrium condition is itself composed of a set of n equations,

$$Q_{di} - Q_{si} = 0 \qquad (i = 1, 2, \ldots, n) \qquad \textbf{(3.18)}$$

When (3.18) is added to (3.17), the model becomes complete. You should therefore count a total of $3n$ equations.

Upon substitution of (3.17) into (3.18), however, the model can be reduced to a set of n simultaneous equations only:

$$Q_{di}(P_1, P_2, \ldots, P_n) - Q_{si}(P_1, P_2, \ldots, P_n) = 0 \qquad (i = 1, 2, \ldots, n)$$

Besides, inasmuch as $E_i \equiv Q_{di} - Q_{si}$, where E_i is necessarily also a function of all the n prices, the latter set of equations may be written alternatively as

$$E_i(P_1, P_2, \ldots, P_n) = 0 \qquad (i = 1, 2, \ldots, n)$$

Solved simultaneously, these n equations can determine the n equilibrium prices P_i^*—if a solution does indeed exist. And then the Q_i^* may be derived from the demand or supply functions.

Solution of a General-Equation System

If a model comes equipped with numerical coefficients, as in (3.16), the equilibrium values of the variables will be in numerical terms, too. On a more general level, if a model is expressed in terms of parametric constants, as in (3.12), the equilibrium values will also involve parameters and will hence appear as "formulas," as exemplified by (3.14) and (3.15). If, for greater generality, even the function forms are left unspecified in a model, however, as in (3.17), the manner of expressing the solution values will of necessity be exceedingly general as well.

Drawing upon our experience in parametric models, we know that a solution value is always an expression in terms of the parameters. For a general-function model containing, say, a total of m parameters $(a_1, a_2, \ldots, a_m)$—where m is not necessarily equal to n—the n equilibrium prices can be expected to take the general analytical form of

$$P_i^* = P_i^*(a_1, a_2, \ldots, a_m) \qquad (i = 1, 2, \ldots, n) \qquad \textbf{(3.19)}$$

This is a symbolic statement to the effect that the solution value of *each* variable (here, price) is a function of the set of all parameters of the model. As this is a very general statement, it really does not give much detailed information about the solution. But in the general analytical treatment of some types of problem, even this seemingly uninformative way of expressing a solution will prove of use, as will be seen in Chap. 8.

Writing such a solution is an easy task. But an important catch exists: the expression in (3.19) can be justified if and only if a *unique* solution does indeed exist, for then and only then can we map the ordered m-tuple $(a_1, a_2, \ldots, a_m)$ into a determinate value for each price P_i^*. Yet, unfortunately for us, there is no a priori reason to presume that every model will automatically yield a unique solution. In this connection, it needs to be emphasized that the process of "counting equations and unknowns" does not suffice as a test. Some very simple examples should convince us that an equal number of equations and unknowns (endogenous variables) does not necessarily guarantee the existence of a unique solution.

Consider the three simultaneous-equation systems

$$\begin{aligned} x + \ y &= 8 \\ x + \ y &= 9 \end{aligned} \qquad \textbf{(3.20)}$$

$$\begin{aligned} 2x + \ y &= 12 \\ 4x + 2y &= 24 \end{aligned} \qquad \textbf{(3.21)}$$

$$\begin{aligned} 2x + 3y &= 58 \\ y &= 18 \\ x + \ y &= 20 \end{aligned} \qquad \textbf{(3.22)}$$

In (3.20), despite the fact that two unknowns are linked together by exactly two equations, there is nevertheless no solution. These two equations happen to be *inconsistent,* for if the sum of x and y is 8, it cannot possibly be 9 at the same time. In (3.21), another case of two equations in two variables, the two equations are *functionally dependent,* which means that one can be derived from (and is implied by) the other. (Here, the second equation is equal to two times the first equation.) Consequently, one equation is redundant and may be dropped from the system, leaving in effect only one equation in two unknowns. The solution will then be the equation $y = 12 - 2x$, which yields not a unique ordered pair (x^*, y^*) but an infinite number of them, including $(0, 12)$, $(1, 10)$, $(2, 8)$, etc., all of which satisfy that equation. Lastly, the case of (3.22) involves more equations than unknowns, yet the ordered pair $(2, 18)$ does constitute the unique solution to it. The reason is that, in view of the existence of functional dependence among the equations (the first is equal to the second plus twice the third), we have in effect only two independent, consistent equations in two variables.

These simple examples should suffice to convey the importance of *consistency* and *functional independence* as the two prerequisites for application of the process of counting equations and unknowns. In general, in order to apply that process, make sure that (1) the satisfaction of any one equation in the model will not preclude the satisfaction of another and (2) no equation is redundant. In (3.17), for example, the n demand and n supply functions may safely be assumed to be independent of one another, each being derived from a different source—each demand from the decisions of a group of consumers, and each supply from the decisions of a group of firms. Thus each function serves to describe one facet of the market situation, and none is redundant. Mutual consistency may perhaps also be assumed. In addition, the equilibrium-condition equations in (3.18) are also independent and presumably consistent. Therefore the analytical solution as written in (3.19) can in general be considered justifiable.[†]

For simultaneous-equation models, there exist systematic methods of testing the existence of a unique (or determinate) solution. These would involve, for linear models, an application of the concept of *determinants,* to be introduced in Chap. 5. In the case of non-linear models, such a test would also require a knowledge of so-called partial derivatives and a special type of determinant called the *Jacobian determinant,* which will be discussed in Chaps. 7 and 8.

EXERCISE 3.4

1. Work out the step-by-step solution of (3.13′), thereby verifying the results in (3.14) and (3.15).
2. Rewrite (3.14) and (3.15) in terms of the original parameters of the model in (3.12).
3. The demand and supply functions of a two-commodity market model are as follows:

$$Q_{d1} = 18 - 3P_1 + P_2 \qquad Q_{d2} = 12 + P_1 - 2P_2$$
$$Q_{s1} = -2 + 4P_1 \qquad\quad Q_{s2} = -2 \quad\ + 3P_2$$

Find P_i^* and Q_i^* ($i = 1, 2$). (Use fractions rather than decimals.)

[†] This is essentially the way that Léon Walras approached the problem of the existence of a general-market equilibrium. In the modern literature, there can be found a number of sophisticated mathematical proofs of the existence of a competitive market equilibrium under certain postulated economic conditions. But the mathematics used is advanced. The easiest one to understand is perhaps the proof given in Robert Dorfman, Paul A. Samuelson, and Robert M. Solow, *Linear Programming and Economic Analysis,* McGraw-Hill Book Company, New York, 1958, Chap. 13.

3.5   Equilibrium in National-Income Analysis

Even though the discussion of static analysis has hitherto been restricted to *market models* in various guises—linear and nonlinear, one-commodity and multicommodity, specific and general—it, of course, has applications in other areas of economics also. As an example, we may cite the simplest Keynesian national-income model,

$$Y = C + I_0 + G_0 \qquad (a > 0, \quad 0 < b < 1) \qquad \textbf{(3.23)}$$
$$C = a + bY$$

where Y and C stand for the endogenous variables national income and (planned) consumption expenditure, respectively, and I_0 and G_0 represent the exogenously determined investment and government expenditures. The first equation is an equilibrium condition (national income = total planned expenditure). The second, the consumption function, is behavioral. The two parameters in the consumption function, a and b, stand for the autonomous consumption expenditure and the marginal propensity to consume, respectively.

It is quite clear that these two equations in two endogenous variables are neither functionally dependent upon, nor inconsistent with, each other. Thus we would be able to find the equilibrium values of income and consumption expenditure, Y^* and C^*, in terms of the parameters a and b and the exogenous variables I_0 and G_0.

Substitution of the second equation into the first will reduce (3.23) to a single equation in one variable, Y:

$$Y = a + bY + I_0 + G_0$$

or $\qquad (1 - b)Y = a + I_0 + G_0 \qquad$ (collecting terms involving Y)

To find the solution value of Y (equilibrium national income), we only have to divide through by $(1 - b)$:

$$Y^* = \frac{a + I_0 + G_0}{1 - b} \qquad \textbf{(3.24)}$$

Note, again, that the solution value is expressed entirely in terms of the parameters and exogenous variables, the given data of the model. Putting (3.24) into the second equation of (3.23) will then yield the equilibrium level of consumption expenditure:

$$C^* = a + bY^* = a + \frac{b(a + I_0 + G_0)}{1 - b}$$
$$= \frac{a(1 - b) + b(a + I_0 + G_0)}{1 - b} = \frac{a + b(I_0 + G_0)}{1 - b} \qquad \textbf{(3.25)}$$

This is again expressed entirely in terms of the given data.

Both Y^* and C^* have the expression $(1 - b)$ in the denominator; thus a restriction $b \neq 1$ is necessary, to avoid division by zero. Since b, the marginal propensity to consume, has been assumed to be a positive fraction, this restriction is automatically satisfied. For Y^* and C^* to be positive, moreover, the numerators in (3.24) and (3.25) must be positive. Since the exogenous expenditures I_0 and G_0 are normally positive, as is the parameter a (the vertical intercept of the consumption function), the sign of the numerator expressions will work out, too.

As a check on our calculation, we can add the C^* expression in (3.25) to $(I_0 + G_0)$ and verify that the sum is equal to the Y^* expression in (3.24).

This model is obviously one of extreme simplicity and crudity, but other models of national-income determination, in varying degrees of complexity and sophistication, can be constructed as well. In each case, however, the principles involved in the construction and analysis of the model are identical with those already discussed. For this reason, we shall not go into further illustrations here. A more comprehensive national-income model, involving the simultaneous equilibrium of the money market and the goods market, will be discussed in Sec. 8.6.

EXERCISE 3.5

1. Given the following model:

   $Y = C + I_0 + G_0$

   $C = a + b(Y - T)$ $\quad$ $(a > 0, \quad 0 < b < 1)$ $\quad$ [T: taxes]

   $T = d + tY$ $\quad\quad\quad$ $(d > 0, \quad 0 < t < 1)$ $\quad$ [t: income tax rate]

   (a) How many endogenous variables are there?

   (b) Find Y^*, T^*, and C^*.

2. Let the national-income model be:

   $Y = C + I_0 + G$

   $C = a + b(Y - T_0)$ $\quad$ $(a > 0, \quad 0 < b < 1)$

   $G = gY$ $\quad\quad\quad\quad\quad$ $(0 < g < 1)$

   (a) Identify the endogenous variables.

   (b) Give the economic meaning of the parameter g.

   (c) Find the equilibrium national income.

   (d) What restriction on the parameters is needed for a solution to exist?

3. Find Y^* and C^* from the following:

   $Y = C + I_0 + G_0$

   $C = 25 + 6Y^{1/2}$

   $I_0 = 16$

   $G_0 = 14$

Chapter 4

Linear Models and Matrix Algebra

For the one-commodity model (3.1), the solutions P^* and Q^* as expressed in (3.4) and (3.5), respectively, are relatively simple, even though a number of parameters are involved. As more and more commodities are incorporated into the model, such solution formulas quickly become cumbersome and unwieldy. That was why we had to resort to a little shorthand, even for the two-commodity case—in order that the solutions (3.14) and (3.15) can still be written in a relatively concise fashion. We did not attempt to tackle any three- or four-commodity models, even in the linear version, primarily because we did not yet have at our disposal a method suitable for handling a large system of simultaneous equations. Such a method is found in *matrix algebra,* the subject of this chapter and the next.

Matrix algebra can enable us to do many things. In the first place, it provides a compact way of writing an equation system, even an extremely large one. Second, it leads to a way of testing the existence of a solution by evaluation of a *determinant*—a concept closely related to that of a matrix. Third, it gives a method of finding that solution (if it exists). Since equation systems are encountered not only in static analysis but also in comparative-static and dynamic analyses and in optimization problems, you will find ample application of matrix algebra in almost every chapter that is to follow. This is why it is desirable to introduce matrix algebra early.

However, one slight catch is that matrix algebra is applicable only to *linear*-equation systems. How realistically linear equations can describe actual economic relationships depends, of course, on the nature of the relationships in question. In many cases, even if some sacrifice of realism is entailed by the assumption of linearity, an assumed linear relationship can produce a sufficiently close approximation to an actual nonlinear relationship to warrant its use.

In other cases, while preserving the nonlinearity in the model, we can effect a transformation of variables so as to obtain a linear relation to work with. For example, the nonlinear function

$$y = ax^b$$

can be readily transformed, by taking the logarithm on both sides, into the function

$$\log y = \log a + b \log x$$

which is linear in the two variables ($\log y$) and ($\log x$). (Logarithms will be discussed in more detail in Chap. 10.). More importantly, in many applications such as comparative-static analysis and optimization problems, discussed subsequently, although the original formulation of the economic model is nonlinear in nature, linear equation systems will emerge in the course of analysis. Thus the linearity restriction is not nearly as restrictive as it may first appear.

4.1 Matrices and Vectors

The two-commodity market model (3.12) can be written—after eliminating the quantity variables—as a system of two linear equations, as in (3.13'),

$$c_1 P_1 + c_2 P_2 = -c_0$$
$$\gamma_1 P_1 + \gamma_2 P_2 = -\gamma_0$$

where the parameters c_0 and γ_0 appear to the right of the equals sign. In general, a system of m linear equations in n variables $(x_1, x_2, \ldots, x_n)$ can also be arranged into such a format:

$$
\begin{aligned}
a_{11}x_1 + a_{12}x_2 + \cdots + a_{1n}x_n &= d_1 \\
a_{21}x_1 + a_{22}x_2 + \cdots + a_{2n}x_n &= d_2 \\
&\cdots\cdots\cdots\cdots\cdots \\
a_{m1}x_1 + a_{m2}x_2 + \cdots + a_{mn}x_n &= d_m
\end{aligned}
\tag{4.1}
$$

In (4.1), the variable x_1 appears only within the leftmost column, and in general the variable x_j appears only in the jth column on the left side of the equals sign. The double-subscripted parameter symbol a_{ij} represents the coefficient appearing in the ith equation and attached to the jth variable. For example, a_{21} is the coefficient in the second equation, attached to the variable x_1. The parameter d_i which is unattached to any variable, on the other hand, represents the constant term in the ith equation. For instance, d_1 is the constant term in the first equation. All subscripts are therefore keyed to the specific locations of the variables and parameters in (4.1).

Matrices as Arrays

There are essentially three types of ingredients in the equation system (4.1). The first is the set of coefficients a_{ij}; the second is the set of variables $x_1, \ldots, x_n$; and the last is the set of constant terms $d_1, \ldots, d_m$. If we arrange the three sets as three rectangular arrays and label them, respectively, as A, x, and d (without subscripts), then we have

$$
A = \begin{bmatrix} a_{11} & a_{12} & \cdots & a_{1n} \\ a_{21} & a_{22} & \cdots & a_{2n} \\ \cdots\cdots\cdots\cdots\cdots \\ a_{m1} & a_{m2} & \cdots & a_{mn} \end{bmatrix}
\qquad
x = \begin{bmatrix} x_1 \\ x_2 \\ \vdots \\ x_n \end{bmatrix}
\qquad
d = \begin{bmatrix} d_1 \\ d_2 \\ \vdots \\ d_m \end{bmatrix}
\tag{4.2}
$$

As a simple example, given the linear-equation system

$$\begin{aligned} 6x_1 + 3x_2 + x_3 &= 22 \\ x_1 + 4x_2 - 2x_3 &= 12 \\ 4x_1 - x_2 + 5x_3 &= 10 \end{aligned}$$ (4.3)

we can write

$$A = \begin{bmatrix} 6 & 3 & 1 \\ 1 & 4 & -2 \\ 4 & -1 & 5 \end{bmatrix} \qquad x = \begin{bmatrix} x_1 \\ x_2 \\ x_3 \end{bmatrix} \qquad d = \begin{bmatrix} 22 \\ 12 \\ 10 \end{bmatrix}$$ (4.4)

Each of the three arrays in (4.2) or (4.4) constitutes a *matrix.*

A matrix is defined as a rectangular array of numbers, parameters, or variables. The members of the array, referred to as the *elements* of the matrix, are usually enclosed in brackets, as in (4.2), or sometimes in parentheses or with double vertical lines: $\| \ \|$. Note that in matrix A (the *coefficient matrix* of the equation system), the elements are separated not by commas but by blank spaces only. As a shorthand device, the array in matrix A can be written more simply as

$$A = [a_{ij}] \qquad \left(\begin{matrix} i = 1, 2, \ldots, m \\ j = 1, 2, \ldots, n \end{matrix} \right)$$

Inasmuch as the location of each element in a matrix is unequivocally fixed by the subscript, every matrix is an ordered set.

Vectors as Special Matrices

The number of rows and the number of columns in a matrix together define the *dimension* of the matrix. Since matrix A in (4.2) contains m rows and n columns, it is said to be of dimension $m \times n$ (read "m by n"). It is important to remember that the row number always precedes the column number; this is in line with the way the two subscripts in a_{ij} are ordered. In the special case where $m = n$, the matrix is called a *square matrix;* thus the matrix A in (4.4) is a 3×3 square matrix.

Some matrices may contain only one column, such as x and d in (4.2) or (4.4). Such matrices are given the special name *column vectors.* In (4.2), the dimension of x is $n \times 1$, and that of d is $m \times 1$; in (4.4) both x and d are 3×1. If we arranged the variables x_j in a horizontal array, though, there would result a $1 \times n$ matrix, which is called a *row vector.* For notation purposes, a row vector is often distinguished from a column vector by the use of a primed symbol:

$$x' = [x_1 \quad x_2 \quad \cdots \quad x_n]$$

You may observe that a vector (whether row or column) is merely an ordered n-tuple, and as such it may sometimes be interpreted as a point in an n-dimensional space. In turn, the $m \times n$ matrix A can be interpreted as an ordered set of m row vectors or as an ordered set of n column vectors. These ideas will be followed up in Chap. 5.

An issue of more immediate interest is how the matrix notation can enable us, as promised, to express an equation system in a compact way. With the matrices defined in (4.4), we can express the equation system (4.3) simply as

$$Ax = d$$

In fact, if A, x, and d are given the meanings in (4.2), then even the general-equation system in (4.1) can be written as $Ax = d$. The compactness of this notation is thus unmistakable.

However, the equation $Ax = d$ prompts at least two questions. How do we multiply two matrices A and x? What is meant by the equality of Ax and d? Since matrices involve whole blocks of numbers, the familiar algebraic operations defined for single numbers are not directly applicable, and there is a need for a new set of operational rules.

EXERCISE 4.1

1. Rewrite the market model (3.1) in the format of (4.1), and show that, if the three variables are arranged in the order Q_d, Q_s, and P, the coefficient matrix will be

$$\begin{bmatrix} 1 & -1 & 0 \\ 1 & 0 & b \\ 0 & 1 & -d \end{bmatrix}$$

   How would you write the vector of constants?

2. Rewrite the market model (3.12) in the format of (4.1) with the variables arranged in the following order: Q_{d1}, Q_{s1}, Q_{d2}, Q_{s2}, P_1, P_2. Write out the coefficient matrix, the variable vector, and the constant vector.

3. Can the market model (3.6) be rewritten in the format of (4.1)? Why?

4. Rewrite the national-income model (3.23) in the format of (4.1), with Y as the first variable. Write out the coefficient matrix and the constant vector.

5. Rewrite the national-income model of Exercise 3.5-1 in the format of (4.1), with the variables in the order Y, T, and C. [*Hint:* Watch out for the multiplicative expression $b(Y - T)$ in the consumption function.]

4.2 Matrix Operations

As a preliminary, let us first define the word *equality*. Two matrices $A = [a_{ij}]$ and $B = [b_{ij}]$ are said to be *equal* if and only if they have the same dimension and have identical elements in the corresponding locations in the array. In other words, $A = B$ if and only if $a_{ij} = b_{ij}$ for all values of i and j. Thus, for example, we find

$$\begin{bmatrix} 4 & 3 \\ 2 & 0 \end{bmatrix} = \begin{bmatrix} 4 & 3 \\ 2 & 0 \end{bmatrix} \neq \begin{bmatrix} 2 & 0 \\ 4 & 3 \end{bmatrix}$$

As another example, if $\begin{bmatrix} x \\ y \end{bmatrix} = \begin{bmatrix} 7 \\ 4 \end{bmatrix}$, this will mean that $x = 7$ and $y = 4$.

Addition and Subtraction of Matrices

Two matrices can be added if and only if they have the same dimension. When this dimensional requirement is met, the matrices are said to be *conformable for addition*. In that case, the addition of $A = [a_{ij}]$ and $B = [b_{ij}]$ is defined as the addition of each pair of corresponding elements.

Example 1

$$\begin{bmatrix} 4 & 9 \\ 2 & 1 \end{bmatrix} + \begin{bmatrix} 2 & 0 \\ 0 & 7 \end{bmatrix} = \begin{bmatrix} 4+2 & 9+0 \\ 2+0 & 1+7 \end{bmatrix} = \begin{bmatrix} 6 & 9 \\ 2 & 8 \end{bmatrix}$$

Example 2

$$\begin{bmatrix} a_{11} & a_{12} \\ a_{21} & a_{22} \\ a_{31} & a_{32} \end{bmatrix} + \begin{bmatrix} b_{11} & b_{12} \\ b_{21} & b_{22} \\ b_{31} & b_{32} \end{bmatrix} = \begin{bmatrix} a_{11}+b_{11} & a_{12}+b_{12} \\ a_{21}+b_{21} & a_{22}+b_{22} \\ a_{31}+b_{31} & a_{32}+b_{32} \end{bmatrix}$$

In general, we may state the rule thus:

$$[a_{ij}] + [b_{ij}] = [c_{ij}] \qquad \text{where } c_{ij} = a_{ij} + b_{ij}$$

Note that the sum matrix $[c_{ij}]$ must have the same dimension as the component matrices $[a_{ij}]$ and $[b_{ij}]$.

The subtraction operation $A - B$ can be similarly defined if and only if A and B have the same dimension. The operation entails the result

$$[a_{ij}] - [b_{ij}] = [d_{ij}] \qquad \text{where } d_{ij} = a_{ij} - b_{ij}$$

Example 3

$$\begin{bmatrix} 19 & 3 \\ 2 & 0 \end{bmatrix} - \begin{bmatrix} 6 & 8 \\ 1 & 3 \end{bmatrix} = \begin{bmatrix} 19-6 & 3-8 \\ 2-1 & 0-3 \end{bmatrix} = \begin{bmatrix} 13 & -5 \\ 1 & -3 \end{bmatrix}$$

The subtraction operation $A - B$ may be considered alternatively as an addition operation involving a matrix A and another matrix $(-1)B$. This, however, raises the question of what is meant by the multiplication of a matrix by a single number (here, -1).

Scalar Multiplication

To multiply a matrix by a number—or in matrix-algebra terminology, by a *scalar*—is to multiply *every* element of that matrix by the given scalar.

Example 4

$$7\begin{bmatrix} 3 & -1 \\ 0 & 5 \end{bmatrix} = \begin{bmatrix} 21 & -7 \\ 0 & 35 \end{bmatrix}$$

Example 5

$$\frac{1}{2}\begin{bmatrix} a_{11} & a_{12} \\ a_{21} & a_{22} \end{bmatrix} = \begin{bmatrix} \frac{1}{2}a_{11} & \frac{1}{2}a_{12} \\ \frac{1}{2}a_{21} & \frac{1}{2}a_{22} \end{bmatrix}$$

From these examples, the rationale of the name scalar should become clear, for it "scales up (or down)" the matrix by a certain multiple. The scalar can, of course, be a negative number as well.

Example 6

$$-1\begin{bmatrix} a_{11} & a_{12} & d_1 \\ a_{21} & a_{22} & d_2 \end{bmatrix} = \begin{bmatrix} -a_{11} & -a_{12} & -d_1 \\ -a_{21} & -a_{22} & -d_2 \end{bmatrix}$$

Note that if the matrix on the left represents the coefficients *and* the constant terms in the simultaneous equations

$$a_{11}x_1 + a_{12}x_2 = d_1$$
$$a_{21}x_1 + a_{22}x_2 = d_2$$

then multiplication by the scalar -1 will amount to multiplying both sides of both equations by -1, thereby changing the sign of every term in the system.

Multiplication of Matrices

Whereas a scalar can be used to multiply a matrix of any dimension, the multiplication of two matrices is contingent upon the satisfaction of a different dimensional requirement.

Suppose that, given two matrices A and B, we want to find the product AB. The conformability condition for multiplication is that the *column* dimension of A (the "lead" matrix in the expression AB) must be equal to the row dimension of B (the "lag" matrix). For instance, if

$$\underset{(1 \times 2)}{A} = [a_{11} \quad a_{12}] \qquad \underset{(2 \times 3)}{B} = \begin{bmatrix} b_{11} & b_{12} & b_{13} \\ b_{21} & b_{22} & b_{23} \end{bmatrix} \qquad \textbf{(4.5)}$$

the product AB then *is* defined, since A has *two columns* and B has *two rows*—precisely the same number.[†] This can be checked at a glance by comparing the *second* number in the dimension indicator for A, which is (1×2), with the *first* number in the dimension indicator for A, which is (1×2), with the *first* number in the dimension indicator for B, (2×3). On the other hand, the reverse product BA is *not* defined in this case, because B (now the lead matrix) has *three* columns while A (the lag matrix) has only *one* row; hence the conformability condition is violated.

In general, if A is of dimension $m \times n$ and B is of dimension $p \times q$, the matrix product AB will be defined if and only if $n = p$. If defined, moreover, the product matrix AB will have the dimension $m \times q$—the same number of *rows* as the lead matrix A and the same number of *columns* as the lag matrix B. For the matrices given in (4.5), AB will be 1×3.

It remains to define the exact procedure of multiplication. For this purpose, let us take the matrices A and B in (4.5) for illustration. Since the product AB is defined and is expected to be of dimension 1×3, we may write in general (using the symbol C rather than c' for the row vector) that

$$AB = C = [c_{11} \quad c_{12} \quad c_{13}]$$

Each element in the product matrix C, denoted by c_{ij}, is defined as a sum of products, to be computed from the elements in the *i*th *row* of the lead matrix A, and those in the *j*th *column* of the lag matrix B. To find c_{11}, for instance, we should take the *first row* in A (since $i = 1$) and the *first column* in B (since $j = 1$)—as shown in the top panel of Fig. 4.1—and then pair the elements together sequentially, multiply out each pair, and take the sum of the resulting products, to get

$$c_{11} = a_{11}b_{11} + a_{12}b_{21} \qquad \textbf{(4.6)}$$

Similarly, for c_{12}, we take the *first row* in A (since $i = 1$) and the *second column* in B (since $j = 2$), and calculate the indicated sum of products—in accordance with the lower panel of Fig. 4.1—as follows:

$$c_{12} = a_{11}b_{12} + a_{12}b_{22} \qquad \textbf{(4.6′)}$$

By the same token, we should also have

$$c_{13} = a_{11}b_{13} + a_{12}b_{23} \qquad \textbf{(4.6″)}$$

[†] The matrix *A*, being a row vector, would normally be denoted by *a′*. We use the symbol *A* here to stress the fact that the multiplication rule being explained applies to matrices in general, not only to the product of one vector and one matrix.

FIGURE 4.1

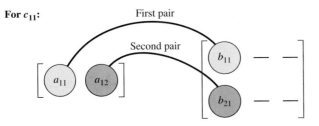

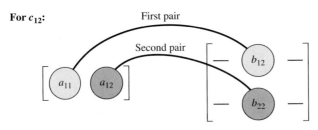

It is the particular pairing requirement in this process which necessitates the matching of the column dimension of the lead matrix and the row dimension of the lag matrix before multiplication can be performed.

The multiplication procedure illustrated in Fig. 4.1 can also be described by using the concept of the *inner product* of two vectors. Given two vectors u and v with n elements each, say, $(u_1, u_2, \ldots, u_n)$ and $(v_1, v_2, \ldots, v_n)$, arranged *either* as two rows *or* as two columns *or* as one row and one column, their inner product, written as $u \cdot v$ (with a dot in the middle), is defined as

$$u \cdot v = u_1 v_1 + u_2 v_2 + \cdots + u_n v_n$$

This is a sum of products of corresponding elements, and hence the inner product of two vectors is a scalar.

Example 7

If, after a shopping trip, we arrange the quantities purchased of n goods as a row vector $Q' = [Q_1 \quad Q_2 \quad \cdots \quad Q_n]$, and list the prices of those goods in a price vector $P' = [P_1 \quad P_2 \quad \cdots \quad P_n]$, then the inner product of these two vectors is

$$Q' \cdot P' = Q_1 P_1 + Q_2 P_2 + \cdots + Q_n P_n = \text{total purchase cost}$$

Using this concept, we can describe the element c_{ij} in the product matrix $C = AB$ simply as the inner product of the ith row of the lead matrix A and the jth column of the lag matrix B. By examining Fig. 4.1, we can easily verify the validity of this description.

The rule of multiplication just outlined applies with equal validity when the dimensions of A and B are other than those illustrated in Fig. 4.1; the only prerequisite is that the conformability condition be met.

Example 8

Given

$$\underset{(3\times2)}{A} = \begin{bmatrix} 1 & 3 \\ 2 & 8 \\ 4 & 0 \end{bmatrix} \quad \text{and} \quad \underset{(2\times1)}{B} = \begin{bmatrix} 5 \\ 9 \end{bmatrix}$$

find *AB*. The product *AB* is indeed defined because *A* has two columns and *B* has two rows. Their product matrix should be 3×1, a column vector:

$$AB = \begin{bmatrix} 1(5) + 3(9) \\ 2(5) + 8(9) \\ 4(5) + 0(9) \end{bmatrix} = \begin{bmatrix} 32 \\ 82 \\ 20 \end{bmatrix}$$

Example 9

Given

$$\underset{(3\times3)}{A} = \begin{bmatrix} 3 & -1 & 2 \\ 1 & 0 & 3 \\ 4 & 0 & 2 \end{bmatrix} \quad \text{and} \quad \underset{(3\times3)}{B} = \begin{bmatrix} 0 & -\frac{1}{5} & \frac{3}{10} \\ -1 & \frac{1}{5} & \frac{7}{10} \\ 0 & \frac{2}{5} & -\frac{1}{10} \end{bmatrix}$$

find *AB*. The same rule of multiplication now yields a very special product matrix:

$$AB = \begin{bmatrix} 0+1+0 & -\frac{3}{5}-\frac{1}{5}+\frac{4}{5} & \frac{9}{10}-\frac{7}{10}-\frac{2}{10} \\ 0+0+0 & -\frac{1}{5}+0+\frac{6}{5} & \frac{3}{10}+0-\frac{3}{10} \\ 0+0+0 & -\frac{4}{5}+0+\frac{4}{5} & \frac{12}{10}+0-\frac{2}{10} \end{bmatrix} = \begin{bmatrix} 1 & 0 & 0 \\ 0 & 1 & 0 \\ 0 & 0 & 1 \end{bmatrix}$$

This last matrix—a square matrix with 1s in its *principal diagonal* (the diagonal running from northwest to southeast) and 0s everywhere else—exemplifies the important type of matrix known as the *identity matrix.* This will be further discussed in Section 4.5.

Example 10

Let us now take the matrix *A* and the vector *x* as defined in (4.4) and find *Ax*. The product matrix is a 3×1 column vector:

$$Ax = \begin{bmatrix} 6 & 3 & 1 \\ 1 & 4 & -2 \\ 4 & -1 & 5 \end{bmatrix} \begin{bmatrix} x_1 \\ x_2 \\ x_3 \end{bmatrix} = \begin{bmatrix} 6x_1 + 3x_2 + x_3 \\ x_1 + 4x_2 - 2x_3 \\ 4x_1 - x_2 + 5x_3 \end{bmatrix}$$

$$\quad (3\times3) \qquad (3\times1) \qquad\qquad (3\times1)$$

Note: The product on the right is a *column* vector, its corpulent appearance notwithstanding! When we write $Ax = d$, therefore, we have

$$\begin{bmatrix} 6x_1 + 3x_2 + x_3 \\ x_1 + 4x_2 - 2x_3 \\ 4x_1 - x_2 + 5x_3 \end{bmatrix} = \begin{bmatrix} 22 \\ 12 \\ 10 \end{bmatrix}$$

which, according to the definition of matrix equality, is equivalent to the statement of the entire equation system in (4.3).

Note that, to use the matrix notation $Ax = d$, it is necessary, because of the conformability condition, to arrange the variables x_j into a *column* vector, even though these variables are listed in a horizontal order in the original equation system.

Example 11

The simple national-income model in two endogenous variables *Y* and *C*,

$$Y = C + I_0 + G_0$$
$$C = a + bY$$

can be rearranged into the standard format of (4.1) as follows:

$$Y - C = I_0 + G_0$$
$$-bY + C = a$$

Hence the coefficient matrix A, the vector of variables x, and the vector of constants d are

$$\underset{(2\times2)}{A} = \begin{bmatrix} 1 & -1 \\ -b & 1 \end{bmatrix} \qquad \underset{(2\times1)}{x} = \begin{bmatrix} Y \\ C \end{bmatrix} \qquad \underset{(2\times1)}{d} = \begin{bmatrix} I_0 + G_0 \\ a \end{bmatrix}$$

Let us verify that this given system can be expressed by the equation $Ax = d$.

By the rule of matrix multiplication, we have

$$Ax = \begin{bmatrix} 1 & -1 \\ -b & 1 \end{bmatrix} \begin{bmatrix} Y \\ C \end{bmatrix} = \begin{bmatrix} 1(Y) + (-1)(C) \\ -b(Y) + 1(C) \end{bmatrix} = \begin{bmatrix} Y - C \\ -bY + C \end{bmatrix}$$

Thus the matrix equation $Ax = d$ would give us

$$\begin{bmatrix} Y - C \\ -bY + C \end{bmatrix} = \begin{bmatrix} I_0 + G_0 \\ a \end{bmatrix}$$

Since matrix equality means the equality between corresponding elements, it is clear that the equation $Ax = d$ does precisely represent the original equation system, as expressed in the (4.1) format.

The Question of Division

While matrices, like numbers, can undergo the operations of addition, subtraction, and multiplication—subject to the conformability conditions—it is not possible to divide one matrix by another. That is, we cannot write A/B.

For two numbers a and b, the quotient a/b (with $b \neq 0$) can be written alternatively as ab^{-1} or $b^{-1}a$, where b^{-1} represents the *inverse* or *reciprocal* of b. Since $ab^{-1} = b^{-1}a$, the quotient expression a/b can be used to represent both ab^{-1} and $b^{-1}a$. The case of matrices is different. Applying the concept of inverses to matrices, we may in certain cases (discussed in Sec. 4.6) define a matrix B^{-1} that is the inverse of matrix B. But from the discussion of the conformability condition it follows that, if AB^{-1} is defined, there can be no assurance that $B^{-1}A$ is also defined. Even if AB^{-1} and $B^{-1}A$ are indeed both defined, they still may not represent the same product. Hence the expression A/B cannot be used without ambiguity, and it must be avoided. Instead, you must specify whether you are referring to AB^{-1} or $B^{-1}A$—provided that the inverse B^{-1} does exist and that the matrix product in question is defined. Inverse matrices will be further discussed in Sec. 4.6.

The Σ Notation

The use of subscripted symbols not only helps in designating the locations of parameters and variables but also lends itself to a flexible shorthand for denoting sums of terms, such as those which arose during the process of matrix multiplication.

The summation shorthand makes use of the Greek letter Σ (sigma, for "sum"). To express the sum of x_1, x_2, and x_3, for instance, we may write

$$x_1 + x_2 + x_3 = \sum_{j=1}^{3} x_j$$

which is read as "the sum of x_j as j ranges from 1 to 3." The symbol j, called the *summation index*, takes only integer values. The expression x_j represents the *summand* (that which is to be summed), and it is in effect a function of j. Aside from the letter j, summation indices are also commonly denoted by i or k, such as

$$\sum_{i=3}^{7} x_i = x_3 + x_4 + x_5 + x_6 + x_7$$

$$\sum_{k=0}^{n} x_k = x_0 + x_1 + \cdots + x_n$$

The application of $\sum$ notation can be readily extended to cases in which the x term is prefixed with a coefficient or in which each term in the sum is raised to some integer power. For instance, we may write:

$$\sum_{j=1}^{3} ax_j = ax_1 + ax_2 + ax_3 = a(x_1 + x_2 + x_3) = a \sum_{j=1}^{3} x_j$$

$$\sum_{j=1}^{3} a_j x_j = a_1 x_1 + a_2 x_2 + a_3 x_3$$

$$\sum_{i=0}^{n} a_i x^i = a_0 x^0 + a_1 x^1 + a_2 x^2 + \cdots + a_n x^n$$

$$= a_0 + a_1 x + a_2 x^2 + \cdots + a_n x^n$$

The last example, in particular, shows that the expression $\sum_{i=0}^{n} a_i x^i$ can in fact be used as a shorthand form of the general polynomial function of (2.4).

It may be mentioned in passing that, whenever the context of the discussion leaves no ambiguity as to the range of summation, the symbol $\sum$ can be used alone, without an index attached (such as $\sum x_i$), or with only the index letter underneath (such as $\sum_i x_i$).

Let us apply the $\sum$ shorthand to matrix multiplication. In (4.6), (4.6'), and (4.6''), each element of the product matrix $C = AB$ is defined as a sum of terms, which may now be rewritten as follows:

$$c_{11} = a_{11}b_{11} + a_{12}b_{21} = \sum_{k=1}^{2} a_{1k}b_{k1}$$

$$c_{12} = a_{11}b_{12} + a_{12}b_{22} = \sum_{k=1}^{2} a_{1k}b_{k2}$$

$$c_{13} = a_{11}b_{13} + a_{12}b_{23} = \sum_{k=1}^{2} a_{1k}b_{k3}$$

In each case, the first subscript of c_{1j} is reflected in the first subscript of a_{1k}, and the second subscript of c_{1j} is reflected in the second subscript of b_{kj} in the $\sum$ expression. The index k, on the other hand, is a "dummy" subscript; it serves to indicate which particular pair of elements is being multiplied, but it does not show up in the symbol c_{1j}.

Extending this to the multiplication of an $m \times n$ matrix $A = [a_{ik}]$ and an $n \times p$ matrix $B = [b_{kj}]$, we may now write the elements of the $m \times p$ product matrix $AB = C = [c_{ij}]$ as

$$c_{11} = \sum_{k=1}^{n} a_{1k}b_{k1} \qquad c_{12} = \sum_{k=1}^{n} a_{1k}b_{k2} \qquad \cdots$$

or more generally,

$$c_{ij} = \sum_{k=1}^{n} a_{ik}b_{kj} \qquad \left(\begin{array}{l} i = 1, 2, \ldots, m \\ j = 1, 2, \ldots, p \end{array} \right)$$

This last equation represents yet another way of stating the rule of multiplication for the matrices defined above.

EXERCISE 4.2

1. Given $A = \begin{bmatrix} 7 & -1 \\ 6 & 9 \end{bmatrix}$, $B = \begin{bmatrix} 0 & 4 \\ 3 & -2 \end{bmatrix}$, and $C = \begin{bmatrix} 8 & 3 \\ 6 & 1 \end{bmatrix}$, find:

   (a) $A + B$ (b) $C - A$ (c) $3A$ (d) $4B + 2C$

2. Given $A = \begin{bmatrix} 2 & 8 \\ 3 & 0 \\ 5 & 1 \end{bmatrix}$, $B = \begin{bmatrix} 2 & 0 \\ 3 & 8 \end{bmatrix}$, and $C = \begin{bmatrix} 7 & 2 \\ 6 & 3 \end{bmatrix}$:

   (a) Is AB defined? Calculate AB. Can you calculate BA? Why?

   (b) Is BC defined? Calculate BC. Is CB defined? If so, calculate CB. Is it true that $BC = CB$?

3. On the basis of the matrices given in Example 9, is the product BA defined? If so, calculate the product. In this case do we have $AB = BA$?

4. Find the product matrices in the following (in each case, append beneath every matrix a dimension indicator):

   (a) $\begin{bmatrix} 0 & 2 & 0 \\ 3 & 0 & 4 \\ 2 & 3 & 0 \end{bmatrix} \begin{bmatrix} 8 & 0 \\ 0 & 1 \\ 3 & 5 \end{bmatrix}$ (c) $\begin{bmatrix} 3 & 5 & 0 \\ 4 & 2 & -7 \end{bmatrix} \begin{bmatrix} x \\ y \\ z \end{bmatrix}$

   (b) $\begin{bmatrix} 6 & 5 & -1 \\ 1 & 0 & 4 \end{bmatrix} \begin{bmatrix} 4 & -1 \\ 5 & 2 \\ 0 & 1 \end{bmatrix}$ (d) $[a \quad b \quad c] \begin{bmatrix} 7 & 0 \\ 0 & 2 \\ 1 & 4 \end{bmatrix}$

5. In Example 7, if we arrange the quantities and prices as column vectors instead of row vectors, is $Q \cdot P$ defined? Can we express the total purchase cost as $Q \cdot P$? As $Q' \cdot P$? As $Q \cdot P'$?

6. Expand the following summation expressions:

   (a) $\displaystyle\sum_{i=2}^{5} x_i$ (d) $\displaystyle\sum_{i=1}^{n} a_i x^{i-1}$

   (b) $\displaystyle\sum_{i=5}^{8} a_i x_i$ (e) $\displaystyle\sum_{i=0}^{3} (x + i)^2$

   (c) $\displaystyle\sum_{i=1}^{4} b x_i$

7. Rewrite the following in $\sum$ notation:

   (a) $x_1(x_1 - 1) + 2x_2(x_2 - 1) + 3x_3(x_3 - 1)$

   (b) $a_2(x_3 + 2) + a_3(x_4 + 3) + a_4(x_5 + 4)$

   (c) $\dfrac{1}{x} + \dfrac{1}{x^2} + \cdots + \dfrac{1}{x^n}$ $(x \neq 0)$

   (d) $1 + \dfrac{1}{x} + \dfrac{1}{x^2} + \cdots + \dfrac{1}{x^n}$ $(x \neq 0)$

8. Show that the following are true:

   (a) $\left(\sum\limits_{i=0}^{n} x_i \right) + x_{n+1} = \sum\limits_{i=0}^{n+1} x_i$

   (b) $\sum\limits_{j=1}^{n} ab_j y_j = a \sum\limits_{j=1}^{n} b_j y_j$

   (c) $\sum\limits_{j=1}^{n} (x_j + y_j) = \sum\limits_{j=1}^{n} x_j + \sum\limits_{j=1}^{n} y_j$

4.3   Notes on Vector Operations

In Secs. 4.1 and 4.2, vectors are considered as a special type of matrix. As such, they qualify for the application of all the algebraic operations discussed. Owing to their dimensional peculiarities, however, some additional comments on vector operations are useful.

Multiplication of Vectors

An $m \times 1$ column vector u, and a $1 \times n$ row vector v', yield a product matrix uv' of dimension $m \times n$.

Example 1   Given $u = \begin{bmatrix} 3 \\ 2 \end{bmatrix}$ and $v' = [1 \quad 4 \quad 5]$, we can get

$$uv' = \begin{bmatrix} 3(1) & 3(4) & 3(5) \\ 2(1) & 2(4) & 2(5) \end{bmatrix} = \begin{bmatrix} 3 & 12 & 15 \\ 2 & 8 & 10 \end{bmatrix}$$

Since each row in u consists of one element only, as does each column in v', each element of uv' turns out to be a single product instead of a sum of products. The product uv' is a 2×3 matrix, even though what we started out with are a pair of vectors.

On the other hand, given a $1 \times n$ row vector u' and an $n \times 1$ column vector v, the product $u'v$ will be of dimension 1×1.

Example 2   Given $u' = [3 \quad 4]$ and $v = \begin{bmatrix} 9 \\ 7 \end{bmatrix}$, we have

$$u'v = [3(9) + 4(7)] = [55]$$

As written, $u'v$ is a matrix, despite the fact that only a single element is present. However, 1×1 matrices behave exactly like scalars with respect to addition and multiplication: $[4] + [8] = [12]$, just as $4 + 8 = 12$; and $[3][7] = [21]$, just as $3(7) = 21$. Moreover, 1×1

matrices possess no major properties that scalars do not have. In fact, there is a one-to-one correspondence between the set of all scalars and the set of all 1×1 matrices whose elements are scalars. For this reason, we may redefine $u'v$ to be the *scalar* corresponding to the 1×1 product matrix. For Example 2, we can accordingly write $u'v = 55$. Such a product is called a *scalar product*.[†] Remember, however, that while a 1×1 matrix can be treated as a scalar, a scalar cannot be replaced by a 1×1 matrix at will if further calculation is to be carried out, because complications regarding conformability conditions may arise.

Example 3   Given a row vector $u' = [3 \quad 6 \quad 9]$, find $u'u$. Since u is merely the column vector with the elements of u' arranged vertically, we have

$$u'u = [3 \quad 6 \quad 9] \begin{bmatrix} 3 \\ 6 \\ 9 \end{bmatrix} = (3)^2 + (6)^2 + (9)^2$$

where we have omitted the brackets from the 1×1 product matrix on the right. Note that the product $u'u$ gives the sum of squares of the elements of u.

In general, if $u' = [u_1 \quad u_2 \quad \cdots \quad u_n]$, then $u'u$ will be the sum of squares (a scalar) of the elements u_j:

$$u'u = u_1^2 + u_2^2 + \cdots + u_n^2 = \sum_{j=1}^{n} u_j^2$$

Had we calculated the inner product $u \cdot u$ (or $u' \cdot u'$), we would have, of course, obtained exactly the same result.

To conclude, it is important to distinguish between the meanings of uv' (a matrix larger than 1×1) and $u'v$ (a 1×1 matrix, or a scalar). Observe, in particular, that a scalar product must have a *row* vector as the lead matrix and a *column* vector as the lag matrix; otherwise the product cannot be 1×1.

Geometric Interpretation of Vector Operations

It was mentioned earlier that a column or row vector with n elements (referred to hereafter as an *n-vector*) can be viewed as an *n*-tuple, and hence as a point in an *n*-dimensional space (referred to hereafter as an *n-space*). Let us elaborate on this idea. In Fig. 4.2*a*, a point $(3, 2)$ is plotted in a 2-space and is labeled u. This is the geometric counterpart of the vector $u = \begin{bmatrix} 3 \\ 2 \end{bmatrix}$ or the vector $u' = [3 \quad 2]$, both of which indicate in this context one and the same ordered pair. If an arrow (a directed-line segment) is drawn from the point of origin $(0, 0)$ to the point u, it will specify the unique straight route by which to reach the destination point u from the point of origin. Since a unique arrow exists for each point, we can regard the vector u as graphically represented *either* by the point $(3, 2)$, *or* by the corresponding arrow. Such an arrow, which emanates from the origin $(0, 0)$ like the hand of a clock, with a definite length and a definite direction, is called a *radius vector*.

[†] The concept of scalar product is thus akin to the concept of inner product of two vectors with the same number of elements in each, which also yields a scalar. Recall, however, that the inner product is exempted from the conformability condition for multiplication, so that we may write it as $u \cdot v$. In the case of scalar product (denoted without a dot between the two vector symbols), on the other hand, we can express it only as a row vector multiplied by a column vector, with the row vector in the lead.

FIGURE 4.2

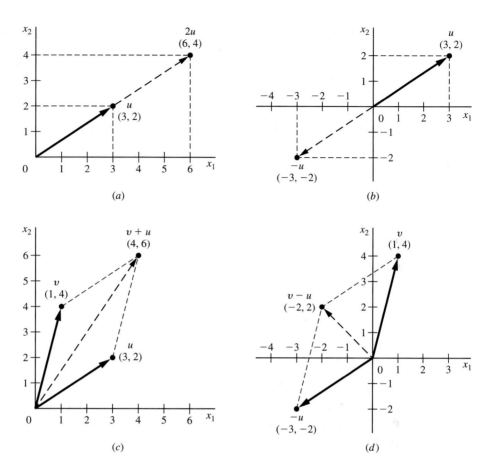

Following this new interpretation of a vector, it becomes possible to give geometric meanings to (*a*) the scalar multiplication of a vector, (*b*) the addition and subtraction of vectors, and more generally, (*c*) the so-called linear combination of vectors.

First, if we plot the vector $\begin{bmatrix} 6 \\ 4 \end{bmatrix} = 2u$ in Fig. 4.2*a*, the resulting arrow will overlap the old one but will be twice as long. In fact, the multiplication of vector u by any scalar k will produce an overlapping arrow, but the arrowhead will be relocated, unless $k = 1$. If the scalar multiplier is $k > 1$, the arrow will be extended out (scaled up); if $0 < k < 1$, the arrow will be shortened (scaled down); if $k = 0$, the arrow will shrink into the point of origin—which represents a *null vector,* $\begin{bmatrix} 0 \\ 0 \end{bmatrix}$. A negative scalar multiplier will even reverse the direction of the arrow. If the vector u is multiplied by -1, for instance, we get $-u = \begin{bmatrix} -3 \\ -2 \end{bmatrix}$, and this plots in Fig. 4.2*b* as an arrow of the same length as u but diametrically opposite in direction.

Next, consider the addition of two vectors, $v = \begin{bmatrix} 1 \\ 4 \end{bmatrix}$ and $u = \begin{bmatrix} 3 \\ 2 \end{bmatrix}$. The sum $v + u = \begin{bmatrix} 4 \\ 6 \end{bmatrix}$ can be directly plotted as the broken arrow in Fig. 4.2*c*. If we construct a parallelogram with the two vectors u and v (solid arrows) as two of its sides, however, the diagonal of the parallelogram will turn out exactly to be the arrow representing the vector sum $v + u$. In general, a vector sum can be obtained geometrically from a parallelogram. Moreover, this method can also give us the *vector difference* $v - u$, since the latter is equivalent to the *sum* of v and $(-1)u$. In Fig. 4.2*d*, we first reproduce the vector v and the negative vector $-u$ from diagrams *c* and *b*, respectively, and then construct a parallelogram. The resulting diagonal represents the vector difference $v - u$.

It takes only a simple extension of these results to interpret geometrically a linear combination (i.e., a linear sum or difference) of vectors. Consider the simple case of

$$3v + 2u = 3\begin{bmatrix} 1 \\ 4 \end{bmatrix} + 2\begin{bmatrix} 3 \\ 2 \end{bmatrix} = \begin{bmatrix} 9 \\ 16 \end{bmatrix}$$

The scalar multiplication aspect of this operation involves the relocation of the respective arrowheads of the two vectors v and u, and the addition aspect calls for the construction of a parallelogram. Beyond these two basic graphical operations, there is nothing new in a linear combination of vectors. This is true even if there are more terms in the linear combination, as in

$$\sum_{i=1}^{n} k_i v_i = k_1 v_1 + k_2 v_2 + \cdots + k_n v_n$$

where k_i are a set of scalars but the subscripted symbols v_i now denote a set of vectors. To form this sum, the first two terms may be added first, and then the resulting sum is added to the third, and so forth, till all terms are included.

Linear Dependence

A set of vectors $v_1, \ldots, v_n$ is said to be *linearly dependent* if (and only if) any one of them can be expressed as a linear combination of the remaining vectors; otherwise they are *linearly independent*.

Example 4   The three vectors $v_1 = \begin{bmatrix} 2 \\ 7 \end{bmatrix}$, $v_2 = \begin{bmatrix} 1 \\ 8 \end{bmatrix}$, and $v_3 = \begin{bmatrix} 4 \\ 5 \end{bmatrix}$ are linearly dependent because v_3 is a linear combination of v_1 and v_2:

$$3v_1 - 2v_2 = \begin{bmatrix} 6 \\ 21 \end{bmatrix} - \begin{bmatrix} 2 \\ 16 \end{bmatrix} = \begin{bmatrix} 4 \\ 5 \end{bmatrix} = v_3$$

Note that this last equation is alternatively expressible as

$$3v_1 - 2v_2 - v_3 = 0$$

where $0 \equiv \begin{bmatrix} 0 \\ 0 \end{bmatrix}$ represents a null vector (also called the *zero vector*).

Example 5   The two row vectors $v_1' = [5 \quad 12]$ and $v_2' = [10 \quad 24]$ are linearly dependent because

$$2v_1' = 2[5 \quad 12] = [10 \quad 24] = v_2'$$

The fact that one vector is a multiple of another vector illustrates the simplest case of linear combination. Note again that this last equation may be written equivalently as

$$2v_1' - v_2' = 0'$$

where $0'$ represents the null row vector $[0 \quad 0]$.

With the introduction of null vectors, linear dependence may be redefined as follows. A set of m-vectors $v_1, \ldots, v_n$ is *linearly dependent* if and only if there exists a set of scalars $k_1, \ldots, k_n$ (not all zero) such that

$$\sum_{i=1}^{n} k_i v_i = \underset{(m \times 1)}{0}$$

If this equation can be satisfied *only when* $k_i = 0$ for all i, on the other hand, these vectors are linearly independent.

The concept of linear dependence admits of an easy geometric interpretation also. Two vectors u and $2u$—one being a multiple of the other—are obviously dependent. Geometrically, in Fig. 4.2*a*, their arrows lie on a single straight line. The same is true of the two dependent vectors u and $-u$ in Fig. 4.2*b*. In contrast, the two vectors u and v of Fig. 4.2*c* are linearly *independent,* because it is impossible to express one as a multiple of the other. Geometrically, their arrows do not lie on a single straight line.

When more than two vectors in the 2-space are considered, there emerges this significant conclusion: once we have found two linearly *independent* vectors in the 2-space (say, u and v), all the other vectors in that space will be expressible as a linear combination of these (u and v). In Fig. 4.2*c* and *d*, it has already been illustrated how the two simple linear combinations $v + u$ and $v - u$ can be found. Furthermore, by extending, shortening, and reversing the given vectors u and v and then combining these into various parallelograms, we can generate an infinite number of new vectors, which will exhaust the set of all 2-vectors. Because of this, any set of three or more 2-vectors (three or more vectors in a 2-space) must be linearly dependent. Two of them can be independent, but then the third must be a linear combination of the first two.

Vector Space

The totality of the 2-vectors generated by the various linear combinations of two independent vectors u and v constitutes the two-dimensional *vector space.* Since we are dealing only with vectors with real-valued elements, this vector space is none other than R^2, the 2-space we have been referring to all along. The 2-space cannot be generated by a single 2-vector, because linear combinations of the latter can only give rise to the set of vectors lying on a single straight line. Nor does the generation of the 2-space require more than two linearly independent 2-vectors—at any rate, it would be impossible to find more than two.

The two linearly independent vectors u and v are said to *span* the 2-space. They are also said to constitute a *basis* for the 2-space. Note that we said *a* basis, not *the* basis, because any pair of 2-vectors can serve in that capacity as long as they are linearly independent. In particular, consider the two vectors [1   0] and [0   1], which are called *unit vectors.* The first one plots as an arrow lying along the horizontal axis, and the second, an arrow lying along the vertical axis. Because they are linearly independent, they can serve as a basis for the 2-space, and we do in fact ordinarily think of the 2-space as spanned by its two axes, which are nothing but the extended versions of the two unit vectors.

By analogy, the three-dimensional vector space is the totality of 3-vectors, and it must be spanned by exactly three linearly independent 3-vectors. As an illustration, consider the set of three unit vectors

$$e_1 \equiv \begin{bmatrix} 1 \\ 0 \\ 0 \end{bmatrix} \qquad e_2 \equiv \begin{bmatrix} 0 \\ 1 \\ 0 \end{bmatrix} \qquad e_3 \equiv \begin{bmatrix} 0 \\ 0 \\ 1 \end{bmatrix} \qquad \textbf{(4.7)}$$

FIGURE 4.3

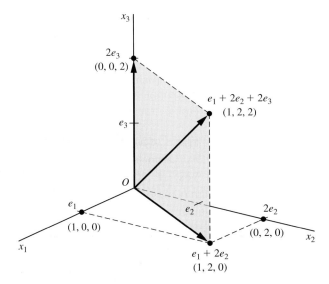

where each e_i is a vector with 1 as its ith element and with zeros elsewhere.[†] These three vectors are obviously linearly independent; in fact, their arrows lie on the three axes of the 3-space in Fig. 4.3. Thus they span the 3-space, which implies that the entire 3-space (R^3, in our framework) can be generated from these unit vectors. For example, the vector $\begin{bmatrix} 1 \\ 2 \\ 2 \end{bmatrix}$ can be considered as the linear combination $e_1 + 2e_2 + 2e_3$. Geometrically, we can first add the vectors e_1 and $2e_2$ in Fig. 4.3 by the parallelogram method, in order to get the vector represented by the point (1, 2, 0) in the x_1x_2 plane, and then add the latter vector to $2e_3$—via the parallelogram constructed in the shaded vertical plane—to obtain the desired final result, at the point (1, 2, 2).

The further extension to n-space should be obvious. The n-space can be defined as the totality of n-vectors. Though nongraphable, we can still think of the n-space as being spanned by a total of n (n-element) unit vectors that are all linearly independent. Each n-vector, being an ordered n-tuple, represents a *point* in the n-space, or an arrow extending from the point of origin (i.e., the n-element null vector) to the said point. And any given set of n linearly independent n-vectors is, in fact, capable of generating the entire n-space. Since, in our discussion, each element of the n-vector is restricted to be a real number, this n-space is in fact R^n.

The n-space we have referred to is sometimes more specifically called the *Euclidean n-space* (named after Euclid). To explain this latter concept, we must first comment briefly on the concept of *distance* between two vector points. For any pair of vector points u and v in a given space, the distance from u to v is some real-valued function

$$d = d(u, v)$$

with the following properties: (1) when u and v coincide, the distance is zero; (2) when the two points are distinct, the distance from u to v and the distance from v to u are represented

---

[†] The symbol e may be associated with the German word *eins*, for "one."

by an identical positive real number; and (3) the distance between u and v is never longer than the distance from u to w (a point distinct from u and v) plus the distance from w to v. Expressed symbolically,

$$d(u, v) = 0 \qquad\qquad \text{(for } u = v\text{)}$$
$$d(u, v) = d(v, u) > 0 \qquad\qquad \text{(for } u \neq v\text{)}$$
$$d(u, v) \leq d(u, w) + d(w, v) \qquad \text{(for } w \neq u, v\text{)}$$

The last property is known as the *triangular inequality,* because the three points u, v, and w together will usually define a triangle.

When a vector space has a distance function defined that fulfills the previous three properties, it is called a *metric space.* However, note that the distance $d(u, v)$ has been discussed only in general terms. Depending on the specific form assigned to the d function, there may result a variety of metric spaces. The so-called Euclidean space is one specific type of metric space, with a distance function defined as follows. Let point u be the n-tuple $(a_1, a_2, \ldots, a_n)$ and point v be the n-tuple $(b_1, b_2, \ldots, b_n)$; then the Euclidean distance function is

$$d(u, v) = \sqrt{(a_1 - b_1)^2 + (a_2 - b_2)^2 + \cdots + (a_n - b_n)^2}$$

where the square root is taken to be positive. As can be easily verified, this specific distance function satisfies all three properties previously enumerated. Applied to the two-dimensional space in Fig. 4.2a, the distance between the two points $(6, 4)$ and $(3, 2)$ is found to be

$$\sqrt{(6 - 3)^2 + (4 - 2)^2} = \sqrt{3^2 + 2^2} = \sqrt{13}$$

This result is seen to be consistent with *Pythagoras's theorem,* which states that the length of the hypotenuse of a right-angled triangle is equal to the (positive) square root of the sum of the squares of the lengths of the other two sides. For if we take $(6, 4)$ and $(3, 2)$ to be u and v, and plot a new point w at $(6, 2)$, we shall indeed have a right-angled triangle with the lengths of its horizontal and vertical sides equal to 3 and 2, respectively, and the length of the hypotenuse (the distance between u and v) equal to $\sqrt{3^2 + 2^2} = \sqrt{13}$.

The Euclidean distance function can also be expressed in terms of the square root of a scalar product of two vectors. Since u and v denote the two n-tuples $(a_1, \ldots, a_n)$ and $(b_1, \ldots, b_n)$, we can write a column vector $u - v$, with elements $a_1 - b_1, a_2 - b_2, \ldots, a_n - b_n$. What goes under the square-root sign in the Euclidean distance function is, of course, simply the sum of squares of these n elements, which, in view of Example 3 of this section, can be written as the scalar product $(u - v)'(u - v)$. Hence we have

$$d(u, v) = \sqrt{(u - v)'(u - v)}$$

EXERCISE 4.3

1. Given $u' = [5 \quad 1 \quad 3]$, $v' = [3 \quad 1 \quad -1]$, $w' = [7 \quad 5 \quad 8]$, and $x' = [x_1 \quad x_2 \quad x_3]$, write out the column vectors, u, v, w, and x, and find

   (a) uv' (c) xx' (e) $u'v$ (g) $u'u$

   (b) uw' (d) $v'u$ (f) $w'x$ (h) $x'x$

2. Given $w = \begin{bmatrix} 3 \\ 2 \\ 16 \end{bmatrix}$, $x = \begin{bmatrix} x_1 \\ x_2 \end{bmatrix}$, $y = \begin{bmatrix} y_1 \\ y_2 \end{bmatrix}$, and $z = \begin{bmatrix} z_1 \\ z_2 \end{bmatrix}$:

(a) Which of the following are defined: $w'x$, $x'y'$, xy', $y'y$, zz', yw', $x \cdot y$?

(b) Find all the products that are defined.

3. Having sold n items of merchandise at quantities $Q_1, \ldots, Q_n$ and prices $P_1, \ldots, P_n$, how would you express the total revenue in (a) $\sum$ notation and (b) vector notation?

4. Given two nonzero vectors w_1 and w_2, the angle θ ($0° \le \theta \le 180°$) they form is related to the scalar product $w_1'w_2$ ($= w_2'w_1$) as follows:

$$\theta \text{ is a(n) } \left\{ \begin{matrix} \text{acute} \\ \text{right} \\ \text{obtuse} \end{matrix} \right\} \text{ angle if and only if } w_1'w_2 \left\{ \begin{matrix} > \\ = \\ < \end{matrix} \right\} 0$$

Verify this by computing the scalar product for each of the following pair of vectors (see Figs. 4.2 and 4.3):

(a) $w_1 = \begin{bmatrix} 3 \\ 2 \end{bmatrix}$, $w_2 = \begin{bmatrix} 1 \\ 4 \end{bmatrix}$

(d) $w_1 = \begin{bmatrix} 1 \\ 0 \\ 0 \end{bmatrix}$, $w_2 = \begin{bmatrix} 0 \\ 2 \\ 0 \end{bmatrix}$

(b) $w_1 = \begin{bmatrix} 1 \\ 4 \end{bmatrix}$, $w_2 = \begin{bmatrix} -3 \\ -2 \end{bmatrix}$

(e) $w_1 = \begin{bmatrix} 1 \\ 2 \\ 2 \end{bmatrix}$, $w_2 = \begin{bmatrix} 1 \\ 2 \\ 0 \end{bmatrix}$

(c) $w_1 = \begin{bmatrix} 3 \\ 2 \end{bmatrix}$, $w_2 = \begin{bmatrix} -3 \\ -2 \end{bmatrix}$

5. Given $u = \begin{bmatrix} 5 \\ 1 \end{bmatrix}$ and $v = \begin{bmatrix} 0 \\ 3 \end{bmatrix}$, find the following graphically:

(a) $2v$ (c) $u - v$ (e) $2u + 3v$

(b) $u + v$ (d) $v - u$ (f) $4u - 2v$

6. Since the 3-space is spanned by the three unit vectors defined in (4.7), any other 3-vector should be expressible as a linear combination of e_1, e_2, and e_3. Show that the following 3-vectors can be so expressed:

(a) $\begin{bmatrix} 4 \\ 7 \\ 0 \end{bmatrix}$ (b) $\begin{bmatrix} 25 \\ -2 \\ 1 \end{bmatrix}$ (c) $\begin{bmatrix} -1 \\ 6 \\ 9 \end{bmatrix}$ (d) $\begin{bmatrix} 2 \\ 0 \\ 8 \end{bmatrix}$

7. In the three-dimensional Euclidean space, what is the distance between the following points?

(a) $(3, 2, 8)$ and $(0, -1, 5)$ (b) $(9, 0, 4)$ and $(2, 0, -4)$

8. The triangular inequality is written with the *weak* inequality sign $\le$, rather than the strict inequality sign $<$. Under what circumstances would the "=" part of the inequality apply?

9. Express the length of a radius vector v in the Euclidean n-space (i.e., the distance from the origin to point v) by using each of the following:

(a) scalars   (b) a scalar product   (c) an inner product

4.4 Commutative, Associative, and Distributive Laws

In ordinary scalar algebra, the additive and multiplicative operations obey the commutative, associative, and distributive laws as follows:

Commutative law of addition: $\qquad\qquad\qquad\qquad\qquad a + b = b + a$
Commutative law of multiplication: $\qquad\qquad\qquad\qquad ab = ba$
Associative law of addition: $\qquad\qquad\qquad\qquad (a + b) + c = a + (b + c)$
Associative law of multiplication: $\qquad\qquad\qquad\quad (ab)c = a(bc)$
Distributive law: $\qquad\qquad\qquad\qquad\qquad\qquad a(b + c) = ab + ac$

These have been referred to during the discussion of the similarly named laws applicable to the union and intersection of sets. Most, but not all, of these laws also apply to matrix operations—the significant exception being the commutative law of multiplication.

Matrix Addition

Matrix addition is commutative as well as associative. This follows from the fact that matrix addition calls only for the addition of the corresponding elements of two matrices, and that the order in which each pair of corresponding elements is added is immaterial. In this context, incidentally, the subtraction operation $A - B$ can simply be regarded as the addition operation $A + (-B)$, and thus no separate discussion is necessary.

The commutative and associative laws can be stated as follows:

Commutative law $\qquad\qquad\qquad\qquad A + B = B + A$

PROOF $\qquad A + B = [a_{ij}] + [b_{ij}] = [a_{ij} + b_{ij}] = [b_{ij} + a_{ij}] = B + A$

Example 1 Given $A = \begin{bmatrix} 3 & 1 \\ 0 & 2 \end{bmatrix}$ and $B = \begin{bmatrix} 6 & 2 \\ 3 & 4 \end{bmatrix}$, we find that

$$A + B = B + A = \begin{bmatrix} 9 & 3 \\ 3 & 6 \end{bmatrix}$$

Associative law $\qquad\qquad\qquad (A + B) + C = A + (B + C)$

PROOF $\qquad (A + B) + C = [a_{ij} + b_{ij}] + [c_{ij}] = [a_{ij} + b_{ij} + c_{ij}]$
$$= [a_{ij}] + [b_{ij} + c_{ij}] = A + (B + C)$$

Example 2 Given $v_1 = \begin{bmatrix} 3 \\ 4 \end{bmatrix}$, $v_2 = \begin{bmatrix} 9 \\ 1 \end{bmatrix}$, and $v_3 = \begin{bmatrix} 2 \\ 5 \end{bmatrix}$, we find that

$$(v_1 + v_2) - v_3 = \begin{bmatrix} 12 \\ 5 \end{bmatrix} - \begin{bmatrix} 2 \\ 5 \end{bmatrix} = \begin{bmatrix} 10 \\ 0 \end{bmatrix}$$

which is equal to

$$v_1 + (v_2 - v_3) = \begin{bmatrix} 3 \\ 4 \end{bmatrix} + \begin{bmatrix} 7 \\ -4 \end{bmatrix} = \begin{bmatrix} 10 \\ 0 \end{bmatrix}$$

Applied to the linear combination of vectors $k_1 v_1 + \cdots + k_n v_n$, the associative law permits us to select any pair of terms for addition (or subtraction) first, instead of having to follow the sequence in which the n terms are listed.

Matrix Multiplication

Matrix multiplication is *not* commutative, that is,

$$AB \neq BA$$

As explained previously, even when AB is defined, BA may not be; but even if both products are defined, the general rule is still $AB \neq BA$.

Example 3 Let $A = \begin{bmatrix} 1 & 2 \\ 3 & 4 \end{bmatrix}$ and $B = \begin{bmatrix} 0 & -1 \\ 6 & 7 \end{bmatrix}$; then

$$AB = \begin{bmatrix} 1(0) + 2(6) & 1(-1) + 2(7) \\ 3(0) + 4(6) & 3(-1) + 4(7) \end{bmatrix} = \begin{bmatrix} 12 & 13 \\ 24 & 25 \end{bmatrix}$$

but

$$BA = \begin{bmatrix} 0(1) - 1(3) & 0(2) - 1(4) \\ 6(1) + 7(3) & 6(2) + 7(4) \end{bmatrix} = \begin{bmatrix} -3 & -4 \\ 27 & 40 \end{bmatrix}$$

Example 4 Let u' be 1×3 (a row vector); then the corresponding column vector u must be 3×1. The product $u'u$ will be 1×1, but the product uu' will be 3×3. Thus, obviously, $u'u \neq uu'$.

In view of the general rule $AB \neq BA$, the terms *premultiply* and *postmultiply* are often used to specify the order of multiplication. In the product AB, the matrix B is said to be *pre*multiplied by A, and A to be *post*multiplied by B.

There do exist interesting exceptions to the rule $AB \neq BA$, however. One such case is when A is a square matrix and B is an identity matrix. Another is when A is the inverse of B, that is, when $A = B^{-1}$. Both of these will be taken up again later. It should also be remarked here that the scalar multiplication of a matrix *does* obey the commutative law; thus, if k is a scalar, then

$$kA = Ak$$

Although it is not in general commutative, matrix multiplication *is* associative.

Associative law $$(AB)C = A(BC) = ABC$$

In forming the product ABC, the conformability condition must naturally be satisfied by each *adjacent* pair of matrices. If A is $m \times n$ and if C is $p \times q$, then conformability requires that B be $n \times p$:

$$\underset{(m \times n)}{A} \quad \underset{(n \times p)}{B} \quad \underset{(p \times q)}{C}$$

Note the dual appearance of n and p in the dimension indicators. If the conformability condition is met, the associative law states that any *adjacent* pair of matrices may be multiplied out first, provided that the product is duly inserted in the exact place of the original pair.

Example 5 If $x = \begin{bmatrix} x_1 \\ x_2 \end{bmatrix}$ and $A = \begin{bmatrix} a_{11} & 0 \\ 0 & a_{22} \end{bmatrix}$, then

$$x'Ax = x'(Ax) = [x_1 \quad x_2] \begin{bmatrix} a_{11}x_1 \\ a_{22}x_2 \end{bmatrix} = a_{11}x_1^2 + a_{22}x_2^2$$

Exactly the same result comes from

$$(x'A)x = [a_{11}x_1 \quad a_{22}x_2] \begin{bmatrix} x_1 \\ x_2 \end{bmatrix} = a_{11}x_1^2 + a_{22}x_2^2$$

In Example 5, the square matrix A has nonzero elements a_{11} and a_{22} in the principal diagonal, and zeros everywhere else. Such a matrix is called a *diagonal matrix*. When a diagonal matrix A appears in the product $x'Ax$, the resulting product gives a "weighted" sum of squares, the weights for the x_1^2 and the x_2^2 terms being supplied by the elements in the diagonal of A. This result is in contrast to the scalar product $x'x$, which yields a simple (unweighted) sum of squares.

Example 6

Let the economic ideal be defined as the national-income level Y^0 coupled with the inflation rate p^0. And suppose that we view any positive deviation of the actual income Y from Y^0 to be equally undesirable as a negative deviation of the same magnitude, and similarly for deviations of the actual inflation rate p from p^0. Then we may write a *social-loss function* such as

$$\Lambda = \alpha(Y - Y^0)^2 + \beta(p - p^0)^2$$

where α and β are the weights assigned to the two sources of social loss. If deviations of Y are considered to be the more serious type of loss, then α should exceed β. Note that the squaring of the deviations produces two effects. First, upon squaring, a positive deviation will receive the same loss value as a negative deviation of the same numerical magnitude. Second, squaring causes the larger deviations to show up much more significantly in the social-loss measure than minor deviations. Such a social-loss function can be expressed, if desired, by the matrix product

$$[Y - Y^0 \quad p - p^0]\begin{bmatrix} \alpha & 0 \\ 0 & \beta \end{bmatrix}\begin{bmatrix} Y - Y^0 \\ p - p^0 \end{bmatrix}$$

Matrix multiplication is also distributive.

Distributive law $A(B + C) = AB + AC$ [premultiplication by A]

$(B + C)A = BA + CA$ [postmultiplication by A]

In each case, the conformability conditions for addition as well as for multiplication must, of course, be observed.

EXERCISE 4.4

1. Given $A = \begin{bmatrix} 3 & 6 \\ 2 & 4 \end{bmatrix}$, $B = \begin{bmatrix} -1 & 7 \\ 8 & 4 \end{bmatrix}$, and $C = \begin{bmatrix} 3 & 4 \\ 1 & 9 \end{bmatrix}$, verify that

   (a) $(A + B) + C = A + (B + C)$
   (b) $(A + B) - C = A + (B - C)$

2. The subtraction of a matrix B may be considered as the addition of the matrix $(-1)B$. Does the commutative law of addition permit us to state that $A - B = B - A$? If not, how would you correct the statement?

3. Test the associative law of multiplication with the following matrices:

$$A = \begin{bmatrix} 5 & 3 \\ 0 & 5 \end{bmatrix} \qquad B = \begin{bmatrix} -8 & 0 & 7 \\ 1 & 3 & 2 \end{bmatrix} \qquad C = \begin{bmatrix} 1 & 0 \\ 0 & 3 \\ 7 & 1 \end{bmatrix}$$

4. Prove that for any two scalars g and k

   (a) $k(A + B) = kA + kB$

   (b) $(g + k)A = gA + kA$

   (*Note:* To *prove* a result, you cannot use specific examples.)

5. For (a) through (d) find $C = AB$.

   (a) $A = \begin{bmatrix} 12 & 14 \\ 20 & 5 \end{bmatrix}$ $B = \begin{bmatrix} 3 & 9 \\ 0 & 2 \end{bmatrix}$

   (b) $A = \begin{bmatrix} 4 & 7 \\ 9 & 1 \end{bmatrix}$ $B = \begin{bmatrix} 3 & 8 & 5 \\ 2 & 6 & 7 \end{bmatrix}$

   (c) $A = \begin{bmatrix} 7 & 11 \\ 2 & 9 \\ 10 & 6 \end{bmatrix}$ $B = \begin{bmatrix} 12 & 4 & 5 \\ 3 & 6 & 1 \end{bmatrix}$

   (d) $A = \begin{bmatrix} 6 & 2 & 5 \\ 7 & 9 & 4 \end{bmatrix}$ $B = \begin{bmatrix} 10 & 1 \\ 11 & 3 \\ 2 & 9 \end{bmatrix}$

   (e) Find (i) $C = AB$, and (ii) $D = BA$, if

   $$A = \begin{bmatrix} -2 \\ 4 \\ 7 \end{bmatrix} \qquad B = [3 \quad 6 \quad -2]$$

6. Prove that $(A + B)(C + D) = AC + AD + BC + BD$.

7. If the matrix A in Example 5 had all its four elements nonzero, would $x'Ax$ still give a weighted sum of squares? Would the associative law still apply?

8. Name some situations or contexts where the notion of a weighted or unweighted sum of squares may be relevant.

4.5 Identity Matrices and Null Matrices

Identity Matrices

We have referred earlier to the term *identity matrix*. Such a matrix is defined as a *square* (repeat: square) matrix with 1s in its principal diagonal and 0s everywhere else. It is denoted by the symbol I, or I_n, in which the subscript n serves to indicate its row (as well as column) dimension. Thus,

$$I_2 = \begin{bmatrix} 1 & 0 \\ 0 & 1 \end{bmatrix} \qquad I_3 = \begin{bmatrix} 1 & 0 & 0 \\ 0 & 1 & 0 \\ 0 & 0 & 1 \end{bmatrix}$$

But both of these can also be denoted by I.

The importance of this special type of matrix lies in the fact that it plays a role similar to that of the number 1 in scalar algebra. For any number a, we have $1(a) = a(1) = a$. Similarly, for any matrix A, we have

$$IA = AI = A \tag{4.8}$$

Example 1   Let $A = \begin{bmatrix} 1 & 2 & 3 \\ 2 & 0 & 3 \end{bmatrix}$, then

$$IA = \begin{bmatrix} 1 & 0 \\ 0 & 1 \end{bmatrix} \begin{bmatrix} 1 & 2 & 3 \\ 2 & 0 & 3 \end{bmatrix} = \begin{bmatrix} 1 & 2 & 3 \\ 2 & 0 & 3 \end{bmatrix} = A$$

$$AI = \begin{bmatrix} 1 & 2 & 3 \\ 2 & 0 & 3 \end{bmatrix} \begin{bmatrix} 1 & 0 & 0 \\ 0 & 1 & 0 \\ 0 & 0 & 1 \end{bmatrix} = \begin{bmatrix} 1 & 2 & 3 \\ 2 & 0 & 3 \end{bmatrix} = A$$

Because A is 2×3, premultiplication and postmultiplication of A by I would call for identity matrices of different dimensions, namely, I_2 and I_3, respectively. But in case A is $n \times n$, then the same identity matrix I_n can be used, so that (4.8) becomes $I_n A = A I_n$, thus illustrating an exception to the rule that matrix multiplication is not commutative.

The special nature of identity matrices makes it possible, during the multiplication process, to *insert* or *delete* an identity matrix without affecting the matrix product. This follows directly from (4.8). Recalling the associative law, we have, for instance,

$$\underset{(m \times n)(n \times n)(n \times p)}{A \quad I \quad B} = (AI)B = \underset{(m \times n)(n \times p)}{A \quad B}$$

which shows that the presence or absence of I does not affect the product. Observe that dimension conformability is preserved whether or not I appears in the product.

An interesting case of (4.8) occurs when $A = I_n$, for then we have

$$A I_n = (I_n)^2 = I_n$$

which states that an identity matrix squared is equal to itself. A generalization of this result is that

$$(I_n)^k = I_n \qquad (k = 1, 2, \ldots)$$

An identity matrix remains unchanged when it is multiplied by itself any number of times. Any matrix with such a property (namely, $AA = A$) is referred to as an *idempotent matrix*.

Null Matrices

Just as an identity matrix I plays the role of the number 1, a *null matrix*—or *zero matrix*—denoted by 0, plays the role of the number 0. A null matrix is simply a matrix whose elements are all zero. Unlike I, the zero matrix is not restricted to being square. Thus it is possible to write

$$\underset{(2 \times 2)}{0} = \begin{bmatrix} 0 & 0 \\ 0 & 0 \end{bmatrix} \qquad \text{and} \qquad \underset{(2 \times 3)}{0} = \begin{bmatrix} 0 & 0 & 0 \\ 0 & 0 & 0 \end{bmatrix}$$

and so forth. A square null matrix is idempotent, but a nonsquare one is not. (Why?)

As the counterpart of the number 0, null matrices obey the following rules of operation (subject to conformability) with regard to addition and multiplication:

$$\underset{(m \times n)}{A} + \underset{(m \times n)}{0} = \underset{(m \times n)}{0} + \underset{(m \times n)}{A} = \underset{(m \times n)}{A}$$

$$\underset{(m \times n)(n \times p)}{A \quad 0} = \underset{(m \times p)}{0} \qquad \text{and} \qquad \underset{(q \times m)(m \times n)}{0 \quad A} = \underset{(q \times n)}{0}$$

Note that, in multiplication, the null matrix to the left of the equals sign and the one to the right may be of different dimensions.

Example 2

$$A + 0 = \begin{bmatrix} a_{11} & a_{12} \\ a_{21} & a_{22} \end{bmatrix} + \begin{bmatrix} 0 & 0 \\ 0 & 0 \end{bmatrix} = \begin{bmatrix} a_{11} & a_{12} \\ a_{21} & a_{22} \end{bmatrix} = A$$

Example 3

$$\underset{(2\times3)}{A}\ \underset{(3\times1)}{0} = \begin{bmatrix} a_{11} & a_{12} & a_{13} \\ a_{21} & a_{22} & a_{23} \end{bmatrix} \begin{bmatrix} 0 \\ 0 \\ 0 \end{bmatrix} = \begin{bmatrix} 0 \\ 0 \end{bmatrix} = \underset{(2\times1)}{0}$$

To the left, the null matrix is a 3×1 null vector; to the right, it is a 2×1 null vector.

Idiosyncrasies of Matrix Algebra

Despite the apparent similarities between matrix algebra and scalar algebra, the case of matrices does display certain idiosyncrasies that serve to warn us not to "borrow" from scalar algebra too unquestioningly. We have already seen that, in general, $AB \neq BA$ in matrix algebra. Let us look at two more such idiosyncrasies of matrix algebra.

For one thing, in the case of scalars, the equation $ab = 0$ always implies that either a or b is zero, but this is not so in matrix multiplication. Thus, we have

$$AB = \begin{bmatrix} 2 & 4 \\ 1 & 2 \end{bmatrix} \begin{bmatrix} -2 & 4 \\ 1 & -2 \end{bmatrix} = \begin{bmatrix} 0 & 0 \\ 0 & 0 \end{bmatrix} = 0$$

although neither A nor B is itself a zero matrix.

As another illustration, for scalars, the equation $cd = ce$ (with $c \neq 0$) implies that $d = e$. The same does not hold for matrices. Thus, given

$$C = \begin{bmatrix} 2 & 3 \\ 6 & 9 \end{bmatrix} \qquad D = \begin{bmatrix} 1 & 1 \\ 1 & 2 \end{bmatrix} \qquad E = \begin{bmatrix} -2 & 1 \\ 3 & 2 \end{bmatrix}$$

we find that

$$CD = CE = \begin{bmatrix} 5 & 8 \\ 15 & 24 \end{bmatrix}$$

even though $D \neq E$.

These strange results actually pertain only to the special class of matrices known as *singular matrices,* of which the matrices A, B, and C are examples. (Roughly, these matrices contain a row which is a multiple of another row.) Nevertheless, such examples do reveal the pitfalls of unwarranted extension of algebraic theorems to matrix operations.

EXERCISE 4.5

Given $A = \begin{bmatrix} -1 & 5 & 7 \\ 0 & -2 & 4 \end{bmatrix}$, $b = \begin{bmatrix} 9 \\ 6 \\ 0 \end{bmatrix}$, and $x = \begin{bmatrix} x_1 \\ x_2 \end{bmatrix}$:

1. Calculate: (*a*) AI (*b*) IA (*c*) Ix (*d*) $x'I$

   Indicate the dimension of the identity matrix used in each case.

2. Calculate: (*a*) *Ab*   (*b*) *AIb*   (*c*) *x'IA*   (*d*) *x'A*
   Does the insertion of *I* in (*b*) affect the result in (*a*)? Does the deletion of *I* in (*d*) affect the result in (*c*)?

3. What is the dimension of the null matrix resulting from each of the following?
   (*a*) Premultiply *A* by a 5 × 2 null matrix.
   (*b*) Postmultiply *A* by a 3 × 6 null matrix.
   (*c*) Premultiply *b* by a 2 × 3 null matrix.
   (*d*) Postmultiply *x* by a 1 × 5 null matrix.

4. Show that the diagonal matrix

$$\begin{bmatrix} a_{11} & 0 & \cdots & 0 \\ 0 & a_{22} & \cdots & 0 \\ \multicolumn{4}{c}{\dotfill} \\ 0 & 0 & \cdots & a_{nn} \end{bmatrix}$$

can be idempotent only if each diagonal element is either 1 or 0. How many different numerical idempotent diagonal matrices of dimension $n \times n$ can be constructed altogether from such a matrix?

4.6 Transposes and Inverses

When the rows and columns of a matrix A are interchanged—so that its first row becomes the first column, and vice versa—we obtain the *transpose* of A, which is denoted by A' or A^T. The prime symbol is by no means new to us; it was used earlier to distinguish a row vector from a column vector. In the newly introduced terminology, a row vector x' constitutes the transpose of the column vector x. The superscript T in the alternative symbol is obviously shorthand for the word transpose.

Example 1   Given $\underset{(2\times 3)}{A} = \begin{bmatrix} 3 & 8 & -9 \\ 1 & 0 & 4 \end{bmatrix}$ and $\underset{(2\times 2)}{B} = \begin{bmatrix} 3 & 4 \\ 1 & 7 \end{bmatrix}$, we can interchange the rows and columns and write

$$\underset{(3\times 2)}{A'} = \begin{bmatrix} 3 & 1 \\ 8 & 0 \\ -9 & 4 \end{bmatrix} \quad \text{and} \quad \underset{(2\times 2)}{B'} = \begin{bmatrix} 3 & 1 \\ 4 & 7 \end{bmatrix}$$

By definition, if a matrix A is $m \times n$, then its transpose A' must be $n \times m$. An $n \times n$ square matrix, however, possesses a transpose with the same dimension.

Example 2   If $C = \begin{bmatrix} 9 & -1 \\ 2 & 0 \end{bmatrix}$ and $D = \begin{bmatrix} 1 & 0 & 4 \\ 0 & 3 & 7 \\ 4 & 7 & 2 \end{bmatrix}$, then

$$C' = \begin{bmatrix} 9 & 2 \\ -1 & 0 \end{bmatrix} \quad \text{and} \quad D' = \begin{bmatrix} 1 & 0 & 4 \\ 0 & 3 & 7 \\ 4 & 7 & 2 \end{bmatrix}$$

Here, the dimension of each transpose is identical with the original matrix.

In D', we also note the remarkable result that D' inherits not only the dimension of D but also the original array of elements! The fact that $D' = D$ is the result of the symmetry of the elements with reference to the principal diagonal. Considering the principal diagonal in D as a mirror, the elements located to its northeast are exact images of the elements to its southwest; hence the first row reads identically with the first column, and so forth. The matrix D exemplifies the special class of square matrices known as *symmetric matrices.* Another example of such a matrix is the identity matrix I, which, as a symmetric matrix, has the transpose $I' = I$.

Properties of Transposes

The following properties characterize transposes:

$$(A')' = A \tag{4.9}$$

$$(A + B)' = A' + B' \tag{4.10}$$

$$(AB)' = B'A' \tag{4.11}$$

The first says that the transpose of the transpose is the original matrix—a rather self-evident conclusion.

The second property may be verbally stated thus: The transpose of a sum is the sum of the transposes.

Example 3　If $A = \begin{bmatrix} 4 & 1 \\ 9 & 0 \end{bmatrix}$ and $B = \begin{bmatrix} 2 & 0 \\ 7 & 1 \end{bmatrix}$, then

$$(A + B)' = \begin{bmatrix} 6 & 1 \\ 16 & 1 \end{bmatrix}' = \begin{bmatrix} 6 & 16 \\ 1 & 1 \end{bmatrix}$$

and

$$A' + B' = \begin{bmatrix} 4 & 9 \\ 1 & 0 \end{bmatrix} + \begin{bmatrix} 2 & 7 \\ 0 & 1 \end{bmatrix} = \begin{bmatrix} 6 & 16 \\ 1 & 1 \end{bmatrix}$$

The third property is that the transpose of a product is the product of the transposes *in reverse order.* To appreciate the necessity for the reversed order, let us examine the dimension conformability of the two products on the two sides of (4.11). If we let A be $m \times n$ and B be $n \times p$, then AB will be $m \times p$, and $(AB)'$ will be $p \times m$. For equality to hold, it is necessary that the right-hand expression $B'A'$ be of the identical dimension. Since B' is $p \times n$ and A' is $n \times m$, the product $B'A'$ is indeed $p \times m$, as required. The dimension of $B'A'$ thus works out. Note that, on the other hand, the product $A'B'$ is not even defined unless $m = p$.

Example 4　Given $A = \begin{bmatrix} 1 & 2 \\ 3 & 4 \end{bmatrix}$ and $B = \begin{bmatrix} 0 & -1 \\ 6 & 7 \end{bmatrix}$, we have

$$(AB)' = \begin{bmatrix} 12 & 13 \\ 24 & 25 \end{bmatrix}' = \begin{bmatrix} 12 & 24 \\ 13 & 25 \end{bmatrix}$$

and

$$B'A' = \begin{bmatrix} 0 & 6 \\ -1 & 7 \end{bmatrix}\begin{bmatrix} 1 & 3 \\ 2 & 4 \end{bmatrix} = \begin{bmatrix} 12 & 24 \\ 13 & 25 \end{bmatrix}$$

This verifies the property.

Inverses and Their Properties

For a given matrix A, the transpose A' is always derivable. On the other hand, its *inverse* matrix—another type of "derived" matrix—may or may not exist. The inverse of matrix A, denoted by A^{-1}, is defined only if A is a square matrix, in which case the inverse is the matrix that satisfies the condition

$$AA^{-1} = A^{-1}A = I \qquad\qquad \textbf{(4.12)}$$

That is, whether A is pre- or postmultiplied by A^{-1}, the product will be the same identity matrix. This is another exception to the rule that matrix multiplication is not commutative.

The following points are worth noting:

1. Not every square matrix has an inverse—squareness is a *necessary* condition, but *not* a *sufficient* condition, for the existence of an inverse. If a square matrix A has an inverse, A is said to be *nonsingular;* if A possesses no inverse, it is called a *singular* matrix.

2. If A^{-1} does exist, then the matrix A can be regarded as the inverse of A^{-1}, just as A^{-1} is the inverse of A. In short, A and A^{-1} are inverses of each other.

3. If A is $n \times n$, then A^{-1} must also be $n \times n$; otherwise it cannot be conformable for *both* pre- and postmultiplication. The identity matrix produced by the multiplication will also be $n \times n$.

4. If an inverse exists, then it is unique. To prove its uniqueness, let us suppose that B has been found to be an inverse for A, so that

$$AB = BA = I$$

Now assume that there is another matrix C such that $AC = CA = I$. By premultiplying both sides of $AB = I$ by C, we find that

$$CAB = CI(= C) \qquad \text{[by (4.8)]}$$

Since $CA = I$ by assumption, the preceding equation is reducible to

$$IB = C \qquad \text{or} \qquad B = C$$

That is, B and C must be one and the same inverse matrix. For this reason, we can speak of *the* (as against *an*) inverse of A.

5. The two parts of condition (4.12)—namely, $AA^{-1} = I$ and $A^{-1}A = I$—actually imply each other, so that satisfying either equation is sufficient to establish the inverse relationship between A and A^{-1}. To prove this, we should show that if $AA^{-1} = I$, and if there is a matrix B such that $BA = I$, then $B = A^{-1}$ (so that $BA = I$ must in effect be the equation $A^{-1}A = I$). Let us postmultiply both sides of the given equation $BA = I$ by A^{-1}; then

$$(BA)A^{-1} = IA^{-1}$$
$$B(AA^{-1}) = IA^{-1} \qquad \text{[associative law]}$$
$$BI = IA^{-1} \qquad [AA^{-1} = I \text{ by assumption}]$$

Therefore, as required,

$$B = A^{-1} \qquad \text{[by (4.8)]}$$

Analogously, it can be demonstrated that, if $A^{-1}A = I$, then the only matrix C which yields $CA^{-1} = I$ is $C = A$.

Example 5

Let $A = \begin{bmatrix} 3 & 1 \\ 0 & 2 \end{bmatrix}$ and $B = \dfrac{1}{6}\begin{bmatrix} 2 & -1 \\ 0 & 3 \end{bmatrix}$; then, since the scalar multiplier $(\frac{1}{6})$ in B can be moved to the rear (commutative law), we can write

$$AB = \begin{bmatrix} 3 & 1 \\ 0 & 2 \end{bmatrix}\begin{bmatrix} 2 & -1 \\ 0 & 3 \end{bmatrix}\frac{1}{6} = \begin{bmatrix} 6 & 0 \\ 0 & 6 \end{bmatrix}\frac{1}{6} = \begin{bmatrix} 1 & 0 \\ 0 & 1 \end{bmatrix}$$

This establishes B as the inverse of A, and vice versa. The reverse multiplication, as expected, also yields the same identity matrix:

$$BA = \frac{1}{6}\begin{bmatrix} 2 & -1 \\ 0 & 3 \end{bmatrix}\begin{bmatrix} 3 & 1 \\ 0 & 2 \end{bmatrix} = \frac{1}{6}\begin{bmatrix} 6 & 0 \\ 0 & 6 \end{bmatrix} = \begin{bmatrix} 1 & 0 \\ 0 & 1 \end{bmatrix}$$

The following three properties of inverse matrices are of interest. If A and B are nonsingular matrices with dimension $n \times n$, then

$$(A^{-1})^{-1} = A \tag{4.13}$$

$$(AB)^{-1} = B^{-1}A^{-1} \tag{4.14}$$

$$(A')^{-1} = (A^{-1})' \tag{4.15}$$

The first says that the inverse of an inverse is the original matrix. The second states that the inverse of a product is the product of the inverses *in reverse order.* And the last one means that the inverse of the transpose is the transpose of the inverse. Note that in these statements the existence of the inverses and the satisfaction of the conformability condition are presupposed.

The validity of (4.13) is fairly obvious, but let us prove (4.14) and (4.15). Given the product AB, let us find its inverse—call it C. From (4.12) we know that $CAB = I$; thus, postmultiplication of both sides by $B^{-1}A^{-1}$ will yield

$$CABB^{-1}A^{-1} = IB^{-1}A^{-1} \,(= B^{-1}A^{-1}) \tag{4.16}$$

But the left side is reducible to

$$CA(BB^{-1})A^{-1} = CAIA^{-1} \qquad \text{[by (4.12)]}$$
$$= CAA^{-1} = CI = C \qquad \text{[by (4.12) and (4.8)]}$$

Substitution of this into (4.16) then tells us that $C = B^{-1}A^{-1}$ or, in other words, that the inverse of AB is equal to $B^{-1}A^{-1}$, as alleged. In this proof, the equation $AA^{-1} = A^{-1}A = I$ was utilized twice. Note that the application of this equation is permissible if and only if a matrix and its inverse are strictly adjacent to each other in a product. We may write $AA^{-1}B = IB = B$, but *never* $ABA^{-1} = B$.

The proof of (4.15) is as follows. Given A', let us find its inverse—call it D. By definition, we then have $DA' = I$. But we know that

$$(AA^{-1})' = I' = I$$

produces the same identity matrix. Thus we may write

$$DA' = (AA^{-1})'$$
$$= (A^{-1})'A' \qquad \text{[by (4.11)]}$$

Postmultiplying both sides by $(A')^{-1}$, we obtain

$$DA'(A')^{-1} = (A^{-1})'A'(A')^{-1}$$

or $\qquad\qquad\qquad D = (A^{-1})' \qquad\qquad$ [by (4.12)]

Thus, the inverse of A' is equal to $(A^{-1})'$, as alleged.

In the proofs just presented, mathematical operations were performed on whole blocks of numbers. If those blocks of numbers had not been treated as mathematical entities (matrices), the same operations would have been much more lengthy and involved. The beauty of matrix algebra lies precisely in its simplification of such operations.

Inverse Matrix and Solution of Linear-Equation System

The application of the concept of inverse matrix to the solution of a simultaneous-equation system is immediate and direct. Referring to the equation system in (4.3), we pointed out earlier that it can be written in matrix notation as

$$\underset{(3\times3)}{A}\ \underset{(3\times1)}{x} = \underset{(3\times1)}{d} \qquad\qquad\textbf{(4.17)}$$

where A, x, and d are as defined in (4.4). Now if the inverse matrix A^{-1} exists, the premultiplication of both sides of the equation (4.17) by A^{-1} will yield

$$A^{-1}Ax = A^{-1}d$$

or $\qquad\qquad \underset{(3\times1)}{x} = \underset{(3\times3)}{A^{-1}}\ \underset{(3\times1)}{d} \qquad\qquad\textbf{(4.18)}$

The left side of (4.18) is a column vector of variables, whereas the right-hand product is a column vector of certain known numbers. Thus, by definition of the equality of matrices or vectors, (4.18) shows the set of values of the variables that satisfy the equation system, i.e., the solution values. Furthermore, since A^{-1} is unique if it exists, $A^{-1}d$ must be a unique vector of solution values. We shall therefore write the x vector in (4.18) as x^*, to indicate its status as a (unique) solution.

Methods of testing the existence of the inverse and of its calculation will be discussed in Chap. 5. It may be stated here, however, that the inverse of the matrix A in (4.4) is

$$A^{-1} = \frac{1}{52}\begin{bmatrix} 18 & -16 & -10 \\ -13 & 26 & 13 \\ -17 & 18 & 21 \end{bmatrix}$$

Thus (4.18) will turn out to be

$$\begin{bmatrix} x_1^* \\ x_2^* \\ x_3^* \end{bmatrix} = \frac{1}{52}\begin{bmatrix} 18 & -16 & -10 \\ -13 & 26 & 13 \\ -17 & 18 & 21 \end{bmatrix}\begin{bmatrix} 22 \\ 12 \\ 10 \end{bmatrix} = \begin{bmatrix} 2 \\ 3 \\ 1 \end{bmatrix}$$

which gives the solution: $x_1^* = 2$, $x_2^* = 3$, and $x_3^* = 1$.

The upshot is that, as one way of finding the solution of a linear-equation system $Ax = d$, where the coefficient matrix A is nonsingular, is to first find the inverse A^{-1}, and then postmultiply A^{-1} by the constant vector d. The product $A^{-1}d$ will then give the solution values of the variables.

Example 6

As shown in Example 11 of Sec. 4.2, the simple national-income model

$$Y = C + I_0 + G_0$$
$$C = a + bY$$

can be written in matrix notation as $Ax = d$, where

$$A = \begin{bmatrix} 1 & -1 \\ -b & 1 \end{bmatrix} \qquad x = \begin{bmatrix} Y \\ C \end{bmatrix} \quad \text{and} \quad d = \begin{bmatrix} I_0 + G_0 \\ a \end{bmatrix}$$

The inverse of matrix A is (see explanation in Sec. 5.6)

$$A^{-1} = \frac{1}{1-b} \begin{bmatrix} 1 & 1 \\ b & 1 \end{bmatrix}$$

Thus the solution of the model is $x^* = A^{-1}d$, or

$$\begin{bmatrix} Y^* \\ C^* \end{bmatrix} = \frac{1}{1-b} \begin{bmatrix} 1 & 1 \\ b & 1 \end{bmatrix} \begin{bmatrix} I_0 + G_0 \\ a \end{bmatrix} = \frac{1}{1-b} \begin{bmatrix} I_0 + G_0 + a \\ b(I_0 + G_0) + a \end{bmatrix}$$

EXERCISE 4.6

1. Given $A = \begin{bmatrix} 0 & 4 \\ -1 & 3 \end{bmatrix}$, $B = \begin{bmatrix} 3 & -8 \\ 0 & 1 \end{bmatrix}$, and $C = \begin{bmatrix} 1 & 0 & 9 \\ 6 & 1 & 1 \end{bmatrix}$, find A', B', and C'.

2. Use the matrices given in Prob. 1 to verify that
   (a) $(A + B)' = A' + B'$ (b) $(AC)' = C'A'$

3. Generalize the result (4.11) to the case of a product of three matrices by proving that, for any conformable matrices A, B, and C, the equation $(ABC)' = C'B'A'$ holds.

4. Given the following four matrices, test whether any one of them is the inverse of another:

$$D = \begin{bmatrix} 1 & 12 \\ 0 & 3 \end{bmatrix} \qquad E = \begin{bmatrix} 1 & 1 \\ 6 & 8 \end{bmatrix} \qquad F = \begin{bmatrix} 1 & -4 \\ 0 & \frac{1}{3} \end{bmatrix} \qquad G = \begin{bmatrix} 4 & -\frac{1}{2} \\ -3 & \frac{1}{2} \end{bmatrix}$$

5. Generalize the result (4.14) by proving that, for any conformable nonsingular matrices A, B, and C, the equation $(ABC)^{-1} = C^{-1}B^{-1}A^{-1}$ holds.

6. Let $A = I - X(X'X)^{-1}X'$.
   (a) Must A be square? Must $(X'X)$ be square? Must X be square?
   (b) Show that matrix A is idempotent. [*Note:* If X' and X are not square, it is inappropriate to apply (4.14).]

4.7 Finite Markov Chains

A common application of matrix algebra is found in what is known as Markov processes or Markov chains. *Markov processes* are used to measure or estimate movements over time. This involves the use of a Markov transition matrix, where each value in the transition matrix is a probability of moving from one state (location, job, etc.) to another state. There is also a vector containing the initial distribution across the various states. By repeatedly multiplying such a vector by the transition matrix, one can estimate changes across states over time.

Consider the problem of internal employee movement within a company that has many different branches, or outlets.[†] A simple illustration using two branches, such as Abbotsford and Burnaby, will help to demonstrate the basics of a Markov process. To determine the number of employees in Abbotsford tomorrow, we take the probability that the employees will stay in the Abbotsford branch multiplied by the total number of employees currently in Abbotsford, which gives the total number of current Abbotsford employees who will remain tomorrow. Added to this number is the number of Burnaby employees transferring to Abbotsford. This number is found by multiplying the total number of current Burnaby employees by the probability of a Burnaby employee transferring to Abbotsford. Similarly the process would be the same for determining the number of employees in the Burnaby region tomorrow, made up of those Burnaby employees who chose to remain and the Abbotsford employees who transfer into the Burnaby region today. The process described involves four probabilities. These four probabilities together can be arranged in a matrix. This is known as a Markov transition matrix (or simply, a "Markov").

Let A_t and B_t denote the populations of Abbotsford and Burnaby, respectively, at some time, t. Further, define the transitional probabilities as follows

$$P_{AA} \equiv \text{probability that a current } A \text{ remains an } A$$

$$P_{AB} \equiv \text{probability that a current } A \text{ moves to } B$$

$$P_{BB} \equiv \text{probability that a current } B \text{ remains a } B$$

$$P_{BA} \equiv \text{probability that a current } B \text{ moves to } A.$$

If we denote the distribution of employees across locations at time t as a vector

$$x'_t = [A_t \quad B_t]$$

and the transitional probabilities in matrix form

$$M = \begin{bmatrix} P_{AA} & P_{AB} \\ P_{BA} & P_{BB} \end{bmatrix}$$

then the distribution of employees across locations in the next period $(t + 1)$ is

$$\underset{(1 \times 2)}{x'_t} \ \underset{(2 \times 2)}{M} = \underset{(1 \times 2)}{x'_{t+1}}$$

$$[A_t \quad B_t] \begin{bmatrix} P_{AA} & P_{AB} \\ P_{BA} & P_{BB} \end{bmatrix} = [(A_t P_{AA} + B_t P_{BA}) \ (A_t P_{AB} + B_t P_{BB})]$$

$$= [A_{t+1} \quad B_{t+1}]$$

[†] We would like to thank Sarah Dunn for this example. This work comes from her final project while a student at the British Columbia Institute of Technology, Burnaby, BC, Canada (June 2003).

To find the distribution of employees after two periods

$$[A_{t+1} \quad B_{t+1}] \begin{bmatrix} P_{AA} & P_{AB} \\ P_{BA} & P_{BB} \end{bmatrix} = [A_{t+2} \quad B_{t+2}]$$

$$[A_t \quad B_t] \begin{bmatrix} P_{AA} & P_{AB} \\ P_{BA} & P_{BB} \end{bmatrix} \begin{bmatrix} P_{AA} & P_{AB} \\ P_{BA} & P_{BB} \end{bmatrix} = [A_{t+2} \quad B_{t+2}]$$

$$[A_t \quad B_t] \begin{bmatrix} P_{AA} & P_{AB} \\ P_{BA} & P_{BB} \end{bmatrix}^2 = [A_{t+2} \quad B_{t+2}]$$

In general, for n periods

$$[A_t \quad B_t] \begin{bmatrix} P_{AA} & P_{AB} \\ P_{BA} & P_{BB} \end{bmatrix}^n = [A_{t+n} \quad B_{t+n}]$$

The 2×2 probability matrix M is known as the *Markov transition matrix*. For the case where n is exogenous, the process is known as a finite Markov chain.

Example 1

Suppose the initial distribution of employees across the two locations at time $t = 0$ is

$$x_0' = [A_0 \quad B_0] = [100 \quad 100]$$

In other words, there are initially equal numbers at each location. Further, let the transitional probabilities in matrix form be as follows:

$$M = \begin{bmatrix} P_{AA} & P_{AB} \\ P_{BA} & P_{BB} \end{bmatrix} = \begin{bmatrix} 0.7 & 0.3 \\ 0.4 & 0.6 \end{bmatrix}$$

Then the distribution of employees across locations in the next period ($t = 1$) is

$$[100 \quad 100] \begin{bmatrix} 0.7 & 0.3 \\ 0.4 & 0.6 \end{bmatrix} = [110 \quad 90] = [A_1 \quad B_1]$$

The distribution after two periods is given by

$$[100 \quad 100] \begin{bmatrix} 0.7 & 0.3 \\ 0.4 & 0.6 \end{bmatrix}^2 = [100 \quad 100] \begin{bmatrix} 0.61 & 0.39 \\ 0.52 & 0.48 \end{bmatrix}$$
$$= [113 \quad 87] = [A_2 \quad B_2]$$

The distribution after 10 periods ($t = 10$) is given by

$$[100 \quad 100] \begin{bmatrix} 0.7 & 0.3 \\ 0.4 & 0.6 \end{bmatrix}^{10} = [100 \quad 100] \begin{bmatrix} 0.5174 & 0.4286 \\ 0.5174 & 0.4286 \end{bmatrix}$$
$$= [114.3 \quad 85.7] = [A_{10} \quad B_{10}]$$

Notice what happens when the Markov transition matrix is raised to higher and higher powers. The new transition matrix found by raising the original matrix to increasingly higher powers converges to a matrix where the rows are identical. This is referred to as the *steady state*. What would you expect the eleventh or higher periods of distribution to look like?

Special Case: Absorbing Markov Chains

Now, let us extend the model by adding a third option: Employees can exit the company, with

$$P_{AE} \equiv \text{probability that a current } A \text{ chooses to exit } (E)$$

$$P_{BE} \equiv \text{probability that a current } B \text{ chooses to exit } (E)$$

At this point, we will add the following assumptions:

$$P_{EA} = 0 \qquad P_{EB} = 0 \qquad P_{EE} = 1$$

where P_{EA}, P_{EB}, and P_{EE} are the probabilities that an employee who is currently an E will go to A, B, or E, respectively. In other words, nobody who leaves the company ever returns. It is also implied by these restrictions that our company never replaces employees that leave (there are no new hires).

Starting at time $t = 0$, our Markov chain now becomes

$$\begin{bmatrix} A_0 & B_0 & E_0 \end{bmatrix} \begin{bmatrix} P_{AA} & P_{AB} & P_{AE} \\ P_{BA} & P_{BB} & P_{BE} \\ P_{EA} & P_{EB} & P_{EE} \end{bmatrix}^n = \begin{bmatrix} A_n & B_n & E_n \end{bmatrix}$$

$$\begin{bmatrix} A_0 & B_0 & E_0 \end{bmatrix} \begin{bmatrix} P_{AA} & P_{AB} & P_{AE} \\ P_{BA} & P_{BB} & P_{BE} \\ 0 & 0 & 1 \end{bmatrix}^n = \begin{bmatrix} A_n & B_n & E_n \end{bmatrix}$$

(Assume $E_0 = 0$.)

This type of Markov process is referred to as an *absorbing Markov chain*. Because of the values of the transition probabilities found in the third row, we see that once an employee becomes an E in one state (time period) that employee will remain there for all future states (time periods). As n goes to infinity, A_n and B_n will approach zero and E_n will approach the value of the total number of workers at time zero (i.e., $A_0 + B_0 + E_0$).

EXERCISE 4.7

1. Consider the situation of a mass layoff (i.e., a factory shuts down) where 1,200 people become unemployed and now begin a job search. In this case there are two states: employed (E) and unemployed (U) with an initial vector

   $$x_0' = \begin{bmatrix} E & U \end{bmatrix} = \begin{bmatrix} 0 & 1{,}200 \end{bmatrix}$$

   Suppose that in any given period an unemployed person will find a job with probability .7 and will therefore remain unemployed with a probability of .3. Additionally, persons who find themselves employed in any given period may lose their job with a probability of .1 (and will have a .9 probability of remaining employed).

   (a) Set up the Markov transition matrix for this problem.

   (b) What will be the number of unemployed people after (i) 2 periods; (ii) 3 periods; (iii) 5 periods; (iv) 10 periods?

   (c) What is the steady-state level of unemployment?

5

Linear Models and Matrix Algebra (Continued)

In Chap. 4, it was shown that a linear-equation system, however large, may be written in a compact matrix notation. Furthermore, such an equation system can be solved by finding the inverse of the coefficient matrix, provided the inverse exists. Now we must address ourselves to the questions of how to test for the existence of the inverse and how to find that inverse. Only after we have answered these questions will it be possible to apply matrix algebra meaningfully to economic models.

5.1 Conditions for Nonsingularity of a Matrix

A given coefficient matrix A can have an inverse (i.e., can be "nonsingular") only if it is square. As was pointed out earlier, however, the squareness condition is necessary but not sufficient for the existence of the inverse A^{-1}. A matrix can be square, but singular (without an inverse) nonetheless.

Necessary versus Sufficient Conditions

The concepts of "necessary condition" and "sufficient condition" are used frequently in economics. It is important that we understand their precise meanings before proceeding further.

A necessary condition is in the nature of a prerequisite: Suppose that a statement p is true *only if* another statement q is true; then q constitutes a necessary condition of p. Symbolically, we express this as follows:

$$p \Rightarrow q \qquad (5.1)$$

which is read as "p only if q," or alternatively, "if p, then q." It is also logically correct to interpret (5.1) to mean "p implies q." It may happen, of course, that we also have $p \Rightarrow w$ at the same time. Then both q and w are necessary conditions for p.

Example 1   If we let p be the statement "a person is a father" and q be the statement "a person is male," then the logical statement $p \Rightarrow q$ applies. A person is a father *only if* he is male, and to be male is a necessary condition for fatherhood. Note, however, that the converse is not true: fatherhood is not a necessary condition for maleness.

A different type of situation is one in which a statement p is true if q is true, but p can also be true when q is not true. In this case, q is said to be a sufficient condition for p. The truth of q suffices to establish the truth of p, but it is not a necessary condition for p. This case is expressed symbolically by

$$p \Leftarrow q \qquad\qquad \textbf{(5.2)}$$

which is read: "p *if* q" (without the word *only*)—or alternatively, "if q, then p," as if reading (5.2) backward. It can also be interpreted to mean "q implies p."

Example 2

If we let p be the statement "one can get to Europe" and q be the statement "one takes a plane to Europe," then $p \Leftarrow q$. Flying can serve to get one to Europe, but since ocean transportation is also feasible, flying is not a prerequisite. We can write $p \Leftarrow q$, but not $p \Rightarrow q$.

In a third possible situation, q is *both* necessary and sufficient for p. In such an event, we write

$$p \Leftrightarrow q \qquad\qquad \textbf{(5.3)}$$

which is read: "p *if and only if* q" (also written as "p iff q"). The double-headed arrow is really a combination of the two types of arrow in (5.1) and (5.2), hence the joint use of the two terms "if" and "only if." Note that (5.3) states not only that p implies q but also that q implies p.

Example 3

If we let p be the statement "there are less than 30 days in the month" and q be the statement "it is the month of February," then $p \Leftrightarrow q$. To have less than 30 days in the month, it is necessary that it be February. Conversely, the specification of February is sufficient to establish that there are less than 30 days in the month. Thus q is a necessary-and-sufficient condition for p.

In order to prove $p \Rightarrow q$, it needs to be shown that q follows logically from p. Similarly, to prove $p \Leftarrow q$ requires a demonstration that p follows logically from q. But to prove $p \Leftrightarrow q$ necessitates a demonstration that p and q follow from each other.

Necessary conditions and sufficient conditions are important as screening devices. Consider a pool of applicants being considered for scholarship awards, or for job positions. Since necessary conditions are in the nature of prerequisites, they serve to separate the candidates into two groups: Those who fail to meet the necessary conditions are automatically disqualified; those who satisfy the necessary conditions remain as admissible candidates. To remain as an admissible candidate, however, carries no guarantee that the candidate will eventually be successful. Thus, necessary conditions are more conclusive in screening out the unsuccessful candidates than in identifying the successful ones. In general, we should bear in mind that necessary conditions are *not* in themselves *sufficient*.

In contrast to necessary conditions, sufficient conditions serve directly to identify successful candidates. A candidate that satisfies a sufficient condition is automatically a successful one. Just as necessary conditions are not in themselves sufficient, sufficient conditions are not in themselves necessary. This is because, along with any given sufficient condition, there may exist other, less stringent, sufficient conditions, and the candidate who fails to satisfy the given sufficient condition may yet qualify under an easier sufficient condition. For example, a grade of A is sufficient for passing a course, but it is not a necessary condition since a grade of B is also sufficient.

The most effective screening device is found in the necessary-and-sufficient conditions. Failure to satisfy such a condition means the candidate is definitely out, and satisfaction of such a condition means the candidate is definitely in. We can find an immediate application of this in our present discussion of nonsingularity of a matrix.

Conditions for Nonsingularity

After the squareness condition (a necessary condition) is already met, a sufficient condition for the nonsingularity of a matrix is that its rows be linearly independent (or, what amounts to the same thing, that its *columns* be linearly independent). When the dual conditions of squareness and linear independence are taken together, they constitute the necessary-and-sufficient condition for nonsingularity (nonsingularity $\Leftrightarrow$ squareness *and* linear independence).

An $n \times n$ coefficient matrix A can be considered as an ordered set of row vectors, i.e., as a column vector whose elements are themselves row vectors:

$$A = \begin{bmatrix} a_{11} & a_{12} & \cdots & a_{1n} \\ a_{21} & a_{22} & \cdots & a_{2n} \\ \cdots & \cdots & \cdots & \cdots \\ a_{n1} & a_{n2} & \cdots & a_{nn} \end{bmatrix} = \begin{bmatrix} v_1' \\ v_2' \\ \vdots \\ v_n' \end{bmatrix}$$

where $v_i' = [a_{i1} \quad a_{i2} \quad \cdots \quad a_{in}]$, $i = 1, 2, \ldots, n$. For the rows (row vectors) to be linearly independent, none must be a linear combination of the rest. More formally, as was mentioned in Sec. 4.3, linear row independence requires that the only set of scalars k_i which can satisfy the vector equation

$$\sum_{i=1}^{n} k_i v_i' = \underset{(1 \times n)}{0} \tag{5.4}$$

be $k_i = 0$ for all i.

Example 4   If the coefficient matrix is

$$A = \begin{bmatrix} 3 & 4 & 5 \\ 0 & 1 & 2 \\ 6 & 8 & 10 \end{bmatrix} = \begin{bmatrix} v_1' \\ v_2' \\ v_3' \end{bmatrix}$$

then, since $[6 \quad 8 \quad 10] = 2[3 \quad 4 \quad 5]$, we have $v_3' = 2v_1' = 2v_1' + 0v_2'$. Thus the third row is expressible as a linear combination of the first two, and the rows are *not* linearly independent. Alternatively, we may write the previous equation as

$$2v_1' + 0v_2' - v_3' = [6 \quad 8 \quad 10] + [0 \quad 0 \quad 0] - [6 \quad 8 \quad 10] = [0 \quad 0 \quad 0]$$

Inasmuch as the set of scalars that led to the zero vector of (5.4) is not $k_i = 0$ for all i, it follows that the rows are linearly dependent.

Unlike the squareness condition, the linear-independence condition cannot normally be ascertained at a glance. Thus a method of testing linear independence among rows (or columns) needs to be developed. Before we concern ourselves with that task, however, it would strengthen our motivation first to have an intuitive understanding of why the linear-independence condition is heaped together with the squareness condition at all. From the discussion of counting equations and unknowns in Sec. 3.4, we recall the general conclusion that, for a system of equations to possess a unique solution, it is not sufficient to have the same number of equations as unknowns. In addition, the *equations* must be consistent with and functionally independent (meaning, in the present context of linear systems, *linearly* independent) of one another. There is a fairly obvious tie-in between the "same number of equations as unknowns" criterion and the *squareness* (same number of rows and columns) of the coefficient matrix. What the "linear independence among the rows" requirement does is to preclude the inconsistency and the linear dependence *among the equations* as well. Taken together, therefore, the dual requirement of squareness and row independence in the coefficient matrix is tantamount to the conditions for the existence of a unique solution enunciated in Sec. 3.4.

Let us illustrate how the linear dependence *among the rows* of the coefficient matrix can cause inconsistency or linear dependence *among the equations* themselves. Let the equation system $Ax = d$ take the form

$$\begin{bmatrix} 10 & 4 \\ 5 & 2 \end{bmatrix} \begin{bmatrix} x_1 \\ x_2 \end{bmatrix} = \begin{bmatrix} d_1 \\ d_2 \end{bmatrix}$$

where the coefficient matrix A contains linearly dependent rows: $v'_1 = 2v'_2$. (Note that its columns are also dependent, the first being $\frac{5}{2}$ of the second.) We have not specified the values of the constant terms d_1 and d_2, but there are only *two* distinct possibilities regarding their relative values: (1) $d_1 = 2d_2$ and (2) $d_1 \neq 2d_2$. Under the first—with, say, $d_1 = 12$ and $d_2 = 6$—the two equations are consistent but *linearly dependent* (just as the two rows of matrix A are), for the first equation is merely the second equation times 2. One equation is then redundant, and the system reduces in effect to a single equation, $5x_1 + 2x_2 = 6$, with an infinite number of solutions. For the second possibility—with, say, $d_1 = 12$ but $d_2 = 0$—the two equations are *inconsistent,* because if the first equation ($10x_1 + 4x_2 = 12$) is true, then, by halving each term, we can deduce that $5x_1 + 2x_2 = 6$; consequently the second equation ($5x_1 + 2x_2 = 0$) cannot possibly be true also. Thus no solution exists.

The upshot is that no unique solution will be available (under either possibility) so long as the rows in the coefficient matrix A are linearly dependent. In fact, the only way to have a unique solution is to have linearly independent rows (or columns) in the coefficient matrix. In that case, matrix A will be nonsingular, which means that the inverse A^{-1} does exist, and that a unique solution $x^* = A^{-1}d$ can be found.

Rank of a Matrix

Even though the concept of row independence has been discussed only with regard to square matrices, it is equally applicable to any $m \times n$ rectangular matrix. If the maximum number of linearly independent rows that can be found in such a matrix is r, the matrix is said to be of *rank r*. (The rank also tells us the maximum number of linearly independent *columns* in the said matrix.) The rank of an $m \times n$ matrix can be at most m or n, whichever is smaller.

Given a matrix with only two rows (or two columns), row independence (or column independence) is easily verified by visual inspection—one only has to check whether one row (column) is the exact multiple of the other. But for a matrix of larger dimension, visual inspection may not be feasible, and a more formal method is needed. One method for finding the rank of a matrix A (not necessarily square), i.e., for determining the number of independent rows in A, involves transforming A into a so-called *echelon matrix* by using certain "elementary row operations." A particular structural feature of the echelon matrix will then tell us the rank of matrix A.

There are only three types of *elementary row operations* on a matrix:[†]

1. Interchange of any two rows in the matrix.
2. Multiplication (or division) of a row by any scalar $k \neq 0$.
3. Addition of "k times any row" to another row.

While each of these operations converts a given matrix A into a different form, none of them alters the rank. It is this characteristic of elementary row operations that enables us to read the rank of A from its echelon matrix. The easiest way to explain the method of echelon matrix is by a specific example.

Example 5

Find the rank of the matrix

$$A = \begin{bmatrix} 0 & -11 & -4 \\ 2 & 6 & 2 \\ 4 & 1 & 0 \end{bmatrix}$$

from its echelon form. First, we check the first column of A for the presence of zero elements. If there are zero elements in column 1, we move those zero elements to the bottom of the matrix. In the case of A, we want to move the 0 (first element of column 1) to the bottom of that column, which can be accomplished by interchanging row 1 and row 3 (using the first elementary row operation). The result is

$$A_1 = \begin{bmatrix} 4 & 1 & 0 \\ 2 & 6 & 2 \\ 0 & -11 & -4 \end{bmatrix}$$

Our next objective is to reshape the first column of A_1 into a unit vector e_1 as defined in (4.7). To transform the element 4 into unity, we divide row 1 of A_1 by the scalar 4 (applying the second elementary row operation), which yields

$$A_2 = \begin{bmatrix} 1 & \frac{1}{4} & 0 \\ 2 & 6 & 2 \\ 0 & -11 & -4 \end{bmatrix}$$

Then, to transform the element 2 in column 1 of A_2 into 0, we multiply row 1 of A_2 by -2, and then add the result to row 2 of A_2 (applying the third elementary row operation). The resulting matrix,

$$A_3 = \begin{bmatrix} 1 & \frac{1}{4} & 0 \\ 0 & 5\frac{1}{2} & 2 \\ 0 & -11 & -4 \end{bmatrix}$$

[†] Similarly to elementary row operations, there can be defined elementary column operations. For our purposes, row operations are sufficient.

now has the desired unit vector e_1 as its first column. Having achieved this, we now exclude the first row of A_3 from further consideration, and continue to work only on the remaining two rows, where we want to create a two-element unit vector in the second column—by transforming the element $5\frac{1}{2}$ into 1, and the element -11 into 0. To this end, we need to divide row 2 of A_3 by $5\frac{1}{2}$, thereby changing the row into the vector $[0 \quad 1 \quad \frac{4}{11}]$, and then add 11 times this vector to row 3 of A_3. The end result, in the form of

$$A_4 = \begin{bmatrix} 1 & \frac{1}{4} & 0 \\ 0 & 1 & \frac{4}{11} \\ 0 & 0 & 0 \end{bmatrix}$$

exemplifies the echelon matrix, which, by definition, possesses three structural features. First, nonzero rows (rows with at least one nonzero element) appear above the zero rows (rows that contain only 0s). Second, in every nonzero row, the first nonzero element is unity. Third, the unit element (the first nonzero element) in any row must appear to the left of the counterpart unit element of the immediately following row. It should be clear by now that all the elementary row operations we have undertaken are designed to produce these features in A_4.

Now, we can simply read the rank of A from the number of nonzero rows present in the echelon matrix A_4. Since A_4 contains two nonzero rows, we can conclude that $r(A) = 2$. This is, of course, also the rank of matrices A_1 through A_4, because elementary row operations do not alter the rank of a matrix.

The method of echelon matrix transformation applies to nonsquare as well as square matrices. We have chosen a square matrix for Example 5 because our immediate objective is to address the question of nonsingularity, which pertains only to square matrices. By definition, for an $n \times n$ matrix A to be nonsingular, it must have n linearly independent rows (or columns); consequently, it must be of rank n, and its echelon matrix must contain exactly n nonzero rows, with no zero rows at all. Conversely, an $n \times n$ matrix having rank n must be nonsingular. Thus an $n \times n$ echelon matrix with no zero rows must be nonsingular, as is the matrix from which the echelon matrix is derived via elementary row operations. In Example 5, the matrix A is 3×3, but $r(A) = 2$; hence, A is not nonsingular.

EXERCISE 5.1

1. In the following paired statements, let p be the first statement and q the second. Indicate for each case whether (5.1), (5.2), or (5.3) applies.

   (a) It is a holiday; it is Thanksgiving Day.

   (b) A geometric figure has four sides; it is a rectangle.

   (c) Two ordered pairs (a, b) and (b, a) are equal; a is equal to b.

   (d) A number is rational; it can be expressed as a ratio of two integers.

   (e) A 4×4 matrix is nonsingular; the rank of the 4×4 matrix is 4.

   (f) The gasoline tank in my car is empty; I cannot start my car.

   (g) The letter is returned to the sender with the marking "addressee unknown"; the sender wrote the wrong address on the envelope.

2. Let p be the statement "a geometric figure is a square," and let q be as follows:
   (*a*) It has four sides.
   (*b*) It has four equal sides.
   (*c*) It has four equal sides each perpendicular to the adjacent one.
   Which is true for each case: $p \Rightarrow q$, $p \Leftarrow q$, or $p \Leftrightarrow q$?

3. Are the rows linearly independent in each of the following?

   (*a*) $\begin{bmatrix} 24 & 8 \\ 9 & -3 \end{bmatrix}$ (*b*) $\begin{bmatrix} 2 & 0 \\ 0 & 2 \end{bmatrix}$ (*c*) $\begin{bmatrix} 0 & 4 \\ 3 & 2 \end{bmatrix}$ (*d*) $\begin{bmatrix} -1 & 5 \\ 2 & -10 \end{bmatrix}$

4. Check whether the columns of each matrix in Prob. 3 are also linearly independent. Do you get the same answer as for row independence?

5. Find the rank of each of the following matrices from its echelon matrix, and comment on the question of nonsingularity.

   (*a*) $A = \begin{bmatrix} 1 & 5 & 1 \\ 0 & 3 & 9 \\ -1 & 0 & 0 \end{bmatrix}$ (*c*) $C = \begin{bmatrix} 7 & 6 & 3 & 3 \\ 0 & 1 & 2 & 1 \\ 8 & 0 & 0 & 8 \end{bmatrix}$

   (*b*) $B = \begin{bmatrix} 0 & -1 & -4 \\ 3 & 1 & 2 \\ 6 & 1 & 0 \end{bmatrix}$ (*d*) $D = \begin{bmatrix} 2 & 7 & 9 & -1 \\ 1 & 1 & 0 & 1 \\ 0 & 5 & 9 & -3 \end{bmatrix}$

6. By definition of linear dependence among rows of a matrix, one or more rows can be expressed as a linear combination of some other rows. In the echelon matrix, linear dependence is signified by the presence of one or more zero rows. What provides the link between the presence of a linear combination of rows in a given matrix and the presence of zero rows in the echelon matrix?

5.2 Test of Nonsingularity by Use of Determinant

To ascertain whether a square matrix is nonsingular, we can also make use of the concept of determinant.

Determinants and Nonsingularity

The determinant of a square matrix A, denoted by $|A|$, is a uniquely defined scalar (number) associated with that matrix. Determinants are defined only for *square* matrices. The smallest possible matrix is, of course, the 1×1 matrix $A = [a_{11}]$. By definition, its determinant is equal to the single element a_{11} itself: $|A| = |a_{11}| = a_{11}$. The symbol $|a_{11}|$ here must not be confused with the look-alike symbol for the absolute value of a number. In the absolute-value context, we have, for instance, not only $|5| = 5$, but also $|-5| = 5$, because the absolute value of a number is its numerical value without regard to the algebraic sign. In contrast, the determinant symbol preserves the sign of the element, so while $|8| = 8$ (a positive number), we have $|-8| = -8$ (a negative number). This distinction proves to be crucial in the later discussion when we apply determinantal tests whose results depend critically on the signs of determinants of various dimensions, including 1×1 ones, such as $|a_{11}| = a_{11}$.

For a 2×2 matrix $A = \begin{bmatrix} a_{11} & a_{12} \\ a_{21} & a_{22} \end{bmatrix}$, its determinant is defined to be the sum of two terms as follows:

$$|A| = \begin{vmatrix} a_{11} & a_{12} \\ a_{21} & a_{22} \end{vmatrix} = a_{11}a_{22} - a_{21}a_{12} \qquad [= \text{a scalar}] \qquad (5.5)$$

which is obtained by multiplying the two elements in the principal diagonal of A and then subtracting the product of the two remaining elements. In view of the dimension of matrix A, the determinant $|A|$ given in (5.5) is called a *second-order determinant.*

Example 1   Given $A = \begin{bmatrix} 10 & 4 \\ 8 & 5 \end{bmatrix}$ and $B = \begin{bmatrix} 3 & 5 \\ 0 & -1 \end{bmatrix}$, their determinants are

$$|A| = \begin{vmatrix} 10 & 4 \\ 8 & 5 \end{vmatrix} = 10(5) - 8(4) = 18$$

and

$$|B| = \begin{vmatrix} 3 & 5 \\ 0 & -1 \end{vmatrix} = 3(-1) - 0(5) = -3$$

While a determinant (enclosed by two vertical bars rather than brackets) is by definition a scalar, a matrix as such does not have a numerical value. In other words, a determinant is reducible to a number, but a matrix is, in contrast, a whole block of numbers. It should also be emphasized that a determinant is defined only for a square matrix, whereas a matrix as such does not have to be square.

Even at this early stage of discussion, it is possible to have an inkling of the relationship between the linear dependence of the rows in a matrix A, on the one hand, and its determinant $|A|$, on the other. The two matrices

$$C = \begin{bmatrix} c_1' \\ c_2' \end{bmatrix} = \begin{bmatrix} 3 & 8 \\ 3 & 8 \end{bmatrix} \qquad \text{and} \qquad D = \begin{bmatrix} d_1' \\ d_2' \end{bmatrix} = \begin{bmatrix} 2 & 6 \\ 8 & 24 \end{bmatrix}$$

both have linearly dependent rows, because $c_1' = c_2'$ and $d_2' = 4d_1'$. Both of their determinants also turn out to be equal to zero:

$$|C| = \begin{vmatrix} 3 & 8 \\ 3 & 8 \end{vmatrix} = 3(8) - 3(8) = 0$$

$$|D| = \begin{vmatrix} 2 & 6 \\ 8 & 24 \end{vmatrix} = 2(24) - 8(6) = 0$$

This result strongly suggests that a "vanishing" determinant (a zero-value determinant) may have something to do with linear dependence. We shall see that this is indeed the case. Furthermore, the value of a determinant $|A|$ can serve not only as a criterion for testing the linear independence of the rows (hence the nonsingularity) of matrix A, but also as an input in the calculation of the inverse A^{-1}, if it exists.

First, however, we must widen our vista by a discussion of higher-order determinants.

Evaluating a Third-Order Determinant

A determinant of order 3 is associated with a 3×3 matrix. Given

$$A = \begin{bmatrix} a_{11} & a_{12} & a_{13} \\ a_{21} & a_{22} & a_{23} \\ a_{31} & a_{32} & a_{33} \end{bmatrix}$$

FIGURE 5.1

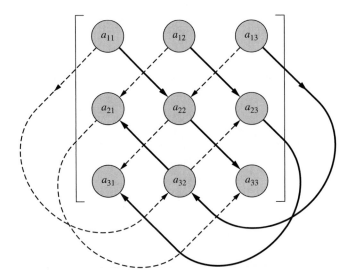

its determinant has the value

$$|A| = \begin{vmatrix} a_{11} & a_{12} & a_{13} \\ a_{21} & a_{22} & a_{23} \\ a_{31} & a_{32} & a_{33} \end{vmatrix} = a_{11} \begin{vmatrix} a_{22} & a_{23} \\ a_{32} & a_{33} \end{vmatrix} - a_{12} \begin{vmatrix} a_{21} & a_{23} \\ a_{31} & a_{33} \end{vmatrix} + a_{13} \begin{vmatrix} a_{21} & a_{22} \\ a_{31} & a_{32} \end{vmatrix}$$

$$= a_{11}a_{22}a_{33} - a_{11}a_{23}a_{32} + a_{12}a_{23}a_{31} - a_{12}a_{21}a_{33}$$
$$+ a_{13}a_{21}a_{32} - a_{13}a_{22}a_{31} \qquad [= \text{a scalar}] \qquad \textbf{(5.6)}$$

Looking first at the lower line of (5.6), we see the value of $|A|$ expressed as a sum of six product terms, three of which are prefixed by minus signs and three by plus signs. Complicated as this sum may appear, there is nonetheless a very easy way of "catching" all these six terms from a given third-order determinant. This is best explained diagrammatically (Fig. 5.1). In the determinant shown in Fig. 5.1, each element in the top row has been linked with two other elements via two *solid* arrows as follows: $a_{11} \rightarrow a_{22} \rightarrow a_{33}$, $a_{12} \rightarrow a_{23} \rightarrow a_{31}$, and $a_{13} \rightarrow a_{32} \rightarrow a_{21}$. Each triplet of elements so linked can be multiplied out, and their product taken as one of the six product terms in (5.6). The solid-arrow product terms are to be prefixed with plus signs.

On the other hand, each top-row element has also been connected with two other elements via two *broken* arrows as follows: $a_{11} \rightarrow a_{32} \rightarrow a_{23}$, $a_{12} \rightarrow a_{21} \rightarrow a_{33}$, and $a_{13} \rightarrow a_{22} \rightarrow a_{31}$. Each triplet of elements so connected can also be multiplied out, and their product taken as one of the six terms in (5.6). Such products are prefixed by minus signs. The sum of all the six products will then be the value of the determinant.

Example 2

$$\begin{vmatrix} 2 & 1 & 3 \\ 4 & 5 & 6 \\ 7 & 8 & 9 \end{vmatrix} = (2)(5)(9) + (1)(6)(7) + (3)(8)(4) - (2)(8)(6) - (1)(4)(9) - (3)(5)(7) = -9$$

Example 3

$$\begin{vmatrix} -7 & 0 & 3 \\ 9 & 1 & 4 \\ 0 & 6 & 5 \end{vmatrix} = (-7)(1)(5) + (0)(4)(0) + (3)(6)(9) - (-7)(6)(4) - (0)(9)(5) - (3)(1)(0)$$
$$= 295$$

This method of cross-diagonal multiplication provides a handy way of evaluating a third-order determinant, but unfortunately it is *not* applicable to determinants of orders higher than 3. For the latter, we must resort to the so-called Laplace expansion of the determinant.

Evaluating an *n*th-Order Determinant by Laplace Expansion

Let us first explain the *Laplace-expansion* process for a third-order determinant. Returning to the first line of (5.6), we see that the value of $|A|$ can also be regarded as a sum of *three* terms, each of which is a product of a first-row element and a particular *second*-order determinant. This latter process of evaluating $|A|$—by means of certain lower-order determinants—illustrates the Laplace expansion of the determinant.

The three second-order determinants in (5.6) are not arbitrarily determined, but are specified by means of a definite rule. The first one, $\begin{vmatrix} a_{22} & a_{23} \\ a_{32} & a_{33} \end{vmatrix}$, is a *sub*determinant of $|A|$ obtained by deleting the *first* row and *first* column of $|A|$. This is called the *minor* of the element a_{11} (the element at the intersection of the deleted row and column) and is denoted by $|M_{11}|$. In general, the symbol $|M_{ij}|$ can be used to represent the minor obtained by deleting the *i*th row and *j*th column of a given determinant. Since a minor is itself a determinant, it has a value. As the reader can verify, the other two second-order determinants in (5.6) are, respectively, the minors $|M_{12}|$ and $|M_{13}|$; that is,

$$|M_{11}| \equiv \begin{vmatrix} a_{22} & a_{23} \\ a_{32} & a_{33} \end{vmatrix} \qquad |M_{12}| \equiv \begin{vmatrix} a_{21} & a_{23} \\ a_{31} & a_{33} \end{vmatrix} \qquad |M_{13}| \equiv \begin{vmatrix} a_{21} & a_{22} \\ a_{31} & a_{32} \end{vmatrix}$$

A concept closely related to the minor is that of the *cofactor*. A cofactor, denoted by $|C_{ij}|$, is a minor with a prescribed algebraic sign attached to it.[†] The rule of sign is as follows. If the sum of the two subscripts *i* and *j* in the minor $|M_{ij}|$ is even, then the cofactor takes the same sign as the minor; that is, $|C_{ij}| \equiv |M_{ij}|$. If it is odd, then the cofactor takes the opposite sign to the minor; that is, $|C_{ij}| \equiv -|M_{ij}|$. In short, we have

$$|C_{ij}| \equiv (-1)^{i+j} |M_{ij}|$$

where it is obvious that the expression $(-1)^{i+j}$ can be positive if and only if $(i + j)$ is even. The fact that a cofactor has a specific sign is of extreme importance and should always be borne in mind.

Example 4

In the determinant $\begin{vmatrix} 9 & 8 & 7 \\ 6 & 5 & 4 \\ 3 & 2 & 1 \end{vmatrix}$, the minor of the element 8 is

$$|M_{12}| = \begin{vmatrix} 6 & 4 \\ 3 & 1 \end{vmatrix} = -6$$

but the cofactor of the same element is

$$|C_{12}| = -|M_{12}| = 6$$

because $i + j = 1 + 2 = 3$ is odd. Similarly, the cofactor of the element 4 is

$$|C_{23}| = -|M_{23}| = -\begin{vmatrix} 9 & 8 \\ 3 & 2 \end{vmatrix} = 6$$

[†] Many writers use the symbols M_{ij} and C_{ij} (without the vertical bars) for minors and cofactors. We add the vertical bars to give visual emphasis to the fact that minors and cofactors are in the nature of determinants and, as such, have scalar values.

Using these new concepts, we can express a third-order determinant as

$$|A| = a_{11}|M_{11}| - a_{12}|M_{12}| + a_{13}|M_{13}|$$

$$= a_{11}|C_{11}| + a_{12}|C_{12}| + a_{13}|C_{13}| = \sum_{j=1}^{3} a_{1j}|C_{1j}| \qquad \textbf{(5.7)}$$

i.e., as a sum of three terms, each of which is the product of a first-row element and its corresponding cofactor. Note the difference in the signs of the $a_{12}|M_{12}|$ and $a_{12}|C_{12}|$ terms in (5.7). This is because $1 + 2$ gives an odd number.

The Laplace expansion of a *third*-order determinant serves to reduce the evaluation problem to one of evaluating only certain *second*-order determinants. A similar reduction is achieved in the Laplace expansion of higher-order determinants. In a fourth-order determinant $|B|$, for instance, the top row will contain four elements, $b_{11} \ldots b_{14}$; thus, in the spirit of (5.7), we may write

$$|B| = \sum_{j=1}^{4} b_{1j}|C_{1j}|$$

where the cofactors $|C_{1j}|$ are of order 3. Each third-order cofactor can then be evaluated as in (5.6). In general, the Laplace expansion of an nth-order determinant will reduce the problem to one of evaluating n cofactors, each of which is of the $(n-1)$st order, and the repeated application of the process will methodically lead to lower and lower orders of determinants, eventually culminating in the basic second-order determinants as defined in (5.5). Then the value of the original determinant can be easily calculated.

Although the process of Laplace expansion has been couched in terms of the cofactors of the first-row elements, it is also feasible to expand a determinant by the cofactor of any row or, for that matter, of any column. For instance, if the first column of a third-order determinant $|A|$ consists of the elements a_{11}, a_{21}, and a_{31}, expansion by the cofactors of these elements will also yield the value of $|A|$:

$$|A| = a_{11}|C_{11}| + a_{21}|C_{21}| + a_{31}|C_{31}| = \sum_{i=1}^{3} a_{i1}|C_{i1}|$$

Example 5

Given $|A| = \begin{vmatrix} 5 & 6 & 1 \\ 2 & 3 & 0 \\ 7 & -3 & 0 \end{vmatrix}$, expansion by the first *row* produces the result

$$|A| = 5 \begin{vmatrix} 3 & 0 \\ -3 & 0 \end{vmatrix} - 6 \begin{vmatrix} 2 & 0 \\ 7 & 0 \end{vmatrix} + \begin{vmatrix} 2 & 3 \\ 7 & -3 \end{vmatrix} = 0 + 0 - 27 = -27$$

But expansion by the first *column* yields the identical answer:

$$|A| = 5 \begin{vmatrix} 3 & 0 \\ -3 & 0 \end{vmatrix} - 2 \begin{vmatrix} 6 & 1 \\ -3 & 0 \end{vmatrix} + 7 \begin{vmatrix} 6 & 1 \\ 3 & 0 \end{vmatrix} = 0 - 6 - 21 = -27$$

Insofar as numerical calculation is concerned, this fact affords us an opportunity to choose some "easy" row or column for expansion. A row or column with the largest number of 0s or 1s is always preferable for this purpose, because a 0 times its cofactor is simply 0, so that the term will drop out, and a 1 times its cofactor is simply the cofactor itself, so that at least one multiplication step can be saved. In Example 5, the easiest way to expand the determinant is by the third column, which consists of the elements 1, 0, and 0. We could therefore have evaluated it thus:

$$|A| = 1 \begin{vmatrix} 2 & 3 \\ 7 & -3 \end{vmatrix} = -6 - 21 = -27$$

To sum up, the value of a determinant $|A|$ of order n can be found by the Laplace expansion of *any row* or *any column* as follows:

$$|A| = \sum_{j=1}^{n} a_{ij}|C_{ij}| \qquad \text{[expansion by the } i\text{th row]}$$

$$= \sum_{i=1}^{n} a_{ij}|C_{ij}| \qquad \text{[expansion by the } j\text{th column]} \qquad \textbf{(5.8)}$$

EXERCISE 5.2

1. Evaluate the following determinants:

   (a) $\begin{vmatrix} 8 & 1 & 3 \\ 4 & 0 & 1 \\ 6 & 0 & 3 \end{vmatrix}$

   (c) $\begin{vmatrix} 4 & 0 & 2 \\ 6 & 0 & 3 \\ 8 & 2 & 3 \end{vmatrix}$

   (e) $\begin{vmatrix} a & b & c \\ b & c & a \\ c & a & b \end{vmatrix}$

   (b) $\begin{vmatrix} 1 & 2 & 3 \\ 4 & 7 & 5 \\ 3 & 6 & 9 \end{vmatrix}$

   (d) $\begin{vmatrix} 1 & 1 & 4 \\ 8 & 11 & -2 \\ 0 & 4 & 7 \end{vmatrix}$

   (f) $\begin{vmatrix} x & 5 & 0 \\ 3 & y & 2 \\ 9 & -1 & 8 \end{vmatrix}$

2. Determine the signs to be attached to the relevant minors in order to get the following cofactors of a determinant: $|C_{13}|$, $|C_{23}|$, $|C_{33}|$, $|C_{41}|$, and $|C_{34}|$.

3. Given $\begin{vmatrix} a & b & c \\ d & e & f \\ g & h & i \end{vmatrix}$, find the minors and cofactors of the elements a, b, and f.

4. Evaluate the following determinants:

   (a) $\begin{vmatrix} 1 & 2 & 0 & 9 \\ 2 & 3 & 4 & 6 \\ 1 & 6 & 0 & -1 \\ 0 & -5 & 0 & 8 \end{vmatrix}$

   (b) $\begin{vmatrix} 2 & 7 & 0 & 1 \\ 5 & 6 & 4 & 8 \\ 0 & 0 & 9 & 0 \\ 1 & -3 & 1 & 4 \end{vmatrix}$

5. In the first determinant of Prob. 4, find the value of the cofactor of the element 9.

6. Find the minors and cofactors of the third row, given

   $$A = \begin{bmatrix} 9 & 11 & 4 \\ 3 & 2 & 7 \\ 6 & 10 & 4 \end{bmatrix}$$

7. Use Laplace expansion to find the determinant of

   $$A = \begin{bmatrix} 15 & 7 & 9 \\ 2 & 5 & 6 \\ 9 & 0 & 12 \end{bmatrix}$$

5.3 Basic Properties of Determinants

We can now discuss some properties of determinants which will enable us to "discover" the connection between linear dependence among the rows of a square matrix and the vanishing of the determinant of that matrix.

Five basic properties will be discussed here. These are properties common to determinants of all orders, although we shall illustrate mostly with second-order determinants:

Property I The interchange of rows and columns does not affect the value of a determinant. In other words, the determinant of a matrix A has the same value as that of its transpose A', that is, $|A| = |A'|$.

Example 1

$$\begin{vmatrix} 4 & 3 \\ 5 & 6 \end{vmatrix} = \begin{vmatrix} 4 & 5 \\ 3 & 6 \end{vmatrix} = 9$$

Example 2

$$\begin{vmatrix} a & b \\ c & d \end{vmatrix} = \begin{vmatrix} a & c \\ b & d \end{vmatrix} = ad - bc$$

Property II The interchange of any *two* rows (or any *two* columns) will alter the sign, but not the numerical value, of the determinant. (This property is obviously related to the first elementary row operation on a matrix.)

Example 3 $\begin{vmatrix} a & b \\ c & d \end{vmatrix} = ad - bc$, but the interchange of the two rows yields

$$\begin{vmatrix} c & d \\ a & b \end{vmatrix} = cb - ad = -(ad - bc)$$

Example 4 $\begin{vmatrix} 0 & 1 & 3 \\ 2 & 5 & 7 \\ 3 & 0 & 1 \end{vmatrix} = -26$, but the interchange of the first and third columns yields

$$\begin{vmatrix} 3 & 1 & 0 \\ 7 & 5 & 2 \\ 1 & 0 & 3 \end{vmatrix} = 26.$$

Property III The multiplication of any *one* row (or *one* column) by a scalar k will change the value of the determinant k-fold. (This property is related to the second elementary row operation on a matrix.)

Example 5 By multiplying the top row of the determinant in Example 3 by k, we get

$$\begin{vmatrix} ka & kb \\ c & d \end{vmatrix} = kad - kbc = k(ad - bc) = k\begin{vmatrix} a & b \\ c & d \end{vmatrix}$$

It is important to distinguish between the two expressions kA and $k|A|$. In multiplying a *matrix A* by a scalar k, all the elements in A are to be multiplied by k. But, if we read the equation in the present example from right to left, it should be clear that, in multiplying a *determinant $|A|$* by k, only a single row (or column) should be multiplied by k. This equation, therefore, in effect gives us a rule for factoring a determinant: whenever any single row or column contains a common divisor, it may be factored out of the determinant.

Example 6

Factoring the first column and the second row in turn, we have

$$\begin{vmatrix} 15a & 7b \\ 12c & 2d \end{vmatrix} = 3 \begin{vmatrix} 5a & 7b \\ 4c & 2d \end{vmatrix} = 3(2) \begin{vmatrix} 5a & 7b \\ 2c & d \end{vmatrix} = 6(5ad - 14bc)$$

The direct evaluation of the original determinant will, of course, produce the same answer.

In contrast, the factoring of a *matrix* requires the presence of a common divisor for *all* its elements, as in

$$\begin{bmatrix} ka & kb \\ kc & kd \end{bmatrix} = k \begin{bmatrix} a & b \\ c & d \end{bmatrix}$$

Property IV The addition (subtraction) of a multiple of any row to (from) another row will leave the value of the determinant unaltered. The same holds true if we replace the word *row* by *column* in the previous statement. (This property is related to the third elementary row operation on a matrix.)

Example 7

Adding k times the top row of the determinant in Example 3 to its second row, we end up with the original determinant:

$$\begin{vmatrix} a & b \\ c + ka & d + kb \end{vmatrix} = a(d + kb) - b(c + ka) = ad - bc = \begin{vmatrix} a & b \\ c & d \end{vmatrix}$$

Property V If one row (or column) is a multiple of another row (or column), the value of the determinant will be zero. As a special case of this, when two rows (or two columns) are *identical*, the determinant will vanish.

Example 8

$$\begin{vmatrix} 2a & 2b \\ a & b \end{vmatrix} = 2ab - 2ab = 0 \qquad \begin{vmatrix} c & c \\ d & d \end{vmatrix} = cd - cd = 0$$

Additional examples of this type of "vanishing" determinant can be found in Exercise 5.2-1.

This important property is, in fact, a logical consequence of Property IV. To understand this, let us apply Property IV to the two determinants in Example 8 and watch the outcome. For the first one, try to subtract twice the second row from the top row; for the second determinant, subtract the second column from the first column. Since these operations do not alter the values of the determinants, we can write

$$\begin{vmatrix} 2a & 2b \\ a & b \end{vmatrix} = \begin{vmatrix} 0 & 0 \\ a & b \end{vmatrix} \qquad \begin{vmatrix} c & c \\ d & d \end{vmatrix} = \begin{vmatrix} 0 & c \\ 0 & d \end{vmatrix}$$

The new (reduced) determinants now contain, respectively, a row and a column of zeros; thus their Laplace expansion must yield a value of zero in both cases. In general, when one row (column) is a multiple of another row (column), the application of Property IV can always reduce all elements of that row (column) to zero, and Property V therefore follows.

The basic properties just discussed are useful in several ways. For one thing, they can be of great help in simplifying the task of evaluating determinants. By subtracting multiples of one row (or column) from another, for instance, the elements of the determinant may be reduced to much smaller and simpler numbers. Factoring, if feasible, can also accomplish the same. If we can indeed apply these properties to transform some row or column into a form containing mostly 0s or 1s, Laplace expansion of the determinant will become a much more manageable task.

Determinantal Criterion for Nonsingularity

Our present concern, however, is primarily to link the linear dependence of rows with the vanishing of a determinant. For this purpose, Property V can be invoked. Consider an equation system $Ax = d$:

$$\begin{bmatrix} 3 & 4 & 2 \\ 15 & 20 & 10 \\ 4 & 0 & 1 \end{bmatrix} \begin{bmatrix} x_1 \\ x_2 \\ x_3 \end{bmatrix} = \begin{bmatrix} d_1 \\ d_2 \\ d_3 \end{bmatrix}$$

This system can have a unique solution if and only if the rows in the coefficient matrix A are linearly independent, so that A is nonsingular. But the second row is five times the first; the rows are indeed *dependent,* and hence no unique solution exists. The detection of this row dependence was by visual inspection, but by virtue of Property V we could also have discovered it through the fact that $|A| = 0$.

The row dependence in a matrix may, of course, assume a more intricate and secretive pattern. For instance, in the matrix

$$B = \begin{bmatrix} 4 & 1 & 2 \\ 5 & 2 & 1 \\ 1 & 0 & 1 \end{bmatrix} = \begin{bmatrix} v_1' \\ v_2' \\ v_3' \end{bmatrix}$$

there exists row dependence because $2v_1' - v_2' - 3v_3' = 0$; yet this fact defies visual detection. Even in this case, however, Property V will give us a vanishing determinant, $|B| = 0$, since by adding three times v_3' to v_2' and subtracting twice v_1' from it, the second row can be reduced to a zero vector. In general, *any* pattern of linear dependence among rows will be reflected in a vanishing determinant—and herein lies the beauty of Property V! Conversely, if the rows are linearly independent, the determinant must have a nonzero value.

We have, in the previous two paragraphs, tied the nonsingularity of a matrix principally to the linear independence among *rows*. But, on occasion, we have made the claim that, for a *square* matrix A, row independence $\Leftrightarrow$ column independence. We are now equipped to prove that claim:

> According to Property I, we know that $|A| = |A'|$. Since row independence in $A \Leftrightarrow |A| \neq 0$, we may also state that row independence in $A \Leftrightarrow |A'| \neq 0$. But $|A'| \neq 0 \Leftrightarrow$ row independence in the transpose $A' \Leftrightarrow$ column independence in A (rows of A' are by definition the columns of A). Therefore, *row* independence in $A \Leftrightarrow$ *column* independence in A.

Our discussion of the test of nonsingularity can now be summarized. Given a linear-equation system $Ax = d$, where A is an $n \times n$ coefficient matrix,

$$|A| \neq 0 \Leftrightarrow \text{there is row (column) independence in matrix } A$$

$$\Leftrightarrow A \text{ is nonsingular}$$

$$\Leftrightarrow A^{-1} \text{ exists}$$

$$\Leftrightarrow \text{a unique solution } x^* = A^{-1}d \text{ exists}$$

Thus the value of the determinant of the coefficient matrix, $|A|$, provides a convenient criterion for testing the nonsingularity of matrix A and the existence of a unique solution to the equation system $Ax = d$. Note, however, that the determinantal criterion says nothing about the algebraic signs of the solution values; i.e., even though we are assured of a unique solution when $|A| \neq 0$, we may sometimes get negative solution values that are economically inadmissible.

Example 9   Does the equation system

$$7x_1 - 3x_2 - 3x_3 = 7$$
$$2x_1 + 4x_2 + x_3 = 0$$
$$-2x_2 - x_3 = 2$$

possess a unique solution? The determinant $|A|$ is

$$\begin{vmatrix} 7 & -3 & -3 \\ 2 & 4 & 1 \\ 0 & -2 & -1 \end{vmatrix} = -8 \neq 0$$

Therefore a unique solution does exist.

Rank of a Matrix Redefined

The rank of a matrix A was earlier defined to be the maximum number of linearly independent rows in A. In view of the link between row independence and the nonvanishing of the determinant, we can redefine the rank of an $m \times n$ matrix as the maximum order of a nonvanishing determinant that can be constructed from the rows and columns of that matrix. The rank of any matrix is a unique number.

Obviously, the rank can at most be m or n, whichever is smaller, because a determinant is defined only for a square matrix, and from a matrix of dimension, say, 3×5, the largest possible determinants (vanishing or not) will be of order 3. Symbolically, this fact may be expressed as follows:

$$r(A) \leq \min \{m, n\}$$

which is read: "The rank of A is less than or equal to the minimum of the set of two numbers m and n." The rank of an $n \times n$ nonsingular matrix A must be n; in that case, we may write $r(A) = n$.

Sometimes, one may be interested in the rank of the product of two matrices. In that case, the following rule can be of use:

$$r(AB) \leq \min \{r(A), r(B)\} \tag{5.9}$$

While this rule does not yield a unique value of $r(AB)$, the application of the rule can nevertheless lead to unique results. In particular, we can use (5.9) to show that if a matrix A, with $r(A) = j$, is multiplied by any (conformable) nonsingular matrix B, the rank of the product matrix AB (or BA, as the case may be), must be j. We shall prove this for the product AB (the case of BA is analogous). First, looking at the right-hand side of (5.9), we see only three possible cases: (i) $r(A) < r(B)$, (ii) $r(A) = r(B)$, and (iii) $r(A) > r(B)$.

For cases (i) and (ii), (5.9) reduces directly to $r(AB) \leq r(A) = j$. For case (iii), we find that $r(AB) \leq r(B) < r(A) = j$. Thus, either way, we get

$$r(AB) \leq r(A) = j \qquad (5.10)$$

Now consider the identity $(AB)B^{-1} = A$. By (5.9), we can write

$$r[(AB)B^{-1}] \leq \min\{r(AB), r(B^{-1})\}$$

Applying the same reasoning that led us to (5.10), we can conclude from this that

$$r[(AB)B^{-1}] \leq r(AB)$$

Since the left-side expression of this inequality is equal to $r(A) = j$, we may write

$$j \leq r(AB) \qquad (5.11)$$

But (5.10) and (5.11) cannot be satisfied simultaneously unless $r(AB) = j$. Thus the rank of the product matrix AB must be j, as asserted.

EXERCISE 5.3

1. Use the determinant $\begin{vmatrix} 4 & 0 & -1 \\ 2 & 1 & -7 \\ 3 & 3 & 9 \end{vmatrix}$ to verify the first four properties of determinants.

2. Show that, when all the elements of an nth-order determinant $|A|$ are multiplied by a number k, the result will be $k^n |A|$.

3. Which properties of determinants enable us to write the following?

   (a) $\begin{vmatrix} 9 & 18 \\ 27 & 56 \end{vmatrix} = \begin{vmatrix} 9 & 18 \\ 0 & 2 \end{vmatrix}$ (b) $\begin{vmatrix} 9 & 27 \\ 4 & 2 \end{vmatrix} = 18 \begin{vmatrix} 1 & 3 \\ 2 & 1 \end{vmatrix}$

4. Test whether the following matrices are nonsingular:

   (a) $\begin{bmatrix} 4 & 0 & 1 \\ 19 & 1 & -3 \\ 7 & 1 & 0 \end{bmatrix}$ (c) $\begin{bmatrix} 7 & -1 & 0 \\ 1 & 1 & 4 \\ 13 & -3 & -4 \end{bmatrix}$

   (b) $\begin{bmatrix} 4 & -2 & 1 \\ -5 & 6 & 0 \\ 7 & 0 & 3 \end{bmatrix}$ (d) $\begin{bmatrix} -4 & 9 & 5 \\ 3 & 0 & 1 \\ 10 & 8 & 6 \end{bmatrix}$

5. What can you conclude about the rank of each matrix in Prob. 4?

6. Can any of the given sets of 3-vectors below span the 3-space? Why or why not?

   (a) [1 2 1]   [2 3 1]   [3 4 2]

   (b) [8 1 3]   [1 2 8]   [−7 1 5]

7. Rewrite the simple national-income model (3.23) in the $Ax = d$ format (with Y as the first variable in the vector x), and then test whether the coefficient matrix A is nonsingular.

8. Comment on the validity of the following statements:

   (a) "Given any matrix A, we can always derive from it a transpose, and a determinant."

   (b) "Multiplying each element of an $n \times n$ determinant by 2 will double the value of that determinant."

   (c) "If a square matrix A vanishes, then we can be sure that the equation system $Ax = d$ is nonsingular."

5.4 Finding the Inverse Matrix

If the matrix A in the linear-equation system $Ax = d$ is nonsingular, then A^{-1} exists, and the solution of the system will be $x^* = A^{-1}d$. We have learned to test the nonsingularity of A by the criterion $|A| \neq 0$. The next question is, How can we find the inverse A^{-1} if A does pass that test?

Expansion of a Determinant by Alien Cofactors

Before answering this query, let us discuss another important property of determinants.

Property VI The expansion of a determinant by *alien cofactors* (the cofactors of a "wrong" row or column) always yields a value of zero.

Example 1

If we expand the determinant $\begin{vmatrix} 4 & 1 & 2 \\ 5 & 2 & 1 \\ 1 & 0 & 3 \end{vmatrix}$ by using its *first*-row elements but the cofactors of the *second*-row elements

$$|C_{21}| = -\begin{vmatrix} 1 & 2 \\ 0 & 3 \end{vmatrix} = -3 \qquad |C_{22}| = \begin{vmatrix} 4 & 2 \\ 1 & 3 \end{vmatrix} = 10 \qquad |C_{23}| = -\begin{vmatrix} 4 & 1 \\ 1 & 0 \end{vmatrix} = 1$$

we get $a_{11}|C_{21}| + a_{12}|C_{22}| + a_{13}|C_{23}| = 4(-3) + 1(10) + 2(1) = 0$.

More generally, applying the same type of expansion by alien cofactors as described in Example 1 to the determinant $|A| = \begin{vmatrix} a_{11} & a_{12} & a_{13} \\ a_{21} & a_{22} & a_{23} \\ a_{31} & a_{32} & a_{33} \end{vmatrix}$ will yield a zero sum of products as follows:

$$\sum_{i=1}^{3} a_{1j}|C_{2j}| = a_{11}|C_{21}| + a_{12}|C_{22}| + a_{13}|C_{23}|$$

$$= -a_{11}\begin{vmatrix} a_{12} & a_{13} \\ a_{32} & a_{33} \end{vmatrix} + a_{12}\begin{vmatrix} a_{11} & a_{13} \\ a_{31} & a_{33} \end{vmatrix} - a_{13}\begin{vmatrix} a_{11} & a_{12} \\ a_{31} & a_{32} \end{vmatrix} \qquad \textbf{(5.12)}$$

$$= -a_{11}a_{12}a_{33} + a_{11}a_{13}a_{32} + a_{11}a_{12}a_{33} - a_{12}a_{13}a_{31}$$
$$\qquad - a_{11}a_{13}a_{32} + a_{12}a_{13}a_{31} = 0$$

The reason for this outcome lies in the fact that the sum of products in (5.12) can be considered as the result of the *regular* expansion by the second row of another determinant $|A^*| \equiv \begin{vmatrix} a_{11} & a_{12} & a_{13} \\ a_{11} & a_{12} & a_{13} \\ a_{31} & a_{32} & a_{33} \end{vmatrix}$, which differs from $|A|$ only in its second row and whose first two rows are identical. As an exercise, write out the cofactors of the second rows of $|A^*|$ and verify that these are precisely the cofactors which appeared in (5.12)—and with the correct signs. Since $|A^*| = 0$, because of its two identical rows, the expansion by alien cofactors shown in (5.12) will of necessity yield a value of zero also.

Property VI is valid for determinants of all orders and applies when a determinant is expanded by the alien cofactors of any row or any column. Thus we may state, in general, that for a determinant of order n the following holds:

$$\sum_{j=1}^{n} a_{ij}|C_{i'j}| = 0 \quad (i \neq i') \qquad \text{[expansion by } i\text{th row and}$$
$$\text{cofactors of } i'\text{th row]}$$

$$\text{(5.13)}$$

$$\sum_{i=1}^{n} a_{ij}|C_{ij'}| = 0 \quad (j \neq j') \qquad \text{[expansion by } j\text{th column and}$$
$$\text{cofactors of } j'\text{th column]}$$

Carefully compare (5.13) with (5.8). In the latter (regular Laplace expansion), the subscripts of a_{ij} and of $|C_{ij}|$ must be identical in each product term in the sum. In the expansion by alien cofactors, such as in (5.13), on the other hand, one of the two subscripts (a chosen value of i' or j') is inevitably "out of place."

Matrix Inversion

Property VI, as summarized in (5.13), is of direct help in developing a method of matrix inversion, i.e., of finding the inverse of a matrix.

Assume that an $n \times n$ nonsingular matrix A is given:

$$\underset{(n \times n)}{A} = \begin{bmatrix} a_{11} & a_{12} & \cdots & a_{1n} \\ a_{21} & a_{22} & \cdots & a_{2n} \\ \cdots\cdots\cdots\cdots\cdots\cdots \\ a_{n1} & a_{n2} & \cdots & a_{nn} \end{bmatrix} \quad (|A| \neq 0) \qquad \text{(5.14)}$$

Since each element of A has a cofactor $|C_{ij}|$, it is possible to form a matrix of cofactors by replacing each element a_{ij} in (5.14) with its cofactor $|C_{ij}|$. Such a cofactor matrix, denoted by $C = [|C_{ij}|]$, must also be $n \times n$. For our present purposes, however, the transpose of C is of more interest. This transpose C' is commonly referred to as the *adjoint* of A and is symbolized by adj A. Written out, the adjoint takes the form

$$\underset{(n \times n)}{C'} \equiv \text{adj } A \equiv \begin{bmatrix} |C_{11}| & |C_{21}| & \cdots & |C_{n1}| \\ |C_{12}| & |C_{22}| & \cdots & |C_{n2}| \\ \cdots\cdots\cdots\cdots\cdots\cdots\cdots \\ |C_{1n}| & |C_{2n}| & \cdots & |C_{nn}| \end{bmatrix} \qquad \text{(5.15)}$$

The matrices A and C' are conformable for multiplication, and their product AC' is another $n \times n$ matrix in which each element is a sum of products. By utilizing the formula for Laplace expansion as well as Property VI of determinants, the product AC' may be expressed as follows:

$$\underset{(n \times n)}{AC'} = \begin{bmatrix} \sum_{j=1}^{n} a_{1j}|C_{1j}| & \sum_{j=1}^{n} a_{1j}|C_{2j}| & \cdots & \sum_{j=1}^{n} a_{1j}|C_{nj}| \\ \sum_{j=1}^{n} a_{2j}|C_{1j}| & \sum_{j=1}^{n} a_{2j}|C_{2j}| & \cdots & \sum_{j=1}^{n} a_{2j}|C_{nj}| \\ \vdots & \vdots & & \vdots \\ \sum_{j=1}^{n} a_{nj}|C_{1j}| & \sum_{j=1}^{n} a_{nj}|C_{2j}| & \cdots & \sum_{j=1}^{n} a_{nj}|C_{nj}| \end{bmatrix}$$

$$
=
\begin{bmatrix}
|A| & 0 & \cdots & 0 \\
0 & |A| & \cdots & 0 \\
\vdots & \vdots & & \vdots \\
0 & 0 & \cdots & |A|
\end{bmatrix}
\qquad \text{[by (5.8) and (5.13)]}
$$

$$
= |A|
\begin{bmatrix}
1 & 0 & \cdots & 0 \\
0 & 1 & \cdots & 0 \\
\vdots & \vdots & & \vdots \\
0 & 0 & \cdots & 1
\end{bmatrix}
= |A| I_n \qquad \text{[factoring]}
$$

As the determinant $|A|$ is a nonzero scalar, it is permissible to divide both sides of the equation $AC' = |A|I$ by $|A|$. The result is

$$
\frac{AC'}{|A|} = I \qquad \text{or} \qquad A\frac{C'}{|A|} = I
$$

Premultiplying both sides of the last equation by A^{-1}, and using the result that $A^{-1}A = I$, we can get $\dfrac{C'}{|A|} = A^{-1}$, or

$$
A^{-1} = \frac{1}{|A|} \text{ adj } A \qquad \text{[by (5.15)]} \tag{5.16}
$$

Now, we have found a way to invert the matrix A!

The general procedure for finding the inverse of a square matrix A thus involves the following steps: (1) find $|A|$ [we need to proceed with the subsequent steps if and only if $|A| \neq 0$, for if $|A| = 0$, the inverse in (5.16) will be undefined]; (2) find the cofactors of all the elements of A, and arrange them as a matrix $C = [|C_{ij}|]$; (3) take the transpose of C to get adj A; and (4) divide adj A by the determinant $|A|$. The result will be the desired inverse A^{-1}.

Example 2   Find the inverse of $A = \begin{bmatrix} 3 & 2 \\ 1 & 0 \end{bmatrix}$. Since $|A| = -2 \neq 0$, the inverse A^{-1} exists. The cofactor of each element is in this case a 1×1 determinant, which is simply defined as the scalar element of that determinant itself (that is, $|a_{ij}| \equiv a_{ij}$). Thus, we have

$$
C = \begin{bmatrix} |C_{11}| & |C_{12}| \\ |C_{21}| & |C_{22}| \end{bmatrix} = \begin{bmatrix} 0 & -1 \\ -2 & 3 \end{bmatrix}
$$

Observe the minus signs attached to 1 and 2, as required for cofactors. Transposing the cofactor matrix yields

$$
\text{adj } A = \begin{bmatrix} 0 & -2 \\ -1 & 3 \end{bmatrix}
$$

so the inverse A^{-1} can be written as

$$
A^{-1} = \frac{1}{|A|} \text{ adj } A = -\frac{1}{2} \begin{bmatrix} 0 & -2 \\ -1 & 3 \end{bmatrix} = \begin{bmatrix} 0 & 1 \\ \frac{1}{2} & -\frac{3}{2} \end{bmatrix}
$$

<u>**Example 3**</u>

Find the inverse of $B = \begin{bmatrix} 4 & 1 & -1 \\ 0 & 3 & 2 \\ 3 & 0 & 7 \end{bmatrix}$. Since $|B| = 99 \neq 0$, the inverse B^{-1} also exists. The cofactor matrix is

$$\begin{bmatrix} \begin{vmatrix} 3 & 2 \\ 0 & 7 \end{vmatrix} & -\begin{vmatrix} 0 & 2 \\ 3 & 7 \end{vmatrix} & \begin{vmatrix} 0 & 3 \\ 3 & 0 \end{vmatrix} \\ -\begin{vmatrix} 1 & -1 \\ 0 & 7 \end{vmatrix} & \begin{vmatrix} 4 & -1 \\ 3 & 7 \end{vmatrix} & -\begin{vmatrix} 4 & 1 \\ 3 & 0 \end{vmatrix} \\ \begin{vmatrix} 1 & -1 \\ 3 & 2 \end{vmatrix} & -\begin{vmatrix} 4 & -1 \\ 0 & 2 \end{vmatrix} & \begin{vmatrix} 4 & 1 \\ 0 & 3 \end{vmatrix} \end{bmatrix} = \begin{bmatrix} 21 & 6 & -9 \\ -7 & 31 & 3 \\ 5 & -8 & 12 \end{bmatrix}$$

Therefore,

$$\text{adj } B = \begin{bmatrix} 21 & -7 & 5 \\ 6 & 31 & -8 \\ -9 & 3 & 12 \end{bmatrix}$$

and the desired inverse matrix is

$$B^{-1} = \frac{1}{|B|} \text{ adj } B = \frac{1}{99} \begin{bmatrix} 21 & -7 & 5 \\ 6 & 31 & -8 \\ -9 & 3 & 12 \end{bmatrix}$$

You can check that the results in Examples 2 and 3 do satisfy $AA^{-1} = A^{-1}A = I$ and $BB^{-1} = B^{-1}B = I$, respectively.

EXERCISE 5.4

1. Suppose that we expand a fourth-order determinant by its *third column* and the cofactors of the *second-column* elements. How would you write the resulting sum of products in $\sum$ notation? What will be the sum of products in $\sum$ notation if we expand it by the *second row* and the cofactors of the *fourth-row* elements?

2. Find the inverse of each of the following matrices:

    (a) $A = \begin{bmatrix} 5 & 2 \\ 0 & 1 \end{bmatrix}$ (b) $B = \begin{bmatrix} -1 & 0 \\ 9 & 2 \end{bmatrix}$ (c) $C = \begin{bmatrix} 3 & 7 \\ 3 & -1 \end{bmatrix}$ (d) $D = \begin{bmatrix} 7 & 6 \\ 0 & 3 \end{bmatrix}$

3. (a) Drawing on your answers to Prob. 2, formulate a two-step rule for finding the adjoint of a given 2×2 matrix A: In the first step, indicate what should be done to the two diagonal elements of A in order to get the diagonal elements of adj A; in the second step, indicate what should be done to the two off-diagonal elements of A. (*Warning:* This rule applies only to 2×2 matrices.)

    (b) Add a third step which, in conjunction with the previous two steps, yields the 2×2 inverse matrix A^{-1}.

4. Find the inverse of each of the following matrices:

    (a) $E = \begin{bmatrix} 4 & -2 & 1 \\ 7 & 3 & 0 \\ 2 & 0 & 1 \end{bmatrix}$ (c) $G = \begin{bmatrix} 1 & 0 & 0 \\ 0 & 0 & 1 \\ 0 & 1 & 0 \end{bmatrix}$

    (b) $F = \begin{bmatrix} 1 & -1 & 2 \\ 1 & 0 & 3 \\ 4 & 0 & 2 \end{bmatrix}$ (d) $H = \begin{bmatrix} 1 & 0 & 0 \\ 0 & 1 & 0 \\ 0 & 0 & 1 \end{bmatrix}$

5. Find the inverse of

$$A = \begin{bmatrix} 4 & 1 & -5 \\ -2 & 3 & 1 \\ 3 & -1 & 4 \end{bmatrix}$$

6. Solve the system $Ax = d$ by matrix inversion, where

(a) $4x + 3y = 28$
$\quad\; 2x + 5y = 42$

(b) $4x_1 + x_2 - 5x_3 = 8$
$\quad -2x_1 + 3x_2 + x_3 = 12$
$\quad\;\; 3x_1 - x_2 + 4x_3 = 5$

7. Is it possible for a matrix to be its own inverse?

5.5   Cramer's Rule

The method of matrix inversion discussed in Sec. 5.4 enables us to derive a practical, if not always efficient, way of solving a linear-equation system, known as *Cramer's rule*.

Derivation of the Rule

Given an equation system $Ax = d$, where A is $n \times n$, the solution can be written as

$$x^* = A^{-1}d = \frac{1}{|A|}(\text{adj }A)d \qquad [\text{by }(5.16)]$$

provided A is nonsingular. According to (5.15), this means that

$$\begin{bmatrix} x_1^* \\ x_2^* \\ \vdots \\ x_n^* \end{bmatrix} = \frac{1}{|A|} \begin{bmatrix} |C_{11}| & |C_{21}| & \cdots & |C_{n1}| \\ |C_{12}| & |C_{22}| & \cdots & |C_{n2}| \\ \multicolumn{4}{c}{\dotfill} \\ |C_{1n}| & |C_{2n}| & \cdots & |C_{nn}| \end{bmatrix} \begin{bmatrix} d_1 \\ d_2 \\ \vdots \\ d_n \end{bmatrix}$$

$$= \frac{1}{|A|} \begin{bmatrix} d_1|C_{11}| + d_2|C_{21}| + \cdots + d_n|C_{n1}| \\ d_1|C_{12}| + d_2|C_{22}| + \cdots + d_n|C_{n2}| \\ \dotfill \\ d_1|C_{1n}| + d_2|C_{2n}| + \cdots + d_n|C_{nn}| \end{bmatrix}$$

$$= \frac{1}{|A|} \begin{bmatrix} \sum_{i=1}^{n} d_i|C_{i1}| \\ \sum_{i=1}^{n} d_i|C_{i2}| \\ \vdots \\ \sum_{i=1}^{n} d_i|C_{in}| \end{bmatrix}$$

Equating the corresponding elements on the two sides of the equation, we obtain the solution values

$$x_1^* = \frac{1}{|A|} \sum_{i=1}^{n} d_i |C_{i1}| \qquad x_2^* = \frac{1}{|A|} \sum_{i=1}^{n} d_i |C_{i2}| \qquad \text{(etc.)} \qquad \textbf{(5.17)}$$

The $\sum$ terms in (5.17) look unfamiliar. What do they mean? From (5.8), we see that the Laplace expansion of a determinant $|A|$ by its first column can be expressed in the form $\sum_{i=1}^{n} a_{i1} |C_{i1}|$. If we replace the first column of $|A|$ by the column vector d but keep all the other columns intact, then a new determinant will result, which we can call $|A_1|$—the subscript 1 indicating that the first column has been replaced by d. The expansion of $|A_1|$ by its first column (the d column) will yield the expression $\sum_{i=1}^{n} d_i |C_{i1}|$, because the elements d_i now take the place of the elements a_{i1}. Returning to (5.17), we see therefore that

$$x_1^* = \frac{1}{|A|} |A_1|$$

Similarly, if we replace the second column of $|A|$ by the column vector d, while retaining all the other columns, the expansion of the new determinant $|A_2|$ by its second column (the d column) will result in the expression $\sum_{i=1}^{n} d_i |C_{i2}|$. When divided by $|A|$, this latter sum will give us the solution value x_2^*, and so on.

This procedure can now be generalized. To find the solution value of the jth variable x_j^*, we can merely replace the jth column of the determinant $|A|$ by the constant terms $d_1 \cdots d_n$ to get a new determinant $|A_j|$ and then divide $|A_j|$ by the original determinant $|A|$. Thus, the solution of the system $Ax = d$ can be expressed as

$$x_j^* = \frac{|A_j|}{|A|} = \frac{1}{|A|} \begin{vmatrix} a_{11} & a_{12} & \cdots & d_1 & \cdots & a_{1n} \\ a_{21} & a_{22} & \cdots & d_2 & \cdots & a_{2n} \\ \vdots & \vdots & & \vdots & & \vdots \\ a_{n1} & a_{n2} & \cdots & d_n & \cdots & a_{nn} \end{vmatrix} \qquad \textbf{(5.18)}$$

$$(j\text{th column replaced by } d)$$

The result in (5.18) is the statement of Cramer's rule. Note that, whereas the matrix inversion method yields the solution values of *all* the endogenous variables at once (x^* is a vector), Cramer's rule can give us the solution value of only a single endogenous variable at a time (x_j^* is a scalar); this is why it may not be efficient.

Example 1

Find the solution of the equation system

$$5x_1 + 3x_2 = 30$$
$$6x_1 - 2x_2 = 8$$

The coefficients and the constant terms give the following determinants:

$$|A| = \begin{vmatrix} 5 & 3 \\ 6 & -2 \end{vmatrix} = -28 \qquad |A_1| = \begin{vmatrix} 30 & 3 \\ 8 & -2 \end{vmatrix} = -84$$

$$|A_2| = \begin{vmatrix} 5 & 30 \\ 6 & 8 \end{vmatrix} = -140$$

Therefore, by virtue of (5.18), we can immediately write

$$x_1^* = \frac{|A_1|}{|A|} = \frac{-84}{-28} = 3 \quad \text{and} \quad x_2^* = \frac{|A_2|}{|A|} = \frac{-140}{-28} = 5$$

Example 2   Find the solution of the equation system

$$7x_1 - x_2 - x_3 = 0$$
$$10x_1 - 2x_2 + x_3 = 8$$
$$6x_1 + 3x_2 - 2x_3 = 7$$

The relevant determinants $|A|$ and $|A_j|$ are found to be

$$|A| = \begin{vmatrix} 7 & -1 & -1 \\ 10 & -2 & 1 \\ 6 & 3 & -2 \end{vmatrix} = -61 \qquad |A_1| = \begin{vmatrix} 0 & -1 & -1 \\ 8 & -2 & 1 \\ 7 & 3 & -2 \end{vmatrix} = -61$$

$$|A_2| = \begin{vmatrix} 7 & 0 & -1 \\ 10 & 8 & 1 \\ 6 & 7 & -2 \end{vmatrix} = -183 \qquad |A_3| = \begin{vmatrix} 7 & -1 & 0 \\ 10 & -2 & 8 \\ 6 & 3 & 7 \end{vmatrix} = -244$$

thus the solution values of the variables are

$$x_1^* = \frac{|A_1|}{|A|} = \frac{-61}{-61} = 1 \qquad x_2^* = \frac{|A_2|}{|A|} = \frac{-183}{-61} = 3 \qquad x_3^* = \frac{|A_3|}{|A|} = \frac{-244}{-61} = 4$$

Notice that in each of these examples we find $|A| \neq 0$. This is a necessary condition for the application of Cramer's rule, as it is for the existence of the inverse A^{-1}. Cramer's rule is, after all, based upon the concept of the inverse matrix, even though in practice it bypasses the process of matrix inversion.

Note on Homogeneous-Equation Systems

The equation systems $Ax = d$ considered before can have any constants in the vector d. If $d = 0$, that is, if $d_1 = d_2 = \cdots = d_n = 0$, however, the equation system will become

$$Ax = 0$$

where 0 is a zero vector. This special case is referred to as a *homogeneous-equation system.* The word *homogeneous* here relates to the property that when all the variables, $x_1, \ldots, x_n$ are multiplied by the same number, the equation system will remain valid. This is possible only if the constant terms of the system—those unattached to any x_i—are all zero.

If the matrix A is nonsingular, a homogeneous-equation system can yield only a "trivial solution," namely, $x_1^* = x_2^* = \cdots = x_n^* = 0$. This follows from the fact that the solution $x^* = A^{-1}d$ will in this case become

$$\underset{(n \times 1)}{x^*} = \underset{(n \times n)}{A^{-1}} \underset{(n \times 1)}{0} = \underset{(n \times 1)}{0}$$

Alternatively, this outcome can be derived from Cramer's rule. The fact that $d = 0$ implies that $|A_j|$, for all j, must contain a whole column of zeros, and thus the solution will turn out to be

$$x_j^* = \frac{|A_j|}{|A|} = \frac{0}{|A|} = 0 \qquad (j = 1, 2, \ldots, n)$$

Curiously enough, the *only* way to get a *non*trivial solution from a homogeneous-equation system is to have $|A| = 0$, that is, to have a *singular* coefficient matrix A! In that event, we have

$$x_j^* = \frac{|A_j|}{|A|} = \frac{0}{0}$$

where the $0/0$ expression is not equal to zero but is, rather, something undefined. Consequently, Cramer's rule is not applicable. This does not mean that we cannot obtain solutions; it means only that we cannot get a unique solution.

Consider the homogeneous-equation system

$$\begin{aligned}
a_{11}x_1 + a_{12}x_2 &= 0 \\
a_{21}x_1 + a_{22}x_2 &= 0
\end{aligned} \qquad\qquad (5.19)$$

It is self-evident that $x_1^* = x_2^* = 0$ is a solution, but that solution is trivial. Now, assume that the coefficient matrix A is singular, so that $|A| = 0$. This implies that the row vector $[a_{11} \quad a_{12}]$ is a multiple of the row vector $[a_{21} \quad a_{22}]$; consequently, one of the two equations is redundant. By deleting, say, the second equation from (5.19), we end up with one (the first) equation in two variables, the solution of which is $x_1^* = (-a_{12}/a_{11})x_2^*$. This solution is nontrivial and well defined if $a_{11} \neq 0$, but it really represents an infinite number of solutions because, for every possible value of x_2^*, there is a corresponding value x_1^* such that the pair constitutes a solution. Thus no unique nontrivial solution exists for this homogeneous-equation system. This last statement is also generally valid for the n-variable case.

Solution Outcomes for a Linear-Equation System

Our discussion of the several variants of the linear-equation system $Ax = d$ reveals that as many as four different types of solution outcome are possible. For a better overall view of these variants, we list them in tabular form in Table 5.1.

As a first possibility, the system may yield a unique, nontrivial solution. This type of outcome can arise only when we have a nonhomogeneous system with a nonsingular coefficient matrix A. The second possible outcome is a unique, trivial solution, and this is

TABLE 5.1
Solution Outcomes for a Linear-Equation System $Ax = d$

Determinant $|A|$	Vector d	
	$d \neq 0$ (nonhomogeneous system)	$d = 0$ (homogeneous system)
$|A| \neq 0$ (matrix A nonsingular)	There exists a unique, nontrivial solution $x^* \neq 0$.	There exists a unique, trivial solution $x^* = 0$.
$|A| = 0$ (matrix A singular)		
Equations dependent	There exist an infinite number of solutions (not including the trivial one).	There exist an infinite number of solutions (including the trivial one).
Equations inconsistent	No solution exists.	[Not possible.]

associated with a homogeneous system with a nonsingular matrix A. As a third possibility, we may have an infinite number of solutions. This eventuality is linked exclusively to a system in which the equations are dependent (i.e., in which there are redundant equations). Depending on whether the system is homogeneous, the trivial solution may or may not be included in the set of infinite number of solutions. Finally, in the case of an inconsistent equation system, there exists no solution at all. From the point of view of a model builder, the most useful and desirable outcome is, of course, that of a unique, nontrivial solution $x^* \neq 0$.

EXERCISE 5.5

1. Use Cramer's rule to solve the following equation systems:

(a) $3x_1 - 2x_2 = 6$
$2x_1 + x_2 = 11$

(b) $-x_1 + 3x_2 = -3$
$4x_1 - x_2 = 12$

(c) $8x_1 - 7x_2 = 9$
$x_1 + x_2 = 3$

(d) $5x_1 + 9x_2 = 14$
$7x_1 - 3x_2 = 4$

2. For each of the equation systems in Prob. 1, find the inverse of the coefficient matrix, and get the solution by the formula $x^* = A^{-1}d$.

3. Use Cramer's rule to solve the following equation systems:

(a) $8x_1 - x_2 = 16$
$2x_2 + 5x_3 = 5$
$2x_1 + 3x_3 = 7$

(b) $-x_1 + 3x_2 + 2x_3 = 24$
$x_1 + x_3 = 6$
$5x_2 - x_3 = 8$

(c) $4x + 3y - 2z = 1$
$x + 2y = 6$
$3x + z = 4$

(d) $-x + y + z = a$
$x - y + z = b$
$x + y - z = c$

4. Show that Cramer's rule can be derived alternatively by the following procedure. Multiply both sides of the first equation in the system $Ax = d$ by the cofactor $|C_{1j}|$, and then multiply both sides of the second equation by the cofactor $|C_{2j}|$, etc. Add all the newly obtained equations. Then assign the values $1, 2, \ldots, n$ to the index j, successively, to get the solution values $x_1^*, x_2^*, \ldots, x_n^*$ as shown in (5.17).

5.6   Application to Market and National-Income Models

Simple equilibrium models such as those discussed in Chap. 3 can be solved with ease by Cramer's rule or by matrix inversion.

Market Model

The two-commodity model described in (3.12) can be written (after eliminating the quantity variables) as a system of two linear equations, as in (3.13′):

$$c_1 P_1 + c_2 P_2 = -c_0$$
$$\gamma_1 P_1 + \gamma_2 P_2 = -\gamma_0$$

The three determinants needed—$|A|$, $|A_1|$, and $|A_2|$—have the following values:

$$|A| = \begin{vmatrix} c_1 & c_2 \\ \gamma_1 & \gamma_2 \end{vmatrix} = c_1\gamma_2 - c_2\gamma_1$$

$$|A_1| = \begin{vmatrix} -c_0 & c_2 \\ -\gamma_0 & \gamma_2 \end{vmatrix} = -c_0\gamma_2 + c_2\gamma_0$$

$$|A_2| = \begin{vmatrix} c_1 & -c_0 \\ \gamma_1 & -\gamma_0 \end{vmatrix} = -c_1\gamma_0 + c_0\gamma_1$$

Therefore the equilibrium prices must be

$$P_1^* = \frac{|A_1|}{|A|} = \frac{c_2\gamma_0 - c_0\gamma_2}{c_1\gamma_2 - c_2\gamma_1} \qquad P_2^* = \frac{|A_2|}{|A|} = \frac{c_0\gamma_1 - c_1\gamma_0}{c_1\gamma_2 - c_2\gamma_1}$$

which are precisely those obtained in (3.14) and (3.15). The equilibrium quantities can be found, as before, by setting $P_1 = P_1^*$ and $P_2 = P_2^*$ in the demand or supply functions.

National-Income Model

The simple national-income model cited in (3.23) can also be solved by the use of Cramer's rule. As written in (3.23), the model consists of the following two simultaneous equations:

$$Y = C + I_0 + G_0$$
$$C = a + bY \qquad (a > 0, \quad 0 < b < 1)$$

These can be rearranged into the form

$$Y - C = I_0 + G_0$$
$$-bY + C = a$$

so that the endogenous variables Y and C appear only on the left of the equals signs, whereas the exogenous variables and the unattached parameter appear only on the right. The coefficient matrix now takes the form $\begin{bmatrix} 1 & -1 \\ -b & 1 \end{bmatrix}$, and the column vector of constants (data), $\begin{bmatrix} I_0 + G_0 \\ a \end{bmatrix}$. Note that the sum $I_0 + G_0$ is considered as a single entity, i.e., a single element in the constant vector.

Cramer's rule now leads immediately to the following solution:

$$Y^* = \frac{\begin{vmatrix} (I_0 + G_0) & -1 \\ a & 1 \end{vmatrix}}{\begin{vmatrix} 1 & -1 \\ -b & 1 \end{vmatrix}} = \frac{I_0 + G_0 + a}{1 - b}$$

$$C^* = \frac{\begin{vmatrix} 1 & (I_0 + G_0) \\ -b & a \end{vmatrix}}{\begin{vmatrix} 1 & -1 \\ -b & 1 \end{vmatrix}} = \frac{a + b(I_0 + G_0)}{1 - b}$$

You should check that the solution values just obtained are identical with those shown in (3.24) and (3.25).

Let us now try to solve this model by inverting the coefficient matrix. Since the coefficient matrix is $A = \begin{bmatrix} 1 & -1 \\ -b & 1 \end{bmatrix}$, its cofactor matrix is $\begin{bmatrix} 1 & b \\ 1 & 1 \end{bmatrix}$, and we therefore have adj $A = \begin{bmatrix} 1 & 1 \\ b & 1 \end{bmatrix}$. It follows that the inverse matrix is

$$A^{-1} = \frac{1}{|A|} \text{adj} A = \frac{1}{1-b} \begin{bmatrix} 1 & 1 \\ b & 1 \end{bmatrix}$$

We know that, for the equation system $Ax = d$, the solution is expressible as $x^* = A^{-1}d$. Applied to the present model, this means that

$$\begin{bmatrix} Y^* \\ C^* \end{bmatrix} = \frac{1}{1-b} \begin{bmatrix} 1 & 1 \\ b & 1 \end{bmatrix} \begin{bmatrix} I_0 + G_0 \\ a \end{bmatrix} = \frac{1}{1-b} \begin{bmatrix} I_0 + G_0 + a \\ b(I_0 + G_0) + a \end{bmatrix}$$

It is easy to see that this is again the same solution as obtained before.

IS-LM Model: Closed Economy

As another linear model of the economy, we can think of the economy as being made up of two sectors: the real goods sector and the monetary sector.

The goods market involves the following equations:

$$Y = C + I + G$$
$$C = a + b(1 - t)Y$$
$$I = d - ei$$
$$G = G_0$$

The endogenous variables are Y, C, I, and i (where i is the rate of interest). The exogenous variable is G_0, while a, d, e, b, and t are structural parameters.

In the newly introduced money market, we have:

$$\text{Equilibrium condition: } M_d = M_s$$

$$\text{Money demand: } M_d = kY - li$$

$$\text{Money supply: } M_s = M_0$$

where M_0 is the exogenous stock of money and k and l are parameters. These three equations can be condensed into:

$$M_0 = kY - li$$

Together, the two sectors give us the following system of equations:

$$Y - C - I = G_0$$
$$b(1 - t)Y - C = -a$$
$$I + ei = d$$
$$kY - li = M_0$$

Note that by further substitution the system could be further reduced to a 2×2 system of equations. For now, we will leave it as a 4×4 system. In matrix form, we have

$$\begin{bmatrix} 1 & -1 & -1 & 0 \\ b(1-t) & -1 & 0 & 0 \\ 0 & 0 & 1 & e \\ k & 0 & 0 & -l \end{bmatrix} \begin{bmatrix} Y \\ C \\ I \\ i \end{bmatrix} = \begin{bmatrix} G_0 \\ -a \\ d \\ M_0 \end{bmatrix}$$

To find the determinant of the coefficient matrix, we can use Laplace expansion on one of the columns (preferably one with the most zeros). Expanding the fourth column, we find

$$|A| = (-e) \begin{vmatrix} 1 & -1 & -1 \\ b(1-t) & -1 & 0 \\ k & 0 & 0 \end{vmatrix} - l \begin{vmatrix} 1 & -1 & -1 \\ b(1-t) & -1 & 0 \\ 0 & 0 & 1 \end{vmatrix}$$

$$= (-e)(k) \begin{vmatrix} -1 & -1 \\ -1 & 0 \end{vmatrix} - l \begin{vmatrix} 1 & -1 \\ b(1-t) & -1 \end{vmatrix}$$

$$= ek - l[(-1) - (-1)b(1-t)]$$

$$= ek + l[1 - b(1-t)]$$

We can use Cramer's rule to find the equilibrium income Y^*. This is done by replacing the first column of the coefficient matrix A with the vector of exogenous variables and taking the ratio of the determinant of the new matrix to the original determinant, or

$$Y^* = \frac{|A_1|}{|A|} = \frac{\begin{vmatrix} G_0 & -1 & -1 & 0 \\ -a & -1 & 0 & 0 \\ d & 0 & 1 & e \\ M_0 & 0 & 0 & -l \end{vmatrix}}{ek + l[1 - b(1-t)]}$$

Using Laplace expansion on the second column of the numerator produces

$$Y^* = \frac{(-1)(-1)^3 \begin{vmatrix} -a & 0 & 0 \\ d & 1 & e \\ M_0 & 0 & -l \end{vmatrix}}{ek + l[1 - b(1-t)]} + \frac{(-1)(-1)^4 \begin{vmatrix} G_0 & -1 & 0 \\ d & 1 & e \\ M_0 & 0 & -l \end{vmatrix}}{ek + l[1 - b(1-t)]}$$

$$= \frac{\begin{vmatrix} -a & 0 & 0 \\ d & 1 & e \\ M_0 & 0 & -l \end{vmatrix} - \begin{vmatrix} G_0 & -1 & 0 \\ d & 1 & e \\ M_0 & 0 & -l \end{vmatrix}}{ek + l[1 - b(1-t)]}$$

By further expansion, we obtain

$$Y^* = \frac{(1) \begin{vmatrix} -a & 0 \\ M_0 & -l \end{vmatrix} - \left\{ (-1)(-1)^3 \begin{vmatrix} d & e \\ M_0 & -l \end{vmatrix} + (-1)^4 \begin{vmatrix} G_0 & 0 \\ M_0 & -l \end{vmatrix} \right\}}{ek + l[1 - b(1-t)]}$$

$$= \frac{al - [d(-l) - eM_0] - G_0(-l)}{ek + l[1 - b(1-t)]}$$

$$= \frac{l(a + d + G_0) + eM_0}{ek + l[1 - b(1-t)]}$$

Since the solution to Y^* is linear with respect to the exogenous variables, we can rewrite Y^* as

$$Y^* = \left(\frac{e}{ek + l[1 - b(1-t)]} \right) M_0 + \left(\frac{l}{ek + l[1 - b(1-t)]} \right) (a + d + G_0)$$

In this form, we can see that the Keynesian policy multipliers with respect to the money supply and government expenditure are the coefficients of M_0 and G_0, that is,

Money-supply multiplier: $\dfrac{e}{ek + l[1 - b(1 - t)]}$

and

Government-expenditure multiplier: $\dfrac{l}{ek + l[l - b(1 - t)]}$

Matrix Algebra versus Elimination of Variables

The economic models used for illustration above involve two or four equations only, and thus only fourth or lower-order determinants need to be evaluated. For large equation systems, higher-order determinants will appear, and their evaluation will be more complicated. And so will be the inversion of large matrices. From the computational point of view, in fact, matrix inversion and Cramer's rule are not necessarily more efficient than the method of successive eliminations of variables.

However, matrix methods have other merits. As we have seen from the preceding pages, matrix algebra gives us a compact notation for any linear-equation system, and also furnishes a determinantal criterion for testing the existence of a unique solution. These are advantages not otherwise available. In addition, it should be noted that, unlike the elimination-of-variable method, which affords no means of analytically expressing the solution, the matrix-inversion method and Cramer's rule do provide the handy solution expressions $x^* = A^{-1}d$ and $x_j^* = |A_j|/|A|$. Such analytical expressions of the solution are useful not only because they are in themselves a summary statement of the actual solution procedure, but also because they make possible the performance of further mathematical operations on the solution as written, if called for.

Under certain circumstances, matrix methods can even claim a computational advantage, such as when the task is to solve at the same time several equation systems having an identical coefficient matrix A but different constant-term vectors. In such cases, the elimination-of-variable method would require that the computational procedure be repeated each time a new equation system is considered. With the matrix-inversion method, however, we are required to find the common inverse matrix A^{-1} *only once;* then the same inverse can be used to premultiply all the constant-term vectors pertaining to the various equation systems involved, in order to obtain their respective solutions. This particular computational advantage will take on great practical significance when we consider the solution of the Leontief input-output models in Sec. 5.7.

EXERCISE 5.6

1. Solve the national-income model in Exercise 3.5-1:
   (*a*) By matrix inversion   (*b*) By Cramer's rule
   (List the variables in the order *Y, C, T.*)
2. Solve the national-income model in Exercise 3.5-2:
   (*a*) By matrix inversion   (*b*) By Cramer's rule
   (List the variables in the order *Y, C, G.*)

3. Let the IS equation be

$$Y = \frac{A}{1-b} - \frac{g}{1-b}i$$

where $1-b$ is the marginal propensity to save, g is the investment sensitivity to interest rates, and A is an aggregate of exogenous variables. Let the LM equation be

$$Y = \frac{M_0}{k} + \frac{l}{k}i$$

where k and l are income and interest sensitivity of money demand, respectively, and M_0 is real money balances.

If $b = 0.7$, $g = 100$, $A = 252$, $k = 0.25$, $l = 200$, and $M_0 = 176$, then

(a) Write the IS-LM system in matrix form.

(b) Solve for Y and i by matrix inversion.

5.7 Leontief Input-Output Models

In its "static" version, the input-output analysis of Professor Wassily Leontief, a Nobel Prize winner,[†] deals with this particular question: "What level of output should each of the n industries in an economy produce, in order that it will just be sufficient to satisfy the total demand for that product?"

The rationale for the term *input-output analysis* is quite plain to see. The output of any industry (say, the steel industry) is needed as an input in many other industries, or even for that industry itself; therefore the "correct" (i.e., shortage-free as well as surplus-free) level of steel output will depend on the input requirements of all the n industries. In turn, the output of many other industries will enter into the steel industry as inputs, and consequently the "correct" levels of the other products will in turn depend partly upon the input requirements of the steel industry. In view of this interindustry dependence, any set of "correct" output levels for the n industries must be one that is consistent with all the input requirements in the economy, so that no bottlenecks will arise anywhere. In this light, it is clear that input-output analysis should be of great use in production planning, such as in planning for the economic development of a country or for a program of national defense.

Strictly speaking, input-output analysis is not a form of the general equilibrium analysis as discussed in Chap. 3. Although the interdependence of the various industries is emphasized, the "correct" output levels envisaged are those which satisfy technical input-output relationships rather than market equilibrium conditions. Nevertheless, the problem posed in input-output analysis also boils down to one of solving a system of simultaneous equations, and matrix algebra can again be of service.

Structure of an Input-Output Model

Since an input-output model normally encompasses a large number of industries, its framework is of necessity rather involved. To simplify the problem, the following assumptions are as a rule adopted: (1) each industry produces only one homogeneous commodity (broadly interpreted, this does permit the case of two or more jointly produced commodities,

[†] Wassily W. Leontief, *The Structure of American Economy 1919–1939*, 2d ed., Oxford University Press, Fair Lawn, N.J., 1951.

TABLE 5.2
Input-
Coefficient
Matrix

Input	Output				
	I	**II**	**III**	$\cdots$	**N**
I	a_{11}	a_{12}	a_{13}	$\cdots$	a_{1n}
II	a_{21}	a_{22}	a_{23}	$\cdots$	a_{2n}
III	a_{31}	a_{32}	a_{33}	$\cdots$	a_{3n}
$\vdots$	$\vdots$	$\vdots$	$\vdots$		$\vdots$
N	a_{n1}	a_{n2}	a_{n3}	$\cdots$	a_{nn}

provided they are produced in a fixed proportion to one another); (2) each industry uses a fixed input ratio (or factor combination) for the production of its output; and (3) production in every industry is subject to constant returns to scale, so that a k-fold change in every input will result in an exactly k-fold change in the output. These assumptions are, of course, unrealistic. A saving grace is that, if an industry produces two different commodities or uses two different possible factor combinations, then that industry may—at least conceptually—be broken down into two separate industries.

From these assumptions we see that, in order to produce each unit of the jth commodity, the input need for the ith commodity must be a fixed amount, which we shall denote by a_{ij}. Specifically, the production of each unit of the jth commodity will require a_{1j} (amount) of the first commodity, a_{2j} of the second commodity, . . . , and a_{nj} of the nth commodity. (The order of the subscripts in a_{ij} is easy to remember: The first subscript refers to the input, and the second to the output, so that a_{ij} indicates how much of the ith commodity is used for the production of each unit of the jth commodity.) For our purposes, we may assume prices to be given and, thus, adopt "a dollar's worth" of each commodity as its unit. Then the statement $a_{32} = 0.35$ will mean that 35 cents' worth of the third commodity is required as an input for producing a dollar's worth of the second commodity. The a_{ij} symbol will be referred to as an *input coefficient.*

For an n-industry economy, the input coefficients can be arranged into a matrix $A = [a_{ij}]$, as in Table 5.2, in which each *column* specifies the input requirements for the production of one unit of the output of a particular industry. The second column, for example, states that to produce a unit (a dollar's worth) of commodity II, the inputs needed are: a_{12} units of commodity I, a_{22} units of commodity II, etc. If no industry uses its own product as an input, then the elements in the principal diagonal of matrix A will all be zero.

The Open Model

If the n industries in Table 5.2 constitute the entirety of the economy, then all their products would be for the sole purpose of meeting the *input demand* of the same n industries (to be used in further production) as against the *final demand* (such as consumer demand, not for further production). At the same time, all the inputs used in the economy would be in the nature of *intermediate inputs* (those supplied by the n industries) as against *primary inputs* (such as labor, not an industrial product). To allow for the presence of final demand and primary inputs, we must include in the model an *open sector* outside of the n-industry network. Such an open sector can accommodate the activities of the consumer households, the government sector, and even foreign countries.

In view of the presence of the open sector, the sum of the elements in each column of the input-coefficient matrix A (or *input matrix A*, for short) must be less than 1. Each column sum represents the *partial* input cost (not including the cost of primary inputs) incurred in producing a dollar's worth of some commodity; if this sum is greater than or equal to $1, therefore, production will not be economically justifiable. Symbolically, this fact may be stated thus:

$$\sum_{i=1}^{n} a_{ij} < 1 \qquad (j = 1, 2, \ldots, n)$$

where the summation is over i, that is, over the elements appearing in the various *rows* of a specific column j. Carrying this line of thought a step further, it may also be stated that, since the value of output ($1) must be fully absorbed by the payments to all factors of production, the amount by which the column sum falls short of $1 must represent the payment to the primary inputs of the open sector. Thus the value of the primary inputs needed in producing a unit of the jth commodity should be $1 - \sum_{i=1}^{n} a_{ij}$.

If industry I is to produce an output just sufficient to meet the input requirements of the n industries as well as the final demand of the open sector, its output level x_1 must satisfy the following equation:

$$x_1 = a_{11}x_1 + a_{12}x_2 + \cdots + a_{1n}x_n + d_1$$

where d_1 denotes the final demand for its output and $a_{1j}x_j$ represents the input demand from the jth industry.[†] By the same token, the output levels of the other industries should satisfy the equations

$$x_2 = a_{21}x_1 + a_{22}x_2 + \cdots + a_{2n}x_n + d_2$$
$$\cdots\cdots\cdots\cdots\cdots\cdots\cdots\cdots\cdots\cdots$$
$$x_n = a_{n1}x_1 + a_{n2}x_2 + \cdots + a_{nn}x_n + d_n$$

After moving all terms that involve the variables x_j to the left of the equals signs, and leaving only the exogenously determined final demands d_j on the right, we can express the "correct" output levels of the n industries by the following system of n linear equations:

$$\begin{aligned}
(1 - a_{11})x_1 - \quad & a_{12}x_2 - \cdots - & a_{1n}x_n &= d_1 \\
-a_{21}x_1 + (1 - a_{22})x_2 - & \cdots - & a_{2n}x_n &= d_2 \\
\cdots\cdots\cdots\cdots & \cdots\cdots\cdots\cdots & & \\
-a_{n1}x_1 - \quad & a_{n2}x_2 - \cdots + (1 - a_{nn})x_n &= d_n
\end{aligned} \qquad \textbf{(5.20)}$$

In matrix notation, this may be written as

$$\begin{bmatrix} (1 - a_{11}) & -a_{12} & \cdots & -a_{1n} \\ -a_{21} & (1 - a_{22}) & \cdots & -a_{2n} \\ \vdots & \vdots & & \vdots \\ -a_{n1} & -a_{n2} & \cdots & (1 - a_{nn}) \end{bmatrix} \begin{bmatrix} x_1 \\ x_2 \\ \vdots \\ x_n \end{bmatrix} = \begin{bmatrix} d_1 \\ d_2 \\ \vdots \\ d_n \end{bmatrix} \qquad \textbf{(5.20')}$$

If the 1s in the principal diagonal of the matrix on the left are ignored, the matrix is simply $-A = [-a_{ij}]$. As it is, on the other hand, the matrix is the *sum* of the identity matrix

[†] Do not ever add up the input coefficients across a row; such a sum—say, $a_{11} + a_{12} + \cdots + a_{1n}$—is devoid of any useful economic meaning. The sum of the products $a_{11}x_1 + a_{12}x_2 + \cdots + a_{1n}x_n$, on the other hand, does have an economic meaning; it represents the total amount of x_1 needed as input for all the n industries.

I_n (with 1s in its principal diagonal and with 0s everywhere else) and the matrix $-A$. Thus (5.20′) can also be written as

$$(I - A)x = d \qquad \textbf{(5.20″)}$$

where x and d are, respectively, the variable vector and the final-demand (constant-term) vector. The matrix $I - A$ is called the *Leontief matrix*. As long as $I - A$ is nonsingular, we shall be able to find its inverse $(I - A)^{-1}$, and obtain the unique solution of the system from the equation

$$x^* = (I - A)^{-1}d \qquad \textbf{(5.21)}$$

A Numerical Example

For purposes of illustration, suppose that there are only three industries in the economy and one primary input, and that the input-coefficient matrix is as follows (let us use decimal values this time):

$$A = \begin{bmatrix} a_{11} & a_{12} & a_{13} \\ a_{21} & a_{22} & a_{23} \\ a_{31} & a_{32} & a_{33} \end{bmatrix} = \begin{bmatrix} 0.2 & 0.3 & 0.2 \\ 0.4 & 0.1 & 0.2 \\ 0.1 & 0.3 & 0.2 \end{bmatrix} \qquad \textbf{(5.22)}$$

Note that each column sum in A is less than 1, as it should be. Further, if we denote by a_{0j} the dollar amount of the primary input used in producing a dollar's worth of the jth commodity, we can write [by subtracting each column sum in (5.22) from 1]:

$$a_{01} = 0.3 \qquad a_{02} = 0.3 \quad \text{and} \quad a_{03} = 0.4 \qquad \textbf{(5.23)}$$

With the matrix A of (5.22), the open input-output system can be expressed in the form $(I - A)x = d$ as follows:

$$\begin{bmatrix} 0.8 & -0.3 & -0.2 \\ -0.4 & 0.9 & -0.2 \\ -0.1 & -0.3 & 0.8 \end{bmatrix} \begin{bmatrix} x_1 \\ x_2 \\ x_3 \end{bmatrix} = \begin{bmatrix} d_1 \\ d_2 \\ d_3 \end{bmatrix} \qquad \textbf{(5.24)}$$

Here we have deliberately not given specific values to the final demands d_1, d_2, and d_3. In this way, by keeping the vector d in parametric form, our solution will appear as a "formula" into which we can feed various specific d vectors to obtain various corresponding specific solutions.

By inverting the 3×3 Leontief matrix, the solution of (5.24) can be found, approximately (because of rounding of decimal figures), to be

$$\begin{bmatrix} x_1^* \\ x_2^* \\ x_3^* \end{bmatrix} = (I - A)^{-1}d = \frac{1}{0.384} \begin{bmatrix} 0.66 & 0.30 & 0.24 \\ 0.34 & 0.62 & 0.24 \\ 0.21 & 0.27 & 0.60 \end{bmatrix} \begin{bmatrix} d_1 \\ d_2 \\ d_3 \end{bmatrix}$$

If the specific final-demand vector (say, the final-output target of a development program) happens to be $d = \begin{bmatrix} 10 \\ 5 \\ 6 \end{bmatrix}$, in billions of dollars, then the following specific solution values will emerge (again in billions of dollars):

$$x_1^* = \frac{1}{0.384}[0.66(10) + 0.30(5) + 0.24(6)] = \frac{9.54}{0.384} = 24.84$$

and similarly,

$$x_2^* = \frac{7.94}{0.384} = 20.68 \quad \text{and} \quad x_3^* = \frac{7.05}{0.384} = 18.36$$

An important question now arises. The production of the output mix x_1^*, x_2^*, and x_3^* must entail a definite required amount of the primary input. Would the amount *required* be consistent with what is *available* in the economy? On the basis of (5.23), the required primary input may be calculated as follows:

$$\sum_{j=1}^{3} a_{0j} x_j^* = 0.3(24.84) + 0.3(20.68) + 0.4(18.36) = \$21.00 \text{ billion}$$

Therefore, the specific final demand $d = \begin{bmatrix} 10 \\ 5 \\ 6 \end{bmatrix}$ will be feasible if and only if the available amount of the primary input is at least $21 billion. If the amount available falls short, then that particular production target will, of course, have to be revised downward accordingly.

One notable feature of the previous analysis is that, as long as the input coefficients remain the same, the inverse $(I - A)^{-1}$ will not change; therefore only *one* matrix inversion needs to be performed, even if we are to consider a hundred or a thousand different final-demand vectors—such as a spectrum of alternative development targets. This economizes the computational effort as compared with the elimination-of-variable method. However, this advantage is not shared by Cramer's rule as outlined in (5.18), because each time a different final-demand vector d is used, we must calculate a new determinant as the numerator in (5.18), which is not as simple as multiplying a known inverse matrix $(I - A)^{-1}$ by a new vector d.

The Existence of Nonnegative Solutions

In the previous numerical example, the Leontief matrix $I - A$ happens to be nonsingular, so solution values of output variables x_j do exist. Moreover, the solution values x_j^* all turn out to be nonnegative, as economic sense would dictate. Such desired results, however, cannot be expected to emerge automatically; they come about only when the Leontief matrix possesses certain properties. These properties are described in the so-called *Hawkins-Simon condition.*[†]

To explain this condition, we need to introduce the mathematical concept of *principal minors* of a matrix, because the algebraic signs of principal minors will provide important clues in guiding our analytical conclusions. We already know that, given a square matrix, say, B, with determinant $|B|$, a minor is a subdeterminant obtained by deleting the *i*th row and *j*th column of $|B|$, where i and j are not necessarily equal. If we now impose the restriction that $i = j$, then the resulting minor is known as a *principal* minor. For example, given a 3×3 matrix B, we can write its determinant generally as

$$|B| = \begin{vmatrix} b_{11} & b_{12} & b_{13} \\ b_{21} & b_{22} & b_{23} \\ b_{31} & b_{32} & b_{33} \end{vmatrix} \qquad \textbf{(5.25)}$$

[†] David Hawkins and Herbert A. Simon, "Note: Some Conditions of Macroeconomic Stability," *Econometrica*, July–October, 1949, pp. 245–48.

The simultaneous deletion of the ith row and the ith column ($i = 3, 2, 1$, successively) results in the following three 2×2 principal minors:

$$\begin{vmatrix} b_{11} & b_{12} \\ b_{21} & b_{22} \end{vmatrix} \qquad \begin{vmatrix} b_{11} & b_{13} \\ b_{31} & b_{33} \end{vmatrix} \qquad \begin{vmatrix} b_{22} & b_{23} \\ b_{32} & b_{33} \end{vmatrix} \qquad \textbf{(5.26)}$$

In view of their 2×2 dimensions, these are referred to as *second-order principal minors.* We can also generate *first-order principal minors* (1×1) by deleting any two rows and the same-numbered columns from $|B|$. They are

$$|b_{11}| = b_{11} \qquad |b_{22}| = b_{22} \qquad |b_{33}| = b_{33} \qquad \textbf{(5.27)}$$

Finally, to complete the picture, we can consider $|B|$ itself as the *third-order principal minor* of $|B|$. Note that in all the minors listed in (5.25) through (5.27), their principal-diagonal elements consist exclusively of the principal-diagonal elements of B. Herein lies the rationale for the name "principal minors."[†]

While certain economic applications require checking the algebraic signs of *all* the principal minors of a matrix B, quite often our conclusion depends only on the sign pattern of a particular subset of the principal minors referred to variously as the *leading principal minors, naturally ordered principal minors,* or *successive principal minors.* In the 3×3 case, this subset consists only of the first members of (5.25) through (5.27):

$$|B_1| \equiv |b_{11}| \qquad |B_2| \equiv \begin{vmatrix} b_{11} & b_{12} \\ b_{21} & b_{22} \end{vmatrix} \qquad |B_3| \equiv \begin{vmatrix} b_{11} & b_{12} & b_{13} \\ b_{21} & b_{22} & b_{23} \\ b_{31} & b_{32} & b_{33} \end{vmatrix} \qquad \textbf{(5.28)}$$

Here, the single subscript m in the symbol $|B_m|$, unlike in the subscript usage in the context of Cramer's rule, is employed to indicate that the leading principal minor is of dimension $m \times m$. An easy way to derive the leading principal minors is to section off the determinant $|B|$ with the successive broken lines as shown:

$$\begin{vmatrix} b_{11} & b_{12} & b_{13} \\ b_{21} & b_{22} & b_{23} \\ b_{31} & b_{32} & b_{33} \end{vmatrix} \qquad \textbf{(5.29)}$$

Taking the top element in the principal diagonal of $|B|$ by itself alone gives us $|B_1|$; taking the first two elements in the principal diagonal, b_{11} and b_{22}, along with their accompanying off-diagonal elements yields $|B_2|$; and so forth.

[†] An alternative definition of principal minors would allow for the various permutations of the subscript indices i, j, and k. This would mean, in the input-output context, the renumbering of the industries (e.g., the first industry becomes the second industry, and vice versa, so that the subscript 11 becomes 22, and the subscript 22 becomes 11, and so on). As a result, in addition to the 2×2 principal minors in (5.26), we would also have

$$\begin{vmatrix} b_{22} & b_{21} \\ b_{12} & b_{11} \end{vmatrix} \qquad \begin{vmatrix} b_{33} & b_{31} \\ b_{13} & b_{11} \end{vmatrix} \qquad \text{and} \qquad \begin{vmatrix} b_{33} & b_{32} \\ b_{23} & b_{22} \end{vmatrix}$$

But these last three, in the order given, exactly match the three listed in (5.26) in value and algebraic sign; thus they can be omitted from consideration for our purposes. Similarly, even though the permutation of subscript indices can generate additional 3×3 principal minors, they merely duplicate the one in (5.25) in value and sign, and thus can also be disregarded.

Given a higher-dimension determinant, say, $n \times n$, there will of course be a larger number of principal minors, but the pattern of their construction is the same. A *k*th-order principal minor is always obtained by deleting any $n - k$ rows and the same-numbered columns from $|B|$. And its leading principal minors $|B_m|$ (with $m = 1, 2, \ldots, n$) are always formed by taking the first m principal-diagonal elements in $|B|$ along with their accompanying off-diagonal elements.

With this background, we are ready to state the following important theorem due to Hawkins and Simon:

> Given (*a*) an $n \times n$ matrix B, with $b_{ij} \le 0$ ($i \ne j$) (i.e., with all off-diagonal elements nonpositive), and (*b*) an $n \times 1$ vector $d \ge 0$ (all elements nonnegative), there exists an $n \times 1$ vector $x^* \ge 0$ such that $Bx^* = d$, if and only if
>
> $$|B_m| > 0 \qquad (m = 1, 2, \ldots, n)$$
>
> i.e., if and only if the leading principal minors of B are all positive.

The relevance of this theorem to input-output analysis becomes clear when we let B represent the Leontief matrix $I - A$ (where $b_{ij} = -a_{ij}$ for $i \ne j$ are indeed all nonpositive), and d, the final-demand vector (where all the elements are indeed nonnegative). Then $Bx^* = d$ is equivalent to $(I - A)x^* = d$, and the existence of $x^* \ge 0$ guarantees nonnegative solution output levels. The necessary-and-sufficient condition for this, known as the *Hawkins-Simon condition*, is that all the principal minors of the Leontief matrix $I - A$ be positive.

The proof of this theorem is too lengthy to be presented here,[†] but it should be worthwhile to explore its economic meaning, which is relatively easy to see in the simple two-industry case ($n = 2$).

Economic Meaning of the Hawkins-Simon Condition

For the two-industry case, the Leontief matrix is

$$I - A = \begin{bmatrix} 1 - a_{11} & -a_{12} \\ -a_{21} & 1 - a_{22} \end{bmatrix}$$

The first part of the Hawkins-Simon condition, $|B_1| > 0$, requires that

$$1 - a_{11} > 0 \qquad \text{or} \qquad a_{11} < 1$$

Economically, this requires the amount of the first commodity used in the production of a dollar's worth of the first commodity to be less than one dollar. The other part of the condition, $|B_2| > 0$, requires that

$$(1 - a_{11})(1 - a_{22}) - a_{12}a_{21} > 0$$

[†] A thorough discussion can be found in Akira Takayama, *Mathematical Economics,* 2d ed., Cambridge University Press, 1985, pp. 380–385.

Some writers use an alternative version of the Hawkins-Simon condition, which requires *all* the principal minors of B (not only the leading ones) to be positive. As Takayama shows, however, in the present case, with the special restriction on $|B|$, it happens that requiring the positivity of the leading principal minors (a less stringent condition) can achieve the same result. Nevertheless, it should be emphasized that, as a general rule, the fact that the leading principal minors satisfy a particular sign requirement does not guarantee that all the principal minors automatically satisfy that requirement, too. Hence, a condition stated in terms of *all* the principal minors must be checked against *all* the principal minors, not only the leading ones.

or, equivalently,

$$a_{11} + a_{12}a_{21} + (1 - a_{11})\, a_{22} < 1$$

Further, since $(1 - a_{11})\, a_{22}$ is positive, the previous inequality implies that

$$a_{11} + a_{12}a_{21} < 1$$

Economically, a_{11} measures the *direct* use of the first commodity as input in the production of the first commodity itself, and $a_{12}a_{21}$ measures the *indirect* use—it gives the amount of the first commodity needed in producing the specific quantity of the second commodity that goes into the production of a dollar's worth of the first commodity. Thus the last inequality mandates that the amount of the first commodity used as direct and indirect inputs in producing a dollar's worth of the commodity itself, must be less than one dollar. Thus, what the Hawkins-Simon condition does is to specify certain practicability and viability restrictions for the production process. If and only if the production process is economically practicable and viable, can it yield meaningful, nonnegative solution output levels.

The Closed Model

If the exogenous sector of the open input-output model is absorbed into the system as just another *industry,* the model will become a *closed model.* In such a model, final demand and primary input do not appear; in their place will be the input requirements and the output of the newly conceived industry. All goods will now be *intermediate* in nature, because everything that is produced is produced only for the sake of satisfying the input requirements of the $(n + 1)$ industries in the model.

At first glance, the conversion of the open sector into an additional industry would not seem to create any significant change in the analysis. Actually, however, since the new industry is assumed to have a fixed input ratio as does any other industry, the supply of what used to be the primary input must now bear a fixed proportion to what used to be called the *final demand.* More concretely, this may mean, for example, that households will consume each commodity in a fixed proportion to the labor service they supply. This certainly constitutes a significant change in the analytical framework involved.

Mathematically, the disappearance of the final demands means that we will now have a homogeneous-equation system. Assuming four industries only (including the new one, designated by the subscript 0), the "correct" output levels will, by analogy to (5.20'), be those which satisfy the equation system:

$$\begin{bmatrix} (1 - a_{00}) & -a_{01} & -a_{02} & -a_{03} \\ -a_{10} & (1 - a_{11}) & -a_{12} & -a_{13} \\ -a_{20} & -a_{21} & (1 - a_{22}) & -a_{23} \\ -a_{30} & -a_{31} & -a_{32} & (1 - a_{33}) \end{bmatrix} \begin{bmatrix} x_0 \\ x_1 \\ x_2 \\ x_3 \end{bmatrix} = \begin{bmatrix} 0 \\ 0 \\ 0 \\ 0 \end{bmatrix}$$

Because this equation system is homogeneous, it can have a nontrivial solution if and only if the 4×4 Leontief matrix $I - A$ has a vanishing determinant. The latter condition is indeed always satisfied: In a closed model, no primary input exists; hence each column sum in the input-coefficient matrix A must now be exactly equal to (rather than less than) 1; that is, $a_{0j} + a_{1j} + a_{2j} + a_{3j} = 1$, or

$$a_{0j} = 1 - a_{1j} - a_{2j} - a_{3j}$$

But this implies that, in every column of the matrix $I - A$, given previously, the top element is always equal to the negative of the sum of the other three elements. Consequently, the four rows are linearly dependent, and we must find $|I - A| = 0$. This guarantees that the system does possess nontrivial solutions; in fact, as indicated in Table 5.1, it has an infinite number of them. This means that in a closed model, with a homogeneous-equation system, no unique "correct" output mix exists. We can determine the output levels $x_1^*, \ldots, x_4^*$ in proportion to one another, but cannot fix their absolute levels unless additional restrictions are imposed on the model.

EXERCISE 5.7

1. On the basis of the model in (5.24), if the final demands are $d_1 = 30$, $d_2 = 15$, and $d_3 = 10$ (all in billions of dollars), what are the solution output levels for the three industries? (Round off answers to two decimal places.)

2. Using the information in (5.23), calculate the total amount of primary input required to produce the solution output levels of Prob. 1.

3. In a two-industry economy, it is known that industry I uses 10 cents of its own product and 60 cents of commodity II to produce a dollar's worth of commodity I; industry II uses none of its own product but uses 50 cents of commodity I in producing a dollar's worth of commodity II; and the open sector demands $1,000 billion of commodity I and $2,000 billion of commodity II.

   (a) Write out the input matrix, the Leontief matrix, and the specific input-output matrix equation for this economy.

   (b) Check whether the data in this problem satisfy the Hawkins-Simon condition.

   (c) Find the solution output levels by Cramer's rule.

4. Given the input matrix and the final-demand vector

$$A = \begin{bmatrix} 0.05 & 0.25 & 0.34 \\ 0.33 & 0.10 & 0.12 \\ 0.19 & 0.38 & 0 \end{bmatrix} \qquad d = \begin{bmatrix} 1800 \\ 200 \\ 900 \end{bmatrix}$$

   (a) Explain the economic meaning of the elements 0.33, 0, and 200.

   (b) Explain the economic meaning (if any) of the third-column sum.

   (c) Explain the economic meaning (if any) of the third-row sum.

   (d) Write out the specific input-output matrix equation for this model.

   (e) Check whether the data given in this problem satisfy the Hawkins-Simon condition.

5. (a) Given a 4×4 matrix $B = [b_{ij}]$, write out all the principal minors.

   (b) Write out all the leading principal minors.

6. Show that, by itself (without other restrictions on matrix B), the Hawkins-Simon condition already guarantees the existence of a unique solution vector x^*, though not necessarily nonnegative.

5.8 Limitations of Static Analysis

In the discussion of static equilibrium in the market or in the national income, our primary concern has been to find the equilibrium values of the endogenous variables in the model. A fundamental point that was ignored in such an analysis is the actual process of adjustments and readjustments of the variables ultimately leading to the equilibrium state (if it is at all attainable). We asked only about where we shall arrive but did not question when or what may happen along the way.

The static type of analysis fails, therefore, to take into account two problems of importance. One is that, since the adjustment process may take a long time to complete, an equilibrium state as determined within a particular frame of static analysis may have lost its relevance before it is even attained, if the exogenous forces in the model have undergone some changes in the meantime. This is the problem of shifts of the equilibrium state. The second is that, even if the adjustment process is allowed to run its course undisturbed, the equilibrium state envisaged in a static analysis may be altogether unattainable. This would be the case of a so-called unstable equilibrium, which is characterized by the fact that the adjustment process will drive the variables further away from, rather than progressively closer to, that equilibrium state. To disregard the adjustment process, therefore, is to assume away the problem of attainability of equilibrium.

The shifts of the equilibrium state (in response to exogenous changes) pertain to a type of analysis called *comparative statics,* and the question of attainability and stability of equilibrium falls within the realm of *dynamic analysis.* Each of these clearly serves to fill a significant gap in the static analysis, and it is thus imperative to inquire into those areas of analysis also. We shall leave the study of dynamic analysis to Part 5 of the book and shall next turn our attention to the problem of comparative statics.

Comparative-Static Analysis

Part 3

Chapter 6

Comparative Statics and the Concept of Derivative

This chapter and Chaps. 7 and 8 will be devoted to the methods of comparative-static analysis.

6.1 The Nature of Comparative Statics

Comparative statics, as the name suggests, is concerned with the comparison of different equilibrium states that are associated with different sets of values of parameters and exogenous variables. For purposes of such a comparison, we always start by assuming a given initial equilibrium state. In the isolated-market model, for example, such an initial equilibrium will be represented by a determinate price P^* and a corresponding quantity Q^*. Similarly, in the simple national-income model of (3.23), the initial equilibrium will be specified by a determinate Y^* and a corresponding C^*. Now if we let a disequilibrating change occur in the model—in the form of a change in the value of some parameter or exogenous variable—the initial equilibrium will, of course, be upset. As a result, the various endogenous variables must undergo certain adjustments. If it is assumed that a new equilibrium state relevant to the new values of the data can be defined and attained, the question posed in the comparative-static analysis is: How would the new equilibrium compare with the old?

It should be noted that in comparative statics we still disregard the process of adjustment of the variables; we merely compare the initial (*pre*change) equilibrium state with the final (*post*change) equilibrium state. Also, we still preclude the possibility of instability of equilibrium, for we assume the new equilibrium to be attainable, just as we do for the old.

A comparative-static analysis can be either qualitative or quantitative in nature. If we are interested only in the question of, say, whether an increase in investment I_0 will increase or decrease the equilibrium income Y^*, the analysis will be qualitative because the *direction* of change is the only matter considered. But if we are concerned with the *magnitude* of the change in Y^* resulting from a given change in I_0 (that is, the size of the investment multiplier), the analysis will obviously be quantitative. By obtaining a quantitative answer, however, we can automatically tell the direction of change from its algebraic sign. Hence the quantitative analysis always embraces the qualitative.

It should be clear that the problem under consideration is essentially one of finding a *rate of change:* the rate of change of the equilibrium value of an endogenous variable with respect to the change in a particular parameter or exogenous variable. For this reason, the mathematical concept of *derivative* takes on preponderant significance in comparative statics, because that concept—the most fundamental one in the branch of mathematics known as *differential calculus*—is directly concerned with the notion of rate of change! Later on, moreover, we shall find the concept of derivative to be of extreme importance for optimization problems as well.

6.2   Rate of Change and the Derivative

Even though our present context is concerned only with the rates of change of the equilibrium values of the variables in a model, we may carry on the discussion in a more general manner by considering the rate of change of any variable y in response to a change in another variable x, where the two variables are related to each other by the function

$$y = f(x)$$

Applied to the comparative-static context, the variable y will represent the equilibrium value of an endogenous variable, and x will be some parameter. Note that, for a start, we are restricting ourselves to the simple case where there is only a single parameter or exogenous variable in the model. Once we have mastered this simplified case, however, the extension to the case of more parameters will prove relatively easy.

The Difference Quotient

Since the notion of "change" figures prominently in the present context, a special symbol is needed to represent it. When the variable x changes from the value x_0 to a new value x_1, the change is measured by the difference $x_1 - x_0$. Hence, using the symbol Δ (the Greek capital delta, for "difference") to denote the change, we write $\Delta x = x_1 - x_0$. Also needed is a way of denoting the value of the function $f(x)$ at various values of x. The standard practice is to use the notation $f(x_i)$ to represent the value of $f(x)$ when $x = x_i$. Thus, for the function $f(x) = 5 + x^2$, we have $f(0) = 5 + 0^2 = 5$; and similarly, $f(2) = 5 + 2^2 = 9$, etc.

When x changes from an initial value x_0 to a new value $(x_0 + \Delta x)$, the value of the function $y = f(x)$ changes from $f(x_0)$ to $f(x_0 + \Delta x)$. The change in y per unit of change in x can be represented by the *difference quotient*.

$$\frac{\Delta y}{\Delta x} = \frac{f(x_0 + \Delta x) - f(x_0)}{\Delta x} \tag{6.1}$$

This quotient, which measures the average rate of change of y, can be calculated if we know the initial value of x, or x_0, and the magnitude of change in x, or Δx. That is, $\Delta y/\Delta x$ is a function of x_0 and Δx.

Example 1   Given $y = f(x) = 3x^2 - 4$, we can write

$$f(x_0) = 3(x_0)^2 - 4 \qquad f(x_0 + \Delta x) = 3(x_0 + \Delta x)^2 - 4$$

Therefore, the difference quotient is

$$\frac{\Delta y}{\Delta x} = \frac{3(x_0 + \Delta x)^2 - 4 - \left(3x_0^2 - 4\right)}{\Delta x} = \frac{6x_0 \, \Delta x + 3(\Delta x)^2}{\Delta x}$$

$$= 6x_0 + 3 \, \Delta x \tag{6.2}$$

which can be evaluated if we are given x_0 and Δx. Let $x_0 = 3$ and $\Delta x = 4$; then the average rate of change of y is $6(3) + 3(4) = 30$. This means that, on the average, as x changes from 3 to 7, the change in y is 30 units per unit change in x.

The Derivative

Frequently, we are interested in the rate of change of y when Δx is very small. In such a case, it is possible to obtain an approximation of $\Delta y/\Delta x$ by dropping all the terms in the difference quotient involving the expression Δx. In (6.2), for instance, if Δx is very small, we may simply take the term $6x_0$ on the right as an approximation of $\Delta y/\Delta x$. The smaller the value of Δx, of course, the closer is the approximation to the true value of $\Delta y/\Delta x$.

As Δx approaches zero (meaning that it gets closer and closer to, but never actually reaches, zero), $(6x_0 + 3 \, \Delta x)$ will approach the value $6x_0$, and by the same token, $\Delta y/\Delta x$ will approach $6x_0$ also. Symbolically, this fact is expressed either by the statement $\Delta y/\Delta x \to 6x_0$ as $\Delta x \to 0$, or by the equation

$$\lim_{\Delta x \to 0} \frac{\Delta y}{\Delta x} = \lim_{\Delta x \to 0} (6x_0 + 3\Delta x) = 6x_0 \tag{6.3}$$

where the symbol $\lim_{\Delta x \to 0}$ is read as "The limit of ... as Δx approaches 0." If, as $\Delta x \to 0$, the limit of the difference quotient $\Delta y/\Delta x$ indeed exists, that limit is called the derivative of the function $y = f(x)$.

Several points should be noted about the derivative if it exists. First, a derivative is a *function;* in fact, in this usage the word *derivative* really means a derived function. The original function $y = f(x)$ is a *primitive function,* and the derivative is another function derived from it. Whereas the difference quotient is a function of x_0 and Δx, you should observe—from (6.3), for instance—that the derivative is a function of x_0 only. This is because Δx is already compelled to approach zero, and therefore it should not be regarded as another variable in the function. Let us also add that so far we have used the subscripted symbol x_0 only in order to stress the fact that a change in x must start from some specific value of x. Now that this is understood, we may delete the subscript and simply state that the derivative, like the primitive function, is itself a function of the independent variable x. That is, for each value of x, there is a unique corresponding value for the derivative function.

Second, since the derivative is merely a limit of the difference quotient, which measures a rate of change of y, the derivative must of necessity also be a measure of some rate of change. In view of the fact that the change in x envisaged in the derivative concept is infinitesimal (that is, $\Delta x \to 0$), the rate measured by the derivative is in the nature of an *instantaneous* rate of change.

Third, there is the matter of notation. Derivative functions are commonly denoted in two ways. Given a primitive function $y = f(x)$, one way of denoting its derivative (if it exists) is to use the symbol $f'(x)$, or simply f'; this notation is attributed to the mathematician

Lagrange. The other common notation is dy/dx, devised by the mathematician Leibniz. [Actually there is a third notation, Dy, or $Df(x)$, but we shall not use it in the following discussion.] The notation $f'(x)$, which resembles the notation for the primitive function $f(x)$, has the advantage of conveying the idea that the derivative is itself a function of x. The reason for expressing it as $f'(x)$—rather than, say, $\phi(x)$—is to emphasize that the function f' is derived from the primitive function f. The alternative notation, dy/dx, serves instead to emphasize that the value of a derivative measures a rate of change. The letter d is the counterpart of the Greek Δ, and dy/dx differs from $\Delta y/\Delta x$ chiefly in that the former is the limit of the latter as Δx approaches zero. In the subsequent discussion, we shall use both of these notations, depending on which seems the more convenient in a particular context.

Using these two notations, we may define the derivative of a given function $y = f(x)$ as follows:

$$\frac{dy}{dx} \equiv f'(x) \equiv \lim_{\Delta x \to 0} \frac{\Delta y}{\Delta x}$$

Example 2   Referring to the function $y = 3x^2 - 4$ again, we have shown its difference quotient to be (6.2), and the limit of that quotient to be (6.3). On the basis of the latter, we may now write (replacing x_0 with x):

$$\frac{dy}{dx} = 6x \qquad \text{or} \qquad f'(x) = 6x$$

Note that different values of x will give the derivative correspondingly different values. For instance, when $x = 3$, we find, by substituting $x = 3$ in the $f'(x)$ expression, that $f'(3) = 6(3) = 18$; similarly, when $x = 4$, we have $f'(4) = 6(4) = 24$. Thus, whereas $f'(x)$ denotes a *derivative function,* the expressions $f'(3)$ and $f'(4)$ each represents a specific *derivative value.*

EXERCISE 6.2

1. Given the function $y = 4x^2 + 9$:
   (a) Find the difference quotient as a function of x and Δx. (Use x in lieu of x_0.)
   (b) Find the derivative dy/dx.
   (c) Find $f'(3)$ and $f'(4)$.
2. Given the function $y = 5x^2 - 4x$:
   (a) Find the difference quotient as a function of x and Δx.
   (b) Find the derivative dy/dx.
   (c) Find $f'(2)$ and $f'(3)$.
3. Given the function $y = 5x - 2$:
   (a) Find the difference quotient $\Delta y/\Delta x$. What type of function is it?
   (b) Since the expression Δx does not appear in the function $\Delta y/\Delta x$ in part (a), does it make any difference to the value of $\Delta y/\Delta x$ whether Δx is large or small? Consequently, what is the limit of the difference quotient as Δx approaches zero?

6.3   The Derivative and the Slope of a Curve

Elementary economics tells us that, given a total-cost function $C = f(Q)$, where C denotes total cost and Q the output, the marginal cost (MC) is defined as the change in total cost resulting from a unit increase in output; that is, $\text{MC} = \Delta C / \Delta Q$. It is understood that ΔQ is an extremely small change. For the case of a product that has discrete units (integers only), a change of one unit is the smallest change possible; but for the case of a product whose quantity is a continuous variable, ΔQ can refer to an infinitesimal change. In this latter case, it is well known that the marginal cost can be measured by the slope of the total-cost curve. But the slope of the total-cost curve is nothing but the limit of the ratio $\Delta C / \Delta Q$, when ΔQ approaches zero. Thus the concept of the slope of a curve is merely the geometric counterpart of the concept of the derivative. Both have to do with the "marginal" notion so extensively used in economics.

In Fig. 6.1, we have drawn a total-cost curve C, which is the graph of the (primitive) function $C = f(Q)$. Suppose that we consider Q_0 as the initial output level from which an increase in output is measured; then the relevant point on the cost curve is the point A. If output is to be raised to $Q_0 + \Delta Q = Q_2$, the total cost will be increased from C_0 to $C_0 + \Delta C = C_2$; thus $\Delta C / \Delta Q = (C_2 - C_0)/(Q_2 - Q_0)$. Geometrically, this is the ratio of two line segments, EB/AE, or the *slope* of the line AB. This particular ratio measures an average rate of change—the *average* marginal cost for the particular ΔQ pictured—and represents a difference quotient. As such, it is a function of the initial value Q_0 and the amount of change ΔQ.

What happens when we vary the magnitude of ΔQ? If a smaller output increment is contemplated (say, from Q_0 to Q_1 only), then the average marginal cost will be measured by the slope of the line AD instead. Moreover, as we reduce the output increment further and further, flatter and flatter lines will result until, in the limit (as $\Delta Q \to 0$), we obtain the line KG (which is the *tangent line* to the cost curve at point A) as the relevant line. The slope

FIGURE 6.1

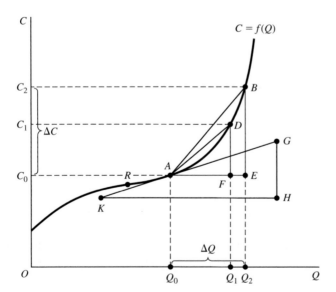

of $KG (= HG/KH)$ measures the slope of the total-cost curve at point A and represents the limit of $\Delta C/\Delta Q$, as $\Delta Q \rightarrow 0$, when initial output is at $Q = Q_0$. Therefore, in terms of the derivative, the slope of the $C = f(Q)$ curve at point A corresponds to the particular derivative value $f'(Q_0)$.

What if the initial output level is changed from Q_0 to, say, Q_2? In that case, point B on the curve will replace point A as the relevant point, and the slope of the curve at the new point B will give us the derivative value $f'(Q_2)$. Analogous results are obtainable for alternative initial output levels. In general, the derivative $f'(Q)$—a function of Q—will vary as Q changes.

6.4 The Concept of Limit

The derivative dy/dx has been defined as the limit of the difference quotient $\Delta y/\Delta x$ as $\Delta x \rightarrow 0$. If we adopt the shorthand symbols $q \equiv \Delta y/\Delta x$ (q for quotient) and $v \equiv \Delta x$ (v for variation in the value of x), we have

$$\frac{dy}{dx} = \lim_{\Delta x \to 0} \frac{\Delta y}{\Delta x} = \lim_{v \to 0} q$$

In view of the fact that the derivative concept relies heavily on the notion of limit, it is imperative that we get a clear idea about that notion.

Left-Side Limit and Right-Side Limit

The concept of limit is concerned with the question: "What value does one variable (say, q) approach as another variable (say, v) approaches a specific value (say, zero)?" In order for this question to make sense, q must, of course, be a function of v; say, $q = g(v)$. Our immediate interest is in finding the limit of q as $v \rightarrow 0$, but we may just as easily explore the more general case of $v \rightarrow N$, where N is any finite real number. Then, $\lim_{v \to 0} q$ will be merely a special case of $\lim_{v \to N} q$ where $N = 0$. In the course of the discussion, we shall actually also consider the limit of q as $v \rightarrow +\infty$ (plus infinity) or as $v \rightarrow -\infty$ (minus infinity).

When we say $v \rightarrow N$, the variable v can approach the number N either from values greater than N, or from values less than N. If, as $v \rightarrow N$ from the left side (from values less than N), q approaches a finite number L, we call L the *left-side limit* of q. On the other hand, if L is the number that q tends to as $v \rightarrow N$ from the right side (from values greater than N), we call L the *right-side limit* of q. The left- and right-side limits may or may not be equal.

The left-side limit of q is symbolized by $\lim_{v \to N^-} q$ (the minus sign signifies from values less than N), and the right-side limit is written as $\lim_{v \to N^+} q$. When—and only when—the two limits have a common finite value (say, L), we consider the limit of q to exist and write it as $\lim_{v \to N} q = L$. Note that L must be a *finite* number. If we have the situation of $\lim_{v \to N} q = \infty$ (or $-\infty$), we shall consider q to possess *no* limit, because $\lim_{v \to N} q = \infty$ means that $q \rightarrow \infty$ as $v \rightarrow N$, and if q will assume *ever-increasing* values as v tends to N, it would be contradictory to say that q has a limit. As a convenient way of expressing the fact that $q \rightarrow \infty$ as $v \rightarrow N$, however, some people do indeed write $\lim_{v \to N} q = \infty$ and speak of q as having an "infinite limit."

In certain cases, only the limit of one side needs to be considered. In taking the limit of q as $v \to +\infty$, for instance, only the left-side limit of q is relevant, because v can approach $+\infty$ only from the left. Similarly, for the case of $v \to -\infty$, only the right-side limit is relevant. Whether the limit of q exists in these cases will depend only on whether q approaches a finite value as $v \to +\infty$, or as $v \to -\infty$.

It is important to realize that the symbol ∞ (infinity) is not a number, and therefore it cannot be subjected to the usual algebraic operations. We cannot have $3 + \infty$ or $1/\infty$; nor can we write $q = \infty$, which is not the same as $q \to \infty$. However, it is acceptable to express the *limit* of q as "=" (as against $\to$) ∞, for this merely indicates that $q \to \infty$.

Graphical Illustrations

Let us illustrate, in Fig. 6.2, several possible situations regarding the limit of a function $q = g(v)$.

Figure 6.2a shows a smooth curve. As the variable v tends to the value N from *either* side on the horizontal axis, the variable q tends to the value L. In this case, the left-side limit is identical with the right-side limit; therefore we can write $\lim\limits_{v \to N} q = L$.

FIGURE 6.2

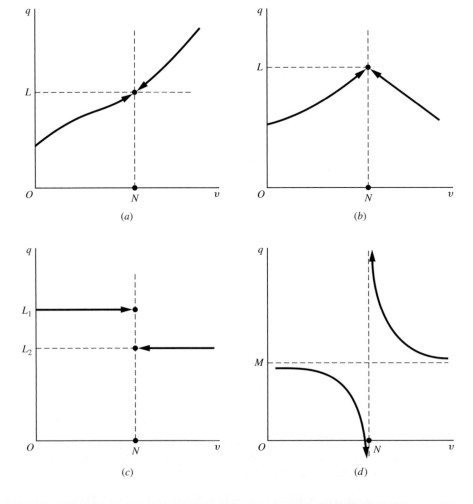

(a)

(b)

(c)

(d)

The curve drawn in Fig. 6.2*b* is not smooth; it has a sharp turning point directly above the point *N*. Nevertheless, as *v* tends to *N* from either side, *q* again tends to an identical value *L*. The limit of *q* again exists and is equal to *L*.

Figure 6.2*c* shows what is known as a *step function*.[†] In this case, as *v* tends to *N*, the left-side limit of *q* is L_1, but the right-side limit is L_2, a different number. Hence, *q* does not have a limit as $v \to N$.

Lastly, in Fig. 6.2*d*, as *v* tends to *N*, the left-side limit of *q* is $-\infty$, whereas the right-side limit is $+\infty$, because the two parts of the (hyperbolic) curve will fall and rise indefinitely while approaching the broken vertical line as an asymptote. Again, $\lim_{v \to N} q$ does not exist. On the other hand, if we are considering a different sort of limit in diagram *d*, namely, $\lim_{v \to +\infty} q$, then only the left-side limit has relevance, and we do find that limit to exist: $\lim_{v \to +\infty} q = M$. Analogously, you can verify that $\lim_{v \to -\infty} q = M$ as well.

It is also possible to apply the concepts of left-side and right-side limits to the discussion of the marginal cost in Fig. 6.1. In that context, the variables *q* and *v* will refer, respectively, to the quotient $\Delta C / \Delta Q$ and to the magnitude of ΔQ, with all changes being measured from point *A* on the curve. In other words, *q* will refer to the slope of such lines as *AB*, *AD*, and *KG*, whereas *v* will refer to the length of such lines as $Q_0 Q_2$ ($=$ line *AE*) and $Q_0 Q_1$ ($=$ line *AF*). We have already seen that, as *v* approaches zero from a positive value, *q* will approach a value equal to the slope of line *KG*. Similarly, we can establish that, if ΔQ approaches zero from a negative value (i.e., as the *decrease* in output becomes less and less), the quotient $\Delta C / \Delta Q$, as measured by the slope of such lines as *RA* (not drawn), will also approach a value equal to the slope of line *KG*. Indeed, the situation here is very much akin to that illustrated in Fig. 6.2*a*. Thus the slope of *KG* in Fig. 6.1 (the counterpart of *L* in Fig. 6.2) is indeed the limit of the quotient *q* as *v* tends to zero, and as such it gives us the marginal cost at the output level $Q = Q_0$.

Evaluation of a Limit

Let us now illustrate the algebraic evaluation of a limit of a given function $q = g(v)$.

Example 1   Given $q = 2 + v^2$, find $\lim_{v \to 0} q$. To take the left-side limit, we substitute the series of negative values $-1, -\frac{1}{10}, -\frac{1}{100}, \ldots$ (in that order) for *v* and find that $(2 + v^2)$ will decrease steadily and approach 2 (because v^2 will gradually approach 0). Next, for the right-side limit, we substitute the series of positive values $1, \frac{1}{10}, \frac{1}{100}, \ldots$ (in that order) for *v* and find the same limit as before. Inasmuch as the two limits are identical, we consider the limit of *q* to exist and write $\lim_{v \to 0} q = 2$.

[†] This name is easily explained by the shape of the curve. But step functions can be expressed algebraically, too. The one illustrated in Fig. 6.2*c* can be expressed by the equation

$$q = \begin{cases} L_1 & \text{(for } 0 \le v < N) \\ L_2 & \text{(for } N \le v) \end{cases}$$

Note that, in each subset of its domain as described, the function appears as a distinct constant function, which constitutes a "step" in the graph.

In economics, step functions can be used, for instance, to show the various prices charged for different quantities purchased (the curve shown in Fig. 6.2*c* pictures *quantity discount*) or the various tax rates applicable to different income brackets.

It is tempting to regard the answer obtained in Example 1 as the outcome of setting $v = 0$ in the equation $q = 2 + v^2$, but this temptation should in general be resisted. In evaluating $\lim_{v \to N} q$, we only let v *tend to N*, but, as a rule, do not let $v = N$. Indeed, we can quite legitimately speak of the limit of q as $v \to N$, even if N is *not* in the domain of the function $q = g(v)$. In this latter case, if we try to set $v = N$, q will clearly be undefined.

Example 2   Given $q = (1 - v^2)/(1 - v)$, find $\lim_{v \to 1} q$. Here, $N = 1$ is not in the domain of the function, and we cannot set $v = 1$ because that would involve division by zero. Moreover, even the limit-evaluation procedure of letting $v \to 1$, as used in Example 1, will cause difficulty, for the denominator $(1 - v)$ will approach zero when $v \to 1$, and we will still have no way of performing the division in the limit.

One way out of this difficulty is to try to transform the given ratio to a form in which v will not appear in the denominator. Since $v \to 1$ implies that $v \neq 1$, so that $(1 - v)$ is nonzero, it is legitimate to divide the expression $(1 - v^2)$ by $(1 - v)$, and write[†]

$$q = \frac{1 - v^2}{1 - v} = 1 + v \qquad (v \neq 1)$$

In this new expression for q, there is no longer a denominator with v in it. Since $(1 + v) \to 2$ as $v \to 1$ from *either* side, we may then conclude that $\lim_{v \to 1} q = 2$.

Example 3   Given $q = (2v + 5)/(v + 1)$, find $\lim_{v \to +\infty} q$. The variable v again appears in *both* the numerator and the denominator. If we let $v \to +\infty$ in both, the result will be a ratio between two infinitely large numbers, which does not have a clear meaning. To get out of the difficulty, we try this time to transform the given ratio to a form in which the variable v will not appear in the numerator.[‡] This, again, can be accomplished by dividing out the given ratio. Since $(2v + 5)$ is not evenly divisible by $(v + 1)$, however, the result will contain a remainder term as follows:

$$q = \frac{2v + 5}{v + 1} = 2 + \frac{3}{v + 1}$$

But, at any rate, this new expression for q no longer has a numerator with v in it. Noting that the remainder $3/(v + 1) \to 0$ as $v \to +\infty$, we can then conclude that $\lim_{v \to +\infty} q = 2$.

There also exist several useful theorems on the evaluation of limits. These will be discussed in Sec. 6.6.

[†] The division can be performed, as in the case of numbers, in the following manner:

$$1 - v \overline{\smash{\big)}\ \begin{array}{r} 1 + v \\ 1 \qquad\quad - v^2 \\ \hline 1 - v \\ \hline v - v^2 \\ v - v^2 \\ \hline \end{array}}$$

Alternatively, we may resort to factoring as follows:

$$\frac{1 - v^2}{1 - v} = \frac{(1 + v)(1 - v)}{1 - v} = 1 + v \qquad (v \neq 1)$$

[‡] Note that, unlike the $v \to 0$ case, where we want to take v out of the *denominator* in order to avoid division by zero, the $v \to \infty$ case is better served by taking v out of the *numerator*. As $v \to \infty$, an expression containing v in the numerator will become infinite but an expression with v in the denominator will, more conveniently for us, approach zero and quietly vanish from the scene.

Formal View of the Limit Concept

The previous discussion should have conveyed some general ideas about the limit concept. Let us now give it a more precise definition. Since such a definition will make use of the concept of *neighborhood* of a point on a line (in particular, a specific number as a point on the line of real numbers), we shall first explain the latter term.

For a given number L, there can always be found a number $(L - a_1) < L$ and another number $(L + a_2) > L$, where a_1 and a_2 are some arbitrary positive numbers. The set of all numbers falling between $(L - a_1)$ and $(L + a_2)$ is called the *interval* between those two numbers. If the numbers $(L - a_1)$ and $(L + a_2)$ are included in the set, the set is a *closed interval;* if they are excluded, the set is an *open interval*. A closed interval between $(L - a_1)$ and $(L + a_2)$ is denoted by the bracketed expression

$$[L - a_1, L + a_2] \equiv \{q \mid L - a_1 \leq q \leq L + a_2\}$$

and the corresponding *open* interval is denoted with parentheses:

$$(L - a_1, L + a_2) \equiv \{q \mid L - a_1 < q < L + a_2\} \tag{6.4}$$

Thus, [ ] relate to the weak inequality sign $\leq$, whereas ( ) relate to the strict inequality sign $<$. But in both types of intervals, the smaller number $(L - a_1)$ is always listed first. Later on, we shall also have occasion to refer to *half-open and half-closed* intervals such as $(3, 5]$ and $[6, \infty)$, which have the following meanings:

$$(3, 5] \equiv \{x \mid 3 < x \leq 5\} \qquad [6, \infty) \equiv \{x \mid 6 \leq x < \infty\}$$

Now we may define a *neighborhood* of L to be an open interval as defined in (6.4), which is an interval "covering" the number L.[†] Depending on the magnitudes of the arbitrary numbers a_1 and a_2, it is possible to construct various neighborhoods for the given number L. Using the concept of neighborhood, the limit of a function may then be defined as follows:

> As v approaches a number N, the limit of $q = g(v)$ is the number L, if, for every neighborhood of L that can be chosen, *however small,* there can be found a corresponding neighborhood of N (excluding the point $v = N$) in the domain of the function such that, for every value of v in that N-neighborhood, its image lies in the chosen L-neighborhood.

This statement can be clarified with the help of Fig. 6.3, which resembles Fig. 6.2a. From what was learned about Fig. 6.2a, we know that $\lim_{v \to N} q = L$ in Fig. 6.3. Let us show that L does indeed fulfill the new definition of a limit. As the first step, select an arbitrary small neighborhood of L, say, $(L - a_1, L + a_2)$. (This should have been made even smaller, but we are keeping it relatively large to facilitate exposition.) Now construct a neighborhood of N, say, $(N - b_1, N + b_2)$, such that the two neighborhoods (when extended into quadrant I) will together define a rectangle (shaded in diagram) with two of its corners lying on the given curve. It can then be verified that, for every value of v in this neighborhood of N (not counting $v = N$), the corresponding value of $q = g(v)$ lies in the

---

[†] The identification of an open interval as the neighborhood of a point is valid only when we are considering a point on a line (one-dimensional space). In the case of a point in a plane (two-dimensional space), its neighborhood must be thought of as an area, say, a circular area that includes the point.

FIGURE 6.3

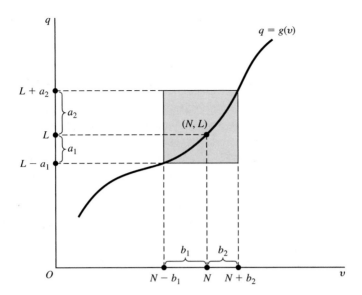

chosen neighborhood of L. In fact, no matter how *small* an L-neighborhood we choose, a (correspondingly small) N-neighborhood can be found with the property just cited. Thus L fulfills the definition of a limit, as was to be demonstrated.

We can also apply the given definition to the step function of Fig. 6.2c in order to show that neither L_1 nor L_2 qualifies as $\lim_{v \to N} q$. If we choose a very small neighborhood of L_1—say, just a hair's width on each side of L_1—then, no matter what neighborhood we pick for N, the rectangle associated with the two neighborhoods cannot possibly enclose the lower step of the function. Consequently, for any value of $v > N$, the corresponding value of q (located on the lower step) will not be in the neighborhood of L_1, and thus L_1 fails the test for a limit. By similar reasoning, L_2 must also be dismissed as a candidate for $\lim_{v \to N} q$. In fact, in this case no limit exists for q as $v \to N$.

The fulfillment of the definition can also be checked algebraically rather than by graph. For instance, consider again the function

$$q = \frac{1 - v^2}{1 - v} = 1 + v \qquad (v \neq 1) \tag{6.5}$$

It has been found in Example 2 that $\lim_{v \to 1} q = 2$; thus, here we have $N = 1$ and $L = 2$. To verify that $L = 2$ is indeed the limit of q, we must demonstrate that, for every chosen neighborhood of L, $(2 - a_1, 2 + a_2)$, there exists a neighborhood of N, $(1 - b_1, 1 + b_2)$, such that, whenever v is in this neighborhood of N, q must be in the chosen neighborhood of L. This means essentially that, for given values of a_1 and a_2, however small, two numbers b_1 and b_2 must be found such that, whenever the inequality

$$1 - b_1 < v < 1 + b_2 \qquad (v \neq 1) \tag{6.6}$$

is satisfied, another inequality of the form

$$2 - a_1 < q < 2 + a_2 \tag{6.7}$$

must also be satisfied. To find such a pair of numbers b_1 and b_2, let us first rewrite (6.7) by substituting (6.5):

$$2 - a_1 < 1 + v < 2 + a_2 \qquad\qquad \textbf{(6.7')}$$

This, in turn, can be transformed (by subtracting 1 from each side) into the inequality

$$1 - a_1 < v < 1 + a_2 \qquad\qquad \textbf{(6.7'')}$$

A comparison of (6.7'')—a variant of (6.7)—with (6.6) suggests that if we choose the two numbers b_1 and b_2 to be $b_1 = a_1$ and $b_2 = a_2$, the two inequalities (6.6) and (6.7) will always be satisfied simultaneously. Thus the neighborhood of N, $(1 - b_1, 1 + b_2)$, as required in the definition of a limit, can indeed be found for the case of $L = 2$, and this establishes $L = 2$ as the limit.

Let us now utilize the definition of a limit in the opposite way, to show that another value (say, 3) cannot qualify as $\lim_{v \to 1} q$ for the function in (6.5). If 3 were that limit, it would have to be true that, for every chosen neighborhood of 3, $(3 - a_1, 3 + a_2)$, there exists a neighborhood of 1, $(1 - b_1, 1 + b_2)$, such that, whenever v is in the latter neighborhood, q must be in the former neighborhood. That is, whenever the inequality

$$1 - b_1 < v < 1 + b_2$$

is satisfied, another inequality of the form

$$3 - a_1 < 1 + v < 3 + a_2$$

or $\qquad\qquad\qquad 2 - a_1 < v < 2 + a_2$

must also be satisfied. The *only* way to achieve this result is to choose $b_1 = a_1 - 1$ and $b_2 = a_2 + 1$. This would imply that the neighborhood of 1 is to be the open interval $(2 - a_1, 2 + a_2)$. According to the definition of a limit, however, a_1 and a_2 can be made arbitrarily small, say, $a_1 = a_2 = 0.1$. In that case, the last-mentioned interval will turn out to be $(1.9, 2.1)$ which lies entirely to the right of the point $v = 1$ on the horizontal axis and, hence, does not even qualify as a neighborhood of 1. Thus the definition of a limit cannot be satisfied by the number 3. A similar procedure can be employed to show that *any* number other than 2 will contradict the definition of a limit in the present case.

In general, if one number satisfies the definition of a limit of q as $v \to N$, then no other number can. If a limit exists, it is unique.

EXERCISE 6.4

1. Given the function $q = (v^2 + v - 56)/(v - 7)$, $(v \neq 7)$, find the left-side limit and the right-side limit of q as v approaches 7. Can we conclude from these answers that q has a limit as v approaches 7?

2. Given $q = [(v + 2)^3 - 8]/v$, $(v \neq 0)$, find:
   (a) $\lim_{v \to 0} q$ (b) $\lim_{v \to 2} q$ (c) $\lim_{v \to a} q$

3. Given $q = 5 - 1/v$, $(v \neq 0)$, find:
   (a) $\lim_{v \to +\infty} q$ (b) $\lim_{v \to -\infty} q$

4. Use Fig. 6.3 to show that we *cannot* consider the number $(L + a_2)$ as the limit of q as v tends to N.

6.5   Digression on Inequalities and Absolute Values

We have encountered inequality signs many times before. In the discussion of Sec. 6.4, we also applied mathematical operations to inequalities. In transforming $(6.7')$ into $(6.7'')$, for example, we subtracted 1 from each side of the inequality. What rules of operations are generally applicable to inequalities (as opposed to equations)?

Rules of Inequalities

To begin with, let us state an important property of inequalities: inequalities are *transitive*. This means that, if $a > b$ and if $b > c$, then $a > c$. Since equalities (equations) are also transitive, the transitivity property should apply to "weak" inequalities ($\geq$ or $\leq$) as well as to "strict" ones ($>$ or $<$). Thus we have

$$a > b, b > c \Rightarrow a > c$$
$$a \geq b, b \geq c \Rightarrow a \geq c$$

This property is what makes possible the writing of a *continued inequality,* such as $3 < a < b < 8$ or $7 \leq x \leq 24$. (In writing a continued inequality, the inequality signs are as a rule arranged in the same direction, usually with the smallest number on the left.)

The most important rules of inequalities are those governing the addition (subtraction) of a number to (from) an inequality, the multiplication or division of an inequality by a number, and the squaring of an inequality. Specifically, these rules are as follows.

Rule I   (addition and subtraction) $a > b \Rightarrow a \pm k > b \pm k$

An inequality will continue to hold if an equal quantity is added to or subtracted from each side. This rule may be generalized thus: If $a > b > c$, then $a \pm k > b \pm k > c \pm k$.

Rule II   (multiplication and division)

$$a > b \Rightarrow \begin{cases} ka > kb & (k > 0) \\ ka < kb & (k < 0) \end{cases}$$

The multiplication of both sides by a *positive* number preserves the inequality, but a *negative* multiplier will cause the *sense* (or *direction*) of the inequality to be reversed.

Example 1   Since $6 > 5$, multiplication by 3 will yield $3(6) > 3(5)$, or $18 > 15$; but multiplication by -3 will result in $(-3)6 < (-3)5$, or $-18 < -15$.

Division of an inequality by a number n is equivalent to multiplication by the number $1/n$; therefore the rule on division is subsumed under the rule on multiplication.

Rule III   (squaring) $a > b, (b \geq 0) \Rightarrow a^2 > b^2$

If its two sides are both nonnegative, the inequality will continue to hold when both sides are squared.

Example 2   Since $4 > 3$ and since both sides are positive, we have $4^2 > 3^2$, or $16 > 9$. Similarly, since $2 > 0$, it follows that $2^2 > 0^2$, or $4 > 0$.

Rules I through III have been stated in terms of strict inequalities, but their validity is unaffected if the $>$ signs are replaced by $\geq$ signs.

Absolute Values and Inequalities

When the domain of a variable x is an open interval (a, b), the domain may be denoted by the set $\{x \mid a < x < b\}$ or, more simply, by the inequality $a < x < b$. Similarly, if it is a closed interval $[a, b]$, it may be expressed by the weak inequality $a \leq x \leq b$. In the special case of an interval of the form $(-a, a)$—say, $(-10, 10)$—it may be represented either by the inequality $-10 < x < 10$ or, alternatively, by the inequality

$$|x| < 10$$

where the symbol $|x|$ denotes the *absolute value* (or *numerical value*) of x.

For any real number n, the absolute value of n is defined as follows:[†]

$$|n| \equiv \begin{cases} n & (\text{if } n > 0) \\ -n & (\text{if } n < 0) \\ 0 & (\text{if } n = 0) \end{cases} \tag{6.8}$$

Note that, if $n = 15$, then $|15| = 15$; but if $n = -15$, we find

$$|-15| = -(-15) = 15$$

also. In effect, therefore, the absolute value of any real number is simply its numerical value after the sign is removed. For this reason, we always have $|n| = |-n|$. The absolute value of n is also called the *modulus* of n.

Given the expression $|x| = 10$, we may conclude from (6.8) that x must be either 10 or -10. By the same token, the expression $|x| < 10$ means that (1) if $x > 0$, then $x \equiv |x| < 10$, so that x must be less than 10; but also (2) if $x < 0$, then according to (6.8) we have $-x \equiv |x| < 10$, or $x > -10$, so that x must be greater than -10. Hence, by combining the two parts of this result, we see that x must lie within the open interval $(-10, 10)$. In general, we can write

$$|x| < n \Leftrightarrow -n < x < n \qquad (n > 0) \tag{6.9}$$

which can also be extended to weak inequalities as follows:

$$|x| \leq n \Leftrightarrow -n \leq x \leq n \qquad (n \geq 0) \tag{6.10}$$

Because they are themselves numbers, the absolute values of two numbers m and n can be added, subtracted, multiplied, and divided. The following properties characterize absolute values:

$$|m| + |n| \geq |m + n|$$
$$|m| \cdot |n| = |m \cdot n|$$
$$\frac{|m|}{|n|} = \left|\frac{m}{n}\right|$$

The first of these, interestingly, involves an inequality rather than an equation. The reason for this is easily seen: whereas the left-hand expression $|m| + |n|$ is definitely a *sum* of two

---

[†] We caution again that, although the absolute-value notation is similar to that of a first-order determinant, these two concepts are entirely different. The definition of a first-order determinant is $|a_{ij}| \equiv a_{ij}$, regardless of the sign of a_{ij}. In the definition of the absolute value $|n|$, on the other hand, the sign of n will make a difference. The context of the discussion should normally make it clear whether an absolute value or a first-order determinant is under consideration.

numerical values (both taken as positive), the expression $|m + n|$ is the numerical value of *either* a sum (if m and n are, say, both positive) *or* a difference (if m and n have opposite signs). Thus the left side may exceed the right side.

Example 3

If $m = 5$ and $n = 3$, then $|m| + |n| = |m + n| = 8$. But if $m = 5$ and $n = -3$, then $|m| + |n| = 5 + 3 = 8$, whereas

$$|m + n| = |5 - 3| = 2$$

is a smaller number.

In the other two properties, on the other hand, it makes no difference whether m and n have identical or opposite signs, since, in taking the absolute value of the product or quotient on the right-hand side, the sign of the latter term will be removed in any case.

Example 4

If $m = 7$ and $n = 8$, then $|m| \cdot |n| = |m \cdot n| = 7(8) = 56$. But even if $m = -7$ and $n = 8$ (opposite signs), we still get the same result from

$$|m| \cdot |n| = |-7| \cdot |8| = 7(8) = 56$$

and

$$|m \cdot n| = |-7(8)| = 7(8) = 56$$

Solution of an Inequality

Like an equation, an inequality containing a variable (say, x) may have a solution; the solution, if it exists, is a set of values of x which make the inequality a true statement. Such a solution will itself usually be in the form of an inequality.

Example 5

Find the solution of the inequality

$$3x - 3 > x + 1$$

As in solving an equation, the variable terms should first be collected on one side of the inequality. By adding $(3 - x)$ to both sides, we obtain

$$3x - 3 + 3 - x > x + 1 + 3 - x$$

or

$$2x > 4$$

Multiplying both sides by $\frac{1}{2}$ (which does not reverse the sense of the inequality, because $\frac{1}{2} > 0$) will then yield the solution

$$x > 2$$

which is itself an inequality. This solution is not a single number, but a set of numbers. Therefore we may also express the solution as the set $\{x \mid x > 2\}$ or as the open interval $(2, \infty)$.

Example 6

Solve the inequality $|1 - x| \leq 3$. First, let us get rid of the absolute-value notation by utilizing (6.10). The given inequality is equivalent to the statement that

$$-3 \leq 1 - x \leq 3$$

or, after subtracting 1 from each side,

$$-4 \leq -x \leq 2$$

Multiplying each side by (-1), we then get

$$4 \geq x \geq -2$$

where the sense of inequality has been duly reversed. Writing the smaller number first, we may express the solution in the form of the inequality

$$-2 \leq x \leq 4$$

or in the form of the set $\{x \mid -2 \leq x \leq 4\}$ or the closed interval $[-2, 4]$.

Sometimes, a problem may call for the satisfaction of several inequalities in several variables simultaneously; then we must solve a system of simultaneous inequalities. This problem arises, for example, in nonlinear programming, which will be discussed in Chap. 13.

EXERCISE 6.5

1. Solve the following inequalities:
   (a) $3x - 1 < 7x + 2$ (c) $5x + 1 < x + 3$
   (b) $2x + 5 < x - 4$ (d) $2x - 1 < 6x + 5$
2. If $8x - 3 < 0$ and $8x > 0$, express these in a continued inequality and find its solution.
3. Solve the following:
   (a) $|x + 1| < 6$ (b) $|4 - 3x| < 2$ (c) $|2x + 3| \leq 5$

6.6 Limit Theorems

Our interest in rates of change led us to the consideration of the concept of derivative, which, being in the nature of the limit of a difference quotient, in turn prompted us to study questions of the existence and evaluation of a limit. The basic process of limit evaluation, as illustrated in Sec. 6.4, involves letting the variable v approach a particular number (say, N) and observing the value that q approaches. When actually evaluating the limit of a function, however, we may draw upon certain established limit theorems, which can materially simplify the task, especially for complicated functions.

Theorems Involving a Single Function

When a single function $q = g(v)$ is involved, the following theorems are applicable.

Theorem I   If $q = av + b$, then $\lim_{v \to N} q = aN + b$ (a and b are constants).

Example 1   Given $q = 5v + 7$, we have $\lim_{v \to 2} q = 5(2) + 7 = 17$. Similarly, $\lim_{v \to 0} q = 5(0) + 7 = 7$.

Theorem II   If $q = g(v) = b$, then $\lim_{v \to N} q = b$.

This theorem, which says that the limit of a constant function is the constant in that function, is merely a special case of Theorem I, with $a = 0$. (You have already encountered an example of this case in Exercise 6.2-3.)

Theorem III   If $q = v$, then $\lim_{v \to N} q = N$.
If $q = v^k$, then $\lim_{v \to N} q = N^k$.

Example 2   Given $q = v^3$, we have $\lim_{v \to 2} q = (2)^3 = 8$.

You may have noted that, in Theorems I through III, what is done to find the limit of q as $v \to N$ is indeed to let $v = N$. But these are special cases, and they do not vitiate the general rule that "$v \to N$" does not mean "$v = N$."

Theorems Involving Two Functions

If we have two functions of the same independent variable v, $q_1 = g(v)$ and $q_2 = h(v)$, and if *both* functions possess limits as follows:

$$\lim_{v \to N} q_1 = L_1 \qquad \lim_{v \to N} q_2 = L_2$$

where L_1 and L_2 are two *finite* numbers, the following theorems are applicable.

Theorem IV   (sum-difference limit theorem)

$$\lim_{v \to N} (q_1 \pm q_2) = L_1 \pm L_2$$

The limit of a sum (difference) of two functions is the sum (difference) of their respective limits.

In particular, we note that

$$\lim_{v \to N} 2q_1 = \lim_{v \to N} (q_1 + q_1) = L_1 + L_1 = 2L_1$$

which is in line with Theorem I.

Theorem V   (product limit theorem)

$$\lim_{v \to N} (q_1 q_2) = L_1 L_2$$

The limit of a product of two functions is the product of their limits.

Applied to the square of a function, this gives

$$\lim_{v \to N} (q_1 q_1) = L_1 L_1 = L_1^2$$

which is in line with Theorem III.

Theorem VI   (quotient limit theorem)

$$\lim_{v \to N} \frac{q_1}{q_2} = \frac{L_1}{L_2} \qquad (L_2 \neq 0)$$

The limit of a quotient of two functions is the quotient of their limits. Naturally, the limit L_2 is restricted to be nonzero; otherwise the quotient is undefined.

Example 3   Find $\lim_{v \to 0} (1 + v)/(2 + v)$. Since we have here $\lim_{v \to 0} (1 + v) = 1$ and $\lim_{v \to 0} (2 + v) = 2$, the desired limit is $\frac{1}{2}$.

Remember that L_1 and L_2 represent finite numbers; otherwise these theorems do not apply. In the case of Theorem VI, furthermore, L_2 must be nonzero as well. If these restrictions are not satisfied, we must fall back on the method of limit evaluation illustrated in Examples 2 and 3 in Sec. 6.4, which relate to the cases, respectively, of L_2 being zero and of L_2 being infinite.

Limit of a Polynomial Function

With the given limit theorems at our disposal, we can easily evaluate the limit of any polynomial function

$$q = g(v) = a_0 + a_1v + a_2v^2 + \cdots + a_nv^n \qquad (6.11)$$

as v tends to the number N. Since the limits of the separate terms are, respectively,

$$\lim_{v \to N} a_0 = a_0 \qquad \lim_{v \to N} a_1v = a_1N \qquad \lim_{v \to N} a_2v^2 = a_2N^2 \qquad \text{(etc.)}$$

the limit of the polynomial function is (by the sum limit theorem)

$$\lim_{v \to N} q = a_0 + a_1N + a_2N^2 + \cdots + a_nN^n \qquad (6.12)$$

This limit is also, we note, actually equal to $g(N)$, that is, equal to the value of the function in (6.11) when $v = N$. This particular result will prove important in discussing the concept of *continuity* of the polynomial function.

EXERCISE 6.6

1. Find the limits of the function $q = 7 - 9v + v^2$:
   - (a) As $v \to 0$
   - (b) As $v \to 3$
   - (c) As $v \to -1$
2. Find the limits of $q = (v + 2)(v - 3)$:
   - (a) As $v \to -1$
   - (b) As $v \to 0$
   - (c) As $v \to 5$
3. Find the limits of $q = (3v + 5)/(v + 2)$:
   - (a) As $v \to 0$
   - (b) As $v \to 5$
   - (c) As $v \to -1$

6.7 Continuity and Differentiability of a Function

The preceding discussion of the concept of limit and its evaluation can now be used to define the continuity and differentiability of a function. These notions bear directly on the derivative of the function, which is what interests us.

Continuity of a Function

When a function $q = g(v)$ possesses a limit as v tends to the point N in the domain, and when this limit is also equal to $g(N)$—that is, equal to the value of the function at $v = N$—the function is said to be *continuous* at N. As defined here, the term *continuity* involves no less than three requirements: (1) the point N must be in the domain of the function; i.e., $g(N)$ is defined; (2) the function must have a limit as $v \to N$; i.e., $\lim_{v \to N} g(v)$ exists; and (3) that limit must be equal in value to $g(N)$; i.e., $\lim_{v \to N} g(v) = g(N)$.

It is important to note that while the point (N, L) was excluded from consideration in discussing the limit of the curve in Fig. 6.3, we are no longer excluding it in the present context. Rather, as the third requirement specifically states, the point (N, L) must be on the graph of the function before the function can be considered as continuous at point N.

Let us check whether the functions shown in Fig. 6.2 are continuous. In diagram *a*, all three requirements are met at point *N*. Point *N* is in the domain; *q* has the limit *L* as $v \to N$; and the limit *L* happens also to be the value of the function at *N*. Thus, the function represented by that curve is continuous at *N*. The same is true of the function depicted in Fig. 6.2*b*, since *L* is the limit of the function as *v* approaches the value *N* in the domain, and since *L* is also the value of the function at *N*. This last graphic example should suffice to establish that the continuity of a function at point *N* does *not* necessarily imply that the graph of the function is "smooth" at $v = N$, for the point (*N, L*) in Fig. 6.2*b* is actually a "sharp" point and yet the function is continuous at that value of *v*.

When a function $q = g(v)$ is continuous at all values of *v* in the interval (*a, b*), it is said to be continuous in that interval. If the function is continuous at all points in a subset *S* of the domain (where the subset *S* may be the union of several disjoint intervals), it is said to be continuous in *S*. And, finally, if the function is continuous at all points in its domain, we say that it is continuous in its domain. Even in this latter case, however, the graph of the function may nevertheless show a discontinuity (a gap) at some value of *v*, say, at $v = 5$, if that value of *v* is *not* in its domain.

Again referring to Fig. 6.2, we see that in diagram *c* the function is *discontinuous* at *N* because a limit does not exist at that point, in violation of the second requirement of continuity. Nevertheless, the function does satisfy the requirements of continuity in the interval (0, *N*) of the domain, as well as in the interval [*N*, ∞). Diagram *d* obviously is also discontinuous at $v = N$. This time, discontinuity emanates from the fact that *N* is excluded from the domain, in violation of the first requirement of continuity.

On the basis of the graphs in Fig. 6.2, it appears that sharp points are consistent with continuity, as in diagram *b*, but that gaps are taboo, as in diagrams *c* and *d*. This is indeed the case. Roughly speaking, therefore, a function that is continuous in a particular interval is one whose graph can be drawn for the said interval without lifting the pencil or pen from the paper—a feat which is possible even if there are sharp points, but impossible when gaps occur.

Polynomial and Rational Functions

Let us now consider the continuity of certain frequently encountered functions. For any polynomial function, such as $q = g(v)$ in (6.11), we have found from (6.12) that $\lim\limits_{v \to N} q$ exists and is equal to the value of the function at *N*. Since *N* is a point (any point) in the domain of the function, we can conclude that any polynomial function is continuous in its domain. This is a very useful piece of information, because polynomial functions will be encountered very often.

What about rational functions? Regarding continuity, there exists an interesting theorem (the continuity theorem) which states that the sum, difference, product, and quotient of any finite number of functions that are continuous in the domain are, respectively, also continuous in the domain. As a result, any rational function (a quotient of two polynomial functions) must also be continuous in its domain.

Example 1	The rational function

$$q = g(v) = \frac{4v^2}{v^2 + 1}$$

is defined for all finite real numbers; thus its domain consists of the interval $(-\infty, \infty)$. For any number N in the domain, the limit of q is (by the quotient limit theorem)

$$\lim_{v \to N} q = \frac{\lim_{v \to N} (4v^2)}{\lim_{v \to N} (v^2 + 1)} = \frac{4N^2}{N^2 + 1}$$

which is equal to $g(N)$. Thus the three requirements of continuity are all met at N. Moreover, we note that N can represent any point in the domain of this function; consequently, this function is continuous in its domain.

<table>
<tr><td>**Example 2**</td><td>The rational function

$$q = \frac{v^3 + v^2 - 4v - 4}{v^2 - 4}$$

is not defined at $v = 2$ and at $v = -2$. Since those two values of v are not in the domain, the function is discontinuous at $v = -2$ and $v = 2$, despite the fact that a limit of q exists as $v \to -2$ or 2. Graphically, this function will display a gap at each of these two values of v. But for other values of v (those which *are* in the domain), this function is continuous.</td></tr>
</table>

Differentiability of a Function

The previous discussion has provided us with the tools for ascertaining whether any function has a limit as its independent variable approaches some specific value. Thus we can try to take the limit of any function $y = f(x)$ as x approaches some chosen value, say, x_0. However, we can also apply the "limit" concept at a different level and take the limit of the difference quotient of that function, $\Delta y / \Delta x$, as Δx approaches zero. The outcomes of limit-taking at these two different levels relate to two different, though related, properties of the function f.

Taking the limit of the function $y = f(x)$ itself, we can, in line with the discussion of the preceding subsection, examine whether the function f is *continuous* at $x = x_0$. The conditions for continuity are (1) $x = x_0$ must be in the domain of the function f, (2) y must have a limit as $x \to x_0$, and (3) the said limit must be equal to $f(x_0)$. When these are satisfied, we can write

$$\lim_{x \to x_0} f(x) = f(x_0) \qquad \text{[continuity condition]} \qquad \textbf{(6.13)}$$

In contrast, when the "limit" concept is applied to the difference quotient $\Delta y / \Delta x$ as $\Delta x \to 0$, we deal instead with the question of whether the function f is *differentiable* at $x = x_0$, i.e., whether the derivative dy/dx exists at $x = x_0$, or whether $f'(x_0)$ exists. The term *differentiable* is used here because the process of obtaining the derivative dy/dx is known as *differentiation* (also called *derivation*). Since $f'(x_0)$ exists if and only if the limit of $\Delta y / \Delta x$ exists at $x = x_0$ as $\Delta x \to 0$, the symbolic expression of the differentiability of f is

$$f'(x_0) = \lim_{\Delta x \to 0} \frac{\Delta y}{\Delta x}$$

$$\equiv \lim_{\Delta x \to 0} \frac{f(x_0 + \Delta x) - f(x_0)}{\Delta x} \qquad \text{[differentiability condition]} \qquad \textbf{(6.14)}$$

These two properties, continuity and differentiability, are very intimately related to each other—the continuity of f is a *necessary* condition for its differentiability (although, as we shall see later, this condition is *not sufficient*). What this means is that, to be differentiable at $x = x_0$, the function must first pass the test of being continuous at $x = x_0$. To prove this, we shall demonstrate that, given a function $y = f(x)$, its continuity at $x = x_0$ follows from its differentiability at $x = x_0$; i.e., condition (6.13) follows from condition (6.14). Before doing this, however, let us simplify the notation somewhat by (1) replacing x_0 with the symbol N and (2) replacing $(x_0 + \Delta x)$ with the symbol x. The latter is justifiable because the postchange value of x can be any number (depending on the magnitude of the change) and hence is a variable denotable by x. The equivalence of the two notation systems is shown in Fig. 6.4, where the old notations appear (in brackets) alongside the new. Note that, with the notational change, Δx now becomes $(x - N)$, so that the expression "$\Delta x \to 0$" becomes "$x \to N$," which is analogous to the expression $v \to N$ used before in connection with the function $q = g(v)$. Accordingly, (6.13) and (6.14) can now be rewritten, respectively, as

$$\lim_{x \to N} f(x) = f(N) \qquad\qquad (6.13')$$

$$f'(N) = \lim_{x \to N} \frac{f(x) - f(N)}{x - N} \qquad\qquad (6.14')$$

What we want to show is, therefore, that the continuity condition (6.13') follows from the differentiability condition (6.14'). First, since the notation $x \to N$ implies that $x \neq N$, so that $x - N$ is a nonzero number, it is permissible to write the following identity:

$$f(x) - f(N) \equiv \frac{f(x) - f(N)}{x - N}(x - N) \qquad\qquad (6.15)$$

FIGURE 6.4

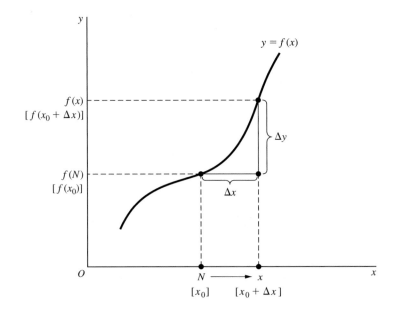

Taking the limit of each side of (6.15) as $x \to N$ yields the following results:

$$\text{Left side} = \lim_{x \to N} f(x) - \lim_{x \to N} f(N) \qquad \text{[difference limit theorem]}$$

$$= \lim_{x \to N} f(x) - f(N) \qquad \text{[} f(N) \text{ is a constant]}$$

$$\text{Right side} = \lim_{x \to N} \frac{f(x) - f(N)}{x - N} \lim_{x \to N} (x - N) \qquad \text{[product limit theorem]}$$

$$= f'(N)(\lim_{x \to N} x - \lim_{x \to N} N) \qquad \text{[by (6.14$'$) and difference limit theorem]}$$

$$= f'(N)(N - N) = 0$$

Note that we could not have written these results, if condition (6.14$'$) had not been granted, for if $f'(N)$ did not exist, then the right-side expression (and hence also the left-side expression) in (6.15) would not possess a limit. If $f'(N)$ does exist, however, the two sides will have limits as shown in the previous equations. Moreover, when the left-side result and the right-side result are equated, we get $\lim_{x \to N} f(x) - f(N) = 0$, which is identical with (6.13$'$). Thus we have proved that continuity, as shown in (6.13$'$), follows from differentiability, as shown in (6.14$'$). In general, if a function is differentiable at every point in its domain, we may conclude that it must be continuous in its domain.

Although differentiability implies continuity, the converse is not true. That is, continuity is a *necessary,* but *not* a *sufficient,* condition for differentiability. To demonstrate this, we merely have to produce a counterexample. Let us consider the function

$$y = f(x) = |x - 2| + 1 \tag{6.16}$$

which is graphed in Fig. 6.5. As can be readily shown, this function is not differentiable, though continuous, when $x = 2$. That the function is continuous at $x = 2$ is easy to establish. First, $x = 2$ is in the domain of the function. Second, the limit of y exists as x tends to 2; to be specific, $\lim_{x \to 2^+} y = \lim_{x \to 2^-} y = 1$. Third, $f(2)$ is also found to be 1. Thus all three requirements of continuity are met. To show that the function f is *not* differentiable at

FIGURE 6.5

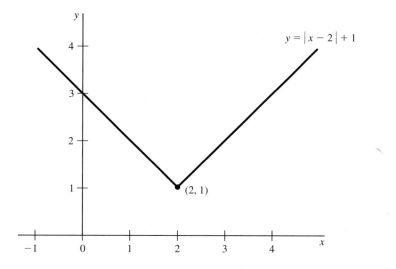

$x = 2$, we must show that the limit of the difference quotient

$$\lim_{x \to 2} \frac{f(x) - f(2)}{x - 2} = \lim_{x \to 2} \frac{|x - 2| + 1 - 1}{x - 2} = \lim_{x \to 2} \frac{|x - 2|}{x - 2}$$

does *not* exist. This involves the demonstration of a disparity between the left-side and the right-side limits. Since, in considering the right-side limit, x must exceed 2, according to the definition of absolute value in (6.8) we have $|x - 2| = x - 2$. Thus the right-side limit is

$$\lim_{x \to 2^+} \frac{|x - 2|}{x - 2} = \lim_{x \to 2^+} \frac{x - 2}{x - 2} = \lim_{x \to 2^+} 1 = 1$$

On the other hand, in considering the left-side limit, x must be less than 2; thus, according to (6.8), $|x - 2| = -(x - 2)$. Consequently, the left-side limit is

$$\lim_{x \to 2^-} = \frac{|x - 2|}{x - 2} = \lim_{x \to 2^-} \frac{-(x - 2)}{x - 2} = \lim_{x \to 2^-} (-1) = -1$$

which is different from the right-side limit. This shows that continuity does not guarantee differentiability. In sum, all differentiable functions are continuous, but not all continuous functions are differentiable.

In Fig. 6.5, the nondifferentiability of the function at $x = 2$ is manifest in the fact that the point $(2, 1)$ has no tangent line defined, and hence no definite slope can be assigned to the point. Specifically, to the left of that point, the curve has a slope of -1, but to the right it has a slope of $+1$, and the slopes on the two sides display no tendency to approach a common magnitude at $x = 2$. The point $(2, 1)$ is, of course, a special point; it is the only sharp point on the curve. At other points on the curve, the derivative is defined and the function is differentiable. More specifically, the function in (6.16) can be divided into two linear functions as follows:

Left part: $y = -(x - 2) + 1 = 3 - x$ $(x \leq 2)$

Right part: $y = (x - 2) + 1 = x - 1$ $(x > 2)$

The left part is differentiable in the interval $(-\infty, 2)$, and the right part is differentiable in the interval $(2, \infty)$ in the domain.

In general, differentiability is a more restrictive condition than continuity, because it requires something beyond continuity. Continuity at a point only rules out the presence of a gap, whereas differentiability rules out "sharpness" as well. Therefore, differentiability calls for "smoothness" of the function (curve) as well as its continuity. Most of the *specific* functions employed in economics have the property that they are differentiable everywhere. When *general* functions are used, moreover, they are often assumed to be everywhere differentiable, as we shall in the subsequent discussion.

EXERCISE 6.7

1. A function $y = f(x)$ is discontinuous at $x = x_0$ when *any* of the three requirements for continuity is violated at $x = x_0$. Construct three graphs to illustrate the violation of each of those requirements.

2. Taking the set of all finite real numbers as the domain of the function $q = g(v) = v^2 - 5v - 2$:

   (a) Find the limit of q as v tends to N (a finite real number).

   (b) Check whether this limit is equal to $g(N)$.

   (c) Check whether the function is continuous at N and continuous in its domain.

3. Given the function $q = g(v) = \dfrac{v+2}{v^2+2}$:

   (a) Use the limit theorems to find $\lim\limits_{v \to N} q$, N being a finite real number.

   (b) Check whether this limit is equal to $g(N)$.

   (c) Check the continuity of the function $g(v)$ at N and in its domain $(-\infty, \infty)$.

4. Given $y = f(x) = \dfrac{x^2 - 9x + 20}{x - 4}$:

   (a) Is it possible to apply the quotient limit theorem to find the limit of this function as $x \to 4$?

   (b) Is this function continuous at $x = 4$? Why?

   (c) Find a function which, for $x \neq 4$, is equivalent to the given function, and obtain from the equivalent function the limit of y as $x \to 4$.

5. In the rational function in Example 2, the numerator is evenly divisible by the denominator, and the quotient is $v + 1$. Can we for that reason replace that function outright by $q = v + 1$? Why or why not?

6. On the basis of the graphs of the six functions in Fig. 2.8, would you conclude that each such function is differentiable at every point in its domain? Explain.

Chapter 7

Rules of Differentiation and Their Use in Comparative Statics

The central problem of comparative-static analysis, that of finding a rate of change, can be identified with the problem of finding the derivative of some function $y = f(x)$, provided only an infinitesimal change in x is being considered. Even though the derivative dy/dx is defined as the limit of the difference quotient $q = g(v)$ as $v \to 0$, it is by no means necessary to undertake the process of limit-taking each time the derivative of a function is sought, for there exist various rules of differentiation (derivation) that will enable us to obtain the desired derivatives directly. Instead of going into comparative-static models immediately, therefore, let us begin by learning some rules of differentiation.

7.1 Rules of Differentiation for a Function of One Variable

First, let us discuss three rules that apply, respectively, to the following types of function of a single independent variable: $y = k$ (constant function) and $y = x^n$ and $y = cx^n$ (power functions). All these have smooth, continuous graphs and are therefore differentiable everywhere.

Constant-Function Rule

The derivative of a constant function $y = k$, or $f(x) = k$, is identically zero, i.e., is zero for all values of x. Symbolically, this rule may be stated as: Given $y = f(x) = k$, the derivative is

$$\frac{dy}{dx} = \frac{dk}{dx} = 0 \qquad \text{or} \qquad f'(x) = 0$$

Alternatively, we may state the rule as: Given $y = f(x) = k$, the derivative is

$$\frac{d}{dx}y = \frac{d}{dx}f(x) = \frac{d}{dx}k = 0$$

where the derivative symbol has been separated into two parts, d/dx on the one hand, and y [or $f(x)$ or k] on the other. The first part, d/dx, is an *operator symbol,* which instructs us to perform a particular mathematical operation. Just as the operator symbol $\sqrt{\ }$ instructs us to take a square root, the symbol d/dx represents an instruction to take the derivative of, or to differentiate, (some function) with respect to the variable x. The function to be operated on (to be differentiated) is indicated in the second part; here it is $y = f(x) = k$.

The proof of the rule is as follows. Given $f(x) = k$, we have $f(N) = k$ for any value of N. Thus the value of $f'(N)$—the value of the derivative at $x = N$—as defined in (6.13) is

$$f'(N) = \lim_{x \to N} \frac{f(x) - f(N)}{x - N} = \lim_{x \to N} \frac{k - k}{x - N} = \lim_{x \to N} 0 = 0$$

Moreover, since N represents any value of x at all, the result $f'(N) = 0$ can be immediately generalized to $f'(x) = 0$. This proves the rule.

It is important to distinguish clearly between the statement $f'(x) = 0$ and the similar-looking but different statement $f'(x_0) = 0$. By $f'(x) = 0$, we mean that the derivative function f' has a zero value for *all* values of x; in writing $f'(x_0) = 0$, on the other hand, we are merely associating the zero value of the derivative with a particular value of x, namely, $x = x_0$.

As discussed before, the derivative of a function has its geometric counterpart in the slope of the curve. The graph of a constant function, say, a fixed-cost function $C_F = f(Q) = \$1,200$, is a horizontal straight line with a zero slope throughout. Correspondingly, the derivative must also be zero for all values of Q:

$$\frac{d}{dQ} C_F = \frac{d}{dQ} 1200 = 0$$

Power-Function Rule

The derivative of a power function $y = f(x) = x^n$ is nx^{n-1}. Symbolically, this is expressed as

$$\frac{d}{dx} x^n = nx^{n-1} \qquad \text{or} \qquad f'(x) = nx^{n-1} \tag{7.1}$$

Example 1   The derivative of $y = x^3$ is $\dfrac{dy}{dx} = \dfrac{d}{dx} x^3 = 3x^2$.

Example 2   The derivative of $y = x^9$ is $\dfrac{d}{dx} x^9 = 9x^8$.

This rule is valid for any real-valued power of x; that is, the exponent can be any real number. But we shall prove it only for the case where n is some positive integer. In the simplest case, that of $n = 1$, the function is $f(x) = x$, and according to the rule, the derivative is

$$f'(x) = \frac{d}{dx} x = 1(x^0) = 1$$

The proof of this result follows easily from the definition of $f'(N)$ in (6.14′). Given $f(x) = x$, the derivative value at any value of x, say, $x = N$, is

$$f'(N) = \lim_{x \to N} \frac{f(x) - f(N)}{x - N} = \lim_{x \to N} \frac{x - N}{x - N} = \lim_{x \to N} 1 = 1$$

Since N represents any value of x, it is permissible to write $f'(x) = 1$. This proves the rule for the case of $n = 1$. As the graphical counterpart of this result, we see that the function $y = f(x) = x$ plots as a 45° line, and it has a slope of $+1$ throughout.

For the cases of larger integers, $n = 2, 3, \ldots$, let us first note the following identities:

$$\frac{x^2 - N^2}{x - N} = x + N \qquad \text{[2 terms on the right]}$$

$$\frac{x^3 - N^3}{x - N} = x^2 + Nx + N^2 \qquad \text{[3 terms on the right]}$$

$$\vdots$$

$$\frac{x^n - N^n}{x - N} = x^{n-1} + Nx^{n-2} + N^2 x^{n-3} + \cdots + N^{n-1}$$
$$\text{[}n \text{ terms on the right]} \qquad \textbf{(7.2)}$$

On the basis of (7.2), we can express the derivative of a power function $f(x) = x^n$ at $x = N$ as follows:

$$f'(N) = \lim_{x \to N} \frac{f(x) - f(N)}{x - N} = \lim_{x \to N} \frac{x^n - N^n}{x - N}$$

$$= \lim_{x \to N} (x^{n-1} + Nx^{n-2} + \cdots + N^{n-1}) \qquad \text{[by (7.2)]}$$

$$= \lim_{x \to N} x^{n-1} + \lim_{x \to N} Nx^{n-2} + \cdots + \lim_{x \to N} N^{n-1} \qquad \text{[sum limit theorem]}$$

$$= N^{n-1} + N^{n-1} + \cdots + N^{n-1} \qquad \text{[a total of } n \text{ terms]}$$

$$= nN^{n-1} \qquad \textbf{(7.3)}$$

Again, N is any value of x; thus this last result can be generalized to

$$f'(x) = nx^{n-1}$$

which proves the rule for n, any positive integer.

As mentioned previously, this rule applies even when the exponent n in the power expression x^n is not a positive integer. The following examples serve to illustrate its application to the latter cases.

Example 3   Find the derivative of $y = x^0$. Applying (7.1), we find

$$\frac{d}{dx} x^0 = 0(x^{-1}) = 0$$

Example 4   Find the derivative of $y = 1/x^3$. This involves the reciprocal of a power, but by rewriting the function as $y = x^{-3}$, we can again apply (7.1) to get the derivative:

$$\frac{d}{dx} x^{-3} = -3x^{-4} \qquad \left[= \frac{-3}{x^4} \right]$$

Example 5

Find the derivative of $y = \sqrt{x}$. A square root is involved in this case, but since $\sqrt{x} = x^{1/2}$, the derivative can be found as follows:

$$\frac{d}{dx}x^{1/2} = \frac{1}{2}x^{-1/2} \qquad \left[= \frac{1}{2\sqrt{x}} = \frac{\sqrt{x}}{2x} \right]$$

Derivatives are themselves functions of the independent variable x. In Example 1, for instance, the derivative is $dy/dx = 3x^2$, or $f'(x) = 3x^2$, so that a different value of x will result in a different value of the derivative, such as

$$f'(1) = 3(1)^2 = 3 \qquad f'(2) = 3(2)^2 = 12$$

These specific values of the derivative can be expressed alternatively as

$$\left.\frac{dy}{dx}\right|_{x=1} = 3 \qquad \left.\frac{dy}{dx}\right|_{x=2} = 12$$

but the notations $f'(1)$ and $f'(2)$ are obviously preferable because of their simplicity.

It is of the utmost importance to realize that, to find the derivative values $f'(1)$, $f'(2)$, etc., we must *first* differentiate the function $f(x)$, to get the derivative function $f'(x)$, and *then* let x assume specific values in $f'(x)$. To substitute specific values of x into the primitive function $f(x)$ prior to differentiation is definitely not permissible. As an illustration, if we let $x = 1$ in the function of Example 1 before differentiation, the function will degenerate into $y = x = 1$—a constant function—which will yield a zero derivative rather than the correct answer of $f'(x) = 3x^2$.

Power-Function Rule Generalized

When a multiplicative constant c appears in the power function, so that $f(x) = cx^n$, its derivative is

$$\frac{d}{dx}cx^n = cnx^{n-1} \qquad \text{or} \qquad f'(x) = cnx^{n-1}$$

This result shows that, in differentiating cx^n, we can simply retain the multiplicative constant c intact and then differentiate the term x^n according to (7.1).

Example 6

Given $y = 2x$, we have $dy/dx = 2x^0 = 2$.

Example 7

Given $f(x) = 4x^3$, the derivative is $f'(x) = 12x^2$.

Example 8

The derivative of $f(x) = 3x^{-2}$ is $f'(x) = -6x^{-3}$.

For a proof of this new rule, consider the fact that for any value of x, say, $x = N$, the value of the derivative of $f(x) = cx^n$ is

$$f'(N) = \lim_{x \to N} \frac{f(x) - f(N)}{x - N} = \lim_{x \to N} \frac{cx^n - cN^n}{x - N} = \lim_{x \to N} c\left(\frac{x^n - N^n}{x - N}\right)$$

$$= \lim_{x \to N} c \lim_{x \to N} \frac{x^n - N^n}{x - N} \qquad \text{[product limit theorem]}$$

$$= c \lim_{x \to N} \frac{x^n - N^n}{x - N} \qquad \text{[limit of a constant]}$$

$$= cnN^{n-1} \qquad \text{[from (7.3)]}$$

In the view that N is any value of x, this last result can be generalized immediately to $f'(x) = cnx^{n-1}$, which proves the rule.

EXERCISE 7.1

1. Find the derivative of each of the following functions:

   (a) $y = x^{12}$ (c) $y = 7x^5$ (e) $w = -4u^{1/2}$

   (b) $y = 63$ (d) $w = 3u^{-1}$ (f) $w = 4u^{1/4}$

2. Find the following:

   (a) $\dfrac{d}{dx}(-x^{-4})$ (c) $\dfrac{d}{dw}5w^4$ (e) $\dfrac{d}{du}au^b$

   (b) $\dfrac{d}{dx}9x^{1/3}$ (d) $\dfrac{d}{dx}cx^2$ (f) $\dfrac{d}{du}-au^{-b}$

3. Find $f'(1)$ and $f'(2)$ from the following functions:

   (a) $y = f(x) = 18x$ (c) $f(x) = -5x^{-2}$ (e) $f(w) = 6w^{1/3}$

   (b) $y = f(x) = cx^3$ (d) $f(x) = \frac{3}{4}x^{4/3}$ (f) $f(w) = -3w^{-1/6}$

4. Graph a function $f(x)$ that gives rise to the derivative function $f'(x) = 0$. Then graph a function $g(x)$ characterized by $g'(x_0) = 0$.

7.2 Rules of Differentiation Involving Two or More Functions of the Same Variable

The three rules presented in Sec. 7.1 are each concerned with a single given function $f(x)$. Now suppose that we have two *differentiable* functions of the same variable x, say, $f(x)$ and $g(x)$, and we want to differentiate the sum, difference, product, or quotient formed with these two functions. In such circumstances, are there appropriate rules that apply? More concretely, given two functions—say, $f(x) = 3x^2$ and $g(x) = 9x^{12}$—how do we get the derivative of, say, $3x^2 + 9x^{12}$, or the derivative of $(3x^2)(9x^{12})$?

Sum-Difference Rule

The derivative of a sum (difference) of two functions is the sum (difference) of the derivatives of the two functions:

$$\frac{d}{dx}[f(x) \pm g(x)] = \frac{d}{dx}f(x) \pm \frac{d}{dx}g(x) = f'(x) \pm g'(x)$$

The proof of this again involves the application of the definition of a derivative and of the various limit theorems. We shall omit the proof and, instead, merely verify its validity and illustrate its application.

Example 1   From the function $y = 14x^3$, we can obtain the derivative $dy/dx = 42x^2$. But $14x^3 = 5x^3 + 9x^3$, so that y may be regarded as the sum of two functions $f(x) = 5x^3$ and $g(x) = 9x^3$. According to the sum rule, we then have

$$\frac{dy}{dx} = \frac{d}{dx}(5x^3 + 9x^3) = \frac{d}{dx}5x^3 + \frac{d}{dx}9x^3 = 15x^2 + 27x^2 = 42x^2$$

which is identical with our earlier result.

This rule, which we stated in terms of two functions, can easily be extended to more functions. Thus, it is also valid to write

$$\frac{d}{dx}[f(x) \pm g(x) \pm h(x)] = f'(x) \pm g'(x) \pm h'(x)$$

Example 2

The function cited in Example 1, $y = 14x^3$, can be written as $y = 2x^3 + 13x^3 - x^3$. The derivative of the latter, according to the sum-difference rule, is

$$\frac{dy}{dx} = \frac{d}{dx}(2x^3 + 13x^3 - x^3) = 6x^2 + 39x^2 - 3x^2 = 42x^2$$

which again checks with the previous answer.

This rule is of great practical importance. With it at our disposal, it is now possible to find the derivative of any polynomial function, since the latter is nothing but a sum of power functions.

Example 3

$$\frac{d}{dx}(ax^2 + bx + c) = 2ax + b$$

Example 4

$$\frac{d}{dx}(7x^4 + 2x^3 - 3x + 37) = 28x^3 + 6x^2 - 3 + 0 = 28x^3 + 6x^2 - 3$$

Note that in Examples 3 and 4 the constants c and 37 do not really produce any effect on the derivative, because the derivative of a constant term is zero. In contrast to the *multiplicative* constant, which is retained during differentiation, the *additive* constant drops out. This fact provides the mathematical explanation of the well-known economic principle that the fixed cost of a firm does not affect its marginal cost. Given a short-run total-cost function

$$C = Q^3 - 4Q^2 + 10Q + 75$$

the marginal-cost function (for infinitesimal output change) is the limit of the quotient $\Delta C/\Delta Q$, or the derivative of the C function:

$$\frac{dC}{dQ} = 3Q^2 - 8Q + 10$$

whereas the fixed cost is represented by the additive constant 75. Since the latter drops out during the process of deriving dC/dQ, the magnitude of the fixed cost obviously cannot affect the marginal cost.

In general, if a primitive function $y = f(x)$ represents a *total* function, then the derivative function dy/dx is its *marginal* function. Both functions can, of course, be plotted against the variable x graphically; and because of the correspondence between the derivative of a function and the slope of its curve, for each value of x the marginal function should show the slope of the total function at that value of x. In Fig. 7.1a, a linear (constant-slope) total function is seen to have a constant marginal function. On the other hand, the nonlinear (varying-slope) total function in Fig. 7.1b gives rise to a curved marginal function, which lies below (above) the horizontal axis when the total function is negatively (positively) sloped. And, finally, the reader may note from Fig. 7.1c (cf. Fig. 6.5) that

FIGURE 7.1

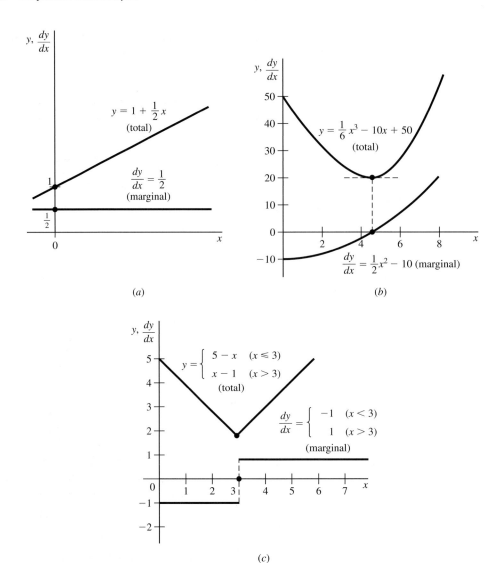

(a)

(b)

(c)

"nonsmoothness" of a total function will result in a gap (discontinuity) in the marginal or derivative function. This is in sharp contrast to the everywhere-smooth total function in Fig. 7.1*b* which gives rise to a continuous marginal function. For this reason, the *smoothness* of a *primitive* function can be linked to the *continuity* of its *derivative* function. In particular, instead of saying that a certain function is smooth (and differentiable) everywhere, we may alternatively characterize it as a function with a continuous derivative function, and refer to it as a *continuously differentiable* function.

The following notations are often used to denote the continuity and the continuous differentiability of a function *f*:

$$f \in C^{(0)} \quad \text{or} \quad f \in C: \qquad f \text{ is continuous}$$

$$f \in C^{(1)} \quad \text{or} \quad f \in C': \qquad f \text{ is continuously differentiable}$$

where $C^{(0)}$, or simply C, is the symbol for the set of all continuous functions, and $C^{(1)}$, or C', is the symbol for the set of all continuously differentiable functions.

Product Rule

The derivative of the product of two (differentiable) functions is equal to the first function times the derivative of the second function plus the second function times the derivative of the first function:

$$\frac{d}{dx}[f(x)g(x)] = f(x)\frac{d}{dx}g(x) + g(x)\frac{d}{dx}f(x)$$

$$= f(x)g'(x) + g(x)f'(x) \qquad (7.4)$$

It is also possible, of course, to rearrange the terms and express the rule as

$$\frac{d}{dx}[f(x)g(x)] = f'(x)g(x) + f(x)g'(x) \qquad (7.4')$$

Example 5 Find the derivative of $y = (2x + 3)(3x^2)$. Let $f(x) = 2x + 3$ and $g(x) = 3x^2$. Then it follows that $f'(x) = 2$ and $g'(x) = 6x$, and according to (7.4) the desired derivative is

$$\frac{d}{dx}[(2x + 3)(3x^2)] = (2x + 3)(6x) + (3x^2)(2) = 18x^2 + 18x$$

This result can be checked by first multiplying out $f(x)g(x)$ and then taking the derivative of the product polynomial. The product polynomial is in this case $f(x)g(x) = (2x + 3)(3x^2) = 6x^3 + 9x^2$, and direct differentiation does yield the same derivative, $18x^2 + 18x$.

The important point to remember is that the derivative of a product of two functions is *not* the simple product of the two separate derivatives. Instead, it is a weighted sum of $f'(x)$ and $g'(x)$, the weights being $g(x)$ and $f(x)$, respectively. Since this differs from what intuitive generalization leads one to expect, let us produce a proof for (7.4). According to (6.13), the value of the derivative of $f(x)g(x)$ when $x = N$ should be

$$\frac{d}{dx}[f(x)g(x)]\Big|_{x=N} = \lim_{x \to N} \frac{f(x)g(x) - f(N)g(N)}{x - N} \qquad (7.5)$$

But, by adding *and* subtracting $f(x)g(N)$ in the numerator (thereby leaving the original magnitude unchanged), we can transform the quotient on the right of (7.5) as follows:

$$\frac{f(x)g(x) - f(x)g(N) + f(x)g(N) - f(N)g(N)}{x - N}$$

$$= f(x)\frac{g(x) - g(N)}{x - N} + g(N)\frac{f(x) - f(N)}{x - N}$$

Substituting this for the quotient on the right of (7.5) and taking its limit, we then get

$$\frac{d}{dx}[f(x)g(x)]\Big|_{x=N} = \lim_{x \to N} f(x) \lim_{x \to N} \frac{g(x) - g(N)}{x - N}$$

$$+ \lim_{x \to N} g(N) \lim_{x \to N} \frac{f(x) - f(N)}{x - N} \qquad (7.5')$$

The four limit expressions in (7.5′) are easily evaluated. The first one is $f(N)$, and the third is $g(N)$ (limit of a constant). The remaining two are, according to (6.13), respectively, $g'(N)$ and $f'(N)$. Thus (7.5′) reduces to

$$\frac{d}{dx}[f(x)g(x)]\Big|_{x=N} = f(N)g'(N) + g(N)f'(N) \qquad \textbf{(7.5″)}$$

And, since N represents any value of x, (7.5″) remains valid if we replace every N symbol by x. This proves the rule.

As an extension of the rule to the case of *three* functions, we have

$$\frac{d}{dx}[f(x)g(x)h(x)] = f'(x)g(x)h(x) + f(x)g'(x)h(x)$$
$$+ f(x)g(x)h'(x) \qquad \text{[cf. (7.4′)]} \qquad \textbf{(7.6)}$$

In words, the derivative of the product of three functions is equal to the product of the second and third functions times the derivative of the first, plus the product of the first and third functions times the derivative of the second, plus the product of the first and second functions times the derivative of the third. This result can be derived by the repeated application of (7.4). First treat the product $g(x)h(x)$ as a single function, say, $\phi(x)$, so that the original product of three functions will become a product of *two* functions, $f(x)\phi(x)$. To this, (7.4) is applicable. After the derivative of $f(x)\phi(x)$ is obtained, we may reapply (7.4) to the product $g(x)h(x) \equiv \phi(x)$ to get $\phi'(x)$. Then (7.6) will follow. The details are left to you as an exercise.

The validity of a rule is one thing; its serviceability is something else. Why do we need the product rule when we can resort to the alternative procedure of multiplying out the two functions $f(x)$ and $g(x)$ and then taking the derivative of the product directly? One answer to this question is that the alternative procedure is applicable only to *specific* (numerical or parametric) functions, whereas the product rule is applicable even when the functions are given in the *general* form. Let us illustrate with an economic example.

Finding Marginal-Revenue Function from Average-Revenue Function

If we are given an average-revenue (AR) function in specific form,

$$\text{AR} = 15 - Q$$

the marginal-revenue (MR) function can be found by first multiplying AR by Q to get the total-revenue (R) function:

$$R \equiv \text{AR} \cdot Q = (15 - Q)Q = 15Q - Q^2$$

and then differentiating R:

$$\text{MR} \equiv \frac{dR}{dQ} = 15 - 2Q$$

But if the AR function is given in the general form $\text{AR} = f(Q)$, then the total-revenue function will also be in a general form:

$$R \equiv \text{AR} \cdot Q = f(Q) \cdot Q$$

and therefore the "multiply out" approach will be to no avail. However, because R is a product of two functions of Q, namely, $f(Q)$ and Q itself, the product rule can be put to work. Thus we can differentiate R to get the MR function as follows:

$$\text{MR} \equiv \frac{dR}{dQ} = f(Q) \cdot 1 + Q \cdot f'(Q) = f(Q) + Qf'(Q) \qquad \textbf{(7.7)}$$

However, can such a general result tell us anything significant about the MR? Indeed it can. Recalling that $f(Q)$ denotes the AR function, let us rearrange (7.7) and write

$$\text{MR} - \text{AR} = \text{MR} - f(Q) = Qf'(Q) \qquad \textbf{(7.7′)}$$

This gives us an important relationship between MR and AR: namely, they will always differ by the amount $Qf'(Q)$.

It remains to examine the expression $Qf'(Q)$. Its first component Q denotes output and is always nonnegative. The other component, $f'(Q)$, represents the slope of the AR curve plotted against Q. Since "average revenue" and "price" are but different names for the same thing:

$$\text{AR} \equiv \frac{R}{Q} \equiv \frac{PQ}{Q} \equiv P$$

the AR curve can also be regarded as a curve relating price P to output Q: $P = f(Q)$. Viewed in this light, the AR curve is simply the *inverse* of the demand curve for the product of the firm, i.e., the demand curve plotted after the P and Q axes are reversed. Under pure competition, the AR curve is a horizontal straight line, so that $f'(Q) = 0$ and, from (7.7′), MR − AR = 0 for all possible values of Q. Thus the MR curve and the AR curve must coincide. Under imperfect competition, on the other hand, the AR curve is normally downward-sloping, as in Fig. 7.2, so that $f'(Q) < 0$ and, from (7.7′), MR − AR < 0 for all positive levels of output. In this case, the MR curve must lie below the AR curve.

The conclusion just stated is *qualitative* in nature; it concerns only the relative positions of the two curves. But (7.7′) also furnishes the *quantitative* information that the MR curve will fall short of the AR curve at any output level Q by precisely the amount $Qf'(Q)$. Let us look at Fig. 7.2 again and consider the particular output level N. For that output, the

FIGURE 7.2

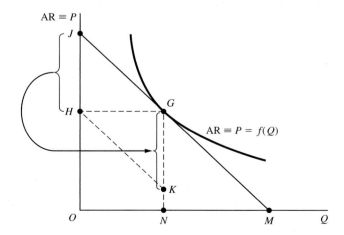

expression $Qf'(Q)$ specifically becomes $Nf'(N)$; if we can find the magnitude of $Nf'(N)$ in the diagram, we shall know how far below the average-revenue point G the corresponding marginal-revenue point must lie.

The magnitude of N is already specified. And $f'(N)$ is simply the slope of the AR curve at point G (where $Q = N$), that is, the slope of the tangent line JM measured by the ratio of two distances OJ/OM. However, we see that $OJ/OM = HJ/HG$; besides, distance HG is precisely the amount of output under consideration, N. Thus the distance $Nf'(N)$, by which the MR curve must lie below the AR curve at output N, is

$$Nf'(N) = HG\frac{HJ}{HG} = HJ$$

Accordingly, if we mark a vertical distance $KG = HJ$ directly below point G, then point K must be a point on the MR curve. (A simple way of accurately plotting KG is to draw a straight line passing through point H and parallel to JG; point K is where that line intersects the vertical line NG.)

The same procedure can be used to locate other points on the MR curve. All we must do, for any chosen point G' on the curve, is first to draw a tangent to the AR curve at G' that will meet the vertical axis at some point J'. Then draw a horizontal line from G' to the vertical axis, and label the intersection with the axis as H'. If we mark a vertical distance $K'G' = H'J'$ directly below point G', then the point K' will be a point on the MR curve. This is the graphical way of deriving an MR curve from a given AR curve. Strictly speaking, the accurate drawing of a tangent line requires a knowledge of the value of the derivative at the relevant output, that is, $f'(N)$; hence the graphical method just outlined cannot quite exist by itself. An important exception is the case of a linear AR curve, where the tangent to any point on the curve is simply the given line itself, so that there is in effect no need to draw any tangent at all. Then the graphical method will apply in a straightforward way.

Quotient Rule

The derivative of the quotient of two functions, $f(x)/g(x)$, is

$$\frac{d}{dx}\frac{f(x)}{g(x)} = \frac{f'(x)g(x) - f(x)g'(x)}{g^2(x)}$$

In the numerator of the right-hand expression, we find two product terms, each involving the derivative of only one of the two original functions. Note that $f'(x)$ appears in the positive term, and $g'(x)$ in the negative term. The denominator consists of the square of the function $g(x)$; that is, $g^2(x) \equiv [g(x)]^2$.

Example 6

$$\frac{d}{dx}\left(\frac{2x-3}{x+1}\right) = \frac{2(x+1) - (2x-3)(1)}{(x+1)^2} = \frac{5}{(x+1)^2}$$

Example 7

$$\frac{d}{dx}\left(\frac{5x}{x^2+1}\right) = \frac{5(x^2+1) - 5x(2x)}{(x^2+1)^2} = \frac{5(1-x^2)}{(x^2+1)^2}$$

Example 8

$$\frac{d}{dx}\left(\frac{ax^2+b}{cx}\right) = \frac{2ax(cx) - (ax^2+b)(c)}{(cx)^2}$$

$$= \frac{c(ax^2-b)}{(cx)^2} = \frac{ax^2-b}{cx^2}$$

This rule can be proved as follows. For any value of $x = N$, we have

$$\frac{d}{dx}\frac{f(x)}{g(x)}\bigg|_{x=N} = \lim_{x \to N} \frac{f(x)/g(x) - f(N)/g(N)}{x - N} \tag{7.8}$$

The quotient expression following the limit sign can be rewritten in the form

$$\frac{f(x)g(N) - f(N)g(x)}{g(x)g(N)} \frac{1}{x - N}$$

By adding *and* subtracting $f(N)g(N)$ in the numerator and rearranging, we can further transform the expression to

$$\frac{1}{g(x)g(N)} \left[\frac{f(x)g(N) - f(N)g(N) + f(N)g(N) - f(N)g(x)}{x - N} \right]$$

$$= \frac{1}{g(x)g(N)} \left[g(N)\frac{f(x) - f(N)}{x - N} - f(N)\frac{g(x) - g(N)}{x - N} \right]$$

Substituting this result into (7.8) and taking the limit, we then have

$$\frac{d}{dx}\frac{f(x)}{g(x)}\bigg|_{x=N} = \lim_{x \to N} \frac{1}{g(x)g(N)} \left[\lim_{x \to N} g(N) \lim_{x \to N} \frac{f(x) - f(N)}{x - N} \right.$$

$$\left. - \lim_{x \to N} f(N) \lim_{x \to N} \frac{g(x) - g(N)}{x - N} \right]$$

$$= \frac{1}{g^2(N)}[g(N)f'(N) - f(N)g'(N)] \qquad \text{[by (6.13)]}$$

which can be generalized by replacing the symbol N with x, because N represents any value of x. This proves the quotient rule.

Relationship Between Marginal-Cost and Average-Cost Functions

As an economic application of the quotient rule, let us consider the rate of change of average cost when output varies.

Given a total-cost function $C = C(Q)$, the average-cost (AC) function is a quotient of two functions of Q, since $\text{AC} \equiv C(Q)/Q$, defined as long as $Q > 0$. Therefore, the rate of change of AC with respect to Q can be found by differentiating AC:

$$\frac{d}{dQ}\frac{C(Q)}{Q} = \frac{[C'(Q) \cdot Q - C(Q) \cdot 1]}{Q^2} = \frac{1}{Q}\left[C'(Q) - \frac{C(Q)}{Q}\right] \tag{7.9}$$

From this it follows that, for $Q > 0$,

$$\frac{d}{dQ}\frac{C(Q)}{Q} \gtreqless 0 \qquad \text{if} \qquad C'(Q) \gtreqless \frac{C(Q)}{Q} \tag{7.10}$$

Since the derivative $C'(Q)$ represents the marginal-cost (MC) function, and $C(Q)/Q$ represents the AC function, the economic meaning of (7.10) is: The slope of the AC

FIGURE 7.3

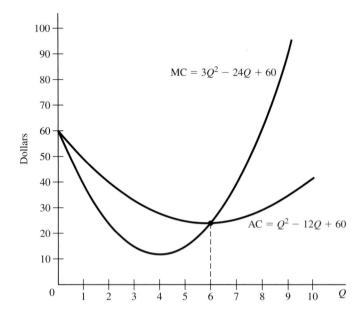

curve will be positive, zero, or negative if and only if the marginal-cost curve lies above, intersects, or lies below the AC curve. This is illustrated in Fig. 7.3, where the MC and AC functions plotted are based on the specific total-cost function

$$C = Q^3 - 12Q^2 + 60Q$$

To the left of $Q = 6$, AC is declining, and thus MC lies below it; to the right, the opposite is true. At $Q = 6$, AC has a slope of zero, and MC and AC have the same value.[†]

The qualitative conclusion in (7.10) is stated explicitly in terms of cost functions. However, its validity remains unaffected if we interpret $C(Q)$ as *any other* differentiable total function, with $C(Q)/Q$ and $C'(Q)$ as its corresponding average and marginal functions. Thus this result gives us a *general* marginal-average relationship. In particular, we may point out, the fact that MR lies below AR when AR is downward-sloping, as discussed in connection with Fig. 7.2, is nothing but a special case of the general result in (7.10).

[†] Note that (7.10) does *not* state that, when AC is negatively sloped, MC must also be negatively sloped; it merely says that AC must exceed MC in that circumstance. At $Q = 5$ in Fig. 7.3, for instance, AC is declining but MC is rising, so that their slopes will have opposite signs.

EXERCISE 7.2

1. Given the total-cost function $C = Q^3 - 5Q^2 + 12Q + 75$, write out a variable-cost (VC) function. Find the derivative of the VC function, and interpret the economic meaning of that derivative.

2. Given the average-cost function $AC = Q^2 - 4Q + 174$, find the MC function. Is the given function more appropriate as a long-run or a short-run function? Why?

3. Differentiate the following by using the product rule:

   (a) $(9x^2 - 2)(3x + 1)$ (c) $x^2(4x + 6)$ (e) $(2 - 3x)(1 + x)(x + 2)$

   (b) $(3x + 10)(6x^2 - 7x)$ (d) $(ax - b)(cx^2)$ (f) $(x^2 + 3)x^{-1}$

4. (a) Given AR $= 60 - 3Q$, plot the average-revenue curve, and then find the MR curve by the method used in Fig. 7.2.

   (b) Find the total-revenue function and the marginal-revenue function mathematically from the given AR function.

   (c) Does the graphically derived MR curve in (a) check with the mathematically derived MR function in (b)?

   (d) Comparing the AR and MR functions, what can you conclude about their relative slopes?

5. Provide a mathematical proof for the general result that, given a *linear* average curve, the corresponding marginal curve must have the same vertical intercept but will be twice as steep as the average curve.

6. Prove the result in (7.6) by first treating $g(x)h(x)$ as a single function, $g(x)h(x) \equiv \phi(x)$, and then applying the product rule (7.4).

7. Find the derivatives of:

   (a) $(x^2 + 3)/x$ (c) $6x/(x + 5)$

   (b) $(x + 9)/x$ (d) $(ax^2 + b)/(cx + d)$

8. Given the function $f(x) = ax + b$, find the derivatives of:

   (a) $f(x)$ (b) $xf(x)$ (c) $1/f(x)$ (d) $f(x)/x$

9. (a) Is it true that $f \in C' \Rightarrow f \in C$?

   (b) Is it true that $f \in C \Rightarrow f \in C'$?

10. Find the marginal and average functions for the following total functions and graph the results.

    Total-cost function:

    (a) $C = 3Q^2 + 7Q + 12$

    Total-revenue function:

    (b) $R = 10Q - Q^2$

    Total-product function:

    (c) $Q = aL + bL^2 - cL^3$ $(a, b, c > 0)$

7.3 Rules of Differentiation Involving Functions of Different Variables

In Sec. 7.2, we discussed the rules of differentiation of a sum, difference, product, or quotient of two (or more) differentiable functions of the same variable. Now we shall consider cases where there are two or more differentiable functions, each of which has a *distinct* independent variable.

Chain Rule

If we have a differentiable function $z = f(y)$, where y is in turn a differentiable function of another variable x, say, $y = g(x)$, then the derivative of z with respect to x is equal to the derivative of z with respect to y, times the derivative of y with respect to x. Expressed symbolically,

$$\frac{dz}{dx} = \frac{dz}{dy}\frac{dy}{dx} = f'(y)g'(x) \tag{7.11}$$

This rule, known as the *chain rule,* appeals easily to intuition. Given a Δx, there must result a corresponding Δy via the function $y = g(x)$, but this Δy will in turn bring about a Δz via the function $z = f(y)$. Thus there is a "chain reaction" as follows:

$$\Delta x \xrightarrow{\text{via } g} \Delta y \xrightarrow{\text{via } f} \Delta z$$

The two links in this chain entail two difference quotients, $\Delta y/\Delta x$ and $\Delta z/\Delta y$, but when they are multiplied, the Δy will cancel itself out, and we end up with

$$\frac{\Delta z}{\Delta y}\frac{\Delta y}{\Delta x} = \frac{\Delta z}{\Delta x}$$

a difference quotient that relates Δz to Δx. If we take the limit of these difference quotients as $\Delta x \to 0$ (which implies $\Delta y \to 0$), each difference quotient will turn into a derivative; i.e., we shall have $(dz/dy)(dy/dx) = dz/dx$. This is precisely the result in (7.11).

In view of the function $y = g(x)$, we can express the function $z = f(y)$ as $z = f[g(x)]$, where the contiguous appearance of the two function symbols f and g indicates that this is a *composite function* (function of a function). It is for this reason that the chain rule is also referred to as the *composite-function rule* or *function-of-a-function rule.*

The extension of the chain rule to three or more functions is straightforward. If we have $z = f(y)$, $y = g(x)$, and $x = h(w)$, then

$$\frac{dz}{dw} = \frac{dz}{dy}\frac{dy}{dx}\frac{dx}{dw} = f'(y)g'(x)h'(w)$$

and similarly for cases in which more functions are involved.

Example 1   If $z = 3y^2$, where $y = 2x + 5$, then

$$\frac{dz}{dx} = \frac{dz}{dy}\frac{dy}{dx} = 6y(2) = 12y = 12(2x + 5)$$

Example 2   If $z = y - 3$, where $y = x^3$, then

$$\frac{dz}{dx} = 1(3x^2) = 3x^2$$

Example 3   The usefulness of this rule can best be appreciated when we must differentiate a function such as $z = (x^2 + 3x - 2)^{17}$. Without the chain rule at our disposal, dz/dx can be found only via the laborious route of first multiplying out the 17th-power expression. With the chain rule, however, we can take a shortcut by defining a new, *intermediate* variable $y = x^2 + 3x - 2$, so that we get in effect two functions linked in a chain:

$$z = y^{17} \quad \text{and} \quad y = x^2 + 3x - 2$$

The derivative dz/dx can then be found as follows:

$$\frac{dz}{dx} = \frac{dz}{dy}\frac{dy}{dx} = 17y^{16}(2x + 3) = 17(x^2 + 3x - 2)^{16}(2x + 3)$$

Example 4

Given a total-revenue function of a firm $R = f(Q)$, where output Q is a function of labor input L, or $Q = g(L)$, find dR/dL. By the chain rule, we have

$$\frac{dR}{dL} = \frac{dR}{dQ}\frac{dQ}{dL} = f'(Q)g'(L)$$

Translated into economic terms, dR/dQ is the MR function and dQ/dL is the marginal-physical-product-of-labor (MPP_L) function. Similarly, dR/dL has the connotation of the marginal-revenue-product-of-labor (MRP_L) function. Thus the result shown constitutes the mathematical statement of the well-known result in economics that $MRP_L = MR \cdot MPP_L$.

Inverse-Function Rule

If the function $y = f(x)$ represents a one-to-one mapping, i.e., if the function is such that each value of y is associated with a unique value of x, the function f will have an *inverse function $x = f^{-1}(y)$* (read: "x is an inverse function of y"). Here, the symbol f^{-1} is a function symbol which, like the derivative-function symbol f', signifies a function related to the function f; it does *not* mean the reciprocal of the function $f(x)$.

What the existence of an inverse function essentially means is that, in this case, not only will a given value of x yield a unique value of y [that is, $y = f(x)$], but also a given value of y will yield a unique value of x. To take a nonnumerical instance, we may exemplify the one-to-one mapping by the mapping from the set of all husbands to the set of all wives in a monogamous society. Each husband has a unique wife, and each wife has a unique husband. In contrast, the mapping from the set of all fathers to the set of all sons is not one-to-one, because a father may have more than one son, albeit each son has a unique father.

When x and y refer specifically to numbers, the property of one-to-one mapping is seen to be unique to the class of functions known as *strictly monotonic* (or *monotone*) *functions*. Given a function $f(x)$, if successively larger values of the independent variable x *always* lead to successively larger values of $f(x)$, that is, if

$$x_1 > x_2 \Rightarrow f(x_1) > f(x_2)$$

then the function f is said to be a *strictly increasing* function. If successive increases in x *always* lead to successive decreases in $f(x)$, that is, if

$$x_1 > x_2 \Rightarrow f(x_1) < f(x_2)$$

on the other hand, the function is said to be a *strictly decreasing* function. In either of these cases, an inverse function f^{-1} exists.[†]

A practical way of ascertaining the strict monotonicity of a given function $y = f(x)$ is to check whether the derivative $f'(x)$ always adheres to the same algebraic sign (not zero) for all values of x. Geometrically, this means that its slope is either always upward or always

---

[†] By omitting the adverb *strictly*, we can define *monotonic* (or *monotone*) functions as follows: An *increasing function* is a function with the property that

$$x_1 > x_2 \Rightarrow f(x_1) \geq f(x_2) \qquad \text{[with the weak inequality } \geq \text{]}$$

and a *decreasing function* is one with the property that

$$x_1 > x_2 \Rightarrow f(x_1) \leq f(x_2) \qquad \text{[with the weak inequality } \leq \text{]}$$

Note that, under this definition, an ascending (descending) step function qualifies as an increasing (decreasing) function, despite the fact that its graph contains horizontal segments. Since such functions do not have a one-to-one mapping, they do not have inverse functions.

downward. Thus a firm's demand curve $Q = f(P)$ that has a negative slope throughout is strictly decreasing. As such, it has an inverse function $P = f^{-1}(Q)$, which, as mentioned previously, gives the average-revenue curve of the firm, since $P \equiv$ AR.

Example 5

The function

$$y = 5x + 25$$

has the derivative $dy/dx = 5$, which is positive regardless of the value of x; thus the function is strictly increasing. It follows that an inverse function exists. In the present case, the inverse function is easily found by solving the given equation $y = 5x + 25$ for x. The result is the function

$$x = \tfrac{1}{5}y - 5$$

It is interesting to note that this inverse function is also strictly increasing, because $dx/dy = \tfrac{1}{5} > 0$ for all values of y.

Generally speaking, if an inverse function exists, the original and the inverse functions must both be strictly monotonic. Moreover, if f^{-1} is the inverse function of f, then f must be the inverse function of f^{-1}; that is, f and f^{-1} must be inverse functions of each other.

It is easy to verify that the graph of $y = f(x)$ and that of $x = f^{-1}(y)$ are one and the same, only with the axes reversed. If one lays the x axis of the f^{-1} graph over the x axis of the f graph (and similarly for the y axis), the two curves will coincide. On the other hand, if the x axis of the f^{-1} graph is laid over the y axis of the f graph (and vice versa), the two curves will become *mirror images* of each other with reference to the 45° line drawn through the origin. This mirror-image relationship provides us with an easy way of graphing the inverse function f^{-1}, once the graph of the original function f is given. (You should try this with the two functions in Example 5.)

For inverse functions, the rule of differentiation is

$$\frac{dx}{dy} = \frac{1}{dy/dx}$$

This means that the derivative of the inverse function is the reciprocal of the derivative of the original function; as such, dx/dy must take the same sign as dy/dx, so that if f is strictly increasing (decreasing), then so must be f^{-1}.

As a verification of this rule, we can refer back to Example 5, where dy/dx was found to be 5, and dx/dy equal to $\tfrac{1}{5}$. These two derivatives are indeed reciprocal to each other and have the same sign.

In that simple example, the inverse function is relatively easy to obtain, so that its derivative dx/dy can be found directly from the inverse function. As Example 6 shows, however, the inverse function is sometimes difficult to express explicitly, and thus direct differentiation may not be practicable. The usefulness of the inverse-function rule then becomes more fully apparent.

Example 6

Given $y = x^5 + x$, find dx/dy. First of all, since

$$\frac{dy}{dx} = 5x^4 + 1 > 0$$

for any value of x, the given function is strictly increasing, and an inverse function exists. To solve the given equation for x may not be such an easy task, but the derivative of the inverse function can nevertheless be found quickly by use of the inverse-function rule:

$$\frac{dx}{dy} = \frac{1}{dy/dx} = \frac{1}{5x^4 + 1}$$

The inverse-function rule is, strictly speaking, applicable only when the function involved is a one-to-one mapping. In fact, however, we do have some leeway. For instance, when dealing with a U-shaped curve (not strictly monotonic), we may consider the downward- and the upward-sloping segments of the curve as representing two *separate* functions, each with a restricted domain, and each being strictly monotonic in the restricted domain. To each of these, the inverse-function rule can then again be applied.

EXERCISE 7.3

1. Given $y = u^3 + 2u$, where $u = 5 - x^2$, find dy/dx by the chain rule.
2. Given $w = ay^2$ and $y = bx^2 + cx$, find dw/dx by the chain rule.
3. Use the chain rule to find dy/dx for the following:
   (a) $y = (3x^2 - 13)^3$ (b) $y = (7x^3 - 5)^9$ (c) $y = (ax + b)^5$
4. Given $y = (16x + 3)^{-2}$, use the chain rule to find dy/dx. Then rewrite the function as $y = 1/(16x + 3)^2$ and find dy/dx by the quotient rule. Are the answers identical?
5. Given $y = 7x + 21$, find its inverse function. Then find dy/dx and dx/dy, and verify the inverse-function rule. Also verify that the graphs of the two functions bear a mirror-image relationship to each other.
6. Are the following functions strictly monotonic?
   (a) $y = -x^6 + 5$ $(x > 0)$
   (b) $y = 4x^5 + x^3 + 3x$
   For each strictly monotonic function, find dx/dy by the inverse-function rule.

7.4 Partial Differentiation

Hitherto, we have considered only the derivatives of functions of a single independent variable. In comparative-static analysis, however, we are likely to encounter the situation in which several parameters appear in a model, so that the equilibrium value of each endogenous variable may be a function of more than one parameter. Therefore, as a final preparation for the application of the concept of derivative to comparative statics, we must learn how to find the derivative of a function of more than one variable.

Partial Derivatives

Let us consider a function

$$y = f(x_1, x_2, \ldots, x_n) \qquad (7.12)$$

where the variables x_i $(i = 1, 2, \ldots, n)$ are all *independent* of one another, so that each can vary by itself without affecting the others. If the variable x_1 undergoes a change Δx_1 while

$x_2, \ldots, x_n$ all remain fixed, there will be a corresponding change in y, namely, Δy. The difference quotient in this case can be expressed as

$$\frac{\Delta y}{\Delta x_1} = \frac{f(x_1 + \Delta x_1, x_2, \ldots, x_n) - f(x_1, x_2, \ldots, x_n)}{\Delta x_1} \qquad (7.13)$$

If we take the limit of $\Delta y / \Delta x_1$ as $\Delta x_1 \to 0$, that limit will constitute a derivative. We call it the *partial derivative* of y with respect to x_1, to indicate that all the other independent variables in the function are held constant when taking this particular derivative. Similar partial derivatives can be defined for infinitesimal changes in the other independent variables. The process of taking partial derivatives is called *partial differentiation.*

Partial derivatives are assigned distinctive symbols. In lieu of the letter d (as in dy/dx), we employ the symbol ∂, which is a variant of the Greek δ (lowercase delta). Thus we shall now write $\partial y / \partial x_i$, which is read: "the partial derivative of y with respect to x_i." The partial-derivative symbol sometimes is also written as $\dfrac{\partial}{\partial x_i} y$; in that case, its $\partial / \partial x_i$ part can be regarded as an operator symbol instructing us to take the partial derivative of (some function) with respect to the variable x_i. Since the function involved here is denoted in (7.12) by f, it is also permissible to write $\partial f / \partial x_i$.

Is there also a partial-derivative counterpart for the symbol $f'(x)$ that we used before? The answer is yes. Instead of f', however, we now use f_1, f_2, etc., where the subscript indicates which independent variable (alone) is being allowed to vary. If the function in (7.12) happens to be written in terms of unsubscripted variables, such as $y = f(u, v, w)$, then the partial derivatives may be denoted by f_u, f_v, and f_w rather than f_1, f_2, and f_3.

In line with these notations, and on the basis of (7.12) and (7.13), we can now define

$$f_1 \equiv \frac{\partial y}{\partial x_1} \equiv \lim_{\Delta x_1 \to 0} \frac{\Delta y}{\Delta x_1}$$

as the first in the set of n partial derivatives of the function f.

Techniques of Partial Differentiation

Partial differentiation differs from the previously discussed differentiation primarily in that we must hold $(n - 1)$ independent variables *constant* while allowing *one* variable to vary. Inasmuch as we have learned how to handle *constants* in differentiation, the actual differentiation should pose little problem.

Example 1

Given $y = f(x_1, x_2) = 3x_1^2 + x_1 x_2 + 4x_2^2$, find the partial derivatives. When finding $\partial y / \partial x_1$, (or f_1), we must bear in mind that x_2 is to be treated as a constant during differentiation. As such, x_2 will drop out in the process if it is an *additive* constant (such as the term $4x_2^2$) but will be retained if it is a *multiplicative* constant (such as in the term $x_1 x_2$). Thus we have

$$\frac{\partial y}{\partial x_1} \equiv f_1 = 6x_1 + x_2$$

Similarly, by treating x_1 as a constant, we find that

$$\frac{\partial y}{\partial x_2} \equiv f_2 = x_1 + 8x_2$$

Note that, like the primitive function f, both partial derivatives are themselves functions of the variables x_1 and x_2. That is, we may write them as two derived functions

$$f_1 = f_1(x_1, x_2) \quad \text{and} \quad f_2 = f_2(x_1, x_2)$$

For the point $(x_1, x_2) = (1, 3)$ in the domain of the function f, for example, the partial derivatives will take the following specific values:

$$f_1(1, 3) = 6(1) + 3 = 9 \quad \text{and} \quad f_2(1, 3) = 1 + 8(3) = 25$$

Example 2   Given $y = f(u, v) = (u + 4)(3u + 2v)$, the partial derivatives can be found by use of the product rule. By holding v constant, we have

$$f_u = (u + 4)(3) + 1(3u + 2v) = 2(3u + v + 6)$$

Similarly, by holding u constant, we find that

$$f_v = (u + 4)(2) + 0(3u + 2v) = 2(u + 4)$$

When $u = 2$ and $v = 1$, these derivatives will take the following values:

$$f_u(2, 1) = 2(13) = 26 \quad \text{and} \quad f_v(2, 1) = 2(6) = 12$$

Example 3   Given $y = (3u - 2v)/(u^2 + 3v)$, the partial derivatives can be found by use of the quotient rule:

$$\frac{\partial y}{\partial u} = \frac{3(u^2 + 3v) - 2u(3u - 2v)}{(u^2 + 3v)^2} = \frac{-3u^2 + 4uv + 9v}{(u^2 + 3v)^2}$$

$$\frac{\partial y}{\partial v} = \frac{-2(u^2 + 3v) - 3(3u - 2v)}{(u^2 + 3v)^2} = \frac{-u(2u + 9)}{(u^2 + 3v)^2}$$

Geometric Interpretation of Partial Derivatives

As a special type of derivative, a partial derivative is a measure of the instantaneous rates of change of some variable, and in that capacity it again has a geometric counterpart in the slope of a particular curve.

Let us consider a production function $Q = Q(K, L)$, where Q, K, and L denote output, capital input, and labor input, respectively. This function is a particular two-variable version of (7.12), with $n = 2$. We can therefore define two partial derivatives $\partial Q / \partial K$ (or Q_K) and $\partial Q / \partial L$ (or Q_L). The partial derivative Q_K relates to the rates of change of output with respect to infinitesimal changes in capital, while labor input is held constant. Thus Q_K symbolizes the marginal-physical-product-of-capital (MPP_K) function. Similarly, the partial derivative Q_L is the mathematical representation of the MPP_L function.

Geometrically, the production function $Q = Q(K, L)$ can be depicted by a *production surface* in a 3-space, such as is shown in Fig. 7.4. The variable Q is plotted vertically, so that for any point (K, L) in the base plane (KL plane), the height of the surface will indicate the output Q. The domain of the function should consist of the entire nonnegative quadrant of the base plane, but for our purposes it is sufficient to consider a subset of it, the

FIGURE 7.4

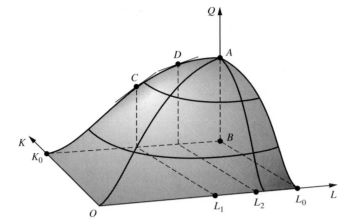

rectangle OK_0BL_0. As a consequence, only a small portion of the production surface is shown in the figure.

Let us now hold capital fixed at the level K_0 and consider only variations in the input L. By setting $K = K_0$, all points in our (curtailed) domain become irrelevant except those on the line segment K_0B. By the same token, only the curve K_0CDA (a cross section of the production surface) is germane to the present discussion. This curve represents a total-physical-product-of-labor (TPP_L) curve for a fixed amount of capital $K = K_0$; thus we may read from its slope the rate of change of Q with respect to changes in L while K is held constant. It is clear, therefore, that the slope of a curve such as K_0CDA represents the geometric counterpart of the partial derivative Q_L. Once again, we note that the slope of a total (TPP_L) curve is its corresponding marginal ($\text{MPP}_L \equiv Q_L$) curve.

As mentioned earlier, a partial derivative is a function of all the independent variables of the primitive function. That Q_L is a function of L is immediately obvious from the K_0CDA curve itself. When $L = L_1$, the value of Q_L is equal to the slope of the curve at point C; but when $L = L_2$, the relevant slope is the one at point D. Why is Q_L also a function of K? The answer is that K can be fixed at various levels, and for each fixed level of K, there results a different TPP_L curve (a different cross section of the production surface), with inevitable repercussions on the derivative Q_L. Hence Q_L is also a function of K.

An analogous interpretation can be given to the partial derivative Q_K. If the labor input is held constant instead of K (say, at the level of L_0), the line segment L_0B will be the relevant subset of the domain, and the curve L_0A will indicate the relevant subset of the production surface. The partial derivative Q_K can then be interpreted as the slope of the curve L_0A—bearing in mind that the K axis extends from southeast to northwest in Fig. 7.4. It should be noted that Q_K is again a function of both the variables L and K.

Gradient Vector

All the partial derivatives of a function $y = f(x_1, x_2, \ldots, x_n)$ can be collected under a single mathematical entity called the *gradient vector*, or simply the *gradient,* of function f:

$$\text{grad } f(x_1, x_2, \ldots, x_n) = (f_1, f_2, \ldots, f_n)$$

where $f_i \equiv \partial y / \partial x_i$. Note that we are using parentheses rather than brackets here in writing the vector. Alternatively, the gradient can be denoted by $\nabla f(x_1, x_2, \ldots, x_n)$, where ∇ (read: "del") is the inverted version of the Greek letter Δ.

Since the function f has n arguments, there are altogether n partial derivatives; hence, grad f is an n-vector. When these derivatives are evaluated at a specific point $(x_{10}, x_{20}, \ldots, x_{n0})$ in the domain, we get grad $f(x_{10}, x_{20}, \ldots, x_{n0})$, a vector of specific derivative *values*.

Example 4	The gradient vector of the production function $Q = Q(K, L)$ is

$$\nabla Q = \nabla Q(K, L) = (Q_K, Q_L)$$

EXERCISE 7.4

1. Find $\partial y / \partial x_1$ and $\partial y / \partial x_2$ for each of the following functions:

   (a) $y = 2x_1^3 - 11x_1^2 x_2 + 3x_2^2$

   (b) $y = 7x_1 + 6x_1 x_2^2 - 9x_2^3$

   (c) $y = (2x_1 + 3)(x_2 - 2)$

   (d) $y = (5x_1 + 3)/(x_2 - 2)$

2. Find f_x and f_y from the following:

   (a) $f(x, y) = x^2 + 5xy - y^3$

   (b) $f(x, y) = (x^2 - 3y)(x - 2)$

   (c) $f(x, y) = \dfrac{2x - 3y}{x + y}$

   (d) $f(x, y) = \dfrac{x^2 - 1}{xy}$

3. From the answers to Prob. 2, find $f_x(1, 2)$—the value of the partial derivative f_x when $x = 1$ and $y = 2$—for each function.

4. Given the production function $Q = 96K^{0.3} L^{0.7}$, find the MPP_K and MPP_L functions. Is MPP_K a function of K alone, or of both K and L? What about MPP_L?

5. If the utility function of an individual takes the form

   $$U = U(x_1, x_2) = (x_1 + 2)^2 (x_2 + 3)^3$$

   where U is total utility, and x_1 and x_2 are the quantities of two commodities consumed:

   (a) Find the marginal-utility function of each of the two commodities.

   (b) Find the value of the marginal utility of the first commodity when 3 units of each commodity are consumed.

6. The total money supply M has two components: bank deposits D and cash holdings C, which we assume to bear a constant ratio $C/D = c, 0 < c < 1$. The high-powered money H is defined as the sum of cash holdings held by the public and the reserves held by the banks. Bank reserves are a fraction of bank deposits, determined by the reserve ratio $r, 0 < r < 1$.

   (a) Express the money supply M as a function of high-powered money H.

   (b) Would an increase in the reserve ratio r raise or lower the money supply?

   (c) How would an increase in the cash-deposit ratio c affect the money supply?

7. Write the gradients of the following functions:

   (a) $f(x, y, z) = x^2 + y^3 + z^4$

   (b) $f(x, y, z) = xyz$

7.5 Applications to Comparative-Static Analysis

Equipped with the knowledge of the various rules of differentiation, we can at last tackle the problem posed in comparative-static analysis: namely, how the equilibrium value of an endogenous variable will change when there is a change in any of the exogenous variables or parameters.

Market Model

First let us consider again the simple one-commodity market model of (3.1). That model can be written in the form of two equations:

$$Q = a - bP \qquad (a, b > 0) \qquad \text{[demand]}$$
$$Q = -c + dP \qquad (c, d > 0) \qquad \text{[supply]}$$

with solutions

$$P^* = \frac{a + c}{b + d} \tag{7.14}$$

$$Q^* = \frac{ad - bc}{b + d} \tag{7.15}$$

These solutions will be referred to as being in the *reduced form:* The two endogenous variables have been reduced to explicit expressions of the four mutually independent parameters a, b, c, and d.

To find how an infinitesimal change in one of the parameters will affect the value of P^*, one has only to differentiate (7.14) partially with respect to each of the parameters. If the *sign* of a partial derivative, say, $\partial P^*/\partial a$, can be determined from the given information about the parameters, we shall know the direction in which P^* will move when the parameter a changes; this constitutes a qualitative conclusion. If the magnitude of $\partial P^*/\partial a$ can be ascertained, it will constitute a quantitative conclusion.

Similarly, we can draw qualitative or quantitative conclusions from the partial derivatives of Q^* with respect to each parameter, such as $\partial Q^*/\partial a$. To avoid misunderstanding, however, a clear distinction should be made between the two derivatives $\partial Q^*/\partial a$ and $\partial Q/\partial a$. The latter derivative is a concept appropriate to the demand function taken alone, and without regard to the supply function. The derivative $\partial Q^*/\partial a$ pertains, on the other hand, to the equilibrium quantity in (7.15) which, being in the nature of a solution of the model, takes into account the interaction of demand and supply together. To emphasize this distinction, we shall refer to the partial derivatives of P^* and Q^* with respect to the parameters as *comparative-static derivatives*. The possibility of confusion between $\partial Q^*/\partial a$ and $\partial Q/\partial a$ is precisely the reason why we have chosen to use the asterisk notation, as in Q^* to denote the equilibrium value.

Concentrating on P^* for the time being, we can get the following four partial derivatives from (7.14):

$$\frac{\partial P^*}{\partial a} = \frac{1}{b + d} \qquad \left[\text{parameter } a \text{ has the coefficient } \frac{1}{b + d}\right]$$

$$\frac{\partial P^*}{\partial b} = \frac{0(b + d) - 1(a + c)}{(b + d)^2} = \frac{-(a + c)}{(b + d)^2} \qquad \text{[quotient rule]}$$

$$\frac{\partial P^*}{\partial c} = \frac{1}{b+d} \left(= \frac{\partial P^*}{\partial a} \right)$$

$$\frac{\partial P^*}{\partial d} = \frac{0(b+d) - 1(a+c)}{(b+d)^2} = \frac{-(a+c)}{(b+d)^2} \left(= \frac{\partial P^*}{\partial b} \right)$$

Since all the parameters are restricted to being positive in the present model, we can conclude that

$$\frac{\partial P^*}{\partial a} = \frac{\partial P^*}{\partial c} > 0 \qquad \text{and} \qquad \frac{\partial P^*}{\partial b} = \frac{\partial P^*}{\partial d} < 0 \qquad \textbf{(7.16)}$$

For a fuller appreciation of the results in (7.16), let us look at Fig. 7.5, where each diagram shows a change in *one* of the parameters. As before, we are plotting Q (rather than P) on the vertical axis.

Figure 7.5a pictures an increase in the parameter a (to a'). This means a higher vertical intercept for the demand curve, and inasmuch as the parameter b (the slope parameter) is unchanged, the increase in a results in a parallel upward shift of the demand curve from D

FIGURE 7.5

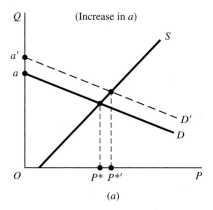

(a)

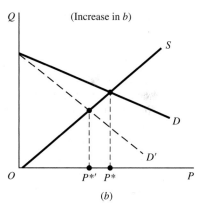

(b)

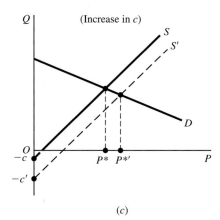

(c)

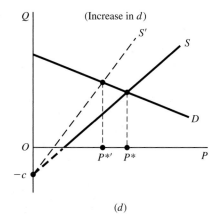

(d)

to D'. The intersection of D' and the supply curve S determines an equilibrium price $P^{*'}$, which is greater than the old equilibrium price P^*. This corroborates the result that $\partial P^*/\partial a > 0$, although for the sake of exposition we have shown in Fig. 7.5a a much larger change in the parameter a than what the concept of derivative implies.

The situation in Fig. 7.5c has a similar interpretation; but since the increase takes place in the parameter c, the result is a parallel shift of the supply curve instead. Note that this shift is downward because the supply curve has a vertical intercept of $-c$; thus an increase in c would mean a change in the intercept, say, from -2 to -4. The graphical comparative-static result, that $P^{*'}$ exceeds P^*, again conforms to what the positive sign of the derivative $\partial P^*/\partial c$ would lead us to expect.

Figures 7.5b and 7.5d illustrate the effects of changes in the slope parameters b and d of the two functions in the model. An increase in b means that the slope of the demand curve will assume a larger numerical (absolute) value; i.e., it will become steeper. In accordance with the result $\partial P^*/\partial b < 0$, we find a decrease in P^* in this diagram. The increase in d that makes the supply curve steeper also results in a decrease in the equilibrium price. This is, of course, again in line with the negative sign of the comparative-static derivative $\partial P^*/\partial d$.

Thus far, all the results in (7.16) seem to have been obtainable graphically. If so, why should we bother to use differentiation at all? The answer is that the differentiation approach has at least two major advantages. First, the graphical technique is subject to a dimensional restriction, but differentiation is not. Even when the number of endogenous variables and parameters is such that the equilibrium state cannot be shown graphically, we can nevertheless apply the differentiation techniques to the problem. Second, the differentiation method can yield results that are on a higher level of generality. The results in (7.16) will remain valid, regardless of the specific values that the parameters a, b, c, and d take, as long as they satisfy the sign restrictions. So the comparative-static conclusions of this model are, in effect, applicable to an infinite number of combinations of (linear) demand and supply functions. In contrast, the graphical approach deals only with some specific members of the family of demand and supply curves, and the analytical result derived therefrom is applicable, strictly speaking, only to the specific functions depicted.

This discussion serves to illustrate the application of partial differentiation to comparative-static analysis of the simple market model, but only half of the task has actually been accomplished, for we can also find the comparative-static derivatives pertaining to Q^*. This we shall leave to you as an exercise.

National-Income Model

In place of the simple national-income model discussed in Chap. 3, let us now work with a slightly enlarged model with three endogenous variables, Y (national income), C (consumption), and T (taxes):

$$
\begin{aligned}
Y &= C + I_0 + G_0 \\
C &= \alpha + \beta(Y - T) \qquad (\alpha > 0; \quad 0 < \beta < 1) \qquad \textbf{(7.17)} \\
T &= \gamma + \delta Y \qquad (\gamma > 0; \quad 0 < \delta < 1)
\end{aligned}
$$

The first equation in this system gives the equilibrium condition for national income, while the second and third equations show, respectively, how C and T are determined in the model.

The restrictions on the values of the parameters α, β, γ, and δ can be explained thus: α is positive because consumption is positive even if disposable income $(Y - T)$ is zero; β is a positive fraction because it represents the marginal propensity to consume; γ is positive because even if Y is zero the government will still have a positive tax revenue (from tax bases other than income); and finally, δ is a positive fraction because it represents an income tax rate, and as such it cannot exceed 100 percent. The exogenous variables I_0 (investment) and G_0 (government expenditure) are, of course, nonnegative. All the parameters and exogenous variables are assumed to be independent of one another, so that any one of them can be assigned a new value without affecting the others.

This model can be solved for Y^* by substituting the third equation of (7.17) into the second and then substituting the resulting equation into the first. The equilibrium income (in reduced form) is

$$Y^* = \frac{\alpha - \beta\gamma + I_0 + G_0}{1 - \beta + \beta\delta} \tag{7.18}$$

Similar equilibrium values can also be found for the endogenous variables C and T, but we shall concentrate on the equilibrium income.

From (7.18), there can be obtained six comparative-static derivatives. Among these, the following three have special policy significance:

$$\frac{\partial Y^*}{\partial G_0} = \frac{1}{1 - \beta + \beta\delta} > 0 \tag{7.19}$$

$$\frac{\partial Y^*}{\partial \gamma} = \frac{-\beta}{1 - \beta + \beta\delta} < 0 \tag{7.20}$$

$$\frac{\partial Y^*}{\partial \delta} = \frac{-\beta(\alpha - \beta\gamma + I_0 + G_0)}{(1 - \beta + \beta\delta)^2} = \frac{-\beta Y^*}{1 - \beta + \beta\delta} < 0 \qquad \text{[by (7.18)]} \tag{7.21}$$

The partial derivative in (7.19) gives us the *government-expenditure multiplier.* It has a positive sign here because β is less than 1, and $\beta\delta$ is greater than zero. If numerical values are given for the parameters β and δ, we can also find the numerical value of this multiplier from (7.19). The derivative in (7.20) may be called the *nonincome-tax multiplier,* because it shows how a change in γ, the government revenue from nonincome-tax sources, will affect the equilibrium income. This multiplier is negative in the present model because the denominator in (7.20) is positive and the numerator is negative. Lastly, the partial derivative in (7.21)—which is not in the nature of a multiplier, since it does not relate a dollar change to another dollar change as the derivatives in (7.19) and (7.20) do—tells us the extent to which an increase in the income tax rate δ will lower the equilibrium income.

Again, note the difference between the two derivatives $\partial Y^*/\partial G_0$ and $\partial Y/\partial G_0$. The former is derived from (7.18), the expression for the equilibrium income. The latter, obtainable from the first equation in (7.17), is $\partial Y/\partial G_0 = 1$, which is altogether different in magnitude and in concept.

Input-Output Model

The solution of an open input-output model appears as a matrix equation $x^* = (I - A)^{-1}d$. If we denote the inverse matrix $(I - A)^{-1}$ by $V = [v_{ij}]$, then, for instance, the solution for a three-industry economy can be written as $x^* = Vd$, or

$$
\begin{bmatrix} x_1^* \\ x_2^* \\ x_3^* \end{bmatrix} = \begin{bmatrix} v_{11} & v_{12} & v_{13} \\ v_{21} & v_{22} & v_{23} \\ v_{31} & v_{32} & v_{33} \end{bmatrix} \begin{bmatrix} d_1 \\ d_2 \\ d_3 \end{bmatrix}
\tag{7.22}
$$

What are the rates of change of the solution values x_j^* with respect to the exogenous final demands d_1, d_2, and d_3? The general answer is that

$$
\frac{\partial x_j^*}{\partial d_k} = v_{jk} \qquad (j, k = 1, 2, 3)
\tag{7.23}
$$

To see this, let us multiply out Vd in (7.22) and express the solution as

$$
\begin{bmatrix} x_1^* \\ x_2^* \\ x_3^* \end{bmatrix} = \begin{bmatrix} v_{11}d_1 + v_{12}d_2 + v_{13}d_3 \\ v_{21}d_1 + v_{22}d_2 + v_{23}d_3 \\ v_{31}d_1 + v_{32}d_2 + v_{33}d_3 \end{bmatrix}
$$

In this system of three equations, each one gives a particular solution value as a function of the exogenous final demands. Partial differentiation of these produces a total of nine comparative-static derivatives:

$$
\frac{\partial x_1^*}{\partial d_1} = v_{11} \qquad \frac{\partial x_1^*}{\partial d_2} = v_{12} \qquad \frac{\partial x_1^*}{\partial d_3} = v_{13}
$$

$$
\frac{\partial x_2^*}{\partial d_1} = v_{21} \qquad \frac{\partial x_2^*}{\partial d_2} = v_{22} \qquad \frac{\partial x_2^*}{\partial d_3} = v_{23}
\tag{7.23'}
$$

$$
\frac{\partial x_3^*}{\partial d_1} = v_{31} \qquad \frac{\partial x_3^*}{\partial d_2} = v_{32} \qquad \frac{\partial x_3^*}{\partial d_3} = v_{33}
$$

This is simply the expanded version of (7.23).

Reading (7.23') as three distinct columns, we may combine the three derivatives in each column into a matrix (vector) derivative:

$$
\frac{\partial x^*}{\partial d_1} \equiv \frac{\partial}{\partial d_1} \begin{bmatrix} x_1^* \\ x_2^* \\ x_3^* \end{bmatrix} = \begin{bmatrix} v_{11} \\ v_{21} \\ v_{31} \end{bmatrix} \qquad \frac{\partial x^*}{\partial d_2} = \begin{bmatrix} v_{12} \\ v_{22} \\ v_{32} \end{bmatrix} \qquad \frac{\partial x^*}{\partial d_3} = \begin{bmatrix} v_{13} \\ v_{23} \\ v_{33} \end{bmatrix}
\tag{7.23''}
$$

Since the three column vectors in (7.23'') are merely the columns of the matrix V, by further consolidation we can summarize the nine derivatives in a single matrix derivative $\partial x^*/\partial d$. Given $x^* = Vd$, we can simply write

$$
\frac{\partial x^*}{\partial d} = \begin{bmatrix} v_{11} & v_{12} & v_{13} \\ v_{21} & v_{22} & v_{23} \\ v_{31} & v_{32} & v_{33} \end{bmatrix} = V \equiv (I - A)^{-1}
$$

Thus, $(I - A)^{-1}$, the inverse of the Leontief matrix, gives us an ordered display of all the comparative-static derivatives of our open input-output model. Obviously, this matrix derivative can easily be extended from the present three-industry model to the general n-industry case.

Comparative-static derivatives of the input-output model are useful as tools of economic planning, for they provide the answer to the question: If the planning targets, as reflected in

$(d_1, d_2, \ldots, d_n)$, are revised, and if we wish to take care of all direct and indirect requirements in the economy so as to be completely free of bottlenecks, how must we change the output goals of the n industries?

EXERCISE 7.5

1. Examine the comparative-static properties of the equilibrium quantity in (7.15), and check your results by graphic analysis.
2. On the basis of (7.18), find the partial derivatives $\partial Y^*/\partial I_0$, $\partial Y^*/\partial \alpha$, and $\partial Y^*/\partial \beta$. Interpret their meanings and determine their signs.
3. The numerical input-output model (5.21) was solved in Sec. 5.7.
   (a) How many comparative-static derivatives can be derived?
   (b) Write out these derivatives in the form of (7.23′) and (7.23″).

7.6   Note on Jacobian Determinants

Our study of partial derivatives was motivated solely by comparative-static considerations. But partial derivatives also provide a means of testing whether there exists functional (linear *or* nonlinear) dependence among a set of n functions in n variables. This is related to the notion of Jacobian determinants (named after Jacobi).

Consider the two functions

$$y_1 = 2x_1 + 3x_2$$
$$y_2 = 4x_1^2 + 12x_1x_2 + 9x_2^2 \tag{7.24}$$

If we get all the four partial derivatives

$$\frac{\partial y_1}{\partial x_1} = 2 \qquad \frac{\partial y_1}{\partial x_2} = 3 \qquad \frac{\partial y_2}{\partial x_1} = 8x_1 + 12x_2 \qquad \frac{\partial y_2}{\partial x_2} = 12x_1 + 18x_2$$

and arrange them into a square matrix in a prescribed order, called a Jacobian matrix and denoted by J, and then take its determinant, the result will be what is known as a *Jacobian determinant* (or a *Jacobian,* for short), denoted by $|J|$:

$$|J| \equiv \begin{vmatrix} \dfrac{\partial y_1}{\partial x_1} & \dfrac{\partial y_1}{\partial x_2} \\ \dfrac{\partial y_2}{\partial x_1} & \dfrac{\partial y_2}{\partial x_2} \end{vmatrix} = \begin{vmatrix} 2 & 3 \\ (8x_1 + 12x_2) & (12x_1 + 18x_2) \end{vmatrix} \tag{7.25}$$

For economy of space, this Jacobian is sometimes also expressed as

$$|J| \equiv \left| \frac{\partial(y_1, y_2)}{\partial(x_1, x_2)} \right|$$

More generally, if we have n differentiable functions in n variables, not necessarily linear,

$$y_1 = f^1(x_1, x_2, \ldots, x_n)$$
$$y_2 = f^2(x_1, x_2, \ldots, x_n)$$
$$\ldots \ldots \ldots \ldots \ldots \ldots \ldots$$
$$y_n = f^n(x_1, x_2, \ldots, x_n) \tag{7.26}$$

where the symbol f^n denotes the nth function (and *not* the function raised to the nth power), we can derive a total of n^2 partial derivatives. Adopting the notation $f_j^i \equiv \partial y^i / \partial x_j$, we can write the Jacobian

$$|J| \equiv \left| \frac{\partial(y_1, y_2, \ldots, y_n)}{\partial(x_1, x_2, \ldots, x_n)} \right|$$

$$\equiv \begin{vmatrix} \partial y_1 / \partial x_1 & \cdots & \partial y_1 / \partial x_n \\ \vdots & & \vdots \\ \partial y_n / \partial x_1 & \cdots & \partial y_n / \partial x_n \end{vmatrix} \equiv \begin{vmatrix} f_1^1 & \cdots & f_n^1 \\ \vdots & & \vdots \\ f_1^n & \cdots & f_n^n \end{vmatrix} \qquad \textbf{(7.27)}$$

A Jacobian test for the existence of functional dependence among a set of n functions is provided by the following theorem: The Jacobian $|J|$ defined in (7.27) will be identically zero for all values of $x_1, \ldots, x_n$ if and only if the n functions $f^1, \ldots, f^n$ in (7.26) are functionally (linearly or nonlinearly) dependent.

As an example, for the two functions in (7.24) the Jacobian as given in (7.25) has the value

$$|J| = (24x_1 + 36x_2) - (24x_1 + 36x_2) = 0$$

That is, the Jacobian vanishes for all values of x_1 and x_2. Therefore, according to the theorem, the two functions in (7.24) must be dependent. You can verify that y_2 is simply y_1 squared; thus they are indeed functionally dependent—here *non*linearly dependent.

Let us now consider the special case of *linear* functions. We have earlier shown that the rows of the coefficient matrix A of a linear-equation system

$$\begin{aligned} a_{11}x_1 + a_{12}x_2 + \cdots + a_{1n}x_n &= d_1 \\ a_{21}x_1 + a_{22}x_2 + \cdots + a_{2n}x_n &= d_2 \\ &\cdots\cdots\cdots\cdots\cdots\cdots\cdots\cdots \\ a_{n1}x_1 + a_{n2}x_2 + \cdots + a_{nn}x_n &= d_n \end{aligned} \qquad \textbf{(7.28)}$$

are linearly dependent if and only if the determinant $|A| = 0$. This result can now be interpreted as a special application of the Jacobian criterion of functional dependence.

Take the left side of each equation in (7.28) as a separate function of the n variables $x_1, \ldots, x_n$, and denote these functions by $y_1, \ldots, y_n$. The partial derivatives of these functions will turn out to be $\partial y_1 / \partial x_1 = a_{11}$, $\partial y_1 / \partial x_2 = a_{12}$, etc., so that we may write, in general, $\partial y_i / \partial x_j = a_{ij}$. In view of this, the elements of the Jacobian of these n functions will be precisely the elements of the coefficient matrix A, already arranged in the correct order. That is, we have $|J| = |A|$, and thus the Jacobian criterion of functional dependence among $y_1, \ldots, y_n$—or, what amounts to the same thing, linear dependence among the rows of the coefficient matrix A—is equivalent to the criterion $|A| = 0$ in the present linear case.

We have discussed the Jacobian in the context of a system of n functions in n variables. It should be pointed out, however, that the Jacobian in (7.27) is defined even if each function in (7.26) contains more than n variables, say, $n + 2$ variables:

$$y_i = f^i(x_1, \ldots, x_n, x_{n+1}, x_{n+2}) \qquad (i = 1, 2, \ldots, n)$$

In such a case, if we hold any two of the variables (say, x_{n+1} and x_{n+2}) constant, or treat them as parameters, we will again have n functions in exactly n variables and can form a

Jacobian. Moreover, by holding a different pair of the x variables constant, we can form a different Jacobian. Such a situation will indeed be encountered in Chap. 8 in connection with the discussion of the implicit-function theorem.

EXERCISE 7.6

1. Use Jacobian determinants to test the existence of functional dependence between the paired functions.

   (a) $y_1 = 3x_1^2 + x_2$

   $y_2 = 9x_1^4 + 6x_1^2(x_2 + 4) + x_2(x_2 + 8) + 12$

   (b) $y_1 = 3x_1^2 + 2x_2^2$

   $y_2 = 5x_1 + 1$

2. Consider (7.22) as a set of three functions $x_i^* = f^i(d_1, d_2, d_3)$ (with $i = 1, 2, 3$).

   (a) Write out the 3×3 Jacobian. Does it have some relation to (7.23')? Can we write $|J| = |V|$?

   (b) Since $V \equiv (I - A)^{-1}$, can we conclude that $|V| \neq 0$? What can we infer from this about the three equations in (7.22)?

Chapter 8

Comparative-Static Analysis of General-Function Models

The study of partial derivatives has enabled us, in Chap. 7, to handle the simpler type of comparative-static problems, in which the equilibrium solution of the model can be explicitly stated in the reduced form. In that case, partial differentiation of the solution will directly yield the desired comparative-static information. You will recall that the definition of the partial derivative requires the absence of any functional relationship among the independent variables (say, x_i), so that x_1 can vary without affecting the values of x_2, $x_3, \ldots, x_n$. As applied to comparative-static analysis, this means that the parameters and/or exogenous variables which appear in the reduced-form solution must be mutually independent. Since these are indeed defined as predetermined data for purposes of the model, the possibility of their mutually affecting one another is inherently ruled out. The procedure of partial differentiation adopted in Chap. 7 is therefore fully justifiable.

However, no such expediency should be expected when, owing to the inclusion of general functions in a model, no explicit reduced-form solution can be obtained. In such cases, we will have to find the comparative-static derivatives directly from the originally given equations in the model. Take, for instance, a simple national-income model with two endogenous variables Y and C:

$$Y = C + I_0 + G_0$$
$$C = C(Y, T_0) \qquad [T_0: \text{exogenous taxes}]$$

which is reducible to a single equation (an equilibrium condition)

$$Y = C(Y, T_0) + I_0 + G_0$$

to be solved for Y^*. Because of the general form of the C function, however, no explicit solution is available. We must, therefore, find the comparative-static derivatives directly from this equation. How might we approach the problem? What special difficulty might we encounter?

Let us suppose that an equilibrium solution Y^* does exist. Then, under certain rather general conditions (to be discussed in Section 8.5), we may take Y^* to be a differentiable function of the exogenous variables I_0, G_0, and T_0. Hence we may write the equation

$$Y^* = Y^*(I_0, G_0, T_0)$$

even though we are unable to determine explicitly the form which this function takes. Furthermore, in some neighborhood of the equilibrium value Y^*, the following identical equality will hold:

$$Y^* \equiv C(Y^*, T_0) + I_0 + G_0$$

This type of identity will be referred to as an *equilibrium identity* because it is nothing but the equilibrium condition with the Y variable replaced by its equilibrium value Y^*. Now that Y^* has entered into the picture, it may seem at first blush that simple partial differentiation of this identity will yield any desired comparative-static derivative, say, $\partial Y^*/\partial T_0$. This, unfortunately, is not the case. Since Y^* is a function of T_0, the two arguments of the C function are *not* independent. Specifically, T_0 can in this case affect C not only *directly,* but also *indirectly* via Y^*. Consequently, partial differentiation is no longer appropriate for our purposes. How, then, do we tackle this situation?

The answer is that we must resort to *total differentiation* (as against partial differentiation). Based on the notion of *total differentials,* the process of total differentiation can lead us to the related concept of *total derivative,* which measures the rate of change of a function such as $C(Y^*, T_0)$ with respect to the argument T_0, when T_0 also affects the other argument, Y^*. Thus, once we become familiar with these concepts, we shall be able to deal with functions whose arguments are not all independent, and that would remove the major stumbling block we have so far encountered in our study of the comparative statics of a general-function model. As a prelude to the discussion of these concepts, however, we should first introduce the notion of *differentials.*

8.1   Differentials

The symbol dy/dx, for the derivative of the function $y = f(x)$, has hitherto been regarded as a single entity. We shall now reinterpret it as a ratio of two quantities, dy and dx.

Differentials and Derivatives

By definition, the derivative $dy/dx = f'(x)$ is the limit of a difference quotient:

$$\frac{dy}{dx} = f'(x) = \lim_{\Delta x \to 0} \frac{\Delta y}{\Delta x} \tag{8.1}$$

Thus, by itself, $\Delta y/\Delta x$ (without requiring $\Delta x \to 0$) is not equal to dy/dx. If we denote the discrepancy between the two quotients by δ, we can write

$$\frac{\Delta y}{\Delta x} - \frac{dy}{dx} = \delta \qquad \text{where} \qquad \delta \to 0 \quad \text{as} \quad \Delta x \to 0 \qquad \text{[by (8.1)]} \tag{8.2}$$

Multiplying (8.2) through by Δx, and rearranging, we have

$$\Delta y = \frac{dy}{dx} \Delta x + \delta \, \Delta x \qquad \text{or} \qquad \Delta y = f'(x)\Delta x + \delta \, \Delta x \tag{8.3}$$

This equation describes the change in y (Δy) that results from a specific—not necessarily small—change in x (Δx) from any starting value of x in the domain of the function

FIGURE 8.1

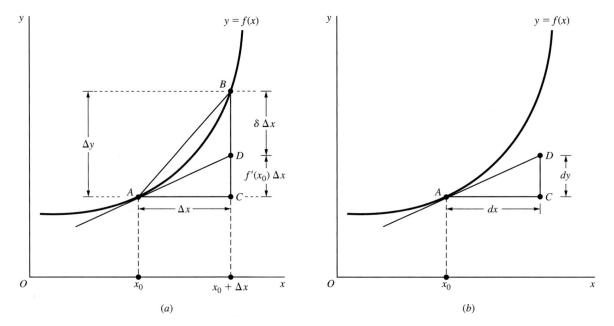

(a)   *(b)*

$y = f(x)$. But it also suggests that we can, by ignoring the discrepancy term $\delta\,\Delta x$, use the $f'(x)\,\Delta x$ term as an approximation to the true Δy value, where the approximation gets progressively better as Δx gets progressively smaller.

In Fig. 8.1a, when x changes from x_0 to $x_0 + \Delta x$, a movement from point A to point B occurs on the graph of $y = f(x)$. The true Δy is measured by the distance CB, and the ratio of the two distances $CB/AC = \Delta y/\Delta x$ can be read from the slope of line segment AB. But if we draw a tangent line AD through point A, and use AD in place of AB to approximate the value of Δy, we obtain distance CD, which leaves distance DB as the discrepancy or error of approximation. Since the slope of AD is $f'(x_0)$, distance CD is equal to $f'(x_0)\,\Delta x$ and, by (8.3), distance DB is equal to $\delta\,\Delta x$. Obviously, as Δx decreases, point B would slide along the curve toward point A, thereby reducing the discrepancy and making $f'(x)$ or dy/dx a better approximation to $\Delta y/\Delta x$.

Focusing on the tangent line AD, and taking the distance CD as an approximation to CB, let us relabel the distances AC and CD by dx and dy, respectively, as in Fig. 8.1b. Then

$$\frac{dy}{dx} = \text{slope of tangent } AD = f'(x)$$

and, after multiplying through by dx, we get

$$dy = f'(x)\,dx \qquad\qquad\qquad \textbf{(8.4)}$$

The derivative $f'(x)$ can then be reinterpreted as the factor of proportionality between the two finite changes dy and dx. Accordingly, given a specific value of dx, we can multiply it by $f'(x)$ to get dy as an approximation to Δy, with the understanding that the smaller the Δx, the better the approximation. The quantities dx and dy are called the *differentials* of x and y, respectively.

A few remarks are in order regarding differentials as mathematical entities. First, while dx is an independent variable, dy is a dependent variable. Specifically, dy is a function of x as well as of dx: It depends on x because a different position for x_0 in Fig. 8.1 would mean a different location for point A and for its tangent line; it depends on dx because a different magnitude of dx would mean a different position for point C as well as a different distance CD. Second, if $dx = 0$, then $dy = 0$, because point B would in that case coincide with point A. But if $dx \neq 0$, then it is possible to divide dy by dx to get $f'(x)$, just as we can multiply dx by $f'(x)$ to get dy. Third, the differential dy can be expressed only in terms of some other differential(s)—here, dx. This is because our context calls for the coupling of a dependent change dy with an independent change dx. While it makes sense to write $dy = f'(x)\, dx$, it is not meaningful to chop away the dx term on the right and write $dy = f'(x)$. The coupling of the two changes is effected through the derivative $f'(x)$, which may be viewed as a "converter" that serves to translate a given change dx into a counterpart change dy.

The process of finding the differential dy from a given function $y = f(x)$ is called *differentiation*. Recall that we have been using this term as a synonym for derivation, without having given an adequate explanation. In light of our interpretation of a derivative as a quotient of two differentials, however, the rationale of the term becomes self-evident. It is still somewhat ambiguous, though, to use the single term "differentiation" to refer to the process of finding the differential dy as well as to that of finding the derivative dy/dx. To avoid confusion, the usual practice is to qualify the word *differentiation* with the phrase "with respect to x" when we take the derivative dy/dx.

Differentials and Point Elasticity

To illustrate the economic application of differentials, let us consider the notion of the elasticity of a function. Given a demand function $Q = f(P)$, for instance, its elasticity is defined as $(\Delta Q/Q)/(\Delta P/P)$. Using the idea of approximation explained in Fig. 8.1, we can replace the independent change ΔP and the dependent change ΔQ with the differentials dP and dQ, respectively, to get an approximation elasticity measure known as the *point elasticity* of demand and denoted by ε_d (the Greek letter epsilon, for "elasticity"):[†]

$$\varepsilon_d \equiv \frac{dQ/Q}{dP/P} = \frac{dQ/dP}{Q/P} \qquad\qquad \textbf{(8.5)}$$

Observe that on the extreme right of the expression we have rearranged the differentials dQ and dP into a ratio dQ/dP, which can be construed as the derivative, or the *marginal* function, of the demand function $Q = f(P)$. Since we can interpret similarly the ratio Q/P in the denominator as the *average* function of the demand function, the point elasticity of demand ε_d in (8.5) is seen to be the ratio of the marginal function to the average function of the demand function.

[†] The point-elasticity measure can alternatively be interpreted as the limit of $\dfrac{\Delta Q/Q}{\Delta P/P} = \dfrac{\Delta Q/\Delta P}{Q/P}$ as $\Delta P \to 0$, which gives the same result as (8.5).

Indeed, this last-described relationship is valid not only for the demand function but also for any other function, because for any given *total* function $y = f(x)$ we can write the formula for the point elasticity of y with respect to x as

$$\varepsilon_{yx} = \frac{dy/dx}{y/x} = \frac{\text{marginal function}}{\text{average function}} \tag{8.6}$$

As a matter of convention, the *absolute* value of the elasticity measure is used in deciding whether the function is elastic at a particular point. In the case of a demand function, for instance, we stipulate:

$$\text{The demand is} \begin{cases} \text{elastic} \\ \text{of unit elasticity} \\ \text{inelastic} \end{cases} \text{at a point when } |\varepsilon_d| \gtreqless 1.$$

Example 1   Find ε_d if the demand function is $Q = 100 - 2P$. The marginal function and the average function of the given demand are

$$\frac{dQ}{dP} = -2 \quad \text{and} \quad \frac{Q}{P} = \frac{100 - 2P}{P}$$

so their ratio will give us

$$\varepsilon_d = \frac{-P}{50 - P}$$

As written, the elasticity is shown as a function of P. As soon as a specific price is chosen, however, the point elasticity will be determinate in magnitude. When $P = 25$, for instance, we have $\varepsilon_d = -1$, or $|\varepsilon_d| = 1$, so that the demand elasticity is unitary at that point. When $P = 30$, in contrast, we have $|\varepsilon_d| = 1.5$; hence, demand is elastic at that price. More generally, it may be verified that we have $|\varepsilon_d| > 1$ for $25 < P < 50$ and $|\varepsilon_d| < 1$ for $0 < P < 25$ in the present example. (Can a price $P > 50$ be considered meaningful here?)

Example 2   Find the point elasticity of supply ε_s from the supply function $Q = P^2 + 7P$, and determine whether the supply is elastic at $P = 2$. Since the marginal and average functions are, respectively,

$$\frac{dQ}{dP} = 2P + 7 \quad \text{and} \quad \frac{Q}{P} = P + 7$$

their ratio gives us the elasticity of supply

$$\varepsilon_s = \frac{2P + 7}{P + 7}$$

When $P = 2$, this elasticity has the value $11/9 > 1$; thus the supply is elastic at $P = 2$.

At the risk of digressing a trifle, it may also be added here that the interpretation of the ratio of two differentials as a derivative—and the consequent transformation of the elasticity formula of a function into a ratio of its marginal to its average—makes possible a quick way of determining the point elasticity graphically. The two diagrams in Fig. 8.2 illustrate the cases, respectively, of a negatively sloped curve and a positively sloped curve. In each case, the value of the marginal function at point A on the curve, or at $x = x_0$ in the domain, is measured by the slope of the tangent line AB. The value of the average function, on the

FIGURE 8.2

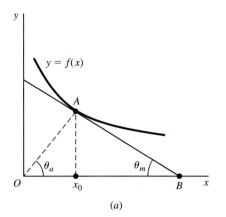 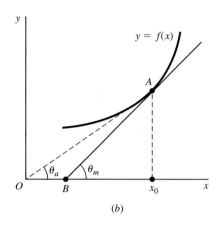

(*a*)   (*b*)

FIGURE 8.3

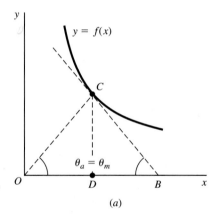 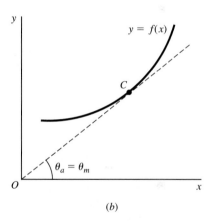

(*a*)   (*b*)

other hand, is in each case measured by the slope of line OA (the line joining the point of origin with the given point A on the curve, like a radius vector), because at point A we have $y = x_0 A$ and $x = Ox_0$, so that the average is $y/x = x_0 A/Ox_0 =$ slope of OA. The elasticity at point A can thus be readily ascertained by comparing the *numerical* values of the two slopes involved: If AB is steeper than OA, the function is elastic at point A; in the opposite case, it is inelastic at A. Accordingly, the function pictured in Fig. 8.2a is inelastic at A (or at $x = x_0$), whereas the one in Fig. 8.2b is elastic at A.

Moreover, the two slopes under comparison are directly dependent on the respective sizes of the two angles θ_m and θ_a (Greek letter theta; the subscripts m and a indicate marginal and average, respectively). Thus we may, alternatively, compare these two angles instead of the two corresponding slopes. Referring to Fig. 8.2 again, you can see that $\theta_m < \theta_a$ at point A in diagram a, indicating that the marginal falls short of the average in numerical value; thus the function is inelastic at point A. The exact opposite is true in Fig. 8.2b.

Sometimes, we are interested in locating a point of unitary elasticity on a given curve. This can now be done easily. If the curve is negatively sloped, as in Fig. 8.3a, we should find a point C such that the line OC and the tangent BC will make the same-sized angle with the x axis, though in the opposite direction. In the case of a positively sloped curve, as in Fig. 8.3b, one has only to find a point C such that the tangent line at C, when properly extended, passes through the point of origin.

We must warn you that the graphical method just described is based on the assumption that the function $y = f(x)$ is plotted with the dependent variable y on the vertical axis. In particular, in applying the method to a demand curve, we should make sure that Q is on the vertical axis. (Now suppose that Q is actually plotted on the horizontal axis. How should our method of reading the point elasticity be modified?)

EXERCISE 8.1

1. Find the differential dy, given:

   (a) $y = -x(x^2 + 3)$ (b) $y = (x - 8)(7x + 5)$ (c) $y = \dfrac{x}{x^2 + 1}$

2. Given the import function $M = f(Y)$, where M is imports and Y is national income, express the income elasticity of imports ε_{MY} in terms of the propensities to import.

3. Given the consumption function $C = a + bY$ (with $a > 0; 0 < b < 1$):

   (a) Find its marginal function and its average function.

   (b) Find the income elasticity of consumption ε_{CY}, and determine its sign, assuming $Y > 0$.

   (c) Show that this consumption function is inelastic at all positive income levels.

4. Find the point elasticity of demand, given $Q = k/P^n$, where k and n are positive constants.

   (a) Does the elasticity depend on the price in this case?

   (b) In the special case where $n = 1$, what is the shape of the demand curve? What is the point elasticity of demand?

5. (a) Find a positively sloped curve with a constant point elasticity everywhere on the curve.

   (b) Write the equation of the curve, and verify by (8.6) that the elasticity is indeed a constant.

6. Given $Q = 100 - 2P + 0.02Y$, where Q is quantity demanded, P is price, and Y is income, and given $P = 20$ and $Y = 5,000$, find the

   (a) Price elasticity of demand.

   (b) Income elasticity of demand.

8.2 Total Differentials

The concept of differentials can easily be extended to a function of two or more independent variables. Consider a saving function

$$S = S(Y, i) \qquad\qquad (8.7)$$

where S is savings, Y is national income, and i is the interest rate. This function is assumed—as all the functions we shall use here will be assumed—to be continuous and to possess continuous (partial) derivatives, or, symbolically, $f \in C'$. The partial derivative $\partial S/\partial Y$ measures the marginal propensity to save. Thus, for any change in Y, dY, the resulting change in S can be approximated by the quantity $(\partial S/\partial Y)\, dY$, which is comparable to the right-hand expression in (8.4). Similarly, given a change in i, di, we may take $(\partial S/\partial i)\, di$

as the approximation to the resulting change in S. The total change in S is then approximated by the differential

$$dS = \frac{\partial S}{\partial Y} dY + \frac{\partial S}{\partial i} di \qquad\qquad (8.8)$$

or, in an alternative notation,

$$dS = S_Y\, dY + S_i\, di$$

Note that the two partial derivatives S_Y and S_i again play the role of "converters" that serve to convert the changes dY and di, respectively, into a corresponding change dS. The expression dS, being the *sum* of the approximate changes from both sources, is called the *total differential* of the saving function. And the process of finding such a total differential is called *total differentiation.* In contrast, the two additive components to the right of the equals sign in (8.8) are referred to as the *partial differentials* of the saving function.

It is possible, of course, that Y may change while i remains constant. In that case, $di = 0$, and the total differential will reduce to $dS = (\partial S/\partial Y)\, dY$. Dividing both sides by dY, we get

$$\frac{\partial S}{\partial Y} = \left(\frac{dS}{dY} \right)_{i\text{ constant}}$$

Thus it is clear that the partial derivative $\partial S/\partial Y$ can also be interpreted, in the spirit of Fig. 8.1*b*, as the ratio of two differentials dS and dY, with the proviso that i, the other independent variable in the function, is held constant. Analogously, we can interpret the partial derivative $\partial S/\partial i$ as the ratio of the differential dS (with Y held constant) to the differential di. Note that although dS and di can now each stand alone as a differential, the expression $\partial S/\partial i$ remains as a single entity.

The more general case of a function of n independent variables can be exemplified by, say, a utility function in the general form

$$U = U(x_1, x_2, \ldots, x_n) \qquad\qquad (8.9)$$

The total differential of this function can be written as

$$dU = \frac{\partial U}{\partial x_1} dx_1 + \frac{\partial U}{\partial x_2} dx_2 + \cdots + \frac{\partial U}{\partial x_n} dx_n \qquad\qquad (8.10)$$

or
$$dU = U_1\, dx_1 + U_2\, dx_2 + \cdots + U_n\, dx_n = \sum_{i=1}^{n} U_i\, dx_i$$

in which each term on the right side indicates the approximate change in U resulting from a change in one of the independent variables. Economically, the first term, $U_1\, dx_1$, means the marginal utility of the first commodity times the increment in consumption of that commodity, and similarly for the other terms. The sum of these, dU, thus represents the total approximate change in utility originating from all possible sources of change. As the reasoning in (8.3) shows, dU, as an approximation, tends toward the true change ΔU as all the dx_i terms tend to zero.

Like any other function, the saving function (8.7) and the utility function (8.9) can both be expected to give rise to point-elasticity measures similar to that defined in (8.6). But each elasticity measure must in these instances be defined in terms of the change in *one* of the independent variables only; there will thus be *two* such elasticity measures to the saving function, and *n* of them to the utility function. These are accordingly called *partial elasticities*. For the saving function, the partial elasticities may be written as

$$\varepsilon_{SY} = \frac{\partial S/\partial Y}{S/Y} = \frac{\partial S}{\partial Y}\frac{Y}{S} \quad\text{and}\quad \varepsilon_{Si} = \frac{\partial S/\partial i}{S/i} = \frac{\partial S}{\partial i}\frac{i}{S}$$

For the utility function, the *n* partial elasticities can be concisely denoted as follows:

$$\varepsilon_{Ux_i} = \frac{\partial U}{\partial x_i}\frac{x_i}{U} \qquad (i = 1, 2, \ldots, n)$$

Example 1

Find the total differential for the following utility functions, where $a, b > 0$:

(a) $U(x_1, x_2) = ax_1 + bx_2$
(b) $U(x_1, x_2) = x_1^2 + x_2^3 + x_1x_2$
(c) $U(x_1, x_2) = x_1^a x_2^b$

The total differentials are as follows:

(a)
$$\frac{\partial U}{\partial x_1} = U_1 = a \qquad \frac{\partial U}{\partial x_2} = U_2 = b$$

and

$$dU = U_1\,dx_1 + U_2\,dx_2 = a\,dx_1 + b\,dx_2$$

(b)
$$\frac{\partial U}{\partial x_1} = U_1 = 2x_1 + x_2 \qquad \frac{\partial U}{\partial x_2} = U_2 = 3x_2^2 + x_1$$

and

$$dU = U_1\,dx_1 + U_2\,dx_2 = (2x_1 + x_2)\,dx_1 + \left(3x_2^2 + x_1\right)dx_2$$

(c)
$$\frac{\partial U}{\partial x_1} = U_1 = ax_1^{a-1}x_2^b = \frac{ax_1^a x_2^b}{x_1} \qquad \frac{\partial U}{\partial x_2} = U_2 = bx_1^a x_2^{b-1} = \frac{bx_1^a x_2^b}{x_2}$$

and

$$dU = \left(\frac{ax_1^a x_2^b}{x_1}\right)dx_1 + \left(\frac{bx_1^a x_2^b}{x_2}\right)dx_2$$

EXERCISE 8.2

1. Express the total differential dU by using the gradient vector ∇U.
2. Find the total differential, given
   (a) $z = 3x^2 + xy - 2y^3$
   (b) $U = 2x_1 + 9x_1x_2 + x_2^2$
3. Find the total differential, given
   (a) $y = \dfrac{x_1}{x_1 + x_2}$ \qquad (b) $y = \dfrac{2x_1 x_2}{x_1 + x_2}$
4. The supply function of a certain commodity is
   $$Q = a + bP^2 + R^{1/2} \qquad (a < 0,\ b > 0) \qquad [R:\text{ rainfall}]$$
   Find the price elasticity of supply ε_{QP}, and the rainfall elasticity of supply ε_{QR}.

5. How do the two partial elasticities in Prob. 4 vary with P and R? In a strictly monotonic fashion (assuming positive P and R)?
6. The foreign demand for our exports X depends on the foreign income Y_f and our price level P: $X = Y_f^{1/2} + P^{-2}$. Find the partial elasticity of foreign demand for our exports with respect to our price level.
7. Find the total differential for each of the following functions:
   (a) $U = -5x^3 - 12xy - 6y^5$
   (b) $U = 7x^2 y^3$
   (c) $U = 3x^3(8x - 7y)$
   (d) $U = (5x^2 + 7y)(2x - 4y^3)$
   (e) $U = \dfrac{9y^3}{x - y}$
   (f) $U = (x - 3y)^3$

8.3   Rules of Differentials

A straightforward way of finding the total differential dy, given a function

$$y = f(x_1, x_2)$$

is to find the partial derivatives f_1 and f_2 and substitute these into the equation

$$dy = f_1 \, dx_1 + f_2 \, dx_2$$

But sometimes it may be more convenient to apply certain rules of differentials which, in view of their striking resemblance to the derivative formulas studied before, are very easy to remember.

Let k be a constant and u and v be two functions of the variables x_1 and x_2. Then the following rules are valid:[†]

Rule I	$dk = 0$	(cf. constant-function rule)
Rule II	$d(cu^n) = cnu^{n-1} \, du$	(cf. power-function rule)
Rule III	$d(u \pm v) = du \pm dv$	(cf. sum-difference rule)
Rule IV	$d(uv) = v \, du + u \, dv$	(cf. product rule)
Rule V	$d\left(\dfrac{u}{v}\right) = \dfrac{1}{v^2}(v \, du - u \, dv)$	(cf. quotient rule)

Instead of proving these rules here, we shall merely illustrate their practical application.

[†] All the rules of differentials discussed in this section are also applicable when u and v are themselves the independent variables (rather than functions of some other variables x_1 and x_2).

Example 1

Find the total differential dy of the function

$$y = 5x_1^2 + 3x_2$$

The straightfoward method calls for the evaluation of the partial derivatives $f_1 = 10x_1$ and $f_2 = 3$, which will then enable us to write

$$dy = f_1\, dx_1 + f_2\, dx_2 = 10x_1\, dx_1 + 3\, dx_2$$

We may, however, let $u = 5x_1^2$ and $v = 3x_2$ and apply the previously given rules to get the identical answer as follows:

$$\begin{aligned}
dy &= d\left(5x_1^2\right) + d(3x_2) && \text{[by Rule III]} \\
&= 10x_1\, dx_1 + 3\, dx_2 && \text{[by Rule II]}
\end{aligned}$$

Example 2

Find the total differential of the function

$$y = 3x_1^2 + x_1 x_2^2$$

Since $f_1 = 6x_1 + x_2^2$ and $f_2 = 2x_1 x_2$, the desired differential is

$$dy = \left(6x_1 + x_2^2\right) dx_1 + 2x_1 x_2\, dx_2$$

By applying the given rules, the same result can be arrived at thus:

$$\begin{aligned}
dy &= d\left(3x_1^2\right) + d\left(x_1 x_2^2\right) && \text{[by Rule III]} \\
&= 6x_1\, dx_1 + x_2^2\, dx_1 + x_1\, d\left(x_2^2\right) && \text{[by Rules II and IV]} \\
&= \left(6x_1 + x_2^2\right) dx_1 + 2x_1 x_2\, dx_2 && \text{[by Rule II]}
\end{aligned}$$

Example 3

Find the total differential of the function

$$y = \frac{x_1 + x_2}{2x_1^2}$$

In view of the fact that the partial derivatives in this case are

$$f_1 = \frac{-(x_1 + 2x_2)}{2x_1^3} \qquad \text{and} \qquad f_2 = \frac{1}{2x_1^2}$$

(check these as an exercise), the desired differential is

$$dy = \frac{-(x_1 + 2x_2)}{2x_1^3} dx_1 + \frac{1}{2x_1^2} dx_2$$

However, the same result may also be obtained by application of the rules as follows:

$$\begin{aligned}
dy &= \frac{1}{4x_1^4}\left[2x_1^2 d(x_1 + x_2) - (x_1 + x_2)\, d\left(2x_1^2\right)\right] && \text{[by Rule V]} \\
&= \frac{1}{4x_1^4}\left[2x_1^2(dx_1 + dx_2) - (x_1 + x_2)4x_1\, dx_1\right] && \text{[by Rules III and II]} \\
&= \frac{1}{4x_1^4}\left[-2x_1(x_1 + 2x_2)\, dx_1 + 2x_1^2\, dx_2\right] \\
&= \frac{-(x_1 + 2x_2)}{2x_1^3} dx_1 + \frac{1}{2x_1^2} dx_2
\end{aligned}$$

These rules can naturally be extended to cases where more than two functions of x_1 and x_2 are involved. In particular, we can add the following two rules to the previous collection:

Rule VI $\qquad\qquad\qquad\qquad d(u \pm v \pm w) = du \pm dv \pm dw$

Rule VII $\qquad\qquad\qquad\qquad d(uvw) = vw\,du + uw\,dv + uv\,dw$

To derive Rule VII, we can employ the familiar trick of first letting $z = vw$, so that

$$d(uvw) = d(uz) = z\,du + u\,dz \qquad \text{[by Rule IV]}$$

Then, by applying Rule IV again to dz, we get the intermediate result

$$dz = d(vw) = w\,dv + v\,dw$$

which, when substituted into the preceding equation, will yield

$$d(uvw) = vw\,du + u(w\,dv + v\,dw) = vw\,du + uw\,dv + uv\,dw$$

as the desired final result. A similar procedure can be employed to derive Rule VI.

EXERCISE 8.3

1. Use the rules of differentials to find (*a*) dz from $z = 3x^2 + xy - 2y^3$ and (*b*) dU from $U = 2x_1 + 9x_1 x_2 + x_2^2$. Check your answers against those obtained for Exercise 8.2-2.
2. Use the rules of differentials to find dy from the following functions:

   (*a*) $y = \dfrac{x_1}{x_1 + x_2}$ $\qquad\qquad$ (*b*) $y = \dfrac{2x_1 x_2}{x_1 + x_2}$

   Check your answers against those obtained for Exercise 8.2-3.
3. Given $y = 3x_1(2x_2 - 1)(x_3 + 5)$
   (*a*) Find dy by Rule VII.
   (*b*) Find the differential of y, if $dx_2 = dx_3 = 0$.
4. Prove Rules II, III, IV, and V, assuming u and v to be the independent variables (rather than functions of some other variables).

8.4 Total Derivatives

We shall now tackle the question posed at the beginning of the chapter; namely, how can we find the rate of change of the function $C(Y^*, T_0)$ with respect to T_0, when Y^* and T_0 are related? As previously mentioned, the answer lies in the concept of total derivative. Unlike a *partial* derivative, a *total* derivative does not require the argument Y^* to remain constant as T_0 varies, and can thus allow for the postulated relationship between the two arguments.

Finding the Total Derivative

To carry on the discussion in a general framework, let us consider any function

$$y = f(x, w) \qquad \text{where} \qquad x = g(w) \qquad\qquad \textbf{(8.11)}$$

FIGURE 8.4

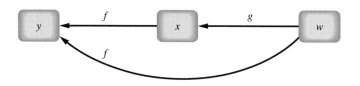

The two functions f and g can also be combined into a composite function

$$y = f[g(w), w] \tag{8.11'}$$

The three variables y, x, and w are related to one another as shown in Fig. 8.4. In this figure, which we shall refer to as a *channel map*, it is clearly seen that w—the ultimate source of change—can affect y through two separate channels: (1) *indirectly*, via the function g and then f (the straight arrows), and (2) *directly*, via the function f (the curved arrow). The direct effect can simply be represented by the partial derivative f_w. But the indirect effect can only be expressed by a product of two derivatives, $f_x \dfrac{dx}{dw}$, or $\dfrac{\partial y}{\partial x} \dfrac{dx}{dw}$, by the chain rule for a composite function. Adding up the two effects gives us the desired total derivative of y with respect to w:

$$\frac{dy}{dw} = f_x \frac{dx}{dw} + f_w$$

$$= \frac{\partial y}{\partial x} \frac{dx}{dw} + \frac{\partial y}{\partial w} \tag{8.12}$$

This total derivative can also be obtained by an alternative method: We may first differentiate the function $y = f(x, w)$ totally, to get the total differential

$$dy = f_x \, dx + f_w \, dw$$

and then divide through by dw. The result is identical with (8.12). Either way, the process of finding the total derivative dy/dw is referred to as the *total differentiation of y with respect to w*.

It is extremely important to distinguish between the two look-alike symbols dy/dw and $\partial y/\partial w$ in (8.12). The former is a *total* derivative, and the latter, a *partial* derivative. The latter is in fact merely a component of the former.

Example 1

Find the total derivative dy/dw, given the function

$$y = f(x, w) = 3x - w^2 \qquad \text{where} \qquad x = g(w) = 2w^2 + w + 4$$

By virtue of (8.12), the total derivative should be

$$\frac{dy}{dw} = 3(4w + 1) + (-2w) = 10w + 3$$

As a check, we may substitute the function g into the function f, to get

$$y = 3(2w^2 + w + 4) - w^2 = 5w^2 + 3w + 12$$

which is now a function of w alone. The derivative dy/dw is then easily found to be $10w + 3$, the identical answer.

FIGURE 8.5

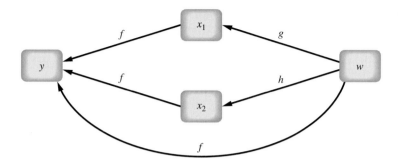

Example 2

If we have a utility function $U = U(c, s)$, where c is the amount of coffee consumed and s is the amount of sugar consumed, and another function $s = g(c)$ indicating the complementarity between these two goods, then we can simply write the composite function

$$U = U[c, g(c)]$$

from which it follows that

$$\frac{dU}{dc} = \frac{\partial U}{\partial c} + \frac{\partial U}{\partial g(c)}g'(c)$$

A Variation on the Theme

The situation is only slightly more complicated when we have

$$y = f(x_1, x_2, w) \qquad \text{where} \begin{cases} x_1 = g(w) \\ x_2 = h(w) \end{cases} \qquad \textbf{(8.13)}$$

The channel map will now appear as in Fig. 8.5. This time, the variable w can affect y through three channels: (1) indirectly, via the function g and then f, (2) again indirectly, via the function h and then f, and (3) directly via f. From our previous experience, these three effects are expected to be expressible, respectively as $\dfrac{\partial y}{\partial x_1}\dfrac{dx_1}{dw}$, $\dfrac{\partial y}{\partial x_2}\dfrac{dx_2}{dw}$, and $\dfrac{\partial y}{\partial w}$. By adding these together, we get the total derivative

$$\frac{dy}{dw} = \frac{\partial y}{\partial x_1}\frac{dx_1}{dw} + \frac{\partial y}{\partial x_2}\frac{dx_2}{dw} + \frac{\partial y}{\partial w}$$

$$= f_1\frac{dx_1}{dw} + f_2\frac{dx_2}{dw} + f_w \qquad \textbf{(8.14)}$$

which is comparable to (8.12). If we take the total differential dy, and then divide through by dw, we can arrive at the same result.

Example 3

Let the production function be

$$Q = Q(K, L, t)$$

where, aside from the two inputs K and L, there is a third argument t, denoting time. The presence of the t argument indicates that the production function can shift over time in reflection of technological changes. Thus this is a dynamic rather than a static production function. Since capital and labor, too, can change over time, we may write

$$K = K(t) \qquad \text{and} \qquad L = L(t)$$

Then the rate of change of output with respect to time can be expressed, in line with the total-derivative formula (8.14), as

$$\frac{dQ}{dt} = \frac{\partial Q}{\partial K}\frac{dK}{dt} + \frac{\partial Q}{\partial L}\frac{dL}{dt} + \frac{\partial Q}{\partial t}$$

or, in an alternative notation,

$$\frac{dQ}{dt} = Q_K K'(t) + Q_L L'(t) + Q_t$$

Another Variation on the Theme

When the ultimate source of change, w in (8.13), is replaced by two coexisting sources, u and v, the situation becomes the following:

$$y = f(x_1, x_2, u, v) \qquad \text{where} \quad \begin{cases} x_1 = g(u, v) \\ x_2 = h(u, v) \end{cases} \qquad \textbf{(8.15)}$$

While the channel map will now contain more arrows, the principle of its construction remains the same; we shall, therefore, leave it to you to draw. To find the total derivative of y with respect to u (while v is held constant), let us take the total differential of y, and then divide through by the differential du, with the result:

$$\frac{dy}{du} = \frac{\partial y}{\partial x_1}\frac{dx_1}{du} + \frac{\partial y}{\partial x_2}\frac{dx_2}{du} + \frac{\partial y}{\partial u}\frac{du}{du} + \frac{\partial y}{\partial v}\frac{dv}{du}$$

$$= \frac{\partial y}{\partial x_1}\frac{dx_1}{du} + \frac{\partial y}{\partial x_2}\frac{dx_2}{du} + \frac{\partial y}{\partial u} \qquad \left[\frac{dv}{du} = 0 \text{ since } v \text{ is held constant}\right]$$

In view of the fact that we are varying u while holding v constant (as a single derivative cannot handle changes in u and v both), however, the result obtained must be modified in two ways: (1) the derivatives dx_1/du and dx_2/du on the right should be rewritten with the partial sign as $\partial x_1/\partial u$ and $\partial x_2/\partial u$, which is in line with the functions g and h in (8.15); and (2) the ratio dy/du on the left should also be interpreted as a *partial* derivative, even though—being derived through the process of total differentiation of y—it is actually in the nature of a *total* derivative. For this reason, we shall refer to it by the explicit name of *partial total derivative,* and denote it by $\S y/\S u$ (with $\S$ rather than ∂), in order to distinguish it from the simple partial derivative $\partial y/\partial u$ which, as our result shows, is but one of three component terms that add up to the partial total derivative.[†]

With these modifications, our result becomes

$$\frac{\S y}{\S u} = \frac{\partial y}{\partial x_1}\frac{\partial x_1}{\partial u} + \frac{\partial y}{\partial x_2}\frac{\partial x_2}{\partial u} + \frac{\partial y}{\partial u} \qquad \textbf{(8.16)}$$

which is comparable to (8.14). Note the appearance of the symbol $\partial y/\partial u$ on the right, which necessitates the adoption of the new symbol $\S y/\S u$ on the left to indicate the broader

---

[†] An alternative way of denoting this partial total derivative is

$$\left.\frac{dy}{du}\right|_{v \text{ constant}} \qquad \text{or} \qquad \left.\frac{dy}{du}\right|_{dv=0}$$

concept of a partial total derivative. In a perfectly analogous manner, we can derive the other partial total derivative, $\S y/\S v$. Inasmuch as the roles of u and v are symmetrical in (8.15), however, a simpler alternative is available to us. All we have to do to obtain $\S y/\S v$ is to replace the symbol u in (8.16) by the symbol v throughout.

The use of the new symbols $\S y/\S u$ and $\S y/\S v$ for the partial total derivatives, if unconventional, serves the good purpose of avoiding confusion with the simple partial derivatives $\partial y/\partial u$ and $\partial y/\partial v$ that can arise from the function f alone in (8.15). However, in the special case where the f function takes the form of $y = f(x_1, x_2)$ without the arguments u and v, the simple partial derivatives $\partial y/\partial u$ and $\partial y/\partial v$ are not defined. Hence, it may not be inappropriate in such a case to use the latter symbols for the partial total derivatives of y with respect to u and v, since no confusion is likely to arise. Even in that event, though, the use of a special symbol is advisable for the sake of greater clarity.

Some General Remarks

To conclude this section, we offer three general remarks regarding total derivative and total differentiation:

1. In the cases we have discussed, the situation involves without exception a variable that is functionally dependent on a second variable, which is in turn dependent functionally on a third variable. As a consequence, the notion of a *chain* inevitably enters the picture, as evidenced by the appearance of a product (or products) of two derivative expressions as the component(s) of a total derivative. For this reason, the total-derivative formulas in (8.12), (8.14), and (8.16) can also be regarded as expressions of the chain rule, or the composite-function rule—a more sophisticated version of the chain rule introduced in Sec. 7.3.

2. The chain of derivatives does not have to be limited to only two "links" (two derivatives being multiplied); the concept of total derivative should be extendible to cases where there are three or more links in the composite function.

3. In all cases discussed, total derivatives—including those which have been called *partial total derivatives*—measure rates of change with respect to some *ultimate* variables in the chain or, in other words, with respect to certain variables which are in a sense *exogenous* and which are *not* expressed as functions of some other variables. The essence of the total derivative and of the process of total differentiation is to make due allowance for *all* the channels, indirect as well as direct, through which the effects of a change in an *ultimate* independent variable can possibly be carried to the particular dependent variable under study.

EXERCISE 8.4

1. Find the total derivative dz/dy, given
    (a) $z = f(x, y) = 5x + xy - y^2$, where $x = g(y) = 3y^2$
    (b) $z = 4x^2 - 3xy + 2y^2$, where $x = 1/y$
    (c) $z = (x + y)(x - 2y)$, where $x = 2 - 7y$
2. Find the total derivative dz/dt, given
    (a) $z = x^2 - 8xy - y^3$, where $x = 3t$ and $y = 1 - t$

(b) $z = 7u + vt$, where $u = 2t^2$ and $v = t + 1$

(c) $z = f(x, y, t)$, where $x = a + bt$ and $y = c + kt$

3. Find the rate of change of output with respect to time, if the production function is $Q = A(t)K^{\alpha}L^{\beta}$, where $A(t)$ is an increasing function of t, and $K = K_0 + at$, and $L = L_0 + bt$.

4. Find the partial total derivatives $\S W/\S u$ and $\S W/\S v$ if

   (a) $W = ax^2 + bxy + cu$, where $x = \alpha u + \beta v$ and $y = \gamma u$

   (b) $W = f(x_1, x_2)$, where $x_1 = 5u^2 + 3v$ and $x_2 = u - 4v^3$

5. Draw a channel map appropriate to the case of (8.15).

6. Derive the expression for $\S y/\S v$ formally from (8.15) by taking the total differential of y and then dividing through by dv.

8.5 Derivatives of Implicit Functions

The concept of total differentials can also enable us to find the derivatives of so-called implicit functions.

Implicit Functions

A function given in the form of $y = f(x)$, say,

$$y = f(x) = 3x^4 \tag{8.17}$$

is called an *explicit function,* because the variable y is explicitly expressed as a function of x. If this function is written alternatively in the equivalent form

$$y - 3x^4 = 0 \tag{8.17'}$$

however, we no longer have an explicit function. Rather, the function (8.17) is then only *implicitly* defined by the equation (8.17'). When we are (only) given an equation in the form of (8.17'), therefore, the function $y = f(x)$ which it implies, and whose specific form may not even be known to us, is referred to as an *implicit function.*

An equation in the form of (8.17') can be denoted in general by $F(y, x) = 0$, because its left side is a function of the two variables y and x. Note that we are using the capital letter F here to distinguish it from the function f; the function F, representing the left-side expression in (8.17'), has two arguments, y and x, whereas the function f, representing the implicit function, has only one argument, x. There may, of course, be more than two arguments in the F function. For instance, we may encounter an equation $F(y, x_1, \ldots, x_m) = 0$. Such an equation *may* also define an implicit function $y = f(x_1, \ldots, x_m)$.

The equivocal word *may* in the last sentence was used advisedly. For, whereas an explicit function, say, $y = f(x)$, can always be transformed into an equation $F(y, x) = 0$ by simply transposing the $f(x)$ expression to the left side of the equals sign, the reverse transformation is not always possible. Indeed, in certain cases, a given equation in the form of $F(y, x) = 0$ may not implicitly define a function $y = f(x)$. For instance, the equation $x^2 + y^2 = 0$ is satisfied only at the point of origin $(0, 0)$, and hence yields no meaningful function to speak of. As another example, the equation

$$F(y, x) = x^2 + y^2 - 9 = 0 \tag{8.18}$$

FIGURE 8.6

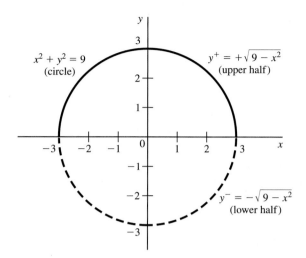

implies not a function, but a relation, because (8.18) plots as a circle, as shown in Fig. 8.6, so that no unique value of y corresponds to each value of x. Note, however, that if we restrict y to nonnegative values, then we will have the upper half of the circle only, and that does constitute a function, namely, $y = +\sqrt{9 - x^2}$. Similarly, the lower half of the circle, with y values nonpositive, constitutes another function, $y = -\sqrt{9 - x^2}$. In contrast, neither the left half nor the right half of the circle can qualify as a function.

In view of this uncertainty, it becomes of interest to ask whether there are known general conditions under which we can be sure that a given equation in the form of

$$F(y, x_1, \ldots, x_m) = 0 \tag{8.19}$$

does indeed define an implicit function

$$y = f(x_1, \ldots, x_m) \tag{8.20}$$

locally, i.e., around some specific point in the domain. The answer to this lies in the so-called implicit-function theorem, which states that:

> Given (8.19), if (a) the function F has continuous partial derivatives $F_y, F_1, \ldots, F_m$, and if (b) at a point $(y_0, x_{10}, \ldots, x_{m0})$ satisfying the equation (8.19), F_y is nonzero, then there exists an m-dimensional neighborhood of $(x_{10}, \ldots, x_{m0})$, N, in which y is an implicitly defined function of the variables $x_1, \ldots, x_m$, in the form of (8.20). This implicit function satisfies $y_0 = f(x_{10}, \ldots, x_{m0})$. It also satisfies the equation (8.19) for *every* m-tuple $(x_1, \ldots, x_m)$ in the neighborhood N—thereby giving (8.19) the status of an *identity* in that neighborhood. Moreover, the implicit function f is continuous and has continuous partial derivatives $f_1, \ldots, f_m$.

Let us apply this theorem to the equation of the circle, (8.18), which contains only one x variable. First, we can duly verify that $F_y = 2y$ and $F_x = 2x$ are continuous, as required. Then we note that F_y is nonzero except when $y = 0$, that is, except at the leftmost point $(-3, 0)$ and the rightmost point $(3, 0)$ on the circle. Thus, around any point on the circle except $(-3, 0)$ and $(3, 0)$, we can construct a neighborhood in which the equation (8.18) defines an implicit function $y = f(x)$. This is easily verifiable in Fig. 8.6, where it is indeed possible to draw, say, a rectangle around any point on the circle—except $(-3, 0)$ and $(3, 0)$—such that the portion of the circle enclosed therein will constitute the graph of a function, with a unique y value for each value of x in that rectangle.

Several things should be noted about the implicit-function theorem. First, the conditions cited in the theorem are in the nature of sufficient (but not necessary) conditions. This means that if we happen to find $F_y = 0$ at a point satisfying (8.19), we cannot use the theorem to deny the existence of an implicit function around that point. For such a function may in fact exist (see Exercise 8.5-7).[†] Second, even if an implicit function f is assured to exist, the theorem gives no clue as to the specific form the function f takes. Nor, for that matter, does it tell us the exact size of the neighborhood N in which the implicit function is defined. However, despite these limitations, this theorem is one of great importance. For whenever the conditions of the theorem are satisfied, it now becomes meaningful to talk about and make use of a function such as (8.20), even if our model may contain an equation (8.19) which is difficult or impossible to solve explicitly for y in terms of the x variables. Moreover, since the theorem also guarantees the existence of the partial derivatives $f_1, \ldots, f_m$, it is now also meaningful to talk about these derivatives of the implicit function.

Derivatives of Implicit Functions

If the equation $F(y, x_1, \ldots, x_m) = 0$ can be solved for y, we can explicitly write out the function $y = f(x_1, \ldots, x_m)$, and find its derivatives by the methods learned before. For instance, (8.18) can be solved to yield two separate functions

$$\begin{aligned} y^+ &= +\sqrt{9 - x^2} \qquad \text{[upper half of circle]} \\ y^- &= -\sqrt{9 - x^2} \qquad \text{[lower half of circle]} \end{aligned} \qquad \textbf{(8.18$'$)}$$

and their derivatives can be found as follows:

$$\begin{aligned} \frac{dy^+}{dx} &= \frac{d}{dx}(9 - x^2)^{1/2} = \tfrac{1}{2}(9 - x^2)^{-1/2}(-2x) \\ &= \frac{-x}{\sqrt{9 - x^2}} = \frac{-x}{y^+} \qquad (y^+ \neq 0) \\ \frac{dy^-}{dx} &= \frac{d}{dx}[-(9 - x^2)^{1/2}] = -\tfrac{1}{2}(9 - x^2)^{-1/2}(-2x) \\ &= \frac{x}{\sqrt{9 - x^2}} = \frac{-x}{y^-} \qquad (y^- \neq 0) \end{aligned} \qquad \textbf{(8.21)}$$

But what if the given equation, $F(y, x_1, \ldots, x_m) = 0$, cannot be solved for y explicitly? In this case, if under the terms of the implicit-function theorem an implicit function is known to exist, we can still obtain the desired derivatives without having to solve for y first. To do this, we make use of the so-called implicit-function rule—a rule that can give us the derivatives of *every* implicit function defined by the given equation. The development of this rule depends on the following basic facts: (1) if two expressions are *identically*

[†] On the other hand, if $F_y = 0$ in an entire neighborhood, then it can be concluded that no implicit function is defined in that neighborhood. By the same token if $F_y = 0$ identically, then no implicit function exists anywhere.

equal, their respective total differentials must be equal;[†] (2) differentiation of an expression that involves $y, x_1, \ldots, x_m$ will yield an expression involving the differentials $dy, dx_1, \ldots, dx_m$; and (3) the differential of y, dy, can be substituted out, so the fact that we cannot solve for y does not matter.

Applying these facts to the equation $F(y, x_1, \ldots, x_m) = 0$—which, we recall, has the status of an *identity* in the neighborhood N in which the implicit function is defined—we can write $dF = d0$, or

$$F_y \, dy + F_1 \, dx_1 + F_2 \, dx_2 + \cdots + F_m \, dx_m = 0 \qquad \textbf{(8.22)}$$

Since the implicit function $y = f(x_1, x_2, \ldots, x_m)$ has the total differential

$$dy = f_1 \, dx_1 + f_2 \, dx_2 + \cdots + f_n \, dx_n$$

we can substitute this dy expression into (8.22) to get (after collecting terms)

$$(F_y \, f_1 + F_1) \, dx_1 + (F_y \, f_2 + F_2) \, dx_2 + \cdots + (F_y \, f_m + F_m) \, dx_m = 0 \quad \textbf{(8.22$'$)}$$

The fact that all the dx_i can vary independently from one another means that, for the equation (8.22$'$) to hold, each parenthesized expression must individually vanish; i.e., we must have

$$F_y \, f_i + F_i = 0 \qquad \text{(for all } i\text{)}$$

Dividing through by F_y, and solving for f_i, we obtain the so-called implicit-function rule for finding the partial derivative f_i of the implicit function $y = f(x_1, x_2, \ldots, x_m)$:

$$f_i \equiv \frac{\partial y}{\partial x_i} = -\frac{F_i}{F_y} \qquad (i = 1, 2, \ldots, m) \qquad \textbf{(8.23)}$$

In the simple case where the given equation is $F(y, x) = 0$, the rule gives

$$\frac{dy}{dx} = -\frac{F_x}{F_y} \qquad \textbf{(8.23$'$)}$$

[†] Take, for example, the identity
$$x^2 - y^2 \equiv (x + y)(x - y)$$
This is an identity because the two sides are equal for *any* values of x and y that one may assign. Taking the total differential of each side, we have
$$d(\text{left side}) = 2x \, dx - 2y \, dy$$
$$d(\text{right side}) = (x - y) \, d(x + y) + (x + y) \, d(x - y)$$
$$= (x - y)(dx + dy) + (x + y)(dx - dy)$$
$$= 2x \, dx - 2y \, dy$$
The two results are indeed equal. If two expressions are *not* identically equal, but are equal only for certain specific values of the variables, however, their total differentials will *not* be equal. The equation
$$x^2 - y^2 = x^2 + y^2 - 2$$
for instance, is valid only for $y = \pm 1$. The total differentials of the two sides are
$$d(\text{left side}) = 2x \, dx - 2y \, dy$$
$$d(\text{right side}) = 2x \, dx + 2y \, dy$$
which are not equal. Note, in particular, that they are not equal even at $y = \pm 1$.

What this rule states is that, even if the specific form of the implicit function is not known to us, we can nevertheless find its derivative(s) by taking the *negative* of the ratio of a pair of partial derivatives of the F function which appears in the given equation that defines the implicit function. Observe that F_y always appears in the denominator of the ratio. This being the case, it is not admissible to have $F_y = 0$. Since the implicit-function theorem specifies that $F_y \neq 0$ at the point around which the implicit function is defined, the problem of a zero denominator is automatically taken care of in the relevant neighborhood of that point.

Example 1

Find dy/dx for the implicit function defined by (8.17′). Since $F(y, x)$ takes the form of $y - 3x^4$, we have, by (8.23′),

$$\frac{dy}{dx} = -\frac{F_x}{F_y} = -\frac{-12x^3}{1} = 12x^3$$

In this particular case, we can easily solve the given equation for y to get $y = 3x^4$. Thus the correctness of the derivative is easily verified.

Example 2

Find dy/dx for the implicit functions defined by the equation of the circle (8.18). This time we have $F(y, x) = x^2 + y^2 - 9$; thus $F_y = 2y$ and $F_x = 2x$. By (8.23′), the desired derivative is

$$\frac{dy}{dx} = -\frac{2x}{2y} = -\frac{x}{y} \qquad (y \neq 0)^\dagger$$

Earlier, it was asserted that the implicit-function rule gives us the derivative of *every* implicit function defined by a given equation. Let us verify this with the two functions in (8.18′) and their derivatives in (8.21). If we substitute y^+ for y in the implicit-function-rule result $dy/dx = -x/y$, we will indeed obtain the derivative dy^+/dx as shown in (8.21); similarly, the substitution of y^- for y will yield the other derivative in (8.21). Thus our earlier assertion is duly verified.

Example 3

Find $\partial y/\partial x$ for any implicit function(s) that may be defined by the equation $F(y, x, w) = y^3x^2 + w^3 + yxw - 3 = 0$. This equation is not easily solved for y. But since F_y, F_x, and F_w are all obviously continuous, and since $F_y = 3y^2x^2 + xw$ is indeed nonzero at a point such as $(1, 1, 1)$ which satisfies the given equation, an implicit function $y = f(x, w)$ assuredly exists around that point at least. It is thus meaningful to talk about the derivative $\partial y/\partial x$. By (8.23), moreover, we can immediately write

$$\frac{\partial y}{\partial x} = -\frac{F_x}{F_y} = -\frac{2y^3x + yw}{3y^2x^2 + xw}$$

At the point $(1, 1, 1)$, this derivative has the value $-\frac{3}{4}$.

Example 4

Assume that the equation $F(Q, K, L) = 0$ implicitly defines a production function $Q = f(K, L)$. Let us find a way of expressing the marginal physical products MPP_K and MPP_L in relation to the function F. Since the marginal products are simply the partial derivatives $\partial Q/\partial K$ and $\partial Q/\partial L$, we can apply the implicit-function rule and write

$$MPP_K \equiv \frac{\partial Q}{\partial K} = -\frac{F_K}{F_Q} \qquad \text{and} \qquad MPP_L \equiv \frac{\partial Q}{\partial L} = -\frac{F_L}{F_Q}$$

---

† The restriction $y \neq 0$ is of course perfectly consistent with our earlier discussion of the equation (8.18) that follows the statement of the implicit-function theorem.

Aside from these, we can obtain yet another partial derivative,

$$\frac{\partial K}{\partial L} = -\frac{F_L}{F_K}$$

from the equation $F(Q, K, L) = 0$. What is the economic meaning of $\partial K/\partial L$? The partial sign implies that the other variable, Q, is being held constant; it follows that the changes in K and L described by this derivative are in the nature of "compensatory" changes designed to keep the output Q constant at a specified level. These are therefore the type of changes pertaining to movements *along* a production *isoquant* drawn with the K variable on the vertical axis and the L variable on the horizontal axis. As a matter of fact, the derivative $\partial K/\partial L$ is the measure of the slope of such an isoquant, which is negative in the normal case. The absolute value of $\partial K/\partial L$, on the other hand, is the measure of the *marginal rate of technical substitution* between the two inputs.

Extension to the Simultaneous-Equation Case

The implicit-function theorem also comes in a more general and powerful version that deals with the conditions under which a set of simultaneous equations

$$\begin{aligned}
F^1(y_1, \ldots, y_n; x_1, \ldots, x_m) &= 0 \\
F^2(y_1, \ldots, y_n; x_1, \ldots, x_m) &= 0 \\
\cdots\cdots\cdots\cdots\cdots\cdots\cdots\cdots\cdots\cdots\cdots \\
F^n(y_1, \ldots, y_n; x_1, \ldots, x_m) &= 0
\end{aligned}$$

(8.24)

will assuredly define a set of implicit functions[†]

$$\begin{aligned}
y_1 &= f^1(x_1, \ldots, x_m) \\
y_2 &= f^2(x_1, \ldots, x_m) \\
\cdots\cdots\cdots\cdots\cdots\cdots \\
y_n &= f^n(x_1, \ldots, x_m)
\end{aligned}$$

(8.25)

The generalized version of the theorem states that:

Given the equation system (8.24), if (*a*) the functions $F^1, \ldots, F^n$ all have continuous partial derivatives with respect to all the y and x variables, and if (*b*) at a point $(y_{10}, \ldots, y_{n0}; x_{10}, \ldots, x_{m0})$ satisfying (8.24), the following Jacobian determinant is nonzero:

$$|J| \equiv \left| \frac{\partial(F^1, \ldots, F^n)}{\partial(y_1, \ldots, y_n)} \right| \equiv \begin{vmatrix} \dfrac{\partial F^1}{\partial y_1} & \dfrac{\partial F^1}{\partial y_2} & \cdots & \dfrac{\partial F^1}{\partial y_n} \\ \dfrac{\partial F^2}{\partial y_1} & \dfrac{\partial F^2}{\partial y_2} & \cdots & \dfrac{\partial F^2}{\partial y_n} \\ \cdots\cdots\cdots\cdots\cdots\cdots\cdots \\ \dfrac{\partial F^n}{\partial y_1} & \dfrac{\partial F^n}{\partial y_2} & \cdots & \dfrac{\partial F^n}{\partial y_n} \end{vmatrix} \neq 0$$

[†] To view it another way, what these conditions serve to do is to assure us that the n equations in (8.24) can *in principle* be solved for the n variables—$y_1, \ldots, y_n$—even if we may not be able to obtain the solution (8.25) in an explicit form.

then there exists an m-dimensional neighborhood of $(x_{10}, \ldots, x_{m0})$, N, in which the variables $y_1, \ldots, y_n$ are functions of the variables $x_1, \ldots, x_m$ in the form of (8.25). These implicit functions satisfy

$$y_{10} = f^1(x_{10}, \ldots, x_{m0})$$
$$\cdots\cdots\cdots\cdots\cdots\cdots\cdots$$
$$y_{n0} = f^n(x_{10}, \ldots, x_{m0})$$

They also satisfy (8.24) for *every* m-tuple $(x_1, \ldots, x_m)$ in the neighborhood N—thereby giving (8.24) the status of a set of *identities* as far as this neighborhood is concerned. Moreover, the implicit functions $f^1, \ldots, f^n$ are continuous and have continuous partial derivatives with respect to all the x variables.

As in the single-equation case, it is possible to find the partial derivatives of the implicit functions directly from the n equations in (8.24), without having to solve them for the y variables. Taking advantage of the fact that, in the neighborhood N, the equations in (8.24) have the status of identities, we can take the total differential of each of these, and write $dF^j = 0\,(j = 1, 2, \ldots, n)$. The result is a set of equations involving the differentials $dy_1, \ldots, dy_n$ and $dx_1, \ldots, dx_m$. Specifically, after transposing the dx_i terms to the right of the equals signs, we have

$$\frac{\partial F^1}{\partial y_1}dy_1 + \frac{\partial F^1}{\partial y_2}dy_2 + \cdots + \frac{\partial F^1}{\partial y_n}dy_n = -\left(\frac{\partial F^1}{\partial x_1}dx_1 + \cdots + \frac{\partial F^1}{\partial x_m}dx_m\right)$$

$$\frac{\partial F^2}{\partial y_1}dy_1 + \frac{\partial F^2}{\partial y_2}dy_2 + \cdots + \frac{\partial F^2}{\partial y_n}dy_n = -\left(\frac{\partial F^2}{\partial x_1}dx_1 + \cdots + \frac{\partial F^2}{\partial x_m}dx_m\right) \qquad \textbf{(8.26)}$$

$$\cdots\cdots\cdots\cdots\cdots\cdots\cdots\cdots\cdots\cdots\cdots\cdots\cdots\cdots\cdots\cdots\cdots$$

$$\frac{\partial F^n}{\partial y_1}dy_1 + \frac{\partial F^n}{\partial y_2}dy_2 + \cdots + \frac{\partial F^n}{\partial y_n}dy_n = -\left(\frac{\partial F^n}{\partial x_1}dx_1 + \cdots + \frac{\partial F^n}{\partial x_m}dx_m\right)$$

Moreover, from (8.25), we can write the differentials of the y_j variables as

$$dy_1 = \frac{\partial y_1}{\partial x_1}dx_1 + \frac{\partial y_1}{\partial x_2}dx_2 + \cdots + \frac{\partial y_1}{\partial x_m}dx_m$$

$$dy_2 = \frac{\partial y_2}{\partial x_1}dx_1 + \frac{\partial y_2}{\partial x_2}dx_2 + \cdots + \frac{\partial y_2}{\partial x_m}dx_m \qquad \textbf{(8.27)}$$

$$\cdots\cdots\cdots\cdots\cdots\cdots\cdots\cdots\cdots\cdots\cdots\cdots\cdots\cdots$$

$$dy_n = \frac{\partial y_n}{\partial x_1}dx_1 + \frac{\partial y_n}{\partial x_2}dx_2 + \cdots + \frac{\partial y_n}{\partial x_m}dx_m$$

and these can be used to eliminate the dy_j expressions in (8.26). But since the result of substitution would be unmanageably messy, let us simplify matters by considering only what would happen when x_1 alone changes while all the other variables $x_2, \ldots, x_m$ remain constant. Letting $dx_1 \neq 0$, but setting $dx_2 = \cdots = dx_m = 0$ in (8.26) and (8.27), then substituting (8.27) into (8.26) and dividing through by $dx_1 \neq 0$, we obtain the equation system

$$\frac{\partial F^1}{\partial y_1}\left(\frac{\partial y_1}{\partial x_1}\right) + \frac{\partial F^1}{\partial y_2}\left(\frac{\partial y_2}{\partial x_1}\right) + \cdots + \frac{\partial F^1}{\partial y_n}\left(\frac{\partial y_n}{\partial x_1}\right) = -\frac{\partial F^1}{\partial x_1}$$

$$\frac{\partial F^2}{\partial y_1}\left(\frac{\partial y_1}{\partial x_1}\right) + \frac{\partial F^2}{\partial y_2}\left(\frac{\partial y_2}{\partial x_1}\right) + \cdots + \frac{\partial F^2}{\partial y_n}\left(\frac{\partial y_n}{\partial x_1}\right) = -\frac{\partial F^2}{\partial x_1} \qquad \textbf{(8.28)}$$

$$\cdots\cdots\cdots\cdots\cdots\cdots\cdots\cdots\cdots\cdots\cdots\cdots\cdots\cdots\cdots$$

$$\frac{\partial F^n}{\partial y_1}\left(\frac{\partial y_1}{\partial x_1}\right) + \frac{\partial F^n}{\partial y_2}\left(\frac{\partial y_2}{\partial x_1}\right) + \cdots + \frac{\partial F^n}{\partial y_n}\left(\frac{\partial y_n}{\partial x_1}\right) = -\frac{\partial F^n}{\partial x_1}$$

Even this result—for the case where x_1 alone changes—looks formidably complex, because it is full of derivatives. But its structure is actually quite easy to comprehend, once we learn to distinguish between the two types of derivatives that appear in (8.28). One type, which we have parenthesized for visual distinction, consists of the partial derivatives of the implicit functions with respect to x_1 that we are seeking. These, therefore, should be viewed as the "variables" to be solved for in (8.28). The other type, on the other hand, consists of the partial derivatives of the F^j functions given in (8.24). Since they would all take specific values when evaluated at the point $(y_{10}, \ldots, y_{n0}; x_{10}, \ldots, x_{m0})$—the point around which the implicit functions are defined—they appear here not as derivative functions but as derivative values. As such, they can be treated as given constants. This fact makes (8.28) a *linear equation system,* with a structure similar to (4.1). What is interesting is that such a linear system has arisen during the process of analysis of a problem that is not necessarily linear in itself, since no linearity restrictions have been placed on the equation system (8.24). Thus we have here an illustration of how linear algebra can come into play even in nonlinear problems.

Being a linear equation system, (8.28) can be written in matrix notation as

$$\begin{bmatrix} \dfrac{\partial F^1}{\partial y_1} & \dfrac{\partial F^1}{\partial y_2} & \cdots & \dfrac{\partial F^1}{\partial y_n} \\ \dfrac{\partial F^2}{\partial y_1} & \dfrac{\partial F^2}{\partial y_2} & \cdots & \dfrac{\partial F^2}{\partial y_n} \\ \cdots\cdots\cdots\cdots\cdots\cdots \\ \dfrac{\partial F^n}{\partial y_1} & \dfrac{\partial F^n}{\partial y_2} & \cdots & \dfrac{\partial F^n}{\partial y_n} \end{bmatrix} \begin{bmatrix} \left(\dfrac{\partial y_1}{\partial x_1}\right) \\ \left(\dfrac{\partial y_2}{\partial x_1}\right) \\ \vdots \\ \left(\dfrac{\partial y_n}{\partial x_1}\right) \end{bmatrix} = \begin{bmatrix} -\dfrac{\partial F^1}{\partial x_1} \\ -\dfrac{\partial F^2}{\partial x_1} \\ \vdots \\ -\dfrac{\partial F^n}{\partial x_1} \end{bmatrix} \qquad \textbf{(8.28')}$$

Since the determinant of the coefficient matrix in (8.28') is nothing but the particular Jacobian determinant $|J|$ which is known to be nonzero under conditions of the implicit-function theorem, and since the system must be nonhomogeneous (why?), there should be a unique nontrivial solution to (8.28'). By Cramer's rule, this solution may be expressed analytically as follows:

$$\left(\frac{\partial y_j}{\partial x_1}\right) = \frac{|J_j|}{|J|} \qquad (j = 1, 2, \ldots, n) \qquad \text{[see (5.18)]} \qquad \textbf{(8.29)}$$

By a suitable adaptation of this procedure, the partial derivatives of the implicit functions with respect to the other variables, $x_2, \ldots, x_m$, can also be obtained. It is a nice feature of this procedure that, each time we allow a particular x_i variable to change, we can obtain in one fell swoop the partial derivatives of all the implicit functions $f^1, \ldots, f^n$ with respect to that particular x_i variable.

Similarly, to the implicit-function rule (8.23) for the single-equation case, the procedure just described calls only for the use of the partial derivatives of the F functions—evaluated at the point $(y_{10}, \ldots, y_{n0}; x_{10}, \ldots, x_{m0})$—in the calculation of the partial derivatives of the implicit functions $f^1, \ldots, f^n$. Thus the matrix equation (8.28') and its analytical solution (8.29) are in effect a statement of the simultaneous-equation version of the implicit-function rule.

Note that the requirement $|J| \neq 0$ rules out a zero denominator in (8.29), just as the requirement $F_y \neq 0$ did in the implicit-function rule (8.23) and (8.23'). Also, the role played by the condition $|J| \neq 0$ in guaranteeing a unique (albeit implicit) solution (8.25) to the general (possibly *nonlinear*) system (8.24) is very similar to the role of the nonsingularity condition $|A| \neq 0$ in a *linear* system $Ax = d$.

| **Example 5** | The following three equations |

$$\begin{array}{ll} xy - w = 0 & F^1 = (x, y, w; z) = 0 \\ y - w^3 - 3z = 0 & F^2 = (x, y, w; z) = 0 \\ w^3 + z^3 - 2zw = 0 & F^3 = (x, y, w; z) = 0 \end{array}$$

are satisfied at point $P: (x, y, w; z) = (\frac{1}{4}, 4, 1, 1)$. The F^i functions obviously possess continuous derivatives. Thus, if the Jacobian $|J|$ is nonzero at point P, we can use the implicit-function theorem to find the comparative-static derivative $(\partial x / \partial z)$.

To do this, we can first take the total differential of the system:

$$y \, dx + x \, dy - dw = 0$$
$$dy - 3w^2 \, dw - 3 \, dz = 0$$
$$(3w^2 - 2z) \, dw + (3z^2 - 2w) \, dz = 0$$

Moving the exogenous differential (and its coefficients) to the right-hand side and writing in matrix form, we get

$$\begin{bmatrix} y & x & -1 \\ 0 & 1 & -3w^2 \\ 0 & 0 & (3w^2 - 2z) \end{bmatrix} \begin{bmatrix} dx \\ dy \\ dw \end{bmatrix} = \begin{bmatrix} 0 \\ 3 \\ 2w - 3z^2 \end{bmatrix} dz$$

where the coefficient matrix on the left-hand side is the Jacobian

$$|J| = \begin{vmatrix} F_x^1 & F_y^1 & F_w^1 \\ F_x^2 & F_y^2 & F_w^2 \\ F_x^3 & F_y^3 & F_w^3 \end{vmatrix} = \begin{vmatrix} y & x & -1 \\ 0 & 1 & -3w^2 \\ 0 & 0 & (3w^2 - 2z) \end{vmatrix} = y(3w^2 - 2z)$$

At the point P, the Jacobian determinant $|J| = 4 \; (\neq 0)$. Therefore, the implicit-function rule applies and

$$\begin{bmatrix} y & x & -1 \\ 0 & 1 & -3w^2 \\ 0 & 0 & (3w^2 - 2z) \end{bmatrix} \begin{bmatrix} \left(\dfrac{\partial x}{\partial z}\right) \\ \left(\dfrac{\partial y}{\partial z}\right) \\ \left(\dfrac{\partial w}{\partial z}\right) \end{bmatrix} = \begin{bmatrix} 0 \\ 3 \\ 2w - 3z^2 \end{bmatrix}$$

Using Cramer's rule to find an expression for $(\partial x/\partial z)$, we obtain

$$\left(\frac{\partial x}{\partial z}\right) = \frac{\begin{vmatrix} 0 & x & -1 \\ 3 & 1 & -3w^2 \\ 2w - 3z^2 & 0 & (3w^2 - 2z) \end{vmatrix}}{|J|} = \frac{\begin{vmatrix} 0 & \frac{1}{4} & -1 \\ 3 & 1 & -3 \\ -1 & 0 & 1 \end{vmatrix}}{4}$$

$$= 0 + (-3)\frac{\begin{vmatrix} \frac{1}{4} & -1 \\ 0 & 1 \end{vmatrix}}{4} + (-1)\frac{\begin{vmatrix} \frac{1}{4} & -1 \\ 1 & -3 \end{vmatrix}}{4}$$

$$= \frac{-3}{16} + \frac{-1}{16}$$

$$= -\frac{1}{4}$$

Example 6

Let the national-income model (7.17) be rewritten in the form

$$Y - C - I_0 - G_0 = 0$$
$$C - \alpha - \beta(Y - T) = 0 \qquad\qquad \textbf{(8.30)}$$
$$T - \gamma - \delta Y = 0$$

If we take the endogenous variables (Y, C, T) to be (y_1, y_2, y_3), and take the exogenous variables and parameters $(I_0, G_0, \alpha, \beta, \gamma, \delta)$ to be $(x_1, x_2, \ldots, x_6)$, then the left-side expression in each equation can be regarded as a specific F function, in the form of $F^i(Y, C, T; I_0, G_0, \alpha, \beta, \gamma, \delta)$. Thus (8.30) is a specific case of (8.24), with $n = 3$ and $m = 6$. Since the functions F^1, F^2, and F^3 do have continuous partial derivatives, and since the relevant Jacobian determinant (the one involving only the endogenous variables),

$$|J| = \begin{vmatrix} \dfrac{\partial F^1}{\partial Y} & \dfrac{\partial F^1}{\partial C} & \dfrac{\partial F^1}{\partial T} \\[2mm] \dfrac{\partial F^2}{\partial Y} & \dfrac{\partial F^2}{\partial C} & \dfrac{\partial F^2}{\partial T} \\[2mm] \dfrac{\partial F^3}{\partial Y} & \dfrac{\partial F^3}{\partial C} & \dfrac{\partial F^3}{\partial T} \end{vmatrix} = \begin{vmatrix} 1 & -1 & 0 \\ -\beta & 1 & \beta \\ -\delta & 0 & 1 \end{vmatrix} = 1 - \beta + \beta\delta \qquad \textbf{(8.31)}$$

is always nonzero (both β and δ being restricted to be positive fractions), we can take Y, C, and T to be implicit functions of $(I_0, G_0, \alpha, \beta, \gamma, \delta)$ at and *around* any point that satisfies (8.30). But a point that satisfies (8.30) would be an equilibrium solution, relating to Y^*, C^* and T^*. Hence, what the implicit-function theorem tells us is that we are justified in writing

$$Y^* = f^1(I_0, G_0, \alpha, \beta, \gamma, \delta)$$
$$C^* = f^2(I_0, G_0, \alpha, \beta, \gamma, \delta)$$
$$T^* = f^3(I_0, G_0, \alpha, \beta, \gamma, \delta)$$

indicating that the equilibrium values of the endogenous variables are implicit functions of the exogenous variables and the parameters.

The partial derivatives of the implicit functions, such as $\partial Y^*/\partial I_0$ and $\partial Y^*/\partial G_0$, are in the nature of comparative-static derivatives. To find these, we need only the partial derivatives of the F functions, evaluated at the equilibrium state of the model. Moreover, since $n = 3$, three of these can be found in one operation. Suppose we now hold all exogenous variables and parameters fixed except G_0. Then, by adapting the result in (8.28′), we may write the equation

$$\begin{bmatrix} 1 & -1 & 0 \\ -\beta & 1 & \beta \\ -\delta & 0 & 1 \end{bmatrix} \begin{bmatrix} \partial Y^*/\partial G_0 \\ \partial C^*/\partial G_0 \\ \partial T^*/\partial G_0 \end{bmatrix} = \begin{bmatrix} 1 \\ 0 \\ 0 \end{bmatrix}$$

from which three comparative-static derivatives (all with respect to G_0) can be calculated. The first one, representing the government-expenditure multiplier, will for instance come out to be

$$\frac{\partial Y^*}{\partial G_0} = \frac{\begin{vmatrix} 1 & -1 & 0 \\ 0 & 1 & \beta \\ 0 & 0 & 1 \end{vmatrix}}{|J|} = \frac{1}{1 - \beta + \beta\delta} \qquad \text{[by (8.31)]}$$

This is, of course, nothing but the result obtained earlier in (7.19). Note, however, that in the present approach we have worked only with implicit functions, and have completely bypassed the step of solving the system (8.30) explicitly for Y^*, C^*, and T^*. It is this particular feature of the method that will now enable us to tackle the comparative statics of general-function models which, by their very nature, can yield no explicit solution.

EXERCISE 8.5

1. For each $F(x, y) = 0$, find dy/dx for each of the following:
   (a) $y - 6x + 7 = 0$
   (b) $3y + 12x + 17 = 0$
   (c) $x^2 + 6x - 13 - y = 0$
2. For each $F(x, y) = 0$ use the implicit-function rule to find dy/dx:
   (a) $F(x, y) = 3x^2 + 2xy + 4y^3 = 0$
   (b) $F(x, y) = 12x^5 - 2y = 0$
   (c) $F(x, y) = 7x^2 + 2xy^2 + 9y^4 = 0$
   (d) $F(x, y) = 6x^3 - 3y = 0$
3. For each $F(x, y, z) = 0$ use the implicit-function rule to find $\partial y/\partial x$ and $\partial y/\partial z$:
   (a) $F(x, y, z) = x^2 y^3 + z^2 + xyz = 0$
   (b) $F(x, y, z) = x^3 z^2 + y^3 + 4xyz = 0$
   (c) $F(x, y, z) = 3x^2 y^3 + xz^2 y^2 + y^3 zx^4 + y^2 z = 0$
4. Assuming that the equation $F(U, x_1, x_2, \ldots, x_n) = 0$ implicitly defines a utility function $U = f(x_1, x_2, \ldots, x_n)$:
   (a) Find the expressions for $\partial U/\partial x_2$, $\partial U/\partial x_n$, $\partial x_3/\partial x_2$, and $\partial x_4/\partial x_n$.
   (b) Interpret their respective economic meanings.
5. For each of the given equations $F(y, x) = 0$, is an implicit function $y = f(x)$ defined around the point $(y = 3, x = 1)$?
   (a) $x^3 - 2x^2 y + 3xy^2 - 22 = 0$
   (b) $2x^2 + 4xy - y^4 + 67 = 0$

If your answer is affirmative, find dy/dx by the implicit-function rule, and evaluate it at the said point.

6. Given $x^2 + 3xy + 2yz + y^2 + z^2 - 11 = 0$, is an implicit function $z = f(x, y)$ defined around the point $(x = 1, y = 2, z = 0)$? If so, find $\partial z/\partial x$ and $\partial z/\partial y$ by the implicit-function rule, and evaluate them at that point.

7. By considering the equation $F(y, x) = (x - y)^3 = 0$ in a neighborhood around the point of origin, prove that the conditions cited in the implicit-function theorem are *not* in the nature of *necessary* conditions.

8. If the equation $F(x, y, z) = 0$ implicitly defines each of the three variables as a function of the other two variables, and if all the derivatives in question exist, find the value of $\dfrac{\partial z}{\partial x} \dfrac{\partial x}{\partial y} \dfrac{\partial y}{\partial z}$.

9. Justify the assertion in the text that the equation system (8.28′) must be nonhomogeneous.

10. From the national-income model (8.30), find the nonincome-tax multiplier by the implicit-function rule. Check your results against (7.20).

8.6 Comparative Statics of General-Function Models

When we first considered the problem of comparative-static analysis in Chap. 7, we dealt with the case where the equilibrium values of the endogenous variables of the model are expressible explicitly in terms of the exogenous variables and parameters. There, the technique of simple partial differentiation was all we needed. When a model contains functions expressed in the general form, however, that technique becomes inapplicable because of the unavailability of explicit solutions. Instead, a new technique must be employed that makes use of such concepts as total differentials, total derivatives, as well as the implicit-function theorem and the implicit-function rule. We shall illustrate this first with a market model, and then move on to national-income models.

Market Model

Consider a single-commodity market, where the quantity demanded Q_d is a function not only of price P but also of an exogenously determined income Y_0. The quantity supplied Q_s, on the other hand, is a function of price alone. If these functions are not given in specific forms, our model may be written generally as follows:

$$Q_d = Q_s$$
$$Q_d = D(P, Y_0) \qquad (\partial D/\partial P < 0;\ \partial D/\partial Y_0 > 0) \qquad \textbf{(8.32)}$$
$$Q_s = S(P) \qquad (dS/dP > 0)$$

Both the D and S functions are assumed to possess continuous derivatives or, in other words, to have smooth graphs. Moreover, in order to ensure economic relevance, we have imposed definite restrictions on the signs of these derivatives. By the restriction $dS/dP > 0$, the supply function is stipulated to be strictly increasing, although it is permitted to be either linear or nonlinear. Similarly, by the restrictions on the two partial derivatives of the demand function, we indicate that it is a strictly decreasing function of price but a strictly increasing function of income. For notational simplicity, the sign restrictions on the derivatives of a function are sometimes indicated with $+$ or $-$ signs placed directly underneath the independent variables. Thus the D and S functions in (8.32) may alternatively be presented as

$$Q_d = D(\underset{-}{P}, \underset{+}{Y_0}) \qquad Q_s = S(\underset{+}{P})$$

These restrictions serve to confine our analysis to the "normal" case we expect to encounter.

In drawing the usual type of two-dimensional demand curve, the income level is assumed to be held fixed. When income changes, it will upset a given equilibrium by causing a shift of the demand curve. Similarly, in (8.32), Y_0 can cause a disequilibrating change through the demand function. Here, Y_0 is the only exogenous variable or parameter; thus the comparative-static analysis of this model will be concerned exclusively with how a change in Y_0 will affect the equilibrium position of the model.

The equilibrium position of the market is defined by the equilibrium condition $Q_d = Q_s$, which, upon substitution and rearrangement, can be expressed by

$$D(P, Y_0) - S(P) = 0 \qquad\qquad \textbf{(8.33)}$$

Even though this equation cannot be solved explicitly for the equilibrium price P^*, we shall assume that there does exist a static equilibrium—for otherwise there would be no point in even raising the question of comparative statics. From our experience with specific-function models, we have learned to expect P^* to be a function of the exogenous variable Y_0:

$$P^* = P^*(Y_0) \qquad\qquad \textbf{(8.34)}$$

But now we can provide a rigorous foundation for this expectation by appealing to the implicit-function theorem. Inasmuch as (8.33) is in the form of $F(P, Y_0) = 0$, the satisfaction of the conditions of the implicit-function theorem will guarantee that every value of Y_0 will yield a unique value of P^* in the neighborhood of a point satisfying (8.33), that is, in the neighborhood of an (initial or "old") equilibrium solution. In that case, we can indeed write the implicit function $P^* = P^*(Y_0)$ and discuss its derivative, dP^*/dY_0—the very comparative-static derivative we desire—which is known to exist. Let us, therefore, check those conditions. First, the function $F(P, Y_0)$ indeed possesses continuous derivatives; this is because, by assumption, its two additive components $D(P, Y_0)$ and $S(P)$ have continuous derivatives. Second, the partial derivative of F with respect to P, namely, $F_P = \partial D/\partial P - dS/dP$, is negative, and hence nonzero, no matter where it is evaluated. Thus the implicit-function theorem applies, and (8.34) is indeed legitimate.

According to the same theorem, the equilibrium condition (8.33) can now be taken to be an identity in some neighborhood of the equilibrium solution. Consequently, we may write the equilibrium identity

$$\underbrace{D(P^*, Y_0) - S(P^*)}_{F(P^*, Y_0)} \equiv 0 \qquad \text{[Excess demand} \equiv 0 \text{ in equilibrium]} \qquad \textbf{(8.35)}$$

It then requires only a straight application of the implicit-function rule to produce the comparative-static derivative, dP^*/dY_0. For visual clarity, we shall from here on enclose comparative-static derivatives in parentheses to distinguish them from the regular derivative expressions that merely constitute part of the model specification. The result from the implicit-function rule is

$$\left(\frac{dP^*}{dY_0}\right) = -\frac{\partial F/\partial Y_0}{\partial F/\partial P^*} = -\frac{\partial D/\partial Y_0}{\partial D/\partial P^* - dS/dP^*} > 0 \qquad \textbf{(8.36)}$$

In this result, the expression $\partial D/\partial P^*$ refers to the derivative $\partial D/\partial P$ evaluated at the initial equilibrium, i.e., at $P = P^*$; a similar interpretation attaches to dS/dP^*. In fact, $\partial D/\partial Y_0$ must be evaluated at the equilibrium point as well. By virtue of the sign specifications in (8.32), (dP^*/dY_0) is invariably positive. Thus our *qualitative* conclusion is that an increase (decrease) in the income level will always result in an increase (decrease) in the equilibrium price. If the values which the derivatives of the demand and supply functions take at the initial equilibrium are known, (8.36) will, of course, yield a *quantitative* conclusion also.

This discussion of market adjustment is concerned with the effect of a change in Y_0 on P^*. Is it possible also to find out the effect on the equilibrium quantity $Q^*(= Q_d^* = Q_s^*)$? The answer is yes. Since, in the equilibrium state, we have $Q^* = S(P^*)$, and since $P^* = P^*(Y_0)$, we may apply the chain rule to get the derivative

$$\left(\frac{dQ^*}{dY_0}\right) = \frac{dS}{dP^*}\left(\frac{dP^*}{dY_0}\right) > 0 \qquad \left[\text{since } \frac{dS}{dP^*} > 0\right] \qquad \textbf{(8.37)}$$

Thus the equilibrium quantity is also positively related to Y_0 in this model. Again, (8.37) can supply a quantitative conclusion if the values which the various derivatives take at the equilibrium are known.

The results in (8.36) and (8.37), which exhaust the comparative-static contents of the model (since the latter contains only one exogenous and two endogenous variables), are not surprising. In fact, they convey no more than the proposition that an upward shift of the demand curve will result in a higher equilibrium price as well as a higher equilibrium quantity. This same proposition, it may seem, could have been arrived at in a flash from a simple graphic analysis! This sounds correct, but one should not lose sight of the far, far more general character of the analytical procedure we have used here. The graphic analysis is by its very nature limited to a specific set of curves (the geometric counterpart of a specific set of functions); its conclusions are therefore, strictly speaking, relevant and applicable to only that set of curves. In sharp contrast, the formulation in (8.32), simplified as it is, covers the entire set of possible combinations of negatively sloped demand curves and positively sloped supply curves. Thus it is vastly more general. Also, the analytical procedure used here can handle many problems of greater complexity that would prove to be beyond the capabilities of the graphic approach.

Simultaneous-Equation Approach

The analysis of model (8.32) was carried out on the basis of a single equation, namely, (8.35). Since only one endogenous variable can fruitfully be incorporated into one equation, the inclusion of P^* means the exclusion of Q^*. As a result, we were compelled to find (dP^*/dY_0) first and then to infer (dQ^*/dY_0) in a subsequent step. Now we shall show how P^* and Q^* can be studied simultaneously. As there are two endogenous variables, we shall accordingly set up a two-equation system. First, letting $Q = Q_d = Q_s$ in (8.32) and rearranging, we can express our market model as

$$F^1(P, Q; Y_0) = D(P, Y_0) - Q = 0$$
$$F^2(P, Q; Y_0) = S(P) - Q = 0$$

(8.38)

which is in the form of (8.24), with $n = 2$ and $m = 1$. It becomes of interest, once again, to check the conditions of the implicit-function theorem. First, since the demand and supply functions are both assumed to possess continuous derivatives, so must the functions F^1 and F^2. Second, the endogenous-variable Jacobian (the one involving P and Q) indeed turns out to be nonzero, regardless of where it is evaluated, because

$$|J| = \begin{vmatrix} \dfrac{\partial F^1}{\partial P} & \dfrac{\partial F^1}{\partial Q} \\[2mm] \dfrac{\partial F^2}{\partial P} & \dfrac{\partial F^2}{\partial Q} \end{vmatrix} = \begin{vmatrix} \dfrac{\partial D}{\partial P} & -1 \\[2mm] \dfrac{dS}{dP} & -1 \end{vmatrix} = \dfrac{dS}{dP} - \dfrac{\partial D}{\partial P} > 0 \quad (8.39)$$

Hence, if an equilibrium solution (P^*, Q^*) exists (as we must assume in order to make it meaningful to talk about comparative statics), the implicit-function theorem tells us that we can write the implicit functions

$$P^* = P^*(Y_0) \qquad \text{and} \qquad Q^* = Q^*(Y_0) \qquad (8.40)$$

even though we cannot solve for P^* and Q^* explicitly. These functions are known to have continuous derivatives. Moreover, (8.38) will have the status of a pair of identities in some neighborhood of the equilibrium state, so that we may also write

$$D(P^*, Y_0) - Q^* \equiv 0 \qquad [\text{i.e., } F^1(P^*, Q^*; Y_0) \equiv 0]$$
$$S(P^*) - Q^* \equiv 0 \qquad [\text{i.e., } F^2(P^*, Q^*; Y_0) \equiv 0]$$

(8.41)

From these, (dP^*/dY_0) and (dQ^*/dY_0) can be found simultaneously by using the implicit-function rule (8.28′).

In the present context, with F^1 and F^2 as defined in (8.41), and with two endogenous variables P^* and Q^* and a single exogenous variable Y_0, the implicit-function rule takes the specific form

$$\begin{bmatrix} \dfrac{\partial F^1}{\partial P^*} & \dfrac{\partial F^1}{\partial Q^*} \\[3mm] \dfrac{\partial F^2}{\partial P^*} & \dfrac{\partial F^2}{\partial Q^*} \end{bmatrix} \begin{bmatrix} \left(\dfrac{dP^*}{dY_0}\right) \\[3mm] \left(\dfrac{dQ^*}{dY_0}\right) \end{bmatrix} = \begin{bmatrix} -\dfrac{\partial F^1}{\partial Y_0} \\[3mm] -\dfrac{\partial F^2}{\partial Y_0} \end{bmatrix}$$

Note that the comparative-static derivatives are written here with the symbol d rather than ∂, because there is only one exogenous variable in the present problem. More specifically, the last equation can be expressed as

$$\begin{bmatrix} \dfrac{\partial D}{\partial P^*} & -1 \\[3mm] \dfrac{dS}{dP^*} & -1 \end{bmatrix} \begin{bmatrix} \left(\dfrac{dP^*}{dY_0}\right) \\[3mm] \left(\dfrac{dQ^*}{dY_0}\right) \end{bmatrix} = \begin{bmatrix} -\dfrac{\partial D}{\partial Y_0} \\[3mm] 0 \end{bmatrix}$$

By Cramer's rule, and using (8.39), we then find the solution to be

$$\left(\frac{dP^*}{dY_0}\right) = \frac{\begin{vmatrix} -\dfrac{\partial D}{\partial Y_0} & -1 \\ 0 & -1 \end{vmatrix}}{|J|} = \frac{\dfrac{\partial D}{\partial Y_0}}{|J|}$$

$$\left(\frac{dQ^*}{dY_0}\right) = \frac{\begin{vmatrix} \dfrac{\partial D}{\partial P^*} & -\dfrac{\partial D}{\partial Y_0} \\ \dfrac{dS}{dP^*} & 0 \end{vmatrix}}{|J|} = \frac{\dfrac{dS}{dP^*}\dfrac{\partial D}{\partial Y_0}}{|J|}$$

(8.42)

where all the derivatives of the demand and supply functions (including those appearing in the Jacobian) are to be evaluated at the initial equilibrium. You can check that the results just obtained are identical with those obtained earlier in (8.36) and (8.37), by means of the single-equation approach.

Instead of directly applying the implicit-function rule, we can also reach the same result by first differentiating totally each identity in (8.41) in turn, to get a linear system of equations in the variables dP^* and dQ^*:

$$\frac{\partial D}{\partial P^*}dP^* - dQ^* = -\frac{\partial D}{\partial Y_0}dY_0$$

$$\frac{dS}{dP^*}dP^* - dQ^* = 0$$

and then dividing through by $dY_0 \neq 0$, and interpreting each quotient of two differentials as a derivative.

Use of Total Derivatives

In both the single-equation and the simultaneous-equation approaches illustrated above, we have taken the *total differentials* of both sides of an equilibrium identity and then equated the two results to arrive at the implicit-function rule. Instead of taking the total differentials, however, it is possible to take, and equate, the *total derivatives* of the two sides of the equilibrium identity with respect to a particular exogenous variable or parameter.

In the single-equation approach, for instance, the equilibrium identity is

$$D(P^*, Y_0) - S(P^*) \equiv 0 \qquad \text{[from (8.35)]}$$

where

$$P^* = P^*(Y_0) \qquad \text{[from (8.34)]}$$

Taking the total derivative of the equilibrium identity with respect to Y_0—which takes into account the indirect as well as the direct effects of a change in Y_0—will therefore give us the equation

$$\underbrace{\frac{\partial D}{\partial P^*}\left(\frac{dP^*}{dY_0}\right)}_{\left(\substack{\text{indirect effect} \\ \text{of } Y_0 \text{ on } D}\right)} + \underbrace{\frac{\partial D}{\partial Y_0}}_{\left(\substack{\text{direct effect} \\ \text{of } Y_0 \text{ on } D}\right)} - \underbrace{\frac{dS}{dP^*}\left(\frac{dP^*}{dY_0}\right)}_{\left(\substack{\text{indirect effect} \\ \text{of } Y_0 \text{ on } S}\right)} = 0$$

When this is solved for (dP^*/dY_0), the result is identical with the one in (8.36).

FIGURE 8.7

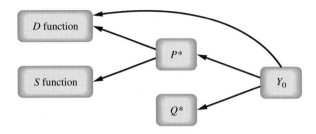

In the simultaneous-equation approach, on the other hand, there is a pair of equilibrium identities:

$$D(P^*, Y_0) - Q^* \equiv 0$$

$$S(P^*) - Q^* \equiv 0 \qquad \text{[from (8.41)]}$$

where $\qquad P^* = P^*(Y_0) \qquad Q^* = Q^*(Y_0) \qquad$ [from (8.40)]

The various effects of Y_0 are now harder to keep track of, but with the help of the channel map in Fig. 8.7, the pattern should become clear. This channel map tells us, for instance, that when differentiating the D function with respect to Y_0, we must allow for the indirect effect of Y_0 upon D through P^*, as well as the direct effect of Y_0 (curved arrow). In differentiating the S function with respect to Y_0, on the other hand, there is only the indirect effect (through P^*) to be taken into account. Thus the result of totally differentiating the two identities with respect to Y_0 is, upon rearrangement, the following pair of equations:

$$\frac{\partial D}{\partial P^*}\left(\frac{dP^*}{dY_0}\right) - \left(\frac{dQ^*}{dY_0}\right) = -\frac{\partial D}{\partial Y_0}$$

$$\frac{dS}{dP^*}\left(\frac{dP^*}{dY_0}\right) - \left(\frac{dQ^*}{dY_0}\right) = 0$$

These are, of course, identical with the equations obtained by the total-differential method, and they lead again to the comparative-static derivatives in (8.42).

National-Income Model (IS-LM)

A typical application of the implicit-function theorem is a general-functional form of the IS-LM model.[†] Equilibrium in this macroeconomic model is characterized by an income level and interest rates that simultaneously produce equilibrium in both the goods market and the money market.

A goods market is described by the following set of equations:

$$Y = C + I + G \qquad C = C(Y - T) \qquad G = G_0$$

$$I = I(r) \qquad T = T(Y)$$

Y is the level of gross domestic product (GDP), or national income. In this form of the model, Y can also be thought of as aggregate supply. C, I, G, and T are consumption, investment, government spending, and taxes, respectively.

[†] IS stands for "investment equals savings" and LM stands for "liquidity preference equals money supply."

1. Consumption is assumed to be a strictly increasing function of disposable income $(Y - T)$. If we denote disposable income as $Y^d = Y - T$, then the consumption function can be expressed as

$$C = C(Y^d)$$

where $dC/dY^d = C'(Y^d)$ is the marginal propensity to consume $(0 < C'(Y^d) < 1)$.

2. Investment spending is assumed to be a strictly decreasing function of the rate of interest, r:

$$\frac{dI}{dr} = I'(r) < 0$$

3. The public sector is described by two variables: government spending (G) and taxes (T). Typically, government spending is assumed to be exogenous (set by policy) whereas taxes are assumed to be an increasing function of income. $\dfrac{dT}{dY} = T'(Y)$ is the marginal tax rate $(0 < T'(Y) < 1)$.

If we substitute the functions for C, I, G into the first equation $Y = C + I + G$, we get

$$Y = C(Y - T(Y)) + I(r) + G_0 \qquad \text{(IS curve)}$$

which gives us a single equation with two endogenous variables: Y and r. This equation gives us all the combinations of Y and r that produce equilibrium in the goods market. This equation implicitly defines the IS curve.

Slope of the IS Curve

If we rewrite the IS equation, which is in the nature of an equilibrium identity,

$$Y - C(Y^d) - I(r) - G_0 \equiv 0$$

then the total differential with respect to Y and r is

$$dY - C'(Y^d)[1 - T'(Y)]\, dY - I'(r)\, dr = 0$$

Note:
$$\frac{dY^d}{dY} = 1 - T'(Y)$$

We can rearrange the dY and dr terms to get an expression for the slope of the IS curve:

$$\frac{dr}{dY} = \frac{1 - C'(Y^d)[1 - T'(Y)]}{I'(r)} < 0$$

Given the restrictions placed on the derivatives of $C, I,$ and T, we can easily verify that the slope of the IS curve is negative.

The money market can be described by the following three equations:

$$M^d = L(Y, r) \qquad \text{[money demand]} \qquad \text{where} \qquad L_Y > 0 \quad \text{and} \quad L_r < 0$$

$$M^s = M_0^s \qquad \text{[money supply]}$$

where the money supply is assumed to be exogenously determined by the central monetary authority, and

$$M^d = M^s \qquad \text{[equilibrium condition]}$$

Substituting the first two equations into the third, we get an expression that implicitly defines the LM curve, which is again in the nature of an equilibrium identity.

$$L(Y, r) \equiv M_0^s$$

Slope of the LM Curve

Since this is an equilibrium identity, we can take the total differential with respect to the two endogenous variables, Y and r:

$$L_Y \, dY + L_r \, dr = 0$$

which can be rearranged to give us an expression for the slope of the LM curve

$$\frac{dr}{dY} = -\frac{L_Y}{L_r} > 0$$

Since $L_Y > 0$ and $L_r < 0$, we can determine that the slope of the LM curve is positive.

The simultaneous macroeconomic equilibrium state of both the goods and money markets can be described by the following system of equations:

$$Y \equiv C(Y^d) + I(r) + G_0$$
$$L(Y, r) \equiv M_0^s$$

which implicitly define the two endogenous variables, Y and r, as functions of the exogenous variables, G_0 and M_0^s. Taking the total differential of the system, we get

$$dY - C'(Y^d)[1 - T'(Y)] \, dY - I'(r) \, dr = dG_0$$
$$L_Y \, dY + L_r \, dr = dM_0^s$$

or, in matrix form,

$$\begin{bmatrix} 1 - C'(Y^d)[1 - T'(Y)] & -I'(r) \\ L_Y & L_r \end{bmatrix} \begin{bmatrix} dY \\ dr \end{bmatrix} = \begin{bmatrix} dG_0 \\ dM_0^s \end{bmatrix}$$

The Jacobian determinant is

$$|J| = \begin{vmatrix} 1 - C'(Y^d)[1 - T'(Y)] & -I'(r) \\ L_Y & L_r \end{vmatrix}$$

$$= \{1 - C'(Y^d)[1 - T'(Y)]\}L_r + L_Y I'(r) < 0$$

Since $|J| \neq 0$, this system satisfies the conditions of the implicit-function theorem and the implicit functions

$$Y^* = Y^*(G_0, M_0^s)$$

and

$$r^* = r^*(G_0, M_0^s)$$

can be written even though we are unable to solve for Y^* and r^* explicitly. Even though we cannot solve for Y^* and r^* explicitly, we can perform comparative-static exercises to determine the effects of a change of one of the exogenous variables (G_0, M_0^s) on the equilibrium values of Y^* and r^*. Consider the comparative-static derivatives $\partial Y^*/\partial G_0$ and

$\partial r^* / \partial G_0$ which we shall derive by applying the implicit-function theorem to our system of total differentials in matrix form

$$\begin{bmatrix} 1 - C'(Y^d)[1 - T'(Y)] & -I'(r) \\ L_Y & L_r \end{bmatrix} \begin{bmatrix} dY \\ dr \end{bmatrix} = \begin{bmatrix} dG_0 \\ dM_0^s \end{bmatrix}$$

First we set $dM_0^s = 0$ and divide both sides by dG_0.

$$\begin{bmatrix} 1 - C' \cdot (1 - T') & -I'(r) \\ L_Y & L_r \end{bmatrix} \begin{bmatrix} \dfrac{dY^*}{dG_0} \\ \dfrac{dr^*}{dG_0} \end{bmatrix} = \begin{bmatrix} 1 \\ 0 \end{bmatrix}$$

Using Cramer's rule, we obtain

$$\frac{dY^*}{dG_0} = \frac{\begin{vmatrix} 1 & -I' \\ 0 & L_r \end{vmatrix}}{|J|} = \frac{L_r}{|J|} = \frac{\ominus}{\ominus} > 0$$

and

$$\frac{dr^*}{dG_0} = \frac{\begin{vmatrix} 1 - C' \cdot (1 - T') & 1 \\ L_Y & 0 \end{vmatrix}}{|J|} = \frac{-L_Y}{|J|} = \frac{\ominus}{\ominus} > 0$$

From the implicit-function theorem, these ratios of differentials, dY^*/dG_0 and dr^*/dG_0, can be interpreted as partial derivatives,

$$\frac{\partial Y^*(G_0, M_0^s)}{\partial G_0} \quad \text{and} \quad \frac{\partial r^*(G_0, M_0^s)}{\partial G_0}$$

which are our desired comparative-static derivatives.

Extending the Model: An Open Economy

One property of a model that economists look for is its robustness; the ability of the model to be applied to different settings. At this point we will extend the basic model to incorporate the foreign sector.

1. *Net exports.* Let X denote exports, M denote imports, and E denote the exchange rate (measured as the domestic price of foreign currency). Exports are an increasing function of the exchange rate.

$$X = X(E) \quad \text{where} \quad X'(E) > 0$$

   Imports are a decreasing function of the exchange rate but an increasing function of income.

$$M = M(Y, E) \quad \text{where} \quad M_Y > 0, \ M_E < 0$$

2. *Capital flows.* The net flow of capital into a country is a function of both the domestic interest rate r and world interest rate r_w. Let K denote net capital inflow such that

$$K = K(r, r_w) \quad \text{where} \quad K_r > 0, K_{r_w} < 0$$

3. *Balance of payments.* The inflows and outflows of foreign currency for a country are typically separated into two accounts: *current* account (net exports of goods and services) and the *capital* account (the purchasing of foreign and domestic bonds). Together, the two accounts make up the balance of payments.

$$BP = \text{current account} + \text{capital account}$$
$$= [X(E) - M(Y, E)] + K(r, r_w)$$

Under flexible exchange rates, the exchange rate adjusts to keep the balance of payments equal to zero. Having the balance of payments equal to zero is the equivalent to saying the supply of foreign currency equals the demand for foreign currency by a country.[†]

Open-Economy Equilibrium

Equilibrium in an open economy is characterized by three conditions: aggregate demand equals aggregate supply; the demand for money equals the supply of money; the balance of payments equals zero. Adding the foreign sector to our basic model gives us the following system of three equations

$$Y = C(Y^d) + I(r) + G_0 + X(E) - M(Y, E)$$
$$L(Y, r) = M_0^s$$
$$X(E) - M(Y, E) + K(r, r_w) = 0$$

Since we have three equations, we need three endogenous variables, which are Y, r, and E. The exogenous variables now become G_0, M_0^s, and r_w. Rewriting the system as equilibrium identities $F^1 \equiv 0$, $F^2 \equiv 0$, $F^3 \equiv 0$ allows us to find the Jacobian:

$$Y - C(Y^d) - I(r) - G_0 - X(E) + M(Y, E) \equiv 0$$
$$L(Y, r) - M_0^s \equiv 0$$
$$X(E) - M(Y, E) + K(r, r_w) \equiv 0$$

$$|J| = \begin{vmatrix} 1 - C' \cdot (1 - T') + M_Y & -I' & M_E - X' \\ L_Y & L_r & 0 \\ -M_Y & K_r & X' - M_E \end{vmatrix}$$

Using Laplace expansion down the third column, we obtain

$$|J| = (M_E - X') \begin{vmatrix} L_Y & L_r \\ -M_Y & K_r \end{vmatrix} + (X' - M_E) \begin{vmatrix} 1 - C' \cdot (1 - T') + M_Y & -I' \\ L_Y & L_r \end{vmatrix}$$

$$= (M_E - X')(L_Y K_r + L_r M_Y) + (X' - M_E)\{[1 - C' \cdot (1 - T') + M_Y]L_r + I' L_Y\}$$

$$= (M_E - X')\{L_Y(K_r - I') + L_r[C'(1 - T') - 1]\}$$

Given the assumptions about the signs of the partial derivatives and the restriction that $0 < C' \cdot (1 - T') < 1$, we can determine that $|J| < 0$. Therefore, we can write the implicit functions

$$Y^* = Y^*(G_0, M_0^s, r_w)$$
$$r^* = r^*(G_0, M_0^s, r_w)$$
$$E^* = E^*(G_0, M_0^s, r_w)$$

[†] Under a fixed exchange rate regime, the balance of payments is not necessarily zero. In such an event, any surpluses or deficits are recorded as *change of official settlements.*

Taking the total differential of the system of equations and writing it in matrix form

$$
\begin{bmatrix}
1 - C' \cdot (1 - T') + M_Y & -I' & M_E - X' \\
L_Y & L_r & 0 \\
-M_Y & K_r & X' - M_E
\end{bmatrix}
\begin{bmatrix}
dY^* \\
dr^* \\
dE^*
\end{bmatrix}
=
\begin{bmatrix}
dG_0 \\
dM_0^s \\
-K_{r_w}\, dr_w
\end{bmatrix}
$$

will allow us to carry out a series of comparative-static exercises. Let's consider the impact of change in the world with interest rates r_w on the equilibrium values of Y, r, and E. Setting $dG_0 = dM_0^s = 0$ and dividing both sides by dr_w gives us

$$
\begin{bmatrix}
1 - C' \cdot (1 - T') + M_Y & -I' & M_E - X' \\
L_Y & L_r & 0 \\
-M_Y & K_r & X' - M_E
\end{bmatrix}
\begin{bmatrix}
\dfrac{dY^*}{dr_w} \\[2mm]
\dfrac{dr^*}{dr_w} \\[2mm]
\dfrac{dE^*}{dr_w}
\end{bmatrix}
=
\begin{bmatrix}
0 \\
0 \\
-K_{r_w}
\end{bmatrix}
$$

Using Cramer's rule, we obtain the comparative-static derivatives

$$
\frac{\partial Y^*}{\partial r_w} =
\frac{\begin{vmatrix}
0 & -I' & M_E - X' \\
0 & L_r & 0 \\
-K_{r_w} & K_r & X' - M_E
\end{vmatrix}}{|J|}
= \frac{(-K_{r_w})(-L_r)(M_E - X')}{|J|} > 0
$$

and

$$
\frac{\partial r^*}{\partial r_w} =
\frac{\begin{vmatrix}
1 - C' \cdot (1 - T') + M_Y & 0 & M_E - X' \\
L_Y & 0 & 0 \\
-M_Y & -K_{r_w} & X' - M_E
\end{vmatrix}}{|J|}
= \frac{K_{r_w}(-L_Y)(M_E - X')}{|J|} > 0
$$

and

$$
\frac{\partial E^*}{\partial r_w} =
\frac{\begin{vmatrix}
1 - C' \cdot (1 - T') + M_Y & -I' & 0 \\
L_Y & L_r & 0 \\
-M_Y & K_r & -K_{r_w}
\end{vmatrix}}{|J|}
$$

$$
= \frac{-K_{r_w}\{[1 - C' \cdot (1 - T') + M_Y]L_r + L_Y I'\}}{|J|} > 0
$$

At this point you should compare the results we have derived to the macroeconomic principles. Intuitively, a rise in the world interest rate should lead to an increase in capital outflows and a depreciation of the domestic currency. This, in turn, will lead to an increase in net exports and income. The increase in domestic income will cause an increase in money demand, putting upward pressure on domestic interest rates. This result is illustrated graphically in Fig. 8.8 where a rise in world interest rates leads to a rightward shift of the IS curve.

FIGURE 8.8

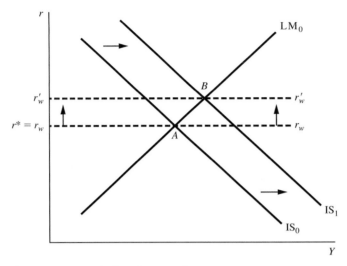

Summary of the Procedure

In the analysis of the general-function market model and national-income model, it is not possible to obtain explicit solution values of the endogenous variables. Instead, we rely on the implicit-function theorem to enable us to write the implicit solutions such as

$$P^* = P^*(Y_0) \qquad \text{and} \qquad r^* = r^*(G_0, M_0^s)$$

Our subsequent search for the comparative-static derivatives such as (dP^*/dY_0) and $(\partial r^*/\partial G_0)$ then rests for its meaningfulness upon the known fact—thanks again to the implicit-function theorem—that the P^* and r^* functions do possess continuous derivatives.

To facilitate the application of that theorem, we make it a standard practice to write the equilibrium condition(s) of the model in the form of (8.19) or (8.24). We then check whether (1) the F function(s) have continuous derivatives and (2) the value of F_y or the endogenous-variable Jacobian determinant (as the case may be) is nonzero at the initial equilibrium of the model. However, as long as the individual functions in the model have continuous derivatives—an assumption which is often adopted as a matter of course in general-function models—the first condition is automatically satisfied. As a practical matter, therefore, it is needed only to check the value of F_y or the endogenous-variable Jacobian. And if it is nonzero at the equilibrium, we may proceed at once to the task of finding the comparative-static derivatives.

To that end, the implicit-function rule is of help. For the single-equation case, simply set the endogenous variables equal to its equilibrium value (e.g., set $P = P^*$) in the equilibrium condition, and then apply the rule as stated in (8.23) to the resulting equilibrium identity. For the simultaneous-equation case, we must also first set all endogenous variables equal to their respective equilibrium values in the equilibrium conditions. Then we can either apply the implicit-function rule as illustrated in (8.29) to the resulting equilibrium identities, or arrive at the same result by carrying out the several steps outlined as follows:

1. Take the total differential of each equilibrium identity in turn.
2. Select one, and only one, exogenous variable (say, X_0) as the sole disequilibrating factor, and set the differentials of *all other* exogenous variables equal to zero. Then divide

all remaining terms in each identity by dX_0, and interpret each quotient of two differentials as a comparative-static derivative—a *partial* one if the model contains two or more exogenous variables.[†]

3. Solve the resulting equation system for the comparative-static derivatives appearing therein, and interpret their economic implications. In this step, if Cramer's rule is used, we can take advantage of the fact that, earlier, in checking the condition $|J| \neq 0$, we have in fact already calculated the determinant of the coefficient matrix of the equation system now being solved.

4. For the analysis of another disequilibrating factor (another exogenous variable), if any, repeat steps 2 and 3. Although a different group of comparative-static derivatives will emerge in the new equation system, the coefficient matrix will be the same as before, and thus the known value of $|J|$ can again be put to use.

Given a model with m exogenous variables, it will take exactly m applications of steps 1, 2, and 3 to catch all the comparative-static derivatives there are.

[†] Instead of taking steps 1 and 2, we may equivalently resort to the total-derivative method by differentiating (both sides of) each equilibrium identity totally with respect to the selected exogenous variable. In so doing, a channel map will prove to be of help.

EXERCISE 8.6

1. Let the equilibrium condition for national income be
$$S(Y) + T(Y) = I(Y) + G_0 \qquad (S', T', I' > 0; \quad S' + T' > I')$$
where S, Y, T, I, and G stand for saving, national income, taxes, investment, and government expenditure, respectively. All derivatives are continuous.
   (a) Interpret the economic meanings of the derivatives S', T', and I'.
   (b) Check whether the conditions of the implicit-function theorem are satisfied. If so, write the equilibrium identity.
   (c) Find (dY^*/dG_0) and discuss its economic implications.

2. Let the demand and supply functions for a commodity be
$$Q_d = D(P, Y_0) \qquad (D_p < 0; \quad D_{Y_0} > 0)$$
$$Q_s = S(P, T_0) \qquad (S_p > 0; \quad S_{T_0} < 0)$$
where Y_0 is income and T_0 is the tax on the commodity. All derivatives are continuous.
   (a) Write the equilibrium condition in a single equation.
   (b) Check whether the implicit-function theorem is applicable. If so, write the equilibrium identity.
   (c) Find $(\partial P^*/\partial Y_0)$ and $(\partial P^*/\partial T_0)$, and discuss their economic implications.
   (d) Using a procedure similar to (8.37), find $(\partial Q^*/\partial Y_0)$ from the supply function and $(\partial Q^*/\partial T_0)$ from the demand function. (Why not use the demand function for the former, and the supply function for the latter?)

3. Solve Prob. 2 by the simultaneous-equation approach.

4. Let the demand and supply functions for a commodity be
$$Q_d = D(P, t_0) \qquad \text{and} \qquad Q_s = Q_{s0}$$
$${}_{-}{}_{+}$$

where t_0 is consumers' taste for the commodity, and where both partial derivatives are continuous.

(a) What is the meaning of the $-$ and $+$ signs beneath the independent variables P and t_0?

(b) Write the equilibrium condition as a single equation.

(c) Is the implicit-function theorem applicable?

(d) How would the equilibrium price vary with consumers' taste?

5. Consider the following national-income model (with taxes ignored):

$$Y - C(Y) - I(i) - G_0 = 0 \qquad (0 < C' < 1; \quad I' < 0)$$
$$kY + L(i) - M_{s0} = 0 \qquad (k = \text{positive constant}; \quad L' < 0)$$

(a) Is the first equation in the nature of an equilibrium condition?

(b) What is the total quantity demanded for money in this model?

(c) Analyze the comparative statics of the model when money supply changes (monetary policy) and when government expenditure changes (fiscal policy).

6. In Prob. 5, suppose that while the demand for money still depends on Y as specified, it is now no longer affected by the interest rate.

(a) How should the model statement be revised?

(b) Write the new Jacobian, call it $|J|'$. Is $|J|'$ numerically (in absolute value) larger or smaller than $|J|$?

(c) Would the implicit-function rule still apply?

(d) Find the new comparative-static derivatives.

(e) Comparing the new $(\partial Y^*/\partial G_0)$ with that in Prob. 5, what can you conclude about the effectiveness of fiscal policy in the new model where Y is independent of i?

(f) Comparing the new $(\partial Y^*/\partial M_{s0})$ with that in Prob. 5, what can you say about the effectiveness of monetary policy in the new model?

8.7 Limitations of Comparative Statics

Comparative statics is a useful area of study, because in economics we are often interested in finding out how a disequilibrating change in a parameter will affect the equilibrium state of a model. It is important to realize, however, that by its very nature comparative statics ignores the process of adjustment from the old equilibrium to the new and also neglects the length of time required in that adjustment process. As a consequence, it must of necessity also disregard the possibility that, because of the inherent instability of the model, the new equilibrium may not be attainable ever. The study of the process of adjustment per se belongs to the field of *economic dynamics.* When we come to that, particular attention will be directed toward the manner in which a variable will change over time, and explicit consideration will be given to the question of stability of equilibrium.

The important topic of dynamics, however, must wait its turn. Meanwhile, in Part 4, we shall undertake to study the problem of *optimization,* an exceedingly important special variety of equilibrium analysis with attendant comparative-static implications (and complications) of its own.

Part 4

Optimization Problems

Chapter 9

Optimization: A Special Variety of Equilibrium Analysis

When we first introduced the term equilibrium in Chap. 3, we made a broad distinction between goal and nongoal equilibrium. In the latter type, exemplified by our study of market and national-income models, the interplay of certain opposing forces in the model—e.g., the forces of demand and supply in the market models and the forces of leakages and injections in the income models—dictates an equilibrium state, if any, in which these opposing forces are just balanced against each other, thus obviating any further tendency to change. The attainment of this type of equilibrium is the outcome of the impersonal balancing of these forces and does not require the conscious effort on the part of anyone to accomplish a specified goal. True, the consuming households behind the forces of demand and the firms behind the forces of supply are each striving for an optimal position under the given circumstances, but as far as the market itself is concerned, no one is aiming at any particular equilibrium price or equilibrium quantity (unless, of course, the government happens to be trying to peg the price). Similarly, in national-income determination, the impersonal balancing of leakages and injections is what brings about an equilibrium state, and no conscious effort at reaching any particular goal (such as an attempt to alter an undesirable income level by means of monetary or fiscal policies) needs to be involved at all.

In the present part of the book, however, our attention will be turned to the study of *goal equilibrium,* in which the equilibrium state is defined as the optimum position for a given economic unit (a household, a business firm, or even an entire economy) and in which the said economic unit will be deliberately striving for attainment of that equilibrium. As a result, in this context—but only in this context—our earlier warning that equilibrium does not imply desirability becomes irrelevant and immaterial. In this part of the book, our primary focus will be on the classical techniques for locating optimum positions—those using differential calculus. More modern developments, known as mathematical programming, will be discussed in Chap. 13.

9.1 Optimum Values and Extreme Values

Economics is essentially a science of choice. When an economic project is to be carried out, such as the production of a specified level of output, there are normally a number of alternative ways of accomplishing it. One (or more) of these alternatives will, however, be more desirable than others from the standpoint of some criterion, and it is the essence of the optimization problem to choose, on the basis of that specified criterion, the best alternative available.

The most common criterion of choice among alternatives in economics is the goal of *maximizing* something (such as maximizing a firm's profit, a consumer's utility, or the rate of growth of a firm or of a country's economy) or of *minimizing* something (such as minimizing the cost of producing a given output). Economically, we may categorize such maximization and minimization problems under the general heading of *optimization,* meaning "the quest for the best." From a purely mathematical point of view, however, the terms *maximum* and *minimum* do not carry with them any connotation of optimality. Therefore, the collective term for maximum and minimum, as mathematical concepts, is the more matter-of-fact designation *extremum,* meaning an extreme value.

In formulating an optimization problem, the first order of business is to delineate an *objective function* in which the dependent variable represents the object of maximization or minimization and in which the set of independent variables indicates the objects whose magnitudes the economic unit in question can pick and choose, with a view to optimizing. We shall therefore refer to the independent variables as *choice variables.*[†] The essence of the optimization process is simply to find the set of values of the choice variables that will lead us to the desired extremum of the objective function.

For example, a business firm may seek to maximize profit π, that is, to maximize the difference between total revenue R and total cost C. Since, within the framework of a given state of technology and a given market demand for the firm's product, R and C are both functions of the output level Q, it follows that π is also expressible as a function of Q:

$$\pi(Q) = R(Q) - C(Q)$$

This equation constitutes the relevant objective function, with π as the object of maximization and Q as the (only) choice variable. The optimization problem is then that of choosing the level of Q that maximizes π. Note that while the *optimal* level of π is by definition its *maximal* level, the optimal level of the choice variable Q is itself not required to be either a maximum or a minimum.

To cast the problem into a more general mold for further discussion (though still confining ourselves to objective functions of one variable only), let us consider the general function

$$y = f(x)$$

and attempt to develop a procedure for finding the level of x that will maximize or minimize the value of y. It will be assumed in our discussion that the function f is continuously differentiable.

[†] They can also be called *decision variables,* or *policy variables.*

9.2 Relative Maximum and Minimum: First-Derivative Test

Since the objective function $y = f(x)$ is stated in the general form, there is no restriction as to whether it is linear or nonlinear or whether it is monotonic or contains both increasing and decreasing parts. From among the many possible types of function compatible with the objective-function form discussed in Sec. 9.1, we have selected three specific cases to be depicted in Fig. 9.1. Simple as they may be, the graphs in Fig. 9.1 should give us valuable insight into the problem of locating the maximum or minimum value of the function $y = f(x)$.

Relative versus Absolute Extremum

If the objective function is a constant function, as in Fig. 9.1*a*, all values of the choice variable x will result in the same value of y, and the height of each point on the graph of the function (such as A or B or C) may be considered a maximum or, for that matter, a minimum—or, indeed, neither. In this case, there is in effect no significant choice to be made regarding the value of x for the maximization or minimization of y.

In Fig. 9.1*b*, the function is strictly increasing, and there is no finite maximum if the set of nonnegative real numbers is taken to be its domain. However, we may consider the end point D on the left (the y intercept) as representing a minimum; in fact, it is in this case the *absolute* (or *global*) minimum in the range of the function.

The points E and F in Fig. 9.1*c*, on the other hand, are examples of a *relative* (or *local*) extremum, in the sense that each of these points represents an extremum in the immediate neighborhood of the point only. The fact that point F is a relative minimum is, of course, no guarantee that it is also the global minimum of the function, although this may happen to be the case. Similarly, a relative maximum point such as E may or may not be a global maximum. Note also that a function can very well have several relative extrema, some of which may be maxima while others are minima.

In most economic problems that we shall be dealing with, our primary, if not exclusive, concern will be with extreme values other than end-point values, for with most such problems the domain of the objective function is restricted to be the set of nonnegative real numbers, and thus an end point (on the left) will represent the zero level of the choice variable, which is often of no practical interest. Actually, the type of function most frequently encountered in economic analysis is that shown in Fig. 9.1*c*, or some variant thereof that contains only a single bend in the curve. We shall therefore continue our discussion mainly with reference to the search for *relative* extrema such as points E and F. This will, however, by no means foreclose the knowledge of an absolute maximum if we want it, because an absolute maximum must be either a relative maximum or one of the end points of the

FIGURE 9.1

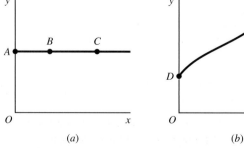

(a)

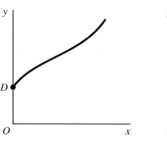

(b)

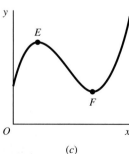

(c)

FIGURE 9.2

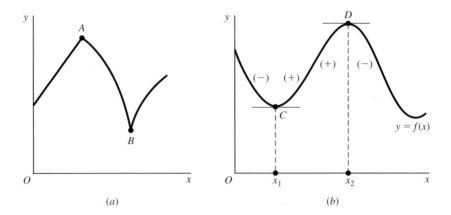

(a)   (b)

function. Thus if we know all the relative maxima, it is necessary only to select the largest of these and compare it with the end points in order to determine the absolute maximum. The absolute minimum of a function can be found analogously. Hereafter, the extreme values considered will be *relative* or *local* ones, unless indicated otherwise.

First-Derivative Test

As a matter of terminology, from now on we shall refer to the derivative of a function alternatively as its *first* derivative (short for *first-order* derivative). The reason for this will become apparent shortly.

Given a function $y = f(x)$, the first derivative $f'(x)$ plays a major role in our search for its extreme values. This is due to the fact that, if a relative extremum of the function occurs at $x = x_0$, then either (1) $f'(x_0)$ does not exist, or (2) $f'(x_0) = 0$. The first eventuality is illustrated in Fig. 9.2a, where both points A and B depict relative extreme values of y, and yet no derivative is defined at either of these sharp points. Since in the present discussion we are assuming that $y = f(x)$ is continuous and possesses a continuous derivative, however, we are in effect ruling out sharp points. For smooth functions, relative extreme values can occur only where the first derivative has a zero value. This is illustrated by points C and D in Fig. 9.2b, both of which represent extreme values, and both of which are characterized by a zero slope—$f'(x_1) = 0$ and $f'(x_2) = 0$. It is also easy to see that when the slope is nonzero we cannot possibly have a relative minimum (the bottom of a valley) or a relative maximum (the peak of a hill). For this reason, we can, in the context of smooth functions, take the condition $f'(x) = 0$ to be a *necessary* condition for a relative extremum (either maximum or minimum).

We must hasten to add, however, that a zero slope, while *necessary*, is *not sufficient* to establish a relative extremum. An example of the case where a zero slope is not associated with an extremum will be presented shortly. By appending a certain proviso to the zero-slope condition, however, we can obtain a decisive test for a relative extremum. This may be stated as follows:

First-derivative test for relative extremum If the first derivative of a function $f(x)$ at $x = x_0$ is $f'(x_0) = 0$, then the value of the function at x_0, $f(x_0)$, will be

a. A relative *maximum* if the derivative $f'(x)$ changes its sign from positive to negative from the immediate left of the point x_0 to its immediate right.

b. A relative *minimum* if $f'(x)$ changes its sign from negative to positive from the immediate left of x_0 to its immediate right.

c. Neither a relative maximum nor a relative minimum if $f'(x)$ has the same sign on both
the immediate left and the immediate right of point x_0.

Let us call the value x_0 a *critical value* of x if $f'(x_0) = 0$, and refer to $f(x_0)$ as a *stationary value* of y (or of the function f). The point with coordinates x_0 and $f(x_0)$ can,
accordingly, be called a *stationary point*. (The rationale for the word *stationary* should be
self-evident—wherever the slope is zero, the point in question is never situated on an
upward or downward incline, but is rather at a standstill position.) Then, graphically, the
first possibility listed in this test will establish the stationary point as the peak of a hill, such
as point D in Fig. 9.2b, whereas the second possibility will establish the stationary point as
the bottom of a valley, such as point C in the same diagram. Note, however, that in view of
the existence of a third possibility, yet to be discussed, we are unable to regard the condition $f'(x) = 0$ as a *sufficient condition* for a relative extremum. But we now see that, *if* the
necessary condition $f'(x) = 0$ is satisfied, *then* the change-of-derivative-sign proviso can
serve as a *sufficient condition* for a relative maximum or minimum, depending on the
direction of the sign change.

Let us now explain the third possibility. In Fig. 9.3a, the function f is shown to attain
a zero slope at point J (when $x = j$). Even though $f'(j)$ is zero—which makes $f(j)$ a
stationary value—the derivative does not change its sign from one side of $x = j$ to the
other; therefore, according to the first-derivative test, point J gives neither a maximum nor

FIGURE 9.3

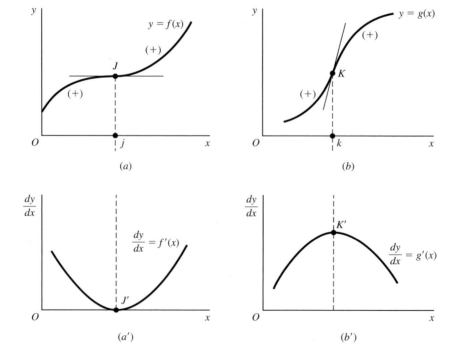

a minimum, as is duly confirmed by the graph of the function. Rather, it exemplifies what is known as an *inflection point.*

The characteristic feature of an inflection point is that, at that point, the derivative (as against the primitive) function reaches an extreme value. Since this extreme value can be either a maximum or a minimum, we have two types of inflection points. In Fig. 9.3*a'*, where we have plotted the derivative $f'(x)$, we see that its value is zero when $x = j$ (see point *J'*) but is positive on both sides of point *J'*; this makes *J'* a *minimum* point of the derivative function $f'(x)$.

The other type of inflection point is portrayed in Fig. 9.3*b*, where the slope of the function $g(x)$ increases till the point k is reached and decreases thereafter. Consequently, the graph of the derivative function $g'(x)$ will assume the shape shown in Fig. 9.3*b'*, where point *K'* gives a *maximum* value of the derivative function $g'(x)$.[†]

To sum up: A relative extremum must be a stationary value, but a stationary value may be associated with either a relative extremum or an inflection point. To find the relative maximum or minimum of a given function, therefore, the procedure should be first to find the stationary values of the function where the condition $f'(x) = 0$ is satisfied, and then to apply the first-derivative test to determine whether each of the stationary values is a relative maximum, a relative minimum, or neither.

Example 1	Find the relative extrema of the function

$$y = f(x) = x^3 - 12x^2 + 36x + 8$$

First, we find the derivative function to be

$$f'(x) = 3x^2 - 24x + 36$$

To get the critical values, i.e., the values of x satisfying the condition $f'(x) = 0$, we set the quadratic derivative function equal to zero and get the quadratic equation

$$3x^2 - 24x + 36 = 0$$

By factoring the polynomial or by applying the quadratic formula, we then obtain the following pair of roots (solutions):

$$x_1^* = 6 \qquad \text{[at which we have } f'(6) = 0 \text{ and } f(6) = 8\text{]}$$
$$x_2^* = 2 \qquad \text{[at which we have } f'(2) = 0 \text{ and } f(2) = 40\text{]}$$

Since $f'(6) = f'(2) = 0$, these two values of x are the critical values we desire.

It is easy to verify that, in the immediate neighborhood of $x = 6$, we have $f'(x) < 0$ for $x < 6$, and $f'(x) > 0$ for $x > 6$; thus the value of the function $f(6) = 8$ is a relative minimum. Similarly, since, in the immediate neighborhood of $x = 2$, we find $f'(x) > 0$ for $x < 2$, and $f'(x) < 0$ for $x > 2$, the value of the function $f(2) = 40$ is a relative maximum.

[†] Note that a zero derivative value, while a necessary condition for a relative extremum, is *not* required for an inflection point; for the derivative $g'(x)$ has a positive value at $x = k$, and yet point *K* is an inflection point.

FIGURE 9.4

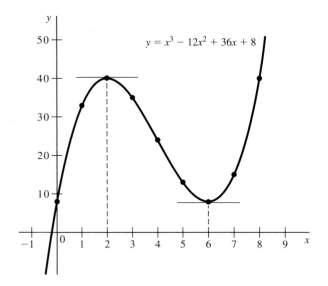

Figure 9.4 shows the graph of the function of this example. Such a graph may be used to verify the location of extreme values obtained through use of the first-derivative test. But, in reality, in most cases "helpfulness" flows in the opposite direction—the mathematically derived extreme values will help in plotting the graph. The accurate plotting of a graph ideally requires knowledge of the value of the function at every point in the domain; but as a matter of actual practice, only a few points in the domain are selected for purposes of plotting, and the rest of the points typically are filled in by interpolation. The pitfall of this practice is that, unless we hit upon the stationary point(s) by coincidence, we shall miss the exact location of the turning point(s) in the curve. Now, with the first-derivative test at our disposal, it becomes possible to locate these turning points precisely.

Example 2

Find the relative extremum of the average-cost function

$$AC = f(Q) = Q^2 - 5Q + 8$$

The derivative here is $f'(Q) = 2Q - 5$, a linear function. Setting $f'(Q)$ equal to zero, we get the linear equation $2Q - 5 = 0$, which has the single root $Q^* = 2.5$. This is the only critical value in this case. To apply the first-derivative test, let us find the values of the derivative at, say, $Q = 2.4$ and $Q = 2.6$, respectively. Since $f'(2.4) = -0.2 < 0$ whereas $f'(2.6) = 0.2 > 0$, we can conclude that the stationary value $AC = f(2.5) = 1.75$ represents a relative minimum. The graph of the function of this example is actually a U-shaped curve, so that the relative minimum already found will also be the absolute minimum. Our knowledge of the exact location of this point should be of great help in plotting the AC curve.

EXERCISE 9.2

1. Find the stationary values of the following (check whether they are relative maxima or minima or inflection points), assuming the domain to be the set of all real numbers:
    (a) $y = -2x^2 + 8x + 7$ (b) $y = 5x^2 + x$ (c) $y = 3x^2 + 3$ (d) $y = 3x^2 - 6x + 2$

2. Find the stationary values of the following (check whether they are relative maxima or minima or inflection points), assuming the domain to be the interval $[0, \infty)$:

   (a) $y = x^3 - 3x + 5$

   (b) $y = \frac{1}{3}x^3 - x^2 + x + 10$

   (c) $y = -x^3 + 4.5x^2 - 6x + 6$

3. Show that the function $y = x + 1/x$ (with $x \neq 0$) has two relative extrema, one a maximum and the other a minimum. Is the "minimum" larger or smaller than the "maximum"? How is this paradoxical result possible?

4. Let $T = \phi(x)$ be a *total* function (e.g., total product or total cost):

   (a) Write out the expressions for the *marginal* function M and the *average* function A.

   (b) Show that, when A reaches a relative extremum, M and A must have the same value.

   (c) What general principle does this suggest for the drawing of a marginal curve and an average curve in the same diagram?

   (d) What can you conclude about the elasticity of the total function T at the point where A reaches an extreme value?

9.3 Second and Higher Derivatives

Hitherto we have considered only the first derivative $f'(x)$ of a function $y = f(x)$; now let us introduce the concept of *second derivative* (short for *second-order derivative*), and derivatives of even higher orders. These will enable us to develop alternative criteria for locating the relative extrema of a function.

Derivative of a Derivative

Since the first derivative $f'(x)$ is itself a function of x, it, too, should be differentiable with respect to x, provided that it is continuous and smooth. The result of this differentiation, known as the second derivative of the function f, is denoted by

$f''(x)$ where the double prime indicates that $f(x)$ has been differentiated with respect to x twice, and where the expression (x) following the double prime suggests that the second derivative is again a function of x

or

$\dfrac{d^2y}{dx^2}$ where the notation stems from the consideration that the second derivative means, in fact, $\dfrac{d}{dx}\left(\dfrac{dy}{dx}\right)$; hence, the d^2 (read: "*d*-two") in the numerator and dx^2 (read: "*dx* squared") in the denominator of this symbol.

If the second derivative $f''(x)$ exists for all x values in the domain, the function $f(x)$ is said to be *twice differentiable;* if, in addition, $f''(x)$ is continuous, the function $f(x)$ is said to be *twice continuously differentiable.* Just as the notation $f \in C^{(1)}$ or $f \in C'$ is often used to indicate that the function f is continuously differentiable, an analogous notation

$$f \in C^{(2)} \qquad \text{or} \qquad f \in C''$$

can be used to signify that f is twice continuously differentiable.

As a function of x the second derivative can be differentiated with respect to x again to produce a *third* derivative, which in turn can be the source of a *fourth* derivative, and so on ad infinitum, as long as the differentiability condition is met. These higher-order derivatives are symbolized along the same line as the second derivative:

$$f'''(x), f^{(4)}(x), \ldots, f^{(n)}(x) \qquad \text{[with superscripts enclosed in ( )]}$$

or
$$\frac{d^3 y}{dx^3}, \frac{d^4 y}{dx^4}, \ldots, \frac{d^n y}{dx^n}$$

The last of these can also be written as $\dfrac{d^n}{dx^n} y$, where the $\dfrac{d^n}{dx^n}$ part serves as an operator symbol instructing us to take the nth derivative of (some function) with respect to x.

Almost all the *specific* functions we shall be working with possess continuous derivatives up to any order we desire; i.e., they are continuously differentiable any number of times. Whenever a *general* function is used, such as $f(x)$, we always assume that it has derivatives up to any order we need.

<hr/>

Example 1

Find the first through the fifth derivatives of the function
$$y = f(x) = 4x^4 - x^3 + 17x^2 + 3x - 1$$

The desired derivatives are as follows:
$$f'(x) = 16x^3 - 3x^2 + 34x + 3$$
$$f''(x) = 48x^2 - 6x + 34$$
$$f'''(x) = 96x - 6$$
$$f^{(4)}(x) = 96$$
$$f^{(5)}(x) = 0$$

In this particular (polynomial) example, we note that each successive derivative function emerges as a lower-order polynomial—from cubic to quadratic, to linear, to constant. We note also that the fifth derivative, being the derivative of a constant, is equal to zero for all values of x; we could therefore have written it as $f^{(5)}(x) \equiv 0$ as well. The equation $f^{(5)}(x) = 0$ should be carefully distinguished from the equation $f^{(5)}(x_0) = 0$ (zero at x_0 only). Also, understand that the statement $f^{(5)}(x) \equiv 0$ does not mean that the fifth derivative does not exist; it indeed exists, and has the value zero.

<hr/>

Example 2

Find the first four derivatives of the rational function
$$y = g(x) = \frac{x}{1 + x} \qquad (x \neq -1)$$

These derivatives can be found either by use of the quotient rule, or, after rewriting the function as $y = x(1 + x)^{-1}$, by the product rule:

$$\left.\begin{array}{l} g'(x) = (1 + x)^{-2} \\ g''(x) = -2(1 + x)^{-3} \\ g'''(x) = 6(1 + x)^{-4} \\ g^{(4)}(x) = -24(1 + x)^{-5} \end{array}\right\} \qquad (x \neq -1)$$

In this case, repeated derivation evidently does not tend to simplify the subsequent derivative expressions.

Note that, like the primitive function $g(x)$, all the successive derivatives obtained are themselves functions of x. Given specific values of x, however, these derivative functions will then take specific values. When $x = 2$, for instance, the second derivative in Example 2 can be evaluated as

$$g''(2) = -2(3)^{-3} = \frac{-2}{27}$$

and similarly for other values of x. It is of the utmost importance to realize that to evaluate this second derivative $g''(x)$ at $x = 2$, as we did, we must first obtain $g''(x)$ from $g'(x)$ and then substitute $x = 2$ into the equation for $g''(x)$. It is *incorrect* to substitute $x = 2$ into $g(x)$ or $g'(x)$ *prior* to the differentiation process leading to $g''(x)$.

Interpretation of the Second Derivative

The derivative function $f'(x)$ measures the rate of change of the function f. By the same token, the second-derivative function f'' is the measure of the rate of change of the first derivative f'; in other words, the second derivative measures the *rate of change* of the *rate of change* of the original function f. To put it differently, with a given infinitesimal increase in the independent variable x from a point $x = x_0$,

$$\left.\begin{array}{l} f'(x_0) > 0 \\ f'(x_0) < 0 \end{array}\right\} \text{means that the } \textit{value of the function} \text{ tends to } \left\{\begin{array}{l} \text{increase} \\ \text{decrease} \end{array}\right.$$

whereas, with regard to the second derivative,

$$\left.\begin{array}{l} f''(x_0) > 0 \\ f''(x_0) < 0 \end{array}\right\} \text{means that the } \textit{slope of the curve} \text{ tends to } \left\{\begin{array}{l} \text{increase} \\ \text{decrease} \end{array}\right.$$

Thus a positive first derivative coupled with a positive second derivative at $x = x_0$ implies that the slope of the curve at that point is *positive and increasing.* In other words, the value of the function is increasing at an increasing rate. Likewise, a positive first derivative with a negative second derivative indicates that the slope of the curve is *positive but decreasing*—the value of the function is increasing at a decreasing rate. The case of a negative first derivative can be interpreted analogously, but a warning is in order in this case: When $f'(x_0) < 0$ and $f''(x_0) > 0$, the slope of the curve is *negative and increasing,* but this does *not* mean that the slope is changing, say, from (-10) to (-11); on the contrary, the change should be from (-11), a smaller number, to (-10), a larger number. In other words, the negative slope must tend to be *less* steep as x increases. Lastly, when $f'(x_0) < 0$ and $f''(x_0) < 0$, the slope of the curve must be *negative and decreasing.* This refers to a negative slope that tends to become *steeper* as x increases.

All of this can be further clarified with a graphical explanation. Figure 9.5*a* illustrates a function with $f''(x) < 0$ throughout. Since the slope must steadily decrease as x increases on the graph, we will, when we move from left to right, pass through a point A with a positive slope, then a point B with zero slope, and then a point C with a negative slope. It may happen, of course, that a function with $f''(x) < 0$ is characterized by $f'(x) > 0$ everywhere, and thus plots only as the rising portion of an inverse U-shaped curve, or, with $f'(x) < 0$ everywhere, plots only as the declining portion of that curve.

The opposite case of a function with $f''(x) > 0$ throughout is illustrated in Fig. 9.5*b*. Here, as we pass through points D to E to F, the slope steadily increases and changes from

FIGURE 9.5

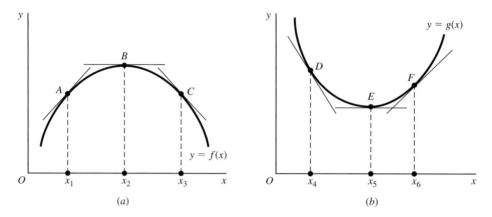

(a)   (b)

negative to zero to positive. Again, we add that a function characterized by $f''(x) > 0$ throughout may, depending on the first-derivative specification, plot only as the declining or the rising portion of a U-shaped curve.

From Fig. 9.5, it is evident that the second derivative $f''(x)$ relates to the *curvature* of a graph; it determines how the curve tends to bend itself. To describe the two types of differing curvatures discussed, we refer to the one in Fig. 9.5a as *strictly concave,* and the one in Fig. 9.5b as *strictly convex.* And, understandably, a function whose graph is strictly concave (strictly convex) is called a *strictly concave (strictly convex) function.* The precise geometric characterization of a strictly concave function is as follows. If we pick any pair of points M and N on its curve and join them by a straight line, the line segment MN must lie entirely *below* the curve, except at points M and N. The characterization of a strictly convex function can be obtained by substituting the word *above* for the word *below* in the last statement. Try this out in Fig. 9.5. If the characterizing condition is relaxed somewhat, so that the line segment MN is allowed to lie *either* below the curve, *or* along (coinciding with) the curve, then we will be describing instead a *concave function,* without the adverb *strictly.* Similarly, if the line segment MN *either* lies above, *or* lies along the curve, then the function is *convex,* again without the adverb *strictly.* Note that, since the line segment MN may coincide with a (nonstrictly) concave or convex curve, the latter may very well contain a linear segment. In contrast, a *strictly* concave or convex curve can never contain a linear segment anywhere. It follows that while a strictly concave (convex) function is automatically a concave (convex) function, the converse is not true.[†]

From our earlier discussion of the second derivative, we may now infer that if the second derivative $f''(x)$ is negative for *all* x, then the primitive function $f(x)$ must be a strictly concave function. Similarly, $f(x)$ must be strictly convex, if $f''(x)$ is positive for *all* x. Despite this, it is *not* valid to reverse this inference and say that, if $f(x)$ is strictly concave (strictly convex), then $f''(x)$ must be negative (positive) for all x. This is because, in certain exceptional cases, the second derivative may have a *zero* value at a stationary point on such a curve. An example of this can be found in the function $y = f(x) = x^4$, which plots as a strictly convex curve, but whose derivatives

$$f'(x) = 4x^3 \qquad f''(x) = 12x^2$$

[†] We shall discuss these concepts further in Sec. 11.5.

indicate that, at the stationary point where $x = 0$, the value of the second derivative is $f''(0) = 0$. Note, however, that at any other point, with $x \neq 0$, the second derivative of this function does have the (expected) positive sign. Aside from the possibility of a zero value at a stationary point, therefore, the second derivative of a strictly concave or convex function may be expected in general to adhere to a single algebraic sign.

For other types of function, the second derivative may take both positive and negative values, depending on the value of x. In Fig. 9.3a and b, for instance, both $f(x)$ and $g(x)$ undergo a sign change in the second derivative at their respective inflection points J and K. According to Fig. 9.3a', the slope of $f'(x)$—that is, the value of $f''(x)$—changes from negative to positive at $x = j$; the exact opposite occurs with the slope of $g'(x)$—that is, the value of $g''(x)$—on the basis of Fig. 9.3b'. Translated into curvature terms, this means that the graph of $f(x)$ turns from strictly concave to strictly convex at point J, whereas the graph of $g(x)$ has the reverse change at point K. Consequently, instead of characterizing an inflection point as a point where the first derivative reaches an extreme value, we may alternatively characterize it as a point where the function undergoes a change in curvature or a change in the sign of its second derivative.

An Application

The two curves in Fig. 9.5 exemplify the graphs of quadratic functions, which may be expressed generally in the form

$$y = ax^2 + bx + c \qquad (a \neq 0)$$

From our discussion of the second derivative, we can now derive a convenient way of determining whether a given quadratic function will have a strictly convex (U-shaped) or a strictly concave (inverse U-shaped) graph.

Since the second derivative of the quadratic function cited is $d^2y/dx^2 = 2a$, this derivative will always have the same algebraic sign as the coefficient a. Recalling that a positive second derivative implies a strictly convex curve, we can infer that a positive coefficient a in the preceding quadratic function gives rise to a U-shaped graph. In contrast, a negative coefficient a leads to a strictly concave curve, shaped like an inverted U.

As intimated at the end of Sec. 9.2, the relative extremum of this function will also prove to be its absolute extremum, because in a quadratic function there can be found only a single valley or peak, evident in a U or inverted U, respectively.

Attitudes toward Risk

The most common application of the concept of marginal utility is to the context of goods consumption. But in another useful application, we consider the marginal utility of *income,* or more to the point of the present discussion, the *payoff* to a betting game, and use this concept to distinguish between different individuals' attitudes toward risk.

Consider the game where, for a fixed sum of money paid in advance (the *cost* of the game), you can throw a die and collect $10 if an odd number shows up, or $20 if the number is even. In view of the equal probability of the two outcomes, the mathematically *expected value of payoff* is

$$EV = 0.5 \times \$10 + 0.5 \times \$20 = \$15$$

FIGURE 9.6

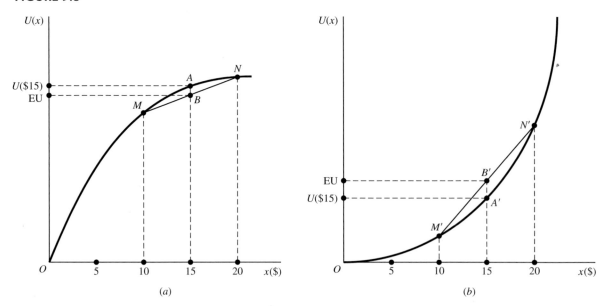

(a)

(b)

The game is deemed a *fair game,* or *fair bet,* if the cost of the game is exactly $15. Despite its fairness, playing such a game still involves a risk, for even though the probability distribution of the two possible outcomes is known, the actual result of any individual play is not. Hence, people who are "risk-averse" would consistently decline to play such a game. On the other hand, there are "risk-loving" or "risk-preferring" people who would welcome fair games, or even games with odds set against them (i.e., with the cost of the game exceeding the expected value of payoff).

The explanation for such diverse attitudes toward risk is easily found in the differing utility functions people possess. Assume that a potential player has the strictly concave utility function $U = U(x)$ depicted in Fig. 9.6a, where x denotes the payoff, with $U(0) = 0$, $U'(x) > 0$ (positive marginal utility of income or payoff), and $U''(x) < 0$ (diminishing marginal utility) for all x. The economic decision facing this person involves the choice between two courses of action: First, by not playing the game, the person saves the $15 cost of the game ($= EV$) and thus enjoys the utility level $U(\$15)$, measured by the height of point A on the curve. Second, by playing, the person has a .5 probability of receiving $10 and thus enjoying $U(\$10)$ (see point M), plus a .5 probability of receiving $20 and thus enjoying $U(\$20)$ (see point N). The *expected utility from playing* is, therefore, equal to

$$EU = 0.5 \times U(\$10) + 0.5 \times U(\$20)$$

which, being the average of the height of M and that of N, is measured by the height of point B, the midpoint on the line segment MN. Since, by the defining property of a strictly concave utility function, line segment MN must lie below arc MN, point B must be lower than point A; that is, EU, the expected utility from playing, falls short of the utility of the cost of the game, and the game should be avoided. For this reason, a strictly concave utility function is associated with risk-averse behavior.

For a risk-loving person, the decision process is analogous, but the opposite choice will be made, because now the relevant utility function is a strictly convex one. In Fig. 9.6b,

$U(\$15)$, the utility of keeping the \$15 by not playing the game, is shown by point A' on the curve, and EU, the expected utility from playing, is given by B', the midpoint on the line segment $M'N'$. But this time line segment $M'N'$ lies above arc $M'N'$, and point B' is above point A'. Thus there definitely is a positive incentive to play the game. In contrast to the situation in Fig. 9.6a, we can thus associate a strictly convex utility function with risk-loving behavior.

EXERCISE 9.3

1. Find the second and third derivatives of the following functions:

    (a) $ax^2 + bx + c$

    (b) $7x^4 - 3x - 4$

    (c) $\dfrac{3x}{1-x}$ $\quad$ $(x \neq 1)$

    (d) $\dfrac{1+x}{1-x}$ $\quad$ $(x \neq 1)$

2. Which of the following quadratic functions are strictly convex?

    (a) $y = 9x^2 - 4x + 8$
    (b) $w = -3x^2 + 39$
    (c) $u = 9 - 2x^2$
    (d) $v = 8 - 5x + x^2$

3. Draw (a) a concave curve which is *not* strictly concave, and (b) a curve which qualifies simultaneously as a concave curve and a convex curve.

4. Given the function $y = a - \dfrac{b}{c+x}$ $\quad$ $(a, b, c > 0; x \geq 0)$, determine the general shape of its graph by examining (a) its first and second derivatives, (b) its vertical intercept, and (c) the limit of y as x tends to infinity. If this function is to be used as a consumption function, how should the parameters be restricted in order to make it economically sensible?

5. Draw the graph of a function $f(x)$ such that $f'(x) \equiv 0$, and the graph of a function $g(x)$ such that $g'(3) = 0$. Summarize in one sentence the essential difference between $f(x)$ and $g(x)$ in terms of the concept of stationary point.

6. A person who is neither risk-averse nor risk-loving (indifferent toward a fair game) is said to be "risk-neutral."

    (a) What kind of utility function would you use to characterize such a person?

    (b) Using the die-throwing game detailed in the text, describe the relationship between $U(\$15)$ and EU for the risk-neutral person.

9.4 Second-Derivative Test

Returning to the pair of extreme points B and E in Fig. 9.5 and remembering the newly established relationship between the second derivative and the curvature of a curve, we should be able to see the validity of the following criterion for a relative extremum:

Second-derivative test for relative extremum If the value of the first derivative of a function f at $x = x_0$ is $f'(x_0) = 0$, then the value of the function at x_0, $f(x_0)$, will be

a. A relative *maximum* if the second-derivative value at x_0 is $f''(x_0) < 0$.

b. A relative *minimum* if the second-derivative value at x_0 is $f''(x_0) > 0$.

This test is in general more convenient to use than the first-derivative test, because it does not require us to check the derivative sign to both the left and the right of x_0. But it has the drawback that no unequivocal conclusion can be drawn in the event that $f''(x_0) = 0$. For then the stationary value $f(x_0)$ can be *either* a relative maximum, *or* a relative minimum, *or* even an inflectional value.[†] When the situation of $f''(x_0) = 0$ is encountered, we must either revert to the first-derivative test, or resort to another test, to be developed in Sec. 9.6, that involves the third or even higher derivatives. For most problems in economics, however, the second-derivative test would usually be adequate for determining a relative maximum or minimum.

Example 1

Find the relative extremum of the function

$$y = f(x) = 4x^2 - x$$

The first and second derivatives are

$$f'(x) = 8x - 1 \qquad \text{and} \qquad f''(x) = 8$$

Setting $f'(x)$ equal to zero and solving the resulting equation, we find the (only) critical value to be $x^* = \frac{1}{8}$, which yields the (only) stationary value $f\left(\frac{1}{8}\right) = -\frac{1}{16}$. Because the second derivative is positive (in this case it is indeed positive for any value of x), the extremum is established as a minimum. Further, since the given function plots as a U-shaped curve, the relative minimum is also the absolute minimum.

Example 2

Find the relative extrema of the function

$$y = g(x) = x^3 - 3x^2 + 2$$

The first two derivatives of this function are

$$g'(x) = 3x^2 - 6x \qquad \text{and} \qquad g''(x) = 6x - 6$$

Setting $g'(x)$ equal to zero and solving the resulting quadratic equation, $3x^2 - 6x = 0$, we obtain the critical values $x_1^* = 2$ and $x_2^* = 0$, which in turn yield the two stationary values:

$$g(2) = -2 \qquad \text{[a minimum because } g''(2) = 6 > 0]$$
$$g(0) = 2 \qquad \text{[a maximum because } g''(0) = -6 < 0]$$

Necessary versus Sufficient Conditions

As was the case with the first-derivative test, the zero-slope condition $f'(x) = 0$ plays the role of a *necessary* condition in the second-derivative test. Since this condition is based on the first-order derivative, it is often referred to as the *first-order condition*. Once we find the first-order condition satisfied at $x = x_0$, the negative (positive) sign of $f''(x_0)$ is *sufficient* to establish the stationary value in question as a relative maximum (minimum). These sufficient conditions, which are based on the second-order derivative, are often referred to as *second-order conditions*.

[†] To see that an inflection point is possible when $f''(x_0) = 0$, let us refer back to Fig. 9.3a and 9.3a'. Point *J* in the upper diagram is an inflection point, with $x = j$ as its critical value. Since the $f'(x)$ curve in the lower diagram attains a minimum at $x = j$, the slope of $f'(x)$ [i.e., $f''(x)$] must be zero at the critical value $x = j$. Thus point *J* illustrates an inflection point occurring when $f''(x_0) = 0$.

To see that a relative extremum is also consistent with $f''(x_0) = 0$, consider the function $y = x^4$. This function plots as a U-shaped curve and has a minimum, $y = 0$, attained at the critical value $x = 0$. Since the second derivative of this function is $f''(x) = 12x^2$, we again obtain a zero value for this derivative at the critical value $x = 0$. Thus this function illustrates a relative extremum occurring when $f''(x_0) = 0$.

TABLE 9.1
**Conditions for
a Relative
Extremum:**
y = f(x)

Condition	Maximum	Minimum
First-order necessary	$f'(x) = 0$	$f'(x) = 0$
Second-order necessary[†]	$f''(x) \leq 0$	$f''(x) \geq 0$
Second-order sufficient[†]	$f''(x) < 0$	$f''(x) > 0$

[†]Applicable only after the first-order necessary condition has been satisfied.

It bears repeating that the first-order condition is *necessary,* but *not sufficient,* for a relative maximum or minimum. (Remember inflection points?) In sharp contrast, the second-order condition that $f''(x)$ be negative (positive) at the critical value x_0 is *sufficient* for a relative maximum (minimum), but it is *not necessary.* [Remember the relative extremum that occurs when $f''(x_0) = 0$?] For this reason, one should carefully guard against the following line of argument: "Since the stationary value $f(x_0)$ is already known to be a minimum, we must have $f''(x_0) > 0$." The reasoning here is faulty because it incorrectly treats the positive sign of $f''(x_0)$ as a necessary condition for $f(x_0)$ to be a minimum.

This is not to say that second-order derivatives can never be used in stating *necessary* conditions for relative extrema. Indeed they can. But care must then be taken to allow for the fact that a relative maximum (minimum) can occur not only when $f''(x_0)$ is negative (positive), but also when $f''(x_0)$ is zero. Consequently, *second-order necessary conditions* must be couched in terms of weak inequalities: for a stationary value $f(x_0)$ to be a relative $\begin{Bmatrix} \text{maximum} \\ \text{minimum} \end{Bmatrix}$, it is necessary that $f''(x_0) \begin{Bmatrix} \leq \\ \geq \end{Bmatrix} 0$.

The preceding discussion can be summed up in Table 9.1. All the equations and inequalities in the table are in the nature of conditions (requirements) to be met, rather than descriptive specifications of a given function. In particular, the equation $f'(x) = 0$ does not signify that function f has a zero slope everywhere; rather, it states the stipulation that only those values of x that satisfy this requirement can qualify as critical values.

Conditions for Profit Maximization

We shall now present an economic example of extreme-value problems, i.e., problems of optimization.

One of the first things that a student of economics learns is that, in order to maximize profit, a firm must equate marginal cost and marginal revenue. Let us show the mathematical derivation of this condition. To keep the analysis on a general level, we shall work with the total-revenue function $R = R(Q)$ and total-cost function $C = C(Q)$, both of which are functions of a single variable Q. From these it follows that a profit function (the objective function) may also be formulated in terms of Q (the choice variable):

$$\pi = \pi(Q) = R(Q) - C(Q) \tag{9.1}$$

To find the profit-maximizing output level, we must satisfy the first-order necessary condition for a maximum: $d\pi/dQ = 0$. Accordingly, let us differentiate (9.1) with respect to Q and set the resulting derivative equal to zero: The result is

$$\frac{d\pi}{dQ} \equiv \pi'(Q) = R'(Q) - C'(Q)$$

$$= 0 \quad \text{iff} \quad R'(Q) = C'(Q) \tag{9.2}$$

Thus the *optimum* output (*equilibrium* output) Q^* must satisfy the equation $R'(Q^*) = C'(Q^*)$, or MR = MC. This condition constitutes the first-order condition for profit maximization.

However, the first-order condition may lead to a minimum rather than a maximum; thus we must check the second-order condition next. We can obtain the second derivative by differentiating the first derivative in (9.2) with respect to Q:

$$\frac{d^2\pi}{dQ^2} \equiv \pi''(Q) = R''(Q) - C''(Q)$$

$$\leq 0 \qquad \text{iff} \qquad R''(Q) \leq C''(Q)$$

This last inequality is the second-order necessary condition for maximization. If it is not met, then Q^* cannot possibly maximize profit; in fact, it minimizes profit. If $R''(Q^*) = C''(Q^*)$, then we are unable to reach a definite conclusion. The best scenario is to find $R''(Q^*) < C''(Q^*)$, which satisfies the second-order sufficient condition for a maximum. In that case, we can conclusively take Q^* to be a profit-maximizing output. Economically, this would mean that, if the rate of change of MR is less than the rate of change of MC at the output where MC = MR, then that output will maximize profit.

These conditions are illustrated in Fig. 9.7. In Fig. 9.7*a* we have drawn a total-revenue and a total-cost curve, which are seen to intersect twice, at output levels of Q_2 and Q_4. In the open interval (Q_2, Q_4), total revenue R exceeds total cost C, and thus π is positive. But in the intervals $[0, Q_2)$ and $(Q_4, Q_5]$, where Q_5 represents the upper limit of the firm's productive capacity, π is negative. This fact is reflected in Fig. 9.7*b*, where the profit curve—obtained by plotting the vertical distance between the R and C curves for each level of output—lies above the horizontal axis only in the interval (Q_2, Q_4).

When we set $d\pi/dQ = 0$, in line with the first-order condition, it is our intention to locate the peak point K on the profit curve, at output Q_3, where the slope of the curve is zero. However, the relative-minimum point M (output Q_1) will also offer itself as a candidate, because it, too, meets the zero-slope requirement. Below, we shall resort to the second-order condition to eliminate the "wrong" kind of extremum.

The first-order condition $d\pi/dQ = 0$ is equivalent to the condition $R'(Q) = C'(Q)$. In Fig. 9.7*a*, the output level Q_3 satisfies this, because the R and C curves do have the same slope at Q_3 (the tangent lines drawn to the two curves at H and J are parallel to each other). The same is true for output Q_1. Since the equality of the slopes of R and C means the equality of MR and MC, outputs Q_3 and Q_1 must obviously be where the MR and MC curves intersect, as illustrated in Fig. 9.7*c*.

How does the second-order condition enter into the picture? Let us first look at Fig. 9.7*b*. At point K, the second derivative of the π function will (barring the exceptional zero-value case) have a negative value, $\pi''(Q_3) < 0$, because the curve is inverse U-shaped around K; this means that Q_3 will maximize profit. At point M, on the other hand, we would expect that $\pi''(Q_1) > 0$; thus Q_1 provides a relative minimum for π instead. The second-order sufficient condition for a maximum can, of course, be stated alternatively as $R''(Q) < C''(Q)$, that is, that the slope of the MR curve be less than the slope of the MC curve. From Fig. 9.7*c*, it is immediately apparent that output Q_3 satisfies this condition, since the slope of MR is negative while that of MC is positive at point L. But output Q_1 violates this condition because both MC and MR have negative slopes, and that of MR is *numerically smaller* than that of MC at point N, which implies that $R''(Q_1)$ is *greater* than

FIGURE 9.7

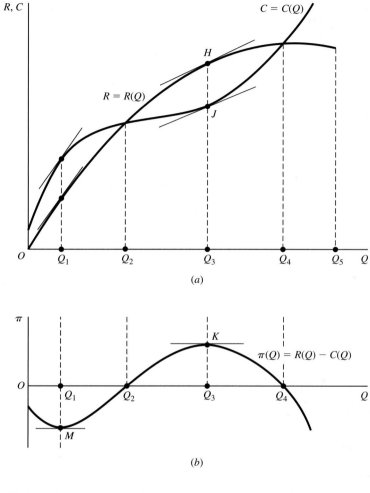

(a)

(b)

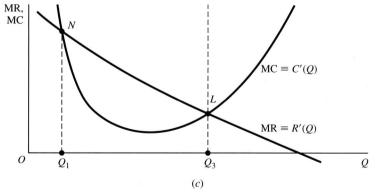

(c)

$C''(Q_1)$ instead. In fact, therefore, output Q_1 also violates the second-order *necessary* condition for a relative maximum, but satisfies the second-order *sufficient* condition for a relative minimum.

Example 3

Let the $R(Q)$ and $C(Q)$ functions be

$$R(Q) = 1{,}200Q - 2Q^2$$
$$C(Q) = Q^3 - 61.25Q^2 + 1{,}528.5Q + 2{,}000$$

Then the profit function is

$$\pi(Q) = -Q^3 + 59.25Q^2 - 328.5Q - 2{,}000$$

where R, C, and π are all in dollar units and Q is in units of (say) tons per week. This profit function has two critical values, $Q = 3$ and $Q = 36.5$, because

$$\frac{d\pi}{dQ} = -3Q^2 + 118.5Q - 328.5 = 0 \qquad \text{when } Q = \begin{cases} 3 \\ 36.5 \end{cases}$$

But since the second derivative is

$$\frac{d^2\pi}{dQ^2} = -6Q + 118.5 \qquad \begin{cases} > 0 & \text{when } Q = 3 \\ < 0 & \text{when } Q = 36.5 \end{cases}$$

the profit-maximizing output is $Q^* = 36.5$ (tons per week). (The other output minimizes profit.) By substituting Q^* into the profit function, we can find the maximized profit to be $\pi^* = \pi(36.5) = 16{,}318.44$ (dollars per week).

As an alternative approach to the preceding, we can first find the MR and MC functions and then equate the two, i.e., find their intersection. Since

$$R'(Q) = 1{,}200 - 4Q$$
$$C'(Q) = 3Q^2 - 122.5Q + 1{,}528.5$$

equating the two functions will result in a quadratic equation identical with $d\pi/dQ = 0$ which has yielded the two critical values of Q cited previously.

Coefficients of a Cubic Total-Cost Function

In Example 3, a cubic function is used to represent the total-cost function. The traditional total-cost curve $C = C(Q)$, as illustrated in Fig. 9.7a, is supposed to contain two wiggles that form a concave segment (decreasing marginal cost) and a subsequent convex segment (increasing marginal cost). Since the graph of a cubic function always contains exactly two wiggles, as illustrated in Fig. 9.4, it should suit that role well. However, Fig. 9.4 immediately alerts us to a problem: the cubic function can possibly produce a downward-sloping segment in its graph, whereas the total-cost function, to make economic sense, should be upward-sloping everywhere (a larger output always entails a higher total cost). If we wish to use a cubic total-cost function such as

$$C = C(Q) = aQ^3 + bQ^2 + cQ + d \qquad \qquad \textbf{(9.3)}$$

therefore, it is essential to place appropriate restrictions on the parameters so as to prevent the C curve from ever bending downward.

An equivalent way of stating this requirement is that the MC function should be positive throughout, and this can be ensured only if the *absolute minimum* of the MC function turns out to be positive. Differentiating (9.3) with respect to Q, we obtain the MC function

$$MC = C'(Q) = 3aQ^2 + 2bQ + c \qquad \qquad \textbf{(9.4)}$$

which, because it is a quadratic, plots as a parabola as in Fig. 9.7c. In order for the MC curve to stay positive (above the horizontal axis) everywhere, it is necessary that the parabola be U-shaped (otherwise, with an inverse U, the curve is bound to extend itself into the second quadrant). Hence the coefficient of the Q^2 term in (9.4) has to be positive; i.e., we must impose the restriction $a > 0$. This restriction, however, is by no means sufficient, because the minimum value of a U-shaped MC curve—call it MC_{min} (a relative minimum which also happens to be an absolute minimum)—may still occur below the horizontal axis. Thus we must next find MC_{min} and ascertain the parameter restrictions that would make it positive.

According to our knowledge of relative extremum, the minimum of MC will occur where

$$\frac{d}{dQ}MC = 6aQ + 2b = 0$$

The output level that satisfies this first-order condition is

$$Q^* = \frac{-2b}{6a} = \frac{-b}{3a}$$

This minimizes (rather than maximizes) MC because the second derivative $d^2(MC)/dQ^2 = 6a$ is assuredly positive in view of the restriction $a > 0$. The knowledge of Q^* now enables us to calculate MC_{min}, but we may first infer the sign of coefficient b from it. Inasmuch as negative output levels are ruled out, we see that b can never be positive (given $a > 0$). Moreover, since the law of diminishing returns is assumed to set in at a positive output level (that is, MC is assumed to have an initial declining segment), Q^* should be positive (rather than zero). Consequently, we must impose the restriction $b < 0$.

It is a simple matter now to substitute the MC-minimizing output Q^* into (9.4) to find that

$$MC_{min} = 3a\left(\frac{-b}{3a}\right)^2 + 2b\frac{-b}{3a} + c = \frac{3ac - b^2}{3a}$$

Thus, to guarantee the positivity of MC_{min}, we must impose the restriction[†] $b^2 < 3ac$. This last restriction, we may add, in effect also implies the restriction $c > 0$. (Why?)

The preceding discussion has involved the three parameters a, b, and c. What about the other parameter, d? The answer is that there is need for a restriction on d also, but that has nothing to do with the problem of keeping the MC positive. If we let $Q = 0$ in (9.3), we find

---

[†] This restriction may also be obtained by the method of *completing the square*. The MC function can be successively transformed as follows:

$$MC = 3aQ^2 + 2bQ + c$$

$$= \left(3aQ^2 + 2bQ + \frac{b^2}{3a}\right) - \frac{b^2}{3a} + c$$

$$= \left(\sqrt{3a}Q + \sqrt{\frac{b^2}{3a}}\right)^2 + \frac{-b^2 + 3ac}{3a}$$

Since the squared expression can possibly be zero, we must, in order to ensure the positivity of MC, require that $b^2 < 3ac$ on the knowledge that $a > 0$.

that $C(0) = d$. The role of d is thus to determine the vertical intercept of the C curve only, with no bearing on its slope. Since the economic meaning of d is the fixed cost of a firm, the appropriate restriction (in the short-run context) would be $d > 0$.

In sum, the coefficients of the total-cost function (9.3) should be restricted as follows (assuming the short-run context):

$$a, c, d > 0 \qquad b < 0 \qquad b^2 < 3ac \qquad \textbf{(9.5)}$$

As you can readily verify, the $C(Q)$ function in Example 3 does satisfy (9.5).

Upward-Sloping Marginal-Revenue Curve

The marginal-revenue curve in Fig. 9.7c is shown to be downward-sloping throughout. This, of course, is how the MR curve is traditionally drawn for a firm under imperfect competition. However, the possibility of the MR curve being partially, or even wholly, upward-sloping can by no means be ruled out a priori.[†]

Given an average-revenue function $AR = f(Q)$, the marginal-revenue function can be expressed by

$$MR = f(Q) + Qf'(Q) \qquad \text{[from (7.7)]}$$

The slope of the MR curve can thus be ascertained from the derivative

$$\frac{d}{dQ}MR = f'(Q) + f'(Q) + Qf''(Q) = 2f'(Q) + Qf''(Q)$$

As long as the AR curve is downward-sloping (as it would be under imperfect competition), the $2f'(Q)$ term is assuredly negative. But the $Qf''(Q)$ term can be either negative, zero, or positive, depending on the sign of the second derivative of the AR function, i.e., depending on whether the AR curve is strictly concave, linear, or strictly convex. If the AR curve is strictly convex either in its entirety (as illustrated in Fig. 7.2) or along a specific segment, the possibility will exist that the (positive) $Qf''(Q)$ term may dominate the (negative) $2f'(Q)$ term, thereby causing the MR curve to be wholly or partially upward-sloping.

Example 4   Let the average-revenue function be

$$AR = f(Q) = 8,000 - 23Q + 1.1Q^2 - 0.018Q^3$$

As can be verified (see Exercise 9.4-7), this function gives rise to a downward-sloping AR curve, as is appropriate for a firm under imperfect competition. Since

$$MR = f(Q) + Qf'(Q) = 8,000 - 46Q + 3.3Q^2 - 0.072Q^3$$

it follows that the slope of MR is

$$\frac{d}{dQ}MR = -46 + 6.6Q - 0.216Q^2$$

Because this is a quadratic function and since the coefficient of Q^2 is negative, dMR/dQ must plot as an inverse-U-shaped curve against Q, such as shown in Fig. 9.5a. If a segment of this curve happens to lie above the horizontal axis, the slope of MR will take positive values.

[†] This point is emphatically brought out in John P. Formby, Stéphen Layson, and W. James Smith, "The Law of Demand, Positive Sloping Marginal Revenue, and Multiple Profit Equilibria," *Economic Inquiry,* April 1982, pp. 303–311.

Setting $dMR/dQ = 0$, and applying the quadratic formula, we find the two zeros of the quadratic function to be $Q_1 = 10.76$ and $Q_2 = 19.79$ (approximately). This means that, for values of Q in the open interval (Q_1, Q_2), the dMR/dQ curve does lie above the horizontal axis. Thus the marginal-revenue curve indeed is positively sloped for output levels between Q_1 and Q_2.

The presence of a positively sloped segment on the MR curve has interesting implications. Such an MR curve may produce more than one intersection with the MC curve satisfying the second-order sufficient condition for profit maximization. While all such intersections constitute local optima, however, only one of them is the global optimum that the firm is seeking.

EXERCISE 9.4

1. Find the relative maxima and minima of y by the second-derivative test:

   (a) $y = -2x^2 + 8x + 25$

   (b) $y = x^3 + 6x^2 + 9$

   (c) $y = \frac{1}{3}x^3 - 3x^2 + 5x + 3$

   (d) $y = \dfrac{2x}{1 - 2x}$ $\left(x \neq \dfrac{1}{2} \right)$

2. Mr. Greenthumb wishes to mark out a rectangular flower bed, using a wall of his house as one side of the rectangle. The other three sides are to be marked by wire netting, of which he has only 64 ft available. What are the length L and width W of the rectangle that would give him the largest possible planting area? How do you make sure that your answer gives the largest, not the smallest area?

3. A firm has the following total-cost and demand functions:

   $$C = \tfrac{1}{3}Q^3 - 7Q^2 + 111Q + 50$$

   $$Q = 100 - P$$

   (a) Does the total-cost function satisfy the coefficient restrictions of (9.5)?

   (b) Write out the total-revenue function R in terms of Q.

   (c) Formulate the total-profit function π in terms of Q.

   (d) Find the profit-maximizing level of output Q^*.

   (e) What is the maximum profit?

4. If coefficient b in (9.3) were to take a zero value, what would happen to the marginal-cost and total-cost curves?

5. A quadratic profit function $\pi(Q) = hQ^2 + jQ + k$ is to be used to reflect the following assumptions:

   (a) If nothing is produced, the profit will be negative (because of fixed costs).

   (b) The profit function is strictly concave.

   (c) The maximum profit occurs at a positive output level Q^*.

   What parameter restrictions are called for?

6. A purely competitive firm has a single variable input L (labor), with the wage rate W_0 per period. Its fixed inputs cost the firm a total of F dollars per period. The price of the product is P_0.

   (a) Write the production function, revenue function, cost function, and profit function of the firm.

(b) What is the first-order condition for profit maximization? Give this condition an economic interpretation.

(c) What economic circumstances would ensure that profit is maximized rather than minimized?

7. Use the following procedure to verify that the AR curve in Example 4 is negatively sloped:

(a) Denote the slope of AR by S. Write an expression for S.

(b) Find the maximum value of S, S_{max}, by using the second-derivative test.

(c) Then deduce from the value of S_{max} that the AR curve is negatively sloped throughout.

9.5 Maclaurin and Taylor Series

The time has now come for us to develop a test for relative extrema that can apply even when the second derivative turns out to have a zero value at the stationary point. Before we can do that, however, it is first necessary to discuss the so-called expansion of a function $y = f(x)$ into what are known, respectively, as a *Maclaurin series* (expansion around the point $x = 0$) and a *Taylor series* (expansion around any point $x = x_0$).

To *expand* a function $y = f(x)$ around a point x_0 means, in the present context, to transform that function into a *polynomial* form, in which the coefficients of the various terms are expressed in terms of the derivative values $f'(x_0)$, $f''(x_0)$, etc.—all evaluated at the point of expansion x_0. In the Maclaurin series, these will be evaluated at $x = 0$; thus we have $f'(0)$, $f''(0)$, etc., in the coefficients. The result of expansion is a *power series* because, being a polynomial, it consists of a sum of power functions.

Maclaurin Series of a Polynomial Function

Let us consider first the expansion of a *polynomial* function of the nth degree,

$$f(x) = a_0 + a_1 x + a_2 x^2 + a_3 x^3 + a_4 x^4 + \cdots + a_n x^n \qquad \textbf{(9.6)}$$

into an equivalent nth-degree polynomial where the coefficients (a_0, a_1, etc.) are expressed instead in terms of the derivative values $f'(0)$, $f''(0)$, etc. Since this involves the transformation of one polynomial into another of the same degree, it may seem a sterile and purposeless exercise, but actually it will serve to shed much light on the whole idea of expansion.

Since the power series after expansion will involve the derivatives of various orders of the function f, let us first find these. By successive differentiation of (9.6), we can get the derivatives as follows:

$$f'(x) = a_1 + 2a_2 x + 3a_3 x^2 + 4a_4 x^3 + \cdots + na_n x^{n-1}$$

$$f''(x) = 2a_2 + 3(2)a_3 x + 4(3)a_4 x^2 + \cdots + n(n-1)a_n x^{n-2}$$

$$f'''(x) = 3(2)a_3 + 4(3)(2)a_4 x + \cdots + n(n-1)(n-2)a_n x^{n-3}$$

$$f^{(4)}(x) = 4(3)(2)a_4 + 5(4)(3)(2)a_5 x + \cdots + n(n-1)(n-2)(n-3)a_n x^{n-4}$$

$$\vdots$$

$$f^{(n)}(x) = n(n-1)(n-2)(n-3)\cdots(3)(2)(1)a_n$$

Note that each successive differentiation reduces the number of terms by one—the additive constant in front drops out—until, in the nth derivative, we are left with a single product term (a constant term). These derivatives can be evaluated at various values of x; here we shall evaluate them at $x = 0$, with the result that all terms involving x will drop out. We are then left with the following exceptionally neat derivative values:

$$f'(0) = a_1 \qquad f''(0) = 2a_2 \qquad f'''(0) = 3(2)a_3 \qquad f^{(4)}(0) = 4(3)(2)a_4$$

$$\cdots \qquad f^{(n)}(0) = n(n-1)(n-2)(n-3)\cdots(3)(2)(1)a_n \tag{9.7}$$

If we now adopt a shorthand symbol $n!$ (read: "n factorial"), defined as

$$n! \equiv n(n-1)(n-2)\cdots(3)(2)(1) \qquad (n = \text{a positive integer})$$

so that, for example, $2! = 2 \times 1 = 2$ and $3! = 3 \times 2 \times 1 = 6$, etc. (with $0!$ defined as equal to 1), then the result in (9.7) can be rewritten as

$$a_1 = \frac{f'(0)}{1!} \qquad a_2 = \frac{f''(0)}{2!} \qquad a_3 = \frac{f'''(0)}{3!} \qquad a_4 = \frac{f^{(4)}(0)}{4!} \qquad \cdots \qquad a_n = \frac{f^{(n)}(0)}{n!}$$

Substituting these into (9.6) and utilizing the obvious fact that $f(0) = a_0$, we can now express the given function $f(x)$ as a new, but equivalent, same-degree polynomial in which the coefficients are expressed in terms of derivatives evaluated at $x = 0$:[†]

$$f(x) = \frac{f(0)}{0!} + \frac{f'(0)}{1!}x + \frac{f''(0)}{2!}x^2 + \frac{f'''(0)}{3!}x^3$$

$$+ \cdots + \frac{f^{(n)}(0)}{n!}x^n \qquad \text{[Maclaurin's formula]} \tag{9.8}$$

This new polynomial, called the Maclaurin series of the polynomial function $f(x)$, represents the expansion of the function $f(x)$ around zero ($x = 0$). Note that the point of expansion (here, 0) is simply the value of x that will be used to evaluate $f(x)$ and all its derivatives.

| **Example 1** | Find the Maclaurin series for the function |

$$f(x) = 2 + 4x + 3x^2 \tag{9.9}$$

This function has the derivatives

$$\begin{aligned} f'(x) &= 4 + 6x \\ f''(x) &= 6 \end{aligned} \qquad \text{so that} \qquad \left\{ \begin{aligned} f'(0) &= 4 \\ f''(0) &= 6 \end{aligned} \right.$$

Thus the Maclaurin series is

$$f(x) = f(0) + f'(0)x + \frac{f''(0)}{2}x^2$$

$$= 2 + 4x + 3x^2$$

The previous line verifies that the Maclaurin series does indeed correctly represent the given function.

[†] Since $0! = 1$ and $1! = 1$, the first two terms on the right of the equals sign in (9.8) can be written more simply as $f(0)$, and $f'(0)x$, respectively. We have included the denominators $0!$ and $1!$ here to call attention to the symmetry among the various terms in the expansion.

Taylor Series of a Polynomial Function

More generally, the polynomial function in (9.6) can be expanded around any point x_0, not necessarily zero. In the interest of simplicity, we shall explain this by means of the specific quadratic function in (9.9) and generalize the result later.

For the purpose of expansion around a specific point x_0, we may first interpret any given value of x as a *deviation* from x_0. More specifically, we shall let $x = x_0 + \delta$, where δ represents the deviation from the value x_0. Upon such interpretation, the given function (9.9) and its derivatives now become

$$f(x) = 2 + 4(x_0 + \delta) + 3(x_0 + \delta)^2$$
$$f'(x) = 4 + 6(x_0 + \delta) \qquad\qquad\qquad\qquad \textbf{(9.10)}$$
$$f''(x) = 6$$

We know that the expression $(x_0 + \delta) = x$ is a variable in the function, but since x_0 in the present context is a *fixed* (chosen) number, only δ can be properly regarded as a variable in (9.10). Consequently, $f(x)$ is in fact a function of δ, say, $g(\delta)$:

$$g(\delta) = 2 + 4(x_0 + \delta) + 3(x_0 + \delta)^2 \qquad [\equiv f(x)]$$

with derivatives

$$g'(\delta) = 4 + 6(x_0 + \delta) \quad [\equiv f'(x)]$$
$$g''(\delta) = 6 \qquad\qquad\qquad [\equiv f''(x)]$$

We already know how to expand $g(\delta)$ around zero ($\delta = 0$). According to (9.8), such an expansion will yield the following Maclaurin series:

$$g(\delta) = \frac{g(0)}{0!} + \frac{g'(0)}{1!}\delta + \frac{g''(0)}{2!}\delta^2 \qquad\qquad \textbf{(9.11)}$$

But since we have let $x = x_0 + \delta$, the fact that $\delta = 0$ implies $x = x_0$; hence, on the basis of the identity $g(\delta) \equiv f(x)$, we can write for the case of $\delta = 0$:

$$g(0) = f(x_0) \qquad g'(0) = f'(x_0) \qquad g''(0) = f''(x_0)$$

Upon substituting these into (9.11), we find the result to represent the expansion of $f(x)$ around the point x_0, because the coefficients now involve the derivatives $f'(x_0)$, $f''(x_0)$, etc., all evaluated at $x = x_0$:

$$f(x)[=g(\delta)] = \frac{f(x_0)}{0!} + \frac{f'(x_0)}{1!}(x - x_0) + \frac{f''(x_0)}{2!}(x - x_0)^2 \qquad \textbf{(9.12)}$$

You should compare this result—the Taylor polynomial of $f(x)$—with the Maclaurin polynomial of $g(\delta)$ in (9.11).

Since for the specific function under consideration, (9.9), we have

$$f(x_0) = 2 + 4x_0 + 3x_0^2 \qquad f'(x_0) = 4 + 6x_0 \qquad f''(x_0) = 6$$

the Taylor polynomial in (9.12) becomes

$$f(x) = 2 + 4x_0 + 3x_0^2 + (4 + 6x_0)(x - x_0) + \tfrac{6}{2}(x - x_0)^2$$
$$= 2 + 4x + 3x^2$$

This verifies that the Taylor polynomial does correctly represent the given function.

The expansion formula in (9.12) can be generalized to apply to the nth-degree polynomial of (9.6). The generalized formula is

$$f(x) = \frac{f(x_0)}{0!} + \frac{f'(x_0)}{1!}(x - x_0) + \frac{f''(x_0)}{2!}(x - x_0)^2 + \cdots$$
$$+ \frac{f^{(n)}(x_0)}{n!}(x - x_0)^n \qquad \text{[Taylor's formula]} \qquad \textbf{(9.13)}$$

This differs from Maclaurin's formula in (9.8) only in the replacement of zero by x_0 as the point of expansion, and in the replacement of x by the expression $(x - x_0)$. What (9.13) tells us is that, given an nth-degree polynomial $f(x)$, if we let $x = 7$ (say) in the terms on the right of (9.13), select an arbitrary number x_0, then evaluate and add these terms, we will end up exactly with $f(7)$—the value of $f(x)$ at $x = 7$.

Example 2   Taking $x_0 = 3$ as the point of expansion, we can rewrite (9.6) equivalently as

$$f(x) = f(3) + f'(3)(x - 3) + \frac{f''(3)}{2}(x - 3)^2 + \cdots + \frac{f^{(n)}(3)}{n!}(x - 3)^n$$

Expansion of an Arbitrary Function

Heretofore, we have shown how an nth-degree polynomial function can be expressed in another, equivalent, nth-degree polynomial form. As it turns out, it is also possible to express any *arbitrary* function $\phi(x)$—one that is not necessarily a polynomial—in a polynomial form similar to (9.13), provided $\phi(x)$ has finite, continuous derivatives up to the desired order at the expansion point x_0.

According to a mathematical proposition known as *Taylor's theorem*, given an arbitrary function $\phi(x)$, if we know the value of the function at $x = x_0$ [that is, $\phi(x_0)$] and the values of its derivatives at x_0 [that is, $\phi'(x_0)$, $\phi''(x_0)$, etc.], then this function can be expanded around the point x_0 as follows ($n = $ a fixed positive integer arbitrarily chosen):

$$\phi(x) = \left[\frac{\phi(x_0)}{0!} + \frac{\phi'(x_0)}{1!}(x - x_0) + \frac{\phi''(x_0)}{2!}(x - x_0)^2 \right.$$
$$\left. + \cdots + \frac{\phi^{(n)}(x_0)}{n!}(x - x_0)^n \right] + R_n$$
$$\equiv P_n + R_n \qquad \text{[Taylor's formula with remainder]} \qquad \textbf{(9.14)}$$

where P_n represents the (bracketed) nth-degree polynomial [the first $(n + 1)$ terms on the right], and R_n denotes a *remainder*, to be explained on page 248.[†] The presence of R_n is what distinguishes (9.14) from Taylor's formula (9.13), and for this reason (9.14) is called *Taylor's formula with remainder*. The form of the polynomial P_n and the size of the remainder R_n will depend on the value of n we choose. The larger the n, the more terms there will be in P_n; accordingly, R_n will in general assume a different value for each different n. This fact explains the need for the subscript n in these two symbols. As a memory aid, we can identify n as the order of the highest derivative in P_n. (In the special case of $n = 0$, no derivative will appear in P_n at all.)

[†] The symbol R_n (remainder) is not to be confused with the symbol R^n (n-space).

The appearance of R_n in (9.14) is due to the fact that we are here dealing with an arbitrary function ϕ which cannot always be transformed *exactly* into, but can only be approximated by, the polynomial form shown in (9.13). Therefore, a remainder term is included as a supplement to the P_n part, to represent the discrepancy between $\phi(x)$ and P_n. Thus, P_n constitutes a polynomial approximation to $\phi(x)$, with the term R_n as a measure of the error of approximation. If we choose $n = 1$, for example, we have

$$\phi(x) = [\phi(x_0) + \phi'(x_0)(x - x_0)] + R_1 = P_1 + R_1$$

where P_1 consists of $n + 1 = 2$ terms and constitutes a *linear* approximation to $\phi(x)$. If we choose $n = 2$, a second-power term will appear, so that

$$\phi(x) = \left[\phi(x_0) + \phi'(x_0)(x - x_0) + \frac{\phi''(x_0)}{2!}(x - x_0)^2\right] + R_2 = P_2 + R_2$$

where P_2, consisting of $n + 1 = 3$ terms, is a *quadratic* approximation to $\phi(x)$. And so forth. The fact that we can create polynomial approximations to any arbitrary function (provided it has finite, continuous derivatives) is of great practical significance. Polynomial functions—even higher-degree ones—are relatively easy to work with, and if they can serve as good approximations to some difficult functions, much convenience is to be gained, as the next two examples will illustrate.

We should point out that the arbitrary function $\phi(x)$ could obviously encompass the nth-degree polynomial of (9.6) as a special case. For this latter case, if the expansion is into another nth-degree polynomial, the result of (9.13) will exactly apply; or in other words, we can use the result in (9.14), with $R_n \equiv 0$. However, if the given nth-degree polynomial $f(x)$ is to be expanded into a polynomial of a *lesser* degree, then the latter can only be considered an approximation to $f(x)$, and a remainder must appear; in that case, the result in (9.14) can be applied with a nonzero remainder. Thus Taylor's formula in the form of (9.14) is perfectly general.

Example 3

Expand the nonpolynomial function

$$\phi(x) = \frac{1}{1 + x}$$

around the point $x_0 = 1$, with $n = 4$. We shall need the first four derivatives of $\phi(x)$, which are

$$\phi'(x) = -(1 + x)^{-2} \qquad \text{so that} \qquad \phi'(1) = -(2)^{-2} = \frac{-1}{4}$$

$$\phi''(x) = 2(1 + x)^{-3} \qquad\qquad\qquad \phi''(1) = 2(2)^{-3} = \frac{1}{4}$$

$$\phi'''(x) = -6(1 + x)^{-4} \qquad\qquad\qquad \phi'''(1) = -6(2)^{-4} = \frac{-3}{8}$$

$$\phi^{(4)}(x) = 24(1 + x)^{-5} \qquad\qquad\qquad \phi^{(4)}(1) = 24(2)^{-5} = \frac{3}{4}$$

Also, we see that $\phi(1) = \frac{1}{2}$. Thus, setting $x_0 = 1$ in (9.14) and utilizing the obtained derivatives, we arrive at the following Taylor series with remainder:

$$\phi(x) = \frac{1}{2} - \frac{1}{4}(x - 1) + \frac{1}{8}(x - 1)^2 - \frac{1}{16}(x - 1)^3 + \frac{1}{32}(x - 1)^4 + R_4$$

$$= \frac{31}{32} - \frac{13}{16}x + \frac{1}{2}x^2 - \frac{3}{16}x^3 + \frac{1}{32}x^4 + R_4$$

It is possible, of course, to choose $x_0 = 0$ as the point of expansion here, too. In that case, with x_0 set equal to zero in (9.14), the expansion will result in a *Maclaurin series with remainder.*

Example 4

Expand the quadratic function

$$\phi(x) = 5 + 2x + x^2$$

around $x_0 = 1$, with $n = 1$. This function is, like (9.9) in Example 1, a second-degree polynomial. But since $n = 1$, our assigned task is to expand it into a *first*-degree polynomial, i.e., to find a linear approximation to the given quadratic function; thus a remainder term is bound to appear. For this reason, $\phi(x)$ should be viewed as an "arbitrary" function for the purpose of this Taylor expansion.

To carry out this expansion, we need only the first derivative $\phi'(x) = 2 + 2x$. Evaluated at $x_0 = 1$, the given function and its derivative yield

$$\phi(x_0) = \phi(1) = 8 \qquad \phi'(x_0) = \phi'(1) = 4$$

Thus Taylor's formula with remainder gives us

$$\phi(x) = \phi(x_0) + \phi'(x_0)(x - x_0) + R_1$$
$$= 8 + 4(x - 1) + R_1 = 4 + 4x + R_1$$

where the $(4 + 4x)$ term is a linear approximation and the R_1 term represents the error of approximation.

In Fig. 9.8, $\phi(x)$ plots as a parabola, and its linear approximation as a straight line tangent to the $\phi(x)$ curve at the point (1, 8). The occurrence of the point of tangency at $x = 1$ is not a matter of coincidence; rather, it is the direct consequence of the fact that the point of expansion is set at that particular value of x. This suggests that, when an arbitrary function $\phi(x)$ is approximated by a polynomial, the latter will give the exact value of $\phi(x)$ *at* (and only *at*) the point of expansion, with zero error of approximation ($R_1 = 0$). Elsewhere, R_1 is strictly nonzero and, in fact, shows increasingly larger errors of approximation as we

FIGURE 9.8

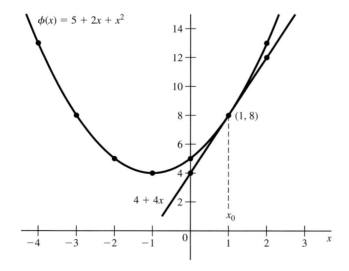

try to approximate $\phi(x)$ for x values farther and farther away from the point of expansion x_0. Thus, when attempting to approximate any function $\phi(x)$ by a polynomial, if we are most interested in obtaining an accurate approximation in the neighborhood of a specific value of x, say x_0, then we ought to choose x_0 as the point of expansion.

The construction of Fig. 9.8 is strongly reminiscent of Fig. 8.1. Indeed, both figures are concerned with "approximations." But there is a difference in the scope of approximation. In Fig. 8.1, we attempt to approximate Δy by the differential dy with the help of a tangent line drawn at x_0, a given starting value of x. In Fig. 9.8, on the other hand, we aim more broadly to approximate an entire curve by a particular straight line, i.e., to approximate the height of the curve at any value of x, say, x_1, by the corresponding height of the straight line at x_1. Note that, in both cases, the error of approximation varies with the value of x. In Fig. 8.1, the error (the difference between dy and Δy) gets smaller as Δx gets smaller, or as x gets closer to x_0, at which the tangent line is drawn. In Fig. 9.8, the error (the vertical discrepancy between the straight line and the curve) gets smaller as x approaches x_0, the chosen point of expansion.

Lagrange Form of the Remainder

Now we must comment further on the remainder term. According to the *Lagrange form of the remainder*, we can express R_n as

$$R_n = \frac{\phi^{(n+1)}(p)}{(n+1)!}(x - x_0)^{n+1} \tag{9.15}$$

where p is some number between x (the point where we wish to evaluate the arbitrary function ϕ) and x_0 (the point where we expand the function ϕ). Note that this expression closely resembles the term which should logically follow the last term in P_n in (9.14), except that the derivative involved is here to be evaluated at a point p instead of x_0. Since the point p is, unfortunately, not otherwise specified, this formula does not really enable us to calculate R_n; nevertheless, it does have great analytical significance. Let us therefore illustrate its meaning graphically, although we shall do it only for the simple case of $n = 0$.

When $n = 0$, no derivatives whatever will appear in the polynomial part P_0; therefore (9.14) reduces to

$$\phi(x) = P_0 + R_0 = \phi(x_0) + \phi'(p)(x - x_0)$$

or $\qquad \phi(x) - \phi(x_0) = \phi'(p)(x - x_0)$

This result, a simple version of the *mean-value theorem,* states that the difference between the value of the function ϕ at x_0 and at any other x value can be expressed as the product of the difference $(x - x_0)$ and the derivative ϕ' evaluated at p (with p being some point between x and x_0). Let us look at Fig. 9.9, where the function $\phi(x)$ is shown as a continuous curve with derivative values defined at all points. Let x_0 be the chosen point of expansion, and let x be *any* point on the horizontal axis. If we try to approximate $\phi(x)$, or distance xB, by $\phi(x_0)$, or distance $x_0 A$, it will involve an error equal to $\phi(x) - \phi(x_0)$, or the distance CB. What the mean-value theorem says is that the error CB—which constitutes the value of the remainder term R_0 in the expansion—can be expressed as $\phi'(p)(x - x_0)$, where p is some point between x and x_0. First we locate, on the curve between points

FIGURE 9.9

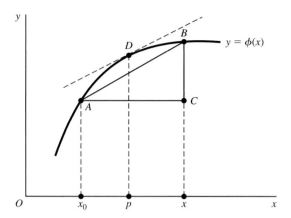

A and *B*, a point *D* such that the tangent line at *D* is parallel to line *AB*; such a point *D* must exist, since the curve passes from *A* to *B* in a continuous and smooth manner. Then, the remainder will be

$$R_0 = CB = \frac{CB}{AC}AC = (\text{slope of } AB) \cdot AC$$
$$= (\text{slope of tangent at } D) \cdot AC$$
$$= (\text{slope of curve at } x = p) \cdot AC$$
$$= \phi'(p)(x - x_0)$$

where the point *p* is between *x* and x_0, as required. This demonstrates the rationale of the Lagrange form of the remainder for the case $n = 0$. We can always express R_0 as $\phi'(p)(x - x_0)$ because, even though *p* cannot be assigned a specific value, we can be sure that such a point exists.

Equation (9.15) provides a way of expressing the remainder term R_n, but it does not eliminate R_n as a source of discrepancy between $\phi(x)$ and the polynomial P_n. However, if it happens that as we increase *n* (thus raising the degree of the polynomial) indefinitely, we find that

$$R_n \to 0 \text{ as } n \to \infty \qquad \text{so that} \qquad P_n \to \phi(x) \text{ as } n \to \infty$$

then the Taylor series is said to be convergent to $\phi(x)$ at the point of expansion, and the Taylor series can be written as a *convergent infinite series* as follows:

$$\phi(x) = \frac{\phi(x_0)}{0!} + \frac{\phi'(x_0)}{1!}(x - x_0) + \frac{\phi''(x_0)}{2!}(x - x_0)^2 + \cdots \quad \textbf{(9.16)}$$

Note that the R_n term is no longer shown; in its place is an ellipsis signifying that the polynomial contains an infinite number of subsequent terms whose mathematical structures follow the pattern indicated by the previous terms. In this (convenient) event, it will be possible to make P_n as accurate an approximation to $\phi(x)$ as we desire by choosing a large enough value for *n*, that is, by including a large enough number of terms in the polynomial P_n. An important example of this will be discussed in Sec. 10.2.

EXERCISE 9.5

1. Find the value of the following factorial expressions:

(a) $5!$

(b) $8!$

(c) $\dfrac{4!}{3!}$

(d) $\dfrac{6!}{4!}$

(e) $\dfrac{(n+2)!}{n!}$

2. Find the first five terms of the Maclaurin series (i.e., choose $n = 4$ and let $x_0 = 0$) for:

(a) $\phi(x) = \dfrac{1}{1-x}$

(b) $\phi(x) = \dfrac{1-x}{1+x}$

3. Find the Taylor series with $n = 4$ and $x_0 = -2$, for the two functions in Prob. 2.

4. On the basis of Taylor's formula with the Lagrange form of the remainder [see (9.14) and (9.15)], show that at the point of expansion ($x = x_0$) the Taylor series will always give *exactly* the value of the function at that point, $\phi(x_0)$, not merely an approximation.

9.6 Nth-Derivative Test for Relative Extremum of a Function of One Variable

The expansion of a function into a Taylor (or Maclaurin) series is useful as an approximation device in the circumstance that $R_n \to 0$ as $n \to \infty$, but our present concern is with its application in the development of a general test for a relative extremum.

Taylor Expansion and Relative Extremum

As a preparatory step for that task, let us redefine a relative extremum as follows:

A function $f(x)$ attains a relative maximum (minimum) value at x_0 if $f(x) - f(x_0)$ is negative (positive) for values of x in the immediate neighborhood of x_0, both to its left and to its right.

This can be made clear by reference to Fig. 9.10, where x_1 is a value of x to the left of x_0, and x_2 is a value of x to the right of x_0. In Fig. 9.10a, $f(x_0)$ is a relative maximum; thus $f(x_0)$ exceeds both $f(x_1)$ and $f(x_2)$. In short, $f(x) - f(x_0)$ is negative for any value of x in the immediate neighborhood of x_0. The opposite is true of Fig. 9.10b, where $f(x_0)$ is a relative minimum, and thus $f(x) - f(x_0) > 0$.

Assuming $f(x)$ to have finite, continuous derivatives up to the desired order at the point $x = x_0$, the function $f(x)$—not necessarily polynomial—can be expanded around the point x_0 as a Taylor series. On the basis of (9.14) (after duly changing ϕ to f), and using the Lagrange form of the remainder, we can write

$$f(x) - f(x_0) = f'(x_0)(x - x_0) + \frac{f''(x_0)}{2!}(x - x_0)^2 + \cdots$$

$$+ \frac{f^{(n)}(x_0)}{n!}(x - x_0)^n + \frac{f^{(n+1)}(p)}{(n+1)!}(x - x_0)^{n+1} \qquad \textbf{(9.17)}$$

FIGURE 9.10

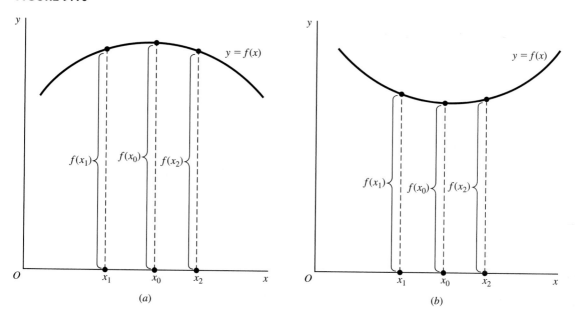

If the sign of the expression $f(x) - f(x_0)$ can be determined for values of x to the immediate left and right of x_0, we can readily come to a conclusion as to whether $f(x_0)$ is an extremum, and if so, whether it is a maximum or a minimum. For this, it is necessary to examine the right-hand sum of (9.17). Altogether, there are $(n + 1)$ terms in this sum—n terms from P_n, plus the remainder which is in the $(n + 1)$st degree—and thus the actual number of terms is indefinite, being dependent upon the value of n we choose. However, by properly choosing n, we can always make sure that there will exist only a single term on the right. This will drastically simplify the task of evaluating the sign of $f(x) - f(x_0)$ and ascertaining whether $f(x_0)$ is an extremum, and if so, which kind.

Some Specific Cases

This can be made clearer through some specific illustrations.

Case 1 $\qquad\qquad\qquad\qquad\qquad\qquad f'(x_0) \neq 0$

If the first derivative at x_0 is nonzero, let us choose $n = 0$, so that the remainder will be in the first degree. Then there will be only $n + 1 = 1$ term on the right side, implying that only the remainder R_0 will be there. That is, we have

$$f(x) - f(x_0) = \frac{f'(p)}{1!}(x - x_0) = f'(p)(x - x_0)$$

where p is some number between x_0 and a value of x in the immediate neighborhood of x_0. Note that p must accordingly be very, very close to x_0.

What is the sign of the expression on the right? Because of the continuity of the derivative, $f'(p)$ will have the same sign as $f'(x_0)$ since, as mentioned before, p is very, very close to x_0. In the present case, $f'(p)$ must be nonzero; in fact, it must be a specific positive or negative number. But what about the $(x - x_0)$ part? When we go from the left of x_0 to its right, x shifts from a magnitude $x_1 < x_0$ to a magnitude $x_2 > x_0$ (see Fig. 9.10). Consequently, the expression $(x - x_0)$ must turn from negative to positive as we move, and $f(x) - f(x_0) = f'(p)(x - x_0)$ must also change sign from the left of x_0 to its right. However, this violates our new definition of a relative extremum; accordingly, there cannot exist a relative extremum at $f(x_0)$ when $f'(x_0) \neq 0$—a fact that is already well known to us.

Case 2 $\qquad\qquad\qquad\qquad f'(x_0) = 0; \ f''(x_0) \neq 0$

In this case, choose $n = 1$, so that the remainder will be in the second degree. Then initially there will be $n + 1 = 2$ terms on the right. But one of these terms will vanish because $f'(x_0) = 0$, and we shall again be left with only one term to evaluate:

$$f(x) - f(x_0) = f'(x_0)(x - x_0) + \frac{f''(p)}{2!}(x - x_0)^2$$
$$= \tfrac{1}{2}f''(p)(x - x_0)^2 \qquad [\text{because } f'(x_0) = 0]$$

As before, $f''(p)$ will have the same sign as $f''(x_0)$, a sign that is specified and unvarying, whereas the $(x - x_0)^2$ part, being a square, is invariably positive. Thus the expression $f(x) - f(x_0)$ must take the same sign as $f''(x_0)$ and, according to the earlier definition of relative extremum, will specify

$$\begin{array}{ll} \text{A relative maximum of } f(x) \text{ if } f''(x_0) < 0 \\ \text{A relative minimum of } f(x) \text{ if } f''(x_0) > 0 \end{array} \qquad [\text{with } f'(x_0) = 0]$$

You will recognize this as the second-derivative test introduced earlier.

Case 3 $\qquad\qquad\qquad\qquad f'(x_0) = f''(x_0) = 0, \text{ but } f'''(x_0) \neq 0$

Here we are encountering a situation that the second-derivative test is incapable of handling, for $f''(x_0)$ is now zero. With the help of the Taylor series, however, a conclusive result can be established without difficulty.

Let us choose $n = 2$; then three terms will initially appear on the right. But two of these will drop out because $f'(x_0) = f''(x_0) = 0$, so that we again have only one term to evaluate:

$$f(x) - f(x_0) = f'(x_0)(x - x_0) + \frac{1}{2!}f''(x_0)(x - x_0)^2 + \frac{1}{3!}f'''(p)(x - x_0)^3$$
$$= \frac{1}{6}f'''(p)(x - x_0)^3 \qquad [\text{because } f'(x_0) = 0, \ f''(x_0) = 0]$$

As previously, the sign of $f'''(p)$ is identical with that of $f'''(x_0)$ because of the continuity of the derivative and because p is very close to x_0. But the $(x - x_0)^3$ part has a varying sign. Specifically, since $(x - x_0)$ is negative to the left of x_0, so also will be $(x - x_0)^3$; yet, to the right of x_0, the $(x - x_0)^3$ part will be positive. Thus there is a change in the sign of $f(x) - f(x_0)$ as we pass through x_0, which violates the definition of a relative extremum. However, we know that x_0 is a critical value $[f'(x_0) = 0]$, and thus it must give an inflection point, inasmuch as it does not give a relative extremum.

Case 4 $\qquad\qquad f'(x_0) = f''(x_0) = \cdots = f^{(N-1)}(x_0) = 0, \text{ but } f^{(N)}(x_0) \neq 0$

This is a very general case, and we can therefore derive a general result from it. Note that here all the derivative values are zero until we arrive at the Nth one.

Analogously to the preceding three cases, the Taylor series for Case 4 will reduce to

$$f(x) - f(x_0) = \frac{1}{N!} f^{(N)}(p)(x - x_0)^N$$

Again, $f^{(N)}(p)$ takes the same sign as $f^{(N)}(x_0)$, which is unvarying. The sign of the $(x - x_0)^N$ part, on the other hand, will *vary* if N is *odd* (cf. Cases 1 and 3) and will *remain unchanged* (positive) if N is *even* (cf. Case 2). When N is odd, accordingly, $f(x) - f(x_0)$ will change sign as we pass through the point x_0, thereby violating the definition of a relative extremum (which means that x_0 must give us an inflection point on the curve). But when N is even, $f(x) - f(x_0)$ will not change sign from the left of x_0 to its right, and this will establish the stationary value $f(x_0)$ as a relative maximum or minimum, depending on whether $f^{(N)}(x_0)$ is negative or positive.

Nth-Derivative Test

At last, then, we may state the following general test.

Nth-Derivative test for relative extremum of a function of one variable If the first derivative of a function $f(x)$ at x_0 is $f'(x_0) = 0$ and if the first *nonzero* derivative value at x_0 encountered in successive derivation is that of the Nth derivative, $f^{(N)}(x_0) \neq 0$, then the stationary value $f(x_0)$ will be

a. A relative *maximum* if N is an even number and $f^{(N)}(x_0) < 0$.
b. A relative *minimum* if N is an even number but $f^{(N)}(x_0) > 0$.
c. An *inflection point* if N is odd.

It should be clear from the preceding statement that the Nth-derivative test can work if and only if the function $f(x)$ is capable of yielding, sooner or later, a nonzero derivative value at the critical value x_0. While there do exist exceptional functions that fail to satisfy this condition, most of the functions we are likely to encounter will indeed produce nonzero $f^{(N)}(x_0)$ in successive differentiation.[†] Thus the test should prove serviceable in most instances.

[†] If $f(x)$ is a constant function, for instance, then obviously $f'(x) = f''(x) = \cdots = 0$, so that no nonzero derivative value can ever be found. This, however, is a trivial case, since a constant function requires no test for extremum anyway. As a nontrivial example, consider the function

$$y = \begin{cases} e^{-1/x^2} & \text{(for } x \neq 0) \\ 0 & \text{(for } x = 0) \end{cases}$$

where the function $y = e^{-1/x^2}$ is an exponential function, yet to be introduced (Chap. 10). By itself, $y = e^{-1/x^2}$ is discontinuous at $x = 0$, because $x = 0$ is not in the domain (division by zero is undefined). However, since $\lim_{x \to 0} y = 0$, we can, by appending the stipulation that $y = 0$ for $x = 0$, fill the gap in the domain and thereby obtain a continuous function. The graph of this function shows that it attains a minimum at $x = 0$. But it turns out that, at $x = 0$, all the derivatives (up to any order) have zero values. Thus we are unable to apply the Nth-derivative test to confirm the graphically ascertainable fact that the function has a minimum at $x = 0$. For further discussion of this exceptional case, see R. Courant, *Differential and Integral Calculus* (translated by E. J. McShane), Interscience, New York, vol. I, 2d ed., 1937, pp. 196, 197, and 336.

Example 1 Examine the function $y = (7 - x)^4$ for its relative extremum. Since $f'(x) = -4(7 - x)^3$ is zero when $x = 7$, we take $x = 7$ as the critical value for testing, with $y = 0$ as the stationary value of the function. By successive derivation (continued until we encounter a nonzero derivative value at the point $x = 7$), we get

$$f''(x) = 12(7 - x)^2 \qquad \text{so that} \qquad f''(7) = 0$$

$$f'''(x) = -24(7 - x) \qquad\qquad\qquad f'''(7) = 0$$

$$f^{(4)}(x) = 24 \qquad\qquad\qquad\qquad f^{(4)}(7) = 24$$

Since 4 is an even number and since $f^{(4)}(7)$ is positive, we conclude that the point (7, 0) represents a relative minimum.

As is easily verified, this function plots as a strictly convex curve. Inasmuch as the second derivative at $x = 7$ is zero (rather than positive), this example serves to illustrate our earlier statement regarding the second derivative and the curvature of a curve (Sec. 9.3) to the effect that, while a positive $f''(x)$ for all x does imply a strictly convex $f(x)$, a strictly convex $f(x)$ does *not* imply a positive $f''(x)$ for all x. More importantly, it also serves to illustrate the fact that, given a strictly convex (strictly concave) curve, the extremum found on that curve must be a minimum (maximum), because such an extremum will *either* satisfy the second-order sufficient condition, *or*, failing that, satisfy another (higher-order) sufficient condition for a minimum (maximum).

EXERCISE 9.6

1. Find the stationary values of the following functions:
   (a) $y = x^3$ (b) $y = -x^4$ (c) $y = x^6 + 5$

   Determine by the Nth-derivative test whether they represent relative maxima, relative minima, or inflection points.

2. Find the stationary values of the following functions:
   (a) $y = (x - 1)^3 + 16$ (c) $y = (3 - x)^6 + 7$
   (b) $y = (x - 2)^4$ (d) $y = (5 - 2x)^4 + 8$

   Use the Nth-derivative test to determine the exact nature of these stationary values.

Chapter 10

Exponential and Logarithmic Functions

The Nth-derivative test developed in Chap. 9 equips us for the task of locating the extreme values of any objective function, as long as it involves only one choice variable, possesses derivatives to the desired order, and sooner or later yields a nonzero derivative value at the critical value x_0. In the examples cited in Chap. 9, however, we made use only of polynomial and rational functions, for which we know how to obtain the necessary derivatives. Suppose that our objective function happened to be an *exponential* one, such as

$$y = 8^{x - \sqrt{x}}$$

Then we are still helpless in applying the derivative criterion, because we have yet to learn how to differentiate such a function. This is what we shall do in the present chapter.

Exponential functions, as well as the closely related logarithmic functions, have important applications in economics, especially in connection with growth problems, and in economic dynamics in general. The particular application relevant to the present part of the book, however, involves a class of optimization problems in which the choice variable is *time*. For example, a certain wine dealer may have a stock of wine, the market value of which is known to increase with time in some prescribed fashion. The problem is to determine the best time to sell that stock on the basis of the wine-value function, after taking into account the interest cost involved in having the money capital tied up in that stock. Exponential functions may enter into such a problem in two ways. First, the value of the wine may increase with time according to some *exponential law of growth*. In that event, we would have an exponential wine-value function. Second, when we consider the interest cost, the presence of interest compounding will surely introduce an exponential function into the picture. Thus we must study the nature of exponential functions before we can discuss this type of optimization problem.

Since our primary purpose is to deal with time as a choice variable, let us now switch to the symbol t—in lieu of x—to indicate the independent variable in the subsequent discussion. (However, this same symbol t can very well represent variables other than time also.)

10.1   The Nature of Exponential Functions

As introduced in connection with polynomial functions, the term *exponent* means an indicator of the power to which a variable is to be raised. In power expressions such as x^3 or x^5, the exponents are *constants;* but there is no reason why we cannot also have a *variable* exponent, such as in 3^x or 3^t, where the number 3 is to be raised to varying powers (various values of x or t). A function whose *independent* variable appears in the role of an exponent is called an *exponential function.*

Simple Exponential Function

In its simple version, the exponential function may be represented in the form

$$y = f(t) = b^t \qquad (b > 1) \tag{10.1}$$

where y and t are the dependent and independent variables, respectively, and b denotes a fixed *base* of the exponent. The domain of such a function is the set of all real numbers. Thus, unlike the exponents in a polynomial function, the variable exponent t in (10.1) is not limited to positive integers—unless we wish to impose such a restriction.

But why the restriction of $b > 1$? The explanation is as follows. Since the domain of the function in (10.1) consists of the set of all real numbers, it is possible for t to take a value such as $\frac{1}{2}$. If b is allowed to be negative, the half power of b will involve taking the square root of a negative number. While this is not an impossible task, we would certainly prefer to take the easy way out by restricting b to be positive. Once we adopt the restriction $b > 0$, however, we might as well go all the way to the restriction $b > 1$: The restriction $b > 1$ differs from $b > 0$ only in the further exclusion of the cases of (1) $0 < b < 1$ and (2) $b = 1$; but as will be shown, the first case can be subsumed under the restriction $b > 1$, whereas the second case can be dismissed outright. Consider the first case. If $b = \frac{1}{5}$, then we have

$$y = \left(\frac{1}{5}\right)^t = \frac{1}{5^t} = 5^{-t}$$

This shows that a function with a fractional base can easily be rewritten into one with a base greater than 1. As for the second case, the fact that $b = 1$ will give us the function $y = 1^t = 1$, so that the exponential function actually degenerates into a constant function; it may therefore be disqualified as a member of the exponential family.

Graphical Form

The graph of the exponential function in (10.1) takes the general shape of the curve in Fig. 10.1. The curve drawn is based on the value $b = 2$; but even for other values of b, the same general configuration will prevail.

Several salient features of this type of exponential curve may be noted. First, it is continuous and smooth everywhere; thus the function should be everywhere differentiable. As a matter of fact, it is continuously differentiable any number of times. Second, it is strictly increasing, and in fact y increases at an increasing rate throughout. Consequently, both the first and second derivatives of the function $y = b^t$ should be positive—a fact we should

FIGURE 10.1

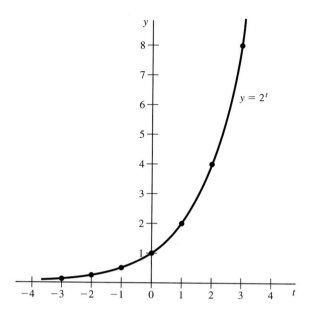

be able to confirm after we have developed the relevant differentiation formulas. Third, we note that, even though the domain of the function contains negative as well as positive numbers, the range of the function is limited to the open interval $(0, \infty)$. That is, the dependent variable y is invariably *positive*, regardless of the sign of the independent variable t.

The strict monotonicity of the exponential function has at least two interesting and significant implications. First, we may infer that the exponential function must have an inverse function, which is itself strictly monotonic. This inverse function, we shall find, turns out to be a *logarithmic* function. Second, since strict monotonicity means that there is a unique value of t for a given value of y and since the range of the exponential function is the interval $(0, \infty)$, it follows that we should be able to express *any positive number* as a unique power of a base $b > 1$. This can be seen from Fig. 10.1, where the curve of $y = 2^t$ covers all the positive values of y in its range; therefore any positive value of y must be expressible as some unique power of the number 2. Actually, even if the base is changed to some other real number greater than 1, the same range holds, so that it is possible to express any positive number y as a power of any base $b > 1$.

Generalized Exponential Function

This last point deserves closer scrutiny. If a positive y can indeed be expressed as powers of various alternative bases, then there must exist a general procedure of *base conversion*. In the case of the function $y = 9^t$, for instance, we can readily transform it into $y = (3^2)^t = 3^{2t}$, thereby converting the base from 9 to 3, provided the exponent is duly altered from t to $2t$. This change in exponent, necessitated by the base conversion, does not create any new type of function, for, if we let $w = 2t$, then $y = 3^{2t} = 3^w$ is still in the form of (10.1). From the point of view of the base 3, however, the exponent is now $2t$ rather than t. What is the effect of adding a numerical coefficient (here, 2) to the exponent t?

FIGURE 10.2

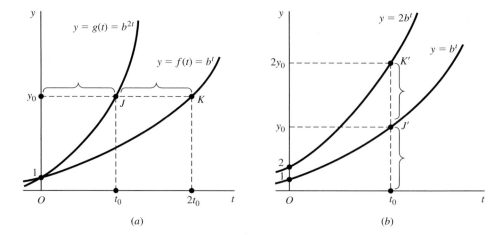

(a)   (b)

The answer is to be found in Fig. 10.2*a*, where two curves are drawn—one for the function $y = f(t) = b^t$ and one for another function $y = g(t) = b^{2t}$. Since the exponent in the latter is exactly twice that of the former, and since the identical base is adopted for the two functions, the assignment of an arbitrary value $t = t_0$ in the function g and $t = 2t_0$ in the function f must yield the same value:

$$f(2t_0) = g(t_0) = b^{2t_0} = y_0$$

Thus the distance $y_0 J$ will be half of $y_0 K$. By similar reasoning, for any value of y, the function g should be exactly halfway between the function f and the vertical axis. It may be concluded, therefore, that the *doubling* of the exponent has the effect of compressing the exponential curve *halfway* toward the y axis, whereas *halving* the exponent will extend the curve away from the y axis to *twice* the horizontal distance.

It is of interest that both functions share the same vertical intercept

$$f(0) = g(0) = b^0 = 1$$

The change of the exponent t to $2t$, or to any other multiple of t, will leave the vertical intercept unaffected. In terms of *compressing,* this is because compressing a zero horizontal distance will still yield a zero distance.

The change of exponent is one way of modifying—and generalizing—the exponential function of (10.1); another way is to attach a coefficient to b^t, such as $2b^t$. [*Warning:* $2b^t \neq (2b)^t$.] The effect of such a coefficient is also to compress or extend the curve, except that this time the direction is vertical. In Fig. 10.2*b*, the higher curve represents $y = 2b^t$, and the lower one is $y = b^t$. For every value of t, the former must obviously be twice as high, because it has a y value twice as large as the latter. Thus we have $t_0 J' = J'K'$. Note that the vertical intercept, too, is changed in the present case. We may conclude that *doubling* the coefficient (here, from 1 to 2) serves to extend the curve away from the horizontal axis to *twice* the vertical distance, whereas *halving* the coefficient will compress the curve *halfway* toward the t axis.

With the knowledge of the two modifications just discussed, the exponential function $y = b^t$ can now be generalized to the form

$$y = ab^{ct} \tag{10.2}$$

where a and c are "compressing" or "extending" agents. When assigned various values, they will alter the position of the exponential curve, thus generating a whole family of exponential curves (functions). If a and c are positive, the general configuration shown in Fig. 10.2 will prevail; if a or c or both are *negative,* however, then fundamental modifications will occur in the configuration of the curve (see Exercise 10.1-5).

A Preferred Base

What prompted the discussion of the change of exponent from t to ct was the question of base conversion. But, granting the feasibility of base conversion, why would one want to do it anyhow? One answer is that some bases are more convenient than others as far as mathematical manipulations are concerned.

Curiously enough, in calculus, the preferred base happens to be a certain irrational number denoted by the symbol e:

$$e = 2.71828\ldots$$

When this base e is used in an exponential function, it is referred to as a *natural exponential function,* examples of which are

$$y = e^t \qquad y = e^{3t} \qquad y = Ae^{rt}$$

These illustrative functions can also be expressed by the alternative notations

$$y = \exp(t) \qquad y = \exp(3t) \qquad y = A\exp(rt)$$

where the abbreviation exp (for exponential) indicates that e is to have as its exponent the expression in parentheses.

The choice of such an outlandish number as $e = 2.71828\ldots$ as the preferred base no doubt seems bewildering. But there is an excellent reason for this choice, for the function e^t possesses the remarkable property of being its own derivative! That is,

$$\frac{d}{dt}e^t = e^t$$

a fact that reduces the work of differentiation to no work at all. Moreover, armed with this differentiation rule—to be proved in Section 10.5—it will also be easy to find the derivative of a more complicated natural exponential function such as $y = Ae^{rt}$. To do this, first let $w = rt$, so that the function becomes

$$y = Ae^w \qquad \text{where } w = rt, \text{ and } A, r \text{ are constants}$$

Then, by the chain rule, we can write

$$\frac{dy}{dt} = \frac{dy}{dw}\frac{dw}{dt} = Ae^w(r) = rAe^{rt}$$

That is,

$$\frac{d}{dt}Ae^{rt} = rAe^{rt} \tag{10.3}$$

The mathematical convenience of the base e should thus be amply clear.

EXERCISE 10.1

1. Plot in a single diagram the graphs of the exponential functions $y = 3^t$ and $y = 3^{2t}$.
   (a) Do the two graphs display the same general positional relationship as shown in Fig. 10.2a?
   (b) Do these two curves share the same y intercept? Why?
   (c) Sketch the graph of the function $y = 3^{3t}$ in the same diagram.
2. Plot in a single diagram the graphs of the exponential functions $y = 4^t$ and $y = 3(4^t)$.
   (a) Do the two graphs display the general positional relationship suggested in Fig. 10.2b?
   (b) Do the two curves have the same y intercept? Why?
   (c) Sketch the graph of the function $y = \frac{3}{2}(4^t)$ in the same diagram.
3. Taking for granted that e^t is its own derivative, use the chain rule to find dy/dt for the following:
   (a) $y = e^{5t}$ (b) $y = 4e^{3t}$ (c) $y = 6e^{-2t}$
4. In view of our discussion about (10.1), do you expect the function $y = e^t$ to be strictly increasing at an increasing rate? Verify your answer by determining the signs of the first and second derivatives of this function. In doing so, remember that the domain of this function is the set of all real numbers, i.e., the interval $(-\infty, \infty)$.
5. In (10.2), if negative values are assigned to a and c, the general shape of the curves in Fig. 10.2 will no longer prevail. Examine the change in curve configuration by contrasting (a) the case of $a = -1$ against the case of $a = 1$, and (b) the case of $c = -1$ against the case of $c = 1$.

10.2 Natural Exponential Functions and the Problem of Growth

The pertinent questions still unanswered are: How is the number e defined? Does it have any economic meaning in addition to its mathematical significance as a convenient base? And, in what ways do natural exponential functions apply to economic analysis?

The Number e

Let us consider the following function:

$$f(m) = \left(1 + \frac{1}{m}\right)^m \qquad\qquad (10.4)$$

If larger and larger values are assigned to m, then $f(m)$ will also assume larger values; specifically, we find that

$$f(1) = \left(1 + \tfrac{1}{1}\right)^1 = 2$$
$$f(2) = \left(1 + \tfrac{1}{2}\right)^2 = 2.25$$
$$f(3) = \left(1 + \tfrac{1}{3}\right)^3 = 2.37037\ldots$$
$$f(4) = \left(1 + \tfrac{1}{4}\right)^4 = 2.44141\ldots$$
$$\vdots$$

Moreover, if m is increased indefinitely, then $f(m)$ will converge to the number $2.71828\ldots \equiv e$; thus e may be defined as the limit of (10.4) as $m \to \infty$:

$$e \equiv \lim_{m\to\infty} f(m) = \lim_{m\to\infty} \left(1 + \frac{1}{m}\right)^m \tag{10.5}$$

That the approximate value of e is 2.71828 can be verified by finding the Maclaurin series of the function $\phi(x) = e^x$—with x used here to facilitate the direct application of the expansion formula (9.14). Such a series will give us a polynomial approximation to e^x, and thus the value of e ($= e^1$) may be approximated by setting $x = 1$ in that polynomial. If the remainder term R_n approaches zero as the number of terms in the series is increased indefinitely, i.e., if the series is convergent to $\phi(x)$, then we can indeed approximate the value of e to any desired degree of accuracy by making the number of included terms sufficiently large.

To this end, we need to have derivatives of various orders for the function. Accepting the fact that the first derivative of e^x is e^x itself, we can see that the derivative of $\phi(x)$ is simply e^x and, similarly, that the second, third, or any higher-order derivatives must be e^x as well. Hence, when we evaluate all the derivatives at the expansion point ($x_0 = 0$), we have the gratifyingly neat result

$$\phi'(0) = \phi''(0) = \cdots = \phi^{(n)}(0) = e^0 = 1$$

Consequently, by setting $x_0 = 0$ in (9.14), the Maclaurin series of e^x is

$$e^x = \phi(x) = \phi(0) + \phi'(0)x + \frac{\phi''(0)}{2!}x^2 + \frac{\phi'''(0)}{3!}x^3 + \cdots + \frac{\phi^{(n)}(0)}{n!}x^n + R_n$$

$$= 1 + x + \frac{1}{2!}x^2 + \frac{1}{3!}x^3 + \cdots + \frac{1}{n!}x^n + R_n$$

The remainder term R_n, according to (9.15), can be written as

$$R_n = \frac{\phi^{(n+1)}(p)}{(n+1)!}x^{n+1} = \frac{e^p}{(n+1)!}x^{n+1} \qquad [\phi^{(n+1)}(x) = e^x; \ \therefore \phi^{(n+1)}(p) = e^p]$$

Inasmuch as the factorial expression $(n+1)!$ increases in value more rapidly than the power expression x^{n+1} (for a finite x) as n increases, it follows that $R_n \to 0$ as $n \to \infty$. Thus the Maclaurin series converges, and the value of e^x may, as a result, be expressed as a convergent infinite series as follows:

$$e^x = 1 + x + \frac{1}{2!}x^2 + \frac{1}{3!}x^3 + \frac{1}{4!}x^4 + \frac{1}{5!}x^5 + \cdots \tag{10.6}$$

As a special case, for $x = 1$, we find that

$$e = 1 + 1 + \frac{1}{2!} + \frac{1}{3!} + \frac{1}{4!} + \frac{1}{5!} + \cdots$$

$$= 2 + 0.5 + 0.1666667 + 0.0416667 + 0.0083333 + 0.0013889$$
$$\quad + 0.0001984 + 0.0000248 + 0.0000028 + 0.0000003 + \cdots$$

$$= 2.7182819$$

Thus, if we want a figure accurate to five decimal places, we can write $e = 2.71828$. Note that we need not worry about the subsequent terms in the infinite series, because they will be of negligible magnitude if we are concerned only with five decimal places.

An Economic Interpretation of e

Mathematically, the number e is the limit expression in (10.5). But does it also possess some economic meaning? The answer is that it can be interpreted as the result of a special mode of interest compounding.

Suppose that, starting out with a principal (or capital) of $1, we find a hypothetical banker to offer us the unusual interest rate of 100 percent per annum ($1 interest per year). If interest is to be compounded once a year, the value of our asset at the end of the year will be $2; we shall denote this value by $V(1)$, where the number in parentheses indicates the frequency of compounding within 1 year:

$$V(1) = \text{initial principal } (1 + \text{interest rate})$$
$$= 1(1 + 100\%) = \left(1 + \tfrac{1}{1}\right)^1 = 2$$

If interest is compounded semiannually, however, an interest amounting to 50 percent (half of 100 percent) of principal will accrue at the end of 6 months. We shall therefore have $1.50 as the new principal during the second 6-month period, in which interest will be calculated at 50 percent of $1.50. Thus our year-end asset value will be $1.50(1 + 50\%)$; that is,

$$V(2) = (1 + 50\%)(1 + 50\%) = \left(1 + \tfrac{1}{2}\right)^2$$

By analogous reasoning, we can write $V(3) = (1 + \tfrac{1}{3})^3$, $V(4) = (1 + \tfrac{1}{4})^4$, etc.; or, in general,

$$V(m) = \left(1 + \frac{1}{m}\right)^m \tag{10.7}$$

where m represents the frequency of compounding in 1 year.

In the limiting case, when interest is compounded *continuously* during the year, i.e., when m becomes infinite, the value of the asset will grow in a "snowballing" fashion, becoming at the end of 1 year

$$\lim_{m \to \infty} V(m) = \lim_{m \to \infty} \left(1 + \frac{1}{m}\right)^m = e \text{ (dollars)} \qquad [\text{by } (10.5)]$$

Thus, the number $e = 2.71828$ can be interpreted as the year-end value to which a principal of $1 will grow if interest at the rate of 100 percent per annum is compounded continuously.

Note that the interest rate of 100 percent is only a *nominal interest rate,* for if $1 becomes $e = $2.718 after 1 year, the *effective interest rate* is in this case approximately 172 percent per annum.

Interest Compounding and the Function Ae^{rt}

The continuous interest-compounding process just discussed can be generalized in three directions, to allow for: (1) more years of compounding, (2) a principal other than $1, and (3) a nominal interest rate other than 100 percent.

If a principal of \$1 becomes \$$e$ after 1 year of continuous compounding and if we let \$$e$ be the new principal in the second year (during which every dollar will again grow into \$$e$), our asset value at the end of 2 years will obviously become \$$e$ $(e) = $ \$$e^2$. By the same token, it will become \$$e^3$ at the end of 3 years or, more generally, will become \$$e^t$ after t years.

Next, let us change the principal from \$1 to an unspecified amount, \$$A$. This change is easily taken care of: if \$1 will grow into \$$e^t$ after t years of continuous compounding at the nominal rate of 100 percent per annum, it stands to reason that \$$A$ will grow into \$$Ae^t$.

How about a nominal interest rate of other than 100 percent, for instance, $r = 0.05$ ($= 5$ percent)? The effect of this rate change is to alter the expression Ae^t to Ae^{rt}, as can be verified from the following. With an initial principal of \$$A$, to be invested for t years at a nominal interest rate r, the compound-interest formula (10.7) must be modified to the form

$$V(m) = A\left(1 + \frac{r}{m}\right)^{mt} \tag{10.8}$$

The insertion of the coefficient A reflects the change of principal from the previous level of \$1. The quotient expression r/m means that, in each of the m compounding periods in a year, only $1/m$ of the nominal rate r will actually be applicable. Finally, the exponent mt tells us that, since interest is to be compounded m times a year, there should be a total of mt compoundings in t years.

The formula (10.8) can be transformed into an alternative form

$$V(m) = A\left[\left(1 + \frac{r}{m}\right)^{m/r}\right]^{rt}$$
$$= A\left[\left(1 + \frac{1}{w}\right)^{w}\right]^{rt} \quad \text{where } w \equiv \frac{m}{r} \tag{10.8'}$$

As the frequency of compounding m is increased, the newly created variable w must increase pari passu; thus, as $m \to \infty$, we have $w \to \infty$, and the bracketed expression in (10.8'), by virtue of (10.5), tends to the number e. Consequently, we find the asset value in the generalized continuous-compounding process to be

$$V \equiv \lim_{m \to \infty} V(m) = Ae^{rt} \tag{10.8''}$$

as anticipated.

Note that, in (10.8), t is a *discrete* (as against a *continuous*) variable: It can only take values that are integral multiples of $1/m$. For example, if $m = 4$ (compounding on a quarterly basis), then t can only take the values of $\frac{1}{4}, \frac{1}{2}, \frac{3}{4}, 1$, etc., indicating that $V(m)$ will assume a new value only at the end of each new quarter. When $m \to \infty$, as in (10.8''), however, $1/m$ becomes infinitesimal, and accordingly the variable t will become continuous. In that case, it becomes legitimate to speak of fractions of a year and to let t be, say, 1.2 or 2.35.

The upshot is that the expressions e, e^t, Ae^t, and Ae^{rt} can all be interpreted economically in connection with continuous interest compounding, as summarized in Table 10.1.

Instantaneous Rate of Growth

It should be pointed out, however, that interest compounding is an illustrative, but not exclusive, interpretation of the natural exponential function Ae^{rt}. Interest compounding

TABLE 10.1
Continuous
Interest
Compounding

Principal, $	Nominal Interest Rate	Years of Continuous Compounding	Asset Value, at the End of Compounding Process, $
1	100% (= 1)	1	e
1	100%	t	e^t
A	100%	t	Ae^t
A	r	t	Ae^{rt}

merely exemplifies the general process of *exponential growth* (here, the growth of a sum of money capital over time), and we can apply the function equally well to the growth of population, wealth, or real capital.

Applied to some context other than interest compounding, the coefficient r in Ae^{rt} no longer denotes the nominal interest rate. What economic meaning does it then take? The answer is that r can be reinterpreted as the *instantaneous rate of growth* of the function Ae^{rt}. (In fact, this is why we have adopted the symbol r, for rate of growth, in the first place.) Given the function $V = Ae^{rt}$, which gives the value of V at each point of time t, the rate of change of V is to be found in the derivative

$$\frac{dV}{dt} = r Ae^{rt} = rV \qquad \text{[see (10.3)]}$$

But the *rate of growth* of V is simply the *rate of change* in V expressed in relative (percentage) terms, i.e., expressed as a ratio to the value of V itself. Thus, for any given point of time, we have

$$\text{Rate of growth of } V \equiv \frac{dV/dt}{V} = \frac{rV}{V} = r \qquad \textbf{(10.9)}$$

as was stated previously.

Several observations should be made about this rate of growth. But, first, let us clarify a fundamental point regarding the concept of time, namely, the distinction between a *point* of time and a *period* of time. The variable V (denoting a sum of money, or the size of population, etc.) is a *stock* concept, which is concerned with the question: How much of it *exists* at a given moment? As such, V is related to the *point* concept of time; at each point of time, V takes a unique value. The change in V, on the other hand, represents a *flow*, which involves the question: How much of it *takes place* during a given time span? Hence a change in V and, by the same token, the rate of change of V must have reference to some specified period of time, say, per year.

With this understanding, let us return to (10.9) for some comments:

1. The rate of growth defined in (10.9) is an *instantaneous* rate of growth. Since the derivative $dV/dt = r Ae^{rt}$ takes a different value at a different point of t, as will $V = Ae^{rt}$, their ratio must also have reference to a specific point (or *instant*) of t. In this sense, the rate of growth is instantaneous.

2. In the present case, however, the instantaneous rate of growth happens to be a constant r, with the rate of growth thus remaining uniform at all points of time. This may not, of course, be true of all growth situations actually encountered.

3. Even though the rate of growth r is measured at a particular point of time, its magnitude nevertheless has the connotation of so many percent *per unit of time,* say, per year (if t is measured in year units). Growth, by its very nature, can occur only over a time interval. This is why a single still picture (recording the situation at one instant) could never portray, say, the growth of a child, whereas two still pictures taken at different times—say, a year apart—can accomplish this. To say that V has a rate of growth of r at the instant $t = t_0$, therefore, really means that, if the rate of change $dV/dt(= rV)$ prevailing at $t = t_0$ is allowed to continue undisturbed for one whole unit of time (1 year), then V will have grown by the amount rV at the end of the year.

4. For the exponential function $V = Ae^{rt}$, the *percentage rate* of growth is constant at all points of t, but the *absolute amount* of increment of V increases as time goes on, because the percentage rate will be calculated on larger and larger bases.

Upon interpreting r as the instantaneous rate of growth, it is clear that little effort will henceforth be required to find the rate of growth of a natural exponential function of the form $y = Ae^{rt}$, provided r is a constant. Given a function $y = 75e^{0.02t}$, for instance, we can immediately read off the rate of growth of y as 0.02 or 2 percent per period.

Continuous versus Discrete Growth

The preceding discussion, though analytically interesting, is still open to question insofar as economic relevance is concerned, because in actuality growth does not always take place on a *continuous* basis—not even in interest compounding. Fortunately, however, even for cases of *discrete* growth, where changes occur only once per period rather than from instant to instant, the continuous exponential growth function can be justifiably used.

For one thing, in cases where the frequency of compounding is relatively high, though not infinite, the continuous pattern of growth may be regarded as an approximation to the true growth pattern. But, more importantly, we can show that a problem of discrete or discontinuous growth can always be transformed into an equivalent continuous version.

Suppose that we have a geometric pattern of growth (say, the *discrete* compounding of interest) as shown by the following sequence:

$$A, \ A(1+i), \ A(1+i)^2, \ A(1+i)^3, \ldots$$

where the effective interest rate per period is denoted by i and where the exponent of the expression $(1 + i)$ denotes the number of periods covered in the compounding. If we consider $(1 + i)$ to be the base b in an exponential expression, then the given sequence may be summarized by the exponential function Ab^t—except that, because of the discrete nature of the problem, t is restricted to integer values only. Moreover, $b = 1 + i$ is a positive number (positive even if i is a *negative* interest rate, say, -0.04), so that it can always be expressed as a power of any real number greater than 1, including e. This means that there must exist a number r such that[†]

$$1 + i = b = e^r$$

[†] The method of finding the number t, given a specific value of b, will be discussed in Sec. 10.4.

Thus we can transform Ab^t into a natural exponential function:

$$A(1+i)^t = Ab^t = Ae^{rt}$$

For any given value of t—in this context, integer values of t—the function Ae^{rt} will, of course, yield exactly the same value as $A(1+i)^t$, such as $A(1+i) = Ae^r$ and $A(1+i)^2 = Ae^{2r}$. Consequently, even though a *discrete* case $A(1+i)^t$ is being considered, we may still work with the *continuous* natural exponential function Ae^{rt}. This explains why natural exponential functions are extensively applied in economic analysis despite the fact that not all growth patterns may actually be continuous.

Discounting and Negative Growth

Let us now turn briefly from interest compounding to the closely related concept of *discounting*. In a compound-interest problem, we seek to compute the *future value V* (principal plus interest) from a given *present value A* (initial principal). The problem of *discounting* is the opposite one of finding the present value A of a given sum V which is to be available t years from now.

Let us take the discrete case first. If the amount of principal A will grow into the future value of $A(1+i)^t$ after t years of annual compounding at the interest rate i per annum, i.e., if

$$V = A(1+i)^t$$

then, by dividing both sides of the equation by the nonzero expression $(1+i)^t$, we can get the discounting formula:

$$A = \frac{V}{(1+i)^t} = V(1+i)^{-t} \tag{10.10}$$

which involves a negative exponent. It should be realized that in this formula the roles of V and A have been reversed: V is now a given, whereas A is the unknown, to be computed from i (the rate of discount) and t (the number of years), as well as V.

Similarly, for the continuous case, if the principal A will grow into Ae^{rt} after t years of continuous compounding at the rate r in accordance with the formula

$$V = Ae^{rt}$$

then we can derive the corresponding continuous-discounting formula simply by dividing both sides of the last equation by e^{rt}:

$$A = \frac{V}{e^{rt}} = Ve^{-rt} \tag{10.11}$$

Here again, we have A (rather than V) as the unknown, to be computed from the given future value V, the nominal rate of discount r, and the number of years t. The expression e^{-rt} is often referred to as the *discount factor*.

Taking (10.11) as an exponential growth function, we can immediately read $-r$ as the instantaneous rate of growth of A. Being negative, this rate is in effect a *rate of decay*. Just as interest compounding exemplifies the process of growth, discounting illustrates *negative growth*.

EXERCISE 10.2

1. Use the infinite-series form of e^x in (10.6) to find the approximate value of:

   (a) e^2 (b) $\sqrt{e} \ (= e^{1/2})$

   (Round off your calculation of each term to three decimal places, and continue with the series till you get a term 0.000.)

2. Given the function $\phi(x) = e^{2x}$:

   (a) Write the polynomial part P_n of its Maclaurin series.

   (b) Write the Lagrange form of the remainder R_n. Determine whether $R_n \to 0$ as $n \to \infty$, that is, whether the series is convergent to $\phi(x)$.

   (c) If convergent, so that $\phi(x)$ may be expressed as an infinite series, write out this series.

3. Write an exponential expression for the value:

   (a) \$70, compounded continuously at the interest rate of 4% for 3 years

   (b) \$690, compounded continuously at the interest rate of 5% for 2 years

   (These interest rates are nominal rates per annum.)

4. What is the instantaneous rate of growth of y in each of the following?

   (a) $y = e^{0.07t}$ (c) $y = Ae^{0.4t}$

   (b) $y = 15e^{0.03t}$ (d) $y = 0.03e^{t}$

5. Show that the two functions $y_1 = Ae^{rt}$ (interest compounding) and $y_2 = Ae^{-rt}$ (discounting) are mirror images of each other with reference to the y axis [cf. Exercise 10.1-5, part (b)].

10.3   Logarithms

Exponential functions are closely related to *logarithmic functions* (*log functions,* for short). Before we can discuss log functions, we must first understand the meaning of the term *logarithm.*

The Meaning of Logarithm

When we have two numbers such as 4 and 16, which can be related to each other by the equation $4^2 = 16$, we define the *exponent* 2 to be the *logarithm* of 16 to the base of 4, and write

$$\log_4 16 = 2$$

It should be clear from this example that the logarithm is nothing but the *power* to which a base (4) must be raised to attain a particular number (16). In general, we may state that

$$y = b^t \quad \Leftrightarrow \quad t = \log_b y \qquad\qquad \textbf{(10.12)}$$

which indicates that the log of y to the base b (denoted by $\log_b y$) is the power to which the base b must be raised in order to attain the value y. For this reason, it is correct, though tautological, to write

$$b^{\log_b y} = y$$

Given y, the process of finding its logarithm $\log_b y$ is referred to as *taking the* log *of y to the base b.* The reverse process, that of finding y from a known value of its logarithm $\log_b y$, is referred to as *taking the antilog of* $\log_b y$.

In the discussion of exponential functions, we emphasized that the function $y = b^t$ (with $b > 1$) is strictly increasing. This means that, for any positive value of y, there is a *unique* exponent t (not necessarily positive) such that $y = b^t$; moreover, the larger the value of y, the larger must be t, as can be seen from Fig. 10.2. Translated into logarithms, the strict monotonicity of the exponential function implies that any positive number y must possess a *unique* logarithm t to a base $b > 1$ such that the larger the y, the larger its logarithm. As Figs. 10.1 and 10.2 show, y is necessarily positive in the exponential function $y = b^t$; consequently, a negative number or zero cannot possess a logarithm.

Common Log and Natural Log

The base of the logarithm, $b > 1$, does not have to be restricted to any particular number, but in actual log applications two numbers are widely chosen as bases—the number 10 and the number e. When 10 is the base, the logarithm is known as the *common logarithm,* symbolized by $\log_{10}$ (or if the context is clear, simply by log). With e as the base, on the other hand, the logarithm is referred to as the *natural logarithm* and is denoted either by $\log_e$ or by ln (for natural log). We may also use the symbol log (without subscript e) if it is not ambiguous in the particular context.

Common logarithms, used frequently in *computational* work, are exemplified by the following:

$$\log_{10} 1{,}000 = 3 \qquad [\text{because } 10^3 = 1{,}000]$$
$$\log_{10} 100 \;\; = 2 \qquad [\text{because } 10^2 = 100]$$
$$\log_{10} 10 \;\; = 1 \qquad [\text{because } 10^1 = 10]$$
$$\log_{10} 1 \;\; = 0 \qquad [\text{because } 10^0 = 1]$$
$$\log_{10} 0.1 \;\; = -1 \qquad [\text{because } 10^{-1} = 0.1]$$
$$\log_{10} 0.01 \;\; = -2 \qquad [\text{because } 10^{-2} = 0.01]$$

Observe the close relation between the set of numbers immediately to the left of the equals signs and the set of numbers immediately to the right. From these, it should be apparent that the common logarithm of a number between 10 and 100 must be between 1 and 2 and that the common logarithm of a number between 1 and 10 must be a positive fraction, etc. The exact logarithms can easily be obtained from a table of common logarithms or electronic calculators with log capabilities.[†]

In *analytical* work, however, natural logarithms prove vastly more convenient to use than common logarithms. Since, by the definition of logarithm, we have the relationship

$$y = e^t \quad \Leftrightarrow \quad t = \log_e y \quad (\text{or } t = \ln y) \qquad (10.13)$$

it is easy to see that the analytical convenience of e in exponential functions will automatically extend into the realm of logarithms with e as the base.

[†] More fundamentally, the value of a logarithm, like the value of e, can be calculated (or approximated) by resorting to a Maclaurin expansion of a log function, in a manner similar to that outlined in (10.6). However, we shall not venture into this derivation here.

The following examples will serve to illustrate natural logarithms:

$$\ln e^3 = \log_e e^3 = 3$$
$$\ln e^2 = \log_e e^2 = 2$$
$$\ln e^1 = \log_e e^1 = 1$$
$$\ln 1 = \log_e e^0 = 0$$
$$\ln \frac{1}{e} = \log_e e^{-1} = -1$$

The general principle emerging from these examples is that, given an expression e^k, where k is any real number, we can automatically read the exponent k as the natural log of e^k. In general, therefore, we have the result that $\ln e^k = k$.[†]

The common log and natural log are convertible into each other; i.e., the base of a logarithm can be changed, just as the base of an exponential expression can. A pair of conversion formulas will be developed after we have studied the basic rules of logarithms.

Rules of Logarithms

Logarithms are in the nature of exponents; therefore, they obey certain rules closely related to the rules of exponents introduced in Sec. 2.5. These can be of great help in simplifying mathematical operations. The first three rules are stated only in terms of the natural log, but they are also valid when the symbol ln is replaced by $\log_b$.

Rule I   (log of a product) $\qquad\qquad \ln(uv) = \ln u + \ln v \qquad (u, v > 0)$

Example 1
$$\ln(e^6 e^4) = \ln e^6 + \ln e^4 = 6 + 4 = 10$$

Example 2
$$\ln(Ae^7) = \ln A + \ln e^7 = \ln A + 7$$

PROOF   By definition, $\ln u$ is the power to which e must be raised to attain the value of u; thus $e^{\ln u} = u$.[‡] Similarly, we have $e^{\ln v} = v$ and $e^{\ln(uv)} = uv$. The latter is an exponential expression for uv. However, another expression of uv is obtainable by direct multiplication of u and v:

$$uv = e^{\ln u} e^{\ln v} = e^{\ln u + \ln v}$$

Thus, by equating the two expressions for uv above, we find

$$e^{\ln(uv)} = e^{\ln u + \ln v} \qquad \text{and hence} \qquad \ln(uv) = \ln u + \ln v$$

Rule II   (log of a quotient) $\qquad\qquad \ln(u/v) = \ln u - \ln v \qquad (u, v > 0)$

[†] As a mnemonic device, observe that when the symbol ln (or $\log_e$) is placed at the left of the expression e^k, the symbol ln seems to cancel out the symbol e, leaving k as the answer.

[‡] Note that when e is raised to the power ln u, the symbol e and the symbol ln again seem to cancel out, leaving u as the answer.

Example 3

$$\ln(e^2/c) = \ln e^2 - \ln c = 2 - \ln c$$

Example 4

$$\ln(e^2/e^5) = \ln e^2 - \ln e^5 = 2 - 5 = -3$$

The proof of this rule is very similar to that of Rule I and is therefore left to you as an exercise.

Rule III   (log of a power) $\ln u^a = a \ln u$ $(u > 0)$

Example 5

$$\ln e^{15} = 15 \ln e = 15$$

Example 6

$$\ln A^3 = 3 \ln A$$

PROOF   By definition, $e^{\ln u} = u$; and similarly, $e^{\ln u^a} = u^a$. However, another expression for u^a can be formed as follows:

$$u^a = (e^{\ln u})^a = e^{a \ln u}$$

By equating the exponents in the two expressions for u^a, we obtain the desired result, $\ln u^a = a \ln u$.

These three rules are useful devices for simplifying the mathematical operations in certain types of problems. Rule I serves to convert, via logarithms, a multiplicative operation (uv) into an additive one $(\ln u + \ln v)$; Rule II turns a division (u/v) into a subtraction $(\ln u - \ln v)$; and Rule III enables us to reduce a power to a multiplicative constant. Moreover, these rules can be used in combination. Also, they can be read backward, and applied in reverse.

Example 7

$$\ln(uv^a) = \ln u + \ln v^a = \ln u + a \ln v$$

Example 8

$$\ln u + a \ln v = \ln u + \ln v^a = \ln(uv^a)   \text{[Example 7 in reverse]}$$

You are warned, however, that when we have *additive* expressions to begin with, logarithms may be of no help at all. In particular, it should be remembered that

$$\ln(u \pm v) \neq \ln u \pm \ln v$$

Let us now introduce two additional rules concerned with changes in the base of a logarithm.

Rule IV   (conversion of log base) $\log_b u = (\log_b e)(\log_e u)$ $(u > 0)$

This rule, which resembles the chain rule in spirit (witness the "chain" $b \nearrow^e \searrow_e \nearrow^u$), enables us to derive a logarithm $\log_e u$ (to base e) from the logarithm $\log_b u$ (to base b), or vice versa.

PROOF   Let $u = e^p$, so that $p = \log_e u$. Then it follows that

$$\log_b u = \log_b e^p = p \log_b e = (\log_e u)(\log_b e)$$

Rule IV can readily be generalized to

$$\log_b u = (\log_b c)(\log_c u)$$

where c is some base other than b.

Rule V   **(inversion of log base)** $\qquad\qquad\qquad$ $\log_b e = \dfrac{1}{\log_e b}$

This rule, which resembles the inverse-function rule of differentiation, enables us to obtain the log of b to the base e immediately upon being given the log of e to the base b, and vice versa. (This rule can also be generalized to the form $\log_b c = 1/\log_c b$.)

PROOF   As an application of Rule IV, let $u = b$; then we have

$$\log_b b = (\log_b e)(\log_e b)$$

But the left-side expression is $\log_b b = 1$; therefore $\log_b e$ and $\log_e b$ must be reciprocal to each other, as Rule V asserts.

From the last two rules, it is easy to derive the following pair of conversion formulas between common log and natural log:

$$\log_{10} N = (\log_{10} e)(\log_e N) = 0.4343 \log_e N$$
$$\log_e N = (\log_e 10)(\log_{10} N) = 2.3026 \log_{10} N$$

(10.14)

for N a positive real number. The first equals sign in each formula is easily justified by Rule IV. In the first formula, the value 0.4343 (the common log of 2.71828) can be found from a table of common logarithms or an electronic calculator; in the second, the value 2.3026 (the natural log of 10) is merely the reciprocal of 0.4343, so calculated because of Rule V.

Example 9 $\log_e 100 = 2.3026(\log_{10} 100) = 2.3026(2) = 4.6052$. Conversely, we have $\log_{10} 100 = 0.4343(\log_e 100) = 0.4343(4.6052) = 2$.

An Application

The preceding rules of logarithms enable us to solve with ease certain simple *exponential equations* (exponential *functions* set equal to zero). For instance, if we seek to find the value of x that satisfies the equation

$$ab^x - c = 0 \qquad (a, b, c > 0)$$

we can first try to transform this exponential equation, by the use of logarithms, into a *linear* equation and then solve it as such. For this purpose, the c term should first be transposed to the right side:

$$ab^x = c$$

This is because there is no simple log expression for the additive expression $(ab^x - c)$, but there do exist convenient log expressions for the multiplicative term ab^x and for c individually. Thus, after the transposition of c and upon taking the log (say, to base 10) of both sides, we have

$$\log a + x \log b = \log c$$

which is a linear equation in the variable x, with the solution

$$x = \frac{\log c - \log a}{\log b}$$

EXERCISE 10.3

1. What are the values of the following logarithms?
   - (a) $\log_{10} 10,000$
   - (b) $\log_{10} 0.0001$
   - (c) $\log_3 81$
   - (d) $\log_5 3,125$

2. Evaluate the following:
   - (a) $\ln e^7$
   - (b) $\log_e e^{-4}$
   - (c) $\ln(1/e^3)$
   - (d) $\log_e(1/e^2)$
   - (e) $(e^{\ln 3})!$
   - (f) $\ln e^x - e^{\ln x}$

3. Evaluate the following by application of the rules of logarithms:
   - (a) $\log_{10}(100)^{13}$
   - (b) $\log_{10} \frac{1}{100}$
   - (c) $\ln(3/B)$
   - (d) $\ln Ae^2$
   - (e) $\ln ABe^{-4}$
   - (f) $(\log_4 e)(\log_e 64)$

4. Which of the following are valid?
   - (a) $\ln u - 2 = \ln \dfrac{u}{e^2}$
   - (b) $3 + \ln v = \ln \dfrac{e^3}{v}$
   - (c) $\ln u + \ln v - \ln w = \ln \dfrac{uv}{w}$
   - (d) $\ln 3 + \ln 5 = \ln 8$

5. Prove that $\ln(u/v) = \ln u - \ln v$.

10.4 Logarithmic Functions

When a variable is expressed as a function of the logarithm of another variable, the function is referred to as a *logarithmic function*. We have already seen two versions of this type of function in (10.12) and (10.13), namely,

$$t = \log_b y \qquad \text{and} \qquad t = \log_e y \; (= \ln y)$$

which differ from each other only in regard to the base of the logarithm.

Log Functions and Exponential Functions

As we stated earlier, log functions are inverse functions of certain exponential functions. An examination of the previous two log functions will confirm that they are indeed the respective inverse functions of the exponential functions

$$y = b^t \qquad \text{and} \qquad y = e^t$$

because the log functions cited are the results of reversing the roles of the dependent and independent variables of the corresponding exponential functions. You should realize, of course, that the symbol t is being used here as a general symbol, and it does not necessarily stand for *time*. Even when it does, its appearance as a *dependent* variable does not mean that time is determined by some variable y; it means only that a given value of y is associated with a unique point of time.

As inverse functions of strictly increasing (exponential) functions, logarithmic functions must also be strictly increasing, which is consistent with our earlier statement that the larger a number, the larger is its logarithm to any given base. This property may be expressed symbolically in terms of the following two propositions: For two positive values of y (y_1, and y_2),

$$\ln y_1 = \ln y_2 \qquad \Leftrightarrow \qquad y_1 = y_2$$
$$\ln y_1 > \ln y_2 \qquad \Leftrightarrow \qquad y_1 > y_2 \qquad\qquad \textbf{(10.15)}$$

These propositions are also valid, of course, if we replace ln by $\log_b$.

The Graphical Form

The monotonicity and other general properties of logarithmic functions can be clearly observed from their graphs. Given the graph of the exponential function $y = e^t$, we can obtain the graph of the corresponding log function by replotting the original graph with the two axes transposed. The result of such replotting is illustrated in Fig. 10.3. Note that if the graph of Fig. 10.3b were laid over the graph of Fig. 10.3a, with y axis on y axis and t axis on t axis, the two curves should coincide exactly. As they actually appear in Fig. 10.3—with interchanged axes—on the other hand, the two curves are seen to be mirror images of each other (as the graphs of any pair of inverse functions must be) with reference to the 45° line drawn through the origin.

This mirror-image relationship has several noteworthy implications. For one, although both are strictly increasing, the log curve shows y increasing at a *decreasing rate* (second derivative negative), in contradistinction to the exponential curve, which shows y increasing at an increasing rate. Another interesting contrast is that, while the exponential function has a positive *range,* the log function has a positive *domain* instead. (This latter restriction

FIGURE 10.3

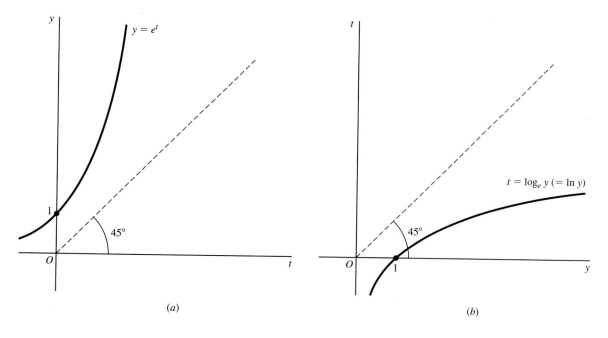

(a)

(b)

on the domain of the log function is, of course, merely another way of stating that only positive numbers possess logarithms.) A third consequence of the mirror-image relationship is that, just as $y = e^t$ has a vertical intercept at 1, the log function $t = \log_e y$ must cross the horizontal axis at $y = 1$, indicating that $\log_e 1 = 0$. Inasmuch as this horizontal intercept is unaffected by the base of the logarithm—for instance, $\log_{10} 1 = 0$, too—we may infer from the general shape of the log curve in Fig. 10.3b that, for *any* base,

$$\left.\begin{array}{r} 0 < y < 1 \\ y = 1 \\ y > 1 \end{array}\right\} \quad \Leftrightarrow \quad \left\{\begin{array}{l} \log y < 0 \\ \log y = 0 \\ \log y > 0 \end{array}\right. \tag{10.16}$$

For verification, we can check the two sets of examples of common and natural logarithms given in Sec. 10.3. Furthermore, we may note that

$$\log y \to \left\{\begin{array}{r} \infty \\ -\infty \end{array}\right\} \quad \text{as } y \to \left\{\begin{array}{l} \infty \\ 0^+ \end{array}\right. \tag{10.16'}$$

The graphical comparison of the logarithmic function and the exponential function in Fig. 10.3 is based on the simple functions $y = e^t$ and $t = \ln y$. The same general result will prevail if we compare the generalized exponential function $y = Ae^{rt}$ with its corresponding log function. With the (positive) constants A and r to *compress* or *extend* the exponential curve, it will nevertheless resemble the general shape of Fig. 10.3a, except that its vertical intercept will be at $y = A$ rather than at $y = 1$ (when $t = 0$, we have $y = Ae^0 = A$). Its inverse function, accordingly, must have a *horizontal* intercept at $y = A$. In general, with reference to the 45° line, the corresponding log curve will be a mirror image of the exponential curve.

If the specific algebraic expression of the inverse of $y = Ae^{rt}$ is desired, it can be obtained by taking the natural log of both sides of this exponential function [which, according to the first proposition in (10.15), will leave the equation undisturbed] and then solving for t:

$$\ln y = \ln(Ae^{rt}) = \ln A + rt \ln e = \ln A + rt$$

Hence,

$$t = \frac{\ln y - \ln A}{r} \qquad (r \neq 0) \tag{10.17}$$

This result, a log function, constitutes the inverse of the exponential function $y = Ae^{rt}$. As claimed earlier, the function in (10.17) has a horizontal intercept at $y = A$, because when $y = A$, we have $\ln y = \ln A$, and therefore $t = 0$.

Base Conversion

In Sec. 10.2, it was stated that the exponential function $y = Ab^t$ can always be converted into a *natural* exponential function $y = Ae^{rt}$. We are now ready to derive a conversion formula. Instead of Ab^t, however, let us consider the conversion of the more general expression Ab^{ct} into Ae^{rt}. Since the essence of the problem is to find an r from given values of b and c such that

$$e^r = b^c$$

all that is necessary is to express r as a function of b and c. Such a task is easily accomplished by taking the natural log of both sides of the last equation:

$$\ln e^r = \ln b^c$$

The left side can immediately be read as equal to r, so that the desired function (conversion formula) emerges as

$$r = \ln b^c = c \ln b \qquad\qquad \textbf{(10.18)}$$

This indicates that the function $y = Ab^{ct}$ can always be rewritten in the natural-base form, $y = Ae^{(c \ln b)t}$.

<table>
<tr><td>

Example 1
</td><td>

Convert $y = 2^t$ to a natural exponential function. Here, we have $A = 1$, $b = 2$, and $c = 1$. Hence $r = c \ln b = \ln 2$, and the desired exponential function is

$$y = Ae^{rt} = e^{(\ln 2)t}$$

If we like, we can also calculate the numerical value of $\ln 2$ by use of (10.14) and a table of common logarithms as follows:

$$\ln 2 = 2.3026 \log_{10} 2 = 2.3026(0.3010) = 0.6931 \qquad \textbf{(10.19)}$$

Then we may express the earlier result alternatively as $y = e^{0.6931t}$.
</td></tr>
</table>

<table>
<tr><td>

Example 2
</td><td>

Convert $y = 3(5)^{2t}$ to a natural exponential function. In this example, $A = 3$, $b = 5$, and $c = 2$, and formula (10.18) gives us $r = 2 \ln 5$. Therefore the desired function is

$$y = Ae^{rt} = 3e^{(2 \ln 5)t}$$

Again, if we like, we can calculate that

$$2 \ln 5 = \ln 25 = 2.3026 \log_{10} 25 = 2.3026(1.3979) = 3.2188$$

so the earlier result can be alternatively expressed as $y = 3e^{3.2188t}$.
</td></tr>
</table>

It is also possible, of course, to convert log functions of the form $t = \log_b y$ into equivalent natural log functions. To that end, it is sufficient to apply Rule IV of logarithms, which may be expressed as

$$\log_b y = (\log_b e)(\log_e y)$$

The direct substitution of this result into the given log function immediately gives us the desired natural log function:

$$
\begin{aligned}
t = \log_b y &= (\log_b e)(\log_e y) \\
&= \frac{1}{\log_e b} \log_e y \qquad \text{[by Rule V of logarithms]} \\
&= \frac{\ln y}{\ln b}
\end{aligned}
$$

By the same procedure, we can transform the more general log function $t = a \log_b(cy)$ into the equivalent form

$$t = a(\log_b e)(\log_e cy) = \frac{a}{\log_e b} \log_e(cy) = \frac{a}{\ln b} \ln(cy)$$

Example 3

Convert the function $t = \log_2 y$ into the natural log form. Since in this example we have $b = 2$ and $a = c = 1$, the desired function is

$$t = \frac{1}{\ln 2} \ln y$$

By (10.19), however, we may also express it as $t = (1/0.6931) \ln y$.

Example 4

Convert the function $t = 7 \log_{10}(2y)$ into a natural logarithmic function. The values of the constants are in this case $a = 7$, $b = 10$, and $c = 2$; consequently, the desired function is

$$t = \frac{7}{\ln 10} \ln(2y)$$

But since $\ln 10 = 2.3026$, as (10.14) indicates, this function can be rewritten as $t = (7/2.3026) \ln(2y) = 3.0400 \ln(2y)$.

In the preceding discussion, we have followed the practice of expressing t as a function of y when the function is logarithmic. The only reason for doing so is our desire to stress the inverse-function relationship between the exponential and logarithmic functions. When a log function is studied *by itself*, we shall write $y = \ln t$ (rather than $t = \ln y$), as is customary. Naturally, nothing in the analytical aspect of the discussion will be affected by such an interchange of symbols.

EXERCISE 10.4

1. The form of the inverse function of $y = Ae^{rt}$ in (10.17) requires r to be nonzero. What is the meaning of this requirement when viewed in reference to the original exponential function $y = Ae^{rt}$?
2. (*a*) Sketch a graph of the exponential function $y = Ae^{rt}$; indicate the value of the vertical intercept.
   (*b*) Then sketch the graph of the log function $t = \dfrac{\ln y - \ln A}{r}$, and indicate the value of the horizontal intercept.
3. Find the inverse function of $y = ab^{ct}$.
4. Transform the following functions to their natural exponential forms:
   (*a*) $y = 8^{3t}$ (*c*) $y = 5(5)^t$
   (*b*) $y = 2(7)^{2t}$ (*d*) $y = 2(15)^{4t}$
5. Transform the following functions to their natural logarithmic forms:
   (*a*) $t = \log_7 y$ (*c*) $t = 3 \log_{15}(9y)$
   (*b*) $t = \log_8(3y)$ (*d*) $t = 2 \log_{10} y$
6. Find the continuous-compounding nominal interest rate per annum (r) that is equivalent to a discrete-compounding interest rate (i) of
   (*a*) 5 percent per annum, compounded annually.
   (*b*) 5 percent per annum, compounded semiannually.
   (*c*) 6 percent per annum, compounded semiannually.
   (*d*) 6 percent per annum, compounded quarterly.

7. (*a*) In describing Fig. 10.3, the text states that, if the two curves are laid over each other, they show a mirror-image relationship. Where is the "mirror" located?

(*b*) If we plot a function $f(x)$ and its negative, $-f(x)$, in the same diagram, will the two curves display a mirror-image relationship, too? If so, where is the "mirror" located in this case?

(*c*) If we plot the graphs of Ae^{rt} and Ae^{-rt} in the same diagram, will the two curves be mirror images of each other? If so, where is the "mirror" located?

10.5   Derivatives of Exponential and Logarithmic Functions

Earlier it was claimed that the function e^t is its own derivative. As it turns out, the natural log function, $\ln t$, possesses a rather convenient derivative also, namely, $d(\ln t)/dt = 1/t$. This fact reinforces our preference for the base e. Let us now prove the validity of these two derivative formulas, and then we shall deduce the derivative formulas for certain variants of the exponential and log expressions e^t and $\ln t$.

Log-Function Rule

The derivative of the log function $y = \ln t$ is

$$\frac{d}{dt} \ln t = \frac{1}{t}$$

To prove this, we recall that, by definition, the derivative of $y = \psi(t) = \ln t$ has the following value at $t = N$ (assuming $t \to N^+$):

$$\psi'(N) = \lim_{t \to N^+} \frac{\psi(t) - \psi(N)}{t - N} = \lim_{t \to N^+} \frac{\ln t - \ln N}{t - N}$$

$$= \lim_{t \to N^+} \frac{\ln(t/N)}{t - N} \qquad \text{[by Rule II of logarithms]}$$

Now let us introduce a shorthand symbol $m \equiv \dfrac{N}{t - N}$. Then we can write $\dfrac{1}{t - N} = \dfrac{m}{N}$, and also $\dfrac{t}{N} = 1 + \dfrac{t - N}{N} = 1 + \dfrac{1}{m}$. Thus the expression to the right of the limit sign in the previous equation can be converted to the form

$$\frac{1}{t - N} \ln \frac{t}{N} = \frac{m}{N} \ln \left(1 + \frac{1}{m}\right) = \frac{1}{N} \ln \left(1 + \frac{1}{m}\right)^m \qquad \text{[by Rule III of logarithms]}$$

Note that, as $t \to N^+$, m tends to infinity. Thus, to find the desired derivative value, we may take the limit of the last expression in the preceding equation as $m \to \infty$:

$$\psi'(N) = \lim_{m \to \infty} \frac{1}{N} \ln \left(1 + \frac{1}{m}\right)^m = \frac{1}{N} \ln e = \frac{1}{N} \qquad \text{[by (10.5)]}$$

Since N can be any number for which a logarithm is defined, however, we can generalize this result, and write $\psi'(t) = d(\ln t)/dt = 1/t$. This proves the log-function rule for $t \to N^+$.

The case of $t \to N^-$ needs some modifications, but the essence of the proof is similar. Now the derivative of $y = \ln t$ has the value

$$\psi'(N) = \lim_{t \to N^-} \frac{\psi(t) - \psi(N)}{t - N} = \lim_{t \to N^-} \frac{\psi(N) - \psi(t)}{N - t}$$

$$= \lim_{t \to N^-} \frac{\ln N - \ln t}{N - t} = \lim_{t \to N^-} \frac{\ln(N/t)}{N - t}$$

Let $\mu = t/(N - t)$; then $1/(N - t) = \mu/t$, and $N/t = 1 + (N - t)/t = 1 + 1/\mu$. These equations enable us to rewrite the expression to the right of the last limit sign in the preceding equation for $\psi'(N)$ as

$$\frac{1}{N - t} \ln \frac{N}{t} = \frac{\mu}{t} \ln \left(1 + \frac{1}{\mu}\right) = \frac{1}{t} \ln \left(1 + \frac{1}{\mu}\right)^\mu$$

As $t \to N^-$, $\mu \to \infty$. Thus the desired derivative value is

$$\psi'(N) = \lim_{t \to N^-} \frac{1}{N} \ln e = \frac{1}{N}$$

the same result as for the case of $t \to N^+$. This completes the proof of the log-function rule. Notice, once more, that in the proof process, no specific numerical values are employed, and the result is therefore generally applicable.

Exponential-Function Rule

The derivative of the function $y = e^t$ is

$$\frac{d}{dt} e^t = e^t$$

This result follows easily from the log-function rule. We know that the inverse function of the function $y = e^t$ is $t = \ln y$, with derivative $dt/dy = 1/y$. Thus, by the inverse-function rule, we may write immediately

$$\frac{d}{dt} e^t = \frac{dy}{dt} = \frac{1}{dt/dy} = \frac{1}{1/y} = y = e^t$$

The Rules Generalized

The log-function and exponential-function rules can be generalized to cases where the variable t in the expression e^t and $\ln t$ is replaced by some *function* of t, say, $f(t)$. The generalized versions of the two rules are

$$\frac{d}{dt} e^{f(t)} = f'(t) e^{f(t)} \qquad \left[\text{or } \frac{d}{dt} e^u = e^u \frac{du}{dt}\right]$$

$$\frac{d}{dt} \ln f(t) = \frac{f'(t)}{f(t)} \qquad \left[\text{or } \frac{d}{dt} \ln v = \frac{1}{v} \frac{dv}{dt}\right]$$

(10.20)

The proofs for (10.20) involve nothing more than the straightforward application of the chain rule. Given a function $y = e^{f(t)}$, we can first let $u = f(t)$, so that $y = e^u$. Then, by the chain rule, the derivative emerges as

$$\frac{d}{dt} e^{f(t)} = \frac{d}{dt} e^u = \frac{de^u}{du} \frac{du}{dt} = e^u \frac{du}{dt} = e^{f(t)} f'(t)$$

Similarly, given a function $y = \ln f(t)$, we can first let $v = f(t)$, so as to form a chain: $y = \ln v$, where $v = f(t)$. Then, by the chain rule, we have

$$\frac{d}{dt} \ln f(t) = \frac{d}{dt} \ln v = \frac{d \ln v}{dv} \frac{dv}{dt} = \frac{1}{v} \frac{dv}{dt} = \frac{1}{f(t)} f'(t)$$

Note that the only real modification introduced in (10.20) beyond the simpler rules $de^t/dt = e^t$ and $d(\ln t)/dt = 1/t$ is the multiplicative factor $f'(t)$.

Example 1   Find the derivative of the function $y = e^{rt}$. Here, the exponent is $rt = f(t)$, with $f'(t) = r$; thus

$$\frac{dy}{dt} = \frac{d}{dt} e^{rt} = r e^{rt}$$

Example 2   Find dy/dt from the function $y = e^{-t}$. In this case, $f(t) = -t$, so that $f'(t) = -1$. As a result,

$$\frac{dy}{dt} = \frac{d}{dt} e^{-t} = -e^{-t}$$

Example 3   Find dy/dt from the function $y = \ln(at)$. Since in this case $f(t) = at$, with $f'(t) = a$, the derivative is

$$\frac{d}{dt} \ln(at) = \frac{a}{at} = \frac{1}{t}$$

which is, interestingly enough, identical with the derivative of $y = \ln t$.

This example illustrates the fact that a multiplicative constant for t *within* a log expression drops out in the process of derivation. But note that, for a constant k, we have

$$\frac{d}{dt} k \ln t = k \frac{d}{dt} \ln t = \frac{k}{t}$$

thus a multiplicative constant *outside* the log expression is still retained in derivation.

Example 4   Find the derivative of the function $y = \ln t^c$. With $f(t) = t^c$ and $f'(t) = ct^{c-1}$, the formula in (10.20) yields

$$\frac{d}{dt} \ln t^c = \frac{ct^{c-1}}{t^c} = \frac{c}{t}$$

Example 5   Find dy/dt from $y = t^3 \ln t^2$. Because this function is a product of two terms t^3 and $\ln t^2$, the product rule should be used:

$$\frac{dy}{dt} = t^3 \frac{d}{dt} \ln t^2 + (\ln t^2) \frac{d}{dt} t^3$$

$$= t^3 \left(\frac{2t}{t^2} \right) + (\ln t^2)(3t^2)$$

$$= 2t^2 + 3t^2(2 \ln t) \qquad \text{[Rule III of logarithms]}$$

$$= 2t^2(1 + 3 \ln t)$$

The Case of Base b

For exponential and log functions with base b, the derivatives are

$$\frac{d}{dt}b^t = b^t \ln b \qquad \left[\text{Warning: } \frac{d}{dt}b^t \neq tb^{t-1}\right]$$

$$\frac{d}{dt}\log_b t = \frac{1}{t \ln b}$$

(10.21)

Note that in the special case of base e (when $b = e$), we have $\ln b = \ln e = 1$, so that these two derivatives reduce to the basic exponential-function rule $(d/dt)e^t = e^t$ and the basic log-function rule $(d/dt)\ln t = 1/t$, respectively.

The proofs for (10.21) are not difficult. For the case of b^t, the proof is based on the identity $b \equiv e^{\ln b}$, which enables us to write

$$b^t = e^{(\ln b)t} = e^{t \ln b}$$

(We write $t \ln b$, instead of $\ln bt$, in order to emphasize that t is not a part of the log expression.) Hence

$$\frac{d}{dt}b^t = \frac{d}{dt}e^{t \ln b} = (\ln b)(e^{t \ln b}) \qquad \text{[by (10.20)]}$$

$$= (\ln b)(b^t) = b^t \ln b$$

To prove the second part of (10.21), on the other hand, we rely on the basic log property that

$$\log_b t = (\log_b e)(\log_e t) = \frac{1}{\ln b}\ln t$$

which leads us to the derivative

$$\frac{d}{dt}\log_b t = \frac{d}{dt}\left(\frac{1}{\ln b}\ln t\right) = \frac{1}{\ln b}\frac{d}{dt}\ln t = \frac{1}{\ln b}\left(\frac{1}{t}\right)$$

The more general versions of these two formulas are

$$\frac{d}{dt}b^{f(t)} = f'(t)b^{f(t)}\ln b$$

(10.21′)

$$\frac{d}{dt}\log_b f(t) = \frac{f'(t)}{f(t)}\frac{1}{\ln b}$$

Again, it is seen that if $b = e$, then $\ln b = 1$, and these formulas reduce to (10.20).

Example 6   Find the derivative of the function $y = 12^{1-t}$. Here, $b = 12$, $f(t) = 1 - t$, and $f'(t) = -1$; thus

$$\frac{dy}{dt} = -(12)^{1-t}\ln 12$$

Higher Derivatives

Higher derivatives of exponential and log functions, like those of other types of functions, are merely the results of repeated differentiation.

Example 7

Find the *second* derivative of $y = b^t$ (with $b > 1$). The first derivative, by (10.21), is $y'(t) = b^t \ln b$ (where $\ln b$ is, of course, a constant); thus, by differentiating once more with respect to t, we have

$$y''(t) = \frac{d}{dt}y'(t) = \left(\frac{d}{dt}b^t\right)\ln b = (b^t \ln b)\ln b = b^t(\ln b)^2$$

Note that $y = b^t$ is always positive and $\ln b$ (for $b > 1$) is also positive [by (10.16)]; thus $y'(t) = b^t \ln b$ must be positive. And $y''(t)$, being a product of b^t and a squared number, is also positive. These facts confirm our previous assertion that the exponential function $y = b^t$ increases monotonically at an increasing rate.

Example 8

Find the *second* derivative of $y = \ln t$. The first derivative is $y' = 1/t = t^{-1}$; hence, the second derivative is

$$y'' = -t^{-2} = \frac{-1}{t^2}$$

Inasmuch as the domain of this function consists of the open interval $(0, \infty)$, $y' = 1/t$ must be a positive number. On the other hand, y'' is always negative. Together, these conclusions serve to confirm our earlier assertion that the log function $y = \ln t$ increases monotonically at a decreasing rate.

An Application

One of the prime virtues of the logarithm is its ability to convert a multiplication into an addition, and a division into a subtraction. This property can be exploited when we are differentiating a complicated *product* or *quotient* of any type of functions (not necessarily exponential or logarithmic).

Example 9

Find dy/dx from

$$y = \frac{x^2}{(x+3)(2x+1)}$$

Instead of applying the product and quotient rules, we may first take the natural log of both sides of the equation to reduce the function to the form

$$\ln y = \ln x^2 - \ln(x+3) - \ln(2x+1)$$

According to (10.20), the derivative of the left side with respect to x is

$$\frac{d}{dx}(\text{left side}) = \frac{1}{y}\frac{dy}{dx}$$

whereas the right side gives

$$\frac{d}{dx}(\text{right side}) = \frac{2x}{x^2} - \frac{1}{x+3} - \frac{2}{2x+1} = \frac{7x+6}{x(x+3)(2x+1)}$$

When the two results are equated and both sides are multiplied by y, we get the desired derivative as follows:

$$\frac{dy}{dx} = \frac{7x+6}{x(x+3)(2x+1)}y$$

$$= \frac{7x+6}{x(x+3)(2x+1)}\frac{x^2}{(x+3)(2x+1)} = \frac{x(7x+6)}{(x+3)^2(2x+1)^2}$$

Example 10   Find dy/dx from $y = x^a e^{kx-c}$. Taking the natural log of both sides, we have

$$\ln y = a \ln x + \ln e^{kx-c} = a \ln x + kx - c$$

Differentiating both sides with respect to x, and using (10.20), we then get

$$\frac{1}{y}\frac{dy}{dx} = \frac{a}{x} + k$$

and

$$\frac{dy}{dx} = \left(\frac{a}{x} + k\right) y = \left(\frac{a}{x} + k\right) x^a e^{kx-c}$$

Note, however, that if the given function contains additive terms, then it may *not* be desirable to convert the function into the log form.

EXERCISE 10.5

1. Find the derivatives of:
   (a) $y = e^{2t+4}$
   (b) $y = e^{1-9t}$
   (c) $y = e^{t^2+1}$
   (d) $y = 5e^{2-t^2}$
   (e) $y = e^{ax^2+bx+c}$
   (f) $y = xe^x$
   (g) $y = x^2 e^{2x}$
   (h) $y = axe^{bx+c}$

2. (a) Verify the derivative in Example 3 by utilizing the equation $\ln(at) = \ln a + \ln t$.
   (b) Verify the result in Example 4 by utilizing the equation $\ln t^c = c \ln t$.

3. Find the derivatives of:
   (a) $y = \ln(7t^5)$
   (b) $y = \ln(at^c)$
   (c) $y = \ln(t+19)$
   (d) $y = 5\ln(t+1)^2$
   (e) $y = \ln x - \ln(1+x)$
   (f) $y = \ln[x(1-x)^8]$
   (g) $y = \ln\left(\frac{2x}{1+x}\right)$
   (h) $y = 5x^4 \ln x^2$

4. Find the derivatives of:
   (a) $y = 5^t$
   (b) $y = \log_2(t+1)$
   (c) $y = 13^{2t+3}$
   (d) $y = \log_7 7x^2$
   (e) $y = \log_2(8x^2 + 3)$
   (f) $y = x^2 \log_3 x$

5. Prove the two formulas in (10.21').

6. Show that the function $V = Ae^{rt}$ (with $A, r > 0$) and the function $A = Ve^{-rt}$ (with $V, r > 0$) are both strictly monotonic, but in opposite directions, and that they are both strictly convex in shape (cf. Exercise 10.2-5).

7. Find the derivatives of the following by first taking the natural log of both sides:
   (a) $y = \dfrac{3x}{(x+2)(x+4)}$
   (b) $y = (x^2 + 3)e^{x^2+1}$

10.6 Optimal Timing

What we have learned about exponential and log functions can now be applied to some simple problems of optimal timing.

A Problem of Wine Storage

Suppose that a certain wine dealer is in possession of a particular quantity (say, a case) of wine, which he can either sell at the present time ($t = 0$) for a sum of $\$K$ or else store for some length of time and then sell at a higher value. The growing value (V) of the wine is known to be the following function of time:

$$V = Ke^{\sqrt{t}} \quad [= K\exp(t^{1/2})] \qquad (10.22)$$

so that if $t = 0$ (sell now), then $V = K$. The problem is to ascertain when he should sell it in order to maximize profit, assuming the storage cost to be nil.[†]

Since the cost of wine is a "sunk" cost—the wine is already paid for by the dealer—and since storage cost is assumed to be nonexistent, to maximize profit is the same as maximizing the sales revenue, or the value of V. There is one catch, however. Each value of V corresponding to a specific point of t represents a dollar sum receivable at a different date and, because of the interest element involved, is not directly comparable with the V value of another date. The way out of this difficulty is to *discount* each V figure to its *present-value* equivalent (the value at time $t = 0$), for then all the V values will be on a comparable footing.

Let us assume that the interest rate on the continuous-compounding basis is at the level of r. Then, according to (10.11), the present value of V can be expressed as

$$A(t) = Ve^{-rt} = Ke^{\sqrt{t}}e^{-rt} = Ke^{\sqrt{t}-rt} \qquad (10.22')$$

where A, denoting the present value of V, is itself a function of t. Therefore our problem amounts to finding the value of t that maximizes A.

Maximization Conditions

The first-order condition for maximizing A is to have $dA/dt = 0$. To find this derivative, we can either differentiate (10.22') directly with respect to t, or do it indirectly by first taking the natural log of both sides of (10.22') and then differentiating with respect to t. Let us illustrate the latter procedure.

First, we obtain from (10.22') the equation

$$\ln A(t) = \ln K + \ln e^{\sqrt{t}-rt} = \ln K + (t^{1/2} - rt)$$

Upon differentiating both sides with respect to t, we then get

$$\frac{1}{A}\frac{dA}{dt} = \frac{1}{2}t^{-1/2} - r$$

or

$$\frac{dA}{dt} = A\left(\frac{1}{2}t^{-1/2} - r\right)$$

Since $A \neq 0$, the condition $dA/dt = 0$ can be satisfied if and only if

$$\frac{1}{2}t^{-1/2} = r \quad \text{or} \quad \frac{1}{2\sqrt{t}} = r \quad \text{or} \quad \frac{1}{2r} = \sqrt{t}$$

This implies that the optimum length of storage time is

$$t^* = \left(\frac{1}{2r}\right)^2 = \frac{1}{4r^2}$$

[†] The consideration of storage cost will entail a difficulty we are not yet equipped to handle. Later, in Chap. 14, we shall return to this problem.

If $r = 0.10$, for instance, then $t^* = 25$, and the dealer should store the case of wine for 25 years. Note that the higher the rate of interest (rate of discount) is, the shorter the optimum storage period will be.

The first-order condition, $1/(2\sqrt{t}) = r$, admits of an easy economic interpretation. The left-hand expression merely represents the rate of growth of wine value V, because from (10.22)

$$\frac{dV}{dt} = \frac{d}{dt} K \exp(t^{1/2}) = K \frac{d}{dt} \exp(t^{1/2}) \qquad [K \text{ constant}]$$

$$= K \left(\frac{1}{2} t^{-1/2}\right) \exp(t^{1/2}) \qquad [\text{by } (10.20)]$$

$$= \left(\frac{1}{2} t^{-1/2}\right) V \qquad [\text{by } (10.22)]$$

so that the rate of growth of V is indeed the left-hand expression in the first-order condition:

$$r_V \equiv \frac{dV/dt}{V} = \frac{1}{2} t^{-1/2} = \frac{1}{2\sqrt{t}}$$

The right-hand expression r is, in contrast, the rate of interest or the rate of compound-interest growth of the cash fund receivable *if* the wine is sold right away—an *opportunity-cost* aspect of storing the wine. Thus, the equating of the two instantaneous rates, as illustrated in Fig. 10.4, is an attempt to hold onto the wine until the advantage of storage is completely wiped out, i.e., to wait till the moment when the (declining) rate of growth of wine value is just matched by the (constant) interest rate on cash sales receipts.

The next order of business is to check whether the value of t^* satisfies the second-order condition for maximization of A. The second derivative of A is

$$\frac{d^2 A}{dt^2} = \frac{d}{dt} A \left(\frac{1}{2} t^{-1/2} - r\right) = A \frac{d}{dt} \left(\frac{1}{2} t^{-1/2} - r\right) + \left(\frac{1}{2} t^{-1/2} - r\right) \frac{dA}{dt}$$

FIGURE 10.4

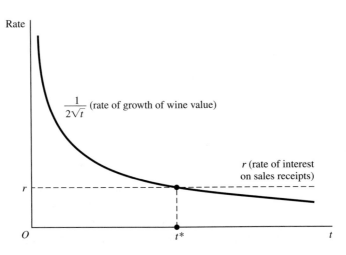

But, since the final term drops out when we evaluate it at the equilibrium (optimum) point, where $dA/dt = 0$, we are left with

$$\frac{d^2 A}{dt^2} = A \frac{d}{dt} \left(\frac{1}{2} t^{-1/2} - r \right) = A \left(-\frac{1}{4} t^{-3/2} \right) = \frac{-A}{4\sqrt{t^3}}$$

In view that $A > 0$, this second derivative is negative when evaluated at $t^* > 0$, thereby ensuring that the solution value t^* is indeed profit-maximizing.

A Problem of Timber Cutting

A similar problem, which involves a choice of the best time to take action, is that of timber cutting.

Suppose the value of timber (already planted on some given land) is the following increasing function of time:

$$V = 2^{\sqrt{t}}$$

expressed in units of $1,000. Assuming a discount rate of r (on the continuous basis) and also assuming zero upkeep cost during the period of timber growth, what is the optimal time to cut the timber for sale?

As in the wine problem, we should first convert V into its present value:

$$A(t) = V e^{-rt} = 2^{\sqrt{t}} e^{-rt}$$

thus
$$\ln A = \ln 2^{\sqrt{t}} + \ln e^{-rt} = \sqrt{t} \ln 2 - rt = t^{1/2} \ln 2 - rt$$

To maximize A, we must set $dA/dt = 0$. The first derivative is obtainable by differentiating $\ln A$ with respect to t and then multiplying by A:

$$\frac{1}{A} \frac{dA}{dt} = \frac{1}{2} t^{-1/2} \ln 2 - r$$

thus
$$\frac{dA}{dt} = A \left(\frac{\ln 2}{2\sqrt{t}} - r \right)$$

Since $A \neq 0$, the condition $dA/dt = 0$ can be met if and only if

$$\frac{\ln 2}{2\sqrt{t}} = r \qquad \text{or} \qquad \sqrt{t} = \frac{\ln 2}{2r}$$

Consequently, the optimum number of years of growth is

$$t^* = \left(\frac{\ln 2}{2r} \right)^2$$

It is evident from this solution that, the higher the rate of discount, the earlier the timber should be cut.

To make sure that t^* is a maximizing (instead of minimizing) solution, the second-order condition should be checked. But this will be left to you as an exercise.

In this example, we have abstracted from planting cost by assuming that the trees are already planted, in which case the (sunk) planting cost is legitimately excludable from consideration in the optimization decision. If the decision is not one of when to harvest but one of whether or not to plant at all, then the planting cost (incurred at the *present*) must be duly compared with the *present* value of the timber output, computed with t set at the optimum value t^*. For instance, if $r = 0.05$, then we have

$$t^* = \left(\frac{0.6931}{0.10}\right)^2 = (6.931)^2 = 48.0 \text{ years}$$

and

$$A^* = 2^{6.931}e^{-0.05(48.0)} = (122.0222)e^{-2.40}$$

$$= 122.0222(0.0907) = \$11.0674 \text{ (in thousands)}$$

So only a planting cost lower than A^* will make the venture worthwhile—again, provided that upkeep cost is nil.

EXERCISE 10.6

1. If the value of wine grows according to the function $V = Ke^{2\sqrt{t}}$, instead of as in (10.22), how long should the dealer store the wine?
2. Check the second-order condition for the timber-cutting problem.
3. As a generalization of the optimization problem illustrated in the present section, show that:
    (a) With any value function $V = f(t)$ and a given continuous rate of discount r, the first-order condition for the present value A of V to reach a maximum is that the rate of growth of V be equal to r.
    (b) The second-order sufficient condition for a maximum really amounts to the stipulation that the rate of growth of V be strictly decreasing with time.
4. Analyze the comparative statics of the wine-storage problem.

10.7 Further Applications of Exponential and Logarithmic Derivatives

Aside from their use in optimization problems, the derivative formulas of Sec. 10.5 have further useful economic applications.

Finding the Rate of Growth

When a variable y is a function of time, $y = f(t)$, its instantaneous rate of growth is defined as[†]

$$r_y \equiv \frac{dy/dt}{y} = \frac{f'(t)}{f(t)} = \frac{\text{marginal function}}{\text{total function}} \qquad \textbf{(10.23)}$$

But, from (10.20), we see that this ratio is precisely the derivative of $\ln f(t) = \ln y$. Thus, to find the instantaneous rate of growth of a function of time $f(t)$, we can—instead of differentiating it with respect to t, and then dividing by $f(t)$—simply take its natural log

---

[†] If the variable t does *not* denote time, the expression $(dy/dt)/y$ is referred to as the *proportional rate of change* of y with respect to t.

and then differentiate ln $f(t)$ with respect to time.[†] This alternative method may turn out to be the simpler approach, if $f(t)$ is a multiplicative or divisional expression which, upon logarithm-taking, will reduce to a sum or difference of additive terms.

Example 1

Find the rate of growth of $V = Ae^{rt}$, where t denotes time. It is already known to us that the rate of growth of V is r, but let us check it by finding the derivative of ln V:

$$\ln V = \ln A + rt \ln e = \ln A + rt \qquad \text{[A constant]}$$

Therefore,

$$r_V = \frac{d}{dt} \ln V = 0 + \frac{d}{dt} rt = r$$

as was to be demonstrated.

Example 2

Find the rate of growth of $y = 4^t$. In this case, we have

$$\ln y = \ln 4^t = t \ln 4$$

Hence

$$r_y = \frac{d}{dt} \ln y = \ln 4$$

This is as it should be, because $e^{\ln 4} \equiv 4$, and consequently, $y = 4^t$ can be rewritten as $y = e^{(\ln 4)t}$, which would immediately enable us to read (ln 4) as the rate of growth of y.

Rate of Growth of a Combination of Functions

To carry this discussion a step further, let us examine the instantaneous rate of growth of a *product* of two functions of time:

$$y = uv \quad \text{where} \begin{cases} u = f(t) \\ v = g(t) \end{cases}$$

Taking the natural log of y, we obtain

$$\ln y = \ln u + \ln v$$

Thus the desired rate of growth is

$$r_y = \frac{d}{dt} \ln y = \frac{d}{dt} \ln u + \frac{d}{dt} \ln v$$

But the two terms on the right side are the rates of growth of u and v, respectively. Thus we have the rule

$$r_{(uv)} = r_u + r_v \qquad\qquad \textbf{(10.24)}$$

Expressed in words, the instantaneous rate of growth of a *product* is the *sum* of the instantaneous rates of growth of the components.

By a similar procedure, the rate of growth of a *quotient* can be shown to be the *difference* between the rates of growth of the components (see Exercise 10.7-4):

$$r_{(u/v)} = r_u - r_v \qquad\qquad \textbf{(10.25)}$$

[†] If we plot the natural log of a function $f(t)$ against t in a two-dimensional diagram, the slope of the curve, accordingly, will tell us the rate of growth of $f(t)$. This provides the rationale for the so-called semilog scale charts, which are used for comparing the rates of growth of different variables, or the rates of growth of the same variable in different countries.

Example 3   If consumption C is growing at the rate α, and if population H (for "heads") is growing at the rate β, what is the rate of growth of per capita consumption? Since per capita consumption is equal to C/H, its rate of growth should be

$$r_{(C/H)} = r_C - r_H = \alpha - \beta$$

Now consider the instantaneous rate of growth of a *sum* of two functions of time:

$$z = u + v \qquad \text{where} \begin{cases} u = f(t) \\ v = g(t) \end{cases}$$

This time, the natural log will be

$$\ln z = \ln(u + v) \qquad [\neq \ln u + \ln v]$$

Thus

$$r_z = \frac{d}{dt} \ln z = \frac{d}{dt} \ln(u + v)$$

$$= \frac{1}{u + v} \frac{d}{dt}(u + v) \qquad \text{[by (10.20)]}$$

$$= \frac{1}{u + v}[f'(t) + g'(t)]$$

But from (10.23) we have $r_u = f'(t)/f(t)$, so that $f'(t) = f(t)r_u = ur_u$. Similarly, we have $g'(t) = vr_v$. As a result, we can write the rule

$$r_{(u+v)} = \frac{u}{u + v}r_u + \frac{v}{u + v}r_v \qquad \textbf{(10.26)}$$

which shows that the rate of growth of a *sum* is a *weighted average* of the rates of growth of the components.

By the same token, we have (see Exercise 10.7-5)

$$r_{(u-v)} = \frac{u}{u - v}r_u - \frac{v}{u - v}r_v \qquad \textbf{(10.27)}$$

Example 4   The exports of goods of a country, $G = G(t)$, has a growth rate of a/t, and its exports of services, $S = S(t)$, has a growth rate of b/t. What is the growth rate of its total exports? Since total exports is $X(t) = G(t) + S(t)$, a sum, its rate of growth should be

$$r_X = \frac{G}{X}r_G + \frac{S}{X}r_S$$

$$= \frac{G}{X}\left(\frac{a}{t}\right) + \frac{S}{X}\left(\frac{b}{t}\right) = \frac{Ga + Sb}{Xt}$$

Finding the Point Elasticity

We have seen that, given $y = f(t)$, the derivative of $\ln y$ measures the instantaneous rate of growth of y. Now let us see what happens when, given a function $y = f(x)$, we differentiate $\ln y$ with respect to $\ln x$, rather than to x.

To begin with, let us define $u \equiv \ln y$ and $v \equiv \ln x$. Then we can observe a chain of relationship linking u to y, and thence to x and v as follows:

$$u \equiv \ln y \qquad y = f(x) \qquad x \equiv e^{\ln x} \equiv e^{v}$$

Accordingly, the derivative of $\ln y$ with respect to $\ln x$ is

$$\frac{d(\ln y)}{d(\ln x)} = \frac{du}{dv} = \frac{du}{dy}\frac{dy}{dx}\frac{dx}{dv}$$

$$= \left(\frac{d}{dy}\ln y\right)\left(\frac{dy}{dx}\right)\left(\frac{d}{dv}e^{v}\right) = \frac{1}{y}\frac{dy}{dx}e^{v} = \frac{1}{y}\frac{dy}{dx}x = \frac{dy}{dx}\frac{x}{y}$$

But this expression is precisely that of the point elasticity of the function. Hence we have established the general principle that, for a function $y = f(x)$, the point elasticity of y with respect to x is

$$\varepsilon_{yx} = \frac{d(\ln y)}{d(\ln x)} \tag{10.28}$$

It should be noted that the subscript yx in this symbol is an indicator that y and x are the two variables involved and does not imply the multiplication of y and x. This is unlike the case of $r_{(uv)}$, where the subscript *does* denote a product. Again, we now have an alternative way of finding the point elasticity of a function by use of logarithms, which may often prove to be an easier approach, *if* the given function comes in the form of a multiplicative or divisional expression.

Example 5

Find the point elasticity of demand, given that $Q = k/P$, where k is a positive constant. This is the equation of a rectangular hyperbola (see Fig. 2.8d); and, as is well known, a demand function of this form has a unitary point elasticity at all points. To show this, we shall apply (10.28). Since the natural log of the demand function is

$$\ln Q = \ln k - \ln P$$

the elasticity of demand (Q with respect to P) is indeed

$$\varepsilon_d = \frac{d(\ln Q)}{d(\ln P)} = -1 \qquad \text{or} \qquad |\varepsilon_d| = 1$$

The result in (10.28) was derived by use of the chain rule of derivatives. It is of interest that a similar chain rule holds for elasticities; i.e., given a function $y = g(w)$, where $w = h(x)$, we have

$$\varepsilon_{yx} = \varepsilon_{yw}\varepsilon_{wx} \tag{10.29}$$

The proof is as follows:

$$\varepsilon_{yw}\varepsilon_{wx} = \left(\frac{dy}{dw}\frac{w}{y}\right)\left(\frac{dw}{dx}\frac{x}{w}\right) = \frac{dy}{dw}\frac{dw}{dx}\frac{w}{y}\frac{x}{w} = \frac{dy}{dx}\frac{x}{y} = \varepsilon_{yx}$$

EXERCISE 10.7

1. Find the instantaneous rate of growth:

   (a) $y = 5t^2$ (c) $y = ab^t$ (e) $y = t/3^t$

   (b) $y = at^c$ (d) $y = 2^t(t^2)$

2. If population grows according to the function $H = H_0(2)^{bt}$ and consumption by the function $C = C_0 e^{at}$, find the rates of growth of population, of consumption, and of per capita consumption by using the natural log.

3. If y is related to x by $y = x^k$, how will the rates of growth r_y and r_x, be related?

4. Prove that if $y = u/v$, where $u = f(t)$ and $v = g(t)$, then the rate of growth of y will be $r_y = r_u - r_v$, as shown in (10.25).

5. The real income y is defined as the nominal income Y deflated by the price level P. How is r_y (for real income) related to r_Y (for nominal income)?

6. Prove the rate-of-growth rule (10.27).

7. Given the demand function $Q_d = k/P^n$, where k and n are positive constants, find the point elasticity of demand ε_d by using (10.28) (cf. Exercise 8.1-4).

8. (a) Given $y = wz$, where $w = g(x)$ and $z = h(x)$, establish that $\varepsilon_{yx} = \varepsilon_{wx} + \varepsilon_{zx}$.

   (b) Given $y = u/v$, where $u = G(x)$ and $v = H(x)$, establish that $\varepsilon_{yx} = \varepsilon_{ux} - \varepsilon_{vx}$.

9. Given $y = f(x)$, show that the derivative $d(\log_b y)/d(\log_b x)$—log to base b rather than e—also measures the point elasticity ε_{yx}.

10. Show that, if the demand for money M_d is a function of the national income $Y = Y(t)$ and the interest rate $i = i(t)$, the rate of growth of M_d can be expressed as a weighted sum of r_Y and r_i,

$$r_{M_d} = \varepsilon_{M_d Y} r_Y + \varepsilon_{M_d i} r_i$$

where the weights are the elasticities of M_d with respect to Y and i, respectively.

11. Given the production function $Q = F(K, L)$, find a general expression for the rate of growth of Q in terms of the rates of growth of K and L.

Chapter 11

The Case of More than One Choice Variable

The problem of optimization was discussed in Chap. 9 within the framework of an objective function with a single choice variable. In Chap. 10 the discussion was extended to exponential objective functions, but we still dealt with one choice variable only. Now we must develop a way of finding the extreme values of an objective function that involves two or more choice variables. Only then will we be able to tackle the type of problem confronting, say, a multi-product firm, where the profit-maximizing decision consists of the choice of optimal output levels for several commodities and the optimal combination of several different inputs.

We shall discuss first the case of an objective function of two choice variables, $z = f(x, y)$, in order to take advantage of its graphability. Later the analytical results can be generalized to the nongraphable n-variable case. Regardless of the number of variables, however, we shall assume in general that, when written in a general form, our objective function possesses continuous partial derivatives to any desired order. This will ensure the smoothness and differentiability of the objective function as well as its partial derivatives.

For functions of several variables, extreme values are again of two kinds: (1) absolute or global and (2) relative or local. As before, our attention will be focused heavily on relative extrema, and for this reason we shall often drop the adjective "relative," with the understanding that, unless otherwise specified, the extrema referred to are *relative*. However, in Sec. 11.5, conditions for *absolute* extrema will be given due consideration.

11.1 The Differential Version of Optimization Conditions

The discussion in Chap. 9 of optimization conditions for problems with a single choice variable was couched entirely in terms of *derivatives,* as against differentials. To prepare for the discussion of problems with two or more choice variables, it would be helpful also to know how those conditions can equivalently be expressed in terms of *differentials.*

First-Order Condition

Given a function $z = f(x)$, we can, as explained in Sec. 8.1, write the differential

$$dz = f'(x) \, dx \tag{11.1}$$

FIGURE 11.1

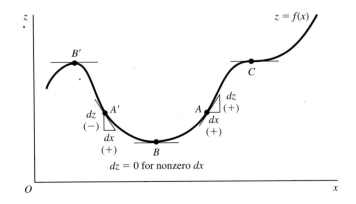

and use dz as an approximation to the actual change, Δz, induced by the change of x from x_0 to $x_0 + \Delta x$; the smaller the Δx, the better the approximation. From (11.1), it is clear that if $f'(x) > 0$, dz and dx must take the same algebraic sign; this is illustrated by point A in Fig. 11.1 (cf. Fig. 8.1b). In the opposite case where $f'(x) < 0$, exemplified by point A', dz and dx take opposite algebraic signs. Since points like A and A'—where $f'(x) \neq 0$ and hence $dz \neq 0$—cannot qualify as stationary points, it stands to reason that a necessary condition for z to attain an extremum (a stationary value) is $dz = 0$. More accurately, the condition should be stated as "$dz = 0$ for an arbitrary nonzero dx," since a zero dx (no change in x) has no relevance in our present context. In Fig. 11.1, a minimum of z occurs at point B, and a maximum of z occurs at point B'. In both cases, with the tangent line horizontal, i.e., with $f'(x) = 0$ there, dz (the vertical side of the triangle formed with the tangent line as the hypotenuse) indeed reduces to zero. Thus the first-order *derivative* condition "$f'(x) = 0$" can be translated into the first-order *differential* condition "$dz = 0$ for an arbitrary nonzero dx." Bear in mind, however, that while this differential condition is necessary for an extremum, it is by no means sufficient, because an inflection point such as C in Fig. 11.1 can also satisfy the condition that $dz = 0$ for an arbitrary nonzero dx.

Second-Order Condition

The second-order sufficient conditions for extrema of z are, in terms of derivatives, $f''(x) < 0$ (for a maximum) and $f''(x) > 0$ (for a minimum) at the stationary point. To translate these conditions into differential equivalents, we need the notion of *second-order differential,* defined as the differential of a differential, i.e., $d(dz)$, commonly denoted by d^2z (read: "d-two z").

Given that $dz = f'(x)\,dx$, we can obtain d^2z merely by further differentiation of dz. In so doing, however, we should bear in mind that dx, representing in this context an arbitrary or given nonzero change in x, is to be treated as a constant during differentiation. Consequently, dz can vary only with $f'(x)$, but since $f'(x)$ is in turn a function of x, dz can in the final analysis vary only with x. In view of this, we have

$$d^2z \equiv d(dz) = d[f'(x)\,dx] \qquad [\text{by } (11.1)]$$
$$= [df'(x)]\,dx \qquad [dx \text{ is constant}]$$
$$= [f''(x)\,dx]\,dx = f''(x)\,dx^2 \qquad \textbf{(11.2)}$$

Note that the exponent 2 appears in (11.2) in two fundamentally different ways. In the symbol d^2z, the exponent 2 (read: "two") indicates the *second-order* differential of z; but in the symbol $dx^2 \equiv (dx)^2$, the exponent 2 (read: "squared") denotes the *squaring* of the first-order differential dx. The result in (11.2) provides a direct link between d^2z and $f''(x)$. Inasmuch as we are considering nonzero values of dx only, the dx^2 term is always positive; thus d^2z and $f''(x)$ must take the same algebraic sign. Just as a positive (negative) $f''(x)$ at a stationary point delineates a valley (peak), so must a positive (negative) d^2z at such a point.

It follows that the *derivative* condition "$f''(x) < 0$ is sufficient for a maximum of z" can equivalently be stated as the *differential* condition "$d^2z < 0$ for an arbitrary nonzero dx is sufficient for a maximum of z." The translation of condition for a minimum of z is analogous; we just need to reverse the sense of inequality in the preceding sentence. Going one step further, we may also conclude on the basis of (11.2) that the second-order *necessary* conditions are

For maximum of z: $\quad f''(x) \leq 0$

For minimum of z: $\quad f''(x) \geq 0$

can be translated, respectively, into

$$\left. \begin{array}{ll} \text{For maximum of } z: & d^2z \leq 0 \\ \text{For minimum of } z: & d^2z \geq 0 \end{array} \right\} \text{ for arbitrary nonzero values of } dx$$

Differential Conditions versus Derivative Conditions

Now that we have demonstrated the possibility of expressing the derivative version of first- and second-order conditions in terms of dz and d^2z, you may very well ask why we bothered to develop a new set of differential conditions when derivative conditions were already available. The answer is that differential conditions—but not derivative conditions—are stated in forms that can be directly generalized from the one-variable case to cases with two or more choice variables. To be more specific, the first-order condition (zero value for dz) and the second-order condition (negativity or positivity for d^2z) are applicable with equal validity to all cases, provided the phrase "for arbitrary nonzero values of dx" is duly modified to reflect the change in the number of choice variables.

This does not mean, however, that derivative conditions will have no further role to play. To the contrary, since derivative conditions are operationally more convenient to apply, we shall—after the generalization process is carried out by means of the differential conditions to cases with more choice variables—still attempt to develop and make use of derivative conditions appropriate to those cases.

11.2 Extreme Values of a Function of Two Variables

For a function of one choice variable, an extreme value is represented graphically by the peak of a hill or the bottom of a valley in a two-dimensional graph. With *two* choice variables, the graph of the function—$z = f(x, y)$—becomes a surface in a 3-space, and while the extreme values are still to be associated with peaks and bottoms, these "hills" and "valleys" themselves now take on a three-dimensional character. They will, in this new

FIGURE 11.2

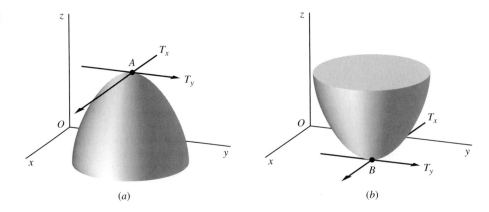

(a)   (b)

context, be shaped like domes and bowls, respectively. The two diagrams in Fig. 11.2 serve to illustrate. Point A in diagram a, the peak of a dome, constitutes a maximum; the value of z at this point is larger than at any other point in its immediate neighborhood. Similarly, point B in diagram b, the bottom of a bowl, represents a minimum; everywhere in its immediate neighborhood the value of the function exceeds that at point B.

First-Order Condition

For the function

$$z = f(x, y)$$

the first-order necessary condition for an extremum (either maximum or minimum) again involves $dz = 0$. But since there are two independent variables here, dz is now a *total* differential; thus the first-order condition should be modified to the form

$$dz = 0 \text{ for arbitrary values of } dx \text{ and } dy, \text{ not both zero} \qquad \textbf{(11.3)}$$

The rationale behind (11.3) is similar to the explanation of the condition $dz = 0$ for the one-variable case: an extremum point must be a stationary point, and at a stationary point, dz as an approximation to the actual change Δz must be zero for arbitrary dx and dy, not both zero.

In the present two-variable case, the total differential is

$$dz = f_x\, dx + f_y\, dy \qquad \textbf{(11.4)}$$

In order to satisfy condition (11.3), it is necessary-and-sufficient that the two partial derivatives f_x and f_y be simultaneously equal to zero. Thus the equivalent derivative version of the first-order condition (11.3) is

$$f_x = f_y = 0 \qquad \left[\text{or} \quad \frac{\partial z}{\partial x} = \frac{\partial z}{\partial y} = 0 \right] \qquad \textbf{(11.5)}$$

There is a simple graphical interpretation of this condition. With reference to point A in Fig. 11.2a, to have $f_x = 0$ at that point means that the tangent line T_x, drawn through A and

FIGURE 11.3

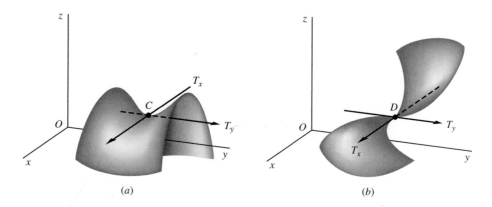

(a)   (b)

parallel to the xz plane (holding y constant), must have a zero slope. By the same token, to have $f_y = 0$ at point A means that the tangent line T_y, drawn through A and parallel to the yz plane (holding x constant), must also have a zero slope. You can readily verify that these tangent-line requirements actually also apply to the minimum point B in Fig. 11.2b. This is because condition (11.5), like condition (11.3), is a necessary condition for *both* a maximum and a minimum.

As in the earlier discussion, the first-order condition is *necessary*, but *not sufficient*. That it is not sufficient to establish an extremum can be seen from the two diagrams in Fig. 11.3. At point C in diagram a, both T_x and T_y have zero slopes, but this point does not qualify as an extremum: Whereas it is a *minimum* when viewed against the background of the yz plane, it turns out to be a *maximum* when looked at against the xz plane! A point with such a "dual personality" is referred to, for graphical reasons, as a *saddle point.* Similarly, point D in Fig. 11.3b, while characterized by flat T_x and T_y, is no extremum, either; its location on the twisted surface makes it an *inflection point,* whether viewed against the xz or the yz plane. These counterexamples decidedly rule out the first-order condition as a sufficient condition for an extremum.

To develop a sufficient condition, we must look to the second-order total differential, which is related to second-order partial derivatives.

Second-Order Partial Derivatives

The function $z = f(x, y)$ can give rise to *two* first-order partial derivatives,

$$f_x \equiv \frac{\partial z}{\partial x} \qquad \text{and} \qquad f_y \equiv \frac{\partial z}{\partial y}$$

Since f_x is itself a function of x (as well as of y), we can measure the rate of change of f_x with respect to x, while y remains fixed, by a particular second-order (or second) partial derivative denoted by either f_{xx} or $\partial^2 z/\partial x^2$:

$$f_{xx} \equiv \frac{\partial}{\partial x}(f_x) \qquad \text{or} \qquad \frac{\partial^2 z}{\partial x^2} \equiv \frac{\partial}{\partial x}\left(\frac{\partial z}{\partial x}\right)$$

The notation f_{xx} has a double subscript signifying that the primitive function f has been differentiated partially with respect to x twice, whereas the notation $\partial^2 z/\partial x^2$ resembles that of d^2z/dx^2 except for the use of the partial symbol. In a perfectly analogous manner, we can use the second partial derivative

$$f_{yy} \equiv \frac{\partial}{\partial y}(f_y) \qquad \text{or} \qquad \frac{\partial^2 z}{\partial y^2} = \frac{\partial}{\partial y}\left(\frac{\partial z}{\partial y}\right)$$

to denote the rate of change of f_y with respect to y, while x is held constant.

Recall, however, that f_x is also a function of y and that f_y is also a function of x. Hence, there can be written two more second partial derivatives:

$$f_{xy} \equiv \frac{\partial^2 z}{\partial x\, \partial y} \equiv \frac{\partial}{\partial x}\left(\frac{\partial z}{\partial y}\right) \qquad \text{and} \qquad f_{yx} \equiv \frac{\partial^2 z}{\partial y\, \partial x} \equiv \frac{\partial}{\partial y}\left(\frac{\partial z}{\partial x}\right)$$

These are called *cross* (or *mixed*) *partial derivatives* because each measures the rate of change of one first-order partial derivative with respect to the "other" variable.

It bears repeating that the second-order partial derivatives of $z = f(x, y)$, like z and the first derivatives f_x and f_y, are also functions of the variables x and y. When that fact requires emphasis, we can write f_{xx} as $f_{xx}(x, y)$, and f_{xy} as $f_{xy}(x, y)$, etc. And, along the same line, we can use the notation $f_{yx}(1, 2)$ to denote the value of f_{yx} evaluated at $x = 1$ and $y = 2$, etc.

Even though f_{xy} and f_{yx} have been separately defined, they will—according to a proposition known as *Young's theorem*—have identical values, as long as the two cross partial derivatives are both continuous. In that case, the sequential order in which partial differentiation is undertaken becomes immaterial, because $f_{xy} = f_{yx}$. For the ordinary types of *specific* functions with which we work, this continuity condition is usually met; for *general* functions, as mentioned earlier, we always assume the continuity condition to hold. Hence, we may in general expect to find identical cross partial derivatives. In fact, the theorem applies also to functions of three or more variables. Given $z = g(u, v, w)$, for instance, the mixed partial derivatives will be characterized by $g_{uv} = g_{vu}, g_{vw} = g_{wv}$, etc., provided these partial derivatives are all continuous.

Example 1

Find the four second-order partial derivatives of

$$z = x^3 + 5xy - y^2$$

The first partial derivatives of this function are

$$f_x = 3x^2 + 5y \qquad \text{and} \qquad f_y = 5x - 2y$$

Therefore, upon further differentiation, we get

$$f_{xx} = 6x \qquad f_{yx} = 5 \qquad f_{xy} = 5 \qquad f_{yy} = -2$$

As expected, f_{yx} and f_{xy} are identical.

Example 2

Find all the second partial derivatives of $z = x^2 e^{-y}$. In this case, the first partial derivatives are

$$f_x = 2xe^{-y} \qquad \text{and} \qquad f_y = -x^2 e^{-y}$$

Thus we have

$$f_{xx} = 2e^{-y} \qquad f_{yx} = -2xe^{-y} \qquad f_{xy} = -2xe^{-y} \qquad f_{yy} = x^2 e^{-y}$$

Again, we see that $f_{yx} = f_{xy}$.

Note that the second partial derivatives are all functions of the original variables x and y. This fact is clear enough in Example 2, but it is true even for Example 1, although some second partial derivatives happen to be *constant* functions in that case.

Second-Order Total Differential

Given the total differential dz in (11.4), and with the concept of second-order partial derivatives at our command, we can derive an expression for the second-order total differential d^2z by further differentiation of dz. In so doing, we should remember that in the equation $dz = f_x\,dx + f_y\,dy$, the symbols dx and dy represent arbitrary or given changes in x and y; so they must be treated as constants during differentiation. As a result, dz depends only on f_x and f_y, and since f_x and f_y are themselves functions of x and y, dz, like z itself, is a function of x and y.

To obtain d^2z, we merely apply the definition of a differential—as shown in (11.4)—to dz itself. Thus,

$$d^2z \equiv d(dz) = \frac{\partial(dz)}{\partial x}\,dx + \frac{\partial(dz)}{\partial y}\,dy \qquad [\text{cf. (11.4)}]$$

$$= \frac{\partial}{\partial x}(f_x\,dx + f_y\,dy)\,dx + \frac{\partial}{\partial y}(f_x\,dx + f_y\,dy)\,dy$$

$$= (f_{xx}\,dx + f_{xy}\,dy)\,dx + (f_{yx}\,dx + f_{yy}\,dy)\,dy$$

$$= f_{xx}\,dx^2 + f_{xy}\,dy\,dx + f_{yx}\,dx\,dy + f_{yy}\,dy^2$$

$$= f_{xx}\,dx^2 + 2f_{xy}\,dx\,dy + f_{yy}\,dy^2 \qquad [f_{xy} = f_{yx}] \qquad \textbf{(11.6)}$$

Note, again, that the exponent 2 appears in (11.6) in two different ways. In the symbol d^2z, the exponent 2 indicates the *second-order* total differential of z; but in the symbol $dx^2 \equiv (dx)^2$, the exponent denotes the *squaring* of the first-order differential dx.

The result in (11.6) shows the magnitude of d^2z in terms of given values of dx and dy, measured from some point (x_0, y_0) in the domain. In order to calculate d^2z, however, we also need to know the second-order partial derivatives f_{xx}, f_{xy}, and f_{yy}, all evaluated at (x_0, y_0)—just as we need to know the first-order partial derivatives to calculate dz from (11.4).

Example 3   Given $z = x^3 + 5xy - y^2$, find dz and d^2z. This function is the same as the one in Example 1. Thus, substituting the various derivatives already obtained there into (11.4) and (11.6), we find[†]

$$dz = (3x^2 + 5y)\,dx + (5x - 2y)\,dy$$

[†] An alternative way of reaching these results is by direct differentiation of the function:

$$dz = d(x^3) + d(5xy) - d(y^2)$$
$$= 3x^2\,dx + 5y\,dx + 5x\,dy - 2y\,dy$$

Further differentiation of dz (bearing in mind that dx and dy are constants) will then yield

$$d^2z = d(3x^2)\,dx + d(5y)\,dx + d(5x)\,dy - d(2y)\,dy$$
$$= (6x\,dx)\,dx + (5\,dy)\,dx + (5\,dx)\,dy - (2\,dy)\,dy$$
$$= 6x\,dx^2 + 10\,dx\,dy - 2\,dy^2$$

and

$$d^2z = 6x\, dx^2 + 10\, dx\, dy - 2\, dy^2$$

We can also calculate dz and d^2z at specific points in the domain. At the point $x = 1$ and $y = 2$, for instance, we have

$$dz = 13\, dx + dy \qquad \text{and} \qquad d^2z = 6\, dx^2 + 10\, dx\, dy - 2\, dy^2$$

Second-Order Condition

In the one-variable case, $d^2z < 0$ at a stationary point identifies the point as the peak of a hill in a 2-space. Similarly, in the two-variable case, $d^2z < 0$ at a stationary point would identify the point as the peak of a dome in a 3-space. Thus, once the first-order necessary condition is satisfied, the second-order sufficient condition for a maximum of $z = f(x, y)$ is

maximum: $\quad d^2z < 0$ for arbitrary values of dx and dy, not both zero $\qquad$ **(11.7)**

A positive d^2z value at a stationary point, on the other hand, is associated with the bottom of a bowl. The second-order sufficient condition for a minimum of $z = f(x, y)$ is

minimum: $\quad d^2z > 0$ for arbitrary values of dx and dy, not both zero $\qquad$ **(11.8)**

The reason why (11.7) and (11.8) are only sufficient, but not necessary, conditions is that it is again possible for d^2z to take a zero value at a maximum or a minimum. For this reason, second-order *necessary* conditions must be stated with weak inequalities as follows:

For maximum of z: $\qquad d^2z \le 0$

For minimum of z: $\qquad d^2z \ge 0$ $\Bigg\}$ for arbitrary values of dx and dy, not both zero

$$\text{(11.9)}$$

In the following, however, we shall pay more attention to the second-order sufficient conditions.

For operational convenience, second-order differential conditions can be translated into equivalent conditions on second-order derivatives. In the two-variable case, (11.6) shows that this would entail restrictions on the signs of the second-order partial derivatives f_{xx}, f_{xy}, and f_{yy}. The actual translation would require a knowledge of quadratic forms, which will be discussed in Sec. 11.3. But we may first introduce the main result here: For any values of dx and dy, not both zero,

$$d^2z \begin{cases} < 0 & \text{iff} \quad f_{xx} < 0; \quad f_{yy} < 0; \quad \text{and} \quad f_{xx}f_{yy} > f_{xy}^2 \\ > 0 & \text{iff} \quad f_{xx} > 0; \quad f_{yy} > 0; \quad \text{and} \quad f_{xx}f_{yy} > f_{xy}^2 \end{cases}$$

Note that the sign of d^2z hinges not only on f_{xx} and f_{yy}, which have to do with the surface configuration around point A (Fig. 11.4) in the two basic directions shown by T_x (east-west) and T_y (north-south), but also on the cross partial derivative f_{xy}. The role played by this latter partial derivative is to ensure that the surface in question will yield (two-dimensional) cross sections with the same type of configuration (hill or valley, as the case may be) not only in the two basic directions (east-west and north-south), but in all other possible directions (such as northeast-southwest) as well.

FIGURE 11.4

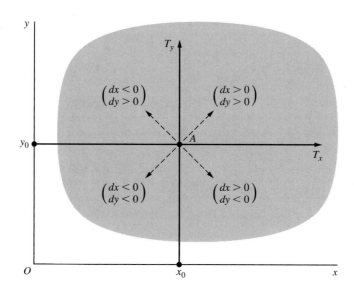

This result, together with the first-order condition (11.5), enables us to construct Table 11.1. It should be understood that all the second partial derivatives therein are to be evaluated at the stationary point where $f_x = f_y = 0$. It should also be stressed that the second-order sufficient condition is *not necessary* for an extremum. In particular, if a stationary value is characterized by $f_{xx} f_{yy} = f_{xy}^2$ in violation of that condition, that stationary value may nevertheless turn out to be an extremum. On the other hand, in the case of another type of violation, with a stationary point characterized by $f_{xx} f_{yy} < f_{xy}^2$, we can identify that point as a saddle point, because the sign of d^2z will in that case be indefinite (positive for some values of dx and dy, but negative for others).

Example 4

Find the extreme value(s) of $z = 8x^3 + 2xy - 3x^2 + y^2 + 1$. First let us find all the first and second partial derivatives:

$$f_x = 24x^2 + 2y - 6x \qquad f_y = 2x + 2y$$
$$f_{xx} = 48x - 6 \qquad f_{yy} = 2 \qquad f_{xy} = 2$$

The first-order condition calls for satisfaction of the simultaneous equations $f_x = 0$ and $f_y = 0$; that is,

$$24x^2 + 2y - 6x = 0$$
$$2y + 2x = 0$$

The second equation implies that $y = -x$, and when this information is substituted into the first equation, we get $24x^2 - 8x = 0$, which yields the pair of solutions

$$x_1^* = 0 \qquad [\text{implying } y_1^* = -x_1^* = 0]$$
$$x_2^* = \tfrac{1}{3} \qquad \left[\text{implying } y_2^* = -\tfrac{1}{3}\right]$$

To apply the second-order condition, we note that, when

$$x_1^* = y_1^* = 0$$

TABLE 11.1
Conditions for Relative Extremum:
$z = f(x, y)$

Condition	Maximum	Minimum
First-order necessary condition	$f_x = f_y = 0$	$f_x = f_y = 0$
Second-order sufficient condition†	$f_{xx}, f_{yy} < 0$ and $f_{xx} f_{yy} > f_{xy}^2$	$f_{xx}, f_{yy} > 0$ and $f_{xx} f_{yy} > f_{xy}^2$

† Applicable only after the first-order necessary condition has been satisfied.

f_{xx} turns out to be -6, while f_{yy} is 2, so that $f_{xx} f_{yy}$ is negative and is necessarily less than a squared value f_{xy}^2. This fails the second-order condition. The fact that f_{xx} and f_{yy} have opposite signs suggests, of course, that the surface in question will curl upward in one direction but downward in another, thereby giving rise to a saddle point.

What about the other solution? When evaluated at $x_2^* = \frac{1}{3}$, we find that $f_{xx} = 10$, which, together with the fact that $f_{yy} = f_{xy} = 2$, meets all three parts of the second-order sufficient condition for a minimum. Therefore, by setting $x = \frac{1}{3}$ and $y = -\frac{1}{3}$ in the given function, we can obtain as a minimum of z the value $z^* = \frac{23}{27}$. In the present example, there thus exists only one relative extremum (a minimum), which can be represented by the ordered triple

$$(x^*, y^*, z^*) = \left(\frac{1}{3}, \frac{-1}{3}, \frac{23}{27} \right)$$

Example 5

Find the extreme value(s) of $z = x + 2ey - e^x - e^{2y}$. The relevant derivatives of this function are

$$f_x = 1 - e^x \qquad f_y = 2e - 2e^{2y}$$
$$f_{xx} = -e^x \qquad f_{yy} = -4e^{2y} \qquad f_{xy} = 0$$

To satisfy the necessary condition, we must have

$$1 - e^x = 0$$
$$2e - 2e^{2y} = 0$$

which has only one solution, namely, $x^* = 0$ and $y^* = \frac{1}{2}$. To ascertain the status of the value of z corresponding to this solution (the stationary value), we evaluate the second-order derivatives at $x = 0$ and $y = \frac{1}{2}$, and find that $f_{xx} = -1$, $f_{yy} = -4e$, and $f_{xy} = 0$. Since f_{xx} and f_{yy} are both negative and since, in addition, $(-1)(-4e) > 0$, we may conclude that the z value in question, namely,

$$z^* = 0 + e - e^0 - e^1 = -1$$

is a maximum value of the function. This maximum point on the given surface can be denoted by the ordered triple $(x^*, y^*, z^*) = (0, \frac{1}{2}, -1)$.

Again, note that, to evaluate the second partial derivatives at x^* and y^*, differentiation must be undertaken first, and then the specific values of x^* and y^* are to be substituted into the derivatives as the final step.

EXERCISE 11.2

Use Table 11.1 to find the extreme value(s) of each of the following four functions, and determine whether they are maxima or minima:

1. $z = x^2 + xy + 2y^2 + 3$
2. $z = -x^2 - y^2 + 6x + 2y$

3. $z = ax^2 + by^2 + c$; consider each of the three subcases:

    (a) $a > 0, b > 0$ (b) $a < 0, b < 0$ (c) a and b opposite in sign

4. $z = e^{2x} - 2x + 2y^2 + 3$

5. Consider the function $z = (x - 2)^4 + (y - 3)^4$.

    (a) Establish by intuitive reasoning that z attains a minimum ($z^* = 0$) at $x^* = 2$ and $y^* = 3$.

    (b) Is the first-order necessary condition in Table 11.1 satisfied?

    (c) Is the second-order sufficient condition in Table 11.1 satisfied?

    (d) Find the value of d^2z. Does it satisfy the second-order necessary condition for a minimum in (11.9)?

11.3 Quadratic Forms—An Excursion

The expression for d^2z on the last line of (11.6) exemplifies what are known as *quadratic forms,* for which there exist established criteria for determining whether their signs are always positive, negative, nonpositive, or nonnegative, for arbitrary values of dx and dy, not both zero. Since the second-order condition for extremum hinges directly on the sign of d^2z, those criteria are of direct interest.

To begin with, we define a *form* as a polynomial expression in which each component term has a uniform degree. Our earlier encounter with polynomials was confined to the case of a single variable: $a_0 + a_1x + \cdots + a_nx^n$. When more variables are involved, each term of a polynomial may contain either one variable or several variables, each raised to a nonnegative integer power, such as $3x + 4x^2y^3 - 2yz$. In the special case where each term has a uniform degree—i.e., where the sum of exponents in each term is uniform—the polynomial is called a *form*. For example, $4x - 9y + z$ is a *linear form* in three variables, because each of its terms is of the first degree. On the other hand, the polynomial $4x^2 - xy + 3y^2$, in which each term is of the second degree (sum of integer exponents $= 2$), constitutes a *quadratic form* in two variables. We may also encounter quadratic forms in three variables, such as $x^2 + 2xy - yw + 7w^2$, or indeed in n variables.

Second-Order Total Differential as a Quadratic Form

If we consider the differentials dx and dy in (11.6) as variables and the partial derivatives as coefficients, i.e., if we let

$$u \equiv dx \qquad v \equiv dy$$
$$a \equiv f_{xx} \qquad b \equiv f_{yy} \qquad h \equiv f_{xy}[= f_{yx}] \tag{11.10}$$

then the second-order total differential

$$d^2z = f_{xx}\, dx^2 + 2f_{xy}\, dx\, dy + f_{yy}\, dy^2$$

can easily be identified as a quadratic form q in the two variables u and v:

$$q = au^2 + 2huv + bv^2 \tag{11.6'}$$

Note that, in this quadratic form, $dx \equiv u$ and $dy \equiv v$ are cast in the role of variables, whereas the second partial derivatives are treated as constants—the exact opposite of the situation when we were differentiating dz to get d^2z. The reason for this role reversal lies in the changed nature of the problem we are now dealing with. The second-order sufficient condition for extremum stipulates d^2z to be definitely positive (for a minimum) and definitely negative (for a maximum), regardless of the values that dx and dy may take (so long as they are not both zero). It is obvious, therefore, that in the present context dx and dy must be considered as *variables*. The second partial derivatives, on the other hand, will assume specific values at the points we are examining as possible extremum points, and thus may be regarded as *constants*.

The major question becomes, then: What restrictions must be placed upon a, b, and h in (11.6′), while u and v are allowed to take any values, in order to ensure a definite sign for q?

Positive and Negative Definiteness

As a matter of terminology, let us remark that a quadratic form q is said to be

$$
\left.
\begin{array}{l}
\textit{Positive definite} \\
\textit{Positive semidefinite} \\
\textit{Negative semidefinite} \\
\textit{Negative definite}
\end{array}
\right\}
\text{ if } q \text{ is invariably }
\left\{
\begin{array}{ll}
\text{positive} & (> 0) \\
\text{nonnegative} & (\geq 0) \\
\text{nonpositive} & (\leq 0) \\
\text{negative} & (< 0)
\end{array}
\right.
$$

regardless of the values of the variables in the quadratic form, not all zero. If q changes signs when the variables assume different values, on the other hand, q is said to be *indefinite*. Clearly, the cases of positive and negative definiteness of $q = d^2z$ are related to the second-order *sufficient* conditions for a minimum and a maximum, respectively. The cases of *semi*definiteness, on the other hand, relate to second-order *necessary* conditions. When $q = d^2z$ is indefinite, we have the symptom of a saddle point.

Determinantal Test for Sign Definiteness

A widely used test for the sign definiteness of q calls for the examination of the signs of certain determinants. This test happens to be more easily applicable to positive and negative definiteness (as against semidefiniteness); that is, it applies more easily to second-order sufficient (as against necessary) conditions. We shall confine our discussion here to the sufficient conditions only.[†]

For the two-variable case, determinantal conditions for the sign definiteness of q are relatively easy to derive. In the first place, we see that the signs of the first and third terms in (11.6′) are independent of the values of the variables u and v, because these variables appear in squares. Thus it is easy to specify the condition for the positive or negative definiteness of these terms alone, by restricting the signs of a and b. The trouble spot lies in the middle term. But if we can convert the entire polynomial into an expression such that the variables u and v appear only in some squares, the definiteness of the sign of q will again become tractable.

[†] For a discussion of a determinantal test for second-order necessary conditions, see Alpha C. Chiang, *Elements of Dynamic Optimization,* Waveland Press Inc., 1992, pp. 85–90.

The device that will do the trick is that of completing the square. By adding h^2v^2/a to, and subtracting the same quantity from, the right side of (11.6′), we can rewrite the quadratic form as follows:

$$q = au^2 + 2huv + \frac{h^2}{a}v^2 + bv^2 - \frac{h^2}{a}v^2$$

$$= a\left(u^2 + \frac{2h}{a}uv + \frac{h^2}{a^2}v^2\right) + \left(b - \frac{h^2}{a}\right)v^2$$

$$= a\left(u + \frac{h}{a}v\right)^2 + \frac{ab - h^2}{a}(v^2)$$

Now that the variables u and v appear only in squares, we can predicate the sign of q entirely on the values of the coefficients a, b, and h as follows:

$$q \text{ is } \begin{Bmatrix} \text{positive definite} \\ \text{negative definite} \end{Bmatrix} \quad \text{iff} \quad \begin{Bmatrix} a > 0 \\ a < 0 \end{Bmatrix} \quad \text{and} \quad ab - h^2 > 0 \quad \textbf{(11.11)}$$

Now that (1) $ab - h^2$ should be *positive* in both cases and (2) as a prerequisite for the positivity of $ab - h^2$, the product ab must be positive (since it must exceed the squared term h^2); hence, this condition automatically implies that a and b must take the identical algebraic sign.

The condition just derived may be stated more succinctly by the use of determinants. We observe first that the quadratic form in (11.6′) can be rearranged into the following square, symmetric format:

$$q = \quad a(u^2) + h(uv)$$
$$+ \, h(vu) + b(v^2)$$

with the squared terms placed on the diagonal and with the $2huv$ term split into two equal parts and placed off the diagonal. The coefficients now form a symmetric matrix, with a and b on the principal diagonal and h off the diagonal. Viewed in this light, the quadratic form is also easily seen to be the 1×1 matrix (a scalar) resulting from the following matrix multiplication:

$$q = [u \quad v]\begin{bmatrix} a & h \\ h & b \end{bmatrix}\begin{bmatrix} u \\ v \end{bmatrix}$$

Note that this is a more generalized case of the matrix product $x'Ax$ discussed in Sec. 4.4, Example 5. In that example, with a so-called diagonal matrix (a symmetric matrix with only zeros as its off-diagonal elements) as A, the product $x'Ax$ represents a weighted sum of squares. Here, with any symmetric matrix as A (allowing nonzero off-diagonal elements to appear), the product $x'Ax$ is a quadratic form.

The determinant of the 2×2 coefficient matrix, $\begin{vmatrix} a & h \\ h & b \end{vmatrix}$—which is referred to as the *discriminant* of the quadratic form q, and which we shall therefore denote by $|D|$—supplies the clue to the criterion in (11.11), for the latter can be alternatively expressed as:

$$q \text{ is } \begin{Bmatrix} \text{positive definite} \\ \text{negative definite} \end{Bmatrix} \quad \text{iff} \quad \begin{Bmatrix} |a| > 0 \\ |a| < 0 \end{Bmatrix} \quad \text{and} \quad \begin{vmatrix} a & h \\ h & b \end{vmatrix} > 0 \quad \textbf{(11.11′)}$$

The determinant $|a| = a$ is simply the *first leading principal minor* of $|D|$. The determinant $\begin{vmatrix} a & h \\ h & b \end{vmatrix}$ is, on the other hand, the *second leading principal minor* of $|D|$. In the present case, there are only two leading principal minors available, and their signs will serve to determine the positive or negative definiteness of q.

When (11.11′) is translated, via (11.10), into terms of the second-order total differential d^2z, we have

$$d^2z \text{ is} \begin{Bmatrix} \text{positive definite} \\ \text{negative definite} \end{Bmatrix} \quad \text{iff} \quad \begin{Bmatrix} f_{xx} > 0 \\ f_{xx} < 0 \end{Bmatrix} \quad \text{and} \quad \begin{vmatrix} f_{xx} & f_{xy} \\ f_{xy} & f_{yy} \end{vmatrix} = f_{xx}f_{yy} - f_{xy}^2 > 0$$

Recalling that the latter inequality implies that f_{xx} and f_{yy} are required to take the *same* sign, we see that this is precisely the second-order sufficient condition presented in Table 11.1.

In general, the discriminant of a quadratic form

$$q = au^2 + 2huv + bv^2$$

is the symmetric determinant $\begin{vmatrix} a & h \\ h & b \end{vmatrix}$. In the particular case of the quadratic form

$$d^2z = f_{xx}\,dx^2 + 2f_{xy}\,dx\,dy + f_{yy}\,dy^2$$

the discriminant is a determinant with the second-order partial derivatives as its elements. Such a determinant is called a *Hessian determinant* (or simply a *Hessian*). In the two-variable case, the Hessian is

$$|H| = \begin{vmatrix} f_{xx} & f_{xy} \\ f_{yx} & f_{yy} \end{vmatrix}$$

which, in view of Young's theorem ($f_{xy} = f_{yx}$), is symmetric—as a discriminant should be. You should carefully distinguish the Hessian determinant from the Jacobian determinant discussed in Sec. 7.6.

Example 1

Is $q = 5u^2 + 3uv + 2v^2$ either positive or negative definite? The discriminant of q is $\begin{vmatrix} 5 & 1.5 \\ 1.5 & 2 \end{vmatrix}$, with leading principal minors

$$5 > 0 \quad \text{and} \quad \begin{vmatrix} 5 & 1.5 \\ 1.5 & 2 \end{vmatrix} = 7.75 > 0$$

Therefore q is positive definite.

Example 2

Given $f_{xx} = -2$, $f_{xy} = 1$, and $f_{yy} = -1$ at a certain point on a function $z = f(x, y)$, does d^2z have a definite sign at that point regardless of the values of dx and dy? The discriminant of the quadratic form d^2z is in this case $\begin{vmatrix} -2 & 1 \\ 1 & -1 \end{vmatrix}$, with leading principal minors

$$-2 < 0 \quad \text{and} \quad \begin{vmatrix} -2 & 1 \\ 1 & -1 \end{vmatrix} = 1 > 0$$

Thus d^2z is negative definite.

Three-Variable Quadratic Forms

Can similar conditions be obtained for a quadratic form in *three* variables?

A quadratic form with three variables u_1, u_2, and u_3 may be generally represented as

$$
\begin{aligned}
q(u_1, u_2, u_3) = \quad & d_{11}(u_1^2) \quad + d_{12}(u_1 u_2) + d_{13}(u_1 u_3) \\
+ \; & d_{21}(u_2 u_1) + d_{22}(u_2^2) \quad + d_{23}(u_2 u_3) \\
+ \; & d_{31}(u_3 u_1) + d_{32}(u_3 u_2) + d_{33}(u_3^2) \\
= \; & \sum_{i=1}^{3} \sum_{j=1}^{3} d_{ij} u_i u_j
\end{aligned}
\tag{11.12}
$$

where the double-$\sum$ (double-sum) notation means that both the index i and the index j are allowed to take the values 1, 2, and 3; and thus the double-sum expression is equivalent to the 3×3 array shown in Eq. (11.12). Such a square array of the quadratic form is, incidentally, always to be considered a symmetric one, even though we have written the pair of coefficients (d_{12}, d_{21}) or (d_{23}, d_{32}) as if the two members of each pair were different. For if the term in the quadratic form involving the variables u_1 and u_2 happens to be, say, $12 u_1 u_2$, we can let $d_{12} = d_{21} = 6$, so that $d_{12} u_1 u_2 = d_{21} u_2 u_1$, and a similar procedure may be applied to make the other off-diagonal elements symmetrical.

Actually, this three-variable quadratic form is again expressible as a product of three matrices:

$$
q(u_1, u_2, u_3) = [u_1 \quad u_2 \quad u_3] \begin{bmatrix} d_{11} & d_{12} & d_{13} \\ d_{21} & d_{22} & d_{23} \\ d_{31} & d_{32} & d_{33} \end{bmatrix} \begin{bmatrix} u_1 \\ u_2 \\ u_3 \end{bmatrix} \equiv u'Du \tag{11.12'}
$$

As in the two-variable case, the first matrix (a row vector) and the third matrix (a column vector) merely list the variables, and the middle one (D) is a symmetric coefficient matrix from the square-array version of the quadratic form in (11.12). This time, however, a total of *three* leading principal minors can be formed from its discriminant, namely,

$$
|D_1| \equiv d_{11} \qquad |D_2| \equiv \begin{vmatrix} d_{11} & d_{12} \\ d_{21} & d_{22} \end{vmatrix} \qquad |D_3| \equiv \begin{vmatrix} d_{11} & d_{12} & d_{13} \\ d_{21} & d_{22} & d_{23} \\ d_{31} & d_{32} & d_{33} \end{vmatrix}
$$

where $|D_i|$ denotes the ith leading principal minor of the discriminant $|D|$.[†] It turns out that the conditions for positive or negative definiteness can again be stated in terms of certain sign restrictions on these principal minors.

By the now-familiar device of completing the square, the quadratic form in (11.12) can be converted into an expression in which the three variables appear only as components of

---

[†] We have so far viewed the ith leading principal minor $|D_i|$ as a subdeterminant formed by retaining the first i principal-diagonal elements of $|D|$. Since the notion of a *minor* implies the *deletion* of something from the original determinant, however, you may prefer to view the ith leading principal minor alternatively as a subdeterminant formed by deleting the last $(n - i)$ rows and columns of $|D|$.

some squares. Specifically, recalling that $a_{12} = a_{21}$, etc., we have

$$q = d_{11}\left(u_1 + \frac{d_{12}}{d_{11}}u_2 + \frac{d_{13}}{d_{11}}u_3\right)^2 + \frac{d_{11}d_{22} - d_{12}^2}{d_{11}}\left(u_2 + \frac{d_{11}d_{23} - d_{12}d_{13}}{d_{11}d_{22} - d_{12}^2}u_3\right)^2$$

$$+ \frac{d_{11}d_{22}d_{33} - d_{11}d_{23}^2 - d_{22}d_{13}^2 - d_{33}d_{12}^2 + 2d_{12}d_{13}d_{23}}{d_{11}d_{22} - d_{12}^2}(u_3)^2$$

This sum of squares will be positive (negative) for any values of u_1, u_2, and u_3, not all zero, if and only if the coefficients of the three squared expressions are all positive (negative). But the three coefficients (in the order given) can be expressed in terms of the three leading principal minors as follows:

$$|D_1| \qquad \frac{|D_2|}{|D_1|} \qquad \frac{|D_3|}{|D_2|}$$

Hence, for *positive definiteness,* the necessary-and-sufficient condition is threefold:

$$|D_1| > 0$$
$$|D_2| > 0 \qquad \text{[given that } |D_1| > 0 \text{ already]}$$
$$|D_3| > 0 \qquad \text{[given that } |D_2| > 0 \text{ already]}$$

In other words, the three leading principal minors must all be positive. For *negative definiteness,* on the other hand, the necessary-and-sufficient condition becomes:

$$|D_1| < 0$$
$$|D_2| > 0 \qquad \text{[given that } |D_1| < 0 \text{ already]}$$
$$|D_3| < 0 \qquad \text{[given that } |D_2| > 0 \text{ already]}$$

That is, the three leading principal minors must alternate in sign in the specified manner.

Example 3   Determine whether $q = u_1^2 + 6u_2^2 + 3u_3^2 - 2u_1u_2 - 4u_2u_3$ is either positive or negative definite. The discriminant of q is

$$\begin{vmatrix} 1 & -1 & 0 \\ -1 & 6 & -2 \\ 0 & -2 & 3 \end{vmatrix}$$

with leading principal minors as follows:

$$1 > 0 \qquad \begin{vmatrix} 1 & -1 \\ -1 & 6 \end{vmatrix} = 5 > 0 \qquad \text{and} \qquad \begin{vmatrix} 1 & -1 & 0 \\ -1 & 6 & -2 \\ 0 & -2 & 3 \end{vmatrix} = 11 > 0$$

Therefore, the quadratic form is positive definite.

Example 4   Determine whether $q = 2u^2 + 3v^2 - w^2 + 6uv - 8uw - 2vw$ is either positive or negative definite. The discriminant may be written as $\begin{vmatrix} 2 & 3 & -4 \\ 3 & 3 & -1 \\ -4 & -1 & -1 \end{vmatrix}$, and we find its first leading principal minor to be $2 > 0$, but the second leading principal minor is $\begin{vmatrix} 2 & 3 \\ 3 & 3 \end{vmatrix} = -3 < 0$.

This violates the condition for both positive and negative definiteness; thus q is neither positive nor negative definite.

n-Variable Quadratic Forms

As an extension of the preceding result to the n-variable case, we shall state without proof that, for the quadratic form

$$q(u_1, u_2, \ldots, u_n) = \sum_{i=1}^{n} \sum_{j=1}^{n} d_{ij} u_i u_j \qquad \text{[where } d_{ij} = d_{ji}\text{]}$$

$$= \underset{(1 \times n)}{u'} \underset{(n \times n)}{D} \underset{(n \times 1)}{u} \qquad \text{[cf. (11.12')]}$$

the necessary-and-sufficient condition for *positive definiteness* is that the leading principal minors of $|D|$, namely,

$$|D_1| \equiv d_{11} \qquad |D_2| \equiv \begin{vmatrix} d_{11} & d_{12} \\ d_{21} & d_{22} \end{vmatrix} \qquad \cdots \qquad |D_n| \equiv \begin{vmatrix} d_{11} & d_{12} & \cdots & d_{1n} \\ d_{21} & d_{22} & \cdots & d_{2n} \\ \cdots\cdots\cdots\cdots\cdots \\ d_{n1} & d_{n2} & \cdots & d_{nn} \end{vmatrix}$$

all be positive. The corresponding necessary-and-sufficient condition for *negative definiteness* is that the leading principal minors alternate in sign as follows:

$$|D_1| < 0 \qquad |D_2| > 0 \qquad |D_3| < 0 \qquad \text{(etc.)}$$

so that all the *odd*-numbered ones are negative and all *even*-numbered ones are positive. The nth leading principal minor, $|D_n| = |D|$, should be positive if n is even, but negative if n is odd. This can be expressed succinctly by the inequality $(-1)^n |D_n| > 0$.

Characteristic-Root Test for Sign Definiteness

Aside from the preceding determinantal test for the sign definiteness of a quadratic form $u'Du$, there is an alternative test that utilizes the concept of the so-called characteristic roots of the matrix D. This concept arises in a problem of the following nature. Given an $n \times n$ matrix D, can we find a scalar r, and an $n \times 1$ vector $x \neq 0$, such that the matrix equation

$$\underset{(n \times n)}{D} \underset{(n \times 1)}{x} = r \underset{(n \times 1)}{x} \qquad\qquad \textbf{(11.13)}$$

is satisfied? If so, the scalar r is referred to as a *characteristic root* of matrix D and x as a *characteristic vector* of that matrix.[†]

The matrix equation $Dx = rx$ can be rewritten as $Dx - rIx = 0$, or

$$(D - rI)x = 0 \qquad \text{where 0 is } n \times 1 \qquad\qquad \textbf{(11.13')}$$

[†] Characteristic roots are also known by the alternative names of *latent roots,* or *eigenvalues.* Characteristic vectors are also called *eigenvectors.*

This, of course, represents a system of n homogeneous linear equations. Since we want a nontrivial solution for x, the coefficient matrix $(D - rI)$—called the *characteristic matrix* of D—is required to be singular. In other words, its determinant must be made to vanish:

$$|D - rI| = \begin{vmatrix} d_{11} - r & d_{12} & \cdots & d_{1n} \\ d_{21} & d_{22} - r & \cdots & d_{2n} \\ \cdots & \cdots & \cdots & \cdots \\ d_{n1} & d_{n2} & \cdots & d_{nn} - r \end{vmatrix} = 0 \qquad \textbf{(11.14)}$$

Equation (11.14) is called the *characteristic equation* of matrix D. Since the determinant $|D - rI|$ will yield, upon Laplace expansion, an nth-degree polynomial in the variable r, (11.14) is in fact an nth-degree polynomial equation. There will thus be a total of n roots, $(r_1, \ldots, r_n)$, each of which qualifies as a characteristic root. If D is symmetric, as is the case in the quadratic-form context, the characteristic roots will always turn out to be real numbers, but they can take either algebraic sign, or be zero.

Inasmuch as these values of r will all make the determinant $|D - rI|$ vanish, the substitution of any of these (say, r_i) into the equation system (11.13') will produce a corresponding vector $x|_{r=r_i}$. More accurately, the system being homogeneous, it will yield an infinite number of vectors corresponding to the root r_i. We shall, however, apply a process of *normalization* (to be explained in Example 5) and select a particular member of that infinite set as *the* characteristic vector corresponding to r_i; this vector will be denoted by v_i. With a total of n characteristic roots, there should be a total of n such corresponding characteristic vectors.

Example 5

Find the characteristic roots and vectors of the matrix $\begin{bmatrix} 2 & 2 \\ 2 & -1 \end{bmatrix}$. By substituting the given matrix for D in (11.14), we get the equation

$$\begin{vmatrix} 2 - r & 2 \\ 2 & -1 - r \end{vmatrix} = r^2 - r - 6 = 0$$

with roots $r_1 = 3$ and $r_2 = -2$. When the first root is used, the matrix equation (11.13') takes the form of

$$\begin{bmatrix} 2 - 3 & 2 \\ 2 & -1 - 3 \end{bmatrix} \begin{bmatrix} x_1 \\ x_2 \end{bmatrix} = \begin{bmatrix} -1 & 2 \\ 2 & -4 \end{bmatrix} \begin{bmatrix} x_1 \\ x_2 \end{bmatrix} = \begin{bmatrix} 0 \\ 0 \end{bmatrix}$$

The two rows of the coefficient matrix being linearly dependent, as we would expect in view of (11.14), there is an infinite number of solutions, which can be expressed by the equation $x_1 = 2x_2$. To force out a unique solution, we *normalize* the solution by imposing the restriction $x_1^2 + x_2^2 = 1$.[†] Then, since

$$x_1^2 + x_2^2 = (2x_2)^2 + x_2^2 = 5x_2^2 = 1$$

we can obtain (by taking the positive square root) $x_2 = 1/\sqrt{5}$, and also $x_1 = 2x_2 = 2/\sqrt{5}$. Thus the first characteristic vector is

$$v_1 = \begin{bmatrix} 2/\sqrt{5} \\ 1/\sqrt{5} \end{bmatrix}$$

[†] More generally, for the n-variable case, we require that $\sum_{i=1}^{n} x_i^2 = 1$.

Similarly, by using the second root $r_2 = -2$ in (11.13'), we get the equation

$$\begin{bmatrix} 2-(-2) & 2 \\ 2 & -1-(-2) \end{bmatrix} \begin{bmatrix} x_1 \\ x_2 \end{bmatrix} = \begin{bmatrix} 4 & 2 \\ 2 & 1 \end{bmatrix} \begin{bmatrix} x_1 \\ x_2 \end{bmatrix} = \begin{bmatrix} 0 \\ 0 \end{bmatrix}$$

which has the solution $x_1 = -\frac{1}{2}x_2$. Upon normalization, we find

$$x_1^2 + x_2^2 = \left(-\frac{1}{2}x_2\right)^2 + x_2^2 = \frac{5}{4}x_2^2 = 1$$

which yields $x_2 = 2/\sqrt{5}$ and $x_1 = -1/\sqrt{5}$. Thus the second characteristic vector is

$$v_2 = \begin{bmatrix} -1/\sqrt{5} \\ 2/\sqrt{5} \end{bmatrix}$$

The set of characteristic vectors obtained in this manner possesses two important properties: First, the scalar product $v_i'v_i$ $(i = 1, 2, \ldots, n)$ must be equal to unity, since

$$v_i'v_i = [x_1 \quad x_2 \quad \cdots \quad x_n] \begin{bmatrix} x_1 \\ x_2 \\ \vdots \\ x_n \end{bmatrix} = \sum_{i=1}^{n} x_i^2 = 1 \qquad \text{[by normalization]}$$

Second, the scalar product $v_i'v_j$ (where $i \neq j$) can always be taken to be zero.[†] In sum, therefore, we may write that

$$v_i'v_i = 1 \qquad \text{and} \qquad v_i'v_j = 0 \qquad (i \neq j) \tag{11.15}$$

These properties will prove useful later (see Example 6). As a matter of terminology, when two vectors yield a zero-valued scalar product, the vectors are said to be *orthogonal* (perpendicular) to each other.[‡] Hence each pair of characteristic vectors of matrix D must be orthogonal. The other property, $v_i'v_i = 1$, is indicative of normalization. Together, these two properties account for the fact that the characteristic vectors $(v_1, \ldots, v_n)$ are said to

---

[†] To demonstrate this, we note that, by (11.13), we may write $Dv_j = r_jv_j$, and $Dv_i = r_iv_i$. By premultiplying both sides of each of these equations by an appropriate row vector, we have

$$v_i'Dv_j = v_i'r_jv_j = r_jv_i'v_j \qquad \text{[r_j is a scalar]}$$
$$v_j'Dv_i = v_j'r_iv_i = r_iv_j'v_i = r_iv_i'v_j \qquad \text{[$v_j'v_i = v_i'v_j$]}$$

Since $v_i'Dv_j$ and $v_j'Dv_i$ are both 1×1, and since they are transposes of each other (recall that $D' = D$ because D is symmetric), they must represent the same scalar. It follows that the extreme-right expressions in these two equations are equal; hence, by subtracting, we have

$$(r_j - r_i)v_i'v_j = 0$$

Now if $r_j \neq r_i$ (distinct roots), then $v_i'v_j$ has to be zero in order for the equation to hold, and this establishes our claim. If $r_j = r_i$ (repeated roots), moreover, it will always be possible, as it turns out, to find two linearly independent normalized vectors satisfying $v_i'v_j = 0$. Thus, we may state in general that $v_i'v_j = 0$, whenever $i \neq j$.

[‡] As a simple illustration of this, think of the two unit vectors of a 2-space, $e_1 = \begin{bmatrix} 1 \\ 0 \end{bmatrix}$ and $e_2 = \begin{bmatrix} 0 \\ 1 \end{bmatrix}$. These vectors lie, respectively, on the two axes, and are thus perpendicular. At the same time, we do find that $e_1'e_2 = e_2'e_1 = 0$. See also Exercise 4.3-4.

be a set of *orthonormal* vectors. You should try to verify the orthonormality of the two characteristic vectors found in Example 5.

Now we are ready to explain how the characteristic roots and characteristic vectors of matrix D can be of service in determining the sign definiteness of the quadratic form $u'Du$. In essence, the idea is again to transform $u'Du$ (which involves not only squared terms $u_1^2, \ldots, u_n^2$, but also cross-product terms such as u_1u_2 and u_2u_3) into a form that contains only squared terms. Thus the approach is similar in intent to the completing-the-square process used before in deriving the determinantal test. However, in the present case, the transformation possesses the additional feature that each squared term has as its coefficient one of the characteristic roots, so that the signs of the n roots will provide sufficient information for determining the sign definiteness of the quadratic form.

The transformation that will do the trick is as follows. Let the characteristic vectors $v_1, \ldots, v_n$ constitute the columns of a matrix T:

$$\underset{(n\times n)}{T} = [v_1 \quad v_2 \quad \cdots \quad v_n]$$

and then apply the transformation $\underset{(n\times 1)}{u} = \underset{(n\times n)}{T} \underset{(n\times 1)}{y}$ to the quadratic form $u'Du$:

$$u'Du = (Ty)'D(Ty) = y'T'DTy \qquad \text{[by (4.11)]}$$
$$= y'Ry \qquad \text{where} \qquad R \equiv T'DT$$

As a result, the original quadratic form in the variables u_i is now turned into another quadratic form in the variables y_i. Since the u_i variables and the y_i variables take the same range of values, the transformation does not affect the sign definiteness of the quadratic form. Thus we may now just as well consider the sign of the quadratic form $y'Ry$ instead. What makes this latter quadratic form intriguing is that the matrix R will turn out to be a diagonal one, with the roots $r_1, \ldots, r_n$ of matrix D displayed along its diagonal, and with zeros everywhere else, so that we have in fact

$$u'Du = y'Ry = [y_1 \quad y_2 \quad \cdots \quad y_n] \begin{bmatrix} r_1 & 0 & \cdots & 0 \\ 0 & r_2 & \cdots & 0 \\ \cdots\cdots\cdots\cdots\cdots \\ 0 & 0 & \cdots & r_n \end{bmatrix} \begin{bmatrix} y_1 \\ y_2 \\ \vdots \\ y_n \end{bmatrix}$$

$$= r_1 y_1^2 + r_2 y_2^2 + \cdots + r_n y_n^2 \qquad\qquad (11.16)$$

which is an expression involving squared terms only. The transformation $R \equiv T'DT$ provides us, therefore, with a procedure for *diagonalizing* the symmetric matrix D into the special diagonal matrix R.

<hr>

Example 6   Verify that the matrix $\begin{bmatrix} 2 & 2 \\ 2 & -1 \end{bmatrix}$ given in Example 5 can be diagonalized into the matrix $\begin{bmatrix} r_1 & 0 \\ 0 & r_2 \end{bmatrix} = \begin{bmatrix} 3 & 0 \\ 0 & -2 \end{bmatrix}$. On the basis of the characteristic vectors found in Example 5, the transformation matrix T should be

$$T = [v_1 \quad v_2] = \begin{bmatrix} 2/\sqrt{5} & -1/\sqrt{5} \\ 1/\sqrt{5} & 2/\sqrt{5} \end{bmatrix}$$

Thus we may write

$$
R \equiv T'DT = \begin{bmatrix} \dfrac{2}{\sqrt{5}} & \dfrac{1}{\sqrt{5}} \\[2mm] -\dfrac{1}{\sqrt{5}} & \dfrac{2}{\sqrt{5}} \end{bmatrix} \begin{bmatrix} 2 & 2 \\ 2 & -1 \end{bmatrix} \begin{bmatrix} \dfrac{2}{\sqrt{5}} & -\dfrac{1}{\sqrt{5}} \\[2mm] \dfrac{1}{\sqrt{5}} & \dfrac{2}{\sqrt{5}} \end{bmatrix} = \begin{bmatrix} 3 & 0 \\ 0 & -2 \end{bmatrix}
$$

which duly verifies the diagonalization process.

To prove the diagonalization result in (11.16), let us (partially) write out the matrix R as follows:

$$
R \equiv T'DT = \begin{bmatrix} v'_1 \\ v'_2 \\ \vdots \\ v'_n \end{bmatrix} D[v_1 \quad v_2 \quad \cdots \quad v_n]
$$

We may easily verify that $D[v_1 \quad v_2 \quad \cdots \quad v_n]$ can be rewritten as $[Dv_1 \quad Dv_2 \quad \cdots \quad Dv_n]$. Besides, by (11.13), we can further rewrite this as $[r_1v_1 \quad r_2v_2 \quad \cdots \quad r_nv_n]$. Hence, we see that

$$
R = \begin{bmatrix} v'_1 \\ v'_2 \\ \vdots \\ v'_n \end{bmatrix} [r_1v_1 \quad r_2v_2 \quad \cdots \quad r_nv_n] = \begin{bmatrix} r_1v'_1v_1 & r_2v'_1v_2 & \cdots & r_nv'_1v_n \\ r_1v'_2v_1 & r_2v'_2v_2 & \cdots & r_nv'_2v_n \\ \cdots\cdots\cdots\cdots\cdots\cdots\cdots\cdots \\ r_1v'_nv_1 & r_2v'_nv_2 & \cdots & r_nv'_nv_n \end{bmatrix}
$$

$$
= \begin{bmatrix} r_1 & 0 & \cdots & 0 \\ 0 & r_2 & \cdots & 0 \\ \vdots & \vdots & & \vdots \\ 0 & 0 & \cdots & r_n \end{bmatrix} \qquad \text{[by (11.15)]}
$$

which is precisely what we intended to show.

In view of the result in (11.16), we may formally state the characteristic-root test for the sign definiteness of a quadratic form as follows:

1. $q = u'Du$ is positive (negative) definite, if and only if *every* characteristic root of D is positive (negative).
2. $q = u'Du$ is positive (negative) semidefinite, if and only if *all* characteristic roots of D are nonnegative (nonpositive).
3. $q = u'Du$ is indefinite, if and only if some of the characteristic roots of D are positive and some are negative.

Note that, in applying this test, all we need are the characteristic roots; the characteristic vectors are not required unless we wish to find the transformation matrix T. Note, also, that this test, unlike the determinantal test previously outlined, permits us to check the second-order necessary conditions (part 2 of the test) simultaneously with the sufficient conditions (part 1 of the test). However, it does have a drawback. When the matrix D is of a high dimension, the polynomial equation (11.14) may not be easily solvable for the characteristic roots needed for the test. In such cases, the determinantal test might yet be preferable.

EXERCISE 11.3

1. By direct matrix multiplication, express each of the following matrix products as a quadratic form:

   (a) $[u \quad v] \begin{bmatrix} 4 & 2 \\ 2 & 3 \end{bmatrix} \begin{bmatrix} u \\ v \end{bmatrix}$ (c) $[x \quad y] \begin{bmatrix} 5 & 2 \\ 4 & 0 \end{bmatrix} \begin{bmatrix} x \\ y \end{bmatrix}$

   (b) $[u \quad v] \begin{bmatrix} -2 & 3 \\ 1 & -4 \end{bmatrix} \begin{bmatrix} u \\ v \end{bmatrix}$ (d) $[dx \quad dy] \begin{bmatrix} f_{xx} & f_{xy} \\ f_{yx} & f_{yy} \end{bmatrix} \begin{bmatrix} dx \\ dy \end{bmatrix}$

2. In Prob.1b and c, the coefficient matrices are not symmetric with respect to the principal diagonal. Verify that by averaging the off-diagonal elements and thus converting them, respectively, into $\begin{bmatrix} -2 & 2 \\ 2 & -4 \end{bmatrix}$ and $\begin{bmatrix} 5 & 3 \\ 3 & 0 \end{bmatrix}$ we will get the same quadratic forms as before.

3. On the basis of their coefficient matrices (the *symmetric* versions), determine by the determinantal test whether the quadratic forms in Prob.1a, b, and c are either positive definite or negative definite.

4. Express each of the following quadratic forms as a matrix product involving a *symmetric* coefficient matrix:

   (a) $q = 3u^2 - 4uv + 7v^2$ (d) $q = 6xy - 5y^2 - 2x^2$

   (b) $q = u^2 + 7uv + 3v^2$ (e) $q = 3u_1^2 - 2u_1 u_2 + 4u_1 u_3 + 5u_2^2 + 4u_3^2 - 2u_2 u_3$

   (c) $q = 8uv - u^2 - 31v^2$ (f) $q = -u^2 + 4uv - 6uw - 4v^2 - 7w^2$

5. From the discriminants obtained from the symmetric coefficient matrices of Prob. 4, ascertain by the determinantal test which of the quadratic forms are positive definite and which are negative definite.

6. Find the characteristic roots of each of the following matrices:

   (a) $D = \begin{bmatrix} 4 & 2 \\ 2 & 3 \end{bmatrix}$ (b) $E = \begin{bmatrix} -2 & 2 \\ 2 & -4 \end{bmatrix}$ (c) $F = \begin{bmatrix} 5 & 3 \\ 3 & 0 \end{bmatrix}$

   What can you conclude about the signs of the quadratic forms $u'Du$, $u'Eu$, and $u'Fu$? (Check your results against Prob. 3.)

7. Find the characteristic vectors of the matrix $\begin{bmatrix} 4 & 2 \\ 2 & 1 \end{bmatrix}$.

8. Given a quadratic form $u'Du$, where D is 2×2, the characteristic equation of D can be written as

   $$\begin{vmatrix} d_{11} - r & d_{12} \\ d_{21} & d_{22} - r \end{vmatrix} = 0 \quad (d_{12} = d_{21})$$

   Expand the determinant; express the roots of this equation by use of the quadratic formula; and deduce the following:

   (a) No imaginary number (a number involving $\sqrt{-1}$) can occur in r_1 and r_2.

   (b) To have repeated roots, matrix D must be in the form of $\begin{bmatrix} c & 0 \\ 0 & c \end{bmatrix}$.

   (c) To have either positive or negative semidefiniteness, the discriminant of the quadratic form may vanish, that is, $|D| = 0$ is possible.

11.4   Objective Functions with More than Two Variables

When there appear in an objective function $n > 2$ choice variables, it is no longer possible to graph the function, although we can still speak of a *hypersurface* in an $(n + 1)$-dimensional space. On such a (nongraphable) hypersurface, there again may exist $(n + 1)$-dimensional analogs of peaks of domes and bottoms of bowls. How do we identify them?

First-Order Condition for Extremum

Let us specifically consider a function of three choice variables,

$$z = f(x_1, x_2, x_3)$$

with first partial derivatives f_1, f_2, and f_3 and second partial derivatives f_{ij} ($\equiv \partial^2 z / \partial x_i \partial x_j$), with $i, j = 1, 2, 3$. By virtue of Young's theorem, we have $f_{ij} = f_{ji}$.

Our earlier discussion suggests that, to have a maximum or a minimum of z, it is necessary that $dz = 0$ for arbitrary values of dx_1, dx_2, and dx_3, not all zero. Since the value of dz is now

$$dz = f_1 \, dx_1 + f_2 \, dx_2 + f_3 \, dx_3 \qquad\qquad \textbf{(11.17)}$$

and since dx_1, dx_2, and dx_3 are arbitrary changes in the independent variables, not all zero, the only way to guarantee a zero dz is to have $f_1 = f_2 = f_3 = 0$. Thus, again, the necessary condition for extremum is that all the first-order partial derivatives be zero, the same as for the two-variable case.[†]

Second-Order Condition

The satisfaction of the first-order condition earmarks certain values of z as the stationary values of the objective function. If at a stationary value of z we find that d^2z is positive definite, this will suffice to establish that value of z as a minimum. Analogously, the negative definiteness of d^2z is a sufficient condition for the stationary value to be a maximum. This raises the questions of how to express d^2z when there are three variables in the function and how to determine its positive or negative definiteness.

The expression for d^2z can be obtained by differentiating dz in (11.17). In such a process, as in (11.6), we should treat the derivatives f_i as variables and the differentials dx_i

---

[†] As a special case, note that if we happen to be working with a function $z = f(x_1, x_2, x_3)$ implicitly defined by an equation $F(z, x_1, x_2, x_3) = 0$, where

$$f_i \equiv \frac{\partial z}{\partial x_i} = \frac{-\partial F / \partial x_i}{\partial F / \partial z} \qquad (i = 1, 2, 3)$$

then the first-order condition $f_1 = f_2 = f_3 = 0$ will amount to the condition

$$\frac{\partial F}{\partial x_1} = \frac{\partial F}{\partial x_2} = \frac{\partial F}{\partial x_3} = 0$$

since the value of the denominator $\partial F / \partial z \neq 0$ makes no difference.

as constants. Thus we have

$$d^2z = d(dz) = \frac{\partial(dz)}{\partial x_1} dx_1 + \frac{\partial(dz)}{\partial x_2} dx_2 + \frac{\partial(dz)}{\partial x_3} dx_3$$

$$= \frac{\partial}{\partial x_1}(f_1 \, dx_1 + f_2 \, dx_2 + f_3 \, dx_3) \, dx_1$$

$$+ \frac{\partial}{\partial x_2}(f_1 \, dx_1 + f_2 \, dx_2 + f_3 \, dx_3) \, dx_2$$

$$+ \frac{\partial}{\partial x_3}(f_1 \, dx_1 + f_2 \, dx_2 + f_3 \, dx_3) \, dx_3$$

$$= \quad f_{11} \, dx_1^2 \quad + f_{12} \, dx_1 \, dx_2 + f_{13} \, dx_1 \, dx_3$$
$$+ f_{21} \, dx_2 \, dx_1 + f_{22} \, dx_2^2 \quad + f_{23} \, dx_2 \, dx_3$$
$$+ f_{31} \, dx_3 \, dx_1 + f_{32} \, dx_3 \, dx_2 + f_{33} \, dx_3^2 \qquad \textbf{(11.18)}$$

which is a quadratic form similar to (11.12). Consequently, the criteria for positive and negative definiteness we learned earlier are directly applicable here.

In determining the positive or negative definiteness of d^2z, we must again, as we did in (11.6'), regard dx_i as variables that can take any values (though not all zero), while considering the derivatives f_{ij} as coefficients upon which to impose certain restrictions. The coefficients in (11.18) give rise to the symmetric Hessian determinant

$$|H| = \begin{vmatrix} f_{11} & f_{12} & f_{13} \\ f_{21} & f_{22} & f_{23} \\ f_{31} & f_{32} & f_{33} \end{vmatrix}$$

whose leading principal minors may be denoted by

$$|H_1| = f_{11} \qquad |H_2| = \begin{vmatrix} f_{11} & f_{12} \\ f_{21} & f_{22} \end{vmatrix} \qquad |H_3| = |H|$$

Thus, on the basis of the determinantal criteria for positive and negative definiteness, we may state the second-order sufficient condition for an extremum of z as follows:

$$z^* \text{ is a } \begin{Bmatrix} \text{maximum} \\ \text{minimum} \end{Bmatrix}$$

$$\text{if } \begin{cases} |H_1| < 0; \quad |H_2| > 0; \quad |H_3| < 0 \quad (d^2z \text{ negative definite}) \\ |H_1| > 0; \quad |H_2| > 0; \quad |H_3| > 0 \quad (d^2z \text{ positive definite}) \end{cases} \qquad \textbf{(11.19)}$$

In using this condition, we must evaluate all the leading principal minors at the stationary point where $f_1 = f_2 = f_3 = 0$.

We may, of course, also apply the characteristic-root test and associate the positive definiteness (negative definiteness) of d^2z with the positivity (negativity) of all the characteristic roots of the *Hessian matrix* $\begin{bmatrix} f_{11} & f_{12} & f_{13} \\ f_{21} & f_{22} & f_{23} \\ f_{31} & f_{32} & f_{33} \end{bmatrix}$. In fact, instead of saying that the second-order total differential d^2z is positive (negative) definite, it is also acceptable to state that the Hessian matrix H (to be distinguished from the Hessian determinant $|H|$) is positive (negative) definite. In this usage, however, note that the sign definiteness of H refers to the sign of the quadratic form d^2z with which H is associated, *not* to the signs of the elements of H per se.

Example 1

Find the extreme value(s) of

$$z = 2x_1^2 + x_1 x_2 + 4x_2^2 + x_1 x_3 + x_3^2 + 2$$

The first-order condition for extremum involves the simultaneous satisfaction of the following three equations:

$$(f_1 =)\ 4x_1 +\ x_2 +\ x_3 = 0$$
$$(f_2 =)\ x_1 + 8x_2 \qquad\quad = 0$$
$$(f_3 =)\ x_1 \qquad\quad + 2x_3 = 0$$

Because this is a homogeneous linear-equation system, in which all the three equations are independent (the determinant of the coefficient matrix does not vanish), there exists only the single solution $x_1^* = x_2^* = x_3^* = 0$. This means that there is only one stationary value, $z^* = 2$.

The Hessian determinant of this function is

$$|H| = \begin{vmatrix} f_{11} & f_{12} & f_{13} \\ f_{21} & f_{22} & f_{23} \\ f_{31} & f_{32} & f_{33} \end{vmatrix} = \begin{vmatrix} 4 & 1 & 1 \\ 1 & 8 & 0 \\ 1 & 0 & 2 \end{vmatrix}$$

whose leading principal minors are all positive:

$$|H_1| = 4 \qquad |H_2| = 31 \qquad |H_3| = 54$$

Thus we can conclude, by (11.9), that $z^* = 2$ is a minimum.

Example 2

Find the extreme value(s) of

$$z = -x_1^3 + 3x_1 x_3 + 2x_2 - x_2^2 - 3x_3^2$$

The first partial derivatives are found to be

$$f_1 = -3x_1^2 + 3x_3 \qquad f_2 = 2 - 2x_2 \qquad f_3 = 3x_1 - 6x_3$$

By setting all f_i equal to zero, we get three simultaneous equations, one nonlinear and two linear:

$$-3x_1^2 \qquad\quad + 3x_3 = 0$$
$$- 2x_2 \qquad\quad = -2$$
$$3x_1 \qquad\quad - 6x_3 = 0$$

Since the second equation gives $x_2^* = 1$ and the third equation implies $x_1^* = 2x_3^*$, substitution of these into the first equation yields two solutions:

$$(x_1^*, x_2^*, x_3^*) = \begin{cases} (0, 1, 0), \text{ implying } z^* = 1 \\ \left(\frac{1}{2}, 1, \frac{1}{4}\right), \text{ implying } z^* = \frac{17}{16} \end{cases}$$

The second-order partial derivatives, properly arranged, give us the Hessian

$$|H| = \begin{vmatrix} -6x_1 & 0 & 3 \\ 0 & -2 & 0 \\ 3 & 0 & -6 \end{vmatrix}$$

in which the first element $(-6x_1)$ reduces to 0 under the first solution (with $x_1^* = 0$) and to -3 under the second $\left(\text{with } x_1^* = \frac{1}{2}\right)$. It is immediately obvious that the first solution does not satisfy the second-order sufficient condition, since $|H_1| = 0$. We may, however, resort to the characteristic-root test for further information. For this purpose, we apply the characteristic equation (11.14). Since the quadratic form being tested is d^2z, whose discriminant is the Hessian determinant, we should, of course, substitute the elements of the Hessian for the d_{ij} elements in that equation. Hence the characteristic equation is (for the first solution)

$$\begin{vmatrix} -r & 0 & 3 \\ 0 & -2-r & 0 \\ 3 & 0 & -6-r \end{vmatrix} = 0$$

which, upon expansion, becomes the cubic equation

$$r^3 + 8r^2 + 3r - 18 = 0$$

Using Theorem I in Sec. 3.3, we are able to find an integer root -2. Thus the cubic function should be divisible by $(r + 2)$, and we can factor the cubic function and rewrite the preceding equation as

$$(r + 2)(r^2 + 6r - 9) = 0$$

It is clear from the $(r + 2)$ term that one of the characteristic roots is $r_1 = -2$. The other two roots can be found by applying the quadratic formula to the other term; they are $r_2 = -3 + \frac{1}{2}\sqrt{72}$, and $r_3 = -3 - \frac{1}{2}\sqrt{72}$. Inasmuch as r_1 and r_3 are negative but r_2 is positive, the quadratic form d^2z is indefinite, thereby violating the second-order necessary conditions for both a maximum and a minimum z. Thus the first solution ($z^* = 1$) is not an extremum at all.

As for the second solution, the situation is simpler. Since the leading principal minors

$$|H_1| = -3 \qquad |H_2| = 6 \qquad \text{and} \qquad |H_3| = -18$$

duly alternate in sign, the determinantal test is conclusive. According to (11.19), the solution $z^* = \frac{17}{16}$ is a maximum.

n-Variable Case

When there are n choice variables, the objective function may be expressed as

$$z = f(x_1, x_2, \ldots, x_n)$$

The total differential will then be

$$dz = f_1 \, dx_1 + f_2 \, dx_2 + \cdots + f_n \, dx_n$$

so that the necessary condition for extremum ($dz = 0$ for arbitrary dx_i, not all zero) means that all the n first-order partial derivatives are required to be zero.

The second-order differential d^2z will again be a quadratic form, derivable analogously to (11.18) and expressible by an $n \times n$ array. The coefficients of that array, properly arranged, will now give the (symmetric) Hessian

$$|H| = \begin{vmatrix} f_{11} & f_{12} & \cdots & f_{1n} \\ f_{21} & f_{22} & \cdots & f_{2n} \\ \cdots\cdots\cdots\cdots\cdots\cdots\cdots \\ f_{n1} & f_{n2} & \cdots & f_{nn} \end{vmatrix}$$

TABLE 11.2

Determinantal Test for Relative Extremum: $z = f(x_1, x_2, \ldots, x_n)$

Condition	Maximum	Minimum
First-order necessary condition	$f_1 = f_2 = \cdots = f_n = 0$	$f_1 = f_2 = \cdots = f_n = 0$
Second-order sufficient condition[†]	$|H_1| < 0; |H_2| > 0;$ $|H_3| < 0; \ldots; (-1)^n|H_n| > 0$	$|H_1|, |H_2|, \ldots, |H_n| > 0$

[†] Applicable only after the first-order necessary condition has been satisfied.

with leading principal minors $|H_1|, |H_2|, \ldots, |H_n|$, as defined before. The second-order sufficient condition for extremum is, as before, that all those principal minors be positive (for a minimum in z) and that they duly alternate in sign (for a maximum in z), the first one being negative.

In summary, then—if we concentrate on the determinantal test—we have the criteria as listed in Table 11.2, which is valid for an objective function of any number of choice variables. As special cases, we can have $n = 1$ or $n = 2$. When $n = 1$, the objective function is $z = f(x)$, and the conditions for maximization, $f_1 = 0$ and $|H_1| < 0$, reduce to $f'(x) = 0$ and $f''(x) < 0$, exactly as we learned in Sec. 9.4. Similarly, when $n = 2$, the objective function is $z = f(x_1, x_2)$, so that the first-order condition for maximum is $f_1 = f_2 = 0$, whereas the second-order sufficient condition becomes

$$f_{11} < 0 \qquad \text{and} \qquad \begin{vmatrix} f_{11} & f_{12} \\ f_{21} & f_{22} \end{vmatrix} = f_{11}f_{22} - f_{12}^2 > 0$$

which is merely a restatement of the information presented in Table 11.1.

EXERCISE 11.4

Find the extreme values, if any, of the following four functions. Check whether they are maxima or minima by the determinantal test.

1. $z = x_1^2 + 3x_2^2 - 3x_1 x_2 + 4x_2 x_3 + 6x_3^2$
2. $z = 29 - \left(x_1^2 + x_2^2 + x_3^2\right)$
3. $z = x_1 x_3 + x_1^2 - x_2 + x_2 x_3 + x_2^2 + 3x_3^2$
4. $z = e^{2x} + e^{-y} + e^{w^2} - (2x + 2e^w - y)$

Then answer the following questions regarding Hessian matrices and their characteristic roots.

5. (a) Which of Probs. 1 through 4 yield diagonal Hessian matrices? In each such case, do the diagonal elements possess a uniform sign?
   (b) What can you conclude about the characteristic roots of each diagonal Hessian matrix found? About the sign definiteness of $d^2 z$?
   (c) Do the results of the characteristic-root test check with those of the determinantal test?
6. (a) Find the characteristic roots of the Hessian matrix for Prob. 3.
   (b) What can you conclude from your results?
   (c) Is your answer to (b) consistent with the result of the determinantal test for Prob. 3?

11.5   Second-Order Conditions in Relation to Concavity and Convexity

Second-order conditions—whether stated in terms of the principal minors of the Hessian determinant or the characteristic roots of the Hessian matrix—are always concerned with the question of whether a stationary point is the peak of a hill or the bottom of a valley. In other words, they relate to how a curve, surface, or hypersurface (as the case may be) bends itself around a stationary point. In the single-choice-variable case, with $z = f(x)$, the hill (valley) configuration is manifest in an inverse (U-shaped) curve. For the two-variable function $z = f(x, y)$, the hill (valley) configuration takes the form of a dome-shaped (bowl-shaped) surface, as illustrated in Fig. 11.2a (Fig. 11.2b). When three or more choice variables are present, the hills and valleys are no longer graphable, but we may nevertheless think of "hills" and "valleys" on hypersurfaces.

A function that gives rise to a hill (valley) over the entire domain is said to be a *concave* (*convex*) function.[†] For the present discussion, we shall take the domain to be the entire R^n, where n is the number of choice variables. Inasmuch as the hill and valley characterizations refer to the entire domain, concavity and convexity are, of course, global concepts. For a finer classification, we may also distinguish between concavity and convexity on the one hand, and *strict* concavity and *strict* convexity on the other hand. In the *non*strict case, the hill or valley is allowed to contain one or more flat (as against curved) portions, such as line segments (on a curve) or plane segments (on a surface). The presence of the word *strict,* however, rules out such line or plane segments. The two surfaces shown in Fig. 11.2 illustrate strictly concave and strictly convex functions, respectively. The curve in Fig. 6.5, on the other hand, is convex (it shows a valley) but not strictly convex (it contains line segments). A strictly concave (strictly convex) function must be concave (convex), but the converse is not true.

In view of the association of concavity and strict concavity with a global hill configuration, an extremum of a concave function must be a peak—a maximum (as against minimum). Moreover, that maximum must be an absolute maximum (as against relative maximum), since the hill covers the entire domain. However, that absolute maximum may not be unique, because multiple maxima may occur if the hill contains a flat horizontal top. The latter possibility can be dismissed only when we specify strict concavity. For only then will the peak consist of a single point and the absolute maximum be *unique*. A unique (nonunique) absolute maximum is also referred to as a *strong (weak)* absolute maximum.

By analogous reasoning, an extremum of a *convex* function must be an absolute (or global) minimum, which may not be unique. But an extremum of a *strictly convex* function must be a unique absolute minimum.

In the preceding paragraphs, the properties of concavity and convexity are taken to be global in scope. If they are valid only for a portion of the curve or surface (only on a subset S of the domain), then the associated maximum and minimum are relative (or local) to that subset of the domain, since we cannot be certain of the situation outside of subset S. In our earlier discussion of the sign definiteness of d^2z (or of the Hessian matrix H), we evaluated the leading principal minors of the Hessian determinant only at the stationary point. By thus limiting the verification of the hill or valley configuration to a small neighborhood of the stationary point, we could discuss only *relative* maxima and minima. But it may

---

[†] If the hill (valley) pertains only to a subset S of the domain, the function is said to be *concave (convex) on S.*

happen that d^2z has a definite sign everywhere, regardless of where the leading principal minors are evaluated. In that event, the hill or valley would cover the entire domain, and the maximum or minimum found would be absolute in nature. More specifically, if d^2z is *everywhere* negative (positive) semidefinite, the function $z = f(x_1, x_2, \ldots, x_n)$ must be concave (convex), and if d^2z is *everywhere* negative (positive) definite, the function f must be strictly concave (strictly convex).

The preceding discussion is summarized in Fig. 11.5 for a twice continuously differen-tiable function $z = f(x_1, x_2, \ldots, x_n)$. For clarity, we concentrate exclusively on concavity and maximum; however, the relationships depicted will remain valid if the words *concave, negative,* and *maximum* are replaced, respectively, by *convex, positive,* and *minimum.* To read

FIGURE 11.5

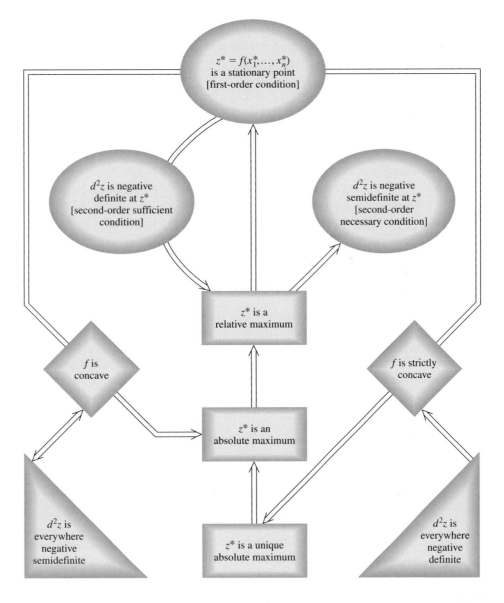

Fig. 11.5, recall that the $\Rightarrow$ symbol (here elongated and even bent) means "implies." When that symbol extends from one enclosure (say, a rectangle) to another (say, an oval), it means that the former implies (is sufficient for) the latter; it also means that the latter is necessary for the former. And when the $\Rightarrow$ symbol extends from one enclosure through a second to a third, it means that the first enclosure, when accompanied by the second, implies the third.

In this light, the middle column in Fig. 11.5, read from top to bottom, states that the first-order condition is necessary for z^* to be a relative maximum, and the relative-maximum status of z^* is, in turn, necessary for z^* to be an absolute maximum, and so on. Alternatively, reading that column from bottom to top, we see that the fact that z^* is a unique absolute maximum is sufficient to establish z^* as an absolute maximum, and the absolute-maximum status of z^* is, in turn, sufficient for z^* to be a relative maximum, and so forth. The three ovals at the top have to do with the first- and second-order conditions at the stationary point z^*. Hence they relate only to a relative maximum. The diamonds and triangles in the lower part, on the other hand, describe global properties that enable us to draw conclusions about an absolute maximum. Note that while our earlier discussion indicated only that the everywhere negative semidefiniteness of d^2z is *sufficient* for the concavity of function f, we have added in Fig. 11.5 the information that the condition is *necessary*, too. In contrast, the stronger property of everywhere negative definiteness of d^2z is *sufficient*, but *not necessary*, for the strict concavity of f—because strict concavity of f is compatible with a zero value of d^2z at a stationary point.

The most important message conveyed by Fig. 11.5, however, lies in the two extended $\Rightarrow$ symbols passing through the two diamonds. The one on the left states that, given a *concave* objective function, any stationary point can immediately be identified as an absolute maximum. Proceeding a step further, we see that the one on the right indicates that if the objective function is *strictly* concave, the stationary point must in fact be a unique absolute maximum. In either case, once the first-order condition is met, concavity or strict concavity effectively replaces the second-order condition as a sufficient condition for maximum—nay, for an absolute maximum. The powerfulness of this new sufficient condition becomes clear when we recall that d^2z can happen to be zero at a peak, causing the second-order sufficient condition to fail. Concavity or strict concavity, however, can take care of even such troublesome peaks, because it guarantees that a higher-order sufficient condition is satisfied even if the second-order one is not. It is for this reason that economists often assume concavity from the very outset when a maximization model is to be formulated with a *general* objective function (and, similarly, convexity is often assumed for a minimization model). For then all one needs to do is to apply the first-order condition. Note, however, that if a *specific* objective function is used, the property of concavity or convexity can no longer simply be assumed. Rather, it must be checked.

Checking Concavity and Convexity

Concavity and convexity, strict or nonstrict, can be defined (and checked) in several ways. We shall first introduce a geometric definition of concavity and convexity for a two-variable function $z = f(x_1, x_2)$, similar to the one-variable version discussed in Sec. 9.3:

> The function $z = f(x_1, x_2)$ is *concave (convex)* iff, for any pair of distinct points M and N on its graph—a surface—line segment MN lies either *on* or *below (above)* the surface. The function is *strictly concave (strictly convex)* iff line segment MN lies entirely *below (above)* the surface, except at M and N.

FIGURE 11.6

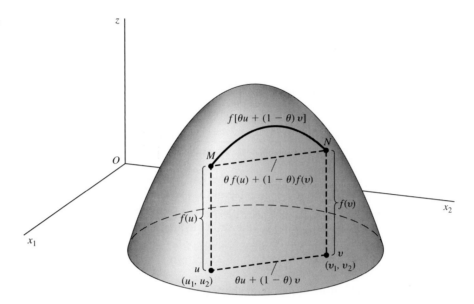

The case of a strictly concave function is illustrated in Fig. 11.6, where M and N, two arbitrary points on the surface, are joined together by a broken line segment as well as a solid arc, with the latter consisting of points on the surface that lie directly above the line segment. Since strict concavity requires line segment MN to lie entirely below arc MN (except at M and N) for *any* pair of points M and N, the surface must typically be dome-shaped. Analogously, the surface of a strictly convex function must typically be bowl-shaped. As for (nonstrictly) concave and convex functions, since line segment MN is allowed to lie on the surface itself, some portion of the surface, or even the entire surface, may be a plane—flat, rather than curved.

   To facilitate generalization to the nongraphable *n*-dimensional case, the geometric definition needs to be translated into an equivalent algebraic version. Returning to Fig. 11.6, let $u = (u_1, u_2)$ and $v = (v_1, v_2)$ be any two distinct ordered pairs (2-vectors) in the domain of $z = f(x_1, x_2)$. Then the z values (height of surface) corresponding to these will be $f(u) = f(u_1, u_2)$ and $f(v) = f(v_1, v_2)$, respectively. We have assumed that the variables can take all real values, so if u and v are in the domain, then all the points on the line segment uv are also in the domain. Now each point on the said line segment is in the nature of a "weighted average" of u and v. Thus we can denote this line segment by $\theta u + (1 - \theta)v$, where θ (the Greek letter theta)—unlike u and v—is a (variable) scalar with the range of values $0 \le \theta \le 1$.[†] By the same token, line segment MN, representing the set of all weighted averages of $f(u)$ and $f(v)$, can be expressed by $\theta f(u) + (1 - \theta)f(v)$, with θ again varying from 0 to 1. What about arc MN along the surface? Since that arc shows the

---

[†] The weighted-average expression $\theta u + (1 - \theta)v$, for any specific value of θ between 0 and 1, is technically known as a *convex combination* of the two vectors u and v. Leaving a more detailed explanation of this to a later point of this section, we may note here that when $\theta = 0$, the given expression reduces to vector v and similarly that when $\theta = 1$, the expression reduces to vector u. An intermediate value of θ, on the other hand, gives us an average of the two vectors u and v.

values of the function f evaluated at the various points on line segment uv, it can be written simply as $f[\theta u + (1 - \theta)v]$. Using these expressions, we may now state the following algebraic definition:

A function f is $\begin{Bmatrix} \text{concave} \\ \text{convex} \end{Bmatrix}$ iff, for any pair of distinct points u and v in the domain of f, and

for $0 < \theta < 1$,

$$\underbrace{\theta f(u) + (1 - \theta)f(v)}_{\text{height of line segment}} \begin{Bmatrix} \leq \\ \geq \end{Bmatrix} \underbrace{f[\theta u + (1 - \theta)v]}_{\text{height of arc}} \tag{11.20}$$

Note that, in order to exclude the two end points M and N from the height comparison, we have restricted θ to the open interval $(0, 1)$ only.

This definition is easily adaptable to *strict* concavity and convexity by changing the weak inequalities $\leq$ and $\geq$ to the strict inequalities $<$ and $>$, respectively. The advantage of the algebraic definition is that it can be applied to a function of any number of variables, for the vectors u and v in the definition can very well be interpreted as n-vectors instead of 2-vectors.

From (11.20), the following three theorems on concavity and convexity can be deduced fairly easily. These will be stated in terms of functions $f(x)$ and $g(x)$, but x can be interpreted as a vector of variables; that is, the theorems are valid for functions of any number of variables.

Theorem I (linear function) If $f(x)$ is a linear function, then it is a concave function as well as a convex function, but not strictly so.

Theorem II (negative of a function) If $f(x)$ is a concave function, then $-f(x)$ is a convex function, and vice versa. Similarly, if $f(x)$ is a strictly concave function, then $-f(x)$ is a strictly convex function, and vice versa.

Theorem III (sum of functions) If $f(x)$ and $g(x)$ are both concave (convex) functions, then $f(x) + g(x)$ is also a concave (convex) function. If $f(x)$ and $g(x)$ are both concave (convex) and, in addition, either one or both of them are strictly concave (strictly convex), then $f(x) + g(x)$ is strictly concave (strictly convex).

Theorem I follows from the fact that a linear function plots as a straight line, plane, or hyperplane, so that "line segment MN" always coincides with "arc MN." Consequently, the equality part of the two weak inequalities in (11.20) are simultaneously satisfied, making the function qualify as both concave and convex. However, since it fails the strict-inequality part of the definition, the linear function is neither strictly concave nor strictly convex.

Underlying Theorem II is the fact that the definitions of concavity and convexity differ only in the sense of inequality. Suppose that $f(x)$ is concave; then

$$\theta f(u) + (1 - \theta)f(v) \leq f[\theta u + (1 - \theta)v]$$

Multiplying through by -1, and duly reversing the sense of the inequality, we get

$$\theta[-f(u)] + (1 - \theta)[-f(v)] \geq -f[\theta u + (1 - \theta)v]$$

This, however, is precisely the condition for $-f(x)$ to be convex. Thus the theorem is proved for the concave $f(x)$ case. The geometric interpretation of this result is very simple: the mirror image of a hill with reference to the base plane or hyperplane is a valley. The opposite case can be proved similarly.

To see the reason behind Theorem III, suppose that $f(x)$ and $g(x)$ are both concave. Then the following two inequalities hold:

$$\theta f(u) + (1 - \theta) f(v) \leq f[\theta u + (1 - \theta)v] \qquad \textbf{(11.21)}$$

$$\theta g(u) + (1 - \theta) g(v) \leq g[\theta u + (1 - \theta)v] \qquad \textbf{(11.22)}$$

Adding these, we obtain a new inequality

$$\theta[f(u) + g(u)] + (1 - \theta)[f(v) + g(v)]$$
$$\leq f[\theta u + (1 - \theta)v] + g[\theta u + (1 - \theta)v] \qquad \textbf{(11.23)}$$

But this is precisely the condition for $[f(x) + g(x)]$ to be concave. Thus the theorem is proved for the concave case. The proof for the convex case is similar.

Moving to the second part of Theorem III, let $f(x)$ be *strictly* concave. Then (11.21) becomes a *strict* inequality:

$$\theta f(u) + (1 - \theta) f(v) < f[\theta u + (1 - \theta)v] \qquad \textbf{(11.21′)}$$

Adding this to (11.22), we find the sum of the left-side expressions in these two inequalities to be *strictly* less than the sum of the right-side expressions, regardless of whether the $<$ sign or the $=$ sign holds in (11.22). This means that (11.23) now becomes a *strict* inequality, too, thereby making $[f(x) + g(x)]$ *strictly* concave. Besides, the same conclusion emerges a fortiori, if $g(x)$ is made strictly concave along with $f(x)$, that is, if (11.22) is converted into a strict inequality along with (11.21). This proves the second part of the theorem for the concave case. The proof for the convex case is similar.

This theorem, which is also valid for a sum of more than two concave (convex) functions, may prove useful sometimes because it makes possible the compartmentalization of the task of checking concavity or convexity of a function that consists of additive terms. If the additive terms are found to be individually concave (convex), that would be sufficient for the sum function to be concave (convex).

Example 1

Check $z = x_1^2 + x_2^2$ for concavity or convexity. To apply (11.20), let $u = (u_1, u_2)$ and $v = (v_1, v_2)$ be any two distinct points in the domain. Then we have

$$f(u) = f(u_1, u_2) = u_1^2 + u_2^2$$
$$f(v) = f(v_1, v_2) = v_1^2 + v_2^2$$

and
$$f[\theta u + (1 - \theta)v] = f\left[\underbrace{\theta u_1 + (1 - \theta)v_1}_{\text{value of } x_1}, \underbrace{\theta u_2 + (1 - \theta)v_2}_{\text{value of } x_2}\right]$$

$$= [\theta u_1 + (1 - \theta)v_1]^2 + [\theta u_2 + (1 - \theta)v_2]^2$$

Substituting these into (11.20), subtracting the right-side expression from the left-side one, and collecting terms, we find their difference to be

$$\theta(1 - \theta)\left(u_1^2 + u_2^2\right) + \theta(1 - \theta)\left(v_1^2 + v_2^2\right) - 2\theta(1 - \theta)(u_1 v_1 + u_2 v_2)$$

$$= \theta(1 - \theta)[(u_1 - v_1)^2 + (u_2 - v_2)^2]$$

Since θ is a positive fraction, $\theta(1 - \theta)$ must be positive. Moreover, since (u_1, u_2) and (v_1, v_2) are distinct points, so that either $u_1 \neq v_1$ or $u_2 \neq v_2$ (or both), the bracketed expression must also be positive. Thus the strict > inequality holds in (11.20), and $z = x_1^2 + x_2^2$ is strictly convex.

Alternatively, we may check the x_1^2 and x_2^2 terms separately. Since each of them is individually strictly convex, their sum is also strictly convex.

Because this function is strictly convex, it possesses a unique absolute minimum. It is easy to verify that the said minimum is $z^* = 0$, attained at $x_1^* = x_2^* = 0$, and that it is indeed absolute and unique because any ordered pair $(x_1, x_2) \neq (0, 0)$ yields a z value greater than zero.

Example 2   Check $z = -x_1^2 - x_2^2$ for concavity or convexity. This function is the negative of the function in Example 1. Thus, by Theorem II, it is strictly concave.

Example 3   Check $z = (x + y)^2$ for concavity or convexity. Even though the variables are denoted by x and y instead of x_1 and x_2, we can still let $u = (u_1, u_2)$ and $v = (v_1, v_2)$ denote two distinct points in the domain, with the subscript i referring to the ith variable. Then we have

$$f(u) = f(u_1, u_2) = (u_1 + u_2)^2$$
$$f(v) = f(v_1, v_2) = (v_1 + v_2)^2$$

and
$$f[\theta u + (1 - \theta)v] = [\theta u_1 + (1 - \theta)v_1 + \theta u_2 + (1 - \theta)v_2]^2$$
$$= [\theta(u_1 + u_2) + (1 - \theta)(v_1 + v_2)]^2$$

Substituting these into (11.20), subtracting the right-side expression from the left-side one, and simplifying, we find their difference to be

$$\theta(1 - \theta)(u_1 + u_2)^2 - 2\theta(1 - \theta)(u_1 + u_2)(v_1 + v_2) + \theta(1 - \theta)(v_1 + v_2)^2$$
$$= \theta(1 - \theta)[(u_1 + u_2) - (v_1 + v_2)]^2$$

As in Example 1, $\theta(1 - \theta)$ is positive. The square of the bracketed expression is nonnegative (zero cannot be ruled out this time). Thus the $\geq$ inequality holds in (11.20), and the function $(x + y)^2$ is convex, though not strictly so.

Accordingly, this function has an absolute minimum that may not be unique. It is easy to verify that the absolute minimum is $z^* = 0$, attained whenever $x^* + y^* = 0$. That this is an absolute minimum is clear from the fact that whenever $x + y \neq 0$, z will be greater than $z^* = 0$. That it is not unique follows from the fact that an infinite number of (x^*, y^*), pairs can satisfy the condition $x^* + y^* = 0$.

Differentiable Functions

As stated in (11.20), the definition of concavity and convexity uses no derivatives and thus does not require differentiability. If the function *is* differentiable, however, concavity and convexity can also be defined in terms of its first derivatives. In the one-variable case, the definition is:

A differentiable function $f(x)$ is $\left\{ \begin{matrix} \text{concave} \\ \text{convex} \end{matrix} \right\}$ iff, for any given point u and any other point v in the domain,

$$f(v) \left\{ \begin{matrix} \leq \\ \geq \end{matrix} \right\} f(u) + f'(u)(v - u) \qquad \qquad \text{(11.24)}$$

FIGURE 11.7

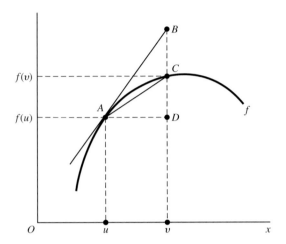

Concavity and convexity will be *strict,* if the weak inequalities in (11.24) are replaced by the *strict* inequalities < and >, respectively. Interpreted geometrically, this definition depicts a concave (convex) curve as one that lies on or below (above) all its tangent lines. To qualify as a strictly concave (strictly convex) curve, on the other hand, the curve must lie strictly below (above) all the tangent lines, except at the points of tangency.

In Fig. 11.7, let point A be any given point on the curve, with height $f(u)$ and with tangent line AB. Let x increase from the value u. Then a strictly concave curve (as drawn) must, in order to form a hill, curl progressively away from the tangent line AB, so that point C, with height $f(v)$, has to lie below point B. In this case, the slope of line segment AC is less than that of tangent AB. If the curve is *non*strictly concave, on the other hand, it may contain a line segment, so that, for instance, arc AC may turn into a line segment and be coincident with line segment AB, as a linear portion of the curve. In the latter case the slope of AC is equal to that of AB. Together, these two situations imply that

$$\left(\text{Slope of line segment } AC = \frac{DC}{AD} =\right) \frac{f(v) - f(u)}{v - u} \leq (\text{slope of } AB =) f'(u)$$

When multiplied through by the positive quantity $(v - u)$, this inequality yields the result in (11.24) for the concave function. The same result can be obtained, if we consider instead x values less than u.

When there are two or more independent variables, the definition needs a slight modification:

A differentiable function $f(x) = f(x_1, \ldots, x_n)$ is $\left\{\begin{array}{c}\text{concave}\\\text{convex}\end{array}\right\}$ iff, for any given point $u = (u_1, \ldots, u_n)$ and any other point $v = (v_1, \ldots, v_n)$ in the domain,

$$f(v) \left\{\begin{array}{c}\leq\\\geq\end{array}\right\} f(u) + \sum_{j=1}^{n} f_j(u)(v_j - u_j) \qquad \text{(11.24')}$$

where $f_j(u) \equiv \partial f / \partial x_j$ is evaluated at $u = (u_1, \ldots, u_n)$.

This definition requires the graph of a concave (convex) function $f(x)$ to lie on or below (above) all its tangent planes or hyperplanes. For *strict* concavity and convexity, the weak inequalities in (11.24') should be changed to *strict* inequalities, which would require the graph of a strictly concave (strictly convex) function to lie strictly below (above) all its tangent planes or hyperplanes, except at the points of tangency.

Finally, consider a function $z = f(x_1, \ldots, x_n)$ which is twice continuously differentiable. For such a function, second-order partial derivatives exist, and thus d^2z is defined. Concavity and convexity can then be checked by the sign of d^2z:

A twice continuously differentiable function $z = f(x_1, \ldots, x_n)$ is $\begin{Bmatrix} \text{concave} \\ \text{convex} \end{Bmatrix}$ if, and only

if, d^2z is everywhere $\begin{Bmatrix} \text{negative} \\ \text{positive} \end{Bmatrix}$ semidefinite. The said function is strictly $\begin{Bmatrix} \text{concave} \\ \text{convex} \end{Bmatrix}$ if

(but *not* only if) d^2z is everywhere $\begin{Bmatrix} \text{negative} \\ \text{positive} \end{Bmatrix}$ definite. **(11.25)**

You will recall that the concave and strictly concave aspects of (11.25) have already been incorporated into Fig. 11.5.

Example 4

Check $z = -x^4$ for concavity or convexity by the derivative conditions. We first apply (11.24). The left- and right-side expressions in that inequality are in the present case $-v^4$ and $-u^4 - 4u^3(v - u)$, respectively. Subtracting the latter from the former, we find their difference to be

$$-v^4 + u^4 + 4u^3(v - u) = (v - u)\left(-\frac{v^4 - u^4}{v - u} + 4u^3 \right) \qquad \text{[factoring]}$$

$$= (v - u)[-(v^3 + v^2u + vu^2 + u^3) + 4u^3] \qquad \text{[by (7.2)]}$$

It would be nice if the bracketed expression turned out to be divisible by $(v - u)$, for then we could again factor out $(v - u)$ and obtain a squared term $(v - u)^2$ to facilitate the evaluation of sign. As it turns out, this is indeed the case. Thus the preceding difference equation can be written as

$$-(v - u)^2[v^2 + 2vu + 3u^2] = -(v - u)^2[(v + u)^2 + 2u^2]$$

Given that $v \neq u$, the sign of this expression must be negative. With the strict $<$ inequality holding in (11.24), the function $z = -x^4$ is strictly concave. This means that it has a unique absolute maximum. As can be easily verified, that maximum is $z^* = 0$, attained at $x^* = 0$.

Because this function is twice continuously differentiable, we may also apply (11.25). Since there is only one variable, (11.25) gives us

$$d^2z = f''(x)\, dx^2 = -12x^2\, dx^2 \qquad \text{[by (11.2)]}$$

We know that dx^2 is positive (only nonzero changes in x are being considered); but $-12x^2$ can be either negative or zero. Thus the best we can do is to conclude that d^2z is everywhere negative *semi*definite, and that $z = -x^4$ is (nonstrictly) concave. This conclusion from (11.25) is obviously weaker than the one obtained earlier from (11.24); namely, $z = -x^4$ is strictly concave. What limits us to the weaker conclusion in this case is the same culprit that causes the second-derivative test to fail on occasions—the fact that d^2z may take a zero value at a stationary point of a function known to be strictly concave, or strictly convex. This is why, of course, the negative (positive) definiteness of d^2z is presented in (11.25) as only a sufficient, but not necessary, condition for strict concavity (strict convexity).

Example 5   Check $z = x_1^2 + x_2^2$ for concavity or convexity by the derivative conditions. This time we have to use (11.24′) instead of (11.24). With $u = (u_1, u_2)$ and $v = (v_1, v_2)$ as any two points in the domain, the two sides of (11.24′) are

$$\text{Left side} = v_1^2 + v_2^2$$
$$\text{Right side} = u_1^2 + u_2^2 + 2u_1(v_1 - u_1) + 2u_2(v_2 - u_2)$$

Subtracting the latter from the former, and simplifying, we can express their difference as

$$v_1^2 - 2v_1 u_1 + u_1^2 + v_2^2 - 2v_2 u_2 + u_2^2 = (v_1 - u_1)^2 + (v_2 - u_2)^2$$

Given that $(v_1, v_2) \neq (u_1, u_2)$, this difference is always positive. Thus the strict $>$ inequality holds in (11.24′), and $z = x_1^2 + x_2^2$ is strictly convex. Note that the present result merely reaffirms what we have previously found in Example 1.

As for the use of (11.25), since $f_1 = 2x_1$, and $f_2 = 2x_2$, we have

$$f_{11} = 2 > 0 \qquad \text{and} \qquad \begin{vmatrix} f_{11} & f_{12} \\ f_{21} & f_{22} \end{vmatrix} = \begin{vmatrix} 2 & 0 \\ 0 & 2 \end{vmatrix} = 4 > 0$$

regardless of where the second-order partial derivatives are evaluated. Thus $d^2 z$ is everywhere positive definite, which duly satisfies the sufficient condition for strict convexity. In the present example, therefore, (11.24′) and (11.25) do yield the same conclusion.

Convex Functions versus Convex Sets

Having clarified the meaning of the adjective *convex* as applied to a function, we must hasten to explain its meaning when used to describe a *set*. Although convex sets and convex functions are not unrelated, they are distinct concepts, and it is important not to confuse them.

For easier intuitive grasp, let us begin with the geometric characterization of a convex set. Let S be a set of points in a 2-space or 3-space. If, for any two points in set S, the line segment connecting these two points lies entirely in S, then S is said to be a *convex set*. It should be obvious that a straight line satisfies this definition and constitutes a convex set. By convention, a set consisting of a single point is also considered as a convex set, and so is the null set (with no point). For additional examples, let us look at Fig. 11.8. The disk—namely, the "solid" circle, a circle plus all the points within it—is a convex set, because a line joining any two points in the disk lies entirely in the disk, as exemplified by *ab* (linking two boundary points) and *cd* (linking two interior points). Note, however, that a

FIGURE 11.8

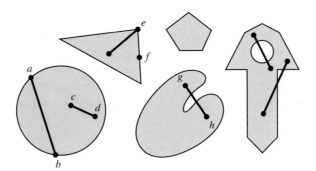

FIGURE 11.9

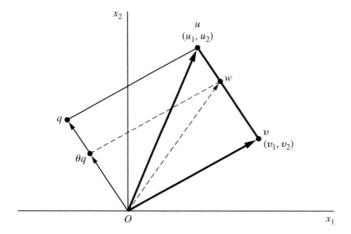

(hollow) circle is *not* in itself a convex set. Similarly, a triangle, or a pentagon, is not in itself a convex set, but its solid version is. The remaining two solid figures in Fig. 11.8 are not convex sets. The palette-shaped figure is reentrant (indented); thus a line segment such as *gh* does not lie entirely in the set. In the key-shaped figure, moreover, we find not only the feature of reentrance, but also the presence of a hole, which is yet another cause of nonconvexity. Generally speaking, to qualify as a convex set, the set of points must contain no holes, and its boundary must not be indented anywhere.

The geometric definition of convexity also applies readily to point sets in a 3-space. For instance, a solid cube is a convex set, whereas a hollow cylinder is not. When a 4-space or a space of higher dimension is involved, however, the geometric interpretation becomes less obvious. We then need to turn to the algebraic definition of convex sets.

To this end, it is useful to introduce the concept of *convex combination* of vectors (points), which is a special type of linear combination. A linear combination of two vectors *u* and *v* can be written as

$$k_1 u + k_2 v$$

where k_1 and k_2 are two scalars. When these two scalars both lie in the closed interval $[0, 1]$ and add up to unity, the linear combination is said to be a convex combination, and can be expressed as

$$\theta u + (1 - \theta)v \qquad (0 \leq \theta \leq 1) \tag{11.26}$$

As an illustration, the combination $\dfrac{1}{3}\begin{bmatrix} 2 \\ 0 \end{bmatrix} + \dfrac{2}{3}\begin{bmatrix} 4 \\ 9 \end{bmatrix}$ is a convex combination. In view of the fact that these two scalar multipliers are positive fractions adding up to 1, such a convex combination may be interpreted as a *weighted average* of the two vectors.[†]

The unique characteristic of the combination in (11.26) is that, for every acceptable value of θ, the resulting sum vector lies on the line segment connecting the points *u* and *v*. This can be demonstrated by means of Fig. 11.9, where we have plotted two vectors $u = \begin{bmatrix} u_1 \\ u_2 \end{bmatrix}$ and $v = \begin{bmatrix} v_1 \\ v_2 \end{bmatrix}$ as two points with coordinates (u_1, u_2) and (v_1, v_2), respectively.

[†] This interpretation has been made use of earlier in the discussion of concave and convex functions.

If we plot another vector q such that $Oquv$ forms a parallelogram, then we have (by virtue of the discussion in Fig. 4.3)

$$u = q + v \qquad \text{or} \qquad q = u - v$$

It follows that a convex combination of vectors u and v (let us call it w) can be expressed in terms of vector q, because

$$w = \theta u + (1 - \theta)v = \theta u + v - \theta v = \theta(u - v) + v = \theta q + v$$

Hence, to plot the vector w, we can simply add θq and v by the familiar parallelogram method. If the scalar θ is a positive fraction, the vector θq will merely be an abridged version of vector q; thus θq must lie on the line segment Oq. Adding θq and v, therefore, we must find vector w lying on the line segment uv, for the new, smaller parallelogram is nothing but the original parallelogram with the qu side shifted downward. The exact location of vector w will, of course, vary according to the value of the scalar θ; by varying θ from zero to unity, the location of w will shift from v to u. Thus the set of all points on the line segment uv, including u and v themselves, corresponds to the set of all convex combinations of vectors u and v.

In view of the preceding, a convex set may now be redefined as follows: A set S is convex if and only if, for any two points $u \in S$ and $v \in S$, and for every scalar $\theta \in [0, 1]$, it is true that $w = \theta u + (1 - \theta)v \in S$. Because this definition is algebraic, it is applicable regardless of the dimension of the space in which the vectors u and v are located. Comparing this definition of a convex set with that of a convex function in (11.20), we see that even though the same adjective *convex* is used in both, the meaning of this word changes radically from one context to the other. In describing a *function,* the word *convex* specifies how a curve or surface bends itself—it must form a valley. But in describing a *set,* the word specifies how the points in the set are "packed" together—they must not allow any holes to arise, and the boundary must not be indented. Thus convex functions and convex sets are clearly distinct mathematical entities.

Yet convex functions and convex sets are not unrelated. For one thing, in defining a convex function, we need a convex set for the domain. This is because the definition (11.20) requires that, for any two points u and v in the domain, all the convex combinations of u and v—specifically, $\theta u + (1 - \theta)v, 0 \le \theta \le 1$—must also be in the domain, which is, of course, just another way of saying that the domain must be a convex set. To satisfy this requirement, we adopted earlier the rather strong assumption that the domain consists of the entire n-space (where n is the number of choice variables), which is indeed a convex set. However, with the concept of convex sets at our disposal, we can now substantially weaken that assumption. For all we need to assume is that the domain is a convex subset of R^n, rather than R^n itself.

There is yet another way in which convex functions are related to convex sets. If $f(x)$ is a convex function, then for any constant k, it can give rise to a convex set

$$S^{\le} \equiv \{x \mid f(x) \le k\} \qquad [f(x) \text{ convex}] \qquad \textbf{(11.27)}$$

This is illustrated in Fig. 11.10*a* for the one-variable case. The set $S^{\le}$ consists of all the x values associated with the segment of the $f(x)$ curve lying on or below the broken horizontal line. Hence it is the line segment on the horizontal axis marked by the heavy dots,

FIGURE 11.10

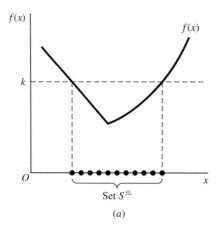

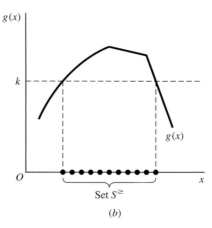

(a)

(b)

which is a convex set. Note that if the k value is changed, the $S^\leq$ set will become a different line segment on the horizontal axis, but it will still be a convex set.

Going a step further, we may observe that even a *concave* function is related to convex sets in ways similar. First, the definition of a concave function in (11.20) is, like the convex-function case, predicated upon a domain that is a convex set. Moreover, even a concave function—say, $g(x)$—can generate an associated convex set, given some constant k. That convex set is

$$S^\geq \equiv \{x \mid g(x) \geq k\} \qquad [g(x) \text{ concave}] \qquad \textbf{(11.28)}$$

in which the $\geq$ sign appears instead of $\leq$. Geometrically, as shown in Fig. 11.10b for the one-variable case, the set $S^\geq$ contains all the x values corresponding to the segment of the $g(x)$ curve lying on or above the broken horizontal line. Thus it is again a line segment on the horizontal axis—a convex set.

Although Fig. 11.10 specifically illustrates the one-variable case, the definitions of $S^\leq$ and $S^\geq$ in (11.27) and (11.28) are not limited to functions of a single variable. They are equally valid if we interpret x to be a vector, i.e., let $x = (x_1, \ldots, x_n)$. In that case, however, (11.27) and (11.28) will define convex sets in the n-space instead. It is important to remember that while a convex function implies (11.27), and a concave function implies (11.28), the converse is not true—for (11.27) can also be satisfied by a nonconvex function and (11.28) by a nonconcave function. This is discussed further in Sec. 12.4.

EXERCISE 11.5

1. Use (11.20) to check whether the following functions are concave, convex, strictly concave, strictly convex, or neither:

   (a) $z = x^2$ (b) $z = x_1^2 + 2x_2^2$ (c) $z = 2x^2 - xy + y^2$

2. Use (11.24) or (11.24′) to check whether the following functions are concave, convex, strictly concave, strictly convex, or neither:

   (a) $z = -x^2$ (b) $z = (x_1 + x_2)^2$ (c) $z = -xy$

3. In view of your answer to Prob. 2c, could you have made use of Theorem III of this section to compartmentalize the task of checking the function $z = 2x^2 - xy + y^2$ in Prob. 1c? Explain your answer.

4. Do the following constitute convex sets in the 3-space?

   (*a*) A doughnut   (*b*) A bowling pin   (*c*) A perfect marble

5. The equation $x^2 + y^2 = 4$ represents a circle with center at $(0, 0)$ and with a radius of 2.

   (*a*) Interpret geometrically the set $\{(x, y) \mid x^2 + y^2 \leq 4\}$.

   (*b*) Is this set convex?

6. Graph each of the following sets, and indicate whether it is convex:

   (*a*) $\{(x, y) \mid y = e^x\}$ (*c*) $\{(x, y) \mid y \leq 13 - x^2\}$

   (*b*) $\{(x, y) \mid y \geq e^x\}$ (*d*) $\{(x, y) \mid xy \geq 1; x > 0, y > 0\}$

7. Given $u = \begin{bmatrix} 10 \\ 6 \end{bmatrix}$ and $v = \begin{bmatrix} 4 \\ 8 \end{bmatrix}$, which of the following are *convex* combinations of u and v?

   (*a*) $\begin{bmatrix} 7 \\ 7 \end{bmatrix}$ (*b*) $\begin{bmatrix} 5.2 \\ 7.6 \end{bmatrix}$ (*c*) $\begin{bmatrix} 6.2 \\ 8.2 \end{bmatrix}$

8. Given two vectors u and v in the 2-space, find and sketch:

   (*a*) The set of all linear combinations of u and v.

   (*b*) The set of all nonnegative linear combinations of u and v.

   (*c*) The set of all convex combinations of u and v.

9. (*a*) Rewrite (11.27) and (11.28) specifically for the cases where the f and g functions have n independent variables.

   (*b*) Let $n = 2$, and let the function f be shaped like a (vertically held) ice-cream cone whereas the function g is shaped like a pyramid. Describe the sets $S^{\leq}$ and $S^{\geq}$.

11.6 Economic Applications

At the beginning of this chapter, the case of a multiproduct firm was cited as an illustration of the general problem of optimization with more than one choice variable. We are now equipped to handle that problem and others of a similar nature.

Problem of a Multiproduct Firm

Example 1

Let us first postulate a two-product firm under circumstances of pure competition. Since with pure competition the prices of both commodities must be taken as exogenous, these will be denoted by P_{10} and P_{20}, respectively. Accordingly, the firm's revenue function will be

$$R_1 = P_{10} Q_1 + P_{20} Q_2$$

where Q_i represents the output level of the *i*th product per unit of time. The firm's cost function is assumed to be

$$C = 2Q_1^2 + Q_1 Q_2 + 2Q_2^2$$

Note that $\partial C / \partial Q_1 = 4Q_1 + Q_2$ (the marginal cost of the first product) is a function not only of Q_1 but also of Q_2. Similarly, the marginal cost of the second product also depends, in part, on the output level of the first product. Thus, according to the assumed cost function, the two commodities are seen to be technically related in production.

The profit function of this hypothetical firm can now be written readily as

$$\pi = R - C = P_{10} Q_1 + P_{20} Q_2 - 2Q_1^2 - Q_1 Q_2 - 2Q_2^2$$

a function of two choice variables (Q_1 and Q_2) and two price parameters. It is our task to find the levels of Q_1 and Q_2 which, in combination, will maximize π. For this purpose, we first find the first-order partial derivatives of the profit function:

$$\pi_1 \left(\equiv \frac{\partial \pi}{\partial Q_1} \right) = P_{10} - 4Q_1 - Q_2$$

$$\pi_2 \left(\equiv \frac{\partial \pi}{\partial Q_2} \right) = P_{20} - Q_1 - 4Q_2$$

(11.29)

Setting both equal to zero, to satisfy the necessary condition for a maximum, we get the two simultaneous equations

$$4Q_1 + Q_2 = P_{10}$$
$$Q_1 + 4Q_2 = P_{20}$$

which yield the unique solution

$$Q_1^* = \frac{4P_{10} - P_{20}}{15} \quad \text{and} \quad Q_2^* = \frac{4P_{20} - P_{10}}{15}$$

Thus, if $P_{10} = 12$ and $P_{20} = 18$, for example, we have $Q_1^* = 2$ and $Q_2^* = 4$, implying an optimal profit $\pi^* = 48$ per unit of time.

To be sure that this does represent a maximum profit, let us check the second-order condition. The second partial derivatives, obtainable by partial differentiation of (11.29), give us the following Hessian:

$$|H| = \begin{vmatrix} \pi_{11} & \pi_{12} \\ \pi_{21} & \pi_{22} \end{vmatrix} = \begin{vmatrix} -4 & -1 \\ -1 & -4 \end{vmatrix}$$

Since $|H_1| = -4 < 0$ and $|H_2| = 15 > 0$, the Hessian matrix (or $d^2 z$) is negative definite, and the solution does maximize the profit. In fact, since the signs of the leading principal minors do not depend on where they are evaluated, $d^2 z$ is in this case *everywhere* negative definite. Thus, according to (11.25), the objective function must be strictly concave, and the maximum profit just found is actually a unique absolute maximum.

Example 2   Let us now transplant the problem of Example 1 into the setting of a monopolistic market. By virtue of this new market-structure assumption, the revenue function must be modified to reflect the fact that the prices of the two products will now vary with their output levels (which are assumed to be identical with their sales levels, no inventory accumulation being contemplated in the model). The exact manner in which prices will vary with output levels is, of course, to be found in the demand functions for the firm's two products.

Suppose that the demands facing the monopolist firm are as follows:

$$Q_1 = 40 - 2P_1 + P_2$$
$$Q_2 = 15 + P_1 - P_2$$

(11.30)

These equations reveal that the two commodities are related in *consumption;* specifically, they are substitute goods, because an increase in the price of one will raise the demand for the other. As given, (11.30) expresses the quantities demanded Q_1 and Q_2 as functions of prices, but for our present purposes it will be more convenient to have prices P_1 and P_2 expressed in terms of the sales volumes Q_1 and Q_2, that is, to have average-revenue functions for the two products. Since (11.30) can be rewritten as

$$-2P_1 + P_2 = Q_1 - 40$$
$$P_1 - P_2 = Q_2 - 15$$

$$3P_1 = Q_1 - Q_2 - 55$$

we may (considering Q_1 and Q_2 as parameters) apply Cramer's rule to solve for P_1 and P_2 as follows:

$$P_1 = 55 - Q_1 - \ \ Q_2$$
$$P_2 = 70 - Q_1 - 2Q_2 \qquad \textbf{(11.30')}$$

These constitute the desired average-revenue functions, since $P_1 \equiv AR_1$ and $P_2 \equiv AR_2$. Consequently, the firm's total-revenue function can be written as

$$
\begin{aligned}
R &= P_1 Q_1 + P_2 Q_2 \\
&= (55 - Q_1 - Q_2)Q_1 + (70 - Q_1 - 2Q_2)Q_2 \qquad \text{[by (11.30')]} \\
&= 55Q_1 + 70Q_2 - 2Q_1 Q_2 - Q_1^2 - 2Q_2^2
\end{aligned}
$$

If we again assume the total-cost function to be

$$C = Q_1^2 + Q_1 Q_2 + Q_2^2$$

then the profit function will be

$$\pi = R - C = 55Q_1 + 70Q_2 - 3Q_1 Q_2 - 2Q_1^2 - 3Q_2^2 \qquad \textbf{(11.31)}$$

which is an objective function with two choice variables. Once the profit-maximizing output levels Q_1^* and Q_2^* are found, however, the optimal prices P_1^* and P_2^* are easy enough to find from (11.30').

The objective function yields the following first and second partial derivatives:

$$\pi_1 = 55 - 3Q_2 - 4Q_1 \qquad \pi_2 = 70 - 3Q_1 - 6Q_2$$
$$\pi_{11} = -4 \qquad \pi_{12} = \pi_{21} = -3 \qquad \pi_{22} = -6$$

To satisfy the first-order condition for a maximum of π, we must have $\pi_1 = \pi_2 = 0$; that is,

$$4Q_1 + 3Q_2 = 55$$
$$3Q_1 + 6Q_2 = 70$$

Thus the solution output levels (per unit of time) are

$$(Q_1^*, Q_2^*) = \left(8, 7\tfrac{2}{3}\right)$$

Upon substitution of this result into (11.30') and (11.31), respectively, we find that

$$P_1^* = 39\tfrac{1}{3} \qquad P_2^* = 46\tfrac{2}{3} \qquad \text{and} \qquad \pi^* = 488\tfrac{1}{3} \qquad \text{(per unit of time)}$$

Inasmuch as the Hessian is $\begin{vmatrix} -4 & -3 \\ -3 & -6 \end{vmatrix}$, we have

$$|H_1| = -4 < 0 \qquad \text{and} \qquad |H_2| = 15 > 0$$

so that the value of π^* does represent the maximum profit. Here, the signs of the leading principal minors are again independent of where they are evaluated. Thus the Hessian matrix is everywhere negative definite, implying that the objective function is strictly concave and that it has a unique absolute maximum.

Price Discrimination

Even in a single-product firm, there can arise an optimization problem involving two or more choice variables. Such would be the case, for instance, when a monopolistic firm sells a single product in two or more separate markets (e.g., domestic and foreign) and therefore must decide upon the quantities (Q_1, Q_2, etc.) to be supplied to the respective markets in order to maximize profit. The several markets will, in general, have different demand conditions, and if demand elasticities differ in the various markets, profit maximization will entail the practice of price discrimination. Let us derive this familiar conclusion mathematically.

Example 3

For a change of pace, this time let us use three choice variables, i.e., assume three separate markets. Also, let us work with general rather than numerical functions. Accordingly, our monopolistic firm will simply be assumed to have total-revenue and total-cost functions as follows:

$$R = R_1(Q_1) + R_2(Q_2) + R_3(Q_3)$$
$$C = C(Q) \quad \text{where} \quad Q = Q_1 + Q_2 + Q_3$$

Note that the symbol R_i represents here the revenue function of the *i*th market, rather than a derivative in the sense of f_i. Each such revenue function naturally implies a particular demand structure, which will generally be different from those prevailing in the other two markets. On the cost side, on the other hand, only one cost function is postulated, since a single firm is producing for all three markets. In view of the fact that $Q = Q_1 + Q_2 + Q_3$, total cost C is also basically a function of Q_1, Q_2, and Q_3, which constitute the choice variables of the model. We can, of course, rewrite $C(Q)$ as $C(Q_1 + Q_2 + Q_3)$. It should be noted, however, that even though the latter version contains three independent variables, the function should nevertheless be considered as having a single argument only, because the sum of Q_i is really a single entity. In contrast, if the function appears in the form $C(Q_1, Q_2, Q_3)$, then there can be counted as many arguments as independent variables.

Now the profit function is

$$\pi = R_1(Q_1) + R_2(Q_2) + R_3(Q_3) - C(Q)$$

with first partial derivatives $\pi_i \equiv \partial\pi/\partial Q_i$ (for $i = 1, 2, 3$) as follows:[†]

$$\pi_1 = R_1'(Q_1) - C'(Q)\frac{\partial Q}{\partial Q_1} = R_1'(Q_1) - C'(Q) \quad \left[\text{since } \frac{\partial Q}{\partial Q_1} = 1\right]$$

$$\pi_2 = R_2'(Q_2) - C'(Q)\frac{\partial Q}{\partial Q_2} = R_2'(Q_2) - C'(Q) \quad \left[\text{since } \frac{\partial Q}{\partial Q_2} = 1\right] \quad \textbf{(11.32)}$$

$$\pi_3 = R_3'(Q_3) - C'(Q)\frac{\partial Q}{\partial Q_3} = R_3'(Q_3) - C'(Q) \quad \left[\text{since } \frac{\partial Q}{\partial Q_3} = 1\right]$$

Setting these equal to zero simultaneously will give us

$$C'(Q) = R_1'(Q_1) = R_2'(Q_2) = R_3'(Q_3)$$

That is,

$$MC = MR_1 = MR_2 = MR_3$$

Thus the levels of Q_1, Q_2, and Q_3 should be chosen such that the marginal revenue in each market is equated to the marginal cost of the total output Q.

[†] Note that, to find $\partial C/\partial Q_i$, the chain rule is used:

$$\frac{\partial C}{\partial Q_i} = \frac{dC}{dQ}\frac{\partial Q}{\partial Q_i}$$

To see the implications of this condition with regard to price discrimination, let us first find out how the MR in any market is specifically related to the price in that market. Since the revenue in each market is $R_i = P_i Q_i$, it follows that the marginal revenue must be

$$MR_i \equiv \frac{dR_i}{dQ_i} = P_i \frac{dQ_i}{dQ_i} + Q_i \frac{dP_i}{dQ_i}$$

$$= P_i \left(1 + \frac{dP_i}{dQ_i} \frac{Q_i}{P_i}\right) = P_i \left(1 + \frac{1}{\varepsilon_{di}}\right) \qquad \text{[by (8.4)]}$$

where ε_{di}, the point elasticity of demand in the ith market, is normally negative. Consequently, the relationship between MR_i and P_i can be expressed alternatively by the equation

$$MR_i = P_i \left(1 - \frac{1}{|\varepsilon_{di}|}\right) \tag{11.33}$$

Recall that $|\varepsilon_{di}|$ is, in general, a function of P_i, so that when Q_i^* is chosen, and P_i^* thus specified, $|\varepsilon_{di}|$ will also assume a specific value, which can be either greater than, or less than, or equal to one. But if $|\varepsilon_{di}| < 1$ (demand being inelastic at a point), then its reciprocal will exceed one, and the parenthesized expression in (11.33) will be negative, thereby implying a negative value for MR_i. Similarly, if $|\varepsilon_{di}| = 1$ (unitary elasticity), then MR_i will take a zero value. Inasmuch as a firm's MC is positive, the first-order condition $MC = MR_i$ requires the firm to operate at a positive level of MR_i. Hence the firm's chosen sales levels Q_i must be such that the corresponding point elasticity of demand in each market is greater than one.

The first-order condition $MR_1 = MR_2 = MR_3$ can now be translated, via (11.33), into the following:

$$P_1 \left(1 - \frac{1}{|\varepsilon_{d1}|}\right) = P_2 \left(1 - \frac{1}{|\varepsilon_{d2}|}\right) = P_3 \left(1 - \frac{1}{|\varepsilon_{d3}|}\right)$$

From this it can readily be inferred that the *smaller* the value of $|\varepsilon_d|$ (at the chosen level of output) in a particular market, the *higher* the price charged in that market must be—hence, price discrimination—if profit is to be maximized.

To ensure maximization, let us examine the second-order condition. From (11.32), the second partial derivatives are found to be

$$\pi_{11} = R_1''(Q_1) - C''(Q) \frac{\partial Q}{\partial Q_1} = R_1''(Q_1) - C''(Q)$$

$$\pi_{22} = R_2''(Q_2) - C''(Q) \frac{\partial Q}{\partial Q_2} = R_2''(Q_2) - C''(Q)$$

$$\pi_{33} = R_3''(Q_3) - C''(Q) \frac{\partial Q}{\partial Q_3} = R_3''(Q_3) - C''(Q)$$

and $\qquad \pi_{12} = \pi_{21} = \pi_{13} = \pi_{31} = \pi_{23} = \pi_{32} = -C''(Q) \qquad \left[\text{since } \frac{\partial Q}{\partial Q_i} = 1\right]$

so that we have (after shortening the second-derivative notation)

$$|H| = \begin{vmatrix} R_1'' - C'' & -C'' & -C'' \\ -C'' & R_2'' - C'' & -C'' \\ -C'' & -C'' & R_3'' - C'' \end{vmatrix}$$

The second-order sufficient condition will thus be duly satisfied, provided we have:

1. $|H_1| = R_1'' - C'' < 0$; that is, the slope of MR_1 is less than the slope of MC of the entire output [cf. the situation of point L in Fig. 9.6c]. (Since any of the three markets can be taken as the "first" market, this in effect also implies $R_2'' - C'' < 0$ and $R_3'' - C'' < 0$.)
2. $|H_2| = (R_1'' - C'')(R_2'' - C'') - (C'')^2 > 0$; or, $R_1'' R_2'' - (R_1'' + R_2'')C'' > 0$.
3. $|H_3| = R_1'' R_2'' R_3'' - (R_1'' R_2'' + R_1'' R_3'' + R_2'' R_3'')C'' < 0$.

The last two parts of this condition are not as easy to interpret economically as the first. Note that had we assumed that the general $R_i(Q_i)$ functions are all concave and the general $C(Q)$ function is convex, so that $-C(Q)$ is concave, then the profit function—the sum of concave functions—could have been taken to be concave, thereby obviating the need to check the second-order condition.

<table>
<tr><td>**Example 4**</td><td>To make the above example more concrete, let us now give a numerical version. Suppose that our monopolistic firm has the specific average-revenue functions</td></tr>
</table>

$$P_1 = 63 - 4Q_1 \qquad \text{so that} \qquad R_1 = P_1 Q_1 = 63Q_1 - 4Q_1^2$$
$$P_2 = 105 - 5Q_2 \qquad\qquad R_2 = P_2 Q_2 = 105Q_2 - 5Q_2^2$$
$$P_3 = 75 - 6Q_3 \qquad\qquad R_3 = P_3 Q_3 = 75Q_3 - 6Q_3^2$$

and that the total-cost function is

$$C = 20 + 15Q$$

Then the marginal functions will be

$$R_1' = 63 - 8Q_1 \qquad R_2' = 105 - 10Q_2 \qquad R_3' = 75 - 12Q_3 \qquad C' = 15$$

When each marginal revenue R_i' is set equal to the marginal cost C' of the total output, the equilibrium quantities are found to be

$$Q_1^* = 6 \qquad Q_2^* = 9 \qquad \text{and} \qquad Q_3^* = 5$$

Thus
$$Q^* = \sum_{i=1}^{3} Q_1^* = 20$$

Substituting these solutions into the revenue and cost equations, we get $\pi^* = 679$ as the total profit from the triple-market business operation.

Because this is a specific model, we do have to check the second-order condition (or the concavity of the objective function). Since the second derivatives are

$$R_1'' = -8 \qquad R_2'' = -10 \qquad R_3'' = -12 \qquad C'' = 0$$

all three parts of the second-order sufficient conditions given in Example 3 are duly satisfied.

It is easy to see from the average-revenue functions that the firm should charge the discriminatory prices $P_1^* = 39$, $P_2^* = 60$, and $P_3^* = 45$ in the three markets. As you can readily verify, the point elasticity of demand is lowest in the second market, in which the highest price is charged.

Input Decisions of a Firm

Instead of output levels Q_i, the choice variables of a firm may also appear in the guise of input levels.

<table>
<tr><td>**Example 5**</td><td>Consider a competitive firm with the following profit function</td></tr>
</table>

$$\pi = R - C = PQ - wL - rK \qquad (11.34)$$

where
     P = price
     Q = output
     L = labor
     K = capital
     w, r = input prices for L and K, respectively

Since the firm operates in a competitive market, the exogenous variables are P, w, and r (written here without the zero subscript). There are three endogenous variables, K, L, and Q. However output Q is in turn a function of K and L via the production function

$$Q = Q(K, L)$$

We shall assume it to be a Cobb-Douglas function (further discussed in Sec. 12.6) of the form

$$Q = L^\alpha K^\beta$$

where α and β are positive parameters. If we further assume decreasing returns to scale, then $\alpha + \beta < 1$. For simplicity, we shall consider the symmetric case where $\alpha = \beta < \frac{1}{2}$

$$Q = L^\alpha K^\alpha \qquad (11.35)$$

Substituting (11.35) into (11.34) gives us

$$\pi(K, L) = P L^\alpha K^\alpha - wL - rK$$

The first-order condition for profit maximization is

$$\frac{\partial \pi}{\partial L} = P\alpha L^{\alpha-1} K^\alpha - w = 0$$
$$\frac{\partial \pi}{\partial K} = P\alpha L^\alpha K^{\alpha-1} - r = 0 \qquad (11.36)$$

This system of equations defines the optimal L and K for profit maximization. But first, let us check the second-order condition to verify that we do have a maximum.

The Hessian for this problem is

$$|H| = \begin{vmatrix} \pi_{LL} & \pi_{LK} \\ \pi_{KL} & \pi_{KK} \end{vmatrix} = \begin{vmatrix} P\alpha(\alpha-1)L^{\alpha-2}K^\alpha & P\alpha^2 L^{\alpha-1}K^{\alpha-1} \\ P\alpha^2 L^{\alpha-1}K^{\alpha-1} & P\alpha(\alpha-1)L^\alpha K^{\alpha-2} \end{vmatrix}$$

The sufficient condition for a maximum is that $|H_1| < 0$ and $|H| > 0$:

$$|H_1| = P\alpha(\alpha-1)L^{\alpha-2}K^\alpha < 0$$
$$|H| = P^2\alpha^2(\alpha-1)^2 L^{2\alpha-2}K^{2\alpha-2} - P^2\alpha^4 L^{2\alpha-2}K^{2\alpha-2}$$
$$= P^2\alpha^2 L^{2\alpha-2}K^{2\alpha-2}(1 - 2\alpha) > 0$$

Therefore, for $\alpha < \frac{1}{2}$, the second-order sufficient condition is satisfied.

We can now return to the first-order condition to solve for the optimal K and L. Rewriting the first equation in (11.36) to isolate K, we get

$$P\alpha L^{\alpha-1} K^\alpha = w$$

$$K = \left(\frac{w}{P\alpha} L^{1-\alpha} \right)^{\frac{1}{\alpha}}$$

Substituting this into the second equation of (11.36), we have

$$P\alpha L^{\alpha}K^{\alpha-1} - r = P\alpha L^{\alpha}\left[\left(\frac{w}{P\alpha}L^{1-\alpha}\right)^{\frac{1}{\alpha}}\right]^{\alpha-1} - r = 0$$

or

$$P^{\frac{1}{\alpha}}\alpha^{\frac{1}{\alpha}}w^{(\alpha-1)/\alpha}L^{(2\alpha-1)/\alpha} = r$$

Rearranging to solve for L then gives us

$$L^* = (P\alpha w^{\alpha-1}r^{-\alpha})^{1/(1-2\alpha)}$$

Taking advantage of the symmetry of the model, we can quickly write the optimal K as

$$K^* = (P\alpha r^{\alpha-1}w^{-\alpha})^{1/(1-2\alpha)}$$

L^* and K^* are the firm's input demand equations.

If we substitute L^* and K^* into the production function, we find that

$$Q^* = (L^*)^{\alpha}(K^*)^{\alpha}$$
$$= (P\alpha w^{\alpha-1}r^{-\alpha})^{\alpha/(1-2\alpha)}(P\alpha r^{\alpha-1}w^{-\alpha})^{\alpha/(1-2\alpha)}$$
$$= \left(\frac{\alpha^2 P^2}{wr}\right)^{\alpha/(1-2\alpha)} \tag{11.37}$$

This gives us an expression for the optimal output as a function of the exogenous variables P, w, and r.

Example 6 Let us assume the following circumstances: (1) Two inputs a and b are used in the production of a single product Q of a hypothetical firm. (2) The prices of both inputs, P_a and P_b, are beyond the control of the firm, as is the output price P; here we shall denote them by P_{a0}, P_{b0}, and P_0, respectively. (3) The production process takes t_0 years (t_0 being some positive constant) to complete; thus the revenue from sales should be duly discounted before it can be properly compared with the cost of production incurred at the present time. The rate of discount, on a continuous basis, is assumed to be given at r_0.

Upon assumption 1, we can write a general production function $Q = Q(a, b)$, with marginal physical products Q_a and Q_b. Assumption 2 enables us to express the total cost as

$$C = P_{a0}a + P_{b0}b$$

and the total revenue as

$$R = P_0 Q(a, b)$$

To write the profit function, however, we must first discount the revenue by multiplying it by the constant $e^{-r_0t_0}$—which, to avoid complicated superscripts with subscripts, we shall write as e^{-rt}. Thus, the profit function is

$$\pi = P_0 Q(a, b)e^{-rt} - P_{a0}a - P_{b0}b$$

in which a and b are the only choice variables.

To maximize profit, it is necessary that the first partial derivatives

$$\pi_a\left(\equiv \frac{\partial \pi}{\partial a}\right) = P_0 Q_a e^{-rt} - P_{a0}$$

$$\pi_b\left(\equiv \frac{\partial \pi}{\partial b}\right) = P_0 Q_b e^{-rt} - P_{b0} \tag{11.38}$$

both be zero. This means that

$$P_0 Q_a e^{-rt} = P_{a0} \qquad \text{and} \qquad P_0 Q_b e^{-rt} = P_{b0} \qquad \textbf{(11.39)}$$

Since $P_0 Q_a$ (the price of the product times the marginal product of input *a*) represents the *value of marginal product of input a* (VMP$_a$), the first equation merely says that the present value of VMP$_a$ should be equated to the given price of input *a*. The second equation is the same prerequisite applied to input *b*.

Note that, to satisfy (11.39), both marginal physical products Q_a and Q_b must be positive, because P_0, P_{a0}, P_{b0}, and e^{-rt} all have positive values. This has an important interpretation in terms of an *isoquant*, defined as the locus of input combinations that yield the same output level. When plotted in the *ab* plane, isoquants will generally appear like those drawn in Fig. 11.11. Inasmuch as each of them pertains to a fixed output level, along any isoquant we must have

$$dQ = Q_a \, da + Q_b \, db = 0$$

which implies that the slope of an isoquant is expressible as

$$\frac{db}{da} = -\frac{Q_a}{Q_b} \qquad \left(= -\frac{\text{MPP}_a}{\text{MPP}_b} \right) \qquad \textbf{(11.40)}$$

Thus, to have both Q_a and Q_b positive is to confine the firm's input choice to the negatively sloped segments of the isoquants only. In Fig. 11.11, the relevant region of operation is accordingly restricted to the shaded area defined by the two so-called ridge lines. Outside the shaded area, where the isoquants are characterized by positive slopes, the marginal product of one input must be negative. The movement from the input combination at *M* to the one at *N*, for instance, indicates that with input *b* held constant the *increase* in input *a* leads us to a *lower* isoquant (a smaller output); thus, Q_a must be negative. Similarly, a movement from M' to N' illustrates the negativity of Q_b. Note that when we confine our attention to the shaded area, each isoquant can be taken as a function of the form $b = \phi(a)$, because for every admissible value of *a*, the isoquant determines a unique value of *b*.

FIGURE 11.11

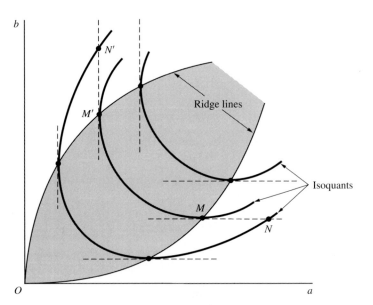

The second-order condition revolves around the second partial derivatives of π, obtainable from (11.38). Bearing in mind that Q_a and Q_b, being derivatives, are themselves functions of the variables a and b, we can find π_{aa}, $\pi_{ab} = \pi_{ba}$, and π_{bb}, and arrange them into a Hessian:

$$|H| = \begin{vmatrix} \pi_{aa} & \pi_{ab} \\ \pi_{ab} & \pi_{bb} \end{vmatrix} = \begin{vmatrix} P_0 Q_{aa} e^{-rt} & P_0 Q_{ab} e^{-rt} \\ P_0 Q_{ab} e^{-rt} & P_0 Q_{bb} e^{-rt} \end{vmatrix} \qquad \textbf{(11.41)}$$

For a stationary value of π to be a maximum, it is sufficient that

$$|H_1| < 0 \qquad \text{[that is, } \pi_{aa} < 0 \text{, which can occur iff } Q_{aa} < 0 \text{]}$$

$$|H_2| = |H| > 0 \qquad \left[\text{that is, } \pi_{aa} \pi_{bb} > \pi_{ab}^2, \text{ which can occur iff } Q_{aa} Q_{bb} > Q_{ab}^2 \right]$$

Thus, we note, the second-order condition can be tested either with the π_{ij} derivatives or the Q_{ij} derivatives, whichever are more convenient.

The symbol Q_{aa} denotes the rate of change of Q_a ($\equiv$ MPP$_a$) as input a changes while input b is fixed; similarly, Q_{bb} denotes the rate of change of Q_b ($\equiv$ MPP$_b$) as input b changes alone. So the second-order sufficient condition stipulates, in part, that the MPP of both inputs be *diminishing* at the chosen input levels a^* and b^*. Observe, however, that diminishing MPP$_a$ and MPP$_b$ does *not* guarantee the satisfaction of the second-order condition, because the latter condition also involves the magnitude of $Q_{ab} = Q_{ba}$, which measures the rate of change of MPP of one input as the amount of the other input varies.

Upon further examination it emerges that, just as the first-order condition specifies the isoquant to be negatively sloped at the chosen input combination (as shown in the shaded area of Fig. 11.11), the second-order sufficient condition serves to specify that same isoquant to be strictly convex at the chosen input combination. The curvature of the isoquant is associated with the sign of the second derivative d^2b/da^2. To obtain the latter, (11.40) must be differentiated totally with respect to a, bearing in mind that both Q_a and Q_b are derivative functions of a and b and yet, on an isoquant, b is itself a function of a; that is,

$$Q_a = Q_a(a, b) \qquad Q_b = Q_b(a, b) \qquad \text{and} \qquad b = \phi(a)$$

The total differentiation thus proceeds as follows:

$$\frac{d^2 b}{da^2} = \frac{d}{da}\left(-\frac{Q_a}{Q_b} \right) = -\frac{1}{Q_b^2}\left[Q_b \frac{dQ_a}{da} - Q_a \frac{dQ_b}{da} \right] \qquad \textbf{(11.42)}$$

Since b is a function of a on the isoquant, the total-derivative formula (8.9) gives us

$$\frac{dQ_a}{da} = \frac{\partial Q_a}{\partial b}\frac{db}{da} + \frac{\partial Q_a}{\partial a} = Q_{ba}\frac{db}{da} + Q_{aa}$$

$$\frac{dQ_b}{da} = \frac{\partial Q_b}{\partial b}\frac{db}{da} + \frac{\partial Q_b}{\partial a} = Q_{bb}\frac{db}{da} + Q_{ab}$$

$$\textbf{(11.43)}$$

After substituting (11.40) into (11.43) and then substituting the latter into (11.42), we can rewrite the second derivative as

$$\frac{d^2 b}{da^2} = -\frac{1}{Q_b^2}\left[Q_{aa}Q_b - Q_{ba}Q_a - Q_{ab}Q_a + Q_{bb}Q_a^2\left(\frac{1}{Q_b} \right) \right]$$

$$= -\frac{1}{Q_b^3}[Q_{aa}(Q_b)^2 - 2Q_{ab}(Q_a)(Q_b) + Q_{bb}(Q_a)^2] \qquad \textbf{(11.44)}$$

It is to be noted in (11.44) that the expression in brackets (last line) is a quadratic form in the two variables Q_a and Q_b. If the second-order sufficient condition is satisfied, so that

$$Q_{aa} < 0 \quad \text{and} \quad \begin{vmatrix} Q_{aa} & -Q_{ab} \\ -Q_{ab} & Q_{bb} \end{vmatrix} > 0$$

then, by virtue of (11.11'), the said quadratic form must be negative definite. This will in turn make $d^2 b/da^2$ positive, because Q_b has been constrained to be positive by the first-order condition. Thus the satisfaction of the second-order sufficient condition means that the relevant (negatively sloped) isoquant is strictly convex at the chosen input combination, as was asserted.

The concept of strict convexity, as applied to an isoquant $b = \phi(a)$, which is drawn in the two-dimensional ab plane, should be carefully distinguished from the same concept as applied to the production function $Q(a, b)$ itself, which is drawn in the three-dimensional abQ space. Note, in particular, that if we are to apply the concept of strict concavity or convexity to the production function in the present context, then, to produce the desired isoquant shape, the appropriate stipulation is that $Q(a, b)$ be strictly *concave* in the 3-space (be dome-shaped), which is in sharp contradistinction to the stipulation that the relevant isoquant be strictly *convex* in the 2-space (be U-shaped, or shaped like a part of a U).

Example 7

Next, suppose that interest is compounded *quarterly* instead, at a given interest rate of i_0 per quarter. Also suppose that the production process takes exactly a quarter of a year. The profit function then becomes

$$\pi = P_0 Q(a, b)(1 + i_0)^{-1} - P_{a0}a - P_{b0}b$$

The first-order condition is now found to be

$$P_0 Q_a (1 + i_0)^{-1} - P_{a0} = 0$$
$$P_0 Q_b (1 + i_0)^{-1} - P_{b0} = 0$$

with an analytical interpretation entirely the same as in Example 6, except for the different manner of discounting.

You can readily see that the same sufficient condition derived in Example 6 must apply here as well.

EXERCISE 11.6

1. If the competitive firm of Example 1 has the cost function $C = 2Q_1^2 + 2Q_2^2$ instead, then:
   (a) Will the production of the two goods still be technically related?
   (b) What will be the new optimal levels of Q_1 and Q_2?
   (c) What is the value of π_{12}? What does this imply economically?

2. A two-product firm faces the following demand and cost functions:
   $$Q_1 = 40 - 2P_1 - P_2 \qquad Q_2 = 35 - P_1 - P_2 \qquad C = Q_1^2 + 2Q_2^2 + 10$$
   (a) Find the output levels that satisfy the first-order condition for maximum profit. (Use fractions.)
   (b) Check the second-order sufficient condition. Can you conclude that this problem possesses a unique absolute maximum?
   (c) What is the maximal profit?

3. On the basis of the equilibrium price and quantity in Example 4, calculate the point elasticity of demand $|\varepsilon_{di}|$ (for $i = 1, 2$). Which market has the highest and the lowest demand elasticities?

4. If the cost function of Example 4 is changed to $C = 20 + 15Q + Q^2$
   (a) Find the new marginal-cost function.
   (b) Find the new equilibrium quantities. (Use fractions.)
   (c) Find the new equilibrium prices.
   (d) Verify that the second-order sufficient condition is met.

5. In Example 7, how would you rewrite the profit function if the following conditions hold?
   (a) Interest is compounded semiannually at an interest rate of i_0 per annum, and the production process takes 1 year.
   (b) Interest is compounded quarterly at an interest rate of i_0 per annum, and the production process takes 9 months.

6. Given $Q = Q(a, b)$, how would you express algebraically the isoquant for the output. level of, say, 260?

11.7 Comparative-Static Aspects of Optimization

Optimization, which is a special variety of static equilibrium analysis, is naturally also subject to investigations of the comparative-static sort. The idea is, again, to find out how a change in any parameter will affect the equilibrium position of the model, which in the present context refers to the optimal values of the choice variables (and the optimal value of the objective function). Since no new technique is involved beyond those discussed in Part 3, we may proceed directly with some illustrations, based on the examples introduced in Sec. 11.6.

Reduced-Form Solutions

Example 1 of Sec. 11.6 contains two parameters (or exogenous variables), P_{10} and P_{20}; it is not surprising, therefore, that the optimal output levels of this two-product firm are expressed strictly in terms of these parameters:

$$Q_1^* = \frac{4P_{10} - P_{20}}{15} \qquad \text{and} \qquad Q_2^* = \frac{4P_{20} - P_{10}}{15}$$

These are reduced-form solutions, and simple partial differentiation alone is sufficient to tell us all the comparative-static properties of the model, namely,

$$\frac{\partial Q_1^*}{\partial P_{10}} = \frac{4}{15} \qquad \frac{\partial Q_1^*}{\partial P_{20}} = -\frac{1}{15} \qquad \frac{\partial Q_2^*}{\partial P_{10}} = -\frac{1}{15} \qquad \frac{\partial Q_2^*}{\partial P_{20}} = \frac{4}{15}$$

For maximum profit, each product of the firm should be produced in a larger quantity if its market price rises or if the market price of the other product falls.

Of course, these conclusions follow only from the particular assumptions of the model in question. We may point out, in particular, that the effects of a change in P_{10} on Q_2^* and of P_{20} on Q_1^*, are consequences of the assumed technical relation on the production side of these two commodities, and that in the absence of such a relation we shall have

$$\frac{\partial Q_1^*}{\partial P_{20}} = \frac{\partial Q_2^*}{\partial P_{10}} = 0$$

Moving on to Example 2, we note that the optimal output levels are there stated, numerically, as $Q_1^* = 8$ and $Q_2^* = 7\frac{2}{3}$—no parameters appear. In fact, all the constants in the equations of the model are numerical rather than parametric, so that by the time we reach the solution stage those constants have all lost their respective identities through the process of arithmetic manipulation. What this serves to underscore is the fundamental lack of generality in the use of numerical constants and the consequent lack of comparative-static content in the equilibrium solution.

On the other hand, the *non*use of numerical constants is no guarantee that a problem will automatically become amenable to comparative-static analysis. The price-discrimination problem (Example 3), for instance, was primarily set up for the study of the equilibrium (profit-maximization) condition, and no parameter was introduced at all. Accordingly, even though stated in terms of general functions, a reformulation will be necessary if a comparative-static study is contemplated.

General-Function Models

The input-decision problem of Example 6 illustrates the case where a general-function formulation does embrace several parameters—in fact, no less than five (P_0, P_{a0}, P_{b0}, r, and t), where we have, as before, omitted the 0 subscripts from the exogenous variables r_0 and t_0. How do we derive the comparative-static properties of this model?

The answer lies again in the application of the implicit-function theorem. But, unlike the cases of nongoal-equilibrium models of the market or of national-income determination, where we worked with the equilibrium conditions of the model, the present context of goal equilibrium dictates that we work with the first-order conditions of optimization. For Example 6, these conditions are stated in (11.39). Collecting all terms in (11.39) to the left of the equals signs, and making explicit that Q_a and Q_b are both functions of the endogenous (choice) variables a and b, we can rewrite the first-order conditions in the format of (8.24) as follows:

$$F^1(a, b; P_0, P_{a0}, P_{b0}, r, t) = P_0 Q_a(a, b)e^{-rt} - P_{a0} = 0$$
$$F^2(a, b; P_0, P_{a0}, P_{b0}, r, t) = P_0 Q_b(a, b)e^{-rt} - P_{b0} = 0 \tag{11.45}$$

The functions F^1 and F^2 are assumed to possess continuous derivatives. Thus it would be possible to apply the implicit-function theorem, provided the Jacobian of this system with respect to the endogenous variables a and b does not vanish at the initial equilibrium. The said Jacobian turns out to be nothing but the Hessian determinant of the π function of Example 6:

$$|J| = \begin{vmatrix} \dfrac{\partial F^1}{\partial a} & \dfrac{\partial F^1}{\partial b} \\[2mm] \dfrac{\partial F^2}{\partial a} & \dfrac{\partial F^2}{\partial b} \end{vmatrix} = \begin{vmatrix} P_0 Q_{aa}e^{-rt} & P_0 Q_{ab}e^{-rt} \\ P_0 Q_{ab}e^{-rt} & P_0 Q_{bb}e^{-rt} \end{vmatrix} = |H| \quad \text{[by (11.41)]} \tag{11.46}$$

Hence, if we assume that the second-order sufficient condition for profit-maximization is satisfied, then $|H|$ must be positive, and so must be $|J|$, at the initial equilibrium or optimum. In that event, the implicit-function theorem will enable us to write the pair of implicit functions

$$
\begin{aligned}
a^* &= a^*(P_0, P_{a0}, P_{b0}, r, t) \\
b^* &= b^*(P_0, P_{a0}, P_{b0}, r, t)
\end{aligned}
$$

(11.47)

as well as the pair of identities

$$
\begin{aligned}
P_0 Q_a(a^*, b^*)e^{-rt} - P_{a0} &\equiv 0 \\
P_0 Q_b(a^*, b^*)e^{-rt} - P_{b0} &\equiv 0
\end{aligned}
$$

(11.48)

To study the comparative statics of the model, first take the total differential of each identity in (11.48). For the time being, we shall permit all the exogenous variables to vary, so that the result of total differentiation will involve da^*, db^*, as well as dP_0, dP_{a0}, dP_{b0}, dr, and dt. If we place on the left side of the equals sign only those terms involving da^* and db^*, the result will be

$$
\begin{aligned}
P_0 Q_{aa}e^{-rt}da^* + P_0 Q_{ab}e^{-rt}db^* &= - Q_a e^{-rt}dP_0 + dP_{a0} \\
&\quad + P_0 Q_a t e^{-rt}dr + P_0 Q_a r e^{-rt}dt \\
P_0 Q_{ab}e^{-rt}da^* + P_0 Q_{bb}e^{-rt}db^* &= - Q_b e^{-rt}dP_0 + dP_{b0} \\
&\quad + P_0 Q_b t e^{-rt}dr + P_0 Q_b r e^{-rt}dt
\end{aligned}
$$

(11.49)

where, be it noted, the first and second derivatives of Q are all to be evaluated at the equilibrium, i.e., at a^* and b^*. You will also note that the coefficients of da^* and db^* on the left are precisely the elements of the Jacobian in (11.46).

To derive the specific comparative-static derivatives—of which there are a total of 10 (why?)—we now shall allow only a single exogenous variable to vary at a time. Suppose we let P_0 vary, alone. Then $dP_0 \neq 0$, but $dP_{a0} = dP_{b0} = dr = dt = 0$, so that only the first term will remain on the right side of each equation in (11.49). Dividing through by dP_0, and interpreting the ratio da^*/dP_0 to be the comparative-static derivative $(\partial a^*/\partial P_0)$, and similarly for the ratio db^*/dP_0, we can write the matrix equation

$$
\begin{bmatrix} P_0 Q_{aa}e^{-rt} & P_0 Q_{ab}e^{-rt} \\ P_0 Q_{ab}e^{-rt} & P_0 Q_{bb}e^{-rt} \end{bmatrix} \begin{bmatrix} (\partial a^*/\partial P_0) \\ (\partial b^*/\partial P_0) \end{bmatrix} = \begin{bmatrix} -Q_a e^{-rt} \\ -Q_b e^{-rt} \end{bmatrix}
$$

The solution, by Cramer's rule, is found to be

$$
\begin{aligned}
\left(\frac{\partial a^*}{\partial P_0} \right) &= \frac{(Q_b Q_{ab} - Q_a Q_{bb})P_0 e^{-2rt}}{|J|} \\
\left(\frac{\partial b^*}{\partial P_0} \right) &= \frac{(Q_a Q_{ab} - Q_b Q_{aa})P_0 e^{-2rt}}{|J|}
\end{aligned}
$$

(11.50)

If you prefer, an alternative method is available for obtaining these results: You may simply differentiate the two identities in (11.48) *totally* with respect to P_0 (while holding the other four exogenous variables fixed), bearing in mind that P_0 can affect a^* and b^* via (11.47).

Let us now analyze the signs of the comparative-static derivatives in (11.50). On the assumption that the second-order sufficient condition is satisfied, the Jacobian in the denominator must be positive. The second-order condition also implies that Q_{aa} and Q_{bb} are negative, just as the first-order condition implies that Q_a and Q_b are positive. Moreover, the expression P_0e^{-2rt} is certainly positive. Thus, if $Q_{ab} > 0$ (if increasing one input will raise the MPP of the other input), we can conclude that both $(\partial a^*/\partial P_0)$ and $(\partial b^*/\partial P_0)$ will be positive, implying that an increase in the product price will result in increased employment of both inputs in equilibrium. If $Q_{ab} < 0$, on the other hand, the sign of each derivative in (11.50) will depend on the relative strength of the negative force and the positive force in the parenthetical expression on the right.

Next, let the exogenous variable r vary, alone. Then all the terms on the right of (11.49) will vanish except those involving dr. Dividing through by $dr \neq 0$, we now obtain the following matrix equation

$$\begin{bmatrix} P_0 Q_{aa}e^{-rt} & P_0 Q_{ab}e^{-rt} \\ P_0 Q_{ab}e^{-rt} & P_0 Q_{bb}e^{-rt} \end{bmatrix} \begin{bmatrix} (\partial a^*/\partial r) \\ (\partial b^*/\partial r) \end{bmatrix} = \begin{bmatrix} P_0 Q_a te^{-rt} \\ P_0 Q_b te^{-rt} \end{bmatrix}$$

with the solution

$$\left(\frac{\partial a^*}{\partial r} \right) = \frac{t(Q_a Q_{bb} - Q_b Q_{ab})(P_0 e^{-rt})^2}{|J|}$$

$$\left(\frac{\partial b^*}{\partial r} \right) = \frac{t(Q_b Q_{aa} - Q_a Q_{ab})(P_0 e^{-rt})^2}{|J|}$$

(11.51)

Both of these comparative-static derivatives will be negative if Q_{ab} is positive, but indeterminate in sign if Q_{ab} is negative.

By a similar procedure, we may find the effects of changes in the remaining parameters. Actually, in view of the symmetry between r and t in (11.48) it is immediately obvious that both $(\partial a^*/\partial t)$ and $(\partial b^*/\partial t)$ must be similar in appearance to (11.51).

The effects of changes in P_{a0} and P_{b0} are left to you to analyze. As you will find, the sign restriction of the second-order sufficient condition will again be useful in evaluating the comparative-static derivatives, because it can tell us the signs of Q_{aa} and Q_{bb} as well as the Jacobian $|J|$ at the initial equilibrium (optimum). Thus, aside from distinguishing between maximum and minimum, the second-order condition also has a vital role to play in the study of shifts in equilibrium positions as well.

EXERCISE 11.7

For Probs.1 through 3, assume that $Q_{ab} > 0$.

1. On the basis of the model described in (11.45) through (11.48), find the comparative-static derivatives $(\partial a^*/\partial P_{a0})$ and $(\partial b^*/\partial P_{a0})$. Interpret the economic meaning of the result. Then analyze the effects on a^* and b^* of a change in P_{b0}.

2. For the problem of Example 7 in Sec. 11.6:

   (a) How many parameters are there? Enumerate them.

   (b) Following the procedure described in (11.45) through (11.50), and assuming that the second-order sufficient condition is satisfied, find the comparative-static derivatives $(\partial a^*/\partial P_0)$ and $(\partial b^*/\partial P_0)$. Evaluate their signs and interpret their economic meanings.

(c) Find $(\partial a^*/\partial i_0)$ and $(\partial b^*/\partial i_0)$, evaluate their signs, and interpret their economic meanings.

3. Show that the results in (11.50) can be obtained alternatively by differentiating the two identities in (11.48) *totally* with respect to P_0, while holding the other exogenous variables fixed. Bear in mind that P_0 can affect a^* and b^* by virtue of (11.47).

4. A Jacobian determinant, as defined in (7.27), is made up of *first*-order partial derivatives. On the other hand, a Hessian determinant, as defined in Secs. 11.3 and 11.4, has as its elements *second*-order partial derivatives. How, then, can it turn out that $|J| = |H|$, as in (11.46)?

Chapter 12

Optimization with Equality Constraints

Chapter 11 presented a general method for finding the relative extrema of an objective function of two or more choice variables. One important feature of that discussion is that all the choice variables are *independent* of one another, in the sense that the decision made regarding one variable does not impinge upon the choices of the remaining variables. For instance, a two-product firm can choose any value for Q_1 and any value for Q_2 it wishes, without the two choices limiting each other.

If the said firm is somehow required to observe a restriction (such as a production quota) in the form of $Q_1 + Q_2 = 950$, however, the independence between the choice variables will be lost. In that event, the firm's profit-maximizing output levels Q_1^* and Q_2^* will be not only simultaneous but also dependent, because the higher Q_1^* is, the lower Q_2^* must correspondingly be, in order to stay within the combined quota of 950. The new optimum satisfying the production quota constitutes a *constrained optimum,* which, in general, may be expected to differ from the *free optimum* discussed in Chap. 11.

A restriction, such as the production quota mentioned before, establishes a relationship between the two variables in their roles as choice variables, but this should be distinguished from other types of relationships that may link the variables together. For instance, in Example 2 of Sec. 11.6, the two products of the firm are related in consumption (substitutes) as well as in production (as is reflected in the cost function), but that fact does not qualify the problem as one of constrained optimization, since the two output variables are still *independent as choice variables*. Only the dependence of the variables qua choice variables gives rise to a constrained optimum.

In the present chapter, we shall consider equality constraints only, such as $Q_1 + Q_2 = 950$. Our primary concern will be with *relative* constrained extrema, although *absolute* ones will also be discussed in Sec. 12.4.

12.1 Effects of a Constraint

The primary purpose of imposing a constraint is to give due cognizance to certain limiting factors present in the optimization problem under discussion.

We have already seen the limitation on output choices that result from a production quota. For further illustration, let us consider a consumer with the simple utility (index) function

$$U = x_1 x_2 + 2x_1 \qquad\qquad (12.1)$$

Since the marginal utilities—the partial derivatives $U_1 \equiv \partial U / \partial x_1$ and $U_2 \equiv \partial U / \partial x_2$—are positive for all positive levels of x_1 and x_2 here, to have U maximized without any constraint, the consumer should purchase an *infinite* amount of both goods, a solution that obviously has little practical relevance. To render the optimization problem meaningful, the purchasing power of the consumer must also be taken into account; i.e., a *budget constraint* should be incorporated into the problem. If the consumer intends to spend a given sum, say, $60, on the two goods and if the current prices are $P_{10} = 4$ and $P_{20} = 2$, then the budget constraint can be expressed by the linear equation

$$4x_1 + 2x_2 = 60 \qquad\qquad (12.2)$$

Such a constraint, like the production quota referred to earlier, renders the choices of x_1^* and x_2^* mutually dependent.

The problem now is to maximize (12.1), subject to the constraint stated in (12.2). Mathematically, what the constraint (variously called *restraint, side relation,* or *subsidiary condition*) does is to narrow the domain, and hence the range of the objective function. The domain of (12.1) would normally be the set $\{(x_1, x_2) \mid x_1 \geq 0, x_2 \geq 0\}$. Graphically, the domain is represented by the nonnegative quadrant of the $x_1 x_2$ plane in Fig. 12.1a. After the budget constraint (12.2) is added, however, we can admit only those values of the variables which satisfy this latter equation, so that the domain is immediately reduced to the set of points lying on the budget line. This will automatically affect the range of the objective function, too; only that subset of the utility surface lying directly above the budget-constraint line will now be relevant. The said subset (a cross section of the surface) may look like the curve in Fig. 12.1b, where U is plotted on the vertical axis, with the budget line of diagram *a* placed on the horizontal axis. Our interest, then, is only in locating the maximum on the curve in diagram *b*.

In general, for a function $z = f(x, y)$, the difference between a constrained extremum and a free extremum may be illustrated in the three-dimensional graph of Fig. 12.2. The free extremum in this particular graph is the peak point of the entire dome, but the constrained extremum is at the peak of the inverse U-shaped curve situated on top of (i.e., lying

FIGURE 12.1

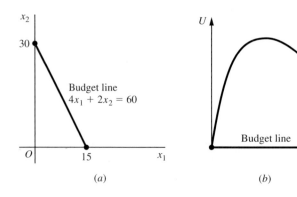

(a)

(b)

FIGURE 12.2

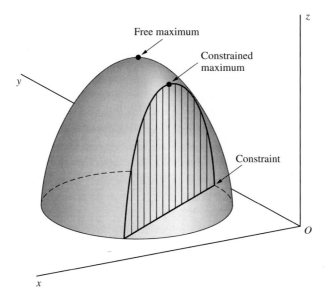

directly above) the constraint line. In general, a constrained maximum can be expected to have a lower value than the free maximum, although, by coincidence, the two maxima may happen to have the same value. But the constrained maximum can never exceed the free maximum.

It is interesting to note that, had we added another constraint intersecting the first constraint at a single point in the xy plane, the two constraints together would have restricted the domain to that single point. Then the locating of the extremum would become a trivial matter. In a meaningful problem, the number and the nature of the constraints should be such as to restrict, but not eliminate, the possibility of choice. Generally, the number of constraints should be less than the number of choice variables.

12.2 Finding the Stationary Values

Even without any new technique of solution, the constrained maximum in the simple example defined by (12.1) and (12.2) can easily be found. Since the constraint (12.2) implies

$$x_2 = \frac{60 - 4x_1}{2} = 30 - 2x_1 \qquad \textbf{(12.2')}$$

we can combine the constraint with the objective function by substituting (12.2') into (12.1). The result is an objective function in one variable only:

$$U = x_1(30 - 2x_1) + 2x_1 = 32x_1 - 2x_1^2$$

which can be handled with the method already learned. By setting $dU/dx_1 = 32 - 4x_1$ equal to zero, we get the solution $x_1^* = 8$, which by virtue of (12.2') immediately leads to $x_2^* = 30 - 2(8) = 14$. From (12.1), we can then find the stationary value $U^* = 128$; and since the second derivative is $d^2U/dx_1^2 = -4 < 0$, that stationary value constitutes a (constrained) maximum of U.[†]

When the constraint is itself a complicated function, or when there are several constraints to consider, however, the technique of substitution and elimination of variables could become a burdensome task. More importantly, when the constraint comes in a form such that we cannot solve it to express one variable (x_2) as an explicit function of the other (x_1), the elimination method would in fact be of no avail—even if x_2 were known to be an implicit function of x_1, that is, even if the conditions of the implicit-function theorem were satisfied. In such cases, we may resort to a method known as the *method of Lagrange (undetermined) multiplier*, which, as we shall see, has distinct analytical advantages.

Lagrange-Multiplier Method

The essence of the Lagrange-multiplier method is to convert a constrained-extremum problem into a form such that the first-order condition of the free-extremum problem can still be applied.

Given the problem of maximizing $U = x_1x_2 + 2x_1$, subject to the constraint $4x_1 + 2x_2 = 60$ [from (12.1) and (12.2)], let us write what is referred to as the *Lagrangian function*, which is a modified version of the objective function that incorporates the constraint as follows:

$$Z = x_1x_2 + 2x_1 + \lambda(60 - 4x_1 - 2x_2) \tag{12.3}$$

The symbol λ (the Greek letter lambda), representing some as yet undetermined number, is called a *Lagrange (undetermined) multiplier.* If we can somehow be assured that $4x_1 + 2x_2 = 60$, so that the constraint will be satisfied, then the last term in (12.3) will vanish regardless of the value of λ. In that event, Z will be identical with U. Moreover, with the constraint out of the way, we only have to seek the *free* maximum of Z, in lieu of the *constrained* maximum of U, with respect to the two variables x_1 and x_2. The question is: How can we make the parenthetical expression in (12.3) vanish?

The tactic that will accomplish this is simply to treat λ as an additional choice variable in (12.3), i.e., to consider $Z = Z(\lambda, x_1, x_2)$. For then the first-order condition for free extremum will consist of the set of simultaneous equations

$$\begin{aligned}
Z_\lambda (\equiv \partial Z/\partial\lambda) &= 60 - 4x_1 - 2x_2 = 0 \\
Z_1 (\equiv \partial Z/\partial x_1) &= x_2 + 2 - 4\lambda = 0 \\
Z_2 (\equiv \partial Z/\partial x_2) &= x_1 - 2\lambda = 0
\end{aligned} \tag{12.4}$$

and the first equation will automatically guarantee the satisfaction of the constraint. Thus, by incorporating the constraint into the Lagrangian function Z and by treating the Lagrange multiplier as an extra variable, we can obtain the constrained extremum U^* (two choice variables) simply by screening the stationary values of Z, taken as a *free* function of three choice variables.

Solving (12.4) for the critical values of the variables, we find $x_1^* = 8$, $x_2^* = 14$ (and $\lambda^* = 4$). As expected, the values of x_1^* and x_2^* check with the answers already obtained by

[†] You may recall that for the flower-bed problem of Exercise 9.4-2 the same technique of substitution was applied to find the maximum area, using a constraint (the available quantity of wire netting) to eliminate one of the two variables (the length or the width of the flower bed).

the substitution method. Furthermore, it is clear from (12.3) that $Z^* = 128$; this is identical with the value of U^* found earlier, as it should be.

In general, given an objective function

$$z = f(x, y) \tag{12.5}$$

subject to the constraint

$$g(x, y) = c \tag{12.6}$$

where c is a constant,[†] we can write the Lagrangian function as

$$Z = f(x, y) + \lambda[c - g(x, y)] \tag{12.7}$$

For stationary values of Z, regarded as a function of the three variables λ, x, and y, the necessary condition is

$$
\begin{aligned}
Z_\lambda &= c - g(x, y) = 0 \\
Z_x &= f_x - \lambda g_x = 0 \\
Z_y &= f_y - \lambda g_y = 0
\end{aligned} \tag{12.8}
$$

Since the first equation in (12.8) is simply a restatement of (12.6), the stationary values of the Lagrangian function Z will automatically satisfy the constraint of the original function z. And since the expression $\lambda[c - g(x, y)]$ is now assuredly zero, the stationary values of Z in (12.7) must be identical with those of (12.5), subject to (12.6).

Let us illustrate the method with two more examples.

Example 1

Find the extremum of

$$z = xy \qquad \text{subject to} \qquad x + y = 6$$

The first step is to write the Lagrangian function

$$Z = xy + \lambda(6 - x - y)$$

For a stationary value of Z, it is necessary that

$$
\left.
\begin{aligned}
Z_\lambda &= 6 - x - y = 0 \\
Z_x &= y - \lambda = 0 \\
Z_y &= x - \lambda = 0
\end{aligned}
\right\}
\quad \text{or} \quad
\left\{
\begin{aligned}
x + y &= 6 \\
-\lambda + y &= 0 \\
-\lambda + x &= 0
\end{aligned}
\right.
$$

Thus, by Cramer's rule or some other method, we can find

$$\lambda^* = 3 \qquad x^* = 3 \qquad y^* = 3$$

The stationary value is $Z^* = z^* = 9$, which needs to be tested against a second-order condition before we can tell whether it is a maximum or minimum (or neither). That will be taken up in Sec. 12.3.

[†] It is also possible to subsume the constant c under the constraint function so that (12.6) appears instead as $G(x, y) = 0$, where $G(x, y) = g(x, y) - c$. In that case, (12.7) should be changed to $Z = f(x, y) + \lambda[0 - G(x, y)] = f(x, y) - \lambda G(x, y)$. The version in (12.6) is chosen because it facilitates the study of the comparative-static effect of a change in the constraint constant later [see (12.16)].

Example 2

Find the extremum of

$$z = x_1^2 + x_2^2 \qquad \text{subject to} \qquad x_1 + 4x_2 = 2$$

The Lagrangian function is

$$Z = x_1^2 + x_2^2 + \lambda(2 - x_1 - 4x_2)$$

for which the necessary condition for a stationary value is

$$\left. \begin{array}{l} Z_\lambda = 2 - x_1 - 4x_2 = 0 \\ Z_1 = 2x_1 - \lambda = 0 \\ Z_2 = 2x_2 - 4\lambda = 0 \end{array} \right\} \quad \text{or} \quad \left\{ \begin{array}{l} x_1 + 4x_2 = 2 \\ -\lambda + 2x_1 \qquad = 0 \\ -4\lambda \qquad + 2x_2 = 0 \end{array} \right.$$

The stationary value of Z, defined by the solution

$$\lambda^* = \tfrac{4}{17} \qquad x_1^* = \tfrac{2}{17} \qquad x_2^* = \tfrac{8}{17}$$

is therefore $Z^* = z^* = \tfrac{4}{17}$. Again, a second-order condition should be consulted before we can tell whether z^* is a maximum or a minimum.

Total-Differential Approach

In the discussion of the free extremum of $z = f(x, y)$, it was learned that the first-order necessary condition may be stated in terms of the total differential dz as follows:

$$dz = f_x \, dx + f_y \, dy = 0 \qquad\qquad \textbf{(12.9)}$$

This statement remains valid after a constraint $g(x, y) = c$ is added. However, with the constraint in the picture, we can no longer take both dx and dy as "arbitrary" changes as before. For if $g(x, y) = c$, then dg must be equal to dc, which is zero since c is a constant. Hence,

$$(dg =)g_x \, dx + g_y \, dy = 0 \qquad\qquad \textbf{(12.10)}$$

and this relation makes dx and dy dependent on each other. The first-order necessary condition therefore becomes $dz = 0$ [(12.9)], subject to $g = c$, and hence also subject to $dg = 0$ [(12.10)]. By visual inspection of (12.9) and (12.10), it should be clear that, in order to satisfy this necessary condition, we must have

$$\frac{f_x}{g_x} = \frac{f_y}{g_y} \qquad\qquad \textbf{(12.11)}$$

This result can be verified by solving (12.10) for dy and substituting the result into (12.9). The condition (12.11), together with the constraint $g(x, y) = c$, will provide two equations from which to find the critical values of x and y.[†]

Does the total-differential approach yield the same first-order condition as the Lagrange-multiplier method? Let us compare (12.8) with the result just obtained. The first equation

---

[†] Note that the constraint $g = c$ is still to be considered along with (12.11), even though we have utilized the equation $dg = 0$—that is, (12.10)—in deriving (12.11). While $g = c$ necessarily implies $dg = 0$, the converse is not true: $dg = 0$ merely implies $g = a$ constant (not necessarily c). Unless the constraint is explicitly considered, therefore, some information will be unwittingly left out of the problem.

in (12.8) merely repeats the constraint; the new result requires its satisfaction also. The last two equations in (12.8) can be rewritten, respectively, as

$$\frac{f_x}{g_x} = \lambda \qquad \text{and} \qquad \frac{f_y}{g_y} = \lambda \qquad\qquad \textbf{(12.11')}$$

and these convey precisely the same information as (12.11). Note, however, that whereas the total-differential approach yields only the values of x^* and y^*, the Lagrange-multiplier method also gives the value of λ^* as a direct by-product. As it turns out, λ^* provides a measure of the sensitivity of Z^* (and z^*) to a shift of the constraint, as we shall presently demonstrate. Therefore, the Lagrange-multiplier method offers the advantage of containing certain built-in comparative-static information in the solution.

An Interpretation of the Lagrange Multiplier

To show that λ^* indeed measures the sensitivity of Z^* to changes in the constraint, let us perform a comparative-static analysis on the first-order condition (12.8). Since λ, x, and y are endogenous, the only available exogenous variable is the constraint parameter c. A change in c would cause a shift of the constraint curve in the xy plane and thereby alter the optimal solution. In particular, the effect of an *increase* in c (a larger budget, or a larger production quota) would indicate how the optimal solution is affected by a *relaxation* of the constraint.

To do the comparative-static analysis, we again resort to the implicit-function theorem. Taking the three equations in (12.8) to be in the form of $F^j(\lambda, x, y; c) = 0$ (with $j = 1, 2, 3$), and assuming them to have continuous partial derivatives, we must first check that the following endogenous-variable Jacobian (where $f_{xy} = f_{yx}$, and $g_{xy} = g_{yx}$)

$$|J| = \begin{vmatrix} \dfrac{\partial F^1}{\partial \lambda} & \dfrac{\partial F^1}{\partial x} & \dfrac{\partial F^1}{\partial y} \\[2mm] \dfrac{\partial F^2}{\partial \lambda} & \dfrac{\partial F^2}{\partial x} & \dfrac{\partial F^2}{\partial y} \\[2mm] \dfrac{\partial F^3}{\partial \lambda} & \dfrac{\partial F^3}{\partial x} & \dfrac{\partial F^3}{\partial y} \end{vmatrix} = \begin{vmatrix} 0 & -g_x & -g_y \\ -g_x & f_{xx} - \lambda g_{xx} & f_{xy} - \lambda g_{xy} \\ -g_y & f_{xy} - \lambda g_{xy} & f_{yy} - \lambda g_{yy} \end{vmatrix} \qquad \textbf{(12.12)}$$

does not vanish in the optimal state. At this moment, there is certainly no inkling that this would be the case. But our previous experience with the comparative statics of optimization problems [see the discussion of (11.46)] would suggest that this Jacobian is closely related to the second-order sufficient condition, and that if the sufficient condition is satisfied, then the Jacobian will be nonzero at the equilibrium (optimum). Leaving the full demonstration of this fact to Sec. 12.3, let us proceed on the assumption that $|J| \neq 0$. If so, then we can express λ^*, x^*, and y^* all as implicit functions of the parameter c:

$$\lambda^* = \lambda^*(c) \qquad x^* = x^*(c) \qquad \text{and} \qquad y^* = y^*(c) \qquad \textbf{(12.13)}$$

all of which will have continuous derivatives. Also, we have the equilibrium identities

$$c - g(x^*, y^*) \equiv 0$$
$$f_x(x^*, y^*) - \lambda^* g_x(x^*, y^*) \equiv 0 \qquad \textbf{(12.14)}$$
$$f_y(x^*, y^*) - \lambda^* g_y(x^*, y^*) \equiv 0$$

Now since the optimal value of Z depends on λ^*, x^*, and y^*, that is,

$$Z^* = f(x^*, y^*) + \lambda^*[c - g(x^*, y^*)] \tag{12.15}$$

we may, in view of (12.13), consider Z^* to be a function of c alone. Differentiating Z^* totally with respect to c, we find

$$\frac{dZ^*}{dc} = f_x \frac{dx^*}{dc} + f_y \frac{dy^*}{dc} + [c - g(x^*, y^*)]\frac{d\lambda^*}{dc} + \lambda^* \left(1 - g_x \frac{dx^*}{dc} - g_y \frac{dy^*}{dc}\right)$$

$$= (f_x - \lambda^* g_x)\frac{dx^*}{dc} + (f_y - \lambda^* g_y)\frac{dy^*}{dc} + [c - g(x^*, y^*)]\frac{d\lambda^*}{dc} + \lambda^*$$

where f_x, f_y, g_x, and g_y are all to be evaluated at the optimum. By (12.14), however, the first three terms on the right will all drop out. Thus we are left with the simple result

$$\frac{dZ^*}{dc} = \lambda^* \tag{12.16}$$

which validates our claim that the solution value of the Lagrange multiplier constitutes a measure of the effect of a change in the constraint via the parameter c on the optimal value of the objective function.

A word of caution, however, is perhaps in order here. For this interpretation of λ^*, you must express Z specifically as in (12.7). In particular, write the last term as $\lambda[c - g(x, y)]$, *not* $\lambda[g(x, y) - c]$.

n-Variable and Multiconstraint Cases

The generalization of the Lagrange-multiplier method to n variables can be easily carried out if we write the choice variables in subscript notation. The objective function will then be in the form

$$z = f(x_1, x_2, \ldots, x_n)$$

subject to the constraint

$$g(x_1, x_2, \ldots, x_n) = c$$

It follows that the Lagrangian function will be

$$Z = f(x_1, x_2, \ldots, x_n) + \lambda[c - g(x_1, x_2, \ldots, x_n)]$$

for which the first-order condition will consist of the following $(n + 1)$ simultaneous equations:

$$Z_\lambda = c - g(x_1, x_2, \ldots, x_n) = 0$$
$$Z_1 = f_1 - \lambda g_1 = 0$$
$$Z_2 = f_2 - \lambda g_2 = 0$$
$$\cdots\cdots\cdots\cdots\cdots$$
$$Z_n = f_n - \lambda g_n = 0$$

Again, the first of these equations will assure us that the constraint is met, even though we are to focus our attention on the *free* Lagrangian function.

When there is more than one constraint, the Lagrange-multiplier method is equally applicable, provided we introduce as many such multipliers as there are constraints in the Lagrangian function. Let an n-variable function be subject simultaneously to the two constraints

$$g(x_1, x_2, \ldots, x_n) = c \quad \text{and} \quad h(x_1, x_2, \ldots, x_n) = d$$

Then, adopting λ and μ (the Greek letter mu) as the two undetermined multipliers, we may construct a Lagrangian function as follows:

$$Z = f(x_1, x_2, \ldots, x_n) + \lambda[c - g(x_1, x_2, \ldots, x_n)] + \mu[d - h(x_1, x_2, \ldots, x_n)]$$

This function will have the same value as the original objective function f if both constraints are satisfied, i.e., if the last two terms in the Lagrangian function both vanish. Considering λ and μ as choice variables, we now count $(n + 2)$ variables, thus the first-order condition will in this case consist of the following $(n + 2)$ simultaneous equations:

$$Z_\lambda = c - g(x_1, x_2, \ldots, x_n) = 0$$
$$Z_\mu = d - h(x_1, x_2, \ldots, x_n) = 0$$
$$Z_i = f_i - \lambda g_i - \mu h_i = 0 \quad (i = 1, 2, \ldots, n)$$

These should normally enable us to solve for all the x_i as well as λ and μ. As before, the first two equations of the necessary condition represent essentially a mere restatement of the two constraints.

EXERCISE 12.2

1. Use the Lagrange-multiplier method to find the stationary values of z:
   (a) $z = xy$, subject to $x + 2y = 2$.
   (b) $z = x(y + 4)$, subject to $x + y = 8$.
   (c) $z = x - 3y - xy$, subject to $x + y = 6$.
   (d) $z = 7 - y + x^2$, subject to $x + y = 0$.

2. In Prob. 1, find whether a slight relaxation of the constraint will increase or decrease the optimal value of z. At what rate?

3. Write the Lagrangian function and the first-order condition for stationary values (without solving the equations) for each of the following:
   (a) $z = x + 2y + 3w + xy - yw$, subject to $x + y + 2w = 10$.
   (b) $z = x^2 + 2xy + yw^2$, subject to $2x + y + w^2 = 24$ and $x + w = 8$.

4. If, instead of $g(x, y) = c$, the constraint is written in the form of $G(x, y) = 0$, how should the Lagrangian function and the first-order condition be modified as a consequence?

5. In discussing the total-differential approach, it was pointed out that, given the constraint $g(x, y) = c$, we may deduce that $dg = 0$. By the same token, we can further deduce that $d^2g = d(dg) = d(0) = 0$. Yet, in our earlier discussion of the unconstrained extremum of a function $z = f(x, y)$, we had a situation where $dz = 0$ is accompanied by either a positive definite or a negative definite d^2z, rather than $d^2z = 0$. How would you account for this disparity of treatment in the two cases?

6. If the Lagrangian function is written as $Z = f(x, y) + \lambda[g(x, y) - c]$ rather than as in (12.7), can we still interpret the Lagrange multiplier as in (12.16)? Give the new interpretation, if any.

12.3　Second-Order Conditions

The introduction of a Lagrange multiplier as an additional variable makes it possible to apply to the constrained-extremum problem the same first-order condition used in the free-extremum problem. It is tempting to go a step further and borrow the second-order necessary-and-sufficient conditions as well. This, however, should not be done. For even though Z^* is indeed a standard type of extremum with respect to the choice variables, it is *not* so with respect to the Lagrange multiplier. Specifically, we can see from (12.15) that, unlike x^* and y^*, if λ^* is replaced by any other value of λ, no effect will be produced on Z^*, since $[c - g(x^*, y^*)]$ is identically zero. Thus the role played by λ in the optimal solution differs basically from that of x and y.[†] While it is harmless to treat λ as just another choice variable in the discussion of the first-order condition, we must be careful not to apply blindly the second-order conditions developed for the free-extremum problem to the present constrained case. Rather, we must derive a set of new ones. As we shall see, the new conditions can again be stated in terms of the second-order total differential d^2z. However, the presence of the constraint will entail certain significant modifications of the criterion.

Second-Order Total Differential

It has been mentioned that, inasmuch as the constraint $g(x, y) = c$ means $dg = g_x \, dx + g_y \, dy = 0$, as in (12.10), dx and dy no longer are both arbitrary. We may, of course, still take (say) dx as an arbitrary change, but then dy must be regarded as dependent on dx, always to be chosen so as to satisfy (12.10), i.e., to satisfy $dy = -(g_x/g_y) \, dx$. Viewed differently, once the value of dx is specified, dy will depend on g_x and g_y, but since the latter derivatives in turn depend on the variables x and y, dy will also depend on x and y. Obviously, then, the earlier formula for d^2z in (11.6), which is based on the arbitrariness of both dx and dy, can no longer apply.

To find an appropriate new expression for d^2z, we must treat dy as a variable dependent on x and y during differentiation (if dx is to be considered a constant). Thus,

$$
\begin{aligned}
d^2z = d(dz) &= \frac{\partial(dz)}{\partial x} \, dx + \frac{\partial(dz)}{\partial y} \, dy \\
&= \frac{\partial}{\partial x}(f_x \, dx + f_y \, dy)dx + \frac{\partial}{\partial y}(f_x \, dx + f_y \, dy)\,dy \\
&= \left[f_{xx} \, dx + \left(f_{xy} \, dy + f_y \frac{\partial dy}{\partial x} \right) \right] dx + \left[f_{yx} \, dx + \left(f_{yy} \, dy + f_y \frac{\partial dy}{\partial y} \right) \right] dy \\
&= f_{xx} \, dx^2 + f_{xy} \, dy \, dx + f_y \frac{\partial(dy)}{\partial x} \, dx + f_{yx} \, dx \, dy + f_{yy} \, dy^2 + f_y \frac{\partial(dy)}{\partial y} \, dy
\end{aligned}
$$

[†] In a more general framework of constrained optimization known as "nonlinear programming," to be discussed in Chap. 13, it will be shown that, with inequality constraints, if Z^* is a maximum (minimum) with respect to x and y, then it will in fact be a minimum (maximum) with respect to λ. In other words, the point (λ^*, x^*, y^*) is a saddle point. The present case—where Z^* is a genuine extremum with respect to x and y, but is invariant with respect to λ—may be considered as a degenerate case of the saddle point. The saddle-point nature of the solution (λ^*, x^*, y^*) also leads to the important concept of "duality." But this subject is best to be pursued later.

Since the third and the sixth terms can be reduced to

$$f_y \left[\frac{\partial(dy)}{\partial x} dx + \frac{\partial(dy)}{\partial y} dy \right] = f_y \, d(dy) = f_y \, d^2 y$$

the desired expression for $d^2 z$ is

$$d^2 z = f_{xx} \, dx^2 + 2 f_{xy} \, dx \, dy + f_{yy} \, dy^2 + f_y \, d^2 y \qquad \textbf{(12.17)}$$

which differs from (11.6) only by the last term, $f_y \, d^2 y$.

It should be noted that this last term is in the *first* degree [$d^2 y$ is *not* the same as $(dy)^2$]; thus its presence in (12.17) disqualifies $d^2 z$ as a quadratic form. However, $d^2 z$ can be transformed into a quadratic form by virtue of the constraint $g(x, y) = c$. Since the constraint implies $dg = 0$ and also $d^2 g = d(dg) = 0$, then by the procedure used in obtaining (12.17) we can get

$$(d^2 g =) g_{xx} \, dx^2 + 2 g_{xy} \, dx \, dy + g_{yy} \, dy^2 + g_y \, d^2 y = 0$$

Solving this last equation for $d^2 y$ and substituting the result in (12.17), we are able to eliminate the first-degree expression $d^2 y$ and write $d^2 z$ as the following quadratic form:

$$d^2 z = \left(f_{xx} - \frac{f_y}{g_y} g_{xx} \right) dx^2 + 2 \left(f_{xy} - \frac{f_y}{g_y} g_{xy} \right) dx \, dy + \left(f_{yy} - \frac{f_y}{g_y} g_{yy} \right) dy^2$$

Because of (12.11′), the first parenthetical coefficient is reducible to $(f_{xx} - \lambda g_{xx})$, and similarly for the other terms. However, by partially differentiating the derivatives in (12.8), you will find that the following second derivatives

$$\begin{aligned}
Z_{xx} &= f_{xx} - \lambda g_{xx} \\
Z_{xy} &= f_{xy} - \lambda g_{xy} = Z_{yx} \qquad \textbf{(12.18)} \\
Z_{yy} &= f_{yy} - \lambda g_{yy}
\end{aligned}$$

are precisely equal to these parenthetical coefficients. Hence, by making use of the Lagrangian function, we can finally express $d^2 z$ more neatly as follows:

$$\begin{aligned}
d^2 z = \quad & Z_{xx} \, dx^2 \quad + Z_{xy} \, dx \, dy \\
& + Z_{yx} \, dy \, dx + Z_{yy} \, dy^2 \qquad \textbf{(12.17′)}
\end{aligned}$$

The coefficients of (12.17′) are simply the second partial derivatives of Z with respect to the choice variables x and y; together, therefore, they can give rise to a Hessian determinant.

Second-Order Conditions

For a constrained extremum of $z = f(x, y)$, subject to $g(x, y) = c$, the second-order necessary-and-sufficient conditions still revolve around the algebraic sign of the second-order total differential $d^2 z$, evaluated at a stationary point. However, there is one important change. In the present context, we are concerned with the sign definiteness or semidefiniteness of $d^2 z$, *not* for all possible values of dx and dy (not both zero), but *only* for those

dx and dy values (not both zero) satisfying the linear constraint (12.10), $g_x dx + g_y dy = 0$. Thus the second-order *necessary* conditions are

For maximum of z: d^2z negative semidefinite, subject to $dg = 0$

For minimum of z: d^2z positive semidefinite, subject to $dg = 0$

and the second-order *sufficient* conditions are

For maximum of z: d^2z negative definite, subject to $dg = 0$

For minimum of z: d^2z positive definite, subject to $dg = 0$

In the following, we shall concentrate on the second-order sufficient conditions.

Inasmuch as the (dx, dy) pairs satisfying the constraint $g_x\, dx + g_y\, dy = 0$ constitute merely a subset of the set of all possible dx and dy, the constrained sign definiteness is less stringent—that is, easier to satisfy—than the unconstrained sign definiteness discussed in Chap. 11. In other words, the second-order sufficient condition for a constrained-extremum problem is a weaker condition than that for a free-extremum problem. This is welcome news because, unlike necessary conditions which must be stringent in order to serve as effective screening devices, sufficient conditions should be weak to be truly serviceable.[†]

The Bordered Hessian

As in the case of free extremum, it is possible to express the second-order sufficient condition in determinantal form. In place of the Hessian determinant $|H|$, however, in the constrained-extremum case we shall encounter what is known as a *bordered Hessian*.

In preparation for the development of this idea, let us first analyze the conditions for the sign definiteness of a two-variable quadratic form, subject to a linear constraint, say,

$$q = au^2 + 2\,huv + bv^2 \qquad \text{subject to} \qquad \alpha u + \beta v = 0$$

Since the constraint implies $v = -(\alpha/\beta)u$, we can rewrite q as a function of one variable only:

$$q = au^2 - 2h\frac{\alpha}{\beta}u^2 + b\frac{\alpha^2}{\beta^2}u^2 = (a\beta^2 - 2h\alpha\beta + b\alpha^2)\frac{u^2}{\beta^2}$$

It is obvious that q is positive (negative) definite if and only if the expression in parentheses is positive (negative). Now, it so happens that the following symmetric determinant

$$\begin{vmatrix} 0 & \alpha & \beta \\ \alpha & a & h \\ \beta & h & b \end{vmatrix} = 2h\alpha\beta - a\beta^2 - b\alpha^2$$

is exactly the *negative* of the said parenthetical expression. Consequently, we can state that

$$q \text{ is } \begin{Bmatrix} \text{positive definite} \\ \text{negative definite} \end{Bmatrix} \text{ subject to } \alpha u + \beta v = 0 \qquad \text{iff} \qquad \begin{vmatrix} 0 & \alpha & \beta \\ \alpha & a & h \\ \beta & h & b \end{vmatrix} \begin{Bmatrix} < 0 \\ > 0 \end{Bmatrix}$$

[†] "A million-dollar bank deposit" is clearly a sufficient condition for "being able to afford a steak dinner." But the extremely limited applicability of that condition renders it practically useless. A more meaningful sufficient condition might be something like "fifty dollars in one's wallet," which is a much less stringent financial requirement.

It is noteworthy that the determinant used in this criterion is nothing but the discriminant of the original quadratic form $\begin{vmatrix} a & h \\ h & b \end{vmatrix}$, with a border placed on top and a similar border on the left. Furthermore, the border is merely composed of the two coefficients α and β from the constraint, plus a zero in the principal diagonal. This bordered discriminant is symmetric.

Example 1

Determine whether $q = 4u^2 + 4uv + 3v^2$, subject to $u - 2v = 0$, is either positive or negative definite. We first form the bordered discriminant $\begin{vmatrix} 0 & 1 & -2 \\ 1 & 4 & 2 \\ -2 & 2 & 3 \end{vmatrix}$, which is made symmetric by splitting the coefficient of uv into two equal parts for insertion into the determinant. Inasmuch as the determinant has a negative value (-27), q must be positive definite.

When applied to the quadratic form d^2z in (12.17′), the variables u and v become dx and dy, respectively, and the (plain) discriminant consists of the Hessian $\begin{vmatrix} Z_{xx} & Z_{xy} \\ Z_{yx} & Z_{yy} \end{vmatrix}$. Moreover, the constraint to the quadratic form being $g_x\,dx + g_y\,dy = 0$, we have $\alpha = g_x$ and $\beta = g_y$. Thus, for values of dx and dy that satisfy the said constraint, we now have the following determinantal criterion for the sign definiteness of d^2z:

$$d^2z \text{ is} \begin{Bmatrix} \text{positive definite} \\ \text{negative definite} \end{Bmatrix} \text{subject to } dg = 0 \qquad \text{iff} \qquad \begin{vmatrix} 0 & g_x & g_y \\ g_x & Z_{xx} & Z_{xy} \\ g_y & Z_{yx} & Z_{yy} \end{vmatrix} \begin{Bmatrix} < 0 \\ > 0 \end{Bmatrix}$$

The determinant to the right, often referred to as a bordered Hessian, shall be denoted by $|\overline{H}|$, where the bar on top symbolizes the border. On the basis of this, we may conclude that, given a stationary value of $z = f(x, y)$ or of $Z = f(x, y) + \lambda[c - g(x, y)]$, a positive $|\overline{H}|$ is sufficient to establish it as a relative maximum of z; similarly, a negative $|\overline{H}|$ is sufficient to establish it as a minimum—all the derivatives involved in $|\overline{H}|$ being evaluated at the critical values of x and y.

Now that we have derived the second-order sufficient condition, it is an easy matter to verify that, as earlier claimed, the satisfaction of this condition will guarantee that the endogenous-variable Jacobian (12.12) does not vanish in the optimal state. Substituting (12.18) into (12.12), and multiplying both the first column and the first row of the Jacobian by -1 (which will leave the value of the determinant unaltered), we see that

$$|J| = \begin{vmatrix} 0 & g_x & g_y \\ g_x & Z_{xx} & Z_{xy} \\ g_y & Z_{yx} & Z_{yy} \end{vmatrix} = |\overline{H}| \qquad\qquad \textbf{(12.19)}$$

That is, the endogenous-variable Jacobian is identical with the bordered Hessian—a result similar to (11.42) where it was shown that, in the free-extremum context, the endogenous-variable Jacobian is identical with the plain Hessian. If, in fulfillment of the sufficient condition, we have $|\overline{H}| \neq 0$ at the optimum, then $|J|$ must also be nonzero. Consequently, in applying the implicit-function theorem to the present context, it would not be amiss to substitute the condition $|\overline{H}| \neq 0$ for the usual condition $|J| \neq 0$. This practice will be followed when we analyze the comparative statics of constrained-optimization problems in Sec. 12.5.

Example 2

Let us now return to Example 1 of Sec. 12.2 and ascertain whether the stationary value found there gives a maximum or a minimum. Since $Z_x = y - \lambda$ and $Z_y = x - \lambda$, the second-order partial derivatives are $Z_{xx} = 0$, $Z_{xy} = Z_{yx} = 1$, and $Z_{yy} = 0$. The border elements we need are $g_x = 1$ and $g_y = 1$. Thus we find that

$$|\bar{H}| = \begin{vmatrix} 0 & 1 & 1 \\ 1 & 0 & 1 \\ 1 & 1 & 0 \end{vmatrix} = 2 > 0$$

which establishes the value $z^* = 9$ as a maximum.

Example 3

Continuing on to Example 2 of Sec. 12.2, we see that $Z_1 = 2x_1 - \lambda$ and $Z_2 = 2x_2 - 4\lambda$. These yield $Z_{11} = 2$, $Z_{12} = Z_{21} = 0$, and $Z_{22} = 2$. From the constraint $x_1 + 4x_2 = 2$, we obtain $g_1 = 1$ and $g_2 = 4$. It follows that the bordered Hessian is

$$|\bar{H}| = \begin{vmatrix} 0 & 1 & 4 \\ 1 & 2 & 0 \\ 4 & 0 & 2 \end{vmatrix} = -34 < 0$$

and the value $z^* = \frac{4}{17}$ is a minimum.

Example 4

Consider a simple two-period model where a consumer's utility is a function of consumption in both periods. Let the consumer's utility function be

$$U(x_1, x_2) = x_1 x_2$$

where x_1 is consumption in period 1 and x_2 is consumption in period 2. The consumer is also endowed with a budget B at the beginning of period 1.

Let r denote a market interest rate at which the consumer can choose to borrow or lend across the two periods. The consumer's intertemporal budget constraint is that x_1 and the present value of x_2 add up to B. Thus,

$$x_1 + \frac{x_2}{1 + r} = B$$

The Lagrangian for this utility maximization problem is

$$Z = x_1 x_2 + \lambda \left(B - x_1 - \frac{x_2}{1 + r} \right)$$

with first-order conditions

$$\frac{\partial Z}{\partial \lambda} = B - x_1 - \frac{x_2}{1 + r} = 0$$

$$\frac{\partial Z}{\partial x_1} = x_2 - \lambda = 0$$

$$\frac{\partial Z}{\partial x_2} = x_1 - \frac{\lambda}{1 + r} = 0$$

Combining the last two first-order equations to eliminate λ gives us

$$\frac{x_2}{x_1} = \frac{\lambda}{\lambda/(1 + r)} = 1 + r$$

Substituting this equation into the budget constraint then yields the solution

$$x_1^* = \frac{B}{2} \quad \text{and} \quad x_2^* = \frac{B(1 + r)}{2}$$

Next, we should check the second-order sufficient condition for a maximum. The bordered Hessian for this problem is

$$|\bar{H}| = \begin{vmatrix} 0 & -1 & -\dfrac{1}{1+r} \\ -1 & 0 & 1 \\ -\dfrac{1}{1+r} & 1 & 0 \end{vmatrix} = \dfrac{2}{1+r} > 0$$

Thus the second-order sufficient condition is satisfied for a maximum U.

n-Variable Case

When the objective function takes the form

$$z = f(x_1, x_2, \ldots, x_n) \qquad \text{subject to} \qquad g(x_1, x_2, \ldots, x_n) = c$$

the second-order condition still hinges on the sign of d^2z. Since the latter is a constrained quadratic form in the variables $dx_1, dx_2, \ldots, dx_n$, subject to the relation

$$(dg =) g_1\, dx_1 + g_2\, dx_2 + \cdots + g_n\, dx_n = 0$$

the conditions for the positive or negative definiteness of d^2z again involve a bordered Hessian. But this time these conditions must be expressed in terms of the bordered leading principal minors of the Hessian.

Given a bordered Hessian

$$|\bar{H}| = \begin{vmatrix} 0 & g_1 & g_2 & \cdots & g_n \\ g_1 & Z_{11} & Z_{12} & \cdots & Z_{1n} \\ g_2 & Z_{21} & Z_{22} & \cdots & Z_{2n} \\ \cdots\cdots\cdots\cdots\cdots\cdots\cdots\cdots\cdots \\ g_n & Z_{n1} & Z_{n2} & \cdots & Z_{nn} \end{vmatrix}$$

its bordered leading principal minors can be defined as

$$|\bar{H}_2| \equiv \begin{vmatrix} 0 & g_1 & g_2 \\ g_1 & Z_{11} & Z_{12} \\ g_2 & Z_{21} & Z_{22} \end{vmatrix} \qquad |\bar{H}_3| \equiv \begin{vmatrix} 0 & g_1 & g_2 & g_3 \\ g_1 & Z_{11} & Z_{12} & Z_{13} \\ g_2 & Z_{21} & Z_{22} & Z_{23} \\ g_3 & Z_{31} & Z_{32} & Z_{33} \end{vmatrix} \qquad \text{(etc.)}$$

with the last one being $|\bar{H}_n| = |\bar{H}|$. In the newly introduced symbols, the horizontal bar above H again means bordered, and the subscript indicates the order of the leading principal minor being bordered. For instance, $|\bar{H}_2|$ involves the second leading principal minor of the (plain) Hessian, bordered with 0, g_1, and g_2; and similarly for the others. The conditions for positive and negative definiteness of d^2z are then

$$d^2z \text{ is } \left\{ \begin{array}{l} \text{positive definite} \\ \text{negative definite} \end{array} \right\} \text{ subject to } dg = 0 \quad \text{iff} \quad \left\{ \begin{array}{l} |\bar{H}_2|, |\bar{H}_3|, \ldots, |\bar{H}_n| < 0 \\ |\bar{H}_2| > 0; |\bar{H}_3| < 0; |\bar{H}_4| > 0; \text{etc.} \end{array} \right.$$

In the former, all the bordered leading principal minors, starting with $|\bar{H}_2|$, must be negative; in the latter, they must alternate in sign. As previously, a positive definite d^2z is

TABLE 12.1 **Determinantal Test for Relative Constrained Extremum:** $z = f(x_1, x_2, \ldots, x_n)$, **Subject to** $g(x_1, x_2, \ldots, x_n) = c$; **with** $Z = f(x_1, x_2, \ldots, x_n) + \lambda[c - g(x_1, x_2, \ldots, x_n)]$

Condition	Maximum	Minimum
First-order necessary condition	$Z_\lambda = Z_1 = Z_2 = \cdots = Z_n = 0$	$Z_\lambda = Z_1 = Z_2 = \cdots = Z_n = 0$
Second-order sufficient condition[†]	$\|\bar{H}_2\| > 0; \|\bar{H}_3\| < 0;$ $\|\bar{H}_4\| > 0; \ldots; (-1)^n\|\bar{H}_n\| > 0$	$\|\bar{H}_2\|, \|\bar{H}_3\|, \ldots, \|\bar{H}_n\| < 0$

[†] Applicable only after the first-order necessary condition has been satisfied.

sufficient to establish a stationary value of z as its minimum, whereas a negative definite d^2z is sufficient to establish it as a maximum.

Drawing the threads of the discussion together, we may summarize the conditions for a constrained relative extremum in Table 12.1. You will recognize, however, that the criterion stated in the table is not complete. Because the second-order sufficient condition is *not* necessary, failure to satisfy the criteria stated does not preclude the possibility that the stationary value is nonetheless a maximum or a minimum as the case may be. In many economic applications, however, this (relatively less stringent) second-order sufficient condition is either satisfied, or assumed to be satisfied, so that the information in the table is adequate. It should prove instructive for you to compare the results contained in Table 12.1 with those in Table 11.2 for the free-extremum case.

Multiconstraint Case

When more than one constraint appears in the problem, the second-order condition involves a Hessian with more than one border. Suppose that there are n choice variables and m constraints ($m < n$) of the form $g^j(x_1, \ldots, x_n) = c_j$. Then the Lagrangian function will be

$$Z = f(x_1, \ldots, x_n) + \sum_{j=1}^{m} \lambda_j[c_j - g^j(x_1, \ldots, x_n)]$$

and the bordered Hessian will appear as

$$|\bar{H}| \equiv \begin{vmatrix} 0 & 0 & \cdots & 0 & g_1^1 & g_2^1 & \cdots & g_n^1 \\ 0 & 0 & \cdots & 0 & g_1^2 & g_2^2 & \cdots & g_n^2 \\ \cdots & & & & & & & \cdots \\ 0 & 0 & \cdots & 0 & g_1^m & g_2^m & \cdots & g_n^m \\ \hline g_1^1 & g_1^2 & \cdots & g_1^m & Z_{11} & Z_{12} & \cdots & Z_{1n} \\ g_2^1 & g_2^2 & \cdots & g_2^m & Z_{21} & Z_{22} & \cdots & Z_{2n} \\ \cdots & & & & & & & \cdots \\ g_n^1 & g_n^2 & \cdots & g_n^m & Z_{n1} & Z_{n2} & \cdots & Z_{nn} \end{vmatrix}$$

where $g_i^j \equiv \partial g^j / \partial x_i$ are the partial derivatives of the constraint functions, and the double-subscripted Z symbols denote, as before, the second-order partial derivatives of the Lagrangian function. Note that we have partitioned the bordered Hessian into four *areas* for visual clarity. The upper-left area consists of zeros only, and the lower-right area is simply the plain Hessian. The other two areas, containing the g_i^j derivatives, bear a mirror-image relationship to each other with reference to the principal diagonal, thereby resulting in a symmetric array of elements in the entire bordered Hessian.

Various bordered leading principal minors can be formed from $|\overline{H}|$. The one that contains Z_{22} as the last element of its principal diagonal may be denoted by $|\overline{H}_2|$, as before. By including one more row and one more column, so that Z_{33} enters into the scene, we will have $|\overline{H}_3|$, and so forth. With this symbology, we can state the second-order sufficient condition in terms of the signs of the following $(n - m)$ bordered leading principal minors:

$$|\overline{H}_{m+1}|, |\overline{H}_{m+2}|, \ldots, |\overline{H}_n|(= |\overline{H}|)$$

For a maximum of z, a sufficient condition is that these bordered leading principal minors alternate in sign, the sign of $|\overline{H}_{m+1}|$ being that of $(-1)^{m+1}$. For a minimum of z, a sufficient condition is that these principal minors all take the same sign, namely, that of $(-1)^m$.

Note that it makes an important difference whether we have an odd or even number of constraints, because (-1) raised to an odd power will yield the opposite sign to the case of an even power. Note, also, that when $m = 1$, the condition just stated reduces to that presented in Table 12.1.

EXERCISE 12.3

1. Use the bordered Hessian to determine whether the stationary value of z obtained in each part of Exercise 12.2-1 is a maximum or a minimum.

2. In stating the second-order sufficient conditions for constrained maximum and minimum, we specified the algebraic signs of $|\overline{H}_2|$, $|\overline{H}_3|$, $|\overline{H}_4|$, etc., but not of $|\overline{H}_1|$. Write out an appropriate expression for $|\overline{H}_1|$, and verify that it invariably takes the negative sign.

3. Recalling Property II of determinants (Sec. 5.3), show that:

   (a) By appropriately interchanging two rows and/or two columns of $|\overline{H}_2|$ and duly altering the sign of the determinant after each interchange, it can be transformed into

   $$\begin{vmatrix} Z_{11} & Z_{12} & g_1 \\ Z_{21} & Z_{22} & g_2 \\ g_1 & g_2 & 0 \end{vmatrix}$$

   (b) By a similar procedure, $|\overline{H}_3|$ can be transformed into

   $$\begin{vmatrix} Z_{11} & Z_{12} & Z_{13} & g_1 \\ Z_{21} & Z_{22} & Z_{23} & g_2 \\ Z_{31} & Z_{32} & Z_{33} & g_3 \\ g_1 & g_2 & g_3 & 0 \end{vmatrix}$$

   What alternative way of "bordering" the principal minors of the Hessian do these results suggest?

4. Write out the bordered Hessian for a constrained optimization problem with four choice variables and two constraints. Then state specifically the second-order sufficient condition for a maximum and for a minimum of z, respectively.

12.4 Quasiconcavity and Quasiconvexity

In Sec. 11.5 it was shown that, for a problem of free extremum, a knowledge of the concavity or convexity of the objective function obviates the need to check the second-order condition. In the context of constrained optimization, it is again possible to dispense with the second-order condition if the surface or hypersurface has the appropriate type of configuration. But this time the desired configuration is quasiconcavity (rather than concavity) for a maximum, and quasiconvexity (rather than convexity) for a minimum. As we shall demonstrate, quasiconcavity (quasiconvexity) is a weaker condition than concavity (convexity). This is only to be expected, since the second-order sufficient condition to be dispensed with is also weaker for the constrained optimization problem (d^2z definite in sign only for those dx_i satisfying $dg = 0$) than for the free one (d^2z definite in sign for *all* dx_i).

Geometric Characterization

Quasiconcavity and quasiconvexity, like concavity and convexity, can be either strict or nonstrict. We shall first present the geometric characterization of these concepts:

> Let u and v be any two distinct points in the domain (a convex set) of a function f, and let line segment uv in the domain give rise to arc MN on the graph of the function, such that point N is higher than or equal in height to point M. Then function f is said to be *quasiconcave* (*quasiconvex*) if all points on arc MN other than M and N are higher than or equal in height to point M (lower than or equal in height to point N). The function f is said to be *strictly quasiconcave* (*strictly quasiconvex*) if all the points on arc MN other than M and N are strictly higher than point M (strictly lower than point N).

It should be clear from this that any strictly quasiconcave (strictly quasiconvex) function is quasiconcave (quasiconvex), but the converse is not true.

For a better grasp, let us examine the illustrations in Fig. 12.3, all drawn for the one-variable case. In Fig.12.3a, line segment uv in the domain gives rise to arc MN on the curve such that N is higher than M. Since all the points between M and N on the said arc are strictly higher than M, this particular arc satisfies the condition for strict quasiconcavity. For the curve to qualify as strictly quasiconcave, however, *all* possible (u, v) pairs must have arcs that satisfy the same condition. This is indeed the case for the function in Fig. 12.3a. Note that this function also satisfies the condition for (nonstrict) quasiconcavity. But it fails the condition for quasiconvexity, because some points on arc MN are higher than N, which is forbidden for a quasiconvex function. The function in Fig. 12.3b has the opposite configuration. All the points on arc $M'N'$ are lower than N', the higher of the two ends, and the same is true of all arcs that can be drawn. Thus the function in Fig. 12.3b is strictly

FIGURE 12.3

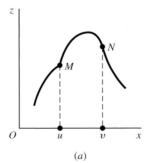

(a)

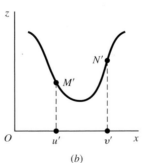

(b)

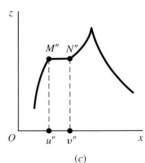

(c)

FIGURE 12.4

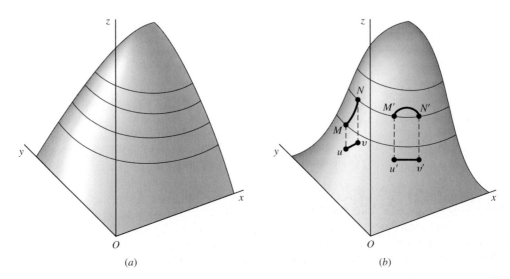

(a)   (b)

quasiconvex. As you can verify, it also satisfies the condition for (nonstrict) quasiconvex-ity, but fails the condition for quasiconcavity. What distinguishes Fig. 12.3*c* is the presence of a horizontal line segment $M''N''$, where all the points have the same height. As a result, that line segment—and hence the entire curve—can only meet the condition for quasicon-cavity, but not strict quasiconcavity.

Generally speaking, a quasiconcave function that is not also concave has a graph roughly shaped like a bell, or a portion thereof, and a quasiconvex function has a graph shaped like an inverted bell, or a portion thereof. On the bell, it is admissible (though not required) to have both concave and convex segments. This more permissive nature of the characterization makes quasiconcavity (quasiconvexity) a weaker condition than concavity (convexity). In Fig. 12.4, we contrast strict concavity against strict quasiconcavity for the two-variable case. As drawn, both surfaces depict increasing functions, as they contain only the ascending por-tions of a dome and a bell, respectively. The surface in Fig. 12.4*a* is strictly concave, but the one in Fig. 12.4*b* is certainly not, since it contains convex portions near the base of the bell. Yet it is strictly quasiconcave; all the arcs on the surface, exemplified by MN and $M'N'$, sat-isfy the condition that all the points on each arc between the two end points are higher than the lower end point. Returning to Fig. 12.4*a*, we should note that the surface therein is also strictly quasiconcave. Although we have not drawn any illustrative arcs MN and $M'N'$ in Fig. 12.4*a*, it is not difficult to check that all possible arcs do indeed satisfy the condition for strict quasi-concavity. In general, a strictly concave function must be strictly quasiconcave, although the converse is not true. We shall demonstrate this more formally in the paragraphs that follow.

Algebraic Definition

The preceding geometric characterization can be translated into an algebraic definition for easier generalization to higher-dimensional cases:

A function f is $\begin{Bmatrix} \text{quasiconcave} \\ \text{quasiconvex} \end{Bmatrix}$ iff, for any pair of distinct points u and v in the (convex-set) domain of f, and for $0 < \theta < 1$,

$$f(v) \geq f(u) \Rightarrow f[\theta u + (1-\theta)v] \begin{Bmatrix} \geq f(u) \\ \leq f(v) \end{Bmatrix} \qquad \textbf{(12.20)}$$

To adapt this definition to *strict* quasiconcavity and quasiconvexity, the two weak inequalities on the right should be changed into strict inequalities $\left\{ \begin{array}{c} > f(u) \\ < f(v) \end{array} \right\}$. You may find it instructive to compare (12.20) with (11.20).

From this definition, the following three theorems readily follow. These will be stated in terms of a function $f(x)$, where x can be interpreted as a vector of variables, $x = (x_1, \ldots, x_n)$.

Theorem I **(negative of a function)** If $f(x)$ is quasiconcave (strictly quasiconcave), then $-f(x)$ is quasiconvex (strictly quasiconvex).

Theorem II **(concavity versus quasiconcavity)** Any concave (convex) function is quasiconcave (quasiconvex), but the converse is not true. Similarly, any strictly concave (strictly convex) function is strictly quasiconcave (strictly quasiconvex), but the converse is not true.

Theorem III **(linear function)** If $f(x)$ is a linear function, then it is quasiconcave as well as quasiconvex.

Theorem I follows from the fact that multiplying an inequality by -1 reverses the sense of inequality. Let $f(x)$ be quasiconcave, with $f(v) \geq f(u)$. Then, by (12.20), $f[\theta u + (1 - \theta)v] \geq f(u)$. As far as the function $-f(x)$ is concerned, however, we have (after multiplying the two inequalities through by -1) $- f(u) \geq -f(v)$ and $-f[\theta u + (1 - \theta)v] \leq -f(u)$. Interpreting $-f(u)$ as the height of point N, and $-f(v)$ as the height of M, we see that the function $-f(x)$ satisfies the condition for quasiconvexity in (12.20). This proves one of the four cases cited in Theorem I; the proofs for the other three are similar.

For Theorem II, we shall only prove that concavity implies quasiconcavity. Let $f(x)$ be concave. Then, by (11.20),

$$f[\theta u + (1 - \theta)v] \geq \theta f(u) + (1 - \theta)f(v)$$

Now assume that $f(v) \geq f(u)$; then any weighted average of $f(v)$ and $f(u)$ cannot possibly be less than $f(u)$, i.e.,

$$\theta f(u) + (1 - \theta)f(v) \geq f(u)$$

Combining these two results, we find that, by transitivity,

$$f[\theta u + (1 - \theta)v] \geq f(u) \qquad \text{for } f(v) \geq f(u)$$

which satisfies the definition of quasiconcavity in (12.20). Note, however, that the condition for quasiconcavity cannot guarantee concavity.

Once Theorem II is established, Theorem III follows immediately. We already know that a linear function is both concave and convex, though not strictly so. In view of Theorem II, a linear function must also be both quasiconcave and quasiconvex, though not strictly so.

In the case of concave and convex functions, there is a useful theorem to the effect that the sum of concave (convex) functions is also concave (convex). Unfortunately, this theorem cannot be generalized to quasiconcave and quasiconvex functions. For instance, a sum of two quasiconcave functions is *not necessarily* quasiconcave (see Exercise 12.4-3).

FIGURE 12.5

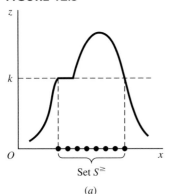

Set $S^\geqq$

(a)

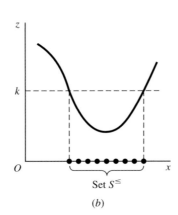

Set $S^\leqq$

(b)

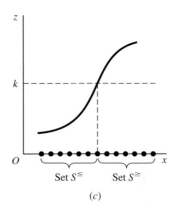

Set $S^\leqq$ Set $S^\geqq$

(c)

Sometimes it may prove easier to check quasiconcavity and quasiconvexity by the following alternative definition:

A function $f(x)$, where x is a vector of variables, is $\left\{ \begin{array}{l} \text{quasiconcave} \\ \text{quasiconvex} \end{array} \right\}$ iff, for any constant k, the set

$$\left. \begin{array}{l} S^\geqq \equiv \{x \mid f(x) \geq k\} \\ S^\leqq \equiv \{x \mid f(x) \leq k\} \end{array} \right\} \text{ is a convex set} \qquad \textbf{(12.21)}$$

The sets $S^\geqq$ and $S^\leqq$, which are subsets of the domain, were introduced earlier (Fig. 11.10) to show that a convex function (or even a concave function) can give rise to a convex set. Here we are employing these two sets as tests for quasiconcavity and quasiconvexity. The three functions in Fig. 12.5 all contain concave as well as convex segments and hence are neither convex nor concave. But the function in Fig. 12.5a is quasiconcave, because for any value of k (only one of which has been illustrated), the set $S^\geqq$ is convex. The function in Fig. 12.5b is, on the other hand, quasiconvex since the set $S^\leqq$ is convex. The function in Fig. 12.5c—a monotonic function—differs from the other two in that both $S^\geqq$ and $S^\leqq$ are convex sets. Hence that function is quasiconcave as well as quasiconvex.

Note that while (12.21) can be used to check quasiconcavity and quasiconvexity, it is incapable of distinguishing between strict and nonstrict varieties of these properties. Note, also, that the defining properties in (12.21) are in themselves not sufficient for concavity and convexity, respectively. In particular, given a concave function which must perforce be quasiconcave, we can conclude that $S^\geqq$ is a convex set; but given that $S^\geqq$ is a convex set, we can conclude only that the function f is *quasi*concave (but not necessarily concave).

Example 1   Check $z = x^2$ $(x \geq 0)$ for quasiconcavity and quasiconvexity. This function is easily verified geometrically to be convex, in fact strictly so. Hence it is quasiconvex. Interestingly, it is also quasiconcave. For its graph—the right half of a U-shaped curve, initiating from the point of origin and increasing at an increasing rate—is, similarly to Fig. 12.5c, capable of generating a convex $S^\geqq$ as well as a convex $S^\leqq$.

If we wish to apply (12.20) instead, we first let u and v be any two distinct nonnegative values of x. Then

$$f(u) = u^2 \quad f(v) = v^2 \quad \text{and} \quad f[\theta u + (1-\theta)v] = [\theta u + (1-\theta)v]^2$$

Suppose that $f(v) \geq f(u)$, that is, $v^2 \geq u^2$; then $v \geq u$, or more specifically, $v > u$ (since u and v are distinct). Inasmuch as the weighted average $[\theta u + (1 - \theta)v]$ must lie between u and v, we may write the continuous inequality

$$v^2 > [\theta u + (1 - \theta)v]^2 > u^2 \qquad \text{for } 0 < \theta < 1$$

or
$$f(v) > f[\theta u + (1 - \theta)v] > f(u) \qquad \text{for } 0 < \theta < 1$$

By (12.20), this result makes the function f *both* quasiconcave and quasiconvex—indeed strictly so.

Example 2

Show that $z = f(x, y) = xy$ (with $x, y \geq 0$) is quasiconcave. We shall use the criterion in (12.21) and establish that the set $S^{\geq} = \{(x, y) \mid xy \geq k\}$ is a convex set for any k. For this purpose, we set $xy = k$ to obtain an isovalue curve for each value of k. Like x and y, k should be nonnegative. In case $k > 0$, the isovalue curve is a rectangular hyperbola in the first quadrant of the xy plane. The set $S^{\geq}$, consisting of all the points on or above a rectangular hyperbola, is a convex set. In the other case, with $k = 0$, the isovalue curve as defined by $xy = 0$ is L-shaped, with the L coinciding with the nonnegative segments of the x and y axes. The set $S^{\geq}$, consisting this time of the entire nonnegative quadrant, is again a convex set. Thus, by (12.21), the function $z = xy$ (with $x, y \geq 0$) is quasiconcave.

You should be careful not to confuse the shape of the isovalue curves $xy = k$ (which is defined in the xy plane) with the shape of the surface $z = xy$ (which is defined in the xyz space). The characteristic of the z surface (quasiconcave in 3-space) is what we wish to ascertain; the shape of the isovalue curves (convex in 2-space for positive k) is of interest here only as a means to delineate the sets $S^{\geq}$ in order to apply the criterion in (12.21).

Example 3

Show that $z = f(x, y) = (x - a)^2 + (y - b)^2$ is quasiconvex. Let us again apply (12.21). Setting $(x - a)^2 + (y - b)^2 = k$, we see that k must be nonnegative. For each k, the isovalue curve is a circle in the xy plane with its center at (a, b) and with radius $\sqrt{k}$. Since $S^{\leq} = \{(x, y) \mid (x - a)^2 + (y - b)^2 \leq k\}$ is the set of all points on or inside a circle, it constitutes a convex set. This is true even when $k = 0$—when the circle degenerates into a single point, (a, b)—since by convention a single point is considered as a convex set. Thus the given function is quasiconvex.

Differentiable Functions

The definitions (12.20) and (12.21) do not require differentiability of the function f. If f is differentiable, however, quasiconcavity and quasiconvexity can alternatively be defined in terms of its first derivatives:

A differentiable function of one variable, $f(x)$, is $\begin{Bmatrix} \text{quasiconcave} \\ \text{quasiconvex} \end{Bmatrix}$ iff, for any pair of distinct points u and v in the domain,

$$f(v) \geq f(u) \Rightarrow \begin{Bmatrix} f'(u)(v - u) \\ f'(v)(v - u) \end{Bmatrix} \geq 0 \qquad \textbf{(12.22)}$$

Quasiconcavity and quasiconvexity will be *strict*, if the weak inequality on the right is changed to the strict inequality > 0. When there are two or more independent variables, the definition is to be modified as follows:

A differentiable function $f(x_1, \ldots, x_n)$ is $\begin{Bmatrix} \text{quasiconcave} \\ \text{quasiconvex} \end{Bmatrix}$ iff, for any two distinct points

$u = (u_1, \ldots, u_n)$ and $v = (v_1, \ldots, v_n)$ in the domain,

$$f(v) \geq f(u) \Rightarrow \left\{ \begin{array}{c} \displaystyle\sum_{j=1}^{n} f_j(u)(v_j - u_j) \\[4mm] \displaystyle\sum_{j=1}^{n} f_j(v)(v_j - u_j) \end{array} \right\} \geq 0 \qquad (12.22')$$

where $f_j \equiv \partial f / \partial x_j$, to be evaluated at u or v as the case may be.

Again, for *strict* quasiconcavity and quasiconvexity, the weak inequality on the right should be changed to the strict inequality > 0.

Finally, if a function $z = f(x_1, \ldots, x_n)$ is twice continuously differentiable, quasiconcavity and quasiconvexity can be checked by means of the first and second partial derivatives of the function, arranged into the bordered determinant

$$|B| = \begin{vmatrix} 0 & f_1 & f_2 & \cdots & f_n \\ f_1 & f_{11} & f_{12} & \cdots & f_{1n} \\ f_2 & f_{21} & f_{22} & \cdots & f_{2n} \\ \multicolumn{5}{c}{\dotfill} \\ f_n & f_{n1} & f_{n2} & \cdots & f_{nn} \end{vmatrix} \qquad (12.23)$$

This bordered determinant resembles the bordered Hessian $|\overline{H}|$ introduced in Sec. 12.3. But unlike the latter, the border in $|B|$ is composed of the first derivatives of the function f rather than an extraneous constraint function g. It is because $|B|$ depends exclusively on the derivatives of function f itself that we can use $|B|$, along with its leading principal minors

$$|B_1| = \begin{vmatrix} 0 & f_1 \\ f_1 & f_{11} \end{vmatrix} \quad |B_2| = \begin{vmatrix} 0 & f_1 & f_2 \\ f_1 & f_{11} & f_{12} \\ f_2 & f_{21} & f_{22} \end{vmatrix} \quad \cdots \quad |B_n| = |B| \quad (12.24)$$

to characterize the configuration of that function.

We shall state here two conditions; one is necessary, and the other is sufficient. Both relate to quasiconcavity on a domain consisting only of the *nonnegative orthant* (the n-dimensional analog of the nonnegative quadrant), that is, with $x_1, \ldots, x_n \geq 0$.[†]

For $z = f(x_1, \ldots, x_n)$ to be quasiconcave on the nonnegative orthant, it is necessary that

$$|B_1| \leq 0, \quad |B_2| \geq 0, \quad \cdots, \quad |B_n| \left\{ \begin{array}{c} \leq \\ \geq \end{array} \right\} 0 \text{ if } n \text{ is } \left\{ \begin{array}{c} \text{odd} \\ \text{even} \end{array} \right. \qquad (12.25)$$

wherever the partial derivatives are evaluated in the nonnegative orthant.

[†] Whereas concavity (convexity) of a function on a convex domain can always be extended to concavity (convexity) over the entire space, quasiconcavity and quasiconvexity cannot. For instance, our conclusions in Examples 1 and 2 will not hold if the variables are allowed to take negative values. The two conditions given here are based on Kenneth J. Arrow and Alain C. Enthoven, "Quasi-Concave Programming," *Econometrica,* October 1961, p. 797 (Theorem 5), and Akira Takayama, *Analytical Methods in Economics,* University of Michigan Press, 1993, p. 65 (Theorem 1.12).

A sufficient condition for f to be strictly quasiconcave on the nonnegative orthant is that

$$|B_1| < 0, \quad |B_2| > 0, \quad \ldots, \quad |B_n| \begin{Bmatrix} < \\ > \end{Bmatrix} 0 \text{ if } n \text{ is } \begin{Bmatrix} \text{odd} \\ \text{even} \end{Bmatrix} \quad \textbf{(12.26)}$$

wherever the partial derivatives are evaluated in the nonnegative orthant.

Note that the condition $|B_1| \leq 0$ in (12.25) is automatically satisfied because $|B_1| = -f_1^2$; it is listed here only for the sake of symmetry. So is the condition $|B_1| < 0$ in (12.26).

Example 4

The function $z = f(x_1, x_2) = x_1 x_2$ $(x_1, x_2 \geq 0)$ is quasiconcave (cf. Example 2). We shall now check this by (12.22′). Let $u = (u_1, u_2)$ and $v = (v_1, v_2)$ be any two points in the domain. Then $f(u) = u_1 u_2$ and $f(v) = v_1 v_2$. Assume that

$$f(v) \geq f(u) \quad \text{or} \quad v_1 v_2 \geq u_1 u_2 \quad (v_1, v_2, u_1, u_2 \geq 0) \quad \textbf{(12.27)}$$

Since the partial derivatives of f are $f_1 = x_2$ and $f_2 = x_1$, (12.22′) amounts to the condition that

$$f_1(u)(v_1 - u_1) + f_2(u)(v_2 - u_2) = u_2(v_1 - u_1) + u_1(v_2 - u_2) \geq 0$$

or, upon rearrangement,

$$u_2(v_1 - u_1) \geq u_1(u_2 - v_2) \quad \textbf{(12.28)}$$

We need to consider four possibilities regarding the values of u_1 and u_2. First, if $u_1 = u_2 = 0$, then (12.28) is trivially satisfied. Second, if $u_1 = 0$ but $u_2 > 0$, then (12.28) reduces to the condition $u_2 v_1 \geq 0$, which is again satisfied since u_2 and v_1 are both nonnegative. Third, if $u_1 > 0$ and $u_2 = 0$, then (12.28) reduces to the condition $0 \geq -u_1 v_2$, which is still satisfied. Fourth and last, suppose that u_1 and u_2 are both positive, so that v_1 and v_2 are also positive. Subtracting $v_2 u_1$ from both sides of (12.27), we obtain

$$v_2(v_1 - u_1) \geq u_1(u_2 - v_2) \quad \textbf{(12.29)}$$

Three subpossibilities now present themselves:

1. If $u_2 = v_2$, then $v_1 \geq u_1$. In fact, we should have $v_1 > u_1$ since (u_1, u_2) and (v_1, v_2) are distinct points. The fact that $u_2 = v_2$ and $v_1 > u_1$ implies that condition (12.28) is satisfied.
2. If $u_2 > v_2$, then we must also have $v_1 > u_1$ by (12.29). Multiplying both sides of (12.29) by u_2/v_2, we get

$$u_2(v_1 - u_1) \geq \frac{u_2}{v_2} u_1(u_2 - v_2) > u_1(u_2 - v_2) \quad \left[\text{since} \frac{u_2}{v_2} > 1 \right] \quad \textbf{(12.30)}$$

Thus (12.28) is again satisfied.

3. The final subpossibility is that $u_2 < v_2$, implying that u_2/v_2 is a positive fraction. In this case, the first line of (12.30) still holds. The second line also holds, but now for a different reason: a fraction (u_2/v_2) of a negative number $(u_2 - v_2)$ is greater than the latter number itself.

Inasmuch (12.28) is satisfied in every possible situation that can arise, the function $z = x_1 x_2$ $(x_1, x_2 \geq 0)$ is quasiconcave. Therefore, the necessary condition (12.25) should hold. Because the partial derivatives of f are

$$f_1 = x_2 \quad f_2 = x_1 \quad f_{11} = f_{22} = 0 \quad f_{12} = f_{21} = 1$$

the relevant leading principal minors turn out to be

$$|B_1| = \begin{vmatrix} 0 & x_2 \\ x_2 & 0 \end{vmatrix} = -x_2^2 \leq 0 \quad |B_2| = \begin{vmatrix} 0 & x_2 & x_1 \\ x_2 & 0 & 1 \\ x_1 & 1 & 0 \end{vmatrix} = 2x_1 x_2 \geq 0$$

Thus (12.25) is indeed satisfied. Note, however, that the sufficient condition (12.26) is satisfied only over the positive orthant.

Example 5 Show that $z = f(x, y) = x^a y^b$ $(x, y > 0; 0 < a, b < 1)$ is strictly quasiconcave. The partial derivatives of this function are

$$f_x = ax^{a-1} y^b \quad f_y = bx^a y^{b-1}$$
$$f_{xx} = a(a-1)x^{a-2} y^b \quad f_{xy} = f_{yx} = abx^{a-1} y^{b-1} \quad f_{yy} = b(b-1)x^a y^{b-2}$$

Thus the leading principal minors of $|B|$ have the following signs:

$$|B_1| = \begin{vmatrix} 0 & f_x \\ f_x & f_{xx} \end{vmatrix} = -(ax^{a-1} y^b)^2 < 0$$

$$|B_2| = \begin{vmatrix} 0 & f_x & f_y \\ f_x & f_{xx} & f_{xy} \\ f_y & f_{yx} & f_{yy} \end{vmatrix} = [2a^2 b^2 - a(a-1)b^2 - a^2 b(b-1)]x^{3a-2} y^{3b-2} > 0$$

This satisfies the sufficient condition for strict quasiconcavity in (12.26).

A Further Look at the Bordered Hessian

The bordered determinant $|B|$, as defined in (12.23), differs from the bordered Hessian

$$|\overline{H}| = \begin{vmatrix} 0 & g_1 & g_2 & \cdots & g_n \\ g_1 & Z_{11} & Z_{12} & \cdots & Z_{1n} \\ g_2 & Z_{21} & Z_{22} & \cdots & Z_{2n} \\ \cdots & \cdots & \cdots & \cdots & \cdots \\ g_n & Z_{n1} & Z_{n2} & \cdots & Z_{nn} \end{vmatrix}$$

in two ways: (1) the border elements in $|B|$ are the first-order partial derivatives of function f rather than g; and (2) the remaining elements in $|B|$ are the second-order partial derivatives of f rather than the Lagrangian function Z. However, in the special case of a linear constraint equation, $g(x_1, \ldots, x_n) = a_1 x_1 + \cdots + a_n x_n = c$—a case frequently encountered in economics (see Sec. 12.5)—Z_{ij} reduces to f_{ij}. For then the Lagrangian function is

$$Z = f(x_1, \ldots, x_n) + \lambda(c - a_1 x_1 - \cdots - a_n x_n)$$

so that

$$Z_j = f_j - \lambda a_j \quad \text{and} \quad Z_{ij} = f_{ij}$$

Turning to the borders, we note that the linear constraint function yields the first derivative $g_j = a_j$. Moreover, when the first-order condition is satisfied, we have $Z_j = f_j - \lambda a_j = 0$, so that $f_j = \lambda a_j$, or $f_j = \lambda g_j$. Thus the border in $|B|$ is simply that of $|\overline{H}|$ multiplied by a positive scalar λ. By factoring out λ successively from the horizontal and vertical borders of $|\overline{H}|$ (see Sec. 5.3, Example 5), we have

$$|B| = \lambda^2 |\overline{H}|$$

Consequently, in the linear-constraint case, the two bordered determinants always possess the same sign at the stationary point of Z. By the same token, the leading principal minors $|B_i|$ and $|\overline{H}_i|$ ($i = 1, \ldots, n$) must also share the same sign at that point. It then follows that if the bordered determinant $|B|$ satisfies the sufficient condition for strict quasiconcavity in (12.26), the bordered Hessian $|\overline{H}|$ must then satisfy the second-order sufficient condition for constrained maximization in Table 12.1.

Absolute versus Relative Extrema

A more comprehensive picture of the relationship between quasiconcavity and second-order conditions is presented in Fig. 12.6. (A suitable modification will adapt the figure for quasiconvexity.) Constructed in the same spirit—and to be read in the same manner—as Fig. 11.5, this figure relates quasiconcavity to *absolute* as well as *relative* constrained maxima of a twice-differentiable function $z = f(x_1, \ldots, x_n)$. The three ovals in the upper part summarize the first- and second-order conditions for a relative constrained maximum. And the rectangles in the middle column, like those in Fig. 11.5, tie the concepts of relative maximum, absolute maximum, and unique absolute maximum to one another.

But the really interesting information are those in the two diamonds and the elongated $\Rightarrow$ symbols passing through them. The one on the left tells us that, once the first-order condition is satisfied, and if the two provisos listed in the diamond are also satisfied, we have a sufficient condition for an absolute constrained maximum. The first proviso is that the function f be explicitly quasiconcave—a new term which we must hasten to define.

A quasiconcave function f is *explicitly quasiconcave* if it has the further property that

$$f(v) > f(u) \Rightarrow f[\theta u + (1 - \theta)v] > f(u)$$

This defining property means that whenever a point on the surface, $f(v)$, is higher than another, $f(u)$, then all the intermediate points—the points on the surface lying directly above line segment uv in the domain—must also be higher than $f(u)$. What such a stipulation does is to rule out any *horizontal* plane segments on the surface except for a plateau at the top of the surface.[†] Note that the condition for *explicit* quasiconcavity is not as strong as the condition for *strict* quasiconcavity, since the latter requires $f[\theta u + (1 - \theta)v] > f(u)$ even for $f(v) = f(u)$, implying that *non*horizontal plane segments are ruled out, too.[‡] The other

---

[†] Let the surface contain a horizontal plane segment P such that $f(u) \in P$ and $f(v) \notin P$. Then those intermediate points that are located on P will be of equal height to $f(u)$, thereby violating the first proviso.

[‡] Let the surface contain a slanted plane segment P' such that $f(u) = f(v)$ are both located on P'. Then all the intermediate points will also be on P' and be of equal height to $f(u)$, thereby violating the cited requirement for strict quasiconcavity.

FIGURE 12.6

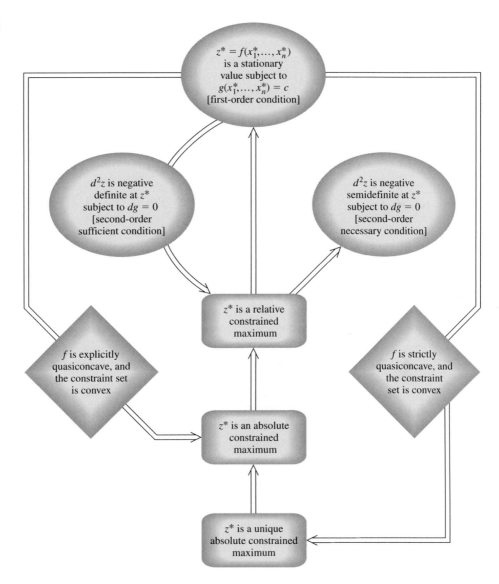

proviso in the left-side diamond is that the set $\{(x_1, \ldots, x_n) \mid g(x_1, \ldots, x_n) = c\}$ be convex. When both provisos are met, we shall be dealing with that portion of a bell-shaped, horizontal-segment-free surface (or hypersurface) lying directly above a convex set in the domain. A local maximum found on such a subset of the surface must be an absolute constrained maximum.

The diamond on the right in Fig. 12.6 involves the stronger condition of *strict* quasiconcavity. A strictly quasiconcave function must be explicitly quasiconcave, although the converse is not true. Hence, when strict quasiconcavity replaces explicit quasiconcavity, an absolute constrained maximum is still ensured. But this time that absolute constrained maximum must also be unique, since the absence of any plane segment anywhere on the surface decidedly precludes the possibility of multiple constrained maxima.

EXERCISE 12.4

1. Draw a strictly quasiconcave curve $z = f(x)$ which is
   (a) also quasiconvex   (d) not concave
   (b) not quasiconvex   (e) neither concave nor convex
   (c) not convex   (f) both concave and convex

2. Are the following functions quasiconcave? Strictly so? First check graphically, and then algebraically by (12.20). Assume that $x \geq 0$.
   (a) $f(x) = a$ (b) $f(x) = a + bx$ $(b > 0)$ (c) $f(x) = a + cx^2$ $(c < 0)$

3. (a) Let $z = f(x)$ plot as a negatively sloped curve shaped like the right half of a bell in the first quadrant, passing through the points $(0, 5)$, $(2, 4)$, $(3, 2)$, and $(5, 1)$. Let $z = g(x)$ plot as a positively sloped $45°$ line. Are $f(x)$ and $g(x)$ quasiconcave?
   (b) Now plot the sum $f(x) + g(x)$. Is the sum function quasiconcave?

4. By examining their graphs, and using (12.21), check whether the following functions are quasiconcave, quasiconvex, both, or neither:
   (a) $f(x) = x^3 - 2x$ (b) $f(x_1, x_2) = 6x_1 - 9x_2$ (c) $f(x_1, x_2) = x_2 - \ln x_1$

5. (a) Verify that a cubic function $z = ax^3 + bx^2 + cx + d$ is in general neither quasiconcave nor quasiconvex.
   (b) Is it possible to impose restrictions on the parameters such that the function becomes both quasiconcave and quasiconvex for $x \geq 0$?

6. Use (12.22) to check $z = x^2 (x \geq 0)$ for quasiconcavity and quasiconvexity.

7. Show that $z = xy$ $(x, y \geq 0)$ is not quasiconvex.

8. Use bordered determinants to check the following functions for quasiconcavity and quasiconvexity:
   (a) $z = -x^2 - y^2$ $(x, y > 0)$ (b) $z = -(x + 1)^2 - (y + 2)^2$ $(x, y > 0)$

12.5 Utility Maximization and Consumer Demand

The maximization of a utility function was cited in Sec. 12.1 as an example of constrained optimization. Let us now reexamine this problem in more detail. For simplicity, we shall still allow our hypothetical consumer the choice of only two goods, both of which have continuous, positive marginal-utility functions. The prices of both goods are market-determined, hence exogenous, although in this section we shall omit the zero subscript from the price symbols. If the purchasing power of the consumer is a given amount B (for budget), the problem posed will be that of maximizing a smooth utility (index) function

$$U = U(x, y) \qquad (U_x, U_y > 0)$$

subject to

$$x P_x + y P_y = B$$

First-Order Condition

The Lagrangian function of this optimization model is

$$Z = U(x, y) + \lambda(B - xP_x - yP_y)$$

As the first-order condition, we have the following set of simultaneous equations:

$$\begin{aligned} Z_\lambda &= B - xP_x - yP_y = 0 \\ Z_x &= U_x - \lambda P_x = 0 \\ Z_y &= U_y - \lambda P_y = 0 \end{aligned} \qquad \textbf{(12.31)}$$

Since the last two equations are equivalent to

$$\frac{U_x}{P_x} = \frac{U_y}{P_y} = \lambda \qquad \textbf{(12.31$'$)}$$

the first-order condition in effect calls for the satisfaction of (12.31$'$), subject to the budget constraint—the first equation in (12.31). What (12.31$'$) states is merely the familiar proposition in classical consumer theory that, in order to maximize utility, consumers must allocate their budgets so as to equalize the ratio of marginal utility to price for every commodity. Specifically, in the equilibrium or optimum, these ratios should have the common value λ^*. As we learned earlier, λ^* measures the comparative-static effect of the constraint constant on the optimal value of the objective function. Hence, we have in the present context $\lambda^* = (\partial U^*/\partial B)$; that is, the optimal value of the Lagrange multiplier can be interpreted as the *marginal utility of money* (budget money) when the consumer's utility is maximized.

If we restate the condition in (12.31$'$) in the form

$$\frac{U_x}{U_y} = \frac{P_x}{P_y} \qquad \textbf{(12.31$''$)}$$

the first-order condition can be given an alternative interpretation, in terms of indifference curves.

An *indifference curve* is defined as the locus of the combinations of x and y that will yield a constant level of U. This means that on an indifference curve we must find

$$dU = U_x \, dx + U_y \, dy = 0$$

with the implication that $dy/dx = -U_x/U_y$. Accordingly, if we plot an indifference curve in the xy plane, as in Fig. 12.7, its slope, dy/dx, must be equal to the negative of the marginal-utility ratio U_x/U_y. (Since we assume $U_x, U_y > 0$, the slope of the indifference curve must be negative.) Note that U_x/U_y, the negative of the indifference-curve slope, is called the *marginal rate of substitution* between the two goods.

What about the meaning of P_x/P_y? As we shall presently see, this ratio represents the negative of the slope of the graph of the budget constraint. The budget constraint, $xP_x + yP_y = B$, can be written alternatively as

$$y = \frac{B}{P_y} - \frac{P_x}{P_y}x$$

so that, when plotted in the xy plane as in Fig. 12.7, it emerges as a straight line with slope $-P_x/P_y$ (and vertical intercept B/P_y).

FIGURE 12.7

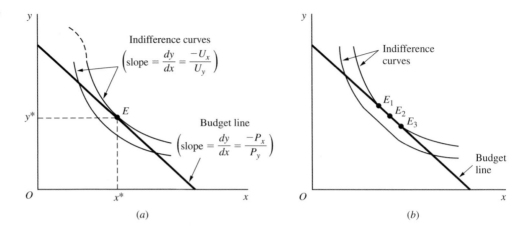

(a)

(b)

In this light, the new version of the first-order condition—(12.31″) plus the budget constraint—discloses that, to maximize utility, a consumer must allocate the budget such that the slope of the budget line (on which the consumer must remain) is equal to the slope of some indifference curve. This condition is met at point E in Fig. 12.7a, where the budget line is tangent to an indifference curve.

Second-Order Condition

If the bordered Hessian in the present problem is positive, i.e., if

$$|\overline{H}| = \begin{vmatrix} 0 & P_x & P_y \\ P_x & U_{xx} & U_{xy} \\ P_y & U_{yx} & U_{yy} \end{vmatrix} = 2P_x P_y U_{xy} - P_y^2 U_{xx} - P_x^2 U_{yy} > 0 \quad \textbf{(12.32)}$$

(with all the derivatives evaluated at the critical values x^* and y^*), then the stationary value of U will assuredly be a maximum. The presence of the derivatives U_{xx}, U_{yy}, and U_{xy} in (12.32) clearly suggests that meeting this condition would entail certain restrictions on the utility function and, hence, on the shape of the indifference curves. What are these restrictions?

Considering first the shape of the indifference curves, we can show that a positive $|\overline{H}|$ means the strict convexity of the (downward-sloping) indifference curve at the point of tangency E. Just as the downward slope of an indifference curve is guaranteed by a negative dy/dx ($= -U_x/U_y$), its strict convexity would be ensured by a positive d^2y/dx^2. To get the expression for d^2y/dx^2, we can differentiate $-U_x/U_y$ with respect to x; but in doing so, we should bear in mind not only that both U_x and U_y (being derivatives) are functions of x and y but also that, along a given indifference curve, y is itself a function of x. Accordingly, both U_x and U_y can be considered as functions of x alone; therefore, we can get a total derivative

$$\frac{d^2y}{dx^2} = \frac{d}{dx}\left(-\frac{U_x}{U_y}\right) = -\frac{1}{U_y^2}\left(U_y \frac{dU_x}{dx} - U_x \frac{dU_y}{dx}\right) \quad \textbf{(12.33)}$$

Since x can affect U_x and U_y not only directly but also indirectly, via the intermediary of y, we have

$$\frac{dU_x}{dx} = U_{xx} + U_{yx}\frac{dy}{dx} \qquad \frac{dU_y}{dx} = U_{xy} + U_{yy}\frac{dy}{dx} \quad \textbf{(12.34)}$$

where dy/dx refers to the slope of the indifference curve. Now, at the point of tangency E—the only point relevant to the discussion of the second-order condition—this slope is identical with that of the budget constraint; that is, $dy/dx = -P_x/P_y$. Thus we can rewrite (12.34) as

$$\frac{dU_x}{dx} = U_{xx} - U_{yx}\frac{P_x}{P_y} \qquad \frac{dU_y}{dx} = U_{xy} - U_{yy}\frac{P_x}{P_y} \qquad \textbf{(12.34')}$$

Substituting (12.34') into (12.33) and utilizing the information that

$$U_x = \frac{U_y P_x}{P_y} \quad [\text{from } (12.31'')]$$

and then factoring out U_y/P_y^2, we can finally transform (12.33) into

$$\frac{d^2 y}{dx^2} = \frac{2 P_x P_y U_{xy} - P_y^2 U_{xx} - P_x^2 U_{yy}}{U_y P_y^2} = \frac{|\overline{H}|}{U_y P_y^2} \qquad \textbf{(12.33')}$$

It is clear that when the second-order sufficient condition (12.32) is satisfied, the second derivative in (12.33') is positive, and the relevant indifference curve is strictly convex at the point of tangency. In the present context, it is also true that the strict convexity of the indifference curve at the tangency implies the satisfaction of the sufficient condition (12.32). This is because, given that the indifference curves are negatively sloped, with no stationary points anywhere, the possibility of a zero $d^2 y/dx^2$ value on a strictly convex curve is ruled out. Thus strict convexity can now result only in a positive $d^2 y/dx^2$, and hence a positive $|\overline{H}|$, by (12.33').

Recall, however, that the derivatives in $|\overline{H}|$ are to be evaluated at the critical values x^* and y^* only. Thus the strict convexity of the indifference curve, as a sufficient condition, pertains only to the point of tangency, and it is not inconceivable for the curve to contain a concave segment away from point E, as illustrated by the broken curve segment in Fig. 12.7a. On the other hand, if the utility function is known to be a smooth, increasing, strictly quasiconcave function, then every indifference curve will be everywhere strictly convex. Such a utility function has a surface like the one in Fig. 12.4b. When such a surface is cut with a plane parallel to the xy plane, we obtain for each of such cuts a cross section which, when projected onto the xy plane, becomes a strictly convex, downward-sloping indifference curve. In that event, no matter where the point of tangency may occur, the second-order sufficient condition will always be satisfied. Besides, there can exist only one point of tangency, one that yields the unique absolute maximum level of utility attainable on the given linear budget. This result, of course, conforms perfectly to what the diamond on the right of Fig. 12.6 states.

You have been repeatedly reminded that the second-order sufficient condition is not necessary. Let us illustrate here the maximization of utility while (12.32) fails to hold. Suppose that, as illustrated in Fig. 12.7b, the relevant indifference curve contains a linear segment that coincides with a portion of the budget line. Then clearly we have multiple maxima, since the first-order condition $U_x/U_y = P_x/P_y$ is now satisfied at every point on the linear segment of the indifference curve, including E_1, E_2, and E_3. In fact, these are absolute constrained maxima. But since on a line segment $d^2 y/dx^2$ is zero, we have $|\overline{H}| = 0$ by (12.33'). Thus maximization is achieved in this case even though the second-order sufficient condition (12.32) is violated.

The fact that a linear segment appears on the indifference curve suggests the presence of a slanted plane segment on the utility surface. This occurs when the utility function is explicitly quasiconcave rather than strictly quasiconcave. As Fig. 12.7*b* shows, points E_1, E_2, and E_3, all of which are located on the same (highest attainable) indifference curve, yield the same absolute maximum utility under the given linear budget constraint. Refer- ring to Fig. 12.6 again, we note that this result is perfectly consistent with the message conveyed by the diamond on the left.

Comparative-Static Analysis

In our consumer model, the prices P_x and P_y are exogenous, as is the amount of the bud- get B. If we assume the satisfaction of the second-order sufficient condition, we can analyze the comparative-static properties of the model on the basis of the first-order condition (12.31), viewed as a set of equations $F^j = 0 \, (j = 1, 2, 3)$, where each F^j function has continuous partial derivatives. As pointed out in (12.19), the endogenous-variable Jacobian of this set of equations must have the same value as the bordered Hessian; that is, $|J| = |\bar{H}|$. Thus, when the second-order condition (12.32) is met, $|J|$ must be positive and it does not vanish at the initial optimum. Consequently, the implicit-function theorem is applicable, and we may express the optimal values of the endogenous variables as implicit functions of the exogenous variables:

$$\begin{aligned}
\lambda^* &= \lambda^*(P_x, P_y, B) \\
x^* &= x^*(P_x, P_y, B) \\
y^* &= y^*(P_x, P_y, B)
\end{aligned}$$
(12.35)

These are known to possess continuous derivatives that give comparative-static informa- tion. In particular, the derivatives of the last two functions x^* and y^*, which are descriptive of the consumer's demand behavior, can tell us how the consumer will react to changes in prices and in the budget. To find these derivatives, however, we must first convert (12.31) into a set of equilibrium identities as follows:

$$\begin{aligned}
B - x^* P_x - y^* P_y &\equiv 0 \\
U_x(x^*, y^*) - \lambda^* P_x &\equiv 0 \\
U_y(x^*, y^*) - \lambda^* P_y &\equiv 0
\end{aligned}$$
(12.36)

By taking the total differential of each identity in turn (allowing every variable to change), and noting that $U_{xy} = U_{yx}$, we then arrive at the linear system

$$\begin{aligned}
-P_x \, dx^* - P_y \, dy^* &= x^* dP_x + y^* dP_y - dB \\
-P_x \, d\lambda^* + U_{xx} \, dx^* + U_{xy} \, dy^* &= \lambda^* dP_x \\
-P_y \, d\lambda^* + U_{yx} \, dx^* + U_{yy} \, dy^* &= \lambda^* dP_y
\end{aligned}$$
(12.37)

To study the effect of a change in the budget size (also referred to as the *income* of the consumer), let $dP_x = dP_y = 0$, but keep $dB \neq 0$. Then, after dividing (12.37) through by dB, and interpreting each ratio of differentials as a partial derivative, we can write the matrix equation[†]

$$\begin{bmatrix} 0 & -P_x & -P_y \\ -P_x & U_{xx} & U_{xy} \\ -P_y & U_{yx} & U_{yy} \end{bmatrix} \begin{bmatrix} (\partial \lambda^*/\partial B) \\ (\partial x^*/\partial B) \\ (\partial y^*/\partial B) \end{bmatrix} = \begin{bmatrix} -1 \\ 0 \\ 0 \end{bmatrix}$$
(12.38)

[†] The matrix equation (12.38) can also be obtained by totally differentiating (12.36) with respect to *B*, while bearing in mind the implicit solutions in (12.35).

As you can verify, the array of elements in the coefficient matrix is exactly the same as what would appear in the Jacobian $|J|$, which has the same value as the bordered Hessian $|\overline{H}|$ although the latter has P_x and P_y (rather than $-P_x$ and $-P_y$) in the first row and the first column. By Cramer's rule, we can solve for all three comparative-static derivatives, but we shall confine our attention to the following two:

$$
\left(\frac{\partial x^*}{\partial B}\right) = \frac{1}{|J|} \begin{vmatrix} 0 & -1 & -P_y \\ -P_x & 0 & U_{xy} \\ -P_y & 0 & U_{yy} \end{vmatrix} = \frac{1}{|J|} \begin{vmatrix} -P_x & U_{xy} \\ -P_y & U_{yy} \end{vmatrix} \tag{12.39}
$$

$$
\left(\frac{\partial y^*}{\partial B}\right) = \frac{1}{|J|} \begin{vmatrix} 0 & -P_x & -1 \\ -P_x & U_{xx} & 0 \\ -P_y & U_{yx} & 0 \end{vmatrix} = \frac{-1}{|J|} \begin{vmatrix} -P_x & U_{xx} \\ -P_y & U_{yx} \end{vmatrix} \tag{12.40}
$$

By the second-order condition, $|J| = |\overline{H}|$ is positive, as are P_x and P_y. Unfortunately, in the absence of additional information about the relative magnitudes of P_x, P_y, and the U_{ij}, we are still unable to ascertain the signs of these two comparative-static derivatives. This means that, as the consumer's budget (or income) increases, his or her optimal purchases x^* and y^* may *either* increase *or* decrease. In case, say, x^* decreases as B increases, product x is referred to as an *inferior good* as against a *normal good*.

Next, we may analyze the effect of a change in P_x. Letting $dP_y = dB = 0$ this time, but keeping $dP_x \neq 0$, and then dividing (12.37) through by dP_x, we obtain another matrix equation:

$$
\begin{bmatrix} 0 & -P_x & -P_y \\ -P_x & U_{xx} & U_{xy} \\ -P_y & U_{yx} & U_{yy} \end{bmatrix} \begin{bmatrix} (\partial\lambda^*/\partial P_x) \\ (\partial x^*/\partial P_x) \\ (\partial y^*/\partial P_x) \end{bmatrix} = \begin{bmatrix} x^* \\ \lambda^* \\ 0 \end{bmatrix} \tag{12.41}
$$

From this, the following comparative-static derivatives emerge:

$$
\left(\frac{\partial x^*}{\partial P_x}\right) = \frac{1}{|J|} \begin{vmatrix} 0 & x^* & -P_y \\ -P_x & \lambda^* & U_{xy} \\ -P_y & 0 & U_{yy} \end{vmatrix}
$$

$$
= \frac{-x^*}{|J|} \begin{vmatrix} -P_x & U_{xy} \\ -P_y & U_{yy} \end{vmatrix} + \frac{\lambda^*}{|J|} \begin{vmatrix} 0 & -P_y \\ -P_y & U_{yy} \end{vmatrix}
$$

$$
\equiv T_1 + T_2 \qquad [T_i \text{ means the } i\text{th term}] \tag{12.42}
$$

$$
\left(\frac{\partial y^*}{\partial P_x}\right) = \frac{1}{|J|} \begin{vmatrix} 0 & -P_x & x^* \\ -P_x & U_{xx} & \lambda^* \\ -P_y & U_{yx} & 0 \end{vmatrix}
$$

$$
= \frac{x^*}{|J|} \begin{vmatrix} -P_x & U_{xx} \\ -P_y & U_{yx} \end{vmatrix} - \frac{\lambda^*}{|J|} \begin{vmatrix} 0 & -P_x \\ -P_y & U_{yx} \end{vmatrix}
$$

$$
\equiv T_3 + T_4 \tag{12.43}
$$

How do we interpret these two results? The first one, $(\partial x^*/\partial P_x)$, tells how a change in P_x affects the optimal purchase of x; it thus provides the basis for the study of our consumer's demand function for x. There are two component terms in this effect. The first term, T_1, can be rewritten, by using (12.39), as $-(\partial x^*/\partial B)x^*$. In this light, T_1 seems to be a measure of the effect of a change in B (budget, or income) upon the optimal purchase x^*, with x^* itself serving as a weighting factor. However, since this derivative obviously is concerned with a price change, T_1 must be interpreted as the *income effect* of a *price change*. As P_x rises, the decline in the consumer's real income will produce an effect on x^* similar to that of an actual decrease in B; hence the use of the term $-(\partial x^*/\partial B)$. Understandably, the more prominent the place of commodity x in the total budget, the greater this income effect will be—and hence the appearance of the weighting factor x^* in T_1. This interpretation can be demonstrated more formally by expressing the consumer's effective income loss by the differential $dB = -x^* dP_x$. Then we have

$$x^* = -\frac{dB}{dP_x} \tag{12.44}$$

and

$$T_1 = -\left(\frac{\partial x^*}{\partial B}\right) x^* = \left(\frac{\partial x^*}{\partial B}\right) \frac{dB}{dP_x}$$

which shows T_1 to be the measure of the effect of dP_x on x^* via B, that is, the income effect.

If we now compensate the consumer for the effective income loss by a cash payment numerically equal to dB, then, because of the neutralization of the income effect, the remaining component in the comparative-static derivative $(\partial x^*/\partial P_x)$, namely, T_2, will measure the change in x^* due entirely to price-induced substitution of one commodity for another, i.e., the *substitution effect* of the change in P_x. To see this more clearly, let us return to (12.37), and consider how the income compensation will modify the situation. When studying the effect of dP_x only (with $dP_y = dB = 0$), the first equation in (12.37) can be written as $-P_x\, dx^* - P_y\, dy^* = x^*\, dP_x$. Since the indication of the effective income loss to the consumer lies in the expression $x^* dP_x$ (which, incidentally, appears only in the first equation), to compensate the consumer means to set this term equal to zero. If so, the

vector of constants in (12.41) must be changed from $\begin{bmatrix} x^* \\ \lambda^* \\ 0 \end{bmatrix}$ to $\begin{bmatrix} 0 \\ \lambda^* \\ 0 \end{bmatrix}$, and the income-

compensated version of the derivative $(\partial x^*/\partial P_x)$ will be

$$\left(\frac{\partial x^*}{\partial P_x}\right)_{\text{compensated}} = \frac{1}{|J|} \begin{vmatrix} 0 & 0 & -P_y \\ -P_x & \lambda^* & U_{xy} \\ -P_y & 0 & U_{yy} \end{vmatrix} = \frac{\lambda^*}{|J|} \begin{vmatrix} 0 & -P_y \\ -P_y & U_{yy} \end{vmatrix} = T_2$$

Hence, we may express (12.42) in the form

$$\left(\frac{\partial x^*}{\partial P_x}\right) = T_1 + T_2 = \underbrace{-\left(\frac{\partial x^*}{\partial B}\right) x^*}_{\text{income effect}} + \underbrace{\left(\frac{\partial x^*}{\partial P_x}\right)_{\text{compensated}}}_{\text{substitution effect}} \tag{12.42'}$$

This result, which decomposes the comparative-static derivative $(\partial x^*/\partial P_x)$ into two components, an income effect and a substitution effect, is the two-good version of the so-called Slutsky equation.

What can we say about the sign of $(\partial x^*/\partial P_x)$? The substitution effect T_2 is clearly negative, because $|J| > 0$ and $\lambda^* > 0$ [see (12.31')]. The income effect T_1, on the other hand, is indeterminate in sign according to (12.39). Should it be negative, it would reinforce T_2; in that event, an increase in P_x must decrease the purchase of x, and the demand curve of the utility-maximizing consumer would be negatively sloped. Should it be positive, but relatively small in magnitude, it would dilute the substitution effect, though the overall result would still be a downward-sloping demand curve. But in case T_1 is positive and dominates T_2 (such as when x^* is a significant item in the consumer budget, thus providing an overwhelming weighting factor), then a rise in P_x will actually lead to a *larger* purchase of x, a special demand situation characteristic of what are called *Giffen goods*. Normally, of course, we would expect $(\partial x^*/\partial P_x)$ to be negative.

Finally, let us examine the comparative-static derivative in (12.43), $(\partial y^*/\partial P_x) = T_3 + T_4$, which has to do with the *cross effect* of a change in the price of x on the optimal purchase of y. The term T_3 bears a striking resemblance to term T_1 and again has the interpretation of an income effect.[†] Note that the weighting factor here is again x^* (rather than y^*); this is because we are studying the effect of a change in P_x on effective income, which depends for its magnitude upon the relative importance of x^* (not y^*) in the consumer budget. Naturally, the remaining term, T_4, is again a measure of the substitution effect.

The sign of T_3 is, according to (12.40), dependent on such factors as U_{xx}, U_{yx}, etc., and is indeterminate without further restrictions on the model. However, the substitution effect T_4 will surely be positive in our model, since λ^*, P_x, P_y and $|J|$ are all positive. This means that, unless more than offset by a negative income effect, an increase in the price of x will always increase the purchase of y in our two-commodity model. In other words, in the context of the present model, where the consumer can choose only between two goods, these goods must bear a relationship to each other as substitutes.

Even though the preceding analysis relates to the effects of a change in P_x, our results are readily adaptable to the case of a change in P_y. Our model happens to be such that the positions occupied by the variables x and y are perfectly symmetrical. Thus, to infer the effects of a change in P_y, all that it takes is to interchange the roles of x and y in the results already obtained.

Proportionate Changes in Prices and Income

It is also of interest to ask how x^* and y^* will be affected when all three parameters P_x, P_y, and B are changed in the same proportion. Such a question still lies within the realm of comparative statics, but unlike the preceding analysis, the present inquiry now involves the simultaneous change of all the parameters.

When both prices are raised, along with income, by the same multiple j, every term in the budget constraint will increase j-fold, to become

$$jB - jxP_x - jyP_y = 0$$

Inasmuch as the common factor j can be canceled out, however, this new constraint is in fact identical with the old. The utility function, moreover, is independent of these parameters. Consequently, the old equilibrium levels of x and y will continue to prevail; that is, the consumer equilibrium position in our model is invariant to *equal* proportionate changes in all the prices and in the income. Thus, in the present model, the consumer is seen to be free from any "money illusion."

[†] If you need a stronger dose of assurance that T_3 represents the income effect, you can use (12.40) and (12.44) to write

$$T_3 = -\left(\frac{\partial y^*}{\partial B}\right)x^* = \left(\frac{\partial y^*}{\partial B}\right)\frac{dB}{dP_x}$$

Thus T_3 is the effect of a change in P_x on y^* via the income factor B.

Symbolically, this situation can be described by the equations

$$x^*(P_x, P_y, B) = x^*(jP_x, jP_y, jB)$$
$$y^*(P_x, P_y, B) = y^*(jP_x, jP_y, jB)$$

The functions x^* and y^*, with the *invariance* property just cited, are no ordinary functions; they are examples of a special class of function known as *homogeneous functions*, which have interesting economic applications. We shall therefore examine these in Sec. 12.6.

EXERCISE 12.5

1. Given $U = (x + 2)(y + 1)$ and $P_x = 4$, $P_y = 6$, and $B = 130$:
   (a) Write the Lagrangian function.
   (b) Find the optimal levels of purchase x^* and y^*.
   (c) Is the second-order sufficient condition for maximum satisfied?
   (d) Does the answer in (b) give any comparative-static information?

2. Assume that $U = (x + 2)(y + 1)$, but this time assign no specific numerical values to the price and income parameters.
   (a) Write the Lagrangian function.
   (b) Find x^*, y^*, and λ^* in terms of the parameters P_x, P_y, and B.
   (c) Check the second-order sufficient condition for maximum.
   (d) By setting $P_x = 4$, $P_y = 6$, and $B = 130$, check the validity of your answer to Prob. 1.

3. Can your solution (x^* and y^*) in Prob. 2 yield any comparative-static information? Find all the comparative-static derivatives you can, evaluate their signs, and interpret their economic meanings.

4. From the utility function $U = (x + 2)(y + 1)$ and the constraint $xP_x + yP_y = B$ of Prob. 2, we have already found the U_{ij} and $|\bar{H}|$, as well as x^* and λ^*. Moreover, we recall that $|J| = |\bar{H}|$.
   (a) Substitute these into (12.39) and (12.40) to find $(\partial x^*/\partial B)$ and $(\partial y^*/\partial B)$.
   (b) Substitute into (12.42) and (12.43) to find $(\partial x^*/\partial P_x)$ and $(\partial y^*/\partial P_x)$.
   Do these results check with those obtained in Prob. 3?

5. Comment on the validity of the statement: "If the derivative $(\partial x^*/\partial P_x)$ is negative, then x cannot possibly represent an inferior good."

6. When studying the effect of dP_x alone, the first equation in (12.37) reduces to $-P_x\,dx^* - P_y\,dy^* = x^*\,dP_x$, and when we compensate for the consumer's effective income loss by dropping the term x^*dP_x, the equation becomes $-P_x\,dx^* - P_y\,dy^* = 0$. Show that this last result can be obtained alternatively from a compensation procedure whereby we try to keep the consumer's optimal utility level U^* (rather than effective income) unchanged, so that the term T_2 can alternatively be interpreted as $(\partial x^*/\partial P_x)_{U^*=\text{constant}}$. [*Hint:* Make use of (12.31″).]

7. (a) Does the assumption of diminishing marginal utility to goods x and y imply strictly convex indifference curves?
   (b) Does the assumption of strict convexity in the indifference curves imply diminishing marginal utility to goods x and y?

12.6   Homogeneous Functions

A function is said to be homogeneous of degree r, if multiplication of each of its independent variables by a constant j will alter the value of the function by the proportion j^r, that is, if

$$f(jx_1, \ldots, jx_n) = j^r f(x_1, \ldots, x_n)$$

In general, j can take any value. However, in order for the preceding equation to make sense, $(jx_1, \ldots, jx_n)$ must not lie outside the domain of the function f. For this reason, in economic applications the constant j is usually taken to be positive, as most economic variables do not admit negative values.

Example 1   Given the function $f(x, y, w) = x/y + 2w/3x$, if we multiply each variable by j, we get

$$f(jx, jy, jw) = \frac{(jx)}{(jy)} + \frac{2(jw)}{3(jx)} = \frac{x}{y} + \frac{2w}{3x} = f(x, y, w) = j^0 f(x, y, w)$$

In this particular example, the value of the function will *not* be affected at all by equal proportionate changes in all the independent variables; or, one might say, the value of the function is changed by a multiple of j^0 ($= 1$). This makes the function f a homogeneous function of degree zero.

You will observe that the functions x^* and y^* cited at the end of Sec. 12.5 are both homogeneous of degree zero.

Example 2   When we multiply each variable in the function

$$g(x, y, w) = \frac{x^2}{y} + \frac{2w^2}{x}$$

by j, we get

$$g(jx, jy, jw) = \frac{(jx)^2}{(jy)} + \frac{2(jw)^2}{(jx)} = j\left(\frac{x^2}{y} + \frac{2w^2}{x}\right) = jg(x, y, w)$$

The function g is homogeneous of degree one (or, of the first degree); multiplication of each variable by j will alter the value of the function exactly j-fold as well.

Example 3   Now, consider the function $h(x, y, w) = 2x^2 + 3yw - w^2$. A similar multiplication this time will give us

$$h(jx, jy, jw) = 2(jx)^2 + 3(jy)(jw) - (jw)^2 = j^2 h(x, y, w)$$

Thus the function h is homogeneous of degree two; in this case, a doubling of all variables, for example, will quadruple the value of the function.

Linear Homogeneity

In the discussion of production functions, wide use is made of homogeneous functions of the first degree. These are often referred to as *linearly homogeneous* functions, the adverb *linearly* modifying the adjective *homogeneous*. Some writers, however, seem to prefer the somewhat misleading terminology *linear* homogeneous functions, or even *linear and* homogeneous functions, which tends to convey, wrongly, the impression that the functions themselves are linear. On the basis of the function g in Example 2, we know that a function which is homogeneous of the first degree is *not necessarily* linear in itself. Hence you should avoid using the terms "linear homogeneous functions" and "linear and homogeneous functions" unless, of course, the functions in question are indeed linear. Note, however, that it is not incorrect to speak of "linear homogeneity," meaning homogeneity of degree one, because to modify a noun (homogeneity) does call for the use of an adjective (linear).

Since the primary field of application of linearly homogeneous functions is in the theory of production, let us adopt as the framework of our discussion a production function in the form, say,

$$Q = f(K, L) \tag{12.45}$$

Whether applied at the *micro* or the *macro* level, the mathematical assumption of linear homogeneity would amount to the economic assumption of constant returns to scale, because linear homogeneity means that raising all inputs (independent variables) j-fold will always raise the output (value of the function) exactly j-fold also.

What unique properties characterize this linearly homogeneous production function?

Property I Given the linearly homogeneous production function $Q = f(K, L)$, the average physical product of labor (APP_L) and of capital (APP_K) can be expressed as functions of the capital–labor ratio, $k \equiv K/L$, alone.

To prove this, we multiply each independent variable in (12.45) by a factor $j = 1/L$. By virtue of linear homogeneity, this will change the output from Q to $jQ = Q/L$. The right side of (12.45) will correspondingly become

$$f\left(\frac{K}{L}, \frac{L}{L}\right) = f\left(\frac{K}{L}, 1\right) = f(k, 1)$$

Since the variables K and L in the original function are to be replaced (whenever they appear) by k and 1, respectively, the right side in effect becomes a function of the capital–labor ratio k alone, say, $\phi(k)$, which is a function with a single argument, k, even though two independent variables K and L are actually involved in that argument. Equating the two sides, we have

$$\text{APP}_L \equiv \frac{Q}{L} = \phi(k) \tag{12.46}$$

The expression for APP_K is then found to be

$$\text{APP}_K \equiv \frac{Q}{K} = \frac{Q}{L}\frac{L}{K} = \frac{\phi(k)}{k} \tag{12.47}$$

Since both average products depend on k alone, linear homogeneity implies that, as long as the K/L ratio is kept constant (whatever the absolute levels of K and L), the average products will be constant, too. Therefore, while the production function is homogeneous of degree one, both APP_L and APP_K are homogeneous of degree *zero* in the variables K and L, since equal proportionate changes in K and L (maintaining a constant k) will not alter the magnitudes of the average products.

Property II Given a linearly homogeneous production function $Q = f(K, L)$, the marginal physical products MPP_L and MPP_K can be expressed as functions of k alone.

To find the marginal products, we first write the total product as

$$Q = L\phi(k) \qquad \text{[by (12.46)]} \qquad\qquad \textbf{(12.45')}$$

and then differentiate Q with respect to K and L. For this purpose, we shall find the following two preliminary results to be of service:

$$\frac{\partial k}{\partial K} = \frac{\partial}{\partial K}\left(\frac{K}{L}\right) = \frac{1}{L} \qquad \frac{\partial k}{\partial L} = \frac{\partial}{\partial L}\left(\frac{K}{L}\right) = \frac{-K}{L^2} \qquad \textbf{(12.48)}$$

The results of differentiation are

$$\text{MPP}_K \equiv \frac{\partial Q}{\partial K} = \frac{\partial}{\partial K}[L\phi(k)]$$

$$= L\frac{\partial\phi(k)}{\partial K} = L\frac{d\phi(k)}{dk}\frac{\partial k}{\partial K} \qquad \text{[chain rule]}$$

$$= L\phi'(k)\left(\frac{1}{L}\right) = \phi'(k) \qquad \text{[by(12.48)]} \qquad \textbf{(12.49)}$$

$$\text{MPP}_L \equiv \frac{\partial Q}{\partial L} = \frac{\partial}{\partial L}[L\phi(k)]$$

$$= \phi(k) + L\frac{\partial\phi(k)}{\partial L} \qquad \text{[product rule]}$$

$$= \phi(k) + L\phi'(k)\frac{\partial k}{\partial L} \qquad \text{[chain rule]}$$

$$= \phi(k) + L\phi'(k)\frac{-K}{L^2} \qquad \text{[by (12.48)]}$$

$$= \phi(k) - k\phi'(k) \qquad\qquad \textbf{(12.50)}$$

which indeed show that MPP_K and MPP_L are functions of k alone.

Like average products, the marginal products will remain the same as long as the capital–labor ratio is held constant; they are homogeneous of degree zero in the variables K and L.

Property III   **(Euler's theorem)** If $Q = f(K, L)$ is linearly homogeneous, then

$$K\frac{\partial Q}{\partial K} + L\frac{\partial Q}{\partial L} \equiv Q$$

PROOF

$$K\frac{\partial Q}{\partial K} + L\frac{\partial Q}{\partial L} = K\phi'(k) + L[\phi(k) - k\phi'(k)] \qquad \text{[by (12.49), (12.50)]}$$

$$= K\phi'(k) + L\phi(k) - K\phi'(k) \qquad [k \equiv K/L]$$

$$= L\phi(k) = Q \qquad\qquad \text{[by (12.45')]}$$

Note that this result is valid for *any* values of K and L; this is why the property can be written as an identical equality. What this property says is that the value of a linearly homogeneous function can always be expressed as a sum of terms, each of which is the product of one of the independent variables and the first-order partial derivative with respect to that variable, regardless of the levels of the two inputs actually employed. Be careful, however, to distinguish between the identity $K\dfrac{\partial Q}{\partial K} + L\dfrac{\partial Q}{\partial L} \equiv Q$ [Euler's theorem, which applies only to the constant-returns-to-scale case of $Q = f(K, L)$] and the equation $dQ = \dfrac{\partial Q}{\partial K}dK + \dfrac{\partial Q}{\partial L}dL$ [total differential of Q, for *any* function $Q = f(K, L)$].

Economically, this property means that under conditions of constant returns to scale, if each input factor is paid the amount of its marginal product, the total product will be exactly exhausted by the distributive shares for all the input factors, or, equivalently, the pure economic profit will be zero. Since this situation is descriptive of the long-run equilibrium under pure competition, it was once thought that only linearly homogeneous production functions would make sense in economics. This, of course, is not the case. The zero economic profit in the long-run equilibrium is brought about by the forces of competition through the entry and exit of firms, regardless of the specific nature of the production functions actually prevailing. Thus it is not mandatory to have a production function that ensures product exhaustion for any and all (K, L) pairs. Moreover, when imperfect competition exists in the factor markets, the remuneration to the factors may not be equal to the marginal products, and, consequently, Euler's theorem becomes irrelevant to the distribution picture. However, linearly homogeneous production functions are often convenient to work with because of the various nice mathematical properties they are known to possess.

Cobb-Douglas Production Function

One specific production function widely used in economic analysis (earlier cited in Sec. 11.6, Example 5) is the *Cobb-Douglas production function:*

$$Q = AK^\alpha L^{1-\alpha} \tag{12.51}$$

where A is a positive constant, and α is a positive fraction. What we shall consider here first is a generalized version of this function, namely,

$$Q = AK^\alpha L^\beta \tag{12.52}$$

where β is another positive fraction which may or may not be equal to $1 - \alpha$. Some of the major features of this function are: (1) it is homogeneous of degree $(\alpha + \beta)$; (2) in the special case of $\alpha + \beta = 1$, it is linearly homogeneous; (3) its isoquants are negatively sloped throughout and strictly convex for positive values of K and L; and (4) it is strictly quasi-concave for positive K and L.

Its homogeneity is easily seen from the fact that, by changing K and L to jK and jL, respectively, the output will be changed to

$$A(jK)^\alpha (jL)^\beta = j^{\alpha+\beta}(AK^\alpha L^\beta) = j^{\alpha+\beta}Q$$

That is, the function is homogeneous of degree $(\alpha + \beta)$. In case $\alpha + \beta = 1$, there will be constant returns to scale, because the function will be linearly homogeneous. (Note, however, that this function is *not* linear! It would thus be confusing to refer to it as a "*linear* homogeneous" or "*linear* and *homogeneous*" function.) That its isoquants have negative slopes and strict convexity can be verified from the signs of the derivatives dK/dL and

d^2K/dL^2 (or the signs of dL/dK and d^2L/dK^2). For any positive output Q_0, (12.52) can be written as

$$AK^\alpha L^\beta = Q_0 \qquad (A, K, L, Q_0 > 0)$$

Taking the natural log of both sides and transposing, we find that

$$\ln A + \alpha \ln K + \beta \ln L - \ln Q_0 = 0$$

which implicitly defines K as a function of L.[†] By the implicit-function rule and the log rule, therefore, we have

$$\frac{dK}{dL} = -\frac{\partial F/\partial L}{\partial F/\partial K} = -\frac{(\beta/L)}{(\alpha/K)} = -\frac{\beta K}{\alpha L} < 0$$

Then it follows that

$$\frac{d^2K}{dL^2} = \frac{d}{dL}\left(-\frac{\beta K}{\alpha L}\right) = -\frac{\beta}{\alpha}\frac{d}{dL}\left(\frac{K}{L}\right) = -\frac{\beta}{\alpha}\frac{1}{L^2}\left(L\frac{dK}{dL} - K\right) > 0$$

The signs of these derivatives establish the isoquant (any isoquant) to be downward-sloping throughout and strictly convex in the LK plane for positive values of K and L. This, of course, is only to be expected from a function that is strictly quasiconcave for positive K and L. For the strict quasiconcavity feature of this function, see Example 5 of Sec. 12.4, where a similar function was discussed.

Let us now examine the $\alpha + \beta = 1$ case (the Cobb-Douglas function proper), to verify the three properties of linear homogeneity cited earlier. First of all, the total product in this special case is expressible as

$$Q = AK^\alpha L^{1-\alpha} = A\left(\frac{K}{L}\right)^\alpha L = LAk^\alpha \qquad \text{(12.51′)}$$

where the expression Ak^α is a specific version of the general expression $\phi(k)$ used before. Therefore, the average products are

$$\text{APP}_L = \frac{Q}{L} = Ak^\alpha$$

$$\text{APP}_K = \frac{Q}{K} = \frac{Q}{L}\frac{L}{K} = \frac{Ak^\alpha}{k} = Ak^{\alpha-1} \qquad \text{(12.53)}$$

both of which are now functions of k alone.

Second, differentiation of $Q = AK^\alpha L^{1-\alpha}$ yields the marginal products:

$$\frac{\partial Q}{\partial K} = A\alpha K^{\alpha-1}L^{-(\alpha-1)} = A\alpha\left(\frac{K}{L}\right)^{\alpha-1} = A\alpha k^{\alpha-1}$$

$$\frac{\partial Q}{\partial L} = AK^\alpha(1-\alpha)L^{-\alpha} = A(1-\alpha)\left(\frac{K}{L}\right)^\alpha = A(1-\alpha)k^\alpha \qquad \text{(12.54)}$$

and these are also functions of k alone.

[†] The conditions of the implicit-function theorem are satisfied, because F (the left-side expression) has continuous partial derivatives, and because $\partial F/\partial K = \alpha/K \neq 0$ for positive values of K.

Last, we can verify Euler's theorem by using (12.54) as follows:

$$K\frac{\partial Q}{\partial K} + L\frac{\partial Q}{\partial L} = KA\alpha k^{\alpha-1} + LA(1-\alpha)k^{\alpha}$$

$$= LAk^{\alpha}\left(\frac{K\alpha}{Lk} + 1 - \alpha\right)$$

$$= LAk^{\alpha}(\alpha + 1 - \alpha) = LAk^{\alpha} = Q \qquad [\text{by } (12.51')]$$

Interesting economic meanings can be assigned to the exponents α and $(1-\alpha)$ in the linearly homogeneous Cobb-Douglas production function. If each input is assumed to be paid by the amount of its marginal product, the relative share of total product accruing to capital will be

$$\frac{K(\partial Q/\partial K)}{Q} = \frac{KA\alpha k^{\alpha-1}}{LAk^{\alpha}} = \alpha$$

Similarly, labor's relative share will be

$$\frac{L(\partial Q/\partial L)}{Q} = \frac{LA(1-\alpha)k^{\alpha}}{LAk^{\alpha}} = 1 - \alpha$$

Thus the exponent of each input variable indicates the relative share of that input in the total product. Looking at it another way, we can also interpret the exponent of each input variable as the partial elasticity of output with respect to that input. This is because the capital-share expression just given is equivalent to the expression $\dfrac{\partial Q/\partial K}{Q/K} \equiv \varepsilon_{QK}$ and, similarly, the labor-share expression just given is precisely that of ε_{QL}.

What about the meaning of the constant A? For given values of K and L, the magnitude of A will proportionately affect the level of Q. Hence A may be considered as an *efficiency parameter,* i.e., as an indicator of the state of technology.

Extensions of the Results

We have discussed linear homogeneity in the specific context of production functions, but the properties cited are equally valid in other contexts, provided the variables K, L, and Q are properly reinterpreted.

Furthermore it is possible to extend our results to the case of more than two variables. With a linearly homogeneous function

$$y = f(x_1, x_2, \ldots, x_n)$$

we can again divide each variable by x_1 (that is, multiply by $1/x_1$) and get the result

$$y = x_1\phi\left(\frac{x_2}{x_1}, \frac{x_3}{x_1}, \ldots, \frac{x_n}{x_1}\right) \qquad [\text{homogeneity of degree 1}]$$

which is comparable to (12.45'). Moreover, Euler's theorem is easily extended to the form

$$\sum_{i=1}^{n} x_i f_i \equiv y \qquad [\text{Euler's theorem}]$$

where the partial derivatives of the original function f (namely, f_i) are again homogeneous of degree zero in the variables x_i, as in the two-variable case.

The preceding extensions can, in fact, also be generalized with relative ease to a homogeneous function of degree r. In the first place, by definition of homogeneity, we can in the present case write

$$y = x_1^r \phi \left(\frac{x_2}{x_1}, \frac{x_3}{x_1}, \ldots, \frac{x_n}{x_1} \right) \qquad \text{[homogeneity of degree } r\text{]}$$

The modified version of Euler's theorem will now appear in the form

$$\sum_{i=1}^{n} x_i f_i \equiv ry \qquad \text{[Euler's theorem]}$$

where a multiplicative constant r has been attached to the dependent variable y on the right. And, finally, the partial derivatives of the original function f, the f_i, will all be homogeneous of degree $(r - 1)$ in the variables x_i. You can thus see that the linear-homogeneity case is merely a special case thereof, in which $r = 1$.

EXERCISE 12.6

1. Determine whether the following functions are homogeneous. If so, of what degree?

   (a) $f(x, y) = \sqrt{xy}$

   (b) $f(x, y) = (x^2 - y^2)^{1/2}$

   (c) $f(x, y) = x^3 - xy + y^3$

   (d) $f(x, y) = 2x + y + 3\sqrt{xy}$

   (e) $f(x, y, w) = \dfrac{xy^2}{w} + 2xw$

   (f) $f(x, y, w) = x^4 - 5yw^3$

2. Show that the function (12.45) can be expressed alternatively as $Q = K \psi \left(\dfrac{L}{K} \right)$ instead of $Q = L\phi \left(\dfrac{K}{L} \right)$.

3. Deduce from Euler's theorem that, with constant returns to scale:

   (a) When $MPP_K = 0$, APP_L is equal to MPP_L.

   (b) When $MPP_L = 0$, APP_K is equal to MPP_K.

4. On the basis of (12.46) through (12.50), check whether the following are true under conditions of constant returns to scale:

   (a) An APP_L curve can be plotted against k ($= K/L$) as the independent variable (on the horizontal axis).

   (b) MPP_K is measured by the slope of that APP_L curve.

   (c) APP_K is measured by the slope of the radius vector to the APP_L curve.

   (d) $MPP_L = APP_L - k(MPP_K) = APP_L - k$ (slope of APP_L).

5. Use (12.53) and (12.54) to verify that the relations described in Prob. 4b, c, and d are obeyed by the Cobb-Douglas production function.

6. Given the production function $Q = AK^\alpha L^\beta$, show that:

   (a) $\alpha + \beta > 1$ implies increasing returns to scale.

   (b) $\alpha + \beta < 1$ implies decreasing returns to scale.

   (c) α and β are, respectively, the partial elasticities of output with respect to the capital and labor inputs.

7. Let output be a function of three inputs: $Q = AK^aL^bN^c$.
   - (a) Is this function homogeneous? If so, of what degree?
   - (b) Under what condition would there be constant returns to scale? Increasing returns to scale?
   - (c) Find the share of product for input N, if it is paid by the amount of its marginal product.
8. Let the production function $Q = g(K, L)$ be homogeneous of degree 2.
   - (a) Write an equation to express the second-degree homogeneity property of this function.
   - (b) Find an expression for Q in terms of $\phi(k)$, in the vein of (12.45').
   - (c) Find the MPP$_K$ function. Is MPP$_K$ still a function of k alone, as in the linear-homogeneity case?
   - (d) Is the MPP$_K$ function homogeneous in K and L? If so, of what degree?

12.7 Least-Cost Combination of Inputs

As another example of constrained optimization, let us discuss the problem of finding the least-cost input combination for the production of a specified level of output Q_0 representing, say, a customer's special order. Here we shall work with a general production function; later on, however, reference will be made to homogeneous production functions.

First-Order Condition

Assuming a smooth production function with two variable inputs, $Q = Q(a, b)$, where $Q_a, Q_b > 0$, and assuming both input prices to be exogenous (though again omitting the zero subscript), we may formulate the problem as one of minimizing the cost

$$C = aP_a + bP_b$$

subject to the output constraint

$$Q(a, b) = Q_0$$

Hence, the Lagrangian function is

$$Z = aP_a + bP_b + \mu[Q_0 - Q(a, b)]$$

To satisfy the first-order condition for a minimum C, the input levels (the choice variables) must satisfy the following simultaneous equations:

$$Z_\mu = Q_0 - Q(a, b) = 0$$
$$Z_a = P_a - \mu Q_a = 0$$
$$Z_b = P_b - \mu Q_b = 0$$

The first equation in this set is merely the constraint restated, and the last two imply the condition

$$\frac{P_a}{Q_a} = \frac{P_b}{Q_b} = \mu \qquad (12.55)$$

FIGURE 12.8

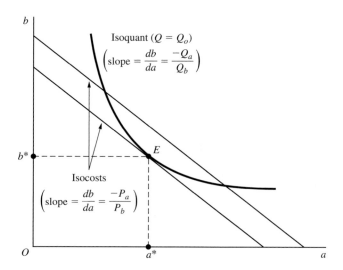

At the point of optimal input combination, the input-price–marginal-product ratio must be the same for each input. Since this ratio measures the amount of outlay per unit of marginal product of the input in question, the Lagrange multiplier can be given the interpretation of the marginal cost of production in the optimum state. This interpretation is, of course, entirely consistent with our earlier discovery in (12.16) that the optimal value of the Lagrange multiplier measures the comparative-static effect of the constraint constant on the optimal value of the objective function, that is, $\mu^* = (\S C^*/\S Q_0)$, where the $\S$ symbol indicates that this is a partial total derivative.

Equation (12.55) can be alternatively written in the form

$$\frac{P_a}{P_b} = \frac{Q_a}{Q_b} \qquad (12.55')$$

which you should compare with (12.31″). Presented in this form, the first-order condition can be explained in terms of isoquants and isocosts. As we learned in (11.36), the Q_a/Q_b ratio is the negative of the slope of an isoquant; that is, it is a measure of the *marginal rate of technical substitution of a for b* (MRTS$_{ab}$). In the present model, the output level is specified at Q_0; thus only one isoquant is involved, as shown in Fig. 12.8, with a negative slope.

The P_a/P_b ratio, on the other hand, represents the negative of the slope of *isocosts* (a notion comparable with the budget line in consumer theory). An isocost, defined as the locus of the input combinations that entail the same total cost, is expressible by the equation

$$C_0 = aP_a + bP_b \qquad \text{or} \qquad b = \frac{C_0}{P_b} - \frac{P_a}{P_b}a$$

where C_0 stands for a (parametric) cost figure. When plotted in the ab plane, as in Fig. 12.8, therefore, it yields a family of straight lines with (negative) slope $-P_a/P_b$ (and vertical intercept C_0/P_b). The equality of the two ratios therefore amounts to the equality of the slopes of the isoquant and a selected isocost. Since we are compelled to stay on the given isoquant, this condition leads us to the point of tangency E and the input combination (a^*, b^*).

Second-Order Condition

To ensure a *minimum* cost, it is sufficient (after the first-order condition is met) to have a negative bordered Hessian, i.e., to have

$$|\overline{H}| = \begin{vmatrix} 0 & Q_a & Q_b \\ Q_a & -\mu Q_{aa} & -\mu Q_{ab} \\ Q_b & -\mu Q_{ba} & -\mu Q_{bb} \end{vmatrix} = \mu(Q_{aa}Q_b^2 - 2Q_{ab}Q_aQ_b + Q_{bb}Q_a^2) < 0$$

Since the optimal value of μ (marginal cost) is positive, this reduces to the condition that the expression in parentheses be negative when evaluated at E.

From (11.44), we recall that the curvature of an isoquant is represented by the second derivative

$$\frac{d^2b}{da^2} = \frac{-1}{Q_b^3}(Q_{aa}Q_b^2 - 2Q_{ab}Q_aQ_b + Q_{bb}Q_a^2)$$

in which the same parenthetical expression appears. Inasmuch as Q_b is positive, the satisfaction of the second-order sufficient condition would imply that d^2b/da^2 is positive—that is, the isoquant is strictly convex—at the point of tangency. In the present context, the strict convexity of the isoquant would also imply the satisfaction of the second-order sufficient condition. For, since the isoquant is negatively sloped, strict convexity can mean only a positive d^2b/da^2 (zero d^2b/da^2 is possible only at a stationary point on the isoquant), which would in turn ensure that $|\overline{H}| < 0$. However, it should again be borne in mind that the sufficient condition $|\overline{H}| < 0$ (and hence the strict convexity of the isoquant) at the tangency is, per se, not necessary for the minimization of C. Specifically, C can be minimized even when the isoquant is (nonstrictly) convex, in a multiple-minimum situation analogous to Fig. 12.7b, with $d^2b/da^2 = 0$ and $|\overline{H}| = 0$ at each minimum.

In discussing the utility-maximization model (Sec. 12.5), it was pointed out that a smooth, increasing, strictly quasiconcave utility function $U = U(x, y)$ gives rise to everywhere strictly convex, downward-sloping indifference curves in the xy plane. Since the notion of isoquants is almost identical with that of indifference curves,[†] we can reason by analogy that a smooth, increasing, strictly quasiconcave production function $Q = Q(a, b)$ can generate everywhere strictly convex, downward-sloping isoquants in the ab plane. If such a production function is assumed, then obviously the second-order sufficient condition will always be satisfied. Moreover, it should be clear that the resulting C^* will be a unique absolute constrained minimum.

The Expansion Path

Let us now turn to one of the comparative-static aspects of this model. Assuming a *fixed* ratio of the two input prices, let us postulate successive increases of Q_0 (ascent to higher and higher isoquants) and trace the effect on the least-cost combination b^*/a^*. Each shift of the isoquant, of course, will result in a new point of tangency, with a higher isocost. The locus of such points of tangency, known as the *expansion path* of the firm, serves to describe the least-cost combinations required to produce varying levels of Q_0. Two possible shapes of the expansion path are shown in Fig. 12.9.

[†] Both are in the nature of "isovalue" curves. They differ only in the field of application; indifference curves are used in models of consumption, and isoquants, in models of production.

FIGURE 12.9

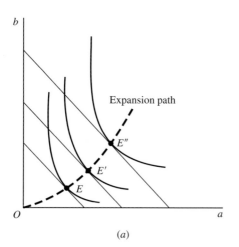

(a)

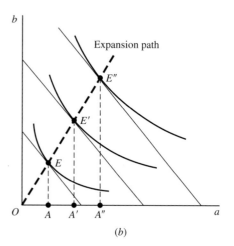

(b)

If we assume the strict convexity of the isoquants (hence, satisfaction of the second-order condition), the expansion path will be derivable directly from the first-order condition (12.55'). Let us illustrate this for the generalized version of the Cobb-Douglas production function.

The condition (12.55') requires the equality of the input-price ratio and the marginal-product ratio. For the function $Q = Aa^\alpha b^\beta$, this means that each point on the expansion path must satsify

$$\frac{P_a}{P_b} = \frac{Q_a}{Q_b} = \frac{A\alpha a^{\alpha-1}b^\beta}{Aa^\alpha \beta b^{\beta-1}} = \frac{\alpha b}{\beta a} \qquad (12.56)$$

implying that the optimal input ratio should be

$$\frac{b^*}{a^*} = \frac{\beta P_a}{\alpha P_b} = \text{a constant} \qquad (12.57)$$

since α, β, and the input prices are all constant. As a result, all points on the expansion path must show the same *fixed* input ratio; i.e., the expansion path must be a straight line emanating from the point of origin. This is illustrated in Fig. 12.9*b*, where the input ratios at the various points of tangency (AE/OA, $A'E'/OA'$, and $A''E''/OA''$) are all equal.

The linearity of the expansion path is characterisitc of the generalized Cobb-Douglas function whether or not $\alpha + \beta = 1$, because the derivation of the result in (12.57) does not rely on the assumption $\alpha + \beta = 1$. As a matter of fact, any homogeneous production function (not necessarily the Cobb-Douglas) will give rise to a linear expansion path for each set of input prices, because of the following reason: if it is homogeneous of (say) degree r, both marginal-product functions Q_a and Q_b must be homogeneous of degree $(r-1)$ in the inputs a and b; thus a j-fold increase in both inputs will produce a j^{r-1}-fold change in the values of *both* Q_a and Q_b, which will leave the Q_a/Q_b ratio intact. Therefore, if the first-order condition $P_a/P_b = Q_a/Q_b$ is satisfied at given input prices by a particular input combination (a_0, b_0), it must also be satisfied by a combination (ja_0, jb_0)—precisely as is depicted by the linear expansion path in Fig. 12.9*b*.

Although *any* homogeneous production function can give rise to a linear expansion path, the specific degree of homogeneity does make a significant difference in the interpretation of the expansion path. In Fig. 12.9*b*, we have drawn the distance OE equal to that EE', so that point E' involves a doubling of the scale of point E. Now if the production function is homogeneous of degree *one,* the output at E' must be twice ($2^1 = 2$) that of E. But if the degree of homogeneity is *two,* the output at E' will be four times ($2^2 = 4$) that of E. Thus, the spacing of the isoquants for $Q = 1, Q = 2, \ldots,$ will be widely different for different degrees of homogeneity.

Homothetic Functions

We have explained that, given a set of input prices, homogeneity (of any degree) of the production function produces a linear expansion path. But linear expansion paths are not unique to homogeneous production functions, for a more general class of functions, known as *homothetic functions,* can produce them, too.

Homotheticity can arise from a composite function in the form

$$H = h[Q(a, b)] \qquad [h'(Q) \neq 0] \qquad \textbf{(12.58)}$$

where $Q(a, b)$ is homogeneous of degree r. Although derived from a homogeneous function, the function $H = H(a, b)$ is in general *not* homogeneous in the variables a and b. Nonetheless, the expansion paths of $H(a, b)$, like those of $Q(a, b)$, are linear. The key to this result is that, at any given point in the ab plane, the H isoquant shares the same slope as the Q isoquant:

$$\text{Slope of } H \text{ isoquant} = -\frac{H_a}{H_b} = -\frac{h'(Q)Q_a}{h'(Q)Q_b}$$

$$= -\frac{Q_a}{Q_b} = \text{slope of } Q \text{ isoquant} \qquad \textbf{(12.59)}$$

Now the linearity of the expansion paths of $Q(a, b)$ implies, and is implied by, the condition

$$-\frac{Q_a}{Q_b} = \text{constant for any given } \frac{b}{a}$$

In view of (12.59), however, we immediately have

$$-\frac{H_a}{H_b} = \text{constant for any given } \frac{b}{a} \qquad \textbf{(12.60)}$$

as well. And this establishes that $H(a, b)$ also produces linear expansion paths.

The concept of homotheticity is more general than that of homogeneity. In fact, every homogeneous function is automatically a member of the homothetic family, but a homothetic function may be a function outside the homogeneous family. The fact that a homogeneous function is always homothetic can be seen from (12.58), where if we let the function $H = h(Q)$ take the specific form $H = Q$—with $h'(Q) = dH/dQ = 1$—then the function Q, being identical with the function H itself, is obviously homothetic. That a homothetic function may not be homogeneous will be illustrated in Example 2, which follows.

In defining the homothetic function H, we specified in (12.58) that $h'(Q) \neq 0$. This enables us to avoid division by zero in (12.59). While the specification $h'(Q) \neq 0$ is the only requirement from the mathematical standpoint, economic considerations would suggest the stronger restriction $h'(Q) > 0$. For if $H(a, b)$ is, like $Q(a, b)$, to serve as a production function, that is, if H is to denote output, then H_a and H_b should, respectively, be made to go in the same direction as Q_a and Q_b in the $Q(a, b)$ function. Thus $H(a, b)$ needs to be restricted to be a monotonically increasing transformation of $Q(a, b)$.

Homothetic production functions (including the special case of homogeneous ones) possess the interesting property that the (partial) elasticity of optimal input level with respect to the output level is uniform for all inputs. To see this, recall that the linearity of expansion paths of homothetic functions means that the optimal input ratio b^*/a^* is unaffected by a change in the exogenous output level H_0. Thus $\partial(b^*/a^*)/\partial H_0 = 0$ or

$$\frac{1}{a^{*2}} \left(a^* \frac{\partial b^*}{\partial H_0} - b^* \frac{\partial a^*}{\partial H_0} \right) = 0 \qquad \text{[quotient rule]}$$

Multiplying through by $a^{*2} H_0$, and rearranging, we then get

$$\frac{\partial a^*}{\partial H_0} \frac{H_0}{a^*} = \frac{\partial b^*}{\partial H_0} \frac{H_0}{b^*} \qquad \text{or} \qquad \varepsilon_{a^* H_0} = \varepsilon_{b^* H_0}$$

which is what we previously asserted.

Example 1

Let $H = Q^2$, where $Q = Aa^\alpha b^\beta$. Since $Q(a, b)$ is homogeneous and $h'(Q) = 2Q$ is positive for positive output, $H(a, b)$ is homothetic for $Q > 0$. We shall verify that it satisfies (12.60). First, by substitution, we have

$$H = Q^2 = (Aa^\alpha b^\beta)^2 = A^2 a^{2\alpha} b^{2\beta}$$

Thus the slope of the isoquants of H is expressed by

$$-\frac{H_a}{H_b} = -\frac{A^2 2\alpha a^{2\alpha-1} b^{2\beta}}{A^2 a^{2\alpha} 2\beta b^{2\beta-1}} = -\frac{\alpha b}{\beta a} \tag{12.61}$$

This result satisfies (12.60) and implies linear expansion paths. A comparison of (12.61) with (12.56) also shows that the function H satisfies (12.59).

In this example, $Q(a, b)$ is homogeneous of degree $(\alpha + \beta)$. As it turns out, $H(a, b)$ is also homogeneous, but of degree $2(\alpha + \beta)$. As a rule, however, a homothetic function is not necessarily homogeneous.

Example 2

Let $H = e^Q$, where $Q = Aa^\alpha b^\beta$. Since $Q(a, b)$ is homogeneous and $h'(Q) = e^Q$ is positive, $H(a, b)$ is homothetic. From this function,

$$H(a, b) = \exp(Aa^\alpha b^\beta)$$

it is easily found that

$$-\frac{H_a}{H_b} = -\frac{A\alpha a^{\alpha-1} b^\beta \exp(Aa^\alpha b^\beta)}{Aa^\alpha \beta b^{\beta-1} \exp(Aa^\alpha b^\beta)} = -\frac{\alpha b}{\beta a}$$

This result is, of course, identical with (12.61) in Example 1. This time, however, the homothetic function is *not* homogeneous, because

$$H(ja, jb) = \exp[A(ja)^\alpha (jb)^\beta] = \exp(Aa^\alpha b^\beta j^{\alpha+\beta})$$
$$= [\exp(Aa^\alpha b^\beta)]^{j^{\alpha+\beta}} = [H(a, b)]^{j^{\alpha+\beta}} \neq j^r H(a, b)$$

Elasticity of Substitution

Another aspect of comparative statics has to do with the effect of a change in the P_a/P_b ratio upon the least-cost input combination b^*/a^* for producing the same given output Q_0 (that is, while we stay on the same isoquant).

When the (exogenous) input-price ratio P_a/P_b rises, we can normally expect the optimal input ratio b^*/a^* also to rise, because input b (now relatively cheaper) will tend to be substituted for input a. The *direction* of substitution is clear, but what about its *extent*? The extent of input substitution can be measured by the following point-elasticity expression, called the *elasticity of substitution* and denoted by σ (lowercase Greek letter sigma, for "substitution"):

$$\sigma \equiv \frac{\text{relative change in } (b^*/a^*)}{\text{relative change in } (P_a/P_b)} = \frac{\dfrac{d(b^*/a^*)}{b^*/a^*}}{\dfrac{d(P_a/P_b)}{P_a/P_b}} = \frac{\dfrac{d(b^*/a^*)}{d(P_a/P_b)}}{\dfrac{b^*/a^*}{P_a/P_b}} \quad \textbf{(12.62)}$$

The value of σ can be anywhere between 0 and ∞; the larger the σ, the greater the substitutability between the two inputs. The limiting case of $\sigma = 0$ is where the two inputs must be used in a fixed proportion as complements to each other. The other limiting case, with σ infinite, is where the two inputs are perfect substitutes for each other. Note that, if (b^*/a^*) is considered as a function of (P_a/P_b), then the elasticity σ will again be the ratio of a *marginal* function to an *average* function.[†]

For illustration, let us calculate the elasticity of substitution for the generalized Cobb-Douglas production function. We learned earlier that, for this case, the least-cost input combination is specified by

$$\left(\frac{b^*}{a^*}\right) = \frac{\beta}{\alpha}\left(\frac{P_a}{P_b}\right) \qquad \text{[from (12.57)]}$$

This equation is in the form $y = ax$, for which dy/dx (the marginal) and y/x (the average) are both equal to the constant a. That is,

$$\frac{d(b^*/a^*)}{d(P_a/P_b)} = \frac{\beta}{\alpha} \qquad \text{and} \qquad \frac{b^*/a^*}{P_a/P_b} = \frac{\beta}{\alpha}$$

Substituting these values into (12.62), we immediately find that $\sigma = 1$; that is, the generalized Cobb-Douglas production function is characterized by a *constant, unitary* elasticity of substitution. Note that the derivation of this result in no way relies upon the assumption that $\alpha + \beta = 1$. Thus the elasticity of substitution of the production function $Q = Aa^\alpha b^\beta$ will be unitary even if $\alpha + \beta \neq 1$.

[†] There is an alternative way of expressing σ. Since, at the point of tangency, we always have

$$\frac{P_a}{P_b} = \frac{Q_a}{Q_b} = \text{MRTS}_{ab}$$

the elasticity of substitution can be defined equivalently as

$$\sigma = \frac{\text{relative change in } (b^*/a^*)}{\text{relative change in MRTS}_{ab}} = \frac{\dfrac{d(b^*/a^*)}{b^*/a^*}}{\dfrac{d(Q_a/Q_b)}{Q_a/Q_b}} = \frac{\dfrac{d(b^*/a^*)}{d(Q_a/Q_b)}}{\dfrac{b^*/a^*}{Q_a/Q_b}} \qquad \textbf{(12.62')}$$

CES Production Function

More recently, there has come into common use another form of production function which, while still characterized by a constant elasticity of substitution (CES), can yield as a σ with a (constant) value other than 1.[†] The equation of this function, known as the *CES production function,* is

$$Q = A[\delta K^{-\rho} + (1-\delta)L^{-\rho}]^{-1/\rho} \quad (A > 0; 0 < \delta < 1; -1 < \rho \neq 0) \quad \textbf{(12.63)}$$

where K and L represent two factors of production, and A, δ, and ρ (lowercase Greek letter rho) are three parameters. The parameter A (the *efficiency parameter*) plays the same role as the coefficient A in the Cobb-Douglas function; it serves as an indicator of the state of technology. The parameter δ (the *distribution parameter*), like the α in the Cobb-Douglas function, has to do with the relative factor shares in the product. And the parameter ρ (the *substitution parameter*)—which has no counterpart in the Cobb-Douglas function—is what determines the value of the (constant) elasticity of substitution, as will be shown later in this section.

First, however, let us observe that this function is homogeneous of degree one. If we replace K and L by jK and jL, respectively, the output will change from Q to

$$A[\delta(jK)^{-\rho} + (1-\delta)(jL)^{-\rho}]^{-1/\rho} = A\{j^{-\rho}[\delta K^{-\rho} + (1-\delta)L^{-\rho}]\}^{-1/\rho}$$
$$= (j^{-\rho})^{-1/\rho}Q = jQ$$

Consequently, the CES function, like all linearly homogeneous production functions, displays constant returns to scale, qualifies for the application of Euler's theorem, and possesses average products and marginal products that are homogeneous of degree zero in the variables K and L.

We may also note that the isoquants generated by the CES production function are always negatively sloped and strictly convex for positive values of K and L. To show this, let us first find the expressions for the marginal products Q_L and Q_K. Using the notation $[\cdots]$ as a shorthand for $[\delta K^{-\rho} + (1-\delta)L^{-\rho}]$, we have

$$Q_L \equiv \frac{\partial Q}{\partial L} = A\left(-\frac{1}{\rho}\right)[\cdots]^{-(1/\rho)-1}(1-\delta)(-\rho)L^{-\rho-1}$$

$$= (1-\delta)A[\cdots]^{-(1+\rho)/\rho}L^{-(1+\rho)}$$

$$= (1-\delta)\frac{A^{1+\rho}}{A^{\rho}}[\cdots]^{-(1+\rho)/\rho}L^{-(1+\rho)}$$

$$= \frac{(1-\delta)}{A^{\rho}}\left(\frac{Q}{L}\right)^{1+\rho} > 0 \qquad \text{[by (12.63)]} \qquad \textbf{(12.64)}$$

and similarly,

$$Q_K \equiv \frac{\partial Q}{\partial K} = \frac{\delta}{A^{\rho}}\left(\frac{Q}{K}\right)^{1+\rho} > 0 \qquad \textbf{(12.65)}$$

[†] K. J. Arrow, H. B. Chenery, B. S. Minhas, and R. M. Solow, "Capital-Labor Substitution and Economic Efficiency," *Review of Economics and Statistics,* August 1961, pp. 225–250.

which are defined for positive values of K and L. Thus the slope of isoquants (with K plotted vertically and L horizontally) is

$$\frac{dK}{dL} = -\frac{Q_L}{Q_K} = -\frac{(1-\delta)}{\delta}\left(\frac{K}{L}\right)^{1+\rho} < 0 \qquad \text{[see (11.36)]} \quad \textbf{(12.66)}$$

It can then be easily checked that $d^2K/dL^2 > 0$ (which we leave to you as an exercise), implying that the isoquants are strictly convex for positive K and L.

It can also be shown that the CES production function is strictly quasiconcave for positive K and L. Further differentiation of (12.64) and (12.65) shows that the second derivatives of the function have the following signs:

$$Q_{LL} = \frac{\partial}{\partial L}Q_L = \frac{(1-\delta)(1+\rho)}{A^\rho}\left(\frac{Q}{L}\right)^\rho \frac{Q_L L - Q}{L^2} < 0$$

$$[Q_L L - Q < 0, \text{ by Euler's theorem}]$$

$$Q_{KK} = \frac{\partial}{\partial K}Q_K = \frac{\delta(1+\rho)}{A^\rho}\left(\frac{Q}{K}\right)^\rho \frac{Q_K K - Q}{K^2} < 0$$

$$[Q_K K - Q < 0, \text{ by Euler's theorem}]$$

$$Q_{KL} = Q_{LK} = \frac{(1-\delta)(1+\rho)}{A^\rho}\left(\frac{Q}{L}\right)^\rho \frac{Q_K}{L} > 0$$

These derivative signs, valid for positive K and L, enable us to check the sufficient condition for strict quasiconcavity (12.26). As you can verify,

$$|B_1| = -Q_K^2 < 0$$

and

$$|B_2| = 2Q_K Q_L Q_{KL} - Q_K^2 Q_{LL} - Q_L^2 Q_{KK} > 0$$

Thus the CES function is strictly quasiconcave for positive K and L.

Last, we shall use the marginal products in (12.64) and (12.65) to find the elasticity of substitution of the CES function. To satisfy the least-cost combination condition $Q_L/Q_K = P_L/P_K$, where P_L and P_K denote the prices of labor service (wage rate) and capital service (rental charge for capital goods), respectively, we must have

$$\frac{1-\delta}{\delta}\left(\frac{K}{L}\right)^{1+\rho} = \frac{P_L}{P_K} \qquad \text{[see (12.66)]}$$

Thus the optimal input ratio is (introducing a shorthand symbol c)

$$\left(\frac{K^*}{L^*}\right) = \left(\frac{\delta}{1-\delta}\right)^{1/(1+\rho)}\left(\frac{P_L}{P_K}\right)^{1/(1+\rho)} \equiv c\left(\frac{P_L}{P_K}\right)^{1/(1+\rho)} \qquad \textbf{(12.67)}$$

Taking (K^*/L^*) to be a function of (P_L/P_K), we find the associated marginal and average functions to be

$$\text{Marginal function} = \frac{d(K^*/L^*)}{d(P_L/P_K)} = \frac{c}{1+\rho}\left(\frac{P_L}{P_K}\right)^{1/(1+\rho)-1}$$

$$\text{Average function} = \frac{K^*/L^*}{P_L/P_K} = c\left(\frac{P_L}{P_K}\right)^{1/(1+\rho)-1}$$

Therefore the elasticity of substitution is[†]

$$\sigma = \frac{\text{Marginal function}}{\text{Average function}} = \frac{1}{1 + \rho} \qquad \textbf{(12.68)}$$

What this shows is that σ is a constant whose magnitude depends on the value of the parameter ρ as follows:

$$\left.\begin{array}{r} -1 < \rho < 0 \\ \rho = 0 \\ 0 < \rho < \infty \end{array}\right\} \quad \Rightarrow \quad \left\{\begin{array}{l} \sigma > 1 \\ \sigma = 1 \\ \sigma < 1 \end{array}\right.$$

Cobb-Douglas Function as a Special Case of the CES Function

In this last result, the middle case of $\rho = 0$ leads to a unitary elasticity of substitution which, as we know, is characteristic of the Cobb-Douglas function. This suggests that the (linearly homogeneous) Cobb-Douglas function is a special case of the (linearly homogeneous) CES function. The difficulty is that the CES function, as given in (12.63), is undefined when $\rho = 0$, because division by zero is not possible. Nevertheless, we can demonstrate that, as $\rho \to 0$, the CES function approaches the Cobb-Douglas function.

For this demonstration, we shall rely on a technique known as *L'Hôpital's rule*. This rule has to do with the evaluation of the limit of a function $f(x) = \dfrac{m(x)}{n(x)}$ as $x \to a$ (where a can be either finite or infinite), when the numerator $m(x)$ and the denominator $n(x)$ either (1) both tend to zero as $x \to a$, thus resulting in an expression of the 0/0 form, or (2) both tend to $\pm\infty$ as $x \to a$, thus resulting in an expression in the form of ∞/∞ (or $\infty/-\infty$, or $-\infty/\infty$, or $-\infty/-\infty$). Even though the limit of $f(x)$ cannot be evaluated as the expression stands under these two circumstances, its value can nevertheless be found by using the formula

$$\lim_{x \to a} \frac{m(x)}{n(x)} = \lim_{x \to a} \frac{m'(x)}{n'(x)} \qquad \text{[L'Hôpital's rule]} \qquad \textbf{(12.69)}$$

Example 3   Find the limit of $(1 - x^2)/(1 - x)$ as $x \to 1$. Here, both $m(x)$ and $n(x)$ approach zero as x approaches unity, thus exemplifying circumstance (1). Since $m'(x) = -2x$ and $n'(x) = -1$, we can write

$$\lim_{x \to 1} \frac{1 - x^2}{1 - x} = \lim_{x \to 1} \frac{-2x}{-1} = \lim_{x \to 1} 2x = 2$$

This answer is identical with that obtained by another method in Example 2 of Sec. 6.4.

[†] Of course, we could also have obtained the same result by first taking the logarithms of both sides of (12.67):

$$\ln\left(\frac{K^*}{L^*}\right) = \ln c + \frac{1}{1 + \rho} \ln\left(\frac{P_L}{P_K}\right)$$

and then applying the formula for elasticity in (10.28), to get

$$\sigma = \frac{d\,(\ln K^*/L^*)}{d\,(\ln P_L/P_K)} = \frac{1}{1 + \rho}$$

Example 4

Find the limit of $(2x + 5)/(x + 1)$ as $x \to \infty$. When x becomes infinite, both $m(x)$ and $n(x)$ become infinite in the present case; thus we have here an example of circumstance (2). Since $m'(x) = 2$ and $n'(x) = 1$, we can write

$$\lim_{x \to \infty} \frac{2x + 5}{x + 1} = \lim_{x \to \infty} \frac{2}{1} = 2$$

Again, this answer is identical with that obtained by another method in Example 3 of Sec. 6.4.

It may turn out that the right-side expression in (12.69) again falls into the 0/0 or the ∞/∞ format, same as the left-side expression. In such an event, we may reapply L'Hôpital's rule, i.e., we may look for the limit of $m''(x)/n''(x)$ as $x \to a$, and take that limit as our answer. It may also turn out that even though the given function $f(x)$, whose limit we wish to evaluate, is originally not in the form of $m(x)/n(x)$ that falls into the 0/0 or the ∞/∞ format upon limit-taking, a suitable transformation will make $f(x)$ amenable to the application of the rule in (12.69). This latter possibility can be illustrated by the problem of finding the limit of the CES function (12.63)—now viewed as a function $Q(\rho)$—as $\rho \to 0$.

As given, $Q(\rho)$ is not in the form of $m(\rho)/n(\rho)$. Dividing both sides of (12.63) by A, and taking the natural log, however, we do get an expression in that form, namely,

$$\ln \frac{Q}{A} = \frac{-\ln[\delta K^{-\rho} + (1 - \delta)L^{-\rho}]}{\rho} \equiv \frac{m(\rho)}{n(\rho)} \qquad \textbf{(12.70)}$$

Moreover, as $\rho \to 0$, we find that $m(\rho) \to -\ln(\delta + 1 - \delta) = -\ln 1 = 0$, and $n(\rho) \to 0$, too. Thus L'Hôpital's rule can be used to find the limit of $\ln(Q/A)$. Once that is done, the limit of Q can also be found: since $Q/A = e^{\ln(Q/A)}$, so that $Q = Ae^{\ln(Q/A)}$, it follows that

$$\lim Q = \lim Ae^{\ln(Q/A)} = Ae^{\lim \ln(Q/A)} \qquad \textbf{(12.71)}$$

From (12.70), let us first find $m'(\rho)$ and $n'(\rho)$, as required by L'Hôpital's rule. The latter is simply $n'(\rho) = 1$. The former is

$$m'(\rho) = \frac{-1}{[\delta K^{-\rho} + (1 - \delta)L^{-\rho}]} \frac{d}{d\rho}[\delta K^{-\rho} + (1 - \delta)L^{-\rho}] \qquad \text{[chain rule]}$$

$$= \frac{-[-\delta K^{-\rho} \ln K - (1 - \delta)L^{-\rho} \ln L]}{[\delta K^{-\rho} + (1 - \delta)L^{-\rho}]} \qquad \text{[by (10.21$'$)]}$$

By L'Hôpital's rule, therefore, we have

$$\lim_{\rho \to 0} \ln \frac{Q}{A} = \lim_{\rho \to 0} \frac{m'(\rho)}{n'(\rho)} = \frac{\delta \ln K + (1 - \delta) \ln L}{1} = \ln(K^\delta L^{1-\delta})$$

In view of this result, when e is raised to the power of $\lim_{\rho \to 0} \ln(Q/A)$, the outcome is simply $K^\delta L^{1-\delta}$. Hence, by (12.71), we finally arrive at the result

$$\lim_{\rho \to 0} Q = AK^\delta L^{1-\delta}$$

showing that, as $\rho \to 0$, the CES function indeed tends to the Cobb-Douglas function.

EXERCISE 12.7

1. Suppose that the isoquants in Fig. 12.9b are derived from a particular homogeneous production function $Q = Q(a, b)$. Noting that $OE = EE' = E'E''$, what must be the ratios between the output levels represented by the three isoquants if the function Q is homogeneous

   (a) of degree one?   (b) of degree two?

2. For the generalized Cobb-Douglas case, if we plot the ratio b^*/a^* against the ratio P_a/P_b, what type of curve will result? Does this result depend on the assumption that $\alpha + \beta = 1$? Read the elasticity of substitution graphically from this curve.

3. Is the CES production function characterized by diminishing returns to each input for all positive levels of input?

4. Show that, on an isoquant of the CES function, $d^2 K / dL^2 > 0$.

5. (a) For the CES function, if each factor of production is paid according to its marginal product, what is the ratio of labor's share of product to capital's share of product? Would a larger value of δ mean a larger relative share for capital?

   (b) For the Cobb-Douglas function, is the ratio of labor's share to capital's share dependent on the K/L ratio? Does the same answer apply to the CES function?

6. (a) The CES production function rules out $\rho = -1$. If $\rho = -1$, however, what would be the general shape of the isoquants for positive K and L?

   (b) Is σ defined for $\rho = -1$? What is the limit of σ as $\rho \to -1$?

   (c) Interpret economically the results for parts (a) and (b).

7. Show that by writing the CES function as $Q = A[\delta K^{-\rho} + (1 - \delta)L^{-\rho}]^{-r/\rho}$, where $r > 0$ is a new parameter, we can introduce increasing returns to scale and decreasing returns to scale.

8. Evaluate the following:

   (a) $\lim\limits_{x \to 4} \dfrac{x^2 - x - 12}{x - 4}$ (c) $\lim\limits_{x \to 0} \dfrac{5^x - e^x}{x}$

   (b) $\lim\limits_{x \to 0} \dfrac{e^x - 1}{x}$ (d) $\lim\limits_{x \to \infty} \dfrac{\ln x}{x}$

9. By use of L'Hôpital's rule, show that

   (a) $\lim\limits_{x \to \infty} \dfrac{x^n}{e^x} = 0$ (b) $\lim\limits_{x \to 0^+} x \ln x = 0$ (c) $\lim\limits_{x \to 0^+} x^x = 1$

Chapter 13

Further Topics in Optimization

This chapter deals with two major topics. The first is nonlinear programming, which extends the techniques of constrained optimization of Chap. 12 by allowing *inequality constraints* into the problem. In Chap. 12, the constraints must be satisfied as strict equalities; i.e., the constraints are always binding. Now we shall consider constraints that may not be binding in the solution; i.e., they may be satisfied as inequalities in the solution.

In the second part of this chapter, we revert back to the realm of classical-constrained optimization to discuss some topics left untouched in the previous chapters. These include the indirect objective function, the envelope theorem, and the concept of duality.

13.1 Nonlinear Programming and Kuhn-Tucker Conditions

In the history of methodological development, the first attempts at dealing with inequality constraints were concentrated on linear ones only. With linearity prevailing in the constraints as well as in the objective function, the resulting methodology is quite naturally christened *linear programming*. Despite the limitation of linearity, however, we could for the first time, explicitly specify the choice variables to be nonnegative, as is appropriate in most economic analysis. This represents a significant advance. Nonlinear programming, a later development, makes it possible even to handle nonlinear inequality constraints and nonlinear objective function. Thus it occupies a most important place in optimization methodology.

In the classical optimization problem, with no explicit restrictions on the signs of the choice variables, and with no inequalities in the constraints, the first-order condition for a relative or local extremum is simply that the first partial derivatives of the (smooth) Lagrangian function with respect to all the choice variables and the Lagrange multipliers be zero. In nonlinear programming, there exists a similar type of first-order condition, known as the *Kuhn-Tucker conditions.*[†] As we shall see, however, while the classical first-order condition is always necessary, the Kuhn-Tucker conditions cannot be accorded the

---

[†] H. W. Kuhn and A. W. Tucker, "Nonlinear Programming," in J. Neyman (ed.), *Proceedings of the Second Berkeley Symposium on Mathematical Statistics and Probability*, University of California Press, Berkeley, California, 1951, pp. 481–492.

status of necessary conditions unless a certain proviso is satisfied. On the other hand, under certain specific circumstances, the Kuhn-Tucker conditions turn out to be *sufficient conditions,* or even *necessary-and-sufficient* conditions as well.

Since the Kuhn-Tucker conditions are the single most important analytical result in nonlinear programming, it is essential to have a proper understanding of those conditions as well as their implications. For the sake of expository convenience, we shall develop these conditions in two steps.

Step 1: Effect of Nonnegativity Restrictions

As the first step, consider a problem with nonnegativity restrictions on the choice variables, but with no other constraints. Taking the single-variable case, in particular, we have

$$\text{Maximize} \quad \pi = f(x_1)$$
$$\text{subject to} \quad x_1 \geq 0 \tag{13.1}$$

where the function f is assumed to be differentiable. In view of the restriction $x_1 \geq 0$, three possible situations may arise. First, if a local maximum of π occurs in the interior of the shaded feasible region in Fig. 13.1, such as point A in Fig. 13.1a, then we have an *interior solution.* The first-order condition in this case is $d\pi/dx_1 = f'(x_1) = 0$, same as in the classical problem. Second, as illustrated by point B in Fig. 13.1b, a local maximum can also occur on the vertical axis, where $x_1 = 0$. Even in this second case, where we have a *boundary solution,* the first-order condition $f'(x_1) = 0$ nevertheless remains valid. However, as a third possibility, a local maximum may in the present context take the position of point C or point D in Fig. 13.1c, because to qualify as a local maximum in problem (13.1), the candidate point merely has to be higher than the neighboring points *within* the feasible region. In view of this last possibility, the maximum point in a problem like (13.1) can be characterized, not only by the equation $f'(x_1) = 0$, but also by the inequality $f'(x_1) < 0$. Note on the other hand, that the opposite inequality $f'(x_1) > 0$ can safely be ruled out, for at a point where the curve is upward-sloping, we can never have a maximum, even if that point is located on the vertical axis, such as point E in Fig. 13.1a.

The upshot of the preceding discussion is that, in order for a value of x_1 to give a local maximum of π in problem (13.1), it must satisfy one of the following three conditions

$$f'(x_1) = 0 \quad \text{and} \quad x_1 > 0 \quad [\text{point } A] \tag{13.2}$$
$$f'(x_1) = 0 \quad \text{and} \quad x_1 = 0 \quad [\text{point } B] \tag{13.3}$$
$$f'(x_1) < 0 \quad \text{and} \quad x_1 = 0 \quad [\text{points } C \text{ and } D] \tag{13.4}$$

FIGURE 13.1

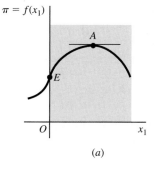

(a)

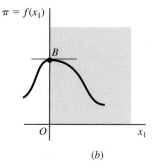

(b)

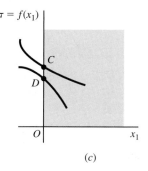

(c)

Actually, these three conditions can be consolidated into a single statement

$$f'(x_1) \leq 0 \qquad x_1 \geq 0 \qquad \text{and} \qquad x_1 f'(x_1) = 0 \qquad \textbf{(13.5)}$$

The first inequality in (13.5) is a summary of the information regarding $f'(x_1)$ enumerated in (13.2) through (13.4). The second inequality is a similar summary for x_1; in fact, it merely reiterates the nonnegativity restriction of the problem. And, as for the third part of (13.5), we have an equation which expresses an important feature common to (13.2) through (13.4), namely, that of the two quantities x_1 and $f'(x_1)$, *at least one* must take a zero value, so that the product of the two must be zero. This feature is referred to as the *complementary slackness* between x_1 and $f'(x_1)$. Taken together, the three parts of (13.5) constitute the first-order necessary condition for a local maximum in a problem where the choice variable must be nonnegative. But going a step further, we can also take them to be necessary for a *global* maximum. This is because a global maximum must also be a local maximum and, as such, must also satisfy the necessary condition for a local maximum.

When the problem contains n choice variables:

$$
\begin{aligned}
\text{Maximize} &\qquad \pi = f(x_1, x_2, \ldots, x_n) \\
\text{subject to} &\qquad x_j \geq 0 \qquad (j = 1, 2, \ldots, n)
\end{aligned}
\qquad \textbf{(13.6)}
$$

The classical first-order condition $f_1 = f_2 = \cdots = f_n = 0$ must be similarly modified. To do this, we can apply the same type of reasoning underlying (13.5) to each choice variable x_j taken by itself. Graphically, this amounts to viewing the horizontal axis in Fig. 13.1 as representing each x_j in turn. The required modification of the first-order condition then readily suggests itself:

$$f_j \leq 0 \qquad x_j \geq 0 \qquad \text{and} \qquad x_j f_j = 0 \qquad (j = 1, 2, \ldots, n) \quad \textbf{(13.7)}$$

where f_j is the partial derivative $\partial \pi / \partial x_j$.

Step 2: Effect of Inequality Constraints

With this background, we now proceed to the second step, and try to include inequality constraints as well. For simplicity, let us first deal with a problem with three choice variables ($n = 3$) and two constraints ($m = 2$):

$$
\begin{aligned}
\text{Maximize} &\qquad \pi = f(x_1, x_2, x_3) \\
\text{subject to} &\qquad g^1(x_1, x_2, x_3) \leq r_1 \\
&\qquad g^2(x_1, x_2, x_3) \leq r_2 \\
\text{and} &\qquad x_1, x_2, x_3 \geq 0
\end{aligned}
\qquad \textbf{(13.8)}
$$

which, with the help of two dummy variables s_1 and s_2, can be transformed into the equivalent form

$$
\begin{aligned}
\text{Maximize} &\qquad \pi = f(x_1, x_2, x_3) \\
\text{subject to} &\qquad g^1(x_1, x_2, x_3) + s_1 = r_1 \\
&\qquad g^2(x_1, x_2, x_3) + s_2 = r_2 \\
\text{and} &\qquad x_1, x_2, x_3, s_1, s_2 \geq 0
\end{aligned}
\qquad \textbf{(13.8')}
$$

If the nonnegativity restrictions are absent, we may, in line with the classical approach, form the Lagrangian function:

$$Z' = f(x_1, x_2, x_3) + \lambda_1[r_1 - g^1(x_1, x_2, x_3) - s_1]$$
$$+ \lambda_2[r_2 - g^2(x_1, x_2, x_3) - s_2] \tag{13.9}$$

and write the first-order condition as

$$\frac{\partial Z'}{\partial x_1} = \frac{\partial Z'}{\partial x_2} = \frac{\partial Z'}{\partial x_3} = \frac{\partial Z'}{\partial s_1} = \frac{\partial Z'}{\partial s_2} = \frac{\partial Z'}{\partial \lambda_1} = \frac{\partial Z'}{\partial \lambda_2} = 0$$

But since the x_j and s_i variables do have to be nonnegative, the first-order condition on those variables should be modified in accordance with (13.7). Consequently, we obtain the following set of conditions instead:

$$\frac{\partial Z'}{\partial x_j} \leq 0 \qquad x_j \geq 0 \qquad \text{and} \qquad x_j \frac{\partial Z'}{\partial x_j} = 0$$

$$\frac{\partial Z'}{\partial s_i} \leq 0 \qquad s_i \geq 0 \qquad \text{and} \qquad s_i \frac{\partial Z'}{\partial s_i} = 0 \tag{13.10}$$

$$\frac{\partial Z'}{\partial \lambda_i} = 0 \qquad\qquad \begin{pmatrix} i = 1, 2 \\ j = 1, 2, 3 \end{pmatrix}$$

Note that the derivatives $\partial Z'/\partial \lambda_i$ are still to be set strictly equal to zero. (Why?)

Each line of (13.10) relates to a different type of variable. But we can consolidate the last two lines and, in the process, eliminate the dummy variable s_i from the first-order condition. Inasmuch as $\partial Z'/\partial s_i = -\lambda_i$, the second line of (13.10) tells us that we must have $-\lambda_i \leq 0$, $s_i \geq 0$, and $-s_i\lambda_i = 0$, or equivalently,

$$s_i \geq 0 \qquad \lambda_i \geq 0 \qquad \text{and} \qquad s_i\lambda_i = 0 \tag{13.11}$$

But the third line—a restatement of the constraints in (13.8′)—means that $s_i = r_i - g^i(x_1, x_2, x_3)$. By substituting the latter into (13.11), therefore, we can combine the second and third lines of (13.10) into

$$r_i - g^i(x_1, x_2, x_3) \geq 0 \qquad \lambda_i \geq 0 \qquad \text{and} \qquad \lambda_i[r_i - g^i(x_1, x_2, x_3)] = 0$$

This enables us to express the first-order condition (13.10) in an equivalent form *without* the dummy variables. Using the symbol g_j^i to denote $\partial g^i/\partial x_j$, we now write

$$\frac{\partial Z'}{\partial x_j} = f_j - (\lambda_1 g_j^1 + \lambda_2 g_j^2) \leq 0 \qquad x_j \geq 0 \qquad \text{and} \qquad x_j \frac{\partial Z'}{\partial x_j} = 0$$

$$r_i - g^i(x_1, x_2, x_3) \geq 0 \qquad\qquad \lambda_i \geq 0 \qquad \text{and} \qquad \lambda_i[r_i - g^i(x_1, x_2, x_3)] = 0 \tag{13.12}$$

These, then, are the Kuhn-Tucker conditions for problem (13.8), or, more accurately, one version of the Kuhn-Tucker conditions, expressed in terms of the Lagrangian function Z' in (13.9).

Now that we know the results, though, it is possible to obtain the same set of conditions more directly by using a different Lagrangian function. Given the problem (13.9), let us ignore the nonnegativity restrictions as well as the inequality signs in the constraints and write the purely classical type of Lagrangian function Z:

$$Z = f(x_1, x_2, x_3) + \lambda_1[r_1 - g^1(x_1, x_2, x_3)] + \lambda_2[r_2 - g^2(x_1, x_2, x_3)] \tag{13.13}$$

Then let us do the following: (1) set the partial derivatives $\partial Z/\partial x_j \leq 0$, but $\partial Z/\partial \lambda_i \geq 0$, (2) impose nonnegativity restrictions on x_j and λ_i, and (3) require complementary slackness to prevail between each variable and the partial derivative of Z with respect to that variable, that is, require their product to vanish. Since the results of these steps, namely,

$$\frac{\partial Z}{\partial x_j} = f_j - (\lambda_1 g_j^1 + \lambda_2 g_j^2) \leq 0 \qquad x_j \geq 0 \qquad \text{and} \qquad x_j \frac{\partial Z}{\partial x_j} = 0$$

$$\frac{\partial Z}{\partial \lambda_i} = r_i - g^i(x_1, x_2, x_3) \geq 0 \qquad \lambda_i \geq 0 \qquad \text{and} \qquad \lambda_i \frac{\partial Z}{\partial \lambda_i} = 0$$

$$(13.14)$$

are identical with (13.12), the Kuhn-Tucker conditions are expressible also in terms of the Lagrangian function Z (as against Z'). Note that, by switching from Z' to Z, we can not only arrive at the Kuhn-Tucker conditions more directly, but also identify the expression $r_i - g^i(x_1, x_2, x_3)$—which was left nameless in (13.12)—as the partial derivative $\partial Z/\partial \lambda_i$. In the subsequent discussion, therefore, we shall only use the (13.14) version of the Kuhn-Tucker conditions, based on the Lagrangian function Z.

Example 1

If we cast the familiar problem of utility maximization into the nonlinear programming mold, we may have a problem with an inequality constraint as follows:

$$\begin{aligned} \text{Maximize} \quad & U = U(x, y) \\ \text{subject to} \quad & P_x x + P_y y \leq B \\ \text{and} \quad & x, y \geq 0 \end{aligned}$$

Note that, with the inequality constraint, the consumer is no longer required to spend the entire amount B.

To add a new twist to the problem, however, let us suppose that a ration has been imposed on commodity x equal to X_0. Then the consumer would face a second constraint, and the problem changes to

$$\begin{aligned} \text{Maximize} \quad & U = U(x, y) \\ \text{subject to} \quad & P_x x + P_y y \leq B \\ & x \leq X_0 \\ \text{and} \quad & x, y \geq 0 \end{aligned}$$

The Lagrangian function is

$$Z = U(x, y) + \lambda_1(B - P_x x - P_y y) + \lambda_2(X_0 - x)$$

and the Kuhn-Tucker conditions are

$$\begin{aligned} Z_x = U_x - P_x \lambda_1 - \lambda_2 \leq 0 \qquad & x \geq 0 \qquad \text{and} \qquad x Z_x = 0 \\ Z_y = U_y - P_y \lambda_1 \leq 0 \qquad & y \geq 0 \qquad \text{and} \qquad y Z_y = 0 \\ Z_{\lambda_1} = B - P_x y - P_y y \geq 0 \qquad & \lambda_1 \geq 0 \qquad \text{and} \qquad \lambda_1 Z_{\lambda_1} = 0 \\ Z_{\lambda_2} = X_0 - x \geq 0 \qquad & \lambda_2 \geq 0 \qquad \text{and} \qquad \lambda_2 Z_{\lambda_2} = 0 \end{aligned}$$

It is useful to examine the implications of the third column of the Kuhn-Tucker conditions. The condition $\lambda_1 Z_{\lambda_1} = 0$, in particular, requires that

$$\lambda_1(B - P_x x - P_y y) = 0$$

Therefore, we must have either

$$\lambda_1 = 0 \quad \text{or} \quad B - P_x x - P_y y = 0$$

If we interpret λ_1 as the marginal utility of budget money (income), and if the budget constraint is nonbinding (satisfied as an inequality in the solution, with money left over), the marginal utility of B should be zero ($\lambda_1 = 0$).

Similarly, the condition $\lambda_2 Z_{\lambda_2} = 0$ requires that either

$$\lambda_2 = 0 \quad \text{or} \quad X_0 - x = 0$$

Since λ_2 can be interpreted as the marginal utility of relaxing the constraint, we see that if the ration constraint is nonbinding, the marginal utility of relaxing the constraint should be zero ($\lambda_2 = 0$).

This feature, referred to as complementary slackness, plays an essential role in the search for a solution. We shall now illustrate this with a numerical example:

$$
\begin{aligned}
\text{Maximize} \quad & U = xy \\
\text{subject to} \quad & x + y \le 100 \\
& x \le 40 \\
\text{and} \quad & x, y \ge 0
\end{aligned}
$$

The Lagrangian is

$$Z = xy + \lambda_1(100 - x - y) + \lambda_2(40 - x)$$

and the Kuhn-Tucker conditions become

$$
\begin{array}{llll}
Z_x = y - \lambda_1 - \lambda_2 \le 0 & x \ge 0 & \text{and} & x Z_x = 0 \\
Z_y = x - \lambda_1 \le 0 & y \ge 0 & \text{and} & y Z_y = 0 \\
Z_{\lambda_1} = 100 - x - y \ge 0 & \lambda_1 \ge 0 & \text{and} & \lambda_1 Z_{\lambda_1} = 0 \\
Z_{\lambda_2} = 40 - x \ge 0 & \lambda_2 \ge 0 & \text{and} & \lambda_2 Z_{\lambda_2} = 0
\end{array}
$$

To solve a nonlinear programming problem, the typical approach is one of trial and error. We can, for example, start by trying a zero value for a choice variable. Setting a variable equal to zero always simplifies the marginal conditions by causing certain terms to drop out. If appropriate nonnegative values of Lagrange multipliers can then be found that satisfy all the marginal inequalities, the zero solution will be optimal. If, on the other hand, the zero solution violates some of the inequalities, then we must let one or more choice variables be positive. For every positive choice variable, we may, by complementary slackness, convert a weak inequality marginal condition into a strict equality. Properly solved, such an equality will lead us either to a solution, or to a contradiction that would then compel us to try something else. If a solution exists, such trials will eventually enable us to uncover it. We can also start by assuming one of the constraints to be nonbinding. Then the related Lagrange multiplier will be zero by complementary slackness and we have thus eliminated a variable. If this assumption leads to a contradiction, then we must treat the said constraint as a strict equality and proceed on that basis.

For the present example, it makes no sense to try $x = 0$ or $y = 0$, for then we would have $U = xy = 0$. We therefore assume both x and y to be nonzero, and deduce $Z_x = Z_y = 0$ from complementary slackness. This means

$$y - \lambda_1 - \lambda_2 = x - \lambda_1 (= 0)$$

so that

$$y - \lambda_2 = x.$$

Now, assume the ration constraint to be nonbinding in the solution, which implies that $\lambda_2 = 0$. Then we have $x = y$, and the given budget $B = 100$ yields the trial solution $x = y = 50$. But this solution violates the ration constraint $x \leq 40$. Hence we must adopt the alternative assumption that the ration constraint is binding with $x^* = 40$. The budget constraint then allows the consumer to have $y^* = 60$. Moreover, since complementary slackness dictates that $Z_x = Z_y = 0$, we can readily calculate that $\lambda_1^* = 40$, and $\lambda_2^* = 20$.

Interpretation of the Kuhn-Tucker Conditions

Parts of the Kuhn-Tucker conditions (13.14) are merely a restatement of certain aspects of the given problem. Thus the conditions $x_j \geq 0$ merely repeat the nonnegativity restrictions, and the conditions $\partial Z/\partial \lambda_i \geq 0$ merely reiterate the constraints. To include these in (13.14), however, has the important advantage of revealing more clearly the remarkable symmetry between the two types of variables, x_j (choice variable) and λ_i (Lagrange multipliers). To each variable in each category, there corresponds a marginal condition—$\partial Z/\partial x_j \leq 0$ or $\partial Z/\partial \lambda_i \geq 0$—to be satisfied by the optimal solution. Each of the variables must be non-negative as well. And, finally, each variable is characterized by complementary slackness in relation to a particular partial derivative of the Lagrangian function Z. This means that, for each x_j, we must find in the optimal solution that *either* the marginal condition holds as an equality, as in the classical context, *or* the choice variable in question must take a zero value, *or* both. Analogously, for each λ_i, we must find in the optimal solution that *either* the marginal condition holds as an equality—meaning that the *i*th constraint is exactly satisfied—*or* the Lagrange multiplier vanishes, *or* both.

An even more explicit interpretation is possible when we look at the expanded expressions for $\partial Z/\partial x_j$ and $\partial Z/\partial \lambda_i$ in (13.14). Assume the problem to be the familiar production problem. Then we have

$f_j \equiv$ marginal gross profit of *j*th product

$\lambda_i \equiv$ shadow price of *i*th resource (the opportunity cost of using a unit of the *i*th resource)

$g_j^i \equiv$ amount of *i*th resource used up in producing the marginal unit of *j*th product

$\lambda_i g_j^i \equiv$ marginal imputed cost of *i*th resource incurred in producing a unit of *j*th product

$\sum_i \lambda_i g_j^i \equiv$ aggregate marginal imputed cost of *j*th product

Thus the marginal condition

$$\frac{\partial Z}{\partial x_j} = f_j - \sum_i \lambda_i g_j^i \leq 0$$

requires that the marginal gross profit of the *j*th product be no greater than its aggregate marginal imputed cost; i.e., no *under*imputation is permitted. The complementary-slackness condition then means that, if the optimal solution calls for the active production of the *j*th product ($x_j^* > 0$), the marginal gross profit must be exactly equal to the aggregate marginal imputed cost ($\partial Z/\partial x_j^* = 0$), as would be the situation in the classical optimization problem. If, on the other hand, the marginal gross profit optimally falls short of the aggregate imputed cost ($\partial Z/\partial x_j^* < 0$), entailing *excess* imputation, then that product must not be produced ($x_j^* = 0$).[†] This latter situation is something that can never occur in the classical context, for if the marginal gross profit is less than the marginal imputed cost, then the output should in that framework be reduced all the way to the level where the marginal condition is satisfied as an equality. What causes the situation of $\partial Z / \partial x_j^* < 0$ to qualify as an optimal one here, is the explicit specification of nonnegativity in the present framework. For then the most we can do in the way of output reduction is to lower production to the level $x_j^* = 0$, and if we still find $\partial Z / \partial x_j^* < 0$ at the zero output, we stop there anyway.

As for the remaining conditions, which relate to the variables λ_i, their meanings are even easier to perceive. First of all, the marginal condition $\partial Z / \partial \lambda_i \geq 0$ merely requires the firm to stay within the capacity limitation of every resource in the plant. The complementary-slackness condition then stipulates that, if the ith resource is not fully used in the optimal solution ($\partial Z / \partial \lambda_i^* > 0$), the shadow price of that resource—which is never allowed to be negative—must be set equal to zero ($\lambda_i^* = 0$). On the other hand, if a resource has a positive shadow price in the optimal solution ($\lambda_i^* > 0$), then it is perforce a fully utilized resource ($\partial Z / \partial \lambda_i^* = 0$).

It is also possible, of course, to take the Lagrange-multiplier value λ_i^* to be a measure of how the optimal value of the objective function reacts to a slight relaxation of the ith constraint. In that light, complementary slackness would mean that, if the ith constraint is optimally not binding ($\partial Z / \partial \lambda_i^* > 0$), then relaxing that particular constraint will not affect the optimal value of the gross profit ($\lambda_i^* = 0$)—just as loosening a belt which is not constricting one's waist to begin with will not produce any greater comfort. If, on the other hand, a slight relaxation of the ith constraint (increasing the endowment of the ith resource) does increase the gross profit ($\lambda_i^* > 0$), then that resource constraint must in fact be binding in the optimal solution ($\partial Z / \partial \lambda_i^* = 0$).

The n-Variable, m-Constraint Case

The preceding discussion can be generalized in a straightforward manner to when there are n choice variables and m constraints. The Lagrangian function Z will appear in the more general form

$$Z = f(x_1, x_2, \ldots, x_n) + \sum_{i=1}^{m} \lambda_i [r_i - g^i(x_1, x_2, \ldots, x_n)] \quad \textbf{(13.15)}$$

And the Kuhn-Tucker conditions will simply be

$$\frac{\partial Z}{\partial x_j} \leq 0 \qquad x_j \geq 0 \qquad \text{and} \qquad x_j \frac{\partial Z}{\partial x_j} = 0 \qquad \text{[maximization]}$$

$$\frac{\partial Z}{\partial \lambda_i} \geq 0 \qquad \lambda_i \geq 0 \qquad \text{and} \qquad \lambda_i \frac{\partial Z}{\partial \lambda_i} = 0 \qquad \left(\begin{array}{l} i = 1, 2, \ldots, m \\ j = 1, 2, \ldots, n \end{array} \right)$$

$$\textbf{(13.16)}$$

Here, in order to avoid a cluttered appearance, we have not written out the expanded expressions for the partial derivatives $\partial Z / \partial x_j$ and $\partial Z / \partial \lambda_i$. But you are urged to write them out for a more detailed view of the Kuhn-Tucker conditions, similar to what was given in (13.14). Note that, aside from the change in the dimension of the problem, the Kuhn-Tucker conditions remain entirely the same. The interpretation of these conditions should naturally also remain the same.

[†] Remember that, given the equation $ab = 0$, where a and b are real numbers, we can legitimately infer that $a \neq 0$ implies $b = 0$, but it is not true that $a = 0$ implies $b \neq 0$, since $b = 0$ is also consistent with $a = 0$.

What if the problem is one of *minimization?* One way of handling it is to convert the problem into a maximization problem and then apply (13.6). To minimize C is equivalent to *maximizing* $-C$, so such a conversion is always feasible. But we must, of course, also reverse the constraint inequalities by multiplying every constraint through by -1. Instead of going through the conversion process, however, we may—again using the Lagrangian function Z as defined in (13.15)—directly apply the minimization version of the Kuhn-Tucker conditions as follows:

$$\frac{\partial Z}{\partial x_j} \geq 0 \qquad x_j \geq 0 \qquad \text{and} \qquad x_j \frac{\partial Z}{\partial x_j} = 0 \qquad \text{[minimization]}$$

$$\frac{\partial Z}{\partial \lambda_i} \leq 0 \qquad \lambda_i \geq 0 \qquad \text{and} \qquad \lambda_i \frac{\partial Z}{\partial \lambda_i} = 0 \qquad \begin{pmatrix} i = 1, 2, \dots, m \\ j = 1, 2, \dots, n \end{pmatrix}$$

(13.17)

This you should compare with (13.16).

Reading (13.16) and (13.17) horizontally (*row*wise), we see that the Kuhn-Tucker conditions for both maximization and minimization problems consist of a set of conditions relating to the choice variables x_j (first row) and another set relating to the Lagrange multipliers λ_i (second row). Reading them vertically (*column*wise) on the other hand, we note that, for each x_j and λ_i, there is a marginal condition (first column), a nonnegativity restriction (second column), and a complementary-slackness condition (third column). In any given problem, the marginal conditions pertaining to the choice variables always differ, as a group, from the marginal conditions for the Lagrange multipliers in the sense of inequality they take.

Subject to the proviso to be explained in Sec. 13.2, the Kuhn-Tucker maximum conditions (13.16) and minimum conditions (13.17) are necessary conditions for a local maximum and local minimum, respectively. But since a global maximum (minimum) must also be a local maximum (minimum), the Kuhn-Tucker conditions can also be taken as necessary conditions for a global maximum (minimum), subject to the same proviso.

Example 2

Let us apply the Kuhn-Tucker conditions to solve a minimization problem:

$$\begin{aligned} \text{Minimize} \qquad & C = (x_1 - 4)^2 + (x_2 - 4)^2 \\ \text{subject to} \qquad & 2x_1 + 3x_2 \geq 6 \\ & -3x_1 - 2x_2 \geq -12 \\ \text{and} \qquad & x_1, x_2 \geq 0 \end{aligned}$$

The Lagrangian function for this problem is

$$Z = (x_1 - 4)^2 + (x_2 - 4)^2 + \lambda_1(6 - 2x_1 - 3x_2) + \lambda_2(-12 + 3x_1 + 2x_2)$$

Since the problem is one of minimization, the appropriate conditions are (13.17), which include the four marginal conditions

$$\frac{\partial Z}{\partial x_1} = 2(x_1 - 4) - 2\lambda_1 + 3\lambda_2 \geq 0$$

$$\frac{\partial Z}{\partial x_2} = 2(x_2 - 4) - 3\lambda_1 + 2\lambda_2 \geq 0$$

(13.18)

$$\frac{\partial Z}{\partial \lambda_1} = 6 - 2x_1 - 3x_2 \leq 0$$

$$\frac{\partial Z}{\partial \lambda_2} = -12 + 3x_1 + 2x_2 \leq 0$$

plus the nonnegativity and complementary-slackness conditions.

To find a solution, we again use the trial-and-error approach, realizing that the first few trials may lead us into a blind alley. Suppose we first try $\lambda_1 > 0$ and $\lambda_2 > 0$ and check whether we can find corresponding x_1 and x_2 values that satisfy both constraints. With positive Lagrange multipliers, we must have $\partial Z/\partial\lambda_1 = \partial Z/\partial\lambda_2 = 0$. From the last two lines of (13.18), we can thus write

$$2x_1 + 3x_2 = 6 \qquad \text{and} \qquad 3x_1 + 2x_2 = 12$$

These two equations yield the trial solution $x_1 = 4\frac{4}{5}$ and $x_2 = -1\frac{1}{5}$, which violates the nonnegativity restriction on x_2.

Let us next try $x_1 > 0$ and $x_2 > 0$, which would imply $\partial Z/\partial x_1 = \partial Z/\partial x_2 = 0$ by complementary slackness. Then, from the first two lines of (13.18), we can write

$$2(x_1 - 4) - 2\lambda_1 + 3\lambda_2 = 0 \qquad \text{and} \qquad 2(x_2 - 4) - 3\lambda_1 + 2\lambda_2 = 0 \quad \textbf{(13.19)}$$

Multiplying the first equation by 2, and the second equation by 3, then subtracting the latter from the former, we can eliminate λ_2 and obtain the result

$$4x_1 - 6x_2 + 5\lambda_1 + 8 = 0$$

By further assuming $\lambda_1 = 0$, we can derive the following relationship between x_1 and x_2:

$$x_1 - \frac{3}{2}x_2 = -2 \qquad\qquad \textbf{(13.20)}$$

In order to solve for the two variables, however, we need another relationship between x_1 and x_2. For this purpose, let us assume that $\lambda_2 \neq 0$, so that $\partial Z/\partial\lambda_2 = 0$. Then, from the last two lines of (13.18), we can write (after rearrangement)

$$3x_1 + 2x_2 = 12 \qquad\qquad \textbf{(13.21)}$$

Together, (13.20) and (13.21) yield another trial solution

$$x_1 = \frac{28}{13}\left(= 2\frac{2}{13}\right) > 0 \qquad x_2 = \frac{36}{13}\left(= 2\frac{10}{13}\right) > 0$$

Substituting these values into (13.19), and solving for the Lagrange multipliers, we get

$$\lambda_1 = 0 \qquad \lambda_2 = \frac{16}{13}\left(= 1\frac{3}{13}\right) > 0$$

Since the solution values for the four variables are all nonnegative and satisfy both constraints, they are acceptable as the final solution.

EXERCISE 13.1

1. Draw a set of diagrams similar to those in Fig. 13.1 for the minimization case, and deduce a set of necessary conditions for a local minimum corresponding to (13.2) through (13.4). Then condense these conditions into a single statement similar to (13.5).

2. (*a*) Show that, in (13.16), instead of writing

$$\lambda_i \frac{\partial Z}{\partial\lambda_i} = 0 \qquad (i = 1, \dots, m)$$

as a set of m separate conditions, it is sufficient to write a single equation in the form of

$$\sum_{i=1}^{m} \lambda_i \frac{\partial Z}{\partial\lambda_i} = 0$$

(b) Can we do the same for the following set of conditions?

$$x_j \frac{\partial Z}{\partial x_j} = 0 \qquad (j = 1, \ldots, n)$$

3. Based on the reasoning used in Prob. 2, which set (or sets) of conditions in (13.17) can be condensed into a single equation?

4. Suppose the problem is

Minimize $C = f(x_1, x_2, \ldots, x_n)$

subject to $g^i(x_1, x_2, \ldots, x_n) \geq r_i$

and $x_j \geq 0 \qquad \begin{pmatrix} i = 1, 2, \ldots, m \\ j = 1, 2, \ldots, n \end{pmatrix}.$

Write the Lagrangian function, take the derivatives $\partial Z / \partial x_j$ and $\partial Z / \partial \lambda_i$ and write out the expanded version of the Kuhn-Tucker minimum conditions (13.17).

5. Convert the minimization problem in Prob. 4 into a maximization problem, formulate the Lagrangian function, take the derivatives with respect to x_j and λ_i, and apply the Kuhn-Tucker maximum conditions (13.16). Are the results consistent with those obtained in Prob. 4?

13.2   The Constraint Qualification

The Kuhn-Tucker conditions are necessary conditions *only if* a particular proviso is satisfied. That proviso, called the *constraint qualification,* imposes a certain restriction on the constraint functions of a nonlinear programming problem, for the specific purpose of ruling out certain irregularities on the boundary of the feasible set, that would invalidate the Kuhn-Tucker conditions should the optimal solution occur there.

Irregularities at Boundary Points

Let us first illustrate the nature of such irregularities by means of some concrete examples.

Example 1

Maximize $\pi = x_1$

subject to $x_2 - (1 - x_1)^3 \leq 0$

and $x_1, x_2 \geq 0$

As shown in Fig. 13.2, the feasible region is the set of points that lie in the first quadrant on or below the curve $x_2 = (1 - x_1)^3$. Since the objective function directs us to maximize x_1, the optimal solution is the point $(1, 0)$. But the solution fails to satisfy the Kuhn-Tucker maximum conditions. To check this, we first write the Lagrangian function

$$Z = x_1 + \lambda_1[-x_2 + (1 - x_1)^3]$$

As the first marginal condition, we should then have

$$\frac{\partial Z}{\partial x_1} = 1 - 3\lambda_1(1 - x_1)^2 \leq 0$$

In fact, since $x_1^* = 1$ is positive, complementary slackness requires that this derivative vanish when evaluated at the point $(1, 0)$. However, the actual value we get happens to be $\partial Z / \partial x_1^* = 1$, thus violating the given marginal condition.

FIGURE 13.2

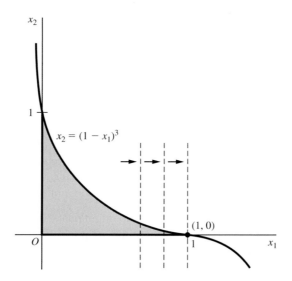

$x_2 = (1 - x_1)^3$

$(1, 0)$

The reason for this anomaly is that the optimal solution (1, 0) occurs in this example at an outward-pointing *cusp,* which constitutes one type of irregularity that can invalidate the Kuhn-Tucker conditions at a boundary optimal solution. A *cusp* is a sharp point formed when a curve takes a sudden reversal in direction, such that the slope of the curve on one side of the point is the same as the slope of the curve on the other side of the point. Here, the boundary of the feasible region at first follows the constraint curve, but when the point (1, 0) is reached, it takes an abrupt turn westward and follows the trail of the horizontal axis thereafter. Since the slopes of both the curved side and the horizontal side of the boundary are zero at the point (1, 0), that point is a cusp.

Cusps are the most frequently cited culprits for the failure of the Kuhn-Tucker conditions, but the truth is that the presence of a cusp is neither necessary nor sufficient to cause those conditions to fail at an optimal solution. Examples 2 and 3 will confirm this.

Example 2

To the problem of Example 1, let us add a new constraint

$$2x_1 + x_2 \leq 2$$

whose border, $x_2 = 2 - 2x_1$, plots as a straight line with slope -2 which passes through the optimal point in Fig. 13.2. Clearly, the feasible region remains the same as before, and so does the optimal solution at the cusp. But if we write the new Lagrangian function

$$Z = x_1 + \lambda_1[-x_2 + (1 - x_1)^3] + \lambda_2[2 - 2x_1 - x_2]$$

and the marginal conditions

$$\frac{\partial Z}{\partial x_1} = 1 - 3\lambda_1(1 - x_1)^2 - 2\lambda_2 \leq 0$$

$$\frac{\partial Z}{\partial x_2} = -\lambda_1 - \lambda_2 \leq 0$$

$$\frac{\partial Z}{\partial \lambda_1} = -x_2 + (1 - x_1)^3 \geq 0$$

$$\frac{\partial Z}{\partial \lambda_2} = 2 - 2x_1 - x_2 \geq 0$$

it turns out that the values $x_1^* = 1$, $x_2^* = 0$, $\lambda_1^* = 1$, and $\lambda_2^* = \frac{1}{2}$ do satisfy these four inequalities, as well as the nonnegativity and complementary-slackness conditions. As a matter of fact, λ_1^* can be assigned any nonnegative value (not just 1), and all the conditions can still be satisfied—which goes to show that the optimal value of a Lagrange multiplier is not necessarily unique. More importantly, however, this example shows that the Kuhn-Tucker conditions can remain valid despite the cusp.

Example 3

The feasible region of the problem

$$
\begin{aligned}
\text{Maximize} \quad & \pi = x_2 - x_1^2 \\
\text{subject to} \quad & -\left(10 - x_1^2 - x_2\right)^3 \leq 0 \\
& -x_1 \leq -2 \\
\text{and} \quad & x_1, x_2 \geq 0
\end{aligned}
$$

as shown in Fig. 13.3, contains no cusp anywhere. Yet, at the optimal solution, (2, 6), the Kuhn-Tucker conditions nonetheless fail to hold. For, with the Lagrangian function

$$
Z = x_2 - x_1^2 + \lambda_1\left(10 - x_1^2 - x_2\right)^3 + \lambda_2(-2 + x_1)
$$

the second marginal condition would require that

$$
\frac{\partial Z}{\partial x_2} = 1 - 3\lambda_1\left(10 - x_1^2 - x_2\right)^2 \leq 0
$$

Indeed, since x_2^* is positive, this derivative should vanish when evaluated at the point (2, 6). But actually we get $\partial Z/\partial x_2 = 1$, regardless of the value assigned to λ_1. Thus the Kuhn-Tucker conditions can fail even in the absence of a cusp—nay, even when the feasible region is a convex set as in Fig. 13.3. The fundamental reason why cusps are neither necessary nor sufficient for the failure of the Kuhn-Tucker conditions is that the preceding irregularities referred to before relate, not to the shape of the feasible region per se, but to the forms of the constraint functions themselves.

FIGURE 13.3

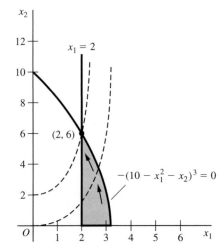

The Constraint Qualification

Boundary irregularities—cusp or no cusp—will not occur if a certain constraint qualification is satisfied.

To explain this, let $x^* \equiv (x_1^*, x_2^*, \ldots, x_n^*)$ be a boundary point of the feasible region and a possible candidate for a solution, and let $dx \equiv (dx_1, dx_2, \ldots, dx_n)$ represent a particular direction of movement from the said boundary point. The direction-of-movement interpretation of the vector dx is perfectly in line with our earlier interpretation of a vector as a directed line segment (an arrow), but here, the point of departure is the point x^* instead of the point of origin, and so the vector dx is *not* in the nature of a radius vector. We shall now impose two requirements on the vector dx. First, if the jth choice variable has a zero value at the point x^*, then we shall only permit a nonnegative change on the x_j axis, that is,

$$dx_j \geq 0 \qquad \text{if} \qquad x_j^* = 0 \qquad \textbf{(13.22)}$$

Second, if the ith constraint is exactly satisfied at the point x^*, then we shall only allow values of $dx_1, \ldots, dx_n$ such that the value of the constraint function $g^i(x^*)$ will not increase (for a maximization problem) or will not decrease (for a minimization problem), that is,

$$dg^i(x^*) = g_1^i \, dx_1 + g_2^i \, dx_2 + \cdots + g_n^i \, dx_n \quad \begin{cases} \leq 0 \, (\text{max.}) \\ \geq 0 \, (\text{min.}) \end{cases} \quad \text{if} \quad g^i(x^*) = r_i$$

$$\textbf{(13.23)}$$

where all the partial derivatives of g_j^i are to be evaluated at x^*. If a vector dx satisfies (13.22) and (13.23), we shall refer to it as a *test vector*. Finally, if there exists a differentiable arc that (1) emanates from the point x^*, (2) is contained entirely in the feasible region, and (3) is tangent to a given test vector, we shall call it a *qualifying arc* for that test vector. With this background, the constraint qualification can be stated simply as follows:

The constraint qualification is satisfied if, for any point x^* on the boundary of the feasible region, there exists a qualifying arc for every test vector dx.

Example 4

We shall show that the optimal point (1, 0) of Example 1 in Fig. 13.2, which fails the Kuhn-Tucker conditions, also fails the constraint qualification. At that point, $x_2^* = 0$; thus the test vector must satisfy

$$dx_2 \geq 0 \qquad [\text{by (13.22)}]$$

Moreover, since the (only) constraint, $g^1 = x_2 - (1 - x_1)^3 \leq 0$, is exactly satisfied at (1, 0), we must let [by (13.23)]

$$g_1^1 \, dx_1 + g_2^1 \, dx_2 = 3(1 - x_1^*)^2 \, dx_1 + dx_2 = dx_2 \leq 0$$

These two requirements together imply that we must let $dx_2 = 0$. In contrast, we are free to choose dx_1. Thus, for instance, the vector $(dx_1, dx_2) = (2, 0)$ is an acceptable test vector, as is $(dx_1, dx_2) = (-1, 0)$. The latter test vector would plot in Fig. 13.2 as an arrow starting from (1, 0) and pointing in the due-west direction (not drawn), and it is clearly possible to draw a qualifying arc for it. (The curved boundary of the feasible region itself can serve as a qualifying arc.) On the other hand, the test vector $(dx_1, dx_2) = (2, 0)$ would plot as an arrow starting from (1, 0) and pointing in the due-east direction (not drawn). Since there is no way to draw a smooth arc tangent to this vector and lying entirely within the feasible region, no qualifying arcs exist for it. Hence the optimal solution point (1, 0) violates the constraint qualification.

Example 5

Referring to Example 2, let us illustrate that, after an additional constraint $2x_1 + x_2 \leq 2$ is added to Fig. 13.2, the point $(1, 0)$ will satisfy the constraint qualification, thereby revalidating the Kuhn-Tucker conditions.

As in Example 4, we have to require $dx_2 \geq 0$ (because $x_2^* = 0$) and $dx_2 \leq 0$ (because the first constraint is exactly satisfied); thus, $dx_2 = 0$. But the second constraint is also exactly satisfied, thereby requiring

$$g_1^2\, dx_1 + g_2^2\, dx_2 = 2dx_1 + dx_2 = 2dx_1 \leq 0 \qquad \text{[by (13.23)]}$$

With nonpositive dx_1 and zero dx_2, the only admissible test vectors—aside from the null vector itself—are those pointing in the due-west direction in Fig. 13.2 from $(1, 0)$. All of these lie along the horizontal axis in the feasible region, and it is certainly possible to draw a qualifying arc for each test vector. Hence, this time the constraint qualification indeed is satisfied.

Linear Constraints

Earlier, in Example 3, it was demonstrated that the convexity of the feasible set does not guarantee the validity of the Kuhn-Tucker conditions as necessary conditions. However, if the feasible region is a convex set formed by *linear* constraints only, then the constraint qualification will invariably be met, and the Kuhn-Tucker conditions will always hold at an optimal solution. This being the case, we need never worry about boundary irregularities when dealing with a nonlinear programming problem with linear constraints.

Example 6

Let us illustrate the linear-constraint result in the two-variable, two-constraint framework. For a maximization problem, the linear constraints can be written as

$$a_{11}x_1 + a_{12}x_2 \leq r_1$$
$$a_{21}x_1 + a_{22}x_2 \leq r_2$$

where we shall take all the parameters to be positive. Then, as indicated in Fig. 13.4, the first constraint border will have a slope of $-a_{11}/a_{12} < 0$, and the second, a slope of $-a_{21}/a_{22} < 0$. The boundary points of the shaded feasible region fall into the following five types: (1) the point of origin, where the two axes intersect, (2) points that lie on one axis segment, such

FIGURE 13.4

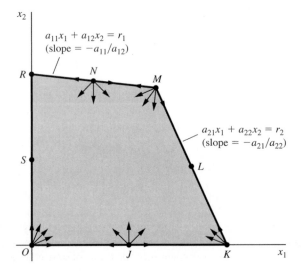

as J and S, (3) points at the intersection of one axis and one constraint border, namely, K and R, (4) points lying on a single constraint border, such as L and N, (5) the point of intersection of the two constraints, M. We may briefly examine each type in turn with reference to the satisfaction of the constraint qualification.

1. At the origin, no constraint is exactly satisfied, so we may ignore (13.23). But since $x_1 = x_2 = 0$, we must choose test vectors with $dx_1 \geq 0$ and $dx_2 \geq 0$, by (13.22). Hence all test vectors from the origin must point in the due-east, due-north, or northeast directions, as depicted in Fig. 13.4. These vectors all happen to fall within the feasible set, and a qualifying arc clearly can be found for each.

2. At a point like J, we can again ignore (13.23). The fact that $x_2 = 0$ means that we must choose $dx_2 \geq 0$, but our choice of dx_1 is free. Hence all vectors would be acceptable except those pointing southward ($dx_2 < 0$). Again all such vectors fall within the feasible region, and there exists a qualifying arc for each. The analysis of point S is similar.

3. At points K and R, both (13.22) and (13.23) must be considered. Specifically, at K, we have to choose $dx_2 \geq 0$ since $x_2 = 0$, so that we must rule out all southward arrows. The second constraint being exactly satisfied, moreover, the test vectors for point K must satisfy

$$g_1^2 \, dx_1 + g_2^2 \, dx_2 = a_{21} \, dx_1 + a_{22} \, dx_2 \leq 0 \qquad \textbf{(13.24)}$$

Since at K we also have $a_{21} x_1 + a_{22} x_2 = r_2$ (second constraint border), however, we may add this equality to (13.24) and modify the restriction on the test vector to the form

$$a_{21}(x_1 + dx_1) + a_{22}(x_2 + dx_2) \leq r_2 \qquad \textbf{(13.24$'$)}$$

Interpreting $(x_j + dx_j)$ to be the new value of x_j attained at the arrowhead of a test vector, we may construe (13.24$'$) to mean that all test vectors must have their arrowheads located on or below the second constraint border. Consequently, all these vectors must again fall within the feasible region, and a qualifying arc can be found for each. The analysis of point R is analogous.

4. At points such as L and N, neither variable is zero and (13.22) can be ignored. However, for point N, (13.23) dictates that

$$g_1^1 \, dx_1 + g_2^1 \, dx_2 = a_{11} \, dx_1 + a_{12} \, dx_2 \leq 0 \qquad \textbf{(13.25)}$$

Since point N satisfies $a_{11} \, dx_1 + a_{12} \, dx_2 = r_1$ (first constraint border), we may add this equality to (13.25) and write

$$a_{11}(x_1 + dx_1) + a_{12}(x_2 + dx_2) \leq r_1 \qquad \textbf{(13.25$'$)}$$

This would require the test vectors to have arrowheads located on or below the first constraint border in Fig. 13.4. Thus we obtain essentially the same kind of result encountered in the other cases. This analysis of point L is analogous.

5. At point M, we may again disregard (13.22), but this time (13.23) requires all test vectors to satisfy both (13.24) and (13.25). Since we may modify the latter conditions to the forms in (13.24$'$) and (13.25$'$), all test vectors must now have their arrowheads located on or below the first as well as the second constraint borders. The result thus again duplicates those of the previous cases.

In this example, it so happens that, for every type of boundary point considered, the test vectors all lie within the feasible region. While this locational feature makes the qualifying arcs easy to find, it is by no means a prerequisite for their existence. In a problem with a nonlinear constraint border, in particular, the constraint border itself may serve as a qualifying arc for some test vector that lies outside of the feasible region. An example of this can be found in one of the problems below.

EXERCISE 13.2

1. Check whether the solution point $(x_1^*, x_2^*) = (2, 6)$ in Example 3 satisfies the constraint qualification.

2. Maximize $\quad \pi = x_1$

   subject to $\quad x_1^2 + x_2^2 \leq 1$

   and $\quad x_1, x_2 \geq 0$

   Solve graphically and check whether the optimal-solution point satisfies (*a*) the constraint qualification and (*b*) the Kuhn-Tucker conditions.

3. Minimize $\quad C = x_1$

   subject to $\quad x_1^2 - x_2 \geq 0$

   and $\quad x_1, x_2 \geq 0$

   Solve graphically. Does the optimal solution occur at a cusp? Check whether the optimal solution satisfies (*a*) the constraint qualification and (*b*) the Kuhn-Tucker minimum conditions.

4. Minimize $\quad C = x_1$

   subject to $\quad -x_2 - (1 - x_1)^3 \geq 0$

   and $\quad x_1, x_2 \geq 0$

   Show that (*a*) the optimal solution $(x_1^*, x_2^*) = (1, 0)$ does not satisfy the Kuhn-Tucker conditions, but (*b*) by introducing a new multiplier $\lambda_0 \geq 0$, and modifying the Lagrangian function (13.15) to the form

   $$Z_0 = \lambda_0 f(x_1, x_2, \ldots, x_n) + \sum_{i=1}^{m} \lambda_1 [r_i - g^i(x_1, x_2, \ldots, x_n)]$$

   the Kuhn-Tucker conditions can be satisfied at (1, 0). (*Note:* The Kuhn-Tucker conditions on the multipliers extend to only $\lambda_1, \ldots, \lambda_m$, but not to λ_0.)

13.3 Economic Applications

War-Time Rationing

Typically during times of war the civilian population is subject to some form of rationing of basic consumer goods. Usually, the method of rationing is through the use of redeemable coupons used by the government. The government will supply each consumer with an allotment of coupons each month. In turn, the consumer will have to redeem a certain number of coupons at the time of purchase of a rationed good. This effectively means the consumer pays *two* prices at the time of the purchase. He or she pays both the coupon price and the monetary price of the rationed good. This requires the consumer to have both sufficient funds and sufficient coupons in order to buy a unit of the rationed good.

Consider the case of a two-good world where both goods, x and y, are rationed. Let the consumer's utility function be $U = U(x, y)$. The consumer has a fixed money budget of B

and faces exogenous prices P_x and P_y. Further, the consumer has an allotment of coupons, denoted C, which can be used to purchase either x or y at a coupon price of c_x and c_y. Therefore the consumer's maximization problem is

$$\text{Maximize} \quad U = U(x, y)$$
$$\text{subject to} \quad P_x x + P_y y \leq B$$
$$c_x x + c_y y \leq C$$
$$\text{and} \quad x, y \geq 0$$

The Lagrangian for the problem is

$$Z = U(x, y) + \lambda_1(B - P_x x - P_y y) + \lambda_2(C - c_x x + c_y y)$$

where λ_1 and λ_2 are the Lagrange multipliers. Since both constraints are linear, the constraint qualification is satisfied and the Kuhn-Tucker conditions are necessary:

$$
\begin{array}{llll}
Z_x &= U_x - \lambda_1 P_x - \lambda_2 c_x \leq 0 & x \geq 0 & x Z_x = 0 \\
Z_y &= U_y - \lambda_1 P_y - \lambda_2 c_y \leq 0 & y \geq 0 & y Z_y = 0 \\
Z_{\lambda_1} &= B - P_x x - P_y y \geq 0 & \lambda_1 \geq 0 & \lambda_1 Z_{\lambda_1} = 0 \\
Z_{\lambda_2} &= C - c_x x - c_y y \geq 0 & \lambda_2 \geq 0 & \lambda_2 Z_{\lambda_2} = 0
\end{array}
$$

Example 1

Suppose the utility function is of the form $U = xy^2$. Further, let $B = 100$ and $P_x = P_y = 1$ while $C = 120$, $c_x = 2$, and $c_y = 1$.
   The Lagrangian takes the specific form

$$Z = xy^2 + \lambda_1(100 - x - y) + \lambda_2(120 - 2x - y)$$

The Kuhn-Tucker conditions are now

$$
\begin{array}{llll}
Z_x = y^2 - \lambda_1 - 2\lambda_2 \leq 0 & x \geq 0 & x Z_x = 0 \\
Z_y = 2xy - \lambda_1 - \lambda_2 \leq 0 & y \geq 0 & y Z_y = 0 \\
Z_{\lambda_1} = 100 - x - y \geq 0 & \lambda_1 \geq 0 & \lambda_1 Z_{\lambda_1} = 0 \\
Z_{\lambda_2} = 120 - 2x - y \geq 0 & \lambda_2 \geq 0 & \lambda_2 Z_{\lambda_2} = 0
\end{array}
$$

Again, the solution procedure involves a certain amount of trial and error. We can first choose one of the constraints to be nonbinding and solve for x and y. Once found, use these values to test if the constraint chosen to be nonbinding is violated. If it is, then redo the procedure choosing another constraint to be nonbinding. If violation of the nonbinding constraint occurs again, then we can assume both constraints bind and the solution is determined only by the constraints.
   Step 1: Assume that the second (ration) constraint is nonbinding in the solution, so that $\lambda_2 = 0$ by complementary slackness. But let x, y, and λ_1 be positive so that complementary slackness would give us the following three equations:

$$Z_x = y^2 - \lambda_1 = 0$$
$$Z_y = 2xy - \lambda_1 = 0$$
$$Z_{\lambda_1} = 100 - x - y = 0$$

Solving for x and y yields a trial solution

$$x = 33^1/_3 \qquad y = 66^2/_3$$

However, when we substitute these solutions into the coupon constraint we find that

$$2(33^1/_3) + 66^2/_3 = 133^1/_3 > 120$$

This solution violates the coupon constraint, and must be rejected.

Step 2: Now let us reverse the assumptions on λ_1 and λ_2 so that $\lambda_1 = 0$, but let $\lambda_2, x, y > 0$. Then, from the marginal conditions, we have

$$Z_x = y^2 - 2\lambda_2 = 0$$
$$Z_y = 2xy - \lambda_2 = 0$$
$$Z_{\lambda_1} = 120 - 2x - y = 0$$

Solving this system of equations yields another trial solution

$$x = 20 \qquad y = 80$$

which implies that $\lambda_2 = 2xy = 3,200$. These solution values, together with $\lambda_1 = 0$, satisfy both the budget and ration constraints. Thus we can accept them as the final solution to the Kuhn-Tucker conditions.

This optimal solution, however, contains a curious abnormality. With the budget constraint binding in the solution, we would normally expect the related Lagrange multiplier to be positive, yet we actually have $\lambda_1 = 0$. Thus, in this example, while the budget constraint is *mathematically* binding (satisfied as a strict equality in the solution), it is *economically* nonbinding (not calling for a positive marginal utility of money).

Peak-Load Pricing

Peak and off-peak pricing and planning problems are commonplace for firms with capacity-constrained production processes. Usually the firm has invested in capacity in order to target a primary market. However there may exist a secondary market in which the firm can often sell its product. Once the capital equipment has been purchased to service the firm's primary market, it is freely available (up to capacity) to be used in the secondary market. Typical examples include schools and universities that build to meet daytime needs (peak), but may offer night-school classes (off-peak); theaters that offer shows in the evening (peak) and matinees (off-peak); and trucking companies that have dedicated routes but may choose to enter "back-haul" markets. Since the capacity cost is a factor in the profit-maximizing decision for the peak market and is already paid, it normally should not be a factor in calculating optimal price and quantity for the smaller, off-peak market. However, if the secondary market's demand is close to the same size as the primary market, capacity constraints may be an issue, especially since it is a common practice to price discriminate and charge lower prices in off-peak periods. Even though the secondary market is smaller than the primary, it is possible that, at the lower (profit-maximizing) price, off-peak demand exceeds capacity. In such cases capacity choices must be made taking both markets into account, making the problem a classic application of nonlinear programming.

Consider a profit-maximizing company that faces two average-revenue curves

$$P_1 = P^1(Q_1) \qquad \text{in the day time (peak period)}$$
$$P_2 = P^2(Q_2) \qquad \text{in the night time (off-peak period)}$$

To operate, the firm must pay b per unit of output, whether it is day or night. Furthermore, the firm must purchase capacity at a cost of c per unit of capacity. Let K denote total capacity measured in units of Q. The firm must pay for capacity, regardless of whether it operates in the off-peak period. Who should be charged for the capacity costs: peak, off-peak, or both sets of customers? The firm's maximization problem becomes

$$\text{Maximize}_{Q_1, Q_2, K} \quad \pi = P_1 Q_1 + P_2 Q_2 - b(Q_1 + Q_2) - cK$$

$$\text{subject to} \quad Q_1 \leq K$$
$$Q_2 \leq K$$

$$\text{where} \quad P_1 = P^1(Q_1)$$
$$P_2 = P^2(Q_2)$$

$$\text{and} \quad Q_1, Q_2, K \geq 0$$

In view that the total revenue for Q_i,

$$R_i \equiv P_i Q_i = P^i(Q_i)Q_i$$

is a function of Q_i alone, we can simplify the statement of the problem to

$$\text{Maximize} \quad \pi = R_1(Q_1) + R_2(Q_2) - b(Q_1 + Q_2) - cK$$

$$\text{subject to} \quad Q_1 \leq K$$
$$Q_2 \leq K$$

$$\text{and} \quad Q_1, Q_2, K \geq 0$$

Note that both constraints are linear; thus the constraint qualification is satisfied and the Kuhn-Tucker conditions are necessary.

The Lagrangian function is

$$Z = R_1(Q_1) + R_2(Q_2) - b(Q_1 + Q_2) - cK + \lambda_1(K - Q_1) + \lambda_2(K - Q_2)$$

and the Kuhn-Tucker conditions are

$$Z_1 = MR_1 - b - \lambda_1 \leq 0 \qquad Q_1 \geq 0 \qquad Q_1 Z_1 = 0$$
$$Z_2 = MR_2 - b - \lambda_2 \leq 0 \qquad Q_2 \geq 0 \qquad Q_2 Z_2 = 0$$
$$Z_K = -c + \lambda_1 + \lambda_2 \leq 0 \qquad K \geq 0 \qquad K Z_K = 0$$
$$Z_{\lambda_1} = K - Q_1 \geq 0 \qquad \lambda_1 \geq 0 \qquad \lambda_1 Z_{\lambda_1} = 0$$
$$Z_{\lambda_2} = K - Q_2 \geq 0 \qquad \lambda_2 \geq 0 \qquad \lambda_2 Z_{\lambda_2} = 0$$

where MR_i is the marginal revenue of Q_i ($i = 1, 2$).

The solution procedure again entails trial and error. Let us first assume that $Q_1, Q_2, K > 0$. Then, by complementary slackness, we have

$$MR_1 - b - \lambda_1 = 0$$
$$MR_2 - b - \lambda_2 = 0 \qquad \qquad \textbf{(13.26)}$$
$$-c + \lambda_1 + \lambda_2 = 0 \quad (\lambda_1 = c - \lambda_2)$$

which can be condensed into two equations after eliminating λ_1:

$$MR_1 = b + c - \lambda_2$$
$$MR_2 = b + \lambda_2 \qquad \qquad \textbf{(13.26')}$$

Then we proceed in two steps.

FIGURE 13.5

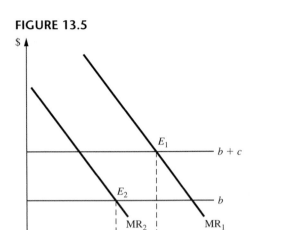

(*a*) Off-peak constraint nonbinding

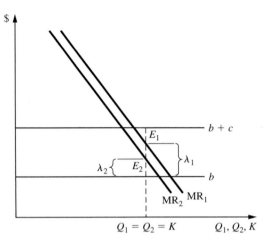

(*b*) Off-peak constraint binding

Step 1: Since the off-peak market is a secondary market, its marginal-revenue function (MR_2) can be expected to lie below that of the primary market (MR_1) as illustrated in Fig. 13.5. Moreover, the capacity constraint is more likely to be nonbinding in the secondary market so that λ_2 is more likely to be zero. So we try $\lambda_2 = 0$. Then (13.26′) becomes

$$MR_1 = b + c$$
$$MR_2 = b$$

(13.26″)

The fact that the primary market absorbs the entire capacity cost c implies that $Q_1 = K$. However, we still need to check whether the constraint $Q_2 \leq K$ is satisfied. If so, we have found a valid solution. Figure 13.5(a) illustrates the case where $Q_1 = K$ and $Q_2 < K$ in the solution. The MR_1 curve intersects the $b + c$ line at point E_1, and the MR_2 curve intersects the b line at point E_2.

What if the previous trial solution entails $Q_2 > K$, as would occur if the MR_2 curve is very close to MR_1, so as to intersect the b line at an output larger than K? Then, of course, the second constraint is violated, and we must reject the assumption of $\lambda_2 = 0$, and proceed to the next step.

Step 2: Now let us assume both Lagrange multipliers to be positive, and thus $Q_1 = Q_2 = K$. Then, unable to eliminate any variables from (13.26), we have

$$MR_1 = b + \lambda_1$$
$$MR_2 = b + \lambda_2$$
$$c = \lambda_1 + \lambda_2$$

(13.26‴)

This case is illustrated in Fig. 13.5(b), where points E_1 and E_2 satisfy the first two equations in (13.26‴). From the third equation, we see that the capacity cost c is the sum of the two Lagrange multipliers. This means λ_1 and λ_2 represent the portions of the capacity cost borne respectively by the two markets.

Example 2   Suppose the average-revenue function during peak hours is

$$P_1 = 22 - 10^{-5} Q_1$$

and that during off-peak hours it is

$$P_2 = 18 - 10^{-5} Q_2$$

To produce a unit of output per half-day requires a unit of capacity costing 8 cents per day. The cost of a unit of capacity is the same whether it is used at peak times only, or off-peak also. In addition to the costs of capacity, it costs 6 cents in operating costs (labor and fuel) to produce 1 unit per half-day (both day and evening).

If we assume that the capacity constraint is nonbinding in the secondary market ($\lambda_2 = 0$), then the given Kuhn-Tucker conditions become

$$\lambda_1 = c = 8$$

$$\underbrace{\begin{aligned} 22 - 2 \times 10^{-5} Q_1 \\ 18 - 2 \times 10^{-5} Q_2 \end{aligned}}_{\text{MR}} \quad \underbrace{\begin{aligned} = b + c \\ = b \end{aligned}}_{\text{MC}} \quad \begin{aligned} = 14 \\ = 6 \end{aligned}$$

Solving this system gives us

$$Q_1 = 400{,}000$$

$$Q_2 = 600{,}000$$

which violates the assumption that the second constraint is nonbinding because $Q_2 > Q_1 = K$.

Therefore, let us assume that both constraints are binding. Then $Q_1 = Q_2 = Q$ and the Kuhn-Tucker conditions become

$$\lambda_1 + \lambda_2 = 8$$

$$22 - 2 \times 10^{-5} Q = 6 + \lambda_1$$

$$18 - 2 \times 10^{-5} Q = 6 + \lambda_2$$

which yield the following solution

$$Q_1 = Q_2 = K = 500{,}000$$

$$\lambda_1 = 6 \qquad \lambda_2 = 2$$

$$P_1 = 17 \qquad P_2 = 13$$

Since the capacity constraint is binding in both markets, the primary market pays $\lambda_1 = 6$ of the capacity cost and the secondary market pays $\lambda_2 = 2$.

EXERCISE 13.3

1. Suppose in Example 2 a unit of capacity costs only 3 cents per day.
   (*a*) What would be the profit-maximizing peak and off-peak prices and quantities?
   (*b*) What would be the values of the Lagrange multipliers? What interpretation do you put on their values?
2. A consumer lives on an island where she produces two goods, x and y, according to the production possibility frontier $x^2 + y^2 \leq 200$, and she consumes all the goods herself. Her utility function is

$$U = xy^3$$

The consumer also faces an environmental constraint on her total output of both goods. The environmental constraint is given by $x + y \leq 20$.

(a) Write out the Kuhn-Tucker first-order conditions.

(b) Find the consumer's optimal x and y. Identify which constraints are binding.

3. An electric company is setting up a power plant in a foreign country, and it has to plan its capacity. The peak-period demand for power is given by $P_1 = 400 - Q_1$ and the off-peak demand is given by $P_2 = 380 - Q_2$. The variable cost is 20 per unit (paid in both markets) and capacity costs 10 per unit which is only paid once and is used in both periods.

(a) Write out the Lagrangian and Kuhn-Tucker conditions for this problem.

(b) Find the optimal outputs and capacity for this problem.

(c) How much of the capacity is paid for by each market (i.e., what are the values of λ_1 and λ_2)?

(d) Now suppose capacity cost is 30 cents per unit (paid only once). Find quantities, capacity, and how much of the capacity is paid for by each market (i.e., λ_1 and λ_2).

13.4 Sufficiency Theorems in Nonlinear Programming

In the previous sections, we have introduced the Kuhn-Tucker conditions and illustrated their applications *as necessary* conditions in optimization problems with inequality constraints. Under certain circumstances, the Kuhn-Tucker conditions can also be taken as sufficient conditions.

The Kuhn-Tucker Sufficiency Theorem: Concave Programming

In classical optimization problems, the sufficient conditions for maximum and minimum are traditionally expressed in terms of the signs of second-order derivatives or differentials. As we have shown in Sec. 11.5, however, these second-order conditions are closely related to the concepts of concavity and convexity of the objective function. Here, in nonlinear programming, the sufficient conditions can also be stated directly in terms of concavity and convexity. And, in fact, these concepts will be applied not only to the objective function $f(x)$ but to the constraint functions $g^i(x)$ as well.

For the *maximization* problem, Kuhn and Tucker offer the following statement of sufficient conditions (sufficiency theorem):

Given the nonlinear programming problem

$$\begin{aligned}
\text{Maximize} \quad & \pi = f(x) \\
\text{subject to} \quad & g^i(x) \leq r_i \qquad (i = 1, 2, \ldots, m) \\
\text{and} \quad & x \geq 0
\end{aligned}$$

if the following conditions are satisfied:

(a) the objective function $f(x)$ is differentiable and *concave* in the nonnegative orthant

(b) each constraint function $g^i(x)$ is differentiable and *convex* in the nonnegative orthant

(c) the point x^* satisfies the Kuhn-Tucker maximum conditions

then x^* gives a global maximum of $\pi = f(x)$.

Note that, in this theorem, the constraint qualification is nowhere mentioned. This is because we have already assumed, in condition (c), that the Kuhn-Tucker conditions are

satisfied at x^* and, consequently, the question of the constraint qualification is no longer an issue.

As it stands, the above theorem indicates that conditions (a), (b), and (c) are sufficient to establish x^* to be an optimal solution. Looking at it differently, however, we may also interpret it to mean that given (a) and (b), then the Kuhn-Tucker maximum conditions are sufficient for a maximum. In the preceding section, we learned that the Kuhn-Tucker conditions, though not necessary *per se,* become necessary when the constraint qualification is satisfied. Combining this information with the sufficiency theorem, we may now state that if the constraint qualification is satisfied and if conditions (a) and (b) are realized, then the Kuhn-Tucker maximum conditions will be *necessary-and-sufficient* for a maximum. This would be the case, for instance, when all the constraints are linear inequalities, which is sufficient for satisfying the constraint qualification.

The maximization problem dealt with in the sufficiency theorem above is often referred to as *concave programming*. This name arises because Kuhn and Tucker adopt the $\geq$ inequality instead of the $\leq$ inequality in every constraint, so that condition (b) would require the $g^i(x)$ functions to be *all concave*, like the $f(x)$ function. But we have modified the formulation in order to convey the idea that in a maximization problem, a constraint is imposed to "rein in" (hence, $\leq$) the attempt to ascend to higher points on the objective function. Though different in form, the two formulations are equivalent in substance. For brevity, we omit the proof.

As stated above, the sufficiency theorem deals only with maximization problems. But adaptation to *minimization* problems is by no means difficult. Aside from the appropriate changes in the theorem to reflect the reversal of the problem itself, all we have to do is to interchange the two words *concave* and *convex* in conditions (a) and (b) and to use the Kuhn-Tucker *minimum* conditions in condition (c). (See Exercise 13.4-1.)

The Arrow-Enthoven Sufficiency Theorem: Quasiconcave Programming

To apply the Kuhn-Tucker sufficiency theorem, certain concavity-convexity specifications must be met. These constitute quite stringent requirements. In another sufficiency theorem— the Arrow-Enthoven sufficiency theorem[†]—these specifications are relaxed to the extent of requiring only *quasiconcavity* and *quasiconvexity* in the objective and constraint functions. With the requirements thus weakened, the scope of applicability of the sufficient conditions is correspondingly widened.

In the original formulation of the Arrow-Enthoven paper, with a maximization problem and with constraints in the $\geq$ form, the $f(x)$ and $g^i(x)$ functions must uniformly be quasiconcave in order for their theorem to be applicable. This gives rise to the name *quasiconcave programming*. In our discussion here, however, we shall again use the $\leq$ inequality in the constraints of a maximization problem and the $\geq$ inequality in the minimization problem.

The theorem is as follows:

Given the nonlinear programming problem

$$\text{Maximize} \quad \pi = f(x)$$
$$\text{subject to} \quad g^i(x) \leq r_i \qquad (i = 1, 2, \ldots, m)$$
$$\text{and} \quad x \geq 0$$

[†] Kenneth J. Arrow and Alain C. Enthoven, "Quasi-concave Programming," *Econometrica,* October, 1961, pp. 779–800.

if the following conditions are satisfied:

(*a*) the objective function $f(x)$ is differentiable and *quasiconcave* in the nonnegative orthant

(*b*) each constraint function $g^i(x)$ is differentiable and *quasiconvex* in the nonnegative orthant

(*c*) the point x^* satisfies the Kuhn-Tucker maximum conditions

(*d*) any *one* of the following is satisfied:

    (*d-i*) $f_j(x^*) < 0$ for at least one variable x_j

    (*d-ii*) $f_j(x^*) > 0$ for some variable x_j that can take on a positive value without violating the constraints

    (*d-iii*) the n derivatives $f_j(x^*)$ are not all zero, and the function $f(x)$ is twice differentiable in the neighborhood of x^* [i.e., all the second-order partial derivatives of $f(x)$ exist at x^*]

    (*d-iv*) the function $f(x)$ is concave

then x^* gives a global maximum of $\pi = f(x)$.

Since the proof of this theorem is quite lengthy, we shall omit it here. However, we do want to call your attention to a few important features of this theorem. For one thing, while Arrow and Enthoven have succeeded in weakening the concavity-convexity specifications to their quasiconcavity-quasiconvexity counterparts, they find it necessary to append a new requirement, (*d*). Note, though, that only *one* of the four alternatives listed under (*d*) is required to form a complete set of sufficient conditions. In effect, therefore, the above theorem contains as many as *four* different sets of sufficient conditions for a maximum. In the case of (*d-iv*), with $f(x)$ concave, it would apear that the Arrow-Enthoven sufficiency theorem becomes identical with the Kuhn-Tucker sufficiency theorem. But this is not true. Inasmuch as Arrow and Enthoven only require the constraint functions $g^i(x)$ to be *quasiconvex,* their sufficient conditions are still weaker.

As stated, the theorem lumps together the conditions (*a*) through (*d*) as a set of sufficient conditions. But it is also possible to interpret it to mean that, when (*a*), (*b*), and (*d*) are satisfied, then the Kuhn-Tucker maximum conditions become sufficient conditions for a maximum. Furthermore, if the constraint qualification is also satisfied, then the Kuhn-Tucker conditions will become necessary-and-sufficient for a maximum.

Like the Kuhn-Tucker theorem, the Arrow-Enthoven theorem can be adapted with ease to the *minimization* framework. Aside from the obvious changes that are needed to reverse the direction of optimization, we simply have to interchange the words *quasiconcave* and *quasiconvex* in conditions (*a*) and (*b*), replace the Kuhn-Tucker maximum conditions by the minimum conditions, reverse the inequalities in (*d-i*) and (*d-ii*), and change the word *concave* to *convex* in (*d-iv*).

A Constraint-Qualification Test

It was mentioned in Sec. 13.2 that if all constraint functions are linear, then the constraint qualification is satisfied. In case the $g^i(x)$ functions are nonlinear, the following test offered by Arrow and Enthoven may prove useful in determining whether the constraint qualification is satisfied:

For a maximization problem, if

(*a*) every constraint function $g^i(x)$ is differentiable and quasiconvex

(*b*) there exists a point x^0 in the nonnegative orthant such that all the constraints are satisfied as strict inequalities at x^0

(*c*) *one* of the following is true:

(*c-i*) every $g^i(x)$ function is convex

(*c-ii*) the partial derivatives of every $g^i(x)$ are not all zero when evaluated at every point x in the feasible region

then the constraint qualification is satisfied.

Again, this test can be adapted to the minimization problem with ease. To do so, just change the word *quasiconvex* to *quasiconcave* in condition (*a*), and change the word *convex* to *concave* in (*c-i*).

EXERCISE 13.4

1. Given: Minimize $C = F(x)$

      subject to $G^i(x) \geq r_i$ $(i = 1, 2, \ldots, m)$

      and $x > 0$

   (*a*) Convert it into a maximization problem.

   (*b*) What in the present problem are the equivalents of the f and g^i functions in the Kuhn-Tucker sufficiency theorem?

   (*c*) Hence, what concavity-convexity conditions should be placed on the F and G^i functions to make the sufficient conditions for a maximum applicable here?

   (*d*) On the basis of the above, how would you state the Kuhn-Tucker sufficient conditions for a *minimum*?

2. Is the Kuhn-Tucker sufficiency theorem applicable to:

   (*a*) Maximize $\pi = x_1$

      subject to $x_1^2 + x_3^2 \leq 1$

      and $x_1, x_2 \geq 0$

   (*b*) Minimize $C = (x_1 - 3)^2 + (x_2 - 4)^2$

      subject to $x_1 + x_2 \geq 4$

      and $x_1, x_2 \geq 0$

   (*c*) Minimize $C = 2x_1 + x_2$

      subject to $x_1^2 - 4x_1 + x_2 \geq 0$

      and $x_1, x_2 \geq 0$

3. Which of the following functions are mathematically acceptable as the objective function of a *maximization* problem which qualifies for the application of the Arrow-Enthoven sufficiency theorem?

   (*a*) $f(x) = x^3 - 2x$

   (*b*) $f(x_1, x_2) = 6x_1 - 9x_2$

   (*c*) $f(x_1, x_2) = x_2 - \ln x_1$ (*Note:* See Exercise 12.4-4.)

4. Is the Arrow-Enthoven constraint qualification satisfied, given that the constraints of a *maximization* problem are:

(a) $x_1^2 + (x_2 - 5)^2 \le 4$ and $5x_1 + x_2 < 10$

(b) $x_1 + x_2 \le 8$ and $-x_1 x_2 \le -8$ (*Note:* $-x_1 x_2$ is not convex.)

13.5 Maximum-Value Functions and the Envelope Theorem[†]

A maximum-value function is an objective function where the choice variables have been assigned their optimal values. These optimal values of the choice variables are, in turn, functions of the exogenous variables and parameters of the problem. Once the optimal values of the choice variables have been substituted into the original objective function, the function indirectly becomes a function of the parameters only (through the parameters' influence on the optimal values of the choice variables). Thus the maximum-value function is also referred to as the *indirect objective function*.

The Envelope Theorem for Unconstrained Optimization

What is the significance of the indirect objective function? Consider that in any optimization problem the direct objective function is maximized (or minimized) for a given set of parameters. The indirect objective function traces out all the maximum values of the objective function as these parameters vary. Hence the indirect objective function is an "envelope" of the set of optimized objective functions generated by varying the parameters of the model. For most students of economics the first illustration of this notion of an envelope arises in the comparison of short-run and long-run cost curves. Students are typically taught that the long-run average cost curve is an envelope of all the short-run average cost curves (what parameter is varying along the envelope in this case?). A formal derivation of this concept is one of the exercises we will be doing in this section.

To illustrate, consider the following unconstrained maximization problem with two choice variables x and y and one parameter ϕ:

$$\text{Maximize} \quad U = f(x, y, \phi) \tag{13.27}$$

The first-order necessary condition is

$$f_x(x, y, \phi) = f_y(x, y, \phi) = 0 \tag{13.28}$$

If second-order conditions are met, these two equations implicitly define the solutions

$$x^* = x^*(\phi) \qquad y^* = y^*(\phi) \tag{13.29}$$

If we substitute these solutions into the objective function, we obtain a new function

$$V(\phi) = f(x^*(\phi), \ y^*(\phi), \phi) \tag{13.30}$$

where this function is the value of f when the values of x and y are those that maximize $f(x, y, \phi)$. Therefore, $V(\phi)$ is *the maximum-value function* (or indirect objective function).

[†] This section of the chapter presents an overview of the envelope theorem. A richer treatment of this topic can be found in Chap. 7 of *The Structure of Economics: A Mathematical Analysis* (3rd ed.) by Eugene Silberberg and Wing Suen (McGraw-Hill, 2001) on which parts of this section are based.

If we differentiate V with respect to ϕ, its only argument, we get

$$\frac{dV}{d\phi} = f_x \frac{\partial x^*}{\partial \phi} + f_y \frac{\partial y^*}{\partial \phi} + f_\phi \tag{13.31}$$

However, from the first-order conditions we know $f_x = f_y = 0$. Therefore, the first two terms disappear and the result becomes

$$\frac{dV}{d\phi} = f_\phi \tag{13.31'}$$

This result says that, at the optimum, as ϕ varies, with x^* and y^* allowed to adjust, the derivative $dV/d\phi$ gives the same result as if x^* and y^* are treated as constants. Note that ϕ enters the maximum-value function (13.30) in three places: one direct and two indirect (through x^* and y^*). Equation (13.31') shows that, at the optimum, only the direct effect of ϕ on the objective function matters. This is the essence of the envelope theorem. The envelope theorem says that only the direct effects of a change in an exogenous variable need be considered, even though the exogenous variable may also enter the maximum-value function indirectly as part of the solution to the endogenous choice variables.

The Profit Function

Let us now apply the notion of the maximum-value function to derive the profit function of a competitive firm. Consider the case where a firm uses two inputs: capital K and labor L. The profit function is

$$\pi = Pf(K, L) - wL - rK \tag{13.32}$$

where P is the output price and w and r are the wage rate and rental rate, respectively.

The first-order conditions are

$$\begin{aligned} \pi_L &= Pf_L(K, L) - w = 0 \\ \pi_K &= Pf_K(K, L) - r = 0 \end{aligned} \tag{13.33}$$

which respectively define the input-demand equations

$$\begin{aligned} L^* &= L^*(w, r, P) \\ K^* &= K^*(w, r, P) \end{aligned} \tag{13.34}$$

Substituting the solutions K^* and L^* into the objective function gives us

$$\pi^*(w, r, P) = Pf(K^*, L^*) - wL^* - rK^* \tag{13.35}$$

where $\pi^*(w, r, P)$ is the *profit function* (an indirect objective function). The profit function gives the maximum profit as a function of the exogenous variables w, r, and P.

Now consider the effect of a change in w on the firm's profits. If we differentiate the original profit function (13.32) with respect to w, holding all other variables constant, we get

$$\frac{\partial \pi}{\partial w} = -L \tag{13.36}$$

However, this result does not take into account the profit-maximizing firm's ability to make a substitution of capital for labor and adjust the level of output in accordance with profit-maximizing behavior.

In contrast, since $\pi^*(w, r, P)$ is the maximum value of profits for any values of w, r, and P, changes in π^* from a change in w takes all capital-for-labor substitutions into account. To evaluate a change in the maximum profit function caused by a change in w, we differentiate $\pi^*(w, r, P)$ with respect to w to obtain

$$\frac{\partial \pi^*}{\partial w} = (Pf_L - w)\frac{\partial L^*}{\partial w} + (Pf_K - r)\frac{\partial K^*}{\partial w} - L^* \qquad \textbf{(13.37)}$$

From the first-order conditions (13.33), the two terms in parentheses are equal to zero. Therefore, the equation becomes

$$\frac{\partial \pi^*}{\partial w} = -L^*(w, r, P) \qquad \textbf{(13.38)}$$

This result says that, at the profit-maximizing position, a change in profits with respect to a change in the wage rate is the same whether or not the factors are held constant or allowed to vary as the factor price changes. In this case, (13.38) shows that the derivative of the profit function with respect to w is the negative of the factor demand function $L^*(w, r, P)$. Following the preceding procedure, we can also show the additional comparative-static results:

$$\frac{\partial \pi^*(w, r, P)}{\partial r} = -K^*(w, r, P) \qquad \textbf{(13.39)}$$

and

$$\frac{\partial \pi^*(w, r, P)}{\partial P} = f(K^*, L^*) \qquad \textbf{(13.40)}$$

Equations (13.38), (13.39), and (13.40) are collectively known as *Hotelling's lemma*. We have obtained these comparative-static derivatives from the profit function by allowing K^* and L^* to adjust to any parameter change. But it is easy to see that the same results will emerge if we differentiate the profit function (13.35) with respect to each parameter while holding K^* and L^* constant. Thus Hotelling's lemma is simply another manifestation of the envelope theorem that we encountered earlier in (13.31').

Reciprocity Condition

Consider again our two-variable unconstrained maximization problem

$$\text{Maximize} \qquad U = f(x, y, \phi) \qquad \text{[from (13.27)]}$$

where x and y are the choice variables and ϕ is a parameter. The first-order conditions are $f_x = f_y = 0$, which imply $x^* = x^*(\phi)$ and $y^* = y^*(\phi)$.

We are interested in the comparative statics regarding the directions of change in $x^*(\phi)$ and $y^*(\phi)$ as ϕ changes and the effects on the value function. The maximum-value function is

$$V(\phi) = f(x^*(\phi), y^*(\phi), \phi) \qquad \textbf{(13.41)}$$

By definition, $V(\phi)$ gives the maximum value of f for any given ϕ.

Now consider a new function that depicts the difference between the actual value and the maximum value of U:

$$\Omega(x, y, \phi) = f(x, y, \phi) - V(\phi) \qquad \textbf{(13.42)}$$

This new function Ω has a maximum value of zero when $x = x^*$ and $y = y^*$; for any $x \neq x^*, y \neq y^*$ we have $f \leq V$. In this framework $\Omega(x, y, \phi)$ can be considered a function

of three independent variables, x, y, and ϕ. The maximum of $\Omega(x, y, \phi) = f(x, y, \phi) - V(\phi)$ can be determined by the first- and second-order conditions.

The first-order conditions are

$$\Omega_x(x, y, \phi) = f_x = 0$$
$$\Omega_y(x, y, \phi) = f_y = 0$$

(13.43)

and

$$\Omega_\phi(x, y, \phi) = f_\phi - V_\phi = 0$$

(13.44)

We can see that the first-order conditions of our new function Ω in (13.43) are nothing but the original maximum conditions for $f(x, y, \phi)$ in (13.28), whereas the condition in (13.44) really restates the envelope theorem (13.31'). These first-order conditions hold whenever $x = x^*(\phi)$ and $y = y^*(\phi)$. The second-order sufficient conditions are satisfied if the Hessian of Ω

$$H = \begin{vmatrix} f_{xx} & f_{xy} & f_{x\phi} \\ f_{yx} & f_{yy} & f_{y\phi} \\ f_{\phi x} & f_{\phi y} & f_{\phi\phi} - V_{\phi\phi} \end{vmatrix}$$

is characterized by

$$f_{xx} < 0 \qquad f_{xx}f_{yy} - f_{xy}^2 > 0 \qquad H < 0$$

In deriving the Hessian above, we listed the variables in the order (x, y, ϕ) and, consequently, the first entry in the second-order conditions, $(\Omega_{xx} =) f_{xx} < 0$ relates to the variable x. Had we adopted an alternative listing order, then the first entry could have been $\Omega_{yy} = f_{yy} < 0$, or

$$\Omega_{\phi\phi} = f_{\phi\phi} - V_{\phi\phi} < 0$$

(13.45)

It turns out that (13.45) can lead us to a result that provides a quick way to reach a comparative-static conclusion. First, we know from (13.41) that

$$V_\phi(\phi) = f_\phi(x^*(\phi), y^*(\phi), \phi)$$

Differentiating both sides with respect to ϕ yields

$$V_{\phi\phi} = f_{\phi x} \frac{\partial x^*}{\partial \phi} + f_{\phi y} \frac{\partial y^*}{\partial \phi} + f_{\phi\phi}$$

(13.46)

Using (13.45) and Young's theorem, we can write

$$V_{\phi\phi} - f_{\phi\phi} = f_{x\phi} \frac{\partial x^*}{\partial \phi} + f_{y\phi} \frac{\partial y^*}{\partial \phi} > 0$$

(13.47)

Suppose that ϕ enters only in the first-order condition for x, such that $f_{y\phi} = 0$. Then (13.47) reduces to

$$f_{x\phi} \frac{\partial x^*}{\partial \phi} > 0$$

(13.48)

which implies that $f_{x\phi}$ and $\partial x^*/\partial \phi$ will have the same sign. Thus, whenever we see the parameter ϕ appearing only in the first-order condition relating to x, and once we have determined the sign of the derivative $f_{x\phi}$ from the objective function $U = f(x, y, \phi)$, we can immediately tell the sign of the comparative-static derivative $\partial x^*/\partial \phi$ without further ado.

For example, in the profit-maximization model:

$$\pi = Pf(K, L) - wL - rK$$

where the first-order conditions are

$$\pi_L = Pf_L - w = 0$$
$$\pi_K = Pf_K - r = 0$$

the exogenous variable w enters only the first-order condition $Pf_L - w = 0$, with

$$\frac{\partial \pi_L}{\partial w} = -1$$

Therefore, by (13.48), we can conclude that $\partial L^*/\partial w$ will also be negative.

Further, if we combine the envelope theorem with Young's theorem, we can derive a relation known as the *reciprocity condition*: $\partial L^*/\partial r = \partial K^*/\partial w$. From the indirect profit function $\pi^*(w, r, P)$, Hotelling's lemma gives us

$$\pi_w^* = \frac{\partial \pi^*}{\partial w} = -L^*(w, r, P)$$

$$\pi_r^* = \frac{\partial \pi^*}{\partial r} = -K^*(w, r, P)$$

Differentiating again and applying Young' theorem, we have

$$\pi_{wr}^* = -\frac{\partial L^*}{\partial r} = -\frac{\partial K^*}{\partial w} = \pi_{rw}^*$$

or

$$\frac{\partial L^*}{\partial r} = \frac{\partial K^*}{\partial w} \qquad \text{(13.49)}$$

This result is referred to as the *reciprocity condition* because it shows the symmetry between the comparative-static cross effect produced by the price of one input on the demand for the "other" input. Specifically, in the comparative-static sense, the effect of r (the rental rate for capital K) on the optimal demand for labor L is the same as the effect of w (the wage rate for labor L) on the optimal demand for capital K.

The Envelope Theorem for Constrained Optimization

The envelope theorem can also be derived for the case of constrained optimization. Again we will have an objective function (U), two choice variables (x and y) and one parameter (ϕ); except now we introduce the following constraint:

$$g(x, y; \phi) = 0$$

The problem becomes:

$$\begin{array}{ll} \text{Maximize} & U = f(x, y; \phi) \\ \text{subject to} & g(x, y; \phi) = 0 \end{array} \qquad \text{(13.50)}$$

The Lagrangian for this problem is

$$Z = f(x, y; \phi) + \lambda[0 - g(x, y; \phi)] \qquad \text{(13.51)}$$

with first-order conditions

$$Z_x = f_x - \lambda g_x = 0$$
$$Z_y = f_y - \lambda g_y = 0$$
$$Z_\lambda = -g(x, y; \phi) = 0$$

Solving this system of equations gives us

$$x = x^*(\phi) \qquad y = y^*(\phi) \qquad \lambda = \lambda^*(\phi)$$

Substituting the solutions into the objective function, we get

$$U^* = f(x^*(\phi), y^*(\phi), \phi) = V(\phi) \tag{13.52}$$

where $V(\phi)$ is the indirect objective function, a maximum-value function. This is the maximum value of y for any ϕ and x_i's that satisfy the constraint.

How does $V(\phi)$ change as ϕ changes? First, we differentiate V with respect to ϕ:

$$\frac{dV}{d\phi} = f_x \frac{\partial x^*}{\partial \phi} + f_y \frac{\partial y^*}{\partial \phi} + f_\phi \tag{13.53}$$

In this case, however, (13.53) will not simplify to $dV/d\phi = f_\phi$ since in constrained optimization, it is not necessary to have $f_x = f_y = 0$ (see Table 12.1). But if we substitute the solutions to x and y into the constraint (producing an identity), we get

$$g(x^*(\phi), y^*(\phi), \phi) \equiv 0$$

and differentiating this with respect to ϕ yields

$$g_x \frac{\partial x^*}{\partial \phi} + g_y \frac{\partial y^*}{\partial \phi} + g_\phi \equiv 0 \tag{13.54}$$

If we multiply (13.54) by λ, combine the result with (13.53), and rearrange terms, we get

$$\frac{dV}{d\phi} = (f_x - \lambda g_x) \frac{\partial x^*}{\partial \phi} + (f_y - \lambda g_y) \frac{\partial y^*}{\partial \phi} + f_\phi - \lambda g_\phi = Z_\phi \tag{13.55}$$

where Z_ϕ is the partial derivative of the Lagrangian function with respect to ϕ, holding all other variables constant. This result is in the same spirit as (13.31), and by virtue of the first-order conditions, it reduces to

$$\frac{dV}{d\phi} = Z_\phi \tag{13.55'}$$

which represents the envelope theorem in the framework of constrained optimization. Note, however, in the present case, the Lagrangian function replaces the objective function in deriving the indirect objective function.

While the results in (13.55) nicely parallel the unconstrained case, it is important to note that some of the comparative-static results depend critically on whether the parameters enter only the objective function, or only the constraints, or enter both. If a parameter enters only in the objective function, then the comparative-static results are the same as for the unconstrained case. However, if the parameter enters the constraint, the relation

$$V_{\phi\phi} \geq f_{\phi\phi}$$

will no longer hold.

Interpretation of the Lagrange Multiplier

In the consumer choice problem in Chap. 12 we derived the result that the Lagrange multiplier λ represented the change in the value of the Lagrange function when the consumer's budget changed. We interpreted λ as the marginal utility of income. Now let us derive a more general interpretation of the Lagrange multiplier with the assistance of the envelope theorem. Consider the problem

$$\text{Maximize} \qquad U = f(x, y)$$
$$\text{subject to} \qquad g(x, y) = c$$

where c is a constant. The Lagrangian for this problem is

$$Z = f(x, y) + \lambda[c - g(x, y)] \qquad \textbf{(13.56)}$$

The first-order conditions are

$$\begin{aligned} Z_x &= f_x(x, y) - \lambda g_x(x, y) = 0 \\ Z_y &= f_y(x, y) - \lambda g_y(x, y) = 0 \\ Z_\lambda &= c - g(x, y) = 0 \end{aligned} \qquad \textbf{(13.57)}$$

From the first two equations in (13.57), we get

$$\lambda = \frac{f_x}{g_x} = \frac{f_y}{g_y} \qquad \textbf{(13.58)}$$

which gives us the condition that the slope of the level curve (indifference curve) of the objective function must equal the slope of the constraint at the optimum.

Equations (13.57) implicitly define the solutions

$$x^* = x^*(c) \qquad y^* = y^*(c) \qquad \lambda^* = \lambda^*(c) \qquad \textbf{(13.59)}$$

Substituting (13.59) back into the Lagrangian yields the maximum-value function,

$$V(c) = Z^*(c) = f(x^*(c), y^*(c)) + \lambda^*(c)[c - g(x_1^*(c), y^*(c))] \qquad \textbf{(13.60)}$$

Differentiating with respect to c yields

$$\begin{aligned} \frac{dV}{dc} = \frac{dZ^*}{dc} &= f_x \frac{\partial x^*}{\partial c} + f_y \frac{\partial y^*}{\partial c} + [c - g(x^*(c), y^*(c))] \frac{\partial \lambda^*}{\partial c} \\ &\quad - \lambda^*(c) g_x \frac{\partial x^*}{\partial c} - \lambda^*(c) g_y \frac{\partial y^*}{\partial c} + \lambda^*(c) \frac{dc}{dc} \end{aligned}$$

By rearranging we get

$$\frac{dZ^*}{dc} = [f_x - \lambda^* g_x] \frac{\partial x^*}{\partial c} + [f_y - \lambda^* g_y] \frac{\partial y^*}{\partial c} + [c - g(x^*, y^*)] \frac{\partial \lambda^*}{\partial c} + \lambda^*$$

By (13.57), the three terms in brackets are all equal to zero. Therefore this expression simplifies to

$$\frac{dV}{dc} = \frac{dZ^*}{dc} = \lambda^* \qquad \textbf{(13.61)}$$

which shows that the optimal value λ^* measures the rate of change of the maximum value of the objective function when c changes, and is for this reason referred to as the "shadow price" of c. Note that, in this case, c enters the problem only through the constraint; it is not an argument of the original objective function.

13.6   Duality and the Envelope Theorem

A consumer's expenditure function and his or her indirect utility function exemplify the minimum- and maximum-value functions for *dual problems.*[†] An expenditure function specifies the minimum expenditure required to obtain a fixed level of utility given the utility function and the prices of consumption goods. An indirect utility function specifies the maximum utility that can be obtained given prices, income, and the utility function.

The Primal Problem

Let $U(x, y)$ be a utility function where x and y are consumption goods. The consumer has a budget B and faces market prices P_x and P_y for goods x and y, respectively. This problem will be considered the *primal problem:*

$$\begin{array}{ll} \text{Maximize} & U = U(x, y) \\ \text{subject to} & P_x x + P_y y = B \end{array} \qquad \text{[Primal]} \qquad \textbf{(13.62)}$$

For this problem, we have the familiar Lagrangian

$$Z = U(x, y) + \lambda(B - P_x x - P_y y)$$

The first-order conditions are

$$\begin{aligned} Z_x &= U_x - \lambda P_x = 0 \\ Z_y &= U_y - \lambda P_y = 0 \\ Z_\lambda &= B - P_x x - P_y y = 0 \end{aligned} \qquad \textbf{(13.63)}$$

This system of equations implicitly defines a solution for x^m, y^m, and λ^m as a function of the exogenous variables B, P_x, P_y:

$$\begin{aligned} x^m &= x^m(P_x, P_y, B) \\ y^m &= y^m(P_x, P_y, B) \\ \lambda^m &= \lambda^m(P_x, P_y, B) \end{aligned}$$

The solutions x^m and y^m are the consumer's ordinary demand functions, sometimes called the "Marshallian" demand functions, hence the superscript m.

Substituting the solutions x^m and y^m into the utility function yields

$$U^* = U^*(x^m(P_x, P_y, B), y^m(P_x, P_y, B)) \equiv V(P_x, P_y, B) \qquad \textbf{(13.64)}$$

where V is the indirect utility function—a maximum-value function showing the maximum attainable utility in problem (13.62). We shall return to this function later.

[†] Duality in economic theory is the relationship between two constrained optimization problems. If one of the problems requires constrained maximization, the other problem will require constrained minimization. The structure and solution of either problem can provide information about the structure and solution of the other problem.

The Dual Problem

Now consider a related *dual problem* for the consumer with the objective of minimizing the expenditure on x and y while maintaining a fixed utility level U^* derived from (13.64) of the primal problem:

$$\text{Minimize} \qquad E = P_x x + P_y y$$
$$\text{subject to} \qquad U(x, y) = U^* \qquad \text{[Dual]} \qquad \textbf{(13.65)}$$

Its Lagrangian is

$$Z^d = P_x x + P_y y + \mu \, [U^* - U(x, y)]$$

and the first-order conditions are

$$Z^d_x = P_x - \mu U_x = 0$$
$$Z^d_y = P_y - \mu U_y = 0 \qquad \textbf{(13.66)}$$
$$Z^d_\lambda = U^* - U(x, y) = 0$$

This system of equations implicitly defines a set of solution values to be labeled x^h, y^h, and λ^h:

$$x^h = x^h(P_x, P_y, U^*)$$
$$y^h = y^h(P_x, P_y, U^*)$$
$$\mu^h = \mu^h(P_x, P_y, U^*)$$

Here x^h and y^h are the compensated ("real income" held constant) demand functions. They are commonly referred to as "Hicksian" demand functions, hence the h superscript.

Substituting x^h and y^h into the objective function of the dual problem yields

$$P_x x^h(P_x, P_y, U^*) + P_y y^h(P_x, P_y, U^*) \equiv E(P_x, P_y, U^*) \quad \textbf{(13.67)}$$

where E is the expenditure function—a minimum-value function showing the minimum expenditure needed to attain the utility level U^*.

Duality

If we take the first two equations in (13.63) and in (13.64), and eliminate the Lagrange multipliers, we can write

$$\frac{Px}{Py} = \frac{Ux}{Uy} \qquad \textbf{(13.68)}$$

This is the tangency condition in which the consumer chooses the optimal bundle where the slope of the indifference curve equals the slope of the budget constraint. The tangency condition is identical for both problems. Thus, when the target level of utility in the minimization problem is set equal to the value U^* obtained from the maximization problem, we get

$$x^m(P_x, P_y, B) = x^h(P_x, P_y, U^*)$$
$$y^m(P_x, P_y, B) = y^h(P_x, P_y, U^*) \qquad \textbf{(13.69)}$$

i.e., the solutions to both the maximization problem and the minimization problem produce identical values for x and y. However, the solutions are functions of different exogenous variables, so comparative-static exercises will generally produce different results.

The fact that the solution values for x and y in the primal and dual problems are determined by the tangency point of the same indifference curve and budget-constraint line means that the minimized expenditure in the dual problem is equal to the given budget B of the primal problem:

$$E(P_x, P_y, U^*) = B \qquad \textbf{(13.70)}$$

This result is parallel to the result in (13.64), which reveals that the maximized value of utility V in the primal problem is equal to the given target level of utility U^* in the dual problem.

While the solution values of x and y are identical in the two problems, the same cannot be said about the Lagrange multipliers. From the first equation in (13.63) and in (13.66), we can calculate $\lambda = U_x/P_x$, but $\mu = P_x/U_x$. Thus, the solution values of λ and μ are reciprocal to each other:

$$\lambda = \frac{1}{\mu} \qquad \text{or} \qquad \lambda^m = \frac{1}{\mu^h} \qquad \textbf{(13.71)}$$

Roy's Identity

One application of the envelope theorem is the derivation of Roy's identity. Roy's identity states that the individual consumer's Marshallian demand function is equal to negative of the ratio of two partial derivatives of the maximum-value function.

Substituting the optimal values x^m, y^m, and λ^m into the Lagrangian of (13.62) gives us

$$V(P_x, P_y, B) = U(x^m, y^m) + \lambda^m (B - P_x x^m - P_y y^m) \qquad \textbf{(13.72)}$$

When we differentiate (13.72) with respect to P_x we find

$$\frac{\partial V}{\partial P_x} = (U_x - \lambda^m P_x)\frac{\partial x^m}{\partial P_x} + (U_y - \lambda^m P_y)\frac{\partial y^m}{\partial P_x}$$
$$+ (B - P_x x^m - P_y y^m)\frac{\partial \lambda^m}{\partial P_x} - \lambda^m x^m$$

At the optimum, the first-order conditions (13.63) enable us to simplify this to

$$\frac{\partial V}{\partial P_x} = -\lambda^m x^m$$

Next, differentiate the value function with respect to B to get

$$\frac{\partial V}{\partial B} = (U_x - \lambda^m P_x)\frac{\partial x^m}{\partial B} + (U_y - \lambda^m P_y)\frac{\partial y^m}{\partial B}$$
$$+ (B - P_x x^m - P_y y^m)\frac{\partial \lambda^m}{\partial B} + \lambda^m$$

Again, at the optimum, (13.63) enables us to simplify this to

$$\frac{\partial V}{\partial B} = \lambda^m$$

By taking the ratio of these two partial derivatives, we find that

$$\frac{\partial V/\partial P_x}{\partial V/\partial B} = -x^m \qquad \textbf{(13.73)}$$

This result, known as *Roy's identity,* shows that the Marshallian demand for commodity x is the negative of the ratio of two partial derivatives of the maximum-value function V with respect to P_x and B, respectively. In view of the symmetry between x and y in the problem, a result similar to (13.73) can also be written for y^m, the Marshallian demand for y. Of course, this result could be arrived at directly by applying the envelope theorem.

Shephard's Lemma

In Sec. 13.5, we derived Hotelling's lemma, which states that the partial derivatives of the maximum value of the profit function yields the firm's input-demand functions and the supply functions. A similar approach applied to the expenditure function yields Shephard's lemma.

Consider the consumer's minimization problem (13.65). The Lagrangian is

$$Z^d = P_x x + P_y y + \mu[U^* - U(x, y)]$$

From the first-order conditions, the following solutions are implicitly defined

$$x^h = x^h(P_x, P_y, U^*)$$
$$y^h = y^h(P_x, P_y, U^*)$$
$$\mu^h = \mu^h(P_x, P_y, U^*)$$

Substituting these solutions into the Lagrangian yields the expenditure function:

$$E(P_x, P_y, U^*) = P_x x^h + P_y y^h + \mu^h[U^* - U(x^h, y^h)]$$

Taking the partial derivatives of this function with respect to P_x and P_y and evaluating them at the optimum, we find that $\partial E/\partial P_x$ and $\partial E/\partial P_y$ represent the consumer's Hicksian demands:

$$\frac{\partial E}{\partial P_x} = (P_x - \mu^h U_x)\frac{\partial x^h}{\partial P_x} + (P_y - \mu^h U_y)\frac{\partial y^h}{\partial P_x} + [U^* - U(x^h, y^h)]\frac{\partial \mu^h}{\partial P_x} + x^h$$

$$= (0)\frac{\partial x^h}{\partial P_x} + (0)\frac{\partial y^h}{\partial P_x} + (0)\frac{\partial \mu^h}{\partial P_x} + x^h = x^h \qquad (13.74)$$

and

$$\frac{\partial E}{\partial P_y} = (P_x - \mu^h U_x)\frac{\partial x^h}{\partial P_y} + (P_y - \mu^h U_y)\frac{\partial y^h}{\partial P_y} + [U^* - U(x^h, y^h)]\frac{\partial \mu^h}{\partial P_y} + y^h$$

$$= (0)\frac{\partial x^h}{\partial P_y} + (0)\frac{\partial y^h}{\partial P_y} + (0)\frac{\partial \mu^h}{\partial P_y} + y^h = y^h \qquad (13.74')$$

Finally, differentiating E with respect to the constraint U^* yields μ^h, the marginal cost of the constraint

$$\frac{\partial E}{\partial U^*} = (P_x - \mu^h U_x)\frac{\partial x^h}{\partial U^*} + (P_y - \mu^h U_y)\frac{\partial y^h}{\partial P_y}$$

$$+ [U^* - U(x^h, y^h)]\frac{\partial \mu^h}{\partial U^*} + \mu^h$$

$$= (0)\frac{\partial x^h}{\partial U^*} + (0)\frac{\partial y^h}{\partial U^*} + (0)\frac{\partial \mu^h}{\partial U^*} + \mu^h = \mu^h \qquad (13.74'')$$

Together, the three partial derivatives (13.74), (13.74'), and (13.74") are referred to as Shephard's lemma.

Example 1

Consider a consumer with the utility function $U = xy$, who faces a budget constraint of B and is given prices P_x and P_y.

The choice problem is

$$\text{Maximize} \quad U = xy$$
$$\text{subject to} \quad P_x x + P_y y = B$$

The Lagrangian for this problem is

$$Z = xy + \lambda(B - P_x x - P_y y)$$

The first-order conditions are

$$Z_x = y - \lambda P_x = 0$$
$$Z_y = x - \lambda P_y = 0$$
$$Z_\lambda = B - P_x x - P_y y = 0$$

Solving the first-order conditions yields the following solutions:

$$x^m = \frac{B}{2P_x} \qquad y^m = \frac{B}{2P_y} \qquad \lambda^m = \frac{B}{2P_x P_y}$$

where x^m and y^m are the consumer's Marshallian demand functions. For the second-order condition, since the bordered Hessian is

$$|\overline{H}| = \begin{vmatrix} 0 & 1 & -P_x \\ 1 & 0 & -P_y \\ -P_x & -P_y & 0 \end{vmatrix} = 2P_x P_y > 0$$

the solution does represent a maximum.[†]

We can now derive the indirect utility function for this problem by substituting x^m and y^m into the utility function:

$$V(P_x, P_y, B) = \left(\frac{B}{2P_x}\right)\left(\frac{B}{2P_y}\right) = \frac{B^2}{4P_x P_y} \tag{13.75}$$

where V denotes the maximized utility. Since V represents the maximized utility, we can set $V = U^*$ in (13.75) to get $B^2/4P_x P_y = U^*$, and then rearrange terms to express B as

$$B = (4P_x P_y U^*)^{1/2} = 2P_x^{1/2} P_y^{1/2} U^{*1/2}$$

Now, think of the consumer's dual problem of expenditure minimization. In the dual problem, the minimum-expenditure function E should be equal to the given budget amount B of the primal problem. Therefore, we can immediately conclude from the preceding equation that

$$E(P_x, P_y, U^*) = B = 2P_x^{1/2} P_y^{1/2} U^{*1/2} \tag{13.76}$$

[†] Note that the bordered Hessian is written here (and in Example 2 on page 440) with the borders in the third row and column, instead of in the first row and column as in (12.19). This is the result of listing the Lagrange multiplier as the last rather than the first variable as we did in previous chapters. Exercise 12.3-3 shows that the two alternative expressions for the bordered Hessian are transformable into each other by elementary row operations without affecting its value. However, when more than two choice variables appear in a problem, it is preferable to use the (12.19) format because that makes it easier to write out the bordered leading principal minors.

Let's now use this example to verify Roy's identity (13.73)

$$x^m = -\frac{\partial V / \partial P_x}{\partial V / \partial B}$$

Taking the relevant partial derivatives of V, we find

$$\frac{\partial V}{\partial P_x} = -\frac{B^2}{4 P_x^2 P_y}$$

and

$$\frac{\partial V}{\partial B} = \frac{B}{2 P_x P_y}$$

The negative of the ratio of these two partials is

$$-\frac{\frac{\partial V}{\partial P_x}}{\frac{\partial V}{\partial B}} = -\frac{\left(\dfrac{B^2}{4 P_x^2 P_y}\right)}{\left(\dfrac{B}{2 P_x P_y}\right)} = \frac{B}{2 P_x} = x^m$$

Thus we find that Roy's identity does hold.

Example 2

Now consider the dual problem of cost minimization given a fixed level of utility related to Example 1. Letting U^* denote the target level of utility, the problem is:

$$\begin{aligned} &\text{Minimize} &&P_x x + P_y y \\ &\text{subject to} &&xy = U^* \end{aligned}$$

The Lagrangian for the problem is

$$Z^d = P_x x + P_y y + \mu(U^* - xy)$$

The first-order conditions are

$$Z_x^d = P_x - \mu y = 0$$
$$Z_y^d = P_y - \mu x = 0$$
$$Z_\mu^d = U^* - xy = 0$$

Solving the system of equations for x, y, and μ, we get

$$x^h = \left(\frac{P_y U^*}{P_x}\right)^{\frac{1}{2}}$$

$$y^h = \left(\frac{P_x U^*}{P_y}\right)^{\frac{1}{2}} \tag{13.77}$$

$$\mu^h = \left(\frac{P_x P_y}{U^*}\right)^{\frac{1}{2}}$$

where x^h and y^h are the consumer's compensated (Hicksian) demand functions. Checking the second-order condition for a minimum, we find

$$|\overline{H}| = \begin{vmatrix} 0 & -\mu & -y \\ -\mu & 0 & -x \\ -y & -x & 0 \end{vmatrix} = -2xy\mu < 0$$

Thus the sufficient condition for a minimum is satisfied.

Substituting x^h and y^h into the original objective function gives us the minimum-value function, or expenditure function

$$E = P_x x^h + P_y y^h = P_x \left(\frac{P_y U^*}{P_x} \right)^{1/2} + P_y \left(\frac{P_x U^*}{P_y} \right)^{1/2}$$

$$= (P_x P_y U^*)^{1/2} + (P_x P_y U^*)^{1/2}$$

$$= 2 P_x^{1/2} P_y^{1/2} U^{*1/2} \tag{13.76'}$$

Note that this result is identical with (13.76) in Example 1. The only difference lies in the process used to derive the result. Equation (13.76') is obtained directly from an expenditure-minimization problem, whereas (13.76) is indirectly deduced, via the duality relationship, from a utility-maximization problem.

We shall now use this example to test the validity of Shephard's lemma (13.74), (13.74'), and (13.74''). Differentiating the expenditure function in (13.76') with respect to P_x, P_y, and U^*, respectively, and relating the resulting partial derivatives to (13.77), we find

$$\frac{\partial E(P_x, P_y, U^*)}{\partial P_x} = \frac{P_y^{1/2} U^{*1/2}}{P_x^{1/2}} = x^h$$

$$\frac{\partial E(P_x, P_y, U^*)}{\partial P_y} = \frac{P_x^{1/2} U^{*1/2}}{P_y^{1/2}} = y^h$$

$$\frac{\partial E(P_x, P_y, U^*)}{\partial U^*} = \frac{P_x^{1/2} P_y^{1/2}}{U^{*1/2}} = \mu^h$$

Thus, Shephard's Lemma holds in this example.

EXERCISE 13.6

1. A consumer has the following utility function: $U(x, y) = x(y + 1)$, where x and y are quantities of two consumption goods whose prices are P_x and P_y, respectively. The consumer also has a budget of B. Therefore, the consumer's Lagrangian is

   $$x(y + 1) + \lambda(B - P_x x - P_y y)$$

   (a) From the first-order conditions find expressions for the demand functions. What kind of good is y? In particular what happens when $P_y > B$?

   (b) Verify that this is a maximum by checking the second-order conditions. By substituting x^* and y^* into the utility function, find an expression for the indirect utility function

   $$U^* = U(P_x, P_y, B)$$

   and derive an expression for the expenditure function

   $$E = E(P_x, P_y, U^*)$$

   (c) This problem could be recast as the following dual problem

   Minimize $P_x x + P_y y$

   subject to $x(y + 1) = U^*$

   Find the values of x and y that solve this minimization problem and show that the values of x and y are equal to the partial derivatives of the expenditure function, $\partial E / \partial P_x$ and $\partial E / \partial P_y$, respectively.

13.7 Some Concluding Remarks

In the present part of the book, we have covered the basic techniques of optimization. The somewhat arduous journey has taken us (1) from the case of a single choice variable to the more general *n*-variable case, (2) from the polynomial objective function to the exponential and logarithmic, and (3) from the unconstrained to the constrained variety of extremum.

Most of this discussion consists of the "classical" methods of optimization, with differential calculus as the mainstay, and derivatives of various orders as the primary tools. One weakness of the calculus approach to optimization is its essentially myopic nature. While the first- and second-order conditions in terms of derivatives or differentials can normally locate relative or local extrema without difficulty, additional information or further investigation is often required for identification of absolute or global extrema. Our detailed discussion of concavity, convexity, quasiconcavity, and quasiconvexity is intended as a useful stepping-stone from the realm of relative extrema to that of absolute ones.

A more serious limitation of the calculus approach is its inability to cope with constraints in the inequality form. For this reason, the budget constraint in the utility-maximization model, for instance, is stated in the form that the total expenditure be exactly *equal to* (and not "less than or equal to") a specified sum. In other words, the limitation of the calculus approach makes it necessary to deny the consumer the option of saving part of the available funds. And, for the same reason, the classical approach does not allow us to specify explicitly that the choice variables must be nonnegative as is appropriate in most economic analysis.

Fortunately, we are liberated from these limitations when we introduce the modern optimization technique known as nonlinear programming. Here we can openly admit inequality constraints, including nonnegativity restrictions on the choice variables, into the problem. This obviously represents a giant step forward in the development of optimization methodology.

Still, even in nonlinear programming, the analytical framework remains static. The problem and its solution relate only to the optimal state at one point of time and cannot address the question of how an optimizing agent should, under given circumstances, behave over a period of time. The latter question pertains to the realm of *dynamic optimization,* which we are unable to handle until we have learned the basics of dynamic analysis—the analysis of movements of variables over time. In fact, aside from its application to dynamic optimization, dynamic analysis is, in itself, an important branch of economic analysis. For this reason, we shall now turn our attention to the subject of dynamic analysis in Part 5.

Dynamic Analysis

Part 5

Chapter 14

Economic Dynamics and Integral Calculus

The term *dynamics,* as applied to economic analysis, has had different meanings at different times and for different economists.[†] In standard usage today, however, the term refers to the type of analysis in which the object is either to trace and study the specific time paths of the variables or to determine whether, given sufficient time, these variables will tend to converge to certain (equilibrium) values. This type of information is important because it fills a major gap that marred our study of statics and comparative statics. In the latter, we always make the arbitrary assumption that the process of economic adjustment inevitably leads to an equilibrium. In a dynamic analysis, the question of "attainability" is to be squarely faced, rather than assumed away.

One salient feature of dynamic analysis is the *dating* of the variables, which introduces the explicit consideration of *time* into the picture. This can be done in two ways: time can be considered either as a *continuous* variable or as a *discrete* variable. In the former case, something is happening to the variable at each *point* of time (such as in continuous interest compounding); whereas in the latter, the variable undergoes a change only once within a *period* of time (e.g., interest is added only at the end of every 6 months). One of these time concepts may be more appropriate than the other in certain contexts.

We shall discuss first the continuous-time case, to which the mathematical techniques of *integral calculus* and *differential equations* are pertinent. Later, in Chaps. 17 and 18, we shall turn to the discrete-time case, which utilizes the methods of *difference equations.*

14.1 Dynamics and Integration

In a static model, generally speaking, the problem is to find the values of the endogenous variables that satisfy some specified equilibrium condition(s). Applied to the context of optimization models, the task becomes one of finding the values of the choice variables that maximize (or minimize) a specific objective function—with the first-order condition serving as the equilibrium condition. In a dynamic model, by contrast, the problem

---

[†] Fritz Machlup, "Statics and Dynamics: Kaleidoscopic Words," *Southern Economic Journal,* October 1959, pp. 91–110; reprinted in Machlup, *Essays on Economic Semantics,* Prentice-Hall, Inc., Englewood Cliffs, N.J., 1963, pp. 9–42.

involves instead the delineation of the time path of some variable, on the basis of a known pattern of change (say, a given instantaneous rate of change).

An example should make this clear. Suppose that population size H is known to change over time at the rate

$$\frac{dH}{dt} = t^{-1/2} \tag{14.1}$$

We then try to find what time path(s) of population $H = H(t)$ can yield the rate of change in (14.1).

You will recognize that, if we know the function $H = H(t)$ to begin with, the derivative dH/dt can be found by differentiation. But in the problem now confronting us, the shoe is on the other foot: we are called upon to uncover the *primitive* function from a given *derived* function, rather than the reverse. Mathematically, we now need the exact opposite of the method of differentiation, or of differential calculus.

The relevant method, known as *integration,* or *integral calculus,* will be studied in this chapter. For the time being, let us be content with the observation that the function $H(t) = 2t^{1/2}$ does indeed have a derivative of the form in (14.1), thus apparently qualifying as a solution to our problem. The trouble is that there also exist similar functions, such as $H(t) = 2t^{1/2} + 15$ or $H(t) = 2t^{1/2} + 99$ or, more generally,

$$H(t) = 2t^{1/2} + c \qquad (c = \text{an arbitrary constant}) \tag{14.2}$$

which all possess exactly the same derivative (14.1). No unique time path can be determined, therefore, unless the value of the constant c can somehow be made definite. To accomplish this, additional information must be introduced into the model, usually in the form of what is known as an *initial condition* or *boundary condition.*

If we have knowledge of the initial population $H(0)$—that is, the value of H at $t = 0$, let us say, $H(0) = 100$—then the value of the constant c can be made determinate. Setting $t = 0$ in (14.2), we get

$$H(0) = 2(0)^{1/2} + c = c$$

But if $H(0) = 100$, then $c = 100$, and (14.2) becomes

$$H(t) = 2t^{1/2} + 100 \tag{14.2'}$$

where the constant is no longer arbitrary. More generally, for any given initial population $H(0)$, the time path will be

$$H(t) = 2t^{1/2} + H(0) \tag{14.2''}$$

Thus the population size H at any point of time will, in the present example, consist of the sum of the initial population $H(0)$ and another term involving the time variable t. Such a time path indeed charts the complete itinerary of the variable H over time, and thus it truly constitutes the solution to our dynamic model. [Equation (14.1) is also a function of t. Why can't *it* be considered a solution as well?]

Simple as it is, this population example illustrates the quintessence of the problems of economic dynamics. Given the pattern of behavior of a variable over time, we seek to find a function that describes the time path of the variable. In the process, we shall encounter one or more arbitrary constants, but if we possess sufficient additional information in the form of *initial conditions,* it will be possible to definitize these arbitrary constants.

In the simpler types of problem, such as the one just cited, the solution can be found by the method of integral calculus, which deals with the process of tracing a given derivative function back to its primitive function. In more complicated cases, we can also resort to the known techniques of the closely related branch of mathematics known as *differential equations*. Since a differential equation is defined as any equation containing differential or derivative expressions, (14.1) surely qualifies as one; consequently, by finding its solution, we have in fact already solved a differential equation, albeit an exceedingly simple one.

Let us now proceed to the study of the basic concepts of integral calculus. Since we discussed differential calculus with x (rather than t) as the independent variable, for the sake of symmetry we shall use x here, too. For convenience, however, we shall in the present discussion denote the primitive and derived functions by $F(x)$ and $f(x)$, respectively, rather than distinguish them by the use of a prime.

14.2   Indefinite Integrals

The Nature of Integrals

It has been mentioned that integration is the reverse of differentiation. If differentiation of a given primitive function $F(x)$ yields the derivative $f(x)$, we can "integrate" $f(x)$ to find $F(x)$, provided appropriate information is available to definitize the arbitrary constant that will arise in the process of integration. The function $F(x)$ is referred to as an *integral* (or *antiderivative*) of the function $f(x)$. These two types of process may thus be likened to two ways of studying a family tree: *integration* involves the tracing of the parentage of the function $f(x)$, whereas *differentiation* seeks out the progeny of the function $F(x)$. But note this difference—while the (differentiable) primitive function $F(x)$ invariably produces a lone offspring, namely, a unique derivative $f(x)$, the derived function $f(x)$ is traceable to an infinite number of possible parents through integration, because if $F(x)$ is an integral of $f(x)$, then so also must be $F(x)$ plus any constant, as we saw in (14.2).

We need a special notation to denote the required integration of $f(x)$ with respect to x. The standard one is

$$\int f(x)\, dx$$

The symbol on the left—an elongated S (with the connotation of sum, to be explained later)—is called the *integral sign,* whereas the $f(x)$ part is known as the *integrand* (the function to be integrated), and the dx part—similar to the dx in the differentiation operator d/dx—reminds us that the operation is to be performed with respect to the variable x. However, you may also take $f(x)\, dx$ as a single entity and interpret it as the differential of the primitive function $F(x)$ [that is, $dF(x) = f(x)\, dx$]. Then, the integral sign in front can be viewed as an instruction to reverse the differentiation process that gave rise to the differential. With this new notation, we can write that

$$\frac{d}{dx} F(x) = f(x) \quad \Rightarrow \quad \int f(x)\, dx = F(x) + c \qquad \textbf{(14.3)}$$

where the presence of c, an arbitrary *constant of integration,* serves to indicate the multiple parentage of the integrand.

The integral $\int f(x)\,dx$ is, more specifically, known as the *indefinite integral* of $f(x)$ (as against the *definite integral* to be discussed in Sec. 14.2), because it has no definite numerical value. Because it is equal to $F(x) + c$, its value will in general vary with the value of x (even if c is definitized). Thus, like a derivative, an indefinite integral is itself a function of the variable x.

Basic Rules of Integration

Just as there are rules of derivation, we can also develop certain rules of integration. As may be expected, the latter are heavily dependent on the rules of derivation with which we are already familiar. From the following derivative formula for a power function,

$$\frac{d}{dx}\left(\frac{x^{n+1}}{n+1}\right) = x^n \qquad (n \neq -1)$$

for instance, we see that the expression $x^{n+1}/(n+1)$ is the primitive function for the derivative function x^n; thus, by substituting these for $F(x)$ and $f(x)$ in (14.3), we may state the result as a rule of integration.

Rule I   (the power rule)

$$\int x^n\,dx = \frac{1}{n+1}x^{n+1} + c \qquad (n \neq -1)$$

Example 1   Find $\int x^3\,dx$. Here, we have $n = 3$, and therefore

$$\int x^3\,dx = \frac{1}{4}x^4 + c$$

Example 2   Find $\int x\,dx$. Since $n = 1$, we have

$$\int x\,dx = \frac{1}{2}x^2 + c$$

Example 3   What is $\int 1\,dx$? To find this integral, we recall that $x^0 = 1$; so we can let $n = 0$ in the power rule and get

$$\int 1\,dx = x + c$$

[$\int 1\,dx$ is sometimes written simply as $\int dx$, since $1\,dx = dx$.]

Example 4   Find $\int \sqrt{x^3}\,dx$. Since $\sqrt{x^3} = x^{3/2}$, we have $n = \frac{3}{2}$; therefore,

$$\int \sqrt{x^3}\,dx = \frac{x^{5/2}}{\frac{5}{2}} + c = \frac{2}{5}\sqrt{x^5} + c$$

Example 5   Find $\int \frac{1}{x^4}\,dx,\ (x \neq 0)$. Since $1/x^4 = x^{-4}$, we have $n = -4$. Thus the integral is

$$\int \frac{1}{x^4}\,dx = \frac{x^{-4+1}}{-4+1} + c = -\frac{1}{3x^3} + c$$

Note that the correctness of the results of integration can always be checked by differentiation; if the integration process is correct, the derivative of the integral must be equal to the integrand.

The derivative formulas for simple exponential and logarithmic functions have been shown to be

$$\frac{d}{dx}e^x = e^x \qquad \text{and} \qquad \frac{d}{dx}\ln x = \frac{1}{x} \qquad (x > 0)$$

From these, two other basic rules of integration emerge.

Rule II   (the exponential rule)

$$\int e^x \, dx = e^x + c$$

Rule III   (the logarithmic rule)

$$\int \frac{1}{x} \, dx = \ln x + c \qquad (x > 0)$$

It is of interest that the integrand involved in Rule III is $1/x = x^{-1}$, which is a special form of the power function x^n with $n = -1$. This particular integrand is inadmissible under the power rule, but now is duly taken care of by the logarithmic rule.

As stated, the logarithmic rule is placed under the restriction $x > 0$, because logarithms do not exist for nonpositive values of x. A more general formulation of the rule, which can take care of negative values of x, is

$$\int \frac{1}{x} \, dx = \ln |x| + c \qquad (x \neq 0)$$

which also implies that $(d/dx) \ln |x| = 1/x$, just as $(d/dx) \ln x = 1/x$. You should convince yourself that the replacement of x (with the restriction $x > 0$) by $|x|$ (with the restriction $x \neq 0$) does not vitiate the formula in any way.

Also, as a matter of notation, it should be pointed out that the integral $\int \frac{1}{x} \, dx$ is sometimes also written as $\int \frac{dx}{x}$.

As variants of Rules II and III, we also have the following two rules.

Rule IIa

$$\int f'(x)e^{f(x)} \, dx = e^{f(x)} + c$$

Rule IIIa

$$\int \frac{f'(x)}{f(x)} \, dx = \ln f(x) + c \qquad [f(x) > 0]$$

or

$$\ln |f(x)| + c \qquad [f(x) \neq 0]$$

The bases for these two rules can be found in the derivative rules in (10.20).

Rules of Operation

The three preceding rules amply illustrate the spirit underlying all rules of integration. Each rule always corresponds to a certain derivative formula. Also, an arbitrary constant is always appended at the end (even though it is to be definitized later by using a given boundary condition) to indicate that a whole family of primitive functions can give rise to the given integrand.

To be able to deal with more complicated integrands, however, we shall also find the following two rules of operation with regard to integrals helpful.

Rule IV   (the integral of a sum) The integral of the sum of a finite number of functions is the sum of the integrals of those functions. For the two-function case, this means that

$$\int [f(x) + g(x)]\, dx = \int f(x)\, dx + \int g(x)\, dx$$

This rule is a natural consequence of the fact that

$$\underbrace{\frac{d}{dx}[F(x) + G(x)]}_{A} = \underbrace{\frac{d}{dx}F(x) + \frac{d}{dx}G(x)}_{B} = \underbrace{f(x) + g(x)}_{C}$$

Inasmuch as $A = C$, on the basis of (14.3) we can write

$$\int [f(x) + g(x)]\, dx = F(x) + G(x) + c \qquad\qquad \textbf{(14.4)}$$

But, from the fact that $B = C$, it follows that

$$\int f(x)\, dx = F(x) + c_1 \qquad \text{and} \qquad \int g(x)\, dx = G(x) + c_2$$

Thus we can obtain (by addition)

$$\int f(x)\, dx + \int g(x)\, dx = F(x) + G(x) + c_1 + c_2 \qquad\qquad \textbf{(14.5)}$$

Since the constants c, c_1, and c_2 are arbitrary in value, we can let $c = c_1 + c_2$. Then the right sides of (14.4) and (14.5) become equal, and as a consequence, their left sides must be equal also. This proves Rule IV.

Example 6   Find $\int (x^3 + x + 1)\, dx$. By Rule IV, this integral can be expressed as a sum of three integrals: $\int x^3\, dx + \int x\, dx + \int 1\, dx$. Since the values of these three integrals have previously been found in Examples 1, 2, and 3, we can simply combine those results to get

$$\int (x^3 + x + 1)\, dx = \left(\frac{x^4}{4} + c_1\right) + \left(\frac{x^2}{2} + c_2\right) + (x + c_3) = \frac{x^4}{4} + \frac{x^2}{2} + x + c$$

In the final answer, we have lumped together the three subscripted constants into a single constant c.

As a general practice, all the additive arbitrary constants of integration that emerge during the process can always be combined into a single arbitrary constant in the final answer.

Example 7   Find $\int \left(2e^{2x} + \frac{14x}{7x^2 + 5}\right) dx$. By Rule IV, we can integrate the two additive terms in the integrand separately, and then sum the results. Since the $2e^{2x}$ term is in the format of $f'(x)e^{f(x)}$ in Rule IIa, with $f(x) = 2x$, the integral is $e^{2x} + c_1$. Similarly, the other term,

$14x/(7x^2 + 5)$, takes the form of $f'(x)/f(x)$, with $f(x) = 7x^2 + 5 > 0$. Thus, by Rule IIIa, the integral is $\ln(7x^2 + 5) + c_2$. Hence we can write

$$\int \left(2e^{2x} + \frac{14x}{7x^2 + 5} \right) dx = e^{2x} + \ln(7x^2 + 5) + c$$

where we have combined c_1 and c_2 into one arbitrary constant c.

Rule V   (the integral of a multiple) The integral of k times an integrand (k being a constant) is k times the integral of that integrand. In symbols,

$$\int kf(x)\, dx = k \int f(x)\, dx$$

What this rule amounts to, operationally, is that a multiplicative constant can be "factored out" of the integral sign. (*Warning:* A *variable* term *cannot* be factored out in this fashion!) To prove this rule (for the case where k is an integer), we recall that k times $f(x)$ merely means adding $f(x)$ k times; therefore, by Rule IV,

$$\int kf(x)\, dx = \int \underbrace{[f(x) + f(x) + \cdots + f(x)]}_{k \text{ terms}} dx$$

$$= \underbrace{\int f(x)\, dx + \int f(x)\, dx + \cdots + \int f(x)\, dx}_{k \text{ terms}} = k \int f(x)\, dx$$

Example 8   Find $\int -f(x)\, dx$. Here $k = -1$, and thus

$$\int -f(x)\, dx = - \int f(x)\, dx$$

That is, the integral of the negative of a function is the negative of the integral of that function.

Example 9   Find $\int 2x^2\, dx$. Factoring out the 2 and applying Rule I, we have

$$\int 2x^2\, dx = 2 \int x^2\, dx = 2 \left(\frac{x^3}{3} + c_1 \right) = \frac{2}{3}x^3 + c$$

Example 10   Find $\int 3x^2\, dx$. In this case, factoring out the multiplicative constant yields

$$\int 3x^2\, dx = 3 \int x^2\, dx = 3 \left(\frac{x^3}{3} + c_1 \right) = x^3 + c$$

Note that, in contrast to the preceding example, the term x^3 in the final answer does not have any fractional expression attached to it. This neat result is due to the fact that 3 (the multiplicative constant of the integrand) happens to be precisely equal to 2 (the power of the function) plus 1. Referring to the power rule (Rule I), we see that the multiplicative constant $(n + 1)$ will in such a case cancel out the fraction $1/(n + 1)$, thereby yielding $(x^{n+1} + c)$ as the answer.

In general, whenever we have an expression $(n + 1)x^n$ as the integrand, there is really no need to factor out the constant $(n + 1)$ and then integrate x^n; instead, we may write $x^{n+1} + c$ as the answer right away.

Example 11   Find $\int \left(5e^x - x^{-2} + \dfrac{3}{x}\right) dx$, $(x \neq 0)$. This example illustrates both Rules IV and V; actually, it illustrates the first three rules as well:

$$\int \left(5e^x - \frac{1}{x^2} + \frac{3}{x}\right) dx = 5 \int e^x\, dx - \int x^{-2}\, dx + 3 \int \frac{1}{x}\, dx \qquad \text{[by Rules IV and V]}$$

$$= (5e^x + c_1) - \left(\frac{x^{-1}}{-1} + c_2\right) + (3 \ln |x| + c_3)$$

$$= 5e^x + \frac{1}{x} + 3 \ln |x| + c$$

The correctness of the result can again be verified by differentiation.

Rules Involving Substitution

Now we shall introduce two more rules of integration which seek to simplify the process of integration, when the circumstances are appropriate, by a substitution of the original variable of integration. Whenever the newly introduced variable of integration makes the integration process easier than under the old, these rules will become of service.

Rule VI   (the substitution rule) The integral of $f(u)(du/dx)$ with respect to the variable x is the integral of $f(u)$ with respect to the variable u:

$$\int f(u) \frac{du}{dx}\, dx = \int f(u)\, du = F(u) + c$$

where the operation $\int du$ has been substituted for the operation $\int dx$.

This rule, the integral-calculus counterpart of the chain rule, may be proved by means of the chain rule itself. Given a function $F(u)$, where $u = u(x)$, the chain rule states that

$$\frac{d}{dx} F(u) = \frac{d}{du} F(u) \frac{du}{dx} = F'(u) \frac{du}{dx} = f(u) \frac{du}{dx}$$

Since $f(u)(du/dx)$ is the derivative of $F(u)$, it follows from (14.3) that the integral (anti-derivative) of the former must be

$$\int f(u) \frac{du}{dx}\, dx = F(u) + c$$

You may note that this result, in fact, follows also from the *canceling* of the two dx expressions on the left.

Example 12   Find $\int 2x(x^2 + 1)\, dx$. The answer to this can be obtained by first multiplying out the integrand:

$$\int 2x(x^2 + 1)\, dx = \int (2x^3 + 2x)dx = \frac{x^4}{2} + x^2 + c$$

but let us now do it by the substitution rule. Let $u = x^2 + 1$; then $du/dx = 2x$, or $dx = du/2x$. Substitution of $du/2x$ for dx will yield

$$\int 2x(x^2 + 1)\, dx = \int 2xu \frac{du}{2x} = \int u\, du = \frac{u^2}{2} + c_1$$

$$= \frac{1}{2}(x^4 + 2x^2 + 1) + c_1 = \frac{1}{2}x^4 + x^2 + c$$

where $c = \frac{1}{2} + c_1$. The same answer can also be obtained by substituting du/dx for $2x$ (instead of $du/2x$ for dx).

Example 13 Find $\int 6x^2(x^3 + 2)^{99}\, dx$. The integrand of this example is not easily multiplied out, and thus the substitution rule now has a better opportunity to display its effectiveness. Let $u = x^3 + 2$; then $du/dx = 3x^2$, so that

$$\int 6x^2(x^3 + 2)^{99}\, dx = \int \left(2\frac{du}{dx}\right) u^{99}\, dx = \int 2u^{99}\, du$$

$$= \frac{2}{100} u^{100} + c = \frac{1}{50}(x^3 + 2)^{100} + c$$

Example 14 Find $\int 8e^{2x+3}\, dx$. Let $u = 2x + 3$; then $du/dx = 2$, or $dx = du/2$. Hence,

$$\int 8e^{2x+3}\, dx = \int 8e^u \frac{du}{2} = 4\int e^u\, du = 4e^u + c = 4e^{2x+3} + c$$

As these examples show, this rule is of help whenever we can—by the judicious choice of a function $u = u(x)$—express the integrand (a function of x) as the product of $f(u)$ (a function of u) and du/dx (the derivative of the u function which we have chosen). However, as illustrated by the last two examples, this rule can be used also when the original integrand is transformable into a constant multiple of $f(u)(du/dx)$. This would not affect the applicability because the constant multiplier can be factored out of the integral sign, which would then leave an integrand of the form $f(u)(du/dx)$, as required in the substitution rule. When the substitution of variables results in a *variable* multiple of $f(u)(du/dx)$, say, x times the latter, however, factoring is not permissible, and this rule will be of no help. In fact, there exists no general formula giving the integral of a product of two functions in terms of the separate integrals of those functions; nor do we have a general formula giving the integral of a quotient of two functions in terms of their separate integrals. Herein lies the reason why integration, on the whole, is more difficult than differentiation and why, with complicated integrands, it is more convenient to look up the answer in prepared tables of integration formulas rather than to undertake the integration by oneself.

Rule VII   **(integration by parts)** The integral of v with respect to u is equal to uv less the integral of u with respect to v:

$$\int v\, du = uv - \int u\, dv$$

The essence of this rule is to replace the operation $\int du$ by the operation $\int dv$.

The rationale behind this result is relatively simple. First, the product rule of differentials gives us

$$d(uv) = v\, du + u\, dv$$

If we integrate both sides of the equation (i.e., integrate each differential), we get a new equation

$$\int d(uv) = \int v\, du + \int u\, dv$$

or $uv = \int v\, du + \int u\, dv$ [no constant is needed on the left (why?)]

Then, by subtracting $\int u\, dv$ from both sides, the previously stated result emerges.

Example 15 Find $\int x(x+1)^{1/2}\,dx$. Unlike Examples 12 and 13, the present example is not amenable to the type of substitution used in Rule VI. (Why?) However, we may consider the given integral to be in the form of $\int v\,du$, and apply Rule VII. To this end, we shall let $v = x$, implying $dv = dx$, and also let $u = \frac{2}{3}(x+1)^{3/2}$, so that $du = (x+1)^{1/2}\,dx$. Then we can find the integral to be

$$\int x(x+1)^{1/2}\,dx = \int v\,du = uv - \int u\,dv$$

$$= \frac{2}{3}(x+1)^{3/2}x - \int \frac{2}{3}(x+1)^{3/2}\,dx$$

$$= \frac{2}{3}(x+1)^{3/2}x - \frac{4}{15}(x+1)^{5/2} + c$$

Example 16 Find $\int \ln x\,dx,\ (x > 0)$. We cannot apply the logarithmic rule here, because that rule deals with the integrand $1/x$, not $\ln x$. Nor can we use Rule VI. But if we let $v = \ln x$, implying $dv = (1/x)\,dx$, and also let $u = x$, so that $du = dx$, then the integration can be performed as follows:

$$\int \ln x\,dx = \int v\,du = uv - \int u\,dv$$

$$= x \ln x - \int dx = x \ln x - x + c = x(\ln x - 1) + c$$

Example 17 Find $\int xe^x\,dx$. In this case, we shall simply let $v = x$, and $u = e^x$, so that $dv = dx$ and $du = e^x\,dx$. Applying Rule VII, we then have

$$\int xe^x\,dx = \int v\,du = uv - \int u\,dv$$

$$= e^x x - \int e^x\,dx = e^x x - e^x + c = e^x(x - 1) + c$$

The validity of this result, like those of the preceding examples, can of course be readily checked by differentiation.

EXERCISE 14.2

1. Find the following:

(a) $\int 16x^{-3}\,dx \qquad (x \neq 0)$

(b) $\int 9x^8\,dx$

(c) $\int (x^5 - 3x)\,dx$

(d) $\int 2e^{-2x}\,dx$

(e) $\int \frac{4x}{x^2 + 1}\,dx$

(f) $\int (2ax + b)(ax^2 + bx)^7\,dx$

2. Find:

(a) $\int 13e^x\,dx$

(b) $\int \left(3e^x + \frac{4}{x}\right)dx \qquad (x > 0)$

(c) $\int \left(5e^x + \frac{3}{x^2}\right)dx \qquad (x \neq 0)$

(d) $\int 3e^{-(2x+7)}\,dx$

(e) $\int 4xe^{x^2+3}\,dx$

(f) $\int xe^{x^2+9}\,dx$

3. Find:

(a) $\displaystyle\int \frac{3dx}{x}$ $(x \neq 0)$

(c) $\displaystyle\int \frac{2x}{x^2 + 3}\, dx$

(b) $\displaystyle\int \frac{dx}{x - 2}$ $(x \neq 2)$

(d) $\displaystyle\int \frac{x}{3x^2 + 5}\, dx$

4. Find:

(a) $\displaystyle\int (x + 3)(x + 1)^{1/2}\, dx$

(b) $\displaystyle\int x \ln x\, dx$ $(x > 0)$

5. Given n constants k_i (with $i = 1, 2, \ldots, n$) and n functions $f_i(x)$, deduce from Rules IV and V that

$$\int \sum_{i=1}^{n} k_i f_i(x)\, dx = \sum_{i=1}^{n} k_i \int f_i(x)\, dx$$

14.3   Definite Integrals

Meaning of Definite Integrals

All the integrals cited in Sec. 14.2 are of the *indefinite* variety: each is a function of a variable and, hence, possesses no definite numerical value. Now, for a given indefinite integral of a continuous function $f(x)$,

$$\int f(x)\, dx = F(x) + c$$

if we choose two values of x in the domain, say, a and b $(a < b)$, substitute them successively into the right side of the equation, and form the difference

$$[F(b) + c] - [F(a) + c] = F(b) - F(a)$$

we get a specific numerical value, free of the variable x as well as the arbitrary constant c. This value is called the *definite integral* of $f(x)$ from a to b. We refer to a as the *lower limit of integration* and to b as the *upper limit of integration*.

In order to indicate the limits of integration, we now modify the integral sign to the form $\displaystyle\int_a^b$. The evaluation of the definite integral is then symbolized in the following steps:

$$\int_a^b f(x)\, dx = F(x) \bigg]_a^b = F(b) - F(a) \tag{14.6}$$

where the symbol $]_a^b$ (also written $|_a^b$ or $[\cdots]_a^b$) is an instruction to substitute b and a, successively, for x in the result of integration to get $F(b)$ and $F(a)$, and then take their difference, as indicated on the right of (14.6). As the first step, however, we must find the indefinite integral, although we may omit the constant c, since the latter will drop out in the process of difference-taking anyway.

Example 1   Evaluate $\displaystyle\int_1^5 3x^2\, dx$. Since the indefinite integral is $x^3 + c$, this definite integral has the value

$$\int_1^5 3x^2\, dx = x^3 \bigg]_1^5 = (5)^3 - (1)^3 = 125 - 1 = 124$$

Example 2	Evaluate $\int_a^b ke^x\,dx$. Here, the limits of integration are given in symbols; consequently, the result of integration is also in terms of those symbols:

$$\int_a^b ke^x\,dx = ke^x\Big]_a^b = k(e^b - e^a)$$

Example 3	Evaluate $\int_0^4 \left(\dfrac{1}{1+x} + 2x\right) dx, (x \neq -1)$. The indefinite integral is $\ln|1+x| + x^2 + c$; thus the answer is

$$\int_0^4 \left(\frac{1}{1+x} + 2x\right) dx = \Big[\ln|1+x| + x^2\Big]_0^4$$
$$= (\ln 5 + 16) - (\ln 1 + 0)$$
$$= \ln 5 + 16 \qquad [\text{since } \ln 1 = 0]$$

It is important to realize that the limits of integration a and b both refer to values of the variable x. Were we to use the substitution-of-variables technique (Rules VI and VII) during integration and introduce a variable u, care should be taken *not* to consider a and b as the limits of u. Example 4 will illustrate this point.

Example 4	Evaluate $\int_1^2 (2x^3 - 1)^2(6x^2)\,dx$. Let $u = 2x^3 - 1$; then $du/dx = 6x^2$, or $du = 6x^2\,dx$. Now notice that, when $x = 1$, u will be 1 but that, when $x = 2$, u will be 15; in other words, the limits of integration in terms of the variable u should be 1 (lower) and 15 (upper). Rewriting the given integral in u will therefore give us not $\int_1^2 u^2\,du$ but

$$\int_1^{15} u^2\,du = \frac{1}{3}u^3\Big]_1^{15} = \frac{1}{3}(15^3 - 1^3) = 1{,}124\tfrac{2}{3}$$

Alternatively, we may first convert u back to x and then use the original limits of 1 and 2 to get the identical answer:

$$\left[\frac{1}{3}u^3\right]_{u=1}^{u=15} = \left[\frac{1}{3}(2x^3 - 1)^3\right]_{x=1}^{x=2} = \frac{1}{3}(15^3 - 1^3) = 1{,}124\tfrac{2}{3}$$

A Definite Integral as an Area under a Curve

Every definite integral has a definite value. That value may be interpreted geometrically to be a particular area under a given curve.

The graph of a continuous function $y = f(x)$ is drawn in Fig. 14.1. If we seek to measure the (shaded) area A enclosed by the curve and the x axis between the two points a and b in the domain, we may proceed in the following manner. First, we divide the interval $[a, b]$ into n subintervals (not necessarily equal in length). Four of these are drawn in Fig. 14.1a—that is, $n = 4$—the first being $[x_1, x_2]$ and the last, $[x_4, x_5]$. Since each of these represents a change in x, we may refer to them as $\Delta x_1, \ldots, \Delta x_4$, respectively. Now, on the subintervals let us construct four rectangular blocks such that the height of each block is equal to the highest value of the function attained in that block (which happens to occur at the left-side boundary of each rectangle here). The first block thus has the height $f(x_1)$ and

FIGURE 14.1

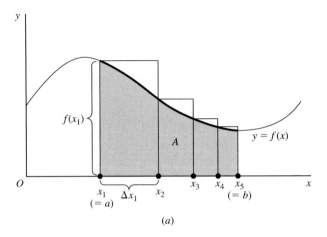

(a)

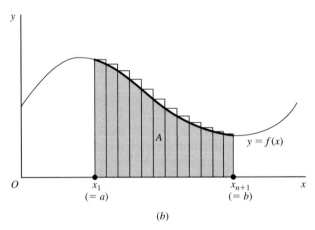

(b)

the width Δx_1, and, in general, the *i*th block has the height $f(x_i)$ and the width Δx_i. The total area A^* of this set of blocks is the sum

$$A^* = \sum_{i=1}^{n} f(x_i)\,\Delta x_i \qquad (n = 4 \text{ in Fig.14.1}a)$$

This, though, is obviously *not* the area under the curve we seek, but only a very rough approximation thereof.

What makes A^* deviate from the true value of A is the unshaded portion of the rectangular blocks; these make A^* an *over*estimate of A. If the unshaded portion can be shrunk in size and be made to approach zero, however, the approximation value A^* will correspondingly approach the true value A. This result will materialize when we try a finer and finer segmentation of the interval $[a, b]$, so that n is increased and Δx_i is shortened indefinitely. Then the blocks will become more slender (if more numerous), and the protrusion beyond the curve will diminish, as can be seen in Fig. 14.1*b*. Carried to the limit, this "slenderizing" operation yields

$$\lim_{n\to\infty}\sum_{i=1}^{n} f(x_i)\,\Delta x_i = \lim_{n\to\infty} A^* = \text{area } A \qquad (14.7)$$

provided this limit exists. (It does in the present case.) This equation, indeed, constitutes the formal definition of an area under a curve.

The summation expression in (14.7), $\sum_{i=1}^{n} f(x_i)\, \Delta x_i$, bears a certain resemblance to the definite integral expression $\int_{a}^{b} f(x)\, dx$. Indeed, the latter is based on the former. The replacement of Δx_i by the differential dx is done in the same spirit as in our earlier discussion of "approximation" in Sec. 8.1. Thus, we rewrite $f(x_i)\, \Delta x_i$ into $f(x)\, dx$. What about the summation sign? The $\sum_{i=1}^{n}$ notation represents the sum of a *finite* number of terms. When we let $n \to \infty$, and take the limit of that sum, the regular notation for such an operation is rather cumbersome. Thus a simpler substitute is needed. That substitute is $\int_{a}^{b}$, where the elongated S symbol also indicates a sum, and where a and b (just as $i = 1$ and n) serve to specify the lower and upper limits of this sum. In short the definite integral is a shorthand for the limit-of-a-sum expression in (14.7). That is,

$$\int_{a}^{b} f(x)\, dx \equiv \lim_{n \to \infty} \sum_{i=1}^{n} f(x_i)\, \Delta x_i = \text{area } A$$

Thus the said definite integral (referred to as a *Riemann integral*) now has an *area* connotation as well as a *sum* connotation, because $\int_{a}^{b}$ is the continuous counterpart of the discrete concept of $\sum_{i=1}^{n}$.

In Fig. 14.1, we attempted to approximate area A by systematically reducing an *over*-estimate A^* by finer segmentation of the interval $[a, b]$. The resulting limit of the sum of block areas is called the *upper integral*—an approximation from above. We could also have approximated area A from below by forming rectangular blocks inscribed by the curve rather than protruding beyond it (see Exercise 14.3-3). The total area A^{**} of this new set of blocks will *under*estimate A, but as the segmentation of $[a, b]$ becomes finer and finer, we shall again find $\lim_{n \to \infty} A^{**} = A$. The last-cited limit of the sum of block areas is called the *lower integral*. If, and only if, the upper integral and lower integral are equal in value, then the Riemann integral $\int_{a}^{b} f(x)\, dx$ is defined, and the function $f(x)$ is said to be *Riemann integrable*. There exist theorems specifying the conditions under which a function $f(x)$ is integrable. According to the fundamental theorem of calculus, a function is integrable in $[a, b]$ if it is continuous in that interval. As long as we are working with continuous functions, therefore, we should have no worries in this regard.

Another point may be noted. Although the area A in Fig. 14.1 happens to lie entirely under a decreasing portion of the curve $y = f(x)$, the conceptual equating of a definite integral with an area is valid also for upward-sloping portions of the curve. In fact, both types of slope may be present simultaneously; e.g., we can calculate $\int_{0}^{b} f(x)\, dx$ as the area under the curve in Fig. 14.1 above the line Ob.

FIGURE 14.2

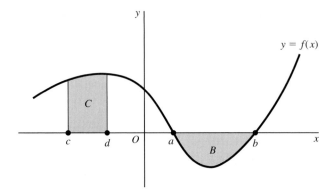

Note that, if we calculate the area B in Fig. 14.2 by the definite integral $\int_a^b f(x)\,dx$, the answer will come out negative, because the height of each rectangular block involved in this area is negative. This gives rise to the notion of a *negative area,* an area that lies *below* the x axis and *above* a given curve. In case we are interested in the numerical rather than the algebraic value of such an area, therefore, we should take the absolute value of the relevant definite integral. The area $C = \int_c^d f(x)\,dx$, on the other hand, has a positive sign even though it lies in the negative region of the x axis; this is because each rectangular block has a positive height as well as a positive width when we are moving from c to d. From this, the implication is clear that interchange of the two limits of integration would, by reversing the direction of movement, alter the sign of Δx_i and of the definite integral. Applied to area B, we see that the definite integral $\int_b^a f(x)\,dx$ (from b to a) will give the negative of the area B; this will measure the numerical value of this area.

Some Properties of Definite Integrals

The discussion in the preceding paragraph leads us to the following property of definite integrals.

Property I The interchange of the limits of integration changes the sign of the definite integral:

$$\int_b^a f(x)\,dx = -\int_a^b f(x)\,dx$$

This can be proved as follows:

$$\int_b^a f(x)\,dx = F(a) - F(b) = -[F(b) - F(a)] = -\int_a^b f(x)\,dx$$

Definite integrals also possess some other interesting properties.

Property II A definite integral has a value of zero when the two limits of integration are identical:

$$\int_a^a f(x)\,dx = F(a) - F(a) = 0$$

Under the "area" interpretation, this means that the area (under a curve) above any single *point* in the domain is nil. This is as it should be, because on top of a point on the x axis, we can draw only a (one-dimensional) *line,* never a (two-dimensional) *area.*

Property III A definite integral can be expressed as a sum of a finite number of definite subintegrals as follows:

$$\int_a^d f(x)\,dx = \int_a^b f(x)\,dx + \int_b^c f(x)\,dx + \int_c^d f(x)\,dx \qquad (a < b < c < d)$$

Only three subintegrals are shown in this equation, but the extension to the case of n subintegrals is also valid. This property is sometimes described as the *additivity property.*

In terms of area, this means that the area (under the curve) lying above the interval $[a, d]$ on the x axis can be obtained by summing the areas lying above the subintervals in the set $\{[a, b], [b, c], [c, d]\}$. Note that, since we are dealing with closed intervals, the border points b and c have each been included in *two* areas. Is this not double counting? It indeed is. But fortunately no damage is done, because by Property II the area above a single point is zero, so that the double counting produces no effect on the calculation. But, needless to say, the double counting of any *interval* is never permitted.

Earlier, it was mentioned that all continuous functions are Riemann integrable. Now, by Property III, we can also find the definite integrals (areas) of certain discontinuous functions. Consider the step function in Fig. 14.3*a*. In spite of the discontinuity at point b in the interval $[a, c]$, we can find the shaded area from the sum

$$\int_a^b f(x)\,dx + \int_b^c f(x)\,dx$$

The same also applies to the curve in Fig. 14.3*b*.

Property IV

$$\int_a^b -f(x)\,dx = -\int_a^b f(x)\,dx$$

Property V

$$\int_a^b kf(x)\,dx = k\int_a^b f(x)\,dx$$

FIGURE 14.3

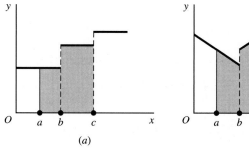
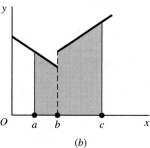

(*a*)   (*b*)

Property VI

$$\int_a^b [f(x) + g(x)]\, dx = \int_a^b f(x)\, dx + \int_a^b g(x)\, dx$$

Property VII **(integration by parts)** Given $u(x)$ and $v(x)$,

$$\int_{x=a}^{x=b} v\, du = uv \Big|_{x=a}^{x=b} - \int_{x=a}^{x=b} u\, dv$$

These last four properties, all borrowed from the rules of indefinite integration, should require no further explanation.

Another Look at the Indefinite Integral

We introduced the definite integral by way of attaching two limits of integration to an indefinite integral. Now that we know the meaning of the definite integral, let us see how we can revert from the latter to the indefinite integral.

Suppose that, instead of fixing the upper limit of integration at b, we allow it to be a variable, designated simply as x. Then the integral will take the form

$$\int_a^x f(x)\, dx = F(x) - F(a)$$

which, now being a function of x, denotes a *variable* area under the curve of $f(x)$. But since the last term on the right is a constant, this integral must be a member of the family of primitive functions of $f(x)$, which we denoted earlier as $F(x) + c$. If we set $c = -F(a)$, then the above integral becomes exactly the indefinite integral $\int f(x)\, dx$.

From this point of view, therefore, we may consider the $\int$ symbol to mean the same as $\int_a^x$, provided it is understood that in the latter version of the symbol the lower limit of integration is related to the constant of integration by the equation $c = -F(a)$.

EXERCISE 14.3

1. Evaluate the following:

(a) $\int_1^3 \frac{1}{2} x^2\, dx$

(b) $\int_0^1 x(x^2 + 6)\, dx$

(c) $\int_1^3 3\sqrt{x}\, dx$

(d) $\int_2^4 (x^3 - 6x^2)\, dx$

(e) $\int_{-1}^1 (ax^2 + bx + c)\, dx$

(f) $\int_4^2 x^2 \left(\frac{1}{3} x^3 + 1 \right) dx$

2. Evaluate the following:

(a) $\int_1^2 e^{-2x}\, dx$

(b) $\int_{-1}^{e-2} \frac{dx}{x+2}$

(c) $\int_2^3 (e^{2x} + e^x)\, dx$

(d) $\int_e^6 \left(\frac{1}{x} + \frac{1}{1+x} \right) dx$

3. In Fig. 14.1*a*, take the lowest value of the function attained in each subinterval as the height of the rectangular block, i.e., take $f(x_2)$ instead of $f(x_1)$ as the height of the first block, though still retaining Δx_1 as its width, and do likewise for the other blocks.

   (*a*) Write a summation expression for the total area A^{**} of the new rectangles.

   (*b*) Does A^{**} overestimate or underestimate the desired area A?

   (*c*) Would A^{**} tend to approach or to deviate further from A if a finer segmentation of $[a, b]$ were introduced? (*Hint:* Try a diagram.)

   (*d*) In the limit, when the number n of subintervals approaches ∞, would the approximation value A^{**} approach the true value A, just as the approximation value A^* did?

   (*e*) What can you conclude from (*a*) to (*d*) about the Riemann integrability of the function $f(x)$ in Fig. 14.1a?

4. The definite integral $\displaystyle\int_a^b f(x)\,dx$ is said to represent an area under a curve. Does this curve refer to the graph of the integrand $f(x)$, or of the primitive function $F(x)$? If we plot the graph of the $F(x)$ function, how can we show the given definite integral on it—by an area, a line segment, or a point?

5. Verify that a constant c can be equivalently expressed as a definite integral:

   (*a*) $\displaystyle c \equiv \int_0^b \frac{c}{b}\,dx$ (*b*) $\displaystyle c \equiv \int_0^c 1\,dt$

14.4   Improper Integrals

Certain integrals are said to be "improper." We shall briefly discuss two varieties thereof.

Infinite Limits of Integration

When we have definite integrals of the form

$$\int_a^\infty f(x)\,dx \qquad \text{and} \qquad \int_{-\infty}^b f(x)\,dx$$

with one limit of integration being infinite, we refer to them as *improper integrals.* In these cases, it is not possible to evaluate the integrals as, respectively,

$$F(\infty) - F(a) \qquad \text{and} \qquad F(b) - F(-\infty)$$

because ∞ is not a number, and therefore it cannot be substituted for x in the function $F(x)$. Instead, we must resort once more to the concept of limits.

The first improper integral we cited can be defined to be the limit of another (proper) integral as the latter's upper limit of integration tends to ∞; that is,

$$\int_a^\infty f(x)\,dx \equiv \lim_{b\to\infty} \int_a^b f(x)\,dx \qquad\qquad \textbf{(14.8)}$$

If this limit exists, the improper integral is said to be convergent (or to converge), and the limiting process will yield the value of the integral. If the limit does not exist, the improper integral is said to be divergent and is in fact meaningless. By the same token, we can define

$$\int_{-\infty}^b f(x)\,dx \equiv \lim_{a\to-\infty} \int_a^b f(x)\,dx \qquad\qquad \textbf{(14.8$'$)}$$

with the same criterion of convergence and divergence.

Example 1   Evaluate $\int_1^\infty \frac{dx}{x^2}$. First we note that

$$\int_1^b \frac{dx}{x^2} = \frac{-1}{x}\Big]_1^b = \frac{-1}{b} + 1$$

Hence, in line with (14.8), the desired integral is

$$\int_1^\infty \frac{dx}{x^2} = \lim_{b\to\infty} \int_1^b \frac{dx}{x^2} = \lim_{b\to\infty}\left(\frac{-1}{b}+1\right) = 1$$

This improper integral does converge, and it has a value of 1.

Since the limit expression is cumbersome to write, some people prefer to omit the "lim" notation and write simply

$$\int_1^\infty \frac{dx}{x^2} = \frac{-1}{x}\Big]_1^\infty = 0 + 1 = 1$$

Even when written in this form, however, the improper integral should nevertheless be interpreted with the limit concept in mind.

Graphically, this improper integral still has the connotation of an area. But since the upper limit of integration is allowed to take on increasingly larger values in this case, the right-side boundary must be extended eastward indefinitely, as shown in Fig. 14.4*a*. Despite this, we are able to consider the area to have the definite (limit) value of 1.

Example 2   Evaluate $\int_1^\infty \frac{dx}{x}$. As before, we first find

$$\int_1^b \frac{dx}{x} = \ln x\Big]_1^b = \ln b - \ln 1 = \ln b$$

When we let $b \to \infty$, by (10.16') we have $\ln b \to \infty$. Thus the given improper integral is divergent.

Figure 14.4*b* shows the graph of the function $1/x$, as well as the area corresponding to the given integral. The indefinite eastward extension of the right-side boundary will result this time in an infinite area, even though the shape of the graph displays a superficial similarity to that of Fig. 14.4*a*.

FIGURE 14.4

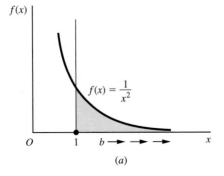

(*a*)

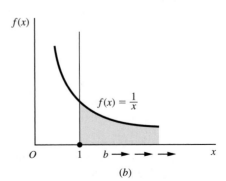

(*b*)

What if both limits of integration are infinite? A direct extension of (14.8) and (14.8′) would suggest the definition

$$\int_{-\infty}^{\infty} f(x)\, dx = \lim_{\substack{b \to +\infty \\ a \to -\infty}} \int_{a}^{b} f(x)\, dx \qquad\qquad (14.8'')$$

Again, this improper integral is said to converge if and only if the limit in question exists.

Infinite Integrand

Even with finite limits of integration, an integral can still be improper if the integrand becomes infinite somewhere in the interval of integration $[a, b]$. To evaluate such an integral, we must again rely upon the concept of a limit.

Example 3   Evaluate $\int_{0}^{1} \dfrac{1}{x}\, dx$. This integral is improper because, as Fig. 14.4*b* shows, the integrand is infinite at the lower limit of integration ($1/x \to \infty$ as $x \to 0^+$). Therefore we should first find the integral

$$\int_{a}^{1} \frac{1}{x}\, dx = \ln x \Big]_{a}^{1} = \ln 1 - \ln a = -\ln a \qquad \text{[for } a > 0\text{]}$$

and then evaluate its limit as $a \to 0^+$:

$$\int_{0}^{1} \frac{1}{x}\, dx \equiv \lim_{a \to 0^+} \int_{a}^{1} \frac{1}{x}\, dx = \lim_{a \to 0^+} (-\ln a)$$

Since this limit does not exist (as $a \to 0^+$, $\ln a \to -\infty$), the given integral is divergent.

Example 4   Evaluate $\int_{0}^{9} x^{-1/2}\, dx$. When $x \to 0^+$, the integrand $1/\sqrt{x}$ becomes infinite; the integral is improper. Again, we can first find

$$\int_{a}^{9} x^{-1/2}\, dx = 2x^{1/2} \Big]_{a}^{9} = 6 - 2\sqrt{a}$$

The limit of this expression as $a \to 0^+$ is $6 - 0 = 6$. Thus the given integral is convergent (to 6).

The situation where the integrand becomes infinite at the *upper* limit of integration is perfectly similar. It is an altogether different proposition, however, when an infinite value of the integrand occurs in the open interval (a, b) rather than at a or b. In this eventuality, it is necessary to take advantage of the additivity of definite integrals and first decompose the given integral into subintegrals. Assume that $f(x) \to \infty$ as $x \to p$, where p is a point in the interval (a, b); then, by the additivity property, we have

$$\int_{a}^{b} f(x)\, dx = \int_{a}^{p} f(x)\, dx + \int_{p}^{b} f(x)\, dx$$

The given integral on the left can be considered as convergent if and only if each subintegral has a limit.

Example 5

Evaluate $\int_{-1}^{1} \frac{1}{x^3}\, dx$. The integrand tends to infinity when x approaches zero; thus we must write the given integral as the sum

$$\int_{-1}^{1} x^{-3}\, dx = \int_{-1}^{0} x^{-3}\, dx + \int_{0}^{1} x^{-3}\, dx \qquad (\text{say, } \equiv I_1 + I_2)$$

The integral I_1 is divergent, because

$$\lim_{b\to 0^-} \int_{-1}^{b} x^{-3}\, dx = \lim_{b\to 0^-} \left[\frac{-1}{2} x^{-2}\right]_{-1}^{b} = \lim_{b\to 0^-} \left(-\frac{1}{2b^2} + \frac{1}{2}\right) = -\infty$$

Thus, we can conclude immediately, without having to evaluate I_2, that the given integral is divergent.

EXERCISE 14.4

1. Check the definite integrals given in Exercises 14.3-1 and 14.3-2 to determine whether any of them is improper. If improper, indicate which variety of improper integral each one is.

2. Which of the following integrals are improper, and why?

   (a) $\int_{0}^{\infty} e^{-rt}\, dt$ (d) $\int_{-\infty}^{0} e^{rt}\, dt$

   (b) $\int_{2}^{3} x^4\, dx$ (e) $\int_{1}^{5} \frac{dx}{x-2}$

   (c) $\int_{0}^{1} x^{-2/3}\, dx$ (f) $\int_{-3}^{4} 6\, dx$

3. Evaluate all the *improper* integrals in Prob. 2.

4. Evaluate the integral I_2 of Example 5, and show that it is also divergent.

5. (a) Graph the function $y = ce^{-t}$ for nonnegative t, $(c > 0)$, and shade the area under the curve.

   (b) Write a mathematical expression for this area, and determine whether it is a finite area.

14.5 Some Economic Applications of Integrals

Integrals are used in economic analysis in various ways. We shall illustrate a few simple applications in the present section and then show the application to the Domar growth model in Sec. 14.6.

From a Marginal Function to a Total Function

Given a total function (e.g., a total-cost function), the process of differentiation can yield the marginal function (e.g., the marginal-cost function). Because the process of integration is the opposite of differentiation, it should enable us, conversely, to infer the total function from a given marginal function.

Example 1

If the marginal cost (MC) of a firm is the following function of output, $C'(Q) = 2e^{0.2Q}$, and if the fixed cost is $C_F = 90$, find the total-cost function $C(Q)$. By integrating $C'(Q)$ with respect to Q, we find that

$$\int 2e^{0.2Q}\, dQ = 2\frac{1}{0.2}e^{0.2Q} + c = 10e^{0.2Q} + c \qquad (14.9)$$

This result may be taken as the desired $C(Q)$ function except that, in view of the arbitrary constant c, the answer appears indeterminate. Fortunately, the information that $C_F = 90$ can be used as an initial condition to definitize the constant. When $Q = 0$, total cost C will consist solely of C_F. Setting $Q = 0$ in the result of (14.9), therefore, we should get a value of 90; that is, $10e^0 + c = 90$. But this would imply that $c = 90 - 10 = 80$. Hence, the total-cost function is

$$C(Q) = 10e^{0.2Q} + 80$$

Note that, unlike the case of (14.2), where the arbitrary constant c has the same value as the initial value of the variable $H(0)$, in the present example we have $c = 80$ but $C(0) \equiv C_F = 90$, so that the two take different values. In general, it should *not* be assumed that the arbitrary constant c will always be equal to the initial value of the total function.

Example 2

If the marginal propensity to save (MPS) is the following function of income, $S'(Y) = 0.3 - 0.1Y^{-1/2}$, and if the aggregate savings S is nil when income Y is 81, find the saving function $S(Y)$. As the MPS is the derivative of the S function, the problem now calls for the integration of $S'(Y)$:

$$S(Y) = \int (0.3 - 0.1Y^{-1/2})\, dY = 0.3Y - 0.2Y^{1/2} + c$$

The specific value of the constant c can be found from the fact that $S = 0$ when $Y = 81$. Even though, strictly speaking, this is not an *initial* condition (not relating to $Y = 0$), substitution of this information into the preceding integral will nevertheless serve to definitize c. Since

$$0 = 0.3(81) - 0.2(9) + c \qquad \Rightarrow \qquad c = -22.5$$

the desired saving function is

$$S(Y) = 0.3Y - 0.2Y^{1/2} - 22.5$$

The technique illustrated in Examples 1 and 2 can be extended directly to other problems involving the search for total functions (such as total revenue, total consumption) from given marginal functions. It may also be reiterated that in problems of this type the validity of the answer (an integral) can always be checked by differentiation.

Investment and Capital Formation

Capital formation is the process of adding to a given stock of capital. Regarding this process as continuous over time, we may express capital stock as a function of time, $K(t)$, and use the derivative dK/dt to denote the rate of capital formation.[†] But the rate of capital

---

[†] As a matter of notation, the derivative of a variable with respect to *time* often is also denoted by a dot placed over the variable, such as $\dot{K} \equiv dK/dt$. In dynamic analysis, where derivatives with respect to *time* occur in abundance, this more concise symbol can contribute substantially to notational simplicity. However, a dot, being such a tiny mark, is easily lost sight of or misplaced; thus, great care is required in using this symbol.

formation at time t is identical with the rate of *net investment* flow at time t, denoted by $I(t)$. Thus, capital stock K and net investment I are related by the following two equations:

$$\frac{dK}{dt} \equiv I(t)$$

and
$$K(t) = \int I(t)\, dt = \int \frac{dK}{dt}\, dt = \int dK$$

The first of the preceding equations is an identity; it shows the synonymity between net investment and the increment of capital. Since $I(t)$ is the derivative of $K(t)$, it stands to reason that $K(t)$ is the integral or antiderivative of $I(t)$, as shown in the second equation. The transformation of the integrand in the latter equation is also easy to comprehend: The switch from I to dK/dt is by definition, and the next transformation is by cancellation of two identical differentials, i.e., by the substitution rule.

Sometimes the concept of *gross investment* is used together with that of net investment in a model. Denoting gross investment by I_g and net investment by I, we can relate them to each other by the equation.

$$I_g = I + \delta K$$

where δ represents the rate of depreciation of capital and δK, the rate of *replacement investment*.

<table>
<tr><td>

Example 3

</td><td>

Suppose that the net investment flow is described by the equation $I(t) = 3t^{1/2}$ and that the initial capital stock, at time $t = 0$, is $K(0)$. What is the time path of capital K? By integrating $I(t)$ with respect to t, we obtain

</td></tr>
</table>

$$K(t) = \int I(t)\, dt = \int 3t^{1/2}\, dt = 2t^{3/2} + c$$

Next, letting $t = 0$ in the leftmost and rightmost expressions, we find $K(0) = c$. Therefore, the time path of K is

$$K(t) = 2t^{3/2} + K(0) \tag{14.10}$$

Observe the basic similarity between the results in (14.10) and in (14.2″).

The concept of definite integral enters into the picture when one desires to find the amount of capital formation during some interval of time (rather than the time path of K). Since $\int I(t)\, dt = K(t)$, we may write the definite integral

$$\int_a^b I(t)\, dt = K(t) \Big]_a^b = K(b) - K(a)$$

to indicate the total capital accumulation during the time interval $[a, b]$. Of course, this also represents an area under the $I(t)$ curve. It should be noted, however, that in the graph of the $K(t)$ function, this definite integral would appear instead as a vertical distance—more specifically, as the difference between the two vertical distances $K(b)$ and $K(a)$. (cf. Exercise 14.3-4.)

To appreciate this distinction between $K(t)$ and $I(t)$ more fully, let us emphasize that capital K is a *stock* concept, whereas investment I is a *flow* concept. Accordingly, while $K(t)$ tells us the *amount* of K existing at each point of time, $I(t)$ gives us the information about the *rate* of (net) investment per year (or per period of time) which is prevailing at each point of time. Thus, in order to calculate the *amount* of net investment undertaken (capital accumulation), we must first specify the length of the interval involved. This fact can also be seen when we rewrite the identity $dK/dt \equiv I(t)$ as $dK \equiv I(t)\, dt$, which states that dK, the increment in K, is based not only on $I(t)$, the rate of flow, but also on dt, the time that elapsed. It is this need to specify the time interval in the expression $I(t)\, dt$ that brings the definite integral into the picture, and gives rise to the *area* representation under the $I(t)$—as against the $K(t)$—curve.

Example 4

If net investment is a constant flow at $I(t) = 1{,}000$ (dollars per year), what will be the total net investment (capital formation) during a year, from $t = 0$ to $t = 1$? Obviously, the answer is \$1,000; this can be obtained formally as follows:

$$\int_0^1 I(t)\, dt = \int_0^1 1{,}000\, dt = 1{,}000t \Big]_0^1 = 1{,}000$$

You can verify that the same answer will emerge if, instead, the year involved is from $t = 1$ to $t = 2$.

Example 5

If $I(t) = 3t^{1/2}$ (thousands of dollars per year)—a nonconstant flow—what will be the capital formation during the time interval [1, 4], that is, during the second, third, and fourth years? The answer lies in the definite integral

$$\int_1^4 3t^{1/2}\, dt = 2t^{3/2} \Big]_1^4 = 16 - 2 = 14$$

On the basis of the preceding examples, we may express the amount of capital accumulation during the time interval [0, t], for any investment rate $I(t)$, by the definite integral

$$\int_0^t I(t)\, dt = K(t) \Big]_0^t = K(t) - K(0)$$

Figure 14.5 illustrates the case of the time interval [0, t_0]. Viewed differently, the preceding equation yields the following expression for the time path $K(t)$:

$$K(t) = K(0) + \int_0^t I(t)\, dt$$

The amount of K at any time t is the initial capital plus the total capital accumulation that has occurred since.

FIGURE 14.5

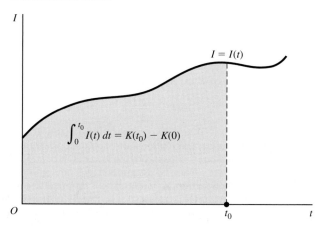

Present Value of a Cash Flow

Our earlier discussion of discounting and present value, limited to the case of a *single* future value V, led us to the discounting formulas

$$A = V(1 + i)^{-t} \qquad [discrete \text{ case}]$$

and
$$A = Ve^{-rt} \qquad [continuous \text{ case}]$$

Now suppose that we have a stream or flow of future values—a series of revenues receivable at various times or of cost outlays payable at various times. How do we compute the present value of the entire cash stream, or cash flow?

In the *discrete* case, if we assume three future revenue figures R_t ($t = 1, 2, 3$) available at the end of the tth year and also assume an interest rate of i per annum, the present values of R_t will be, respectively,

$$R_1(1 + i)^{-1} \qquad R_2(1 + i)^{-2} \qquad R_3(1 + i)^{-3}$$

It follows that the total present value is the sum

$$\Pi = \sum_{t=1}^{3} R_t(1 + i)^{-t} \tag{14.11}$$

(Π is the uppercase Greek letter pi, here signifying *present*.) This differs from the single-value formula only in the replacement of V by R_t and in the insertion of the Σ sign.

The idea of the sum readily carries over to the case of a continuous cash flow, but in the latter context the Σ symbol must give way, of course, to the definite integral sign. Consider a continuous revenue stream at the rate of $R(t)$ dollars per year. This means that at $t = t_1$ the rate of flow is $R(t_1)$ dollars per year, but at another point of time $t = t_2$ the rate will be $R(t_2)$ dollars per year—with t taken as a continuous variable. At any point of time, the amount of revenue during the interval $[t, t + dt]$ can be written as $R(t)\,dt$ [cf. the previous discussion of $dK \equiv I(t)\,dt$]. When continuously discounted at the rate of r per year, its present value should be $R(t)e^{-rt}\,dt$. If we let our problem be that of finding the total present value of a 3-year stream, our answer is to be found in the following definite integral:

$$\Pi = \int_0^3 R(t)e^{-rt}\,dt \tag{14.11'}$$

This expression, the continuous version of the sum in (14.11), differs from the single-value formula only in the replacement of V by $R(t)$ and in the appending of the definite integral sign.[†]

[†] It may be noted that, whereas the upper summation index and the upper limit of integration are identical at 3, the lower summation index 1 differs from the lower limit of integration 0. This is because the first revenue in the discrete stream, by assumption, will not be forthcoming until $t = 1$ (end of first year), but the revenue flow in the continuous case is assumed to commence immediately after $t = 0$.

Example 6   What is the present value of a continuous revenue flow lasting for y years at the constant rate of D dollars per year and discounted at the rate of r per year? According to (14.11'), we have

$$\Pi = \int_0^y De^{-rt}\,dt = D\int_0^y e^{-rt}\,dt = D\left[\frac{-1}{r}e^{-rt}\right]_0^y$$

$$= \frac{-D}{r}e^{-rt}\Big]_{t=0}^{t=y} = \frac{-D}{r}(e^{-ry}-1) = \frac{D}{r}(1-e^{-ry}) \qquad \textbf{(14.12)}$$

Thus, Π depends on D, r and y. If $D = \$3{,}000$, $r = 0.06$, and $y = 2$, for instance, we have

$$\Pi = \frac{3{,}000}{0.06}(1-e^{-0.12}) = 50{,}000(1-0.8869) = \$5{,}655 \qquad \text{[approximately]}$$

The value of Π naturally is always positive; this follows from the positivity of D and r, as well as $(1-e^{-ry})$. (The number e raised to any negative power will always give a positive fractional value, as can be seen from the second quadrant of Fig. 10.3a.)

Example 7   In the wine-storage problem of Sec. 10.6, we assumed zero storage cost. That simplifying assumption was necessitated by our ignorance of a way to compute the present value of a cost flow. With this ignorance behind us, we are now ready to permit the wine dealer to incur storage costs.

Let the purchase cost of the case of wine be an amount C, incurred at the present time. Its (future) sale value, which varies with time, may be generally denoted as $V(t)$—its present value being $V(t)e^{-rt}$. Whereas the sale value represents a single future value (there can be only one sale transaction on this case of wine), the storage cost is a stream. Assuming this cost to be a constant stream at the rate of s dollars per year, the total present value of the storage cost incurred in a total of t years will amount to

$$\int_0^t se^{-rt}\,dt = \frac{s}{r}(1-e^{-rt}) \qquad \text{(cf. (14.12)]}$$

Thus the *net* present value—what the dealer would seek to maximize—can be expressed as

$$N(t) = V(t)e^{-rt} - \frac{s}{r}(1-e^{-rt}) - C = \left[V(t)+\frac{s}{r}\right]e^{-rt} - \frac{s}{r} - C$$

which is an objective function in a single choice variable t.

To maximize $N(t)$, the value of t must be chosen such that $N'(t) = 0$. This first derivative is

$$N'(t) = V'(t)e^{-rt} - r\left[V(t)+\frac{s}{r}\right]e^{-rt} \qquad \text{[product rule]}$$

$$= [V'(t) - rV(t) - s]e^{-rt}$$

and it will be zero if and only if

$$V'(t) = rV(t) + s$$

Thus, this last equation may be taken as the necessary optimization condition for the choice of the time of sale t^*.

The economic interpretation of this condition appeals easily to intuitive reasoning: $V'(t)$ represents the rate of change of the sale value, or the increment in V, if sale is postponed for a year, while the two terms on the right indicate, respectively, the increments in the interest cost and the storage cost entailed by such a postponement of sale (revenue and cost are both reckoned at time t^*). So, the idea of the equating of the two sides is to us just some "old wine in a new bottle," for it is nothing but the same MC = MR condition in a different guise!

Present Value of a Perpetual Flow

If a cash flow were to persist forever—a situation exemplified by the interest from a perpetual bond or the revenue from an indestructible capital asset such as land—the present value of the flow would be

$$\Pi = \int_0^\infty R(t)e^{-rt}\,dt$$

which is an improper integral.

<table>
<tr><td>**Example 8**</td><td>Find the present value of a perpetual income stream flowing at the uniform rate of D dollars per year, if the continuous rate of discount is r. Since, in evaluating an improper integral, we simply take the limit of a proper integral, the result in (14.12) can still be of help. Specifically, we can write</td></tr>
</table>

$$\Pi = \int_0^\infty De^{-rt}\,dt = \lim_{y\to\infty}\int_0^y De^{-rt}\,dt = \lim_{y\to\infty}\frac{D}{r}(1 - e^{-ry}) = \frac{D}{r}$$

Note that the y parameter (number of years) has disappeared from the final answer. This is as it should be, for here we are dealing with a *perpetual* flow. You may also observe that our result (present value = rate of revenue flow ÷ rate of discount) corresponds precisely to the familiar formula for the so-called capitalization of an asset with a perpetual yield.

EXERCISE 14.5

1. Given the following marginal-revenue functions:
   (a) $R'(Q) = 28Q - e^{0.3Q}$ (b) $R'(Q) = 10(1 + Q)^{-2}$
   find in each case the total-revenue function $R(Q)$. What initial condition can you introduce to definitize the constant of integration?

2. (a) Given the marginal propensity to import $M'(Y) = 0.1$ and the information that $M = 20$ when $Y = 0$, find the import function $M(Y)$.
   (b) Given the marginal propensity to consume $C'(Y) = 0.8 + 0.1Y^{-1/2}$ and the information that $C = Y$ when $Y = 100$, find the consumption function $C(Y)$.

3. Assume that the rate of investment is described by the function $I(t) = 12t^{1/3}$ and that $K(0) = 25$:
   (a) Find the time path of capital stock K.
   (b) Find the amount of capital accumulation during the time intervals $[0, 1]$ and $[1, 3]$, respectively.

4. Given a continuous income stream at the constant rate of $1,000 per year:
   (a) What will be the present value Π if the income stream lasts for 2 years and the continuous discount rate is 0.05 per year?
   (b) What will be the present value Π if the income stream terminates after exactly 3 years and the discount rate is 0.04?

5. What is the present value of a perpetual cash flow of:
   (a) $1,450 per year, discounted at $r = 5\%$?
   (b) $2,460 per year, discounted at $r = 8\%$?

14.6   Domar Growth Model

In the population-growth problem of (14.1) and (14.2) and the capital-formation problem of (14.10), the common objective is to delineate a time path on the basis of some given pattern of change of a variable. In the classic growth model of Professor Domar,[†] on the other hand, the idea is to stipulate the type of time path required to prevail if a certain equilibrium condition of the economy is to be satisfied.

The Framework

The basic premises of the Domar model are as follows:

1. Any change in the rate of investment flow per year $I(t)$ will produce a dual effect: it will affect the aggregate demand as well as the productive capacity of the economy.

2. The demand effect of a change in $I(t)$ operates through the multiplier process, assumed to work instantaneously. Thus an increase in $I(t)$ will raise the rate of income flow per year $Y(t)$ by a multiple of the increment in $I(t)$. The multiplier is $k = 1/s$, where s stands for the given (constant) marginal propensity to save. On the assumption that $I(t)$ is the only (parametric) expenditure flow that influences the rate of income flow, we can then state that

$$\frac{dY}{dt} = \frac{dI}{dt}\frac{1}{s} \qquad \textbf{(14.13)}$$

3. The capacity effect of investment is to be measured by the change in the rate of *potential* output the economy is capable of producing. Assuming a constant capacity-capital ratio, we can write

$$\frac{\kappa}{K} \equiv \rho \qquad (= \text{a constant})$$

where κ (the Greek letter kappa) stands for capacity or potential output flow per year, and ρ (the Greek letter rho) denotes the given capacity-capital ratio. This implies, of course, that with a capital stock $K(t)$ the economy is potentially capable of producing an annual product, or income, amounting to $\kappa \equiv \rho K$ dollars. Note that, from $\kappa \equiv \rho K$ (the production function), it follows that $d\kappa = \rho\, dK$, and

$$\frac{d\kappa}{dt} = \rho\frac{dK}{dt} = \rho I \qquad \textbf{(14.14)}$$

In Domar's model, equilibrium is defined to be a situation in which productive capacity is fully utilized. To have equilibrium is, therefore, to require the aggregate demand to be exactly equal to the potential output producible in a year; that is, $Y = \kappa$. If we start initially from an equilibrium situation, however, the requirement will reduce to the balancing of the respective *changes* in capacity and in aggregate demand; that is,

$$\frac{dY}{dt} = \frac{d\kappa}{dt} \qquad \textbf{(14.15)}$$

[†] Evsey D. Domar, "Capital Expansion, Rate of Growth, and Employment," *Econometrica*, April 1946, pp. 137–147; reprinted in Domar, *Essays in the Theory of Economic Growth*, Oxford University Press, Fair Lawn, N.J., 1957, pp. 70–82.

What kind of time path of investment $I(t)$ can satisfy this equilibrium condition at all times?

Finding the Solution

To answer this question, we first substitute (14.13) and (14.14) into the equilibrium condition (14.15). The result is the following differential equation:

$$\frac{dI}{dt}\frac{1}{s} = \rho I \qquad \text{or} \qquad \frac{1}{I}\frac{dI}{dt} = \rho s \qquad \textbf{(14.16)}$$

Since (14.16) specifies a definite pattern of change for I, we should be able to find the equilibrium (or required) investment path from it.

In this simple case, the solution is obtainable by directly integrating both sides of the second equation in (14.16) with respect to t. The fact that the two sides are identical in equilibrium assures the equality of their integrals. Thus,

$$\int \frac{1}{I}\frac{dI}{dt}\, dt = \int \rho s\, dt$$

By the substitution rule and the log rule, the left side gives us

$$\int \frac{dI}{I} = \ln\,|I| + c_1 \qquad (I \neq 0)$$

whereas the right side yields (ρs being a constant)

$$\int \rho s\, dt = \rho s t + c_2$$

Equating the two results and combining the two constants, we have

$$\ln\,|I| = \rho s t + c \qquad \textbf{(14.17)}$$

To obtain $|I|$ from $\ln\,|I|$, we perform an operation known as "taking the antilog of $\ln\,|I|$," which utilizes the fact that $e^{\ln x} = x$. Thus, letting each side of (14.17) become the exponent of the constant e, we obtain

$$e^{\ln\,|I|} = e^{(\rho st + c)}$$

or
$$|I| = e^{\rho st}e^{c} = Ae^{\rho st} \qquad \text{where } A \equiv e^{c}$$

If we take investment to be positive, then $|I| = I$, so that the preceding result becomes $I(t) = Ae^{\rho st}$, where A is arbitrary. To get rid of this arbitrary constant, we set $t = 0$ in the equation $I(t) = Ae^{\rho st}$, to get $I(0) = Ae^{0} = A$. This definitizes the constant A, and enables us to express the solution—the required investment path—as

$$I(t) = I(0)e^{\rho st} \qquad \textbf{(14.18)}$$

where $I(0)$ denotes the initial rate of investment.[†]

This result has a disquieting economic meaning. In order to maintain the balance between capacity and demand over time, the rate of investment flow must grow precisely

---

[†] The solution (14.18) will remain valid even if we let investment be negative in the result $|I| = Ae^{\rho st}$. See Exercise 14.6-3.

FIGURE 14.6

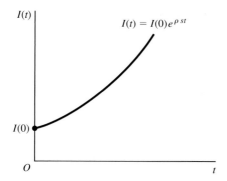

at the exponential rate of ρs, along a path such as illustrated in Fig. 14.6. Obviously, the larger the capacity-capital ratio or the marginal propensity to save, the larger the required rate of growth will be. But at any rate, once the values of ρ and s are known, the required growth path of investment becomes very rigidly set.

The Razor's Edge

It now becomes relevant to ask what will happen if the *actual* rate of growth of investment—call that rate r—differs from the *required* rate ρs.

Domar's approach is to define a *coefficient of utilization*

$$u = \lim_{t \to \infty} \frac{Y(t)}{\kappa(t)} \qquad [u = 1 \text{ means full utilization of capacity}]$$

and show that $u = r/\rho s$, so that $u \gtrless 1$ as $r \gtrless \rho s$. In other words, if there is a discrepancy between the actual and required rates ($r \neq \rho s$), we will find in the end (as $t \to \infty$) either a shortage of capacity ($u > 1$) or a surplus of capacity ($u < 1$), depending on whether r is greater or less than ρs.

We can show, however, that the conclusion about capacity shortage and surplus really applies at any time t, not only as $t \to \infty$. For a given growth rate r implies that

$$I(t) = I(0)e^{rt} \qquad \text{and} \qquad \frac{dI}{dt} = r I(0)e^{rt}$$

Therefore, by (14.13) and (14.14), we have

$$\frac{dY}{dt} = \frac{1}{s}\frac{dI}{dt} = \frac{r}{s}I(0)e^{rt}$$
$$\frac{d\kappa}{dt} = \rho I(t) = \rho I(0)e^{rt}$$

The ratio between these two derivatives,

$$\frac{dY/dt}{d\kappa/dt} = \frac{r}{\rho s}$$

should tell us the relative magnitudes of the demand-creating effect and the capacity-generating effect of investment at any time t, under the actual growth rate of r. If r (the actual rate) exceeds ρs (the required rate), then $dY/dt > d\kappa/dt$, and the demand effect will outstrip the capacity effect, causing a shortage of capacity. Conversely, if $r < \rho s$, there will be a deficiency in aggregate demand and, hence, a surplus of capacity.

The curious thing about this conclusion is that if investment actually grows at a *faster* rate than required ($r > \rho s$), the end result will be a *shortage* rather than a surplus of capacity. It is equally curious that if the actual growth of investment lags behind the required rate ($r < \rho s$), we will encounter a capacity *surplus* rather than a shortage. Indeed, because of such paradoxical results, if we now allow the entrepreneurs to adjust the actual growth rate r (hitherto taken to be a constant) according to the prevailing capacity situation, they will most certainly make the "wrong" kind of adjustment. In the case of $r > \rho s$, for instance, the emergent capacity shortage will motivate an even faster rate of investment. But this would mean an increase in r, instead of the reduction called for under the circumstances. Consequently, the discrepancy between the two rates of growth would be intensified rather than reduced.

The upshot is that, given the parametric constants ρ and s, the only way to avoid both shortage and surplus of productive capacity is to guide the investment flow ever so carefully along the equilibrium path with a growth rate $r^* = \rho s$. And, as we have shown, any deviation from such a "razor's edge" time path will bring about a persistent failure to satisfy the norm of full utilization which Domar envisaged in this model. This is perhaps not too cheerful a prospect to contemplate. Fortunately, more flexible results become possible when certain assumptions of the Domar model are modified, as we shall see from the growth model of Professor Solow, to be discussed in Chap. 15.

EXERCISE 14.6

1. How many factors of production are explicitly considered in the Domar model? What does this fact imply with regard to the capital-labor ratio in production?

2. We learned in Sec. 10.2 that the constant r in the exponential function Ae^{rt} represents the rate of growth of the function. Apply this to (14.16), and deduce (14.18) without going through integration.

3. Show that even if we let investment be negative in the equation $|I| = Ae^{\rho st}$, upon definitizing the arbitrary constant A we will still end up with the solution (14.18).

4. Show that the result in (14.18) can be obtained alternatively by finding—and equating—the *definite* integrals of both sides of (14.16),

$$\frac{1}{I}\frac{dI}{dt} = \rho s$$

with respect to the variable t, with limits of integration $t = 0$ and $t = t$. Remember that when we change the variable of integration from t to I, the limits of integration will change from $t = 0$ and $t = t$, respectively, to $I = I(0)$ and $I = I(t)$.

Chapter 15

Continuous Time: First-Order Differential Equations

In the Domar growth model, we have solved a simple differential equation by direct integration. For more complicated differential equations, there are various established methods of solution. Even in the latter cases, however, the fundamental idea underlying the methods of solution is still the techniques of integral calculus. For this reason, the solution to a differential equation is often referred to as the *integral* of that equation.

Only *first-order* differential equations will be discussed in the present chapter. In this context, the word *order* refers to the highest order of the derivatives (or differentials) appearing in the differential equation; thus a first-order differential equation can contain only the first derivative, say, dy/dt.

15.1 First-Order Linear Differential Equations with Constant Coefficient and Constant Term

The first derivative dy/dt is the only one that can appear in a first-order differential equation, but it may enter in various powers: dy/dt, $(dy/dt)^2$, or $(dy/dt)^3$. The highest power attained by the derivative in the equation is referred to as the *degree* of the differential equation. In case the derivative dy/dt appears only in the first degree, and so does the dependent variable y, and furthermore, no product of the form $y(dy/dt)$ occurs, then the equation is said to be *linear*. Thus a first-order linear differential equation will generally take the form[†]

$$\frac{dy}{dt} + u(t)y = w(t) \qquad \textbf{(15.1)}$$

[†] Note that the derivative term dy/dt in (15.1) has a unit coefficient. This is not to imply that it can never actually have a coefficient other than one, but when such a coefficient appears, we can always "normalize" the equation by dividing each term by the said coefficient. For this reason, the form given in (15.1) may nonetheless be regarded as a *general* representation.

475

where u and w are two functions of t, as is y. In contrast to dy/dt and y, however, no restriction whatsoever is placed on the independent variable t. Thus the functions u and w may very well represent such expressions as t^2 and e^t or some more complicated functions of t; on the other hand, u and w may also be constants.

This last point leads us to a further classification. When the function u (the coefficient of the dependent variable y) is a constant, and when the function w is a constant additive term, (15.1) reduces to the special case of a first-order linear differential equation with *constant coefficient and constant term*. In this section, we shall deal only with this simple variety of differential equations.

The Homogeneous Case

If u and w are constant functions and if w happens to be identically zero, (15.1) will become

$$\frac{dy}{dt} + ay = 0 \qquad\qquad \textbf{(15.2)}$$

where a is some constant. This differential equation is said to be *homogeneous* on account of the zero constant term (compare with homogeneous-equation systems). The defining characteristic of a homogeneous equation is that when all the variables (here, dy/dt and y) are multiplied by a given constant, the equation remains valid. This characteristic holds if the constant term is zero, but will be lost if the constant term is not zero.

Equation (15.2) can be written alternatively as

$$\frac{1}{y}\frac{dy}{dt} = -a \qquad\qquad \textbf{(15.2$'$)}$$

But you will recognize that the differential equation (14.16) we met in the Domar model is precisely of this form. Therefore, by analogy, we should be able to write the solution of (15.2) or (15.2$'$) immediately as follows:

$$y(t) = Ae^{-at} \qquad \text{[\textit{general} solution]} \qquad \textbf{(15.3)}$$

or

$$y(t) = y(0)e^{-at} \qquad \text{[\textit{definite} solution]} \qquad \textbf{(15.3$'$)}$$

In (15.3), there appears an arbitrary constant A; therefore it is a *general solution.* When any particular value is substituted for A, the solution becomes a *particular solution* of (15.2). There is an infinite number of particular solutions, one for each possible value of A, including the value $y(0)$. This latter value, however, has a special significance: $y(0)$ is the only value that can make the solution satisfy the initial condition. Since this represents the result of definitizing the arbitrary constant, we shall refer to (15.3$'$) as the *definite solution* of the differential equation (15.2) or (15.2$'$).

You should observe two things about the solution of a differential equation: (1) the solution is not a numerical value, but rather a function $y(t)$—a time path if t symbolizes time; and (2) the solution $y(t)$ is free of any derivative or differential expressions, so that as soon as a specific value of t is substituted into it, a corresponding value of y can be calculated directly.

The Nonhomogeneous Case

When a nonzero constant takes the place of the zero in (15.2), we have a *nonhomogeneous* linear differential equation

$$\frac{dy}{dt} + ay = b \qquad\qquad \textbf{(15.4)}$$

The solution of this equation will consist of the sum of two terms, one of which is called the *complementary function* (which we shall denote by y_c), and the other known as the *particular integral* (to be denoted by y_p). As will be shown, each of these has a significant economic interpretation. Here, we shall present only the method of solution; its rationale will become clear later.

Even though our objective is to solve the *non*homogeneous equation (15.4), frequently we shall have to refer to its homogeneous version, as shown in (15.2). For convenient reference, we call the latter the *reduced equation* of (15.4). The nonhomogeneous equation (15.4) itself can accordingly be referred to as the *complete equation*. It turns out that the complementary function y_c is nothing but the general solution of the reduced equation, whereas the particular integral y_p is simply *any* particular solution of the complete equation.

Our discussion of the homogeneous case has already given us the general solution of the reduced equation, and we may therefore write

$$y_c = Ae^{-at} \qquad \text{[by (15.3)]}$$

What about the particular integral? Since the particular integral is *any* particular solution of the complete equation, we can first try the simplest possible type of solution, namely, y being some constant ($y = k$). If y is a constant, then it follows that $dy/dt = 0$, and (15.4) will become $ay = b$, with the solution $y = b/a$. Therefore, the constant solution will work as long as $a \neq 0$. In that case, we have

$$y_p = \frac{b}{a} \qquad (a \neq 0)$$

The sum of the complementary function and the particular integral then constitutes the general solution of the complete equation (15.4):

$$y(t) = y_c + y_p = Ae^{-at} + \frac{b}{a} \qquad \text{[general solution, case of } a \neq 0] \quad \textbf{(15.5)}$$

What makes this a general solution is the presence of the arbitrary constant A. We may, of course, definitize this constant by means of an initial condition. Let us say that y takes the value $y(0)$ when $t = 0$. Then, by setting $t = 0$ in (15.5), we find that

$$y(0) = A + \frac{b}{a} \qquad \text{and} \qquad A = y(0) - \frac{b}{a}$$

Thus we can rewrite (15.5) into

$$y(t) = \left[y(0) - \frac{b}{a} \right] e^{-at} + \frac{b}{a} \qquad \text{[definite solution, case of } a \neq 0] \quad \textbf{(15.5')}$$

It should be noted that the use of the initial condition to definitize the arbitrary constant is—and should be—undertaken as the *final* step, after we have found the general solution to the complete equation. Since the values of both y_c and y_p are related to the value of $y(0)$, both of these must be taken into account in definitizing the constant A.

Example 1   Solve the equation $dy/dt + 2y = 6$, with the initial condition $y(0) = 10$. Here, we have $a = 2$ and $b = 6$; thus, by (15.5'), the solution is

$$y(t) = (10 - 3)e^{-2t} + 3 = 7e^{-2t} + 3$$

Example 2

Solve the equation $dy/dt + 4y = 0$, with the initial condition $y(0) = 1$. Since $a = 4$ and $b = 0$, we have

$$y(t) = (1 - 0)e^{-4t} + 0 = e^{-4t}$$

The same answer could have been obtained from (15.3′), the formula for the homogeneous case. The homogeneous equation (15.2) is merely a special case of the nonhomogeneous equation (15.4) when $b = 0$. Consequently, the formula (15.3′) is also a special case of formula (15.5′) under the circumstance that $b = 0$.

What if $a = 0$, so that the solution in (15.5′) is undefined? In that case, the differential equation is of the extremely simple form

$$\frac{dy}{dt} = b \qquad \qquad \textbf{(15.6)}$$

By straight integration, its general solution can be readily found to be

$$y(t) = bt + c \qquad \qquad \textbf{(15.7)}$$

where c is an arbitrary constant. The two component terms in (15.7) can, in fact, again be identified as the complementary function and the particular integral of the given differential equation, respectively. Since $a = 0$, the complementary function can be expressed simply as

$$y_c = Ae^{-at} = Ae^0 = A \qquad (A = \text{an arbitrary constant})$$

As to the particular integral, the fact that the constant solution $y = k$ fails to work in the present case of $a = 0$ suggests that we should try instead a *nonconstant* solution. Let us consider the simplest possible type of the latter, namely, $y = kt$. If $y = kt$, then $dy/dt = k$, and the complete equation (15.6) will reduce to $k = b$, so that we may write

$$y_p = bt \qquad (a = 0)$$

Our new trial solution indeed works! The general solution of (15.6) is therefore

$$y(t) = y_c + y_p = A + bt \qquad \text{[general solution, case of } a = 0] \quad \textbf{(15.7′)}$$

which is identical with the result in (15.7), because c and A are but alternative notations for an arbitrary constant. Note, however, that in the present case, y_c is a constant whereas y_p is a function of time—the exact opposite of the situation in (15.5).

By definitizing the arbitrary constant, we find the definite solution to be

$$y(t) = y(0) + bt \qquad \text{[definite solution, case of } a = 0] \quad \textbf{(15.7″)}$$

Example 3

Solve the equation $dy/dt = 2$, with the initial condition $y(0) = 5$. The solution is, by (15.7″),

$$y(t) = 5 + 2t$$

Verification of the Solution

It is true of all solutions of differential equations that their validity can always be checked by differentiation.

If we try that on the solution (15.5′), we can obtain the derivative

$$\frac{dy}{dt} = -a \left[y(0) - \frac{b}{a} \right] e^{-at}$$

When this expression for dy/dt and the expression for $y(t)$ as shown in (15.5′) are substituted into the left side of the differential equation (15.4), that side should reduce exactly to the value of the constant term b on the right side of (15.4) if the solution is correct. Performing this substitution, we indeed find that

$$-a \left[y(0) - \frac{b}{a} \right] e^{-at} + a \left\{ \left[y(0) - \frac{b}{a} \right] e^{-at} + \frac{b}{a} \right\} = b$$

Thus our solution is correct, provided it also satisfies the initial condition. To check the latter, let us set $t = 0$ in the solution (15.5′). Since the result

$$y(0) = \left[y(0) - \frac{b}{a} \right] + \frac{b}{a} = y(0)$$

is an identity, the initial condition is indeed satisfied.

It is recommended that, as a final step in the process of solving a differential equation, you make it a habit to check the validity of your answer by making sure (1) that the derivative of the time path $y(t)$ is consistent with the given differential equation and (2) that the definite solution satisfies the initial condition.

EXERCISE 15.1

1. Find y_c, y_p, the general solution, and the definite solution, given:

   (a) $\dfrac{dy}{dt} + 4y = 12;\ y(0) = 2$ (c) $\dfrac{dy}{dt} + 10y = 15;\ y(0) = 0$

   (b) $\dfrac{dy}{dt} - 2y = 0;\ y(0) = 9$ (d) $2\dfrac{dy}{dt} + 4y = 6;\ y(0) = 1\frac{1}{2}$

2. Check the validity of your answers to Prob. 1.
3. Find the solution of each of the following by using an appropriate formula developed in the text:

   (a) $\dfrac{dy}{dt} + y = 4;\ y(0) = 0$ (d) $\dfrac{dy}{dt} + 3y = 2;\ y(0) = 4$

   (b) $\dfrac{dy}{dt} = 23;\ y(0) = 1$ (e) $\dfrac{dy}{dt} - 7y = 7;\ y(0) = 7$

   (c) $\dfrac{dy}{dt} - 5y = 0;\ y(0) = 6$ (f) $3\dfrac{dy}{dt} + 6y = 5;\ y(0) = 0$

4. Check the validity of your answers to Prob. 3.

15.2   Dynamics of Market Price

In the (macro) Domar growth model, we found an application of the *homogeneous* case of linear differential equations of the first order. To illustrate the *nonhomogeneous* case, let us present a (micro) dynamic model of the market.

The Framework

Suppose that, for a particular commodity, the demand and supply functions are as follows:

$$Q_d = \alpha - \beta P \qquad (\alpha, \beta > 0)$$
$$Q_s = -\gamma + \delta P \qquad (\gamma, \delta > 0)$$

$$(15.8)$$

Then, according to (3.4), the equilibrium price should be[†]

$$P^* = \frac{\alpha + \gamma}{\beta + \delta} \qquad (= \text{some positive constant}) \qquad (15.9)$$

If it happens that the initial price $P(0)$ is precisely at the level of P^*, the market will clearly be in equilibrium already, and no dynamic analysis will be needed. In the more interesting case of $P(0) \neq P^*$, however, P^* is attainable (if ever) only after a due process of adjustment, during which not only will price change over time but Q_d and Q_s, being functions of P, must change over time as well. In this light, then, the price and quantity variables can *all* be taken to be *functions of time*.

Our dynamic question is this: Given sufficient time for the adjustment process to work itself out, does it tend to bring price to the equilibrium level P^*? That is, does the time path $P(t)$ tend to converge to P^*, as $t \to \infty$?

The Time Path

To answer this question, we must first find the time path $P(t)$. But that, in turn, requires a specific pattern of price change to be prescribed first. In general, price changes are governed by the relative strength of the demand and supply forces in the market. Let us assume, for the sake of simplicity, that the rate of price change (with respect to time) at any moment is always directly proportional to the *excess demand* $(Q_d - Q_s)$ prevailing at that moment. Such a pattern of change can be expressed symbolically as

$$\frac{dP}{dt} = j(Q_d - Q_s) \qquad (j > 0) \qquad (15.10)$$

where j represents a (constant) *adjustment coefficient*. With this pattern of change, we can have $dP/dt = 0$ if and only if $Q_d = Q_s$. In this connection, it may be instructive to note two senses of the term *equilibrium price*: the intertemporal sense (P being constant over time) and the market-clearing sense (the equilibrium price being one that equates Q_d and Q_s). In the present model, the two senses happen to coincide with each other, but this may not be true of all models.

By virtue of the demand and supply functions in (15.8), we can express (15.10) specifically in the form

$$\frac{dP}{dt} = j(\alpha - \beta P + \gamma - \delta P) = j(\alpha + \gamma) - j(\beta + \delta)P$$

or

$$\frac{dP}{dt} + j(\beta + \delta)P = j(\alpha + \gamma) \qquad (15.10')$$

[†] We have switched from the symbols (a, b, c, d) of (3.4) to $(\alpha, \beta, \gamma, \delta)$ here to avoid any possible confusion with the use of a and b as parameters in the differential equation (15.4) which we shall presently apply to the market model.

Since this is precisely in the form of the differential equation (15.4), and since the coefficient of P is nonzero, we can apply the solution formula (15.5′) and write the solution—the time path of price—as

$$P(t) = \left[P(0) - \frac{\alpha + \gamma}{\beta + \delta}\right] e^{-j(\beta + \delta)t} + \frac{\alpha + \gamma}{\beta + \delta}$$

$$= [P(0) - P^*]e^{-kt} + P^* \qquad \text{[by (15.9); } k \equiv j(\beta + \delta)] \qquad \textbf{(15.11)}$$

The Dynamic Stability of Equilibrium

In the end, the question originally posed, namely, whether $P(t) \to P^*$ as $t \to \infty$, amounts to the question of whether the first term on the right of (15.11) will tend to zero as $t \to \infty$. Since $P(0)$ and P^* are both constant, the key factor will be the exponential expression e^{-kt}. In view of the fact that $k > 0$, that expression does tend to zero as $t \to \infty$. Consequently, on the assumptions of our model, the time path will indeed lead the price toward the equilibrium position. In a situation of this sort, where the time path of the relevant variable $P(t)$ *converges* to the level P^*—interpreted here in its role as the intertemporal (rather than market-clearing) equilibrium—the equilibrium is said to be *dynamically stable.*

The concept of dynamic stability is an important one. Let us examine it further by a more detailed analysis of (15.11). Depending on the relative magnitudes of $P(0)$ and P^*, the solution (15.11) really encompasses three possible cases. The first is $P(0) = P^*$, which implies $P(t) = P^*$. In that event, the time path of price can be drawn as the horizontal straight line in Fig. 15.1. As mentioned earlier, the attainment of equilibrium is in this case a fait accompli. Second, we may have $P(0) > P^*$. In this case, the first term on the right of (15.11) is positive, but it will decrease as the increase in t lowers the value of e^{-kt}. Thus the time path will approach the equilibrium level P^* from above, as illustrated by the top curve in Fig. 15.1. Third, in the opposite case of $P(0) < P^*$, the equilibrium level P^* will be approached from below, as illustrated by the bottom curve in the same figure. In general, to have dynamic stability, the *deviation* of the time path from equilibrium must either be identically zero (as in case 1) or steadily decrease with time (as in cases 2 and 3).

A comparison of (15.11) with (15.5′) tells us that the P^* term, the counterpart of b/a, is nothing but the particular integral y_p, whereas the exponential term is the (definitized) complementary function y_c. Thus, we now have an economic interpretation for y_c and y_p; y_p represents the *intertemporal equilibrium level* of the relevant variable, and y_c is the *deviation from equilibrium.* Dynamic stability requires the asymptotic vanishing of the complementary function as t becomes infinite.

FIGURE 15.1

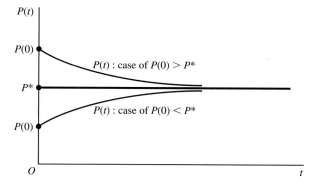

In this model, the particular integral is a constant, so we have a *stationary equilibrium* in the intertemporal sense, represented by P^*. If the particular integral is nonconstant, as in (15.7′), on the other hand, we may interpret it as a *moving equilibrium*.

An Alternative Use of the Model

What we have done in the preceding is to analyze the dynamic stability of equilibrium (the convergence of the time path), given certain sign specifications for the parameters. An alternative type of inquiry is: In order to ensure dynamic stability, what specific restrictions must be imposed upon the parameters?

The answer to that is contained in the solution (15.11). If we allow $P(0) \neq P^*$, we see that the first (y_c) term in (15.11) will tend to zero as $t \to \infty$ if and only if $k > 0$—that is, if and only if

$$j(\beta + \delta) > 0$$

Thus, we can take this last inequality as the required restriction on the parameters j (the adjustment coefficient of price), β (the negative of the slope of the demand curve, plotted with Q on the *vertical* axis), and δ (the slope of the supply curve, plotted similarly).

In case the price adjustment is of the "normal" type, with $j > 0$, so that excess demand drives price up rather than down, then this restriction becomes merely $(\beta + \delta) > 0$ or, equivalently,

$$\delta > -\beta$$

To have dynamic stability in that event, the slope of the supply must exceed the slope of the demand. When both demand and supply are normally sloped $(-\beta < 0, \ \delta > 0)$, as in (15.8), this requirement is obviously met. But even if one of the curves is sloped "perversely," the condition may still be fulfilled, such as when $\delta = 1$ and $-\beta = 1/2$ (positively sloped demand). The latter situation is illustrated in Fig. 15.2, where the equilibrium price P^* is, as usual, determined by the point of intersection of the two curves. If the initial price happens to be at P_1, then Q_d (distance $P_1 G$) will exceed Q_s (distance $P_1 F$), and the excess demand (FG) will drive price up. On the other hand, if price is initially at P_2, then

FIGURE 15.2

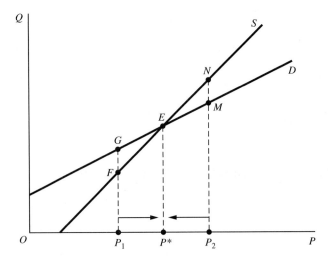

there will be a *negative* excess demand *MN*, which will drive the price down. As the two arrows in the figure show, therefore, the price adjustment in this case will be *toward* the equilibrium, no matter which side of P^* we start from. We should emphasize, however, that while these arrows can display the direction, they are incapable of indicating the magnitude of change. Thus Fig. 15.2 is basically static, not dynamic, in nature, and can serve only to illustrate, not to replace, the dynamic analysis presented.

EXERCISE 15.2

1. If both the demand and supply in Fig. 15.2 are negatively sloped instead, which curve should be steeper in order to have dynamic stability? Does your answer conform to the criterion $\delta > -\beta$?

2. Show that (15.10′) can be rewritten as $dP/dt + k(P - P^*) = 0$. If we let $P - P^* \equiv \Delta$ (signifying deviation), so that $d\Delta/dt = dP/dt$, the differential equation can be further rewritten as

$$\frac{d\Delta}{dt} + k\Delta = 0$$

Find the time path $\Delta(t)$, and discuss the condition for dynamic stability.

3. The dynamic market model discussed in this section is closely patterned after the static one in Sec. 3.2. What specific new feature is responsible for transforming the static model into a dynamic one?

4. Let the demand and supply be

$$Q_d = \alpha - \beta P + \sigma \frac{dP}{dt} \qquad Q_s = -\gamma + \delta P \qquad (\alpha, \beta, \gamma, \delta > 0)$$

   (a) Assuming that the rate of change of price over time is directly proportional to the excess demand, find the time path $P(t)$ (general solution).

   (b) What is the intertemporal equilibrium price? What is the market-clearing equilibrium price?

   (c) What restriction on the parameter σ would ensure dynamic stability?

5. Let the demand and supply be

$$Q_d = \alpha - \beta P - \eta \frac{dP}{dt} \qquad Q_s = \delta P \qquad (\alpha, \beta, \eta, \delta > 0)$$

   (a) Assuming that the market is cleared at every point of time, find the time path $P(t)$ (general solution).

   (b) Does this market have a dynamically stable intertemporal equilibrium price?

   (c) The assumption of the present model that $Q_d = Q_s$ for all t is identical with that of the static market model in Sec. 3.2. Nevertheless, we still have a dynamic model here. How come?

15.3 Variable Coefficient and Variable Term

In the more general case of a first-order linear differential equation

$$\frac{dy}{dt} + u(t)y = w(t) \tag{15.12}$$

$u(t)$ and $w(t)$ represent a variable coefficient and a variable term, respectively. How do we find the time path $y(t)$ in this case?

The Homogeneous Case

For the homogeneous case, where $w(t) = 0$, the solution is still easy to obtain. Since the differential equation is in the form

$$\frac{dy}{dt} + u(t)y = 0 \qquad \text{or} \qquad \frac{1}{y}\frac{dy}{dt} = -u(t) \qquad \textbf{(15.13)}$$

we have, by integrating both sides in turn with respect to t,

$$\text{Left side} = \int \frac{1}{y}\frac{dy}{dt}\,dt = \int \frac{dy}{y} = \ln y + c \qquad \text{(assuming } y > 0)$$

$$\text{Right side} = \int -u(t)\,dt = -\int u(t)\,dt$$

In the latter, the integration process cannot be carried further because $u(t)$ has not been given a specific form; thus we have to settle for just a general integral expression. When the two sides are equated, the result is

$$\ln y = -c - \int u(t)\,dt$$

Then the desired y path can be obtained by taking the antilog of $\ln y$:

$$y(t) = e^{\ln y} = e^{-c}e^{-\int u(t)\,dt} = Ae^{-\int u(t)\,dt} \qquad \text{where } A \equiv e^{-c} \quad \textbf{(15.14)}$$

This is the general solution of the differential equation (15.13).

To highlight the variable nature of the coefficient $u(t)$, we have so far explicitly written out the argument t. For notational simplicity, however, we shall from here on omit the argument and shorten $u(t)$ to u.

As compared with the general solution (15.3) for the constant-coefficient case, the only modification in (15.14) is the replacement of the e^{-at} expression by the more complicated expression $e^{-\int u\,dt}$. The rationale behind this change can be better understood if we interpret the at term in e^{-at} as an integral: $\int a\,dt = at$ (plus a constant which can be absorbed into the A term, since e raised to a constant power is again a constant). In this light, the difference between the two general solutions in fact turns into a similarity. For in both cases we are taking the coefficient of the y term in the differential equation—a constant term a in one case, and a variable term u in the other—and integrating that with respect to t, and then taking the negative of the resulting integral as the exponent of e.

Once the general solution is obtained, it is a relatively simple matter to get the definite solution with the help of an appropriate initial condition.

| **Example 1** | Find the general solution of the equation $\dfrac{dy}{dt} + 3t^2 y = 0$. Here we have $u = 3t^2$, and $\int u\,dt = \int 3t^2\,dt = t^3 + c$. Therefore, by (15.14), we may write the solution as |

$$y(t) = Ae^{-(t^3+c)} = Ae^{-t^3}e^{-c} = Be^{-t^3} \qquad \text{where } B \equiv Ae^{-c}$$

Observe that if we had omitted the constant of integration c, we would have lost no information, because then we would have obtained $y(t) = Ae^{-t^3}$, which is really the identical solution since A and B both represent arbitrary constants. In other words, the expression e^{-c}, where the constant c makes its only appearance, can always be subsumed under the other constant A.

The Nonhomogeneous Case

For the nonhomogeneous case, where $w(t) \neq 0$, the solution is not as easy to obtain. We shall try to find that solution via the concept of exact differential equations, to be discussed in Sec. 15.4. It does no harm, however, to state the result here first: Given the differential equation (15.12), the general solution is

$$y(t) = e^{-\int u\,dt}\left(A + \int we^{\int u\,dt}\,dt\right) \qquad \textbf{(15.15)}$$

where A is an arbitrary constant that can be definitized if we have an appropriate initial condition.

It is of interest that this general solution, like the solution in the constant-coefficient constant-term case, again consists of two additive components. Furthermore, one of these two, $Ae^{-\int u\,dt}$, is nothing but the general solution of the reduced (homogeneous) equation, derived earlier in (15.14), and is therefore in the nature of a complementary function.

Example 2   Find the general solution of the equation $\dfrac{dy}{dt} + 2ty = t$. Here we have

$$u = 2t \qquad w = t \qquad \text{and} \qquad \int u\,dt = t^2 + k \qquad (k \text{ arbitrary})$$

Thus, by (15.15), we have

$$y(t) = e^{-(t^2+k)}\left(A + \int te^{t^2+k}\,dt\right)$$

$$= e^{-t^2}e^{-k}\left(A + e^k\int te^{t^2}\,dt\right)$$

$$= Ae^{-k}e^{-t^2} + e^{-t^2}\left(\frac{1}{2}e^{t^2} + c\right) \qquad [e^{-k}e^k = 1]$$

$$= (Ae^{-k} + c)e^{-t^2} + \frac{1}{2}$$

$$= Be^{-t^2} + \frac{1}{2} \qquad \text{where } B \equiv Ae^{-k} + c \text{ is arbitrary}$$

The validity of this solution can again be checked by differentiation.

It is interesting to note that, in this example, we could again have omitted the constant of integration k, as well as the constant of integration c, without affecting the final outcome. This is because both k and c may be subsumed under the arbitrary constant B in the final solution. You are urged to try out the simpler process of applying (15.15) without using the constants k and c, and verify that the same solution will emerge.

Example 3   Solve the equation $\dfrac{dy}{dt} + 4ty = 4t$. This time we shall omit the constants of integration. Since

$$u = 4t \qquad w = 4t \qquad \text{and} \qquad \int u\,dt = 2t^2 \qquad [\text{constant omitted}]$$

the general solution is, by (15.15),

$$y(t) = e^{-2t^2}\left(A + \int 4te^{2t^2}\,dt\right) = e^{-2t^2}\left(A + e^{2t^2}\right) \qquad [\text{constant omitted}]$$

$$= Ae^{-2t^2} + 1$$

As may be expected, the omission of the constants of integration serves to simplify the procedure substantially.

The differential equation $\dfrac{dy}{dt} + uy = w$ in (15.12) is more general than the equation $\dfrac{dy}{dt} + ay = b$ in (15.4), since u and w are not necessarily constant, as are a and b. Accordingly, solution formula (15.15) is also more general than solution formula (15.5). In fact, when we set $u = a$ and $w = b$, (15.15) should reduce to (15.5). This is indeed the case. For when we have

$$u = a \qquad w = b \qquad \text{and} \qquad \int u\, dt = at \qquad \text{[constant omitted]}$$

then (15.15) becomes

$$y(t) = e^{-at}\left(A + \int be^{at}\, dt\right) = e^{-at}\left(A + \frac{b}{a}e^{at}\right) \qquad \text{[constant omitted]}$$

$$= Ae^{-at} + \frac{b}{a}$$

which is identical with (15.5).

EXERCISE 15.3

Solve the following first-order linear differential equations; if an initial condition is given, definitize the arbitrary constant:

1. $\dfrac{dy}{dt} + 5y = 15$

2. $\dfrac{dy}{dt} + 2ty = 0$

3. $\dfrac{dy}{dt} + 2ty = t;\ y(0) = \dfrac{3}{2}$

4. $\dfrac{dy}{dt} + t^2 y = 5t^2;\ y(0) = 6$

5. $2\dfrac{dy}{dt} + 12y + 2e^t = 0;\ y(0) = \dfrac{6}{7}$

6. $\dfrac{dy}{dt} + y = t$

15.4 Exact Differential Equations

We shall now introduce the concept of exact differential equations and use the solution method pertaining thereto to obtain the solution formula (15.15) previously cited for the differential equation (15.12). Even though our immediate purpose is to use it to solve a *linear* differential equation, an exact differential equation can be either linear or nonlinear by itself.

Exact Differential Equations

Given a function of two variables $F(y, t)$, its total differential is

$$dF(y, t) = \frac{\partial F}{\partial y}\, dy + \frac{\partial F}{\partial t}\, dt$$

When this differential is set equal to zero, the resulting equation

$$\frac{\partial F}{\partial y} dy + \frac{\partial F}{\partial t} dt = 0$$

is known as an *exact differential equation,* because its left side is exactly the differential of the function $F(y, t)$. For instance, given

$$F(y, t) = y^2 t + k \qquad (k \text{ a constant})$$

the total differential is

$$dF = 2yt \, dy + y^2 \, dt$$

thus the differential equation

$$2yt \, dy + y^2 \, dt = 0 \qquad \text{or} \qquad \frac{dy}{dt} + \frac{y^2}{2yt} = 0 \qquad \textbf{(15.16)}$$

is exact.

In general, a differential equation

$$M \, dy + N \, dt = 0 \qquad \textbf{(15.17)}$$

is exact if and only if there exists a function $F(y, t)$ such that $M = \partial F/\partial y$ and $N = \partial F/\partial t$. By Young's theorem, which states that $\partial^2 F/\partial t \, \partial y = \partial^2 F/\partial y \, \partial t$, however, we can also state that (15.17) is exact if and only if

$$\frac{\partial M}{\partial t} = \frac{\partial N}{\partial y} \qquad \textbf{(15.18)}$$

This last equation gives us a simple test for the exactness of a differential equation. Applied to (15.16), where $M = 2yt$ and $N = y^2$, this test yields $\partial M/\partial t = 2y = \partial N/\partial y$; thus the exactness of the said differential equation is duly verified.

Note that no restrictions have been placed on the terms M and N with regard to the manner in which the variable y occurs. Thus an exact differential equation may very well be *nonlinear* (in y). Nevertheless, it will always be of the first order and the first degree.

Being exact, the differential equation merely says

$$dF(y, t) = 0$$

Thus its general solution should clearly be in the form

$$F(y, t) = c$$

To solve an exact differential equation is basically, therefore, to search for the (primitive) function $F(y, t)$ and then set it equal to an arbitrary constant. Let us outline a method of finding this for the equation $M \, dy + N \, dt = 0$.

Method of Solution

To begin with, since $M = \partial F/\partial y$, the function F must contain the integral of M with respect to the variable y; hence we can write out a preliminary result—in a yet indeterminate form—as follows:

$$F(y, t) = \int M \, dy + \psi(t) \qquad \textbf{(15.19)}$$

Here M, a *partial* derivative, is to be integrated with respect to y only; that is, t is to be treated as a constant in the integration process, just as it was treated as a constant in the partial differentiation of $F(y, t)$ that resulted in $M = \partial F/\partial y$.[†] Since, in differentiating $F(y, t)$ partially with respect to y, any additive term containing only the variable t and/or some constants (but with no y) would drop out, we must now take care to reinstate such terms in the integration process. This explains why we have introduced in (15.19) a general term $\psi(t)$, which, though not exactly the same as a constant of integration, has a precisely identical role to play as the latter. It is relatively easy to get $\int M \, dy$; but how do we pin down the exact form of this $\psi(t)$ term?

The trick is to utilize the fact that $N = \partial F/\partial t$. But the procedure is best explained with the help of specific examples.

Example 1

Solve the exact differential equation

$$2yt \, dy + y^2 \, dt = 0 \qquad \text{[reproduced from (15.16)]}$$

In this equation, we have

$$M = 2yt \qquad \text{and} \qquad N = y^2$$

STEP i   By (15.19), we can first write the preliminary result

$$F(y, t) = \int 2yt \, dy + \psi(t) = y^2 t + \psi(t)$$

Note that we have omitted the constant of integration, because it can automatically be merged into the expression $\psi(t)$.

STEP ii   If we differentiate the result from Step i partially with respect to t, we can obtain

$$\frac{\partial F}{\partial t} = y^2 + \psi'(t)$$

But since $N = \partial F/\partial t$, we can equate $N = y^2$ and $\partial F/\partial t = y^2 + \psi'(t)$, to get

$$\psi'(t) = 0$$

STEP iii   Integration of the last result gives us

$$\psi(t) = \int \psi'(t) \, dt = \int 0 \, dt = k$$

and now we have a specific form of $\psi(t)$. It happens in the present case that $\psi(t)$ is simply a constant; more generally, it can be a nonconstant function of t.

STEP iv   The results of Steps i and iii can be combined to yield

$$F(y, t) = y^2 t + k$$

The solution of the exact differential equation should then be $F(y, t) = c$. But since the constant k can be merged into c, we may write the solution simply as

$$y^2 t = c \qquad \text{or} \qquad y(t) = ct^{-1/2}$$

where c is arbitrary.

[†] Some writers employ the operator symbol $\int (\cdots) \, \partial y$ to emphasize that the integration is with respect to y only. We shall still use the symbol $\int (\cdots) \, dy$ here, since there is little possibility of confusion.

Example 2

Solve the equation $(t + 2y)\, dy + (y + 3t^2)\, dt = 0$. First let us check whether this is an exact differential equation. Setting $M = t + 2y$ and $N = y + 3t^2$, we find that $\partial M/\partial t = 1 = \partial N/\partial y$. Thus the equation passes the exactness test. To find its solution, we again follow the procedure outlined in Example 1.

STEP i Apply (15.19) and write

$$F(y, t) = \int (t + 2y)\, dy + \psi(t) = yt + y^2 + \psi(t) \qquad \text{[constant merged into } \psi(t)]$$

STEP ii Differentiate this result with respect to t, to get

$$\frac{\partial F}{\partial t} = y + \psi'(t)$$

Then, equating this to $N = y + 3t^2$, we find that

$$\psi'(t) = 3t^2$$

STEP iii Integrate this last result to get

$$\psi(t) = \int 3t^2\, dt = t^3 \qquad \text{[constant may be omitted]}$$

STEP iv Combine the results of Steps i and iii to get the complete form of the function $F(y, t)$:

$$F(y, t) = yt + y^2 + t^3$$

which implies that the solution of the given differential equation is

$$yt + y^2 + t^3 = c$$

You should verify that setting the total differential of this equation equal to zero will indeed produce the given differential equation.

   This four-step procedure can be used to solve any exact differential equation. Interestingly, it may even be applicable when the given equation is *not* exact. To see this, however, we must first introduce the concept of integrating factor.

Integrating Factor

Sometimes an inexact differential equation can be made exact by multiplying every term of the equation by a particular common factor. Such a factor is called an *integrating factor.*

Example 3

The differential equation

$$2t\, dy + y\, dt = 0$$

is not exact, because it does not satisfy (15.18):

$$\frac{\partial M}{\partial t} = \frac{\partial}{\partial t}(2t) = 2 \neq \frac{\partial N}{\partial y} = \frac{\partial}{\partial y}(y) = 1$$

However, if we multiply each term by y, the given equation will turn into (15.16), which has been established to be exact. Thus y is an integrating factor for the differential equation in the present example.

When an integrating factor can be found for an inexact differential equation, it is always possible to render it exact, and then the four-step solution procedure can be readily put to use.

Solution of First-Order Linear Differential Equations

The general first-order linear differential equation

$$\frac{dy}{dt} + uy = w$$

which, in the format of (15.17), can be expressed as

$$dy + (uy - w)\, dt = 0 \qquad \textbf{(15.20)}$$

has the integrating factor

$$e^{\int u\, dt} \equiv \exp\left(\int u\, dt\right)$$

This integrating factor, whose form is by no means intuitively obvious, can be "discovered" as follows. Let I be the (yet unknown) integrating factor. Multiplication of (15.20) through by I should convert it into an exact differential equation

$$\underbrace{I}_{M}\, dy + \underbrace{I(uy - w)}_{N}\, dt = 0 \qquad \textbf{(15.20$'$)}$$

The exactness test dictates that $\partial M/\partial t = \partial N/\partial y$. Visual inspection of the M and N expressions suggests that, since M consists of I only, and since u and w are functions of t alone, the exactness test will reduce to a very simple condition if I is also a function of t alone. For then the test $\partial M/\partial t = \partial N/\partial y$ becomes

$$\frac{dI}{dt} = Iu \qquad \text{or} \qquad \frac{dI/dt}{I} = u$$

Thus the special form $I = I(t)$ can indeed work, provided it has a rate of growth equal to u, or more explicitly, $u(t)$. Accordingly, $I(t)$ should take the specific form

$$I(t) = Ae^{\int u\, dt} \qquad \text{[cf. (15.13) and (15.14)]}$$

As can be easily verified, however, the constant A can be set equal to 1 without affecting the ability of $I(t)$ to meet the exactness test. Thus we can use the simpler form $e^{\int u\, dt}$ as the integrating factor.

Substitution of this integrating factor into (15.20$'$) yields the exact differential equation

$$e^{\int u\, dt}\, dy + e^{\int u\, dt}(uy - w)\, dt = 0 \qquad \textbf{(15.20$''$)}$$

which can then be solved by the four-step procedure.

STEP i First, we apply (15.19) to obtain

$$F(y, t) = \int e^{\int u\, dt}\, dy + \psi(t) = ye^{\int u\, dt} + \psi(t)$$

The result of integration emerges in this simple form because the integrand is independent of the variable y.

STEP ii Next, we differentiate the result from Step i with respect to t, to get

$$\frac{\partial F}{\partial t} = yue^{\int u\,dt} + \psi'(t) \qquad \text{[chain rule]}$$

And, since this can be equated to $N = e^{\int u\,dt}(uy - w)$, we have

$$\psi'(t) = -we^{\int u\,dt}$$

STEP iii Straight integration now yields

$$\psi(t) = -\int we^{\int u\,dt}\,dt$$

Inasmuch as the functions $u = u(t)$ and $w = w(t)$ have not been given specific forms, nothing further can be done about this integral, and we must be contented with this rather general expression for $\psi(t)$.

STEP iv Substituting this $\psi(t)$ expression into the result of Step i, we find that

$$F(y, t) = ye^{\int u\,dt} - \int we^{\int u\,dt}\,dt$$

So the general solution of the exact differential equation (15.20″)—and of the equivalent, though inexact, first-order linear differential equation (15.20)—is

$$ye^{\int u\,dt} - \int we^{\int u\,dt}\,dt = c$$

Upon rearrangement and substitution of the (arbitrary constant) symbol c by A, this can be written as

$$y(t) = e^{-\int u\,dt}\left(A + \int we^{\int u\,dt}\,dt\right) \qquad\qquad \textbf{(15.21)}$$

which is exactly the result given earlier in (15.15).

EXERCISE 15.4

1. Verify that each of the following differential equations is exact, and solve by the four-step procedure:
   (a) $2yt^3\,dy + 3y^2t^2\,dt = 0$
   (b) $3y^2t\,dy + (y^3 + 2t)\,dt = 0$
   (c) $t(1 + 2y)\,dy + y(1 + y)\,dt = 0$
   (d) $\dfrac{dy}{dt} + \dfrac{2y^4t + 3t^2}{4y^3t^2} = 0$ \qquad [*Hint:* First convert to the form of (15.17).]

2. Are the following differential equations exact? If not, try t, y, and y^2 as possible integrating factors.
   (a) $2(t^3 + 1)\,dy + 3yt^2\,dt = 0$
   (b) $4y^3t\,dy + (2y^4 + 3t)\,dt = 0$

3. By applying the four-step procedure to the general exact differential equation $M\,dy + N\,dt = 0$, derive the following formula for the general solution of an exact differential equation:

$$\int M\,dy + \int N\,dt - \int \left(\frac{\partial}{\partial t}\int M\,dy\right)dt = c$$

15.5 Nonlinear Differential Equations of the First Order and First Degree

In a *linear* differential equation, we restrict to the *first degree* not only the derivative dy/dt, but also the dependent variable y, and we do not allow the product $y(dy/dt)$ to appear. When y appears in a power higher than one, the equation becomes *nonlinear* even if it only contains the derivative dy/dt in the first degree. In general, an equation in the form

$$f(y, t)\, dy + g(y, t)\, dt = 0 \qquad\qquad \textbf{(15.22)}$$

or

$$\frac{dy}{dt} = h(y, t) \qquad\qquad \textbf{(15.22')}$$

where there is no restriction on the powers of y and t, constitutes a first-order first-degree nonlinear differential equation because dy/dt is a first-order derivative in the first power. Certain varieties of such equations can be solved with relative ease by more or less routine procedures. We shall briefly discuss three cases.

Exact Differential Equations

The first is the now-familiar case of exact differential equations. As was pointed out earlier, the y variable can appear in an exact equation in a high power, as in (15.16)—$2yt\, dy + y^2\, dt = 0$—which you should compare with (15.22). True, the cancellation of the common factor y from both terms on the left will reduce the equation to a linear form, but the exactness property will be lost in that event. As an *exact* differential equation, therefore, it must be regarded as nonlinear.

Since the solution method for exact differential equations has already been discussed, no further comment is necessary here.

Separable Variables

The differential equation in (15.22)

$$f(y, t)\, dy + g(y, t)\, dt = 0$$

may happen to possess the convenient property that the function f is in the variable y alone, while the function g involves only the variable t, so that the equation reduces to the special form

$$f(y)\, dy + g(t)\, dt = 0 \qquad\qquad \textbf{(15.23)}$$

In such an event, the variables are said to be *separable,* because the terms involving y—consolidated into $f(y)$—can be mathematically separated from the terms involving t, which are collected under $g(t)$. To solve this special type of equation, only simple integration techniques are required.

Example 1 Solve the equation $3y^2\, dy - t\, dt = 0$. First let us rewrite the equation as

$$3y^2\, dy = t\, dt$$

Integrating the two sides (each of which is a differential) and equating the results, we get

$$\int 3y^2\, dy = \int t\, dt \qquad \text{or} \qquad y^3 + c_1 = \frac{1}{2}t^2 + c_2$$

Thus the general solution can be written as

$$y^3 = \frac{1}{2}t^2 + c \quad \text{or} \quad y(t) = \left(\frac{1}{2}t^2 + c\right)^{1/3}$$

The notable point here is that the integration of each term is performed with respect to a different variable; it is this which makes the separable-variable equation comparatively easy to handle.

Example 2   Solve the equation $2t\,dy + y\,dt = 0$. At first glance, this differential equation does not seem to belong in this spot, because it fails to conform to the general form of (15.23). To be specific, the coefficients of dy and dt are seen to involve the "wrong" variables. However, a simple transformation—dividing through by $2yt$ ($\neq 0$)—will reduce the equation to the separable-variable form

$$\frac{1}{y}\,dy + \frac{1}{2t}\,dt = 0$$

From our experience with Example 1, we can work toward the solution (without first transposing a term) as follows:[†]

$$\int \frac{1}{y}\,dy + \int \frac{1}{2t}\,dt = c$$

so

$$\ln y + \frac{1}{2}\ln t = c \quad \text{or} \quad \ln(yt^{1/2}) = c$$

Thus the solution is

$$yt^{1/2} = e^c = k \quad \text{or} \quad y(t) = kt^{-1/2}$$

where k is an arbitrary constant, as are the symbols c and A employed elsewhere.

Note that, instead of solving the equation in Example 2 as we did, we could also have transformed it first into an exact differential equation (by the integrating factor y) and then solved it as such. The solution, already given in Example 1 of Sec. 15.4, must of course be identical with the one just obtained by separation of variables. The point is that a given differential equation can often be solvable in more than one way, and therefore one may have a choice of the method to be used. In other cases, a differential equation that is not amenable to a particular method may nonetheless become so after an appropriate transformation.

Equations Reducible to the Linear Form

If the differential equation $dy/dt = h(y, t)$ happens to take the specific nonlinear form

$$\frac{dy}{dt} + Ry = Ty^m \tag{15.24}$$

where R and T are two functions of t, and m is any number other than 0 and 1 (what if $m = 0$ or $m = 1$?), then the equation—referred to as a *Bernoulli equation*—can always be reduced to a linear differential equation and be solved as such.

[†] In the integration result, we should, strictly speaking, have written $\ln|y|$ and $\frac{1}{2}\ln|t|$. If y and t can be assumed to be positive, as is appropriate in the majority of economic contexts, then the result given in the text will occur.

The reduction procedure is relatively simple. First, we can divide (15.24) by y^m, to get

$$y^{-m}\frac{dy}{dt} + Ry^{1-m} = T$$

If we adopt a shorthand variable z as follows:

$$z = y^{1-m} \qquad \left[\text{so that } \frac{dz}{dt} = \frac{dz}{dy}\frac{dy}{dt} = (1-m)y^{-m}\frac{dy}{dt}\right]$$

then the preceding equation can be written as

$$\frac{1}{1-m}\frac{dz}{dt} + Rz = T$$

Moreover, after multiplying through by $(1-m)\,dt$ and rearranging, we can transform the equation into

$$dz + [(1-m)Rz - (1-m)T]\,dt = 0 \qquad\qquad \textbf{(15.24')}$$

This is seen to be a first-order linear differential equation of the form (15.20), in which the variable z has taken the place of y.

Clearly, we can apply formula (15.21) to find its solution $z(t)$. Then, as a final step, we can translate z back to y by reverse substitution.

Example 3
Solve the equation $dy/dt + ty = 3ty^2$. This is a Bernoulli equation, with $m = 2$ (giving us $z = y^{1-m} = y^{-1}$), $R = t$, and $T = 3t$. Thus, by (15.24'), we can write the linearized differential equation as

$$dz + (-tz + 3t)\,dt = 0$$

By applying formula (15.21), the solution can be found to be

$$z(t) = A\exp\left(\tfrac{1}{2}t^2\right) + 3$$

(As an exercise, trace out the steps leading to this solution.)

Since our primary interest lies in the solution $y(t)$ rather than $z(t)$, we must perform a reverse transformation using the equation $z = y^{-1}$, or $y = z^{-1}$. By taking the reciprocal of $z(t)$, therefore, we get

$$y(t) = \frac{1}{A\exp\left(\tfrac{1}{2}t^2\right) + 3}$$

as the desired solution. This is a general solution, because an arbitrary constant A is present.

Example 4
Solve the equation $dy/dt + (1/t)y = y^3$. Here, we have $m = 3$ (thus $z = y^{-2}$), $R = 1/t$, and $T = 1$; thus the equation can be linearized into the form

$$dz + \left(\frac{-2}{t}z + 2\right)dt = 0$$

As you can verify, by the use of formula (15.21), the solution of this differential equation is

$$z(t) = At^2 + 2t$$

It then follows, by the reverse transformation $y = z^{-1/2}$, that the general solution in the original variable is to be written as

$$y(t) = (At^2 + 2t)^{-1/2}$$

As an exercise, check the validity of the solutions of these last two examples by differentiation.

EXERCISE 15.5

1. Determine, for each of the following, (1) whether the variables are separable and (2) whether the equation is linear or else can be linearized:

   (a) $2t\,dy + 2y\,dt = 0$ (c) $\dfrac{dy}{dt} = -\dfrac{t}{y}$

   (b) $\dfrac{y}{y+t}\,dy + \dfrac{2t}{y+t}\,dt = 0$ (d) $\dfrac{dy}{dt} = 3y^2t$

2. Solve (a) and (b) in Prob. 1 by separation of variables, taking y and t to be positive. Check your answers by differentiation.
3. Solve (c) in Prob. 1 as a separable-variable equation and, also, as a Bernoulli equation.
4. Solve (d) in Prob. 1 as a separable-variable equation and, also, as a Bernoulli equation.
5. Verify the correctness of the intermediate solution $z(t) = At^2 + 2t$ in Example 4 by showing that its derivative dz/dt is consistent with the linearized differential equation.

15.6   The Qualitative-Graphic Approach

The several cases of nonlinear differential equations previously discussed (exact differential equations, separable-variable equations, and Bernoulli equations) have all been solved *quantitatively*. That is, we have in every case sought and found a time path $y(t)$ which, for each value of t, tells the specific corresponding value of the variable y.

At times, we may not be able to find a quantitative solution from a given differential equation. Yet, in such cases, it may nonetheless be possible to ascertain the *qualitative* properties of the time path—primarily, whether $y(t)$ converges—by directly observing the differential equation itself or by analyzing its graph. Even when quantitative solutions are available, moreover, we may still employ the techniques of qualitative analysis if the qualitative aspect of the time path is our principal or exclusive concern.

The Phase Diagram

Given a first-order differential equation in the general form

$$\frac{dy}{dt} = f(y)$$

either linear or nonlinear in the variable y, we can plot dy/dt against y as in Fig. 15.3. Such a geometric representation, feasible whenever dy/dt is a function of y alone, is called a *phase diagram,* and the graph representing the function f, a *phase line.* (A differential equation of this form—in which the time variable t does not appear as a separate argument of

FIGURE 15.3

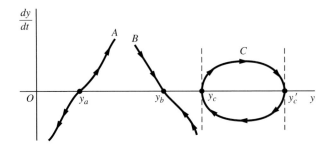

the function *f*—is said to be an *autonomous* differential equation.) Once a phase line is known, its configuration will impart significant qualitative information regarding the time path $y(t)$. The clue to this lies in the following two general remarks:

1. Anywhere *above* the horizontal axis (where $dy/dt > 0$), y must be increasing over time and, as far as the y axis is concerned, must be moving from left to right. By analogous reasoning, any point *below* the horizontal axis must be associated with a leftward movement in the variable y, because the negativity of dy/dt means that y decreases over time. These directional tendencies explain why the arrowheads on the illustrative phase lines in Fig. 15.3 are drawn as they are. Above the horizontal axis, the arrows are uniformly pointed toward the right—toward the northeast or southeast or due east, as the case may be. The opposite is true below the y axis. Moreover, these results are independent of the algebraic sign of y; even if phase line A (or any other) is transplanted to the left of the vertical axis, the direction of the arrows will not be affected.

2. An equilibrium level of y—in the intertemporal sense of the term—if it exists, can occur only on the horizontal axis, where $dy/dt = 0$ (y stationary over time). To find an equilibrium, therefore, it is necessary only to consider the intersection of the phase line with the y axis.[†] To test the dynamic stability of equilibrium, on the other hand, we should also check whether, regardless of the initial position of y, the phase line will always guide it toward the equilibrium position at the said intersection.

Types of Time Path

On the basis of the preceding general remarks, we may observe three different types of time path from the illustrative phase lines in Fig. 15.3.

Phase line A has an equilibrium at point y_a; but *above* as well as *below* that point, the arrowheads consistently lead away from equilibrium. Thus, although equilibrium can be attained if it happens that $y(0) = y_a$, the more usual case of $y(0) \neq y_a$ will result in y being ever-increasing [if $y(0) > y_a$] or ever-decreasing [if $y(0) < y_a$]. Besides, in this case the deviation of y from y_a tends to grow at an increasing pace because, as we follow the arrowheads on the phase line, we deviate farther from the y axis, thereby encountering ever-increasing numerical values of dy/dt as well. The time path $y(t)$ implied by phase line A can therefore be represented by the curves shown in Fig. 15.4a, where y is plotted against t (rather than dy/dt against y). The equilibrium y_a is dynamically unstable.

[†] However, not all intersections represent equilibrium positions. We shall see this when we discuss phase line C in Fig. 15.3.

FIGURE 15.4

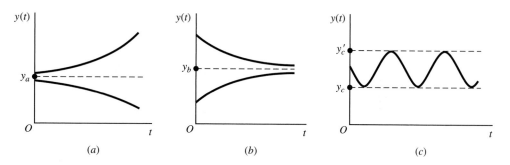

(a)   (b)   (c)

In contrast, phase line B implies a stable equilibrium at y_b. If $y(0) = y_b$, equilibrium prevails at once. But the important feature of phase line B is that, even if $y(0) \neq y_b$, the movement along the phase line will guide y toward the level of y_b. The time path $y(t)$ corresponding to this type of phase line should therefore be of the form shown in Fig. 15.4b, which is reminiscent of the dynamic market model.

The preceding discussion suggests that, in general, it is the slope of the phase line at its intersection point which holds the key to the dynamic stability of equilibrium or the convergence of the time path. A (finite) *positive* slope, such as at point y_a, makes for dynamic *instability;* whereas a (finite) *negative* slope, such as at y_b, implies dynamic *stability.*

This generalization can help us to draw qualitative inferences about given differential equations without even plotting their phase lines. Take the linear differential equation in (15.4), for instance:

$$\frac{dy}{dt} + ay = b \qquad \text{or} \qquad \frac{dy}{dt} = -ay + b$$

Since the phase line will obviously have the (constant) slope $-a$, here assumed nonzero, we may immediately infer (without drawing the line) that

$$a \gtrless 0 \quad \Leftrightarrow \quad y(t) \begin{Bmatrix} \text{converges to} \\ \text{diverges from} \end{Bmatrix} \text{equilibrium}$$

As we may expect, this result coincides perfectly with what the quantitative solution of this equation tells us:

$$y(t) = \left[y(0) - \frac{b}{a} \right] e^{-at} + \frac{b}{a} \qquad \text{[from (15.5$'$)]}$$

We have learned that, starting from a nonequilibrium position, the convergence of $y(t)$ hinges on the prospect that $e^{-at} \to 0$ as $t \to \infty$. This can happen if and only if $a > 0$; if $a < 0$, then $e^{-at} \to \infty$ as $t \to \infty$, and $y(t)$ cannot converge. Thus, our conclusion is one and the same, whether it is arrived at quantitatively or qualitatively.

It remains to discuss phase line C, which, being a closed loop sitting across the horizontal axis, does not qualify as a *function* but shows instead a *relation* between dy/dt and y.[†] The interesting new element that emerges in this case is the possibility of a periodically fluctuating time path. The way that phase line C is drawn, we shall find y fluctuating between the two values y_c and y'_c in a perpetual motion. In order to generate the periodic

---

[†] This can arise from a second-degree differential equation $(dy/dt)^2 = f(y)$.

fluctuation, the loop must, of course, straddle the horizontal axis in such a manner that dy/dt can alternately be positive and negative. Besides, at the two intersection points y_c and y'_c, the phase line should have an infinite slope; otherwise the intersection will resemble either y_a or y_b, neither of which permits a continual flow of arrowheads. The type of time path $y(t)$ corresponding to this looped phase line is illustrated in Fig. 15.4c. Note that, whenever $y(t)$ hits the upper bound y'_c or the lower bound y_c, we have $dy/dt = 0$ (local extrema); but these values certainly do not represent equilibrium values of y. In terms of Fig. 15.3, this means that not all intersections between a phase line and the y axis are equilibrium positions.

In sum, for the study of the dynamic stability of equilibrium (or the convergence of the time path), one has the alternative either of finding the time path itself or else of simply drawing the inference from its phase line. We shall illustrate the application of the latter approach with the Solow growth model. Henceforth, we shall denote the intertemporal equilibrium value of y by $\bar{y}$, as distinct from y^*.

EXERCISE 15.6

1. Plot the phase line for each of the following, and discuss its qualitative implications:

   (a) $\dfrac{dy}{dt} = y - 7$

   (c) $\dfrac{dy}{dt} = 4 - \dfrac{y}{2}$

   (b) $\dfrac{dy}{dt} = 1 - 5y$

   (d) $\dfrac{dy}{dt} = 9y - 11$

2. Plot the phase line for each of the following and interpret:

   (a) $\dfrac{dy}{dt} = (y + 1)^2 - 16 \qquad (y \geq 0)$

   (b) $\dfrac{dy}{dt} = \dfrac{1}{2}y - y^2 \qquad (y \geq 0)$

3. Given $dy/dt = (y - 3)(y - 5) = y^2 - 8y + 15$:

   (a) Deduce that there are two possible equilibrium levels of y, one at $y = 3$ and the other at $y = 5$.

   (b) Find the sign of $\dfrac{d}{dy}\left(\dfrac{dy}{dt}\right)$ at $y = 3$ and $y = 5$, respectively. What can you infer from these?

15.7 Solow Growth Model

The growth model of Professor Robert Solow,[†] a Nobel laureate, is purported to show, among other things, that the razor's-edge growth path of the Domar model is primarily a result of the particular production-function assumption adopted therein and that, under alternative circumstances, the need for delicate balancing may not arise.

The Framework

In the Domar model, output is explicitly stated as a function of capital alone: $\kappa = \rho K$ (the productive capacity, or potential output, is a constant multiple of the stock of capital). The

[†] Robert M. Solow, "A Contribution to the Theory of Economic Growth," *Quarterly Journal of Economics*, February 1956, pp. 65–94.

absence of a labor input in the production function carries the implication that labor is always combined with capital in a *fixed* proportion, so that it is feasible to consider explicitly only one of these factors of production. Solow, in contrast, seeks to analyze the case where capital and labor can be combined in *varying* proportions. Thus his production function appears in the form

$$Q = f(K, L) \qquad (K, L > 0)$$

where Q is output (net of depreciation), K is capital, and L is labor—all being used in the *macro* sense. It is assumed that f_K and f_L are positive (positive marginal products), and f_{KK} and f_{LL} are negative (diminishing returns to each input). Furthermore, the production function f is taken to be linearly homogeneous (constant returns to scale). Consequently, it is possible to write

$$Q = Lf\left(\frac{K}{L}, 1\right) = L\phi(k) \qquad \text{where } k \equiv \frac{K}{L} \qquad \textbf{(15.25)}$$

In view of the assumed signs of f_K and f_{KK}, the newly introduced ϕ function (which, be it noted, has only a single argument, k) must be characterized by a positive first derivative and a negative second derivative. To verify this claim, we first recall from (12.49) that

$$f_K \equiv \text{MPP}_K = \phi'(k)$$

hence $f_K > 0$ automatically means $\phi'(k) > 0$. Then, since

$$f_{KK} = \frac{\partial}{\partial K}\phi'(k) = \frac{d\phi'(k)}{dk}\frac{\partial k}{\partial K} = \phi''(k)\frac{1}{L} \qquad \text{[see (12.48)]}$$

the assumption $f_{KK} < 0$ leads directly to the result $\phi''(k) < 0$. Thus the ϕ function—which, according to (12.46), gives the APP_L for every capital–labor ratio—is one that increases with k at a decreasing rate.

Given that Q depends on K and L, it is necessary now to stipulate how the latter two variables themselves are determined. Solow's assumptions are:

$$\dot{K}\left(\equiv \frac{dK}{dt}\right) = sQ \qquad \text{[constant proportion of } Q \text{ is invested]} \qquad \textbf{(15.26)}$$

$$\frac{\dot{L}}{L}\left(\equiv \frac{dL/dt}{L}\right) = \lambda \qquad (\lambda > 0) \qquad \text{[labor force grows exponentially]} \qquad \textbf{(15.27)}$$

The symbol s represents a (constant) marginal propensity to save, and λ, a (constant) rate of growth of labor. Note the dynamic nature of these assumptions; they specify not how the *levels* of K and L are determined, but how their *rates of change* are.

Equations (15.25) through (15.27) constitute a complete model. To solve this model, we shall first condense it into a single equation in one variable. To begin with, substitute (15.25) into (15.26) to get

$$\dot{K} = sL\phi(k) \qquad \textbf{(15.28)}$$

Since $k \equiv K/L$, and $K \equiv kL$, however, we can obtain another expression for $\dot{K}$ by differentiating the latter identity:

$$\begin{aligned} \dot{K} &= L\dot{k} + k\dot{L} \qquad \text{[product rule]} \\ &= L\dot{k} + k\lambda L \qquad \text{[by (15.27)]} \end{aligned} \qquad \textbf{(15.29)}$$

When (15.29) is equated to (15.28) and the common factor L eliminated, the result emerges that

$$\dot{k} = s\phi(k) - \lambda k \qquad\qquad (15.30)$$

This equation—a differential equation in the variable k, with two parameters s and λ—is the fundamental equation of the Solow growth model.

A Qualitative-Graphic Analysis

Because (15.30) is stated in a general-function form, no specific quantitative solution is available. Nevertheless, we can analyze it qualitatively. To this end, we should plot a phase line, with $\dot{k}$ on the vertical axis and k on the horizontal.

Since (15.30) contains two terms on the right, however, let us first plot these as two separate curves. The λk term, a linear function of k, will obviously show up in Fig. 15.5a as a straight line, with a zero vertical intercept and a slope equal to λ. The $s\phi(k)$ term, on the other hand, plots as a curve that increases at a decreasing rate, like $\phi(k)$, since $s\phi(k)$ is merely a constant fraction of the $\phi(k)$ curve. If we consider K to be an indispensable factor of production, we must start the $s\phi(k)$ curve from the point of origin; this is because if $K = 0$ and thus $k = 0$, Q must also be zero, as will be $\phi(k)$ and $s\phi(k)$. The way the curve is actually drawn also reflects the implicit assumption that there exists a set of k values for which $s\phi(k)$ exceeds λk, so that the two curves intersect at some positive value of k, namely $\bar{k}$.

Based upon these two curves, the value of $\dot{k}$ for each value of k can be measured by the vertical distance between the two curves. Plotting the values of $\dot{k}$ against k, as in Fig. 15.5b, will then yield the phase line we need. Note that, since the two curves in Fig. 15.5a intersect when the capital–labor ratio is $\bar{k}$, the phase line in Fig. 15.5b must cross the horizontal axis at $\bar{k}$. This marks $\bar{k}$ as the intertemporal equilibrium capital–labor ratio.

Inasmuch as the phase line has a negative slope at $\bar{k}$, the equilibrium is readily identified as a stable one; given any (positive) initial value of k, the dynamic movement of the model

FIGURE 15.5

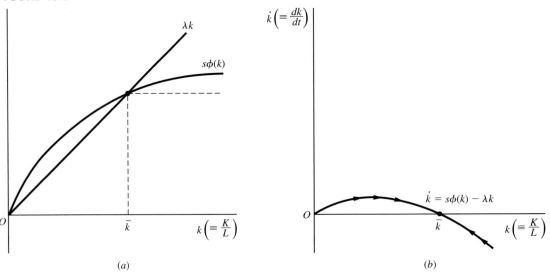

(a) (b)

must lead us convergently to the equilibrium level $\bar{k}$. The significant point is that once this equilibrium is attained—and thus the capital–labor ratio is (by definition) unvarying over time—capital must thereafter grow apace with labor, at the identical rate λ. This will imply, in turn, that net investment must grow at the rate λ (see Exercise 15.7-2). Note, however, that the word *must* is used here not in the sense of requirement, but with the implication of automaticity. Thus, what the Solow model serves to show is that, given a rate of growth of labor λ, the economy by itself, and without the delicate balancing à la Domar, can eventually reach a state of steady growth in which investment will grow at the rate λ, the same as K and L. Moreover, in order to satisfy (15.25), Q must grow at the same rate as well because $\phi(k)$ is a constant when the capital–labor ratio remains unvarying at the level $\bar{k}$. Such a situation, in which the relevant variables all grow at an identical rate, is called a *steady state*—a generalization of the concept of *stationary state* (in which the relevant variables all remain constant, or in other words all grow at the zero rate).

Note that, in the preceding analysis, the production function is assumed for convenience to be invariant over time. If the state of technology is allowed to improve, on the other hand, the production function will have to be duly modified. For instance, it may be written instead in the form

$$Q = T(t)f(K, L) \qquad \left(\frac{dT}{dt} > 0\right)$$

where T, some measure of technology, is an increasing function of time. Because of the increasing multiplicative term $T(t)$, a fixed amount of K and L will turn out a larger output at a future date than at present. In this event, the $s\phi(k)$ curve in Fig. 15.5 will be subject to a secular upward shift, resulting in successively higher intersections with the λk ray and also in larger values of $\bar{k}$. With technological improvement, therefore, it will become possible, in a succession of steady states, to have a larger and larger amount of capital equipment available to each representative worker in the economy, with a concomitant rise in productivity.

A Quantitative Illustration

The preceding analysis had to be qualitative, owing to the presence of a general function $\phi(k)$ in the model. But if we specify the production function to be a linearly homogeneous Cobb-Douglas function, for instance, then a quantitative solution can be found as well.

Let us write the production function as

$$Q = K^{\alpha}L^{1-\alpha} = L\left(\frac{K}{L}\right)^{\alpha} = Lk^{\alpha}$$

so that $\phi(k) = k^{\alpha}$. Then (15.30) becomes

$$\dot{k} = sk^{\alpha} - \lambda k \qquad \text{or} \qquad \dot{k} + \lambda k = sk^{\alpha}$$

which is a Bernoulli equation in the variable k [see (15.24)], with $R = \lambda$, $T = s$, and $m = \alpha$. Letting $z = k^{1-\alpha}$, we obtain its linearized version

$$dz + [(1 - \alpha)\lambda z - (1 - \alpha)s] \, dt = 0$$

or

$$\frac{dz}{dt} + \underbrace{(1 - \alpha)\lambda z}_{a} = \underbrace{(1 - \alpha)s}_{b}$$

This is a linear differential equation with a constant coefficient a and a constant term b. Thus, by formula (15.5′), we have

$$z(t) = \left[z(0) - \frac{s}{\lambda}\right]e^{-(1-\alpha)\lambda t} + \frac{s}{\lambda}$$

The substitution of $z = k^{1-\alpha}$ will then yield the final solution

$$k^{1-\alpha} = \left[k(0)^{1-\alpha} - \frac{s}{\lambda}\right]e^{-(1-\alpha)\lambda t} + \frac{s}{\lambda}$$

where $k(0)$ is the initial value of the capital–labor ratio k.

This solution is what determines the time path of k. Recalling that $(1 - \alpha)$ and λ are both positive, we see that as $t \to \infty$ the exponential expression will approach zero; consequently,

$$k^{1-\alpha} \to \frac{s}{\lambda} \qquad \text{or} \qquad k \to \left(\frac{s}{\lambda}\right)^{1/(1-\alpha)} \qquad \text{as } t \to \infty$$

Therefore, the capital–labor ratio will approach a constant as its equilibrium value. This equilibrium or steady-state value, $(s/\lambda)^{1/(1-\alpha)}$, varies directly with the propensity to save s, and inversely with the rate of growth of labor λ.

EXERCISE 15.7

1. Divide (15.30) through by k, and interpret the resulting equation in terms of the growth rates of k, K, and L.
2. Show that, if capital is growing at the rate λ (that is, $K = Ae^{\lambda t}$), net investment I must also be growing at the rate λ.
3. The original input variables of the Solow model are K and L, but the fundamental equation (15.30) focuses on the capital–labor ratio k instead. What assumption(s) in the model is(are) responsible for (and make possible) this shift of focus? Explain.
4. Draw a phase diagram for each of the following, and discuss the qualitative aspects of the time path $y(t)$:
   (a) $\dot{y} = 3 - y - \ln y$ (b) $\dot{y} = e^y - (y + 2)$

Chapter 16

Higher-Order Differential Equations

In Chap. 15, we discussed the methods of solving a *first-order* differential equation, one in which there appears no derivative (or differential) of orders higher than 1. At times, however, the specification of a model may involve the second derivative or a derivative of an even higher order. We may, for instance, be given a function describing "the rate of change of the rate of change" of the income variable Y, say,

$$\frac{d^2 Y}{dt^2} = kY$$

from which we are supposed to find the time path of Y. In this event, the given function constitutes a *second-order* differential equation, and the task of finding the time path $Y(t)$ is that of *solving* the second-order differential equation. The present chapter is concerned with the methods of solution and the economic applications of such higher-order differential equations, but we shall confine our discussion to the *linear* case only.

A simple variety of linear differential equations of order n is of the following form:

$$\frac{d^n y}{dt^n} + a_1 \frac{d^{n-1} y}{dt^{n-1}} + \cdots + a_{n-1} \frac{dy}{dt} + a_n y = b \qquad \textbf{(16.1)}$$

or, in an alternative notation,

$$y^{(n)}(t) + a_1 y^{(n-1)}(t) + \cdots + a_{n-1} y'(t) + a_n y = b \qquad \textbf{(16.1')}$$

This equation is of *order n*, because the nth derivative (the first term on the left) is the highest derivative present. It is *linear,* since all the derivatives, as well as the dependent variable y, appear only in the first degree, and moreover, no product term occurs in which y and any of its derivatives are multiplied together. You will note, in addition, that this differential equation is characterized by *constant coefficients* (the a's) and a *constant term* (b). The constancy of the coefficients is an assumption we shall retain throughout this chapter. The constant term b, on the other hand, is adopted here as a first approach; later, in Sec. 16.5, we shall drop it in favor of a variable term.

16.1 Second-Order Linear Differential Equations with Constant Coefficients and Constant Term

For pedagogic reasons, let us first discuss the method of solution for the *second-order* case ($n = 2$). The relevant differential equation is then the simple one

$$y''(t) + a_1 y'(t) + a_2 y = b \qquad (16.2)$$

where a_1, a_2, and b are all constants. If the term b is identically zero, we have a *homogeneous* equation, but if b is a nonzero constant, the equation is *nonhomogeneous*. Our discussion will proceed on the assumption that (16.2) is nonhomogeneous; in solving the nonhomogeneous version of (16.2), the solution of the homogeneous version will emerge automatically as a by-product.

In this connection, we recall a proposition introduced in Sec. 15.1 which is equally applicable here: If y_c is the *complementary function,* i.e., the general solution (containing arbitrary constants) of the reduced equation of (16.2) and if y_p is the *particular integral,* i.e., any particular solution (containing no arbitrary constants) of the complete equation (16.2), then $y(t) = y_c + y_p$ will be the general solution of the complete equation. As was explained previously, the y_p component provides us with the equilibrium value of the variable y in the intertemporal sense of the term, whereas the y_c component reveals, for each point of time, the deviation of the time path $y(t)$ from the equilibrium.

The Particular Integral

For the case of constant coefficients and constant term, the particular integral is relatively easy to find. Since the particular integral can be *any* solution of (16.2), i.e., any value of y that satisfies this nonhomogeneous equation, we should always try the simplest possible type: namely, $y =$ a constant. If $y =$ a constant, it follows that

$$y'(t) = y''(t) = 0$$

so that (16.2) in effect becomes $a_2 y = b$, with the solution $y = b/a_2$. Thus, the desired particular integral is

$$y_p = \frac{b}{a_2} \qquad \text{(case of } a_2 \neq 0\text{)} \qquad (16.3)$$

Since the process of finding the value of y_p involves the condition $y'(t) = 0$, the rationale for considering that value as an intertemporal equilibrium becomes self-evident.

Example 1   Find the particular integral of the equation

$$y''(t) + y'(t) - 2y = -10$$

The relevant coefficients here are $a_2 = -2$ and $b = -10$. Therefore, the particular integral is $y_p = -10/(-2) = 5$.

What if $a_2 = 0$—so that the expression b/a_2 is not defined? In such a situation, since the constant solution for y_p fails to work, we must try some *nonconstant* form of solution. Taking the simplest possibility, we may try $y = kt$. Since $a_2 = 0$, the differential equation is now

$$y''(t) + a_1 y'(t) = b$$

but if $y = kt$, which implies $y'(t) = k$ and $y''(t) = 0$, this equation reduces to $a_1 k = b$. This determines the value of k as b/a_1, thereby giving us the particular integral

$$y_p = \frac{b}{a_1} t \qquad \text{(case of } a_2 = 0; \ a_1 \neq 0\text{)} \qquad \textbf{(16.3')}$$

Inasmuch as y_p is in this case a nonconstant function of time, we shall regard it as a moving equilibrium.

Example 2 Find the y_p of the equation $y''(t) + y'(t) = -10$. Here, we have $a_2 = 0$, $a_1 = 1$, and $b = -10$. Thus, by (16.3'), we can write

$$y_p = -10t$$

If it happens that a_1 is also zero, then the solution form of $y = kt$ will also break down, because the expression bt/a_1 will now be undefined. We ought, then, to try a solution of the form $y = kt^2$. With $a_1 = a_2 = 0$, the differential equation now reduces to the extremely simple form

$$y''(t) = b$$

and if $y = kt^2$, which implies $y'(t) = 2kt$ and $y''(t) = 2k$, the differential equation can be written as $2k = b$. Thus, we find $k = b/2$, and the particular integral is

$$y_p = \frac{b}{2} t^2 \qquad \text{(case of } a_1 = a_2 = 0\text{)} \qquad \textbf{(16.3'')}$$

The equilibrium represented by this particular integral is again a moving equilibrium.

Example 3 Find the y_p of the equation $y''(t) = -10$. Since the coefficients are $a_1 = a_2 = 0$ and $b = -10$, formula (16.3'') is applicable. The desired answer is $y_p = -5t^2$.

The Complementary Function

The complementary function of (16.2) is defined to be the general solution of its reduced (homogeneous) equation

$$y''(t) + a_1 y'(t) + a_2 y = 0 \qquad \textbf{(16.4)}$$

This is why we stated that the solution of a homogeneous equation will always be a *by-product* in the process of solving a complete equation.

Even though we have never tackled such an equation before, our experience with the complementary function of the first-order differential equations can supply us with a useful hint. From the solutions (15.3), (15.3'), (15.5), and (15.5'), it is clear that exponential expressions of the form Ae^{rt} figure very prominently in the complementary functions of first-order differential equations with constant coefficients. Then why not try a solution of the form $y = Ae^{rt}$ in the second-order equation, too?

If we adopt the trial solution $y = Ae^{rt}$, we must also accept

$$y'(t) = rAe^{rt} \qquad \text{and} \qquad y''(t) = r^2 Ae^{rt}$$

as the derivatives of y. On the basis of these expressions for y, $y'(t)$, and $y''(t)$, the reduced differential equation (16.4) can be transformed into

$$Ae^{rt}(r^2 + a_1r + a_2) = 0 \qquad \textbf{(16.4')}$$

As long as we choose those values of A and r that satisfy (16.4'), the trial solution $y = Ae^{rt}$ should work. Since e^{rt} can never be zero, we must either let $A = 0$ or see to it that r satisfies the equation

$$r^2 + a_1r + a_2 = 0 \qquad \textbf{(16.4'')}$$

Since the value of the (arbitrary) constant A is to be definitized by use of the initial conditions of the problem, however, we cannot simply set $A = 0$ at will. Therefore, it is essential to look for values of r that satisfy (16.4'').

Equation (16.4'') is known as the *characteristic equation* (or *auxiliary equation*) of the homogeneous equation (16.4), or of the complete equation (16.2). Because it is a quadratic equation in r, it yields two roots (solutions), referred to in the present context as *characteristic roots,* as follows:[†]

$$r_1, r_2 = \frac{-a_1 \pm \sqrt{a_1^2 - 4a_2}}{2} \qquad \textbf{(16.5)}$$

These two roots bear a simple but interesting relationship to each other, which can serve as a convenient means of checking our calculation: The *sum* of the two roots is always equal to $-a_1$, and their *product* is always equal to a_2. The proof of this statement is straightforward:

$$r_1 + r_2 = \frac{-a_1 + \sqrt{a_1^2 - 4a_2}}{2} + \frac{-a_1 - \sqrt{a_1^2 - 4a_2}}{2} = \frac{-2a_1}{2} = -a_1$$

$$r_1 r_2 = \frac{(-a_1)^2 - (a_1^2 - 4a_2)}{4} = \frac{4a_2}{4} = a_2 \qquad \textbf{(16.6)}$$

The values of these two roots are the only values we may assign to r in the solution $y = Ae^{rt}$. But this means that, in effect, there are *two* solutions which will work, namely,

$$y_1 = A_1e^{r_1t} \qquad \text{and} \qquad y_2 = A_2e^{r_2t}$$

where A_1 and A_2 are two arbitrary constants, and r_1 and r_2 are the characteristic roots found from (16.5). Since we want only *one* general solution, however, there seems to be one too many. Two alternatives are now open to us: (1) pick either y_1 or y_2 at random, or (2) combine them in some fashion.

The first alternative, though simpler, is unacceptable. There is only one arbitrary constant in y_1 or y_2, but to qualify as a general solution of a *second-order* differential equation, the expression must contain *two* arbitrary constants. This requirement stems from the fact that, in proceeding from a function $y(t)$ to its second derivative $y''(t)$, we "lose" two constants during the two rounds of differentiation; therefore, to revert from a second-order differential equation to the primitive function $y(t)$, two constants should be reinstated. That leaves us only the alternative of combining y_1 and y_2, so as to include both constants

---

[†] Note that the quadratic equation (16.4'') is in the normalized form; the coefficient of the r^2 term is 1. In applying formula (16.5) to find the characteristic roots of a differential equation, we must first make sure that the characteristic equation is indeed in the normalized form.

A_1 and A_2. As it turns out, we can simply take their *sum*, $y_1 + y_2$, as the general solution of (16.4). Let us demonstrate that, if y_1 and y_2, respectively, satisfy (16.4), then the sum $(y_1 + y_2)$ will also do so. If y_1 and y_2 are indeed solutions of (16.4), then by substituting each of these into (16.4), we must find that the following two equations hold:

$$y_1''(t) + a_1 y_1'(t) + a_2 y_1 = 0$$
$$y_2''(t) + a_1 y_2'(t) + a_2 y_2 = 0$$

By adding these equations, however, we find that

$$\underbrace{[y_1''(t) + y_2''(t)]}_{=\frac{d^2}{dt^2}(y_1+y_2)} + a_1 \underbrace{[y_1'(t) + y_2'(t)]}_{=\frac{d}{dt}(y_1+y_2)} + a_2(y_1 + y_2) = 0$$

Thus, like y_1 or y_2, the sum $(y_1 + y_2)$ satisfies the equation (16.4) as well. Accordingly, the general solution of the homogeneous equation (16.4) or the complementary function of the complete equation (16.2) can, in general, be written as $y_c = y_1 + y_2$.

A more careful examination of the characteristic-root formula (16.5) indicates, however, that as far as the values of r_1 and r_2 are concerned, three possible cases can arise, some of which may necessitate a modification of our result $y_c = y_1 + y_2$.

Case 1 (distinct real roots)   When $a_1^2 > 4a_2$, the square root in (16.5) is a real number, and the two roots r_1 and r_2 will take *distinct* real values, because the square root is added to $-a_1$ for r_1, but subtracted from $-a_1$ for r_2. In this case, we can indeed write

$$y_c = y_1 + y_2 = A_1 e^{r_1 t} + A_2 e^{r_2 t} \qquad (r_1 \neq r_2) \qquad \textbf{(16.7)}$$

Because the two roots are distinct, the two exponential expressions must be linearly independent (neither is a multiple of the other); consequently, A_1 and A_2 will always remain as separate entities and provide us with two constants, as required.

Example 4   Solve the differential equation

$$y''(t) + y'(t) - 2y = -10$$

The particular integral of this equation has already been found to be $y_p = 5$, in Example 1. Let us find the complementary function. Since the coefficients of the equation are $a_1 = 1$ and $a_2 = -2$, the characteristic roots are, by (16.5),

$$r_1, r_2 = \frac{-1 \pm \sqrt{1 + 8}}{2} = \frac{-1 \pm 3}{2} = 1, -2$$

(Check: $r_1 + r_2 = -1 = -a_1$; $r_1 r_2 = -2 = a_2$.) Since the roots are distinct real numbers, the complementary function is $y_c = A_1 e^t + A_2 e^{-2t}$. Therefore, the general solution can be written as

$$y(t) = y_c + y_p = A_1 e^t + A_2 e^{-2t} + 5 \qquad \textbf{(16.8)}$$

In order to definitize the constants A_1 and A_2, there is need now for *two* initial conditions. Let these conditions be $y(0) = 12$ and $y'(0) = -2$. That is, when $t = 0$, $y(t)$ and $y'(t)$ are, respectively, 12 and -2. Setting $t = 0$ in (16.8), we find that

$$y(0) = A_1 + A_2 + 5$$

Differentiating (16.8) with respect to t and then setting $t = 0$ in the derivative, we find that

$$y'(t) = A_1 e^t - 2A_2 e^{-2t} \quad \text{and} \quad y'(0) = A_1 - 2A_2$$

To satisfy the two initial conditions, therefore, we must set $y(0) = 12$ and $y'(0) = -2$, which results in the following pair of simultaneous equations:

$$A_1 + A_2 = 7$$
$$A_1 - 2A_2 = -2$$

with solutions $A_1 = 4$ and $A_2 = 3$. Thus the definite solution of the differential equation is

$$y(t) = 4e^t + 3e^{-2t} + 5 \tag{16.8'}$$

As before, we can check the validity of this solution by differentiation. The first and second derivatives of (16.8') are

$$y'(t) = 4e^t - 6e^{-2t} \quad \text{and} \quad y''(t) = 4e^t + 12e^{-2t}$$

When these are substituted into the given differential equation along with (16.8'), the result is an identity $-10 = -10$. Thus the solution is correct. As you can easily verify, (16.8') also satisfies both of the initial conditions.

Case 2 (repeated real roots)   When the coefficients in the differential equation are such that $a_1^2 = 4a_2$, the square root in (16.5) will vanish, and the two characteristic roots take an identical value:

$$r(= r_1 = r_2) = -\frac{a_1}{2}$$

Such roots are known as *repeated roots,* or *multiple* (here, *double*) *roots.*

If we attempt to write the complementary function as $y_c = y_1 + y_2$, the sum will in this case collapse into a single expression

$$y_c = A_1 e^{rt} + A_2 e^{rt} = (A_1 + A_2)e^{rt} = A_3 e^{rt}$$

leaving us with only one constant. This is not sufficient to lead us from a second-order differential equation back to its primitive function. The only way out is to find another eligible component term for the sum—a term which satisfies (16.4) and yet which is linearly independent of the term $A_3 e^{rt}$, so as to preclude such "collapsing."

An expression that will satisfy these requirements is $A_4 t e^{rt}$. Since the variable t has entered into it multiplicatively, this component term is obviously linearly independent of the $A_3 e^{rt}$ term; thus it will enable us to introduce another constant, A_4. But does $A_4 t e^{rt}$ qualify as a solution of (16.4)? If we try $y = A_4 t e^{rt}$, then, by the product rule, we can find its first and second derivatives to be

$$y'(t) = (rt + 1)A_4 e^{rt} \quad \text{and} \quad y''(t) = (r^2 t + 2r)A_4 e^{rt}$$

Substituting these expressions of y, y', and y'' into the left side of (16.4), we get the expression

$$[(r^2 t + 2r) + a_1(rt + 1) + a_2 t]A_4 e^{rt}$$

Inasmuch as, in the present context, we have $a_1^2 = 4a_2$ and $r = -a_1/2$, this last expression vanishes identically and thus is always equal to the right side of (16.4); this shows that A_4te^{rt} does indeed qualify as a solution.

Hence, the complementary function of the double-root case can be written as

$$y_c = A_3e^{rt} + A_4te^{rt} \tag{16.9}$$

Example 5   Solve the differential equation

$$y''(t) + 6y'(t) + 9y = 27$$

Here, the coefficients are $a_1 = 6$ and $a_2 = 9$; since $a_1^2 = 4a_2$, the roots will be repeated. According to formula (16.5), we have $r = -a_1/2 = -3$. Thus, in line with the result in (16.9), the complementary function may be written as

$$y_c = A_3e^{-3t} + A_4te^{-3t}$$

The general solution of the given differential equation is now also readily obtainable. Trying a constant solution for the particular integral, we get $y_p = 3$. It follows that the general solution of the complete equation is

$$y(t) = y_c + y_p = A_3e^{-3t} + A_4te^{-3t} + 3$$

The two arbitrary constants can again be definitized with two initial conditions. Suppose that the initial conditions are $y(0) = 5$ and $y'(0) = -5$. By setting $t = 0$ in the preceding general solution, we should find $y(0) = 5$; that is,

$$y(0) = A_3 + 3 = 5$$

This yields $A_3 = 2$. Next, by differentiating the general solution and then setting $t = 0$ and also $A_3 = 2$, we must have $y'(0) = -5$. That is,

$$y'(t) = -3A_3e^{-3t} - 3A_4te^{-3t} + A_4e^{-3t}$$

and

$$y'(0) = -6 + A_4 = -5$$

This yields $A_4 = 1$. Thus we can finally write the definite solution of the given equation as

$$y(t) = 2e^{-3t} + te^{-3t} + 3$$

Case 3 (complex roots)   There remains a third possibility regarding the relative magnitude of the coefficients a_1 and a_2, namely, $a_1^2 < 4a_2$. When this eventuality occurs, formula (16.5) will involve the square root of a *negative* number, which cannot be handled before we are properly introduced to the concepts of *imaginary* and *complex* numbers. For the time being, therefore, we shall be content with the mere cataloging of this case and shall leave the full discussion of it to Secs. 16.2 and 16.3.

The three cases cited can be illustrated by the three curves in Fig. 16.1, each of which represents a different version of the quadratic function $f(r) = r^2 + a_1r + a_2$. As we learned earlier, when such a function is set equal to zero, the result is a quadratic *equation* $f(r) = 0$, and to solve the latter equation is merely to "find the zeros of the quadratic *function*." Graphically, this means that the roots of the equation are to be found on the horizontal axis, where $f(r) = 0$.

The position of the lowest curve in Fig. 16.1, is such that the curve intersects the horizontal axis twice; thus we can find two distinct roots r_1 and r_2, both of which satisfy the

FIGURE 16.1

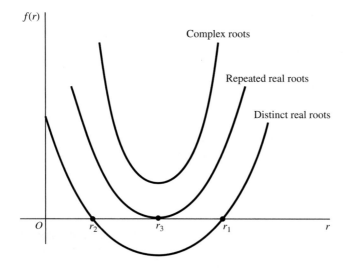

quadratic equation $f(r) = 0$ and both of which, of course, are real-valued. Thus the lowest curve illustrates Case 1. Turning to the middle curve, we note that it meets the horizontal axis only once, at r_3. This latter is the only value of r that can satisfy the equation $f(r) = 0$. Therefore, the middle curve illustrates Case 2. Last, we note that the top curve does not meet the horizontal axis at all, and there is thus no real-valued root to the equation $f(r) = 0$. While there exist no real roots in such a case, there are nevertheless two complex numbers that can satisfy the equation, as will be shown in Sec. 16.2.

The Dynamic Stability of Equilibrium

For Cases 1 and 2, the condition for dynamic stability of equilibrium again depends on the algebraic signs of the characteristic roots.

For Case 1, the complementary function (16.7) consists of the two exponential expressions $A_1 e^{r_1 t}$ and $A_2 e^{r_2 t}$. The coefficients A_1 and A_2 are arbitrary constants; their values hinge on the initial conditions of the problem. Thus we can be sure of a dynamically stable equilibrium ($y_c \to 0$ as $t \to \infty$), regardless of what the initial conditions happen to be, if and only if the roots r_1 and r_2 are *both* negative. We emphasize the word *both* here, because the condition for dynamic stability does *not* permit even *one* of the roots to be positive or zero. If $r_1 = 2$ and $r_2 = -5$, for instance, it might appear at first glance that the second root, being larger in absolute value, can outweigh the first. In actuality, however, it is the *positive* root that must eventually dominate, because as t increases, e^{2t} will grow increasingly larger, but e^{-5t} will steadily dwindle away.

For Case 2, with repeated roots, the complementary function (16.9) contains not only the familiar e^{rt} expression, but also a multiplicative expression te^{rt}. For the former term to approach zero whatever the initial conditions may be, it is necessary-and-sufficient to have $r < 0$. But would that also ensure the vanishing of te^{rt}? As it turns out, the expression te^{rt} (or, more generally, $t^k e^{rt}$) possesses the same general type of time path as does e^{rt} ($r \neq 0$). Thus the condition $r < 0$ is indeed necessary-and-sufficient for the entire complementary function to approach zero as $t \to \infty$, yielding a dynamically stable intertemporal equilibrium.

EXERCISE 16.1

1. Find the particular integral of each equation:
   (a) $y''(t) - 2y'(t) + 5y = 2$ (d) $y''(t) + 2y'(t) - y = -4$
   (b) $y''(t) + y'(t) = 7$ (e) $y''(t) = 12$
   (c) $y''(t) + 3y = 9$

2. Find the complementary function of each equation:
   (a) $y''(t) + 3y'(t) - 4y = 12$ (c) $y''(t) - 2y'(t) + y = 3$
   (b) $y''(t) + 6y'(t) + 5y = 10$ (d) $y''(t) + 8y'(t) + 16y = 0$

3. Find the general solution of each differential equation in Prob. 2, and then definitize the solution with the initial conditions $y(0) = 4$ and $y'(0) = 2$.

4. Are the intertemporal equilibriums found in Prob. 3 dynamically stable?

5. Verify that the definite solution in Example 5 indeed (a) satisfies the two initial conditions and (b) has first and second derivatives that conform to the given differential equation.

6. Show that, as $t \to \infty$, the limit of te^{rt} is zero if $r < 0$, but is infinite if $r \geq 0$.

16.2   Complex Numbers and Circular Functions

When the coefficients of a second-order linear differential equation, $y''(t) + a_1 y'(t) + a_2 y = b$, are such that $a_1^2 < 4a_2$, the characteristic-root formula (16.5) would call for taking the square root of a *negative* number. Since the square of any positive or negative real number is invariably positive, whereas the square of zero is zero, only a *nonnegative* real number can ever yield a real-valued square root. Thus, if we confine our attention to the real number system, as we have so far, no characteristic roots are available for this case (Case 3). This fact motivates us to consider numbers outside of the real-number system.

Imaginary and Complex Numbers

Conceptually, it is possible to define a number $i \equiv \sqrt{-1}$, which when squared will equal -1. Because i is the square root of a negative number, it is obviously not real-valued; it is therefore referred to as an *imaginary number*. With it at our disposal, we may write a host of other imaginary numbers, such as $\sqrt{-9} = \sqrt{9}\sqrt{-1} = 3i$ and $\sqrt{-2} = \sqrt{2}i$.

Extending its application a step further, we may construct yet another type of number—one that contains a *real* part as well as an *imaginary* part, such as $(8 + i)$ and $(3 + 5i)$. Known as *complex numbers,* these can be represented generally in the form $(h + vi)$, where h and v are two real numbers.[†] Of course, in case $v = 0$, the complex number will reduce to a real number, whereas if $h = 0$, it will become an imaginary number. Thus the *set of all real numbers* (call it **R**) constitutes a subset of the *set of all complex numbers* (call it **C**). Similarly, the *set of all imaginary numbers* (call it **I**) also constitutes a subset of **C**. That is, $\mathbf{R} \subset \mathbf{C}$, and $\mathbf{I} \subset \mathbf{C}$. Furthermore, since the terms *real* and *imaginary* are mutually exclusive, the sets **R** and **I** must be disjoint; that is $\mathbf{R} \cap \mathbf{I} = \varnothing$.

[†] We employ the symbols h (for horizontal) and v (for vertical) in the general complex-number notation, because we shall presently plot the values of h and v, respectively, on the horizontal and vertical axes of a two-dimensional diagram.

FIGURE 16.2

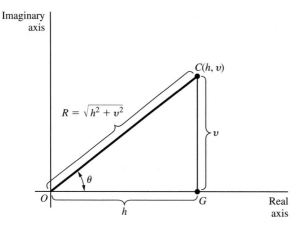

A complex number $(h + vi)$ can be represented graphically in what is called an *Argand diagram,* as illustrated in Fig. 16.2. By plotting h horizontally on the *real axis* and v vertically on the *imaginary axis,* the number $(h + vi)$ can be specified by the point (h, v), which we have alternatively labeled C. The values of h and v are algebraically signed, of course, so that if $h < 0$, the point C will be to the left of the point of origin; similarly, a negative v will mean a location below the horizontal axis.

Given the values of h and v, we can also calculate the length of the line OC by applying Pythagoras's theorem, which states that the square of the hypotenuse of a right-angled triangle is the sum of the squares of the other two sides. Denoting the length of OC by R (for radius vector), we have

$$R^2 = h^2 + v^2 \qquad \text{and} \qquad R = \sqrt{h^2 + v^2} \qquad \textbf{(16.10)}$$

where the square root is always taken to be positive. The value of R is sometimes called the *absolute value,* or *modulus,* of the complex number $(h + vi)$. (Note that changing the signs of h and v will produce no effect on the absolute value of the complex number, R.) Like h and v, then, R is real-valued, but unlike these other values, R is always positive. We shall find the number R to be of great importance in the ensuing discussion.

Complex Roots

Meanwhile, let us return to formula (16.5) and examine the case of complex characteristic roots. When the coefficients of a second-order differential equation are such that $a_1^2 < 4a_2$, the square-root expression in (16.5) can be written as

$$\sqrt{a_1^2 - 4a_2} = \sqrt{4a_2 - a_1^2}\sqrt{-1} = \sqrt{4a_2 - a_1^2}\,i$$

Hence, if we adopt the shorthand

$$h = \frac{-a_1}{2} \qquad \text{and} \qquad v = \frac{\sqrt{4a_2 - a_1^2}}{2}$$

the two roots can be denoted by a pair of *conjugate complex numbers:*

$$r_1, r_2 = h \pm vi$$

These two complex roots are said to be "conjugate" because they always appear together, one being the *sum* of h and vi, and the other being the *difference* between h and vi. Note that they share the same absolute value R.

Example 1

Find the roots of the characteristic equation $r^2 + r + 4 = 0$. Applying the familiar formula, we have

$$r_1, r_2 = \frac{-1 \pm \sqrt{-15}}{2} = \frac{-1 \pm \sqrt{15}\sqrt{-1}}{2} = \frac{-1}{2} \pm \frac{\sqrt{15}}{2} i$$

which constitute a pair of conjugate complex numbers.

As before, we can use (16.6) to check our calculations. If correct, we should have $r_1 + r_2 = -a_1 \,(= -1)$ and $r_1 r_2 = a_2 \,(= 4)$. Since we do find

$$r_1 + r_2 = \left(\frac{-1}{2} + \frac{\sqrt{15}i}{2} \right) + \left(\frac{-1}{2} - \frac{\sqrt{15}i}{2} \right)$$

$$= \frac{-1}{2} + \frac{-1}{2} = -1$$

and

$$r_1 r_2 = \left(\frac{-1}{2} + \frac{\sqrt{15}i}{2} \right) \left(\frac{-1}{2} - \frac{\sqrt{15}i}{2} \right)$$

$$= \left(\frac{-1}{2} \right)^2 - \left(\frac{\sqrt{15}i}{2} \right)^2 = \frac{1}{4} - \frac{-15}{4} = 4$$

our calculation is indeed validated.

Even in the complex-root case (Case 3), we may express the complementary function of a differential equation according to (16.7); that is,

$$y_c = A_1 e^{(h+vi)t} + A_2 e^{(h-vi)t} = e^{ht}(A_1 e^{vit} + A_2 e^{-vit}) \qquad \textbf{(16.11)}$$

But a new feature has been introduced: the number i now appears in the exponents of the two expressions in parentheses. How do we interpret such imaginary exponential functions?

To facilitate their interpretation, it will prove helpful first to transform these expressions into equivalent *circular-function* forms. As we shall presently see, the latter functions characteristically involve periodic fluctuations of a variable. Consequently, the complementary function (16.11), being translatable into circular-function forms, can also be expected to generate a cyclical type of time path.

Circular Functions

Consider a circle with its center at the point of origin and with a radius of length R, as shown in Fig. 16.3. Let the radius, like the hand of a clock, rotate in the counterclockwise direction. Starting from the position OA, it will gradually move into the position OP, followed successively by such positions as OB, OC, and OD; and at the end of a cycle, it will return to OA. Thereafter, the cycle will simply repeat itself.

When in a specific position—say, OP—the clock hand will make a definite angle θ with line OA, and the tip of the hand (P) will determine a vertical distance v and a horizontal distance h. As the angle θ changes during the process of rotation, v and h will vary, although

FIGURE 16.3

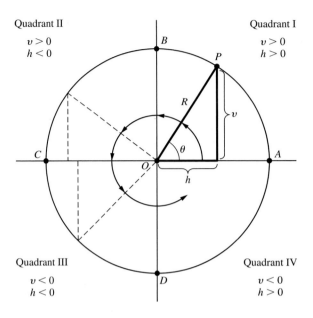

Quadrant II
$v > 0$
$h < 0$

Quadrant I
$v > 0$
$h > 0$

Quadrant III
$v < 0$
$h < 0$

Quadrant IV
$v < 0$
$h > 0$

R will not. Thus the ratios v/R and h/R must change with θ; that is, these two ratios are both functions of the angle θ. Specifically, v/R and h/R are called, respectively, the *sine* (function) of θ and the *cosine* (function) of θ:

$$\sin \theta \equiv \frac{v}{R} \qquad\qquad (16.12)$$

$$\cos \theta \equiv \frac{h}{R} \qquad\qquad (16.13)$$

In view of their connection with a circle, these functions are referred to as *circular functions*. Since they are also associated with a triangle, however, they are alternatively called *trigonometric functions*. Another (and fancier) name for them is *sinusoidal functions*. The sine and cosine functions are not the only circular functions; another frequently encountered one is the *tangent* function, defined as

$$\tan \theta = \frac{\sin \theta}{\cos \theta} = \frac{v}{h} \qquad (h \neq 0)$$

Our major concern here, however, will be with the sine and cosine functions.

The independent variable in a circular function is the angle θ, so the mapping involved here is from an *angle* to a *ratio of two distances*. Usually, angles are measured in *degrees* (for example, 30, 45, and 90°); in analytical work, however, it is more convenient to measure angles in *radians* instead. The advantage of the radian measure stems from the fact that, when θ is so measured, the derivatives of circular functions will come out in neater expressions—much as the base e gives us neater derivatives for exponential and logarithmic functions. But just how much is a radian? To explain this, let us return to Fig. 16.3, where we have drawn the point P so that the length of the *arc AP* is exactly equal to the radius R. A *radian* (abbreviated as *rad*) can then be defined as the size of the angle θ

(in Fig. 16.3) formed by such an R-length arc. Since the circumference of the circle has a total length of $2\pi R$ (where $\pi = 3.14159\ldots$), a complete circle must involve an angle of 2π rad altogether. In terms of degrees, however, a complete circle makes an angle of $360°$; thus, by equating $360°$ to 2π rad, we can arrive at the following conversion table:

Degrees	360	270	180	90	45	0
Radians	2π	$\dfrac{3\pi}{2}$	π	$\dfrac{\pi}{2}$	$\dfrac{\pi}{4}$	0

Properties of the Sine and Cosine Functions

Given the length of R, the value of $\sin\theta$ hinges upon the way the value of v changes in response to changes in the angle θ. In the starting position OA, we have $v = 0$. As the clock hand moves counterclockwise, v starts to assume an increasing positive value, culminating in the maximum value of $v = R$ when the hand coincides with OB, that is, when $\theta = \pi/2$ rad $(= 90°)$. Further movement will gradually shorten v, until its value becomes zero when the hand is in the position OC, i.e., when $\theta = \pi$ rad $(= 180°)$. As the hand enters the third quadrant, v begins to assume negative values; in the position OD, we have $v = -R$. In the fourth quadrant, v is still negative, but it will increase from the value of $-R$ toward the value of $v = 0$, which is attained when the hand returns to OA—that is, when $\theta = 2\pi$ rad $(= 360°)$. The cycle then repeats itself.

When these illustrative values of v are substituted into (16.12), we can obtain the results shown in the "$\sin\theta$" row of Table 16.1. For a more complete description of the sine function, however, see the graph in Fig. 16.4a, where the values of $\sin\theta$ are plotted against those of θ (expressed in radians).

The value of $\cos\theta$, in contrast, depends instead upon the way that h changes in response to changes in θ. In the starting position OA, we have $h = R$. Then h gradually shrinks, till $h = 0$ when $\theta = \pi/2$ (position OB). In the second quadrant, h turns negative, and when $\theta = \pi$ (position OC), $h = -R$. The value of h gradually increases from $-R$ to zero in the third quadrant, and when $\theta = 3\pi/2$ (position OD), we find that $h = 0$. In the fourth quadrant, h turns positive again, and when the hand returns to position OA ($\theta = 2\pi$), we again have $h = R$. The cycle then repeats itself.

The substitution of these illustrative values of h into (16.13) yields the results in the bottom row of Table 16.1, but Fig. 16.4b gives a more complete depiction of the cosine function.

The $\sin\theta$ and $\cos\theta$ functions share the same domain, namely, the set of all real numbers (radian measures of θ). In this connection, it may be pointed out that a *negative* angle simply refers to the reverse rotation of the clock hand; for instance, a clockwise movement

TABLE 16.1

θ	0	$\dfrac{1}{2}\pi$	π	$\dfrac{3}{2}\pi$	2π
$\sin\theta$	0	1	0	-1	0
$\cos\theta$	1	0	-1	0	1

FIGURE 16.4

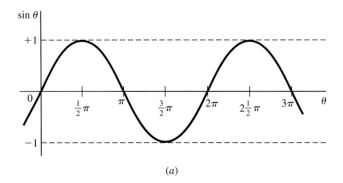

(a)

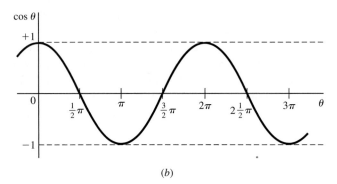

(b)

from OA to OD in Fig. 16.3 generates an angle of $-\pi/2$ rad $(= -90°)$. There is also a common range for the two functions, namely, the closed interval $[-1, 1]$. For this reason, the graphs of $\sin\theta$ and $\cos\theta$ are, in Fig. 16.4, confined to a definite horizontal band.

A major distinguishing property of the sine and cosine functions is that both are *periodic;* their values will repeat themselves for every 2π rad (a complete circle) the angle θ travels through. Each function is therefore said to have a *period* of 2π. In view of this periodicity feature, the following equations hold (for any integer n):

$$\sin(\theta + 2n\pi) = \sin\theta \qquad \cos(\theta + 2n\pi) = \cos\theta$$

That is, adding (or subtracting) any integer multiple of 2π to any angle θ will affect neither the value of $\sin\theta$ nor that of $\cos\theta$.

The graphs of the sine and cosine functions indicate a constant range of fluctuation in each period, namely, ± 1. This is sometimes alternatively described by saying that the *amplitude* of fluctuation is 1. By virtue of the identical period and the identical amplitude, we see that the $\cos\theta$ curve, if shifted rightward by $\pi/2$, will be exactly coincident with the $\sin\theta$ curve. These two curves are therefore said to differ only in *phase,* i.e., to differ only in the location of the peak in each period. Symbolically, this fact may be stated by the equation

$$\cos\theta = \sin\left(\theta + \frac{\pi}{2}\right)$$

The sine and cosine functions obey certain identities. Among these, the more frequently used are

$$\sin(-\theta) \equiv -\sin\theta$$
$$\cos(-\theta) \equiv \cos\theta \tag{16.14}$$

$$\sin^2\theta + \cos^2\theta \equiv 1 \qquad [\text{where } \sin^2\theta \equiv (\sin\theta)^2, \text{ etc.}] \tag{16.15}$$

$$\sin(\theta_1 \pm \theta_2) \equiv \sin\theta_1 \cos\theta_2 \pm \cos\theta_1 \sin\theta_2$$
$$\cos(\theta_1 \pm \theta_2) \equiv \cos\theta_1 \cos\theta_2 \mp \sin\theta_1 \sin\theta_2 \tag{16.16}$$

The pair of identities (16.14) serves to underscore the fact that the cosine function is symmetrical with respect to the vertical axis (that is, θ and $-\theta$ always yield the same cosine value), while the sine function is not. Shown in (16.15) is the fact that, for any magnitude of θ, the sum of the squares of its sine and cosine is always unity. And the set of identities in (16.16) gives the sine and cosine of the sum and difference of two angles θ_1 and θ_2.

Finally, a word about derivatives. Being continuous and smooth, both $\sin\theta$ and $\cos\theta$ are differentiable. The derivatives, $d(\sin\theta)/d\theta$ and $d(\cos\theta)/d\theta$, are obtainable by taking the limits, respectively, of the difference quotients $\Delta(\sin\theta)/\Delta\theta$ and $\Delta(\cos\theta)/\Delta\theta$ as $\Delta\theta \to 0$. The results, stated here without proof, are

$$\frac{d}{d\theta}\sin\theta = \cos\theta \tag{16.17}$$

$$\frac{d}{d\theta}\cos\theta = -\sin\theta \tag{16.18}$$

It should be emphasized, however, that these derivative formulas are valid only when θ is measured in radians; if measured in degrees, for instance, (16.17) will become $d(\sin\theta)/d\theta = (\pi/180)\cos\theta$ instead. It is for the sake of getting rid of the factor $(\pi/180)$ that radian measures are preferred to degree measures in analytical work.

Example 2   Find the slope of the $\sin\theta$ curve at $\theta = \pi/2$. The slope of the sine curve is given by its derivative ($= \cos\theta$). Thus, at $\theta = \pi/2$, the slope should be $\cos(\pi/2) = 0$. You may refer to Fig. 16.4 for verification of this result.

Example 3   Find the second derivative of $\sin\theta$. From (16.17), we know that the first derivative of $\sin\theta$ is $\cos\theta$, therefore the desired second derivative is

$$\frac{d^2}{d\theta^2}\sin\theta = \frac{d}{d\theta}\cos\theta = -\sin\theta$$

Euler Relations

In Sec. 9.5, it was shown that any function which has finite, continuous derivatives up to the desired order can be expanded into a polynomial function. Moreover, if the remainder term R_n in the resulting Taylor series (expansion at any point x_0) or Maclaurin series (expansion at $x_0 = 0$) happens to approach zero as the number of terms n becomes infinite, the polynomial may be written as an infinite series. We shall now expand the sine and cosine functions and then attempt to show how the imaginary exponential expressions encountered in (16.11) can be transformed into circular functions having equivalent expansions.

For the sine function, write $\phi(\theta) = \sin\theta$; it then follows that $\phi(0) = \sin 0 = 0$. By successive derivation, we can get

$$
\left.\begin{array}{l}
\phi'(\theta) = \cos\theta \\
\phi''(\theta) = -\sin\theta \\
\phi'''(\theta) = -\cos\theta \\
\phi^{(4)}(\theta) = \sin\theta \\
\phi^{(5)}(\theta) = \cos\theta \\
\quad\vdots \qquad \vdots
\end{array}\right\}
\Rightarrow
\left\{\begin{array}{l}
\phi'(0) = \cos 0 = 1 \\
\phi''(0) = -\sin 0 = 0 \\
\phi'''(0) = -\cos 0 = -1 \\
\phi^{(4)}(0) = \sin 0 = 0 \\
\phi^{(5)}(0) = \cos 0 = 1 \\
\quad\vdots \qquad \vdots
\end{array}\right.
$$

When substituted into (9.14), where θ now replaces x, these will give us the following Maclaurin series with remainder:

$$
\sin\theta = 0 + \theta + 0 - \frac{\theta^3}{3!} + 0 + \frac{\theta^5}{5!} + \cdots + \frac{\phi^{(n+1)}(p)}{(n+1)!}\theta^{n+1}
$$

Now, the expression $\phi^{(n+1)}(p)$ in the last (remainder) term, which represents the $(n+1)$st derivative evaluated at $\theta = p$, can only take the form of $\pm\cos p$ or $\pm\sin p$ and, as such, can only take a value in the interval $[-1, 1]$, regardless of how large n is. On the other hand, $(n+1)!$ will grow rapidly as $n \to \infty$—in fact, much more rapidly than θ^{n+1} as n increases. Hence, the remainder term will approach zero as $n \to \infty$, and we can therefore express the Maclaurin series as an infinite series:

$$
\sin\theta = \theta - \frac{\theta^3}{3!} + \frac{\theta^5}{5!} - \frac{\theta^7}{7!} + \cdots \tag{16.19}
$$

Similarly, if we write $\psi(\theta) = \cos\theta$, then $\psi(0) = \cos 0 = 1$, and the successive derivatives will be

$$
\left.\begin{array}{l}
\psi'(\theta) = -\sin\theta \\
\psi''(\theta) = -\cos\theta \\
\psi'''(\theta) = \sin\theta \\
\psi^{(4)}(\theta) = \cos\theta \\
\psi^{(5)}(\theta) = -\sin\theta \\
\quad\vdots \qquad \vdots
\end{array}\right\}
\Rightarrow
\left\{\begin{array}{l}
\psi'(0) = -\sin 0 = 0 \\
\psi''(0) = -\cos 0 = -1 \\
\psi'''(0) = \sin 0 = 0 \\
\psi^{(4)}(0) = \cos 0 = 1 \\
\psi^{(5)}(0) = -\sin 0 = 0 \\
\quad\vdots \qquad \vdots
\end{array}\right.
$$

On the basis of these derivatives, we can expand $\cos\theta$ as follows:

$$
\cos\theta = 1 + 0 - \frac{\theta^2}{2!} + 0 + \frac{\theta^4}{4!} + \cdots + \frac{\psi^{(n+1)}(p)}{(n+1)!}\theta^{n+1}
$$

Since the remainder term will again tend toward zero as $n \to \infty$, the cosine function is also expressible as an infinite series, as follows:

$$
\cos\theta = 1 - \frac{\theta^2}{2!} + \frac{\theta^4}{4!} - \frac{\theta^6}{6!} + \cdots \tag{16.20}
$$

You must have noticed that, with (16.19) and (16.20) at hand, we are now capable of constructing a table of sine and cosine values for all possible values of θ (in radians). However, our immediate interest lies in finding the relationship between imaginary exponential expressions and circular functions. To this end, let us now expand the two exponential expressions $e^{i\theta}$ and $e^{-i\theta}$. The reader will recognize that these are but special cases of the expression e^x, which has previously been shown, in (10.6), to have the expansion

$$e^x = 1 + x + \frac{1}{2!}x^2 + \frac{1}{3!}x^3 + \frac{1}{4!}x^4 + \cdots$$

Letting $x = i\theta$, therefore, we can immediately obtain

$$e^{i\theta} = 1 + i\theta + \frac{(i\theta)^2}{2!} + \frac{(i\theta)^3}{3!} + \frac{(i\theta)^4}{4!} + \frac{(i\theta)^5}{5!} + \cdots$$

$$= 1 + i\theta - \frac{\theta^2}{2!} - \frac{i\theta^3}{3!} + \frac{\theta^4}{4!} + \frac{i\theta^5}{5!} - \cdots$$

$$= \left(1 - \frac{\theta^2}{2!} + \frac{\theta^4}{4!} - \cdots\right) + i\left(\theta - \frac{\theta^3}{3!} + \frac{\theta^5}{5!} - \cdots\right)$$

Similarly, by setting $x = -i\theta$, the following result will emerge:

$$e^{-i\theta} = 1 - i\theta + \frac{(-i\theta)^2}{2!} + \frac{(-i\theta)^3}{3!} + \frac{(-i\theta)^4}{4!} + \frac{(-i\theta)^5}{5!} + \cdots$$

$$= 1 - i\theta - \frac{\theta^2}{2!} + \frac{i\theta^3}{3!} + \frac{\theta^4}{4!} - \frac{i\theta^5}{5!} - \cdots$$

$$= \left(1 - \frac{\theta^2}{2!} + \frac{\theta^4}{4!} - \cdots\right) - i\left(\theta - \frac{\theta^3}{3!} + \frac{\theta^5}{5!} - \cdots\right)$$

By substituting (16.19) and (16.20) into these two results, the following pair of identities—known as the *Euler relations*—can readily be established:

$$e^{i\theta} \equiv \cos\theta + i\sin\theta \qquad\qquad \textbf{(16.21)}$$

$$e^{-i\theta} \equiv \cos\theta - i\sin\theta \qquad\qquad \textbf{(16.21$'$)}$$

These will enable us to translate any imaginary exponential function into an equivalent linear combination of sine and cosine functions, and vice versa.

Example 4   Find the value of $e^{i\pi}$. First let us convert this expression into a trigonometric expression. By setting $\theta = \pi$ in (16.21), it is found that $e^{i\pi} = \cos\pi + i\sin\pi$. Since $\cos\pi = -1$ and $\sin\pi = 0$, it follows that $e^{i\pi} = -1$.

Example 5   Show that $e^{-i\pi/2} = -i$. Setting $\theta = \pi/2$ in (16.21$'$), we have

$$e^{-i\pi/2} = \cos\frac{\pi}{2} - i\sin\frac{\pi}{2} = 0 - i(1) = -i$$

Alternative Representations of Complex Numbers

So far, we have represented a pair of conjugate complex numbers in the general form $(h \pm vi)$. Since h and v refer to the abscissa and ordinate in the Cartesian coordinate system of an Argand diagram, the expression $(h \pm vi)$ represents the *Cartesian form* of a pair of conjugate complex numbers. As a by-product of the discussion of circular functions and Euler relations, we can now express $(h \pm vi)$ in two other ways.

Referring to Fig. 16.2, we see that as soon as h and v are specified, the angle θ and the value of R also become determinate. Since a given θ and a given R can together identify a unique point in the Argand diagram, we may employ θ and R to specify the particular pair of complex numbers. By rewriting the definitions of the sine and cosine functions in (16.12) and (16.13) as

$$v = R \sin \theta \quad \text{and} \quad h = R \cos \theta \tag{16.22}$$

the conjugate complex numbers $(h \pm vi)$ can be transformed as follows:

$$h \pm vi = R \cos \theta \pm Ri \sin \theta = R(\cos \theta \pm i \sin \theta)$$

In so doing, we have in effect switched from the Cartesian coordinates of the complex numbers (h and v) to what are called their *polar coordinates* (R and θ). The right-hand expression in the preceding equation, accordingly, exemplifies the *polar form* of a pair of conjugate complex numbers.

Furthermore, in view of the Euler relations, the polar form may also be rewritten into the *exponential form* as follows: $R(\cos \theta \pm i \sin \theta) = Re^{\pm i\theta}$. Hence, we have a total of three alternative representations of the conjugate complex numbers:

$$h \pm vi = R(\cos \theta \pm i \sin \theta) = Re^{\pm i\theta} \tag{16.23}$$

If we are given the values of R and θ, the transformation to h and v is straightforward: we use the two equations in (16.22). What about the reverse transformation? With given values of h and v, no difficulty arises in finding the corresponding value of R, which is equal to $\sqrt{h^2 + v^2}$. But a slight ambiguity arises in regard to θ: the desired value of θ (in radians) is that which satisfies the two conditions $\cos \theta = h/R$ and $\sin \theta = v/R$; but for given values of h and v, θ is not unique! (Why?) Fortunately, the problem is not serious, for by confining our attention to the interval $[0, 2\pi)$ in the domain, the indeterminacy is quickly resolved.

Example 6 Find the Cartesian form of the complex number $5e^{3i\pi/2}$. Here we have $R = 5$ and $\theta = 3\pi/2$; hence, by (16.22) and Table 16.1,

$$h = 5 \cos \frac{3\pi}{2} = 0 \quad \text{and} \quad v = 5 \sin \frac{3\pi}{2} = -5$$

The Cartesian form is thus simply $h + vi = -5i$.

Example 7 Find the polar and exponential forms of $(1 + \sqrt{3}i)$. In this case, we have $h = 1$ and $v = \sqrt{3}$; thus $R = \sqrt{1 + 3} = 2$. Table 16.1 is of no use in locating the value of θ this time, but Table 16.2, which lists some additional selected values of $\sin \theta$ and $\cos \theta$, will help. Specifically,

TABLE 16.2

θ	$\dfrac{\pi}{6}$	$\dfrac{\pi}{4}$	$\dfrac{\pi}{3}$	$\dfrac{3\pi}{4}$
$\sin \theta$	$\dfrac{1}{2}$	$\dfrac{1}{\sqrt{2}}\left(=\dfrac{\sqrt{2}}{2}\right)$	$\dfrac{\sqrt{3}}{2}$	$\dfrac{1}{\sqrt{2}}\left(=\dfrac{\sqrt{2}}{2}\right)$
$\cos \theta$	$\dfrac{\sqrt{3}}{2}$	$\dfrac{1}{\sqrt{2}}\left(=\dfrac{\sqrt{2}}{2}\right)$	$\dfrac{1}{2}$	$\dfrac{-1}{\sqrt{2}}\left(=\dfrac{-\sqrt{2}}{2}\right)$

we are seeking the value of θ such that $\cos\theta = h/R = 1/2$ and $\sin\theta = v/R = \sqrt{3}/2$. The value $\theta = \pi/3$ meets the requirements. Thus, according to (16.23), the desired transformation is

$$1 + \sqrt{3}i = 2\left(\cos\frac{\pi}{3} + i\sin\frac{\pi}{3}\right) = 2e^{i\pi/3}$$

Before leaving this topic, let us note an important extension of the result in (16.23). Supposing that we have the nth power of a complex number—say, $(h + vi)^n$—how do we write its polar and exponential forms? The exponential form is the easier to derive. Since $h + vi = Re^{i\theta}$, it follows that

$$(h + vi)^n = (Re^{i\theta})^n = R^n e^{in\theta}$$

Similarly, we can write

$$(h - vi)^n = (Re^{-i\theta})^n = R^n e^{-in\theta}$$

Note that the power n has brought about two changes: (1) R now becomes R^n, and (2) θ now becomes $n\theta$. When these two changes are inserted into the polar form in (16.23), we find that

$$(h \pm vi)^n = R^n(\cos n\theta \pm i\sin n\theta) \qquad (16.23')$$

That is,

$$[R(\cos\theta \pm i\sin\theta)]^n = R^n(\cos n\theta \pm i\sin n\theta)$$

Known as *De Moivre's theorem,* this result indicates that, to raise a complex number to the nth power, one must simply modify its polar coordinates by raising R to the nth power and multiplying θ by n.

EXERCISE 16.2

1. Find the roots of the following quadratic equations:
   (a) $r^2 - 3r + 9 = 0$ (c) $2x^2 + x + 8 = 0$
   (b) $r^2 + 2r + 17 = 0$ (d) $2x^2 - x + 1 = 0$
2. (a) How many degrees are there in a radian?
   (b) How many radians are there in a degree?
3. With reference to Fig. 16.3, and by using Pythagoras's theorem, prove that
   (a) $\sin^2\theta + \cos^2\theta \equiv 1$ (b) $\sin\dfrac{\pi}{4} = \cos\dfrac{\pi}{4} = \dfrac{1}{\sqrt{2}}$
4. By means of the identities (16.14), (16.15), and (16.16), show that:
   (a) $\sin 2\theta \equiv 2\sin\theta\cos\theta$
   (b) $\cos 2\theta \equiv 1 - 2\sin^2\theta$
   (c) $\sin(\theta_1 + \theta_2) + \sin(\theta_1 - \theta_2) \equiv 2\sin\theta_1\cos\theta_2$
   (d) $1 + \tan^2\theta \equiv \dfrac{1}{\cos^2\theta}$
   (e) $\sin\left(\dfrac{\pi}{2} - \theta\right) \equiv \cos\theta$ (f) $\cos\left(\dfrac{\pi}{2} - \theta\right) \equiv \sin\theta$
5. By applying the chain rule:
   (a) Write out the derivative formulas for $\dfrac{d}{d\theta}\sin f(\theta)$ and $\dfrac{d}{d\theta}\cos f(\theta)$, where $f(\theta)$ is a function of θ.
   (b) Find the derivatives of $\cos\theta^3$, $\sin(\theta^2 + 3\theta)$, $\cos e^\theta$, and $\sin(1/\theta)$.

6. From the Euler relations, deduce that:

(a) $e^{-i\pi} = -1$ (c) $e^{i\pi/4} = \dfrac{\sqrt{2}}{2}(1+i)$

(b) $e^{i\pi/3} = \dfrac{1}{2}(1 + \sqrt{3}i)$ (d) $e^{-3i\pi/4} = -\dfrac{\sqrt{2}}{2}(1+i)$

7. Find the Cartesian form of each complex number:

(a) $2\left(\cos\dfrac{\pi}{6} + i \sin\dfrac{\pi}{6}\right)$ (b) $4e^{i\pi/3}$ (c) $\sqrt{2}e^{-i\pi/4}$

8. Find the polar and exponential forms of the following complex numbers:

(a) $\dfrac{3}{2} + \dfrac{3\sqrt{3}}{2}i$ (b) $4(\sqrt{3} + i)$

16.3   Analysis of the Complex-Root Case

With the concepts of complex numbers and circular functions at our disposal, we are now prepared to approach the complex-root case (Case 3), referred to in Sec. 16.1. You will recall that the classification of the three cases, according to the nature of the characteristic roots, is concerned only with the complementary function of a differential equation. Thus, we can continue to focus our attention on the reduced equation

$$y''(t) + a_1 y'(t) + a_2 y = 0 \qquad \text{[reproduced from (16.4)]}$$

The Complementary Function

When the values of the coefficients a_1 and a_2 are such that $a_1^2 < 4a_2$, the characteristic roots will be the pair of conjugate complex numbers

$$r_1, r_2 = h \pm vi$$

where $\qquad h = -\dfrac{1}{2}a_1 \qquad$ and $\qquad v = \dfrac{1}{2}\sqrt{4a_2 - a_1^2}$

The complementary function, as was already previewed, will thus be in the form

$$y_c = e^{ht}(A_1 e^{vit} + A_2 e^{-vit}) \qquad \text{[reproduced from (16.11)]}$$

Let us first transform the imaginary exponential expressions in the parentheses into equivalent trigonometric expressions, so that we may interpret the complementary function as a circular function. This may be accomplished by using the Euler relations. Letting $\theta = vt$ in (16.21) and (16.21'), we find that

$$e^{vit} = \cos vt + i \sin vt \quad \text{and} \quad e^{-vit} = \cos vt - i \sin vt$$

From these, it follows that the complementary function in (16.11) can be rewritten as

$$y_c = e^{ht}[A_1(\cos vt + i \sin vt) + A_2(\cos vt - i \sin vt)]$$
$$= e^{ht}[(A_1 + A_2)\cos vt + (A_1 - A_2)i \sin vt] \qquad \textbf{(16.24)}$$

FIGURE 16.5

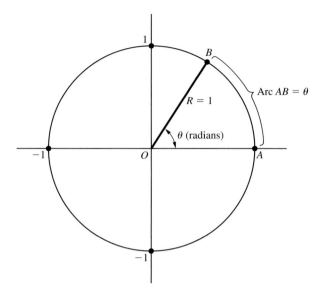

Furthermore, if we employ the shorthand symbols

$$A_5 \equiv A_1 + A_2 \quad \text{and} \quad A_6 \equiv (A_1 - A_2)i$$

it is possible to simplify (16.24) into[†]

$$y_c = e^{ht}(A_5 \cos vt + A_6 \sin vt) \tag{16.24'}$$

where the new arbitrary constants A_5 and A_6 are later to be definitized.

If you are meticulous, you may feel somewhat uneasy about the substitution of θ by vt in the foregoing procedure. The variable θ measures an angle, but vt is a magnitude in units of t (in our context, time). Therefore, how can we make the substitution $\theta = vt$? The answer to this question can best be explained with reference to the *unit circle* (a circle with radius $R = 1$) in Fig. 16.5. True, we have been using θ to designate an angle; but since the angle is measured in radian units, the value of θ is always the ratio of the length of arc AB to the radius R. When $R = 1$, we have specifically

$$\theta \equiv \frac{\text{arc } AB}{R} \equiv \frac{\text{arc } AB}{1} \equiv \text{arc } AB$$

In other words, θ is not only the radian measure of the angle, but also the length of the arc AB, which is a number rather than an angle. If the passing of time is charted on the circumference of the unit circle (counterclockwise), rather than on a straight line as we do in plotting a time series, it really makes no difference whatsoever whether we consider the

---

[†] The fact that in defining A_6, we include in it the imaginary number i is by no means an attempt to "sweep the dirt under the rug." Because A_6 is an arbitrary constant, it can take an imaginary as well as a real value. Nor is it true that, as defined, A_6 will necessarily turn out to be imaginary. Actually, if A_1 and A_2 are a pair of conjugate complex numbers, say, $m \pm ni$, then A_5 and A_6 will both be real: $A_5 = A_1 + A_2 = (m + ni) + (m - ni) = 2m$, and $A_6 = (A_1 - A_2)i = [(m + ni) - (m - ni)]i = (2ni)i = -2n$.

lapse of time as an increase in the radian measure of the angle θ or as a lengthening of the arc AB. Even if $R \neq 1$, moreover, the same line of reasoning can apply, except that in that case θ will be equal to $(\text{arc } AB)/R$ instead; i.e., the angle θ and the arc AB will bear a fixed proportion to each other, instead of being equal. Thus, the substitution $\theta = vt$ is indeed legitimate.

An Example of Solution

Let us find the solution of the differential equation

$$y''(t) + 2y'(t) + 17y = 34$$

with the initial conditions $y(0) = 3$ and $y'(0) = 11$.

Since $a_1 = 2$, $a_2 = 17$, and $b = 34$, we can immediately find the particular integral to be

$$y_p = \frac{b}{a_2} = \frac{34}{17} = 2 \qquad [\text{by (16.3)}]$$

Moreover, since $a_1^2 = 4 < 4a_2 = 68$, the characteristic roots will be the pair of conjugate complex numbers $(h \pm vi)$, where

$$h = -\frac{1}{2}a_1 = -1 \qquad \text{and} \qquad v = \frac{1}{2}\sqrt{4a_2 - a_1^2} = \frac{1}{2}\sqrt{64} = 4$$

Hence, by (16.24'), the complementary function is

$$y_c = e^{-t}(A_5 \cos 4t + A_6 \sin 4t)$$

Combining y_c and y_p, the general solution can be expressed as

$$y(t) = e^{-t}(A_5 \cos 4t + A_6 \sin 4t) + 2$$

To definitize the constants A_5 and A_6, we utilize the two initial conditions. First, by setting $t = 0$ in the general solution, we find that

$$y(0) = e^0(A_5 \cos 0 + A_6 \sin 0) + 2$$
$$= (A_5 + 0) + 2 = A_5 + 2 \qquad [\cos 0 = 1; \sin 0 = 0]$$

By the initial condition $y(0) = 3$, we can thus specify $A_5 = 1$. Next, let us differentiate the general solution with respect to t—using the product rule and the derivative formulas (16.17) and (16.18) while bearing in mind the chain rule [Exercise 16.2-5]—to find $y'(t)$ and then $y'(0)$:

$$y'(t) = -e^{-t}(A_5 \cos 4t + A_6 \sin 4t) + e^{-t}[A_5(-4 \sin 4t) + 4A_6 \cos 4t]$$

so that

$$y'(0) = -(A_5 \cos 0 + A_6 \sin 0) + (-4A_5 \sin 0 + 4A_6 \cos 0)$$
$$= -(A_5 + 0) + (0 + 4A_6) = 4A_6 - A_5$$

By the second initial condition $y'(0) = 11$, and in view that $A_5 = 1$, it then becomes clear that $A_6 = 3$.[†] The definite solution is, therefore,

$$y(t) = e^{-t}(\cos 4t + 3 \sin 4t) + 2 \qquad \qquad \textbf{(16.25)}$$

[†] Note that, here, A_6 indeed turns out to be a real number, even though we have included the imaginary number i in its definition.

As before, the y_p component ($= 2$) can be interpreted as the intertemporal equilibrium level of y, whereas the y_c component represents the deviation from equilibrium. Because of the presence of circular functions in y_c, the time path (16.25) may be expected to exhibit a fluctuating pattern. But what specific pattern will it involve?

The Time Path

We are familiar with the paths of a simple sine or cosine function, as shown in Fig. 16.4. Now we must study the paths of certain variants and combinations of sine and cosine functions so that we can interpret, in general, the complementary function (16.24′)

$$y_c = e^{ht}(A_5 \cos vt + A_6 \sin vt)$$

and, in particular, the y_c component of (16.25).

Let us first examine the term ($A_5 \cos vt$). By itself, the expression ($\cos vt$) is a circular function of (vt), with period 2π ($= 6.2832$) and amplitude 1. The period of 2π means that the graph will repeat its configuration every time that (vt) increases by 2π. When t alone is taken as the independent variable, however, repetition will occur every time t increases by $2\pi/v$, so that with reference to t—as is appropriate in dynamic economic analysis—we shall consider the period of ($\cos vt$) to be $2\pi/v$. (The amplitude, however, remains at 1.) Now, when a multiplicative constant A_5 is attached to ($\cos vt$), it causes the range of fluctuation to change from ± 1 to $\pm A_5$. Thus the amplitude now becomes A_5, though the period is unaffected by this constant. In short, ($A_5 \cos vt$) is a cosine function of t, with period $2\pi/v$ and amplitude A_5. By the same token, ($A_6 \sin vt$) is a sine function of t, with period $2\pi/v$ and amplitude A_6.

There being a common period, the sum ($A_5 \cos vt + A_6 \sin vt$) will also display a repeating cycle every time t increases by $2\pi/v$. To show this more rigorously, let us note that for given values of A_5 and A_6 we can always find two constants A and ε, such that

$$A_5 = A \cos \varepsilon \qquad \text{and} \qquad A_6 = -A \sin \varepsilon$$

Thus we may express the said sum as

$$
\begin{aligned}
A_5 \cos vt + A_6 \sin vt &= A \cos \varepsilon \cos vt - A \sin \varepsilon \sin vt \\
&= A(\cos vt \cos \varepsilon - \sin vt \sin \varepsilon) \\
&= A \cos(vt + \varepsilon) \qquad \text{[by (16.16)]}
\end{aligned}
$$

This is a modified cosine function of t, with amplitude A and period $2\pi/v$, because every time that t increases by $2\pi/v$, ($vt + \varepsilon$) will increase by 2π, which will complete a cycle on the cosine curve.

Had y_c consisted only of the expression ($A_5 \cos vt + A_6 \sin vt$), the implication would have been that the time path of y would be a never-ending, constant-amplitude fluctuation around the equilibrium value of y, as represented by y_p. But there is, in fact, also the multiplicative term e^{ht} to consider. This latter term is of major importance, for, as we shall see, it holds the key to the question of whether the time path will converge.

If $h > 0$, the value of e^{ht} will increase continually as t increases. This will produce a magnifying effect on the amplitude of ($A_5 \cos vt + A_6 \sin vt$) and cause ever-greater deviations from the equilibrium in each successive cycle. As illustrated in Fig. 16.6a, the time path will in this case be characterized by *explosive fluctuation*. If $h = 0$, on the other hand,

FIGURE 16.6

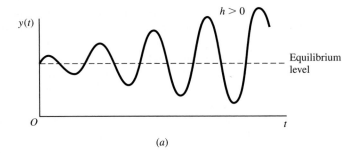

(a)

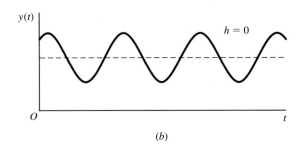

(b)

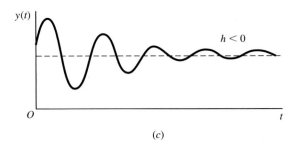

(c)

then $e^{ht} = 1$, and the complementary function will simply be $(A_5 \cos vt + A_6 \sin vt)$, which has been shown to have a constant amplitude. In this second case, each cycle will display a uniform pattern of deviation from the equilibrium as illustrated by the time path in Fig. 16.6*b*. This is a time path with *uniform fluctuation*. Last, if $h < 0$, the term e^{ht} will continually decrease as *t* increases, and each successive cycle will have a smaller amplitude than the preceding one, much as the way a ripple dies down. This case is illustrated in Fig. 16.6*c*, where the time path is characterized by *damped fluctuation*. The solution in (16.25), with $h = -1$, exemplifies this last case. It should be clear that only the case of damped fluctuation can produce a *convergent* time path; in the other two cases, the time path is *nonconvergent* or *divergent*.[†]

In all three diagrams of Fig. 16.6, the intertemporal equilibrium is assumed to be stationary. If it is a moving one, the three types of time path depicted will still fluctuate around it, but since a moving equilibrium generally plots as a curve rather than a horizontal straight

[†] We shall use the two words *nonconvergent* and *divergent* interchangeably, although the latter is more strictly applicable to the explosive than to the uniform variety of nonconvergence.

line, the fluctuation will take on the nature of, say, a series of business cycles around a secular trend.

The Dynamic Stability of Equilibrium

The concept of convergence of the time path of a variable is inextricably tied to the concept of dynamic stability of the intertemporal equilibrium of that variable. Specifically, the equilibrium is dynamically stable if, and only if, the time path is convergent. The condition for convergence of the $y(t)$ path, namely, $h < 0$ (Fig. 16.6c), is therefore also the condition for dynamic stability of the intertemporal equilibrium of y.

You will recall that, for Cases 1 and 2 where the characteristic roots are real, the condition for dynamic stability of equilibrium is that every characteristic root be negative. In the present case (Case 3), with complex roots, the condition seems to be more specialized; it stipulates only that the real part (h) of the complex roots ($h \pm vi$) be negative. However, it is possible to unify all three cases and consolidate the seemingly different conditions into a single, generally applicable one. Just interpret any real root r as a complex root whose imaginary part is zero ($v = 0$). Then the condition "the *real* part of every characteristic root be negative" clearly becomes applicable to all three cases and emerges as the only condition we need.

EXERCISE 16.3

Find the y_p and the y_c, the general solution, and the definite solution of each of the following:

1. $y''(t) - 4y'(t) + 8y = 0$; $y(0) = 3$, $y'(0) = 7$
2. $y''(t) + 4y'(t) + 8y = 2$; $y(0) = 2\frac{1}{4}$, $y'(0) = 4$
3. $y''(t) + 3y'(t) + 4y = 12$; $y(0) = 2$, $y'(0) = 2$
4. $y''(t) - 2y'(t) + 10y = 5$; $y(0) = 6$, $y'(0) = 8\frac{1}{2}$
5. $y''(t) + 9y = 3$; $y(0) = 1$, $y'(0) = 3$
6. $2y''(t) - 12y'(t) + 20y = 40$; $y(0) = 4$, $y'(0) = 5$
7. Which of the differential equations in Probs. 1 to 6 yield time paths with (*a*) damped fluctuation; (*b*) uniform fluctuation; (*c*) explosive fluctuation?

16.4 A Market Model with Price Expectations

In the earlier formulation of the dynamic market model, both Q_d and Q_s are taken to be functions of the current price P alone. But sometimes buyers and sellers may base their market behavior not only on the current price but also on the price *trend* prevailing at the time, for the price trend is likely to lead them to certain *expectations* regarding the price level in the future, and these expectations can, in turn, influence their demand and supply decisions.

Price Trend and Price Expectations

In the continuous-time context, the price-trend information is to be found primarily in the two derivatives dP/dt (whether price is rising) and d^2P/dt^2 (whether increasing at an increasing rate). To take the price trend into account, let us now include these derivatives as additional arguments in the demand and supply functions:

$$Q_d = D[P(t), P'(t), P''(t)]$$
$$Q_s = S[P(t), P'(t), P''(t)]$$

If we confine ourselves to the linear version of these functions and simplify the notation for the independent variables to P, P', and P'', we can write

$$Q_d = \alpha - \beta P + m P' + n P'' \qquad (\alpha, \beta > 0)$$
$$Q_s = -\gamma + \delta P + u P' + w P'' \qquad (\gamma, \delta > 0)$$

(16.26)

where the parameters α, β, γ, and δ are merely carryovers from the previous market models, but m, n, u, and w are new.

The four new parameters, whose signs have not been restricted, embody the buyers' and sellers' price expectations. If $m > 0$, for instance, a rising price will cause Q_d to increase. This would suggest that buyers expect the rising price to *continue* to rise and, hence, prefer to increase their purchases now, when the price is still relatively low. The opposite sign for m would, on the other hand, signify the expectation of a prompt reversal of the price trend, so the buyers would prefer to cut back current purchases and wait for a lower price to materialize later. The inclusion of the parameter n makes the buyers' behavior depend also on the rate of change of dP/dt. Thus the new parameters m and n inject a substantial element of price speculation into the model. The parameters u and w carry a similar implication on the sellers' side of the picture.

A Simplified Model

For simplicity, we shall assume that only the demand function contains price expectations. Specifically, we let m and n be nonzero, but let $u = w = 0$ in (16.26). Further assume that the market is cleared at every point of time. Then we may equate the demand and supply functions to obtain (after normalizing) the differential equation

$$P'' + \frac{m}{n} P' - \frac{\beta + \delta}{n} P = -\frac{\alpha + \gamma}{n}$$

(16.27)

This equation is in the form of (16.2) with the following substitutions:

$$y = P \qquad a_1 = \frac{m}{n} \qquad a_2 = -\frac{\beta + \delta}{n} \qquad b = -\frac{\alpha + \gamma}{n}$$

Since this pattern of change of P involves the second derivative P'' as well as the first derivative P', the present model is certainly distinct from the dynamic market model presented in Sec. 15.2.

Note, however, that the present model differs from the previous model in yet another way. In Sec. 15.2, a dynamic adjustment mechanism, $dP/dt = j(Q_d - Q_s)$ is present. Since that equation implies that $dP/dt = 0$ if and only if $Q_d = Q_s$, the intertemporal sense and the market-clearing sense of equilibrium are coincident in that model. In contrast, the present model assumes market clearance at every moment of time. Thus every price attained in the market is an equilibrium price in the market-clearing sense, although it may not qualify as the intertemporal equilibrium price. In other words, the two senses of equilibrium are now disparate. Note, also, that the adjustment mechanism $dP/dt = j(Q_d - Q_s)$, containing a derivative, is what makes the previous market model dynamic.

In the present model, with no adjustment mechanism, the dynamic nature of the model emanates instead from the expectation terms mP' and nP''.

The Time Path of Price

The intertemporal equilibrium price of this model—the particular integral P_p (formerly y_p)—is easily found by using (16.3). It is

$$P_p = \frac{b}{a_2} = \frac{\alpha + \gamma}{\beta + \delta}$$

Because this is a (positive) constant, it represents a stationary equilibrium.

As for the complementary function P_c (formerly y_c), there are three possible cases.

Case 1 (distinct real roots)

$$\left(\frac{m}{n}\right)^2 > -4\left(\frac{\beta + \delta}{n}\right)$$

The complementary function of this case is, by (16.7),

$$P_c = A_1 e^{r_1 t} + A_2 e^{r_2 t}$$

where

$$r_1, r_2 = \frac{1}{2}\left[-\frac{m}{n} \pm \sqrt{\left(\frac{m}{n}\right)^2 + 4\left(\frac{\beta + \delta}{n}\right)}\right] \qquad \textbf{(16.28)}$$

Accordingly, the general solution is

$$P(t) = P_c + P_p = A_1 e^{r_1 t} + A_2 e^{r_2 t} + \frac{\alpha + \gamma}{\beta + \delta} \qquad \textbf{(16.29)}$$

Case 2 (double real roots)

$$\left(\frac{m}{n}\right)^2 = -4\left(\frac{\beta + \delta}{n}\right)$$

In this case, the characteristic roots take the single value

$$r = -\frac{m}{2n}$$

thus, by (16.9), the general solution may be written as

$$P(t) = A_3 e^{-mt/2n} + A_4 t e^{-mt/2n} + \frac{\alpha + \gamma}{\beta + \delta} \qquad \textbf{(16.29')}$$

Case 3 (complex roots)

$$\left(\frac{m}{n}\right)^2 < -4\left(\frac{\beta + \delta}{n}\right)$$

In this third and last case, the characteristic roots are the pair of conjugate complex numbers

$$r_1, r_2 = h \pm vi$$

where

$$h = -\frac{m}{2n} \quad \text{and} \quad v = \frac{1}{2}\sqrt{-4\left(\frac{\beta+\delta}{n}\right) - \left(\frac{m}{n}\right)^2}$$

Therefore, by (16.24'), we have the general solution

$$P(t) = e^{-mt/2n}(A_5 \cos\ vt + A_6 \sin\ vt) + \frac{\alpha+\gamma}{\beta+\delta} \qquad \textbf{(16.29'')}$$

A couple of general conclusions can be deduced from these results. First, if $n > 0$, then $-4(\beta+\delta)/n$ must be negative and hence less than $(m/n)^2$. Hence Cases 2 and 3 can immediately be ruled out. Moreover, with n positive (as are β and δ), the expression under the square-root sign in (16.28) necessarily exceeds $(m/n)^2$, and thus the square root must be greater than $|m/n|$. The $\pm$ sign in (16.28) would then produce one positive root (r_1) and one negative root (r_2). Consequently, the intertemporal equilibrium is dynamically unstable, unless the definitized value of the constant A_1 happens to be zero in (16.29).

Second, if $n < 0$, then all three cases become feasible. Under Case 1, we can be sure that both roots will be negative if m is negative. (Why?) Interestingly, the repeated root of Case 2 will also be negative if m is negative. Moreover, since h, the real part of the complex roots in Case 3, takes the same value as the repeated root r in Case 2, the negativity of m will also guarantee that h is negative. In short, for all three cases, the dynamic stability of equilibrium is ensured when the parameters m and n are both negative.

Example 1   Let the demand and supply functions be

$$Q_d = 42 - 4P - 4P' + P''$$
$$Q_s = -6 + 8P$$

with initial conditions $P(0) = 6$ and $P'(0) = 4$. Assuming market clearance at every point of time, find the time path $P(t)$.

In this example, the parameter values are

$$\alpha = 42 \quad \beta = 4 \quad \gamma = 6 \quad \delta = 8 \quad m = -4 \quad n = 1$$

Since n is positive, our previous discussion suggests that only Case 1 can arise, and that the two (real) roots r_1 and r_2 will take opposite signs. Substitution of the parameter values into (16.28) indeed confirms this, for

$$r_1, r_2 = \frac{1}{2}(4 \pm \sqrt{16 + 48}) = \frac{1}{2}(4 \pm 8) = 6, -2$$

The general solution is, then, by (16.29),

$$P(t) = A_1 e^{6t} + A_2 e^{-2t} + 4$$

By taking the initial conditions into account, moreover, we find that $A_1 = A_2 = 1$, so the definite solution is

$$P(t) = e^{6t} + e^{-2t} + 4$$

In view of the positive root $r_1 = 6$, the intertemporal equilibrium ($P_p = 4$) is dynamically unstable.

The preceding solution is found by use of formulas (16.28) and (16.29). Alternatively, we can first equate the given demand and supply functions to obtain the differential equation

$$P'' - 4P' - 12P = -48$$

and then solve this equation as a specific case of (16.2).

Example 2 Given the demand and supply functions

$$Q_d = 40 - 2P - 2P' - P''$$
$$Q_s = -5 + 3P$$

with $P(0) = 12$ and $P'(0) = 1$, find $P(t)$ on the assumption that the market is always cleared.

Here the parameters m and n are both negative. According to our previous general discussion, therefore, the intertemporal equilibrium should be dynamically stable. To find the specific solution, we may first equate Q_d and Q_s to obtain the differential equation (after multiplying through by -1)

$$P'' + 2P' + 5P = 45$$

The intertemporal equilibrium is given by the particular integral

$$P_p = \frac{45}{5} = 9$$

From the characteristic equation of the differential equation,

$$r^2 + 2r + 5 = 0$$

we find that the roots are complex:

$$r_1, r_2 = \frac{1}{2}(-2 \pm \sqrt{4 - 20}) = \frac{1}{2}(-2 \pm 4i) = -1 \pm 2i$$

This means that $h = -1$ and $v = 2$, so the general solution is

$$P(t) = e^{-t}(A_5 \cos 2t + A_6 \sin 2t) + 9$$

To definitize the arbitrary constants A_5 and A_6, we set $t = 0$ in the general solution, to get

$$P(0) = e^0(A_5 \cos 0 + A_6 \sin 0) + 9 = A_5 + 9 \qquad [\cos 0 = 1; \sin 0 = 0]$$

Moreover, by differentiating the general solution and then setting $t = 0$, we find that

$$P'(t) = -e^{-t}(A_5 \cos 2t + A_6 \sin 2t) + e^{-t}(-2A_5 \sin 2t + 2A_6 \cos 2t)$$

$$[\text{product rule and chain rule}]$$

and

$$P'(0) = -e^0(A_5 \cos 0 + A_6 \sin 0) + e^0(-2A_5 \sin 0 + 2A_6 \cos 0)$$
$$= -(A_5 + 0) + (0 + 2A_6) = -A_5 + 2A_6$$

Thus, by virtue of the initial conditions $P(0) = 12$ and $P'(0) = 1$, we have $A_5 = 3$ and $A_6 = 2$. Consequently, the definite solution is

$$P(t) = e^{-t}(3 \cos 2t + 2 \sin 2t) + 9$$

This time path is obviously one with periodic fluctuation; the period is $2\pi/v = \pi$. That is, there is a complete cycle every time that t increases by $\pi = 3.14159\ldots$. In view of the multiplicative term e^{-t}, the fluctuation is damped. The time path, which starts from the initial price $P(0) = 12$, converges to the intertemporal equilibrium price $P_p = 9$ in a cyclical fashion.

EXERCISE 16.4

1. Let the parameters $m, n, u,$ and w in (16.26) be all nonzero.

    (a) Assuming market clearance at every point of time, write the new differential equation of the model.

    (b) Find the intertemporal equilibrium price.

    (c) Under what circumstances can periodic fluctuation be ruled out?

2. Let the demand and supply functions be as in (16.26), but with $u = w = 0$ as in the text discussion.

    (a) If the market is not always cleared, but adjusts according to

    $$\frac{dP}{dt} = j(Q_d - Q_s) \qquad (j > 0)$$

    write the appropriate new differential equation.

    (b) Find the intertemporal equilibrium price $\overline{P}$ and the market-clearing equilibrium price P^*.

    (c) State the condition for having a fluctuating price path. Can fluctuation occur if $n > 0$?

3. Let the demand and supply be

    $$Q_d = 9 - P + P' + 3P'' \qquad Q_s = -1 + 4P - P' + 5P''$$

    with $P(0) = 4$ and $P'(0) = 4$.

    (a) Find the price path, assuming market clearance at every point of time.

    (b) Is the time path convergent? With fluctuation?

16.5 The Interaction of Inflation and Unemployment

In this section, we illustrate the use of a second-order differential equation with a macro model dealing with the problem of inflation and unemployment.

The Phillips Relation

One of the most widely used concepts in the modern analysis of the problem of inflation and unemployment is the Phillips relation.[†] In its original formulation, this relation depicts an empirically based negative relation between the rate of growth of money wage and the rate of unemployment:

$$w = f(U) \qquad [f'(U) < 0] \tag{16.30}$$

[†] A. W. Phillips, "The Relationship Between Unemployment and the Rate of Change of Money Wage Rates in the United Kingdom, 1861–1957," *Economica*, November 1958, pp. 283–299.

where the lowercase letter w denotes the rate of growth of money wage W (i.e., $w \equiv \dot{W}/W$) and U is the rate of unemployment. It thus pertains only to the labor market. Later usage, however, has adapted the Phillips relation into a function that links the *rate of inflation* (instead of w) to the rate of unemployment. This adaptation may be justified by arguing that mark-up pricing is in wide use, so that a positive w, reflecting growing money-wage cost, would necessarily carry inflationary implications. And this makes the rate of inflation, like w, a function of U. The inflationary pressure of a positive w can, however, be offset by an increase in labor productivity, assumed to be exogenous, and denoted here by T. Specifically, the inflationary effect can materialize only to the extent that money wage grows faster than productivity. Denoting the rate of inflation—that is, the rate of growth of the price level P—by the lowercase letter p, $(p \equiv \dot{P}/P)$, we may thus write

$$p = w - T \qquad (16.31)$$

Combining (16.30) and (16.31), and adopting the linear version of the function $f(U)$, we then get an adapted Phillips relation

$$p = \alpha - T - \beta U \qquad (\alpha, \beta > 0) \qquad (16.32)$$

The Expectations-Augmented Phillips Relation

More recently, economists have preferred to use the *expectations-augmented* version of the Phillips relation

$$w = f(U) + g\pi \qquad (0 < g \le 1) \qquad (16.30')$$

where π denotes the expected rate of inflation. The underlying idea of (16.30′), as propounded by the Nobel laureate Professor Friedman,[†] is that if an inflationary trend has been in effect long enough, people are apt to form certain inflation expectations which they then attempt to incorporate into their money-wage demands. Thus w should be an increasing function of π. Carried over to (16.32), this idea results in the equation

$$p = \alpha - T - \beta U + g\pi \qquad (0 < g \le 1) \qquad (16.33)$$

With the introduction of a new variable to denote the expected rate of inflation, it becomes necessary to hypothesize how inflation expectations are specifically formed.[‡] Here we adopt the *adaptive expectations* hypothesis

$$\frac{d\pi}{dt} = j(p - \pi) \qquad (0 < j \le 1) \qquad (16.34)$$

Note that, rather than explain the absolute magnitude of π, this equation describes instead its pattern of change over time. If the actual rate of inflation p turns out to exceed the expected rate π, the latter, having now been proven to be too low, is revised upward $(d\pi/dt > 0)$. Conversely, if p falls short of π, then π is revised in the downward direction. In format, (16.34) closely resembles the adjustment mechanism $dP/dt = j(Q_d - Q_s)$ of

[†] Milton Friedman, "The Role of Monetary Policy," *American Economic Review*, March 1968, pp. 1–17.

[‡] This is in contrast to Sec. 16.4, where price expectations were discussed without introducing a new variable to represent the expected price. As a result, the assumptions regarding the formation of expectations were only implicitly embedded in the parameters *m, n, u,* and *w* in (16.26).

the market model. But here the driving force behind the adjustment is the discrepancy between the *actual* and *expected* rates of inflation, rather than Q_d and Q_s.

The Feedback from Inflation to Unemployment

It is possible to consider (16.33) and (16.34) as constituting a complete model. Since there are three variables in a two-equation system, however, one of the variables has to be taken as exogenous. If π and p are considered endogenous, for instance, then U must be treated as exogenous. A more satisfying alternative is to introduce a third equation to explain the variable U, so that the model will be richer in behavioral characteristics. More significantly, this will provide us with an opportunity to take into account the feedback effect of inflation on unemployment. Equation (16.33) tells us how U affects p—largely from the supply side of the economy. But p surely can affect U in return. For example, the rate of inflation may influence the consumption-saving decisions of the public, hence also the aggregate demand for domestic production, and the latter will, in turn, affect the rate of unemployment. Even in the conduct of government policies of demand management, the rate of inflation can make a difference in their effectiveness. Depending on the rate of inflation, a given level of money expenditure (fiscal policy) could translate into varying levels of real expenditure, and similarly, a given rate of nominal-money expansion (monetary policy) could mean varying rates of real-money expansion. And these, in turn, would imply differing effects on output and unemployment.

For simplicity, we shall only take into consideration the feedback through the conduct of monetary policy. Denoting the nominal money balance by M and its rate of growth by $m \equiv \dot{M}/M$, let us postulate that[†]

$$\frac{dU}{dt} = -k(m - p) \qquad (k > 0) \qquad \textbf{(16.35)}$$

Recalling (10.25), and applying it backward, we see that the expression $(m - p)$ represents the rate of growth of *real* money:

$$m - p = \frac{\dot{M}}{M} - \frac{\dot{P}}{P} = r_M - r_P = r_{(M/P)}$$

Thus (16.35) stipulates that dU/dt is negatively related to the rate of growth of real-money balance. Inasmuch as the variable p now enters into the determination of dU/dt, the model now contains a feedback from inflation to unemployment.

The Time Path of π

Together, (16.33) through (16.35) constitute a closed model in the three variables π, p, and U. By eliminating two of the three variables, however, we can condense the model into a single differential equation in a single variable. Suppose that we let that single variable be π. Then we may first substitute (16.33) into (16.34) to get

$$\frac{d\pi}{dt} = j(\alpha - T - \beta U) - j(1 - g)\pi \qquad \textbf{(16.36)}$$

[†] In an earlier discussion, we denoted the money supply by M_s, to distinguish it from the demand for money M_d. Here, we can simply use the unsubscripted letter M, since there is no fear of confusion.

Had this equation contained the expression dU/dt instead of U, we could have substituted (16.35) into (16.36) directly. But as (16.36) stands, we must first deliberately create a dU/dt term by differentiating (16.36) with respect to t, with the result

$$\frac{d^2\pi}{dt^2} = -j\beta\frac{dU}{dt} - j(1-g)\frac{d\pi}{dt} \tag{16.37}$$

Substitution of (16.35) into this then yields

$$\frac{d^2\pi}{dt^2} = j\beta km - j\beta kp - j(1-g)\frac{d\pi}{dt} \tag{16.37'}$$

There is still a p variable to be eliminated. To achieve that, we note that (16.34) implies

$$p = \frac{1}{j}\frac{d\pi}{dt} + \pi \tag{16.38}$$

Using this result in (16.37′), and simplifying, we finally obtain the desired differential equation in the variable π alone:

$$\frac{d^2\pi}{dt^2} + \underbrace{[\beta k + j(1-g)]}_{a_1}\frac{d\pi}{dt} + \underbrace{(j\beta k)}_{a_2}\pi = \underbrace{j\beta km}_{b} \tag{16.37''}$$

The particular integral of this equation is simply

$$\pi_p = \frac{b}{a_2} = m$$

Thus, in this model, the intertemporal equilibrium value of the expected rate of inflation hinges exclusively on the rate of growth of nominal money.

For the complementary function, the two roots are, as before,

$$r_1, r_2 = \frac{1}{2}\left(-a_1 \pm \sqrt{a_1^2 - 4a_2}\right) \tag{16.39}$$

where, as may be noted from (16.37″), both a_1 and a_2 are positive. On a priori grounds, it is not possible to determine whether a_1^2 would exceed, equal, or be less than $4a_2$. Thus all three cases of characteristic roots—distinct real roots, repeated real roots, or complex roots—can conceivably arise. Whichever case presents itself, however, the intertemporal equilibrium will prove dynamically stable in the present model. This can be explained as follows: Suppose, first, that Case 1 prevails, with $a_1^2 > 4a_2$. Then the square root in (16.39) yields a real number. Since a_2 is positive, $\sqrt{a_1^2 - 4a_2}$ is necessarily less than $\sqrt{a_1^2} = a_1$. It follows that r_1 is negative, as is r_2, implying a dynamically stable equilibrium. What if $a_1^2 = 4a_2$ (Case 2)? In that event, the square root is zero, so that $r_1 = r_2 = -a_1/2 < 0$. And the negativity of the repeated roots again implies dynamic stability. Finally, for Case 3, the real part of the complex roots is $h = -a_1/2$. Since this has the same value as the repeated roots under Case 2, the identical conclusion regarding dynamic stability applies.

Although we have only studied the time path of π, the model can certainly yield information on the other variables, too. To find the time path of, say, the U variable, we can *either* start off by condensing the model into a differential equation in U rather than π (see Exercise 16.5-2) *or* deduce the U path from the π path already found (see Example 1).

Example 1

Let the three equations of the model take the specific forms

$$p = \frac{1}{6} - 3U + \pi \qquad (16.40)$$

$$\frac{d\pi}{dt} = \frac{3}{4}(p - \pi) \qquad (16.41)$$

$$\frac{dU}{dt} = -\frac{1}{2}(m - p) \qquad (16.42)$$

Then we have the parameter values $\beta = 3$, $h = 1$, $j = \frac{3}{4}$, and $k = \frac{1}{2}$; thus, with reference to (16.37''), we find

$$a_1 = \beta k + j(1 - g) = \frac{3}{2} \qquad a_2 = j\beta k = \frac{9}{8} \qquad \text{and} \qquad b = j\beta km = \frac{9}{8}m$$

The particular integral is $b/a_2 = m$. With $a_1^2 < 4a_2$, the characteristic roots are complex:

$$r_1, r_2 = \frac{1}{2}\left(-\frac{3}{2} \pm \sqrt{\frac{9}{4} - \frac{9}{2}}\right) = \frac{1}{2}\left(-\frac{3}{2} \pm \frac{3}{2}i\right) = -\frac{3}{4} \pm \frac{3}{4}i$$

That is, $h = -\frac{3}{4}$ and $v = \frac{3}{4}$. Consequently, the general solution for the expected rate of inflation is

$$\pi(t) = e^{-3t/4}\left(A_5 \cos \frac{3}{4}t + A_6 \sin \frac{3}{4}t\right) + m \qquad (16.43)$$

which depicts a time path with damped fluctuation around the equilibrium value m.

From this, we can also deduce the time paths for the p and U variables. According to (16.41), p can be expressed in terms of π and $d\pi/dt$ by the equation

$$p = \frac{4}{3}\frac{d\pi}{dt} + \pi$$

The π path in the general solution (16.43) implies the derivative

$$\frac{d\pi}{dt} = -\frac{3}{4}e^{-3t/4}\left(A_5 \cos \frac{3}{4}t + A_6 \sin \frac{3}{4}t\right)$$

$$+ e^{-3t/4}\left(-\frac{3}{4}A_5 \sin \frac{3}{4}t + \frac{3}{4}A_6 \cos \frac{3}{4}t\right) \qquad \text{[product rule and chain rule]}$$

Using the solution (16.43) and its derivative, we thus have

$$p(t) = e^{-3t/4}\left(A_6 \cos \frac{3}{4}t - A_5 \sin \frac{3}{4}t\right) + m \qquad (16.44)$$

Like the *expected* rate of inflation π, the *actual* rate of inflation p also has a fluctuating time path converging to the equilibrium value m.

As for the U variable, (16.40) tells us that it can be expressed in terms of π and p as follows:

$$U = \frac{1}{3}(\pi - p) + \frac{1}{18}$$

By virtue of the solutions (16.43) and (16.44), therefore, we can write the time path of the rate of unemployment as

$$U(t) = \frac{1}{3}e^{-3t/4}\left[(A_5 - A_6)\cos \frac{3}{4}t + (A_5 + A_6)\sin \frac{3}{4}t\right] + \frac{1}{18} \qquad (16.45)$$

This path is, again, one with damped fluctuation, with $\frac{1}{18}$ as $\overline{U}$, the dynamically stable intertemporal equilibrium value of U.

Because the intertemporal equilibrium values of π and p are both equal to the monetary-policy parameter m, the value of m—the rate of growth of nominal money—provides the axis around which the time paths of π and p fluctuate. If a change occurs in m, a new equilibrium value of π and p will immediately replace the old one, and whatever values the π and p variables happen to take at the moment of the monetary-policy change will become the initial values from which the new π and p paths emanate.

In contrast, the intertemporal equilibrium value $\overline{U}$ does not depend on m. According to (16.45), U converges to the constant $\frac{1}{18}$ regardless of the rate of growth of nominal money, and hence regardless of the equilibrium rate of inflation. This constant equilibrium value of U is referred to as the *natural rate of unemployment*. The fact that the natural rate of unemployment is consistent with any equilibrium rate of inflation can be represented in the Up space by a vertical straight line parallel to the p axis. That vertical line relating the equilibrium values of U and p to each other, is known as the *long-run Phillips curve*. The vertical shape of this curve, however, is contingent upon a special parameter value assumed in this example. When that value is altered, as in Exercise 16.5-4, the long-run Phillips curve may no longer be vertical.

EXERCISE 16.5

1. In the inflation-unemployment model, retain (16.33) and (16.34) but delete (16.35) and let U be exogenous instead.

    (a) What kind of differential equation will now arise?

    (b) How many characteristic roots can you obtain? Is it possible now to have periodic fluctuation in the complementary function?

2. In the text discussion, we condensed the inflation-unemployment model into a differential equation in the variable π. Show that the model can alternatively be condensed into a second-order differential equation in the variable U, with the same a_1 and a_2 coefficients as in (16.37''), but a different constant term $b = kj[\alpha - T - (1 - g)m]$.

3. Let the adaptive expectations hypothesis (16.34) be replaced by the so-called perfect foresight hypothesis $\pi = p$, but retain (16.33) and (16.35).

    (a) Derive a differential equation in the variable p.

    (b) Derive a differential equation in the variable U.

    (c) How do these equations differ fundamentally from the one we obtained under the adaptive expectations hypothesis?

    (d) What change in parameter restriction is now necessary to make the new differential equations meaningful?

4. In Example 1, retain (16.41) and (16.42) but replace (16.40) by

$$p = \frac{1}{6} - 3U + \frac{1}{3}\pi$$

    (a) Find $p(t)$, $\pi(t)$, and $U(t)$.

    (b) Are the time paths still fluctuating? Still convergent?

    (c) What are $\overline{p}$ and $\overline{U}$, the intertemporal equilibrium values of p and U?

    (d) Is it still true that $\overline{U}$ is functionally unrelated to $\overline{p}$? If we now link these two equilibrium values to each other in a long-run Phillips curve, can we still get a vertical curve? What assumption in Example 1 is thus crucial for deriving a vertical long-run Phillips curve?

16.6 Differential Equations with a Variable Term

In the differential equations considered in Sec. 16.1,

$$y''(t) + a_1 y'(t) + a_2 y = b$$

the right-hand term b is a constant. What if, instead of b, we have on the right a *variable term*: i.e., some function of t such as bt^2, e^{bt}, or $b \sin t$? The answer is that we must then modify our particular integral y_p. Fortunately, the complementary function is not affected by the presence of a variable term, because y_c deals only with the reduced equation, whose right side is always zero.

Method of Undetermined Coefficients

We shall explain a method of finding y_p, known as the *method of undetermined coefficients*, which is applicable to constant-coefficient variable-term differential equations, as long as the variable term and its successive derivatives together contain only a *finite* number of distinct types of expression (apart from multiplicative constants). The explanation of this method can best be carried out with a concrete illustration.

Example 1   Find the particular integral of

$$y''(t) + 5y'(t) + 3y = 6t^2 - t - 1 \tag{16.46}$$

By definition, the particular integral is a value of y satisfying the given equation, i.e., a value of y that will make the left side identically equal to the right side regardless of the value of t. Since the left side contains the function $y(t)$ and the derivatives $y'(t)$ and $y''(t)$—whereas the right side contains multiples of the expressions t^2, t, and a constant—we ask: What general function form of $y(t)$, along with its first and second derivatives, will give us the three types of expression t^2, t, and a constant? The obvious answer is a function of the form $B_1 t^2 + B_2 t + B_3$ (where B_i are coefficients yet to be determined), for if we write the particular integral as

$$y(t) = B_1 t^2 + B_2 t + B_3$$

we can derive

$$y'(t) = 2B_1 t + B_2 \qquad \text{and} \qquad y''(t) = 2B_1 \tag{16.47}$$

and these three equations are indeed composed of the said types of expression. Substituting these into (16.46) and collecting terms, we get

$$\text{Left side} = (3B_1)t^2 + (10B_1 + 3B_2)t + (2B_1 + 5B_2 + 3B_3)$$

And when this is equated term by term to the right side, we can determine the coefficients B_i as follows:

$$\left. \begin{array}{r} 3B_1 = 6 \\ 10B_1 + 3B_2 = -1 \\ 2B_1 + 5B_2 + 3B_3 = -1 \end{array} \right\} \quad \Rightarrow \quad \left\{ \begin{array}{l} B_1 = 2 \\ B_2 = -7 \\ B_3 = 10 \end{array} \right.$$

Thus the desired particular integral can be written as

$$y_p = 2t^2 - 7t + 10$$

This method can work only when the number of expression types is finite. (See Exercise 16.6-1.) In general, when this prerequisite is met, the particular integral may be taken as being in the form of a linear combination of all the distinct expression types contained in the given variable term, as well as in all its derivatives. Note, in particular, that a constant expression should be included in the particular integral, if the original variable term or any of its successive derivatives contains a constant term.

Example 2

As a further illustration, let us find the general form for the particular integral suitable for the variable term $(b \sin t)$. Repeated differentiation yields, in this case, the successive derivatives $(b \cos t)$, $(-b \sin t)$, $(-b \cos t)$, $(b \sin t)$, etc., which involve only two distinct types of expression. We may therefore try a particular integral of the form $(B_1 \sin t + B_2 \cos t)$.

A Modification

In certain cases, a complication arises in applying the method. When the coefficient of the y term in the given differential equation is zero, such as in

$$y''(t) + 5y'(t) = 6t^2 - t - 1$$

the previously used trial form for the y_p, namely, $B_1 t^2 + B_2 t + B_3$, will fail to work. The cause of this failure is that, since the $y(t)$ term is out of the picture and since only derivatives $y'(t)$ and $y''(t)$ as shown in (16.47) will be substituted into the left side, no $B_1 t^2$ term will ever appear on the left to be equated to the $6t^2$ term on the right. The way out of this kind of difficulty is to use instead the trial solution $t(B_1 t^2 + B_2 t + B_3)$; or if this too fails (e.g., given the equation $y''(t) = 6t^2 - t - 1$), to use $t^2(B_1 t^2 + B_2 t + B_3)$, and so on.

Indeed, the same trick may be employed in yet another difficult circumstance, as is illustrated in Example 3.

Example 3

Find the particular integral of

$$y''(t) + 3y'(t) - 4y = 2e^{-4t} \qquad \text{(16.48)}$$

Here, the variable term is in the form of e^{-4t}, but all of its successive derivatives (namely, $-8e^{-4t}$, $32e^{-4t}$, $-128e^{-4t}$, etc.) take the same form as well. If we try the solution

$$y(t) = Be^{-4t} \qquad \text{[with } y'(t) = -4Be^{-4t} \text{ and } y''(t) = 16Be^{-4t} \text{]}$$

and substitute these into (16.48), we obtain the inauspicious result that

$$\text{Left side} = (16 - 12 - 4)Be^{-4t} = 0 \qquad \text{(16.49)}$$

which obviously cannot be equated to the right-side term $2e^{-4t}$.

What causes this to happen is the fact that the exponential coefficient in the variable term (-4) happens to be equal to one of the roots of the characteristic equation of (16.48):

$$r^2 + 3r - 4 = 0 \qquad \text{(roots } r_1, r_2 = 1, -4)$$

The characteristic equation, it will be recalled, is obtained through a process of differentiation;[†] but the expression $(16 - 12 - 4)$ in (16.49) is derived through the same process. Not surprisingly, therefore, $(16 - 12 - 4)$ is merely a specific version of $(r^2 + 3r - 4)$ with r set equal to -4. Since -4 happens to be a characteristic root, the quadratic expression

$$r^2 + 3r - 4 = 16 - 12 - 4$$

must of necessity be identically zero.

[†] See the text discussion leading to (16.4″).

To cope with this situation, let us try instead the solution

$$y(t) = Bte^{-4t}$$

with derivatives

$$y'(t) = (1 - 4t)Be^{-4t} \quad \text{and} \quad y''(t) = (-8 + 16t)Be^{-4t}$$

Substituting these into (16.48) will now yield: left side $= -5Be^{-4t}$. When this is equated to the right side, we determine the coefficient to be $B = -2/5$. Consequently, the desired particular integral of (16.48) can be written as

$$y_p = \frac{-2}{5}te^{-4t}$$

EXERCISE 16.6

1. Show that the method of undetermined coefficients is inapplicable to the differential equation $y''(t) + ay'(t) + by = t^{-1}$.
2. Find the particular integral of each of the following equations by the method of undetermined coefficients:

   (a) $y''(t) + 2y'(t) + y = t$ (c) $y''(t) + y'(t) + 2y = e^t$

   (b) $y''(t) + 4y'(t) + y = 2t^2$ (d) $y''(t) + y'(t) + 3y = \sin t$

16.7 Higher-Order Linear Differential Equations

The methods of solution introduced in the previous sections are readily extended to an nth-order linear differential equation. With constant coefficients and a constant term, such an equation can be written generally as

$$y^{(n)}(t) + a_1 y^{(n-1)}(t) + \cdots + a_{n-1} y'(t) + a_n y = b \qquad \textbf{(16.50)}$$

Finding the Solution

In this case of constant coefficients and constant term, the presence of the higher derivatives does not materially affect the method of finding the particular integral discussed earlier.

If we try the simplest possible type of solution, $y = k$, we can see that all the derivatives from $y'(t)$ to $y^{(n)}(t)$ will be zero; hence (16.50) will reduce to $a_n k = b$, and we can write

$$y_p = k = \frac{b}{a_n} \qquad (a_n \neq 0) \qquad [\text{cf. (16.3)}]$$

In case $a_n = 0$, however, we must try a solution of the form $y = kt$. Then, since $y'(t) = k$, all the higher derivatives will vanish, (16.50) can be reduced to $a_{n-1}k = b$, thereby yielding the particular integral

$$y_p = kt = \frac{b}{a_{n-1}}t \qquad (a_n = 0; a_{n-1} \neq 0) \qquad [\text{cf. (16.3$'$)}]$$

If it happens that $a_n = a_{n-1} = 0$, then this last solution will fail, too; instead, a solution of the form $y = kt^2$ must be tried. Further adaptations of this procedure should be obvious.

As for the complementary function, inclusion of the higher-order derivatives in the differential equation has the effect of raising the degree of the characteristic equation. The complementary function is defined as the general solution of the reduced equation

$$y^{(n)}(t) + a_1 y^{(n-1)}(t) + \cdots + a_{n-1} y'(t) + a_n y = 0 \qquad \textbf{(16.51)}$$

Trying $y = Ae^{rt} (\neq 0)$ as a solution and utilizing the knowledge that this implies $y'(t) = r Ae^{rt}, y''(t) = r^2 Ae^{rt}, \ldots, y^{(n)}(t) = r^n Ae^{rt}$, we can rewrite (16.51) as

$$Ae^{rt}(r^n + a_1 r^{n-1} + \cdots + a_{n-1} r + a_n) = 0$$

This equation is satisfied by any value of r which satisfies the following (nth-degree polynomial) characteristic equation

$$r^n + a_1 r^{n-1} + \cdots + a_{n-1} r + a_n = 0 \qquad \textbf{(16.51')}$$

There will, of course, be n roots to this polynomial, and each of these should be included in the general solution of (16.51). Thus our complementary function should in general be in the form

$$y_c = A_1 e^{r_1 t} + A_2 e^{r_2 t} + \cdots + A_n e^{r_n t} \qquad \left(= \sum_{i=1}^{n} A_i e^{r_i t} \right)$$

As before, however, some modifications must be made in case the n roots are not all real and distinct. First, suppose that there are repeated roots, say, $r_1 = r_2 = r_3$. Then, to avoid "collapsing," we must write the first three terms of the solutions as $A_1 e^{r_1 t} + A_2 t e^{r_1 t} + A_3 t^2 e^{r_1 t}$ [cf. (16.9)]. In case we have $r_4 = r_1$ as well, the fourth term must be altered to $A_4 t^3 e^{r_1 t}$, etc.

Second, suppose that two of the roots are complex, say,

$$r_5, r_6 = h \pm vi$$

then the fifth and sixth terms in the preceding solution should be combined into the following expression:

$$e^{ht}(A_5 \cos vt + A_6 \sin vt) \qquad [\text{cf. } (16.24')]$$

By the same token, if two *distinct* pairs of complex roots are found, there must be two such trigonometric expressions (with a different set of values of h, v, and two arbitrary constants for each).[†] As a further possibility, if there happen to be two pairs of *repeated* complex roots, then we should use e^{ht} as the multiplicative term for one but use te^{ht} for the other. Also, even though h and v have identical values in the repeated complex roots, a different pair of arbitrary constants must now be assigned to each.

Once y_p and y_c are found, the general solution of the complete equation (16.50) follows easily. As before, it is simply the sum of the complementary function and the particular integral: $y(t) = y_c + y_p$. In this general solution, we can count a total of n arbitrary constants. Thus, to definitize the solution, as many as n initial conditions will be required.

[†] It is of interest to note that, inasmuch as complex roots always come in conjugate pairs, we can be sure of having *at least one* real root when the differential equation is of an *odd* order, i.e., when n is an odd number.

Example 1

Find the general solution of

$$y^{(4)}(t) + 6y'''(t) + 14y''(t) + 16y'(t) + 8y = 24$$

The particular integral of this fourth-order equation is simply

$$y_p = \frac{24}{8} = 3$$

Its characteristic equation is, by (16.51'),

$$r^4 + 6r^3 + 14r^2 + 16r + 8 = 0$$

which can be factored into the form

$$(r + 2)(r + 2)(r^2 + 2r + 2) = 0$$

From the first two parenthetical expressions, we can obtain the double roots $r_1 = r_2 = -2$, but the last (quadratic) expression yields the pair of complex roots $r_3, r_4 = -1 \pm i$, with $h = -1$ and $v = 1$. Consequently, the complementary function is

$$y_c = A_1 e^{-2t} + A_2 t e^{-2t} + e^{-t}(A_3 \cos t + A_4 \sin t)$$

and the general solution is

$$y(t) = A_1 e^{-2t} + A_2 t e^{-2t} + e^{-t}(A_3 \cos t + A_4 \sin t) + 3$$

The four constants A_1, A_2, A_3, and A_4 can be definitized, of course, if we are given four initial conditions.

Note that all the characteristic roots in this example either are real and negative or are complex and with a negative real part. The time path must therefore be convergent, and the intertemporal equilibrium is dynamically stable.

Convergence and the Routh Theorem

The solution of a high-degree characteristic equation is not always an easy task. For this reason, it should be of tremendous help if we can find a way of ascertaining the convergence or divergence of a time path without having to solve for the characteristic roots. Fortunately, there does exist such a method, which can provide a qualitative (though non-graphic) analysis of a differential equation.

This method is to be found in the *Routh theorem*,[†] which states that:

The real parts of all of the roots of the nth-degree polynomial equation

$$a_0 r^n + a_1 r^{n-1} + \cdots + a_{n-1} r + a_n = 0$$

are negative if and only if the first n of the following sequence of determinants

$$|a_1|; \quad \begin{vmatrix} a_1 & a_3 \\ a_0 & a_2 \end{vmatrix}; \quad \begin{vmatrix} a_1 & a_3 & a_5 \\ a_0 & a_2 & a_4 \\ 0 & a_1 & a_3 \end{vmatrix}; \quad \begin{vmatrix} a_1 & a_3 & a_5 & a_7 \\ a_0 & a_2 & a_4 & a_6 \\ 0 & a_1 & a_3 & a_5 \\ 0 & a_0 & a_2 & a_4 \end{vmatrix}; \quad \cdots$$

all are positive.

In applying this theorem, it should be remembered that $|a_1| \equiv a_1$. Further, it is to be understood that we should take $a_m = 0$ for all $m > n$. For example, given a third-degree

---

[†] For a discussion of this theorem, and a sketch of its proof, see Paul A. Samuelson, *Foundations of Economic Analysis,* Harvard University Press, 1947, pp. 429–435, and the references there cited.

polynomial equation ($n = 3$), we need to examine the signs of the first *three* determinants listed in the Routh theorem; for that purpose, we should set $a_4 = a_5 = 0$.

The relevance of this theorem to the convergence problem should become self-evident when we recall that, in order for the time path $y(t)$ to converge regardless of what the initial conditions happen to be, all the characteristic roots of the differential equation must have negative real parts. Since the characteristic equation (16.51′) is an nth-degree polynomial equation, with $a_0 = 1$, the Routh theorem can be of direct help in the testing of convergence. In fact, we note that the coefficients of the characteristic equation (16.51′) are wholly identical with those of the given differential equation (16.51), so it is perfectly acceptable to substitute the coefficients of (16.51) directly into the sequence of determinants shown in the Routh theorem for testing, provided that we always take $a_0 = 1$. Inasmuch as the condition cited in the theorem is given on the "if and only if" basis, it obviously constitutes a necessary-and-sufficient condition.

Example 2

Test by the Routh theorem whether the differential equation of Example 1 has a convergent time path. This equation is of the fourth order, so $n = 4$. The coefficient are $a_0 = 1$, $a_1 = 6$, $a_2 = 14$, $a_3 = 16$, $a_4 = 8$, and $a_5 = a_6 = a_7 = 0$. Substituting these into the first four determinants, we find their values to be 6, 68, 800, and 6,400, respectively. Because they are all positive, we can conclude that the time path is convergent.

EXERCISE 16.7

1. Find the particular integral of each of the following:
   (a) $y'''(t) + 2y''(t) + y'(t) + 2y = 8$
   (b) $y'''(t) + y''(t) + 3y'(t) = 1$
   (c) $3y'''(t) + 9y''(t) = 1$
   (d) $y^{(4)}(t) + y''(t) = 4$

2. Find the y_p and the y_c (and hence the general solution) of:
   (a) $y'''(t) - 2y''(t) - y'(t) + 2y = 4$
      [Hint: $r^3 - 2r^2 - r + 2 = (r - 1)(r + 1)(r - 2)$]
   (b) $y'''(t) + 7y''(t) + 15y'(t) + 9y = 0$
      [Hint: $r^3 + 7r^2 + 15r + 9 = (r + 1)(r^2 + 6r + 9)$]
   (c) $y'''(t) + 6y''(t) + 10y'(t) + 8y = 8$
      [Hint: $r^3 + 6r^2 + 10r + 8 = (r + 4)(r^2 + 2r + 2)$]

3. On the basis of the signs of the characteristic roots obtained in Prob. 2, analyze the dynamic stability of equilibrium. Then check your answer by the Routh theorem.

4. Without finding their characteristic roots, determine whether the following differential equations will give rise to convergent time paths:
   (a) $y'''(t) - 10y''(t) + 27y'(t) - 18y = 3$
   (b) $y'''(t) + 11y''(t) + 34y'(t) + 24y = 5$
   (c) $y'''(t) + 4y''(t) + 5y'(t) - 2y = -2$

5. Deduce from the Routh theorem that, for the second-order linear differential equation $y''(t) + a_1 y'(t) + a_2 y = b$, the solution path will be convergent regardless of initial conditions if and only if the coefficients a_1 and a_2 are both positive.

Chapter 17

Discrete Time: First-Order Difference Equations

In the continuous-time context, the pattern of change of a variable y is embodied in the derivatives $y'(t)$, $y''(t)$, etc. The time change involved in these is occurring continuously. When time is, instead, taken to be a *discrete* variable, so that the variable t is allowed to take integer values only, the concept of the derivative obviously will no longer be appropriate. Then, as we shall see, the pattern of change of the variable y must be described by so-called differences, rather than by derivatives or differentials, of $y(t)$. Accordingly, the techniques of differential equations will give way to those of *difference equations*.

When we are dealing with discrete time, the value of variable y will change only when the variable t changes from one integer value to the next, such as from $t = 1$ to $t = 2$. Meanwhile, nothing is supposed to happen to y. In this light, it becomes more convenient to interpret the values of t as referring to *periods*—rather than *points*—of time, with $t = 1$ denoting period 1 and $t = 2$ denoting period 2, and so forth. Then we may simply regard y as having one unique value in each time period. In view of this interpretation, the discrete-time version of economic dynamics is often referred to as *period analysis*. It should be emphasized, however, that "period" is being used here not in the calendar sense but in the analytical sense. Hence, a period may involve one extent of calendar time in a particular economic model, but an altogether different one in another. Even in the same model, moreover, each successive period should not necessarily be construed as meaning equal calendar time. In the analytical sense, a period is merely a length of time that elapses before the variable y undergoes a change.

17.1 Discrete Time, Differences, and Difference Equations

The change from continuous time to discrete time produces no effect on the fundamental nature of dynamic analysis, although the formulation of the problem must be altered. Basically, our dynamic problem is still to find a time path from some given pattern of change of a variable y over time. But the pattern of change should now be represented by the difference quotient $\Delta y/\Delta t$, which is the discrete-time counterpart of the derivative dy/dt. Recall, however, that t can now take only integer values; thus, when we are comparing the values of y in two consecutive periods, we must have $\Delta t = 1$. For this reason, the difference quotient $\Delta y / \Delta t$ can be simplified to the expression Δy; this is called the *first difference* of y. The symbol Δ, meaning difference, can accordingly be interpreted as a directive to take the first difference of (y). As such, it constitutes the discrete-time counterpart of the operator symbol d/dt.

The expression Δy can take various values, of course, depending on which two consecutive time periods are involved in the difference-taking (or "differencing"). To avoid ambiguity, let us add a time subscript to y and define the first difference more specifically, as follows:

$$\Delta y_t \equiv y_{t+1} - y_t \qquad (17.1)$$

where y_t means the value of y in the tth period, and y_{t+1} is its value in the period immediately following the tth period. With this symbology, we may describe the pattern of change of y by an equation such as

$$\Delta y_t = 2 \qquad (17.2)$$

or

$$\Delta y_t = -0.1 y_t \qquad (17.3)$$

Equations of this type are called *difference equations*. Note the striking resemblance between the last two equations, on the one hand, and the differential equations $dy/dt = 2$ and $dy/dt = -0.1y$ on the other.

Even though difference equations derive their name from difference expressions such as Δy_t, there are alternate equivalent forms of such equations which are completely free of Δ expressions and which are more convenient to use. By virtue of (17.1), we can rewrite (17.2) as

$$y_{t+1} - y_t = 2 \qquad (17.2')$$

or

$$y_{t+1} = y_t + 2 \qquad (17.2'')$$

For (17.3), the corresponding alternate equivalent forms are

$$y_{t+1} - 0.9 y_t = 0 \qquad (17.3')$$

or

$$y_{t+1} = 0.9 y_t \qquad (17.3'')$$

The double-prime-numbered versions will prove convenient when we are calculating a y value from a known y value of the preceding period. In later discussions, however, we shall employ mostly the single-prime-numbered versions, i.e., those of (17.2') and (17.3').

It is important to note that the choice of time subscripts in a difference equation is somewhat arbitrary. For instance, without any change in meaning, (17.2') can be rewritten as $y_t - y_{t-1} = 2$, where $(t - 1)$ refers to the period which immediately precedes the tth. Or, we may express it equivalently as $y_{t+2} - y_{t+1} = 2$.

Also, it may be pointed out that, although we have consistently used subscripted y symbols, it is also acceptable to use $y(t)$, $y(t + 1)$, and $y(t - 1)$ in their stead. In order to avoid using the notation $y(t)$ for both continuous-time and discrete-time cases, however, we shall, in the discussion of period analysis, adhere to the subscript device.

Analogous to differential equations, difference equations can be either linear or nonlinear, homogeneous or nonhomogeneous, and of the first or second (or higher) orders. Take (17.2') for instance. It can be classified as: (1) linear, for no y term (of any period) is raised to the second (or higher) power or is multiplied by a y term of another period; (2) nonhomogeneous, since the right-hand side (where there is no y term) is nonzero; and (3) of the first order, because there exists only a *first difference* Δy_t, involving a one-period time lag only. (In contrast, a second-order difference equation, to be discussed in Chap. 18, involves a two-period lag and thus entails three y terms: y_{t+2}, y_{t+1}, as well as y_t.)

Actually, (17.2') can also be characterized as having constant coefficients and a constant term ($= 2$). Since the constant-coefficient case is the only one we shall consider, this characterization will henceforth be implicitly assumed. Throughout the present chapter, the constant-term feature will also be retained, although a method of dealing with the variable-term case will be discussed in Chap. 18.

Check that the equation (17.3') is also linear and of the first order; but unlike (17.2'), it is homogeneous.

17.2   Solving a First-Order Difference Equation

In solving a differential equation, our objective was to find a time path $y(t)$. As we know, such a time path is a function of time which is totally free from any derivative (or differential) expressions and which is perfectly consistent with the given differential equation as well as with its initial conditions. The time path we seek from a difference equation is similar in nature. Again, it should be a function of t—a formula defining the values of y in every time period—which is consistent with the given difference equation as well as with its initial conditions. Besides, it must not contain any difference expressions such as Δy_t (or expressions like $y_{t+1} - y_t$).

Solving differential equations is, in the final analysis, a matter of integration. How do we solve a difference equation?

Iterative Method

Before developing a general method of attack, let us first explain a relatively pedestrian method, the *iterative method*—which, though crude, will prove immensely revealing of the essential nature of a so-called solution.

In this chapter we are concerned only with the first-order case; thus the difference equation describes the pattern of change of y between *two* consecutive periods only. Once such a pattern is specified, such as by (17.2''), and once we are given an initial value y_0, it is no problem to find y_1 from the equation. Similarly, once y_1 is found, y_2 will be immediately obtainable, and so forth, by repeated application (iteration) of the pattern of change specified in the difference equation. The results of iteration will then permit us to infer a time path.

Example 1

Find the solution of the difference equation (17.2), assuming an initial value of $y_0 = 15$. To carry out the iterative process, it is more convenient to use the alternative form of the difference equation (17.2″), namely, $y_{t+1} = y_t + 2$, with $y_0 = 15$. From this equation, we can deduce step-by-step that

$$y_1 = y_0 + 2$$
$$y_2 = y_1 + 2 = (y_0 + 2) + 2 = y_0 + 2(2)$$
$$y_3 = y_2 + 2 = [y_0 + 2(2)] + 2 = y_0 + 3(2)$$
$$\cdots\cdots\cdots\cdots\cdots\cdots\cdots\cdots\cdots\cdots\cdots\cdots$$

and, in general, for any period t,

$$y_t = y_0 + t(2) = 15 + 2t \qquad (17.4)$$

This last equation indicates the y value of any time period (including the initial period $t = 0$); it therefore constitutes the solution of (17.2).

The process of iteration is crude—it corresponds roughly to solving simple differential equations by straight integration—but it serves to point out clearly the manner in which a time path is generated. In general, the value of y_t will depend in a specified way on the value of y in the immediately preceding period (y_{t-1}); thus a given initial value y_0 will successively lead to $y_1, y_2, \ldots$, via the prescribed pattern of change.

Example 2

Solve the difference equation (17.3); this time, let the initial value be unspecified and denoted simply by y_0. Again it is more convenient to work with the alternative version in (17.3″), namely, $y_{t+1} = 0.9y_t$. By iteration, we have

$$y_1 = 0.9y_0$$
$$y_2 = 0.9y_1 = 0.9(0.9y_0) = (0.9)^2 y_0$$
$$y_3 = 0.9y_2 = 0.9(0.9)^2 y_0 = (0.9)^3 y_0$$
$$\cdots\cdots\cdots\cdots\cdots\cdots\cdots\cdots\cdots\cdots\cdots\cdots$$

These can be summarized into the solution

$$y_t = (0.9)^t y_0 \qquad (17.5)$$

To heighten interest, we can lend some economic content to this example. In the simple multiplier analysis, a single investment expenditure in period 0 will call forth successive rounds of spending, which in turn will bring about varying amounts of income increment in succeeding time periods. Using y to denote *income increment,* we have $y_0 =$ the amount of investment in period 0; but the subsequent income increments will depend on the marginal propensity to consume (MPC). If MPC $= 0.9$ and if the income of each period is consumed only in the next period, then 90 percent of y_0 will be consumed in period 1, resulting in an income increment in period 1 of $y_1 = 0.9y_0$. By similar reasoning, we can find $y_2 = 0.9y_1$, etc. These, we see, are precisely the results of the iterative process cited previously. In other words, the multiplier process of income generation can be described by a difference equation such as (17.3″), and a solution like (17.5) will tell us what the magnitude of income increment is to be in any time period t.

Example 3

Solve the homogeneous difference equation

$$my_{t+1} - ny_t = 0$$

Upon normalizing and transposing, this may be written as

$$y_{t+1} = \left(\frac{n}{m}\right) y_t$$

which is the same as (17.3″) in Example 2 except for the replacement of 0.9 by n/m. Hence, by analogy, the solution should be

$$y_t = \left(\frac{n}{m}\right)^t y_0$$

Watch the term $\left(\dfrac{n}{m}\right)^t$. It is through this term that various values of t will lead to their corresponding values of y. It therefore corresponds to the expression e^{rt} in the solutions to differential equations. If we write it more generally as b^t (b for base) and attach the more general multiplicative constant A (instead of y_0), we see that the solution of the general homogeneous difference equation of Example 3 will be in the form

$$y_t = Ab^t$$

We shall find that this expression Ab^t will play the same important role in difference equations as the expression Ae^{rt} did in differential equations.[†] However, even though both are exponential expressions, the former is to the base b, whereas the latter is to the base e. It stands to reason that, just as the type of the continuous-time path $y(t)$ depends heavily on the value of r, the discrete-time path y_t hinges principally on the value of b.

General Method

By this time, you must have become quite impressed with the various similarities between differential and difference equations. As might be conjectured, the general method of solution presently to be explained will parallel that for differential equations.

Suppose that we are seeking the solution to the first-order difference equation

$$y_{t+1} + ay_t = c \tag{17.6}$$

where a and c are two constants. The general solution will consist of the sum of two components: a *particular solution* y_p, which is *any* solution of the complete nonhomogeneous equation (17.6), and a *complementary function* y_c, which is the general solution of the reduced equation of (17.6):

$$y_{t+1} + ay_t = 0 \tag{17.7}$$

The y_p component again represents the intertemporal equilibrium level of y, and the y_c component, the deviations of the time path from that equilibrium. The sum of y_c and y_p constitutes the *general* solution, because of the presence of an arbitrary constant. As before, in order to definitize the solution, an initial condition is needed.

Let us first deal with the complementary function. Our experience with Example 3 suggests that we may try a solution of the form $y_t = Ab^t$ (with $Ab^t \neq 0$, for otherwise y_t will turn out simply to be a horizontal straight line lying on the t axis); in that case, we also

---

[†] You may object to this statement by pointing out that the solution (17.4) in Example 1 does not contain a term in the form of Ab^t. This latter fact, however, arises only because in Example 1 we have $b = n/m = 1/1 = 1$, so that the term Ab^t reduces to a constant.

have $y_{t+1} = Ab^{t+1}$. If these values of y_t and y_{t+1} hold, the homogeneous equation (17.7) will become

$$Ab^{t+1} + aAb^t = 0$$

which, upon canceling the nonzero common factor Ab^t, yields

$$b + a = 0 \qquad \text{or} \qquad b = -a$$

This means that, for the trial solution to work, we must set $b = -a$; then the complementary function should be written as

$$y_c(= Ab^t) = A(-a)^t$$

Now let us search for the particular solution, which has to do with the complete equation (17.6). In this regard, Example 3 is of no help at all, because that example relates only to a homogeneous equation. However, we note that for y_p we can choose *any* solution of (17.6); thus if a trial solution of the simplest form $y_t = k$ (a constant) can work out, no real difficulty will be encountered. Now, if $y_t = k$, then y will maintain the same constant value over time, and we must have $y_{t+1} = k$ also. Substitution of these values into (17.6) yields

$$k + ak = c \qquad \text{and} \qquad k = \frac{c}{1+a}$$

Since this particular k value satisfies the equation, the particular integral can be written as

$$y_p(= k) = \frac{c}{1+a} \qquad (a \neq -1)$$

This being a constant, a stationary equilibrium is indicated in this case.

If it happens that $a = -1$, as in Example 1, however, the particular solution $c/(1+a)$ is not defined, and some other solution of the nonhomogeneous equation (17.6) must be sought. In this event, we employ the now-familiar trick of trying a solution of the form $y_t = kt$. This implies, of course, that $y_{t+1} = k(t+1)$. Substituting these into (17.6), we find

$$k(t+1) + akt = c \qquad \text{and} \qquad k = \frac{c}{t+1+at} = c \qquad [\text{because } a = -1]$$

thus

$$y_p(= kt) = ct$$

This form of the particular solution is a nonconstant function of t; it therefore represents a moving equilibrium.

Adding y_c and y_p together, we may now write the general solution in one of the two following forms:

$$y_t = A(-a)^t + \frac{c}{1+a} \qquad [\text{general solution, case of } a \neq -1] \quad \textbf{(17.8)}$$

$$y_t = A(-a)^t + ct = A + ct \qquad [\text{general solution, case of } a = -1] \quad \textbf{(17.9)}$$

Neither of these is completely determinate, in view of the arbitrary constant A. To eliminate this arbitrary constant, we resort to the initial condition that $y_t = y_0$ when $t = 0$. Letting $t = 0$ in (17.8), we have

$$y_0 = A + \frac{c}{1+a} \qquad \text{and} \qquad A = y_0 - \frac{c}{1+a}$$

Consequently, the definite version of (17.8) is

$$y_t = \left(y_0 - \frac{c}{1+a}\right)(-a)^t + \frac{c}{1+a} \qquad \text{[definite solution, case of } a \neq -1\text{]} \quad \textbf{(17.8')}$$

Letting $t = 0$ in (17.9), on the other hand, we find $y_0 = A$, so the definite version of (17.9) is

$$y_t = y_0 + ct \qquad \text{[definite solution, case of } a = -1\text{]} \qquad \textbf{(17.9')}$$

If this last result is applied to Example 1, the solution that emerges is exactly the same as the iterative solution (17.4).

You can check the validity of each of these solutions by the following two steps. First, by letting $t = 0$ in (17.8'), see that the latter equation reduces to the identity $y_0 = y_0$, signifying the satisfaction of the initial condition. Second, by substituting the y_t formula (17.8') and a similar y_{t+1} formula—obtained by replacing t with $(t + 1)$ in (17.8')—into (17.6), see that the latter reduces to the identity $c = c$, signifying that the time path is consistent with the given difference equation. The check on the validity of solution (17.9') is analogous.

Example 4   Solve the first-order difference equation

$$y_{t+1} - 5y_t = 1 \qquad \left(y_0 = \tfrac{7}{4}\right)$$

Following the procedure used in deriving (17.8'), we can find y_c by trying a solution $y_t = Ab^t$ (which implies $y_{t+1} = Ab^{t+1}$). Substituting these values into the homogeneous version $y_{t+1} - 5y_t = 0$ and canceling the common factor Ab^t, we get $b = 5$. Thus

$$y_c = A(5)^t$$

To find y_p, try the solution $y_t = k$, which implies $y_{t+1} = k$. Substituting these into the complete difference equation, we find $k = -\tfrac{1}{4}$. Hence

$$y_p = -\tfrac{1}{4}$$

It follows that the general solution is

$$y_t = y_c + y_p = A(5)^t - \tfrac{1}{4}$$

Letting $t = 0$ here and utilizing the initial condition $y_0 = \tfrac{7}{4}$, we obtain $A = 2$. Thus the definite solution may finally be written as

$$y_t = 2(5)^t - \tfrac{1}{4}$$

Since the given difference equation of this example is a special case of (17.6), with $a = -5$, $c = 1$, and $y_0 = \tfrac{7}{4}$, and since (17.8') is the solution "formula" for this type of difference equation, we could have found our solution by inserting the specific parameter values into (17.8'), with the result that

$$y_t = \left(\frac{7}{4} - \frac{1}{1-5}\right)(5)^t + \frac{1}{1-5} = 2(5)^t - \frac{1}{4}$$

which checks perfectly with the earlier answer.

Note that the y_{t+1} term in (17.6) has a unit coefficient. If a given difference equation has a nonunit coefficient for this term, it must be normalized before using the solution formula (17.8').

EXERCISE 17.2

1. Convert the following difference equations into the form of (17.2''):
   (a) $\Delta y_t = 7$
   (b) $\Delta y_t = 0.3 y_t$
   (c) $\Delta y_t = 2 y_t - 9$

2. Solve the following difference equations by iteration:
   (a) $y_{t+1} = y_t + 1$ $(y_0 = 10)$
   (b) $y_{t+1} = \alpha y_t$ $(y_0 = \beta)$
   (c) $y_{t+1} = \alpha y_t - \beta$ $(y_t = y_0$ when $t = 0)$

3. Rewrite the equations in Prob. 2 in the form of (17.6), and solve by applying formula (17.8') or (17.9'), whichever is appropriate. Do your answers check with those obtained by the iterative method?

4. For each of the following difference equations, use the procedure illustrated in the derivation of (17.8') and (17.9') to find y_c, y_p, and the definite solution:
   (a) $y_{t+1} + 3 y_t = 4$ $(y_0 = 4)$
   (b) $2 y_{t+1} - y_t = 6$ $(y_0 = 7)$
   (c) $y_{t+1} = 0.2 y_t + 4$ $(y_0 = 4)$

17.3   The Dynamic Stability of Equilibrium

In the continuous-time case, the dynamic stability of equilibrium depends on the Ae^{rt} term in the complementary function. In period analysis, the corresponding role is played by the Ab^t term in the complementary function. Since its interpretation is somewhat more complicated than Ae^{rt}, let us try to clarify it before proceeding further.

The Significance of b

Whether the equilibrium is dynamically stable is a question of whether or not the complementary function will tend to zero as $t \to \infty$. Basically, we must analyze the path of the term Ab^t as t is increased indefinitely. Obviously, the value of b (the base of this exponential term) is of crucial importance in this regard. Let us first consider its significance alone, by disregarding the coefficient A (by assuming $A = 1$).

For analytical purposes, we can divide the range of possible values of b, $(-\infty, +\infty)$, into seven distinct regions, as set forth in the first two columns of Table 17.1, arranged in descending order of magnitude of b. These regions are also marked off in Fig. 17.1 on a vertical b scale, with the points $+1$, 0, and -1 as the demarcation points. In fact, these latter three points in themselves constitute the regions II, IV, and VI. Regions III and V, on the other hand, correspond to the set of all positive fractions and the set of all negative fractions, respectively. The remaining two regions, I and VII, are where the numerical value of b exceeds unity.

In each region, the exponential expression b^t generates a different type of time path. These are exemplified in Table 17.1 and illustrated in Fig. 17.1. In region I (where $b > 1$), b^t must increase with t at an increasing pace. The general configuration of the time path will therefore assume the shape of the top graph in Fig. 17.1. Note that this graph is shown

TABLE 17.1
A Classification of the Values of b

				Value of b^t in Different Time Periods				
Region	Value of b		Value of b^t	$t = 0$	$t = 1$	$t = 2$	$t = 3$	$t = 4 \cdots$
I	$b > 1$	$(\lvert b \rvert > 1)$	e.g., $(2)^t$	1	2	4	8	16
II	$b = 1$	$(\lvert b \rvert = 1)$	$(1)^t$	1	1	1	1	1
III	$0 < b < 1$	$(\lvert b \rvert < 1)$	e.g., $\left(\frac{1}{2}\right)^t$	1	$\frac{1}{2}$	$\frac{1}{4}$	$\frac{1}{8}$	$\frac{1}{16}$
IV	$b = 0$	$(\lvert b \rvert = 0)$	$(0)^t$	0	0	0	0	0
V	$-1 < b < 0$	$(\lvert b \rvert < 1)$	e.g., $\left(-\frac{1}{2}\right)^t$	1	$-\frac{1}{2}$	$\frac{1}{4}$	$-\frac{1}{8}$	$\frac{1}{16}$
VI	$b = -1$	$(\lvert b \rvert = 1)$	$(-1)^t$	1	-1	1	-1	1
VII	$b < -1$	$(\lvert b \rvert > 1)$	e.g., $(-2)^t$	1	-2	4	-8	16

as a step function rather than as a smooth curve; this is because we are dealing with period analysis. In region II ($b = 1$), b^t will remain at unity for all values of t. Its graph will thus be a horizontal straight line. Next, in region III, b^t represents a positive fraction raised to integer powers. As the power is increased, b^t must decrease, though it will always remain positive. The next case, that of $b = 0$ in region IV, is quite similar to the case of $b = 1$; but here we have $b^t = 0$ rather than $b^t = 1$, so its graph will coincide with the horizontal axis. However, this case is of peripheral interest only, since we have earlier adopted the assumption that $Ab^t \neq 0$.

When we move into the negative regions, an interesting new phenomenon occurs: The value of b^t will *alternate* between positive and negative values from period to period! This fact is clearly brought out in the last three rows of Table 17.1 and in the last three graphs of Fig. 17.1. In region V, where b is a negative fraction, the alternating time path tends to get closer and closer to the horizontal axis (cf. the positive-fraction region, III). In contrast, when $b = -1$ (region VI), a perpetual alternation between $+1$ and -1 results. And finally, when $b < -1$ (region VII), the alternating time path will deviate farther and farther from the horizontal axis.

What is striking is that, whereas the phenomenon of a fluctuating time path cannot possibly arise from a single Ae^{rt} term (the complex-root case of the second-order differential equation requires a *pair* of complex roots), fluctuation can be generated by a single b^t (or Ab^t) term. Note, however, that the character of the fluctuation is somewhat different; unlike the circular-function pattern, the fluctuation depicted in Fig. 17.1 is nonsmooth. For this reason, we shall employ the word *oscillation* to denote the new, nonsmooth type of fluctuation, even though many writers do use the terms fluctuation and oscillation interchangeably.

The essence of the preceding discussion can be conveyed in the following general statement: The time path of b^t ($b \neq 0$) will be

$$\left.\begin{array}{l} \text{Nonoscillatory} \\ \text{Oscillatory} \end{array}\right\} \quad \text{if} \quad \left\{\begin{array}{l} b > 0 \\ b < 0 \end{array}\right.$$

$$\left.\begin{array}{l} \text{Divergent} \\ \text{Convergent} \end{array}\right\} \quad \text{if} \quad \left\{\begin{array}{l} \lvert b \rvert > 1 \\ \lvert b \rvert < 1 \end{array}\right.$$

It is important to note that, whereas the convergence of the expression e^{rt} depends on the *sign* of r, the convergence of the b^t expression hinges, instead, on the *absolute value* of b.

FIGURE 17.1

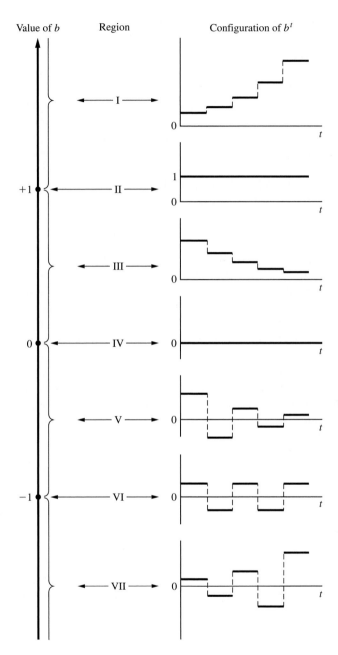

The Role of A

So far we have deliberately left out the multiplicative constant A. But its effects—of which there are two—are relatively easy to take into account. First, the *magnitude* of A can serve to "blow up" (if, say, $A = 3$) or "pare down" (if, say, $A = \frac{1}{5}$) the values of b^t. That is, it can produce a *scale effect* without changing the basic configuration of the time path. The *sign* of A, on the other hand, does materially affect the shape of the path because, if b^t is multiplied by $A = -1$, then each time path shown in Fig. 17.1 will be replaced by its own mirror image with reference to the horizontal axis. Thus, a negative A can produce a *mirror effect* as well as a scale effect.

Convergence to Equilibrium

The preceding discussion presents the interpretation of the Ab^t term in the complementary function, which, as we recall, represents the deviations from some intertemporal equilibrium level. If a term (say) $y_p = 5$ is added to the Ab^t term, the time path must be shifted up vertically by a constant value of 5. This will in no way affect the convergence or divergence of the time path, but it will alter the level with reference to which convergence or divergence in gauged. What Fig. 17.1 pictures is the convergence (or lack of it) of the Ab^t expression to zero. When the y_p is included, it becomes a question of the convergence of the time path $y_t = y_c + y_p$ to the equilibrium level y_p.

In this connection, let us add a word of explanation for the special case of $b = 1$ (region II). A time path such as

$$y_t = A(1)^t + y_p = A + y_p$$

gives the impression that it converges, because the multiplicative term $(1)^t = 1$ produces no explosive effect. Observe, however, that y_t will now take the value $(A + y_p)$ rather than the equilibrium value y_p; in fact, it can never reach y_p (unless $A = 0$). As an illustration of this type of situation, we can cite the time path in (17.9), in which a moving equilibrium $y_p = ct$ is involved. This time path is to be considered divergent, not because of the appearance of t in the particular solution but because, with a nonzero A, there will be a constant deviation from the moving equilibrium. Thus, in stipulating the condition for convergence of time path y_t to the equilibrium y_p, we must rule out the case of $b = 1$.

In sum, the solution

$$y_t = Ab^t + y_p$$

is a convergent path if and only if $|b| < 1$.

Example 1
What kind of time path is represented by $y_t = 2(-\frac{4}{5})^t + 9$? Since $b = -\frac{4}{5} < 0$, the time path is oscillatory. But since $|b| = \frac{4}{5} < 1$, the oscillation is damped, and the time path converges to the equilibrium level of 9.

You should exercise care not to confuse $2(-\frac{4}{5})^t$ with $-2(\frac{4}{5})^t$; they represent entirely different time-path configurations.

Example 2
How do you characterize the time path $y_t = 3(2)^t + 4$? Since $b = 2 > 0$, no oscillation will occur. But since $|b| = 2 > 1$, the time path will diverge from the equilibrium level of 4.

EXERCISE 17.3

1. Discuss the nature of the following time paths:

   (a) $y_t = 3^t + 1$ (c) $y_t = 5\left(-\frac{1}{10}\right)^t + 3$

   (b) $y_t = 2\left(\frac{1}{3}\right)^t$ (d) $y_t = -3\left(\frac{1}{4}\right)^t + 2$

2. What is the nature of the time path obtained from each of the difference equations in Exercise 17.2-4?

3. Find the solutions of the following, and determine whether the time paths are oscillatory and convergent:

(a) $y_{t+1} - \frac{1}{3}y_t = 6$ ($y_0 = 1$)

(b) $y_{t+1} + 2y_t = 9$ ($y_0 = 4$)

(c) $y_{t+1} + \frac{1}{4}y_t = 5$ ($y_0 = 2$)

(d) $y_{t+1} - y_t = 3$ ($y_0 = 5$)

17.4 The Cobweb Model

To illustrate the use of first-order difference equations in economic analysis, we shall cite two variants of the market model for a single commodity. The first variant, known as the *cobweb model,* differs from our earlier market models in that it treats Q_s as a function not of the current price but of the price of the preceding time period.

The Model

Consider a situation in which the producer's output decision must be made one period in advance of the actual sale—such as in agricultural production, where planting must precede by an appreciable length of time the harvesting and sale of the output. Let us assume that the output decision in period t is based on the then-prevailing price P_t. Since this output will not be available for the sale until period $(t + 1)$, however, P_t will determine not Q_{st}, but $Q_{s,t+1}$. Thus we now have a "lagged" supply function.[†]

$$Q_{s,t+1} = S(P_t)$$

or, equivalently, by shifting back the time subscripts by one period,

$$Q_{st} = S(P_{t-1})$$

When such a supply function interacts with a demand function of the form

$$Q_{dt} = D(P_t)$$

interesting dynamic price patterns will result.

Taking the linear versions of these (lagged) supply and (unlagged) demand functions, and assuming that in each time period the market price is always set at a level which clears the market, we have a market model with the following three equations:

$$
\begin{aligned}
Q_{dt} &= Q_{st} \\
Q_{dt} &= \alpha - \beta P_t && (\alpha, \beta > 0) \\
Q_{st} &= -\gamma + \delta P_{t-1} && (\gamma, \delta > 0)
\end{aligned}
\qquad \textbf{(17.10)}
$$

[†] We are making the implicit assumption here that the entire output of a period will be placed on the market, with no part of it held in storage. Such an assumption is appropriate when the commodity in question is perishable or when no inventory is ever kept. A model with inventory will be considered in Sec. 17.5.

By substituting the last two equations into the first, however, the model can be reduced to a single first-order difference equation as follows:

$$\beta P_t + \delta P_{t-1} = \alpha + \gamma$$

In order to solve this equation, it is desirable first to normalize it and shift the time subscripts ahead by one period [alter t to $(t + 1)$, etc.]. The result,

$$P_{t+1} + \frac{\delta}{\beta} P_t = \frac{\alpha + \gamma}{\beta} \tag{17.11}$$

will then be a replica of (17.6), with the substitutions

$$y = P \qquad a = \frac{\delta}{\beta} \qquad \text{and} \qquad c = \frac{\alpha + \gamma}{\beta}$$

Inasmuch as δ and β are both positive, it follows that $a \neq -1$. Consequently, we can apply formula (17.8′), to get the time path

$$P_t = \left(P_0 - \frac{\alpha + \gamma}{\beta + \delta} \right) \left(-\frac{\delta}{\beta} \right)^t + \frac{\alpha + \gamma}{\beta + \delta} \tag{17.12}$$

where P_0 represents the initial price.

The Cobwebs

Three points may be observed in regard to this time path. In the first place, the expression $(\alpha + \gamma)/(\beta + \delta)$, which constitutes the particular integral of the difference equation, can be taken as the intertemporal equilibrium price of the model:[†]

$$\bar{P} = \frac{\alpha + \gamma}{\beta + \delta}$$

Because this is a constant, it is a stationary equilibrium. Substituting $\bar{P}$ into our solution, we can express the time path P_t alternatively in the form

$$P_t = (P_0 - \bar{P}) \left(-\frac{\delta}{\beta} \right)^t + \bar{P} \tag{17.12′}$$

This leads us to the second point, namely, the significance of the expression $(P_0 - \bar{P})$. Since this corresponds to the constant A in the Ab^t term, its sign will bear on the question of whether the time path will commence above or below the equilibrium (mirror effect), whereas its magnitude will decide how far above or below (scale effect). Lastly, there is the expression $(-\delta/\beta)$, which corresponds to the b component of Ab^t. From our model specification that $\beta, \delta > 0$, we can deduce an oscillatory time path. It is this fact which gives rise to the cobweb phenomenon, as we shall presently see. There can, of course, arise *three*

[†] As far as the market-clearing sense of equilibrium is concerned, the price reached in each period is an equilibrium price, because we have assumed that $Q_{dt} - Q_{st}$ for every t.

FIGURE 17.2

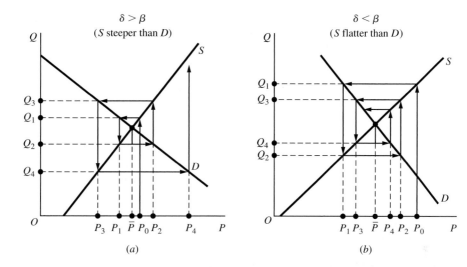

(a)   (b)

possible varieties of oscillation patterns in the model. According to Table 17.1 or Fig. 17.1, the oscillation will be

$$
\left.\begin{array}{l}
\text{Explosive} \\
\text{Uniform} \\
\text{Damped}
\end{array}\right\} \quad \text{if} \quad \delta \gtreqless \beta
$$

where the term *uniform oscillation* refers to the type of path in region VI.

In order to visualize the cobwebs, let us depict the model (17.10) in Fig. 17.2. The second equation of (17.10) plots as a downward-sloping linear demand curve, with its slope numerically equal to β. Similarly, a linear supply curve with a slope equal to δ can be drawn from the third equation, if we let the Q axis represent in this instance a *lagged* quantity supplied. The case of $\delta > \beta$ (S steeper than D) and the case of $\delta < \beta$ (S flatter than D) are illustrated in Fig. 17.2*a* and *b*, respectively. In either case, however, the intersection of D and S will yield the intertemporal equilibrium price $\overline{P}$.

When $\delta > \beta$, as in Fig. 17.2*a*, the interaction of demand and supply will produce an explosive oscillation as follows. Given an initial price P_0 (here assumed above $\overline{P}$), we can follow the arrowhead and read off on the S curve that the quantity supplied in the next period (period 1) will be Q_1. In order to clear the market, the quantity demanded in period 1 must also be Q_1, which is possible if and only if price is set at the level of P_1 (see downward arrow). Now, via the S curve, the price P_1 will lead to Q_2 as the quantity supplied in period 2, and to clear the market in the latter period, price must be set at the level of P_2 according to the demand curve. Repeating this reasoning, we can trace out the prices and quantities in subsequent periods by simply following the arrowheads in the diagram, thereby spinning a "cobweb" around the demand and supply curves. By comparing the price levels, $P_0, P_1, P_2, \ldots$, we observe in this case not only an oscillatory pattern of change but also a tendency for price to widen its deviation from $\overline{P}$ as time goes by. With the cobweb being spun from inside out, the time path is divergent and the oscillation explosive.

By way of contrast, in the case of Fig. 17.2*b*, where $\delta < \beta$, the spinning process will create a cobweb which is centripetal. From P_0, if we follow the arrowheads, we shall be led ever closer to the intersection of the demand and supply curves, where $\overline{P}$ is. While still oscillatory, this price path is convergent.

In Fig. 17.2 we have not shown a third possibility, namely, that of $\delta = \beta$. The procedure of graphical analysis involved, however, is perfectly analogous to the other two cases. It is therefore left to you as an exercise.

The preceding discussion has dealt only with the time path of P (that is, P_t); after P_t is found, however, it takes but a short step to get to the time path of Q. The second equation of (17.10) relates Q_{dt} to P_t, so if (17.12) or (17.12′) is substituted into the demand equation, the time path of Q_{dt} can be obtained immediately. Moreover, since Q_{dt} must be equal to Q_{st} in each time period (clearance of market), we can simply refer to the time path as Q_t rather than Q_{dt}. On the basis of Fig. 17.2, the rationale of this substitution is easily seen. Each point on the D curve relates a P_i to a Q_i pertaining to the same time period; therefore, the demand function can serve to map the time path of price into the time path of quantity.

You should note that the graphical technique of Fig. 17.2 is applicable even when the D and S curves are nonlinear.

EXERCISE 17.4

1. On the basis of (17.10), find the time path of Q, and analyze the condition for its convergence.

2. Draw a diagram similar to those of Fig. 17.2 to show that, for the case of $\delta = \beta$, the price will oscillate uniformly with neither damping nor explosion.

3. Given demand and supply for the cobweb model as follows, find the intertemporal equilibrium price, and determine whether the equilibrium is stable:

   (a) $Q_{dt} = 18 - 3P_t$ $\quad$ $Q_{st} = -3 + 4P_{t-1}$
   (b) $Q_{dt} = 22 - 3P_t$ $\quad$ $Q_{st} = -2 + P_{t-1}$
   (c) $Q_{dt} = 19 - 6P_t$ $\quad$ $Q_{st} = 6P_{t-1} - 5$

4. In model (17.10), let the $Q_{dt} = Q_{st}$ condition and the demand function remain as they are, but change the supply function to

   $$Q_{st} = -\gamma + \delta P_t^*$$

   where P_t^* denotes the *expected price* for period t. Furthermore, suppose that sellers have the "adaptive" type of price expectation:[†]

   $$P_t^* = P_{t-1}^* + \eta(P_{t-1} - P_{t-1}^*) \qquad (0 < \eta \le 1)$$

   where η (the Greek letter eta) is an expectation-adjustment coefficient.

   (a) Give an economic interpretation to the preceding equation. In what respects is it similar to, and different from, the adaptive expectations equation (16.34)?

   (b) What happens if η takes its maximum value? Can we consider the cobweb model as a special case of the present model?

[†] See Marc Nerlove, "Adaptive Expectations and Cobweb Phenomena," *Quarterly Journal of Economics*, May 1958, pp. 227–240.

(c) Show that the new model can be represented by the first-order difference equation

$$P_{t+1} - \left(1 - \eta - \frac{\eta\delta}{\beta}\right) P_t = \frac{\eta(\alpha + \gamma)}{\beta}$$

(*Hint:* Solve the supply function for P_t^*, and then use the information that $Q_{st} = Q_{dt} = \alpha - \beta P_t$.)

(d) Find the time path of price. Is this path necessarily oscillatory? Can it be oscillatory? Under what circumstances?

(e) Show that the time path P_t, if oscillatory, will converge only if $1 - 2/\eta < -\delta/\beta$. As compared with the cobweb solution (17.12) or (17.12'), does the new model have a wider or narrower range for the stability-inducing values of $-\delta/\beta$?

5. The cobweb model, like the previously encountered dynamic market models, is essentially based on the static market model presented in Sec. 3.2. What economic assumption is the dynamizing agent in the present case? Explain.

17.5 A Market Model with Inventory

In the preceding model, price is assumed to be set in such a way as to clear the current output of every time period. The implication of that assumption is either that the commodity is a perishable which cannot be stocked or that, though it is stockable, no inventory is ever kept. Now we shall construct a model in which sellers do keep an inventory of the commodity.

The Model

Let us assume the following:

1. Both the quantity demanded, Q_{dt}, and the quantity currently produced, Q_{st}, are unlagged linear functions of price P_t.

2. The adjustment of price is effected not through market clearance in every period, but through a process of price-setting by the sellers: At the beginning of each period, the sellers set a price for that period after taking into consideration the inventory situation. If, as a result of the preceding-period price, inventory accumulated, the current-period price is set at a lower level than before, in order to "move" the merchandise; but if inventory decumulated instead, the current price is set higher than before.

3. The price adjustment made from period to period is inversely proportional to the observed change in the inventory (stock).

With these assumptions, we can write the following equations:

$$
\begin{aligned}
Q_{dt} &= \alpha - \beta P_t & (\alpha, \beta > 0) \\
Q_{st} &= -\gamma + \delta P_t & (\gamma, \delta > 0) \\
P_{t+1} &= P_t - \sigma(Q_{st} - Q_{dt}) & (\sigma > 0)
\end{aligned}
\qquad \textbf{(17.13)}
$$

where σ denotes the *stock-induced-price-adjustment* coefficient. Note that (17.13) is really nothing but the discrete-time counterpart of the market model of Sec. 15.2, although we have now couched the price-adjustment process in terms of *inventory* $(Q_{st} - Q_{dt})$ rather than *excess demand* $(Q_{dt} - Q_{st})$. Nevertheless, the analytical results will turn out to be much different; for one thing, with discrete time, we may encounter the phenomenon of oscillations. Let us derive and analyze the time path P_t.

The Time Path

By substituting the first two equations into the third, the model can be condensed into a single difference equation:

$$P_{t+1} - [1 - \sigma(\beta + \delta)]P_t = \sigma(\alpha + \gamma) \qquad \textbf{(17.14)}$$

and its solution is given by $(17.8')$:

$$P_t = \left(P_0 - \frac{\alpha + \gamma}{\beta + \delta}\right)[1 - \sigma(\beta + \delta)]^t + \frac{\alpha + \gamma}{\beta + \delta}$$

$$= (P_0 - \overline{P})[1 - \sigma(\beta + \delta)]^t + \overline{P} \qquad \textbf{(17.15)}$$

Obviously, therefore, the dynamic stability of the model will hinge on the expression $1 - \sigma(\beta + \delta)$; for convenience, let us refer to this expression as b.

With reference to Table 17.1, we see that, in analyzing the exponential expression b^t, seven distinct regions of b values may be defined. However, since our model specifications $(\sigma, \beta, \delta > 0)$ have effectually ruled out the first two regions, there remain only five possible cases, as listed in Table 17.2. For each of these regions, the b specification of the second column can be translated into an equivalent σ specification, as shown in the third column. For instance, for region III, the b specification is $0 < b < 1$; therefore, we can write

$$0 < 1 - \sigma(\beta + \delta) < 1$$

$$-1 < -\sigma(\beta + \delta) < 0 \qquad \text{[subtracting 1 from all three parts]}$$

and $\qquad \dfrac{1}{\beta + \delta} > \sigma > 0 \qquad \text{[dividing through by } -(\beta + \delta)]$

TABLE 17.2
Types of Time Path

Region	Value of $b \equiv 1 - \sigma(\beta + \delta)$	Value of σ	Nature of Time Path P_t
III	$0 < b < 1$	$0 < \sigma < \dfrac{1}{\beta + \delta}$	Nonoscillatory and convergent
IV	$b = 0$	$\sigma = \dfrac{1}{\beta + \delta}$	Remaining in equilibrium[†]
V	$-1 < b < 0$	$\dfrac{1}{\beta + \delta} < \sigma < \dfrac{2}{\beta + \delta}$	With damped oscillation
VI	$b = -1$	$\sigma = \dfrac{2}{\beta + \delta}$	With uniform oscillation
VII	$b < -1$	$\sigma > \dfrac{2}{\beta + \delta}$	With explosive oscillation

[†] The fact that price will be remaining in equilibrium in this case can also be seen directly from (17.14). With $\sigma = 1/(\beta + \delta)$, the coefficient of P_t becomes zero, and (17.14) reduces to $P_{t+1} = \sigma(\alpha + \gamma) = (\alpha + \gamma)/(\beta + \delta) = \overline{P}$.

This last gives us the desired equivalent σ specification for region III. The translation for the other regions may be carried out analogously. Since the type of time path pertaining to each region is already known from Fig. 17.1, the σ specification enables us to tell from given values of σ, β, and δ the general nature of the time path P_t, as outlined in the last column of Table 17.2.

Example 1

If the sellers in our model always increase (decrease) the price by 10 percent of the amount of the decrease (increase) in inventory, and if the demand curve has a slope of -1 and the supply curve a slope of 15 (both slopes with respect to the price axis), what type of time path P_t will we find?

Here, we have $\sigma = 0.1$, $\beta = 1$, and $\delta = 15$. Since $1/(\beta + \delta) = \frac{1}{16}$ and $2/(\beta + \delta) = \frac{1}{8}$, the value of σ $(= \frac{1}{10})$ lies between the former two values; it is thus a case of region V. The time path P_t will be characterized by damped oscillation.

Graphical Summary of the Results

The substance of Table 17.2, which contains as many as five different possible cases of σ specification, can be made much easier to grasp if the results are presented graphically. Inasmuch as the σ specification involves essentially a comparison of the relative magnitudes of the parameters σ and $(\beta + \delta)$, let us plot σ against $(\beta + \delta)$, as in Fig. 17.3. Note that we need only concern ourselves with the positive quadrant because, by model specification, σ and $(\beta + \delta)$ are both positive. From Table 17.2, it is clear that regions IV and VI are specified by the equations $\sigma = 1/(\beta + \delta)$ and $\sigma = 2/(\beta + \delta)$, respectively. Since each of these plots as a rectangular hyperbola, the two regions are graphically represented by the two hyperbolic curves in Fig. 17.3. Once we have the two hyperbolas, moreover, the other three regions immediately fall into place. Region III, for instance, is merely the set of points lying below the lower hyperbola, where we have σ less than $1/(\beta + \delta)$. Similarly, region V is represented by the set of points falling between the two hyperbolas, whereas all the points located above the higher hyperbola pertain to region VII.

FIGURE 17.3

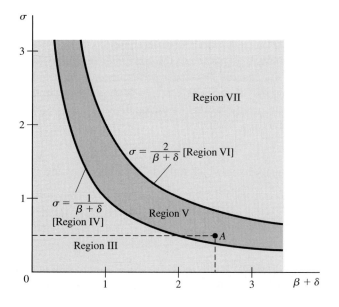

Example 2

If $\sigma = \frac{1}{2}$, $\beta = 1$, and $\delta = \frac{3}{2}$, will our model (17.13) yield a convergent time path P_t? The given parametric values correspond to point A in Fig. 17.3. Since it falls within region V, the time path is convergent, though oscillatory.

You will note that, in the two models just presented, our analytical results are in each instance stated as a set of alternative possible cases—three types of oscillatory path for the cobwebs, and five types of time path in the inventory model. This richness of analytical results stems, of course, from the parametric formulation of the models. The fact that our result cannot be stated in a single unequivocal answer is, of course, a merit rather than a weakness.

EXERCISE 17.5

1. In solving (17.14), why should formula (17.8′) be used instead of (17.9′)?
2. On the basis of Table 17.2, check the validity of the translation from the b specification to the σ specification for regions IV through VII.
3. If model (17.13) has the following numerical form:

$$Q_{dt} = 21 - 2P_t$$
$$Q_{st} = -3 + 6P_t$$
$$P_{t+1} = P_t - 0.3(Q_{st} - Q_{dt})$$

find the time path P_t and determine whether it is convergent.
4. Suppose that, in model (17.13), the supply in each period is a fixed quantity, say, $Q_{st} = k$, instead of a function of price. Analyze the behavior of price over time. What restriction should be imposed on k to make the solution economically meaningful?

17.6   Nonlinear Difference Equations—The Qualitative-Graphic Approach

Thus far we have only utilized *linear* difference equations in our models; but the facts of economic life may not always acquiesce to the convenience of linearity. Fortunately, when nonlinearity occurs in the case of first-order difference-equation models, there exists an easy method of analysis that is applicable under fairly general conditions. This method, graphic in nature, closely resembles that of the qualitative analysis of first-order differential equations presented in Sec. 15.6.

Phase Diagram

Nonlinear difference equations in which only the variables y_{t+1} and y_t appear, such as

$$y_{t+1} + y_t^3 = 5 \qquad \text{or} \qquad y_{t+1} + \sin y_t - \ln y_t = 3$$

can be categorically represented by the equation

$$y_{t+1} = f(y_t) \tag{17.16}$$

where f can be a function of any degree of complexity, as long as it is a function of y_t alone without t as another argument. When the two variables y_{t+1} and y_t are plotted against each other in a Cartesian coordinate plane, the resulting diagram constitutes a *phase diagram,* and the curve corresponding to *f* is a *phase line.* From these, it is possible to analyze the time path of the variable by the process of iteration.

The terms phase diagram and phase line are used here in analogy to the differential-equation case; but note one dissimilarity in the construction of the diagram. In the differential-equation case, we plotted dy/dt against y as in Fig. 15.3, so that, in order to be perfectly analogous in the present case, we should have Δy_t on the vertical axis and y_t on the horizontal. This is not impossible to do, but it is much more convenient to place y_{t+1} on the vertical axis instead, as we have done in Fig. 17.4 where the same scale is used on both axes. Note the presence of a 45° line in each diagram of Fig. 17.4; this line will prove to be of great service in carrying out our graphic analysis.

Let us illustrate the procedure involved by means of Fig. 17.4a, where we have drawn a phase line (labeled f_1) representing a specific difference equation $y_{t+1} = f_1(y_t)$. If we are

FIGURE 17.4

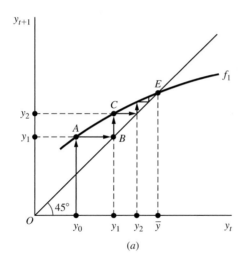

(a)

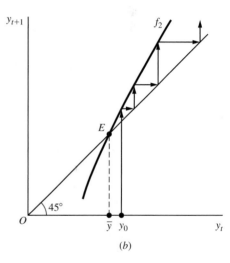

(b)

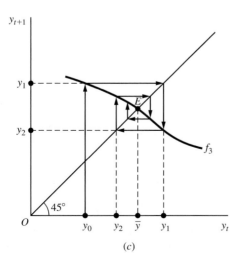

(c)

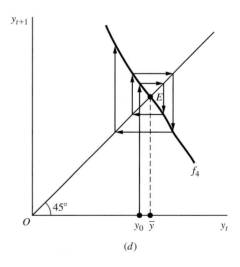

(d)

given an initial value y_0 (plotted on the horizontal axis), by iteration we can trace out all the subsequent values of y as follows. First, since the phase line f_1 maps the initial value y_0 into y_1 according to the equation

$$y_1 = f_1(y_0)$$

we can go straight up from y_0 to the phase line, hit point A, and read its height on the vertical axis as the value of y_1. Next, we seek to map y_1 into y_2 according to the equation

$$y_2 = f_1(y_1)$$

For this purpose, we must first plot y_1 on the horizontal axis—similarly to y_0 during the first mapping. This required transplotting of y_1 from the vertical axis to the horizontal is most easily accomplished by the use of the 45° line, which, having a slope of $+1$, is the locus of points with identical abscissa and ordinate, such as (2, 2) and (5, 5). Thus, to transplot y_1 from the vertical axis, we can simply go across to the 45° line, hit point B, and then turn straight down to the horizontal axis to locate the point y_1. By repeating this process, we can map y_1 to y_2 via point C on the phase line, and then use the 45° line for transplotting y_2, etc.

Now that the nature of the iteration is clear, we may observe that the desired iteration can be achieved simply by following the arrowheads from y_0 to A (on the phase line), to B (on the 45° line), to C (on the phase line), etc.—always alternating between the two lines—without it ever being necessary to resort to the axes again.

Types of Time Path

The graphic iterations just outlined are, of course, equally applicable to the other three diagrams in Fig. 17.4. Actually, these four diagrams serve to illustrate four basic varieties of phase lines, each implying a different type of time path. The first two phase lines, f_1 and f_2, are characterized by positive slopes, with one slope being less than unity and the other one greater than unity:

$$0 < f_1'(y_t) < 1 \qquad \text{and} \qquad f_2'(y_t) > 1$$

The remaining two, on the other hand, are negatively sloped; specifically, we have

$$-1 < f_3'(y_t) < 0 \qquad \text{and} \qquad f_4'(y_t) < -1$$

In each diagram of Fig. 17.4, the intertemporal equilibrium value of y (namely $\bar{y}$) is located at the intersection of the phase line and the 45° line, which we have labeled E. This is so because the point E on the phase line, being simultaneously a point on the 45° line, will map a y_t into a y_{t+1} of identical value; and when $y_{t+1} = y_t$, by definition y must be in equilibrium intertemporally. Our principal task is to determine whether, given an initial value $y_0 \neq \bar{y}$, the pattern of change implied by the phase line will lead us consistently toward $\bar{y}$ (convergent) or away from it (divergent).

For the phase line f_1, the iterative process leads from y_0 to $\bar{y}$ in a steady path, without oscillation. You can verify that, if y_0 is placed to the right of $\bar{y}$, there will also be a steady movement toward $\bar{y}$, although it will be in the leftward direction. These time paths are convergent to equilibrium, and their general configurations would be of the same type as shown in region III of Fig. 17.1.

Given the phase line f_2, whose slope exceeds unity, however, a divergent time path emerges. From an initial value y_0 greater than $\bar{y}$, the arrowheads lead steadily away from the equilibrium to higher and higher y values. As you can verify, an initial value lower than $\bar{y}$ gives rise to a similar steady divergent movement, though in the opposite direction.

When the phase line is negatively inclined, as in f_3 and f_4, the steady movement gives way to oscillation, and there appears now the phenomenon of *overshooting* the equilibrium mark. In diagram *c*, y_0 leads to y_1, which exceeds $\bar{y}$, only to be followed by y_2, which falls short of $\bar{y}$, etc. The convergence of the time path will, in such cases, depend on the slope of the phase line being less than 1 in its absolute value. This is the case of the phase line f_3, where the extent of overshooting tends to diminish in successive periods. For the phase line f_4, whose slope exceeds 1 numerically, on the other hand, the opposite tendency prevails, resulting in a divergent time path.

The oscillatory time paths generated by phase lines f_3 and f_4 are reminiscent of the cobwebs in Fig. 17.2. In Fig. 17.4*c* or *d*, however, the cobweb is spun around a phase line (which contains a lag) and the 45° line, instead of around a demand curve and a (lagged) supply curve. Here, a 45° line is used as a mechanical aid for transplotting a value of y, whereas in Fig. 17.2, the *D* curve (which plays a role similar to that of the 45° line in Fig. 17.4) is an integral part of the model itself. Specifically, once Q_{st} is determined on the supply curve, we let the arrowheads hit the *D* curve for the purpose of finding a price that will "clear the market," as was the rule of the game in the cobweb model. Consequently, there is a basic difference in the labeling of the axes: in Fig. 17.2 there are two entirely different variables, *P* and *Q*, but in Fig. 17.4 the axes represent the values of the same variable y in two consecutive periods. Note however, that if we analyze the graph of the difference equation (17.11) which summarizes the cobweb model, rather than the separate demand and supply functions in (17.10), then the resulting diagram will be a phase line such as shown in Fig. 17.4. In other words, there really exist two alternative ways of graphically analyzing the cobweb model, which will yield the identical result.

The basic rule emerging from the preceding consideration of the phase line is that the *algebraic sign* of its slope determines whether there will be *oscillation,* and the *absolute value* of its slope governs the question of *convergence.* If the phase line happens to contain both positively and negatively sloped segments, and if the absolute value of its slope is at some points greater, and elsewhere less, than 1, the time path will naturally become more complicated. However, even in such cases, the graphic-iterative analysis can be employed with equal ease. Of course, an initial value must be given to us before the iteration can be duly started. Indeed, in these more complicated cases, a different initial value can lead to a time path of an altogether different breed (see Exercises 17.6-2 and 17.6-3).

A Market with a Price Ceiling

We shall now cite an economic example of a nonlinear difference equation. In Fig. 17.4, the four nonlinear phase lines all happen to be of the smooth variety; in the present example, we shall show a nonsmooth phase line.

As a point of departure, let us take the *linear* difference equation (17.11) of the cobweb model and rewrite it as

$$P_{t+1} = \frac{\alpha + \gamma}{\beta} - \frac{\delta}{\beta} P_t \qquad \left(\frac{\delta}{\beta} > 0 \right) \qquad \textbf{(17.17)}$$

FIGURE 17.5

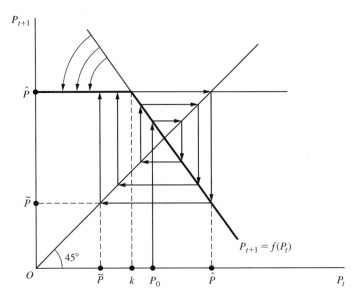

This is in the format of $P_{t+1} = f(P_t)$, with $f'(P_t) = -\delta/\beta < 0$. We have plotted this linear phase line in Fig. 17.5 on the assumption that the slope is greater than 1 in absolute value, implying *explosive* oscillation.

Now let there be imposed a legal price ceiling $\hat{P}$ (read: "P caret" or, less formally, "P hat"). This can be shown in Fig. 17.5 as a horizontal straight line because, irrespective of the level of P_t, P_{t+1} is now forbidden to exceed the level of $\hat{P}$. What this does is to invalidate that part of the phase line lying above $\hat{P}$ or, to view it differently, to bend down the upper part of the phase line to the level of $\hat{P}$, thus resulting in a kinked phase line.[†] In view of the kink, the new (heavy) phase line is not only nonlinear but nonsmooth as well. Like a step function, this kinked line will require more than one equation to express it algebraically:

$$P_{t+1} = \begin{cases} \hat{P} & \text{(for } P_t \le k) \\ \dfrac{\alpha + \gamma}{\beta} - \dfrac{\delta}{\beta} P_t & \text{(for } P_t > k) \end{cases} \qquad \textbf{(17.17$'$)}$$

where k denotes the value of P_t at the kink.

Assuming an initial price P_0, let us trace out the time path of price iteratively. During the first stage of iteration, when the downward-sloping segment of the phase line is in effect, the explosive oscillatory tendency clearly manifests itself. After a few periods, however, the arrowheads begin to hit the ceiling price, and thereafter the time path will develop into a perpetual cyclical movement between $\hat{P}$ and an effective *price floor* $\tilde{P}$ (read: "P tilde" or, less formally, "P wiggle"). Thus, by virtue of the price ceiling, the intrinsic explosive tendency of the model is effectively contained, and the ever-widening oscillation is now tamed into a uniform oscillation producing a so-called limit cycle.

[†] Strictly speaking, we should also "bend" that part of the phase line lying to the right of the point $\hat{P}$ on the horizontal axis. But it does no harm to leave it as it is, as long as the other end has already been bent, because the transplotting of P_{t+1} to the horizontal axis will carry the upper limit of $\hat{P}$ over to the P_t axis automatically.

What is significant about this result is that, whereas in the case of a linear phase line a uniformly oscillatory path can be produced if and only if the slope of the phase line is -1, now after the introduction of nonlinearity the same analytical result can arise even when the phase line has a slope other than -1. The economic implication of this is of considerable import. If one observes a more or less uniform oscillation in the actual time path of a variable and attempts to explain it by means of a *linear* model, one will be forced to rely on the rather special—and implausible—model specification that the phase-line slope is exactly -1. But if nonlinearity is introduced, in either the smooth or the nonsmooth variety, then a host of more reasonable assumptions can be used, each of which can equally account for the observed feature of uniform oscillation.

EXERCISE 17.6

1. In difference-equation models, the variable t can only take integer values. Does this imply that in the phase diagrams of Fig. 17.4 the variables y_t and y_{t+1} must be considered as discrete variables?

2. As a phase line, use the left half of an inverse U-shaped curve, and let it intersect the 45° line at two points L (left) and R (right).
   (*a*) Is this a case of multiple equilibria?
   (*b*) If the initial value y_0 lies to the left of L, what kind of time path will be obtained?
   (*c*) What if the initial value lies between L and R?
   (*d*) What if the initial value lies to the right of R?
   (*e*) What can you conclude about the dynamic stability of equilibrium at L and at R, respectively?

3. As a phase line, use an inverse U-shaped curve. Let its upward-sloping segment intersect the 45° line at point L, and let its downward-sloping segment intersect the 45° line at point R. Answer the same five questions raised in the Prob. 2. (*Note:* Your answer will depend on the particular way the phase line is drawn; explore various possibilities.)

4. In Fig. 17.5, rescind the legal price ceiling and impose a minimum price P_m instead.
   (*a*) How will the phase line change?
   (*b*) Will it be kinked? Nonlinear?
   (*c*) Will there also develop a uniformly oscillatory movement in price?

5. With reference to (17.17′) and Fig. 17.5, show that the constant k can be expressed as

$$k = \frac{\alpha + \gamma}{\delta} - \frac{\beta}{\delta}\hat{P}$$

Chapter 18

Higher-Order Difference Equations

The economic models in Chap. 17 involve difference equations that relate P_t and P_{t-1} to each other. As the P value in one period can uniquely determine the P value in the next, the time path of P becomes fully determinate once an initial value P_0 is specified. It may happen, however, that the value of an economic variable in period t (say, y_t) depends not only on y_{t-1} but also on y_{t-2}. Such a situation will give rise to a difference equation of the second order.

Strictly speaking, a *second-order difference equation* is one that involves an expression $\Delta^2 y_t$, called the *second difference* of y_t, but contains no differences of order higher than 2. The symbol Δ^2, the discrete-time counterpart of the symbol d^2/dt^2, is an instruction to "take the second difference" as follows:

$$\begin{aligned} \Delta^2 y_t = \Delta(\Delta y_t) &= \Delta(y_{t+1} - y_t) && \text{[by (17.1)]} \\ &= (y_{t+2} - y_{t+1}) - (y_{t+1} - y_t) && \text{[again by (17.1)]}^\dagger \\ &= y_{t+2} - 2y_{t+1} + y_t \end{aligned}$$

Thus a second difference of y_t is transformable into a sum of terms involving a two-period time lag. Since expressions like $\Delta^2 y_t$ and Δy_t are quite cumbersome to work with, we shall simply redefine a second-order difference equation as one involving a two-period time lag in the variable. Similarly, a third-order difference equation is one that involves a three-period time lag, etc.

Let us first concentrate on the method of solving a second-order difference equation, leaving the generalization to higher-order equations in Section 18.4. To keep the scope of discussion manageable, we shall only deal with linear difference equations with constant coefficients in the present chapter. However, both the constant-term and variable-term varieties will be examined.

---

† That is, we first move the subscripts in the $(y_{t+1} - y_t)$ expression forward by one period, to get a new expression $(y_{t+2} - y_{t+1})$, and then we subtract from the latter the original expression. Note that, since the resulting difference may be written as $\Delta y_{t+1} - \Delta y_t$, we may infer the following rule of operation:

$$\Delta(y_{t+1} - y_t) = \Delta y_{t+1} - \Delta y_t$$

This is reminiscent of the rule applicable to the derivative of a sum or difference.

18.1   Second-Order Linear Difference Equations with Constant Coefficients and Constant Term

A simple variety of second-order difference equations takes the form

$$y_{t+2} + a_1 y_{t+1} + a_2 y_t = c \tag{18.1}$$

You will recognize this equation to be linear, nonhomogeneous, and with constant coefficients (a_1, a_2) and constant term c.

Particular Solution

As before, the solution of (18.1) may be expected to have two components: a particular solution y_p representing the intertemporal equilibrium level of y, and a complementary function y_c specifying, for every time period, the deviation from the equilibrium. The particular solution, defined as any solution of the complete equation, can sometimes be found simply by trying a solution of the form $y_t = k$. Substituting this constant value of y into (18.1), we obtain

$$k + a_1 k + a_2 k = c \qquad \text{and} \qquad k = \frac{c}{1 + a_1 + a_2}$$

Thus, so long as $(1 + a_1 + a_2) \neq 0$, the particular integral is

$$y_p(= k) = \frac{c}{1 + a_1 + a_2} \qquad \text{(case of } a_1 + a_2 \neq -1) \tag{18.2}$$

Example 1   Find the particular integral of $y_{t+2} - 3y_{t+1} + 4y_t = 6$. Here we have $a_1 = -3$, $a_2 = 4$, and $c = 6$. Since $a_1 + a_2 \neq -1$, the particular solution can be obtained from (18.2) as follows:

$$y_p = \frac{6}{1 - 3 + 4} = 3$$

In case $a_1 + a_2 = -1$, then the trial solution $y_t = k$ breaks down, and we can try $y_t = kt$ instead. Substituting the latter into (18.1) and bearing in mind that we now have $y_{t+1} = k(t + 1)$ and $y_{t+2} = k(t + 2)$, we find that

$$k(t + 2) + a_1 k(t + 1) + a_2 kt = c$$

and $\qquad k = \dfrac{c}{(1 + a_1 + a_2)t + a_1 + 2} = \dfrac{c}{a_1 + 2} \qquad$ [since $a_1 + a_2 = -1$]

Thus we can write the particular solution as

$$y_p(= kt) = \frac{c}{a_1 + 2} t \qquad \text{(case of } a_1 + a_2 = -1; a_1 \neq -2) \tag{18.2'}$$

Example 2   Find the particular solution of $y_{t+2} + y_{t+1} - 2y_t = 12$. Here, $a_1 = 1$, $a_2 = -2$, and $c = 12$. Obviously, formula (18.2) is not applicable, but (18.2′) is. Thus,

$$y_p = \frac{12}{1 + 2} t = 4t$$

This particular solution represents a moving equilibrium.

If $a_1 + a_2 = -1$, but at the same time $a_1 = -2$ (that is, if $a_1 = -2$ and $a_2 = 1$), then we can adopt a trial solution of the form $y_t = kt^2$, which implies $y_{t+1} = k(t+1)^2$, etc. As you may verify, in this case the particular solution turns out to be

$$y_p = kt^2 = \frac{c}{2}t^2 \qquad \text{(case of } a_1 = -2; a_2 = 1) \qquad \textbf{(18.2'')}$$

However, since this formula applies only to the unique case of the difference equation $y_{t+2} - 2y_{t+1} + y_t = c$, its usefulness is rather limited.

Complementary Function

To find the complementary function, we must concentrate on the reduced equation

$$y_{t+2} + a_1 y_{t+1} + a_2 y_t = 0 \qquad \textbf{(18.3)}$$

Our experience with first-order difference equations has taught us that the expression Ab^t plays a prominent role in the general solution of such an equation. Let us therefore try a solution of the form $y_t = Ab^t$, which naturally implies that $y_{t+1} = Ab^{t+1}$, and so on. It is our task now to determine the values of A and b.

Upon substitution of the trial solution into (18.3), the equation becomes

$$Ab^{t+2} + a_1 Ab^{t+1} + a_2 Ab^t = 0$$

or, after canceling the (nonzero) common factor Ab^t,

$$b^2 + a_1 b + a_2 = 0 \qquad \textbf{(18.3')}$$

This quadratic equation—the *characteristic equation* of (18.3) or of (18.1)—which is comparable to (16.4''), possesses the two *characteristic roots*

$$b_1, b_2 = \frac{-a_1 \pm \sqrt{a_1^2 - 4a_2}}{2} \qquad \textbf{(18.4)}$$

each of which is acceptable in the solution Ab^t. In fact, *both b_1 and b_2* should appear in the general solution of the homogeneous difference equation (18.3) because, just as in the case of differential equations, this general solution must consist of two *linearly independent* parts, each with its own multiplicative arbitrary constant.

Three possible situations may be encountered in regard to the characteristic roots, depending on the square-root expression in (18.4). You will find these parallel very closely the analysis of second-order differential equations in Sec. 16.1.

Case 1 (distinct real roots)   When $a_1^2 > 4a_2$, the square root in (18.4) is a real number, and b_1 and b_2 are real and distinct. In that event, b_1^t and b_2^t are linearly independent, and the complementary function can simply be written as a linear combination of these expressions; that is,

$$y_c = A_1 b_1^t + A_2 b_2^t \qquad \textbf{(18.5)}$$

You should compare this with (16.7).

Example 3   Find the solution of $y_{t+2} + y_{t+1} - 2y_t = 12$. This equation has the coefficients $a_1 = 1$ and $a_2 = -2$; from (18.4), the characteristic roots can be found to be $b_1, b_2 = 1, -2$. Thus, the complementary function is

$$y_c = A_1(1)^t + A_2(-2)^t = A_1 + A_2(-2)^t$$

Since, in Example 2, the particular solution of the given difference equation has already been found to be $y_p = 4t$, we can write the general solution as

$$y_t = y_c + y_p = A_1 + A_2(-2)^t + 4t$$

There are still two arbitrary constants A_1 and A_2 to be definitized; to accomplish this, *two* initial conditions are necessary. Suppose that we are given $y_0 = 4$ and $y_1 = 5$. Then, since by letting $t = 0$ and $t = 1$ successively in the general solution we find

$$y_0 = A_1 + A_2 \qquad (= 4 \text{ by the first initial condition})$$
$$y_1 = A_1 - 2A_2 + 4 \qquad (= 5 \text{ by the second initial condition})$$

the arbitrary constants can be definitized to $A_1 = 3$ and $A_2 = 1$. The definite solution then can finally be written as

$$y_t = 3 + (-2)^t + 4t$$

Case 2 (repeated real roots)   When $a_1^2 = 4a_2$, the square root in (18.4) vanishes, and the characteristic roots are repeated:

$$b(= b_1 = b_2) = -\frac{a_1}{2}$$

Now, if we express the complementary function in the form of (18.5), the two components will collapse into a single term:

$$A_1 b_1^t + A_2 b_2^t = (A_1 + A_2)b^t \equiv A_3 b^t$$

This will not do, because we are now short of one constant.

To supply the missing component—which, we recall, should be linearly independent of the term $A_3 b^t$—the old trick of multiplying b^t by the variable t will again work. The new component term is therefore to take the form $A_4 t b^t$. That this is linearly independent of $A_3 b^t$ should be obvious, for we can never obtain the expression $A_4 t b^t$ by attaching a constant coefficient to $A_3 b^t$. That $A_4 t b^t$ does indeed qualify as a solution of the homogeneous equation (18.3), just as $A_3 b^t$ does, can easily be verified by substituting $y_t = A_4 t b^t$ [and $y_{t+1} = A_4(t+1)b^{t+1}$, etc.] into (18.3)[†] and seeing that the latter will reduce to an identity $0 = 0$.

The complementary function for the repeated-root case is therefore

$$y_c = A_3 b^t + A_4 t b^t \tag{18.6}$$

which you should compare with (16.9).

Example 4   Find the complementary function of $y_{t+2} + 6y_{t+1} + 9y_t = 4$. The coefficients being $a_1 = 6$ and $a_2 = 9$, the characteristic roots are found to be $b_1 = b_2 = -3$. We therefore have

$$y_c = A_3(-3)^t + A_4 t(-3)^t$$

If we proceed a step further, we can easily find $y_p = \frac{1}{4}$, so the general solution of the given difference equation is

$$y_t = A_3(-3)^t + A_4 t(-3)^t + \tfrac{1}{4}$$

Given two initial conditions, A_3 and A_4 can again be assigned definite values.

[†] In this substitution it should be kept in mind that we have in the present case $a_1^2 = 4a_2$ and $b = -a_1/2$.

Case 3 (complex roots) Under the remaining possibility of $a_1^2 < 4a_2$, the characteristic roots are conjugate complex. Specifically, they will be in the form

$$b_1, b_2 = h \pm vi$$

where

$$h = -\frac{a_1}{2} \quad \text{and} \quad v = \frac{\sqrt{4a_2 - a_1^2}}{2} \quad \text{(18.7)}$$

The complementary function itself thus becomes

$$y_c = A_1 b_1^t + A_2 b_2^t = A_1(h + vi)^t + A_2(h - vi)^t$$

As it stands, y_c is not easily interpreted. But fortunately, thanks to De Moivre's theorem, given in (16.23'), this complementary function can easily be transformed into trigonometric terms, which we have learned to interpret.

According to the said theorem, we can write

$$(h \pm vi)^t = R^t(\cos \theta t \pm i \sin \theta t)$$

where the value of R (always taken to be positive) is, by (16.10),

$$R = \sqrt{h^2 + v^2} = \sqrt{\frac{a_1^2 + 4a_2 - a_1^2}{4}} = \sqrt{a_2} \quad \text{(18.8)}$$

and θ is the radian measure of the angle in the interval $[0, 2\pi)$, which satisfies the conditions

$$\cos \theta = \frac{h}{R} = \frac{-a_1}{2\sqrt{a_2}} \quad \text{and} \quad \sin \theta = \frac{v}{R} = \sqrt{1 - \frac{a_1^2}{4a_2}} \quad \text{(18.9)}$$

Therefore, the complementary function can be transformed as follows:

$$\begin{aligned} y_c &= A_1 R^t(\cos \theta t + i \sin \theta t) + A_2 R^t(\cos \theta t - i \sin \theta t) \\ &= R^t[(A_1 + A_2) \cos \theta t + (A_1 - A_2)i \sin \theta t] \\ &= R^t(A_5 \cos \theta t + A_6 \sin \theta t) \end{aligned} \quad \text{(18.10)}$$

where we have adopted the shorthand symbols

$$A_5 \equiv A_1 + A_2 \quad \text{and} \quad A_6 \equiv (A_1 - A_2)i$$

The complementary function (18.10) differs from its differential-equation counterpart (16.24') in two important respects. First, the expressions $\cos \theta t$ and $\sin \theta t$ have replaced the previously used $\cos vt$ and $\sin vt$. Second, the multiplicative factor R^t (an exponential with base R) has replaced the natural exponential expression e^{ht}. In short, we have switched from the Cartesian coordinates (h and v) of the complex roots to their polar coordinates (R and θ). The values of R and θ can be determined from (18.8) and (18.9) once h and v become known. It is also possible to calculate R and θ directly from the parameter values a_1 and a_2 via (18.8) and (18.9), provided we first make certain that $a_1^2 < 4a_2$ and that the roots are indeed complex.

Example 5   Find the general solution of $y_{t+2} + \frac{1}{4}y_t = 5$. With coefficients $a_1 = 0$ and $a_2 = \frac{1}{4}$, this constitutes an illustration of the complex-root case of $a_1^2 < 4a_2$. By (18.7), the real and imaginary parts of the roots are $h = 0$ and $v = \frac{1}{2}$. It follows from (18.8) that

$$R = \sqrt{0 + \left(\frac{1}{2}\right)^2} = \frac{1}{2}$$

Since the value of θ is that which can satisfy the two equations

$$\cos\theta = \frac{h}{R} = 0 \qquad \text{and} \qquad \sin\theta = \frac{v}{R} = 1$$

it may be concluded from Table 16.1 that

$$\theta = \frac{\pi}{2}$$

Consequently, the complementary function is

$$y_c = \left(\frac{1}{2}\right)^t \left(A_5 \cos\frac{\pi}{2}t + A_6 \sin\frac{\pi}{2}t\right)$$

To find y_p, let us try a constant solution $y_t = k$ in the complete equation. This yields $k = 4$; thus, $y_p = 4$, and the general solution can be written as

$$y_t = \left(\frac{1}{2}\right)^t \left(A_5 \cos\frac{\pi}{2}t + A_6 \sin\frac{\pi}{2}t\right) + 4 \qquad \textbf{(18.11)}$$

Example 6   Find the general solution of $y_{t+2} - 4y_{t+1} + 16y_t = 0$. In the first place, the particular solution is easily found to be $y_p = 0$. This means that the general solution $y_t\ (= y_c + y_p)$ will be identical with y_c. To find the latter, we note that the coefficients $a_1 = -4$ and $a_2 = 16$ do produce complex roots. Thus we may substitute the a_1 and a_2 values directly into (18.8) and (18.9) to obtain

$$R = \sqrt{16} = 4$$

$$\cos\theta = \frac{4}{2\cdot4} = \frac{1}{2} \qquad \text{and} \qquad \sin\theta = \sqrt{1 - \frac{16}{4\cdot16}} = \sqrt{\frac{3}{4}} = \frac{\sqrt{3}}{2}$$

The last two equations enable us to find from Table 16.2 that

$$\theta = \frac{\pi}{3}$$

It follows that the complementary function—which also serves as the general solution here—is

$$y_c(= y_t) = 4^t \left(A_5 \cos\frac{\pi}{3}t + A_6 \sin\frac{\pi}{3}t\right) \qquad \textbf{(18.12)}$$

The Convergence of the Time Path

As in the case of first-order difference equations, the convergence of the time path y_t hinges solely on whether y_c tends toward zero as $t \to \infty$. What we learned about the various configurations of the expression b^t, in Fig. 17.1, is therefore still applicable, although in the present context we shall have to consider *two* characteristic roots rather than one.

Consider first the case of distinct real roots: $b_1 \neq b_2$. If $|b_1| > 1$ and $|b_2| > 1$, then both component terms in the complementary function (18.5)—$A_1 b_1^t$ and $A_2 b_2^t$—will be explosive, and thus y_c must be divergent. In the opposite case of $|b_1| < 1$ and $|b_2| < 1$, both terms in y_c will converge toward zero as t is indefinitely increased, as will y_c also. What if $|b_1| > 1$ but $|b_2| < 1$? In this intermediate case, it is evident that the $A_2 b_2^t$ term tends to "die down," while the other term tends to deviate farther from zero. It follows that the $A_1 b_1^t$ term must eventually dominate the scene and render the path divergent.

Let us call the root with the higher *absolute* value the *dominant root*. Then it appears that it is the dominant root b_1 which really sets the tone of the time path, at least with regard to its ultimate convergence or divergence. Such is indeed the case. We may state, thus, that a *time path will be convergent—whatever the initial conditions may be—if and only if the dominant root is less than 1 in absolute value*. You can verify that this statement is valid for the cases where both roots are greater than or less than 1 in absolute value (discussed previously), and where one root has absolute value of 1 exactly (*not* discussed previously). Note, however, that even though the eventual convergence depends on the dominant root alone, the *non-dominant* root will exert a definite influence on the time path, too, at least in the beginning periods. Therefore, the exact configuration of y_t is still dependent on both roots.

Turning to the repeated-root case, we find the complementary function to consist of the terms $A_3 b^t$ and $A_4 t b^t$, as shown in (18.6). The former is already familiar to us, but a word of explanation is still needed for the latter, which involves a multiplicative t. If $|b| > 1$, the b^t term will be explosive, and the multiplicative t will simply serve to intensify the explosiveness as t increases. If $|b| < 1$, on the other hand, the b^t part (which tends to zero as t increases) and the t part will run counter to each other; i.e., the value of t will offset rather than reinforce b^t. Which force will prove the stronger? The answer is that the damping force of b^t will always win over the exploding force of t. For this reason, the basic requirement for convergence in the repeated-root case is still that the root be less than 1 in absolute value.

Example 7 Analyze the convergence of the solutions in Examples 3 and 4. For Example 3, the solution is

$$y_t = 3 + (-2)^t + 4t$$

where the roots are 1 and -2, respectively $[3(1)^t = 3]$, and where there is a moving equilibrium $4t$. The dominant root being -2, the time path is divergent.

For Example 4, where the solution is

$$y_t = A_3(-3)^t + A_4 t(-3)^t + \frac{1}{4}$$

and where $|b| = 3$, we also have divergence.

Let us now consider the complex-root case. From the general form of the complementary function in (18.10),

$$y_c = R^t(A_5 \cos \theta t + A_6 \sin \theta t)$$

it is clear that the parenthetical expression, like the one in (16.24′), will produce a fluctuating pattern of a periodic nature. However, since the variable t can only take integer values $0, 1, 2, \ldots$ in the present context, we shall catch and utilize only a subset of the points on the graph of a circular function. The y value at each such point will always prevail for a whole period, till the next relevant point is reached. As illustrated in Fig. 18.1, the resulting path is neither the usual oscillatory type (not alternating between values above and below

FIGURE 18.1

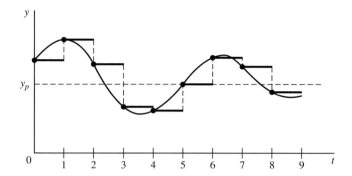

y_p in consecutive periods), nor the usual fluctuating type (not smooth); rather, it displays a sort of *stepped* fluctuation. As far as convergence is concerned, though, the decisive factor is really the R^t term, which, like the e^{ht} term in (16.24′), will dictate whether the stepped fluctuation is to be intensified or mitigated as t increases. In the present case, the fluctuation can be gradually narrowed down if and only if $R < 1$. Since R is by definition the absolute value of the conjugate complex roots ($h \pm vi$), the condition for convergence is again that the characteristic roots be less than unity in absolute value.

To summarize: For all three cases of characteristic roots, the time path will converge to a (stationary or moving) intertemporal equilibrium—regardless of what the initial conditions may happen to be—if and only if the absolute value of every root is less than 1.

Example 8

Are the time paths (18.11) and (18.12) convergent? In (18.11) we have $R = \frac{1}{2}$; therefore the time path will converge to the stationary equilibrium ($= 4$). In (18.12), on the other hand, we have $R = 4$, so the time path will not converge to the equilibrium ($= 0$).

EXERCISE 18.1

1. Write out the characteristic equation for each of the following, and find the characteristic roots:

   (a) $y_{t+2} - y_{t+1} + \frac{1}{2}y_t = 2$

   (c) $y_{t+2} + \frac{1}{2}y_{t+1} - \frac{1}{2}y_t = 5$

   (b) $y_{t+2} - 4y_{t+1} + 4y_t = 7$

   (d) $y_{t+2} - 2y_{t+1} + 3y_t = 4$

2. For each of the difference equations in Prob. 1 state on the basis of its characteristic roots whether the time path involves oscillation or stepped fluctuation, and whether it is explosive.

3. Find the particular solutions of the equations in Prob. 1. Do these represent stationary or moving equilibria?

4. Solve the following difference equations:

   (a) $y_{t+2} + 3y_{t+1} - \frac{7}{4}y_t = 9$ ($y_0 = 6$; $y_1 = 3$)

   (b) $y_{t+2} - 2y_{t+1} + 2y_t = 1$ ($y_0 = 3$; $y_1 = 4$)

   (c) $y_{t+2} - y_{t+1} + \frac{1}{4}y_t = 2$ ($y_0 = 4$; $y_1 = 7$)

5. Analyze the time paths obtained in Prob. 4.

18.2   Samuelson Multiplier-Acceleration Interaction Model

As an illustration of the use of second-order difference equations in economics, let us cite a classic work of Professor Paul Samuelson, the first economist to win the Nobel Prize. We refer to his classic *interaction* model, which seeks to explore the dynamic process of income determination when the acceleration principle is in operation along with the Keynesian multiplier.[†] Among other things, that model serves to demonstrate that the mere interaction of the multiplier and the accelerator is capable of generating cyclical fluctuations endogenously.

The Framework

Suppose that national income Y_t is made up of three component expenditure streams: consumption C_t, investment I_t, and government expenditure G_t. Consumption is envisaged as a function not of current income but of the income of the prior period, Y_{t-1}; for simplicity, it is assumed that C_t is strictly proportional to Y_{t-1}. Investment, which is of the "induced" variety, is a function of the prevailing trend of consumer spending. It is through this induced investment, of course, that the acceleration principle enters into the model. Specifically, we shall assume I_t to bear a fixed ratio to the consumption increment $\Delta C_{t-1} \equiv C_t - C_{t-1}$. The third component, G_t, on the other hand, is taken to be exogenous; in fact, we shall assume it to be a constant and simply denote it by G_0.

These assumptions can be translated into the following set of equations:

$$Y_t = C_t + I_t + G_0$$
$$C_t = \gamma Y_{t-1} \qquad (0 < \gamma < 1) \qquad \textbf{(18.13)}$$
$$I_t = \alpha(C_t - C_{t-1}) \qquad (\alpha > 0)$$

where γ (the Greek letter gamma) represents the marginal propensity to consume, and α stands for the accelerator (short for *acceleration coefficient*). Note that, if induced investment is expunged from the model, we are left with a first-order difference equation which embodies the dynamic multiplier process (cf. Example 2 of Sec. 17.2). With induced investment included, however, we have a second-order difference equation that depicts the interaction of the multiplier and the accelerator.

By virtue of the second equation, we can express I_t in terms of income as follows:

$$I_t = \alpha(\gamma Y_{t-1} - \gamma Y_{t-2}) = \alpha\gamma(Y_{t-1} - Y_{t-2})$$

Upon substituting this and the C_t equation into the first equation in (18.13) and rearranging, the model can be condensed into the single equation

$$Y_t - \gamma(1 + \alpha)Y_{t-1} + \alpha\gamma Y_{t-2} = G_0$$

or, equivalently (after shifting the subscripts forward by two periods),

$$Y_{t+2} - \gamma(1 + \alpha)Y_{t+1} + \alpha\gamma Y_t = G_0 \qquad \textbf{(18.14)}$$

Because this is a second-order linear difference equation with constant coefficients and constant term, it can be solved by the method just learned.

[†] Paul A. Samuelson, "Interactions between the Multiplier Analysis and the Principle of Acceleration," *Review of Economic Statistics*, May 1939, pp. 75–78; reprinted in American Economic Association, *Readings in Business Cycle Theory*, Richard D. Irwin, Inc., Homewood, Ill., 1944, pp. 261–269.

The Solution

As the particular solution, we have, by (18.2),

$$Y_p = \frac{G_0}{1 - \gamma(1 + \alpha) + \alpha\gamma} = \frac{G_0}{1 - \gamma}$$

It may be noted that the expression $1/(1 - \gamma)$ is merely the multiplier that would prevail in the absence of induced investment. Thus $G_0/(1 - \gamma)$—the exogeneous expenditure item times the multiplier—should give us the equilibrium income Y^* in the sense that this income level satisfies the equilibrium condition "national income = total expenditure" [cf. (3.24)]. Being the particular solution of the model, however, it also gives us the intertemporal equilibrium income $\overline{Y}$.

With regard to the complementary function, there are three possible cases. Case 1 $(a_1^2 > 4a_2)$, in the present context, is characterized by

$$\gamma^2(1 + \alpha)^2 > 4\alpha\gamma \qquad \text{or} \qquad \gamma(1 + \alpha)^2 > 4\alpha$$

or

$$\gamma > \frac{4\alpha}{(1 + \alpha)^2}$$

Similarly, to characterize Cases 2 and 3, we only need to change the $>$ sign in the last inequality to $=$ and $<$, respectively. In Fig. 18.2, we have drawn the graph of the equation $\gamma = 4\alpha/(1 + \alpha)^2$. According to the preceding discussion, the (α, γ) pairs that are located exactly *on* this curve pertain to Case 2. On the other hand, the (α, γ) pairs lying *above* this curve (involving higher γ values) have to do with Case 1, and those lying *below* the curve with Case 3.

This tripartite classification, with its graphical representation in Fig. 18.2, is of interest because it reveals clearly the conditions under which cyclical fluctuations can emerge

FIGURE 18.2

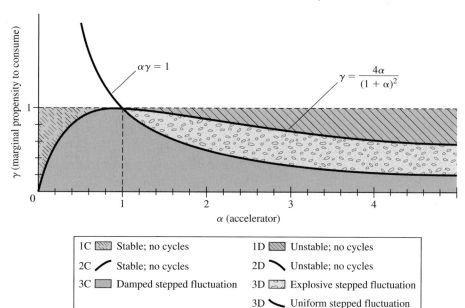

endogenously from the interaction of the multiplier and the accelerator. But this tells nothing about the convergence or divergence of the time path of *Y*. It remains, therefore, for us to distinguish, under each case, between the *damped* and the *explosive* subcases. We could, of course, take the easy way out by simply illustrating such subcases by citing specific numerical examples. But let us attempt the more rewarding, if also more arduous, task of delineating the general conditions under which convergence and divergence will prevail.

Convergence versus Divergence

The difference equation (18.14) has the characteristic equation

$$b^2 - \gamma(1+\alpha)b + \alpha\gamma = 0$$

which yields the two roots

$$b_1, b_2 = \frac{\gamma(1+\alpha) \pm \sqrt{\gamma^2(1+\alpha)^2 - 4\alpha\gamma}}{2}$$

Since the question of convergence versus divergence depends on the values of b_1 and b_2, and since b_1 and b_2, in turn, depend on the values of the parameters α and γ, the conditions for convergence and divergence should be expressible in terms of the values of α and γ. To do this, we can make use of the fact that—by (16.6)—the two characteristic roots are always related to each other by the following two equations:

$$b_1 + b_2 = \gamma(1+\alpha) \tag{18.15}$$
$$b_1 b_2 = \alpha\gamma \tag{18.15'}$$

One the basis of these two equations, we may observe that

$$\begin{aligned}(1 - b_1)(1 - b_2) &= 1 - (b_1 + b_2) + b_1 b_2 \\ &= 1 - \gamma(1+\alpha) + \alpha\gamma = 1 - \gamma \end{aligned} \tag{18.16}$$

In view of the model specification that $0 < \gamma < 1$, it becomes necessary to impose on the two roots the condition

$$0 < (1 - b_1)(1 - b_2) < 1 \tag{18.17}$$

Let us now examine the question of convergence under Case 1, where the roots are real and distinct. Since, by assumption, α and γ are both positive, (18.15') tells us that $b_1 b_2 > 0$, which implies that b_1 and b_2 possess the same algebraic sign. Furthermore, since $\gamma(1+\alpha) > 0$, (18.15) indicates that both b_1 and b_2 must be positive. Hence, the time path Y_t cannot have oscillations in Case 1.

Even though the signs of b_1 and b_2 are now known, there actually exist under Case 1 as many as five possible combinations of (b_1, b_2) values, each with its own implication regarding the corresponding values for α and γ:

$$\begin{array}{llll} (i) & 0 < b_2 < b_1 < 1 & \Rightarrow & 0 < \gamma < 1; \alpha\gamma < 1 \\ (ii) & 0 < b_2 < b_1 = 1 & \Rightarrow & \gamma = 1 \\ (iii) & 0 < b_2 < 1 < b_1 & \Rightarrow & \gamma > 1 \\ (iv) & 1 = b_2 < b_1 & \Rightarrow & \gamma = 1 \\ (v) & 1 < b_2 < b_1 & \Rightarrow & 0 < \gamma < 1; \alpha\gamma > 1 \end{array}$$

Possibility i, where both b_1 and b_2 are positive fractions, duly satisfies condition (18.17) and hence conforms to the model specification $0 < \gamma < 1$. The product of the two roots must also be a positive fraction under this possibility, and this, by (18.15′), implies that $\alpha\gamma < 1$. In contrast, the next three possibilities all violate condition (18.17) and result in inadmissible γ values (see Exercise 18.2-3). Hence they must be ruled out. But Possibility v may still be acceptable. With both b_1 and b_2 greater than one, (18.17) may still be satisfied if $(1 - b_1)(1 - b_2) < 1$. But this time we have $\alpha\gamma > 1$ (rather than < 1) from (18.15′). The upshot is that there are only two admissible subcases under Case 1. The first—Possibility i—involves fractional roots b_1 and b_2, and therefore yields a convergent time path of Y. The other subcase—Possibility v—features roots greater than one, and thus produces a divergent time path. As far as the values of α and γ are concerned, however, the question of convergence and divergence only hinges on whether $\alpha\gamma < 1$ or $\alpha\gamma > 1$. This information is summarized in the top part of Table 18.1, where the convergent subcase is labeled 1C, and the divergent subcase 1D.

The analysis of Case 2, with repeated roots, is similar in nature. The roots are now $b = \gamma(1 + \alpha)/2$, with a positive sign because α and γ are positive. Thus, there is again no oscillation. This time we may classify the value of b into three possibilities only:

$$(vi) \quad 0 < b < 1 \quad \Rightarrow \quad \gamma < 1; \alpha\gamma < 1$$
$$(vii) \quad b = 1 \quad \Rightarrow \quad \gamma = 1$$
$$(viii) \quad b > 1 \quad \Rightarrow \quad \gamma < 1; \alpha\gamma > 1$$

Under Possibility vi, $b\,(= b_1 = b_2)$ is a positive fraction; thus the implications regarding α and γ are entirely identical with those of Possibility i under Case 1. In an analogous manner, Possibility $viii$, with $b\,(= b_1 = b_2)$ greater than one, can satisfy (18.17) only if $1 < b < 2$; if so, it yields the same results as Possibility v. On the other hand, Possibility vii violates (18.17) and must be ruled out. Thus there are again only two admissible subcases. The first—Possibility vi—yields a convergent time path, whereas the other—Possibility $viii$—gives a divergent one. In terms of α and γ, the convergent and divergent subcases are again associated, respectively, with $\alpha\gamma < 1$ and $\alpha\gamma > 1$. These results are listed in the middle part of Table 18.1, where the two subcases are labeled 2C (convergent) and 2D (divergent).

TABLE 18.1
Cases and Subcases of the Samuelson Model

Case	Subcase	Values of α and γ	Time Path Y_t
1. Distinct real roots $\gamma > \dfrac{4\alpha}{(1+\alpha)^2}$	1C: $0 < b_2 < b_1 < 1$ 1D: $1 < b_2 < b_1$	$\alpha\gamma < 1$ $\alpha\gamma > 1$	Nonoscillatory and nonfluctuating
2. Repeated real roots $\gamma = \dfrac{4\alpha}{(1+\alpha)^2}$	2C: $0 < b < 1$ 2D: $b > 1$	$\alpha\gamma < 1$ $\alpha\gamma > 1$	Nonoscillatory and nonfluctuating
3. Complex roots $\gamma < \dfrac{4\alpha}{(1+\alpha)^2}$	3C: $R < 1$ 3D: $R \geq 1$	$\alpha\gamma < 1$ $\alpha\gamma \geq 1$	With stepped fluctuation

Finally, in Case 3, with complex roots, we have stepped fluctuation, and hence endogenous business cycles. In this case, we should look to the absolute value $R = \sqrt{a_2}$ [see (18.8)] for the clue to convergence and divergence, where a_2 is the coefficient of the y_t term in the difference equation (18.1). In the present model, we have $R = \sqrt{\alpha\gamma}$, which gives rise to the following three possibilities:

$$(ix) \quad R < 1 \quad \Rightarrow \quad \alpha\gamma < 1$$
$$(x) \quad R = 1 \quad \Rightarrow \quad \alpha\gamma = 1$$
$$(xi) \quad R > 1 \quad \Rightarrow \quad \alpha\gamma > 1$$

Even though all of these happen to be admissible (see Exercise 18.2-4), only the $R < 1$ possibility entails a convergent time path and qualifies as Subcase 3C in Table 18.1. The other two are thus collectively labeled as Subcase 3D.

In sum, we may conclude from Table 18.1 that a convergent time path can occur if and only if $\alpha\gamma < 1$.

A Graphical Summary

The preceding analysis has resulted in a somewhat complex classification of cases and subcases. It would help to have a visual representation of the classificatory scheme. This is supplied in Fig. 18.2.

The set of all admissible (α, γ) pairs in the model is shown in Fig. 18.2 by the variously shaded rectangular area. Since the values of $\gamma = 0$ and $\gamma = 1$ are excluded, as is the value $\alpha = 0$, the shaded area is a sort of rectangle without sides. We have already graphed the equation $\gamma = 4\alpha/(1+\alpha)^2$ to mark off the three major cases of Table 18.1: The points on that curve pertain to Case 2; the points lying to the north of the curve (representing higher γ values) belong to Case 1; those lying to the south (with lower γ values) are of Case 3. To distinguish between the convergent and divergent subcases, we now add the graph of $\alpha\gamma = 1$ (a rectangular hyperbola) as another demarcation line. The points lying to the north of this rectangular hyperbola satisfy the inequality $\alpha\gamma > 1$, whereas those located below it correspond to $\alpha\gamma < 1$. It is then possible to mark off the subcases easily. Under Case 1, the broken-line shaded region, being below the hyperbola, corresponds to Subcase 1C, but the solid-line shaded region is associated with Subcase 1D. Under Case 2, which relates to the points lying on the curve $\gamma = 4\alpha/(1+\alpha)^2$, Subcase 2C covers the upward-sloping portion of that curve, and Subcase 2D, the downward-sloping portion. Finally, for Case 3, the rectangular hyperbola serves to separate the dot-shaded region (Subcase 3C) from the pebble-shaded region (Subcase 3D). The latter, you should note, also includes the points located *on* the rectangular hyperbola itself, because of the *weak inequality* in the specification $\alpha\gamma \geq 1$.

Since Fig. 18.2 is the repository of all the qualitative conclusions of the model, given any ordered pair (α, γ), we can always find the correct subcase graphically by plotting the ordered pair in the diagram.

Example 1

If the accelerator is 0.8 and the marginal propensity to consume is 0.7, what kind of interaction time path will result? The ordered pair (0.8, 0.7) is located in the dot-shaded region, Subcase 3C; thus the time path is characterized by damped stepped fluctuation.

Example 2

What kind of interaction is implied by $\alpha = 2$ and $\gamma = 0.5$? The ordered pair (2, 0.5) lies exactly on the rectangular hyperbola, under Subcase 3D. The time path of Y will again display stepped fluctuation, but it will be neither explosive nor damped. By analogy to the cases of uniform oscillation and uniform fluctuation, we may term this situation as "uniform stepped fluctuation." However, the uniformity feature in this latter case cannot in general be expected to be a perfect one, because, similarly to what was done in Fig. 18.1, we can only accept those points on a sine or cosine curve that correspond to integer values of *t*, but these values of *t* may hit an entirely different set of points on the curve in each period of fluctuation.

EXERCISE 18.2

1. By consulting Fig. 18.2, find the subcases to which the following sets of values of α and γ pertain, and describe the interaction time path qualitatively.

   (a) $\alpha = 3.5; \gamma = 0.8$ (c) $\alpha = 0.2; \gamma = 0.9$

   (b) $\alpha = 2; \gamma = 0.7$ (d) $\alpha = 1.5; \gamma = 0.6$

2. From the values of α and γ given in parts (a) and (c) of Prob. 1, find the numerical values of the characteristic roots in each instance, and analyze the nature of the time path. Do your results check with those obtained earlier?

3. Verify that Possibilities *ii*, *iii*, and *iv* in Case 1 imply inadmissible values of γ.

4. Show that in Case 3 we can never encounter $\gamma \geq 1$.

18.3 Inflation and Unemployment in Discrete Time

The interaction of inflation and unemployment, discussed earlier in the continuous-time framework, can also be couched in discrete time. Using essentially the same economic assumptions, we shall illustrate in this section how that model can be reformulated as a difference-equation model.

The Model

The earlier continuous-time formulation (Sec. 16.5) consisted of three differential equations:

$$p = \alpha - T - \beta U + g\pi \qquad \text{[expectations-augmented Phillips relation]} \quad \textbf{(16.33)}$$

$$\frac{d\pi}{dt} = j(p - \pi) \qquad \text{[adaptive expectations]} \quad \textbf{(16.34)}$$

$$\frac{dU}{dt} = -k(m - p) \qquad \text{[monetary policy]} \quad \textbf{(16.35)}$$

Three endogenous variables are present: *p* (actual rate of inflation), π (expected rate of inflation), and *U* (rate of unemployment). As many as six parameters appear in the model; among these, the parameter *m*—the rate of growth of nominal money (or, the rate of monetary expansion)—differs from the others in that its magnitude is set as a policy decision.

When cast into the period-analysis mold, the Phillips relation (16.33) simply becomes

$$p_t = \alpha - T - \beta U_t + g\pi_t \qquad (\alpha, \beta > 0; 0 < g \leq 1) \quad \textbf{(18.18)}$$

In the adaptive-expectations equation, the derivative must be replaced by a difference expression:

$$\pi_{t+1} - \pi_t = j(p_t - \pi_t) \qquad (0 < j \leq 1) \quad \textbf{(18.19)}$$

By the same token, the monetary-policy equation should be changed to[†]

$$U_{t+1} - U_t = -k(m - p_{t+1}) \qquad (k > 0) \qquad \textbf{(18.20)}$$

These three equations constitute the new version of the inflation-unemployment model.

The Difference Equation in p

As the first step in the analysis of this new model, we again try to condense the model into a single equation in a single variable. Let that variable be p. Accordingly, we shall focus our attention on (18.18). However, since (18.18)—unlike the other two equations—does not by itself describe a pattern of change, it is up to us to create such a pattern. This is accomplished by *differencing* p_t, i.e., by taking the first difference of p_t, according to the definition

$$\Delta p_t \equiv p_{t+1} - p_t$$

Two steps are involved in this. First, we shift the time subscripts in (18.18) forward one period, to get

$$p_{t+1} = \alpha - T - \beta U_{t+1} + g\pi_{t+1} \qquad \textbf{(18.18$'$)}$$

Then we subtract (18.18) from (18.18$'$), to obtain the first difference of p_t that gives the desired pattern of change:

$$\begin{aligned} p_{t+1} - p_t &= -\beta(U_{t+1} - U_t) + g(\pi_{t+1} - \pi_t) \\ &= \beta k(m - p_{t+1}) + gj(p_t - \pi_t) \qquad \text{[by (18.20) and (18.19)]} \qquad \textbf{(18.21)} \end{aligned}$$

Note that, on the second line of (18.21), the patterns of change of the other two variables as given in (18.19) and (18.20) have been incorporated into the pattern of change of the p variable. Thus (18.21) now embodies all the information in the present model.

However, the π_t term is extraneous to the study of p and needs to be eliminated from (18.21). To that end, we make use of the fact that

$$g\pi_t = p_t - (\alpha - T) + \beta U_t \qquad \text{[by (18.18)]} \qquad \textbf{(18.22)}$$

Substituting this into (18.21) and collecting terms, we obtain

$$(1 + \beta k)p_{t+1} - [1 - j(1 - g)]\, p_t + j\beta U_t = \beta km + j(\alpha - T) \qquad \textbf{(18.23)}$$

But there now appears a U_t term to be eliminated. To do that, we difference (18.23) to get a $(U_{t+1} - U_t)$ term and then use (18.20) to eliminate the latter. Only after this rather lengthy process of substitutions, do we get the desired difference equation in the p variable alone, which, when duly normalized, takes the form

$$p_{t+2} - \underbrace{\frac{1 + gj + (1 - j)(1 + \beta k)}{1 + \beta k}}_{a_1} p_{t+1} + \underbrace{\frac{1 - j(1 - g)}{1 + \beta k}}_{a_2} p_t = \underbrace{\frac{j\beta km}{1 + \beta k}}_{c} \qquad \textbf{(18.24)}$$

[†] We have assumed that the change in U_t depends on $(m - p_{t+1})$, the rate of growth of real money in period $(t + 1)$. As an alternative, it is possible to make it depend on the rate of growth of real money in period t, $(m - p_t)$ (see Exercise 18.3-4).

The Time Path of p

The intertemporal equilibrium value of p, given by the particular integral of (18.24), is

$$\overline{p} = \frac{c}{1 + a_1 + a_2} = \frac{j\beta km}{\beta kj} = m \qquad \text{[by (18.2)]}$$

As in the continuous-time model, therefore, the equilibrium rate of inflation is exactly equal to the rate of monetary expansion.

As to the complementary function, there may arise either distinct real roots (Case 1), or repeated real roots (Case 2), or complex roots (Case 3), depending on the relative magnitudes of a_1^2 and $4a_2$. In the present model,

$$a_1^2 \gtreqless 4a_2 \qquad \text{iff} \qquad [1 + gj + (1 - j)(1 + \beta k)]^2$$
$$\gtreqless 4[1 - j(1 - g)](1 + \beta k) \qquad \textbf{(18.25)}$$

If $g = \frac{1}{2}$, $j = \frac{1}{3}$ and $\beta k = 5$, for instance, then $a_1^2 = (5\frac{1}{6})^2$ whereas $4a_2 = 20$; thus Case 1 results. But if $g = j = 1$, then $a_1^2 = 4$ while $4a_2 = 4(1 + \beta k) > 4$, and we have Case 3 instead. In view of the larger number of parameters in the present model, however, it is not feasible to construct a classificatory graph like Fig. 18.2 in the Samuelson model.

Nevertheless, the analysis of convergence can still proceed along the same line as in Sec. 18.2. Specifically, we recall from (16.6) that the two characteristic roots b_1 and b_2 must satisfy the following two relations:

$$b_1 + b_2 = -a_1 = \frac{1 + gj}{1 + \beta k} + 1 - j > 0 \qquad\qquad \textbf{(18.26)}$$
$$\text{[see (18.24)]}$$
$$b_1 b_2 = a_2 = \frac{1 - j(1 - g)}{1 + \beta k} \in (0, 1) \qquad\qquad \textbf{(18.26$'$)}$$

Furthermore, we have in the present model

$$(1 - b_1)(1 - b_2) = 1 - (b_1 + b_2) + b_1 b_2 = \frac{\beta jk}{1 + \beta k} > 0 \quad \textbf{(18.27)}$$

Now consider Case 1, where the two roots b_1 and b_2 are real and distinct. Since their product $b_1 b_2$ is positive, b_1 and b_2 must take the same sign. Because their sum is positive, moreover, b_1 and b_2 must both be positive, implying that no oscillation can occur. From (18.27), we can infer that neither b_1 nor b_2 can be equal to one; for otherwise $(1 - b_1)(1 - b_2)$ would be zero, in violation of the indicated inequality. This means that, in terms of the various possibilities of (b_1, b_2) combinations enumerated in the Samuelson model, Possibilities *ii* and *iv* cannot arise here. It is also unacceptable to have one root greater, and the other root less, than one; for otherwise $(1 - b_1)(1 - b_2)$ would be negative. Thus Possibility *iii* is ruled out as well. It follows that b_1 and b_2 must be *either* both greater than one, *or* both less than one. If $b_1 > 1$ and $b_2 > 1$ (Possibility *v*), however, (18.26$'$) would be violated. Hence the only viable eventuality is Possibility *i*, with b_1 and b_2 both being positive fractions, so that the time path of p is convergent.

The analysis of Case 2 is basically not much different. By practically identical reasoning, we can conclude that the repeated root b can only turn out to be a positive fraction in this model; that is, Possibility *vi* is feasible, but not Possibilities *vii* and *viii*. The time path of p in Case 2 is again nonoscillatory and convergent.

For Case 3, convergence requires that R (the absolute value of the complex roots) be less than one. By (18.8), $R = \sqrt{a_2}$. Inasmuch as a_2 is a positive fraction [see (18.26′)], we do have $R < 1$. Thus the time path of p in Case 3 is also convergent, although this time there will be stepped fluctuation.

The Analysis of U

If we wish to analyze instead the time path of the rate of unemployment, we may take (18.20) as the point of departure. To get rid of the p term in that equation, we first substitute (18.18′) to get

$$(1 + \beta k)U_{t+1} - U_t = k(\alpha - T - m) + kg\pi_{t+1} \qquad \textbf{(18.28)}$$

Next, to prepare for the substitution of the other equation, (18.19), we difference (18.28) to find that

$$(1 + \beta k)U_{t+2} - (2 + \beta k)U_{t+1} + U_t = kg(\pi_{t+2} - \pi_{t+1}) \qquad \textbf{(18.29)}$$

In view of the presence of a difference expression in π on the right, we can substitute for it a forward-shifted version of the adaptive-expectations equation. The result of this,

$$(1 + \beta k)U_{t+2} - (2 + \beta k)U_{t+1} + U_t = kgj(p_{t+1} - \pi_{t+1}) \qquad \textbf{(18.30)}$$

is the embodiment of all the information in the model.

However, we must eliminate the p and π variables before a proper difference equation in U will emerge. For this purpose, we note from (18.20) that

$$kp_{t+1} = U_{t+1} - U_t + km \qquad \textbf{(18.31)}$$

Moreover, by multiplying (18.22) through by $(-kj)$ and shifting the time subscripts, we can write

$$
\begin{aligned}
-kjg\pi_{t+1} &= -kjp_{t+1} + kj(\alpha - T) - \beta kjU_{t+1} \\
&= -j(U_{t+1} - U_t + km) + kj(\alpha - T) - \beta kjU_{t+1} \\
&\qquad\qquad\qquad\qquad\qquad\qquad \text{[by (18.31)]} \\
&= -j(1 + \beta k)U_{t+1} + jU_t + kj(\alpha - T - m) \qquad \textbf{(18.32)}
\end{aligned}
$$

These two results express p_{t+1} and π_{t+1} in terms of the U variable and can thus enable us, on substitution into (18.30), to obtain—at long last!—the desired difference equation in the U variable alone:

$$
\begin{aligned}
U_{t+2} - \frac{1 + gj + (1 - j)(1 + \beta k)}{1 + \beta k}U_{t+1} &+ \frac{1 - j(1 - g)}{1 + \beta k}U_t \\
&= \frac{kj[\alpha - T - (1 - g)m]}{1 + \beta k} \qquad \textbf{(18.33)}
\end{aligned}
$$

It is noteworthy that the two constant coefficients on the left (a_1 and a_2) are identical with those in the difference equation for p [i.e., (18.24)]. As a result, the earlier analysis of the complementary function of the p path should be equally applicable to the present context. But the constant term on the right of (18.33) does differ from that of (18.24). Consequently, the particular solutions in the two situations will be different. This is as it should be, for, coincidence aside, there is no inherent reason to expect the intertemporal equilibrium rate of unemployment to be the same as the equilibrium rate of inflation.

The Long-Run Phillips Relation

It is readily verified that the intertemporal equilibrium rate of unemployment is

$$\overline{U} = \frac{1}{\beta}[\alpha - T - (1 - g)m]$$

But since the equilibrium rate of inflation has been found to be $\overline{p} = m$, we can link $\overline{U}$ to $\overline{p}$ by the equation

$$\overline{U} = \frac{1}{\beta}[\alpha - T - (1 - g)\overline{p}] \qquad (18.34)$$

Because this equation is concerned only with the *equilibrium* rates of unemployment and inflation, it is said to depict the *long-run* Phillips relation.

A special case of (18.34) has received a great deal of attention among economists: the case of $g = 1$. If $g = 1$, the $\overline{p}$ term will have a zero coefficient and thus drop out of the picture. In other words, $\overline{U}$ will become a constant function of $\overline{p}$. In the standard Phillips diagram, where the rate of unemployment is plotted on the horizontal axis, this outcome gives rise to a vertical long-run Phillips curve. The $\overline{U}$ value in this case, referred to as the *natural rate of unemployment,* is then consistent with any equilibrium rate of inflation, with the notable policy implication that, in the long run, there is no trade-off between the twin evils of inflation and unemployment as exists in the short run.

But what if $g < 1$? In that event, the coefficient of $\overline{p}$ in (18.34) will be negative. Then the long-run Phillips curve will turn out to be downward-sloping, thereby still providing a trade-off relation between inflation and unemployment. Whether the long-run Phillips curve is vertical or negatively sloped is, therefore, critically dependent on the value of the g parameter, which, according to the expectations-augmented Phillips relation, measures the extent to which the expected rate of inflation can work its way into the wage structure and the actual rate of inflation. All of this may sound familiar to you. This is because we discussed the topic in Example 1 in Sec. 16.5, and you have also worked on it in Exercise 16.5-4.

EXERCISE 18.3

1. Supply the intermediate steps leading from (18.23) to (18.24).
2. Show that if the model discussed in this section is condensed into a difference equation in the variable π, the result will be the same as (18.24) except for the substitution of π for p.
3. The time paths of p and U in the model discussed in this section have been found to be consistently convergent. Can divergent time paths arise if we drop the assumption that $g \le 1$? If yes, which divergent "possibilities" in Cases 1, 2, and 3 will now become feasible?
4. Retain equations (18.18) and (18.19), but change (18.20) to
   $$U_{t+1} - U_t = -k(m - p_t)$$
   (*a*) Derive a new difference equation in the variable p.
   (*b*) Does the new difference equation yield a different $\overline{p}$?
   (*c*) Assume that $j = g = 1$. Find the conditions under which the characteristic roots will fall under Cases 1, 2, and 3, respectively.
   (*d*) Let $j = g = 1$. Describe the time path of p (including convergence or divergence) when $\beta k = 3$, 4, and 5, respectively.

18.4   Generalizations to Variable-Term and Higher-Order Equations

We are now ready to extend our methods in two directions, to the variable-term case and to difference equations of higher orders.

Variable Term in the Form of cm^t

When the constant term c in (18.1) is replaced by a variable term—some function of t—the only effect will be on the particular solution. (Why?) To find the new particular solution, we can again apply the method of undetermined coefficients. In the differential-equation context (Sec. 16.6), that method requires that the variable term and its successive derivatives together take only a finite number of distinct types of expression, apart from multiplicative constants. Applied to difference equations, the requirement should be amended to read: "the variable term and its successive *differences* must together take only a finite number of distinct expression types, apart from multiplicative constants." Let us illustrate this method by concrete examples, first taking a variable term in the form cm^t, where c and m are constants.

Example 1   Find the particular solution of

$$y_{t+2} + y_{t+1} - 3y_t = 7^t$$

Here, we have $c = 1$ and $m = 7$. First, let us ascertain whether the variable term 7^t yields a finite number of expression types on successive differencing. According to the rule of differencing ($\Delta y_t = y_{t+1} - y_t$), the *first* difference of the term is

$$\Delta 7^t = 7^{t+1} - 7^t = (7 - 1)7^t = 6(7)^t$$

Similarly, the *second* difference, $\Delta^2(7^t)$, can be expressed as

$$\Delta(\Delta 7^t) = \Delta 6(7^t) = 6(7)^{t+1} - 6(7)^t = 6(7 - 1)7^t = 36(7)^t$$

Moreover, as can be verified, all successive differences will, like the first and second, be some multiple of 7^t. Since there is only a single expression type, we can try a solution $y_t = B(7)^t$ for the particular solution, where B is an undetermined coefficient.

Substituting the trial solution and its corresponding versions for periods $(t + 1)$ and $(t + 2)$ into the given difference equation, we obtain

$$B(7)^{t+2} + B(7)^{t+1} - 3B(7)^t = 7^t \qquad \text{or} \qquad B(7^2 + 7 - 3)(7)^t = 7^t$$

Thus,

$$B = \frac{1}{49 + 7 - 3} = \frac{1}{53}$$

and we can write the particular solution as

$$y_p = B(7)^t = \frac{1}{53}(7)^t$$

This may be taken as a moving equilibrium. You can verify the correctness of the solution by substituting it into the difference equation and seeing to it that there will result an identity, $7^t = 7^t$.

The result reached in Example 1 can be easily generalized from the variable term 7^t to that of cm^t. From our experience, we expect all the successive differences of cm^t to take the same form of expression: namely, Bm^t, where B is some multiplicative constant. Hence we can try a solution $y_t = Bm^t$ for the particular solution, when given the difference equation

$$y_{t+2} + a_1 y_{t+1} + a_2 y_t = cm^t \qquad \textbf{(18.35)}$$

Using the trial solution $y_t = Bm^t$, which implies $y_{t+1} = Bm^{t+1}$, etc., we can rewrite equation (18.35) as

$$Bm^{t+2} + a_1 Bm^{t+1} + a_2 Bm^t = cm^t$$

or
$$B(m^2 + a_1 m + a_2)m^t = cm^t$$

Hence the coefficient B in the trial solution should be

$$B = \frac{c}{m^2 + a_1 m + a_2}$$

and the desired particular solution of (18.35) can be written as

$$y_p = Bm^t = \frac{c}{m^2 + a_1 m + a_2}m^t \qquad (m^2 + a_1 m + a_2 \neq 0) \quad \textbf{(18.36)}$$

Note that the denominator of B is not allowed to be zero. If it happens to be,[†] we must then use the trial solution $y_t = Btm^t$ instead; or, if that too fails, $y_t = Bt^2 m^t$.

Variable Term in the Form of ct^n

Let us now consider variable terms in the form ct^n, where c is any constant, and n is a positive integer.

Example 2   Find the particular solution of

$$y_{t+2} + 5y_{t+1} + 2y_t = t^2$$

The first three differences of t^2 (a special case of ct^n with $c = 1$ and $n = 2$) are found as follows:[‡]

$$\Delta t^2 = (t+1)^2 - t^2 = 2t + 1$$
$$\Delta^2 t^2 = \Delta(\Delta t^2) = \Delta(2t+1) = \Delta 2t + \Delta 1$$
$$= 2(t+1) - 2t + 0 = 2 \qquad [\Delta \text{ constant} = 0]$$
$$\Delta^3 t^2 = \Delta(\Delta^2 t^2) = \Delta 2 = 0$$

Since further differencing will only yield zero, there are altogether three distinct types of expression: t^2 (from the variable term itself), t, and a constant (from the successive differences).

Let us therefore try the solution

$$y_t = B_0 + B_1 t + B_2 t^2$$

[†] Analogous to the situation in Example 3 of Sec. 16.6, this eventuality will materialize when the constant m happens to be equal to a characteristic root of the difference equation. The characteristic roots of the difference equation of (18.35) are the values of b that satisfy the equation $b^2 + a_1 b + a_2 = 0$. If one root happens to have the value m, then it must follow that $m^2 + a_1 m + a_2 = 0$.

[‡] These results should be compared with the first three derivatives of t^2:

$$\frac{d}{dt}t^2 = 2t \qquad \frac{d^2}{dt^2}t^2 = 2 \qquad \text{and} \qquad \frac{d^3}{dt^3}t^2 = 0$$

for the particular solution, with undetermined coefficients B_0, B_1, and B_2. Note that this solution implies

$$
\begin{aligned}
y_{t+1} &= B_0 + B_1(t+1) + B_2(t+1)^2 \\
&= (B_0 + B_1 + B_2) + (B_1 + 2B_2)t + B_2 t^2 \\
y_{t+2} &= B_0 + B_1(t+2) + B_2(t+2)^2 \\
&= (B_0 + 2B_1 + 4B_2) + (B_1 + 4B_2)t + B_2 t^2
\end{aligned}
$$

When these are substituted into the difference equation, we obtain

$$
(8B_0 + 7B_1 + 9B_2) + (8B_1 + 14B_2)t + 8B_2 t^2 = t^2
$$

Equating the two sides term by term, we see that the undetermined coefficients are required to satisfy the following simultaneous equations:

$$
\begin{aligned}
8B_0 + 7B_1 + 9B_2 &= 0 \\
8B_1 + 14B_2 &= 0 \\
8B_2 &= 1
\end{aligned}
$$

Thus, their values must be $B_0 = \frac{13}{256}$, $B_1 = -\frac{7}{32}$, and $B_2 = \frac{1}{8}$, giving us the particular solution

$$
y_p = \frac{13}{256} - \frac{7}{32}t + \frac{1}{8}t^2
$$

Our experience with the variable term t^2 should enable us to generalize the method to the case of ct^n. In the new trial solution, there should obviously be a term $B_n t^n$, to correspond to the given variable term. Furthermore, since successive differencing of the term yields the distinct expressions t^{n-1}, t^{n-2}, ..., t, and B_0 (constant), the new trial solution for the case of the variable term ct^n should be written as

$$
y_t = B_0 + B_1 t + B_2 t^2 + \cdots + B_n t^n
$$

But the rest of the procedure is entirely the same.

It must be added that such a trial solution may also fail to work. In that event, the trick—already employed on countless other occasions—is again to multiply the original trial solution by a sufficiently high power of t. That is, we can instead try $y_t = t(B_0 + B_1 t + B_2 t^2 + \cdots + B_n t^n)$, etc.

Higher-Order Linear Difference Equations

The *order* of a difference equation indicates the highest-order difference present in the equation; but it also indicates the maximum number of periods of time lag involved. An nth-order linear difference equation (with constant coefficients and constant term) may thus be written in general as

$$
y_{t+n} + a_1 y_{t+n-1} + \cdots + a_{n-1} y_{t+1} + a_n y_t = c \tag{18.37}
$$

The method of finding the particular solution of this does not differ in any substantive way. As a starter, we can still try $y_t = k$ (the case of stationary intertemporal equilibrium). Should this fail, we then try $y_t = kt$ or $y_t = kt^2$, etc., in that order.

In the search for the complementary function, however, we shall now be confronted with a characteristic equation which is an nth-degree polynomial equation:

$$
b^n + a_1 b^{n-1} + \cdots + a_{n-1} b + a_n = 0 \tag{18.38}
$$

There will now be n characteristic roots b_i $(i = 1, 2, \ldots, n)$, all of which should enter into the complementary function thus:

$$y_c = \sum_{i=1}^{n} A_i b_i^t \qquad\qquad (18.39)$$

provided, of course, that the roots are all real and distinct. In case there are repeated real roots (say, $b_1 = b_2 = b_3$), then the first three terms in the sum in (18.39) must be modified to

$$A_1 b_1^t + A_2 t b_1^t + A_3 t^2 b_1^t \qquad \text{[cf. (18.6)]}$$

Moreover, if there is a pair of conjugate complex roots—say, b_{n-1}, b_n—then the last two terms in the sum in (18.39) are to be combined into the expression

$$R^t (A_{n-1} \cos \theta t + A_n \sin \theta t)$$

A similar expression can also be assigned to any other pair of complex roots. In case of two *repeated* pairs, however, one of the two must be given a multiplicative factor of $t R^t$ instead of R^t.

After y_p and y_c are both found, the general solution of the complete difference equation (18.37) is again obtained by summing; that is,

$$y_t = y_p + y_c$$

But since there will be a total of n arbitrary constants in this solution, no less than n initial conditions will be required to definitize it.

Example 3

Find the general solution of the third-order difference equation

$$y_{t+3} - \frac{7}{8} y_{t+2} + \frac{1}{8} y_{t+1} + \frac{1}{32} y_t = 9$$

By trying the solution $y_t = k$, the particular solution is easily found to be $y_p = 32$. As for the complementary function, since the cubic characteristic equation

$$b^3 - \frac{7}{8} b^2 + \frac{1}{8} b + \frac{1}{32} = 0$$

can be factored into the form

$$\left(b - \frac{1}{2} \right) \left(b - \frac{1}{2} \right) \left(b + \frac{1}{8} \right) = 0$$

the roots are $b_1 = b_2 = \frac{1}{2}$ and $b_3 = -\frac{1}{8}$. This enables us to write

$$y_c = A_1 \left(\frac{1}{2} \right)^t + A_2 t \left(\frac{1}{2} \right)^t + A_3 \left(-\frac{1}{8} \right)^t$$

Note that the second term contains a multiplicative t; this is due to the presence of repeated roots. The general solution of the given difference equation is then simply the sum of y_c and y_p.

In this example, all three characteristic roots happen to be less than 1 in their absolute values. We can therefore conclude that the solution obtained represents a time path which converges to the stationary equilibrium level 32.

Convergence and the Schur Theorem

When we have a high-order difference equation that is not easily solved, we can nonetheless determine the convergence of the relevant time path qualitatively without having to struggle with its actual quantitative solution. You will recall that the time path can converge if and only if every root of the characteristic equation is less than 1 in absolute value.

In view of this, the following theorem—known as the *Schur theorem*[†]—becomes directly applicable:

The roots of the nth-degree polynomial equation

$$a_0 b^n + a_1 b^{n-1} + \cdots + a_{n-1} b + a_n = 0$$

will all be less than unity in absolute value if and only if the following n determinants

$$\Delta_1 = \begin{vmatrix} a_0 & a_n \\ a_n & a_0 \end{vmatrix} \qquad \Delta_2 = \begin{vmatrix} a_0 & 0 & a_n & a_{n-1} \\ a_1 & a_0 & 0 & a_n \\ a_n & 0 & a_0 & a_1 \\ a_{n-1} & a_n & 0 & a_0 \end{vmatrix} \qquad \cdots$$

$$\Delta_n = \begin{vmatrix} a_0 & 0 & \cdots & 0 & a_n & a_{n-1} & \cdots & a_1 \\ a_1 & a_0 & \cdots & 0 & 0 & a_n & \cdots & a_2 \\ \cdots & \cdots & \cdots & \cdots & \cdots & \cdots & \cdots & \cdots \\ a_{n-1} & a_{n-2} & \cdots & a_0 & 0 & 0 & \cdots & a_n \\ a_n & 0 & \cdots & 0 & a_0 & a_1 & \cdots & a_{n-1} \\ a_{n-1} & a_n & \cdots & 0 & 0 & a_0 & \cdots & a_{n-2} \\ \cdots & \cdots & \cdots & \cdots & \cdots & \cdots & \cdots & \cdots \\ a_1 & a_2 & \cdots & a_n & 0 & 0 & \cdots & a_0 \end{vmatrix}$$

are all positive.

Note that, since the condition in the theorem is given on the "if and only if" basis, it is a necessary-and-sufficient condition. Thus the Schur theorem is a perfect difference-equation counterpart of the Routh theorem introduced earlier in the differential-equation framework.

The construction of these determinants is based on a simple procedure. This is best explained with the aid of the dashed lines which partition each determinant into four *areas*. Each area of the kth determinant, Δ_k, always consists of a $k \times k$ subdeterminant. The *upper-left* area has a_0 alone in the diagonal, zeros above the diagonal, and progressively larger subscripts for the successive coefficients in each column below the diagonal elements. When we transpose the elements of the upper-left area, we obtain the *lower-right* area. Turning to the *upper-right* area, we now place the a_n coefficient alone in the diagonal, with zeros below the diagonal, and progressively smaller subscripts for the successive coefficients as we go up each column from the diagonal. When the elements of this area are transposed, we get the *lower-left* area.

The application of this theorem is straightforward. Since the coefficients of the characteristic equation are the same as those appearing on the left side of the original difference equation, we can introduce them directly into the determinants cited. Note that, in our context, we always have $a_0 = 1$.

Example 4

Does the time path of the equation $y_{t+2} + 3y_{t+1} + 2y_t = 12$ converge? Here we have $n = 2$, and the coefficients are $a_0 = 1$, $a_1 = 3$, and $a_2 = 2$. Thus we get

$$\Delta_1 = \begin{vmatrix} a_0 & a_2 \\ a_2 & a_0 \end{vmatrix} = \begin{vmatrix} 1 & 2 \\ 2 & 1 \end{vmatrix} = -3 < 0$$

[†] For a discussion of this theorem and its history, see John S. Chipman, *The Theory of Inter-Sectoral Money Flows and Income Formation*, The Johns Hopkins Press, Baltimore, 1951, pp. 119–120.

Since this already violates the convergence condition, there is no need to proceed to Δ_2.

Actually, the characteristic roots of the given difference equation are easily found to be $b_1, b_2 = -1, -2$, which indeed imply a divergent time path.

Example 5 Test the convergence of the path of $y_{t+2} + \frac{1}{6}y_{t+1} - \frac{1}{6}y_t = 2$ by the Schur theorem. Here the coefficients are $a_0 = 1$, $a_1 = \frac{1}{6}$, $a_2 = -\frac{1}{6}$ (with $n = 2$). Thus we have

$$\Delta_1 = \begin{vmatrix} a_0 & a_2 \\ a_2 & a_0 \end{vmatrix} = \begin{vmatrix} 1 & -\frac{1}{6} \\ -\frac{1}{6} & 1 \end{vmatrix} = \frac{35}{36} > 0$$

$$\Delta_2 = \begin{vmatrix} a_0 & 0 & a_2 & a_1 \\ a_1 & a_0 & 0 & a_2 \\ a_2 & 0 & a_0 & a_1 \\ a_1 & a_2 & 0 & a_0 \end{vmatrix} = \begin{vmatrix} 1 & 0 & -\frac{1}{6} & \frac{1}{6} \\ \frac{1}{6} & 1 & 0 & -\frac{1}{6} \\ -\frac{1}{6} & 0 & 1 & \frac{1}{6} \\ \frac{1}{6} & -\frac{1}{6} & 0 & 1 \end{vmatrix} = \frac{1,176}{1,296} > 0$$

These do satisfy the necessary-and-sufficient condition for convergence.

EXERCISE 18.4

1. Apply the definition of the "differencing" symbol Δ, to find:
   (a) Δt 　　　　　　　(b) $\Delta^2 t$ 　　　　　　　(c) Δt^3
   Compare the results of differencing with those of differentiation.
2. Find the particular solution of each of the following:
   (a) $y_{t+2} + 2y_{t+1} + y_t = 3^t$
   (b) $y_{t+2} - 5y_{t+1} - 6y_t = 2(6)^t$
   (c) $3y_{t+2} + 9y_t = 3(4)^t$
3. Find the particular solutions of:
   (a) $y_{t+2} - 2y_{t+1} + 5y_t = t$
   (b) $y_{t+2} - 2y_{t+1} + 5y_t = 4 + 2t$
   (c) $y_{t+2} + 5y_{t+1} + 2y_t = 18 + 6t + 8t^2$
4. Would you expect that, when the variable term takes the form $m^t + t^n$, the trial solution should be $B(m)^t + (B_0 + B_1 t + \cdots + B_n t^n)$? Why?
5. Find the characteristic roots and the complementary function of:
   (a) $y_{t+3} - \frac{1}{2}y_{t+2} - y_{t+1} + \frac{1}{2}y_t = 0$
   (b) $y_{t+3} - 2y_{t+2} + \frac{5}{4}y_{t+1} - \frac{1}{4}y_t = 1$
   [*Hint:* Try factoring out $(b - \frac{1}{4})$ in both characteristic equations.]
6. Test the convergence of the solutions of the following difference equations by the Schur theorem:
   (a) $y_{t+2} + \frac{1}{2}y_{t+1} - \frac{1}{2}y_t = 3$
   (b) $y_{t+2} - \frac{1}{9}y_t = 1$
7. In the case of a third-order difference equation
   $$y_{t+3} + a_1 y_{t+2} + a_2 y_{t+1} + a_3 y_t = c$$
   what are the exact forms of the determinants required by the Schur theorem?

19

Simultaneous Differential Equations and Difference Equations

Heretofore, our discussion of economic dynamics has been confined to the analysis of a single dynamic (differential or difference) equation. In the present chapter, methods for analyzing a system of simultaneous dynamic equations are introduced. Because this would entail the handling of several variables at the same time, you might anticipate a great deal of new complications. But the truth is that much of what we have already learned about single dynamic equations can be readily extended to systems of simultaneous dynamic equations. For instance, the solution of a dynamic system would still consist of a set of particular integrals or particular solutions (intertemporal equilibrium values of the various variables) and complementary functions (deviations from equilibriums). The complementary functions would still be based on the reduced equations, i.e., the homogeneous versions of the equations in the system. And the dynamic stability of the system would still depend on the signs (if differential equation system) or the absolute values (if difference equation system) of the characteristic roots in the complementary functions. Thus the problem of a dynamic system is only slightly more complicated than that of a single dynamic equation.

19.1 The Genesis of Dynamic Systems

There are two general ways in which a dynamic system can come into being. It may emanate from a given *set* of interacting patterns of change. Or it may be derived from a *single* given pattern of change, provided the latter consists of a dynamic equation of the second (or higher) order.

Interacting Patterns of Change

The most obvious case of a given set of interacting patterns of change is that of a multisector model where each sector, as described by a dynamic equation, impinges on at least one of the other sectors. A dynamic version of the input-output model, for example, could involve n industries whose output changes produce dynamic repercussions on the other industries. Thus it constitutes a dynamic system. Similarly, a dynamic general-equilibrium market model would involve n commodities that are interrelated in their price adjustments. Thus, there is again a dynamic system.

However, interacting patterns of change can be found even in a single-sector model. The various variables in such a model represent, not different sectors or different commodities, but different *aspects* of an economy. Nonetheless, they can affect one another in their dynamic behavior, so as to provide a network of interactions.[†] A concrete example of this has in fact been encountered in Chap. 18. In the inflation-unemployment model, the expected rate of inflation π follows a pattern of change, (18.19), that depends not only on π, but also on the rate of unemployment U (through the actual rate of inflation p). Reciprocally, the pattern of change of U, (18.20), is dependent on π (again through p). Thus the dynamics of π and U must be simultaneously determined. In retrospect, therefore, the inflation-unemployment model could have been treated as a simultaneous-equation dynamic model. And that would have obviated the long sequence of substitutions and eliminations that were undertaken to condense the model into a single equation in one variable. Below, in Sec. 19.4, we shall indeed rework that model, viewed as a dynamic system. Meanwhile, the notion that the same model can be analyzed either as a single equation or as an equation system supplies a natural cue to the discussion of the second way to have a dynamic system.

The Transformation of a High-Order Dynamic Equation

Suppose that we are given an nth-order differential (or difference) equation in *one* variable. Then, as will be shown, it is always possible to transform that equation into a mathematically equivalent system of n simultaneous *first*-order differential (or difference) equations in n variables. In particular, a second-order differential equation can be rewritten as two simultaneous first-order differential equations in two variables.[‡] Thus, even if we happen to start out with only one (high-order) dynamic equation, a dynamic system can nevertheless be derived through the artifice of mathematical transformation. This fact, incidentally, has an important implication: In the ensuing discussion of dynamic systems, we need only be concerned with systems of *first*-order equations, for if a higher-order equation is present, we can always transform it first into a set of first-order equations. This will result in a larger number of equations in the system, but the order will then be lowered to the minimum.

To illustrate the transformation procedure, let us consider the single difference equation

$$y_{t+2} + a_1 y_{t+1} + a_2 y_t = c \qquad \textbf{(19.1)}$$

If we concoct an artificial new variable x_t, defined by

$$x_t \equiv y_{t+1} \qquad \text{(implying } x_{t+1} \equiv y_{t+2})$$

we can then express the original second-order equation by means of *two* first-order (one-period lag) simultaneous equations as follows:

$$
\begin{aligned}
x_{t+1} &+ a_1 x_t + a_2 y_t = c \\
y_{t+1} &- x_t = 0
\end{aligned}
\qquad \textbf{(19.1′)}
$$

[†] Note that if we have two dynamic equations in the two variables y_1 and y_2 such that the pattern of change of y_1 depends exclusively on y_1 itself, and similarly for y_2, we really do not have a simultaneous-equation system. Instead, we have merely two separate dynamic equations, each of which can be analyzed by itself, with no requirement of "simultaneity."

[‡] Conversely, two first-order differential (or difference) equations in two variables can be consolidated into a single second-order equation in one variable, as we did in Secs. 16.5 and 18.3.

It is easily seen that, as long as the second equation (which defines the variable x_t) is satisfied, the first is identical with the original given equation. By a similar procedure, and using more artificial variables, we can similarly transform a higher-order single equation into an equivalent system of simultaneous first-order equations. You can verify, for instance, that the third-order equation

$$y_{t+3} + y_{t+2} - 3y_{t+1} + 2y_t = 0 \qquad \textbf{(19.2)}$$

can be expressed as

$$
\begin{aligned}
w_{t+1} && + w_t - 3x_t + 2y_t &= 0 \\
x_{t+1} && - w_t &= 0 \qquad \textbf{(19.2')}\\
y_{t+1} && - x_t &= 0
\end{aligned}
$$

where $x_t \equiv y_{t+1}$ (so that $x_{t+1} \equiv y_{t+2}$) and $w_t \equiv x_{t+1}$ (so that $w_{t+1} \equiv x_{t+2} \equiv y_{t+3}$).

By a perfectly similar procedure, we can also transform an *n*th-order *differential* equation into a system of *n* first-order equations. Given the second-order differential equation

$$y''(t) + a_1 y'(t) + a_2 y(t) = 0 \qquad \textbf{(19.3)}$$

for instance, we can introduce a new variable $x(t)$, defined by

$$x(t) \equiv y'(t) \qquad [\text{implying } x'(t) \equiv y''(t)]$$

Then (19.3) can be rewritten as the following system of two first-order equations:

$$
\begin{aligned}
x'(t) && + a_1 x(t) + a_2 y(t) &= 0 \\
y'(t) - && x(t) &= 0
\end{aligned}
\qquad \textbf{(19.3')}
$$

where, you may note, the second equation performs the function of defining the newly introduced x variable, as did the second equation in (19.1'). Essentially the same procedure can also be used to transform a higher-order differential equation. The only modification is that we must introduce a correspondingly larger number of new variables.

19.2 Solving Simultaneous Dynamic Equations

The methods for solving simultaneous differential equations and simultaneous difference equations are quite similar. We shall thus discuss them together in this section. For our present purposes, we shall confine the discussion to linear equations with constant coefficients only.

Simultaneous Difference Equations

Suppose that we are given the following system of linear difference equations:

$$
\begin{aligned}
x_{t+1} && + 6x_t + 9y_t &= 4 \\
y_{t+1} - && x_t &= 0
\end{aligned}
\qquad \textbf{(19.4)}
$$

How do we find the time paths of x and y such that both equations in this system will be satisfied? Essentially, our task is again to seek the particular integrals and complementary functions, and sum these to obtain the desired time paths of the two variables.

Since particular integrals represent intertemporal equilibrium values, let us denote them by $\bar{x}$ and $\bar{y}$. As before, it is advisable first to try constant solutions, namely, $x_{t+1} = x_t = \bar{x}$ and $y_{t+1} = y_t = \bar{y}$. This will indeed work in the present case, for upon substituting these trial solutions into (19.4) we get

$$\left.\begin{array}{r} 7\bar{x} + 9\bar{y} = 4 \\ -\bar{x} + \bar{y} = 0 \end{array}\right\} \quad \Rightarrow \quad \bar{x} = \bar{y} = \frac{1}{4} \tag{19.5}$$

(In case such constant solutions fail to work, however, we must then try solutions of the form $x_t = k_1 t$, $y_t = k_2 t$, etc.)

For the complementary functions, we should, drawing on our previous experience, adopt trial solutions of the form

$$x_t = mb^t \quad \text{and} \quad y_t = nb^t \tag{19.6}$$

where m and n are arbitrary constants and the base b represents the characteristic root. It is then automatically implied that

$$x_{t+1} = mb^{t+1} \quad \text{and} \quad y_{t+1} = nb^{t+1} \tag{19.7}$$

Note that, to simplify matters, we are employing the same base $b \neq 0$ for both variables, although their coefficients are allowed to differ. It is our aim to find the values of b, m, and n that can make the trial solutions (19.6) satisfy the *reduced* (homogeneous) version of (19.4).

Upon substituting the trial solutions into the reduced version of (19.4) and canceling the common factor $b^t \neq 0$, we obtain the two equations

$$\begin{array}{c} (b + 6)m + 9n = 0 \\ -m + bn = 0 \end{array} \tag{19.8}$$

This can be considered as a linear homogeneous-equation system in the two variables m and n—if we are willing to consider b as a parameter for the time being. Because the system (19.8) is homogeneous, it can yield only the trivial solution $m = n = 0$ if its coefficient matrix is nonsingular (see Table 5.1 in Sec. 5.5). In that event, the complementary functions in (19.6) will both be identically zero, signifying that x and y never deviate from their intertemporal equilibrium values. Since that would be an uninteresting special case, we shall try to rule out that trivial solution by requiring the coefficient matrix of the system to be *singular*. That is, we shall require the determinant of that matrix to vanish:

$$\begin{vmatrix} b + 6 & 9 \\ -1 & b \end{vmatrix} = b^2 + 6b + 9 = 0 \tag{19.9}$$

From this quadratic equation, we find that $b(= b_1 = b_2) = -3$ is the only value which can prevent m and n from both being zero in (19.8). We shall therefore only use this value of b. Equation (19.9) is called the *characteristic equation*, and its roots the *characteristic roots*, of the given simultaneous difference-equation system.

Once we have a specific value of b, (19.8) gives us the corresponding solution values of m and n. The system being homogeneous, however, there will actually emerge an infinite number of solutions for (m, n), expressible in the form of an equation $m = kn$, where k is a constant. In fact, for each root b_i, there will in general be a distinct equation $m_i = k_i n_i$. Even with repeated roots, with $b_1 = b_2$, we should still use two such equations, $m_1 = k_1 n_1$

and $m_2 = k_2 n_2$ in the complementary functions. Moreover, with repeated roots, we recall from (18.6) that the complementary functions should be written as

$$x_t = m_1(-3)^t + m_2 t(-3)^t$$
$$y_t = n_1(-3)^t + n_2 t(-3)^t$$

The factors of proportionality between m_i and n_i must, of course, satisfy the given equation system (19.4), which mandates that $y_{t+1} = x_t$, i.e.,

$$n_1(-3)^{t+1} + n_2(t+1)(-3)^{t+1} - m_1(-3)^t + m_2 t(-3)^t$$

Dividing through by $(-3)^t$, we get

$$-3n_1 - 3n_2(t+1) = m_1 + m_2 t$$

or, after rearranging,

$$-3(n_1 + n_2) - 3n_2 t - m_1 + m_2 t$$

Equating the terms with t on the two sides of the equals sign, and similarly for the terms without t, we find

$$m_1 = -3(n_1 + n_2) \qquad \text{and} \qquad m_2 = -3n_2$$

If we now write $n_1 = A_3, n_2 = A_4$, then it follows that

$$m_1 = -3(A_3 + A_4) \qquad m_2 = -3A_4$$

Thus the complementary functions can be written as

$$x_c = -3(A_3 + A_4)(-3)^t - 3A_4 t(-3)^t$$
$$= -3A_3(-3)^t - 3A_4(t+1)(-3)^t \qquad \qquad \textbf{(19.10)}$$
$$y_c = A_3(-3)^t + A_4 t(-3)^t$$

where A_3 and A_4 are arbitrary constants. Then the general solution follows easily by combining the particular solutions in (19.5) with the complementary functions just found. All that remains, then, is to definitize the two arbitrary constants A_3 and A_4 with the help of appropriate initial or boundary conditions.

One significant feature of the preceding solution is that, since both time paths have identical b^t expressions in them, they must either both converge or both diverge. This makes sense because, in a model with dynamically interdependent variables, a general intertemporal equilibrium cannot prevail unless no dynamic motion is present anywhere in the system. In the present case, with repeated roots $b = -3$, the time paths of both x and y will display explosive oscillation.

Matrix Notation

In order to bring out the basic parallelism between the methods of solving a single equation and an equation system, the preceding exposition was carried out without the benefit of matrix notation. Let us now see how the latter can be utilized here. Even though it may seem pointless to apply matrix notation to a simple system of only two equations, the possibility of extending that notation to the n-equation case should make it a worthwhile exercise.

First of all, the given system (19.4) may be expressed as

$$\begin{bmatrix} 1 & 0 \\ 0 & 1 \end{bmatrix} \begin{bmatrix} x_{t+1} \\ y_{t+1} \end{bmatrix} + \begin{bmatrix} 6 & 9 \\ -1 & 0 \end{bmatrix} \begin{bmatrix} x_t \\ y_t \end{bmatrix} = \begin{bmatrix} 4 \\ 0 \end{bmatrix} \qquad \textbf{(19.4')}$$

or, more succinctly, as

$$Iu + Kv = d \qquad \textbf{(19.4'')}$$

where I is the 2×2 identity matrix; K is the 2×2 matrix of the coefficients of the x_t and y_t terms; and u, v, and d are column vectors defined as follows:[†]

$$u = \begin{bmatrix} x_{t+1} \\ y_{t+1} \end{bmatrix} \qquad v = \begin{bmatrix} x_t \\ y_t \end{bmatrix} \qquad d = \begin{bmatrix} 4 \\ 0 \end{bmatrix}$$

The reader may find one feature puzzling: Since we know $Iu = u$, why not drop the I? The answer is that, even though it seems redundant now, the identity matrix will be needed in subsequent operations, and therefore we shall retain it as in (19.4'').

When we try constant solutions $x_{t+1} = x_t = \bar{x}$ and $y_{t+1} = y_t = \bar{y}$ for the particular solutions, we are in effect setting $u = v = \begin{bmatrix} \bar{x} \\ \bar{y} \end{bmatrix}$; this will reduce (19.4'') to

$$(I + K) \begin{bmatrix} \bar{x} \\ \bar{y} \end{bmatrix} = d$$

If the inverse $(I + K)^{-1}$ exists, we can express the particular solutions as

$$\begin{bmatrix} \bar{x} \\ \bar{y} \end{bmatrix} = (I + K)^{-1} d \qquad \textbf{(19.5')}$$

This is of course a general formula, for it is valid for any matrix K and vector d as long as $(I + K)^{-1}$ exists. Applied to our numerical example, we have

$$(I + K)^{-1} d = \begin{bmatrix} 7 & 9 \\ -1 & 1 \end{bmatrix}^{-1} \begin{bmatrix} 4 \\ 0 \end{bmatrix} = \begin{bmatrix} \frac{1}{16} & -\frac{9}{16} \\ \frac{1}{16} & \frac{7}{16} \end{bmatrix} \begin{bmatrix} 4 \\ 0 \end{bmatrix} = \begin{bmatrix} \frac{1}{4} \\ \frac{1}{4} \end{bmatrix}$$

Therefore, $\bar{x} = \bar{y} = \frac{1}{4}$, which checks with (19.5).

Turning to the complementary functions, we see that the trial solutions (19.6) and (19.7) give the u and v vectors the specific forms

$$u = \begin{bmatrix} mb^{t+1} \\ nb^{t+1} \end{bmatrix} = \begin{bmatrix} m \\ n \end{bmatrix} b^{t+1} \qquad \text{and} \qquad v = \begin{bmatrix} mb^t \\ nb^t \end{bmatrix} = \begin{bmatrix} m \\ n \end{bmatrix} b^t$$

When substituted into the reduced equation $Iu + Kv = 0$, these trial solutions will transform the latter into

$$I \begin{bmatrix} m \\ n \end{bmatrix} b^{t+1} + K \begin{bmatrix} m \\ n \end{bmatrix} b^t = 0$$

[†] The symbol v here denotes a vector. Do not confuse it with the v in the complex-number notation $h \pm vi$, where it represents a scalar.

or, after multiplying through by b^{-t} (a scalar) and factoring,

$$(bI + K) \begin{bmatrix} m \\ n \end{bmatrix} = 0 \tag{19.8'}$$

where 0 is a zero vector. It is from this homogeneous-equation system that we are to find the appropriate values of b, m, and n to be used in the trial solutions in order to make the latter determinate.

To avoid trivial solutions for m and n, it is necessary that

$$|bI + K| = 0 \tag{19.9'}$$

And this is the characteristic equation which will give us the characteristic roots b_i. You can verify that if we substitute

$$bI = \begin{bmatrix} b & 0 \\ 0 & b \end{bmatrix} \quad \text{and} \quad K = \begin{bmatrix} 6 & 9 \\ -1 & 0 \end{bmatrix}$$

into this equation, the result will precisely be (19.9), yielding the repeated roots $b = -3$.

In general, each root b_i will elicit from (19.8') a particular set of infinite number of solution values of m and n which are tied to each other by the equation $m_i = k_i n_i$. It is therefore possible to write, for each value of b_i,

$$n_i = A_i \quad \text{and} \quad m_i = k_i A_i$$

where A_i are arbitrary constants to be definitized later. When substituted into the trial solutions, these expressions for n_i and m_i along with the values b_i will lead to specific forms of complementary functions. If all roots are distinct real numbers, we may apply (18.5) and write

$$\begin{bmatrix} x_c \\ y_c \end{bmatrix} = \begin{bmatrix} \Sigma m_i b_i^t \\ \Sigma n_i b_i^t \end{bmatrix} = \begin{bmatrix} \Sigma k_i A_i b_i^t \\ \Sigma A_i b_i^t \end{bmatrix}$$

With repeated roots, however, we must apply (18.6) instead and, as a result, the complementary functions will contain terms with an extra multiplicative t, such as $m_1 b^t + m_2 t b^t$ (for x_c) and $n_1 b^t + n_2 t b^t$ (for y_c). The factors of proportionality between m_i and n_i are to be determined by the relationship between the variables x and y as stipulated in the given equation system, as illustrated in (19.10) in our numerical example. Finally, in the complex-root case, the complementary functions should be written with (18.10) as their prototype.

Finally, to get the general solution, we can simply form the sum

$$\begin{bmatrix} x_t \\ y_t \end{bmatrix} = \begin{bmatrix} x_c \\ y_c \end{bmatrix} + \begin{bmatrix} \bar{x} \\ \bar{y} \end{bmatrix}$$

Then it remains only to definitize the arbitrary constants A_i.

The extension of this procedure to the n-equation system should be self-evident. When n is large, however, the characteristic equation—an nth-degree polynomial equation—may not be easy to solve quantitatively. In that event, we may again find the Schur theorem to be of help in yielding certain qualitative conclusions about the time paths of the variables in the system. All these variables, we recall, are assigned the same base b in the trial solutions, so they must end up with the same b_i^t expressions in the complementary functions and share the same convergence properties. Thus a single application of the Schur theorem will enable us to determine the convergence or divergence of the time path of every variable in the system.

Simultaneous Differential Equations

The method of solution just described can also be applied to a first-order linear *differential-equation* system. About the only major modification needed is to change the trial solutions to

$$x(t) = me^{rt} \quad \text{and} \quad y(t) = ne^{rt} \qquad \textbf{(19.11)}$$

which imply that

$$x'(t) = rme^{rt} \quad \text{and} \quad y'(t) = rne^{rt} \qquad \textbf{(19.12)}$$

In line with our notational convention, the characteristic roots are now denoted by r instead of b.

Suppose that we are given the following equation system:

$$\begin{aligned} x'(t) + 2y'(t) + 2x(t) + 5y(t) &= 77 \\ y'(t) + x(t) + 4y(t) &= 61 \end{aligned} \qquad \textbf{(19.13)}$$

First, let us rewrite it in matrix notation as

$$Ju + Mv = g \qquad \textbf{(19.13′)}$$

where the matrices are

$$J = \begin{bmatrix} 1 & 2 \\ 0 & 1 \end{bmatrix} \quad u = \begin{bmatrix} x'(t) \\ y'(t) \end{bmatrix} \quad M = \begin{bmatrix} 2 & 5 \\ 1 & 4 \end{bmatrix} \quad v = \begin{bmatrix} x(t) \\ y(t) \end{bmatrix} \quad g = \begin{bmatrix} 77 \\ 61 \end{bmatrix}$$

Note, that, in view of the appearance of the $2y'(t)$ term in the first equation of (19.13), we have to use the matrix J in place of the identity matrix I, as in (19.4″). Of course, if J is non-singular (so that J^{-1} exists), then we can in a sense *normalize* (19.13′) by premultiplying every term therein by J^{-1}, to get

$$J^{-1}Ju + J^{-1}Mv = J^{-1}g \quad \text{or} \quad Iu + Kv = d$$
$$(K \equiv J^{-1}M; d \equiv J^{-1}g) \qquad \textbf{(19.13″)}$$

This new format is an exact duplicate of (19.4″), although it must be remembered that the vectors u and v have altogether different meanings in the two different contexts. In the ensuing development, we shall adhere to the $Ju + Mv = g$ formulation given in (19.13′).

To find the particular integrals, let us try constant solutions $x(t) = \bar{x}$ and $y(t) = \bar{y}$—which imply that $x'(t) = y'(t) = 0$. If these solutions hold, the vectors v and u will become $v = \begin{bmatrix} \bar{x} \\ \bar{y} \end{bmatrix}$ and $u = \begin{bmatrix} 0 \\ 0 \end{bmatrix}$, and (19.13′) will reduce to $Mv = g$. Thus the solution for $\bar{x}$ and $\bar{y}$ can be written as

$$\begin{bmatrix} \bar{x} \\ \bar{y} \end{bmatrix} = \bar{v} = M^{-1}g \qquad \textbf{(19.14)}$$

which you should compare with (19.5′). In numerical terms, our present problem yields the following particular integrals:

$$\begin{bmatrix} \bar{x} \\ \bar{y} \end{bmatrix} = \begin{bmatrix} 2 & 5 \\ 1 & 4 \end{bmatrix}^{-1} \begin{bmatrix} 77 \\ 61 \end{bmatrix} = \begin{bmatrix} \frac{4}{3} & -\frac{5}{3} \\ -\frac{1}{3} & \frac{2}{3} \end{bmatrix} \begin{bmatrix} 77 \\ 61 \end{bmatrix} = \begin{bmatrix} 1 \\ 15 \end{bmatrix}$$

Next, let us look for the complementary functions. Using the trial solutions suggested in (19.11) and (19.12), the vectors u and v become

$$u = \begin{bmatrix} m \\ n \end{bmatrix} r e^{rt} \qquad \text{and} \qquad v = \begin{bmatrix} m \\ n \end{bmatrix} e^{rt}$$

Substitution of these into the reduced equation

$$Ju + Mv = 0$$

yields the result

$$J \begin{bmatrix} m \\ n \end{bmatrix} r e^{rt} + M \begin{bmatrix} m \\ n \end{bmatrix} e^{rt} = 0$$

or, after multiplying through by the scalar e^{-rt} and factoring,

$$(rJ + M) \begin{bmatrix} m \\ n \end{bmatrix} = 0 \tag{19.15}$$

You should compare this with (19.8′). Since our objective is to find *nontrivial* solutions of m and n (so that our trial solutions will also be nontrivial), it is necessary that

$$|rJ + M| = 0 \tag{19.16}$$

The analog of (19.9′), this last equation—the characteristic equation of the given equation system—will yield the roots r_i that we need. Then, we can find the corresponding (nontrivial) values of m_i and n_i.

In our present example, the characteristic equation is

$$|rJ + M| = \begin{vmatrix} r+2 & 2r+5 \\ 1 & r+4 \end{vmatrix} = r^2 + 4r + 3 = 0 \tag{19.16′}$$

with roots $r_1 = -1, r_2 = -3$. Substituting these into (19.15), we get

$$\begin{bmatrix} 1 & 3 \\ 1 & 3 \end{bmatrix} \begin{bmatrix} m_1 \\ n_1 \end{bmatrix} = 0 \qquad (\text{for } r_1 = -1)$$

$$\begin{bmatrix} -1 & -1 \\ 1 & 1 \end{bmatrix} \begin{bmatrix} m_2 \\ n_2 \end{bmatrix} = 0 \qquad (\text{for } r_2 = -3)$$

It follows that $m_1 = -3n_1$ and $m_2 = -n_2$, which we may also express as

$$m_1 = 3A_1 \qquad \text{and} \qquad m_2 = A_2$$
$$n_1 = -A_1 \qquad \qquad\quad n_2 = -A_2$$

Now that r_i, m_i, and n_i have all been found, the complementary functions can be written as the following linear combinations of exponential expressions:

$$\begin{bmatrix} x_c \\ y_c \end{bmatrix} = \begin{bmatrix} \Sigma m_i e^{r_i t} \\ \Sigma n_i e^{r_i t} \end{bmatrix} \qquad [\text{distinct real roots}]$$

And the general solution will emerge in the form

$$\begin{bmatrix} x(t) \\ y(t) \end{bmatrix} = \begin{bmatrix} x_c \\ y_c \end{bmatrix} + \begin{bmatrix} \bar{x} \\ \bar{y} \end{bmatrix}$$

In our present example, the solution is

$$\begin{bmatrix} x(t) \\ y(t) \end{bmatrix} = \begin{bmatrix} 3A_1 e^{-t} + A_2 e^{-3t} + 1 \\ -A_1 e^{-t} - A_2 e^{-3t} + 15 \end{bmatrix}$$

Moreover, if we are given the initial conditions $x(0) = 6$ and $y(0) = 12$, the arbitrary constants can be found to be $A_1 = 1$ and $A_2 = 2$. These will serve to definitize the preceding solution.

Once more we may observe that, since the $e^{r_i t}$ expressions are shared by both time paths $x(t)$ and $y(t)$, the latter must either both converge or both diverge. The roots being -1 and -3 in the present case, both time paths converge to their respective equilibria, namely, $\bar{x} = 1$ and $\bar{y} = 15$.

Even though our example consists of a two-equation system only, the method certainly extends to the general n-equation system. When n is large, quantitative solutions may again be difficult, but once the characteristic equation is found, a qualitative analysis will always be possible by resorting to the Routh theorem.

Further Comments on the Characteristic Equation

The term "characteristic equation" has now been encountered in *three* separate contexts: In Sec. 11.3, we spoke of the characteristic equation of a matrix; in Secs. 16.1 and 18.1, the term was applied to a single linear differential equation and difference equation; now, in this section, we have just introduced the characteristic equation of a system of linear difference or differential equations. Is there a connection between the three?

There indeed is, and the connection is a close one. In the first place, given a single equation and an equivalent equation system—as exemplified by the equation (19.1) and the system (19.1′), or the equation (19.3) and the system (19.3′)—their characteristic equations must be identical. For illustration, consider the difference equation (19.1), $y_{t+2} + a_1 y_{t+1} + a_2 y_t = c$. We have earlier learned to write its characteristic equation by directly transplanting its constant coefficients into a quadratic equation:

$$b^2 + a_1 b + a_2 = 0$$

What about the equivalent system (19.1′)? Taking that system to be in the form of $Iu + Kv = d$, as in (19.4″), we have the matrix $K = \begin{bmatrix} a_1 & a_2 \\ -1 & 0 \end{bmatrix}$. So the characteristic equation is

$$|bI + K| = \begin{vmatrix} b + a_1 & a_2 \\ -1 & b \end{vmatrix} = b^2 + a_1 b + a_2 = 0 \qquad \text{[by (19.9′)]} \quad \textbf{(19.17)}$$

which is precisely the same as the one obtained from the single equation as was asserted. Naturally, the same type of result holds also in the differential-equation framework, the only difference being that we would, in accordance with our convention, replace the symbol b by the symbol r in the latter framework.

It is also possible to link the characteristic equation of a difference- (or differential-) equation system to that of a particular square matrix, which we shall call D. Referring to the definition in (11.14), but using the symbol b (instead of r) for the difference-equation framework, we can write the characteristic equation of matrix D as follows:

$$|D - bI| = 0 \qquad\qquad \textbf{(19.18)}$$

In general, if we multiply every element of the determinant $|D - bI|$ by -1, the value of the determinant will be unchanged if matrix D contains an *even* number of rows (or columns), and will change its sign if D contains an *odd* number of rows. In the present case, however, since $|D - bI|$ is to be set equal to zero, multiplying every element by -1 will not matter, regardless of the dimension of matrix D. But to multiply every element of the determinant $|D - bI|$ by -1 is tantamount to multiplying the matrix $(D - bI)$ by -1 (see Example 6 of Sec. 5.3) before taking its determinant. Thus, (19.18) can be rewritten as

$$|bI - D| = 0 \qquad\qquad \textbf{(19.18}'\textbf{)}$$

When this is equated to (19.17), it becomes clear that if we pick the matrix $D = -K$, then its characteristic equation will be identical with that of the system (19.1'). This matrix, $-K$, has a special meaning: If we take the *reduced* version of the system, $Iu + Kv = 0$, and express it in the form of $Iu = -Kv$, or simply $u = -Kv$, we see that $-K$ is the matrix that can transform the vector $v = \begin{bmatrix} x_t \\ y_t \end{bmatrix}$ into the vector $u = \begin{bmatrix} x_{t+1} \\ y_{t+1} \end{bmatrix}$ in that particular equation.

Again, the same reasoning can be adapted to the differential-equation system (19.3'). However, in the case of a system such as (19.13'), $Ju + Mv = g$, where—unlike in the system (19.3')—the first term is Ju rather than Iu, the characteristic equation is in the form

$$|rJ + M| = 0 \qquad [\text{cf. (19.16}'\text{)}]$$

For this case, if we wish to find the expression for the matrix D, we must first normalize the equation $Ju + Mv = g$ into the form of (19.13''), and then take $D = -K = -J^{-1}M$.

In sum, given (1) a single difference or differential equation, and (2) an equivalent equation system, from which we can also obtain (3) an appropriate matrix D, if we try to find the characteristic equations of all three of these, the results must be one and the same.

EXERCISE 19.2

1. Verify that the difference-equation system (19.4) is equivalent to the single equation $y_{t+2} + 6y_{t+1} + 9y_t = 4$, which was solved earlier as Example 4 in Sec. 18.1. How do the solutions obtained by the two different methods compare?

2. Show that the characteristic equation of the difference equation (19.2) is identical with that of the equivalent system (19.2').

3. Solve the following two difference-equation systems:

    (a) $x_{t+1} \qquad\; + \; x_t + 2y_t = 24$

    $\qquad\quad y_{t+1} + 2x_t - 2y_t = \;\; 9 \qquad$ (with $x_0 = 10$ and $y_0 = 9$)

    (b) $x_{t+1} \qquad\quad -x_t - \frac{1}{3}y_t = -1$

    $\qquad\quad x_{t+1} + y_{t+1} \qquad - \frac{1}{6}y_t = \;\; 8\frac{1}{2} \quad$ (with $x_0 = 5$ and $y_0 = 4$)

4. Solve the following two differential-equation systems:

(a) $x'(t) \quad - \quad x(t) - 12y(t) = -60$
$\qquad y'(t) + x(t) + 6y(t) = \quad 36 \qquad$ [with $x(0) = 13$ and $y(0) = 4$]

(b) $x'(t) \qquad - 2x(t) + 3y(t) = \quad 10$
$\qquad y'(t) - x(t) + 2y(t) = \quad 9 \qquad$ [with $x(0) = 8$ and $y(0) = 5$]

5. On the basis of the differential-equation system (19.13), find the matrix D whose characteristic equation is identical with that of the system. Check that the characteristic equations of the two are indeed the same.

19.3 Dynamic Input-Output Models

Our first encounter with input-output analysis was concerned with the question: How much should be produced in each industry so that the input requirements of all industries, as well as the final demand (open system), will be exactly satisfied? The context was static, and the problem was to solve a simultaneous-equation system for the *equilibrium* output levels of all industries. When certain additional economic considerations are incorporated into the model, the input-output system can take on a dynamic character, and there will then result a difference- or differential-equation system of the type discussed in Sec. 19.2.

Three such dynamizing considerations will be considered here. To keep the exposition simple, however, we shall illustrate with two-industry open systems only. Nevertheless, since we shall employ matrix notation, the generalization to the n-industry case should not prove difficult, for it can be accomplished simply by duly changing the dimensions of the matrices involved. For purposes of such generalization, it will prove advisable to denote the variables not by x_t and y_t but by $x_{1,t}$ and $x_{2,t}$, so that we can extend the notation to $x_{n,t}$ when needed. You will recall that, in the input-output context, x_i represents the output (measured in dollars) of the ith industry; the new subscript t will now add a time dimension to it. The input-coefficient symbol a_{ij} will still mean the dollar worth of the ith commodity required in the production of a dollar's worth of the jth commodity, and d_i will again indicate the final demand for the ith commodity.

Time Lag in Production

In a static two-industry open system, the output of industry I should be set at the level of demand as follows:

$$x_1 = a_{11}x_1 + a_{12}x_2 + d_1$$

Now assume a one-period lag in production, so that the amount demanded in period t determines not the current output but the output of period $(t + 1)$. To depict this new situation, we must modify the preceding equation to the form

$$x_{1,t+1} = a_{11}x_{1,t} + a_{12}x_{2,t} + d_{1,t} \qquad \textbf{(19.19)}$$

Similarly, we can write for industry II:

$$x_{2,t+1} = a_{21}x_{1,t} + a_{22}x_{2,t} + d_{2,t} \qquad \textbf{(19.19')}$$

Thus we now have a system of simultaneous difference equations; this constitutes a dynamic version of the input-output model.

In matrix notation, the system consists of the equation

$$x_{t+1} - Ax_t = d_t \qquad (19.20)$$

where $\quad x_{t+1} = \begin{bmatrix} x_{1,t+1} \\ x_{2,t+1} \end{bmatrix} \qquad x_t = \begin{bmatrix} x_{1,t} \\ x_{2,t} \end{bmatrix} \qquad A = \begin{bmatrix} a_{11} & a_{12} \\ a_{21} & a_{22} \end{bmatrix} \qquad d_t = \begin{bmatrix} d_{1,t} \\ d_{2,t} \end{bmatrix}$

Clearly, (19.20) is in the form of (19.4″), with only two exceptions. First, unlike vector u, vector x_{t+1} does not have an identity matrix I as its "coefficient." However, as explained earlier, this really makes no analytical difference. The second, and more substantive, point is that the vector d_t, with a time subscript, implies that the final-demand vector is being viewed as a function of time. If this function is nonconstant, a modification will be required in the method of finding the particular solutions, although the complementary functions will remain unaffected. The following example will illustrate the modified procedure.

Example 1 Given the exponential final-demand vector

$$d_t = \begin{bmatrix} \delta^t \\ \delta^t \end{bmatrix} = \begin{bmatrix} 1 \\ 1 \end{bmatrix} \delta^t \qquad (\delta = \text{a positive scalar})$$

find the particular solutions of the dynamic input-output model (19.20). In line with the method of undetermined coefficients introduced in Sec. 18.4, we should try solutions of the form $x_{1,t} = \beta_1 \delta^t$ and $x_{2,t} = \beta_2 \delta^t$, where β_1 and β_2 are undetermined coefficients. That is, we should try

$$x_t = \begin{bmatrix} \beta_1 \delta^t \\ \beta_2 \delta^t \end{bmatrix} = \begin{bmatrix} \beta_1 \\ \beta_2 \end{bmatrix} \delta^t \qquad (19.21)$$

which implies[†]

$$x_{t+1} = \begin{bmatrix} \beta_1 \delta^{t+1} \\ \beta_2 \delta^{t+1} \end{bmatrix} = \begin{bmatrix} \beta_1 \delta \\ \beta_2 \delta \end{bmatrix} \delta^t = \begin{bmatrix} \delta & 0 \\ 0 & \delta \end{bmatrix} \begin{bmatrix} \beta_1 \\ \beta_2 \end{bmatrix} \delta^t$$

If the indicated trial solutions hold, then the system (19.20) will become

$$\begin{bmatrix} \delta & 0 \\ 0 & \delta \end{bmatrix} \begin{bmatrix} \beta_1 \\ \beta_2 \end{bmatrix} \delta^t - \begin{bmatrix} a_{11} & a_{12} \\ a_{21} & a_{22} \end{bmatrix} \begin{bmatrix} \beta_1 \\ \beta_2 \end{bmatrix} \delta^t = \begin{bmatrix} 1 \\ 1 \end{bmatrix} \delta^t$$

or, on canceling the common scalar multiplier $\delta^t \neq 0$,

$$\begin{bmatrix} \delta - a_{11} & -a_{12} \\ -a_{21} & \delta - a_{22} \end{bmatrix} \begin{bmatrix} \beta_1 \\ \beta_2 \end{bmatrix} = \begin{bmatrix} 1 \\ 1 \end{bmatrix} \qquad (19.22)$$

[†] You will note that the vector $\begin{bmatrix} \beta_1 \delta \\ \beta_2 \delta \end{bmatrix}$ can be rewritten in several equivalent forms:

$$\begin{bmatrix} \beta_1 \\ \beta_2 \end{bmatrix} \delta \quad \text{or} \quad \delta \begin{bmatrix} \beta_1 \\ \beta_2 \end{bmatrix} \quad \text{or} \quad \delta \begin{bmatrix} 1 & 0 \\ 0 & 1 \end{bmatrix} \begin{bmatrix} \beta_1 \\ \beta_2 \end{bmatrix} = \begin{bmatrix} \delta & 0 \\ 0 & \delta \end{bmatrix} \begin{bmatrix} \beta_1 \\ \beta_2 \end{bmatrix}$$

We choose the third alternative here because in a subsequent step we shall want to add $\begin{bmatrix} \delta & 0 \\ 0 & \delta \end{bmatrix}$ to another 2×2 matrix. The first two alternative forms will entail problems of dimension conformability.

Assuming the coefficient matrix on the extreme left to be nonsingular, we can readily find β_1 and β_2 (by Cramer's rule) to be

$$\beta_1 = \frac{\delta - a_{22} + a_{12}}{\Delta} \qquad \text{and} \qquad \beta_2 = \frac{\delta - a_{11} + a_{21}}{\Delta} \qquad \textbf{(19.22')}$$

where $\Delta \equiv (\delta - a_{11})(\delta - a_{22}) - a_{12}a_{21}$. Since β_1 and β_2 are now expressed entirely in the known values of the parameters, we only need to insert them into the trial solution (19.21) to get the definite expressions for the particular solutions.

A more general version of the type of final-demand vector discussed here is given in Exercise 19.3-1.

The procedure for finding the complementary functions of (19.20) is no different from that presented in Sec. 19.2. Since the homogeneous version of the equation system is $x_{t+1} - Ax_t = 0$, the characteristic equation should be

$$|bI - A| = \begin{vmatrix} b - a_{11} & -a_{12} \\ -a_{21} & b - a_{22} \end{vmatrix} = 0 \qquad \text{[cf. (19.9')]}$$

From this we can find the characteristic roots b_1 and b_2 and thence proceed to the remaining steps of the solution process.

Excess Demand and Output Adjustment

The model formulation in (19.20) can also arise from a different economic assumption. Consider the situation in which the excess demand for each product always tends to induce an output increment equal to the excess demand. Since the excess demand for the first product in period t amounts to

$$\underbrace{a_{11}x_{1,t} + a_{12}x_{2,t} + d_{1,t}}_{\text{demanded}} - \underbrace{x_{1,t}}_{\text{supplied}}$$

the output adjustment (increment) $\Delta x_{1,t}$ is to be set exactly equal to that level:

$$\Delta x_{1,t}(\equiv x_{1,t+1} - x_{1,t}) = a_{11}x_{1,t} + a_{12}x_{2,t} + d_{1,t} - x_{1,t}$$

However, if we add $x_{1,t}$ to both sides of this equation, the result will become identical with (19.19). Similarly, our output-adjustment assumption will give an equation the same as (19.19') for the second industry. In short, the same mathematical model can result from altogether different economic assumptions.

So far, the input-output system has been viewed only in the discrete-time framework. For comparison purposes, let us now cast the output-adjustment process in the continuous-time mold.

In the main, this would call for use of the symbol $x_i(t)$ in lieu of $x_{i,t}$, and of the derivative $x_i'(t)$ in lieu of the difference $\Delta x_{i,t}$. With these changes, our output-adjustment assumption will manifest itself in the following pair of differential equations:

$$x_1'(t) = a_{11}x_1(t) + a_{12}x_2(t) + d_1(t) - x_1(t)$$
$$x_2'(t) = a_{21}x_1(t) + a_{22}x_2(t) + d_2(t) - x_2(t)$$

At any instant of time $t = t_0$, the symbol $x_i(t_0)$ tells us the rate of output flow per unit of time (say, per month) that prevails at the said instant, and $d_i(t_0)$ indicates the final demand per month prevailing at that instant. Hence the right-hand sum in each equation indicates the rate of excess demand per month, measured at $t = t_0$. The derivative $x_i'(t_0)$ at the left, on the other hand, represents the rate of output adjustment per month called forth by the excess demand at $t = t_0$. This adjustment will eradicate the excess demand (and bring about equilibrium) in a month's time, but only if both the excess demand and the output adjustment stay unchanged at the current rates. In actuality, the excess demand will vary with time, as will the induced output adjustment, thus resulting in a cat-and-mouse game of chase. The solution of the system, consisting of the time paths of the output x_i, supplies a chronicle of this chase. If the solution is convergent, the cat (output adjustment) will eventually be able to catch the mouse (excess demand), asymptotically (as $t \to \infty$).

After proper rearrangement, this system of differential equations can be written in the format of (19.13') as follows:

$$Ix' + (I - A)x = d \qquad \textbf{(19.23)}$$

where $\quad x' = \begin{bmatrix} x_1'(t) \\ x_2'(t) \end{bmatrix} \qquad x = \begin{bmatrix} x_1(t) \\ x_2(t) \end{bmatrix} \qquad A = \begin{bmatrix} a_{11} & a_{12} \\ a_{21} & a_{22} \end{bmatrix} \qquad d = \begin{bmatrix} d_1(t) \\ d_2(t) \end{bmatrix}$

(the prime denoting derivative, not transpose). The complementary functions can be found by the method discussed earlier. In particular, the characteristic roots are to be found from the equation

$$|rI + (I - A)| = \begin{vmatrix} r + 1 - a_{11} & -a_{12} \\ -a_{21} & r + 1 - a_{22} \end{vmatrix} = 0 \qquad \text{[cf. (19.16)]}$$

As for the particular integrals, if the final-demand vector contains nonconstant functions of time $d_1(t)$ and $d_2(t)$ as its elements, a modification will be needed in the method of solution. Let us illustrate with a simple example.

Example 2

Given the final-demand vector

$$d = \begin{bmatrix} \lambda_1 e^{\rho t} \\ \lambda_2 e^{\rho t} \end{bmatrix} = \begin{bmatrix} \lambda_1 \\ \lambda_2 \end{bmatrix} e^{\rho t}$$

where λ_i and ρ are constants, find the particular integrals of the dynamic model (19.23). Using the method of undetermined coefficients, we can try solutions of the form $x_i(t) = \beta_i e^{\rho t}$, which imply, of course, that $x_i'(t) = \rho \beta_i e^{\rho t}$. In matrix notation, these can be written as

$$x = \begin{bmatrix} \beta_1 \\ \beta_2 \end{bmatrix} e^{\rho t} \qquad \textbf{(19.24)}$$

and $\qquad x' = \rho \begin{bmatrix} \beta_1 \\ \beta_2 \end{bmatrix} e^{\rho t} = \begin{bmatrix} \rho & 0 \\ 0 & \rho \end{bmatrix} \begin{bmatrix} \beta_1 \\ \beta_2 \end{bmatrix} e^{\rho t} \qquad \text{[cf. footnote in Example 1]}$

Upon substituting into (19.23) and canceling the common (nonzero) scalar multiplier $e^{\rho t}$, we obtain

$$\begin{bmatrix} \rho & 0 \\ 0 & \rho \end{bmatrix} \begin{bmatrix} \beta_1 \\ \beta_2 \end{bmatrix} + \begin{bmatrix} 1 - a_{11} & -a_{12} \\ -a_{21} & 1 - a_{22} \end{bmatrix} \begin{bmatrix} \beta_1 \\ \beta_2 \end{bmatrix} = \begin{bmatrix} \lambda_1 \\ \lambda_2 \end{bmatrix}$$

or

$$\begin{bmatrix} \rho + 1 - a_{11} & -a_{12} \\ -a_{21} & \rho + 1 - a_{22} \end{bmatrix} \begin{bmatrix} \beta_1 \\ \beta_2 \end{bmatrix} = \begin{bmatrix} \lambda_1 \\ \lambda_2 \end{bmatrix} \qquad \textbf{(19.25)}$$

If the leftmost matrix is nonsingular, we can apply Cramer's rule and determine the values of the coefficients β_i to be

$$\beta_1 = \frac{\lambda_1(\rho + 1 - a_{22}) + \lambda_2 a_{12}}{\Delta}$$

$$\beta_2 = \frac{\lambda_2(\rho + 1 - a_{11}) + \lambda_1 a_{21}}{\Delta}$$

(19.25′)

where $\Delta \equiv (\rho + 1 - a_{11})(\rho + 1 - a_{22}) - a_{12}a_{21}$. The *undetermined coefficients* having thus been determined, we can introduce these values into the trial solution (19.24) to obtain the desired particular integrals.

Capital Formation

Another economic consideration that can give rise to a dynamic input-output system is capital formation, including the accumulation of inventory.

In the static discussion, we only considered the output level of each product needed to satisfy current demand. The needs for inventory accumulation or capital formation were either ignored, or subsumed under the final-demand vector. To bring capital formation into the open, let us now consider—along with an input-coefficient matrix $A = [a_{ij}]$—a capital-coefficient matrix

$$C = [c_{ij}] = \begin{bmatrix} c_{11} & c_{12} \\ c_{21} & c_{22} \end{bmatrix}$$

where c_{ij} denotes the dollar worth of the ith commodity needed by the jth industry as new capital (either equipment or inventory, depending on the nature of the ith commodity) as a result of an output increment of $1 in the jth industry. For example, if an increase of $1 in the output of the soft-drink (jth) industry induces it to add $2 worth of bottling equipment (ith commodity), then $c_{ij} = 2$. Such a capital coefficient thus reveals a marginal capital-output ratio of sorts, the ratio being limited to one type of capital (the ith commodity) only. Like the input coefficients a_{ij}, the capital coefficients are assumed to be fixed. The idea is for the economy to produce each commodity in such quantity as to satisfy not only the input-requirement demand plus the final demand, but also the capital-requirement demand for it.

If time is *continuous*, output increment is indicated by the derivatives $x_i'(t)$; thus the output of each industry should be set at

$$x_1(t) = \underbrace{a_{11}x_1(t) + a_{12}x_2(t)}_{\text{input requirement}} + \underbrace{c_{11}x_1'(t) + c_{12}x_2'(t)}_{\text{capital requirement}} + \underbrace{d_1(t)}_{\text{final demand}}$$
$$x_2(t) = a_{21}x_1(t) + a_{22}x_2(t) + c_{21}x_1'(t) + c_{22}x_2'(t) + d_2(t)$$

In matrix notation, this is expressible by the equation

$$Ix = Ax + Cx' + d$$

or

$$Cx' + (A - I)x = -d \qquad\qquad \textbf{(19.26)}$$

If time is *discrete,* the capital requirement in period t will be based on the output increment $x_{i,t} - x_{i,t-1}$ ($\equiv \Delta x_{i,t-1}$); thus the output levels should be set at

$$\begin{bmatrix} x_{1,t} \\ x_{2,t} \end{bmatrix} = \underbrace{\begin{bmatrix} a_{11} & a_{12} \\ a_{21} & a_{22} \end{bmatrix} \begin{bmatrix} x_{1,t} \\ x_{2,t} \end{bmatrix}}_{\text{input requirement}} + \underbrace{\begin{bmatrix} c_{11} & c_{12} \\ c_{21} & c_{22} \end{bmatrix} \begin{bmatrix} x_{1,t} - x_{1,t-1} \\ x_{2,t} - x_{2,t-1} \end{bmatrix}}_{\text{capital requirement}} + \underbrace{\begin{bmatrix} d_{1,t} \\ d_{2,t} \end{bmatrix}}_{\text{final demand}}$$

or
$$Ix_t = Ax_t + C(x_t - x_{t-1}) + d_t$$

By shifting the time subscripts forward one period, and collecting terms, however, we can write the equation in the form

$$(I - A - C)x_{t+1} + Cx_t = d_{t+1} \tag{19.27}$$

The differential-equation system (19.26) and the difference-equation system (19.27) can again be solved, of course, by the method of Sec. 19.2. It also goes without saying that these two matrix equations are both extendible to the *n*-industry case simply by an appropriate redefinition of the matrices and a corresponding change in the dimensions thereof.

In the preceding, we have discussed how a dynamic input-output model can arise from such considerations as time lags and adjustment mechanisms. When similar considerations are applied to general-equilibrium market models, the latter will tend to become dynamic in much the same way. But, since the formulation of such models is analogous in spirit to input-output models, we shall dispense with a formal discussion thereof and merely refer you to the illustrative cases in Exercises 19.3-6 and 19.3-7.

EXERCISE 19.3

1. In Example 1, if the final-demand vector is changed to $d_t = \begin{bmatrix} \lambda_1 \delta^t \\ \lambda_2 \delta^t \end{bmatrix}$, what will the particular solutions be? After finding your answers, show that the answers in Example 1 are merely a special case of these, with $\lambda_1 = \lambda_2 = 1$.

2. (a) Show that (19.22) can be written more concisely as
   $$(\delta I - A)\beta = u$$
   (b) Of the five symbols used, which are scalars? Vectors? Matrices?
   (c) Write the solution for β in matrix form, assuming $(\delta I - A)$ to be nonsingular.

3. (a) Show that (19.25) can be written more concisely as
   $$(\rho I + I - A)\beta = \lambda$$
   (b) Which of the five symbols represent scalars, vectors, and matrices, respectively?
   (c) Write the solution for β in matrix form, assuming $(\rho I + I - A)$ to be nonsingular.

4. Given $A = \begin{bmatrix} \frac{3}{10} & \frac{4}{10} \\ \frac{3}{10} & \frac{2}{10} \end{bmatrix}$ and $d_t = \begin{bmatrix} \left(\frac{12}{10}\right)^t \\ \left(\frac{12}{10}\right)^t \end{bmatrix}$ for the discrete-time production-lag input-output model described in (19.20), find (*a*) the particular solutions; (*b*) the complementary functions; and (*c*) the definite time paths, assuming initial outputs $x_{1,0} = \frac{187}{39}$ and $x_{2,0} = \frac{72}{13}$. (Use fractions, not decimals, in all calculations.)

5. Given $A = \begin{bmatrix} \frac{3}{10} & \frac{4}{10} \\ \frac{3}{10} & \frac{2}{10} \end{bmatrix}$ and $d = \begin{bmatrix} e^{t/10} \\ 2e^{t/10} \end{bmatrix}$ for the continuous-time output-adjustment input-output model described in (19.23), find (*a*) the particular integrals; (*b*) the complementary functions; and (*c*) the definite time paths, assuming initial conditions $x_1(0) = \frac{53}{6}$ and $x_2(0) = \frac{25}{6}$. (Use fractions, not decimals, in all calculations.)

6. In an *n*-commodity market, all Q_{di} and Q_{si} (with $i = 1, 2, \ldots, n$) can be considered as functions of the *n* prices $P_1, \ldots, P_n$, and so can the excess demand for each commodity $E_i \equiv Q_{di} - Q_{si}$. Assuming linearity, we can write

$$E_1 = a_{10} + a_{11}P_1 + a_{12}P_2 + \cdots + a_{1n}P_n$$

$$E_2 = a_{20} + a_{21}P_1 + a_{22}P_2 + \cdots + a_{2n}P_n$$

$$\cdots\cdots\cdots\cdots\cdots\cdots\cdots\cdots\cdots\cdots\cdots\cdots\cdots\cdots\cdots$$

$$E_n = a_{n0} + a_{n1}P_1 + a_{n2}P_2 + \cdots + a_{nn}P_n$$

or, in matrix notation,

$$E = a + AP$$

(*a*) What do these last four symbols stand for—scalars, vectors, or matrices? What are their respective dimensions?

(*b*) Consider all prices to be functions of time, and assume that $dP_i/dt = \alpha_i E_i$ ($i = 1, 2, \ldots, n$). What is the economic interpretation of this last set of equations?

(*c*) Write out the differential equations showing each dP_i/dt to be a linear function of the *n* prices.

(*d*) Show that, if we let P' denote the $n \times 1$ column vector of the derivatives dP_i/dt, and if we let α denote an $n \times n$ diagonal matrix, with $\alpha_1, \alpha_2, \ldots, \alpha_n$ (in that order) in the principal diagonal and zeros elsewhere, we can write the preceding differential-equation system in matrix notation as $P' - \alpha AP = \alpha a$.

7. For the *n*-commodity market of Prob. 6, the discrete-time version would consist of a set of difference equations $\Delta P_{i,t} = \alpha_i E_{i,t}$ ($i = 1, 2, \ldots, n$), where $E_{i,t} = a_{i0} + a_{i1}P_{1,t} + a_{i2}P_{2,t} + \cdots + a_{in}P_{n,t}$.

(*a*) Write out the excess-demand equation system, and show that it can be expressed in matrix notation as $E_t = a + AP_t$.

(*b*) Show that the price adjustment equations can be written as $P_{t+1} - P_t = \alpha E_t$, where α is the $n \times n$ diagonal matrix defined in Prob. 6.

(*c*) Show that the difference-equation system of the present discrete-time model can be expressed in the form $P_{t+1} - (I + \alpha A)P_t = \alpha a$.

19.4 The Inflation-Unemployment Model Once More

Having illustrated the multisector type of dynamic systems with input-output models, we shall now provide an economic example of simultaneous dynamic equations in the one-sector setting. For this purpose, the inflation-unemployment model, already encountered twice before in two different guises, can be called back into service once again.

Simultaneous Differential Equations

In Sec. 16.5 the inflation-unemployment model was presented in the continuous-time framework via the following three equations:

$$p = \alpha - T - \beta U + g\pi \qquad (\alpha, \beta > 0; \, 0 < g \leq 1) \qquad \textbf{(16.33)}$$

$$\frac{d\pi}{dt} = j(p - \pi) \qquad (0 < j \leq 1) \qquad \textbf{(16.34)}$$

$$\frac{dU}{dt} = -k(\mu - p) \qquad (k > 0) \qquad \textbf{(16.35)}$$

except that we have adopted the Greek letter μ here to replace m in (16.35) in order to avoid confusion with our earlier usage of the symbol m in the methodological discussion of Sec. 19.2. In the treatment of this model in Sec. 16.5, since we were not yet equipped then to deal with simultaneous dynamic equations, we approached the problem by condensing the model into a single equation in one variable. That necessitated a quite laborious process of substitutions and eliminations. Now, in view of the coexistence of two given patterns of change in the model for π and U, we shall treat the model as one of two simultaneous differential equations.

When (16.33) is substituted into the other two equations, and the derivatives $d\pi/dt \equiv \pi'(t)$ and $dU/dt \equiv U'(t)$ written more simply as π' and U', the model assumes the form

$$\begin{aligned} \pi' \quad + j(1 - g)\pi + j\beta U &= j(\alpha - T) \\ U' - \quad kg\pi + k\beta U &= k(\alpha - T - \mu) \end{aligned} \qquad \textbf{(19.28)}$$

or, in matrix notation,

$$\underbrace{\begin{bmatrix} 1 & 0 \\ 0 & 1 \end{bmatrix}}_{J} \begin{bmatrix} \pi' \\ U' \end{bmatrix} + \underbrace{\begin{bmatrix} j(1-g) & j\beta \\ -kg & k\beta \end{bmatrix}}_{M} \begin{bmatrix} \pi \\ U \end{bmatrix} = \begin{bmatrix} j(\alpha - T) \\ k(\alpha - T - \mu) \end{bmatrix} \qquad \textbf{(19.28')}$$

From this system, the time paths of π and U can be found simultaneously. Then, if desired, we can derive the p path by using (16.33).

Solution Paths

To find the particular integrals, we can simply set $\pi' = U' = 0$ (to make π and U stationary over time) in (19.28') and solve for π and U. In our earlier discussion, in (19.14), such solutions were obtained through matrix inversion, but Cramer's rule can certainly be used, too. Either way, we can find that

$$\bar{\pi} = \mu \qquad \text{and} \qquad \bar{U} = \frac{1}{\beta}[\alpha - T - (1 - g)\mu] \qquad \textbf{(19.29)}$$

The result that $\bar{\pi} = \mu$ (the equilibrium expected rate of inflation equals the rate of monetary expansion) coincides with that reached in Sec. 16.5. As to the rate of unemployment U, we made no attempt to find its equilibrium level in that section. If we did (on the basis of the differential equation in U given in Exercise 16.5-2), however, the answer would be no different from the $\bar{U}$ solution in (19.29).

Turning to the complementary functions, which are based on the trial solutions me^{rt} and ne^{rt}, we can determine m, n, and r from the reduced matrix equation

$$(rJ + M)\begin{bmatrix} m \\ n \end{bmatrix} = 0 \qquad \text{[from (19.15)]}$$

which, in the present context, takes the form

$$\begin{bmatrix} r + j(1-g) & j\beta \\ -kg & r + k\beta \end{bmatrix}\begin{bmatrix} m \\ n \end{bmatrix} = \begin{bmatrix} 0 \\ 0 \end{bmatrix} \tag{19.30}$$

To avoid trivial solutions for m and n from this homogeneous system, the determinant of the coefficient matrix must be made to vanish; that is, we require

$$|rJ + M| = r^2 + [k\beta + j(1-g)]r + k\beta j = 0 \tag{19.31}$$

This quadratic equation, a specific version of the characteristic equation $r^2 + a_1 r + a_2 = 0$, has coefficients

$$a_1 = k\beta + j(1-g) \quad \text{and} \quad a_2 = k\beta j$$

And these, as we would expect, are precisely the a_1 and a_2 values in (16.37″)—a single-equation version of the present model in the variable π. As a result, the previous analysis of the three cases of characteristic roots should apply here with equal validity. Among other conclusions, we may recall that, regardless of whether the roots happen to be real or complex, the real part of each root in the present model turns out to be always negative. Thus the solution paths are always convergent.

| **Example 1** | Find the time paths of π and U, given the parameter values |

$$\alpha - T = \frac{1}{6} \quad \beta = 3 \quad g = 1 \quad j = \frac{3}{4} \quad \text{and} \quad k = \frac{1}{2}$$

Since these parameter values duplicate those in Example 1 in Sec. 16.5, the results of the present analysis can be readily checked against those of the said section.

First, it is easy to determine that the particular integrals are

$$\overline{\pi} = \mu \quad \text{and} \quad \overline{U} = \frac{1}{3}\left(\frac{1}{6}\right) = \frac{1}{18} \quad \text{[by (19.29)]} \tag{19.32}$$

The characteristic equation being

$$r^2 + \frac{3}{2}r + \frac{9}{8} = 0 \quad \text{[by (19.31)]}$$

the two roots turn out to be complex:

$$r_1, r_2 = \frac{1}{2}\left(-\frac{3}{2} \pm \sqrt{\frac{9}{4} - \frac{9}{2}}\right) = -\frac{3}{4} \pm \frac{3}{4}i \quad \left(\text{with } h = -\frac{3}{4} \text{ and } v = \frac{3}{4}\right) \tag{19.33}$$

Substitution of the two roots (along with the parameter values) into (19.30) yields, respectively, the matrix equations

$$\begin{bmatrix} -\frac{3}{4}(1-i) & \frac{9}{4} \\ -\frac{1}{2} & \frac{3}{4}(1+i) \end{bmatrix}\begin{bmatrix} m_1 \\ n_1 \end{bmatrix} = \begin{bmatrix} 0 \\ 0 \end{bmatrix} \quad \left[\text{from } r_1 = -\frac{3}{4} + \frac{3}{4}i\right] \tag{19.34}$$

$$\begin{bmatrix} -\frac{3}{4}(1+i) & \frac{9}{4} \\ -\frac{1}{2} & \frac{3}{4}(1-i) \end{bmatrix}\begin{bmatrix} m_2 \\ n_2 \end{bmatrix} = \begin{bmatrix} 0 \\ 0 \end{bmatrix} \quad \left[\text{from } r_2 = -\frac{3}{4} - \frac{3}{4}i\right] \tag{19.34′}$$

Since r_1 and r_2 are designed—via (19.31)—to make the coefficient matrix singular, each of the preceding two matrix equations actually contains only one independent equation, which can determine only a proportionality relation between the arbitrary constants m_i and n_i. Specifically, we have

$$\frac{1}{3}(1-i)m_1 = n_1 \qquad \text{and} \qquad \frac{1}{3}(1+i)m_2 = n_2$$

The complementary functions can, accordingly, be expressed as

$$\begin{bmatrix} \pi_c \\ U_c \end{bmatrix} = \begin{bmatrix} m_1 e^{r_1 t} + m_2 e^{r_2 t} \\ n_1 e^{r_1 t} + n_2 e^{r_2 t} \end{bmatrix}$$

$$= e^{ht} \begin{bmatrix} m_1 e^{vit} + m_2 e^{-vit} \\ n_1 e^{vit} + n_2 e^{-vit} \end{bmatrix} \qquad \text{[by (16.11)]}$$

$$= e^{ht} \begin{bmatrix} (m_1 + m_2)\cos vt + (m_1 - m_2)i \sin vt \\ (n_1 + n_2)\cos vt + (n_1 - n_2)i \sin vt \end{bmatrix} \qquad \text{[by (16.24)]}$$

If, for notational simplicity, we define new arbitrary constants

$$A_5 \equiv m_1 + m_2 \quad \text{and} \quad A_6 \equiv (m_1 - m_2)i$$

it then follows that[†]

$$n_1 + n_2 = \frac{1}{3}(A_5 - A_6) \qquad (n_1 - n_2)i = \frac{1}{3}(A_5 + A_6)$$

So, using these, and incorporating the h and v values of (19.33) into the complementary functions, we end up with

$$\begin{bmatrix} \pi_c \\ U_c \end{bmatrix} = e^{-3t/4} \begin{bmatrix} A_5 \cos \frac{3}{4}t + A_6 \sin \frac{3}{4}t \\ \frac{1}{3}(A_5 - A_6)\cos \frac{3}{4}t + \frac{1}{3}(A_5 + A_6)\sin \frac{3}{4}t \end{bmatrix} \qquad \textbf{(19.35)}$$

Finally, by combining the particular integrals in (19.32) with the above complementary functions, we can obtain the solution paths of π and U. As may be expected, these paths are exactly the same as those in (16.43) and (16.45) in Sec. 16.5.

Simultaneous Difference Equations

The simultaneous-equation treatment of the inflation-unemployment model in discrete time is similar in spirit to the preceding continuous-time discussion. We shall thus merely give the highlights.

[†] This can be seen from the following:

$$n_1 + n_2 = \frac{1}{3}(1-i)m_1 + \frac{1}{3}(1+i)m_2 = \frac{1}{3}[(m_1 + m_2) - (m_1 - m_2)i]$$

$$= \frac{1}{3}(A_5 - A_6)$$

$$(n_1 - n_2)i = \left[\frac{1}{3}(1-i)m_1 - \frac{1}{3}(1+i)m_2\right]i = \frac{1}{3}[(m_1 - m_2) - (m_1 + m_2)i]i$$

$$= \frac{1}{3}(A_6 + A_5) \qquad [i^2 \equiv -1]$$

The model in question, as given in Sec. 18.3, consists of three equations, two of which describe the patterns of change of π and U, respectively:

$$p_t = \alpha - T - \beta U_t + g\pi_t \tag{18.18}$$

$$\pi_{t+1} - \pi_t = j(p_t - \pi_t) \tag{18.19}$$

$$U_{t+1} - U_t = -k(\mu - p_{t+1}) \tag{18.20}$$

Eliminating p, and collecting terms, we can rewrite the model as the difference-equation system

$$\underbrace{\begin{bmatrix} 1 & 0 \\ -kg & 1 + \beta k \end{bmatrix}}_{J} \begin{bmatrix} \pi_{t+1} \\ U_{t+1} \end{bmatrix} + \underbrace{\begin{bmatrix} -(1 - j + jg) & j\beta \\ 0 & -1 \end{bmatrix}}_{K} \begin{bmatrix} \pi_t \\ U_t \end{bmatrix}$$

$$= \begin{bmatrix} j(\alpha - T) \\ k(\alpha - T - \mu) \end{bmatrix} \tag{19.36}$$

Solution Paths

If stationary equilibriums exist, the particular solutions of (19.36) can be expressed as $\overline{\pi} = \pi_t = \pi_{t+1}$ and $\overline{U} = U_t = U_{t+1}$. Substituting $\overline{\pi}$ and $\overline{U}$ into (19.36), and solving the system (by matrix inversion or Cramer's rule), we obtain

$$\overline{\pi} = \mu \quad \text{and} \quad \overline{U} = \frac{1}{\beta}[\alpha - T - (1 - g)\mu] \tag{19.37}$$

The $\overline{U}$ value is the same as what was found in Sec. 18.3. Although we did not find $\overline{\pi}$ in the latter section, the information in Exercise 18.3-2 indicates that $\overline{\pi} = \mu$, which agrees with (19.37). In fact, you may note, the results in (19.37) are also identical with the intertemporal equilibrium values obtained in the continuous-time framework in (19.29).

The search for the complementary functions, based this time on the trial solutions mb^t and nb^t, involves the reduced matrix equation

$$(bJ + K)\begin{bmatrix} m \\ n \end{bmatrix} = 0$$

or, in view of (19.36),

$$\begin{bmatrix} b - (1 - j + jg) & j\beta \\ -bkg & b(1 + \beta k) - 1 \end{bmatrix}\begin{bmatrix} m \\ n \end{bmatrix} = \begin{bmatrix} 0 \\ 0 \end{bmatrix} \tag{19.38}$$

In order to avoid trivial solutions from this homogeneous system, we require

$$|bJ + K| = (1 + \beta k)b^2 - [1 + gj + (1 - j)(1 + \beta k)]b$$
$$+ (1 - j + jg) = 0 \tag{19.39}$$

The normalized version of this quadratic equation is the characteristic equation $b^2 + a_1 b + a_2 = 0$, with the same a_1 and a_2 coefficients as in (18.24) and (18.33) in Sec. 18.3. Consequently, the analysis of the three cases of characteristic roots undertaken in that section should equally apply here.

For each root, b_i, (19.38) supplies us with a specific proportionality relation between the arbitrary constants m_i and n_i, and these enable us to link the arbitrary constants in the complementary function for U to those in the complementary function for π. Then, by combining the complementary functions and the particular solutions, we can get the time paths of π and U.

EXERCISE 19.4

1. Verify (19.29) by using Cramer's rule.
2. Verify that the same proportionality relation between m_1 and n_1 emerges whether we use the first or the second equation in the system (19.34).
3. Find the time paths (general solutions) of π and U, given:

$$p = \frac{1}{6} - 2U + \frac{1}{3}\pi$$

$$\pi' = \frac{1}{4}(p - \pi)$$

$$U' = -\frac{1}{2}(\mu - p)$$

4. Find the time paths (general solutions) of π and U, given:

(a) $p_t = \frac{1}{2} - 3U_t + \frac{1}{2}\pi_t$ (b) $p_t = \frac{1}{4} - 4U_t + \pi_t$

$\pi_{t+1} - \pi_t = \frac{1}{4}(p_t - \pi_t)$ $\pi_{t+1} - \pi_t = \frac{1}{4}(p_t - \pi_t)$

$U_{t+1} - U_t = -(\mu - p_{t+1})$ $U_{t+1} - U_t = -(\mu - p_{t+1})$

19.5 Two-Variable Phase Diagrams

The preceding sections have dealt with the *quantitative* solutions of *linear* dynamic systems. In the present section, we shall discuss the *qualitative-graphic* (phase-diagram) analysis of a *nonlinear* differential-equation system. More specifically, our attention will be focused on the first-order differential-equation system in two variables, in the general form of

$$x'(t) = f(x, y)$$
$$y'(t) = g(x, y)$$

Note that the time derivatives $x'(t)$ and $y'(t)$ depend only on x and y and that the variable t does not enter into the f and g functions as a separate argument. This feature, which makes the system an *autonomous system,* is a prerequisite for the application of the phase-diagram technique.[†]

The two-variable phase diagram, like the one-variable version in Sec. 15.6, is limited in that it can answer only qualitative questions—those concerning the location and the dynamic stability of the intertemporal equilibrium(s). But, again like the one-variable version, it has the compensating advantages of being able to handle nonlinear systems as comfortably as linear ones and to address problems couched in terms of general functions as readily as those in terms of specific ones.

[†] In the one-variable phase diagram introduced earlier in Sec. 15.6, the equation $dy/dt = f(y)$ is also restricted to be *autonomous,* being forbidden to have the variable t as an explicit argument in the function f.

The Phase Space

When constructing the one-variable phase diagram (Fig. 15.3) for the (autonomous) differential equation $dy/dt = f(y)$, we simply plotted dy/dt against y on the two axes in a two-dimensional phase space. Now that the number of variables is *doubled,* however, how can we manage to meet the apparent need for more axes? The answer, fortunately, is that the 2-space is all we need.

To see why this is feasible, observe that the most crucial task of phase-diagram construction is to determine the direction of movement of the variable(s) over time. It is this information, as embodied in the arrowheads in Fig. 15.3, that enables us to derive the final qualitative inferences. For the drawing of the said arrowheads, only two things are required: (1) a demarcation line—call it the "$dy/dt = 0$" line—that provides the locale for any prospective equilibrium(s) and, more importantly, separates the phase space into two regions, one characterized by $dy/dt > 0$ and the other by $dy/dt < 0$ and (2) a real line on which the increases and decreases of y that are implied by any nonzero values of dy/dt can be indicated. In Fig. 15.3, the demarcation line cited in item 1 is found in the horizontal axis. But that axis actually also serves as the real line cited in item 2. This means that the vertical axis, for dy/dt, can actually be given up without loss, provided we take care to distinguish between the $dy/dt > 0$ region and the $dy/dt < 0$ region—say, by labeling the former with a plus sign, and the latter with a minus sign. This dispensability of one axis is what makes feasible the placement of a two-variable phase diagram in the 2-space. We now need *two* real lines instead of one. But this is automatically taken care of by the standard x and y axes of a two-dimensional diagram. We now also need *two* demarcation lines (or curves), one for $dx/dt = 0$ and the other for $dy/dt = 0$. But these are both graphable in a two-dimensional phase space. And once these are drawn, it would not be difficult to decide which sides of these lines or curves should be marked with plus and minus signs, respectively.

The Demarcation Curves

Given the following autonomous differential-equation system

$$
\begin{aligned}
x' &= f(x, y) \\
y' &= g(x, y)
\end{aligned}
\tag{19.40}
$$

where x' and y' are short for the time derivatives $x'(t)$ and $y'(t)$, respectively, the two demarcation curves—to be denoted by $x' = 0$ and $y' = 0$—represent the graphs of the two equations

$$
\begin{aligned}
f(x, y) &= 0 \qquad [x' = 0 \text{ curve}] \tag{19.41} \\
g(x, y) &= 0 \qquad [y' = 0 \text{ curve}] \tag{19.42}
\end{aligned}
$$

If the specific form of the f function is known, (19.41) can be solved for y in terms of x and the solution plotted in the xy plane as the $x' = 0$ curve. Even if not, however, we can nonetheless resort to the implicit-function rule and ascertain the slope of the $x' = 0$ curve to be

$$
\left. \frac{dy}{dx} \right|_{x'=0} = -\frac{\partial f / \partial x}{\partial f / \partial y} = -\frac{f_x}{f_y} \qquad (f_y \neq 0) \tag{19.43}
$$

FIGURE 19.1

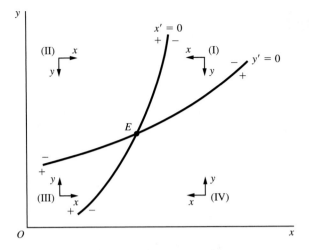

As long as the signs of the partial derivatives f_x and f_y ($\neq 0$) are known, a qualitative clue to the slope of the $x' = 0$ curve is available from (19.43). By the same token, the slope of the $y' = 0$ curve can be inferred from the derivative

$$\left.\frac{dy}{dx}\right|_{y'=0} = -\frac{g_x}{g_y} \qquad (g_y \neq 0) \tag{19.44}$$

For a more concrete illustration, let us assume that

$$f_x < 0 \qquad f_y > 0 \qquad g_x > 0 \qquad \text{and} \qquad g_y < 0 \tag{19.45}$$

Then both the $x' = 0$ and $y' = 0$ curves will be positively sloped. If we further assume that

$$-\frac{f_x}{f_y} > -\frac{g_x}{g_y} \qquad [x' = 0 \text{ curve steeper than } y' = 0 \text{ curve}]$$

then we may encounter a situation such as that shown in Fig. 19.1. Note that the demarcation lines are now possibly curved. Note, also, that they are now no longer required to coincide with the axes.

The two demarcation curves, intersecting at point E, divide the phase space into four distinct regions, labeled I through IV. Point E, where x and y are both stationary ($x' = y' = 0$), represents the intertemporal equilibrium of the system. At any other point, however, either x or y (or both) would be changing over time, in directions dictated by the signs of the time derivatives x' and y' at that point. In the present instance, we happen to have $x' > 0$ ($x' < 0$) to the left (right) of the $x' = 0$ curve; hence the plus (minus) signs on the left (right) of that curve. These signs are based on the fact that

$$\frac{\partial x'}{\partial x} = f_x < 0 \qquad [\text{by (19.40) and (19.45)}] \tag{19.46}$$

which implies that, as we move continually from west to east in the phase space (as x increases), x' undergoes a steady decrease, so that the sign of x' must pass through three stages, in the order $+, 0, -$. Analogously, the derivative

$$\frac{\partial y'}{\partial y} = g_y < 0 \qquad [\text{by (19.40) and (19.45)}] \tag{19.47}$$

implies that, as we move continually from south to north (as y increases), y' steadily decreases, so that the sign of y' must pass through three stages, in the order $+, 0, -$. Thus we are led to append the plus signs below, and the minus signs above, the $y' = 0$ curve in Fig. 19.1.

On the basis of these plus and minus signs, a set of directional arrows can now be drawn to indicate the intertemporal movement of x and y. For any point in region I, x' and y' are both negative. Hence x and y must both decrease over time, producing a *westward* movement for x, and a *southward* movement for y. As indicated by the two arrows in region I, given an initial point located in region I, the intertemporal movement must be in the general southwestward direction. The exact opposite is true in region III, where x' and y' are both positive, so that both the x and y variables must increase over time. In contrast, x' and y' have different signs in region II. With x' positive and y' negative, x should move *eastward* and y *southward*. And region IV displays a tendency exactly opposite to region II.

Streamlines

For a better grasp of the implications of the directional arrows, we can sketch a series of *streamlines* in the phase diagram. Also referred to as *phase trajectories* (or *trajectories* for short) or *phase paths,* these streamlines serve to map out the dynamic movement of the system from any conceivable initial point. A few of these are illustrated in Fig. 19.2, which reproduces the $x' = 0$ and $y' = 0$ curves in Fig 19.1. Since every point in the phase space must be located on one streamline or another, there should exist an infinite number of streamlines, all of which conform to the directional requirements imposed by the xy arrows in every region. For depicting the general qualitative character of the phase diagram, however, a few representative streamlines should normally suffice.

Several features may be noted about the streamlines in Fig. 19.2. First, all of them happen to lead toward point E. This makes E a stable (here, globally stable) intertemporal equilibrium. Later, we shall encounter other types of streamline configurations. Second, while some streamlines never venture beyond a single region (such as the one passing through point A), others may cross over from one region into another (such as those passing through B and C). Third, where a streamline crosses over, it must have either an infinite slope (crossing the $x' = 0$ curve) or a zero slope (crossing the $y' = 0$ curve). This is due to the

FIGURE 19.2

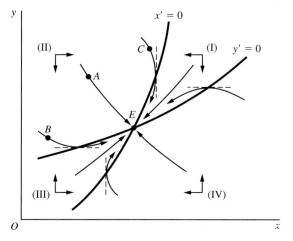

fact that, along the $x' = 0$ $(y' = 0)$ curve, $x(y)$ is stationary over time, so the streamline must not have any horizontal (vertical) movement while crossing that curve. To ensure that these slope requirements are consistently met, it would be advisable, as soon as the demarcation curves have been put in place, to add a few short *vertical* sketching bars across the $x' = 0$ curve and a few *horizontal* ones across the $y' = 0$ curve, as guidelines for the drawing of the streamlines.[†] Fourth, and last, although the streamlines do explicitly point out the directions of movement of x and y over time, they provide no specific information regarding velocity and acceleration, because the phase diagram does not allow for an axis for t (time). It is for this reason, of course, that streamlines carry the alternative name of *phase paths*, as opposed to *time* paths. The only observation we can make about velocity is qualitative in nature: As we move along a streamline closer and closer to the $x' = 0$ $(y' = 0)$ curve, the velocity of approach in the horizontal (vertical) direction must progressively diminish. This is due to the steady decrease in the absolute value of the derivative $x' \equiv dx/dt$ $(y' \equiv dy/dt)$ that occurs as we move toward the demarcation line on which $x'(y')$ takes a zero value.

Types of Equilibrium

Depending on the configurations of the streamlines surrounding a particular intertemporal equilibrium, that equilibrium may fall into one of four categories: (1) nodes, (2) saddle points, (3) foci or focuses, and (4) vortices or vortexes.

A *node* is an equilibrium such that all the streamlines associated with it either flow noncyclically toward it (*stable node*) or flow noncyclically away from it (*unstable node*). We have already encountered a stable node in Fig. 19.2. An unstable node is shown in Fig. 19.3*a*. Note that in this particular illustration, it happens that the streamlines never cross over from region to region. Also, the $x' = 0$ and $y' = 0$ curves happen to be linear, and, in fact, they themselves serve as streamlines.

A *saddle point* is an equilibrium with a double personality—it is stable in some directions, but unstable in others. More accurately, with reference to the illustration in Fig. 19.3*b*, a saddle point has exactly one pair of streamlines—called the *stable branches* of the saddle point—that flow directly and consistently toward the equilibrium, and exactly one pair of streamlines—the *unstable branches*—that flow directly and consistently away from it. All the other trajectories head toward the saddle point initially but sooner or later turn away from it. This double personality, of course, is what inspired the name "saddle point." Since stability is observed only on the stable branches, which are not reachable as a matter of course, a saddle point is generically classified as an *unstable* equilibrium.

The third type of equilibrium, *focus*, is one characterized by whirling trajectories, all of which either flow cyclically toward it (*stable focus*), or flow cyclically away from it (*unstable focus*). Figure 19.3*c* illustrates a stable focus, with only one streamline explicitly drawn in order to avoid clutter. What causes the whirling motion to occur? The answer lies in the way the $x' = 0$ and $y' = 0$ curves are positioned. In Fig. 19.3*c*, the two demarcation curves are sloped in such a way that they take turns in blockading the streamline flowing in a direction prescribed by a particular set of *xy* arrows. As a result, the streamline is frequently compelled to cross over from one region into another, tracing out a spiral. Whether we get

---

[†] To aid your memory, note that the sketching bars across the $x' = 0$ curve should be *perpendicular* to the x axis. Similarly, the sketching bars across the $y' = 0$ curve should be *perpendicular* to the y axis.

FIGURE 19.3

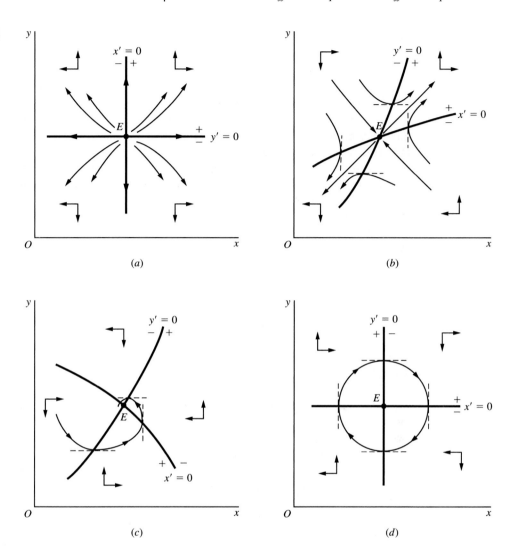

(a)

(b)

(c)

(d)

a stable focus (as is the case here) or an unstable one depends on the relative placement of the two demarcation curves. But in either case, the slope of the streamline at the crossover points must still be either infinite (crossing $x' = 0$) or zero (crossing $y' = 0$).

Finally, we may have a *vortex* (or *center*). This is again an equilibrium with whirling streamlines, but these streamlines now form a family of loops (concentric circles or ovals) orbiting around the equilibrium in a perpetual motion. An example of this is given in Fig. 19.3d, where, again, only a single streamline is shown. Inasmuch as this type of equilibrium is unattainable from any initial position away from point E, a vortex is automatically classified as an unstable equilibrium.

All the illustrations in Fig. 19.3 display a unique equilibrium. When sufficient nonlinearity exists, however, the two demarcation curves may intersect more than once, thereby producing multiple equilibria. In that event, a combination of the previously cited types of intertemporal equilibrium may exist in the same phase diagram. Although there will then be more than four regions to contend with, the underlying principle of phase-diagram analysis will remain basically the same.

Inflation and Monetary Rule à la Obst

As an economic illustration of the two-variable phase diagram, we shall present a model due to Professor Obst,[†] which purports to show the ineffectiveness of the conventional (hence the need for a new) type of countercyclical monetary-policy rule, when an "inflation adjustment mechanism" is at work. Such a model contrasts with our earlier discussion of inflation in that, instead of studying the implications of a *given* rate of monetary expansion, it looks further into the efficacy of two different monetary *rules,* each prescribing a different set of monetary actions to be pursued in the face of various inflationary conditions.

A crucial assumption of the model is the inflation adjustment mechanism

$$\frac{dp}{dt} = h\left(\frac{M_s - M_d}{M_s}\right) = h\left(1 - \frac{M_d}{M_s}\right) \qquad (h > 0) \qquad \textbf{(19.48)}$$

which shows that the effect of an excess supply of money ($M_s > M_d$) is to raise the rate of inflation p, rather than the price level P. The clearance of the money market would thus imply not price stability, but only a stable rate of inflation. To facilitate the analysis, the second equality in (19.48) serves to shift the focus from the excess supply of money to the demand-supply ratio of money, M_d/M_s, which we shall denote by μ. On the assumption that M_d is directly proportional to the nominal national product PQ, we can write

$$\mu \equiv \frac{M_d}{M_s} = \frac{aPQ}{M_s} \qquad (a > 0)$$

The rates of growth of the several variables are then related by

$$\frac{d\mu/dt}{\mu} = \frac{da/dt}{a} + \frac{dP/dt}{P} + \frac{dQ/dt}{Q} - \frac{dM_s/dt}{M_s}$$
$$\text{[by (10.24) and (10.25)]}$$
$$\equiv p + q - m \qquad \text{[}a = \text{a constant]} \qquad \textbf{(19.49)}$$

where the lowercase letters p, q, and m denote, respectively, the rate of inflation, the (exogenous) rate of growth of the real national product, and the rate of monetary expansion.

Equations (19.48) and (19.49), a set of two differential equations, can jointly determine the time paths of p and μ, if, for the time being, m is taken to be exogenous. Using the symbols p' and μ' to represent the time derivatives $p'(t)$ and $\mu'(t)$, we can express this system more concisely as

$$p' = h(1 - \mu)$$
$$\mu' = (p + q - m)\mu \qquad \textbf{(19.50)}$$

[†] Norman P. Obst, "Stabilization Policy with an Inflation Adjustment Mechanism," *Quarterly Journal of Economics,* May 1978, pp. 355–359. No phase diagrams are given in the Obst paper, but they can be readily constructed from the model.

FIGURE 19.4

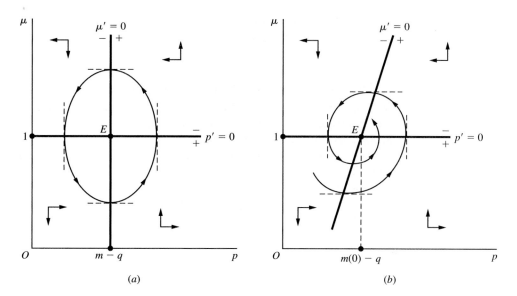

(a)   (b)

Given that h is positive, we can have $p' = 0$ if and only if $1 - \mu = 0$. Similarly, since μ is always positive, $\mu' = 0$ if and only if $p + q - m = 0$. Thus the $p' = 0$ and $\mu' = 0$ demarcation curves are associated with the equations

$$\mu = 1 \qquad [p' = 0 \text{ curve}] \qquad\qquad (19.51)$$

$$p = m - q \qquad [\mu' = 0 \text{ curve}] \qquad\qquad (19.52)$$

As shown in Fig. 19.4a, these plot as a horizontal line and a vertical line, respectively, and yield a unique equilibrium at E. The equilibrium value $\overline{\mu} = 1$ means that in equilibrium M_d and M_s are equal, clearing the money market. The fact that the equilibrium rate of inflation is shown to be positive reflects an implicit assumption that $m > q$.

Since the $p' = 0$ curve corresponds to the $x' = 0$ curve in our previous discussion, it should have vertical sketching bars. And the other curve should have horizontal ones. From (19.50), we find that

$$\frac{\partial p'}{\partial \mu} = -h < 0 \qquad \text{and} \qquad \frac{\partial \mu'}{\partial p} = \mu > 0 \qquad\qquad (19.53)$$

with the implication that a northward movement across the $p' = 0$ curve passes through the $(+, 0, -)$ sequence of signs for p', and an eastward movement across the $\mu' = 0$ curve, the $(-, 0, +)$ sequence of signs for μ'. Thus we obtain the four sets of directional arrows as drawn, which generate streamlines (only one of which is shown) that orbit counterclockwise around point E. This, of course, makes E a vortex. Unless the economy happens initially to be at E, it is impossible to attain equilibrium. Instead, there will be never-ceasing fluctuation.

The preceding conclusion is, however, the consequence of an *exogenous* rate of monetary expansion. What if we now endogenize m by adopting an anti-inflationary monetary rule? The "conventional" monetary rule would call for gearing the rate of monetary expansion negatively to the rate of inflation:

$$m = m(p) \qquad m'(p) < 0 \qquad [\text{conventional monetary rule}] \qquad (19.54)$$

Such a rule would modify the second equation in (19.50) to

$$\mu' = [p + q - m(p)]\mu \qquad \textbf{(19.55)}$$

and alter (19.52) to

$$p = m(p) - q \qquad [\mu' = 0 \text{ curve under conventional monetary rule}] \quad \textbf{(19.56)}$$

Given that $m(p)$ is monotonic, there exists only one value of p—say, p_1—that can satisfy this equation. Hence the new $\mu' = 0$ curve must still emerge as a vertical straight line, although with a different horizontal intercept $p_1 = m(p_1) - q$. Moreover, from (19.55), we find that

$$\frac{\partial \mu'}{\partial p} = [1 - m'(p)]\mu > 0 \qquad [\text{by (19.54)}]$$

which is *qualitatively* no different from the derivative in (19.53). It follows that the directional arrows must also remain as they are in Fig. 19.4a. In short, we would end up with a vortex as before.

The alternative monetary rule proposed by Obst is to gear m to the *rate of change* (rather than the *level*) of the rate of inflation:

$$m = m(p') \qquad m'(p') < 0 \qquad [\text{alternative monetary rule}] \quad \textbf{(19.57)}$$

Under this rule, (19.55) and (19.56) will become, respectively,

$$\mu' = [p + q - m(p')]\mu \qquad \textbf{(19.58)}$$

$$p = m(p') - q \qquad [\mu' = 0 \text{ curve under alternative monetary rule}] \quad \textbf{(19.59)}$$

This time the $\mu' = 0$ curve would become upward-sloping. For, differentiating (19.59) with respect to μ via the chain rule, we have

$$\frac{dp}{d\mu} = m'(p')\frac{dp'}{d\mu} = m'(p')(-h) > 0 \qquad [\text{by (19.50)}]$$

so, by the inverse-function rule, $d\mu/dp$—the slope of the $\mu' = 0$ cruve—is also positive. This new situation is illustrated in Fig. 19.4b, where, for simplicity, the $\mu' = 0$ curve is drawn as a straight line, with an arbitrarily assigned slope.[†] Despite the slope change, the partial derivative

$$\frac{\partial \mu'}{\partial p} = \mu > 0 \qquad [\text{from (19.58)}]$$

is unchanged from (19.53), so the μ arrows should retain their original orientation in Fig. 19.4a. The streamlines (only one of which is shown) will now twirl inwardly toward the equilibrium at $\bar{\mu} = 1$ and $\bar{p} = m(0) - q$, where $m(0)$ denotes $m(p')$ evaluated at $p' = 0$. Thus the alternative monetary rule is seen to be capable of converting a vortex into a stable focus, thereby making possible the asymptotic elimination of the perpetual fluctuation in the rate of inflation. Indeed, with a sufficiently flat $\mu' = 0$ curve, it is even possible to turn the vortex into a stable node.

[†] The slope is inversely proportional to the absolute value of $m'(p')$. The more sensitively the rate of monetary expansion m is made to respond to the rate of change of the rate of inflation p', the flatter the $\mu' = 0$ curve will be in Fig. 19.4b.

EXERCISE 19.5

1. Show that the two-variable phase diagram can also be used, if the model consists of a single second-order differential equation, $y''(t) = f(y', y)$, instead of two first-order equations.

2. The plus and minus signs appended to the two sides of the $x' = 0$ and $y' = 0$ curves in Fig. 19.1 are based on the partial derivatives $\partial x'/\partial x$ and $\partial y'/\partial y$, respectively. Can the same conclusions be obtained from the derivatives $\partial x'/\partial y$ and $\partial y'/\partial x$?

3. Using Fig. 19.2, verify that if a streamline does not have an infinite (zero) slope when crossing the $x' = 0$ ($y' = 0$) curve, it will necessarily violate the directional restrictions imposed by the xy arrows.

4. As special cases of the differential-equation system (19.40), assume that
   (a) $f_x = 0$ $f_y > 0$ $g_x > 0$ and $g_y = 0$
   (b) $f_x = 0$ $f_y < 0$ $g_x < 0$ and $g_y = 0$
   For each case, construct an appropriate phase diagram, draw the streamlines, and determine the nature of the equilibrium.

5. (a) Show that it is possible to produce *either* a stable node *or* a stable focus from the differential-equation system (19.40), if
   $$f_x < 0 \qquad f_y > 0 \qquad g_x < 0 \qquad \text{and} \qquad g_y < 0$$
   (b) What special feature(s) in your phase-diagram construction are responsible for the difference in the outcomes (node versus focus)?

6. With reference to the Obst model, verify that if the positively sloped $\mu' = 0$ curve in Fig. 19.4b is made sufficiently flat, the streamlines, although still characterized by crossovers, will converge to the equilibrium in the manner of a node rather than a focus.

19.6 Linearization of a Nonlinear Differential-Equation System

Another qualitative technique of analyzing a *nonlinear* differential-equation system is to draw inferences from the *linear approximation* to that system, to be derived from the Taylor expansion of the given system around its equilibrium.[†] We learned in Sec. 9.5 that a linear (or even a higher-order polynomial) approximation to an arbitrary function $\phi(x)$ can give us the exact value of $\phi(x)$ at the point of expansion, but will entail progressively larger errors of approximation as we move farther away from the point of expansion. The same is true of the linear approximation to a nonlinear system. At the point of expansion—here, the equilibrium point E—the linear approximation can pinpoint exactly the same equilibrium as the original nonlinear system. And in a sufficiently small neighborhood of E, the linear approximation should have the same general streamline configuration as the original system. As long as we are willing to confine our stability inferences to the immediate neighborhood of the equilibrium, therefore, the linear approximation could serve as an adequate source of information. Such analysis, referred to as *local stability analysis*, can be used

---

[†] In the case of multiple equilibria, each equilibrium requires a separate linear approximation.

either by itself, or as a supplement to the phase-diagram analysis. We shall deal with the two-variable case only.

Taylor Expansion and Linearization

Given an arbitrary (successively differentiable) one-variable function $\phi(x)$, the Taylor expansion around a point x_0 gives the series

$$\phi(x) = \phi(x_0) + \phi'(x_0)(x - x_0) + \frac{\phi''(x_0)}{2!}(x - x_0)^2 + \cdots$$
$$+ \frac{\phi^{(n)}(x_0)}{n!}(x - x_0)^n + R_n$$

where a polynomial involving various powers of $(x - x_0)$ appears on the right. A similar structure characterizes the Taylor expansion of a function of two variables $f(x, y)$ around any point (x_0, y_0). With two variables in the picture, however, the resulting polynomial would comprise various powers of $(y - y_0)$ as well as $(x - x_0)$—in fact, also the products of these two expressions:

$$f(x, y) = f(x_0, y_0) + f_x(x_0, y_0)(x - x_0) + f_y(x_0, y_0)(y - y_0)$$
$$+ \frac{1}{2!}[f_{xx}(x_0, y_0)(x - x_0)^2 + 2f_{xy}(x_0, y_0)(x - x_0)(y - y_0)$$
$$+ f_{yy}(x_0, y_0)(y - y_0)^2] + \cdots + R_n \qquad \textbf{(19.60)}$$

Note that the coefficients of the $(x - x_0)$ and $(y - y_0)$ expressions are now the *partial* derivatives of f, all evaluated at the expansion point (x_0, y_0).

From the Taylor series of a function, the linear approximation—or *linearization* for short—is obtained by simply dropping all terms of order higher than one. Thus, for the one-variable case, the linearization is the following linear function of x:

$$\phi(x_0) + \phi'(x_0)(x - x_0)$$

Similarly, the linearization of (19.60) is the following linear function of x and y:

$$f(x_0, y_0) + f_x(x_0, y_0)(x - x_0) + f_y(x_0, y_0)(y - y_0)$$

Besides, by substituting the function symbol g for f in this result, we can also get the corresponding linearization of $g(x, y)$. It follows that, given the nonlinear system

$$x' = f(x, y)$$
$$y' = g(x, y) \qquad \textbf{(19.61)}$$

its linearization around the expansion point (x_0, y_0) can be written as

$$x' = f(x_0, y_0) + f_x(x_0, y_0)(x - x_0) + f_y(x_0, y_0)(y - y_0)$$
$$y' = g(x_0, y_0) + g_x(x_0, y_0)(x - x_0) + g_y(x_0, y_0)(y - y_0) \qquad \textbf{(19.62)}$$

If the specific forms of the functions f and g are known, then $f(x_0, y_0)$, $f_x(x_0, y_0)$, $f_y(x_0, y_0)$ and their counterparts for the g function can all be assigned specific values and the linear system (19.62) solved quantitatively. However, even if the f and g functions are given in *general* forms, qualitative analysis is still possible, provided only that the signs of f_x, f_y, g_x, and g_y are ascertainable.

The Reduced Linearization

For purposes of local stability analysis, the linearization (19.62) can be put into a simpler form. First, since our point of expansion is to be the equilibrium point $(\bar{x}, \bar{y})$, we should replace (x_0, y_0) by $(\bar{x}, \bar{y})$. More substantively, since at the equilibrium point we have $x' = y' = 0$ by definition, it follows that

$$f(\bar{x}, \bar{y}) = g(\bar{x}, \bar{y}) = 0 \qquad \text{[by (19.61)]}$$

so the first term on the right side of each equation in (19.62) can be dropped. Making these changes, then multiplying out the remaining terms on the right of (19.62) and rearranging, we obtain another version of the linearization:

$$\begin{aligned} x' - f_x(\bar{x}, \bar{y})x - f_y(\bar{x}, \bar{y})y &= -f_x(\bar{x}, \bar{y})\bar{x} - f_y(\bar{x}, \bar{y})\bar{y} \\ y' - g_x(\bar{x}, \bar{y})x - g_y(\bar{x}, \bar{y})y &= -g_x(\bar{x}, \bar{y})\bar{x} - g_y(\bar{x}, \bar{y})\bar{y} \end{aligned} \qquad \textbf{(19.63)}$$

Note that, in (19.63), each term on the right of the equals signs represents a constant. We took the trouble to separate out these constant terms so that we can now drop them all, to get to the reduced equations of the linearization. The result, which may be written in matrix notation as

$$\begin{bmatrix} x' \\ y' \end{bmatrix} - \begin{bmatrix} f_x & f_y \\ g_x & g_y \end{bmatrix}_{(\bar{x}, \bar{y})} \begin{bmatrix} x \\ y \end{bmatrix} = \begin{bmatrix} 0 \\ 0 \end{bmatrix} \qquad \textbf{(19.64)}$$

constitutes the *reduced linearization* of (19.61). Inasmuch as qualitative analysis depends exclusively on the knowledge of the characteristic roots, which, in turn, hinge only on the reduced equations of a system, (19.64) is all we need for the desired local stability analysis.

Going a step further, it may be observed that the only distinguishing property of the reduced linearization lies in the matrix of partial derivatives—the Jacobian matrix of the nonlinear system (19.61)—evaluated at the equilibrium $(\bar{x}, \bar{y})$. Hence, in the final analysis, the local stability or instability of the equilibrium is predicated solely on the makeup of the said Jacobian. For notational convenience in the ensuing discussion, we shall denote the Jacobian evaluated at the equilibrium by J_E and its elements by a, b, c, and d:

$$J_E \equiv \begin{bmatrix} f_x & f_y \\ g_x & g_y \end{bmatrix}_{(\bar{x}, \bar{y})} \equiv \begin{bmatrix} a & b \\ c & d \end{bmatrix} \qquad \textbf{(19.65)}$$

It will be assumed that the two differential equations are functionally independent. Then we shall always have $|J_E| \neq 0$. (For some cases where $|J_E| = 0$, see Exercise 19.6-4.)

Local Stability Analysis

According to (19.16), and using (19.65), the characteristic equation of the reduced linearization should be

$$\begin{vmatrix} r - a & -b \\ -c & r - d \end{vmatrix} = r^2 - (a + d)r + (ad - bc) = 0$$

It is clear that the characteristic roots depend critically on the expressions $(a + d)$ and $(ad - bc)$. The latter is merely the determinant of the Jacobian in (19.65):

$$ad - bc = |J_E|$$

And the former, representing the *sum* of the principal-diagonal elements of that Jacobian, is called the *trace* of J_E, symbolized by tr J_E:

$$a + d = \text{tr } J_E$$

Accordingly, the characteristic roots can be expressed as

$$r_1, r_2 = \frac{\text{tr } J_E \pm \sqrt{(\text{tr } J_E)^2 - 4|J_E|}}{2}$$

The relative magnitudes of $(\text{tr } J_E)^2$ and $4|J_E|$ will determine whether the two roots are real or complex, that is, whether the time paths of x and y are steady or fluctuating. To check the dynamic stability of equilibrium, on the other hand, we need to ascertain the algebraic signs of the two roots. For that purpose, the following two relationships will prove to be most helpful:

$$r_1 + r_2 = \text{tr } J_E \qquad \qquad \textbf{(19.66)}$$
$$\text{[cf. (16.5) and (16.6)]}$$
$$r_1 r_2 = |J_E| \qquad \qquad \textbf{(19.67)}$$

Case 1 (tr $J_E)^2 > 4|J_E|$) In this case, the roots are real and distinct, and no fluctuation is possible. Hence the equilibrium can be either a node or a saddle point, but never a focus or vortex. In view that $r_1 \neq r_2$, there exist three distinct possibilities of sign combination: both roots negative, both roots positive, and two roots with opposite signs.[†] Taking into account the information in (19.66) and (19.67), these three possibilities are characterized by:

$$(i) \quad r_1 < 0, r_2 < 0 \quad \Rightarrow \quad |J_E| > 0; \text{tr } J_E < 0$$
$$(ii) \quad r_1 > 0, r_2 > 0 \quad \Rightarrow \quad |J_E| > 0; \text{tr } J_E > 0$$
$$(iii) \quad r_1 > 0, r_2 < 0 \quad \Rightarrow \quad |J_E| < 0; \text{tr } J_E \gtreqless 0$$

Under Possibility *i*, with both roots negative, both complementary functions x_c and y_c tend to zero as t becomes infinite. The equilibrium is thus a stable node. The opposite is true under Possibility *ii*, which describes an unstable node. In contrast, with two roots of opposite signs, Possibility *iii* yields a saddle point.

To see this last case more clearly, recall that the complementary functions of the two variables under Case 1 take the general form

$$x_c = A_1 e^{r_1 t} + A_2 e^{r_2 t}$$
$$y_c = k_1 A_1 e^{r_1 t} + k_2 A_2 e^{r_2 t}$$

where the arbitrary constants A_1 and A_2 are to be determined from the initial conditions. If the initial conditions are such that $A_1 = 0$, the positive root r_1 will drop out of the picture, leaving it to the negative root r_2 to make the equilibrium stable. Such initial conditions pertain to the points located on the stable branches of the saddle point. On the other hand, if the initial conditions are such that $A_2 = 0$, the negative root r_2 will vanish from the scene, leaving it to the positive root r_1 to make the equilibrium unstable. Such initial conditions relate to the points lying on the unstable branches. Inasmuch as all the other initial conditions also involve $A_1 \neq 0$, they must all give rise to divergent complementary functions, too. Thus Possibility *iii* yields a saddle point.

[†] Since we have ruled out $|J_E| = 0$, no root can take a zero value.

Case 2 (tr $J_E)^2 = 4|J_E|$) As the roots are repeated in this case, only two possibilities of sign combination can arise:

$$(iv) \quad r_1 < 0, r_2 < 0 \quad \Rightarrow \quad |J_E| > 0; \text{ tr } J_E < 0$$
$$(v) \quad r_1 > 0, r_2 > 0 \quad \Rightarrow \quad |J_E| > 0; \text{ tr } J_E > 0$$

These two possibilities are mere duplicates of Possibilities *i* and *ii*. Thus they point to a stable node and an unstable node, respectively.

Case 3 (tr $J_E)^2 < 4|J_E|$) This time, with complex roots $h \pm vi$, cyclical fluctuation is present, and we must encounter either a focus or a vortex. On the basis of (19.66) and (19.67), we have in the present case

$$\text{tr } J_E = r_1 + r_2 = (h + vi) + (h - vi) = 2h$$
$$|J_E| = r_1 r_2 = (h + vi)(h - vi) = h^2 + v^2$$

Thus tr J_E has to take the same sign as h, whereas $|J_E|$ is invariably positive. Consequently, there are three possible outcomes:

$$(vi) \quad h < 0 \quad \Rightarrow \quad |J_E| > 0; \text{ tr } J_E < 0$$
$$(vii) \quad h > 0 \quad \Rightarrow \quad |J_E| > 0; \text{ tr } J_E > 0$$
$$(viii) \quad h = 0 \quad \Rightarrow \quad |J_E| > 0; \text{ tr } J_E = 0$$

These are associated, respectively, with damped fluctuation, explosive fluctuation, and uniform fluctuation. In other word, Possibility *vi* implies a stable focus; Possibility *vii*, an unstable focus; and Possibility *viii*, a vortex.

The conclusions from the preceding discussion are summarized in Table 19.1 to facilitate qualitative inferences from the signs of $|J_E|$ and tr J_E. Three features of the table are especially noteworthy. First, a negative $|J_E|$ is exclusively tied to the saddle-point type of equilibrium. This suggests that $|J_E| < 0$ is a necessary-and-sufficient condition for a saddle point. Second, a zero value for tr J_E occurs only under two circumstances—when there is a saddle point or a vortex. These two circumstances are, however, distinguishable from each other by the sign of $|J_E|$. Accordingly, a zero tr J_E coupled with a positive $|J_E|$ is necessary-and-sufficient for a vortex. Third, while a negative sign for tr J_E is necessary for dynamic stability, it is *not* sufficient, on account of the possibility of a saddle point.

TABLE 19.1
Local Stability Analysis of a Two-Variable Nonlinear Differential-Equation System

Case	Sign of $|J_E|$	Sign of tr J_E	Type of Equilibrium
1. $(\text{tr } J_E)^2 > 4|J_E|$	+	−	Stable node
	+	+	Unstable node
	−	+, 0, −	Saddle point
2. $(\text{tr } J_E)^2 = 4|J_E|$	+	−	Stable node
	+	+	Unstable node
3. $(\text{tr } J_E)^2 < 4|J_E|$	+	−	Stable focus
	+	+	Unstable focus
	+	0	Vortex

Nevertheless, when a negative tr J_E is accompanied by a positive $|J_E|$, we do have a necessary-and-sufficient condition for dynamic stability.

The discussion leading to the summary in Table 19.1 has been conducted in the context of a linear approximation to a *nonlinear* system. However, the contents of that table are obviously applicable also to the qualitative analysis of a system that is *linear* to begin with. In the latter case, the elements of the Jacobian matrix will be a set of given constants, so there is no need to evaluate them at the equilibrium. Since there is no approximation process involved, the stability inferences will no longer be "local" in nature but will have global validity.

Example 1   Analyze the local stability of the nonlinear system

$$x' = f(x, y) = xy - 2$$
$$y' = g(x, y) = 2x - y \qquad (x, y \geq 0)$$

First, setting $x' = y' = 0$, and noting the nonnegativity of x and y, we find a single equilibrium E at $(\bar{x}, \bar{y}) = (1, 2)$. Then, by taking the partial derivatives of x' and y', and evaluating them at E, we obtain

$$J_E = \begin{bmatrix} f_x & f_y \\ g_x & g_y \end{bmatrix}_{(\bar{x}, \bar{y})} = \begin{bmatrix} y & x \\ 2 & -1 \end{bmatrix}_{(1,2)} = \begin{bmatrix} 2 & 1 \\ 2 & -1 \end{bmatrix}$$

Since $|J_E| = -4$ is negative, we can immediately conclude that the equilibrium is locally a saddle point.

Note that while the first row of the Jacobian matrix originally contains the variables y and x, the second row does not. The reason for the difference is that the second equation in the given system is originally linear, and requires no linearization.

Example 2   Given the nonlinear system

$$x' = x^2 - y$$
$$y' = 1 - y$$

we can, by setting $x' = y' = 0$, find two equilibrium points: $E_1 = (1, 1)$ and $E_2 = (-1, 1)$. Thus we need two separate linearizations. Evaluating the Jacobian $\begin{bmatrix} 2x & -1 \\ 0 & -1 \end{bmatrix}$ at the two equilibriums in turn, we obtain

$$J_{E1} = \begin{bmatrix} 2 & -1 \\ 0 & -1 \end{bmatrix} \quad \text{and} \quad J_{E2} = \begin{bmatrix} -2 & -1 \\ 0 & -1 \end{bmatrix}$$

The first of these has a negative determinant; thus $E_1 = (1, 1)$ is locally a saddle point. From the second, we find that $|J_{E2}| = 2$ and tr $J_{E2} = -3$. Hence, by Table 19.1, $E_2 = (-1, 1)$ is locally a stable node under Case 1.

Example 3   Does the linear system

$$x' = x - y + 2$$
$$y' = x + y + 4$$

possess a stable equilibrium? To answer such a qualitative question, we can simply concentrate on the reduced equations and ignore the constants 2 and 4 altogether. As may be expected from a linear system, the Jacobian $\begin{bmatrix} 1 & -1 \\ 1 & 1 \end{bmatrix}$ has as its elements four constants.

Inasmuch as its determinant and trace are both equal to 2, the equilibrium falls under Case 3 and is an unstable focus. Note that this conclusion is reached without having to solve for the equilibrium. Note, also, that the conclusion is in this case globally valid.

Example 4   Analyze the local stability of the Obst model (19.50),

$$p' = h(1 - \mu)$$
$$\mu' = (p + q - m)\mu$$

assuming that the rate of monetary expansion m is exogenous (no monetary rule is followed). According to Fig. 19.4a, the equilibrium of this model occurs at $E = (\bar{p}, \bar{\mu}) = (m - q, 1)$. The Jacobian matrix evaluated at E is

$$J_E = \begin{bmatrix} \dfrac{\partial p'}{\partial p} & \dfrac{\partial p'}{\partial \mu} \\ \dfrac{\partial \mu'}{\partial p} & \dfrac{\partial \mu'}{\partial \mu} \end{bmatrix}_E = \begin{bmatrix} 0 & -h \\ \mu & p+q-m \end{bmatrix}_{(m-q,1)} = \begin{bmatrix} 0 & -h \\ 1 & 0 \end{bmatrix}$$

Since $|J_E| = h > 0$, and tr $J_E = 0$, Table 19.1 indicates that the equilibrium is locally a vortex. This conclusion is consistent with that of the phase-diagram analysis in Sec. 19.5.

Example 5   Analyze the local stability of the Obst model, assuming that the alternative monetary rule is as follows:

$$p' = h(1 - \mu) \qquad \text{[from (19.50)]}$$
$$\mu' = [p + q - m(p')]\mu \qquad \text{[from (19.58)]}$$

Note that since p' is a function of μ, the function $m(p')$ is in the present model also a function of μ. Thus we have to apply the product rule in finding $\partial \mu'/\partial \mu$. At the equilibrium E, where $p' = \mu' = 0$, we have $\bar{\mu} = 1$ and $\bar{p} = m(0) - q$. The Jacobian evaluated at E is, therefore,

$$J_E = \begin{bmatrix} 0 & -h \\ \mu & p+q-m(p')-m'(p')(-h)\mu \end{bmatrix}_E = \begin{bmatrix} 0 & -h \\ 1 & m'(0)h \end{bmatrix}$$

where $m'(0)$ is negative by (19.57). According to Table 19.1, with $|J_E| = h > 0$ and tr $J_E = m'(0)h < 0$, we can have either a stable focus or a stable node, depending on the relative magnitudes of $(\text{tr } J_E)^2$ and $4|J_E|$. To be specific, the larger the absolute value of the derivative $m'(0)$, the larger the absolute value of tr J_E will be and the more likely $(\text{tr } J_E)^2$ will exceed $4|J_E|$, to produce a stable node instead of a stable focus. This conclusion is again consistent with what we learned from the phase-diagram analysis.

EXERCISE 19.6

1. Analyze the local stability of each of the following nonlinear systems:
   (a) $x' = e^x - 1$ (c) $x' = 1 - e^y$
       $y' = ye^x$ $y' = 5x - y$
   (b) $x' = x + 2y$ (d) $x' = x^3 + 3x^2y + y$
       $y' = x^2 + y$ $y' = x(1 + y^2)$

2. Use Table 19.1 to determine the type of equilibrium a nonlinear system would have locally, given that:

(a) $f_x = 0$ $\quad f_y > 0$ $\quad g_x > 0$ $\quad$ and $\quad g_y = 0$
(b) $f_x = 0$ $\quad f_y < 0$ $\quad g_x < 0$ $\quad$ and $\quad g_y = 0$
(c) $f_x < 0$ $\quad f_y > 0$ $\quad g_x < 0$ $\quad$ and $\quad g_y < 0$

Are your results consistent with your answers to Exercises 19.5-4 and 19.5-5?

3. Analyze the local stability of the Obst model, assuming that the conventional monetary rule is followed.

4. The following two systems both possess zero-valued Jacobians. Construct a phase diagram for each, and deduce the locations of all the equilibriums that exist:

(a) $x' = x + y$ $\qquad$ (b) $x' = 0$
  $\quad y' = -x - y$ $\qquad\quad\;\; y' = 0$

Chapter 20

Optimal Control Theory

At the end of Chap. 13, we referred to dynamic optimization as a type of problem we were not ready to tackle because we did not yet have the tools of dynamic analysis such as differential equations. Now that we have acquired such tools, we can finally try a taste of dynamic optimization.

The classical approach to dynamic optimization is called the *calculus of variations*. In the later development of this methodology, however, a more powerful approach known as *optimal control theory* has, for the most part, supplanted the calculus of variations. For this reason, we shall, in this chapter, confine our attention to optimal control theory, explaining its basic nature, introducing the major solution tool called *the maximum principle,* and illustrating its use in some elementary economic models.[†]

20.1 The Nature of Optimal Control

In static optimization, the task is to find a single value for each choice variable, such that a stated objective function will be maximized or minimized, as the case may be. Such a problem is devoid of a time dimension. In contrast, time enters explicitly and prominently in a dynamic optimization problem. In such a problem, we will always have in mind a planning period, say from an initial time $t = 0$ to a terminal time $t = T$, and try to find the best course of action to take during that entire period. Thus the solution for any variable will take the form of not a single value, but a complete time path.

Suppose the problem is one of profit maximization over a time period. At any point of time t, we have to choose the value of some *control variable, $u(t)$,* which will then affect the value of some *state variable, $y(t)$,* via a so-called *equation of motion.* In turn, $y(t)$ will determine the profit $\pi(t)$. Since our objective is to maximize the profit over the entire period, the objective function should take the form of a definite integral of π from $t = 0$ to $t = T$. To be complete, the problem also specifies the initial value of the state variable y,

---

[†] For a more complete treatment of optimal control theory (as well as "calculus of variations"), the student is referred to *Elements of Dynamic Optimization* by Alpha C. Chiang, McGraw-Hill, New York, 1992, now published by Waveland Press, Inc., Prospect Heights, Illinois. This chapter draws heavily from material in this cited book.

$y(0)$, and the terminal value of y, $y(T)$, or alternatively, the range of values that $y(T)$ is allowed to take.

Taking into account the preceding, we can state the simplest problem of optimal control as:

$$\text{Maximize} \quad \int_0^T F(t, y, u)\, dt$$

$$\text{subject to} \quad \frac{dy}{dt} \equiv y' = f(t, y, u) \tag{20.1}$$

$$y(0) = A \qquad y(T) \ \text{free}$$

$$\text{and} \qquad u(t) \in U \qquad \text{for all } t \in [0, T]$$

The first line of (20.1), the objective function, is an integral whose integrand $F(t, y, u)$ stipulates how the choice of the control variable u at time t, along with the resulting y at time t, determines our object of maximization at t. The second line is the equation of motion for the state variable y. What this equation does is to provide the mechanism whereby our choice of control variable u can be translated into a specific pattern of movement of the state variable y. Normally, the linkage between u and y can be adequately described by a first-order differential equation $y' = f(t, y, u)$. However, if it happens that the pattern of change of the state variable requires a second-order differential equation, then we must transform this equation into a pair of first-order differential equations. In that case an additional state variable will be introduced. Both the integrand F and the equation of motion are assumed to be continuous in all their arguments and possess continuous first-order partial derivatives with respect to the state variable y and the time variable t, but not necessarily the control variable u. In the third line, we indicate that the initial state, the value of y at $t = 0$, is a constant A, but the terminal state $y(T)$ is left unrestricted. Finally, the fourth line indicates that the permissible choices of u are limited to a control region U. It may happen, of course, that $u(t)$ is not restricted.

Illustration: A Simple Macroeconomic Model

Consider an economy that produces output Y using capital K and a fixed amount of labor L, according to the production function

$$Y = Y(K, L)$$

Further, output is used either for consumption C or for investment I. If we ignore the problem of depreciation, then

$$I \equiv \frac{dK}{dt}$$

In other words, investment is the change in capital stock over time. Thus we can also write investment as

$$I = Y - C = Y(K, L) - C = \frac{dK}{dt}$$

which gives us a first-order differential equation in the variable K.

If our objective is to maximize some form of social utility over a fixed planning period, then the problem becomes

$$\text{Maximize} \quad \int_0^T U(C)\,dt$$

$$\text{subject to} \quad \frac{dK}{dt} = Y(K, L) - C \qquad \textbf{(20.2)}$$

$$\text{and} \quad K(0) = K_0 \qquad K(T) = K_T$$

where K_0 and K_T are the initial value and terminal (target) value of K. Note that in (20.2), the terminal state is a fixed value, not left free as in (20.1). Here C serves as the control variable and K is the state variable. The problem is to choose the optimal control path $C(t)$ such that its impact on output Y and capital K, and the repercussions therefrom upon C itself, will together maximize the aggregate utility over the planning period.

Pontryagin's Maximum Principle

The key to optimal control theory is a first-order necessary condition known as the *maximum principle*.[†] The statement of the maximum principle involves an approach that is akin to the Lagrangian function and the Lagrangian multiplier variable. For optimal control problems, these are known as the *Hamiltonian function* and *costate variable,* concepts we will now develop.

The Hamiltonian

In (20.1), there are three variables: time t, the state variable y, and the control variable u. We now introduce a new variable known as the costate variable and denoted by $\lambda(t)$. Like the Lagrange multiplier, the costate variable measures the shadow price of the state variable.

The costate variable is introduced into the optimal control problem via a *Hamiltonian function* (or Hamiltonian, for short). The Hamiltonian is defined as

$$H(t, y, u, \lambda) \equiv F(t, y, u) + \lambda(t) f(t, y, u) \qquad \textbf{(20.3)}$$

where H denotes the Hamiltonian and is a function of four variables: t, y, u, and λ.

The Maximum Principle

The maximum principle—the main tool for solving problems of optimal control—is so named because, as a first-order necessary condition it requires us to choose u so as to maximize the Hamiltonian H *at every point of time.*

Since, aside from the control variable, u, H involves the state variable y and costate variable λ, the statement of the maximum principle also stipulates how y and λ should change over time, via an *equation of motion for the state variable y (state equation for*

[†] The term "maximum principle" is attributed to L. S. Pontryagin and his associates, and is often referred to as Pontryagin's maximum principle. See *The Mathematical Theory of Optimal Control Processes* by L. S. Pontryagin, V. G. Boltyanskii, R. V. Gamkrelidze, and E. F. Mishchenko, Interscience, New York, 1962 (translated by K. N. Trirogoff).

short) as well as an *equation of motion for the costate variable* λ (*costate equation* for short). The state equation always comes as part of the problem statement itself, as in the second equation in (20.1). But in the view that (20.3) implies $\partial H/\partial \lambda = f(t, y, u)$, the maximum principle describes the state equation

$$y' = f(t, y, u) \text{ as } y' = \frac{\partial H}{\partial \lambda} \tag{20.4}$$

In contrast, λ does not appear in the problem statement (20.1) and its equation of motion enters into the picture purely as an optimization condition. The costate equation is

$$\lambda' \left(\equiv \frac{d\lambda}{dt} \right) = -\frac{\partial H}{\partial y} \tag{20.5}$$

Note that both equations of motion are stated in terms of the partial derivatives of H, suggesting some symmetry, but there is a negative sign attached to $\partial H/\partial y$ in (20.5).

Equations (20.4) and (20.5) constitute a system of two differential equations. Thus we need two boundary conditions to definitize the two arbitrary constants that will arise in the process of solution. If both the initial state $y(0)$ and the terminal state $y(T)$ are fixed, then these specifications can be used to definitize the constants. But if, as in problem (20.1), the terminal state is not fixed, then something called a *transversality condition* must be included as part of the maximum principle, to fill the gap left by the missing boundary condition.

Summing up the preceding, we can state the various components of the maximum principle for problem (20.1) as follows:

$$
\begin{array}{lll}
(i) & H(t, y, u^*, \lambda) \geq H(t, y, u, \lambda) & \text{for all } t \in [0, T] \\[2mm]
(ii) & y' = \dfrac{\partial H}{\partial \lambda} & \text{(state equation)} \\[3mm]
(iii) & \lambda' = -\dfrac{\partial H}{\partial y} & \text{(costate equation)} \\[3mm]
(iv) & \lambda(T) = 0 & \text{(transversality condition)}
\end{array}
\tag{20.6}
$$

Condition i in (20.6) states that at every time t the value of $u(t)$, the optimal control, must be chosen so as to maximize the value of the Hamiltonian over all admissible values of $u(t)$. In the case where the Hamiltonian is differentiable with respect to u and yields an interior solution, Condition i can be replaced by

$$\frac{\partial H}{\partial u} = 0$$

However, if the control region is a closed set, then boundary solutions are possible and $\partial H/\partial u = 0$ may not apply. In fact, the maximum principle does not even require the Hamiltonian to be differentiable with respect to u.

Conditions ii and iii of the maximum principle, $y' = \partial H/\partial \lambda$ and $\lambda' = -\partial H/\partial y$, give us two equations of motion, referred to as the Hamiltonian system for the given problem. Condition iv, $\lambda(T) = 0$, is the transversality condition appropriate for the free-terminal-state problem only.

Example 1

To illustrate the use of the maximum principle, let us first consider a simple noneconomic example—that of finding the shortest path from a given point A to a given straight line. In Fig. 20.1, we have plotted the point A on the vertical axis in the ty plane, and drawn the straight line as a vertical one at $t = T$. Three (out of an infinite number of) admissible paths are shown, each with a different length. The length of any path is the aggregate of small path segments, each of which can be considered as the hypotenuse (not drawn) of a triangle formed by small movements dt and dy. Denoting the hypotenuse by dh, we have, by Pythagoras's theorem,

$$dh^2 = dt^2 + dy^2$$

Dividing both sides by dt^2 and taking the square root yields

$$\frac{dh}{dt} = \left[1 + \left(\frac{dy}{dt} \right)^2 \right]^{1/2} = [1 + (y')^2]^{1/2} \qquad (20.7)$$

The total length of the path can then be found by integrating (20.7) with respect to t, from $t = 0$ to $t = T$. If we let $y' = u$ be the control variable, (20.7) can be expressed as

$$\frac{dh}{dt} = (1 + u^2)^{1/2} \qquad (20.7')$$

To minimize the integral of (20.7') is, of course, equivalent to maximizing the *negative* of (20.7'). Thus the shortest-path problem is:

$$\text{Maximize} \qquad \int_0^T -(1 + u^2)^{1/2} dt$$

$$\text{subject to} \qquad y' = u$$

$$\text{and} \qquad y(0) = A \qquad y(T) \text{ free}$$

The Hamiltonian for the problem is, by (20.3),

$$H = -(1 + u^2)^{1/2} + \lambda u$$

FIGURE 20.1

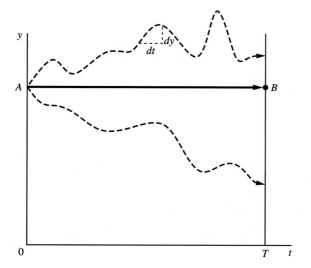

Since H is differentiable in u, and u is unrestricted, the following first-order condition can be used to maximize H:

$$\frac{\partial H}{\partial u} = -\frac{1}{2}(1 + u^2)^{-1/2}(2u) + \lambda = 0$$

or
$$u(t) = \lambda(1 - \lambda^2)^{-1/2}$$

Checking the second-order condition, we find that

$$\frac{\partial^2 H}{\partial u^2} = -(1 + u^2)^{-3/2} < 0$$

which verifies that the solution to $u(t)$ does maximize the Hamiltonian. Since $u(t)$ is a function of λ, we need a solution to the costate variable. From the first-order conditions, the equation of motion for the costate variable is

$$\lambda' = -\frac{\partial H}{\partial y} = 0$$

since H is independent of y. Thus, λ is a constant. To definitize this constant, we can make use of the transversality condition $\lambda(T) = 0$. Since λ can take only a single value, now known to be zero, we actually have $\lambda(t) = 0$ for all t. Thus we can write

$$\lambda^*(t) = 0 \qquad \text{for all } t \in [0, T]$$

It follows that the optimal control is

$$u^*(t) = \lambda^*[1 - (\lambda^*)^2]^{-1/2} = 0$$

Finally, using the equation of motion for the state variable, we see that

$$y' = u = 0$$

or
$$y^*(t) = c_0 \qquad \text{(a constant)}$$

Incorporating the initial condition

$$y(0) = A$$

we can conclude that $c_0 = A$, and write

$$y^*(t) = A \qquad \text{for all } t$$

In Fig. 20.1, this path is the line AB. The shortest path is found to be a straight line with a zero slope.

Example 2   Find the optimal control path that will

$$\text{Maximize} \qquad \int_0^1 (y - u^2)\, dt$$

$$\text{subject to} \qquad y' = u$$

$$\text{and} \qquad y(0) = 5 \qquad y(1) \text{ free}$$

This problem is in the format of (20.1), except that u is unrestricted.
The Hamiltonian for this problem,

$$H = y - u^2 + \lambda u$$

is concave in u, and u is unrestricted, so we can maximize H by applying the first-order condition (also sufficient because of concavity of H):

$$\frac{\partial H}{\partial u} = -2u + \lambda = 0$$

which gives us

$$u(t) = \frac{\lambda}{2} \quad \text{or} \quad y' = \frac{\lambda}{2} \tag{20.8}$$

The equation of motion for λ is

$$\lambda' = -\frac{\partial H}{\partial y} = -1 \tag{20.8'}$$

The last two equations constitute the differential-equation system for this problem.
We can first solve for λ by straight integration of (20.8') to get

$$\lambda(t) = c_1 - t \qquad (c_1 \text{ arbitrary})$$

Moreover, by the transversality condition in (20.6), we must have $\lambda(1) = 0$. Setting $t = 1$ in the last equation yields $c_1 = 1$. Thus the optimal costate path is

$$\lambda^*(t) = 1 - t$$

It follows that $y' = \frac{1}{2}(1 - t)$, by (20.8), and by integration,

$$y(t) = \frac{1}{2}t - \frac{1}{4}t^2 + c_2 \qquad (c_2 \text{ arbitrary})$$

The arbitrary constant can be definitized by using the initial condition $y(0) = 5$. Setting $t = 0$ in the preceding equation, we get $5 = y(0) = c_2$. Thus the optimal path for the state variable is

$$y^*(t) = \frac{1}{2}t - \frac{1}{4}t^2 + 5$$

and the corresponding optimal control path is

$$u^*(t) = \frac{1}{2}(1 - t)$$

Example 3   Find the optimal control path that will

$$\text{Maximize} \quad \int_0^2 (2y - 3u)\, dt$$

$$\text{subject to} \quad y' = y + u$$

$$y(0) = 4 \qquad y(2) \text{ free}$$

$$\text{and} \quad u(t) \in [0, 2]$$

The fact that the control variable is restricted to the closed set $[0, 2]$ gives rise to the possibility of boundary solutions.
The Hamiltonian function

$$H = 2y - 3u + \lambda(y + u) = (2 + \lambda)y + (\lambda - 3)u$$

FIGURE 20.2

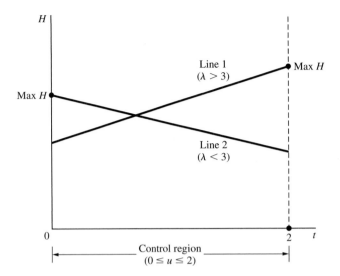

is linear in u. If we plot H against u in the uH plane, we get a straight line with slope $\partial H/\partial u = \lambda - 3$, which is positive if $\lambda > 3$ (Line 1), but negative if $\lambda < 3$ (Line 2), as illustrated in Fig. 20.2. If at any time λ exceeds 3, then the maximum H occurs at the upper boundary of the control region and we must choose $u = 2$. If, on the other hand, λ falls below 3, then in order to maximize H, we must choose $u = 0$. In short, $u^*(t)$ depends on $\lambda(t)$ as follows:

$$u^*(t) = \left\{ \begin{matrix} 2 \\ 0 \end{matrix} \right\} \quad \text{if} \quad \lambda(t) \left\{ \begin{matrix} > \\ < \end{matrix} \right\} 3 \qquad\qquad \textbf{(20.9)}$$

Thus, it is critical to find $\lambda(t)$. To do this, we start from the costate equation

$$\lambda' = -\frac{\partial H}{\partial y} = -2 - \lambda \quad \text{or} \quad \lambda' + \lambda = -2$$

The general solution of this equation is

$$\lambda(t) = Ae^{-t} - 2 \qquad \text{[by (15.5)]}$$

where A is an arbitrary constant. By using the transversality condition $\lambda(T) = \lambda(2) = 0$, we find that $A = 2e^2$. Thus the definite solution for λ is

$$\lambda^*(t) = 2e^{2-t} - 2 \qquad\qquad \textbf{(20.10)}$$

which is a decreasing function of t, falling steadily from the initial value $\lambda^*(0) = 2e^2 - 2 = 12.778$ to a terminal value $\lambda^*(2) = 2e^0 - 2 = 0$. This means that λ^* must pass through the point $\lambda = 3$ at some critical time τ, when the optimal u has to be switched from $u^* = 2$ to $u^* = 0$.

To find this critical time τ, we set $\lambda^*(\tau) = 3$ in (20.10):

$$3 = \lambda^*(\tau) = 2e^{2-\tau} - 2 \quad \text{or} \quad e^{2-\tau} = \frac{5}{2} = 2.5$$

Taking the natural log of both sides, we get

$$\ln e^{2-\tau} = \ln 2.5 \quad \text{or} \quad 2 - \tau = \ln 2.5$$

Thus

$$\tau = 2 - \ln 2.5 = 1.084 \qquad \text{(approx.)}$$

and the optimal control turns out to consist of two phases in the time interval [0, 2]:

$$\text{Phase 1: } u^*[0, \tau) = 2 \qquad \text{Phase 2: } u^*[\tau, 2] = 0$$

20.2 Alternative Terminal Conditions

What happens to the maximum principle when the terminal condition is different from the one in (20.1)? In (20.1), we face a vertical terminal line—with a fixed terminal time but unrestricted terminal state as illustrated in Fig. 20.1. The maximum principle for the maximization problem requires that

$$(i) \quad H(t, y, u^*, \lambda) \geq H(t, y, u, \lambda) \qquad \text{for all } t \in [0, T]$$

$$(ii) \quad y' = \frac{\partial H}{\partial \lambda}$$

$$(iii) \quad \lambda' = -\frac{\partial H}{\partial y}$$

with the transversality condition

$$(iv) \quad \lambda(T) = 0$$

With alternative terminal conditions, Conditions *i*, *ii*, and *iii* will remain the same, but Condition *iv* (the transversality condition) must be duly modified.

Fixed Terminal Point

If the terminal point is fixed so that the terminal condition is $y(T) = y_T$ with both T and y_T given, then the terminal condition itself should provide the information to definitize one constant. In this case, no transversality condition is needed.

Horizontal Terminal Line

Suppose that the terminal state is fixed at a given target level y_T but the terminal time T is free, so that we have the flexibility to reach the target in a hurry or at a leisurely pace. We then have a horizontal terminal line as illustrated in Fig. 20.3a, which allows us to choose between T_1, T_2, T_3, or other terminal times to reach the target level of y. For this case, the transversality condition is a restriction on the Hamiltonian (rather than the costate variable) at $t = T$:

$$H_{t=T} = 0 \qquad\qquad \textbf{(20.11)}$$

Truncated Vertical Terminal Line

If we have a fixed terminal time T, and the terminal state is free but subject to the proviso that $y_T \geq y_{min}$, where y_{min} denotes a given minimum permissible level of y, we face a truncated vertical terminal line, as illustrated in Fig. 20.3b.

FIGURE 20.3

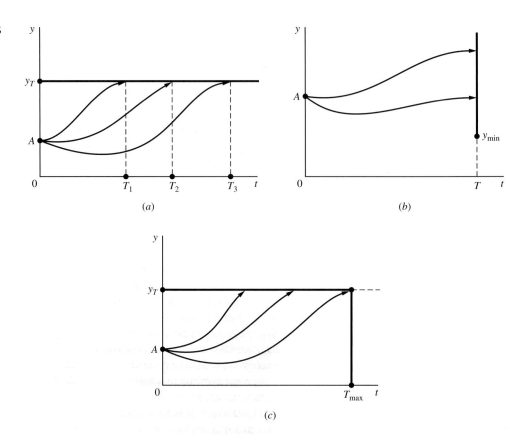

The transversality condition for this case can be stated like the complementary-slackness condition found in the Kuhn-Tucker conditions:

$$\lambda(T) \geq 0 \qquad y_T \geq y_{\min} \qquad (y_T - y_{\min})\lambda(T) = 0 \qquad \textbf{(20.12)}$$

The practical approach for solving this type of problem is to first try $\lambda(T) = 0$ as the transversality condition and test if the resulting y_T^* satisfies the restriction $y_T^* \geq y_{\min}$. If so, the problem is solved. If not, then treat the problem as a given terminal point problem with $y_{\min}$ as the terminal state.

Truncated Horizontal Terminal Line

When the terminal state is fixed at y_T and the terminal time is free but subject to the restriction $T \leq T_{\max}$, where $T_{\max}$ denotes the latest permissible time (a deadline) to reach the given y_T, we face a truncated horizontal terminal line as illustrated in Fig. 20.3c. The transversality condition becomes

$$H_{t=T_{\max}} \geq 0 \qquad T \leq T_{\max} \qquad (T - T_{\max})H_{t=T_{\max}} = 0 \qquad \textbf{(20.13)}$$

This again appears in the format of the complementary-slackness condition.

The practical approach to solving this type of problem is to try $H_{t=T_{\max}} = 0$ first. If the resulting solution value is $T^* \leq T_{\max}$, then the problem is solved. If not, then we must take

T_{max} as a fixed terminal time which, together with the given y_T, defines a fixed end point, and solve the problem as a fixed-end-point problem.

Example 1

In the problem

$$\text{Maximize} \quad \int_0^1 (y - u^2)\, dt$$

$$\text{subject to} \quad y' = u$$

$$\text{and} \quad y(0) = 2 \quad y(1) = a$$

the terminal point is fixed, even though $y(1)$ is assigned a parametric rather than numerical value here.

The Hamiltonian function

$$H = y - u^2 + \lambda u$$

is concave in u, so we can set $\partial H / \partial u = 0$ to maximize H:

$$\frac{\partial H}{\partial u} = -2u + \lambda = 0$$

Thus

$$u = \frac{\lambda}{2}$$

which shows that in order to solve for $u(t)$, we need to solve for $\lambda(t)$ first.

The two equations of motion are

$$y'(=u) = \frac{\lambda}{2}$$

$$\lambda'\left(= -\frac{\partial H}{\partial y}\right) = -1$$

Direct integration of the last equation yields

$$\lambda(t) = c_1 - t \quad (c_1 \text{ arbitrary})$$

which implies that

$$y' = \frac{1}{2}c_1 - \frac{1}{2}t$$

Again, by direct integration, we find that

$$y(t) = \frac{c_1}{2}t - \frac{1}{4}t^2 + c_2 \quad (c_2 \text{ arbitrary})$$

To definitize the two arbitrary constants, we make use of the initial condition $y(0) = 2$, and the terminal condition $y(1) = a$. Setting $t = 0$ and $t = 1$, successively, in the preceding equation, we obtain

$$2 = y(0) = c_2 \quad a = y(1) = \frac{c_1}{2} - \frac{1}{4} + c_2$$

Thus, $c_2 = 2$, and $c_1 = 2a - \frac{7}{2}$.

Therefore, we can write the optimal paths of this problem as:

$$y^*(t) = (a - \frac{7}{4})t - \frac{1}{4}t^2 + 2$$

$$\lambda^*(t) = 2a - \frac{7}{2} - t$$

$$u^*(t) = a - \frac{7}{4} - \frac{1}{2}t$$

Example 2   The problem

$$\text{Maximize} \qquad \int_0^T -(t^2 + u^2)\, dt$$

$$\text{subject to} \qquad y' = u$$

$$\text{and} \qquad y(0)4 \qquad y(T) = 5 \qquad T \text{ free}$$

exemplifies the case of horizontal terminal line where the terminal state is fixed but the time of arrival at the target level of y is unrestricted. In fact, it is one of our tasks to solve for the optimal value of T.

Since the Hamiltonian

$$H = -t^2 - u^2 + \lambda u$$

is concave in u, we can again maximize H by using the first-order condition

$$\frac{\partial H}{\partial u} = -2u + \lambda = 0$$

which gives us

$$u = \frac{\lambda}{2} \qquad\qquad\qquad (20.14)$$

The concavity of H makes it unnecessary to check the second-order condition, but if we wish, it is easy to check that $\partial^2 H / \partial u^2 = -2 < 0$, sufficient for a maximum of H.

The equation of motion for λ is

$$\lambda' = -\frac{\partial H}{\partial y} = 0$$

which implies that λ is a constant. But we cannot yet determine its exact value at this point.

Turning to the equation of motion for y,

$$y' = u = \frac{\lambda}{2} \qquad \text{[by (20.14)]}$$

we can obtain, by direct integration,

$$y(t) = \frac{\lambda}{2}t + c \qquad\qquad\qquad (20.15)$$

Since $y(0) = 4$, we see that $c = 4$. Furthermore, the transversality condition (20.11) requires that

$$H_{t=T} = -T^2 - \frac{\lambda^2}{4} + \frac{\lambda^2}{2} = -T^2 + \frac{\lambda^2}{4} = 0 \qquad \text{[by (20.14)]}$$

Solving the preceding equation for T, and taking the positive square root, we get

$$T = \frac{\lambda}{2} \qquad\qquad (20.16)$$

Since λ is constant, so is T. We try now to find its exact value.

Applying the terminal-state specification $y(T) = 5$ to (20.15), and recalling that $c = 4$, we get

$$y(T) = \frac{\lambda}{2}T + 4 = 5$$

In view of (20.16), the last equation can be rewritten as $T^2 = 1$. Thus, by taking the square root, we can determine the optimal arrival time to be

$$T^* = 1 \qquad \text{(negative root unacceptable)}$$

From this, we can readily deduce that

$$\lambda^*(t) = 2T^* = 2 \qquad \text{[by (20.16)]}$$
$$u^*(t) = \frac{\lambda}{2} = 1 \qquad \text{[by (20.14)]}$$
$$y^*(t) = t + 4 \qquad \text{[by (20.15)]}$$

The last result shows that, in this example, the optimal y path is a straight line going from the given initial point to the horizontal terminal line.

EXERCISE 20.2

Find the optimal paths of the control, state, and costate variables that will

1. Maximize $\displaystyle\int_0^1 (y - u^2)\, dt$

   subject to $\quad y' = u$

   and $\qquad\quad y(0) = 2 \qquad y(1)$ free

2. Maximize $\displaystyle\int_0^8 6y\, dt$

   subject to $\quad y' = y + u$

   $\qquad\qquad\; y(0) = 10 \qquad y(8)$ free

   and $\qquad\quad u(t) \in [0, 2]$

3. Maximize $\displaystyle\int_0^T -(au + bu^2)\, dt$

   subject to $\quad y' = y - u$

   and $\qquad\quad y(0) = y_0 \qquad y(t)$ free

4. Maximize $\displaystyle\int_0^T (yu - u^2 - y^2)\, dt$

   subject to $\quad y' = u$

   and $\qquad\quad y(0) = y_0 \qquad y(t)$ free

5. Maximize $\displaystyle\int_0^{20} -\frac{1}{2}u^2\,dt$

   subject to $y' = u$

   and $y(0) = 10$ $y(20) = 0$

6. Maximize $\displaystyle\int_0^4 3y\,dt$

   subject to $y' = y + u$

   $y(0) = 5$ $y(4) \geq 300$

   and $0 \leq u(t) \leq 2$

7. Maximize $\displaystyle\int_0^1 -u^2\,dt$

   subject to $y' = y + u$

   and $y(0) = 1$ $y(1) = 0$

8. Maximize $\displaystyle\int_1^2 (y + ut - u^2)\,dt$

   subject to $y' = u$

   and $y(1) = 3$ $y(2) = 4$

9. Maximize $\displaystyle\int_0^2 (2y - 3u - au^2)\,dt$

   subject to $y' = u + y$

   and $y(0) = 5$ $y(2)$ free

20.3   Autonomous Problems

In the general control problem framework, the variable t can enter the objective function and state equation directly. The general specification

$$\text{Maximize} \quad \int_0^T F(t, y, u)\,dt$$

$$\text{subject to} \quad y' = f(t, y, u)$$

$$\text{and} \quad \text{boundary conditions}$$

where t explicitly enters into F and f means the date matters. That is, the value generated by the activity $u(t)$ depends not only on the level, but also on exactly when this activity takes place.

Problems in which t is absent from the objective function and state equation such as

$$\text{Maximize} \quad \int_0^T F(y, u)\,dt$$

$$\text{subject to} \quad y' = f(y, u)$$

$$\text{and} \quad \text{boundary conditions}$$

are called *autonomous problems.* In such problems, since the Hamiltonian

$$H = F(y, u) + \lambda f(y, u)$$

does not contain t as an argument, the equations of motion are easier to solve; moreover, they are amenable to the use of phase-diagram analysis.

In still other cases, in an otherwise autonomous problem, time t enters into the picture as part of the discount factor e^{-rt}, but nowhere else, so that the objective function takes the form of

$$\int_0^T G(y, u)e^{-rt}\, dt$$

Strictly speaking, this problem is nonautonomous. However, it is easy to convert the problem into an autonomous one by employing the so-called *current-value Hamiltonian,* defined as:

$$H_c \equiv H e^{rt} = G(y, u) + \mu f(y, u) \tag{20.17}$$

where

$$\mu \equiv \lambda e^{rt} \tag{20.18}$$

is the *current-value Lagrange multiplier.* By focusing on the current (undiscounted) value, we are able to eliminate t from the original Hamiltonian.

Using H_c in lieu of H, we must revise the maximum principle to:

(i) $H_c(y, u^*, \mu) \geq H_c(y, u, \mu)$ for all $t \in [0, T]$

(ii) $y' = \dfrac{\partial H_c}{\partial \mu}$

(iii) $\mu' = -\dfrac{\partial H_c}{\partial y} + r\mu$ (20.19)

(iv) $\mu(T) = 0$ (for vertical terminal line)

or $[H_c]_{t=T} = 0$ (for horizontal terminal line)

20.4 Economic Applications

Lifetime Utility Maximization

Suppose a consumer has the utility function $U(C(t))$, where $C(t)$ is consumption at time t. The consumer's utility function is concave, and has the following properties:

$$U' > 0 \qquad U'' < 0$$

The consumer is also endowed with an initial stock of wealth, or capital, K_0, with income stream derived from the stock of capital according to the following:

$$Y = rK$$

where r is the market rate of interest. The consumer uses the income to purchase C. In addition, the consumer can consume the capital stock. Any income not consumed is added to the capital stock as investment. Thus,

$$K' \equiv I = Y - C = rK - C$$

The consumer's lifetime utility maximization problem is to

$$\text{Maximize} \quad \int_0^T U(C(t))e^{-\delta t}\, dt$$

$$\text{subject to} \quad K' = rK(t) - C(t)$$

$$\text{and} \quad K(0) = K_0 \quad K(T) \geq 0$$

where δ is the consumer's personal rate of time preference ($\delta \geq 0$). It is assumed that $C(t) > 0$ and $K(t) > 0$ for all t.

The Hamiltonian is

$$H = U(C(t))e^{-\delta t} + \lambda(t)\,[rK(t) - C(t)]$$

where C is the control variable, and K is the state variable. Since $U(C)$ is concave, and the constraint is linear in C, we know that the Hamiltonian is concave and the maximization of H can be achieved by simply setting $\partial H/\partial C = 0$. Thus we have

$$\frac{\partial H}{\partial C} = U'(C)e^{-\delta t} - \lambda = 0 \tag{20.20}$$

$$K' = rK(t) - C(t) \tag{20.20$'$}$$

$$\lambda' = -\frac{\partial H}{\partial K} = -r\lambda \tag{20.20$''$}$$

Equation (20.20) states that the discounted marginal utility should be equated to the present shadow price of an additional unit of capital. Differentiating (20.20) with respect to t, we get

$$U''(C)C'e^{-\delta t} - \delta U'(C)e^{-\delta t} = \lambda' \tag{20.21}$$

In view of (20.20) and (20.20$''$) we have

$$\lambda' = -r\lambda = -rU'(C)e^{-\delta t}$$

which can be substituted into (20.21) to yield

$$U''(C)C'(t)e^{-\delta t} - \delta U'(C)e^{-\delta t} = -rU'(C)\,e^{-\delta t}$$

or, after canceling the common factor $e^{-\delta t}$ and rearranging,

$$\frac{-U''(C(t))}{U'(C(t))}C'(t) = r - \delta$$

Since $U' > 0$ and $U'' < 0$, the sign of the derivative $C'(t)$ has to be the same as $(r - \delta)$. Therefore, if $r > \delta$, the optimal consumption will rise over time; if $r < \delta$, the optimal consumption will decline over time.

Solving (20.20$''$) directly gives us

$$\lambda(t) = \lambda_0 e^{-rt}$$

where $\lambda_0 > 0$ is the constant of integration. Combining this with (20.20) gives us

$$U'(C(t)) = \lambda e^{\delta t} = \lambda_0 e^{(\delta - r)t}$$

which shows that the marginal utility of consumption will optimally decrease over time if $r > \delta$, but increase over time if $r < \delta$.

Since the terminal condition $K(T) \geq 0$ identifies the present problem as one with a truncated vertical terminal line, the appropriate transversality condition is, by (20.12),

$$\lambda(T) \geq 0 \quad K(T) \geq 0 \quad K(T)\lambda(T) = 0$$

The key condition is the complementary-slackness stipulation, which means that either the capital stock K must be exhausted on the terminal date, or the shadow price of capital λ must fall to zero on the terminal date. By assumption, $U'(C) > 0$, the marginal utility can never be zero. Therefore, the marginal value of capital cannot be zero. This implies that the capital stock should optimally be exhausted by the terminal date T in this model.

Exhaustible Resource

Let $s(t)$ denote a stock of an exhaustible resource and $q(t)$ be the rate of extraction at any time t such that

$$s' = -q$$

The extracted resource produces a final consumer good c such that

$$c = c(q) \qquad \text{where} \qquad c' > 0, c'' < 0 \qquad \textbf{(20.22)}$$

The consumption good is the sole argument in the utility function of a representative consumer with the following properties:

$$U = U(c) \qquad \text{where} \qquad U' > 0, U'' < 0 \qquad \textbf{(20.22')}$$

The consumer wishes to maximize the utility function over a given interval $[0, T]$. Since c is a function of q, the rate of extraction, q will serve as the control variable. For simplicity, we ignore the issue of discounting over time. The dynamic problem is then to choose the optimal extraction rate that maximizes the utility function subject only to a nonnegativity constraint on the state variable $s(t)$, the stock of the exhaustible resource. The formulation is

$$
\begin{aligned}
\text{Maximize} \qquad & \int_0^T U(c(q))\, dt \\
\text{subject to} \qquad & s' = -q \\
\text{and} \qquad & s(0) = s_0 \qquad s(T) \geq 0
\end{aligned}
\qquad \textbf{(20.23)}
$$

where s_0 and T are given.

The Hamiltonian for the problem is

$$H = U(c(q)) - \lambda q$$

Since H is concave in q by model specifications on the $U(c(q))$ function, we can maximize H by setting $\partial H / \partial q = 0$:

$$\frac{\partial H}{\partial q} = U'(c(q))c'(q) - \lambda = 0 \qquad \textbf{(20.24)}$$

The concavity of H assures us that (20.24) maximizes H, but we can easily check the second-order condition and confirm that $\partial^2 H / \partial q^2$ is negative.

The maximum principle stipulates that

$$\lambda' = -\frac{\partial H}{\partial s} = 0$$

which implies that

$$\lambda(t) = c_0 \qquad \text{a constant} \tag{20.25}$$

To determine c_0, we turn to the transversality conditions. Since the model specifies $K(T) \geq 0$, it has a truncated vertical terminal line, so (20.12) applies:

$$\lambda(T) \geq 0 \qquad s(T) \geq 0 \qquad s(T)\lambda(T) = 0$$

In practical applications, the initial step is to try $\lambda(T) = 0$, solve for q, and see if the solution will work. Since $\lambda(T)$ is a constant, to try $\lambda(T) = 0$ implies $\lambda(t) = 0$ for all t, and $\partial H/\partial q$ in (20.24) reduces to

$$U'(c)c'(q) = 0$$

which (in principle) can be solved for q. Since t is not an explicit argument of U or c, the solution path for q is constant over time:

$$q^*(t) = q^*$$

Now, we check if q^* satisfies the restriction $s(T) \geq 0$. If q^* is a constant, then the equation of motion

$$s' = -q$$

can be readily integrated, yielding

$$s(t) = -qt + c_1 \qquad [c_1 = \text{constant of integration}]$$

Using the initial condition $s(0) = s_0$ yields a solution for the constant of integration

$$c_1 = s_0$$

and the optimal state path is

$$s(t) = s_0 - q^*t \tag{20.26}$$

Without specifying the functional forms for U and c, no numerical solution can be found for q^*. However, from the transversality conditions, we can conclude that if $s(T) \geq 0$, then q^* as derived in the solution is acceptable. But if $s(T) < 0$ for the given q^*, then the extraction rate is too high and we need to find a different solution. Since the trial solution $\lambda(T) = 0$ failed, we now take the alternative of $\lambda(T) > 0$. Even in this case, though, λ is still a constant by (20.25). And (20.24) can still (in principle) yield a constant, but different, solution value q_2^*. It follows that (20.26) remains valid. But this time, with $\lambda(T) > 0$, the transversality condition (20.12) dictates that $s(T) = 0$, or in view of (20.26),

$$s_0 - q_2^*T = 0$$

Thus we can write the revised (constant) optimal rate of extraction as

$$q_2^* = \frac{s_0}{T}$$

This new solution value should represent a lower extraction rate that would not violate the $s(T) \geq 0$ boundary condition.

EXERCISE 20.4

1. Maximize $\quad \int_0^T (K - \alpha K^2 - I^2)\,dt \qquad (\alpha > 0)$

   subject to $\quad K' = I - \delta K \qquad\qquad (\delta > 0)$

   and $\qquad\quad K(0) = K_0 \qquad\qquad\;\; K(T)$ free

2. Solve the following exhaustible resource problem for the optimal extraction path:

   Maximize $\quad \int_0^T \ln(q) e^{-\delta t}\,dt$

   subject to $\quad s' = -q$

   and $\qquad\quad s(0) = s_0 \qquad s(t) \geq 0$

20.5   Infinite Time Horizon

In this section we introduce the problem of dynamic optimization over an infinite planning period. Infinite time horizon models tend to introduce complexities with respect to transversality conditions and optimal time paths that differ from those developed earlier. Rather than address these issues here, we shall illustrate the methodology of such models with a version of the *neoclassical optimal growth model*.

Neoclassical Optimal Growth Model

The standard neoclassical production function expresses output Y as a function of two inputs: labor L and capital K. Its general form is

$$Y = Y(K, L)$$

where $Y(K, L)$ is a linearly homogeneous function with the properties

$$Y_L > 0 \qquad Y_K > 0 \qquad Y_{LL} < 0 \qquad Y_{KK} < 0$$

Rewriting the production function in per capita terms yields

$$y = \phi(k) \qquad \text{with } \phi'(k) > 0 \qquad \text{and} \qquad \phi''(k) < 0$$

where $y = Y/L$ and $k = K/L$. Total output Y is allocated to consumption C or gross investment I. Let δ be the rate of depreciation of the capital stock K. Then net investment or changes to the capital stock can be written as

$$K' = I - \delta K = Y - C - \delta K$$

Denoting per capita consumption as $c \equiv C/L$, we can write as

$$\frac{1}{L} K' = y - c - \delta k \qquad\qquad\qquad \textbf{(20.27)}$$

The right-hand side of (20.27) is in per capita terms, but the left-hand side is not. To unify, we note that

$$K' = \frac{dk}{dt} = \frac{d}{dt}(kL) = k\frac{dL}{dt} + L\frac{dk}{dt} \qquad \textbf{(20.28)}$$

If the population growth rate is[†]

$$\frac{dL/dt}{L} = n \qquad \text{so that} \qquad \frac{dL}{dt} = nL$$

then (20.28) becomes

$$K' = knL + Lk' \qquad \text{or} \qquad \frac{1}{L}K' = kn + k'$$

Substituting this into (20.27) transforms the latter into an equation entirely in per capita terms:

$$k' = y - c - (n + \delta)k = \phi(k) - c - (n + \delta)k \qquad \textbf{(20.27')}$$

Let $U(c)$ be the social welfare function (expressed in per capita terms), where

$$U'(c) > 0 \qquad \text{and} \qquad U''(c) < 0$$

and, to eliminate corner solutions, we also assume

$$U'(c) \to \infty \qquad \text{as } c \to 0$$
$$\text{and} \qquad U'(c) \to 0 \qquad \text{as } c \to \infty$$

If ρ denotes the social discount rate and the initial population is normalized to one, the objective function can be expressed as

$$V = \int_0^\infty U(c)e^{-\rho t} L_0 e^{nt}\, dt = \int_0^\infty U(c)e^{-(\rho - n)t}\, dt$$

$$= \int_0^\infty U(c)e^{-rt}\, dt \qquad \text{where } r = \rho - n$$

In this version of the neoclassical optimal growth model, utility is weighted by a population that grows continuously at a rate of n. However, if $r = \rho - n > 0$, then the model is mathematically no different from one without population weights but with a positive discount rate r.

The optimal growth problem can now be stated as

$$\text{Maximize} \qquad \int_0^\infty U(c)e^{-rt}\, dt$$

$$\text{subject to} \qquad k' = \phi(k) - c - (n + \delta)k \qquad \textbf{(20.29)}$$
$$k(0) = k_0$$
$$\text{and} \qquad 0 \le c(t) \le \phi(k)$$

where k is the state variable and c is the control variable.

[†] In this model we assume labor force and population to be one and the same.

The Hamiltonian for the problem is

$$H = U(c)e^{-rt} + \lambda[\phi(k) - c - (n + \delta)k]$$

Since H is concave in c, the maximum of H corresponds to an interior solution in the control region $[0 < c < f(k)]$, and therefore we can find the maximum of H from

$$\frac{\partial H}{\partial c} = U'(c)e^{-rt} - \lambda = 0$$

or
$$U'(c) = \lambda e^{rt} \tag{20.30}$$

The economic interpretation of (20.30) is that, along the optimal path, the marginal utility of per capita consumption should equal the shadow price of capital (λ) weighted by e^{rt}. Checking second-order conditions, we find

$$\frac{\partial^2 H}{\partial c^2} = U''(c)e^{-rt} < 0$$

Therefore, the Hamiltonian is maximized.

From the maximum principle, we have two equations of motion

$$k' = \frac{\partial H}{\partial \lambda} = \phi(k) - c - (n + \delta)k$$

and
$$\lambda' = -\frac{\partial H}{\partial k} = -\lambda[\phi'(k) - (n + \delta)]$$

The two equations of motion combined with the $U'(c) = \lambda e^{rt}$ should in principle define a solution for c, k, λ. However, at this level of generality we are unable to do more than undertake qualitative analysis of the model. Anything more would require specific forms of both the utility and production functions.

The Current-Value Hamiltonian

Since the preceding model is an example of an autonomous problem (t is not a separate argument in the utility function or state equation but appears only in the discount factor), we may use the current-value Hamiltonian written as

$$H_c = He^{rt} = U(c) + \mu[\phi(k) - c - (n + \delta)k] \qquad \text{[see (20.17)]}$$

where $\mu = \lambda e^{rt}$.

The maximum principle calls for

$$\frac{\partial H_c}{\partial c} = U'(c) - \mu = 0 \qquad \text{or} \qquad \mu = U'(c) \tag{20.31}$$

$$k' = \frac{\partial H_c}{\partial \mu} = \phi(k) - c - (n + \delta)k \tag{20.31'}$$

$$\mu' = -\frac{\partial H_c}{\partial k} + r\mu = -\mu[\phi'(k) - (n + \delta)] + r\mu$$

$$= -\mu[\phi'(k) - (n + \delta + r)] \tag{20.31''}$$

Equations (20.31') and (20.31'') constitute an autonomous differential equation system. This makes possible a qualitative analysis by phase diagram.

Constructing a Phase Diagram

The variables in the differential equations (20.31′) and (20.31″) are k and μ. Since (20.31) involves a function of c, namely $U'(c)$, rather than the plain c itself, it would be simpler to construct a phase diagram in the kc space rather than the $k\mu$ space. To do this, we shall try to eliminate μ. Since $\mu = U'(c)$, by (20.31), differentiation with respect to t gives us

$$\mu' = U''(c)c'$$

Substituting these expressions for μ and μ' into (20.31″) yields

$$c' = -\frac{U'(c)}{U''(c)}[\phi'(k) - (n + \delta + r)]$$

which is a differential equation in c. We now have the autonomous differential equation system

$$k' = \phi(k) - c - (n + \delta)k \tag{20.31′}$$

and $$c' = -\frac{U'(c)}{U''(c)}[\phi'(k) - (n + \delta + r)] \tag{20.32}$$

To construct the phase diagram in the kc space, we first draw the $k' = 0$ and $c' = 0$ curves which are defined by

$$c = \phi(k) - (n + \delta)k \qquad (k' = 0) \tag{20.33}$$

and $$\phi'(k) = n + \delta + r \qquad (c' = 0) \tag{20.34}$$

These two curves are illustrated in Fig. 20.4. The equation for the $k' = 0$ curve, (20.33), has the same structure as the fundamental equation of the Solow growth model, (15.30). Thus the $k' = 0$ curve has the same general shape as the one in Fig. 15.5b. The $c' = 0$ curve, on the other hand, plots as a vertical line because given the model specifications $\phi'(k) > 0$ and $\phi''(k) < 0$, $\phi(k)$ is associated with an upward-sloping concave curve, with a different slope at every point on the curve, so that only a unique value of k can satisfy (20.34). The intersection of the two curves at point E determines the intertemporal equilibrium values of

FIGURE 20.4

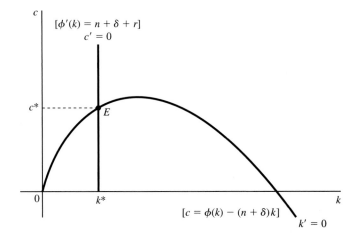

k and c, because at point E, neither k nor c will change in value over time, resulting in a *steady state*. We could label these values as $\bar{k}$ and $\bar{c}$ for intertemporal equilibrium values, but we shall label them as k^* and c^* instead, because they also represent the equilibrium values for optimal growth.

Analyzing the Phase Diagram

The intersection point E in Fig. 20.4 gives us a unique steady state. But what happens if we are initially at some point other than E? Returning to our system of first-order differential equations (20.31′) and (20.32), we can deduce that

$$\frac{\partial k'}{\partial c} = -1 < 0 \qquad \text{and} \qquad \frac{\partial c'}{\partial k} = -\frac{U'(c)}{U''(c)}\phi''(k) < 0$$

Since $\partial k'/\partial c < 0$, all the points below the $k' = 0$ curve are characterized by $k' > 0$ and all the points above the curve by $k' < 0$. Similarly, since $\partial c'/\partial k < 0$, all the points to the left of the $c' = 0$ line are characterized by $c' > 0$ and all the points to the right of the line by $c' < 0$. Thus the $k' = 0$ curve and the $c' = 0$ line divide the phase space into four regions, each with its own distinct pairing of signs of c' and k'. These are reflected in Fig. 20.5 by the right-angled directional arrows in each region.

The streamlines that follow the directional arrows in each region tell us that the steady state at point E is a saddle point. If we have an initial point that lies on one of the two stable branches of the saddle point, the dynamics of the system will lead us to point E. But any initial point that does not lie on a stable branch will make us either skirt around point E, never reaching it, or move steadily away from it. If we follow the streamlines of the latter instances, we will eventually (as $t \to \infty$) end up either with $k = 0$ (exhaustion of capital) or $c = 0$ (per capita consumption dwindling to zero)—both of which are economically unacceptable. Thus, the only viable alternative is to choose a (k, c) pair so as to locate our economy on a stable branch—a "yellow brick road," so to speak—that will take us to the steady state at E. We have not explicitly talked about the transversality condition, but if we had, it would have guided us to the steady state at E, where the per capita consumption can be maintained at a constant level ever after.

FIGURE 20.5

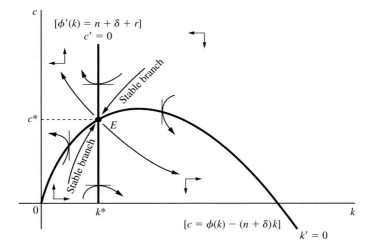

20.6 Limitations of Dynamic Analysis

The static analysis presented in Part 2 of this volume dealt only with the question of what the equilibrium position will be under certain given conditions of a model. The major query was: What values of the variables, *if attained,* will tend to perpetuate themselves? But the *attainability* of the equilibrium position was taken for granted. When we proceeded to the realm of comparative statics, in Part 3, the central question shifted to a more interesting problem: How will the equilibrium position shift in response to a certain change in a parameter? But the attainability aspect was again brushed aside. It was not until we reached the dynamic analysis in Part 5 that we looked the question of attainability squarely in the eye. Here we specifically ask: If initially we are away from an equilibrium position—say, because of a recent disequilibrating parameter change—will the various forces in the model tend to steer us toward the new equilibrium position? Furthermore, in a dynamic analysis, we also learn the particular character of the path (whether steady, fluctuating, or oscillatory) the variable will follow on its way to the equilibrium (if at all). The significance of dynamic analysis should therefore be self-evident.

However, in concluding its discussion, we should also take cognizance of the limitations of dynamic analysis. For one thing, to make the analysis manageable, dynamic models are often formulated in terms of linear equations. While simplicity may thereby be gained, the assumption of linearity will in many cases entail a considerable sacrifice of realism. Since a time path which is germane to a linear model may not always approximate that of a nonlinear counterpart, as we have seen in the price-ceiling example in Sec. 17.6, care must be exercised in the interpretation and application of the results of linear dynamic models. In this connection, however, the qualitative-graphic approach may perform an extremely valuable service, because under quite general conditions it can enable us to incorporate nonlinearity into a model without adding undue complexity to the analysis.

Another shortcoming usually found in dynamic economic models is the use of constant coefficients in differential or difference equations. Inasmuch as the primary role of the coefficients is to specify the parameters of the model, the constancy of coefficients—again assumed for the sake of mathematical manageability—essentially serves to "freeze" the economic environment of the problem under investigation. In other words, it means that the endogenous adjustment of the model is being studied in a sort of economic vacuum, such that no exogenous factors are allowed to intrude. In certain cases, of course, this problem may not be too serious, because many economic parameters do tend to stay relatively constant over long periods of time. And in some other cases, we may be able to undertake a comparative-dynamic type of analysis, to see how the time path of a variable will be affected by a change in certain parameters. Nevertheless, when we are interpreting a time path that extends into the distant future, we should always be careful not to be overconfident about the validity of the path in its more remote stretches, if simplifying assumptions of constancy have been made.

You realize, of course, that to point out its limitations as we have done here is by no means intended to disparage dynamic analysis as such. Indeed, it will be recalled that each type of analysis hitherto presented has been shown to have its own brand of limitations. As long as it is duly interpreted and properly applied, therefore, dynamic analysis—like any other type of analysis—can play an important part in the study of economic phenomena. In particular, the techniques of dynamic analysis have enabled us to extend the study of optimization into the realm of dynamic optimization in this chapter, in which the solution we seek is no longer a static optimum state, but an entire optimal time path.

The Greek Alphabet

A	α	alpha
B	β	beta
Γ	γ	gamma
Δ	δ	delta
E	ε	epsilon
Z	ζ	zeta
H	η	eta
Θ	θ	theta
I	ι	iota
K	κ	kappa
Λ	λ	lambda
M	μ	mu
N	ν	nu
Ξ	ξ	xi
O	o	omicron
Π	π	pi
P	ρ	rho
Σ	σ	sigma
T	τ	tau
Υ	υ	upsilon
Φ	ϕ (or φ)	phi
X	χ	chi
Ψ	ψ	psi
Ω	ω	omega

Mathematical Symbols

1. **Sets**

$a \in S$	a is an element of (belongs to) set S
$b \notin S$	b is not an element of set S
$S \subset T$	set S is a subset of (is contained in) set T
$T \supset S$	set T includes set S
$A \cup B$	the union of set A and set B
$A \cap B$	the intersection of set A and set B
$\tilde{S}$	the complement of set S
$\{\ \}$ or $\varnothing$	the null set (empty set)
$\{a, b, c\}$	the set with elements a, b, and c
$\{x \mid x \text{ has property } P\}$	the set of all objects with property P
$\min\{a, b, c\}$	the smallest element of the specified set
R	the set of all real numbers
R^2	the two-dimensional real space
R^n	the n-dimensional real space
(x, y)	ordered pair
(x, y, z)	ordered triple
(a, b)	open interval from a to b
$[a, b]$	closed interval from a to b

2. **Matrices and Determinants**

A' or A^T	the transpose of matrix A
A^{-1}	the inverse of matrix A
$|A|$	the determinant of matrix A
$|J|$	Jacobian determinant
$|H|$	Hessian determinant
$|\overline{H}|$	bordered Hessian determinant
$r(A)$	the rank of matrix A
$\mathrm{tr}A$	the trace of A

0	null matrix (zero matrix)
$u \cdot v$	the inner product (dot product) of vectors u and v
$u'v$	the scalar product of two vectors

3. Calculus

Given $y = f(x)$, a function of a single variable x:

$\lim\limits_{x \to \infty} f(x)$	the limit of $f(x)$ as x approaches infinity
dy	the first differential of y
d^2y	the second differential of y
$\dfrac{dy}{dx}$ or $f'(x)$	the first derivative of the function $y = f(x)$
$\dfrac{dy}{dx}\bigg|_{x=x_0}$ or $f'(x_0)$	the first derivative evaluated at $x = x_0$
$\dfrac{d^2y}{dx^2}$ or $f''(x)$	the second derivative of $y = f(x)$
$\dfrac{d^n y}{dx^n}$ or $f^{(n)}(x)$	the nth derivative of $y = f(x)$
$\displaystyle\int f(x)\,dx$	indefinite integral of $f(x)$
$\displaystyle\int_a^b f(x)\,dx$	definite integral of $f(x)$ from $x = a$ to $x = b$

Given the function $y = f(x_1, x_2, \ldots, x_n)$:

$\dfrac{\partial y}{\partial x_i}$ or f_i	the partial derivative of f with respect to x_i
$\nabla f \equiv \operatorname{grad} f$	the gradient of f
$\dfrac{dy}{dx_i}$	the total derivative of f with respect to x_i
$\dfrac{\S y}{\S x_i}$	the partial total derivative of f with respect to x_i

4. Differential and Difference Equations

$\dot{y} \equiv \dfrac{dy}{dt}$	the time derivative of y
Δy_t	the first difference of y_t
$\Delta^2 y_t$	the second difference of y_t
y_p	particular integral
y_c	complementary function

5. Others

$\sum\limits_{i=1}^{n} x_i$	the sum of x_i as i ranges from 1 to n

$p \Rightarrow q$	p only if q (p implies q)
$p \Leftarrow q$	p if q (p is implied by q)
$p \Leftrightarrow q$	p if and only if q
iff	if and only if
$|m|$	the absolute value of the number m
$n!$	n factorial $\equiv n(n-1)(n-2)\cdots(3)(2)(1)$
$\log_b x$	the logarithm of x to base b
$\log_e x$ or $\ln x$	the natural logarithm of x (to base e)
e	the base of natural logarithms and natural exponential functions
$\sin \theta$	sine function of θ
$\cos \theta$	cosine function of θ
R_n	the remainder term when the Taylor series involves an nth-degree polynomial

A Short Reading List

Abadie, J. (ed.): *Nonlinear Programming,* North-Holland Publishing Company, Amsterdam, 1967. (A collection of papers on certain theoretical and computational aspects of non-linear programming; Chapter 2, by Abadie, deals with the Kuhn-Tucker theorem in relation to the constraint qualification.)

Allen, R. G. D.: *Mathematical Analysis for Economists,* Macmillan & Co., Ltd., London, 1938. (A clear exposition of differential and integral calculus; determinants are dis-cussed, but not matrices; no set theory, and no mathematical programming.)

_____: *Mathematical Economics,* 2d ed., St. Martin's Press, Inc., New York, 1959. (Dis-cusses a legion of mathematical economic models; explains linear differential and difference equations and matrix algebra.)

Almon, C.: *Matrix Methods in Economics,* Addison-Wesley Publishing Company, Inc., Reading, Mass., 1967. (Matrix methods are discussed in relation to linear-equation systems, input-output models, linear programming, and nonlinear programming. Characteristic roots and characteristic vectors are also covered.)

Baldani, J., J. Bradfield, and R. Turner: *Mathematical Economics,* The Dryden Press, Orlando, 1996.

Baumol, W. J.: *Economic Dynamics: An Introduction,* 3d ed., The Macmillan Company, New York, 1970. (Part IV gives a lucid explanation of simple difference equations; Part V treats simultaneous difference equations; differential equations are only briefly discussed.)

Braun, M.: *Differential Equations and Their Applications: An Introduction to Applied Mathematics,* 4th ed., Springer-Verlag, Inc., New York, 1993. (Contains interesting applications of differential equations, such as the detection of art forgeries, the spread of epidemics, the arms race, and the disposal of nuclear waste.)

Burmeister, E., and A. R. Dobell: *Mathematical Theories of Economic Growth,* The Macmillan Company, New York, 1970. (A thorough exposition of growth models of varying degrees of complexity.)

Chiang, Alpha C.: *Elements of Dynamic Optimization,* McGraw-Hill Book Company, 1992, now published by Waveland Press, Inc., Prospect Heights, Ill.

Clark, Colin W.: *Mathematical Bioeconomics: The Optimal Management of Renewable Resources,* 2nd ed., John Wiley & Sons, Inc., Toronto, 1990. (A thorough explanation of optimal control theory and its use in both renewable and nonrenewable resources.)

Coddington, E. A., and N. Levinson: *Theory of Ordinary Differential Equations,* McGraw-Hill Book Company, New York, 1955. (A basic mathematical text on differential equations.)

Courant, R.: *Differential and Integral Calculus* (trans. E. J. McShane), Interscience Publishers, Inc., New York, vol. I, 2d ed., 1937, vol. II, 1936. (A classic treatise on calculus.)

_____, and F. John: *Introduction to Calculus and Analysis,* Interscience Publishers, Inc., New York, vol. I, 1965, vol. II, 1974. (An updated version of the preceding title.)

Dorfman, R., P. A. Samuelson, and R. M. Solow: *Linear Programming and Economic Analysis,* McGraw-Hill Book Company, New York, 1958. (A detailed treatment of linear programming, game theory, and input-output analysis.)

Franklin, J.: *Methods of Mathematical Economics: Linear and Nonlinear Programming, Fixed-Point Theorems,* Springer-Verlag, Inc., New York, 1980. (A delightful presentation of mathematical programming.)

Frisch, R.: *Maxima and Minima: Theory and Economic Applications* (in collaboration with A. Nataf), Rand McNally & Company, Chicago, Ill., 1966. (A thorough treatment of extremum problems, done primarily in the classical tradition.)

Goldberg, S.: *Introduction to Difference Equations,* John Wiley & Sons, Inc., New York, 1958. (With economic applications.)

Hadley, G.: *Linear Algebra,* Addison-Wesley Publishing Company, Inc., Reading, Mass., 1961. (Covers matrices, determinants, convex sets, etc.)

_____: *Linear Programming,* Addison-Wesley Publishing Company, Inc., Reading, Mass., 1962. (A clearly written, mathematically oriented exposition.)

_____: *Nonlinear and Dynamic Programming,* Addison-Wesley Publishing Company, Inc., Reading, Mass., 1964. (Covers nonlinear programming, stochastic programming, integer programming, and dynamic programming; computational aspects are emphasized.)

Halmos, P. R.: *Naive Set Theory,* D. Van Nostrand Company, Inc., Princeton, N.J., 1960. (An informal and hence readable introduction to the basics of set theory.)

Hands, D. Wade: *Introductory Mathematical Economics,* 2nd ed., Oxford University Press, New York, 2004.

Henderson, J. M., and R. E. Quandt: *Microeconomic Theory: A Mathematical Approach,* 3d ed., McGraw-Hill Book Company, New York, 1980. (A comprehensive mathematical treatment of microeconomic topics.)

Hoy, M., J. Livernois, C. McKenna, R. Rees, and T. Stengos: *Mathematics for Economics,* 2nd ed., The MIT Press, Cambridge, Mass. 2001.

Intriligator, M. D.: *Mathematical Optimization and Economic Theory,* Prentice Hall, Inc., Englewood Cliffs, N.J., 1971. (A thorough discussion of optimization methods, including the classical techniques, linear and nonlinear programming, and dynamic optimization; also applications to the theories of the consumer and the firm, general equilibrium and welfare economics, and theories of growth.)

Kemeny, J. G., J. L. Snell, and G. L. Thompson: *Introduction to Finite Mathematics,* 3d ed., Prentice Hall, Inc., Englewood Cliffs, N.J., 1974. (Covers such topics as sets, matrices, probability, and linear programming.)

Klein, Michael W.: *Mathematical Methods for Economics,* 2nd ed., Addison-Wesley Publishing Company, Inc., Reading, Mass. 2002.

Koo, D.: *Elements of Optimization: With Applications in Economics and Business,* Springer-Verlag, Inc., New York, 1977. (Clear discussion of classical optimization methods, mathematical programming as well as optimal control theory.)

Koopmans, T. C. (ed.): *Activity Analysis of Production and Allocation,* John Wiley & Sons, Inc., New York, 1951, reprinted by Yale University Press, 1972. (Contains a number of important papers on linear programming and activity analysis.)

————: *Three Essays on the State of Economic Science,* McGraw-Hill Book Company, New York, 1957. (The first essay contains a good exposition of convex sets; the third essay discusses the interaction of *tools* and *problems* in economics.)

Lambert, Peter J., *Advanced Mathematics for Economists: Static and Dynamic Optimization,* Blackwell Publishers, New York, 1985.

Leontief, W. W.: *The Structure of American Economy, 1919–1939,* 2d ed., Oxford University Press, Fair Lawn, N.J., 1951. (The pioneering work in input-output analysis.)

Samuelson, P. A.: *Foundations of Economic Analysis,* Harvard University Press, Cambridge, Mass., 1947. (A classic in mathematical economics, but very difficult to read.)

Silberberg, Eugene, and Wing Suen: *The Structure of Economics: A Mathematical Analysis,* 3rd ed., McGraw-Hill Book Company, New York, 2001. (Primarily a microeconomic focus, this book has a strong discussion of the envelope theorem and a wide variety of applications.)

Sydsæter, Knut, and Peter Hammond: *Essential Mathematics for Economic Analysis,* Prentice Hall, Inc., London, 2002.

Takayama, A.: *Mathematical Economics,* 2nd ed., The Dryden Press, Hinsdale, Ill., 1985. (Gives a comprehensive treatment of economic theory in mathematical terms, with concentration on two specific topics: competitive equilibrium and economic growth.)

Thomas, G. B., and R. L. Finney: *Calculus and Analytic Geometry,* 9th ed., Addison-Wesley Publishing Company, Inc., Reading, Mass., 1996. (A clearly written introduction to calculus.)

Answers to Selected Exercises

Exercise 2.3

1. (*a*) $\{x \mid x > 34\}$
3. (*a*) $\{2, 4, 6, 7\}$ (*c*) $\{2, 6\}$ (*e*) $\{2\}$
8. There are 16 subsets.
9. *Hint:* Distinguish between the two symbols $\notin$ and $\not\subset$.

Exercise 2.4

1. (*a*) $\{(3, a), (3, b), (6, a), (6, b), (9, a), (9, b)\}$
3. No.
5. Range $= \{y \mid 8 \le y \le 32\}$

Exercise 2.5

2. (*a*) and (*b*) differ in the sign of the slope measure; (*a*) and (*c*) differ in the vertical intercept.
4. When negative values are permissible, quadrant III has to be used too.
5. (*a*) x^{19}
6. (*a*) x^6

Exercise 3.2

1. $P^* = 2\frac{3}{11}$, and $Q^* = 14\frac{2}{11}$
3. *Note:* In 2(*a*), $c = 10$ (not 6).
5. *Hint:* $b + d = 0$ implies $d = -b$.

Exercise 3.3

1. (*a*) $x_1^* = 5$, and $x_2^* = 3$
3. (*a*) $(x - 6)(x + 1)(x - 3) = 0$, or $x^3 - 8x^2 + 9x + 18 = 0$
5. (*a*) $-1, 2$, and 3   (*c*) $-1, \frac{1}{2}$, and $-\frac{1}{4}$

Exercise 3.4

3. $P_1^* = 3\frac{6}{17}$ $P_2^* = 3\frac{8}{17}$ $Q_1^* = 11\frac{7}{17}$ $Q_2^* = 8\frac{7}{17}$

Exercise 3.5

1. *(b)* $Y^* = (a - bd + I_0 + G_0)/[1 - b(1 - t)]$
$T^* = [d(1 - b) + t(a + I_0 + G_0)]/[1 - b(1 - t)]$
$C^* = [a - bd + b(1 - t)(I_0 + G_0)]/[1 - b(1 - t)]$

3. *Hint:* After substituting the last two equations into the first, consider the resulting equation as a quadratic equation in the variable $w \equiv Y^{1/2}$. Only one root is acceptable, $w_1^* = 11$, giving $Y^* = 121$ and $C^* = 91$. The other root leads to a negative C^*.

Exercise 4.1

1. The elements in the (column) vector of constants are: $0, a, -c$.

Exercise 4.2

1. *(a)* $\begin{bmatrix} 7 & 3 \\ 9 & 7 \end{bmatrix}$ *(c)* $\begin{bmatrix} 21 & -3 \\ 18 & 27 \end{bmatrix}$

3. In this special case, AB happens to be equal to $BA = \begin{bmatrix} 1 & 0 & 0 \\ 0 & 1 & 0 \\ 0 & 0 & 1 \end{bmatrix}$.

4. *(b)* $\begin{bmatrix} 49 & 3 \\ 4 & 3 \end{bmatrix}$ *(c)* $\begin{bmatrix} 3x + 5y \\ 4x + 2y - 7z \end{bmatrix}$
      (2×2) (2×1)

6. *(a)* $x_2 + x_3 + x_4 + x_5$ *(c)* $b(x_1 + x_2 + x_3 + x_4)$

7. *(b)* $\sum_{i=2}^{4} a_i(x_{i+1} + i)$ *(d)* *Hint:* $x^0 = 1$ for $x \neq 0$

Exercise 4.3

1. *(a)* $uv' = \begin{bmatrix} 15 & 5 & -5 \\ 3 & 1 & -1 \\ 9 & 3 & -3 \end{bmatrix}$ *(c)* $xx' = \begin{bmatrix} x_1^2 & x_1x_2 & x_1x_3 \\ x_2x_1 & x_2^2 & x_2x_3 \\ x_3x_1 & x_3x_2 & x_3^2 \end{bmatrix}$

   (e) $u'v = 13$ *(g)* $u'u = 35$

3. *(a)* $\sum_{i=1}^{n} P_i Q_i$ *(b)* $P \cdot Q$ or $P'Q$ or $Q'P$

5. *(a)* $2v = \begin{bmatrix} 0 \\ 6 \end{bmatrix}$ *(c)* $u - v = \begin{bmatrix} 5 \\ -2 \end{bmatrix}$

7. *(a)* $d = \sqrt{27}$

9. *(c)* $d(v, 0) = (v \cdot v)^{1/2}$

Exercise 4.4

1. *(a)* $\begin{bmatrix} 5 & 17 \\ 11 & 17 \end{bmatrix}$

2. No; it should be $A - B = -B + A$.

4. (a) $k(A + B) = k[a_{ij} + b_{ij}] = [ka_{ij} + kb_{ij}] = [ka_{ij}] + [kb_{ij}] = k[a_{ij}] + k[b_{ij}] = kA + kB$ (Can you justify each step?)

Exercise 4.5

1. (a) $AI_3 = \begin{bmatrix} -1 & 5 & 7 \\ 0 & -2 & 4 \end{bmatrix}$ (c) $I_2 x = \begin{bmatrix} x_1 \\ x_2 \end{bmatrix}$

3. (a) 5×3 (c) 2×1

4. *Hint:* Multiply the given diagonal matrix by itself, and examine the resulting product matrix for conditions for idempotency.

Exercise 4.6

1. $A' = \begin{bmatrix} 0 & -1 \\ 4 & 3 \end{bmatrix}$ and $B' = \begin{bmatrix} 3 & 0 \\ -8 & 1 \end{bmatrix}$

3. *Hint:* Define $D \equiv AB$, and apply (4.11).

5. *Hint:* Define $D \equiv AB$, and apply (4.14).

Exercise 5.1

1. (a) (5.2)   (c) (5.3)   (e) (5.3)

3. (a) Yes.   (d) No.

5. (a) $r(A) = 3$; A is nonsingular.   (b) $r(B) = 2$; B is singular.

Exercise 5.2

1. (a) -6 (c) 0   (e) $3abc - a^3 - b^3 - c^3$

3. $|M_b| = \begin{vmatrix} d & f \\ g & i \end{vmatrix}$ $|C_b| = - \begin{vmatrix} d & f \\ g & i \end{vmatrix}$

4. (a) *Hint:* Expand by the third column.

5. 20 (not -20)

Exercise 5.3

3. (a) Property IV.   (b) Property III (applied to both rows).

4. (a) Singular.   (c) Singular.

5. (a) Rank < 3 (c) Rank < 3

7. A is nonsingular because $|A| = 1 - b \neq 0$.

Exercise 5.4

1. $\sum_{i=1}^{4} a_{i3} |C_{i2}|$ $\sum_{j=1}^{4} a_{2j} |C_{4j}|$

3. (a) Interchange the two diagonal elements of A; multiply the two off-diagonal elements of A by -1.

   (b) Divide by $|A|$.

4. (a) $E^{-1} = \dfrac{1}{20}\begin{bmatrix} 3 & 2 & -3 \\ -7 & 2 & 7 \\ -6 & -4 & 26 \end{bmatrix}$ (c) $G^{-1} = \begin{bmatrix} 1 & 0 & 0 \\ 0 & 0 & 1 \\ 0 & 1 & 0 \end{bmatrix}$

Exercise 5.5

1. (a) $x_1^* = 4$, and $x_2^* = 3$ (c) $x_1^* = 2$, and $x_2^* = 1$

2. (a) $A^{-1} = \dfrac{1}{7}\begin{bmatrix} 1 & 2 \\ -2 & 3 \end{bmatrix}; x^* = \begin{bmatrix} 4 \\ 3 \end{bmatrix}$ (c) $A^{-1} = \dfrac{1}{15}\begin{bmatrix} 1 & 7 \\ -1 & 8 \end{bmatrix}; x^* = \begin{bmatrix} 2 \\ 1 \end{bmatrix}$

3. (a) $x_1^* = 2, x_2^* = 0, x_3^* = 1$ (c) $x^* = 0, y^* = 3, z^* = 4$

4. *Hint:* Apply (5.8) and (5.13).

Exercise 5.6

1. (a) $A^{-1} = \dfrac{1}{1 - b + bt}\begin{bmatrix} 1 & 1 & -b \\ b(1 - t) & 1 & -b \\ t & t & 1 - b \end{bmatrix}$

$\begin{bmatrix} Y^* \\ C^* \\ T^* \end{bmatrix} = \dfrac{1}{1 - b + bt}\begin{bmatrix} I_0 + G_0 + a - bd \\ b(1 - t)(I_0 + G_0) + a - bd \\ t(I_0 + G_0) + at + d(1 - b) \end{bmatrix}$

(b) $|A| = 1 - b + bt$ $\qquad\qquad |A_1| = I_0 + G_0 - bd + a$

$|A_2| = a - bd + b(1 - t)(I_0 + G_0)$ $|A_3| = d(1 - b) + t(a + I_0 + G_0)$

Exercise 5.7

1. $x_1^* = 69.53$, $x_2^* = 57.03$, and $x_3^* = 42.58$

3. (a) $A = \begin{bmatrix} 0.10 & 0.50 \\ 0.60 & 0 \end{bmatrix}$; the matrix equation is $\begin{bmatrix} 0.90 & -0.50 \\ -0.60 & 1.00 \end{bmatrix}\begin{bmatrix} x_1 \\ x_2 \end{bmatrix} = \begin{bmatrix} 1,000 \\ 2,000 \end{bmatrix}$.

(c) $x_1^* = 3,333\frac{1}{3}$, and $x_2^* = 4,000$

4. Element 0.33: 33¢ of Commodity II is needed as input for producing $1 of Commodity I.

Exercise 6.2

1. (a) $\Delta y/\Delta x = 8x + 4\Delta x$ (b) $dy/dx = 8x$ (c) $f'(3) = 24, f'(4) = 32$

3. (a) $\Delta y/\Delta x = 5$; a constant function.

Exercise 6.4

1. Left-side limit = right-side limit = 15; the limit is 15.

3. (a) 5   (b) 5

Exercise 6.5

1. (a) $-3/4 < x$ (c) $x < 1/2$

3. (a) $-7 < x < 5$ (c) $-4 \le x \le 1$

Exercise 6.6

1. (a) 7   (c) 17

3. (a) $2\frac{1}{2}$ (c) 2

Exercise 6.7

2. (a) $N^2 - 5N - 2$ (b) Yes.   (c) Yes.

3. (a) $(N+2)/(N^2+2)$ (b) Yes.   (c) Continuous in the domain.

6. Yes; each function is continuous and smooth.

Exercise 7.1

1. (a) $dy/dx = 12x^{11}$ (c) $dy/dx = 35x^4$ (e) $dw/du = -2u^{-1/2}$

3. (a) $f'(x) = 18$; $f'(1) = f'(2) = 18$

   (c) $f'(x) = 10x^{-3}$; $f'(1) = 10$, $f'(2) = 1\frac{1}{4}$

Exercise 7.2

1. $VC = Q^3 - 5Q^2 + 12Q$; $\dfrac{dVC}{dQ} = 3Q^2 - 10Q + 12$ is the MC function.

3. (a) $3(27x^2 + 6x - 2)$ (c) $12x(x+1)$ (e) $-x(9x+14)$

4. (b) $MR = 60 - 6Q$

7. (a) $(x^2 - 3)/x^2$ (c) $30/(x+5)^2$

8. (a) a (c) $-a/(ax+b)^2$

Exercise 7.3

1. $-2x[3(5 - x^2)^2 + 2]$

3. (a) $18x(3x^2 - 13)^2$ (c) $5a(ax+b)^4$

5. $x = \frac{1}{7}y - 3$, $dx/dy = \frac{1}{7}$

Exercise 7.4

1. (a) $\partial y/\partial x_1 = 6x_1^2 - 22x_1x_2$, and $\partial y/\partial x_2 = -11x_1^2 + 6x_2$

   (c) $\partial y/\partial x_1 = 2(x_2 - 2)$, and $\partial y/\partial x_2 = 2x_1 + 3$

3. (a) 12   (c) 10/9

5. (a) $U_1 = 2(x_1 + 2)(x_2 + 3)^3$, and $U_2 = 3(x_1 + 2)^2(x_2 + 3)^2$

Exercise 7.5

1. $\partial Q^*/\partial a = d/(b+d) > 0$ $\partial Q^*/\partial b = -d(a+c)/(b+d)^2 < 0$

   $\partial Q^*/\partial c = -b/(b+d) < 0$ $\partial Q^*/\partial d = b(a+c)/(b+d)^2 > 0$

2. $\partial Y^*/\partial I_0 = \partial Y^*/\partial \alpha = 1/(1 - \beta + \beta\delta) > 0$

Exercise 7.6

1. (a) $|J| = 0$; the functions are dependent.

   (b) $|J| = -20x_2$; the functions are independent.

Exercise 8.1

1. (a) $dy = -3(x^2 + 1)\,dx$ (c) $dy = [(1 - x^2)/(x^2 + 1)^2]\,dx$

3. (a) $dC/dY = b$, and $C/Y = (a + bY)/Y$

Exercise 8.2

2. (a) $dz = (6x + y)\,dx + (x - 6y^2)\,dy$

3. (*a*) $dy = [x_2/(x_1 + x_2)^2] dx_1 - [x_1/(x_1 + x_2)^2] dx_2$

4. $\varepsilon_{QP} = 2bP^2/(a + bP^2 + R^{1/2})$

6. $\varepsilon_{XP} = -2/(Y_f^{1/2} P^2 + 1)$

Exercise 8.3

3. (*a*) $dy = 3[(2x_2 - 1)(x_3 + 5) dx_1 + 2x_1(x_3 + 5) dx_2 + x_1(2x_2 - 1) dx_3]$

4. *Hint:* Apply the definitions of differential and total differential.

Exercise 8.4

1. (*a*) $dz/dy = x + 10y + 6y^2 = 28y + 9y^2$

  (*c*) $dz/dy = -15x + 3y = 108y - 30$

3. $dQ/dt = [a\alpha A/K + b\beta A/L + A'(t)]K^\alpha L^\beta$

4. (*b*) $\S W/\S u = 10u f_1 + f_2$ $\S W/\S v = 3 f_1 - 12v^2 f_2$

Exercise 8.5

5. (*a*) Defined; $dy/dx = -(3x^2 - 4xy + 3y^2)/(-2x^2 + 6xy) = -9/8$

  (*b*) Defined; $dy/dx = -(4x + 4y)/(4x - 4y^3) = 2/13$

7. The condition $F_y \neq 0$ is violated at $(0, 0)$.

8. The product of partial derivatives is equal to -1.

Exercise 8.6

1. (*c*) $(dY^*/dG_0) = 1/(S' + T' - I') > 0$

3. $(\partial P^*/\partial Y_0) = D_{Y_0}/(S_{P*} - D_{P*}) > 0$ $(\partial Q^*/\partial Y_0) = D_{Y_0} S_{P*}/(S_{P*} - D_{P*}) > 0$

  $(\partial P^*/\partial T_0) = -S_{T_0}/(S_{P*} - D_{P*}) > 0$ $(\partial Q^*/\partial T_0) = -S_{T_0} D_{P*}/(S_{P*} - D_{P*}) < 0$

Exercise 9.2

1. (*a*) When $x = 2$, $y = 15$ (a relative maximum).

  (*c*) When $x = 0$, $y = 3$ (a relative minimum).

2. (*a*) The critical value $x = -1$ lies outside the domain; the critical value $x = 1$ leads to $y = 3$ (a relative minimum).

4. (*d*) The elasticity is one.

Exercise 9.3

1. (*a*) $f''(x) = 2a$, $f'''(x) = 0$ (*c*) $f''(x) = 6(1 - x)^{-3}$, $f'''(x) = 18(1 - x)^{-4}$

3. (*b*) A straight line.

5. Every point on $f(x)$ is a stationary point, but the only stationary point on $g(x)$ we know of is at $x = 3$.

Exercise 9.4

1. (*a*) $f(2) = 33$ is a maximum.

  (*c*) $f(1) = 5\frac{1}{3}$ is a maximum; $f(5) = -5\frac{1}{3}$ is a minimum.

2. *Hint:* First write an area function A in terms of one variable (either L or W) alone.

3. (*d*) $Q^* = 11$ (*e*) Maximum profit $= 111\frac{1}{3}$

5. (*a*) $k < 0$ (*b*) $h < 0$ (*c*) $j > 0$

7. (*b*) S is maximized at the output level 20.37 (approximately).

Exercise 9.5

1. (*a*) 120   (*c*) 4   (*e*) $(n + 2)(n + 1)$

2. (*a*) $1 + x + x^2 + x^3 + x^4$

3. (*b*) $-63 - 98x - 62x^2 - 18x^3 - 2x^4 + R_4$

Exercise 9.6

1. (*a*) $f(0) = 0$ is an inflection point.   (*c*) $f(0) = 5$ is a relative minimum.

2. (*b*) $f(2) = 0$ is a relative minimum.

Exercise 10.1

1. (*a*) Yes.   (*b*) Yes.

3. (*a*) $5e^{5t}$ (*c*) $-12e^{-2t}$

5. (*a*) The curve with $a = -1$ is the mirror image of the curve with $a = 1$ with reference to the horizontal axis.

Exercise 10.2

1. (*a*) 7.388   (*b*) 1.649

2. (*c*) $1 + 2x + \dfrac{1}{2!}(2x)^2 + \dfrac{1}{3!}(2x)^3 + \cdots$

3. (*a*) $\$70e^{0.12}$ (*b*) $\$690e^{0.10}$

Exercise 10.3

1. (*a*) 4   (*c*) 4

2. (*a*) 7   (*c*) -3 (*e*) 6

3. (*a*) 26   (*c*) $\ln 3 - \ln B$ (*f*) 3

Exercise 10.4

1. The requirement prevents the function from degenerating into a constant function.

3. *Hint:* Take log to base b.

4. (*a*) $y = e^{(3 \ln 8)t}$ or $y = e^{6.2385t}$ (*c*) $y = 5e^{(\ln 5)t}$ or $y = 5e^{1.6095t}$

5. (*a*) $t = (\ln y)/(\ln 7)$ or $t = 0.5139 \ln y$

(*c*) $t = 3 \ln(9y)/(\ln 15)$ or $t = 1.1078 \ln(9y)$

6. (*a*) $r = \ln 1.05$ (*c*) $r = 2 \ln 1.03$

Exercise 10.5

1. (*a*) $2e^{2t+4}$ (*c*) $2te^{t^2+1}$ (*e*) $(2ax + b)e^{ax^2+bx+c}$

3. (*a*) $5/t$ (*c*) $1/(t + 19)$ (*e*) $1/[x(1 + x)]$

5. *Hint:* Use (10.21), and apply the chain rule.

7. (*a*) $3(8 - x^2)/[(x + 2)^2(x + 4)^2]$

Exercise 10.6

1. $t^* = 1/r^2$

2. $d^2A/dt^2 = -A(\ln 2)/4\sqrt{t^3} < 0$

Exercise 10.7

1. (a) $2/t$ (c) $\ln b$ (e) $1/t - \ln 3$

3. $r_y = kr_x$

7. $|\varepsilon_d| = n$

11. $r_Q = \varepsilon_{QK} r_K + \varepsilon_{QL} r_L$

Exercise 11.2

1. $z^* = 3$ is a minimum.

3. $z^* = c$, which is a minimum in case (a), a maximum in case (b), and a saddle point in case (c).

5. (a) Any pair (x, y) other than $(2, 3)$ yields a positive z value.

    (b) Yes.   (c) No.   (d) Yes ($d^2z = 0$).

Exercise 11.3

1. (a) $q = 4u^2 + 4uv + 3v^2$ (c) $q = 5x^2 + 6xy$

3. (a) Positive definite.   (c) Neither.

5. (a) Positive definite.   (c) Negative definite.   (e) Positive definite.

6. (a) $r_1, r_2 = \frac{1}{2}(7 \pm \sqrt{17})$; $u'Du$ is positive definite.

    (c) $r_1, r_2 = \frac{1}{2}(5 \pm \sqrt{61})$; $u'Fu$ is indefinite.

7. $v_1 = \begin{bmatrix} 2/\sqrt{5} \\ 1/\sqrt{5} \end{bmatrix}$, $v_2 = \begin{bmatrix} -1/\sqrt{5} \\ 2/\sqrt{5} \end{bmatrix}$

Exercise 11.4

1. $z^* = 0$ (minimum)

3. $z^* = -11/40$ (minimum)

4. $z^* = 2 - e$ (minimum), attained at $(x^*, y^*, w^*) = (0, 0, 1)$

5. (b) *Hint:* See (11.16).

6. (a) $r_1 = 2$ $r_2 = 4 + \sqrt{6}$ $r_3 = 4 - \sqrt{6}$

Exercise 11.5

1. (a) Strictly convex.   (c) Strictly convex.

2. (a) Strictly concave.   (c) Neither.

3. No.

5. (a) Disk.   (b) Yes.

7. (a) Convex combination, with $\theta = 0.5$.   (b) Convex combination, with $\theta = 0.2$.

Exercise 11.6

1. (*a*) No.   (*b*) $Q_1^* = P_{10}/4$ and $Q_2^* = P_{20}/4$
3. $|\varepsilon_{d1}| = 1\frac{5}{8}$ $|\varepsilon_{d2}| = 1\frac{1}{3}$ $|\varepsilon_{d3}| = 1\frac{1}{2}$
5. (*a*) $\pi = P_0 Q(a, b)(1 + \frac{1}{2}i_0)^{-2} - P_{a0}a - P_{b0}b$

Exercise 11.7

1. $(\partial a^*/\partial P_{a0}) = P_0 Q_{bb} e^{-rt}/|J| < 0$ $(\partial b^*/\partial P_{a0}) = -P_0 Q_{ab} e^{-rt}/|J| < 0$
2. (*a*) Four.   (*b*) $(\partial a^*/\partial P_0) = (Q_b Q_{ab} - Q_a Q_{bb})P_0(1 + i_0)^{-2}/|J| > 0$
   (*c*) $(\partial a^*/\partial i_0) = (Q_a Q_{bb} - Q_b Q_{ab})P_0^2(1 + i_0)^{-3}/|J| < 0$

Exercise 12.2

1. (*a*) $z^* = 1/2$, attained when $\lambda^* = 1/2$, $x^* = 1$, and $y^* = 1/2$
   (*c*) $z^* = -19$, attained when $\lambda^* = -4$, $x^* = 1$, and $y^* = 5$
4. $Z_\lambda = -G(x, y) = 0$ $Z_x = f_x - \lambda G_x = 0$ $Z_y = f_y - \lambda G_y = 0$
5. *Hint:* Distinguish between identical equality and conditional equality.

Exercise 12.3

1. (*a*) $|\bar{H}| = 4$; z^* is a maximum.   (*c*) $|\bar{H}| = -2$; z^* is a minimum.

Exercise 12.4

2. (*a*) Quasiconcave, but not strictly so.   (*c*) Strictly quasiconcave.
4. (*a*) Neither.   (*c*) Quasiconvex, but not quasiconcave.
5. *Hint:* Review Sec. 9.4.
7. *Hint:* Use either (12.21) or (12.25′).

Exercise 12.5

1. (*b*) $\lambda^* = 3$, $x^* = 16$, $y^* = 11$ (*c*) $|\bar{H}| = 48$; condition is satisfied.
3. $(\partial x^*/\partial B) = 1/2P_x > 0$ $(\partial x^*/\partial P_x) = -(B + P_y)/2P_x^2 < 0$
   $(\partial x^*/\partial P_y) = 1/2P_x > 0$ etc.
5. Not valid.
7. No to both (*a*) and (*b*)—see (12.32) and (12.33′).

Exercise 12.6

1. (*a*) Homogeneous of degree one.   (*c*) Not homogeneous.
   (*e*) Homogeneous of degree two.
4. They are true.
7. (*a*) Homogeneous of degree $a + b + c$.
8. (*a*) $j^2 Q = g(jK, jL)$ (*b*) *Hint:* Let $j = 1/L$.
   (*d*) Homogeneous of degree one in K and L.

Exercise 12.7

1. (*a*) $1:2:3$ (*b*) $1:4:9$

2. *Hint:* Review Figs. 8.2 and 8.3.

4. *Hint:* This is a total derivative.

6. (*a*) Downward-sloping straight lines.   (*b*) $\sigma \to \infty$ as $\rho \to -1$

8. (*a*) 7   (*c*) $\ln 5 - 1$

Exercise 13.1

3. The conditions $x_j(\partial Z/\partial x_j) = 0$ and the conditions $\lambda_i(\partial Z/\partial \lambda_i) = 0$ can be condensed.

5. Consistent.

Exercise 13.2

1. No qualifying arc can be found for a test vector such as $(dx_1, dx_2) = (1, 0)$.

3. $(x_1^*, x_2^*) = (0, 0)$ is a cusp. The constraint qualification is satisfied (all test vectors are horizontal and pointing eastward); the Kuhn-Tucker conditions are satisfied, too.

4. All the conditions can be satisfied by choosing $y_0^* = 0$ and $y_1^* \geq 0$.

Exercise 13.4

2. (*a*) Yes.   (*b*) Yes.   (*c*) No.

4. (*a*) Yes.   (*b*) Yes.

Exercise 14.2

1. (*a*) $-8x^{-2} + c, (x \neq 0)$ (*c*) $\frac{1}{6}x^6 - \frac{3}{2}x^2 + c$

2. (*a*) $13e^x + c$ (*c*) $5e^x - 3x^{-1} + c, (x \neq 0)$

3. (*a*) $3 \ln |x| + c, (x \neq 0)$ (*c*) $\ln(x^2 + 3) + c$

4. (*a*) $\frac{2}{3}(x + 1)^{3/2}(x + 3) - \frac{4}{15}(x + 1)^{5/2} + c$

Exercise 14.3

1. (*a*) $4\frac{1}{3}$ (*b*) $3\frac{1}{4}$ (*e*) $2\left(\dfrac{a}{3} + c\right)$

2. (*a*) $\frac{1}{2}(e^{-2} - e^{-4})$ (*c*) $e^2\left(\frac{1}{2}e^4 - \frac{1}{2}e^2 + e - 1\right)$

3. (*b*) Underestimate.   (*e*) $f(x)$ is Riemann integrable.

Exercise 14.4

1. None.

2. (*a*), (*c*), (*d*) and (*e*).

3. (*a*), (*c*) and (*d*) convergent; (*e*) divergent.

Exercise 14.5

1. (*a*) $R(Q) = 14Q^2 - \frac{10}{3}e^{0.3Q} + \frac{10}{3}$ (*b*) $R(Q) = 10Q/(1 + Q)$

3. (*a*) $K(t) = 9t^{4/3} + 25$

5. (*a*) 29,000

Exercise 14.6

1. Capital alone is considered. Since labor is normally necessary for production as well, the underlying assumption is that K and L are always used in a fixed proportion.
3. *Hint:* Use (6.8).
4. *Hint:* $\ln u - \ln v = \ln \dfrac{u}{v}$

Exercise 15.1

1. (a) $y(t) = -e^{-4t} + 3$ (c) $y(t) = \frac{3}{2}(1 - e^{-10t})$
3. (a) $y(t) = 4(1 - e^{-t})$ (c) $y(t) = 6e^{5t}$ (e) $y(t) = 8e^{7t} - 1$

Exercise 15.2

1. The D curve should be steeper.
3. The price adjustment mechanism generates a differential equation.
5. (a) $P(t) = A \exp\left(-\dfrac{\beta + \delta}{\eta} t\right) + \dfrac{\alpha}{\beta + \delta}$ (b) Yes.

Exercise 15.3

1. $y(t) = Ae^{-5t} + 3$
3. $y(t) = e^{-t^2} + \frac{1}{2}$
5. $y(t) = e^{-6t} - \frac{1}{7}e^t$
6. *Hint:* Review Sec. 14.2, Example 17.

Exercise 15.4

1. (a) $y(t) = (c/t^3)^{1/2}$ (c) $yt + y^2 t = c$

Exercise 15.5

1. (a) Separable; linear when written as $\dfrac{dy}{dt} + \dfrac{1}{t} y = 0$

   (c) Separable; reducible to a Bernoulli equation.
3. $y(t) = (A - t^2)^{1/2}$

Exercise 15.6

1. (a) Upward-sloping phase line; dynamically unstable equilibrium.
   (c) Downward-sloping phase line; dynamically stable equilibrium.
3. The sign of the derivative measures the slope of the phase line.

Exercise 15.7

1. $r_k = r_K - r_L$ [cf. (10.25)]
4. (a) Plot $(3 - y)$ and $\ln y$ as two separate curves, and then subtract. A single equilibrium exists (at a y value between 1 and 3) and is dynamically stable.

Exercise 16.1

1. (a) $y_p = 2/5$ (c) $y_p = 3$ (e) $y_p = 6t^2$
3. (a) $y(t) = 6e^t + e^{-4t} - 3$ (c) $y(t) = e^t + te^t + 3$
6. *Hint:* Apply L'Hôpital's rule.

Exercise 16.2

1. (a) $\frac{3}{2} \pm \frac{3}{2}\sqrt{3}i$ (c) $-\frac{1}{4} \pm \frac{3}{4}\sqrt{7}i$
3. (b) *Hint:* When $\theta = \pi/4$, line OP is a 45° line.
5. (a) $\dfrac{d}{d\theta} \sin f(\theta) = f'(\theta) \cos f(\theta)$ (b) $\dfrac{d}{d\theta} \cos \theta^3 = -3\theta^2 \sin \theta^3$
7. (a) $\sqrt{3} + i$ (c) $1 - i$

Exercise 16.3

1. $y(t) = e^{2t}(3 \cos 2t + \frac{1}{2} \sin 2t)$
3. $y(t) = e^{-3t/2}\left(-\cos \dfrac{\sqrt{7}}{2}t + \dfrac{\sqrt{7}}{7} \sin \dfrac{\sqrt{7}}{2}t\right) + 3$
5. $y(t) = \frac{2}{3} \cos 3t + \sin 3t + \frac{1}{3}$

Exercise 16.4

1. (a) $P'' + \dfrac{m-u}{n-w}P' - \dfrac{\beta+\delta}{n-w} = -\dfrac{\alpha+\gamma}{n-w}$ $(n \neq w)$ (b) $P_p = \dfrac{\alpha+\gamma}{\beta+\delta}$
3. (a) $P(t) = e^{t/2}(2 \cos \frac{3}{2}t + 2 \sin \frac{3}{2}t) + 2$

Exercise 16.5

1. (a) $\dfrac{d\pi}{dt} + j(1-g) = j(\alpha - T - \beta U)$
   (b) No complex roots; no fluctuation.
3. (c) Both are first-order differential equations.   (d) $g \neq 1$
4. (a) $\pi(t) = e^{-t}\left(A_5 \cos \dfrac{\sqrt{2}}{4}t + A_6 \sin \dfrac{\sqrt{2}}{4}t\right) + m$ (c) $\overline{P} = m; \overline{U} = \dfrac{1}{18} - \dfrac{2}{9}m$

Exercise 16.6

2. (a) $y_p = t - 2$ (c) $y_p = \frac{1}{4}e^t$

Exercise 16.7

1. (a) $y_p = 4$ (c) $y_p = \frac{1}{18}t^2$
3. (a) Divergent.   (c) Convergent.

Exercise 17.2

1. (a) $y_{t+1} = y_t + 7$ (c) $y_{t+1} = 3y_t - 9$
3. (a) $y_t = 10 + t$ (c) $y_t = y_0\alpha^t - \beta(1 + \alpha + \alpha^2 + \cdots + \alpha^{t-1})$

Exercise 17.3

1. (*a*) Nonoscillatory; divergent.   (*c*) Oscillatory; convergent.

3. (*a*) $y_t = -8(1/3)^t + 9$ (*c*) $y_t = -2(-1/4)^t + 4$

Exercise 17.4

1. $Q_t = \alpha - \beta(P_0 - \overline{P})(-\delta/\beta)^t - \beta\overline{P}$

3. (*a*) $\overline{P} = 3$; explosive oscillation.   (*c*) $\overline{P} = 2$; uniform oscillation.

5. The lag in the supply function.

Exercise 17.5

1. $a = -1$

3. $P_t = (P_0 - 3)(-1.4)^t + 3$, with explosive oscillation.

Exercise 17.6

1. No.

2. (*b*) Nonoscillatory, explosive downward movement.

   (*d*) Damped, steady downward movement toward R.

4. (*a*) At first downward-sloping, then becoming horizontal.

Exercise 18.1

1. (*a*) $\frac{1}{2} \pm \frac{1}{2}i$ (*c*) $\frac{1}{2}, -1$

3. (*a*) 4 (stationary)   (*c*) 5 (stationary)

4. (*b*) $y_t = \sqrt{2}^t \left(2 \cos \frac{\pi}{4}t + \sin \frac{\pi}{4}t\right) + 1$

Exercise 18.2

1. (*a*) Subcase 1D.   (*c*) Subcase 1C.

3. *Hint:* Use (18.16).

Exercise 18.3

3. Possibilities *v*, *viii*, *x*, and *xi* will become feasible.

4. (*a*) $p_{t+2} - [2 - j(1 - g) - \beta k]p_{t+1} + [1 - j(1 - g) - \beta k(1 - j)]p_t = j\beta km$

   (*c*) $\beta k \gtrless 4$

Exercise 18.4

1. (*a*) 1   (*c*) $3t^2 + 3t + 1$

3. (*a*) $y_p = \frac{1}{4}t$ (*c*) $y_p = 2 - t + t^2$

5. (*a*) $1/2, -1$ and 1

Exercise 19.2

2. $b^3 + b^2 - 3b + 2 = 0$

3. (a) $x_t = -(3)^t + 4(-2)^t + 7$ $\qquad y_t = 2(3)^t + 2(-2)^t + 5$

4. (a) $x(t) = 4e^{-2t} - 3e^{-3t} + 12$ $\qquad y(t) = -e^{-2t} + e^{-3t} + 4$

Exercise 19.3

2. (c) $\beta = (\delta I - A)^{-1} u$

3. (c) $\beta = (\rho I + I - A)^{-1} \lambda$

5. (c) $x_1(t) = 4e^{-4t/10} + 2e^{-11t/10} + \frac{17}{6} e^{t/10}; \quad x_2(t) = 3e^{-4t/10} - 2e^{-11t/10} + \frac{19}{6} e^{t/10}$

Exercise 19.4

4. (a) $\begin{bmatrix} \pi_c \\ U_c \end{bmatrix} = \begin{bmatrix} A_1 \\ \dfrac{23 - \sqrt{193}}{48} A_1 \end{bmatrix} \left(\dfrac{33 + \sqrt{193}}{64} \right)^t + \begin{bmatrix} A_2 \\ \dfrac{23 + \sqrt{193}}{48} A_2 \end{bmatrix} \left(\dfrac{33 - \sqrt{193}}{64} \right)^t$

$\qquad + \begin{bmatrix} \mu \\ \dfrac{1}{6}(1 - \mu) \end{bmatrix}$

Exercise 19.5

1. The single equation can be rewritten as two first-order equations.

2. Yes.

4. (a) Saddle point.

Exercise 19.6

1. (a) $|J_E| = 1$ and tr $J_E = 2$; locally unstable node.

$\qquad$ (c) $|J_E| = 5$ and tr $J_E = -1$; locally stable focus.

2. (a) Locally a saddle point. $\qquad$ (c) Locally stable node or stable focus.

4. (a) The $x' = 0$ and $y' = 0$ curves coincide, and provide a lineful of equilibrium points.

Exercise 20.2

1. $\lambda^* = 1 - t$ $\qquad u^* = \dfrac{1 - t}{2}$ $\qquad y^* = \dfrac{t}{2} - \dfrac{t^2}{4} + 2$

6. $\lambda^*(t) = 3e^{4-t} - 3$ $\qquad u^*(t) = 2$ $\qquad y^*(t) = 7e^t - 2$

Exercise 20.4

1. $\lambda^* = \delta/(\delta^2 + \alpha)$ $\qquad K^* = 1/2(\delta^2 + \alpha)$

Index